Numbers

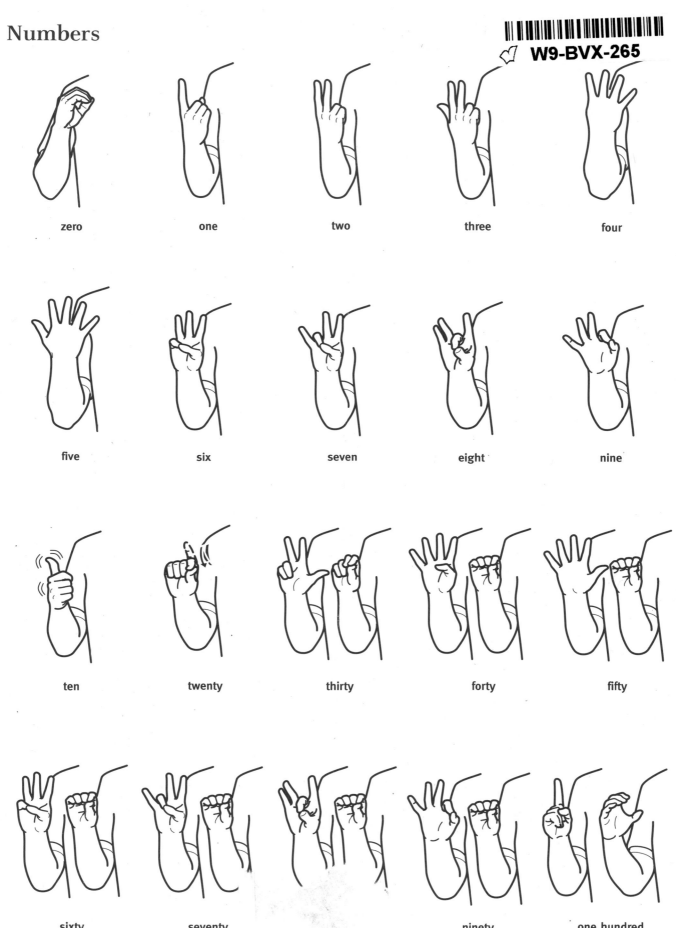

zero   one   two   three   four

five   six   seven   eight   nine

ten   twenty   thirty   forty   fifty

sixty   seventy   ninety   one hundred

The Canadian Dictionary of ASL

Editors-in-Chief

CAROLE SUE BAILEY

KATHY DOLBY

Writers

HILDA CAMPBELL

KATHY DOLBY

Editors

CAROLE SUE BAILEY

HILDA CAMPBELL

KATHY DOLBY

MARY MAHONEY-ROBSON

ASL Consultant

ANGELA STRATIY

Illustrators

DAVID JAMES

ALLAN MOON

VALENTINO SANNA

MEDIA MASTERS

Regional Consultants

CAROLE SUE BAILEY,
Prairie Region

MAUREEN M. DONALD,
Pacific Region

MYLES MURPHY,
Atlantic Region

ROBYN SANDFORD,
Central Region

Support Team

LARAINE COATES

CAROLINE ANNE FRITZ

SHIRLEY HANDLEY

CHARMAINE LETOURNEAU, C.M.

HELEN PIZZACALLA

EDITORS *Carole Sue Bailey & Kathy Dolby*

Developed by
THE CANADIAN
CULTURAL SOCIETY
OF THE DEAF INC.

THE Canadian Dictionary OF ASL

THE UNIVERSITY OF ALBERTA PRESS

Published by
The University of Alberta Press
Ring House 2
Edmonton, Alberta, Canada T6G 2E1

Copyright © The Canadian Cultural Society of the Deaf 2002

ISBN 0–88864–300–4
First edition, sixth printing 2012

NATIONAL LIBRARY OF CANADA CATALOGUING IN PUBLICATION DATA

Bailey, Carole Sue, 1949–
    The Canadian dictionary of ASL

    Co-published by: Canadian Cultural Society of the Deaf.
    ISBN 0–88864–300–4

    1. American Sign Language—Canada—Dictionaries. I. Dolby, Kathy, 1949– II. Campbell, Hilda Marian,
1927– III. Canadian Cultural Society of the Deaf. IV. Title.
HV2475.B34 2002   419/.03   C2002-910615-X

Printed on acid-free paper. ∞

Printed and bound in Canada by Transcontinental Printing Inc., Louiseville, Quebec.

The University of Alberta Press gratefully acknowledges the support received for its publishing program
from The Canada Council for the Arts. In addition, we also gratefully acknowledge the financial support of
the Government of Canada through the Book Publishing Industry Development Program for our
publishing activities.

  Canada Council Conseil des Arts   Government
for the Arts   du Canada   of Alberta ■

Contents

Dedicated to

FORREST CURWIN NICKERSON
(1929–1988)

Founder of the Canadian Cultural Society of the Deaf Inc.

Foreword

DEAF CANADIANS have long recognized a need for the documentation of our signs. In 1982, we rolled up our sleeves and got to work on this monumental task. Today we are proud to share this accomplishment with you.

Our original objective was to provide a comprehensive Canadian reference for students of ASL, most of whom are hearing, but as the project went on, it became more and more important to our writers that we meet the needs of Deaf students of English as well. We must stress, however, that no dictionary can replace face-to-face interaction when learning a language, particularly one such as ASL which is entirely visual in form. While some comments on the grammatical and syntactic structures of ASL appear incidentally throughout *The Canadian Dictionary of ASL*, fluency in the language can only be achieved through association with Deaf people.

Great care has been taken to preserve the sign vocabulary of our language and to respect regional variations across Canada. Material for this extensive work has been drawn from many sources and includes input from a vast number of members of Canada's Deaf Community.

The Canadian Cultural Society of the Deaf wishes to express its sincere gratitude to all who have contributed in either large or small ways to the development and completion of this book. Our language is a very cherished part of our identity as Deaf Canadians and we are touched by the interest you have shown in us through your support of this project.

CHARMAINE LETOURNEAU, C.M.
Past President
Canadian Cultural Society of the Deaf

Preface

U NIVERSALLY, the sign language used by Deaf people, although varied, is unique because it has its own history, cultural aspects, vocabulary and lexicology suited to its particular geographic region. *The Canadian Dictionary of ASL* provides a fundamental description of American Sign Language (ASL), as it was combined with existing Canadian signs to evolve into what has become the preferred sign language used by the majority of Deaf Canadians today.

The origins of ASL can be traced back to nineteenth-century France. In 1816, Laurent Clerc, a Deaf educator, sailed to Hartford, Connecticut, where he helped to establish the very first American school for the Deaf. His French Sign Language, flavoured by the homemade signs already in use by his new American Deaf students, gradually developed into what is now known as American Sign Language and used widely throughout North America.

Just as the sign lexicon in the United States varies slightly from region to region, there are variations across Canada, most notably in the Atlantic provinces, where a British influence is evident. In the Maritimes, for example, one of the signs for **father** is identical to that found in British Sign Language (BSL) and derived from the British two-handed fingerspelled **F**. A study of the regional differences in Canada was undertaken and the results have been incorporated in this *Dictionary*. Regions for which variations have been systematically recorded are categorized as PACIFIC, PRAIRIE, ONTARIO and ATLANTIC.

The *Dictionary* pays special attention to subjects of particular interest to Deaf Canadians—bilingual and bicultural education, residential schools, ice hockey and other winter sports, parliamentary government, weather and geographic features, historical events and geographic place names.

This *Dictionary* also reflects a multicultural society that is the culmination of nearly two hundred years of changing attitudes and lifestyles among Canadians in general, and Deaf Canadians in particular. It represents the codification of common understanding among all Deaf communities where ASL is used, from coast to coast across the nation. This is the living, evolving and vibrant sign language that shows us where Deaf Canadians have been, where they are now, and where they are likely to go next. As such, *The Canadian Dictionary of ASL* is the most reliable and authoritative guide to ASL in Canada today. The editors have attempted to follow Canadian/British spelling and usage, although occasionally, because ASL has its origins in the U.S.A., it was more appropriate to use American references. No attempt was made to incorporate Quebec Sign Language—Langue Signes des Quebecois (LSQ)—into this work.

Technically, the project began with a dream in 1980, when several Canadians attended the National Association of the Deaf's 100th Anniversary celebration in Cincinnati, Ohio. They were so inspired by what they had seen that they began discussing the notion of creating a distinctly Canadian sign language dictionary, because no such body of work had ever existed or been published. The initial meeting was held in Ottawa in December, 1982, under the aegis of the Canadian Coordinating Council on Deafness, but the project was later taken over by the Canadian Cultural Society of the Deaf (CCSD).

Initially, four regional consultants were appointed to plan and begin the work:

Pacific Region	*Prairie Region*
MAUREEN DONALD	CAROLE SUE BAILEY
Central Region	*Atlantic Region*
(Ontario and Quebec)	MYLES MURPHY
ROBYN SANDFORD	DAVID STILL

Their mandate was to collect material and compile a compendium of simple and commonly used ASL signs used by Deaf Canadians, which were to be documented with illustrations and written text. As ideas and suggestions were exchanged, the project began to expand and take on decidedly different proportions. Eventually, regional boards were established as follows:

Pacific Region:	*Prairie Region:*
MAUREEN DONALD *(chair)*	CAROLE SUE BAILEY *(chair)*
LAWRENCE GRANT	KATHY DOLBY
VINCENT KENNEDY	JANE HOOEY
DENNIS MILTON	ROGER SCHMID
DOTTIE RUNDLES	CHRISTINE SPINK-MITCHELL
ELLEN HUGHES	DENNIS ZIMMER
Central Region:	*Atlantic Region:*
ROBYN SANDFORD *(chair)*	MYLES MURPHY *(chair)*
MAUREEN BASKERVILLE	JOHN BARTON
LOUISE FORD	ELIZABETH DOULL
ALMA JOHNSON	KEIR McLEAN
JIM McDERMOTT	DAVID STILL
JOANNE STUMP	

Each regional board was entrusted to research, collect, check, verify and document the signs being used in its specific area. The boards met locally and also, from time to time, they conferred with the regional consultants. In due course, headquarters for the *Dictionary* project were established at the national CCSD office in Edmonton, Alberta, and Carole Sue Bailey was appointed chairperson. From its humble beginnings, the project continued to expand and develop into a significantly more complex undertaking than was originally envisioned. The consultants and boards decided to include such information as parts of speech, definitions, sample sentences and detailed descriptions of how the signs are produced.

In 1990, after the regional research and documentation were completed, a project team settled into a basement office at CCSD headquarters to begin the monumental task of sorting, organizing and refining the material. Hilda Campbell was asked to provide the written text for each entry selected and described by Carole Sue Bailey and Angela Stratiy. A year later, Kathy Dolby joined the team as writer/editor.

Originally, Copp-Clark Pitman Publishing Ltd., of Mississauga, Ontario, contracted to publish the work and provide the necessary artwork. It became a time-consuming and arduous task to exchange drawings and videotapes with their artist by courier and fax in order to edit and ensure accuracy in his illustrations. Eventually, a restructuring of the company led to their phasing out the reference department, and Copp-Clark Pitman withdrew from the project.

With so much time and work already invested in the *Dictionary*, a period of anxiety and doubt followed while CCSD sought another publisher. Happily, a contract was finally entered into with The University of Alberta Press in Edmonton. This had a very positive effect because distance between the project team and the publisher was no longer a problem, and communication became much easier. Consultation between the artists and the editors was also simplified. In the last few years, Carole Sue Bailey and Kathy Dolby put their personal lives aside in order to complete the enormous task of coordinating the text with the artwork, editing and re-editing the material and finally bringing the project to fruition.

One of the most unique features of *The Canadian Dictionary of ASL* is the labelling of the ASL handshapes used in the sign descriptions of the text. This was not a simple task, as new hand configurations cropped up again and again while the work progressed. These labels will enable dictionary users to produce the signs accurately and to have a better understanding of the etymology of ASL as a language. Potential users of the *Dictionary* will include the members of the Deaf Community, and a large proportion of Canada's hearing population—parents and families of Deaf children, professionals working with the Deaf, schools and libraries, professional interpreters and interpreter-training programs, ASL as a second-language programs, teacher-training programs, linguists, researchers and interested individuals from the general public.

With the publication of this *Dictionary*, The University of Alberta Press not only adds another prestigious work to its highly respected range of reference titles; it also becomes an unprecedented pioneer in a unique genre by presenting the first ASL dictionary in Canada.

Acknowledgements

THE CANADIAN CULTURAL SOCIETY OF THE DEAF would like to express its sincere appreciation and thanks to the following individuals and groups for their varied and extensive contributions to our work.

Regional Consultants

The Pacific Regional Board: Maureen Donald, *Chair*, Lawrence Grant, Vincent Kennedy, Dennis Milton, Dottie Rundles, and Ellen Hughes.

The Prairie Regional Board: Carole Sue Bailey, *Chair*, Kathy Dolby, Jane Hooey, Roger Schmid, Christine Spink-Mitchell, and Dennis Zimmer.

The Central Regional Board: Robyn Sandford, *Chair,* Maureen Baskerville, Louise Ford, Alana Johnston, Jim McDermott, and Joanne Stump.

The Atlantic Regional Board: Myles Murphy, *Chair,* John Barton, Elizabeth Doull, Keir McLean, and David Still.

Schools, Colleges, Businesses, Organizations, and Agencies:
Alberta Learning, Alberta School for the Deaf, Bell Canada Communications, Carleton United Church Senior Citizens Place (Saint John, NB), Copp Clark Pitman Publishing Ltd., Deaf Centre Manitoba (Winnipeg), Edmonton Public Schools, Ernest C. Drury School for the Deaf (Milton), Ford Motor Company of Canada, Limited, Grant MacEwan College (Edmonton), Jericho Hill School for the Deaf (Vancouver), Joseph E. Seagram & Sons, Limited, Lafarge Canada Inc., McCain Foods Limited, Media Masters, Mitsubishi Electric Sales Canada Inc., Murphy Oil Company Limited, Mutual Life of Canada, Newfoundland Co-ordinating Council on Deafness, Ontario Cultural Society of the Deaf, Ontario Ministry of Education, PanCanadian Petroleum Limited, Petro-Canada, Quaker Oats Company of Canada Limited, Reader's Digest Foundation of Canada, Saint John Association of the Deaf, Secretary of State, Silent Voice, Society of Deaf/Hard of Hearing Nova Scotians, Sony of Canada Ltd., Sterling Marking Products Inc., Talisman Energy Inc., Vancouver Community College and XentelDM Incorporated.

Individuals Who Contributed in a Variety of Ways:
Clark Archibald, Linda Archibald, Kyle Badree, Shirley Barter, Douglas
Bortoletto, Bob Borys, Wayne Bottlinger, Harvey Bradley, Olga Braem, Avonne
Brooker, John Buckley, Tony Cashin, Vincent Chauvet, Robert Chorniak, Janet
Churchill, Lloyd Clark, Linda Cundy, Brian Dwyer, Aastrid Evensen-Flanjak,
Kirk Ferguson, Marj Filion, Eugene Frost, Mary Fuller, Irene Goulet, Maglorie
Goulet, Marilyn Grant, Cora Gray, Lenora Hare, Mary Hargreaves, Stephen
Harrison, Jean Hetherington, Tracy Hetman, Calvin Holst, Edna Johnston,
David Kerr, Barbara LeDrew, Ron Leduc, Gail Lidkea, Dr. David Mason, Ian
McAllister, Jan McCarthy, Colleen McLaughlin, Joseph McLaughlin, Danny
Murdoch, Dr. Philip Ngai, Margaret Ann Nixon, Helen Pizzacalla, Marg
Pullishy, Alec Ratai, Sandra Reid, Marthe-Yvonne Rikem, Jo-Anne Robinson,
Louise Skirving, Bill Snow, Margaret Sobie, Barbara Staflund, Christine Steele,
David A. Stewart, Lynda Thomas, Frank Wade, Dean Walker, Rick Webster,
Joan Westland, Marjorie Winsor, Vincent Wong, and Kay Zenovitch.

Project Sponsors:
Alberta School for the Deaf and the former Canadian Coordinating Council on
Deafness. Special thanks to the many people from across Canada whose
generous donations have made this project possible. Unfortunately space does
not permit us to include everyone's name.

Editorial, Illustration, Design and Layout:
We also want to acknowledge the work of editors Carole Sue Bailey, Hilda
Campbell, and Kathy Dolby; ASL consultant Angela Stratiy; our administra-
tive secretary, Caroline Anne Fritz, and her assistant, Shirley Handley; Helen
Pizzacalla, President of the Canadian Cultural Society of the Deaf; and our
illustrators, David James, Allan Moon, Valentino Sanna, Shane Chen, and
Nabeal Mansour and his staff at Media Masters, whose collective willingness
and enthusiasm helped to make our dream become a reality. We owe each
and all of them an enormous debt of gratitude. Many people at The
University of Alberta Press also have contributed to this project, especially
Alan Brownoff, Laraine Coates, Brian Kurylo, Mary Mahoney-Robson and
Chris Wangler. Thanks also to Janine Andrews, Linda Cameron, Cathie
Crooks, Glenn Rollans, and Leslie Vermeer at the Press and to the graphic
artists who did the layout, Denise Ahlefeldt, Carol Dragich, Ruth Linka, and
Matthias Reinicke.

Special thanks to Charmaine Letourneau, Past President of the Canadian
Cultural Society of the Deaf, without whose drive and determination, this
monumental project might never have been completed.

An Academic Perspective

THE CANADIAN DICTIONARY OF ASL sets a new standard as being much more than a traditional lexicography of ASL. Rather than assigning ASL signs to arbitrarily chosen English words, the authors make every effort to maintain semantic integrity with each translation. One English word may be conveyed in ASL by one sign or more than one sign. By the same token, one ASL sign may be expressed by one or more English words.

This *Dictionary* preserves ASL and English as distinct languages while functioning as an effective bridge between the two. It serves as an excellent bilingual resource for Deaf children learning English and for anyone interested in learning ASL as a second language. The greatest dividend that I foresee from *The Canadian Dictionary of ASL* is that it will bring hearing and culturally Deaf Canadians one step closer together, and what could be more important than that?

DAVID G. MASON, PH.D.
York University
North York, Ontario

About Using ASL

As MODERN SOCIETY becomes increasingly reliant on information presented in a visual and dynamic format, there has never been a better time for a visual language like ASL to flourish. For most people though, their experience with language has been essentially oral/aural. The majority of people have learned to express themselves by producing vocal sounds and to understand others by interpreting the vocal sounds that they produce.

Entering the community of ASL users is a delightfully different linguistic experience, one that requires a completely new way of thinking about communicating. Newcomers to the visual world of ASL have much to learn. The very best way to familiarize oneself with the language is to spend time with those who regularly use it. The *Canadian Dictionary of ASL* offers an extensive vocabulary of ASL signs for reference, but no dictionary can present the essential nuances that contribute to effective everyday ASL conversation.

ASL has its own unique syntactic structures and grammatical features. To attempt to incorporate an ASL sign into an English sentence would only create confusion. The signs illustrated represent concepts as opposed to English words, and as such, may translate into English words, but may just as often translate into phrases or clauses, or even entire sentences. Users of this *Dictionary* should understand that ASL is a different language than English. In some instances, a literal translation of the ASL sign into English is included in the sign description to illustrate how different the grammatical construction of ASL is.

Certain English terms cannot be found in this *Dictionary* because they are not accorded single-sign-ASL-equivalents. By the same token, certain ASL signs are not accorded single-word-English-equivalents and thus cannot be found in a standard English language dictionary.

The face is the focal point in ASL. The signee* typically takes note of peripheral information provided by the signer's hands and general posture, but the thrust of the message is conveyed by the face. An amazing amount of information can be seen in the eyes, eyebrows and mouth. Punctuation, for example, is evident on the face. Just the raising of the eyebrows can signal a question.

Many signs are accompanied by meaningful positioning of the lips, teeth and/or tongue. When the signer squares his lips as if to produce the syllable 'CHA', the signee will immediately understand that the signer is referring to something very large.

Information can even be registered on the nose. A twitching nose indicates quiet agreement or mutual understanding. Because there is a wealth of information on the face, the signee's eyes should be focused on the signer's face rather than on the hands.

Some signs are iconic in that they actually look like the object or action they represent. Some have evolved from natural gestures; however, for many signs, the hand formation and movement bear no resemblance to the concept being represented. Other concepts are conveyed through the manual spelling (fingerspelling) of the English word.

Communicating in ASL should be a comfortable experience. A novice may find the ASL handshapes somewhat awkward to produce, but with practice, the process should begin to feel more natural. If not, chances are that the production is incorrect. In ASL, awkward hand configurations are virtually nonexistent.

The signing space is also designed with comfort in mind. Most signs are conveniently produced in front of the chest or around the face. Very seldom are signs produced below the waist or above the head.

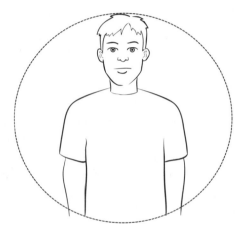

ASL has become an increasingly popular language of study for Canadians of all ages in all walks of life. With the publication of *The Canadian Dictionary of ASL* we have an ASL reference book which is distinctly Canadian, including regional sign variations currently in use from the Atlantic Provinces to Pacific Region. This *Dictionary* is not just a compendium of signs. It also provides valuable information about the syntax and distinctive features of ASL, so that users can gain a greater understanding of the language.

*signee = the person who is watching the signer (the equivalent of a 'listener' in a spoken language).

Sample Entries

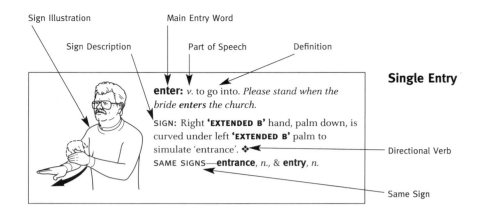

Single Entry

enter: *v.* to go into. *Please stand when the bride enters the church.*

SIGN: Right **'EXTENDED B'** hand, palm down, is curved under left **'EXTENDED B'** palm to simulate 'entrance'. ❖

SAME SIGNS—**entrance**, *n.,* & **entry**, *n.*

— Directional Verb

— Same Sign

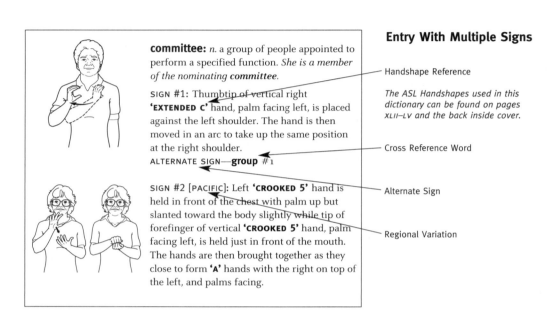

Entry With Multiple Signs

committee: *n.* a group of people appointed to perform a specified function. *She is a member of the nominating committee.*

SIGN #1: Thumbtip of vertical right **'EXTENDED C'** hand, palm facing left, is placed against the left shoulder. The hand is then moved in an arc to take up the same position at the right shoulder.

ALTERNATE SIGN—**group** #1

SIGN #2 [PACIFIC]: Left **'CROOKED 5'** hand is held in front of the chest with palm up but slanted toward the body slightly while tip of forefinger of vertical **'CROOKED 5'** hand, palm facing left, is held just in front of the mouth. The hands are then brought together as they close to form **'A'** hands with the right on top of the left, and palms facing.

— Handshape Reference

The ASL Handshapes used in this dictionary can be found on pages XLII–LV and the back inside cover.

— Cross Reference Word

— Alternate Sign

— Regional Variation

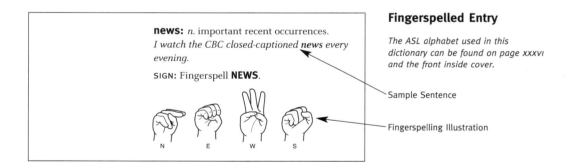

Fingerspelled Entry

news: *n.* important recent occurrences. *I watch the CBC closed-captioned news every evening.*

SIGN: Fingerspell **NEWS**.

The ASL alphabet used in this dictionary can be found on page XXXVI and the front inside cover.

— Sample Sentence

— Fingerspelling Illustration

Entry Without an Illustration

toward: *prep.* in the direction of. *The child is walking toward the water.*

NOTE—**Toward** is generally not accorded a sign of its own but is incorporated in the sign for the verb. The sample sentence would be signed: *CHILD GO-TOWARD WATER.*

Not all signs have a specific sign illustration or fingerspelling. A note explains further.

— ASL Translation

For some entries, translation from English to ASL is complex and a further explanation is included.

A Guide to Using This *Dictionary*

THE CANADIAN DICTIONARY OF ASL was designed for users of ASL and for students learning ASL. Containing over 8700 ASL signs, based on American Sign Language, this *Dictionary* is the only one to contain Canadian terms and regional variants throughout. This guide explains how the entries are organized, and tells where to find other special sections in this *Dictionary*.

General Organization

Main Entry

The main entries in this *Dictionary* define in English the sign illustrated. Often, only one sign illustration corresponds to a specific English word or phrase. If an English word has multiple signs, these follow as part of the same entry. If the English word has a different meaning and a different sign, then a new entry with that specific definition follows the first entry.

Each main entry is identified as to its part of speech. It is then defined and used in a sample English sentence. An illustration of the ASL sign is provided, along with a detailed written description of how the sign is formed, i.e., what shape the hands assume and how they move in relation to each other.

Main entries and their parts of speech appear in **boldface** type. In addition, all main entry words that appear as cross-references in the entries are also in **boldface** type. When a word has multiple signs and multiple meanings, the signs are numbered SIGN #1, SIGN #2, for easy cross-referencing. The English word(s) that equate with the ASL sign illustrated also appear in *italics boldface* type within the sample English sentences.

This *Dictionary* does not supply pronunciation, syllabication, nor inflected forms of the main entry words. Rather, the focus is on English equivalents of the concepts conveyed in the signs. Users can consult an English language dictionary for this information.

While main entries in some sign language dictionaries are organized according to handshapes that characterize the signed language, this *Dictionary* is listed in English alphabetical order, with which the intended audience, specifically Canadians users of ASL, is familiar with. Idiomatic expressions or phrases are listed according to the main word in the phrase. For example, **close (a book)** is listed under C; **(in) order** is listed under O; **(make a) pig of oneself** is listed under P. Abbreviations or acronyms are listed letter-by-letter alphabetically. For example, the order would be **mow, Mr., Mrs., Ms.** [*or* **Ms**], **much; razor, RCMP, reach**.

In general, British/Canadian spelling is used for the main entry word and alternate (American) spelling is indicated in square brackets. For example, **colour** [*also spelled* **color**] is how the main entry would appear in the *Dictionary*.

In the case of a main entry word which can function as either a verb or a noun but the same sign is used for both, this *Dictionary* classifies it under the usage most common to the Deaf. For example, **comb**, *v.*, and **comb**, *n.*, only the verb usage is listed.

Where a main entry word has a variety of meanings and signs, all are entered separately with their appropriate part-of-speech classifications.

Parts of Speech

A part-of-speech label precedes the definition for each main entry word. In some instances, the main entry is longer than just one word. This is because the ASL concept illustrated equates to a phrase in English. The part of speech is then assigned to the phrase rather than just one word. For example, **(take) advantage of**, *v.*, is specified as a verb even though the term is listed in the A's after **advantage**, *n.*

The verb **to be** and its various English forms (am, were, been, etc.) do not appear because they have no ASL equivalents.

Standard parts of speech are indicated by abbreviations as follows:

adj.	adjective
adv.	adverb
conj.	conjunction
inter.	interjection
n.	noun
prep.	preposition
pron.	pronoun
s.s.	sentence substitute
v.	verb
sing.	singular
pl.	plural
phr.	phrase

The label 'sentence substitute' (abbreviated *s.s.*) comprises main entry words such as **amen, okay, (I will) keep it for myself**, etc., which can stand alone as meaningful concepts.

Significant Grammatical Characteristics

The standard English articles (a, an, the) do not exist in ASL. Main entry words that many standard English dictionaries classify as *determiners* are herein labelled according to the function they perform in the given sentence. For example, **more than** is classified as an adverb in the sample sentence *No building in this area can be* **more than** *ten stories high.*

Differences between active and passive voice usages are explained in parentheses where applicable.

aggravated: *v.* provoked or aroused to anger. *He was **aggravated** by the woman's insulting remarks.*

SIGN: Fingertips of right **'CLAWED OPEN EXTENDED A'** hand, palm facing the body, are scraped upward sharply against the chest. Facial expression must clearly convey 'aggravation'. (This sign is used only in a passive voice situation or as an adjective to describe someone's feelings. It would ***not*** be possible to use this sign in an active voice situation: *The woman's insulting remarks **aggravated** him.*)

Verbs including an adverbial component are often repeated in an emphatic, almost rhythmic manner. For example, the concept of 'to work hard over a long period of time', is conveyed using the basic sign for **work**, but this sign is repeated in a circular motion along with a determined facial expression to indicate intensity.

Directional verbs, whose sign descriptions are followed by the symbol ❖, move in different directions depending upon the relative positions of the people represented in the context. For example, the sign illustration and description for **give** indicates a movement from the signer forward.

give: *v.* to place in the possession of another. *I will **give** you some money.*

SIGN #1: Horizontal right **'CONTRACTED B'** hand is held with palm facing leftward/upward and fingers pointing left. The hand then moves forward in a slight arc formation as if giving something to someone. (Handshapes for this sign vary according to the size and shape of the object being given; however, the basic movement remains the same.) ❖

However, the direction of the movement changes according to who is giving what to whom. Thus, the movement may be directed toward the signer from any given position, away from the signer in any given direction, or from some point beyond the signer to any other given point.

Sometimes main entry verbs and their noun equivalents (although they are different words) can be signed in the same way except for movement.

able: *adj.* capable of; having skill. *Wayne Gretzky was **able** to break many National Hockey League records.*

SIGN: **'A'** hands, palms down, are held slightly apart, and are then firmly pushed downward. SAME SIGN—**ability**, *n.*, but the motion is repeated.

In ASL, plurals are generally formed by using numbers or words that indicate quantity, e.g., 'several', followed by the sign for the singular noun. Exceptions do exist; however, space does not permit us to expand further on the subject of plurality in this publication. For plural nouns, which are formed differently than their singular counterparts, separate entries do appear, as in the case of **adult** and **adults**.

adult: *n.* a person who has attained the age of legal majority. *An **adult** has certain rights and responsibilities.*

SIGN: Vertical right **'BENT EXTENDED B'** hand, palm facing left, is held just above shoulder at chin level and moved up level with top of head. (When referring to animals rather than people, **ADULT** is fingerspelled.)

adults: *n.* people who have attained the age of legal majority. *Adults have certain rights and responsibilities.*

SIGN: Vertical **'BENT EXTENDED B'** hands, palms facing each other, are held above eye level, and rotated alternately away from the body.

Certain comparative adjectives are translated into ASL by using the standard sign for the adjective preceded by the sign for **worse**. Facial expression is a key factor in conveying degree. For example, the literal ASL translation for **prettier** is *WORSE PRETTY*, although this may strike English speakers as quite odd.

Similarly, certain aspects of English tend to elude those for whom English is a second language (ESL users). In such cases, explanatory notes are provided.

too: *adv.* excessively; extremely; very. *I have too much work to do.*

NOTE—**Too** in this context is generally not accorded a sign of its own but is incorporated in the sign for the adjective it modifies. In the sample sentence, **much**, *adj.*, is signed relatively slowly using a larger signing space than usual for emphasis. Alternatively, **TOO** may be fingerspelled slowly and emphatically in this context. (ESL USERS: Although **too** may appear to be a positive word, in fact it is not. It means 'more than should be'. If you say that someone was 'too slow', you would mean that you think he should be faster. If you say that someone is 'too talkative', you would prefer that he did not talk so much. If you wish to use a superlative which is positive, use **so** or **very**. Saying that someone is 'so pretty' or 'very pretty' would be a positive comment whereas saying that someone is 'too pretty' implies that you think they should be less pretty.)

Many English adverbs are not included in this *Dictionary* since the adverbial forms of most English words are conveyed through facial expression in conjunction with the sign they modify. To 'drive carefully,' for example, is expressed using the sign for **drive**, along with an intense facial expression and alert posture, while to 'drive carelessly' is expressed using the sign for **drive**, accompanied by a devil-may-care facial expression and laid-back posture. No separate sign is necessary for the adverbs 'carefully' or 'carelessly.'

Explanatory information is generally given for prepositions.

behind: *prep.* in or to the rear of. *He put his old **trophy** behind the new one.*

SIGN #1: Horizontal **'EXTENDED A'** hands are held together with palms facing each other. Right hand is then moved back in a slight outward arc so that it is directly behind the left hand. (Use of this sign is rare as the concept **behind** is usually conveyed by using representative handshapes and positioning the right hand directly behind the left. To show that one car is behind another, horizontal **'3'** hands are held right behind left with extended fingers pointing forward and right palm facing left while left palm faces right. The horizontal **'3'** hand is used to mean 'vehicle' after the type of vehicle has already been specified. The vertical **'ONE'** hand is used to refer to a person.)

Definitions

Each main entry has an English definition to represent the concept of the sign that is illustrated. In many cases, providing an exact English equivalent for the ASL concept is problematic but this *Dictionary* makes every effort to maintain ASL integrity insofar as possible. Where a main entry word has multiple definitions and corresponding signs, each is entered separately. However, regardless of the sign illustrated, ASL and English syntax are so very different that definitions which apply in both languages are often difficult to develop.

Deaf: *adj.* partially or totally unable to hear. *Deaf people communicate as effectively in ASL as hearing people do in spoken English.*

SIGN: Vertical right **'ONE'** hand is held with tip of forefinger just in front of the right ear. The hand is then lowered so that the tip of the forefinger touches the right side of the mouth. Alternatively, this sign may progress from the mouth to the ear. See also **profoundly Deaf**.

Usage in Sample Sentences

Every main entry definition is followed by a sample sentence. The sentences provided strictly reflect the concepts of the signs illustrated. Keep in mind that there might be numerous other English usages which would be inappropriate for a particular sign. For example,

face: *n.* the front of the head from forehead to lower jaw. *She has a pretty face.*

SIGN #1: Forefinger of right **'ONE'** hand, palm toward the face, is used to outline the face in a counter-clockwise direction (from the signer's perspective).

The sign description for **face** cannot be applied to the following usages:

*The images of several presidents are carved on the **face** of Mount Rushmore.*
*No greater risk to the environment exists on the **face** of the earth.*

The sample sentences in this *Dictionary* cannot generally be signed as written because ASL word order differs greatly from that of English. In certain instances, the ASL sign order is provided in the sign description. When this occurs, the literal translation into ASL appears in capital letters.

tear-jerker: *n.* a book, movie or drama that is excessively sentimental. *Last night we watched a movie that was a real tear-jerker.*

SIGN: Vertical **'X'** hands, palms forward, simultaneously stroke downward along the cheeks, then curve forward. Movement is repeated a few times. A sad facial expression must accompany this sign. (The ASL sentence is syntactically different than the English one. In ASL: *LAST NIGHT MOVIE ME **CRY CRY CRY**.*)

Sometimes one sign is used to translate more than one English word. In such cases, the ASL concept is illustrated in boldface type.

deficient: *adj.* having a lack or shortage of. *The doctor told her she was* **deficient** *in calcium.*

SIGN: Thumb of right **'EXTENDED A'** hand, palm facing left, is placed under the chin and is flicked forward firmly. Next, horizontal left **'S'** hand is held in a fixed position with palm facing right. Horizontal right **'EXTENDED B'** hand is held palm down with fingers pointing forward/leftward and is brushed forward/rightward a couple of times across the top of the left hand. (ASL CONCEPT—**not - enough**.)

Sign Illustrations

A three-dimensional language in motion, ASL is difficult to capture and represent adequately on paper. The sign illustrations provided are just 'single captures' of fluid signs, accompanied by sign descriptions, which are intended to clarify and/or reinforce understanding. For more complex signs, multiple drawings are provided. The direction, size and intensity of movement is shown by arrows. A zigzag in the arrow means that the movement is repeated. The initial position of a sign is shown by a dotted line while the final position is represented by a solid line.

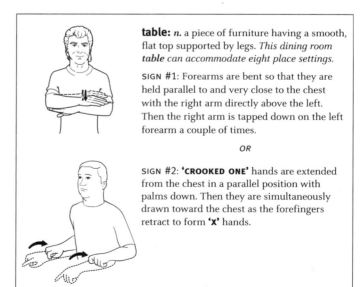

table: *n.* a piece of furniture having a smooth, flat top supported by legs. *This dining room table can accommodate eight place settings.*

SIGN #1: Forearms are bent so that they are held parallel to and very close to the chest with the right arm directly above the left. Then the right arm is tapped down on the left forearm a couple of times.

OR

SIGN #2: **'CROOKED ONE'** hands are extended from the chest in a parallel position with palms down. Then they are simultaneously drawn toward the chest as the forefingers retract to form **'X'** hands.

Note that certain words are not accompanied by illustrations. This is usually because the concept is already incorporated in another sign. This is frequently true of prepositions, which are generally understood from the verb or from the positioning of a noun in the signing space. In such cases, explanatory notes are provided to help the reader understand how the concept is conveyed.

---

toward: *prep.* in the direction of. *The child is walking **toward** the water.*

NOTE—**Toward** is generally not accorded a sign of its own but is incorporated in the sign for the verb. The sample sentence would be signed: *CHILD GO-**TOWARD** WATER.*

Sign Descriptions

A detailed description of how to produce each sign is given. This has been done with the right-handed signer in mind. Signs, which require only one hand, are generally made with the right hand. For many signs, which necessitate two hands, the left hand is held in a fixed position and serves as a base, around which the right hand moves. For left-handed signers, the hands are simply interchanged, the right hand becoming the 'base' hand while the left hand moves.

ASL HANDSHAPES that are commonly used have been given names and are illustrated in charts on pp. XLII–LV and on the back inside cover of the *Dictionary*. In the sign description, the handshapes appear in boldface type for easy reference.

Certain words are not signed but are fingerspelled. FINGERSPELLING can be found on p. XXXVI and on the front inside cover of the *Dictionary*.

---

joke: *n.* a funny anecdote or something that is done for fun. *He always has a **joke** to tell.*

SIGN #1: Fingerspell **JOKE**.

Words for which sign illustrations are given may instead be fingerspelled for emphasis.

Facial expression is a very important component of any sign. Even body posture comes into play in conveying many concepts in ASL. In fact, many signs are accompanied by corresponding lip patterns.

stink: *n.* a strong, foul smell. *If it is threatened, a skunk will create a terrible **stink**.*

SIGN #1: Right **'5'** hand is held with palm facing leftward/downward and thumbtip touching or close to the tip of the nose. The hand is then firmly thrust a short distance forward at a slight downward angle. Meanwhile, a grimace appears on the signer's face and the lips appear to be articulating the syllable 'PO'.

For some entries, tips are provided for English as a Second Language (ESL) users.

let: *v.* to allow; give permission to. *The doctor will not **let** her leave the hospital until Thursday.* (ESL USERS: Although **allow**, *v.,* and **permit**, *v.,* are often followed by the word **to**, **let**, *v., may **not** be followed by **to**; e.g., Allow me to help you. Permit me to help you. Let me help you.*)

SIGN: Horizontal **'EXTENDED B'** hands are held with palms facing and fingers pointing forward. The hands are then swept upward simultaneously from the wrists so that the fingers point upward.
ALTERNATE SIGN—**permit** #1

Frequent reminders that 'signs vary' appear following the sign descriptions. This is because context is critical when selecting signs. The English word 'mean' for example, has a variety of meanings, depending on the context, and each context requires a different ASL sign. Since context possibilities are infinite, it was not feasible to attempt to include ASL sign equivalents for all possible connotations of every English word.

Regional Variation

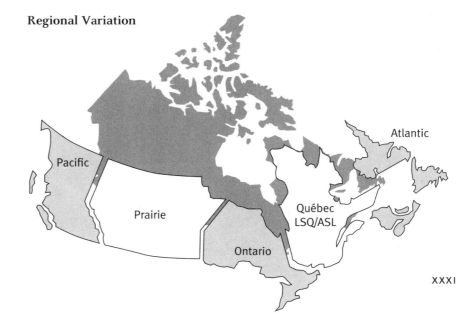

Regional variations are listed under each main entry word to which they apply. For example, the sign description for the main entry word **about** is followed by Atlantic and Ontario sign descriptions.

about: *prep.* in reference to; concerning. *This book is **about** seventeenth century England.*

SIGN #1: Left **'BENT ONE'** hand, palm facing right and forefinger pointing right, remains fixed while forefinger of right **'BENT ONE'** hand circles the left forefinger in a clockwise direction.

SIGN #2 [ATLANTIC]: Horizontal **'MODIFIED G'** hands, left palm facing rightward/backward, and right palm facing leftward/forward, are held so that the thumb and forefinger of the right are between those of the left. Then they are drawn slightly apart as they both change to **'CLOSED MODIFIED G'** hands. Motion is repeated.

SIGN #3 [ONTARIO]: Edge of right **'EXTENDED B'** hand, palm facing left, is brought down, smartly striking the upturned palm of the left **'EXTENDED B'** hand. Motion is repeated.

The regional sign variations illustrated in this *Dictionary* are exclusively Canadian, although ASL vocabulary varies throughout the United States, as well. Signs identified as ATLANTIC, for example, do not appear in the ASL used by New Englanders.

Cross-References

The words SAME SIGN appear after the sign description when another word, which is similar in meaning, is represented by the same sign.

appreciate: *v.* to be grateful for. *I appreciate the help you gave me.*

SIGN #1: Horizontal right **'EXTENDED B'** hand, palm on the chest, is moved in a circular motion, which appears to onlookers to be clockwise.

SAME SIGN—**appreciation**, *n.*

Cross-references appear throughout this *Dictionary*, but only when a given sign represents synonymous concepts. For example, although the same sign might be used for the words democracy and defence, no cross-reference is given due to the vast conceptual difference between the two English terms.

The words ALTERNATE SIGN appear after some sign descriptions.

plenty: *n.* a large number, amount or quantity. *The hostess had **plenty** of food for all the guests.*

SIGN: Horizontal left **'S'** hand, palm facing right, is covered with palm of right **'EXTENDED B'** hand. Then the right hand is brushed firmly forward and slightly to the right. The cheeks are puffed out.

SAME SIGN—**plentiful**, *adj.*

ALTERNATE SIGN—**ample** #1

ALTERNATE SIGNS are provided to give the signer a more varied sign vocabulary where possible. In the context shown here, the alternate sign is synonymous with the sign illustrated, but this would not be true in all contexts.

Other Significant Features of the *Dictionary*

The word 'Deaf' is capitalized throughout this *Dictionary* in recognition of a distinctive group of people, without whom the ASL that appears on the pages of this book would never have evolved. Whether a Deaf individual communicates through ASL or not, s/he is no less Deaf, however, just as a Canadian is Canadian, no matter what his/her cultural values or language of choice. The noun 'deafness' is not capitalized as it connotes a condition rather than an identity.

Words that denote individuals engaged in specific activities or occupations are sometimes expressed using a 'root sign' such as that for **law** followed by an ASL suffix identified in the sign description as an 'Agent Ending'.

law: *n.* an enforceable rule or set of rules established by authority. *The law clearly states that seatbelts must be worn.*

SIGN: Vertical left **'EXTENDED B'** hand is held in a fixed position with palm facing right. Right **'L'** hand, palm facing left, is placed against the fingers of the left hand and then lowered to the heel of the left hand. **LAW** may be finger-spelled for emphasis.

SAME SIGN—**lawyer**, *n.*, and may be followed by the Agent Ending (see p. LIV).

The 'Agent Ending' is formed by lowering the hands from the initial signing position with palms facing each other and fingers pointing forward/upward. Sometimes this is a very noticeable movement but alternatively, it can be a short, subtle movement. An illustration for the 'Agent Ending' can be found in the handshape chart on p. LIV.

Many words beginning with the prefixes **il-**, **im-**, and **in-** do not appear in this *Dictionary* as they simply mean and are signed either **'can't'** or **'not' + root word**.

Many words beginning with the prefix **un-**, meaning **not**, do not appear in this *Dictionary* as they are simply conveyed using the sign for **not** followed by the sign for the root word.

Many signs which exclusively denote 'femaleness' are produced on or near the lower part of the face, whereas signs which exclusively denote 'maleness' are formed on or near the upper part of the face or head.

niece: *n.* a daughter of one's sister or brother. *I have four nephews but only one niece.*

SIGN: Fingertips of right vertical **'BENT U'** hand point leftward and are held close to lower right cheek. The hand then wobbles slightly from the wrist.

nephew: *n.* son of one's brother or sister. *My nephew and my son are the same age.*

SIGN: Fingertips of right vertical **'BENT U'** hand point leftward and are held close to right side of forehead. The hand then wobbles slightly from the wrist.

New signers should be aware that the production of a few signs may vary slightly according to whether the signer is male, female or a child. This is generally attributable to the difference in body builds. For example, the sign for **young** is produced by women in the upper chest region but nearer to the rib cage by men.

From time to time, pronominals appear in ASL to portray certain nouns and/or pronouns which are already understood in the context. For example, a vertical forefinger may be substituted for any noun or pronoun signifying a person. A fist is sometimes substituted for the head of a person.

In certain instances, a sign may incorporate a noun, adjective and verb. For example, if you were giving someone a thick stack of papers, you would indicate this with two hands, one quite far above the other, palms facing, fingers pointing forward as the hands move forward. In such a case, it must already be understood that the noun 'stack' refers to 'paper'.

Special Sections

Charts for FINGERSPELLING and the ASL HANDSHAPES used in this *Dictionary* are found on pages xxxvi and xlii. In addition, the information on these charts are repeated at the front and back of the book for easy reference. Users will find these charts crucial in forming the signs from the written descriptions and the sign illustrations.

Separate sections on NUMBERS (p. lvii), PRONOUNS (p. lxiii), TIME CONCEPTS (p. lxix), and GEOGRAPHIC TERMS (p. lxxv), are also found in this *Dictionary*. They are accorded special placement for quick and easy reference, and also because within each grouping, features unique to ASL are clearly evident.

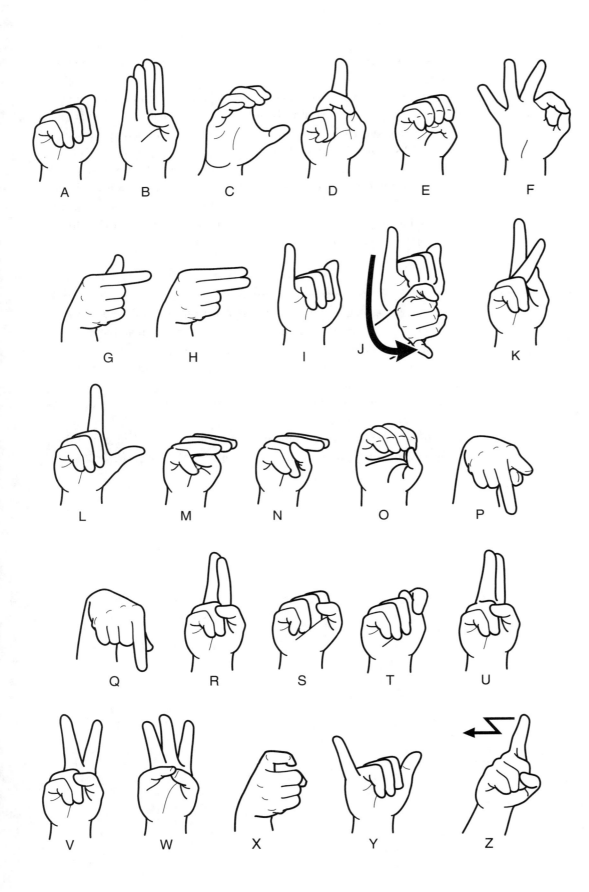

Fingerspelling

MOST ENGLISH WORDS have an ASL sign-equivalent. Others are finger-spelled. In ASL, a one-handed alphabet is used, as opposed to a two-handed alphabet, such as that used in Great Britain. For fingerspelled words, the hand takes on a specific shape to represent each letter of the English alphabet. These handshapes appear also on the inside front cover of the *Dictionary*.

It is very important when fingerspelling that the hand faces the same way as shown in the chart. If the palm is turned toward the body for example, the message will be very difficult to grasp.

The hand should be positioned in front of the right shoulder for right-handers, and in front of the left shoulder for left-handers. The hand and arm essentially remain in a fixed position as the fingers move. Formation of certain letters involves the wrist as well. For example, the wrist must bend for the letter P and rotate for the letter J.

Readers will notice slight variations throughout the *Dictionary* in the formation of the R, T and U. This is because sometimes a relaxed, rather than rigidly formed handshape lends itself better to the particular letter when making the transition to certain other letters to form words.

ASL Handshapes

THE HANDSHAPES USED TO CREATE ASL signs are illustrated in the following seven charts and on the back inside cover of *The Canadian Dictionary of ASL*. These charts may be consulted to assist the user in understanding the written sign descriptions.

In all, 114 handshapes have been identified and named to assist signers with the accurate formation of signs. In the sign descriptions, the handshapes appear in boldface for easy reference. Handshapes generally take the form of fingerspelled letters and numbers with variant combinations. Handshapes are categorized as **'EXTENDED'**, **'BENT'**, **'CLAWED'**, **'COMBINED'**, **'CONTRACTED'**, **'SLANTED'**, **'COVERED'**, **'CROOKED'**, **'FLAT'**, **'INDEX'**, **'MODIFIED'**, **'OFFSET'**, **'OPEN,'** **'CLOSED'** and **'SPREAD'**.

The handshapes, as they appear in the charts, are said to be in the vertical position. When the wrist bends or twists to turn the hand downward or sideways for certain signs, the handshape is described as horizontal.

ASL handshapes may be produced with various palm orientations, depending on the concept being expressed, except in the case of the **'STANDARD BASE'** hand (p. LIV) which is always held palm down with the fingers pointing rightward. In the case of a right-handed signer, the **'STANDARD BASE'** hand is always the left hand. It is important to note that whenever one hand remains in a fixed position while the other moves, it is always the left hand which is fixed and the right hand which moves. Again, this applies specifically to right-handed signers. For left-handed signers, the right hand is held fixed while the left hand moves.

Examples and descriptions of some **'c'** handshape types are shown with sign illustrations so the user can see how the handshapes are used in actual signs.

- In this example, **odd** is signed using the plain **'c'** handshape.

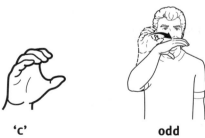

'c'   odd

- When the thumb moves out to the side, the handshape is then said to be **'EXTENDED'**.

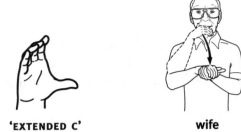

'EXTENDED C'　　　　**wife**

- A **'SPREAD'** handshape is formed when the fingers spread to create space between them.

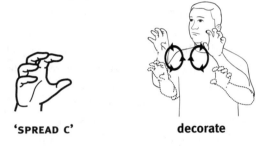

'SPREAD C'　　　　**decorate**

- An **'INDEX'** shape involves only the thumb and forefinger, as opposed to the entire hand.

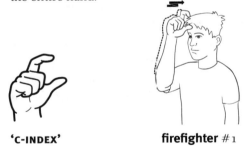

'C-INDEX'　　　　**firefighter** #1

- For a **'CONTRACTED'** handshape, the fingers contract as the descriptor suggests but the fingers involved remain straight.

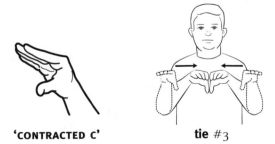

'CONTRACTED C'　　　　**tie** #3

- **'FLAT'** and **'BENT'** hands are compressed to take on a flat appearance.

'FLAT C'   **fall** #5

Other handshapes are also simply made:

- When the fingers are slightly retracted in a relaxed way, the handshape is then referred to as **'CROOKED'**.

- If the fingers are rigidly retracted to resemble the talons on a bird of prey, the handshape is then said to be **'CLAWED'**.

- A tighter handshape is **'CLOSED'** while a less tucked handshape is **'OPEN'**.

- The **'SLANTED'** handshape is slightly askew.

- Putting two shapes together results in a **'COMBINED'** handshape.

- When the fingers overlap slightly, the handshape is **'COVERED'**.

- When the thumb moves just a little to the side of where it normally is for a certain handshape, it is said to be **'OFFSET'**.

- A handshape is **'MODIFIED'** when it has a slightly different look about it.

The handshapes also can be found on a condensed chart on the inside back cover of the *Dictionary* for quick reference.

Handshape	Bent	Clawed	Combined	Contracted/ Slanted	Covered	
A Extended A						
B Extended B	Bent B Bent Extended B			Contracted B		
C Extended C		Clawed Spread C		Contracted C		
D	Bent D Closed Bent D					

Crooked	Flat	Index	Modified	Open/Closed	Spread
		A-Index Closed A-Index		Open A	
Crooked Extended B					
Crooked C	Flat C	C-Index Double C-Index			Spread C Spread Extended C

Handshape	Bent	Clawed	Combined	Contracted/ Slanted	Covered	
E						
F					Covered F	
G						
I	Bent Combined I + One		Combined I + One Combined LY			

Crooked	Flat	Index	Modified/ Offset	Open/Closed	Spread
	Flat F / Flat Open F		Offset F	Open F	
			Modified G / Double Modified G	Closed Modified G / Closed Double Modified G	

Handshape	Bent	Clawed	Combined	Contracted/ Slanted	Covered	
K Extended K						
L	Bent L Bent Thumb L	Clawed L		Contracted L Double Contracted L		
M						
N						

Crooked	Flat	Index	Modified	Open/Closed	Spread
Crooked L					
	Flat M				

Handshape	Bent	Clawed	Combined	Contracted/ Slanted	Covered	
O					Covered O	
R Extended R	Bent R					
S						
T					Covered T	

Crooked	Flat	Index	Modified/ Offset	Open/Closed	Spread
	Flat O	O-Index	Modified O Offset O	Open Spread O Open O-Index	

Handshape	Bent	Clawed	Combined	Contracted/ Slanted	Covered	
U Extended U	Bent U Bent Extended U	Clawed U	Combined U & Y	Contracted U		
V	Bent V Bent Extended V	Clawed V Clawed Extended V		Slanted V		
W		Clawed W				
X						

Crooked	Flat	Index	Modified	Open/Closed	Spread
Crooked U					
Crooked V Crooked Extended V				Closed V	
				Closed W	
				Closed X	

Handshape	Bent	Clawed	Combined	Contracted/ Slanted	Covered	
Y						
One	Bent one					
3		Clawed 3		Contracted 3		
4	Bent 4	Clawed 4		Slanted 4		

Crooked	Flat	Index	Modified	Open/Closed	Spread
			Modified Y		
Crooked one					
Crooked 4					

Handshape	Bent	Clawed	Combined	Contracted/ Slanted	Covered	
5	Bent 5 Bent Midfinger 5	Clawed 5		Contracted 5 Slanted 5		
8					Covered 8	

Standard Base Hand

Agent Ending

Crooked	Flat	Index	Modified	Open/Closed	Spread
Crooked 5 Crooked Slanted 5			Modified 5		
				Open 8	

Numbers

SIGN ILLUSTRATIONS FOR NUMBERS have been consolidated here for quick and easy reference. Numbers can also be found on the inside front cover of the *Dictionary*. Included are the numbers 0 to 30, and multiples of 10 up to 90, as well as 100, 1,000 and 1,000,000. Other numbers are signed as individual digits. For example, the number 36 is expressed as three six. Fractions are expressed by signing the numerator, then lowering the hand slightly while signing the denominator.

Sign Movement

For all numbers above 9, there is definite movement. Movement of the hand and forearm is indicated in the number chart by dotted and solid lines. For the number 22 for example, where the hand actually moves from one place to another, a dotted line outline indicates the initial position while the final position appears in a solid line. When the hand remains in a fixed position, but the handshape changes, two solid-line images appear in order to show the handshapes more clearly. For number 26, there are two solid-line images shown side by side, to show the handshape transition. To produce this sign, the hand and forearm remain in place however.

Palm Orientation

When the numbers 1 to 5 are used as adjectives to quantify nouns, they are formed with the palm facing the body. When the numbers 1 to 5 appear in an address, telephone number, room number, or as an expression of time or age, they are formed with the palm facing forward in the illustration below. The reversal in palm orientation applies only to these 5 numbers.

Palm Facing Forward 1–5

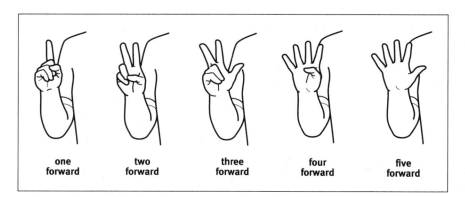

| one forward | two forward | three forward | four forward | five forward |

Hundreds

The sign for 100 is made using the number 1 (palm forward), which is rapidly changed to a **'c'** hand (as in the Roman numeral for 'hundred'). For numbers 101 to 199, the concept of hundred is conveyed by a **'CROOKED ONE'** hand with the forefinger retracting to form an **'x'** hand. The sign for 110 for example, is formed using a **'CROOKED ONE'** hand with the forefinger retracting to form an **'x'** hand, and then the wrist rotating clockwise a quarter turn as the hand assumes the position for the number 10.

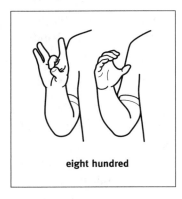

eight hundred

Multiples of One Hundred

Signs for the numbers 200, 300, 400 and 500 are derived from the signs for the numbers 2, 3, 4, and 5 respectively with the modification that the extended fingers in each case are crooked rather than straight and retracted and extended a few times. For the numbers 600, 700, 800, and 900, the base number is used followed by a **'c'** hand. For example, 800 is signed by using the sign for **8**, and then a **'c'** hand.

Numbers in the Thousands

Numbers in the thousands are always expressed as thousands in ASL as opposed to hundreds. Whereas, the number 6,739 could be expressed in English as either 'sixty-seven hundred thirty-nine' or 'six thousand seven hundred thirty-nine', it may only be expressed as 'six thousand seven hundred thirty-nine' in ASL.

6739

Ordinal Numbers (*See also the main entries for:* **first**, **second** *and* **third**.)
Ordinal numbers 1st to 9th are signed as cardinal numbers, palm facing
forward, as the wrist twists clockwise to turn the palm leftward. The ordinal
number 10th is also signed as a cardinal number with a slight clockwise wrist
rotation. Ordinal numbers above 10 are signed as cardinal numbers.

When used to indicate where someone placed in competition, ordinals 1st
to 9th are signed as cardinal numbers which are positioned horizontally with
palm facing left. The hand is then jerked back toward the body. The cardinal
number 10 is signed with a slight wobble to indicate 10th place. Ordinal
numbers above 10 are signed as cardinal numbers in this context.

Expressing Age
There are two ways of expressing age. One way is to use the sign for **old** and
then give the number of years in the usual signing space in front of the chest.
For example, in English the sentence would be: *The dog is five years old.* But
in ASL sentence the sentence is: *DOG OLD FIVE.* The other way to express age
is by positioning the hand with the palm facing relatively forward and the tip
of the forefinger touching the chin. The hand then moves forward a little and
assumes the shape for the appropriate number (of years). If the handshape for
that number is such that the forefinger is required to be in an upright position, as for the number five, then the number will already be formed at the
initial stage when the forefinger touches the chin, in which case, the **'FIVE
HAND'** then moves forward a little.

Expressing Time
Time may be expressed in the usual signing space in front of the chest.
Alternatively, it may be given with the right hand forming the number at the
left wrist just above where the face of a wristwatch would be.

Expressing Money
Dollar amounts of one to ten are expressed by signing the number with a
quarter turn twist of the wrist in a clockwise direction. There is no need to
sign the word **dollar(s)**. For dollar amounts above ten, the number is signed
in its usual way followed by the sign for **dollars**. *Cent* values are typically
expressed at the right side of the forehead.

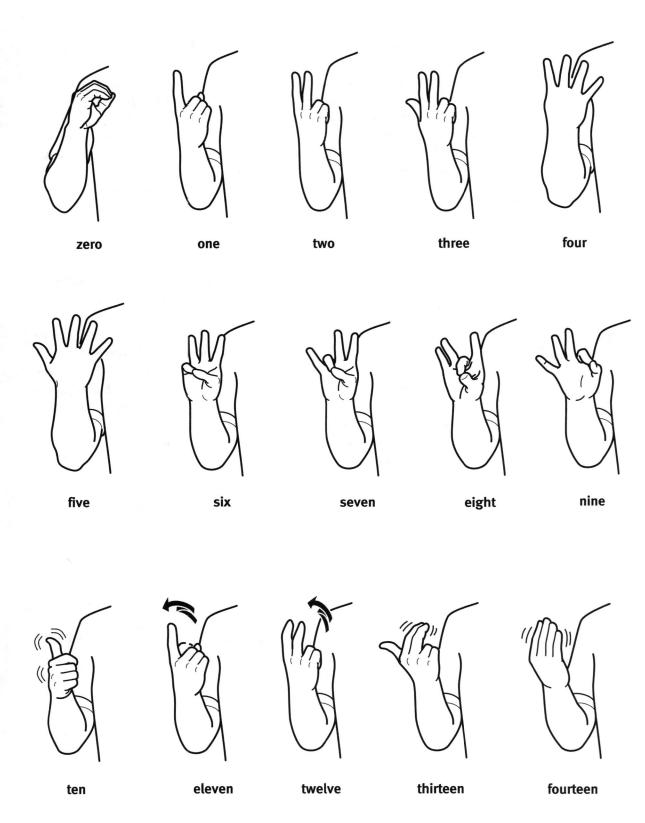

zero   one   two   three   four

five   six   seven   eight   nine

ten   eleven   twelve   thirteen   fourteen

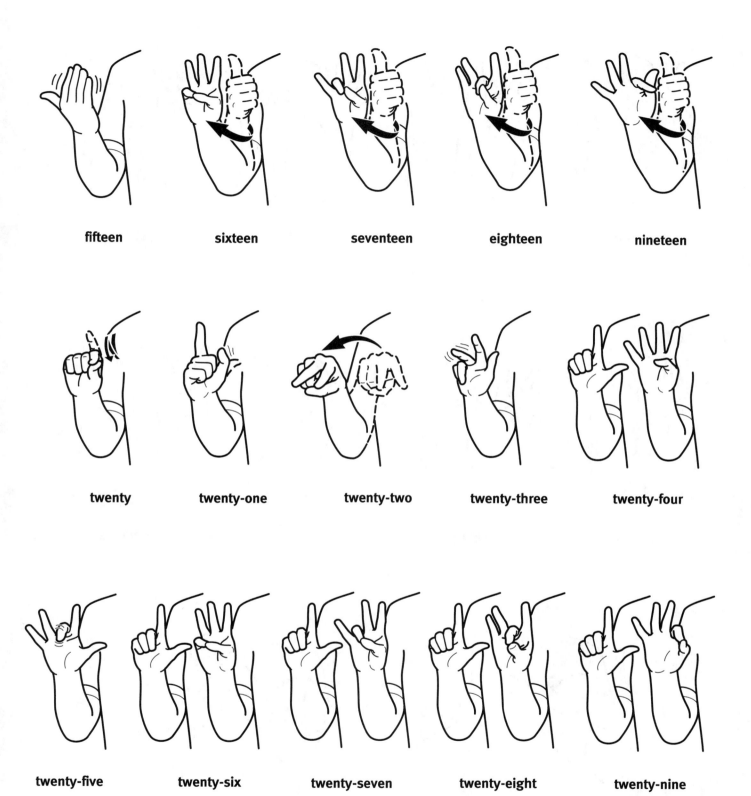

fifteen   sixteen   seventeen   eighteen   nineteen

twenty   twenty-one   twenty-two   twenty-three   twenty-four

twenty-five   twenty-six   twenty-seven   twenty-eight   twenty-nine

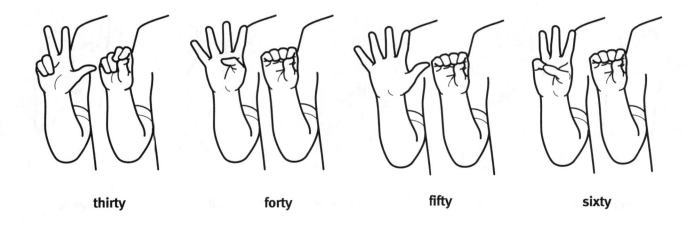

thirty   **forty**   **fifty**   **sixty**

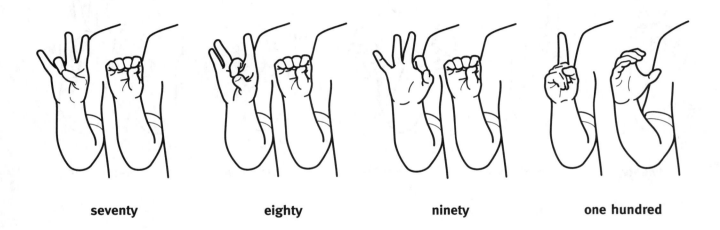

seventy   **eighty**   **ninety**   **one hundred**

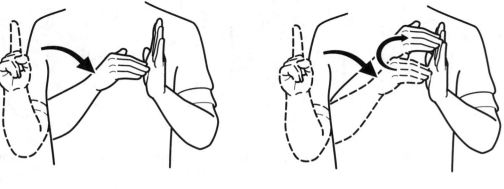

one thousand   **one million**

Pronouns

THE PRONOUNS ILLUSTRATED in this section are those that are most commonly used. Others appear in the *Dictionary* as main entries.

Certain signs are used for more than one English pronoun. **He, she** and **it**, for example, are all represented by the same sign, as are **I** and **me**. Neither gender (male/female), nor case (subjective/objective) is differentiated in the sign.

In general, the signs move in the direction of the person or thing they represent. The signer refers to a man or woman as 'he' or 'she' by pointing to him or her wherever he or she is, or is imagined to be in relation to the signer. Thereafter in a given conversation, that particular man or particular woman is thought to be fixed in space and is referred to by pointing consistently in that direction.

Plurality is generally indicated by a sweeping movement, as shown in the illustration for **you** (*pl.*), as compared to that shown for **you** (*sing.*). It can also be shown by a circular movement, with the handshape indicating the precise number of people and the hand positioned such that the location of the people in relation to the signer is clear, e.g., **you three** (or **the three of you**).

Personal Pronouns— Subjective

I

you (sing.)

he
she
it

we

you (pl.)

they

Personal Pronouns— Objective

me

you (sing.)

him
her
it

us

you (pl.)

them

Personal Pronouns
(Number Specified)

we two (you and I)
us (you and me)

we two (he/she and I)
us (him/her and me)

we three
us

we four
us

we five
us

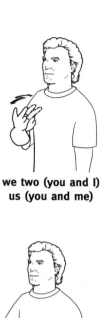

you two

you three

you four

you five

Possessive Pronouns

my
mine

your *(sing.)*
yours

his
her/hers
its

our
ours

your *(pl.)*
yours

their
theirs

Reflexive Pronouns

myself

yourself

himself
herself
itself

ourselves

yourselves

themselves

Relative Pronouns

that
which
who

Demonstrative Pronouns

this #1

this #2

these

that #1

that #2

those

Demonstrative Pronouns
(Number Specified)

those two

those three

those four

those five

Time Concepts

Days of the Week

Sunday   Monday   Tuesday

every Sunday   every Monday   every Tuesday

every other Sunday   every other Monday   every other Tuesday

Days of the Week
(cont.)

| **Wednesday** | **Thursday** | **Friday** | **Saturday** |

| **every Wednesday** | **every Thursday** | **every Friday** | **every Saturday** |

| **every other Wednesday** | **every other Thursday** | **every other Friday** | **every other Saturday** |

General Time Concepts

day

every day

all day

yesterday

today

tomorrow

week

every week

all week

last week

next week

General Time Concepts
(cont.)

month

every month
monthly

year

every year
yearly

all year

last year

next year

morning

every morning

all morning

General Time Concepts
(cont.)

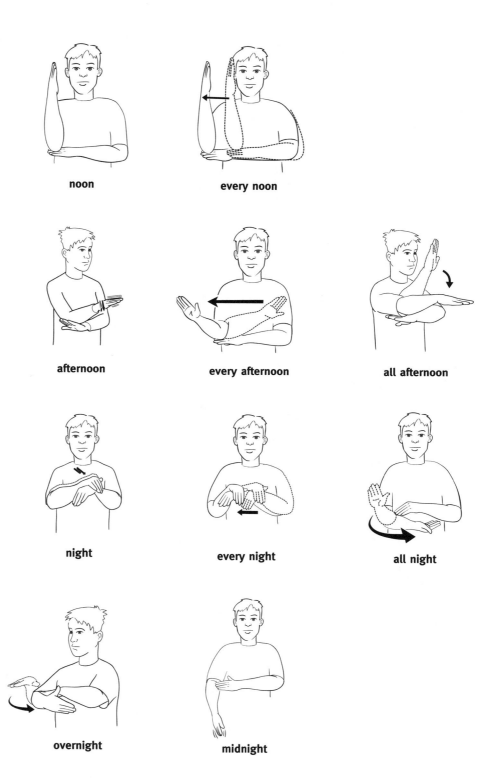

noon

every noon

afternoon

every afternoon

all afternoon

night

every night

all night

overnight

midnight

Geographic Place Names

Provinces and Territories of Canada

Alberta
Albertan

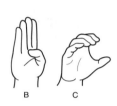

B   C

British Columbia
British Columbian

Manitoba #1
Manitoban

M A N I T O B A

Manitoba #2
Manitoban

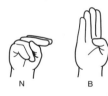

N   B

New Brunswick
New Brunswicker

Newfoundland #1
Newfoundlander

N F L D

Newfoundland #2
Newfoundlander

N W T

Northwest Territories
a person from NWT

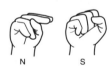

N   S

Nova Scotia
Nova Scotian

N V T

Nunavut
Nunavummiut

Ontario
Ontarian

P   E   I

Prince Edward Island
Prince Edward Islander

Quebec
Quebecer/Quebecois

Saskatchewan
Saskatchewanian/Saskatchewanite

Yukon
Yukoner

Cities of Canada

Amherst
[Nova Scotia]

Belleville
[Ontario]

Burlington
[Ontario]

Burnaby
[British Columbia]

Calgary
[Alberta]
Calgarian

Charlottetown
[Prince Edward Island]

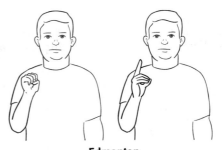

Edmonton
[Alberta]
Edmontonian

Fredericton
[New Brunswick]

Halifax
[Nova Scotia]
Haligonian

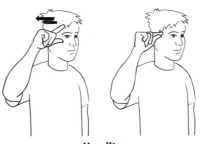

Hamilton
[Ontario]
Hamiltonian

Cities of Canada
(cont.)

Iqaluit
[Nunavut]

London
[Ontario]
Londoner

Milton
[Ontario]
Miltonian

Montreal
[Quebec]
Montrealer

Quebec City
[Quebec]

Regina
[Saskatchewan]

Saskatoon
[Saskatchewan]

St. John
[New Brunswick]

St. John's
[Newfoundland]

Niagara Falls
[Ontario]

Ottawa
[Ontario]

Toronto
[Ontario]
Torontonian

Cities of Canada
(cont.)

Vancouver
[British Columbia]
Vancouverite

Victoria
[British Columbia]
Victorian

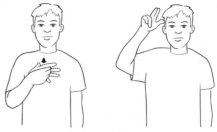

Whitehorse
[Yukon]

Winnipeg
[Manitoba]
Winnipegger

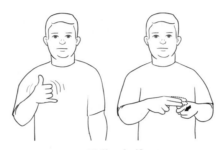

Yellowknife
[Northwest Territories]

Continents

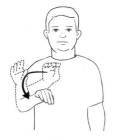

Africa
African

Antarctica

Asia
Asian

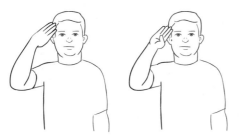

Australia #1
Australian

Australia #2
Australian

Europe
European

North America
North American

South America
South American

Countries

Australia #1
Australian

Australia #2
Australian

Austria
Austrian

Belgium
Belgian

Bulgaria
Bulgarian

Canada
Canadian

China #1
Chinese

China #2
Chinese

Denmark
Danish
Dane

Egypt
Egyptian

England
English

Countries
(cont.)

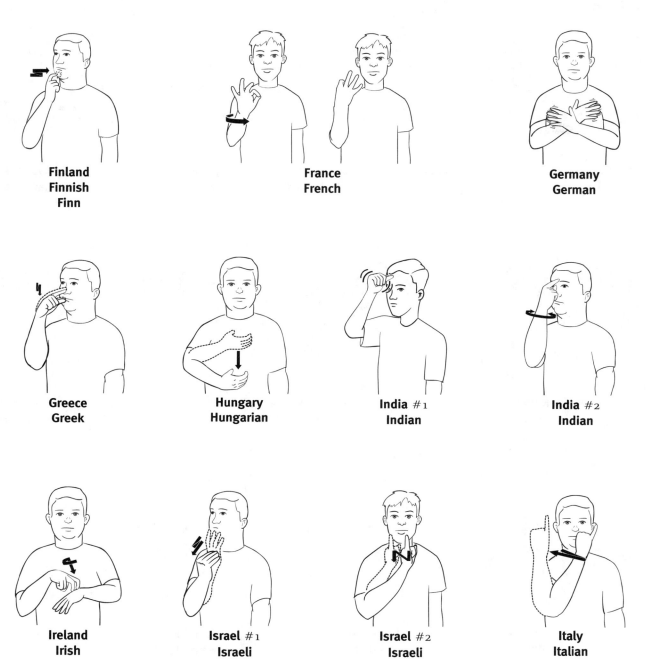

Finland
Finnish
Finn

France
French

Germany
German

Greece
Greek

Hungary
Hungarian

India #1
Indian

India #2
Indian

Ireland
Irish

Israel #1
Israeli

Israel #2
Israeli

Italy
Italian

Countries
(cont.)

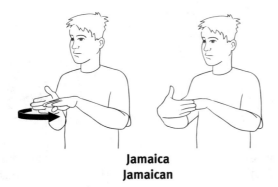

Jamaica
Jamaican

Japan #1
Japanese

Japan #2
Japanese

Korea #1
Korean

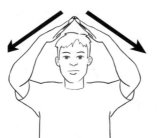

Korea #2
Korean

Malaysia
Malaysian

Mexico
Mexican

Netherlands #1
Netherlander
Dutch

Netherlands #2
Netherlander
Dutch

Countries
(cont.)

New Zealand
New Zealander

Norway
Norwegian

Pakistan
Pakistani

Philippines
Filipino

Poland #1
Polish
Pole

Poland #2
Polish
Pole

Romania
Romanian

Russia
Russian

Scotland #1
Scottish
Scot

Countries
(cont.)

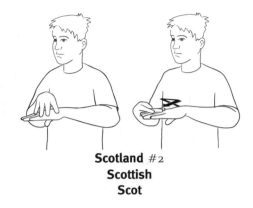

Scotland #2
Scottish
Scot

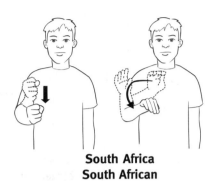

South Africa
South African

Spain
Spanish

Sweden
Swedish
Swede

Switzerland
Swiss

Thailand
Thai

Ukraine
Ukrainian

United States
of America #1
American

United States
of America #2
American

THE
Canadian Dictionary
OF ASL

A

abandon: *v.* to desert; forsake; leave unattended. *The driver **abandoned** his car and walked into town.*

SIGN: **'5'** hands are thrust forward to the left and down from shoulder level, palms facing each other. ❖

abbreviate: *v.* to shorten a word or expression. *You can **abbreviate** American Sign Language to ASL.*

SIGN: **'SPREAD C'** hands are held horizontally and slightly apart, right above left. Then both are closed to form **'S'** hands as the right is brought down to rest on top of the left. SAME SIGN—**abbreviation**, *n.*

abdicate: *v.* to formally surrender or give up one's power or rights. *The Queen might never **abdicate** the throne.*

SIGN: **'OPEN A'** hands, held slightly apart at waist level, palms down, are thrust upward to form **'EXTENDED B'** hands with palms facing forward.

abdomen: *n.* the part of the body containing the stomach, intestines and other digestive organs. *She has a pain in her **abdomen**.*

SIGN: Right **'EXTENDED B'** hand, fingertips pointing leftward and slightly downward, palm toward the body, pats area below the stomach a couple of times.

abduct: *v.* to kidnap; take away by force. *The kidnappers planned to **abduct** the diplomat from his house.*

SIGN: Horizontal right **'SPREAD C'** hand, palm facing left, is pulled backward as it closes to form an **'S'** hand. ❖

abhor: *v.* to hate; loathe. *Many people **abhor** violence.*

SIGN: Thumb of right **'MODIFIED 5'** hand is held at the chin, with palm facing left. Then the hand is thrust forward firmly. Alternatively, this sign may be made two-handed with the left **'MODIFIED 5'** hand in front of the right **'MODIFIED 5'** hand. Facial expression must clearly convey 'abhorrence'.

able: *adj.* capable of; having skill. *Wayne Gretzky was **able** to break many National Hockey League records.*

SIGN: **'A'** hands, palms down, are held slightly apart, and are then firmly pushed downward. SAME SIGN—**ability**, *n.*, but the motion is repeated.

abnormal: *adj.* unusual; irregular. *His behaviour is **abnormal**.*

SIGN: Right **'EXTENDED A'** hand, palm facing left, thumb under chin, is thrust forward (for 'not'). Next, right **'BENT U'** hand, palm down, is circled clockwise over the left **'STANDARD BASE'** hand, and the extended fingers are brought down to rest on it.
(ASL CONCEPT—**not - normal**.)

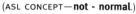

abolish: *v.* to do away with. *The Justice Department decided to **abolish** the outdated laws.*

SIGN: Horizontal right **'A'** hand, palm facing left, is held against right-facing palm of horizontal left **'EXTENDED B'** hand, and is then moved rightward and downward as it opens to become a **'CROOKED 5'** hand with the palm facing down.

abortion: *n.* an induced termination of a pregnancy. *She had an **abortion** during the first trimester of her pregnancy.*

SIGN: Horizontal right **'A'** hand, palm facing left, is held against right-facing palm of horizontal left **'EXTENDED B'** hand, and is then moved rightward and downward as it opens to become a **'CROOKED 5'** hand with the palm facing down.

about: *prep.* in reference to; concerning. *This book is **about** seventeenth century England.*

SIGN #1: Left **'BENT ONE'** hand, palm facing right and forefinger pointing right, remains fixed while forefinger of right **'BENT ONE'** hand circles the left forefinger in a clockwise direction.

about *(cont.)*

SIGN #2 [ATLANTIC]: Horizontal **'MODIFIED G'** hands, left palm facing rightward/backward, and right palm facing leftward/forward, are held so that the thumb and forefinger of the right are between those of the left. Then they are drawn slightly apart as they both change to **'CLOSED MODIFIED G'** hands. Motion is repeated.

SIGN #3 [ONTARIO]: Edge of right **'EXTENDED B'** hand, palm facing left, is brought down, smartly striking the upturned palm of the left **'EXTENDED B'** hand. Motion is repeated.

about: *adv.* approximately. *He is getting married in about three weeks.*

SIGN #4: Vertical right **'5'** hand, palm forward, is circled in front of the right shoulder in a counter-clockwise direction (from the signer's perspective).

above: *adv.* higher than. *The forecast calls for temperatures above normal.*

SIGN: Left **'EXTENDED B'** hand is held palm-down, with fingertips pointing right. Fingertips of right palm-down **'EXTENDED B'** hand rest on and at right angles to back of left hand and are then moved upward from the wrist.

absent: *adj.* not present; not there; away. *He is absent from work because he is sick.*

SIGN: Right **'CONTRACTED 5'** hand, palm up, becomes a **'FLAT O'** hand as it is drawn downward behind the horizontal left **'CROOKED 5'** hand of which the palm is facing the body.
SAME SIGN—**absence**, *n.*

absolute: *adj.* perfect; unquestionable. *The World Winter Games for the Deaf in Banff were an absolute success.*

SIGN #1: Forefinger of vertical right **'ONE'** hand, palm facing left, is held against the lips and the hand is moved sharply forward.

absolute: *adj.* complete; whole. *He told the absolute truth.*

SIGN #2: Right **'EXTENDED B'** hand, palm down with fingers pointing forward/leftward, grazes top of horizontal left **'S'** hand as the right hand is firmly swept leftward.

absorb: *v.* to suck up. *The paper towel will absorb the spill.*

SIGN: **'CONTRACTED 5'** hands are held slightly apart with palms down and are brought up to form **'FLAT O'** hands.

absorbed: *adj.* fully involved; engaged (in). *She was so absorbed in the book she was reading that she missed her bus.*

SIGN: Vertical right **'CLAWED V'** hand, palm facing backward, is thrust forward and slightly downward so that the back of the hand makes contact with the palm of the horizontal left **'SPREAD C'** hand which is held with the palm facing the body.

abstain: *v.* to decline; refrain from; try not to. *He chose to abstain from drinking and smoking.*

SIGN: Right forearm, with **'S'** hand palm down, is thrust forward firmly away from the chest.

abstract: *adj.* theoretical; not concrete; hard to understand. *Mathematics uses abstract concepts.*

SIGN: Fingerspell **ABSTRACT**.

absurd: *adj.* ridiculous; unreasonable; foolish. *It is absurd to go out in such weather.*

SIGN: Vertical right **'Y'** hand, palm toward the nose, is twisted forward so that the palm faces left.

abundance: *n.* plenty; more than enough; full supply. *Canada has an abundance of resources.*

SIGN #1: Right **'5'** hand, palm down, is brushed forward firmly across the top of the horizontal left **'S'** hand, of which the palm faces right. The cheeks are puffed out.

OR

SIGN #2: **'EXTENDED A'** hands, palms slightly facing the body and slightly facing upward, are simultaneously circled outward in opposite directions. The cheeks are puffed out. SAME SIGN—**abundant**, *adj.*

abuse: *n.* wrong or inappropriate use of. *Drug abuse can be fatal.*

SIGN #1: Fingerspell **ABUSE**. (Various signs may be used depending on the context.)

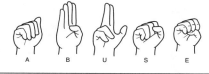

abuse: *v.* to treat badly. *That man is known to abuse his spouse.*

SIGN #2: Horizontal right **'S'** hand, palm facing left, is used to strike back and forth against the upright forefinger of the left **'ONE'** hand, of which the palm faces right. ❖

abuse: *v.* to take sexual advantage of. *The man sexually abused his former girlfriend.*

SIGN #3: Middle finger of the right **'BENT MIDFINGER 5'** hand is stroked toward the body on the upturned left palm. Motion is repeated. ❖

academic: *adj.* scholarly; related to school, college or university study which is theoretical rather than practical. *History is an academic subject.*

SIGN: Right **'EXTENDED B'** hand, palm down, fingers pointing forward and slightly to the left, is brought down twice on the upturned palm of the left **'EXTENDED B'** hand whose fingers point forward and slightly to the right. (**ACADEMIC** is also frequently fingerspelled.)

accelerator: *n.* gas pedal. *He asked the mechanic to check the accelerator.*

SIGN: Right **'EXTENDED B'** hand is held with palm forward/downward. The wrist then bends to lower the hand to a palm down position to simulate the foot movement on the pedal of a car. Motion is repeated.

accept: *v.* to take willingly. *The bride was glad to accept their gift.*

SIGN: Both **'CONTRACTED 5'** hands, palms down, are brought toward the chest while they are being closed to form **'FLAT O'** hands, with fingertips touching the body. SAME SIGN—**accepting**, *adj.*, but the movement is repeated.

access: *n.* the means to approach or be admitted. *Everyone has access to the library.*

SIGN: Right **'EXTENDED B'** hand, palm down, is curved under downturned palm of left **'EXTENDED B'** palm to simulate 'entrance'.

accident: *n.* mishap. *He had a very serious car accident.*

SIGN #1: Horizontal **'S'** hands, palms facing the body, are brought together with force. (The handshapes for this sign vary.)

SIGN #2 [ONTARIO]: Fingertips of horizontal **'BENT EXTENDED B'** hands, palms toward the body, are held parallel and are brought back firmly to touch the chest.

accident (cont.)

OR

SIGN #3 [ONTARIO]: The joined thumbs and forefingers of both **'8'** hands, palms facing, are held slightly apart and are curved upward toward each other, striking each other lightly. The **'8'** hands then continue to curve upward and apart once again.

(by) accident [*or* accidentally]: *n.*

happening by chance. *The caveman discovered fire by accident.*

SIGN #4: **'ONE'** hands, palms facing each other and forefingers pointing forward, are held apart and then turned over so that the palms face down.

OR

SIGN #5: Vertical right **'Y'** hand is held against the right side of the chin with palm facing left. The wrist then rotates to turn the hand so that the palm faces the body. (This sign is used in contexts where something '*unfortunate* but unintentional' has happened.)

acclaim: *n.* praise. *The play about the Deaf received great acclaim.*

SIGN: **'EXTENDED B'** hands, left palm facing upward and right palm facing downward, are brought together twice in a clapping motion.

accommodation: *n.* lodging, with or without meals. *When you travel, it is advisable to reserve accommodation in advance.*

SIGN: Bunched fingertips of vertical right **'MODIFIED O'** hand, palm facing left, touch right cheek. Then the handshape changes to an **'EXTENDED B'** with the fingers held flat against the right cheek.

accompany: *v.* to go with; escort. *We will accompany you to the airport.*

SIGN: **'A'** hands are held together, palms facing each other, and knuckles touching. Then they are thrust forward/downward together from chest level. ❖

accomplish: *v.* to achieve; carry out successfully. *We can accomplish great things if we work cooperatively.*

SIGN: **'ONE'** hands, palms down, forefingers almost touching either side of forehead, are raised so that fingers point upward and palms face away from the body.

SAME SIGN—**accomplishment**, *n.*

accord: *n.* the state of being in spontaneous agreement. *Everyone was in accord regarding the motion.*

SIGN: Left **'ONE'** hand is held at chest level with palm facing right and forefinger pointing away from body. Right **'ONE'** hand, palm facing left, is held slightly higher and then turned downward to match the simultaneously downward-turning left hand.

according to: *prep.* on the authority of; as said by. *According to the weather report, it will snow tonight.*

SIGN: **'ONE'** (or **'K'**) hands, palms down and forefingers pointing forward/leftward, are held in front of the left side of the body, lowered slightly, then moved in an upward arc to the right side of the body.

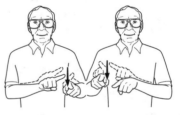

account: *n.* money held in trust. *All the funds were kept in one bank account.*

SIGN #1: Fingerspell **ACCOUNT**.

account: *n.* a report or explanation given either verbally or in writing. *The witness gave a detailed account of the accident.*

SIGN #2: **'F'** hands are held horizontally with palms facing each other, and are alternately moved backward and forward. Motion is repeated.

accounting: *n.* system of recording financial transactions. *You should learn accounting before you set up a business.*

SIGN: Thumb and forefinger of right **'F'** hand, palm down, are used to stroke forward across the upturned palm of the left **'EXTENDED B'** hand. Movement is repeated.
SAME SIGN—**accountant**, *n.*, and may be followed by the Agent Ending (see p. LIV).

accumulate: *v.* to amass; pile up. *They accumulated a stack of old books.*

SIGN: Horizontal right **'SPREAD EXTENDED C'** hand is moved across upturned palm of left **'EXTENDED B'** hand in a circular, counter-clockwise 'gathering' motion, with the palm toward the body.

accurate: *adj.* correct; without error. *The statistics are accurate.*

SIGN #1: **'CLOSED X'** hands are held, right above left, with palms facing. The hands are then brought together sharply so that the joined thumbs and forefingers touch. Alternatively, the right hand sometimes moves in a small clockwise circle before making contact with the left hand.
SAME SIGN—**accuracy**, *n.*

OR

SIGN #2: Right **'ONE'** hand, palm left, is held above left hand, of which the palm faces right. Forefingers point forward. Right hand is then brought down firmly to rest on top of left hand.
SAME SIGN—**accuracy**, *n.*, but the motion is repeated.

accuse: *v.* to blame; bring charges against. *It is a serious allegation to accuse someone of extortion.*

SIGN: Horizontal right **'EXTENDED A'** hand, palm facing left, is thrust forward twice across the back of the left **'A'** hand of which the palm faces downward. Facial expression must be accusatory. ❖
SAME SIGN—**accusation**, *n.*, but the motion is repeated.

accustomed: *adj.* used (to); familiar (with). *Most hearing people are not accustomed to communicating in sign language.*

SIGN: Base of vertical right **'U'** hand, palm facing leftward/forward, is brought down purposefully on the back of the left **'STANDARD BASE'** (or **'U'**) hand, thus lowering it slightly as well.

ache: *n.* pain; distress. *She is suffering from an ache in her stomach.*

SIGN: Horizontal **'BENT ONE'** hands are held apart with right palm down and left palm toward the body while forefingers point toward one another. The hands are then moved toward one another as the right hand twists slightly forward and the left hand twists slightly backward so that the right palm eventually faces the body and the left hand faces downward. This sign is generally made near the afflicted area of the body.

achieve: *v.* to accomplish. *If you work hard, you will achieve your goals.*

SIGN: **'ONE'** hands, palms down, forefingers almost touching either side of forehead, are raised so that fingers point upward and palms face away from the body.
SAME SIGN—**achievement**, *n.*

acid: *n.* sour-tasting, corrosive solution or substance. *Great care must be taken when handling acid.*

SIGN: Fingerspell **ACID**.

acknowledge: *v.* to recognize or avow to be. *Margaret Laurence is acknowledged as an accomplished Canadian author.*

SIGN: Tip of forefinger of right **'CROOKED ONE'** hand is positioned at corner of right eye and brought down to rest on upturned palm of left **'EXTENDED B'** hand.

acorn: *n.* the fruit of an oak tree. *The acorn will grow into a mighty oak.*

SIGN: Thumb of right **'EXTENDED A'** hand, palm facing left, wiggles against the upper front teeth.

acquainted: *adj.* familiar (with). *Are you acquainted with computer terminology?*

SIGN: Fingertips of right **'BENT EXTENDED B'** (or **'EXTENDED B'**) hand, palm toward the head, are tapped against right side of forehead.

acquire: *v.* to get; obtain; gain. *You will acquire great wealth in your new position.*

SIGN: Horizontal **'SPREAD C'** hands, right on top of left, are closed to form **'S'** hands as they are brought toward the chest.

acquit: *v.* to pronounce not guilty; to release from a criminal charge. *Many people think the jury will acquit him of the charges.*

SIGN: Fingers of right **'B'** hand, palm-down, are placed on and at right angles to fingers of upturned palm of left **'EXTENDED B'** hand. Right hand is then slid at a forward/rightward angle across and off the left hand.

SAME SIGN—**acquittal**, *n.*

acronym: *n.* a word formed by combining initial letters. *SLIC is an acronym for 'Sign Language Instructors of Canada'.*

SIGN: Horizontal **'SPREAD C'** hands are held horizontally and slightly apart, right above left. Then both are closed to form **'S'** hands as they come together, the right hand eventually resting on the left hand.

across: *prep.* on or at the other side of. *The store is across the street.*

SIGN: Left **'ONE'** hand is held close to chest with palm facing right and forefinger pointing forward while right **'BENT ONE'** hand is held in front of the left hand with forefinger and palm facing the body. The right hand is then moved forward, thus further separating the two hands.

act: *v.* to behave or conduct oneself. *This dog acts strangely.*

SIGN #1: **'SPREAD C'** hands are held parallel with palms down and are simultaneously swung from side to side.

act: *v.* to play a part; perform a role. *The boy knows how to act on the stage.*

SIGN #2: **'EXTENDED A'** hands, palms facing each other, are rotated alternately in small circles which are brought down against the chest.

SAME SIGNS—**actor**, *n.*, and **actress**, *n.*, and may be followed by the Agent Ending (see p. LIV).

act: *n.* a main section of a drama. *There was an intermission after the second act.*

SIGN #3: Fingerspell **ACT**.

action: *n.* activity and motion. *Deaf people prefer movies with lots of action.*

SIGN: **'SPREAD C'** hands are held parallel with palms down and are simultaneously swung from side to side.

activate: *v.* to start up. *The computer can be activated by pressing this switch.*

SIGN: Left **'5'** hand is held with palm facing right while forefinger of right **'ONE'** hand is inserted between first two fingers of left hand and twisted 180 degrees either to the right or left.

active: *adj.* involved in action. *She is very active in politics.*

SIGN: **'SPREAD C'** hands, palms down, are circled simultaneously in opposite directions (the left counter-clockwise and the right clockwise).

activity: *n.* action or the state of being active. *Many outdoor activities are scheduled during the Quebec Winter Carnival.*

SIGN: **'SPREAD C'** hands are held parallel with palms down and are simultaneously swung from side to side.

actual: *adj.* real; existing. *The copy was less clear than the actual document.*

SIGN: Forefinger of vertical right **'ONE'** hand, palm facing left, is held against the lips and the hand is moved sharply forward.

adapt: *v.* to adjust; modify. *Animals can adapt to changes in the weather.*

SIGN: **'A'** hands, palms facing each other, are twisted 180 degrees.

ALTERNATE SIGN—**accept**, in this context.

add: *v.* to total; find the sum of. *When you add fractions, they must have common denominators.*

SIGN #1: Horizontal **'CONTRACTED 5'** hands, palms facing each other, are brought together as the fingers close to form **'FLAT O'** hands with fingertips touching each other.

SIGN #2 [ATLANTIC]: **'5'** hands, palms toward the body, with the right nearer the chest, are held at a 45° angle. The left hand remains fixed as the right hand moves upward with fingers fluttering.

add: *v.* to increase in length, size, or amount. *She added an extra ingredient to the recipe.*

SIGN #3: Horizontal left **'FLAT O'** hand is held in a fixed position with palm toward the body while the right **'CONTRACTED 5'** hand is held palm-down to the right of and at a lower level than the left hand. The right wrist then rotates rightward/forward as the fingers close to form a **'FLAT O'** hand which is swung upward to touch the underside of the left hand.

addict: *n.* a person who is dependent on something, usually a narcotic. *The victim was a known cocaine addict.*

SIGN: Tip of forefinger of right **'CROOKED ONE'** hand is held at right corner of mouth, and pulled slightly to the right. The head turns rightward at the same time.

SAME SIGN—**addiction**, *n.*

addition: *n.* the adding or totalling of numbers. *A calculator is a time-saving device that can be used for addition.*

SIGN: **'CONTRACTED 5'** hands are held apart, palms facing, and become **'FLAT O'** hands as they are brought together. This movement may be vertical to represent a column of numbers or horizontal to represent numbers in a left to right sequence.

address: *n.* postal designation or place of residence. *She put her new address on the envelope.*

SIGN #1: Horizontal **'EXTENDED A'** hands, palms toward the body, are simultaneously brushed upward twice against the chest.

SIGN #2 [ATLANTIC]: Fingertips of the right **'FLAT O'** hand, palm down, are used to touch the top of the horizontal left **'S'** hand whose palm faces the body. The movement is repeated twice.

address: *v.* to lecture; deliver a speech. *Forrest C. Nickerson then addressed the audience.*

SIGN #3: Right arm is raised and the vertical **'EXTENDED B'** hand, palm facing left, is brought forward sharply from the wrist a couple of times.

address: *v.* attend to. *The executive will address this issue at the next meeting.*

SIGN #4: Vertical **'EXTENDED B'** hands are held one at either side of the face, and are brought forward simultaneously.

adept: *adj.* highly skilled; proficient. *The teacher is an adept mathematician.*

SIGN #1: Left **'EXTENDED B'** hand, palm facing right and fingers pointing upward/forward, is grasped by right **'OPEN A'** hand. Then right hand is pulled forward sharply and closed to form an **'A'** hand.

adept (cont.)

OR

SIGN #2: Tips of joined forefinger and thumb of horizontal right **'F'** hand, palm toward the body, are brought purposefully up to strike the chin.

adequate: *adj.* sufficient to suit the occasion. *An airplane must attain* **adequate** *speed before lifting off.*

SIGN #1: Horizontal left **'S'** hand, palm facing right, is covered with palm of right **'EXTENDED B'** hand. Then the right hand is brushed firmly forward and slightly to the right.

adequate: *adj.* good enough; barely satisfactory. *His photography skills are* **adequate** *for amateur competition.*

SIGN #2: Fingertips of **'BENT EXTENDED B'** hand are positioned at the mouth, then brought forward and down, as hand straightens to assume an **'EXTENDED B'** shape with palm downward as it brushes firmly forward across the horizontal left **'S'** hand. (ASL CONCEPT—**good - enough**.)

adjust: *v.* to settle into or adapt to a new situation. *It takes time for Canadians to* **adjust** *to the tropical climate of Hawaii.*

SIGN: **'X'** hands, palms facing each other, are held right above left and twisted so that left is above right.

SAME SIGN—**adjustment**, *n.* For **adjustable**, *adj.*, the movement is repeated.

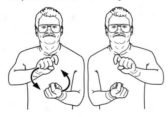

administer: *v.* to direct; control; manage. *There are some Deaf people who* **administer** *schools.*

SIGN: Horizontal **'X'** hands are held slightly apart with left palm facing right and right palm facing left. Then they are alternately moved backward and forward.

SAME SIGN—**administration**, *n.*, in this context. (When it refers to a group of people who manage an operation, **administration**, *n.*, is fingerspelled in the abbreviated form **ADM**.)

admire: *v.* to regard with pleasure and approval. *I* **admire** *her engagement ring.*

SIGN #1: Horizontal right **'OPEN 8'** hand is held with palm toward the chest and tips of thumb and middle finger touching the centre of the chest. The hand then moves forward as the thumb and middle finger close to form an **'8'** hand.

admire: *v.* to have esteem or respect for. *I* **admire** *a person who is honest.*

SIGN #2: **'V'** hands are held apart with one slightly ahead of the other and palms down. The hands then curve forward/upward so that the palms face forward and the extended fingers point upward at a slightly forward angle. ❖

admission: *n.* the act of entry into a place. *They lined up for* **admission** *to the theatre.*

SIGN #1: Right **'EXTENDED B'** hand is curved under left **'EXTENDED B'** palm to simulate 'entrance'.

SIGN #2 [ONTARIO]: Right **'4'** hand, palm facing left, is moved forward two or three times underneath the left **'BENT EXTENDED B'** hand, which is held palm down. This is a wrist movement.

admit: *v.* to allow to enter. *He should not be* **admitted** *to this theatre.*

SIGN #1: Right **'EXTENDED B'** hand is curved under left **'EXTENDED B'** palm to simulate 'entrance'. ❖

admit: *v.* to confess. *She will* **admit** *that she committed the crime.*

SIGN #2: Right **'EXTENDED B'** hand is held with palm against chest, and is brought forward so that the palm faces upward at a slight angle toward the body. Alternatively, this sign may be made with two hands, beginning with one at either side of the chest.

admonish: *v.* to warn or to caution against something to be avoided. *The manager will* ***admonish*** *the clerk for his careless work.*

SIGN: **'EXTENDED B'** hands are held palms down, so that the right hand is above the left and is brought down so that the fingertips are tapped on the back of the left hand. Facial expression must clearly convey 'caution'. ❖

adolescent: *n.* a youth approaching maturity. *An* ***adolescent*** *develops his or her individual tastes.*

SIGN: Fingertips of **'BENT EXTENDED B'** hands, palms facing the body, are brushed upward against the chest.

adopt: *v.* to take another's child as one's own by legal measures. *The couple waited for years to* ***adopt*** *a child.*

SIGN #1: Horizontal right **'SPREAD C'** hand, palm facing left, is brought toward the body as it closes to form an **'S'** hand. Alternatively, **ADOPT** is frequently fingerspelled. ❖
SAME SIGN—**adoption**, *n.*, in this context.

adopt: *v.* to accept by vote or motion. *We will* ***adopt*** *the new policy next year.*

SIGN #2: Both **'CONTRACTED 5'** hands, palms down, are brought toward the chest while closing to form **'FLAT O'** hands with fingertips touching the body.
SAME SIGN—**adoption**, *n.*, in this context.

adore: *v.* to love with intense devotion. *Many people* ***adored*** *Elvis Presley and his music.*

SIGN #1: **'A'** hands, palms facing the body, the right resting on the back of the left, are pressed to the chest and held snugly.

OR

SIGN #2: Back of right **'S'** hand is brought up toward the mouth, kissed, and moved downward at a forward angle.

adult: *n.* a person who has attained the age of legal majority. *An* ***adult*** *has certain rights and responsibilities.*

SIGN: Vertical right **'BENT EXTENDED B'** hand, palm facing left, is held just above shoulder at chin level and moved up level with top of head. (When referring to animals rather than people, **ADULT** is fingerspelled.)

adultery: *n.* unfaithfulness of a married person. *She divorced him on grounds of* ***adultery***.

SIGN: Right **'BENT EXTENDED B'** hand, palm facing left, is moved forward in a semicircle around the vertical left **'EXTENDED B'** hand whose palm faces right.

adults: *n.* people who have attained the age of legal majority. ***Adults*** *have certain rights and responsibilities.*

SIGN: Vertical **'BENT EXTENDED B'** hands, palms facing each other, are held above eye level, and rotated alternately away from the body.

advance: *v.* to be promoted. *If you work hard, you can* ***advance*** *in your career.*

SIGN: Vertical **'BENT EXTENDED B'** hands, held at shoulder level with palms facing each other, are moved upward simultaneously and thrust forward very slightly.

(in) advance: *adv.* beforehand; ahead of time; before due. *Teachers prepare lessons in* ***advance***.

SIGN #1: **'BENT EXTENDED B'** hands are held horizontally with fingers touching, the right hand slightly behind the left, and palms facing each other. The right hand is then curved forward ahead of the left. As a variation, the right **'BENT EXTENDED B'** hand is held in front of the left and then moved straight forward.

OR

SIGN #2: Horizontal **'BENT EXTENDED B'** hands are held with fingers of right hand closest to the body and resting against fingers of left hand. Palms are facing each other. Right hand is then brought back toward the body.

advanced: *adj.* at a high level of difficulty. *He took an advanced course in photography.*

SIGN: Vertical **'BENT EXTENDED B'** hands, held at shoulder level with palms facing each other, are moved upward simultaneously and thrust forward very slightly.

advantage: *n.* benefit; profit. *It might be to your advantage to take a course in business management.*

SIGN: Thumb and forefinger of right **'F'** hand, palm facing down, are brought slightly downward to be inserted into an imaginary pocket at waist level. Alternatively, the imaginary pocket is sometimes located at the left side of the chest.

(take) advantage of: *v.* to make the best of; put to good use. *The young couple took advantage of their last chance to spend time together.*

SIGN #1: Right **'SPREAD C'** hand, palm facing left and toward the body slightly, is transformed to an **'S'** hand, palm facing the body, as it is brushed left twice along the fixed, upturned palm of the left **'EXTENDED B'** hand and finally raised above it.

(take) advantage of: *v.* to make use of for one's own benefit or selfish purpose. *It is unfair to take advantage of someone.*

SIGN #2: Middle finger of right **'BENT MIDFINGER 5'** hand is placed on the upturned palm of the left **'EXTENDED B'** hand, whose fingers point forward/rightward, and is then retracted as it is brought back smartly toward the body.

advertise: *v.* to give public notice of. *The company advertised for a new executive.*

SIGN: **'S'** hands, palms facing downward, are held slightly apart, with right in front of left. Right hand then strikes left hand and moves forward and back to strike it a second time.
SAME SIGN—**advertisement**, *n.*

advise: *v.* to counsel. *Your lawyer will advise you on this matter.*

SIGN: Fingertips of right **'FLAT O'** hand rest on back of left **'STANDARD BASE'** hand. Right hand is then thrust forward as it opens slightly to form a **'CONTRACTED 5'** hand. ❖ SAME SIGN—**advice**, *n.*, but the motion is repeated.

advocate: *v.* to support; defend; recommend. *We must advocate equal rights.*

SIGN: **'S'** hands, palms toward the body, are held at chest level with the left slightly above the right. Then the right is brought upward to strike the left.
SAME SIGN—**advocate**, *n.*, but the motion is repeated.

aerobics: *n.* special fitness exercises. *Some workplaces offer classes in aerobics during lunch hour.*

SIGN: Fingerspell **AEROBICS**.

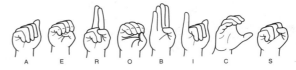

A   E   R   O   B   I   C   S

affect: *v.* to influence. *The new laws will affect the lives of immigrants in Canada.*

SIGN: Right **'FLAT O'** hand is held, palm down, so that the fingertips are resting on the back of the left **'STANDARD BASE'** hand. Then the right hand moves forward as the fingers spread to form a **'5'** hand. ❖ (**AFFECT** is frequently fingerspelled.)

affectionate: *adj.* loving; having or showing fondness. *He is a warm, **affectionate** person.*

SIGN: **'A'** (or **'S'**) hands, palms facing the chest, are crossed left over right at the wrists, and tapped a couple of times against the chest. SAME SIGN—**affection**, *n.*

affiliate: *v.* to be associated with. *The organization, 'American Sign Language Instructors of Canada', is **affiliated** with the Canadian Cultural Society of the Deaf.*

SIGN: **'OPEN F'** hands are brought together so that the thumbs and forefingers are linked to form **'F'** hands. ❖

afford: *v.* to have sufficient means for; have enough money. *They can **afford** to buy a new car.*

SIGN: Tip of forefinger of right **'ONE'** hand, palm toward body, is poked into palm of left **'EXTENDED B'** hand whose palm faces right.

afraid: *adj.* feeling fear or dread. *She is **afraid** of snakes.*

SIGN #1: Horizontal **'5'** hands, palms toward the body, are held out from either side of the chest, and are moved vigorously toward each other, stopping abruptly in front of the chest. Facial expression is important.

SIGN #2 [ONTARIO]: Vertical right **'CONTRACTED 3'** hand is held with palm facing left and tip of forefinger just in front of the nose. The middle finger moves up and down as the hand moves downward/leftward a few times. Facial expression is important. (This sign is used only in contexts where someone feels threatened *physically*.)

afraid: *adj.* a colloquial term meaning sorry; regretful. *I am **afraid** I will have to cancel our appointment.*

SIGN #3: Right **'A'** hand, palm facing the body, is rubbed on the chest with a circular motion which, in the eyes of onlookers, appears clockwise.

after: *conj.* following in time. *After you watch the movie, do not forget to rewind the tape.*

SIGN #1: Right **'EXTENDED B'** hand is held with palm facing left and fingers pointing forward as it curves forward across the back of the left **'STANDARD BASE'** hand.

OR

SIGN #2: **'A'** hands, palms facing each other, are held upright together with knuckles touching. Then the right hand is moved forward and slightly downward.

SIGN #3 [ATLANTIC]: Vertical left **'EXTENDED B'** hand is held in a fixed position with palm right as vertical right **'EXTENDED B'** is held with palm forward and thumbtip resting against the left palm. Then the right hand is changed to a **'BENT EXTENDED B'** shape as the fingers bend downward. Alternatively, the right hand may begin and end with an **'L'** shape.

SIGN #4 [ONTARIO]: Right **'A'** hand, thumb on chin and palm facing left, is stroked downward several times.

after a while: *adv.* later. *After a while, the policeman appeared.*

SIGN: Thumb of vertical right **'L'** hand, palm forward, is rested against right-facing palm of vertical left **'EXTENDED B'** hand. The right wrist then bends to turn the right hand palm downward so that the forefinger eventually points forward.

aftermath: *n.* the results of a momentous event. *There was great confusion in the aftermath of the tornado.*

SIGN: Right **'EXTENDED B'** hand is held with palm facing left and fingers pointing forward as it curves forward across the back of the left **'STANDARD BASE'** hand. Then **'ONE'** hands, palms facing each other and forefingers pointing forward, are held apart and then turned over so that the palms face down. (ASL CONCEPT—**after - happen**.) Sign choices vary according to context.

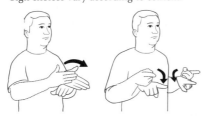

afternoon: *n.* period of time between 12:00 p.m. and sunset. [See TIME CONCEPTS, p. LXXIII.] *The sun is very hot during the afternoon in July.*

SIGN #1: Right **'EXTENDED B'** hand is held out in front of the body with palm down and fingers pointing forward as the forearm rests on the back of the left **'EXTENDED B'** hand and is moved slightly up and down.

SIGN #2 [ATLANTIC]: Right **'B'** hand, palm facing left with fingertips pointing slightly upward and to the left, is held so the side of the forefinger is placed first against middle of forehead, and then brought down against the chin.

afterward: *adv.* subsequently; at a later time. *We had dinner and coffee afterward.*

SIGN: Thumb of vertical right **'L'** hand, palm forward, is rested against right-facing palm of vertical left **'EXTENDED B'** hand. The right wrist then bends to turn the right hand palm downward so that the forefinger eventually points forward.

again: *adv.* once more. *The children saw the same movie again.*

SIGN: Right **'BENT EXTENDED B'** hand, palm up, is overturned and brought downward so that the fingertips touch the upturned palm of the left **'EXTENDED B'** hand.

against: *prep.* in opposition to. *Deaf people are against the idea of being categorized as handicapped or disabled.*

SIGN: Horizontal left **'BENT EXTENDED B'** hand is held with palm facing rightward/backward and fingers pointing to the right. Right **'EXTENDED B'** (or **'B'**) hand is held upright very close to the chest with palm facing left. The right hand then drops from the wrist until it is horizontal with fingertips forcefully striking left hand between the palm and the fingers.

age: *n.* length of one's life. *Canadians who are 18 years of age and over may enter the competition.*

SIGN #1: Right **'S'** hand, slightly open, palm facing left, is brought down a short distance from the chin as it closes. Motion is repeated.

SIGN #2 [ATLANTIC]: The back of the fingers of the right **'BENT EXTENDED B'** hand, palm toward the body, are placed under the chin and brushed forward lightly a couple of times.

agency: *n.* a business or organization that provides a service and/or is authorized to act on someone's behalf. *He found work through the employment agency.*

SIGN: Fingerspell **AGENCY**.

agenda: *n.* a list of items to be discussed or done. *We have a very long agenda planned for the next meeting.*

SIGN: Fingerspell **AGENDA**.

agent: *n.* someone who is authorized to act on behalf of a person, business or organization. *She contacted her insurance agent after the accident.*

SIGN: Fingerspell **AGENT**.

aggravated: *v.* provoked or aroused to anger. *He was **aggravated** by the woman's insulting remarks.*

SIGN: Fingertips of right **'CLAWED OPEN EXTENDED A'** hand, palm facing the body, are scraped upward sharply against the chest. Facial expression must clearly convey 'aggravation'. (This sign is used only in a passive voice situation or as an adjective to describe someone's feelings. It would *not* be possible to use this sign in an active voice situation: *The woman's insulting remarks **aggravated** him*.)

ago: *adv.* in the past. *Years **ago** many Deaf people worked as printers.*

SIGN: Right **'BENT EXTENDED B'** hand, palm toward the body, is moved back to touch right shoulder.

agony: *n.* intense suffering; great pain. *The wounded person was in **agony**.*

SIGN: Thumb of right **'A'** hand, palm facing left, is pressed against the chin and the hand is twisted from the wrist several times. Facial expression must clearly convey 'suffering'.

agree: *v.* to concede; consent; concur. *I **agree** with your suggestion.*

SIGN: Left **'ONE'** hand is held at chest level with palm facing right, and forefinger pointing forward. Right **'ONE'** hand is held slightly higher with palm facing left, and is then turned downward to match the simultaneously downward turning left hand.
SAME SIGN—**agreement**, *n.*

agriculture: See **farm**.

ahead: *adv.* in advance; in front. *He is **ahead** of the class in completing his assignments.*

SIGN: Horizontal **'EXTENDED A'** hands, with left palm facing right and right palm facing left, are positioned so that knuckles of right hand are beside wrist of left hand. Right hand is then curved forward ahead of left hand.

aid: *v.* to help. *The tornado victims were **aided** by other provinces.*

SIGN: Horizontal left **'A'** (or **'EXTENDED A'**) hand, palm facing the body but turned slightly rightward, rests on the upturned palm of the right **'EXTENDED B'** hand. Both hands are moved forward in one motion toward the person receiving help. (For **aid**, *n.*, the horizontal left **'A'** (or **'EXTENDED A'**) hand, palm facing the body but turned slightly rightward, may be positioned on the upturned fingers of the right **'EXTENDED B'** hand. The hands both move as they are tapped together twice in a fixed location.) ❖

aide: *n.* assistant. *She is an **aide** to a top government official.*

SIGN: Horizontal left **'EXTENDED A'** hand is held in a fixed position with palm toward the body. Horizontal right **'L'** hand is positioned so that the thumbtip taps at least twice against the underside of the left hand.

AIDS: *n.* an acronym for acquired immune deficiency syndrome; the body's inability to resist infection. ***AIDS** is a serious illness.*

SIGN: Fingerspell **AIDS**.

ailment: *n.* illness or indisposition of the body or mind. *He missed work today due to a stomach **ailment**.*

SIGN: Horizontal **'ONE'** hands, tips of the forefingers almost touching each other, left palm facing up and right palm facing down are twisted so that palm positions are reversed. **'BENT MIDFINGER 5'** hands are then positioned so that the tip of the right middle finger is in the middle of the forehead and the tip of the left middle finger is on the stomach.
(ASL CONCEPT—**pain - sick**.)

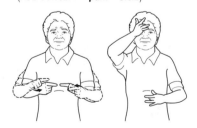

aim: *v.* to strive for a definite goal. *We aim to raise a total of $2000.*

SIGN: Vertical **'ONE'** hands, left palm facing right and right palm facing left, are held out in front of the face, with the left hand directly ahead of the right. The hands are then simultaneously moved forward.

air: *n.* an invisible combination of gases that forms the earth's atmosphere. *The air we breathe is vital for our survival.*

SIGN: Fingerspell **AIR**. (Signs vary, see also **fresh air**.)

A   I   R

airplane: *n.* a flying machine. *One can see many historic airplanes at an aviation museum.*

SIGN: Right **'COMBINED LY'** hand, palm downward and slightly forward, is moved a short distance forward twice.

airport: *n.* a field with structures and equipment where aircraft are maintained, repaired, and operated from. *There are many types of airplanes at an international airport.*

SIGN: Right **'COMBINED LY'** hand, palm downward and slightly forward, is moved a short distance forward twice.

aisle: *n.* a narrow walkway separating seating areas. *Everyone watched as the bride walked down the aisle of the church.*

SIGN: **'EXTENDED B'** hands, held parallel with palms facing one another and fingers pointing forward, are simultaneously moved forward. (When referring to an aisle flanked by high structures such as in a supermarket, vertical, rather than horizontal, **'EXTENDED B'** hands are used to make this sign.)

alarm: *n.* a signal or bell that gives a warning sound or draws attention. *The fire alarm in our apartment building is very loud.*

SIGN: Left side of forefinger of vertical right **'ONE'** hand, palm facing forward, is tapped against right facing palm of vertical left **'EXTENDED B'** hand at least twice. (Flashing lights rather than auditory alarms are used to get the attention of Deaf people. See **flashing light(s)**.)

alcohol: *n.* any liquor containing intoxicating spirits. *Alcohol is heavily taxed.*

SIGN: Horizontal right **'COMBINED I + ONE'** hand is held above and at right angles to horizontal left **'COMBINED I + ONE'** hand, whose palm faces slightly to the right and slightly toward the body. The two hands are then tapped together twice.

SAME SIGN—**alcoholic**, *adj.*, when it means 'containing alcohol'.

alcoholic: *n.* a person who is addicted to alcohol. *He lost his job because he is an alcoholic.*

SIGN: Thumb of right **'A'** hand, palm facing left, is positioned at left shoulder and moved to the right shoulder.

Alcoholics Anonymous: *n.* a self-help organization for recovering alcoholics. *Alcoholics Anonymous has helped many people stop drinking.*

SIGN: Vertical right **'A'** hand, palm forward, is held at shoulder level and appears to knock slightly while moving a little to the right, as it fingerspells **AA**.

alert: *adj.* wide-awake; watchful. *When you drive all night, it is hard to remain alert.*

SIGN: Vertical **'C'** hands, with palms facing each other, are brought up so tips of thumbs touch either side of face at the cheekbones.

algebra: *n.* a branch of mathematics in which calculations are performed using letters and symbols. *He used algebra to solve the equation.*

SIGN: Vertical right **'A'** hand, palm facing forward/leftward, is brushed to the leftward/backward a couple of times across the wrist of the palm-down left **'A'** hand which is simultaneously moving rightward.

alienate: *v.* to cause someone to become unfriendly and to dissociate with others. *He alienated himself from his coworkers when he crossed the picket line.*

SIGN: Left **'ONE'** hand is held upright with palm facing forward/rightward while vertical right **'SPREAD C'** hand is held just behind left hand with palm facing forward/leftward. The right hand is then purposefully moved back toward the body at a slight rightward angle.

alike: *adj.* similar; having a resemblance. *The two brothers were **alike** in appearance.*

SIGN: Vertical right **'Y'** hand is held with palm forward and appears to wobble from side to side as the wrist twists.

alive: *adj.* in a living state. *The people in the car accident were seriously hurt, but still **alive**.*

SIGN #1: Horizontal **'EXTENDED A'** hands are placed at either side, somewhere above the waist, with palms toward the body. They are then raised to a higher position on the chest.

OR

SIGN #2: Horizontal **'L'** hands are placed at either side, somewhere above the waist, with palms toward the body and forefingers pointing toward each other. They are then raised to a higher position on the chest.

SIGN #3 [ATLANTIC]: Tip of midfinger of right **'BENT MIDFINGER 5'** hand, palm toward the body, is used to brush upward lightly on the right side of the chest a couple of times.

all: *pron.* the whole lot, entity or amount. *We were rewarded for **all** of our work on the project.*

SIGN #1: Left **'EXTENDED B'** hand is held with palm facing body and fingertips pointing to the right. Right **'EXTENDED B'** hand is circled around the left hand with the back of the right hand coming to rest in the palm of the left hand.

all: *pron.* the total number. *Instead of choosing one candy, he ate **all** of them.*

SIGN #2: Right **'A'** hand, palm facing forward, twists at the wrist as it is moved smartly to the left, taking on an **'L'** shape with palm facing the body. This sign may be made vertically or horizontally, and with one hand or two, depending on the context.

allergy: *n.* abnormal sensitivity to a specific substance. *He may have an **allergy** to cat hair.*

SIGN #1: Side of crooked forefinger of right **'X'** hand, palm facing left, is tapped against the throat.

OR

SIGN #2: Horizontal **'BENT ONE'** hands are held together, palms facing the body, and tips of forefingers almost touching. Then they are pulled apart with a short, firm motion.
SAME SIGN—**allergic**, *adj.*

alligator: *n.* a large crocodilian reptile. *An **alligator** has a shorter, blunter snout than a crocodile.*

SIGN: **'SPREAD C'** hands are held, right above left, palms facing each other, with fingertips touching. They are then moved apart and back together again to simulate the opening and closing of an alligator's jaws.

allocate: *v.* to assign for a specific use. *The government will **allocate** funds for that project.*

SIGN: Right **'X'** hand is held upright with palm facing left, and is thrust forward and downward to a horizontal position. ❖

allow: *v.* to permit something to occur or to be done. *Most parents do not **allow** their children to behave inappropriately.*

SIGN #1: **'K'** hands, palms down, are held apart, extended fingers pointing downward, and are then flicked upward from the wrists so that the hands are held in either a horizontal or upright position.

OR

SIGN #2: Horizontal **'EXTENDED B'** hands are held with palms facing and fingers pointing forward. The hands are then swept upward simultaneously from the wrists so that the fingers point upward.

all right: *adj.* fine; correct; satisfactory; permissible. *It is **all right** to object.*

SIGN: The edge of the horizontal right **'EXTENDED B'** hand is placed on the upturned palm of the left **'EXTENDED B'** hand, and is pushed forward in a short, upward curving motion so that the fingers point upward. Motion is repeated.

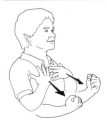

almighty: *adj.* all-powerful; omnipotent. *Most religions teach the concept of an almighty deity.*

SIGN: **'CONTRACTED 5'** hands, palms toward the body and fingers touching either side of the chest, are brought forward as they close to form **'S'** hands.

almost: *adv.* nearly. *The light indicated that the gas tank was almost empty.*

SIGN: Both **'BENT EXTENDED B'** hands are held with palms toward the body. The left hand remains steady, while the fingertips of the right hand are brushed upward from the knuckles of the left.

alone: *adj.* apart from others. *Many old people live alone.*

SIGN: Vertical right **'ONE'** hand, palm facing the body, is moved in a small counter-clockwise circle.

alphabet: *n.* the letters that form the elements of a written language. *Do you know the English manual alphabet used by the Deaf in Canada?*

SIGN: Right hand, palm facing forward, spells **ABC**, and then forms a **'BENT 5'** hand which moves from left to right, fingers fluttering. (AS CONCEPT—**A-B-C - spell**.) **ALPHABET** is frequently fingerspelled.

already: *adv.* before a stated or understood time. *The doctor told me that my foot was broken, but I already knew it.*

SIGN: Vertical **'5'** hands, palms facing the body, are held at chest level, and swung outward, away from the body so that the palms face down.

also: *adv.* as well as. *The school offers courses in Deaf Culture and also in American Sign Language.*

SIGN #1: **'ONE'** hands, palms down, forefingers pointing forward, are firmly brought together twice so that the sides of the forefingers strike each other.

OR

SIGN #2: Vertical right **'Y'** hand is held with palm forward and appears to wobble from side to side as the wrist twists.

---

alter: *v.* to change; modify; cause to be different. *We must alter our plans.*

SIGN: **'X'** hands (or **'A'** hands), palms facing, are twisted 180 degrees.

alternate: *v.* to take place in turns. *Red and black squares alternate on a checkerboard.*

SIGN: Right **'L'** hand is held with forefinger pointing forward and palm down and is turned so that the palm faces left and slightly upward. Motion is repeated.

---

alternative: *n.* an option; choice. *What alternative do we have?*

SIGN #1: Right hand alternates between **'FLAT OPEN F'** and **'F'** as thumb and forefinger pluck first at tip of forefinger of vertical left **'V'** hand (palm facing the body) and then at tip of middle finger.

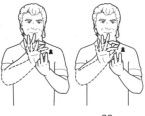

OR

SIGN #2: Right **'EXTENDED A'** hand is held palm down. As the wrist rotates rightward, the hand is turned so that the palm faces left.

although: *conj.* even though; granting that. *Although he is old, he is still active.*

SIGN: Fingers of horizontal **'BENT EXTENDED B'** hands, palms facing the chest, are alternately brushed back and forth against each other.

altogether: *adv.* totally; all told. *Altogether our flight, accommodation, and entertainment made it an expensive holiday.*

SIGN #1: Horizontal **'CONTRACTED 5'** hands, palms facing each other, are brought together as they close to form **'FLAT O'** hands, with fingers of the one hand touching those of the other.

OR

SIGN #2: Right **'CONTRACTED 5'** hand, palm facing down, is circled widely in a clockwise direction over the opening of the horizontal left **'C'** hand whose palm faces right. Right hand is then closed to form a **'FLAT O'** hand of which the fingertips are inserted into the opening of the left hand.

always: *adv.* at all times. *He always visits his mother on her birthday.*

SIGN: Right **'ONE'** hand, palm facing mainly upward but angled toward the body, makes a couple of counter-clockwise circles.

Alzheimer's Disease: *n.* a brain disease that becomes progressively worse. *Living with someone who has Alzheimer's Disease requires much patience and understanding.*

SIGN: Fingerspell **ALZHEIMER**.

amaze: *v.* to surprise; overwhelm. *The magician's tricks will amaze you.*

SIGN: Thumbs and forefingers of **'CLOSED MODIFIED G'** (or **'CLOSED X'**) hands are placed at either cheek, and opened sharply to form **'L'** (or **'CONTRACTED L'**) hands as they move sharply away from the face.
SAME SIGN—**amazement**, *n.*

ambition: *n.* objective; goal. *His ambition is to become the first Deaf dentist in Canada.*

SIGN #1: Vertical **'ONE'** hands, left palm facing right and right palm facing left, are held out in front of the face, with the left hand directly ahead of the right. Both hands are then simultaneously moved forward.

ambition: *n.* a strong desire to achieve or succeed. *His colleagues have noticed that he has a lot of ambition.*

SIGN #2: **'A'** hands are held in front of either side of the chest with palms facing each other and are alternately circled forward, the thumbs brushing upward and forward off the chest with each revolution.

ambitious: *adj.* having a strong desire to achieve or succeed. *He is a very ambitious employee.*

SIGN: **'A'** hands are held in front of either side of the chest with palms facing each other and are alternately circled forward, the thumbs brushing upward and forward off the chest with each revolution.

ambulance: *n.* a vehicle used for transporting the sick and injured. *There is a special phone number for the Deaf to call an ambulance if necessary.*

SIGN #1: Left hand grasps wrist of right **'CONTRACTED 5'** hand. Then right hand is twisted around to the left from the wrist to simulate the action of a flashing light.

SIGN #2 [ONTARIO]: Side of forefinger of vertical right **'U'** hand, palm facing left, touches left side of forehead and then right side. Motion is repeated.

amen: *s.s.* so be it. *At the end of a prayer, people usually say 'amen'.*

SIGN: Vertical **'EXTENDED B'** hands are brought together, palm to palm, and then lowered slightly.

amend: *v.* to revise; change. *He **amended** his motion to include the date.*

SIGN: Left **'EXTENDED B'** hand is held with palm toward the chest and fingers pointing rightward. Right **'FLAT C'** hand, palm toward the body, is brought upward from the wrist to allow the fingers of the left hand to slot into the opening in the right hand.
SAME SIGN—**amendment**, *n.*

American Sign Language (ASL): *n.* a visual-gestural language created by the Deaf and used by Canadians and Americans. *ASL is a vivid, colourful language.*

SIGN: Fingerspell **ASL**.

amiable: *adj.* friendly or pleasing in disposition. *He is always a gracious and **amiable** host.*

SIGN: **'5'** hands, palms facing backward, move backward with fingers fluttering until they come to rest close to either side of the face.

amnesia: *n.* loss or impairment of memory. *She suffered from **amnesia** after the accident.*

SIGN: Fingers of right **'SPREAD C'** hand are placed on the forehead and drawn away to form an **'S'** hand, palm toward the face. Tip of middle finger of vertical right **'BENT MIDFINGER 5'** hand is then drawn across the forehead from left to right. (ASL CONCEPT—**memory - blank**.) Alternatively, only the second part of this sign may be used.

ample: *adj.* more than enough. *We have **ample** food for the party.*

SIGN #1: **'EXTENDED A'** hands, palms slightly facing the body and slightly facing upward, are simultaneously circled outward in opposite directions. The cheeks are puffed out.

OR

SIGN #2: Horizontal left **'S'** hand, palm facing right, is covered with palm of right **'EXTENDED B'** hand. Then the right hand is brushed firmly forward and slightly to the right. The cheeks are puffed out.

amputate: *v.* to remove a body part surgically. *Doctors may have to **amputate** a limb that has gangrene.*

SIGN: Right **'B'** hand is brought down in a chopping motion to strike the left arm. (The location of this sign varies depending on which limb is being discussed.)

amusing: *adj.* funny. *He told an **amusing** story.*

SIGN: The two extended fingers of the **'BENT EXTENDED U'** hand, palm toward the face, stroke the nose at least twice in a downward motion.

analyze: *v.* to investigate; think through; examine. *If you **analyze** the statistics, you will notice some interesting patterns.*

SIGN: **'V'** hands, palms down, extended fingers of one hand pointing toward those of the other hand, are simultaneously moved apart at least twice while the extended fingers retract to take on **'CLAWED V'** handshapes.
SAME SIGN—**analysis**, *n.*

anatomy: *n.* the study of body structure. *Medical students must learn about human anatomy.*

SIGN: Horizontal **'EXTENDED B'** hands, palms toward body, fingertips touching either side of the chest, are moved down and placed at the waist. Next, left **'EXTENDED B'** hand is held in a fixed position with fingers pointing rightward and palm toward the body at a slight upward angle. Right **'BENT 5'** hand is held a little higher and closer to the chest with the palm down and the fingers fluttering as they point toward the left palm. (ASL CONCEPT—**body - study**.)

ancestors: *n.* those from whom descendants are derived. *His ancestors owned a castle in France.*

SIGN: Vertical **'5'** hands, right palm facing left and left palm facing right, are held in front of the right side of the chest, the left hand slightly below and ahead of the right hand. Then they are circled alternately in backward motions over the right shoulder.

ancient: *adj.* very old; belonging to the distant past. *The ancient ruins of Athens are very interesting.*

SIGN: Vertical **'5'** hand is held in front of right shoulder with palm facing left and slightly forward, and is circled backward at least twice.

and: *conj.* a connecting word meaning also, plus, or in addition to. *The Canadian flag is red and white.*

SIGN: Horizontal right **'CONTRACTED 5'** hand, palm facing the body, is drawn from left to right as it closes to form a **'FLAT O'** hand.

anesthetic: *n.* a gas used to produce a loss of feeling prior to surgery. *He was given an anesthetic before his operation.*

SIGN: Right **'SPREAD C'** hand, palm toward the face, is brought upward to cover the nose and mouth.

angel: *n.* a seraphic spirit or divine messenger. *She played an angel in the Christmas pageant.*

SIGN: **'BENT EXTENDED B'** hands, fingertips touching either shoulder, palms down, are swung outward and are then moved up and down slightly as though they were wings.

angle: *n.* the space between two intersecting lines. *Can you draw an angle measuring 90 degrees?*

SIGN: Forefinger of right **'ONE'** hand, palm down, traces the outline of the angle formed by the vertical left **'L'** hand which is held with palm forward at a slight rightward angle.

angry: *adj.* enraged; infuriated. *Her rudeness makes me angry.*

SIGN: **'CLAWED 5'** hands, palms toward body, fingertips touching chest, are swept vigorously upward/outward. Facial expression must clearly convey 'anger'. (The sign shown here may **not** be used as an active voice verb: *His rudeness angers me.* The sign may be used only as an adjective to describe someone's feelings or as a verb in the passive voice as in: *I was angered by his rudeness.*)
SAME SIGN—**anger**, *n.*
ALTERNATE SIGN—**mad** #1

animal: *n.* a living being. *An animal often associated with Canada is the beaver.*

SIGN #1 *(current)*: Without lifting the fingertips of the **'BENT EXTENDED B'** hands from their positions at either side of the chest, the forearms move inward and outward.

OR

SIGN #2 *(used occasionally)*: **'BENT V'** hands are held with palms down, so that the extended fingers of the right hand represent the front legs, and the extended fingers of the left hand represent the hind legs of an animal. Then both hands are moved forward simultaneously with the fingers wiggling so that they appear to be walking.

annihilate: *v.* to destroy completely. *The evil leader meant to annihilate his opponents.*

SIGN: Right **'5'** hand is held palm down, fingertips forward, and as it is thrust forward along the upturned left **'EXTENDED B'** hand, whose fingertips point forward, it assumes the **'S'** handshape.

anniversary: *n.* the date upon which an event occurred at some previous time. *The couple celebrated their 20th wedding anniversary.*

SIGN: Vertical **'COVERED T'** hands are held at either side of the head, palms facing each other, and are swung in small circles above the shoulders.

announce: *v.* to proclaim; make known publicly *The Prime Minister will* **announce** *his cabinet appointments.*

SIGN: **'ONE'** hands, palms down, tips of forefingers touching either side of the mouth, are swung outward so that forefingers point upward and palms face away from the body. SAME SIGN—**announcement**, *n.*

annoy: *v.* to disturb; bother. *Does his teasing* **annoy** *you?*

SIGN: Right **'EXTENDED B'** hand, palm facing slightly left, is positioned above and at right angles to left **'EXTENDED B'** hand which faces slightly right. Then the right hand is brought down sharply between the thumb and forefinger of the left hand. Motion is repeated. ❖

annoyed: *adj.* feeling disturbed or bothered. *I am* **annoyed** *by your constant interruptions.*

SIGN #1: Vertical right **'BENT MIDFINGER 5'** hand is held with palm left and tip of middle finger touching forehead. The wrist then rotates to turn the palm toward the face. Facial expression must clearly convey 'annoyance'. (**Annoyed** #1 and #2 may **not** be used in an active voice situation: *You* **annoy** *me with your constant interruptions.*)

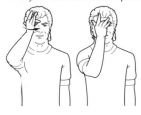

OR

SIGN #2: Middle finger of right **'K'** hand is brought up to touch the tip of the nose. The hand then turns forward and down as it forms an **'F'** hand. Facial expression must clearly convey 'annoyance'.

SIGN #3 [ATLANTIC]: Right **'SPREAD C'** hand is held against the chest with palm down as the fingers close to form an **'S'** shape. Facial expression must clearly convey 'annoyance'

annual: *adj.* occurring once a year. *The* **annual** *staff party will be held on June 10th.*

SIGN #1: Horizontal right **'S'** hand, palm facing left, is placed on top of horizontal left **'S'** hand whose palm faces right. Right forefinger is then flicked forward twice.

SIGN #2 [ATLANTIC]: Left **'ONE'** hand, palm toward body, and forefinger pointing right, remains fixed while forefinger of right **'ONE'** hand circles forward around left forefinger and comes to rest on top of it.

annul: *v.* to cancel or revoke. *The church agreed to* **annul** *their marriage.*

SIGN: Tip of forefinger of right **'ONE'** hand draws an **'X'** across palm of horizontal left **'EXTENDED B'** hand which faces the body at a slight rightward angle.

another: *pron.* one more of the same sort. *My pen does not work so I will get* **another** *one.*

SIGN: Right **'EXTENDED A'** hand is held palm down. As the wrist rotates rightward, the hand is turned so that the palm faces left.

answer: *v.* to reply to. *Please* **answer** *my question.*

SIGN: Vertical **'ONE'** hands, palms facing forward, are held with the tip of the right forefinger near the mouth and the left hand slightly farther forward and downward. Both are moved forward and down, stopping with the palms facing downward. SAME SIGN—**answer**, *n.*

ant: *n.* a type of social insect. *An* **ant** *will sometimes bite.*

SIGN: Fingerspell **ANT**.

anti-: *prefix* against; in opposition to. *He launched an antiwar campaign.*

SIGN: Horizontal left **'BENT EXTENDED B'** hand is held with palm facing rightward/backward and fingers pointing to the right. Right **'EXTENDED B'** (or **'B'**) hand is held upright very close to the chest with palm facing left. The right hand then drops from the wrist until it is horizontal with fingertips forcefully striking left hand between the palm and the fingers. Facial expression is important. (The prefix **ANTI-** may be fingerspelled.)

anticipate: *v.* to expect or regard as likely to happen. *We anticipate better weather soon.*

SIGN: Tip of forefinger of right **'ONE'** hand touches forehead and then, staying in the same place, the hand assumes a vertical **'BENT EXTENDED B'** shape, palm facing left. Vertical left **'BENT EXTENDED B'** hand, palm facing right, is held just in front of left shoulder. Fingers of both hands are then simultaneously moved up and down once or twice. (ASL CONCEPT—**think - expect**.)

antique: *n.* an ancient relic or curio. *The glass vase was a rare antique.*

SIGN #1: Right **'S'** hand, slightly open, palm facing left, is brought down firmly from chin as it closes. (**ANTIQUE** is frequently fingerspelled.)

SIGN #2 [ATLANTIC]: Right **'S'** hand, slightly open, palm facing left, is brought down firmly from the chin as it closes. Then thumb and forefinger of right **'F'** hand are placed at left shoulder.

SIGN #3 [ONTARIO]: Right **'S'** hand, slightly open, palm facing left, is brought down firmly from chin as it closes. Then right **'F'** hand, palm down, is moved sharply from left to right in front of chest.

antlers: *n.* the branched horns of a deer. *The hunters found some antlers that a deer had shed.*

SIGN: Vertical **'5'** hands, palms forward but facing slightly, are placed at either side of the head, thumbs on the forehead. The arms are then moved slightly so that the thumbs tap gently against the forehead.

anxious: *adj.* worried; uneasy. *We are anxious about the missing campers.*

SIGN #1: **'B'** (or **'EXTENDED B'**) hands are held apart in front of the face at such an angle that the palms face each other but slant downward while the fingers of the left hand point upward/rightward and the fingers of the right hand point upward/leftward. The hands are then alternately circled toward each other a few times. Facial expression must clearly convey 'anxiety'.
SAME SIGN—**anxiety**, *n.*

anxious: *adj.* enthusiastic; eager; impatient. *We are anxious to see the competition results.*

SIGN #2: Fingertips of middle fingers of **'BENT MIDFINGER 5'** hands are alternately brushed up and off either side of chest in forward circular motions. Next, **'BENT V'** hands are held apart with one slightly ahead of the other, palms forward/downward and extended fingers pointing forward and slightly upward. The hands are simultaneously jabbed forward twice. Facial expression must clearly convey 'excitement'. (ASL CONCEPT—**excite - look forward**.)

any: *adj.* one or some, regardless of type or amount. *Please give me any information you have.*

SIGN: Right **'EXTENDED A'** hand, palm facing the body, is twisted from the wrist so that the palm faces forward/downward.

anyhow: *adv.* by any means; in any case. *He was tired and injured, but he finally made it home* **anyhow.**

SIGN: Fingers of horizontal **'BENT EXTENDED B'** hands, palms facing the chest, are alternately brushed back and forth against each other.

anyone: *pron.* any person. *Anyone may apply for admission to the college.*

SIGN: Right **'EXTENDED A'** hand, palm facing the body, is twisted from the wrist so that the palm faces forward/downward. Then it is changed to a vertical **'ONE'** hand, and raised so that the palm faces the shoulder.

anything: *pron.* any object or fact. *You can buy* **anything** *at the mall.*

SIGN: Right **'EXTENDED A'** hand, palm facing the body, is twisted from the wrist so that the palm faces forward/downward. Then it is changed to an upturned **'EXTENDED B'** hand, fingers pointing forward, and moved to the right in a small arc.

anyway: *adv.* nevertheless; no matter what happens. *Anyway, the meeting will adjourn soon.*

SIGN: Fingers of horizontal **'BENT EXTENDED B'** hands, palms facing the chest, are alternately brushed back and forth against each other.

anywhere: *adv.* at any location. *You can buy that item* **anywhere.**

SIGN: Right **'EXTENDED A'** hand, palm facing the body, is twisted from the wrist so that the palm faces forward/downward. Then it is changed to a vertical **'ONE'** hand with palm facing forward, and the forefinger is waved from side to side.

apart: *adv.* separated in space or time. *The roosters were kept* **apart.**

SIGN: Horizontal **'BENT EXTENDED B'** hands, palms facing chest and knuckles almost touching each other, are drawn apart.

apartment: *n.* a suite of rooms. *In some apartments, pets are not allowed.*

SIGN #1: Fingerspell **APT**.

SIGN #2 [ONTARIO]: Left **'EXTENDED B'** hand is held in a fixed position with palm up and fingers pointing rightward/forward. Right **'EXTENDED B'** hand is held with palm left and fingers pointing forward and is lowered as it strikes the left palm. The right hand is then raised and bends to assume a **'BENT EXTENDED B'** shape as it twists a quarter turn, then strikes the left palm again as though branding the left palm with a cross.

apathy: *n.* indifference; lack of emotion, enthusiasm or interest. *Apathy can stand in the way of progress.*

SIGN: Fingerspell **APATHY**. (Alternatively, various signs may be used.)

ape: *n.* a large tailless gorilla or chimpanzee. *Apes are primates.*

SIGN: Fingertips of both **'CLAWED 5'** hands, one on either side of the rib-cage, palms toward the body, are brushed upward with a scratching motion.

apologize: *v.* to express regret. *He should apologize for his misconduct.*

SIGN: Right **'A'** (or **'EXTENDED A'**) hand, palm facing the body, is rubbed on the chest with a circular motion which, in the eyes of onlookers, appears clockwise.
SAME SIGN—**apology**, *n.*

apostrophe: *n.* a punctuation mark (') that shows possession, *e.g., Jason's book*, or indicates letter omission(s), *e.g., We're for we are. The apostrophe generally comes after the 's' if the word is plural.*

SIGN: Forefinger of vertical right **'CROOKED ONE'** (or **'BENT ONE'**) hand makes a quarter turn twist to the right to trace the outline of an imaginary apostrophe.

apparatus: *n.* equipment for a particular purpose. *The scientists set up the apparatus for the experiment.*

SIGN: Right **'EXTENDED B'** hand, palm facing up, fingers pointing forward, is moved from left to right in a series of successive short arcs.

apparel: See **clothes**.

apparent: *adj.* clearly perceivable; evident; obvious. *It is apparent that he has a bad cold.*

SIGN: Right **'BENT EXTENDED B'** hand with palm facing forward/left, is twisted slightly from the wrist so that it faces the right shoulder.
ALTERNATE SIGN—**obvious**

appeal: *v.* to ask for a review of a situation by a recognized authority. *The interpreter will appeal the revocation of his professional certificate.*

SIGN: Right **'SPREAD C'** hand is held in a horizontal position as thumb and fingertips thump against chest. (**APPEAL** is frequently fingerspelled.)

appear: *v.* to seem or to be clear. *The students appear to enjoy their class.*

SIGN #1: Right **'BENT EXTENDED B'** hand, palm facing forward/left, is twisted slightly from the wrist so that it faces the right shoulder.

appear: *v.* to show up or come into view. *If you appear on my doorstep tonight, I will be very surprised.*

SIGN #2: Left **'EXTENDED B'** hand is held, palm down, in a fixed position. Right **'ONE'** hand, palm forward, is brought up underneath the left hand and the extended forefinger is thrust upward between the forefinger and middle finger of the left hand.

appearance: *n.* one's looks or outward aspect. *One's appearance is important when applying for work.*

SIGN: Vertical right **'5'** hand, palm toward the face, is circled in what is seen by onlookers as a clockwise direction.

appetite: *n.* a desire to eat or drink. *He has the appetite of three people.*

SIGN: Fingertips of horizontal right **'EXTENDED C'** hand, palm toward the body, are placed against middle of upper chest and the hand is drawn firmly downward. (**APPETITE** is frequently fingerspelled.)

applaud: *v.* to express approval by clapping the hands. *The audience will applaud at the end of the play.*

SIGN: **'EXTENDED B'** hands, palms facing each other, are clapped together.
SAME SIGN—**applause**, *n.*

applaud: *v.* a way in which some Deaf people show their approval of a performance, and offer praise. *The Deaf viewers will applaud at the end of the play.*

SIGN: Both arms, with vertical **'5'** hands, raised above the head, palms facing each other yet facing forward slightly, are twisted back and forth from the wrists so rapidly that all the fingers appear to be fluttering.
SAME SIGN—**applause**, *n.*, in this context.

apple: *n.* a round, firm, fleshy fruit. *British Columbia* **apples** *are delicious.*

SIGN #1: Right **'X'** hand touches right cheek with knuckle of crooked forefinger, which is then twisted back and forth at least twice.

SIGN #2 [ATLANTIC]: Right horizontal **'CLAWED L'** hand, palm toward face, is held near the chin and moved upward a couple of times in front of the mouth to simulate the eating of an apple.

apply: *v.* to make a formal request. *If you* **apply** *for the job, you have a good chance of being hired.*

SIGN #1: Horizontal right **'F'** hand grasps the signer's shirt below the right shoulder between the thumb and forefinger, and is moved back and forth twice.

apply: *v.* to complete an application form. *Job seekers must* **apply** *on this form.*

SIGN #2: Fingertips of right **'FLAT O'** hand are slid from fingertips to heel of upturned left **'EXTENDED B'** hand.

apply: *v.* to pertain to. *The 'no smoking' rule* **applies** *to everyone on this worksite.*

SIGN #3: Thumbs and forefingers of both **'F'** hands interlock and are moved toward the person, place or thing to whom the situation pertains.
ALTERNATE SIGN—**appointment** #1

apply: *v.* to concentrate one's efforts; devote (oneself). *If you* **apply** *yourself, you can become a great musician.*

SIGN #4: Vertical right **'CLAWED V'** hand, palm facing backward, is thrust forward and slightly downward so that the back of the hand makes contact with the palm of the horizontal left **'SPREAD C'** hand which is held with the palm facing the body.

apply: *v.* to put on, or spread onto a surface. *Apply the sunblock to all exposed skin surfaces.*

SIGN #5: Fingertips of **'CROOKED EXTENDED B'** (or **'EXTENDED B'**) hands are moved back and forth in a rubbing motion on various parts of the body. Natural gestures are used rather than a specific sign, depending on what sort of application is intended.

appoint: *v.* to designate or assign to an office. *The president* **appoints** *the committee members.*

SIGN: Thumb and forefinger of right **'OPEN F'** hand are closed to form an **'F'** shape as the hand is brought toward the chest. Alternatively, vertical left **'EXTENDED B'** hand is held with palm facing forward/rightward while thumb and forefinger of right **'OPEN F'** hand are closed to form an **'F'** shape as the hand is brought back against the left palm.
SAME SIGN—**appointment**, *n.*, in this context.

appointment: *n.* an arrangement to be at a certain place at a specific time. *I will cancel my* **appointment** *so I can attend your meeting.*

SIGN #1: Extended fingers of right **'V'** hand are brought downward on either side of forefinger of vertical left **'ONE'** hand, which is held in a fixed position with palm facing right.

OR

SIGN #2: **'S'** hands are held palms down, right hand above left. Right hand is circled clockwise and brought down to rest on back of left hand.

appreciate: *v.* to be grateful for. *I* **appreciate** *the help you gave me.*

SIGN #1: Horizontal right **'EXTENDED B'** hand, palm on the chest, is moved in a circular motion, which appears to onlookers to be clockwise.
SAME SIGN—**appreciation**, *n.*

appreciate: *v.* to realize or understand a problem or situation. *I* **appreciate** *the difficulties you will be facing.*

SIGN #2: Fingertips of right **'BENT EXTENDED B'** hand, with palm toward the face, are tapped against right side of forehead a couple of times.

apprehend: *v.* to arrest; take into custody. *The police hope to* **apprehend** *the thieves at the road block.*

SIGN: Right **'SPREAD C'** hand is held palm down at chest level and is then closed to form an **'S'** hand as it is thrust forward. Alternatively, this sign may be made with two hands held apart in front of the chest. ❖

ALTERNATE SIGNS—**arrest** #2 & #3. Where a *group* of people are being arrested, see **sanction** #2.

apprehensive: *adj.* fearful; uneasy. *She was* **apprehensive** *about driving on icy roads.*

SIGN: Side of forefinger of right **'ONE'** hand, palm facing downward, is tapped twice against left side of chest.

approach: *v.* to make a proposal to. *He must* **approach** *the board members with his suggestions.*

SIGN #1: Vertical left **'EXTENDED B'** hand is held in a fixed position with palm toward face. Vertical right **'EXTENDED B'** hand, palm forward, is moved forward to stop near, but not touching the left hand. ❖

approach: *v.* to move near or nearer to. *I* **approached** *the stranger with caution.*

SIGN #2: Vertical left **'ONE'** hand is held in a fixed position with palm facing the body while vertical right **'ONE'** hand is held closer to the body with palm forward and slightly leftward. The right hand is then moved forward/leftward to meet the left hand. (This sign is sometimes made without the left hand.) ❖

approach: *n.* way; method. *His* **approach** *to coaching is very innovative.*

SIGN #3: **'EXTENDED B'** hands, held parallel with palms facing one another and fingers pointing forward, are simultaneously moved forward.

appropriate: *adj.* suitable; proper; fitting. *This is the* **appropriate** *sign for that concept.*

SIGN: Right **'ONE'** hand, palm facing left, is held above left **'ONE'** hand, palm facing right, with forefingers pointing forward. Then right hand is tapped at least twice on left hand.

approve: *v.* to express acceptance; consider favourably. *Grandma does not* **approve** *of shopping on Sunday.*

SIGN #1: Both **'CONTRACTED 5'** hands, with wrists loosely bent, and palms down, are drawn toward the chest to form **'FLAT O'** hands.

SAME SIGN—**approval**, *n.*, in this context.

approve: *v.* to endorse; show support for. *The city council will* **approve** *the new housing project.*

SIGN #2: Horizontal right **'S'** hand, palm toward the body and facing left slightly, is brought down firmly to rest on the upturned palm of the left **'EXTENDED B'** hand.

SAME SIGN—**approval**, *n.*, in this context.

approximate: *adj.* not necessarily exact, but close to. *The* **approximate** *time of the baby's birth was 2:00 a.m.*

SIGN: Vertical right **'5'** hand, palm forward, is circled in front of the right shoulder with a counter-clockwise motion.

April: *n.* the fourth month of the year. *April showers bring May flowers.*

SIGN: Fingerspell **APRIL**.

apron: *n.* a garment worn to protect a person's clothes. *An* **apron** *should be worn when one is preparing food.*

SIGN: Both **'A'** hands, palms facing the body, are placed together at the middle of the waist. Then they are moved to the sides of the waist and around behind the body before being drawn outward to simulate the tying of apron strings.

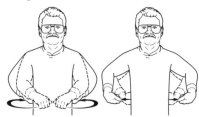

arch: *n.* a bowlike, curved structure. *The bride and groom stood under the arch in the garden.*

SIGN: Right **'EXTENDED B'** (or **'BENT EXTENDED B'**) hand, palm down and fingers pointing forward, is used to inscribe an arch from left to right.

archery: *n.* the sport of shooting with bows and arrows. *He bought a new bow and some arrows to practise archery.*

SIGN: Horizontal left **'S'** hand is held in a fixed position with palm facing right. Horizontal right **'S'** hand, palm facing left, is held just behind the left hand and is then drawn backward and changed to a **'V'** shape as it nears the right shoulder.

architecture: *n.* the structure and design of a building. *The architecture in that city is quite unique.*

SIGN: **'Y'** hands, which are held with palms down and thumbtips touching, alternately wobble slightly.

area: *n.* place; locality; region. *Many older people live in the same area of the city.*

SIGN #1: Right **'5'** hand, palm down, is circled in a counter-clockwise motion.
ALTERNATE SIGN—**region**

area: *n.* specialty; domain; field of interest. *Her area of expertise is fundraising.*

SIGN #2: Left **'B'** hand is held in a fixed position with palm facing right and fingers pointing forward. Right **'B'** hand, palm facing left, and fingers pointing forward, is positioned on top of the left hand and firmly moved forward.

argue: *v.* to debate; present reasons for or against. *It does not help to argue with the referee.*

SIGN: **'BENT ONE'** hands, palms toward the chest, forefingers pointing toward each other, are either simultaneously or alternately moved up and down from the wrist.
SAME SIGN—**argument**, *n.*
ALTERNATE SIGN—**discuss**

arid: *adj.* extremely dry. *Cactuses grow in arid regions.*

SIGN: Side of crooked forefinger of right **'X'** hand, palm facing down, is placed on left side of chin and firmly drawn across to the right side.

arise: *v.* to get out of bed. *Farmers arise very early in the morning.*

SIGN #1: Right **'CROOKED V'** hand, palm upward, is raised and overturned as it is brought downward, extended fingertips coming to rest on upturned palm of left **'EXTENDED B'** hand.

arise: *v.* to occur; come into being. *If you do not check your antifreeze, engine problems could arise.*

SIGN #2: Left **'EXTENDED B'** hand is held, palm down, in a fixed position. Right **'ONE'** hand, palm forward, is brought up underneath the left hand and the extended forefinger is thrust upward between the index and middle finger of the left hand.

arm: *n.* upper limb of the human body. *His arm was stiff after the game.*

SIGN: Right **'CROOKED 5'** hand grasps the upper left arm and moves downward to the wrist of the left **'STANDARD BASE'** hand.

arms: *n.* weapons. *Will there ever be an end to the use of arms?*

SIGN: Fingerspell **ARMS**. (Various signs may be used.)

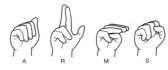

army: *n.* military troops. *The army trains personnel for endurance in the Arctic.*

SIGN: **'A'** hands are placed on the left side of the chest, palms facing the body, with the right hand above the left. Then they are simultaneously moved forward and back to tap twice against the body.

around: *adv.* approximately. *The item costs around fifty or sixty dollars.*

SIGN #1: Vertical right **'5'** hand, palm facing forward, is circled in front of the right shoulder in a counter-clockwise direction.

around: *prep.* in a circular motion. *We walked all the way* **around** *the building.*

NOTE—The English word **around** does not have a one-sign equivalent in ASL. Signs vary considerably depending on several factors. An all-inclusive sign is often used incorporating any combination of the subject, verb, preposition **around**, and the object of the preposition.

aroused: *adj.* excited. *The cat was* **aroused** *by the smell of catnip.*

SIGN: Tips of middle fingers of **'BENT MIDFINGER 5'** hands, palms toward the body, are brushed up and off the chest in alternating circular motions. (This sign is used only in a passive voice situation or as an adjective. It may *not* be used in an active voice situation: *The smell of catnip* **aroused** *the cat.*)

arrange: *v.* to place in proper order; prepare for. *We must* **arrange** *the details of the party.*

SIGN: Horizontal **'EXTENDED B'** hands, palms facing each other and fingers pointing forward, are held slightly apart at the left side of the body and are moved simultaneously toward the right.

(in) arrears: *n.* overdue debts. *His electricity was cut off because his bill was three months* **in arrears.**

SIGN: Tip of forefinger of right **'ONE'** hand, palm toward body, is tapped twice against right-facing palm of horizontal left **'EXTENDED B'** hand.

arrest: *v.* to take into custody. *People are* **arrested** *for breaking the law.*

SIGN #1: Right **'SPREAD C'** hand is held palm down at chest level and is then closed to form an **'S'** hand as it is thrust forward. Alternatively, this sign may be made with two hands held apart in front of the chest. (Where a *group* of people are being arrested, see **sanction** #2. Signs vary considerably.) ❖

OR

SIGN #2: Right **'SPREAD C'** hand, palm facing left, is moved left and becomes an **'S'** hand as it grabs the forefinger of the vertical left **'ONE'** hand whose palm faces right. ❖

OR

SIGN #3: The two clawed fingers of the horizontal right **'CLAWED V'** hand, palm facing left, are moved left to hook around the forefinger of the vertical left **'ONE'** hand whose palm faces right. ❖

arrive: *v.* to reach a destination. *The plane will* **arrive** *at 10:45 a.m.*

SIGN #1: Right **'BENT EXTENDED B'** hand, with palm facing the body, is brought down and laid palm-up on the upturned palm of the left **'EXTENDED B'** hand.

SIGN #2 [ATLANTIC]: **'EXTENDED B'** hands, palms facing away from the body at a 45° angle and fingers pointing forward/upward, are simultaneously brought down to a palms-down position and stopped with a slight bounce. Alternatively, this sign may be made with the right hand only.
SAME SIGN—**arrival**, *n.*

arrogant: *adj.* insolently proud. *Cinderella's sisters were* **arrogant.**

SIGN: **'EXTENDED A'** hand, with thumb pointing downward, is moved upward from stomach to chest. Facial expression must clearly convey 'arrogance'.
SAME SIGN—**arrogance**, *n.*
ALTERNATE SIGN—**conceited**

art: *n.* creative works of beauty or special significance. *The* **art** *on display features paintings by the Group of Seven.*

SIGN: Left **'EXTENDED B'** hand is held in a fixed and relatively fixed position with palm facing the body. The tip of the little finger of the right **'I'** hand is stroked downward twice along the middle of the left palm.
SAME SIGN—**artist**, *n.*, and may be followed by the Agent Ending (see p. LIV).

arthritis: *n.* inflammation of the joint(s). *Arthritis can be a very painful condition.*

SIGN: Vertical right **'A'** hand is held palm forward as the hand wobbles.

article: *n.* a written commentary. *The 'greenhouse effect' was explained in a magazine article.*

SIGN #1: Thumb and forefinger of right **'CLAWED L'** hand, palm facing left, are stroked downward across the right-facing palm of the left **'EXTENDED B'** hand.

article: *n.* item; thing. *A camera can be an expensive article.*

SIGN #2: Right **'EXTENDED B'** hand, palm upward and fingers pointing forward, is moved rightward in an arc formation.

artificial: *adj.* not occurring naturally. *Artificial flowers last a long time.*

SIGN: Side of forefinger of right **'ONE'** hand, palm facing leftward/forward, is lightly brushed forward/downward twice on the right cheek, forefinger either remaining upright or bending slightly to become a **'BENT ONE'**.

as: *conj.* to the same extent. *The deer ran as fast as the wind.*

SIGN #1: **'ONE'** hands, palms down and fingers pointing forward, are brought together.

OR

SIGN #2: Vertical right **'Y'** hand is held with palm forward and appears to wobble from side to side as the wrist twists.

as: *conj.* because. *We assumed you were not coming as we had not heard from you.*

SIGN #3: Fingertips of **'BENT EXTENDED B'** hand are placed against forehead, palm toward face, and are then drawn slightly upward to the right to form an **'A'** hand.
ALTERNATE SIGN—**because** #2

as: *conj.* while. *As her children played in the back yard, she watched them closely.*

SIGN #4: **'ONE'** hands are held apart close to the chest with palms down and forefingers pointing forward. The hands are then moved forward from the body in parallel lines.

ascend: *v.* to rise; to move upward. *The plane is beginning to ascend.*

SIGN: Right **'COMBINED LY'** hand is held palm down with extended fingers pointing forward/leftward. The forearm then moves upward at a forward/rightward angle, the palm of the hand eventually facing upward/rightward. (Sign choice varies considerably, depending on the *size and shape* of the object and the *manner* in which it is ascending.)

ashamed: *adj.* feeling guilt, shame or disgrace. *The girl was ashamed because she cheated on the test.*

SIGN: The backs of the fingers of the right **'BENT EXTENDED B'** hand, palm facing right shoulder, are brushed forward against right cheek as palm faces up.

ask: *v.* to inquire about; make a request. *I will ask for help.*

SIGN #1: Vertical right **'ONE'** hand, palm facing forward is moved firmly forward and slightly downward as the forefinger retracts to form an **'X'** hand. ❖

OR

SIGN #2: Vertical right **'S'** hand is held with palm facing forward. Then the right forefinger is flicked forward to form a **'ONE'** hand, palm facing down. ❖

OR

SIGN #3: **'EXTENDED B'** hands are held with palms together and fingers pointing forward. Then they are tilted upward from the wrists so that the fingers are pointing upward.

SIGN #4 [ATLANTIC]: Vertical right **'OPEN F'** hand, palm facing forward, becomes a **'CLOSED F'** hand as it is moved forward. ❖

asleep: See **sleep**.

asphyxiation: *n.* suffocation. *When his air supply was cut off, the diver died of asphyxiation.*

SIGN: Left **'ONE'** hand is held palm-down with forefinger pointing forward/rightward. The forefinger of the right **'ONE'** hand is held above the left, then brought down sharply to strike the left forefinger. Next, **'5'** hands are held against the chest, right above left, and are moved simultaneously forward and back to simulate breathing. (ASL CONCEPT—**can't - breathe.**)

aspire: *v.* to wish for; strive toward an end. *She aspires to become the prime minister of Canada.*

SIGN: Vertical **'ONE'** hands, left palm facing right and right palm facing left, are held out in front of the face, with the left hand directly ahead of the right. Both hands are then simultaneously moved forward.
SAME SIGN—**aspiration**, *n.*

assassinate: *v.* to murder a well known person. *Someone assassinated the politician.*

SIGN: Vertical left **'EXTENDED B'** hand is held in a fixed position with palm facing rightward and slightly forward. Right **'ONE'** (or **'K'**) hand is held palm down as it moves forward/downward at a slight leftward angle, the forefinger firmly grazing the left palm. ❖
SAME SIGN—**assassination**, *n.*

assault: *n.* a violent physical attack. *Assault is a punishable offence.*

SIGN: Horizontal right **'S'** hand, palm facing left, is used to strike back and forth against the forefinger of the vertical left **'ONE'** hand, of which the palm faces right.

assemble: *v.* to come together. *The skiers will assemble in the hotel lobby.*

SIGN #1: Both **'BENT 5'** hands, palms facing forward, are moved forward and slightly downward from shoulder level, fingers wiggling. ❖

assemble: *v.* to fit parts together. *It takes ten people to assemble one motor.*

SIGN #2: **'FLAT O'** hands, palms facing down, are moved alternately up and down as if fitting components into a specific pattern.

assertive: *adj.* positive; sufficiently confident. *His wishes are often overlooked because he is not assertive.*

SIGN: **'A'** hands, thumbs up, palms facing each other, are brought alternately up against the chest and circled forward.

assessment: *n.* an evaluation; rating. *Interpreters for the Deaf must undergo a comprehensive assessment before becoming certified.*

SIGN: Vertical **'A'** hands are held slightly apart, palms facing forward, and moved alternately up and down.
SAME SIGN—**assess**, *v.*

assign: *v.* to allot a task. *The chairman will assign duties to the board members.*

SIGN: Right **'X'** hand, palm facing left, is held upright and thrust forward and down into a horizontal position. Motion may be repeated in a rightward sweep to indicate the number of people receiving assignments. ❖

assignment: *n.* an allotted task. *The homework assignment was difficult.*

SIGN: Wrist of right **'A'** (or **'S'**) hand, palm facing away from the body, strikes wrist of the left **'A'** (or **'S'**) hand, which is held in front of/below the right hand with palm facing downward. Motion is repeated.

assist: *v.* to help. *The police dog will assist the officers in searching for the lost child.*

SIGN #1: Horizontal left **'A'** (or **'EXTENDED A'**) hand, palm facing the body but turned slightly rightward, rests on the upturned palm of the right **'EXTENDED B'** hand. Both hands are moved forward in one motion toward the person receiving help. ❖
SAME SIGN—**assistance**, *n.*

assist: *n.* in ice hockey, a pass of the puck to another player who scores a goal. *The crowd cheered when the left winger got his sixth assist of the game.*

SIGN #2: Right **'EXTENDED A'** hand is held with palm facing downward/leftward and thumb pointing upward/leftward as it jabs the base of the left **'EXTENDED A'** hand which is also held with palm facing the body and thumb pointing upward/leftward while the hands move slightly apart and back together twice.

---

assistance: See **aid**.

assistant: *n.* a helper. *He is an assistant to the manager.*

SIGN: Horizontal left **'EXTENDED A'** hand is held in a fixed position with palm toward the body. Horizontal right **'L'** hand is positioned so that the thumbtip taps at least twice against the underside of the left hand.

associate: *v.* to mingle; spend time with. *The best way to learn ASL is to associate with native signers, most of whom are Deaf.*

SIGN #1: Right **'EXTENDED A'** hand is held thumb-down above left **'EXTENDED A'** hand which is held thumb-up. The hands then revolve around each other in a counter-clockwise direction.
ALTERNATE SIGNS—**mingle** #1 & #2

---

associate: *v.* to relate or connect things in the mind. *Since the war, he associates thunder with air raids.*

SIGN #2: Tip of forefinger of right **'ONE'** hand, palm toward face, touches right side of forehead. Next, thumbs and forefingers of both **'F'** hands interlock, left palm toward the body while right palm faces away from the body. The hands maintain this position as they purposefully move forward. (ASL CONCEPT—**think - related**.)

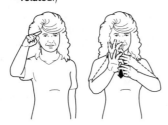

---

association: *n.* an organization. *The SPCA is an association for the prevention of cruelty to animals.*

SIGN: **'EXTENDED A'** (or **'A'**) hands are held, thumbs together, palms facing away from the body, and are curved forward in opposite directions till they come together with palms facing the body.

assorted: *adj.* various. *I bought a package of assorted bows.*

SIGN: **'BENT L'** hands are positioned palms-down with tips of forefingers touching each other, the right finger pointing leftward and the left finger pointing rightward. Then they are moved apart with forefingers fluttering.
SAME SIGN—**assortment**, *n.*

assume: *v.* to take for granted. *Since you have your coat on, I assume you are leaving.*

SIGN: Vertical right **'SPREAD C'** hand is held in front of right side of forehead with palm facing left, and is moved leftward as it closes to form an **'S'** hand.
SAME SIGN—**assumption**, *n.*

assure: *v.* to guarantee; promise. *He assured her that the assignment would be finished on time.*

SIGN: Tip of forefinger of vertical right **'ONE'** hand, palm facing left, is placed just under the lower lip. As the right hand is then brought purposefully forward/downward, it takes on a **'B'** handshape and is pressed against the left **'STANDARD BASE'** hand. (The handshapes for this sign vary.)
SAME SIGN—**assurance**, *n.*, in this context.

astonish: *v.* to surprise. *The magic trick will astonish you.*

SIGN: Thumbs and forefingers of **'CLOSED MODIFIED G'** (or **'CLOSED X'**) hands, palms facing each other, are placed at either cheek, and opened sharply to form **'L'** (or **'CONTRACTED L'**) hands as they move sharply away from the face.
SAME SIGN—**astonishment**, *n.*

astound: *v.* to overwhelm with amazement. *His talents astound his instructors.*

SIGN: Thumbs and forefingers of **'CLOSED MODIFIED G'** (or **'CLOSED X'**) hands, palms facing each other, are placed at either cheek, and opened sharply to form **'L'** (or **'CONTRACTED L'**) hands as they move sharply away from the face.

astounded: *adj.* overwhelmed with amazement. *The student's instructors were astounded by his talents.*

SIGN: **'BENT 5'** hands are held apart, fingertips pointing downward, and are moved sharply downward. (This sign is used only in a passive voice situation or as an adjective. It may **not** be used in an active voice situation: *The student's talents astounded his instructor.*)

astronaut: *n.* a space traveller. *The astronaut was weightless in space.*

SIGN: Heel of vertical right **'R'** hand, palm forward, rests on the back of the left **'STANDARD BASE'** hand. Then the right hand is pushed upward firmly. Agent Ending (see p. LIV) may follow.

at: *prep.* in the location or position of. *The 1991 World Winter Games for the Deaf were held at Banff.*

SIGN: Fingerspell **AT**.

athlete: *n.* one who participates in physical exercise. *About fifty Canadian athletes attended the World Winter Games for the Deaf.*

SIGN: **'A'** hands, palms facing, are held close to one another and moved alternately back and forth. This is a wrist movement. Agent Ending (see p. LIV) may follow.

attach: *v.* to join. *Can you help me attach the trailer to my car?*

SIGN: **'OPEN F'** hands are brought together so that the thumbs and forefingers are linked to form **'F'** hands. ❖

attack: *v.* to assault suddenly. *He attacked someone in a dark alley last night.*

SIGN: Horizontal right **'S'** hand, palm facing left, is moved forward forcefully to strike the forefinger of the vertical left **'ONE'** hand which is held with palm facing right. ❖

attain: *v.* to accomplish; reach; gain through effort. *Deaf people have campaigned to attain recognition of ASL as a legitimate, intricate and colourful language.*

SIGN: **'ONE'** hands, palms down, forefingers almost touching either side of forehead, are raised so that fingers point upward and palms face away from the body.

attempt: *v.* to make an effort; try. *An eighteen-year-old girl will attempt to swim across Lake Ontario.*

SIGN: Horizontal **'EXTENDED A'** (or **'S'**) hands are held apart with palms facing the chest. The wrists then rotate toward the chest, causing the palms to turn downward as the hands curve downward and forward.

attend: *v.* to be present at. *Over 200 people will attend the meeting.*

SIGN: Vertical **'ONE'** hands, palms forward, are staggered so that the right hand is held slightly closer to the chest than the left. The wrists then bend, causing the hands to fall forward so that the palms face downward. ❖ SAME SIGN—**attendance**, *n.*, but the movement is repeated.

(pay) attention: *v.* to heed. *Students must pay attention in class.*

SIGN: Vertical **'EXTENDED B'** hands, one at either side of the face with palms facing each other, are simultaneously moved forward.

attic: *n.* a space just below the roof of a house. *We spent the day in the attic looking through the old trunks and boxes.*

SIGN: Fingerspell **ATTIC**.

attire: See **clothes**.

attitude: *n.* a state of behaviour showing opinion. *A person's attitude can affect his job performance.*

SIGN: Horizontal right **'A'** hand is held with palm toward the left shoulder. The wrist then rotates to turn the hand palm down as it moves backward a short distance so that the thumb pokes into the shoulder.

attorney: *n.* one legally qualified to prosecute and defend actions in a court of law. *The accused man hired an attorney to defend him in court.*

SIGN #1: Vertical left **'EXTENDED B'** hand is held in a fixed position with palm facing right. Right **'L'** hand, palm facing left, is placed against the fingers of the left hand and then lowered to the heel of the left hand. Agent Ending (see p. LIV) may follow.

OR

SIGN #2: With left arm bent at the elbow, the right **'L'** hand is placed first at the wrist, then at the elbow of the left forearm. Agent Ending (see p. LIV) may follow.

attract: *v.* to draw admiration or attention. *Students are often attracted to comics and science fiction.*

SIGN #1: Right **'SPREAD C'** (or **'MODIFIED 5'**) hand is held in front of face, palm facing left, and the fingers are closed to form an **'S'** hand as the forearm moves forward and down.
ALTERNATE SIGN—**drawn to**

attract: *v.* to cause to come near. *A white light will attract moths.*

SIGN #2: Horizontal **'CLAWED L'** hands are held apart with palms up, and forearms are moved sharply back toward the body as hands take on **'A'** shapes.

attractive: *adj.* inviting; pleasing. *The woman looks very attractive in her new gown.*

SIGN: Right **'CONTRACTED 5'** hand is circled counter-clockwise (from the signer's perspective) around the face as the fingers close to form a **'FLAT O'** hand, with palm and fingers toward the chin.

attribute: *n.* a characteristic; quality. *Generosity is a commendable attribute.*

SIGN: Horizontal right **'C'** hand, palm facing the body, is twisted in a circular motion from the wrist so that it becomes upright with palm facing leftward as it is brought back against the left shoulder.

auction: *n.* a public sale of property. *Their belongings will be sold by auction to the highest bidder.*

SIGN: Vertical **'EXTENDED B'** hands, palms facing forward, are held apart and are alternately moved up and down.

audience: *n.* an assembled gathering of listeners (watchers). *The audience was very attentive to the guest speaker.*

SIGN: Both **'CROOKED 5'** hands, with wrists slightly bent, and palms downward, are extended and then drawn upward toward the shoulders.

audiology: *n.* the science and treatment of hearing loss. *Teachers of the Deaf are required to study audiology.*

SIGN: Vertical right **'A'** hand is held with thumb at right ear and palm facing forward. The forearm is circled forward as though turning a handle.
SAME SIGN—**audiologist**, *n.*, and may be followed by the Agent Ending (see p. LIV).

auditorium: *n.* a place where public meetings are held. *The workshop will be held in the auditorium.*

SIGN #1: Fingerspell **AUD**.

A U D

SIGN #2 [ONTARIO]: The joined thumb and forefinger of the horizontal right **'F'** hand, palm down, are used to move in and out of the opening of the horizontal left **'F'** hand of which the palm is facing right. Motion is repeated.

August: *n.* the eighth month of the year. *In August, parents start preparing their children for school.*

SIGN: Fingerspell **AUG**.

aunt: *n.* a parent's sister or sister-in-law. *My mother's youngest sister is my favourite aunt.*

SIGN: Thumb of right **'A'** hand, with palm facing slightly forward and left, is placed on right cheek and drawn slightly downward twice.

authentic: *adj.* genuine; real. *This is an authentic painting by Van Gogh.*

SIGN: Forefinger of vertical right **'ONE'** hand, palm facing left, is held against the lips and the hand is moved sharply forward.

author: *n.* a writer. *Helen Keller was the Deaf and blind author of numerous publications.*

SIGN: Horizontal left **'EXTENDED B'** hand is held in a fixed position with palm facing rightward/backward. Thumb and forefinger of right **'CLOSED X'** hand move forward/rightward twice along the palm of the left hand. Agent Ending (see p. LIV) may follow.

authority: *n.* the right or power to command or enforce obedience. *The police have the authority to arrest drunken drivers.*

SIGN: Thumb of right **'EXTENDED A'** hand, with palm down, is placed against upper part of left arm. Hand is then twisted from the wrist as it is moved in an arc over the bicep area with the palm finally facing backward.

autobody: *adj.* a trade concerned with making repairs to the damaged bodies of motor vehicles. *After the accident, he had his car towed to the autobody shop.*

SIGN: Vertical **'EXTENDED A'** (or **'S'**) hands are held with palms toward the body, and are knocked together a couple of times.

autograph: *v.* to write and give a cherished signature. *He autographed his hockey stick and gave it to the fan.*

SIGN: Right **'U'** hand, palm facing left and extended fingers pointing forward, is twisted from the wrist as it moves in a leftward arc so that the palm faces down and extended fingers come to rest in upturned palm of left **'EXTENDED B'** hand.

automatic: *adj.* working mechanically by itself. *His new car has an automatic transmission.*

SIGN #1: Right **'X'** hand, palm facing the body, is hooked under the horizontal forefinger of the left **'ONE'** hand and moved back and forth.

SIGN #2 [ATLANTIC]: Horizontal **'X'** hands, left palm up and right palm down, are held so the crooked part of the forefinger of the right is used to tap a couple of times on that of the left.

automobile: *n.* a motor car. *The automobile is a major source of air pollution.*

SIGN: **'S'** hands, with palms facing the body, are held in the steering wheel position and are moved up and down alternately to simulate the motion of steering a car. (See also **vehicle** #1 for explanatory notes.)

autopsy: *n.* the post-mortem examination of a human body to determine the cause of death. *Due to the circumstances surrounding the woman's death, the coroner conducted an autopsy.*

autopsy *(cont.)*

SIGN: **'EXTENDED B'** hands are held with fingers pointing forward, left palm facing up and right palm facing down. Then they are flipped over simultaneously so that the palm positions are reversed. Next, horizontal **'EXTENDED B'** hands, palms toward body, fingertips touching either side of the chest, are moved down and placed at the waist. Finally, **'V'** hands, palms down, extended fingers of one hand pointing toward extended fingers of the other hand, are simultaneously moved apart at least twice while the extended fingers retract to take on **'CLAWED V'** handshapes. (ASL CONCEPT—**dead - body - analyze**.)

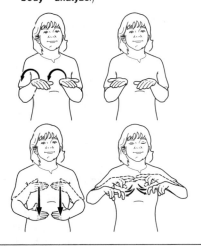

autumn: *n.* the season that comes between summer and winter; fall. *In the northern hemisphere, autumn begins in September.*

SIGN: Side of forefinger of right **'B'** hand, palm down, is brushed downward against bent elbow of the left arm.

available: *adj.* able to be gotten or obtained. *He will be available for work in two weeks.*

SIGN #1: **'A'** hands are held parallel in a palms-down position and simultaneously moved down from the wrists twice as though knocking on a horizontal surface.

available: *adj.* unoccupied; vacant and able to be occupied. *There are still two seats available on the 8:40 flight.*

SIGN #2: Tip of middle finger of right **'BENT MIDFINGER 5'** hand strokes forward/rightward across back of left **'STANDARD BASE'** hand.

avalanche: *n.* the falling of a large mass of snow/ice down a mountain slope. *The highway was closed due to an avalanche near Field, British Columbia.*

SIGN: Horizontal **'5'** hands, bent at the wrists with palms down, are positioned so the left is slightly ahead of the right. Then both hands are simultaneously shoved downward at an angle with a very firm movement. (Signs vary depending on whether the slide consists of rocks, mud, earth, etc.)

avaricious: See **greedy**.

avenue: *n.* a wide street often bordered by trees. *The parade will move along Portage Avenue.*

SIGN: Fingerspell **AVE**.

average: *adj.* the norm; standard. *The graph showed the average rainfall for Vancouver, Toronto and Halifax.*

SIGN #1: Right **'EXTENDED B'** hand, with palm facing left and fingers pointing forward, slides from side to side a few times along forefinger of horizontally held left **'EXTENDED B'** hand, whose palm is facing the body.

average: *v.* to calculate the norm. *The teacher will average the students' marks for their report cards.*

SIGN #2: Edge of right **'EXTENDED B'** hand is placed within the space between the thumb and forefinger of the left **'EXTENDED B'** hand, both palms facing the chest at a slight angle. Then they are separated with a downward curve so that both palms face down.

aviator: *n.* a pilot. *John Payne was the first Deaf Canadian aviator.*

SIGN: Right **'COMBINED LY'** hand, palm downward and slightly forward, is moved a short distance forward twice. Agent Ending (see p. LIV) may follow.

avid: *adj.* intensely eager. *The boy is an avid reader of science fiction.*

SIGN: Horizontal **'EXTENDED B'** hands are held with palms together and fingers pointing forward. The hands are alternately rubbed back and forth against each other.

avoid: *v.* to shun; keep away from. *How did the robbers avoid the guards?*

SIGN: Horizontal right **'EXTENDED A'** hand, palm facing left, is held directly behind horizontal left **'EXTENDED A'** hand whose palm faces right. Right hand then becomes vertical as it is brought back smartly toward the chest.

awake: *adj.* roused from sleep. *He was awake most of the night.*

SIGN: **'C'** hands are held upright with palms facing each other and tips of thumbs touching either side of face at the cheekbones.

award: *n.* a prize; trophy; tribute. *The Canadian Cultural Society of the Deaf's highest award is the Founder's Order of Honour.*

SIGN: Vertical **'X'** hands, with palms facing each other, are thrust forward simultaneously as they move to a horizontal position. (**AWARD** is frequently fingerspelled.)

aware: *adj.* heedful; alert to. *Everyone should be aware of the hazards of smoking.*

SIGN: Fingertips of right **'BENT EXTENDED B'** hand, with palm toward the face, are tapped against right side of forehead a couple of times.
SAME SIGN—**awareness**, *n.*

away: *adv.* not here; at a distance. *He will look after your house while you are away.*

SIGN: Right **'BENT EXTENDED B'** hand with palm facing left, is flung outward from the wrist so that the hand becomes an **'EXTENDED B'** with palm facing downward.

awesome: *adj.* very impressive; having a powerful effect on one's sensibilities. *The special effects for the concert were awesome.*

SIGN #1: Left **'ONE'** hand is held palm down with forefinger pointing forward/rightward. Base of thumb of right **'SPREAD C'** hand, palm facing forward/leftward, slides forward/rightward along back of left hand and off to form an **'S'** hand. Fingers of right hand may flutter while sliding along left hand. Facial expression is important.

OR

SIGN #2: Right **'CROOKED 5'** hand, palm toward face, is held upright and tilted slightly leftward as it is waved leftward, then rightward in front of the face. Motion is repeated. Facial expression is important. Signs vary considerably.
ALTERNATE SIGN—**WOW** #1

awful: *adj.* exceedingly unpleasant. *The blizzard was awful.*

SIGN: Thumb and forefinger of vertical right **'COVERED 8'** hand, which is held near right side of face with palm facing left, are snapped open and thrust slightly forward to form a **'MODIFIED 5'** hand. This sign can be made with either one or two hands, one at either side of the face.

awkward: *adj.* lacking dexterity, efficiency or skill. *He felt awkward the first time he asked a girl for a date.*

SIGN: **'3'** hands, held slightly apart with the palms down, are alternately raised and lowered.

B

baby: *n.* an infant or very young child. *A young **baby** is dependent on adults.*

SIGN: Fingers of palm-up right **'BENT EXTENDED B'** hand point leftward as they rest on rightward-pointing fingers of palm-up left **'BENT EXTENDED B'** hand. The arms are simultaneously moved from side to side as if rocking a baby in one's arms.

babysit: *v.* to take care of a child or children while the parents are absent. *She **babysits** to earn spending money.*

SIGN: Fingers of palm-up right **'EXTENDED B'** hand point leftward as they rest on rightward-pointing fingers of palm-up left **'EXTENDED B'** hand. The arms are simultaneously moved from side to side as if rocking a baby in one's arms. Next, horizontal **'K'** (or **'V'**) hands are held, right above left, with extended fingers pointing forward, the left palm facing rightward and the right palm facing leftward. Then the hands are brought together to strike each other. (ASL CONCEPT—**baby - take care of**.)

bachelor: *n.* an unmarried man. *John was a **bachelor** until he was 40.*

SIGN: Vertical right **'B'** hand, palm facing left and side of forefinger touching left cheek, is moved to the corresponding position on the right cheek.

back: *n.* the rear part of the body from the base of the neck to the base of the spine. *When lifting things, be careful not to injure your **back**.*

SIGN #1: Fingertips of right **'EXTENDED B'** (or **'BENT EXTENDED B'**) hand, palm facing the shoulder, are tapped on the signer's back, over the right shoulder. Alternatively, **BACK** may be fingerspelled.

back: *n.* rear. *We sat at the **back** of the bus.*

SIGN #2: Right **'EXTENDED A'** hand, palm facing left, is held upright and jabbed backward at least twice over the right shoulder.

back: *v.* to support. *He will only **back** honest politicians.*

SIGN #3: **'S'** hands, palms toward the body, are held at chest level with the left slightly above the right. Then the right is brought upward to strike the left.

back and forth: *adv.* to and fro. *The lion paced **back and forth** in his cage.*

SIGN: Horizontal right **'EXTENDED A'** hand is moved back and forth either from left to right with palm facing left, or forward and back with palm facing body.

backpack: *n.* a knapsack; something worn on the back for carrying supplies. *He always carries a **backpack** when he goes hiking.*

SIGN: Thumbs of **'C'** hands, palms facing each other, are tapped on the shoulders.

back up: *v.* to reverse; move backward. *She has to **back up** the car into the garage.*

SIGN #1: Right **'3'** hand, palm facing left, fingers pointing forward, is brought back toward the body to simulate a vehicle backing up. (This handshape is used specifically to indicate that it is a **vehicle** which is backing up. It does not apply to people or animals.) ❖

backup: *adj.* pertaining to a reserve or substitute copy; acting in a supportive role. *The computer operator always makes a **backup** disk for important files.*

SIGN #2: Horizontal left **'EXTENDED A'** hand is held in a fixed position with palm facing right. Right **'EXTENDED A'** hand, palm facing down, is twisted so that the palm faces left as it is brought forward to make contact with left hand just below the thumb.

backward(s): *adv.* towards the rear. *We cannot go backward; we must move forward.*

SIGN: Right **'EXTENDED A'** hand, palm facing left, is held upright and jabbed backward at least twice over the right shoulder. (The concept of 'backward' is usually incorporated with the subject and verb, instead of being a separate sign. To say that 'a car *is moving backward*', a horizontal **'3'** hand is moved backward. To say that a 'person *is moving backward*', a vertical **'ONE'** hand is moved backward.)

bacon: *n.* the salted and smoked back and sides of a hog. *Bacon and eggs are popular breakfast foods.*

SIGN: Vertical **'BENT EXTENDED U'** hands, palms facing each other, and tips of extended fingers touching each other, are moved apart with fingers simultaneously wiggling up and down.

bad: *adj.* not good. *Good behaviour will be rewarded, but bad behaviour will not be condoned.*

SIGN #1: Right **'EXTENDED B'** hand, with fingertips on chin and palm facing body, is turned away, so that palm is facing down.

OR

SIGN #2: Vertical right **'I'** hand is held in front of the right shoulder with palm facing left, and is thrust purposefully forward.

badge: *n.* an emblem worn by an officer of the law as a symbol of authority. *The detective's badge is in the shape of a star.*

SIGN: Vertical right **'C-INDEX'** hand, palm facing left, is tapped a couple of times against the left shoulder.

badminton: *n.* a game played with a net, racquets, and a shuttlecock. *We played badminton until my racquet broke.*

SIGN: Right **'A'** hand is swung back and forth with wrist action to simulate the motion of a badminton racquet in play.

bag: *n.* any flexible container with an opening, usually at the top. *Each member of the tour was allowed to bring only one bag.*

SIGN: Right **'S'** hand is held at one's side, with palm toward body, and the arm is moved up and down to simulate the carrying of a bag. Signs vary according to size, shape and use of the bag. (**BAG** may be fingerspelled.)

baggage: *n.* luggage; the portable personal gear of a traveller. *You must check your baggage before boarding the aircraft.*

SIGN #1: Right **'S'** hand is held at one's side, with palm toward body, and the arm is moved up and down to simulate the carrying of a suitcase.

SIGN #2 [ATLANTIC]: Fingertips of right, palm-down **'FLAT O'** hand (or knuckles of the **'A'** hand) touch top of horizontal left **'S'** hand. Right hand then changes to **'CROOKED 5'** shape, with palm covering left hand.

bake: *v.* to cook by dry heat in an oven. *They baked 200 loaves of bread in the large oven.*

SIGN: Right **'EXTENDED B'** hand, palm up, with fingers pointing forward, slides under left palm-down **'EXTENDED B'** hand whose fingers point rightward.

bakery: *n.* a place where goods such as bread, cake and pastries are baked and/or sold. *She bought some delicious cinnamon buns at the local bakery.*

SIGN: Fingerspell **BAKERY.**

B A K E R Y

balance: *v.* to make equal in weight, amount or extent. *When the weights on both sides of a scale are equal, the scale will balance.*

SIGN: **'EXTENDED B'** hands, palms down and fingers pointing forward, are held apart and alternately raised and lowered.

bald: *adj.* without the usual covering of hair, feathers, etc. *The **bald** man began losing his hair when he was 20.*

SIGN: Tip of middle finger of right **'BENT MIDFINGER 5'** hand, palm facing downward, traces a circle at the top of the head.

ball: *n.* a solid or hollow sphere often used in games. *He got a new bat and **ball** for his birthday.*

SIGN #1: Fingertips and thumbs of **'C'** (or **'SPREAD C'**) hands, palms facing, are tapped together at least twice. (**BALL** is frequently fingerspelled.)

ball: *n.* a social assembly for dancing. *Cinderella danced with the prince at the **ball**.*

SIGN #2: Right **'BENT V'** hand, palm facing downward, is held above upturned palm of left **'EXTENDED B'** hand. Extended fingers of right hand are brushed back and forth lightly across left palm.

(have) a ball: *v.* a colloquial term meaning to enjoy oneself or have a good time. *The students **had a ball** during the week of the Youth Canada Tournament of the Deaf.*

SIGN: Fingertips of right **'EXTENDED B'** hand, palm facing the body, are brought up to the mouth and thrust forward. Tip of right **'CROOKED ONE'** hand then moves downward to tap twice on the wrist of the left **'STANDARD BASE'** hand. (ASL CONCEPT—**good - time**.)

balloon: *n.* an inflatable rubber bag used as a toy or a decoration. *Children love **balloons**.*

SIGN: **'S'** hands are held at the mouth, one behind the other. They are then moved outward and opened to form **'SPREAD C'** hands with right palm facing left and left palm facing right. Cheeks are puffed out.

ballot: *n.* a piece of paper used to register one's vote. *Put an 'X' beside your choice of candidate on the **ballot**.*

SIGN: Joined thumb and forefinger of horizontal right **'F'** hand, palm down, appear to peck at the top of the horizontal left **'S'** hand, whose palm faces right. (**BALLOT** is frequently fingerspelled.)

baloney [*also spelled* **boloney**]: *n.* a colloquial term meaning nonsense. *I think that story is a lot of **baloney**.*

SIGN #1: **'C'** hands are held side by side with palms down. As the hands move apart they close to form **'S'** hands, open to resume the **'C'** shape, close to form **'S'** hands, and so on in a series of simultaneous motions. Facial expression must clearly convey 'disbelief'. (Also used for **baloney** [bologna] meaning 'processed meat' though signs vary.)

SIGN #2 [ONTARIO]: Left **'5'** hand is held palm down with fingers pointing slightly forward and to the right while right **'5'** hand is held palm down with fingers pointing slightly forward and to the left. Both hands are moved toward each other, until thumb and forefinger of each hand are inserted between thumb and forefinger of the other hand. Motion is repeated. Facial expression must clearly convey 'disbelief'.

ban: *n.* an official prohibition. *There is a **ban** on the road for trucks weighing over three tons.*

SIGN: Right **'L'** hand, palm facing left, is tapped smartly against right-facing palm of left **'EXTENDED B'** hand.

SAME SIGN—**ban**, *v.*

banana: *n.* an edible, pulpy, tropical fruit which is crescent-shaped and white in colour with a yellowish or reddish skin. *Monkeys love bananas.*

SIGN: Tips of forefinger and thumb of right **'CONTRACTED L'** hand are held against forefinger of vertical left **'ONE'** hand. Tip of right forefinger then slides downward to form a **'CLOSED MODIFIED G'**. Motion is repeated to simulate the peeling of a banana. (Signs vary.)

band-aid: *n.* an adhesive strip of bandage. *A **band-aid** on her injured hand stopped the bleeding.*

SIGN: Extended fingers of right **'BENT U'** hand, palm facing downward, are drawn backward across back of left **'STANDARD BASE'** hand.

bandage: *v.* to bind or dress a wound. *You should always disinfect a wound before you **bandage** it.*

SIGN: Right **'BENT B'** (or **'B'**) hand, fingers pointing left and palm facing body, is rotated continuously forward around left **'BENT B'** (or **'B'**) hand, whose fingers point right and palm faces the body.

SAME SIGN—**bandage**, *n.*

bandit: *n.* a robber. *A masked **bandit** robbed the train.*

SIGN: Extended fingers of right **'BENT U'** hand, palm facing downward, point leftward as they are drawn from left to right under the nose.

banish: *v.* to dismiss; expel; drive out. *The king will **banish** the traitor from his kingdom.*

SIGN: Fingertips of right **'BENT EXTENDED B'** hand, palm down, are placed on upturned palm of left **'EXTENDED B'** hand and brushed forward to form a straight **'EXTENDED B'** hand. ❖

bank: *n.* a financial institution. *She works as a teller at the **bank**.*

SIGN: Fingerspell **BANK**.

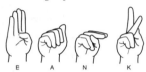

bankrupt: *adj.* legally recognized as being in sufficient financial difficulty that one's debts cannot be paid in full. *The **bankrupt** company had only been in business a short time.*

SIGN: Extended fingers of right **'V'** hand are thrust downward against right-facing palm of vertical left **'EXTENDED B'** hand.
SAME SIGN—**bankruptcy**, *n.*
ALTERNATE SIGN—**broke**

banner: *n.* a flag or symbolic pennant. *The marchers carried a large **banner** with their organization's name on it.*

SIGN: Horizontal right **'EXTENDED B'** hand is waved left and right from the wrist while tip of forefinger of left **'ONE'** hand is held against right forearm. (**BANNER** is frequently fingerspelled.)

banquet: *n.* a sumptuous feast. *Banquets are often held during conventions.*

SIGN: **'FLAT O'** hands, palms facing the body, are circled alternately toward the mouth.

baptize: *v.* to perform the religious ritual of baptism. *The priest will **baptize** the baby.*

SIGN #1: Right **'FLAT O'** hand, palm facing downward, moves back and forth above the head a few times to indicate the sprinkling of water.

OR

SIGN #2: Left **'EXTENDED A'** hand is held palm-up and apart from right **'EXTENDED A'** hand, which is held palm-down. Both hands are then simultaneously overturned once.
SAME SIGN—**baptism**, *n.*

bar: *n.* a place that is stocked with drinks, many of which are alcoholic. *It is customary in an English pub to order drinks at the **bar**.*

SIGN #1: Tip of thumb of right **'Y'** (or **'EXTENDED A'**) hand, palm facing left, is tapped at least twice against the lower lip.

bar: *v.* to block or obstruct. *He was **barred** from taking the exam after missing so many classes.*

SIGN #2: **'EXTENDED B'** hands are held at right angles to one another, the left hand in front of the right, with fingers of left hand pointing upward to the right and fingers of right hand pointing upward to the left. The hands are then pushed firmly forward. ❖

barbecue: *n.* a meal cooked over an outdoor fire. *Everyone enjoyed the steak **barbecue**.*

SIGN: Fingerspell **BBQ**.

bare: *adj.* naked; uncovered. *It is too cold for **bare** feet, so put on some socks and shoes.*

SIGN: Tip of middle finger of right **'BENT MIDFINGER 5'** hand strokes forward/rightward across back of left **'STANDARD BASE'** hand.

barely: *adv.* just; without much room to spare. *He **barely** passed the exam.*

SIGN #1: Tips of thumb and forefinger of right **'F'** (or **'CLOSED X'**) hand, palm toward the face, are held against forehead over right eyebrow and the hand moves sharply forward as if plucking the eyebrow.

barely: *adv.* scarcely; hardly. *He barely touched his food.*

SIGN #2: Right **'CLOSED X'** hand is held palm-up with forefinger tightly crooked as tip of thumb flicks downward against tip of forefinger, thereby changing the hand to a **'CLOSED A-INDEX'**.

bargain: *v.* to negotiate for a mutually acceptable price. *A customer will often bargain with a salesman for a lower price.*

SIGN #1: Vertical **'O'** hands are held with palms facing, thumbs touching and fingertips touching intermittently as they wiggle up and down. At the same time, both hands are repeatedly moved backward and forward.

bargain: *n.* an item which appears to be worth more than the asking price; a good deal. *For $15.00, that dress is a bargain.*

SIGN #2: Side of forefinger of right palm-down **'B'** hand is brushed downward against right-facing palm of left **'EXTENDED B'** hand.

bark: *n.* a noise made by a dog. *That dog has a loud bark.*

SIGN #1: **'BENT EXTENDED B'** hands are held with palms facing (left palm up/right palm down) and fingertips touching. Fingers are then moved apart sharply at least twice so that hands take on straight **'EXTENDED B'** shapes.

bark: *n.* the rind or covering of the branches and trunk of a tree. *Natives made canoes out of birch bark.*

SIGN #2: Left **'5'** hand with arm bent at the elbow, is held upright to represent a tree. The forearm twists slightly a couple of time. Right **'EXTENDED C'** hand is then moved down left forearm or 'tree trunk' which it encloses.

barn: *n.* a building for stabling livestock. *Cows and horses are kept in a barn.*

SIGN: Fingerspell **BARN**.

barrel: *n.* a cylindrical container with rounded sides and flat ends. *The price of a barrel of oil fluctuates markedly.*

SIGN: Horizontal **'EXTENDED C'** hands, palms facing, are curved upward to indicate the shape of a barrel.

barrier: *n.* something that blocks or obstructs the way, or prevents one from going ahead. *The barrier kept the people out.*

SIGN: **'EXTENDED B'** hands are held at right angles to one another, the left hand in front of the right, with fingers of left hand pointing upward to the right and fingers of right hand pointing upward to the left. The hands are then pushed firmly forward.

bartender: *n.* a person employed to mix and serve drinks, particularly alcoholic drinks. *The customer asked the bartender to make him a dry martini.*

SIGN: **'Y'** (or **'EXTENDED A'**) hands are held with thumbs down and palms facing forward/downward. The two hands then circle backward alternately at least twice.
ALTERNATE SIGN—**draft beer**

base: *v.* to establish something on certain grounds. *He bases his theory on evidence collected over many months.*

SIGN #1: Right **'EXTENDED A'** hand is held palm down over left **'STANDARD BASE'** hand, then twisted so that it comes to rest on the back of the left hand with thumb pointing upward and palm facing leftward but slanted toward the body.

base: *n.* one of three corners of the infield playing area of a baseball diamond. *The runner was safe at second base.*

SIGN #2: Fingerspell **BASE**.

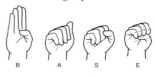

base: *n.* a place at the centre of operations; headquarters. *He is taking firearms training at the military base.*

SIGN #3: Fingerspell **BASE**.

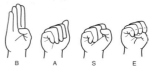

baseball: *n.* a team game played with a ball and bat on a diamond-shaped field. *Baseball is my favourite sport.*

SIGN: **'S'** hands, with right on top of left, are simultaneously tipped forward twice from the wrists, as if holding a bat in readiness to strike at a ball.

basement: *n.* the underground storey of a building. *Let us go down to the basement to play pool.*

SIGN #1: Forefinger of right **'BENT ONE'** hand points downward twice.

OR

SIGN #2: Horizontal right **'EXTENDED A'** hand, palm toward the body, is circled beneath left **'STANDARD BASE'** hand.

bashful: *adj.* shy; shrinking from notice. *The little girl was too bashful to play with other children.*

SIGN: Backs of fingers of right **'BENT EXTENDED B'** hand are held against right cheek. The hand is then twisted forward slightly from the wrist.

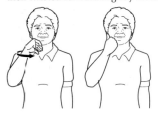

basic: *adj.* essential; fundamental. *It is necessary to understand basic mathematics to do algebra.*

SIGN: Right **'EXTENDED B'** hand, palm down, fingers pointing slightly forward and to the left, is circled counter-clockwise beneath left **'STANDARD BASE'** hand.

basket: *n.* a container usually made of wicker or wood. *The woman carried the fruit in a basket.*

SIGN #1: Horizontal **'C'** hands are held apart with palms facing each other. The hands are then simultaneously raised to indicate the height of the pail. (Signs vary depending on the size and shape of the basket.)

(waste) basket: *n.* a container in which people dispose of things they no longer want. *He threw the broken cup into the wastebasket.*

SIGN #2: Forefinger of right **'ONE'** hand, palm facing forward/left, is moved in an arc in front of left arm from wrist to elbow. As the hand moves, it twists from the wrist so that the palm eventually faces the body.

basketball: *n.* a team game played on a court with a large ball and elevated basket-hoops. *The game of basketball was invented by a Canadian.*

SIGN #1: **'CROOKED 5'** hands are held slightly apart, palms facing each other and fingers pointing forward. Both hands are then simultaneously thrust into an upright position. Motion is repeated.

SIGN #2 [ATLANTIC]: Right **'EXTENDED B'** hand, palm facing down, is bounced downward, moved to the right, and bounced downward again, as if dribbling a basketball.

bastard: *n.* an obnoxious or despicable person. *It is offensive to call someone a bastard.*

SIGN: Side of right **'B'** hand, palm facing left, is brought upward to strike the forehead firmly. Facial expression must clearly convey 'contempt'.

bat: *n.* a nocturnal, mouse-like, flying mammal. *A bat does not have very good eyesight.*

SIGN #1: Forearms are folded across chest with both forefingers flicking out at least twice from **'S'** hands to **'ONE'** hands, palms facing chest. (**BAT** may be fingerspelled.)

bat: *n.* a wooden or metal implement for striking a ball. *The girls took a bat and ball out to the field.*

SIGN #2: **'S'** hands, right on top of left, are moved forward twice from the wrists, as if holding a bat in readiness to strike at a ball.

batch: *n.* a group of things to be dealt with together. *The scientist had a batch of data to analyze.*

SIGN: **'SPREAD C'** hands are held upright and slightly apart with palms facing each other. The wrists then rotate forward, bringing the hands to a horizontal position.

bath: *n.* the act of washing one's body. *The miner had a bath to wash off the coal dust.*

SIGN: Horizontal **'EXTENDED A'** hands, palms facing the body, are held slightly apart, and rubbed up and down simultaneously against the chest.

bathroom: *n.* a room in which to bathe or use a toilet. *The bathroom was being renovated.*

SIGN #1: Right **'A'** hand, with thumbnail on chin and palm facing left, is stroked downward twice.

OR

SIGN #2: Vertical right **'T'** hand is held with palm forward and is jiggled from side to side.

SIGN #3 [ONTARIO]: Fingers of right **'EXTENDED B'** hand, palm down, are brushed twice across and at right angles to fingers of upturned palm of left **'EXTENDED B'** hand.

bathtub: *n.* a tub in which to bathe. *The baby played with his toy duck in the bathtub.*

SIGN: Horizontal **'EXTENDED A'** hands, palms facing the body, are held slightly apart, and rubbed up and down simultaneously against the chest. Then the word **TUB** is fingerspelled.

batter: *n.* a person who hits a ball with a bat. *The batter stood at homeplate and hit the ball.*

SIGN #1: **'S'** hands, with right on top of left, are simultaneously tipped forward from the wrists, as if holding a bat in readiness to strike a ball. Agent Ending (see p. LIV) may follow.

batter: *n.* a beaten mixture of ingredients for cooking. *The cookie batter has raisins in it.*

SIGN #2: Left arm is extended as if curved around a large bowl. Right **'COVERED T'** hand, palm facing the body, is circled clockwise within the opening in a stirring motion.

batter: *v.* to injure by beating or striking repeatedly. *It is a serious crime to batter a person.*

SIGN #3: Horizontal right **'S'** hand, palm facing left, is used to strike back and forth against forefinger of vertical left **'ONE'** hand. ❖

battery: *n.* an apparatus with cells that produce electricity. *A battery is used to provide electricity to start a car.*

SIGN #1: Crooked forefingers of horizontal **'X'** hands, palms facing body, are tapped together at least twice. (**BATTERY** is frequently fingerspelled.)

SIGN #2 [ONTARIO]: The forefinger side of the right vertical **'S'** hand, palm left, is brushed leftward/downward twice from the chin.

battle: *n.* combat involving organized forces. *Twenty soldiers were killed in that battle.*

SIGN #1: **'BENT 4'** hands, are held slightly apart, palms facing each other, with right fingers pointing left and left fingers pointing right. Hands are moved simultaneously to left and right twice.

battle: *n.* a struggle. *For some people, the study of physics is an uphill battle.*

SIGN #2: Horizontal left **'BENT ONE'** hand is held out in front of the body with palm toward the body and forefinger pointing at an upward/rightward angle toward the body. Horizontal right **'BENT ONE'** hand, palm left, is held higher and closer to the body with forefinger pointing directly at tip of left forefinger. The hands then circle forward simultaneously a couple of times. This is a slow, painstaking movement, which is accompanied by an appropriate facial expression.

battle: *v.* to resist or fight against something. *He is battling with a serious illness.*

SIGN #3: Vertical **'S'** hands, palms originally facing each other, are moved vigorously downward so that they come to rest side by side with palms facing down. Motion is repeated.

bawl: *v.* to bellow or cry noisily. *The baby started to bawl when his mother left.*

SIGN: Tips of forefingers of vertical **'CROOKED 4'** hands, palms facing forward, are placed near the eyes and are thrust downward simultaneously so that the palms face downward. Facial expression is important.

bawl out: *v.* a colloquial term meaning to scold or berate. *The woman will bawl out the boys for making such a mess.*

SIGN Horizontal **'S'** hands, with right on top of left, are thrust forward as they open into **'CONTRACTED 5'** hands, palms facing outward in opposite directions. Motion is repeated. Facial expression must clearly convey 'anger'. ❖

beach: *n.* the sandy or pebbly shore of a lake or other large body of water. *We walked along the beach at sunset.*

SIGN: Fingerspell **BEACH**.

beak: *n.* a bird's bill. *The eagle carried a fish in its beak.*

SIGN: Right **'MODIFIED G'** hand, with forefinger on nose and thumb at chin, is brought forward to form a **'CLOSED MODIFIED G'** hand, with palm facing body.

bean: *n.* a legume with kidney-shaped seeds in long pods. *The bean is an inexpensive but rich source of protein.*

SIGN: Fingerspell **BEAN**.

bear: *n.* a large, omnivorous mammal. *Polar bears can be seen around Churchill, Manitoba.*

SIGN #1: Arms are crossed over chest. Fingertips of both **'CLAWED 5'** hands are scraped downward from shoulders, palms facing body.

bear: *v.* to give birth to. *A female sheep often bears twins.*

SIGN #2: Horizontal **'EXTENDED B'** hands, palms facing the body, are positioned with the back of the right hand resting against the left palm. Then the right hand is curved down and under the left until its palm faces downward.

bear: *v.* to endure; tolerate. *Some people cannot bear the sight of snakes.*

SIGN #3: Right **'A'** hand, with thumbnail touching closed lips and palm facing left, is moved slowly down chin.

bear: *v.* to shoulder a burden. *A single parent bears many responsibilities.*

SIGN #4: Fingertips of both **'BENT EXTENDED B'** hands, palms facing the body, are placed on right shoulder. Shoulder is pushed slightly downward to signify the bearing of a burden.

beard: *n.* the hair on a man's face, especially the chin. *He is trying to grow a beard.*

SIGN: Fingertips of **'SPREAD C'** hands are placed on either side of face, palms facing each other, then curved downward along jawlines to outline shape of beard. (Signs vary according to the style of the beard.)

beat: *v.* to strike; pound. *If you beat someone, you could be charged with assault.*

SIGN #1: Horizontal right **'S'** hand strikes back and forth across forefinger of vertical left **'ONE'** hand. ❖

beat: *v.* to overcome; defeat. *The Blue Bombers beat the Stampeders 10 to 7.*

SIGN #2: Vertical right **'S'** hand, palm facing forward, is curved downward from the wrist across the extended finger of the left **'ONE'** hand, which is held horizontally with the palm facing downward. ❖

OR

SIGN #3: Vertical right **'S'** hand, palm facing left, is thrust forward/downward as it is transformed with a flicking motion into a **'U'** hand. ❖

beautiful: *adj.* aesthetically pleasing; very pretty. *A rose is a **beautiful** flower.*

SIGN: Right **'CONTRACTED 5'** hand is circled clockwise (to the onlooker) around face as fingers close at chin to form a **'FLAT O'** hand. SAME SIGN—**beauty**, *n.*

beaver: *n.* a large rodent with soft brown fur, a large broad tail, and webbed hind feet. *A **beaver** cuts down trees by gnawing them with its sharp front teeth.*

SIGN #1: **'CLAWED V'** hands, left palm up and right palm forward/leftward and slightly downward, are positioned so the left remains fixed and the back of the right is in front of the mouth. Then the right is lowered a couple of times as the forefinger and midfinger tap down on those of the left hand.

OR

SIGN #2: **'EXTENDED B'** hands, palms facing, are tented so the fingertips are near the lower lip. The hands are then moved back and forth a few times.

because: *conj.* on account of; for the reason that. *The car ran off the road **because** the surface was slippery.*

SIGN #1: Vertical right **'EXTENDED R'** (or **'R'**) hand, palm toward face, makes small circles (clockwise in the eyes of the onlooker) at right side of forehead. This sign tends to be used in compound sentences.

OR

SIGN #2: Vertical right **'BENT MIDFINGER 5'** hand is held with palm facing right side of forehead and middle finger repeatedly tapping gently in mid-air. This sign tends to be used in compound sentences.

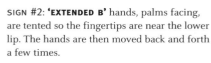

because of: *prep.* on account of. *I will not go **because of** you.*

SIGN #3: Fingertips of **'BENT EXTENDED B'** hand are placed against forehead, palm toward face, and are then drawn slightly upward to the right to form an **'EXTENDED A'** hand.

OR

SIGN #4: Forefinger of right **'L'** hand is placed on forehead, then drawn slightly upward to the right to form an **'EXTENDED A'** hand.

beckon: *v.* to signal or summon by gesture. *The policeman **beckoned** the jaywalker to come with him.*

SIGN: Forefinger of right palm-up **'CROOKED ONE'** hand is further crooked to form an **'X'**. Motion is repeated.

---

become: *v.* to come to be; undergo development. *He will **become** president soon.*

SIGN #1: Palms of **'EXTENDED B'** hands are placed together with right on top of and at right angles to left. Then they are reversed so that left hand is on top of and at right angles to right hand. (This sign is rarely used as it is thought to be unnecessary. The sample sentence in ASL is: *HE PRESIDENT SOON WILL.*)

become: *v.* to suit; look attractive on. *That colour **becomes** you.*

SIGN #2: Left **'ONE'** hand is held at chest level with palm facing right, and forefinger pointing forward. Right **'ONE'** hand is held slightly higher, palm facing left and forefinger pointing forward, and is then turned downward to match the simultaneously downward-turning left hand.

become of: *v.* happen to. *What has **become** of him since he retired from playing professional hockey?*

SIGN: **'ONE'** hands, palms facing each other and forefingers pointing forward, are held apart and then turned over so that the palms face down.

---

bed: *n.* a piece of furniture to sleep or rest on. *The teenager stayed in **bed** until noon.*

SIGN: Head tilts slightly to the right, supported by right **'EXTENDED B'** hand, which is held against right side of face.

bedridden: *adj.* to be confined to bed by sickness or weakness. *The bedridden patient was hospitalized for months.*

SIGN: Head tilts slightly to the right, supported by right **'EXTENDED B'** hand, which is held against right side of face. Then right **'V'** (or **'U'**) hand, with palm up, is laid on upturned palm of left **'EXTENDED B'** hand as both hands move together in forward circular motions. (ASL CONCEPT—**bed - lie-long-time.**)

bedroom: *n.* a room to sleep in. *This house has four bedrooms.*

SIGN: Head tilts slightly to the right, supported by right **'EXTENDED B'** hand, which is held against right side of face. Horizontal **'EXTENDED B'** hands are then held parallel, with palms facing. Finally the hands take on a **'BENT EXTENDED B'** shape as they are swung inward with the right hand positioned ahead of the left, both palms facing the body.

bee: *n.* a stinging insect with wings. *The bee stung him.*

SIGN #1: Right **'CLOSED X'** hand is brushed downward several times against the right cheek as the tips of the thumb and forefinger open and close. (BEE is frequently finger-spelled.)

OR

SIGN #2: Forefinger and thumb of right **'F'** hand are placed against right cheek. **'F'** hand is then changed to a **'B'** hand which lightly slaps right cheek. (Signs vary.)

beef: *n.* the meat of cattle. *My favourite meat is beef.*

SIGN #1: Right **'OPEN F'** hand, palm facing away from the body, is brought down to grasp the skin between thumb and forefinger of horizontal left **'EXTENDED B'** hand whose palm faces body. Hands then make small back and forth movements together. (BEEF is frequently fingerspelled.)

REGIONAL VARIATION—**meat** #2 & #3

beef: *v.* a colloquial term meaning to complain. *He always beefs about being asked to do any extra work.*

SIGN #2: Right **'SPREAD EXTENDED C'** hand is held in a horizontal position as thumb and fingertips thump repeatedly against chest. Facial expression is important.

been to: *v.* While ASL has no equivalent to the English verb 'to be', it does have a transla-tion for the past participle of the verb 'to be' when used with the preposition 'to' preceding nouns of place. *Have you ever been to Ottawa?*

SIGN: Vertical **'5'** hands, palms facing the body, are held at chest level, and swung outward, away from the body so that the palms face down. Next, tip of middle finger of right **'BENT MIDFINGER 5'** hand, palm down, touches down on the back of the left **'STANDARD BASE'** hand. (ASL CONCEPT—**finish - touch.**) The sample sentence in ASL is: *FINISH TOUCH OTTAWA YOU?*

beer: *n.* alcoholic liquor made from fermented malt, hops, etc. *He drank a pint of beer.*

SIGN: Vertical right **'B'** hand, palm facing left-ward/forward, is placed on right cheek and is drawn downward twice. (BEER is frequently fingerspelled.)

before: *prep.* in advance of; prior to. *Cocktails will be served **before** dinner.*

SIGN #1: Vertical left **'B'** hand is held in a fixed position with palm facing forward/rightward and thumb extended slightly. Horizontal right **'EXTENDED B'** hand is held with palm facing backward/leftward and backs of fingers against those of the left hand. The right hand is then moved backward/leftward a couple of times thus creating a circular sort of movement. (To translate, the clauses are reversed so that the sample sentence in ASL is: *DINNER...BEFORE-BEFORE...COCKTAILS.*) Sometimes the right hand is moved in a straight line rather than a circular fashion. This sign is used only in specific contexts.

OR

SIGN #2: (used *rarely* for emphasis where the word order is more akin to English) Back of fingers of horizontal right **'BENT EXTENDED B'** hand are held against fingers of horizontal left **'BENT EXTENDED B'** hand, palms facing each other. Right hand is then moved toward the body.

SIGN #3 [ATLANTIC]: Outside edge of forefinger of horizontal right **'B'** hand, palm facing downward/forward, is laid across fingers of upturned left **'EXTENDED B'** hand at right angles. Right hand is then brushed forward twice.

before: *adv.* at an earlier time. *She had never seen the Rockies **before**.*

SIGN #4: Vertical right **'EXTENDED B'** hand, with palm toward right shoulder, becomes a **'BENT EXTENDED B'** hand as it bends toward the shoulder. Motion may be repeated.

(go) before: *v.* to go in front of; to face. *He has to go **before** the judge next Monday.*

SIGN #5: Vertical left **'EXTENDED B'** hand is held in a fixed position with palm toward face. Vertical right **'EXTENDED B'** hand, palm forward, is moved forward to stop near, but not touching the left hand.

beg: *v.* to ask for something by way of alms or charity. *He **begs** for money and food.*

SIGN #1: Right **'SPREAD EXTENDED C'** hand rests palm up on horizontal forefinger of left **'ONE'** hand, and the hands are bounced against each other a few times.

beg: *v.* to plead; entreat. *She **begged** to be allowed to attend the party.*

SIGN #2: Hands are clasped in an upright position, left **'A'** hand covered with right **'EXTENDED C'** hand, and they are moved forward purposefully.

begin: *v.* to start. *The office employees **begin** work at 9:00 a.m.*

SIGN: Left **'5'** hand is held with palm facing right while forefinger of right **'ONE'** hand is inserted between first two fingers of left hand and twisted 180 degrees to the right.

(on) behalf of: *prep.* speaking in place of; speaking for. *On **behalf of** the membership, the president thanked the woman for her generous donation.*

SIGN: Tip of forefinger of right **'ONE'** hand touches right side of forehead and left **'ONE'** hand is held palm-down at upper chest level with forefinger pointing forward and slightly to the right. Then both forefingers point this way as they move simultaneously forward.

behave: *v.* to act or conduct oneself in a certain way. *He **behaves** like a spoiled child.*

SIGN: **'SPREAD C'** (or **'B'**) hands, palms down, are simultaneously swung from side to side. SAME SIGN—**behaviour**, *n.*

behind: *prep.* in or to the rear of. *He put his old **trophy** behind the new one.*

SIGN #1: Horizontal **'EXTENDED A'** hands are held together with palms facing each other. Right hand is then moved back in a slight outward arc so that it is directly behind the left hand. (Use of this sign is rare as the concept **behind** is usually conveyed by using representative handshapes and positioning the right hand directly behind the left. To show that one car is behind another, horizontal **'3'** hands are held right behind left with extended fingers pointing forward and right palm facing left while left palm faces right. The horizontal **'3'** hand is used to mean 'vehicle' after the type of vehicle has already been specified. The vertical **'ONE'** hand is used to refer to a person.)

47

behind: *prep.* in support of. *The players were behind their coach even though he was criticized by the media.*

SIGN #2: **'S'** hands, palms toward the body, are held at chest level with the left slightly above the right. Then the hands come together to strike each other.

behind: *adv.* late. *She is behind in her correspondence.*

SIGN #3: Horizontal right **'A'** hand, palm facing left, is held directly behind horizontal left **'A'** hand whose palm faces right. Right hand is then brought back smartly toward the chest.

believe: *v.* to accept as true. *Some people believe in miracles.*

SIGN #1: Tip of forefinger of right **'ONE'** hand is placed on forehead. The hand is then brought down as it changes to a **'CROOKED EXTENDED B'** hand and is placed palm down on the upturned palm of the left **'CROOKED EXTENDED B'** hand so that the two hands clasp.

OR

SIGN #2: Edge of forefinger of right **'CROOKED EXTENDED B'** hand is held at forehead and lowered into upturned palm of left **'CROOKED EXTENDED B'** hand so that the two hands clasp.

OR

SIGN #3: Extended fingertips of right **'U'** (or **'CROOKED V'**) hand touch forehead, and are then brought down to rest on back of extended fingers of left **'U'** (or **'CROOKED V'**) hand. Both palms face downward.
SAME SIGN—**belief,** *n.*

bell: *n.* a metal cup that makes a ringing sound when struck. *We could hear the church bells ringing.*

SIGN #1: Right **'S'** hand, palm down, curves leftward in front of chest to strike right-facing palm of vertical left **'EXTENDED B'** hand twice. (Alternatively, the right hand may take the **'COVERED T'** (or **'FLAT O'**) shape.)

bell: *n.* a device that is rung or buzzed by pressing. *Did you hear the bell ring?*

SIGN #2: Right **'EXTENDED A'** hand is brought leftward, and thumb is pressed at least twice against right-facing palm of vertical left **'EXTENDED B'** hand.

belong: *v.* to be a member of. *He belongs to several organizations of the Deaf.*

SIGN #1: **'OPEN F'** hands are held slightly apart, palms facing each other, and are then brought together to form **'F'** hands, with thumbs and forefingers linked.

belong: *v.* to be rightly assigned to. *Does the coat belong to you?*

SIGN #2: Vertical right **'A'** hand, palm facing forward, is pushed firmly forward. ❖

beloved: *adj.* dearly loved. *A beloved pet is like a member of the family.*

SIGN: **'A'** hands are crossed at the wrists, palms facing the body, and are pressed against the chest.

below: *adv.* in a lower position or category. *His work is below average.*

SIGN: Left **'EXTENDED B'** hand, palm down and fingers pointing rightward, is placed on the fingers of the right **'EXTENDED B'** hand of which the palm faces downward and the fingers point forward. The right hand is then moved sharply downward from the wrist.

belt: *n.* a flexible strip of material worn around the waist. *She needs a belt for her jeans.*

SIGN: Thumbs and forefingers of both **'MODIFIED G'** (or **'CLAWED L'**) hands (depending on width of belt) are held in front of waist, palms toward body, and moved together to simulate the fastening of a belt buckle.

bench: *n.* a long seat. *We sat on the bench in the park.*

SIGN #1: **'CLAWED V'** hands are held side by side with palms down and sides of forefingers touching. The hands are then moved apart. (**BENCH** is frequently fingerspelled.)

bench: *n.* the seat occupied by the judge in a courtroom. *The lawyers were asked to approach the bench.*

SIGN #2: Horizontal **'F'** hands, palms facing each other, are alternately raised and lowered a few times.

benched: *v.* kept from participating in a game. *The coach **benched** the pitcher after the other team scored five runs.*

SIGN: Left **'BENT U'** hand is held with palm facing forward/rightward and extended fingers pointing in the same direction. Right **'CLAWED U'** hand is held palm down as forefinger and middle finger are hooked around the extended fingers of the left hand, tugging both hands sharply backward toward the chest.

bend: *v.* to make crooked, curved or bowed. *Be careful not to **bend** the credit card.*

SIGN: **'FLAT O'** hands are held with fingertips touching each other, and palms facing. Fingertips, still touching, are moved toward body to form the point of a **'V'** created as backs of fingers of each hand are brought closer together and palms face body. (Signs vary depending on the shape of what is being bent.)

benefit: *n.* an advantage; profit. *Everyone talked about the **benefits** of the workshop.*

SIGN: Thumb and forefinger of right **'F'** hand, palm facing down, are brought slightly downward to be inserted into an imaginary pocket at waist level. Alternatively, the imaginary pocket is sometimes located at the left side of the chest.
SAME SIGN—**beneficial**, *adj.*

benefits: *n.* financial perks received in addition to one's regular income. *This company offers its employees good **benefits**.*

SIGN: Right **'A-INDEX'** hand is held at an angle with palm facing partially upward and partially toward the body. The forearm is then brought smartly downward toward the body, with the hand taking on a **'CLOSED A-INDEX'** shape as the thumb and forefinger are retracted. Motion is repeated. (**BENEFITS** is frequently fingerspelled.)

benevolent: *adj.* desirous of being good and kind. *The **benevolent** man received praise for his good deeds.*

SIGN: Horizontal **'BENT EXTENDED B'** hands, palms facing each other, are alternately circled forward around each other.
SAME SIGN—**benevolence**, *n.*

benign: *adj.* not malignant or cancerous. *The patient was relieved to hear the tumour was benign.*

SIGN: Fingerspell **BENIGN**.

bequeath: *v.* to give a gift through one's will. *I will **bequeath** my property to my son.*

SIGN: Vertical **'X'** hands, palms facing each other, are held slightly apart, and thrust forward and downward simultaneously. (This sign is often made with one hand slightly ahead of the other.)

beside: *prep.* next to; at the side of. *Come and sit **beside** me.*

SIGN: **'EXTENDED B'** hands are held with palms together and fingers pointing forward. Right hand is then moved in a short arc to the right. (Use of this sign is rare as the concept **beside** is usually conveyed by using representative handshapes and positioning the hands side by side. To show that one car is beside another, horizontal **'3'** hands are held side by side with palms facing and extended fingers pointing forward. The horizontal **'3'** hand is used to mean 'vehicle' after the type of vehicle has already been specified. The vertical **'ONE'** hand is used to refer to a person.)

besides: *prep.* in addition to. *The student read two related books **besides** the assigned text.*

SIGN: Forefinger of right **'ONE'** hand is dropped forward smartly to strike horizontal forefinger of left **'ONE'** hand at right angles.

best: *adj.* having the most outstanding qualities. *Consumer reports rate that car the **best** in its class.*

SIGN #1: Right **'BENT EXTENDED B'** hand, fingers on lips and pointing leftward, palm backward, is drawn upward to the right of the face as the fingers bend to form an **'EXTENDED A'** hand with thumb pointing upward. Appropriate facial expression is essential.

OR

SIGN #2: Horizontal **'EXTENDED A'** hands are held slightly apart with palms facing each other and are simultaneously pulled back sharply toward the chest. Appropriate facial expression is essential.

best man: *n.* the male attendant of the bride-groom at a wedding. *The best man looked after the wedding rings.*

SIGN. Right **'BENT EXTENDED B'** hand, fingers on lips and pointing leftward, palm backward, is drawn upward to the right of the face as the fingers bend to form an **'EXTENDED A'** hand with thumb pointing upward. Then vertical right **'5'** hand, palm facing left, is placed with thumbtip in centre of forehead and is moved down to the middle of the chest.

bet: *v.* to wager or stake money on an uncertain outcome. *Which horse will you bet on in the next race?*

SIGN: **'B'** (or **'EXTENDED B'**) hands are held slightly apart, fingers pointing forward and palms facing upward. They are then turned over simultaneously so that palms are facing down. Alternatively, this sign may be made with one hand only.

betray: *v.* to betray a confidence or be disloyal, often treacherously. *Spies sometimes betray their country.*

SIGN: Fingerspell **BETRAY**.

B E T R A Y

better: *adj.* of higher quality; surpassing in excellence; in an improved state of health. *Are you feeling better now?*

SIGN #1: Right **'BENT EXTENDED B'** hand, fingers on lips and pointing leftward, palm backward, is drawn rightward as the fingers bend to form an **'EXTENDED A'** hand.

SIGN #2 [ATLANTIC]: **'EXTENDED A'** hands are held just above waist level at either side of the body with palms down and thumbs pointing toward the body. As the hands move upward to chest level, they twist upward so that the palms face the body and the thumbs point upward. (Signs vary in the Atlantic provinces. This sign is used to describe one's state of health only.)

between: *prep.* the space or range separating two things. *Saskatchewan is situated between Alberta and Manitoba.*

SIGN #1: Edge of right **'EXTENDED B'** hand, palm facing left, fingers pointing slightly to the left and forward, is inserted between middle finger and forefinger of left **'5'** hand and jiggled.

OR

SIGN #2: Right **'EXTENDED B'** hand, palm facing left and fingers pointing forward, slides from side to side a few times along forefinger of horizontal left **'EXTENDED B'** hand, whose palm is facing the body.

beverage: *n.* a drink. *The flight attendant offered us a choice of beverages.*

SIGN: Right **'C'** hand is held in a horizontal position near the mouth with palm facing left. The hand is then tipped upward slightly. Motion is repeated. If the beverage is alcoholic, this sign is generally made with a **'CLAWED L'** hand.

beyond: *prep.* past; outside of. *Everyone sitting beyond Row H had trouble reading the actors' fingerspelling.*

SIGN: Horizontal **'BENT EXTENDED B'** hands, palms facing each other, the backs of the fingers of the left hand resting against those of the right hand. The right hand is then moved forward.

Bi-Bi-: *adj.* an abbreviation for **Bilingual/Bicultural**, a term used to refer to an environment in which Deaf children are encouraged to develop fluency in both ASL and English, and an understanding of and respect for Deaf Culture as well as the culture of the wider hearing society. *Many Deaf people were excited when Bi-Bi- programs were introduced in schools.*

SIGN: Fingerspell **BIBI**.

B I B I

Bible: *n.* a holy book containing the Old and New Testament. *Have you read the assigned passages in your Bible?*

SIGN: **'BENT MIDFINGER 5'** hands, palms facing, are held slightly apart, fingers pointing forward. Tip of left middle finger is used to tap right palm and vice versa. Then horizontal **'EXTENDED B'** hands, palms together, fingers pointing forward, are opened to the palms-up position. (ASL CONCEPT—**Jesus - book**.)

bicker: *v.* to argue or dispute petulantly. *They bicker constantly over silly things.*

SIGN: **'BENT ONE'** hands, palms toward the chest, forefingers pointing toward each other, are either simultaneously or alternately moved up and down from the wrist. ❖

bicultural: *adj.* involving two different cultures. *Many bicultural people live in Quebec.*

SIGN: Right **'V'** hand is held upright with palm facing the body. Then left **'ONE'** hand is held upright and right **'C'** hand rotates from an upright position to a horizontal position as it moves a quarter turn around the left forefinger. (ASL CONCEPT—**two - culture**.)

bicycle: *n.* a two-wheeled, pedal-driven vehicle. *The boy rode a ten-speed bicycle.*

SIGN #1: **'S'** hands are held palms down, and moved forward alternately in small circles to simulate the pedaling of a bicycle.

SIGN #2 [ATLANTIC]: **'CLAWED L'** hands are held, palms down, tips of thumbs touching, and are twisted up and down alternately.

bid: *n.* an offer or proposal to pay a certain price. *Ours was the lowest bid for the contract.*

SIGN: Right **'B'** (or **'EXTENDED B'**) hand, palm up and fingers pointing forward, is thrust forward.
SAME SIGN—**bid**, *v.*

big: *adj.* large. *We are planning a big celebration.*

SIGN #1: Horizontal **'CLAWED L'** (or **'EXTENDED B'**) hands, with palms facing, are held slightly apart and then simultaneously moved farther apart.

big: *adj.* large in physical stature; grown up. *You are getting to be a big boy now.*

SIGN #2: Vertical right **'BENT EXTENDED B'** hand, palm facing left, is held above shoulder level and is moved further upward in a backward/upward arc.

bilingual: *adj.* able to communicate with reasonably equal skill in two languages. *Deaf people who are fluent in both ASL and English are considered bilingual.*

SIGN: Right **'V'** hand is held upright with palm facing the body. Next, horizontal **'L'** hands are held side by side with palms down, forefingers pointing forward, and tips of thumbs touching. The hands then move apart. (ASL CONCEPT— **two - language**.) Alternatively, see **both**, as the sign for **bilingual** is sometimes formed from **both + language**.

bill: *v.* to present an account of charges; supply a statement showing payment owing. *The new telephone company will bill its customers quarterly.*

SIGN #1: Right **'B'** (or **'EXTENDED B'**) hand, palm up, fingers pointing forward, is thrust forward as if presenting a bill. ❖

bill: *n.* a statement of charges owing. *Have you paid your telephone bill?*

SIGN #2: Tip of forefinger of right **'ONE'** hand, palm toward body, is poked into palm of left **'EXTENDED B'** hand whose palm faces right. (**BILL** is frequently fingerspelled.)

bill: *n.* paper money, as opposed to coins. *Loonies have replaced one dollar **bills** in Canada.*

SIGN #3: Tips of thumbs and forefingers of **'CONTRACTED L'** hands touch. The hands then move apart and the forefingers and thumbs close to form **'CLOSED MODIFIED G'** hands.

bill: *n.* a draft of a law proposed to members of a legislative assembly. *The **bill** was amended.*

SIGN #4: Vertical left **'EXTENDED B'** hand is held in a fixed position with palm facing right. Right **'L'** hand, palm facing left, is placed against the fingers of the left hand and then lowered to the heel of the left hand.

billiards: *n.* a table game played with cues and hard balls. *Billiards is a popular game in England.*

SIGN: Right **'S'** hand, palm toward body, is held near waist and used to simulate holding the handle of a billiard cue. Left **'S'** hand is extended in front of body, palm down, to simulate supporting the imaginary cue, and is held steady while right hand is moved back and forth twice.

bind: *v.* to tie together or secure with a rope or string. *Bind the parcel with some strong cord.*

SIGN #1: **'COVERED T'** hands, palms facing body, are held close together, circled forward around one another, and then drawn firmly apart as though tying something.

bind: *v.* to secure pages within a cover. *The students will bind their essays into a book.*

SIGN #2: Right **'OPEN A'** hand, palm facing left, firmly encloses outer side of upright left **'EXTENDED B'** hand, whose palm faces right.

(in a) bind: *adv.* in an impossible or very difficult situation. *He was **in a bind** after losing his keys because he had lost his duplicate set.*

SIGN: Tips of extended fingers of right **'BENT V'** hand are thrust toward the throat.

binoculars: *n.* opera or field glasses. *People generally take their **binoculars** when they go bird-watching.*

SIGN: **'C'** hands are placed in front of the eyes, palms facing each other. They are then twisted inward twice to simulate the adjustment of binoculars.

biology: *n.* the science of living things. *Biology is a fascinating subject.*

SIGN: **'B'** hands, palms facing forward and slightly downward, are alternately rotated backwards several times.
SAME SIGN—**biological**, *adj.*

birch: *n.* a tree with thin peeling bark. *Natives used the bark of the white **birch** to make their canoes.*

SIGN: Fingerspell **BIRCH**.

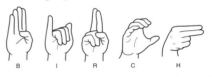

bird: *n.* a feathered vertebrate. *A canary is a tiny yellow song **bird**.*

SIGN: Right **'MODIFIED G'** hand is held at chin, palm facing forward, while thumb and forefinger are opened and closed at least twice to simulate the movement of a bird's beak.

birth: *n.* the bringing forth of offspring. *They are celebrating the **birth** of their grandson.*

SIGN #1: Horizontal **'EXTENDED B'** hands, palms facing the body, are positioned with the back of the right hand resting against the left palm. Then the right hand is curved down and under the left until its palm faces downward.

OR

SIGN #2: Horizontal **'EXTENDED B'** hands are held with palms toward body, the left farther from the body than the right. Right hand then moves forward so that the back of it is laid against the palm of the left hand. (This sign is always used when referring to the birth of 'Christ' and may be used when referring to a 'human' birth but *not* for the birth of an 'animal'. For the birth of an animal, see **birth** #1.)

birthday: *n.* the day on which a person was born. *Her **birthday** is in October.*

SIGN #1: Vertical right **'ONE'** hand is placed so that right elbow rests on back of left **'EXTENDED B'** hand. Right forearm is then lowered until right hand rests near elbow of left arm, with forefinger pointing left. (Alternatively, this sign may be preceded by either **birth** #1 or #2.)

SIGN #2 [ATLANTIC]: Backs of fingers of **'BENT EXTENDED B'** hands are brushed forward against each cheek and brought further forward as they turn over and straighten to become palm-down **'EXTENDED B'** hands with fingers pointing forward. (This sign appears mainly in Newfoundland.)

OR

SIGN #3 [ATLANTIC]: Backs of fingers of **'BENT EXTENDED B'** hands are held against each cheek and brushed forward so that hands take on a **'CROOKED EXTENDED B'** shape with fingers pointing upward and palms facing backward.

SIGN #4 [ONTARIO]: Right **'EXTENDED U'** hand, palm is held at about a 45° angle forward with elbow resting on left **'STANDARD BASE'** hand which is held at the right side of the waist. Extended fingers of right hand then trace a horizontal figure eight.

OR

SIGN #5 [ONTARIO]: The tip of the thumb of the vertical right **'EXTENDED K'** hand, palm facing left, is stroked forward and slightly downward from the right cheek a few times.

SIGN #6 [PRAIRIE]: Right **'BENT MIDFINGER 5'** hand is held with palm facing the body and tip of middle finger touching chin. The hand is then lowered so that the tip of the middle finger touches the centre of the chest.

biscuit: *n.* flat, thin bread which is raised by adding baking powder or soda. *The **biscuit** was served with butter.*

SIGN: Fingerspell **BISCUIT**. (Various signs may be used.)

bisexual: *adj.* sexually attracted to members of either sex. *She belongs to an organization concerned with the interests of **bisexual** people.*

SIGN: Right **'5'** hand is held with palm facing leftward, fingers pointing upward/leftward, and tip of thumb touching the middle of the forehead. The hand is then lowered so that the tip of the thumb comes to rest at about mid-chest. Then thumbtip of vertical right **'5'** hand, palm left, is placed on chin and is lowered to mid-chest. Fingerspell **SEX**. Finally, the right **'CLAWED V'** hand is held with palm down and moved from side to side a few times. (ASL CONCEPT—**man - woman - s-e-x - either.**) BISEXUAL is frequently fingerspelled.

bishop: *n.* the head of a church district. *A **bishop** is a high ranking clergyman.*

SIGN: Vertical **'B'** (or **'EXTENDED B'**) hands, palms facing each other, are placed at either side of head, and then moved upward until the fingertips meet to form the shape of a bishop's mitre. (**BISHOP** is frequently fingerspelled.)

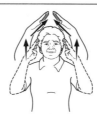

bit: *adj.* a little; a small amount; to a small degree; rather. *She is a **bit** shy.*

SIGN: Right **'X'** hand is held palm-up with forefinger tightly crooked and tip of thumb repeatedly scraping downward against tip of forefinger.

bitch: *n.* a colloquial term used as a vulgar reference to a woman. *She is an actress who enjoys playing the role of a **bitch** in the soap opera.*

SIGN #1: Right **'B'** hand, with palm facing left, is brought upward from a horizontal position in front of chest to a vertical position as it strikes chin sharply. Facial expression must clearly convey 'scorn'.

bitch: *v.* a colloquial term meaning to complain generally about petty matters. *That employee **bitches** about every new policy we try to implement.*

SIGN #2: Fingertips of right **'SPREAD EXTENDED C'** hand are thumped repeatedly against chest. Appropriate facial expression is important.

bite: *v.* to seize with the teeth. *Did your dog bite the postman?*

SIGN: Right **'SPREAD C'** hand becomes a **'CLAWED SPREAD C'** hand as the fingers represent teeth and form a clamp on nearest edge of horizontal left hand, which is held palm-downward. ❖

bitter: *adj.* resentful; marked by ill feeling. *The bitter gambler complained about her losses.*

SIGN #1: Tip of forefinger of right **'ONE'** hand, is brought sharply upward to strike the chin. Facial expression is important.

bitter: *adj.* having an unpalatable, harsh taste. *She did not like the taste of the **bitter** orange peel.*

SIGN #2: Tip of forefinger of right **'ONE'** hand is placed on chin and twisted a quarter turn to the right. Facial expression is important.

bizarre: *adj.* odd or unusual in an interesting or amusing way. *Her rather **bizarre** clothes always attract attention.*

SIGN: Vertical right **'C'** hand, palm facing left, is held near the face and is abruptly dropped downward from the wrist so the palm faces down.

blab: *v.* a colloquial term meaning to reveal information thoughtlessly. *This is a secret, so do not **blab** it to everyone.*

SIGN: **'5'** hands, palms facing forward, are brought down sharply from either side of chin and then moved outward in a series of small arcs with palms facing downward. The lip pattern generally accompanying this sign appears as 'mummummummu'.

black: *adj.* having a colour that is opposite to white. *The woman was dressed in a **black** outfit.*

SIGN: Tip of forefinger of right **'BENT ONE'** hand, palm down, is drawn across forehead from left to right. In the process, the wrist turns so that the forefinger, which originally points leftward, eventually points backward.

blackboard: *n.* a surface for writing upon with chalk. *The teacher wrote the lesson on the **blackboard**.*

SIGN: Tip of forefinger of right **'ONE'** hand, palm down, is drawn across forehead from left to right. In the process, the wrist turns so that the forefinger, which originally points leftward, eventually points backward. Then vertical right **'CLOSED X'** hand, palm forward, is held high and moved in a wavy line from left to right as if writing on a blackboard. (ASL CONCEPT—**black - write on board**.)

blame: *v.* to accuse of fault or error. *The players will **blame** the referee for their defeat.*

SIGN: Horizontal right **'EXTENDED A'** hand, palm facing left, is placed on back of left **'STANDARD BASE'** hand and then pushed sharply forward. ❖

blank: *adj.* empty; free from writing or print. *May I have some **blank** paper?*

SIGN: Tip of middle finger of right **'BENT MIDFINGER 5'** hand strokes forward/rightward across back of left **'STANDARD BASE'** hand.

blanket: *n.* a large covering, as of a bed. *Cover yourself with this **blanket** if you are cold.*

SIGN: **'BENT EXTENDED B'** hands are held apart just in front of the upper chest with palms down and fingers pointing forward but toward each other slightly. The hands are then turned inward from the wrists so that the fingertips touch the chest. Alternatively, this sign may be made with one hand only.

bleed: *v.* to discharge blood. *Did the wound **bleed** profusely?*

SIGN: Fingertips of horizontal right **'5'** hand are placed against back of left **'EXTENDED B'** (or **'5'**) hand, which is held with palm toward body and fingertips pointing to the right. Then right hand, with fingers fluttering, is then lowered to a point below left hand.

blend: *v.* to make a smooth mixture. *Oil and water will not **blend**.*

SIGN #1: Right **'SPREAD C'** hand is held palm down above left **'SPREAD C'** hand, whose palm faces up. They are then alternately circled in a counter-clockwise direction.

blend: *v.* to merge in a harmonious way. *Your suggestion **blends** in perfectly with our plans.*

SIGN #2: With palms facing the body, **'CLAWED 5'** hands are held together so that little fingers interlock. As the hands are simultaneously lowered from the wrists, the corresponding fingers of each hand interlock to simulate the meshing of gears.

bless: *v.* to make holy by religious rite. *The priest will **bless** his congregation.*

SIGN: Tips of thumbs of both **'A'** hands are held almost touching each other at the lips. Then both hands are brought down and out as they open into **'EXTENDED B'** hands, palms facing downward and fingertips pointing forward.

blind: *adj.* sightless. *The **blind** man carries a white cane.*

SIGN #1: Fingertips of right **'CROOKED V'** hand are tapped on either side of nose, near the eyes. (For **legally blind**, see **real** + **blind** #1.)

blind: *n.* something that shuts out the light. *There was no **blind** on the window.*

SIGN #2: Right **'CLOSED X'** hand, with palm facing left, is brought down to simulate motion of lowering a blind.

blinds: *n.* something that shuts out the light. *There were no **blinds** on the window.*

SIGN: **'BENT B'** hands are held, palms down, with right hand slightly above left. Fingers of left hand point right while fingers of right hand point left. The hands are then simultaneously given quarter-turn twists forward and back, from the wrists. (For **vertical blinds**, see **verticals**.)

blink: *v.* to close and immediately reopen one's eye(s), usually involuntarily. *You must not **blink** during this vision test.*

SIGN: **'CONTRACTED L'** hands, with palms facing, are held at each eye. Then thumbs and forefingers are snapped shut to form **'MODIFIED G'** hands and reopened to become **'CONTRACTED L'** hands once again.

block: *v.* to obstruct or stop the progress of. *We tried to get through but the police **blocked** our way.*

SIGN #1: **'EXTENDED B'** hands are crossed but not necessarily quite touching each other, and are moved forward simultaneously. ❖

block: *n.* a solid piece of something, often wood. *The foundation was made of cement blocks.*

SIGN #2: With a slight but deliberate downward thrust horizontal **'EXTENDED B'** hands are held parallel, with palms facing each other and fingers pointing forward. Then the hands take on a **'BENT EXTENDED B'** shape as they are swung inward with a slight downward thrust again, and the right hand positioned ahead of the left, both palms facing the body.

block: *n.* a rectangular section of land bounded by four city streets. *He lives a block from the hospital.*

SIGN #3: Fingerspell **BLOCK**.

block: *n.* a large building which houses separate units such as offices or apartments. *She lives in the apartment block opposite the shopping mall.*

SIGN #4: Fingers of **'BENT EXTENDED B'** (or **'BENT EXTENDED U'** or **'U'**) hands, palms facing each other, are alternately slid up from under to be placed on top of one another as they move upward.

blockhead: *n.* someone who behaves in a stupid manner. *Only a blockhead would swim outside during a thunderstorm.*

SIGN: Thumb and forefinger of right **'MODIFIED G'** hand are pointed at forehead, with palm facing left. Then wrist is twisted, thus rotating **'MODIFIED G'** hand a quarter turn so that palm is toward face. For greater emphasis, this sign may be made with a **'FLAT C'** handshape.

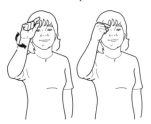

blond *(male)/* **blonde** *(female):* *adj.* flaxen or golden hair colour. *She dyed her hair blonde.*

SIGN: Tip of little finger of right **'Y'** hand, palm toward face, is placed on forehead and then swung outward so that palm faces away from face. (**BLOND** and **BLONDE** are frequently fingerspelled.)

blood: *n.* the vital red fluid that circulates through the body. *He donates blood regularly.*

SIGN: Fingertips of horizontal right **'5'** hand are placed against back of left **'EXTENDED B'** (or **'5'**) hand, which is held with palm toward body and fingertips pointing to the right. Then right hand, with fingers fluttering, is then lowered to a point below left hand. (**BLOOD** is frequently fingerspelled.)

bloom: *v.* to open into a flower. *The roses bloomed in the spring.*

SIGN: Right **'FLAT O'** hand is thrust upward through left **'C'** hand, as fingers open into a **'CONTRACTED 5'** hand.

blossom: *n.* the flower of a plant. *The apple tree is covered with blossoms.*

SIGN: Fingertips of right **'FLAT O'** hand are placed at right side of nose and then moved around to left side.

blouse: *n.* a shirt-like garment. *She wore a white blouse with her new skirt.*

SIGN: Horizontal **'CROOKED 5'** hands are held with palms facing the body and fingertips touching either side of upper chest. Then the hands are simultaneously moved down to waist level.

blow: *v.* to exhale air from the mouth. *The child will blow out the candles on the cake.*

SIGN #1: Back of right **'O'** hand is held at the mouth, and is then thrust forward as fingers spread to form a **'CONTRACTED 5'** hand.

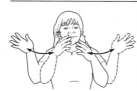

blow: *v.* to send forth a current of air. *The wind will blow harder tomorrow.*

SIGN #2: **'5'** hands, palms facing each other, are waved back and forth with a swaying motion.

blow up: *v.* to explode; burst. *If you set fire to an aerosol can, it might blow up.*

SIGN: **'S'** hands are held with wrists crossed and palms down, the right hand nearest the body. Then both hands are thrust upward forcefully so that the palms face each other.

blue: *adj.* having a colour like that of the sky or deep sea. *He wore a blue shirt.*

SIGN #1: Right **'B'** hand is held almost upright but tilted forward slightly with palm facing left. It is then twisted several times from the wrist.

blue: *adj.* depressed; downhearted. *She was blue after losing the race.*

SIGN #2: Tips of middle fingers of **'BENT MIDFINGER 5'** hands are held at either side of upper chest and are simultaneously lowered. ALTERNATE SIGN—**depressed** #2

bluff: *v.* to deceive in order to gain advantage; fool. *You cannot bluff your way out of this situation.*

SIGN: Vertical right **'A'** hand, with palm forward and slightly leftward, is knocked against forefinger of vertical left **'ONE'** hand whose palm faces right. ❖

blunt: *adj.* frank; straightforward. *His blunt remark was critical of their work.*

SIGN #1: Vertical right **'B'** hand, palm facing left, is held directly in front of the face and thrust forward and slightly downward.

blunt: *adj.* having an end or tip that is not sharp. *The murder victim had been hit over the head with a blunt object.*

SIGN #2: Right **'EXTENDED A'** hand, palm facing left, thumb under chin, is thrust forward. Then tip of middle finger of right **'BENT MIDFINGER 5'** hand, palm facing the body, is placed on the chin. The forearm twists clockwise a quarter turn so that the palm faces leftward/forward. (ASL CONCEPT—**not - sharp**.)

blurry: *adj.* hazy; obscure. *The TV picture is blurry.*

SIGN: Vertical **'5'** hands are held with palms either touching or at least close together. Left hand, palm facing body, is held steady while right hand faces forward and is circled counter-clockwise.

blush: *v.* to become red-faced from shame, embarrassment or modesty. *The children blush when the teacher draws attention to their artwork.*

SIGN: Tip of forefinger of right **'ONE'** hand is stroked downward from lips to form an **'X'** hand, palm facing the body. Next, vertical **'5'** hands, with palms held at either cheek, are pushed upward. (ASL CONCEPT—**red - burn cheeks**.)
ALTERNATE SIGN—**flush** #1

board: *n.* an organized official body or tribunal. *Are you on the advisory board for the college?*

SIGN #1: Vertical right **'B'** hand, palm facing left, is placed on left side of chest and moved straight across to the right side.

board: *n.* a flat piece of rigid material, generally wood, whose length is much greater than its width. *He sawed the board in half.*

SIGN #2: **'EXTENDED C'** hands are held side by side with palms down and are drawn apart.

board: *n.* a flat surface, generally rectangular, for posting messages. *Post a notice on the board.*

SIGN #3: **'ONE'** hands are held with palms forward and forefingers pointing upward/forward, the tips touching. The hands are then drawn apart, moved downward, and back together to outline the shape of a bulletin board.

board: *v.* to go aboard; to get on (a train, airplane, etc.). *He will board the bus at 7:00 a.m.*

SIGN #4: Side of forefinger of palm-down right **'CLAWED V'** hand is thrust against right-facing palm of left **'EXTENDED B'** hand, of which the fingers point forward.

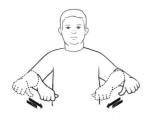

boast: *v.* to brag. *He likes to boast about his job.*

SIGN: **'EXTENDED A'** hands, palms facing downward, are placed at either side of waist and are alternately moved away from the body and then toward the body so that the thumbs jab the signer in the sides. Facial expression is important.

boat: *n.* a water vessel. *The oars are in the boat.*

SIGN: **'CROOKED EXTENDED B'** hands, palms facing each other at a slight angle, are cupped together to form the hull of a boat. Then they are moved up and down in a bobbing motion.

body: *n.* the physical structure of a human or animal. *A healthy body requires good nutrition and daily exercise.*

SIGN: Horizontal **'EXTENDED B'** hands are placed slightly apart, fingertips opposite, with palms on upper chest. Then they are moved simultaneously to waist level.

boil: *v.* to cook in a liquid. *You should boil the water before you drink it.*

SIGN: **'BENT 5'** hands, palms up and fingers fluttering, are alternately circled upward and forward.

bold: *adj.* brave; without fear. *The bold construction worker walked along the girders without hesitation.*

SIGN: **'BENT 5'** hands, with fingertips on either side of chest and palms facing the body, are drawn forward to form **'S'** hands.
REGIONAL VARIATION—**brave** #2

boldface: *adj.* printed in a dark or heavy type face. *The entry words in that dictionary are boldface.*

SIGN: **'CROOKED 5'** hands are held parallel with palms down. They then jerk slightly forward/downward as the fingers retract to form **'CLAWED SPREAD C'** hands.

bomb: *n.* an explosive projectile. *The bomb destroyed the munitions factory when it exploded.*

SIGN: **'S'** hands are held with wrists crossed and palms down, the right hand nearest the body. Then both hands are thrust upward forcefully so that the palms face each other.

bond: *n.* a feeling of closeness; rapport; emotional attachment. *There is a strong bond between my grandfather and me.*

SIGN: Thumbs and forefingers of both **'F'** hands interlock, left palm toward the body while right palm faces away from the body. The hands maintain this position as they move purposefully forward.

bonded: *adj.* insured or bound by law to provide a service in a trustworthy manner. *The bonded moving company is insured against damage.*

SIGN: Fingerspell **BONDED**.

bone: *n.* a hard, dense, porous structure forming the skeleton of a vertebrate. *The femur is the largest bone in the human body.*

SIGN: **'S'** (or **'CLAWED V'**) hands, palms facing chest, are crossed at the wrists, with the right hand nearest the body. The back of the right wrist is tapped twice against the left wrist. (**BONE** is frequently fingerspelled.)

book: *n.* a printed and bound volume. *I have a book about American Sign Language.*

SIGN #1: Horizontal **'EXTENDED B'** hands, palms together, fingers pointing forward, are opened to the palms-up position. Motion is repeated.
See also **close (a book)** and **open (a book)**.

book: *v.* to reserve; arrange beforehand. *Did you book a table at the restaurant?*

SIGN #2: Right **'V'** hand, palm facing forward/leftward, is brought down so that the extended fingers fall one on either side of the forefinger of the vertical left **'ONE'** hand which is held with palm facing right. ❖
ALTERNATE SIGN—**reserve** #3

booklet: *n.* a small book or brochure. *The interpreters' association distributes booklets on how to use interpreters for the Deaf.*

SIGN: Thumb and forefinger of right **'A-INDEX'** (or **'MODIFIED G'**) hand are slid up the edge of left **'EXTENDED B'** hand, which is held with palm facing body. Motion is repeated.

bookshelf: *n.* shelving space for storing books. *Put the vase on the bookshelf.*

SIGN: Horizontal **'EXTENDED B'** hands, palms together, fingers pointing forward, are opened to the palms-up position. Then **'B'** (or **'BENT B'** or **'EXTENDED B'** or **'BENT EXTENDED B'**) hands, positioned side by side, palms down, with fingers pointing forward, are moved apart in a straight line. To indicate that there are a number of shelves, the motion is repeated once or twice, each time at a lower position.

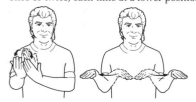

boost: *n.* a method of restarting a rundown car battery. *I will need a boost to get my car started.*

SIGN: **'CLAWED 3'** hands are held slightly apart with palms down and are simultaneously lowered with a firm motion. (Signs vary according to context.)

booster [*or* **booster shot**]: *n.* an injection of vaccine intended to maintain immunity. *In order to prevent tetanus, you should have a booster shot every five years.*

SIGN: Tip of forefinger of right **'BENT L'** hand is jabbed into upper left arm and thumb is repeatedly bent and extended as though depressing a plunger into a syringe.

boot: *n.* a strong outer covering for the foot. *This boot is made of rubber.*

SIGN #1: Thumb of right **'EXTENDED A'** hand, palm facing left, is placed under upper front tooth and flicked forward. Edge of right **'EXTENDED B'** hand is then positioned on wrist of left forearm and brought upward to the elbow. (ASL CONCEPT—**rubber - boot**.) (**BOOT** is frequently fingerspelled.)

SIGN #2 [ONTARIO]: Side of forefinger of right **'X'** hand, palm facing left, is stroked downward on the chin at least twice.

booze: *n.* a colloquial term meaning an alcoholic drink. *Guests brought their own booze to the party.*

SIGN: Horizontal right **'COMBINED I + ONE'** hand is held above and at right angles to horizontal left **'COMBINED I + ONE'** hand, whose palm faces slightly to the right and slightly toward the body. The two hands are then tapped together twice.

bore: *v.* gave birth to. *She bore seven children.*

SIGN #1: Horizontal **'EXTENDED B'** hands, palms facing the body, are positioned with the back of the right hand resting against the left palm. Then the right hand is curved down and under the left until its palm faces downward.

bore: *v.* to make a hole with a revolving tool. *The carpenter used a drill to bore a hole.*

SIGN #2: Forefinger of right **'ONE'** (or **'L'**) hand is jabbed between forefinger and middle finger of vertical left **'EXTENDED B'** hand which is held with palm facing right.

bored/boring: *adj.* the state of feeling disinterested/the quality of being uninteresting. *The students are bored with his boring lectures.*

SIGN #1: Tip of forefinger of right **'ONE'** hand is placed against right side of nose, and is twisted half a turn clockwise. Facial expression must clearly convey 'boredom'.

OR

SIGN #2: With fingers pointing leftward, side of forefinger of right palm-down **'MODIFIED 5'** hand is held at left side of chin. As it is drawn rightward across the chin, it becomes a **'CLAWED 5'** hand, which is then flung forward/downward and becomes a **'5'** hand with palm down. Facial expression must clearly convey 'boredom'.

SAME SIGN—**boredom**, *n.*

born: *v.* was given birth. *Steve was born on Valentine's Day.*

SIGN: Horizontal **'EXTENDED B'** hands, palms facing the body, are positioned with the back of the right hand resting against the left palm. Then the right hand is curved down and under the left until its palm faces downward. ALTERNATE SIGN—**birth** #2

borrow: *v.* to take or use temporarily. *May I borrow your car to drive my sister to the airport?*

SIGN: Right **'V'** (or **'K'**) hand, palm facing left, is placed on left **'V'** (or **'K'**) which is held with palm facing right. The hands are initially positioned horizontally and then tilted back to an upright position. ❖

boss: *n.* an employer. *His boss was pleased with his work.*

SIGN #1: Vertical right **'ONE'** hand is held near the right side of the forehead with palm forward and slightly leftward. The wrist then rotates forward to turn the hand as the forefinger tucks into a **'BENT ONE'** position with the fingertip coming to rest on the right side of the forehead. (**BOSS** is frequently fingerspelled.)

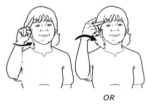

OR

SIGN #2: Fingertips of palm-down right **'SPREAD C'** hand are tapped twice on right shoulder. Alternatively, this sign may be made using both hands, one on each shoulder.

boss: *v.* a colloquial term meaning to give orders, often in a very authoritative manner. *She likes to boss people around.*

SIGN #3: Vertical right **'ONE'** hand is held with palm forward/leftward and tip of forefinger at the right side of the chin while left **'ONE'** hand is held palm down with forefinger pointing forward. The hands then reverse positions with the right wrist dropping so that the hand is palm down with forefinger pointing forward as the left hand moves to a vertical position with palm forward/rightward and tip of forefinger at the side of the chin. Motion is repeated. (**BOSSY**, *adj.*, is fingerspelled.)

both: *pron.* each of two things. *The St. Lawrence and Fraser are both Canadian rivers.*

SIGN #1: Left hand clasps extended fingers of right **'V'** hand which is held upright with palm toward body. As the extended fingers of the right hand are drawn down through the left hand, they close to form a **'U'** (or **'BENT U'**) hand. Alternatively, this sign may be made without the left hand.

both: *pron.* each of two people. *Ryan and Meg are both from Ireland.*

SIGN #2: Horizontal right **'K'** hand is held with palm facing leftward/upward and extended fingers pointing forward. The forearm then moves slightly from side to side several times as if pointing to the two people in question. The positioning of this sign depends on which people are being represented by the word 'both'. If the signer is one of the people being signified, as in 'both of us', the **'K'** hand is held upright and moved back and forth between the signer and the person who makes up the other half of 'us'.

bother: *v.* to be troublesome; disturb. *I would not bother you if it were not important.*

SIGN #1: Edge of right **'EXTENDED B'** hand is brought down twice with a chopping motion between index and middle finger of left **'5'** hand. ❖

OR

SIGN #2: Fingertips of right **'BENT EXTENDED B'** hand, palm down, are tapped smartly a couple of times against back of left **'STANDARD BASE'** hand. ❖

bottle: *n.* a narrow-necked container for liquids. *He brought his host a bottle of wine.*

SIGN: Horizontal right **'C'** hand, palm facing left, is placed on upturned palm of left **'EXTENDED B'** hand. Right hand is then moved upward to outline the shape of a bottle.

bottom: *n.* the lowest part; base. *There are rotten apples at the bottom of the barrel.*

SIGN: **'EXTENDED B'** hands are held with palms facing down, the left above the right, the fingers of the left hand pointing right and those of the right hand pointing left. The right hand is moved up and down slightly.

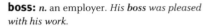

bounce: *v.* to spring up or cause to spring up after striking a surface. *A basketball player must bounce the ball with only one hand.*

SIGN: Right **'EXTENDED B'** hand, palm down and fingers pointing forward, is moved up and down with a bouncing motion.

bow: *n.* a knot with loops. *She made a large bow with the ribbon.*

SIGN #1: Extended fingers of horizontal **'DOUBLE MODIFIED G'** hands, palms toward body, are circled simultaneously forward around one another, pulled outward until fingertips are opposite, and then drawn apart as thumb and extended fingers of each hand come together to form **'CLOSED DOUBLE MODIFIED G'** hands.

bow: *n.* a weapon made of thin wood and a cord that is attached to either end. *An archer uses a bow and arrow to shoot with.*

SIGN #2: Horizontal left **'S'** hand is held in a fixed position with palm facing right. Horizontal right **'S'** hand, palm facing left, is held just behind the left hand and is then drawn backward and changed to a **'V'** shape as it nears the right shoulder.

bow: *v.* to bend the body downward, generally as a courteous gesture. *The entertainer bowed before his audience.*

SIGN #3: Left **'C'** hand clasps forearm of right **'S'** hand which is held with palm facing forward at a slight leftward angle. Right hand is then lowered from the wrist so that palm faces downward. ❖

bowel: *n.* an area below the stomach which is responsible for digestion; intestine. *He had surgery to remove an obstruction from his bowel.*

SIGN: Fingerspell **BOWEL**.

bowel movement: *n.* defecation; the discharge of waste matter from the bowel. *The doctor asked her how often she had a bowel movement.*

SIGN: Horizontal left **'S'** (or **'A'**) hand is held in a fixed position with palm facing right and enclosing thumb of horizontal right **'5'** (or **'EXTENDED A'**) hand, of which the palm faces left. Then the right hand is pulled down sharply. (The frequently fingerspelled abbreviation **BM** is considered a more polite way to express this concept.)

bowl: *n.* a concave dish. *Would you like another bowl of soup?*

SIGN #1: **'CROOKED EXTENDED B'** hands are held side by side with palms up. Then they are moved apart and upward to outline the shape of a bowl.

bowl: *v.* to deliver a bowling ball. *They bowl every Tuesday evening.*

SIGN #2: **'SPREAD C'** hand, is placed near right hip, palm facing forward, and is swung forward.

box: *n.* a case or carton made of cardboard or wood. *I received a box of chocolates for my birthday.*

SIGN #1: Horizontal **'EXTENDED B'** hands are held parallel, with palms facing. Then the hands take on a **'BENT EXTENDED B'** shape as they are swung inward with the right hand positioned ahead of the left.

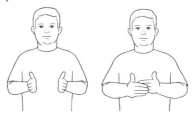

box: *v.* to fight with the fists in a boxing match. *The fighters will box ten rounds.*

SIGN #2: **'S'** hands, are alternately moved in small circles as they are jabbed forward from near the face.

boy: *n.* a male child. *Their first baby was a boy.*

SIGN #1: Right **'FLAT C'** hand is held in front of forehead, with palm facing left, and is closed twice into a **'FLAT O'** hand.

SIGN #2 [ATLANTIC]: Forefinger and thumb of right **'CONTRACTED L'** hand, palm toward the body, are placed one on either side of the chin and are drawn downward to form a **'CLOSED MODIFIED G'** hand. Motion is repeated.

boycott: *v.* to cooperatively refuse to do business with a certain individual or company in order to bring about reform. *Pro-labour activists will boycott the newspaper because of its strong anti-labour bias.*

SIGN: Vertical right **'S'** hand, palm facing backward, is held at or above shoulder level and is forcefully twisted a half turn so that palm faces forward. Alternatively, this sign may be made with two hands.

bra [*abbreviation for* **brassiere**]: *n.* a woman's undergarment worn to support and cover the breasts. *She adjusted the shoulder straps of her bra.*

SIGN: **'EXTENDED C'** hands, with palms facing the body and thumbtips touching, are placed side by side near centre of chest, then moved apart.

braces: *n.* dental wires for straightening crooked teeth. *His upper teeth require braces.*

SIGN #1: Thumb and forefinger of right **'CLAWED L'** hand are placed at either side of mouth, palm toward the body. The hand is then moved slightly forward and back.

OR

SIGN #2: Tips of crossed fingers of vertical right **'R'** hand are moved in an outward arc from left to right side of mouth, palm facing the body.

brag: *v.* to boast. *Many parents brag about their children.*

SIGN: **'EXTENDED A'** hands, palms facing downward, are placed at either side of waist and are alternately moved away from the body and then toward the body so that the thumbs jab the signer in the sides. Facial expression is important.

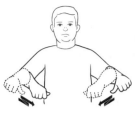

braid: *v.* to weave or intertwine several strands. *Will you braid my hair into two plaits?*

SIGN: Vertical **'R'** hands are held side by side at one side of the head and wobble as they move downward to outline the shape of a braid.

Braille: *n.* a system of writing/printing used by the blind. *Braille consists of raised dots to be read by touch.*

SIGN: Fingers of palm-down right **'5'** hand are fluttered from left to right at least twice across upturned palm of left **'EXTENDED B'** hand.

brain: *n.* the part of the nervous system contained within the cranium. *She used her brain to solve the problem.*

SIGN: Tip of forefinger of right **'CROOKED ONE'** hand, palm toward the head, is tapped against right side of forehead.

brainstorm: *v.* to pool ideas to form a basis for discussion. *Committee members will brainstorm and draw up a plan.*

SIGN: Tip of little finger of right **'I'** hand, palm toward face, touches right side of forehead and is moved purposefully forward and upward. Next, vertical **'S'** hands, palms facing forward, are alternately opened into **'CONTRACTED 5'** hands and thrust forward/ downward to a palms-down position. Motion is repeated several times. (ASL CONCEPT—**idea - throw at many time**.)

brake: *n.* a pedal used for stopping or slowing down a vehicle. *He used the brake to stop the car.*

SIGN: Right **'A'** hand, palm forward/downward, is moved slightly but firmly forward/downward a couple of times while the wrist remains rigid.

branch: *n.* a secondary stem or limb of a tree or shrub. *The squirrel ran along a branch of the oak tree.*

SIGN #1: Left **'5'** hand, with palm facing right, is held upright to represent a tree. Right **'ONE'** hand, is placed palm down against front of left forearm to represent a branch protruding from the tree trunk.

branch: *n.* a department, section or unit within a business or organization. *Which branch of the government does he work for?*

SIGN #2: **'SPREAD C'** hands are held upright and slightly apart with palms facing each other. The wrists then rotate forward, bringing the hands to a horizontal position.

brat: *n.* an impudent child or one who frequently misbehaves. *That little brat is getting on my nerves.*

SIGN: Forefinger and thumb of right palm-down **'A'** (or **'A-INDEX'**) hand grab tip of forefinger of left **'ONE'** hand, and give it a shake. (**BRAT** is frequently fingerspelled.)

brave: *adj.* having or showing courage. *The girl did a brave deed by saving the boy from drowning.*

SIGN #1: **'BENT 5'** hands, with fingertips on either side of chest and palms facing the body, are drawn forward to form **'S'** hands.

SIGN #2 [ATLANTIC]: Side of little finger of right **'BENT EXTENDED B'** hand, palm facing backwards, is placed against lower right cheek and the hand is slid backward toward the shoulder. Alternatively, this sign may be made with two hands, one on either cheek.
SAME SIGN—**bravery**, *n.*

bread: *adj.* a staple food made with flour or meal. *Whole-grain bread is said to be more nutritious than white bread.*

SIGN #1: Fingertips of right horizontal **'CLAWED 5'** or (**'BENT EXTENDED B'**) hand, palm facing body, are brushed downward at least twice against back of **'EXTENDED B'** hand which is held with palm toward the body and fingertips pointing rightward.

SIGN #2 [ATLANTIC]: Right horizontal **'EXTENDED B'** hand, fingers pointing forward/left, is moved back and forth in a cutting motion at right angles to upturned palm of left **'EXTENDED B'** hand, which remains relatively still.

break: *v.* to separate or become separated into two or more pieces; to damage something, making it unusable. *If you break a vase in the store, you must pay for it.*

SIGN #1: **'S'** hands are placed side by side, palms down. Then they are wrenched apart so that palms face one another.

break: *n.* an intermission. *There will be a short break before regular programming continues.*

SIGN #2: Left horizontal **'5'** hand is held with palm facing body while fingers of right palm-down **'EXTENDED B'** hand are inserted between forefinger and middle finger of left hand.

break: *n.* a short rest period. *Let us take a break and finish this later.*

SIGN #3: Thumbs of horizontal **'MODIFIED 5'** hands, palms facing the body, are jabbed into either side of upper chest.

breakdown: *n.* a collapse which causes failure or inability to act or use something effectively. *There has been a breakdown in communication between the committee and the executive.*

SIGN: Fingers of **'CROOKED 5'** hands, palms down, interlock slightly and then drop down so that backs of fingers are almost touching.

breakfast: *n.* the first meal of the day. *He usually eats breakfast at 6:00 a.m.*

SIGN: Fingertips of right **'FLAT O'** hand are brought up to touch the chin just under the lower lip. Left horizontal **'EXTENDED B'** hand is then held with palm facing the body, in the crook of the right elbow. Right **'EXTENDED B'** hand is brought upright until palm faces the body. (ASL CONCEPT—**eat - morning**.) Alternatively, this sign may be made with the first part only, particularly if it is understood that the meal is a 'morning' meal.

breastfeed: *v.* to feed an infant milk from the breast. *Some mothers like to breastfeed their babies.*

SIGN: Fingertips of right **'BENT EXTENDED B'** hand, palm facing body, touch left side of chest, then the right side. **'FLAT O'** hands are then held, palms up, left hand slightly ahead of right, and are moved slightly forward/downward twice.

breasts: *n.* the mammary glands. *A girl's breasts develop during puberty.*

SIGN: Fingertips of right **'BENT EXTENDED B'** hand, palm facing body, touch left side of chest, then the right side.

breathe: *v.* to inhale and exhale air. *She found it hard to breathe on the roller coaster with the wind rushing at her face.*

SIGN: Horizontal **'5'** hands are held, right above left with palms facing the chest, and are moved forward and back. (Signs for **breath**, *n.,* vary according to context.)

breeze: *n.* a gentle current of air. *There is a cool breeze blowing.*

SIGN: **'5'** hands, palms facing each other, are waved simultaneously from side to side.

bribe: *n.* any gift used corruptly to influence another's actions. *The man accepted a bribe for allowing the two women to sit in the front row.*

SIGN: Right **'FLAT O'** hand is furtively slid, palm-up, beneath left **'STANDARD BASE'** hand. ❖ SAME SIGN—**bribery**, *n.*

bride: *n.* a woman who is about to be married or is newly married. *The bride designed her own wedding dress.*

SIGN: Fingerspell **BRIDE**.

bridegroom: *n.* a man who is about to be married or is newly married. *The bridegroom was dressed in a tuxedo.*

SIGN: Fingerspell **BRIDEGROOM**.

bridesmaid: *n.* a woman who attends the bride at a wedding. *She plans to have more than one bridesmaid at her June wedding.*

SIGN #1: Left arm is bent so that the forearm is parallel to the chest. Right horizontal **'S'** hand is held just in front of the left elbow with palm facing backward. The right wrist then rotates to turn the hand palm downward as it moves backward to strike the left forearm near the elbow.

OR

SIGN #2: **'S'** hands are positioned horizontally with the right resting on top of the left as though carrying flowers. The hands are then moved forward together several times in a rhythmic pattern as if keeping time to music while walking up the aisle.

bridge: *n.* a structure that allows passage over a waterway, canyon, railroad, etc. *The bridge spans the South Saskatchewan River.*

SIGN #1: Tips of forefinger and middle finger of right **'V'** (or **'CROOKED V'**) hand are tapped against underside of left forearm at wrist and then again near elbow.

bridge (cont.)

SIGN #2 [ATLANTIC]: Fingertips of 'V' (or 'U') hands, palms down, are placed together. Hands are then drawn apart on a downward slope.

bridge: *n.* a dental device or partial denture. *The dentist made him a temporary bridge to replace the extracted teeth.*

SIGN #3: Thumbnails of 'A' hands are placed side by side on upper teeth and drawn apart to corners of mouth.

brief: *adj.* short in time or space. *There will be a brief meeting in the board room.*

SIGN: Left horizontal 'U' hand is held steady with extended fingers pointing forward/rightward and palm facing backward/ rightward. Right horizontal 'U' hand is held at right angles to the left hand with extended fingers resting on those of the left hand. Extended fingers of right hand are then brushed forward/rightward off the fingers of the left hand. SAME SIGN—**brevity**, *n.*

bright: *adj.* glowing, brilliant or vivid in colour. *She will buy some bright accessories to wear with her grey dress.*

SIGN #1: Vertical 'O' (or 'FLAT O') hands are placed side by side, palms facing forward. Then they are moved apart and slightly upward as the fingers spread to form '5' hands.

bright: *adj.* having quick intelligence or wit. *He was a very bright student.*

SIGN #2: Tip of middle finger of right 'BENT MIDFINGER 5' hand touches forehead and the hand is flung outward so that the palm faces away from face.

brilliant: *adj.* extremely intelligent; clever. *He is a brilliant chemist.*

SIGN #1: Tip of middle finger of right 'BENT MIDFINGER 5' hand, palm toward face, touches right side of forehead, then shimmies outward on an upward angle, giving the impression of a shimmering light.

OR

SIGN #2: Horizontal 'C' hands, which are held with the left directly in front of the right, are pulled backward in a short jerking motion toward the forehead.

bring: *v.* to carry toward a certain place. *Bring me some milk from the refrigerator.*

SIGN: 'EXTENDED B' hands are held parallel with palms up in front of the left side of the body. Then they are simultaneously moved in a slight arc to the right. ❖

broad: *adj.* of great width or extent. *Bilingualism and biculturalism are very broad topics.*

SIGN: Horizontal 'EXTENDED B' hands are held with palms together and fingers pointing forward. The hands are then swung apart so that the palms face mainly forward.

broad-minded: *adj.* accepting or tolerant of other people's opinions. *She felt more comfortable in the company of broad-minded people.*

SIGN: Fingertips of 'B' (or 'EXTENDED B') hands come together in front of forehead and are swung outward so that the palms face mainly forward.

broadcast: *n.* a program whose purpose is to inform a wide audience. *The news broadcast warned of an impending flood.*

SIGN #1: 'ONE' hands, with tips of forefingers touching either side of the mouth, are swung outward so that forefingers point upward and palms face forward.

OR

SIGN #2: 'FLAT O' hands are held with the palms down and sides of tips of forefingers touching. The hands are then opened to form '5' hands as they are moved apart in an outward/forward direction.

brochure: *n.* a pamphlet. *The federal government distributed brochures in both French and English.*

SIGN: Thumb and forefinger of right 'A-INDEX' (or 'MODIFIED G') hand are slid up the edge of the left 'EXTENDED B' hand, which is held with palm facing body. Motion is repeated.

broil: *v.* to cook under high, direct heat. *Broil the chicken pieces at 450 degrees until they are done.*

SIGN: Fingerspell **BROIL**.

broke: *adj.* having no money; bankrupt. *The man was broke after spending all his money at the races.*

SIGN: Right **'BENT EXTENDED B'** hand, fingertips pointing backward, strikes right side of neck sharply. (Alternatively, both hands may be used, one at either side of the neck.)

bronchitis: *n.* an inflammation of the bronchial tubes. *He suffers from chronic bronchitis.*

SIGN: Fingertips of **'BENT EXTENDED B'** hands, palms facing body, are positioned at either side of chest and simultaneously slid up and down.

brood: *v.* to dwell on something or think about it persistently. *It is her nature to brood over things.*

SIGN: Tip of middle finger of right **'BENT MIDFINGER 5'** hand touches centre of forehead and moves downward to rest on back of left **'STANDARD BASE'** hand. Together the two hands then circle forward at least twice. (ASL CONCEPT—**think - touch long time**.)

brook: *n.* a natural freshwater stream. *We set up our camp beside a little brook that would provide us with water.*

SIGN: Forefinger of vertical right **'W'** hand, palm facing left, is tapped against the chin. Next, horizontal **'EXTENDED B'** hands, palms facing each other, are held slightly apart and are simultaneously moved forward in a meandering motion. (ASL CONCEPT—**water - way curve**.)

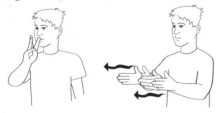

broom: *n.* a brush attached to a long handle for sweeping. *He used a broom to sweep the floor after the party.*

SIGN: Horizontal right **'EXTENDED B'** hand, palm left but slanted toward the body, is brushed back and forth several times across upturned palm of right **'EXTENDED B'** hand, which is held with fingertips pointing forward/rightward.

brother: *n.* one of the sons of the same two parents. *My brother is older than I.*

SIGN #1: Right **'L'** hand is held with palm facing left and thumb touching right side of forehead and is then brought down to rest on back of thumb of horizontal left **'L'** hand which is held with palm facing right and forefinger pointing forward.

SIGN #2 [ATLANTIC]: Knuckles of **'A'** hands, palms facing each other, are rubbed up and down against each other.

brown: *adj.* having a dark colour made up of red, yellow, and black. *She has brown eyes.*

SIGN #1: Vertical right **'BENT 5'** hand is held with palm forward and fingers fluttering as they point forward.

OR

SIGN #2: Right **'B'** hand, palm facing forward/leftward, is brushed downward slightly against the right cheek.

SIGN #3 [ATLANTIC]: Fingertips of right **'U'** hand, palm facing body, take on **'N'** shape as they are stroked downward on chin at least twice.

SIGN #4 [ONTARIO]: Right **'SPREAD C'** hand, palm toward the head, is circled in a clockwise direction near right side of head.

brown-nose: *v.* a colloquial expression meaning to try to get on the good side of someone; to flatter someone for personal gain. *He always brown-noses when the boss is around.*

SIGN: Tip of forefinger of right **'B'** hand, palm facing leftward/downward, rubs up and down on right side of nose.

browse: *v.* to look around without necessarily any definite purpose. *She browsed through the furniture showroom until the rain stopped.*

SIGN: Horizontal **'V'** hands are held parallel with palms down, fingers pointing forward, and are swept to the right in a succession of arcs. Sometimes only the right hand is used.

bruise: *n.* a contusion; a discolouring of the skin resulting from a blow. *He has a bruise on his left knee from sliding into second base.*

SIGN: Inverted right **'K'** hand moves in small clockwise circles. Side of thumb and forefinger of right **'C-INDEX'** hand then touch bruised area of the body. (ASL CONCEPT—**purple - mark**.)

brush: *v.* to use a tool with bristles for smoothing the hair. *Do you brush your hair every night?*

SIGN #1: Right **'A'** hand, palm facing head, is drawn backwards twice as if brushing the hair. SAME SIGN—**brush**, *n.*, meaning *hair brush*. (For **brush**, *n.*, meaning a *paint brush used for large surfaces*, see **paint** #1. For **brush**, *n.*, meaning an *artist's paint brush*, see **paint** #2.)

brush: *v.* to use a toothbrush. *You should brush your teeth after every meal.*

SIGN #2: Forefinger of right **'BENT ONE'** hand, palm facing down, is used to simulate brushing teeth by moving back and forth across open mouth.

bucket: *n.* a pail. *The bucket of water was too heavy for the child to carry.*

SIGN: Right **'S'** hand is held at one's side, with palm toward body, and the arm is moved up and down to simulate the carrying of a bucket. ALTERNATE SIGN—**pail**.

buddy: *n.* a colloquial term meaning a friend or companion. *He and his buddy have gone to Glen Abbey to watch a golf tournament.*

SIGN: Crooked fingers of **'X'** hands are interlocked so that palm of left hand, which is closest to the body, faces up while right palm faces down. Holding this position, the hands are simultaneously and firmly moved forward/downward slightly as interlocked fingers tighten. ALTERNATE SIGN—**friend**, various signs

budge: *v.* to change one's point of view. *The politician refused to budge on the important issue.*

SIGN #1: Left **'V'** hand is held with palm facing upward and angled toward the body while tip of forefinger of vertical right **'V'** hand, palm forward at a leftward-facing angle, touches the centre of the forehead. The right hand is lowered to make contact with the left hand so that the heels of the hands are touching. The right wrist then rotates 180 degrees forward while the left wrist rotates 180 degrees backward so that the right hand ends up with palm facing upward and the palm of the left hand faces downward/rightward, the hands still held together at the heels. (ESL USERS: **Budge** seldom appears in a positive context in English. It is usually preceded by words such as 'refuse to', 'won't', 'hasn't', etc.)

budge: *v.* to move even slightly. *The movers could not budge the heavy piano.*

SIGN #2: Vertical **'EXTENDED C'** hands are held parallel with wrists bent and palms facing forward. They are gradually moved forward as if with great effort. Facial expression must clearly convey the 'effort' expended.

budget: *n.* the amount of money available for one's use. *His budget affords him no luxuries.*

SIGN #1: Back of right **'CONTRACTED B'** (or **'BENT EXTENDED B'**) hand, palm up, is tapped two or three times on upturned palm of left **'EXTENDED B'** hand. (**BUDGET** is frequently fingerspelled.)

budget: *v.* to develop a plan for the spending of one's money. *She will have to budget carefully to save enough money for the down payment on a house.*

SIGN #2: **'CONTRACTED B'** hands, palms up, are circled backward around one another's fingertips.

buffalo: *n.* a bison or large ox with curved horns. *The buffalo is Canada's largest land mammal.*

SIGN #1: Right **'S'** hand, palm facing left, is rubbed against forehead in a circular motion which appears to the onlooker to be clockwise.

OR

SIGN #2: Vertical right **'Y'** hand is placed with palm against forehead and is wobbled slightly. This is a wrist action.

bug: *n.* one of a specific order of insects. *A black bug crawled up the stem of the plant.*

SIGN #1: Thumb of right **'3'** hand is placed on nose, palm facing left, and the two extended fingers are drawn in and out toward the nose. (**BUG** is frequently fingerspelled.)

bug: *n.* fault or defect, as in a computer program. *The computer operator had to work the bugs out of the system.*

SIGN #2: Horizontal **'CLAWED V'** hands are held with palms facing the body and knuckles knocking against each other as the hands are alternately moved up and down.

bug: *v.* to bother; annoy. *I will bug her until she finishes the job.*

SIGN #3: Edge of right **'EXTENDED B'** hand is brought down with a chopping motion between index and middle finger of left **'5'** hand. ❖
ALTERNATE SIGN—**bother** #2

build: *v.* to construct; erect. *We will use this blueprint to build a doghouse.*

SIGN #1: Fingers of **'BENT EXTENDED B'** (or **'BENT EXTENDED U'** or **'U'**) hands, palms facing each other, are alternately slid up from under to be placed on top of one another.
SAME SIGN—**building**, *n.*

build: *n.* body; figure; physical structure. *For what kind of build are these suits designed?*

SIGN #2: Horizontal **'EXTENDED B'** hands are placed slightly apart, fingertips opposite, with palms on upper chest. Then they are moved simultaneously to waist level.

bulb: *n.* a rounded glass object which encloses a light-emitting metal filament and has a metal base which can be screwed into an electrical socket. *I need a new light bulb for my reading lamp.*

SIGN: Fingerspell **BULB**.

bullet: *n.* a small, metal object used as ammunition for a firearm. *The bullet hit the target.*

SIGN: Tips of forefinger and thumb of right **'A-INDEX'** hand, are brushed downward/forward at least twice against end of forefinger of left **'ONE'** hand, which is held with palm facing right and finger pointing forward/upward.

bum: *n.* a tramp, hobo, or other disreputable person. *He was dressed like a bum and needed a shave and haircut.*

SIGN: Right vertical **'SPREAD EXTENDED C'** hand, palm toward the face is positioned so the heel is resting on the right cheek. Then the hand is wiggled slightly.

bump: *n.* a lump or swollen area. *He had a bump on his hand after the ball hit him.*

SIGN: Forefinger of right **'ONE'** hand, palm down, defines a small arc on back of left **'STANDARD BASE'** hand, or anywhere else on the body.

burden: *n.* something heavy that is being carried; load; responsibility. *He found that carrying two mortgages was too much of a financial burden.*

SIGN: Fingertips of both **'BENT EXTENDED B'** hands, are placed on right shoulder. Shoulder is pushed slightly downward to signify the bearing of a burden.

burger: See **hamburger**.

burglar: *n.* one who commits a burglary or theft. *A burglar broke into our house.*

SIGN: Extended fingers of right **'BENT U'** hand, palm facing downward, point leftward as they are drawn from left to right under the nose.

burn: *n.* an injury caused by exposure to fire. *The boy has a very bad* **burn** *on his right shoulder.*

SIGN #1: Fingerspell **BURN**.

B U R N

burn: *v.* to set afire; ignite. *The farmer* **burned** *his old barn.*

SIGN #2: Vertical **'5'** hands with palms facing body, are simultaneously moved upward with fingers fluttering.

burn out: *v.* to become exhausted due to overwork. *He will* **burn out** *if he continues to hold down two full-time jobs.*

SIGN: **'A'** hands are held together with palms facing the chest. The hands then gradually rotate forward with fingers spreading until they take on a **'CROOKED 5'** shape with palms facing upward. Facial expression must clearly convey 'exhaustion'.

burp: *v.* to emit wind noisily from the stomach through the mouth. *Drinking cola tends to make him* **burp**.

SIGN: Right **'S'** hand is held upright in centre of chest with palm facing right. Forefinger flicks upward to form a **'ONE'** hand and back down to form an **'S'** hand again.

bursary: *n.* a scholarship awarded at certain colleges and universities. *She applied for a* **bursary** *to help pay her tuition.*

SIGN: Back of right **'CONTRACTED B'** hand, palm up, is tapped two or three times on upturned palm of left **'EXTENDED B'** hand.

bury: *v.* to put a dead body into a grave or tomb. *My grandfather was* **buried** *in the old cemetery.*

SIGN #1: **'BENT EXTENDED B'** hands are held parallel with palms down and fingers pointing down. The hands are then drawn upward and back toward the body with a curving motion, to form **'EXTENDED B'** hands with palms facing forward/downward.

OR

SIGN #2: **'EXTENDED B'** hands, palms facing each other, fingers pointing forward/downward are moved downward at a slight forward angle.

OR

SIGN #3: Right **'U'** hand, palm down and extended fingers pointing forward, is placed against right-facing palm of left horizontal **'EXTENDED B'** hand and moved downward slowly.
SAME SIGN—**burial**, *n.*

bus: *n.* a long vehicle used for carrying passengers. *She finds it more relaxing to take a* **bus** *than to drive to work.*

SIGN: Fingerspell **BUS**.

B U S

bush: *n.* a small tree or thick shrub. *I planted a rose* **bush** *in the back yard.*

SIGN #1: Fingerspell **BUSH**.

B U S H

bush: *n.* woods; forest. *I love to walk through the* **bush** *in the spring to see all the wildflowers.*

SIGN #2: Both arms drift rightward as right elbow rests on left **'STANDARD BASE'** hand, and vertical right **'5'** hand shimmies or repeatedly twists back and forth in short, jerky movements.

business: *n.* a commercial enterprise. *He owns a large construction* **business**.

SIGN #1: Wrist of vertical right **'B'** hand, palm facing forward/leftward, is brushed back and forth against wrist of left **'STANDARD BASE'** hand.

OR

SIGN #2: Wrist of right **'S'** hand, palm facing forward/leftward, is tapped against wrist of left **'S'** hand which is held with palm down.

(successful or prosperous) business: *n.* a business which makes a very good profit. *He manages a **successful business** in computer software sales.*

SIGN #3: Vertical right **'B'** hand, palm facing forward, is thrust firmly forward until the heel of the hand makes contact with the left **'STANDARD BASE'** hand.

busy: *adj.* working; active. *I am **busy** at the moment so please wait.*

SIGN: Wrist of vertical right **'B'** hand, palm facing forward/leftward, is brushed back and forth against wrist of left **'STANDARD BASE'** hand. (**BUSY** is frequently fingerspelled.)

but: *conj.* although; on the other hand. *The hikers were cold and wet **but** they remained cheerful.*

SIGN #1: Forefingers of **'ONE'** hands are crossed. The hands are then turned outward so that they become vertical with palms facing forward. (**BUT** is frequently fingerspelled.)

but: *prep.* with the exception of. *She will eat anything **but** horse radish.*

SIGN #2: Thumb and forefinger of right **'OPEN F'** hand, palm facing down, grasp tip of forefinger of left **'ONE'** (or **'5'**) hand, which is held with palm toward body. Then right hand is used to pull left hand upward.

butt: *n.* the stubbed end of an extinguished cigarette or cigar. *The smell of the cigarette **butts** in the ashtray was offensive.*

SIGN: Inverted right **'COVERED T'** hand is placed with the knuckle down on the upturned palm of the left **'EXTENDED B'** hand and is twisted back and forth from the wrist several times.

butt in: *v.* a colloquial term meaning to interfere in affairs which should be no one's else's concern. *She was tired of her father-in-law **butting in** every time she had an argument with her husband.*

SIGN #1: Tip of forefinger of right **'CROOKED ONE'** hand touches nose and is then dropped downward and inserted at least twice into the small opening at the top of the horizontal left **'S'** hand which is held with the palm facing right. ❖

butt in: *v.* a colloquial term meaning to interrupt when you should not. *I will not **butt in** while she is talking.*

SIGN #2: Left **'5'** hand is held in a fixed position with palm facing the body while right horizontal **'EXTENDED B'** hand is inserted forcefully between forefinger and middle finger of left hand. ❖

butter: *n.* yellow, fatty food substance churned from cream. *Would you like some **butter** on your toast?*

SIGN #1: Tips of extended fingers of right **'BENT EXTENDED U'** hand, are brushed back twice against right-facing palm of left **'EXTENDED B'** hand.

SIGN #2 [ONTARIO]: Fingertips of right **'BENT EXTENDED B'** hand are brushed back twice against right-facing palm of left **'EXTENDED B'** hand.

butterfly: *n.* an insect with a narrow body and four broad, usually colourful wings. *A monarch **butterfly** flitted among the flowers.*

SIGN: **'EXTENDED B'** hands are crossed at the wrists with palms facing the body. Fingers are then waved back and forth, the hands thus alternating between **'EXTENDED B'** and **'BENT EXTENDED B'** shapes to simulate wing motion.

button: *n.* a round, flat fastener which is forced through a narrow opening. *He lost a **button** off his coat.*

SIGN: Thumb and forefinger of right **'F'** hand are tapped at least twice against chest, with palm facing left.

buy: *v.* to purchase or obtain for a price. *I am planning to **buy** a new car.*

SIGN: Right **'BENT EXTENDED B'** hand is laid, palm up, on upturned palm of left **'EXTENDED B'** hand. Then right hand is moved upward and forward.

by: *prep.* used following a passive verb to indicate agent. *The book, The Call of the Wild, was written **by** Jack London.*

SIGN #1: Fingerspell **BY**.

B   Y

by: *prep.* near. *He left a message by the tele-phone.*

SIGN #2: Horizontal **'BENT EXTENDED B'** hands are held right in front of left with right palm facing leftward and left palm facing right-ward. Right hand is then moved backward so that fingers of right hand touch fingers of left hand to indicate nearness.

bye: *n.* an advantage whereby a competitor has no opponent for a given round and so does not play that round, yet is entitled to advance to the next round. *Because the team had a bye, they had a good rest before their next game.*

SIGN: Fingerspell **BYE**.

bye: See **goodbye**.

byte: *n.* part of a computer's memory storage. *A byte consists of eight consecutive bits.*

SIGN: Fingerspell **BYTE**.

C

cabbage: *n.* a green or reddish vegetable with a round shape and overlapping leaves. *Coleslaw is made from shredded cabbage.*

SIGN: Wrist is bent backward slightly as heel of right **'CLAWED 5'** hand is used to strike right side of forehead a couple of times.

cabin: *n.* a small, simple, often rustic dwelling. *They are building a summer cabin at the lake.*

SIGN: Fingerspell **CABIN**.

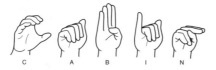

cable: *n.* thick wire or rope. *Always check for underground cables before you dig.*

SIGN: Crooked forefingers of horizontal **'x'** hands, palms facing body, are tapped together at least twice. Then horizontal **'F'** hands are held side by side, palms down and extended fingers pointing forward, and are drawn apart. (ASL CONCEPT—**electric - rope**.) In cases where the cable is not electrically charged, the first part of the sign is removed.

cable television: *n.* a television service that supplies the subscriber with a larger variety of channels through a cable connection. *Cable television provides us with a variety of channels to watch.*

SIGN: Fingerspell **CABLE**.

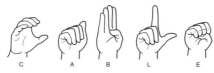

Caesarean section: *n.* a surgical incision made in order to extract a fetus from a mother's womb. *The infant was delivered by Caesarean section.*

SIGN: Thumb of **'EXTENDED A'** hand is placed on the left side of the lower abdomen, palm down, and is drawn across to the right side.

cafeteria: *n.* a restaurant where food is purchased at a counter and carried to a table by the customer. *I will meet you in the cafeteria at noon.*

SIGN: With right **'EXTENDED C'** hand in a more or less vertical position with palm left but slanted downward slightly, the thumb is held against the left lower jaw just to the left of the mouth. The hand then moves rightward so that the thumb comes to rest just to the right of the mouth. (**CAFETERIA** is frequently fingerspelled.)

cake: *n.* a baked mixture of flour, eggs, and other ingredients. *There are 20 candles on the birthday cake.*

SIGN: Fingertips of right **'SPREAD C'** hand are placed on left **'STANDARD BASE'** hand, and the right hand twists to left and right as though using a cookie cutter on the back of the other hand. (**CAKE** is more frequently fingerspelled than signed.)

calculate: *v.* to figure or determine by computation. *Will you calculate your average expenses?*

SIGN: **'K'** hands are held, right above left, somewhere between horizontally and vertically, left palm facing right and right palm facing left yet both palms are angled slightly toward the body. The two hands brush against one another a few times as the right hand repeatedly moves leftward slightly, and the left hand moves rightward.
SAME SIGN—**calculation**, *n.*

calculator: *n.* a small mechanical device used for mathematical computation. *You may use a calculator to do your math assignment.*

SIGN: Fingertips of right **'CLAWED 5'** hand, palm down, are fluttered lightly and circled in a counter-clockwise direction in the upturned palm of the left **'EXTENDED B'** hand.

calendar: *n.* a system for determining the divisions of a year. *Check the calendar to see when spring break is this year.*

SIGN: Left **'EXTENDED B'** hand is held in a fixed position with palm up and fingers pointing rightward. Right **'EXTENDED B'** hand is held palm-down on left hand with fingers pointing leftward. Right hand then flips up so that palm faces the body. Motion is repeated. (**CALENDAR** is frequently fingerspelled.)

calf: *n.* the young of a cow or other bovine animal. *A heifer is a young cow that has not had a calf.*

SIGN: Fingers of palm-up right **'BENT EXTENDED B'** hand point leftward as they rest on rightward-pointing fingers of palm-up left **'BENT EXTENDED B'** hand. The arms are simultaneously moved from side to side as if rocking a baby in one's arms. Then thumb of right **'Y'** hand, palm facing downward, is placed on right temple and is twisted counter-clockwise until palm faces forward and little finger points upward. (ASL CONCEPT—**baby - cow**.)

call: *v.* to summon; to convene (a meeting). *I will call a meeting soon.*

SIGN #1: Fingertips of right **'BENT EXTENDED B'** hand are placed on the back of the left **'STANDARD BASE'** hand. Then as the right hand is drawn slightly upward/rightward and toward the body, the hand closes to form an **'EXTENDED A'** hand. ❖

call: *v.* to designate by name. *What do you call your dog?*

SIGN #2: Horizontal **'U'** hands, left palm facing right and right palm facing left, are held with right middle finger placed on left forefinger at right angles. The hands then move forward together in a small arc. ❖

call: *v.* to send out a cry of appeal. *The drowning boy called for help.*

SIGN #3: Right vertical **'SPREAD C'** hand, palm toward the body, is held near the mouth and is forcefully drawn forward at an upward angle.

call: *v.* to contact by telephone. *She called the ambulance when her son was hurt.*

SIGN #4: Forefinger of right **'X'** hand, palm facing leftward/forward, is moved in a straight line forward/rightward along the forefinger of the left palm-down **'ONE'** hand and beyond. ❖

OR

SIGN #5: Right **'Y'** hand, palm facing forward/leftward, is held upright near right side of face with thumb pointing to the area just to the right of the chin. Then the forearm is moved forward/rightward.

call off: *v.* to cancel an event. *The meeting was called off due to the storm.*

SIGN: Tip of forefinger of right **'ONE'** hand draws an **'X'** across palm of horizontal left **'EXTENDED B'** hand which faces the body at a slight rightward angle.

calm: *adj.* free from motion or disturbance. *The sea was calm and peaceful.*

SIGN: **'B'** (or **'EXTENDED B'**) hands are crossed in front of the mouth, left palm facing rightward/downward and right palm facing leftward/downward with the right hand just behind the left hand. Then they are drawn apart until the palms face completely downward.

calm down: *v.* to make someone calm. *The teacher tried to calm down the excited students.*

SIGN: **'EXTENDED B'** hands are held parallel with palms down and fingers pointing forward. The forearms are then simultaneously moved slowly and deliberately down and up a couple of times.

calmly: *adv.* in a composed, unexcited manner. *Even with deadlines imposed, he goes about his work very* ***calmly***.

SIGN: **'EXTENDED B'** hands are held parallel with palms down and fingers pointing forward. The forearms are simultaneously lowered a short distance, then moved rightward in an arc formation, and back to their original position in a leftward arc.
ALTERNATE SIGN—**calm**

calorie: *n.* a unit for measuring energy created when food is oxidized in one's body. *This soft drink contains only one* ***calorie***.

SIGN: Fingerspell **CALORIE**.

C A L O R I E

camcorder: *n.* a piece of equipment used to record material on a videotape. *He will operate the* ***camcorder*** *at his sister's wedding.*

SIGN: Right horizontal **'3'** (or **'EXTENDED C'**) hand, palm facing left, is moved back and forth a couple of times from the wrist.

camel: *n.* a large desert animal with a humped back and long neck. *The* ***camel*** *is used as a beast of burden in desert regions.*

SIGN: Fingerspell **CAMEL**.

C A M E L

camera: *n.* a device used for taking photographs. *The photographer used an expensive* ***camera*** *for the wedding portraits.*

SIGN: Vertical **'CROOKED L'** (or **'C-INDEX'**) hands are held so as to frame the eyes with a thumb touching either side of face, and palms facing each other, but angled forward slightly. The forefinger of the right hand then makes small up and down movements as if clicking a camera. (**CAMERA** may be fingerspelled.)

camp: *v.* to take up temporary lodging, often in a tent. *They will* ***camp*** *in the mountains.*

SIGN: **'COMBINED I + ONE'** hands are held with palms facing each other but angled downward slightly and extended fingertips of one hand touching the corresponding fingers of the other hand. The hands are then drawn apart with a downward curving motion.
SAME SIGN—**camp** *n.*, but the motion is repeated.

campaign: *n.* a series of activities designed to achieve a social, political, or commercial goal; a promotional plan. *She will be involved in the next election* ***campaign***.

SIGN #1: **'S'** hands, palms facing downward, are held slightly apart, with right in front of left. Right hand then strikes left hand and moves forward and back to strike it a second time. (**CAMPAIGN** is frequently fingerspelled.)

campaign: *n.* a plan designed for a specific purpose. *Her* ***campaign*** *to save the whales has been highly successful.*

SIGN #2: Horizontal **'EXTENDED B'** hands, palms facing each other and fingers pointing forward, are held slightly apart at the left side of the body and are moved simultaneously toward the right.

campaign: *n.* a series of activities designed to register protest against something. *The union will launch a* ***campaign*** *against hiring substitute workers during the strike.*

SIGN #3: Horizontal **'S'** hands, palms toward the chest, are held so the right is resting on the left. Then they are moved back and forth at least twice. This sign is made purposefully along with a look of determination.

campus: *n.* the grounds and buildings of a school, college or university. *When I attended university, I lived in a students' residence on* ***campus***.

SIGN: Fingerspell **CAMPUS**.

C A M P U S

can: *v.* to be able to. *He* ***can*** *lift this box.*

SIGN #1: **'A'** hands, palms down, are held slightly apart, and are then firmly pushed a very short distance downward.

can: *v.* to preserve food in cans or jars. *My mother will* ***can*** *the cherries.*

SIGN #2: Right **'EXTENDED C'** hand is placed, palm down, over the horizontal left **'S'** hand, and twisted clockwise as if screwing a lid onto a jar.

can: *n.* a metal container. *He drank a can of orange pop.*

SIGN #3: Horizontal right **'C'** hand, palm facing left but angled slightly toward the body, is held just above the upturned palm of the left **'EXTENDED B'** hand, which is held with fingers pointing forward/rightward. The right hand is then lowered into the left palm, raised, and lowered once again.

cancel: *v.* to set aside or revoke; to call off. *Please cancel my appointment.*

SIGN: Tip of forefinger of right **'ONE'** hand draws an **'X'** across palm of horizontal left **'EXTENDED B'** hand which faces the body at a slight rightward angle.

cancer: *n.* any type of malignancy caused by uncontrolled cell division. *Scientists are finding new ways to treat cancer.*

SIGN: Fingerspell CANCER.

candid: *adj.* frank or outspoken. *My candid opinion is that their marriage will fail.*

SIGN #1: Vertical right **'B'** hand, palm facing left, is held directly in front of the face and thrust forward and slightly downward.

candid: *adj.* informal or unposed. *The yearbook includes candid photographs taken at school events.*

SIGN #2: Fingerspell CANDID.

candidate: *n.* an applicant or nominee for a position or honour. *He is a good candidate for the presidency.*

SIGN: Horizontal right **'F'** hand grasps the signer's shirt below the right shoulder between the thumb and forefinger, and is moved back and forth twice.

candle: *n.* a cylinder of tallow or wax containing a wick and used to give light. *It is wise to keep a candle on hand in case of a power failure.*

SIGN: Tip of forefinger of vertical left **'ONE'** hand, palm facing right, is placed against the centre of the heel of the right **'CROOKED 5'** hand, which is held upright with palm facing left and fingers fluttering to represent a flickering candle flame.

candy: *n.* a sweet confection. *Jelly beans are Ron's favorite candies.*

SIGN: Fingertips of right **'BENT EXTENDED U'** hand, palm facing body, are stroked downward on chin at least twice. (Signs vary, but are usually located somewhere on the lower part of the face.)

cane: *n.* a rod or stick used to facilitate walking. *Someone who has broken his leg might find it helpful to use a cane.*

SIGN: Horizontal right **'CLOSED A-INDEX'** hand, palm down, is bobbed up and down slightly as the arm moves forward, simulating the arm movement of a person walking with a cane. (Alternatively, CANE may be fingerspelled.)

canine: *n.* any animal belonging to the dog family, such as wolves, foxes, domestic dogs, etc. *Certain canines are trained to assist the police in their work.*

SIGN: Right **'D'** hand is held with palm up but slanted slightly leftward. End of middle finger slides up and down several times against left side of thumb.
ALTERNATE SIGN—**dog** #1

cannon: *n.* a large gun with a heavy metal barrel mounted on a carriage. *The soldiers fired the cannon.*

SIGN: Right **'ONE'** hand is held out from the body with palm facing left and forefinger pointing forward/upward. Left **'C'** hand grasps right forearm near the elbow, as right forearm jerks downward/backward, then jerks back to its original position to show the recoil action of a firearm.

cannot [**can't**]: *v.* is or are not able to. *I cannot believe he is guilty.*

SIGN: Left **'ONE'** hand is held palm-down with forefinger pointing forward/rightward. The forefinger of the right **'ONE'** hand is held above the left, then brought down sharply to strike the left forefinger.

canoe: *n.* a long, narrow, lightweight boat propelled by paddles. *We explored the river in a canoe.*

SIGN: **'CROOKED EXTENDED B'** hands, palms facing each other at a slight angle, are cupped together to form the hull of a boat. Then they are moved up and down in a bobbing motion. Next, **'S'** hands are held, right above left, and are swept downward/backward simultaneously to simulate the paddling of a canoe. The motion is alternated from one side to the other. (ASL CONCEPT—**boat - paddle**.) Once **canoe** has been introduced into the conversation, the first part of this sign may be omitted.

cap: *n.* a head covering, often with a visor. *He always wears a baseball cap.*

SIGN: Right **'CLOSED A-INDEX'** hand is held upright in front of forehead with palm facing leftward/forward, and is moved downward/forward a short distance and back a couple of times as if tugging on the visor. (The same handshape is used for the 'putting on' and 'taking off' of a cap, the movement taking the form of the actual act. In such cases, one sign suffices to convey both **cap**, *n.* and *v.*, which indicates what is being done with the cap.) Alternatively, **CAP** may be fingerspelled.

capable: *adj.* having adequate ability. *She is a capable and efficient secretary.*

SIGN: **'A'** hands, palms down, are held slightly apart, and are lowered and raised a couple of times as if knocking.
SAME SIGN—**capability**, *n.*

capacity: *n.* ability to hold or contain. *The capacity of the tank is 50 litres.*

SIGN: Vertical right **'BENT EXTENDED B'** hand, palm facing left, is held above vertical left **'BENT EXTENDED B'** hand, of which the palm faces right. The hands then move purposefully forward a short distance. (This sign would be inappropriate when referring to the *seating capacity* of a building; instead the sign for **limit** or **maximum** would be used. To refer to someone's *capacity for doing a certain thing*, **ability** would be used.)

capital: *n.* a city where the centre of government is situated. *Ottawa is the capital of Canada.*

SIGN #1: Fingertips of palm-down right **'SPREAD C'** hand are tapped twice on right shoulder.

capital: *n.* available funds. *You will need more capital to start a new business.*

SIGN #2: Back of right **'CONTRACTED B'** hand, palm up, is tapped a couple of times on upturned palm of left **'EXTENDED B'** hand. Then right hand is changed to a **'C'** shape with palm facing leftward/forward, and is placed upright on left palm. The hands are purposefully moved ever so slightly downward/forward together. (ASL CONCEPT—**money - pile**.)

capital letter: See **(upper case) letter**.

capsize: *v.* to overturn. *If you stand up, you will capsize this boat.*

SIGN: Horizontal **'EXTENDED B'** hands, palms facing each other at a slight angle and fingers pointing forward, are cupped together to form the hull of a boat. Then the wrists twist clockwise as the 'boat' is overturned in a rightward direction so that the left palm eventually faces downward while the right palm faces upward. (This sign conveys the three English words 'CAPSIZE THE BOAT'.)

captain: *n.* a commander, leader, or chief. *The player with the "C" on his jersey is the* **captain** *of the hockey team.*

SIGN: Fingertips of palm-down right **'SPREAD C'** hand are tapped twice on right shoulder. Alternatively, this sign may be made using both hands, one on each shoulder.

caption: *n.* a heading, written explanation, or subtitle. *Most of the TV news programs have captions.*

SIGN: Horizontal **'F'** hands, palms facing other, thumbs and forefingers touching, are moved apart with a slight rotation of the wrists so that palms face downward. The movement is generally repeated as this word is usually used in a plural sense by signers to refer to closed captioning on television. (Alternatively, **captions** may be fingerspelled **CC**.)

capture: *v.* to gain possession of or to win control over by using craft or force. *The police will probably* **capture** *the escaped convict.*

SIGN: Right **'SPREAD C'** hand is held palm down at chest level and is then closed to form an **'S'** hand as it is thrust forward. Alternatively, this sign may be made with two hands held apart in front of the chest. ❖

ALTERNATE SIGNS—**arrest** #2 & #3
For contexts where a *group* of people are being captured, see **sanction** #2.

car: *n.* an automobile. *My car is an older model.*

SIGN #1: **'S'** hands, with palms facing the body, are held in the steering wheel position and are moved up and down alternately to simulate the motion of steering a car. **CAR** is frequently fingerspelled. (See also **vehicle** #1 for explanatory notes.)

SIGN #2 [ONTARIO]: Left **'X'** hand is held palm-up and right **'X'** hand is held palm-down as it is lowered so that the crook in the right forefinger comes to rest in the crook of the left forefinger. Motion is repeated a couple of times.

carburetor: *n.* part of a gasoline engine where air mixes with atomized gas and the amount of this mixture that enters the engine is regulated. *The car mechanic fixed the* **carburetor.**

SIGN: Thumb and fingertips of horizontal right **'C'** hand, palm facing the body, are tapped against the throat a couple of times.

card: *n.* a thin, flat, folded piece of heavy paper used to convey a greeting or message. *I received a* **card** *from my colleagues.*

SIGN #1: Fingerspell **CARD**.

card: *n.* a thin, flat piece of heavy paper used to convey information. *Please give me your business* **card.**

SIGN #2: Tips of forefingers and thumbs touch as **'CONTRACTED L'** hands are held together with palms facing forward/downward. The arms are then drawn apart and each forefinger and thumb come together to form **'CLOSED MODIFIED G'** shapes. (Alternatively, **CARD** in this context may be fingerspelled.)

cards: *n.* one of a set of rectangular pieces of cardboard used for playing games or fortune telling. *In bridge, each player is dealt 13* **cards.**

SIGN: Horizontal left **'CLOSED A-INDEX'** hand is held in a fixed position with palm toward the body at a slight rightward angle. While the right hand moves back and forth several times in front of the left hand, the handshape alternates between an **'A-INDEX'** and a **'CLOSED A-INDEX'** as the thumb and forefinger repeatedly open and close. (This sign may be used for **cards**, *n.*, or for the verb phrase **to play cards**.) **CARDS** is frequently fingerspelled. See also **deck (of cards)**.

care: *v.* to have regard or consideration for someone or something. *I* **care** *about you.*

SIGN: Fingerspell **CARE**.

(don't) care: *v.* to be completely indifferent to something. *I will probably lose my job but I don't* **care.**

SIGN: Right **'MODIFIED O'** hand, palm toward the face, is held at the tip of the nose and is turned from the wrist as it is thrust forward/rightward and changed to a **'CONTRACTED 5'** handshape with palm facing downward. Facial expression is important.

care (a great deal): *v.* to have *deep* regard for someone or something. *I care a great deal about you.*

SIGN: Knuckles of vertical right **'OPEN SPREAD O'** hand, palm toward the body, are placed on the chin and are firmly drawn downward, closing to form an **'S'** hand.

care for [*or* **take care of**]: *v.* to look after; to provide physical help. *The nursing home staff care for the elderly residents.*

SIGN: **'K'** (or **'V'**) hands are positioned horizontally with the right one resting on top of the left one. The hands are then moved together in a counter-clockwise motion.

care to: *v.* want to. *Would you care to join us?*

SIGN: **'CROOKED 5'** hands, palms up, are held slightly apart in front of the body. Then they retract to form **'CLAWED 5'** hands as they are simultaneously drawn toward the chest.

career: *n.* a profession or occupation chosen as one's life's work. *She has had a very successful career in politics.*

SIGN: Left **'B'** hand is held in a fixed position with palm facing right and fingers pointing forward. Right **'B'** hand, palm facing left, and fingers pointing forward, is positioned on top of the left hand and firmly moved forward. **CAREER** is frequently fingerspelled.
ALTERNATE SIGN—**job** #2

careful: *adj.* cautious. *He is a very careful driver.*

SIGN: Horizontal **'K'** (or **'V'**) hands are held with right hand resting on left hand and extended fingers pointing forward. Together the hands are circled forward a couple of times. Facial expression is important.

(be) careful: *s.s.* use caution. *Be careful, or you will hurt yourself!*

SIGN: Horizontal **'K'** (or **'V'**) hands are held, right above left, with extended fingers pointing forward, the left palm facing rightward and the right palm facing leftward. The hands are brought together to strike each other a couple of times. Facial expression is important.

careless: *adj.* negligent; not careful. *He is a careless driver.*

SIGN: Extended fingers of right **'V'** hand are waved up and down in front of the forehead with palm alternately facing leftward and downward. Facial expression is important.

caress: *v.* to stroke or to touch in a gentle and/or loving way. *He frequently caresses his wife.*

SIGN: Right **'CROOKED 5'** hand is held palm-down and is twisted gently from the wrist several times so that the palm orientation alternates between downward and leftward/downward. (This sign varies according to context, particularly with regard to location, which depends on which body part is being caressed.)

carpal tunnel syndrome: *n.* a medical condition affecting the bones and joint of the wrist. *Sometimes carpal tunnel syndrome needs to be corrected surgically.*

SIGN: Fingerspell **CTS**.

C   T   S

carpenter: *n.* a person who constructs with timber or wood. *The carpenter built his own house.*

SIGN #1: Left **'CLOSED A-INDEX'** hand is held upright with palm facing right while right **'CLOSED A-INDEX'** hand is held just behind the left hand with palm facing left. Then the right hand makes a tapping motion toward the left hand to simulate the pounding action of a hammer. Agent Ending (see p. LIV) may follow.

SIGN #2 [ATLANTIC]: **'EXTENDED B'** hands are held apart in front of the stomach with palms up and fingers of left hand pointing rightward while fingers of right hand point leftward. The hands are alternately moved backward to strike the stomach a few times. Agent Ending (see p. LIV) may follow.

SIGN [PACIFIC/PRAIRIE]: The bottom of the horizontal right **'S'** hand, palm facing leftward/backward, is brushed forward/rightward several times along the upturned palm of the left **'EXTENDED B'** hand of which the fingers point forward/rightward. Agent Ending (see p. LIV) may follow.

carpet: *n.* a thick floor covering made of wool or synthetic fibres; a rug. *I like the colour of your living room* **carpet.**

SIGN: Fingerspell **CARPET.**

carrot: *n.* a long, tapering, orange-coloured root vegetable. *A raw* **carrot** *makes a nutritious snack.*

SIGN: Fingerspell **CARROT.**

carry: *v.* to transport or to bring from one place to another. *I will help you* **carry** *things when you move.*

SIGN: **'EXTENDED B'** hands are held parallel with palms up in front of the right side of the body. Then they are simultaneously moved in a slight arc to the left.

carry on: *v.* continue; go ahead. *Carry on with your work; do not let me distract you.*

SIGN: Horizontal **'BENT EXTENDED B'** hands are held parallel with palms facing, and are simultaneously moved forward.

ALTERNATE SIGN—**continue**

cartoon: *n.* a comic strip or a humorous picture, either drawn on paper or animated on film by photographing a series of gradually changing drawings to give the impression of movement. *Children enjoy watching the* **cartoons** *on TV.*

SIGN: The two extended fingers of the right **'BENT EXTENDED U'** hand, palm toward the face, stroke the nose at least twice in a downward motion. Alternatively, **CARTOON** may be fingerspelled.

ALTERNATE SIGN—**picture** #2

carve: *v.* to form by cutting or chipping. *The West Coast Indians* **carve** *beautiful totem poles.*

SIGN: Thumb of right **'EXTENDED A'** hand, palm down, is used to jab twice in an upward/backward direction at the fixed palm of the left **'EXTENDED B'** hand, which is held with fingers pointing forward/rightward, and palm facing rightward, but slanted slightly toward the body.

case: *n.* a box-like container. *We buy many of our canned foods by the* **case.**

SIGN #1: With a slight but deliberate downward thrust horizontal **'EXTENDED B'** hands are held parallel, with palms facing each other and fingers pointing forward. Then the hands take on a **'BENT EXTENDED B'** shape as they are swung inward with a slight downward thrust again, and the right hand positioned ahead of the left, both palms facing the body. (**CASE** is frequently fingerspelled.)

case: *n.* a legal action or lawsuit. *The* **case** *was dismissed due to lack of evidence.*

SIGN #2: Fingerspell **CASE.**

(in any) case: *adv.* no matter what happens. *They might be late;* **in any case,** *they will arrive sometime tonight.*

SIGN #3: Fingers of horizontal **'BENT EXTENDED B'** hands, palms facing the chest, are alternately brushed back and forth against each other.

(just in) case: See **just in case.**

cash: *n.* money which is readily available. *He barely had enough* **cash** *to pay for the meal.*

SIGN: Fingerspell **CASH.**

cashier: *n.* a person who receives or handles cash in a business establishment. *The cashier made a mistake when she rang up my purchases.*

SIGN: Fingers of vertical right **'CLAWED 5'** hand, palm forward, flutter as the hand is circled in a counter-clockwise direction to simulate the ringing up of figures on a till or cash register.

casino: *n.* a place where gambling is done. *They won a lot of money last night at the casino.*

SIGN: Fingerspell **CASINO**.
ALTERNATE SIGN—**gamble**

casserole: *n.* food which is baked and served in the same dish. *He will bring a chicken casserole to the potluck luncheon.*

SIGN: Fingerspell **CASSEROLE**.

cast: *n.* the actors who enact roles in a dramatic production. *We went backstage to meet the cast after the play.*

SIGN #1: **'EXTENDED A'** hands, palms facing each other, are rotated alternately in small circles which are brought down against the chest. (**CAST** may be fingerspelled.)

cast: *n.* a rigid casing used to immobilize broken bones while they heal. *She had her broken arm in a cast for six weeks.*

SIGN #2: Fingerspell **CAST**.

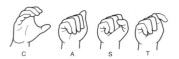

castle: *n.* a fortified medieval structure or a large, magnificent dwelling. *The giant lived in a huge castle at the very top of an enormous, snow-covered mountain.*

SIGN: Left arm is folded in front of chest as right **'S'** hand is lowered palm down onto left arm near the elbow. Then left **'S'** hand is similarly placed on right arm near the elbow. Finally the arms are both raised simultaneously so that the **'S'** hands become upright with palms facing. (This sign is used specifically for storytelling. Otherwise, **CASTLE** is generally fingerspelled.)

casual: *adj.* relaxed and informal. *The invitation indicates that dress for the party is casual.*

SIGN: Right **'ONE'** hand, palm facing left, is held above left **'ONE'** hand, palm facing right, with forefingers pointing forward. Then right hand is tapped at least twice on left hand. (Sign choice depends on context.)

cat: *n.* a small, domesticated, feline mammal. *A cat is an excellent pet.*

SIGN: Vertical right **'FLAT F'** hand, palm facing left, is held near the right corner of the mouth and is drawn backward/rightward several times.

catalogue: *n.* a book which lists items, usually alphabetically, and often describes and/or illustrates them. *I ordered several shirts from a mail-order catalogue.*

SIGN: Thumb and forefinger of right **'A-INDEX'** (or **'MODIFIED G'**) hand are slid up the edge of the left **'EXTENDED B'** hand, which is held with palm facing body. Motion is repeated. (**CATALOGUE** may be fingerspelled.)

catastrophe: *n.* a disaster. *The tornado created a catastrophe.*

SIGN #1: Right **'COVERED 8'** hand, palm facing left, is held upright at about shoulder level. The hand is then thrust backward as the middle finger and thumb flick apart to form a **'MODIFIED 5'** hand.

catastrophe (cont.)

OR

SIGN #2: Left **'CROOKED 5'** hand is held palm-up with fingers pointing forward while right **'CROOKED 5'** hand is held apart and slightly higher with palm down and fingers pointing forward. The arms are then simultaneously moved upward/rightward as the hands are purposefully twisted rightward from the wrist so that the left palm faces right and the right palm faces left.

catch: *v.* to grasp and retain something that has been thrown or struck. *The outfielder will catch the ball.*

SIGN #1: **'CROOKED 5'** hands are held upright, the right hand just behind the left, with palms facing forward. The fingers then retract to form **'SPREAD C'** handshapes as the hands are jerked slightly backward/downward, thus creating a spherical space to accommodate a ball.

catch: *v.* to seize; capture. *The police will catch the thief.*

SIGN #2: Right **'SPREAD C'** hand is held palm down at chest level and is then closed to form an **'S'** hand as it is thrust forward. Alternatively, this sign may be made with two hands held apart in front of the chest. ❖

ALTERNATE SIGNS—**arrest** #2 & #3
For contexts where a *group* of people are being caught, see **sanction** #2.

catch: *v.* to arrive on time to board a public transport vehicle. *You must hurry if you want to catch the next bus.*

SIGN #3: Vertical right **'SPREAD C'** hand, with palm facing forward, is held just above horizontal left **'SPREAD C'** hand, of which the palm faces downward. The hands then come together as they move forward and close to form **'S'** hands.

catch: *v.* to be infected with. *I hope I do not catch your cold.*

SIGN #4: Vertical right **'SPREAD C'** hand, with palm facing forward, is held just above horizontal left **'SPREAD C'** hand, of which the palm faces downward. Then both hands are closed simultaneously to form **'S'** hands as the right hand is brought down to rest on the back of the left hand.

OR

SIGN #5: **'F'** hands, palms facing, are linked by thumbs and forefingers. The hands remain linked as they are brought back toward the body. ❖

catch on: *v.* to comprehend the meaning of. *I finally caught on to the joke.*

SIGN: Vertical right **'SPREAD C'** hand, with palm facing forward, is held just above horizontal left **'SPREAD C'** hand, of which the palm faces downward. Then both hands are closed simultaneously to form **'S'** hands as the right hand is brought down to rest on the back of the left hand. A look of realization accompanies this sign.

 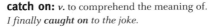

catch up: *v.* to deal with a backlog or to make up for lost ground. *I cannot go out tonight because I need to catch up on my homework.*

SIGN: Horizontal **'EXTENDED A'** hands, left palm facing right and right palm facing left, are held so that the right hand is well behind the left. Then the right hand is curved forward, coming to rest directly behind the left hand.

catcher: *n.* a baseball player who is positioned behind home plate and receives pitches from the pitcher. *The catcher uses hand signals to advise the pitcher how to throw the ball.*

SIGN: Left palm faces forward and right palm faces forward/leftward as **'CROOKED 5'** hands are held upright, the right hand just behind the left. The hands move vigorously together and apart a couple of times. (Agent Ending (see p. LIV) may follow.)

category: *n.* a class of things or people having certain common characteristics. *She will enter the race in the age 16 to 18 category.*

SIGN: **'SPREAD C'** hands are held upright and slightly apart with palms facing each other. The wrists then rotate forward, bringing the hands to a horizontal position.

cater: *v.* to provide food. *This company will cater for the party.*

SIGN: Vertical **'MODIFIED O'** hand, palm facing the body, is brought toward the mouth so that the fingertips touch the lips. Next, left **'EXTENDED B'** hand is held in front of the chest with palm up and fingers pointing forward at a rightward angle while right **'EXTENDED B'** hand is held up high to the right with palm facing left and fingers pointing forward/ upward at a slight rightward angle. The right hand then moves in a downward arc as both hands are moved leftward so that the hands are eventually held parallel with palms up. (ASL CONCEPT—**food - bring**.) **CATERING**, *adj.,* is not signed but fingerspelled.

caterpillar: *n.* the wormlike, often colourful and fuzzy, larva of a butterfly or moth. *The caterpillar will turn into a moth.*

SIGN: Right **'ONE'** hand is placed palm down on the back of the left **'STANDARD BASE'** hand with forefinger pointing left. The right hand moves slowly toward the left elbow as its hand-shape alternates between a **'ONE'** and an **'X'** as it creeps along, simulating the movement of a worm.

ALTERNATE SIGN—**worm**

Caucasian: *n.* a member of the white race. *Caucasians represent many countries and cultures of the world.*

SIGN: Fingertips of right **'FLAT O'** hand, palm toward the body, are placed in the middle of the chest. The hand is then raised to a position in front of the face where it opens to become a **'CONTRACTED 5'** hand with the palm toward the face.

cause: *v.* to make something happen; to produce a certain result. *The inspector wanted to know what caused the fire.*

SIGN #1: Horizontal **'S'** (or **'A'**) hands are held slightly apart with palms facing upward, the left hand slightly ahead of the right hand. The hands are then thrust forward slightly as the fingers open to form **'5'** hands. An inquisitive look accompanies this sign.

cause: *n.* the reason or circumstance which has lead to a certain result. *What is the cause of your anger?*

SIGN #2: Extended fingers of right **'EXTENDED R'** (or **'R'**) hand, palm toward face, make small circles (clockwise in the eyes of the onlooker) at right side of forehead.
ALTERNATE SIGN—**cause** #1

cause: *n.* the ideals or purpose of a group or movement. *They are deeply involved in the cause to save the whales.*

SIGN #3: Tip of forefinger of vertical right **'ONE'** hand, palm toward the face, is used to touch right side of forehead. Then the handshape is changed to a **'BENT V'** and the extended finger-tips are placed against the right-facing palm of the horizontal left **'EXTENDED B'** hand. Next, the fingertips of the right hand are separated from the left hand as the right wrist makes a quarter turn clockwise, the right hand turns slightly toward so that the fingers now point forward/upward, and the fingertips of the right hand re-establish contact with the left palm. (**CAUSE** in this context may be fingerspelled.)
ALTERNATE SIGNS—**cause** #2 or **goal** #1

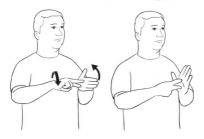

caution: *v.* to warn against possible danger. *The arresting officer **cautioned** the suspect that his statement might be used in evidence.*

SIGN #1: **'EXTENDED B'** hands are held palms down, so that the right hand is above the left and is brought down so that the fingertips are tapped on the back of the left hand. Facial expression must clearly convey 'caution'. ❖

caution: *n.* care or prudence in the face of danger. *This explosive substance must be used with **caution**.*

SIGN #2: Horizontal **'K'** hands are held with right hand resting on left hand and extended fingers pointing forward. Together the hands are circled forward a couple of times. Facial expression is important.
SAME SIGN—**cautious**, *adj.*

cave: *n.* a deep hollow either underground or in the face of a cliff or mountain. *The bear and her cubs came out of the **cave**.*

SIGN: Fingerspell **CAVE**.

cave in: *v.* to collapse or yield completely under pressure. *The walls of the building started to **cave in** when the bomb hit the roof.*

SIGN: Fingers of **'CROOKED 5'** hands, palms down, interlock slightly and then drop down so that backs of fingers are almost touching.

cavity: *n.* a hollow space in a tooth. *The dentist found only one **cavity** when he checked the child's teeth.*

SIGN: Fingerspell **CAVITY**.

cease: *v.* to stop; to bring or come to an end. *This noise must **cease** at once.*

SIGN: Right **'EXTENDED B'** hand, palm facing left, is brought down sharply from a semi-vertical position to strike the upward/ backward facing palm of the rigidly held left **'EXTENDED B'** hand, whose fingers point rightward/forward.

cease-fire: *n.* a military term meaning a period of truce, often temporary. *The commander of the troops ordered a **cease-fire**.*

SIGN: Right **'EXTENDED B'** hand, palm facing left, is brought down sharply from a semi-vertical position to strike the upward/ backward facing palm of the rigidly held left **'EXTENDED B'** hand, whose fingers point rightward/forward. Next, right **'L'** hand, palm facing left, is positioned behind and somewhat lower than left **'L'** hand, of which the palm faces right. Both forefingers point forward/upward. The hands are then simultaneously jerked downward/ forward slightly. (ASL CONCEPT—**stop - shoot**.)

celebrate: *v.* to rejoice in observing or marking a special event. *The team **celebrated** its victory.*

SIGN: Vertical **'COVERED T'** hands are held at either side of the head, palms facing each other, and are swung in small circles above the shoulders.
SAME SIGN—**celebration**, *n.*

celery: *n.* a vegetable with green, leafy stalks. *The recipe calls for chopped **celery**.*

SIGN: Fingerspell **CELERY**.

cell: *n.* a very small room in which a prisoner is housed. *His jail **cell** contained a narrow bed, a toilet and a washbasin.*

SIGN #1: **'4'** (or **'5'**) hands are held with palms facing the body. Back of right hand, whose fingers point slightly upward to the left, is positioned behind palm of left hand at right angles, and is thrust against it.

cell: *n.* the smallest unit of an organism that is able to function independently. *Every body **cell** contains genetic material.*

SIGN #2: Fingerspell **CELL**.

cell: *n.* a device that converts chemical energy to electrical energy. *The battery has a dry **cell** that provides the power to operate this device.*

SIGN #3: Fingerspell **CELL**.

Celsius: *adj.* centigrade; denoting a temperature measurement on the Celsius scale. *In Canada temperature is measured on the **Celsius** scale.*

SIGN: Right **'C'** hand is held upright with palm facing forward/leftward and is wobbled slightly.

cement: *n.* a limestone and clay mixture used to make concrete. *Cement mixed with water can be used as mortar for brickwork.*

SIGN: Tip of forefinger of right **'CROOKED ONE'** hand, palm toward the body, is tapped against the upper front teeth. (**CEMENT** is frequently fingerspelled.)

cemetery: *n.* a place where the dead are buried. *There are many tombstones in the cemetery.*

SIGN: **'BENT EXTENDED B'** hands are held parallel with palms down and fingers pointing down. The hands are then drawn upward and back toward the body with a curving motion, to form **'EXTENDED B'** hands with palms facing forward/downward. (**CEMETERY** is frequently fingerspelled.)

cent: *n.* a penny. *Each piece of bubble gum costs one **cent**.*

SIGN: Vertical right **'ONE'** hand is held with palm toward the face as the tip of the forefinger strokes backward a couple of times on the right side of the forehead just above the temple.

centimetre: *n.* a measurement of length equal to one hundredth of a metre. *Twelve inches is approximately 30 **centimetres**.*

SIGN: Fingerspell **CM**.

centre [*also spelled* **center**]: *n.* the midpoint of a given space or line. *The City Hall is located in the **centre** of the old market square.*

SIGN #1: With palm down, horizontal right **'BENT MIDFINGER 5'** hand is circled clockwise from the wrist above upturned left palm, tip of right midfinger falling in the centre of the left palm.

OR

SIGN #2: Left **'EXTENDED B'** hand is held in a fixed position with palm facing rightward but slanted toward the body, and fingers pointing forward/rightward. With palm down, horizontal right **'BENT EXTENDED B'** hand is held very close to the left hand, and is circled clockwise once from the wrist, the fingertips coming to rest in the palm of the left hand.

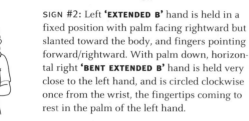

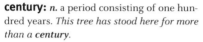

century: *n.* a period consisting of one hundred years. *This tree has stood here for more than a **century**.*

SIGN: Right **'ONE'** hand is held upright with palm facing leftward/forward. The forearm then moves forward slightly as the handshape changes to a **'C'**. Next, horizontal **'S'** hands, palms toward the body, are held so the right is slightly above the left, and the right is circled forward around the left, coming to rest on top of it. (ASL CONCEPT—**one hundred - years**.) In certain contexts, **CENTURY** is fingerspelled, especially when it cannot be directly translated as *100 years*, as in: *Television was unheard of in the nineteenth century*.

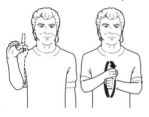

ceramics: *n.* the art of making various forms of pottery from clay. *The Department of Adult Education offers courses in **ceramics**.*

SIGN: Fingerspell **CERAMICS**.

cereal: *n.* any grass that produces an edible grain. *Bran contains more dietary fibre than any other cereal.*

SIGN: Right **'X'** (or **'CROOKED ONE'**) hand is held in a horizontal position with palm facing upward, but angled slightly toward the body. The back of the forefinger is used to brush lightly backward several times in the crook of the bent elbow of the left arm which is held loosely near the left side of the body.

cerebral palsy: *n.* a brain injury which occurs during birth and impairs muscular coordination. *A person with cerebral palsy may have difficulty with speech articulation.*

SIGN: Fingerspell **CP**.

ceremony: *n.* a formal ritual usually based on tradition. *The graduation ceremony will be held in June.*

SIGN: Fingerspell **CEREMONY**.

certain: *adj.* sure; definite; positive and confident about the truth of something. *Are you certain that the meeting is on Saturday?*

SIGN #1: Forefinger of vertical right **'ONE'** hand, palm facing left, is held against the lips and the hand is moved sharply forward.
REGIONAL VARIATION—**sure** #2

certain: *adj.* known but not specified or identified. *Certain aspects of this case are very puzzling.*

SIGN #2: Vertical left **'ONE'** hand is held in a fixed position with palm facing rightward/forward. Horizontal right **'ONE'** hand is held behind left hand with palm facing left. The right hand then makes a slight but firm bounce as if intending to strike the tip of the left forefinger with that of the right forefinger but not quite touching it.

certify: *v.* to affirm qualifications in writing. *CCSD will certify all sign language instructors.*

SIGN: **'C'** hands are held slightly apart in an upright position with palms facing forward, but angled slightly toward each other. Then they are brought together in a single movement so that the thumbs meet.
SAME SIGN—**certificate**, *n.,* and **certification**, *n.,* but the motion is repeated.

chain: *n.* a flexible length of metal links joined together. *She often wears a gold chain around her neck.*

SIGN: Left **'F'** hand is held horizontally with palm facing right while right **'F'** hand is held upright with palm facing forward/ leftward. The two hands are linked by thumbs and forefingers. They are then separated as the left wrist rotates backward bringing the hand to an upright position while the right hand rotates forward to a horizontal position. Thumbs and forefingers are rejoined.

chair: *n.* a seat with a back on it. *This is a comfortable chair.*

SIGN #1: Left **'U'** hand is held palm down with extended fingers pointing forward/rightward. Right **'U'** (or **'CROOKED U'**) hand is held palm down just above the left hand and at right angles to it. The extended fingers of the right hand are then tapped a couple of times on those of the left.

chair: *v.* to run a meeting. *The President will chair the meeting.*

SIGN #2: Horizontal **'X'** hands are held slightly apart with left palm facing right and right palm facing left. Then they are alternately moved backward and forward.

chalk: *n.* a stick of calcium carbonate used for writing on blackboards. *The teacher wrote the assignment on the blackboard with chalk.*

SIGN: Fingertips of right **'CONTRACTED 5'** hand, palm toward the body, are placed against the middle of the chest and the hand is then drawn forward as it closes to form a **'FLAT O'** hand.' Next, vertical right **'CLOSED X'** hand, palm forward, is held high and moved in a wavy line from left to right as if writing on a blackboard. (ASL CONCEPT—**white - write on board**.) If the chalk is a colour other than white, the relevant colour should be used. Alternatively, **CHALK** is frequently fingerspelled.

challenge: *v.* to compete against or to view as a stimulating situation. *He challenged her to a game of chess.*

SIGN: Left horizontal **'EXTENDED A'** hand is held, palm facing the body, just ahead of right **'EXTENDED A'** hand, which is held with palm facing leftward but angled slightly toward the body. Then the wrists are simultaneously twisted so that the thumbs point more emphatically upward as the hands are moved closer together. They may even touch.
SAME SIGN—**challenge**, *n.*

champagne: *n.* an effervescent sparkling wine. *Champagne was served at the reception.*

SIGN: Left **'ONE'** hand is held in a fixed position with palm facing forward/rightward but slanted downward somewhat while the forefinger points rightward/forward at an upward angle. Right **'COVERED T'** hand is held with palm facing the body but slanted upward slightly as the tip of the thumb makes contact with the tip of the left forefinger. The right thumb is then flicked upward at least twice.

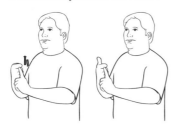

champion: *n.* someone who has defeated all others in a competition. *He is the wrestling champion of Canada.*

SIGN: Left **'ONE'** hand is held in a fixed position with palm facing forward/rightward but slanted downward somewhat while the forefinger points rightward/forward at an upward angle. Right **'CLAWED EXTENDED V'** (or **'SPREAD EXTENDED C'**) hand is then brought downward so that the palm rests on top of the left forefinger.

chance: *n.* likelihood or probability that an event will occur. *Is there any chance that you might support our cause?*

SIGN: **'A'** hands, palms down, are held slightly apart, and are then firmly pushed a very short distance downward. (**CHANCE** is frequently fingerspelled.)

change: *n.* an alteration or transformation. *There has been a change in his appearance.*

SIGN: **'A'** (or **'X'**) hands, palms facing each other, are twisted 180 degrees. (For emphasis, the hands will be held farther apart and the movement will be larger to indicate a big change.)

change (clothes): *v.* to take off one set of clothes and put on another. *I will change clothes before I go to work.*

SIGN: Horizontal left **'COVERED T'** hand, palm facing left but angled toward the body slightly, is held to the left of and just in front of horizontal right **'COVERED T'** hand, of which the palm faces leftward but is angled toward the body. The hands then move simultaneously in circular motions toward the chest. This is a wrist action only so that the hands move but the arms remain stationary.

change one's mind: *v.* to reverse or alter the way one thinks about something. *He had planned to go on a cruise, but he changed his mind when he found out how much it would cost.*

SIGN: Left **'V'** hand is held with palm facing upward and angled toward the body while tip of forefinger of vertical right **'V'** hand, palm forward at a leftward-facing angle, touches the centre of the forehead. The right hand is lowered to make contact with the left hand so that the heels of the hands are touching. The right wrist then rotates 180 degrees forward while the left wrist rotates 180 degrees backward so that the right hand ends up with palm facing upward and the palm of the left hand faces downward/rightward, the hands still held together at the heels.

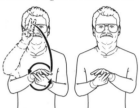

channel: *n.* a specific frequency band used for the transmission of a television signal. *The CBC News is on another channel.*

SIGN: Fingerspell **CHANNEL**.

chaos: *n.* complete disorder and confusion. *There was chaos at the mine site after the explosion.*

SIGN: Left **'CROOKED 5'** hand is held palm-up with fingers pointing forward while right **'CROOKED 5'** hand is held apart and slightly higher with palm down and fingers pointing forward. The arms are then simultaneously moved upward/rightward as the hands are purposefully twisted rightward from the wrist so that the left palm faces right and the right palm faces left.

chapel: *n.* a place of Christian worship. *The funeral home has a small chapel.*

SIGN: Right **'C'** hand is held upright with palm facing forward/leftward as it is tapped up and down on the back of the left **'STANDARD BASE'** hand which is held loosely in front of the chest. (Alternatively, **CHAPEL** may be fingerspelled.)

chapter: *n.* a main section or division of a written work. *I am reading the last chapter of the novel.*

SIGN: Fingerspell **CHAPTER**. (For **chapter** meaning a unit of study in a text book, see **lesson**.)

character: *adj.* related to one's morals or reputation. *Your teacher will provide a character reference for your resume.*

SIGN #1: Horizontal right **'C'** hand, palm facing the body, is twisted in a circular motion from the wrist so that it becomes upright with palm facing leftward as it is brought back against the left shoulder.

SAME SIGN—**character**, *n.*, when a person's reputation is being referred to: *The witness's testimony shed light on the character of the defendant.*

character: *n.* an individual in a story or play. *Hamlet is the main character in Shakespeare's play.*

SIGN #2: Horizontal right **'C'** hand, palm facing the body, is twisted in a circular motion from the wrist so that it becomes upright with palm facing leftward as it is brought back against the left shoulder.

characteristic: *n.* a distinguishing quality, attribute, or trait. *We are studying the characteristics of Inuit art.*

SIGN: Left **'EXTENDED B'** hand is held upright in a fixed position with palm facing forward but angled rightward slightly. Horizontal right **'C'** hand, palm facing the body, is held just in front of left hand and is twisted in a circular motion from the wrist so that it becomes upright with palm facing leftward/forward as it is brought back against the left palm. (This sign is used only for characteristics of inanimate objects. When the characteristic refers to a *human* trait, use **character** #1.)

charge: *v.* to set or demand a certain price. *What did they **charge** you for your car repairs?*

SIGN #1: Forefinger of horizontal right **'x'** hand, palm toward the body at a leftward-facing angle, is brought down smartly across the palm of the horizontal left **'EXTENDED B'** hand, which is facing rightward but angled toward the body.

ALTERNATE SIGN—**bill** #1. This sign is usually used for emphasis when the signer is venting frustration or anger: *If you break that window, I will **charge** you to replace it.*

charge: *v.* to use a credit or account card to pay for something. *I will **charge** it to my credit card account.*

SIGN #2: Horizontal right **'S'** hand, palm toward body at a leftward-facing angle, lies on the upturned palm of the left **'EXTENDED B'** hand, and is pressed back and forth along the length of the left hand as if imprinting a credit card.

charge: *v.* to accuse of a crime or allege that a crime has been committed. *Due to lack of evidence the police could not **charge** him with the theft of my car.*

SIGN #3: Horizontal right **'EXTENDED A'** hand, palm facing left, is thrust forward twice across the back of the left **'A'** hand of which the palm faces downward. (**CHARGE** is frequently fingerspelled.)

ALTERNATE SIGN—**charge** #1

(be in) charge of: *v.* to be responsible for or in command of. *Who **is in charge of** this project?*

SIGN: Horizontal **'x'** hands are held slightly apart with left palm facing right and right palm facing left. Then they are alternately moved backward and forward.

charitable: *adj.* having a kindly attitude towards people; giving or helpful to those in need. *His **charitable** nature led him to do volunteer work with needy children.*

SIGN: Horizontal **'BENT EXTENDED B'** hands, palms facing each other, are alternately circled forward around each other. (**CHARITABLE** is fingerspelled when it describes a thing rather than a person, as in: *Charitable donations may be sent to this address.*)

charity: *n.* money or alms given to the needy. *He does not like to accept **charity**.*

SIGN: Fingerspell **CHARITY**.

chart: *n.* printed information which presents facts in graphical, tabular or diagrammatical form. *A time **chart** lists historical events in the proper sequence.*

SIGN: Fingertips of right **'5'** hand, palm down, are stroked downward across palm of horizontal left **'5'** hand which is facing the chest, but angled rightward. Then the right wrist rotates forward a quarter turn so that the palm is turned toward the body at a leftward-facing angle as the fingertips are stroked across the left palm from left to right. (**CHART** is frequently fingerspelled.) Sign choice varies according to the type of chart under discussion.

chase: *v.* to follow or run after. *Dogs tend to **chase** cats.*

SIGN: Horizontal left **'A'** hand, palm facing right, is held ahead of and to the left of horizontal right **'EXTENDED A'** hand, of which the palm faces the body at a leftward angle. Then the right is moved forward in a series of small clockwise circles to approach the left hand.

chat: *v.* to converse in an easy or gossipy manner. *Drop in later for coffee and we will **chat**.*

SIGN: Horizontal **'CROOKED 5'** hands are held apart with palms facing each other but slanted upward slightly. The hands are simultaneously moved up and down a few times. This is a wrist movement so that only the hands move up and down, as opposed to the arms.

cheap: *adj.* low-priced or inexpensive. *Cheap shoes usually wear out quickly.*

SIGN: Side of forefinger of right palm-down **'B'** hand is brushed downward against right-facing palm of left **'EXTENDED B'** hand.

cheat: *v.* to defraud, trick, or deceive. *He tried to cheat on the final exam.*

SIGN #1 [ATLANTIC]: Thumbtip of right horizontal **'MODIFIED 5'** hand, palm facing left, is held at the tip of the nose. The right hand is then lowered as the wrist rotates to turn the palm downward and the thumb strikes downward against the thumb of the left horizontal **'MODIFIED 5'** hand, of which the palm faces right. Facial expression is important.

SIGN #2 [ONTARIO]: Left forearm is bent so that it is held in front of the chest while the right **'CROOKED L'** hand, palm facing backward, is tapped against the left elbow. This sign is accompanied by a lip pattern such as that used to produce an 'SH' sound.

SIGN #3 [PACIFIC]: Tip of forefinger of right **'CROOKED ONE'** hand, palm facing the body, is tapped against the chin several times. Facial expression is important.

OR

SIGN #4 [PACIFIC]: Left **'ONE'** hand is held in a fixed position with palm down and forefinger pointing rightward/forward while horizontal right **'COMBINED I + ONE'** hand is held with palm down, extended fingers pointing left, and tip of forefinger placed at the end of the nose. Then the right wrist rotates backward as the hand is sharply thrust forward/downward so that the tip of the forefinger brushes past the tip of the left forefinger. Facial expression is important.

SIGN #5 [PRAIRIE]: Left **'ONE'** hand is held in a fixed position with palm down and forefinger pointing rightward/forward while forefinger of right **'ONE'** hand, palm facing the body, is used to touch the nose and is then brought down to strike sharply against the tip of the left forefinger. This sign is accompanied by an appropriate facial expression and a lip pattern such as that used to produce an 'SH' sound.

check: *v.* to inspect, assess or test. *I will check the oil for you.*

SIGN: Left **'EXTENDED B'** hand is held in a fixed position with palm facing rightward but slanted upward and toward the body slightly. Tip of forefinger of right **'ONE'** hand, palm down, is placed at the heel of the left hand, is stroked forward to the centre of the palm and deflected rightward/forward at an upward angle. (For **check**, *n.*, meaning a form of payment, see **cheque**.)

check-out: *n.* a supermarket or department store counter where shoppers pay for their purchases. *Most supermarkets have an express check-out for customers with nine items or less.*

SIGN: Fingers of vertical right **'CLAWED 5'** hand, palm forward, flutter as the hand is circled in a clockwise direction to simulate the ringing up of figures on a till or cash register.

check out: *v.* to investigate or verify. *The police will check out all their alibis.*

SIGN: Left **'EXTENDED B'** hand is held in a fixed position with palm facing rightward but slanted upward and toward the body slightly. Tip of forefinger of right **'ONE'** hand, palm down, is placed at the heel of the left hand, is stroked forward to the centre of the palm and deflected rightward/forward at an upward angle.

check with: *v.* to consult with someone to gain information or to assess a given situation. *I will check with my lawyer to see what my rights are.*

SIGN: Left **'ONE'** hand is held upright in a fixed position while right **'CLAWED V'** hand is held palm down behind it. The right hand is then thrust forward so that the left forefinger is inserted between the clawed right forefinger and middle finger. ❖
ALTERNATE SIGN—**check**

cheek: *n.* either side of the face below the eye and above the mouth. *His right cheek was sore.*

SIGN: Tip of forefinger of right **'ONE'** hand is held at right cheek and is moved in a small circle to outline the cheek. (Sign selection depends on the context. When a description of the cheek is being given, the signer often chooses an all-inclusive sign that conveys **cheek**, *n.*, as well as its description.)

cheer: *n.* a shout of applause or encouragement. *The touchdown brought an enormous cheer from the spectators.*

SIGN: Vertical **'S'** hands are held high with palms facing each other but angled forward. The forearms are then simultaneously thrust forward a slight distance. The mouth is open as if the signer is shouting. **'EXTENDED B'** hands are then vigorously clapped together.

cheerful: *adj.* happy and in good spirits. *They are a **cheerful** group of children.*

SIGN: Horizontal right **'EXTENDED B'** hand, palm toward the body, is brushed up and off the chest twice in a circular motion. ALTERNATE SIGN—**amiable**

cheese: *n.* a solid food made from pressed milk curds, variously prepared and flavoured. *We baited the mousetrap with a piece of **cheese**.*

SIGN: Heel of right **'SPREAD EXTENDED C'** hand is placed on heel of left **'SPREAD EXTENDED C'** hand, and the hands are twisted back and forth a few times in opposite directions.

chef: *n.* a professional cook. *The hotel **chef** prepared an excellent gourmet dinner.*

SIGN: Fingerspell **CHEF**.

chemical: *adj.* pertaining to the laws, operations and results of chemistry. *You must be careful when handling **chemical** substances.*

SIGN: Vertical **'C'** hands, palms facing away from the body, and circled so that the left hand moves clockwise while the right hand moves counter-clockwise. (To the onlooker, the hands are moving the opposite directions, however.) The hands do not move symmetrically, but are offset as they circle.

chemistry: *n.* the science of chemical composition or processes. *He is taking **Chemistry** courses in the evening.*

SIGN: Vertical **'C'** hands, palms facing away from the body, and circled so that the left hand moves clockwise while the right hand moves counter-clockwise. (To the onlooker, the hands are moving the opposite directions, however.) The hands do not move symmetrically, but are offset as they circle. SAME SIGN—**chemist**, *n.,* and may be followed by the Agent Ending (see p. LIV).

cheque [*also spelled* **check**]: *n.* a written order for money drawn upon a bank account. *I will cash my pay **cheque** at the bank.*

SIGN #1: Left **'EXTENDED B'** hand is held in a fixed position with palm facing rightward but slanted upward and toward the body slightly. Backs of extended fingers of right **'BENT U'** hand are placed in left palm and the right hand is moved forward/rightward along the left palm to the fingertips. (Signs vary; see also **card** #2. Alternatively, **CHEQUE** is frequently fingerspelled.)

SIGN #2 [ATLANTIC/ONTARIO]: Left **'U'** hand is held in a fixed position with palm toward the body and extended fingers pointing rightward. Right **'U'** hand is held with palm toward the body and tips of extended fingers touching those of the left hand. The right hand is then lowered with a flourish so that the extended fingers point downward.

cherish: *v.* to value dearly. *I will always **cherish** the memories of my happy childhood.*

SIGN: Knuckles of vertical right **'OPEN SPREAD O'** hand, palm toward the body, are placed on the chin and are firmly drawn downward, closing to form an **'S'** hand.

cherry: *n.* a small, round, fleshy tree fruit containing a hard stone. *There was a **cherry** on top of the sundae.*

SIGN: Left **'ONE'** hand is held in a fixed position with palm facing the body at a downward angle and forefinger pointing rightward. Fingers of right **'OPEN SPREAD O'** hand grasp the end of the left forefinger as the right wrist twists back and forth several times. (**CHERRY** is frequently fingerspelled.)

chess: *n.* a board game for two players, the object being to manoeuvre chess-pieces so that the opponent's king is checkmated. *Planning one's strategy in a game of **chess** is very important.*

SIGN: Fingerspell **CHESS**.

chest: *n.* the part of the body that is enclosed by the ribs. *The man was having severe pains in his **chest**.*

SIGN #1: Palm of horizontal right **'EXTENDED B'** hand is rubbed up and down slightly in the centre of the chest.

chest: *n.* a piece of furniture with drawers in which things can be stored. *Your new shirt is in the top drawer of the chest.*

SIGN #2: **'EXTENDED B'** (or **'B'**) hands are held together at about shoulder level with palms down and fingers pointing forward. The arms move apart to indicate the top of the chest, and as the wrists rotate so that the palms face each other, the hands move straight down to outline the sides of the chest. Next, **'S'** hands are held parallel with palms up at about face level with arms extended away from the body. The hands then move simultaneously toward the body as if opening a drawer. Motion is repeated once or twice, each time at a lower level. (**CHEST**, meaning *chest of drawers*, is frequently fingerspelled.)

chew: *v.* to gnaw or work about between the teeth. *You should chew your food well.*

SIGN: Right **'A'** hand is held palm-down on top of left **'A'** hand, of which the palm faces upward. The hands are rubbed against each other with circular motions in opposite directions.

chicken: *n.* a young domestic fowl. *The chicken was kept in a pen.*

SIGN #1: Right **'MODIFIED G'** hand is held at chin, palm facing forward, while thumb and forefinger are opened and closed at least twice to simulate the movement of a chicken's beak. (In contexts where **chicken** has the colloquial connotation of 'coward', the same sign is used along with a mocking facial expression.)

SIGN #2 [ONTARIO]: **'CONTRACTED 3'** hands are held at either side of the waist, with the thumbs touching the body and the palms facing down. Then the hands are moved forward and back twice. (In contexts where **chicken** has the colloquial connotation of 'coward', the same sign is used along with a mocking facial expression.)

chief: *adj.* main; first in importance or prominence. *The Mackenzie River is the chief waterway in the Northwest Territories.*

SIGN #1: Left **'B'** hand is held in a fixed position with palm facing right and fingers pointing forward. Right **'B'** hand, palm facing left, and fingers pointing forward, is positioned on top of the left hand and firmly moved forward.
ALTERNATE SIGN—**important**

chief: *adj.* referring to the highest ranking person. *He is the Chief Executive Officer of this company.*

SIGN #2: Horizontal right **'EXTENDED A'** hand, palm facing the body at a slight leftward angle, is raised purposefully upward to a level above the right shoulder.

child: *n.* a young human being, either male or female. *He is a very inquisitive child.*

SIGN: Vertical right **'BENT EXTENDED B'** hand is held with palm facing forward and fingers pointing forward. It is then lowered slightly to indicate the relatively low physical stature of a child.

childish: *adj.* behaving in the manner of a child. *Please stop your childish pouting.*

SIGN: Side of forefinger of right **'COMBINED I + ONE'** hand is placed, palm down, under the nose, and the hand is wiggled by twisting the wrist. (**CHILDISH** is frequently fingerspelled.)
ALTERNATE SIGN—**silly**

children: *n.* young humans, either male or female. *The children are playing in the back yard.*

SIGN: Right **'EXTENDED B'** hand is held palm down with fingers pointing forward. The hand then moves rightward in a small arc. Motion may be repeated in a rightward direction to indicate more children. Two hands may be used for this sign, the left hand moving leftward.

chilly: *adj.* cold or cold enough to make one shiver. *Autumn evenings can be quite chilly, so you should wear a sweater.*

SIGN: **'S'** (or **'A'**) hands are held apart, palms facing each other, and are shaken, along with the shoulders, as if the signer is shivering.

chimpanzee: *n.* an intelligent species of ape. *A* **chimpanzee** *has been trained to use a few ASL signs.*

SIGN: Fingertips of both **'CLAWED A'** hands, one on either side of the rib-cage, palms toward the body, are brushed upward with a scratching motion.

chin: *n.* the central and anterior part of the lower jaw; the area just under the lower lip. *He has a sore* **chin**.

SIGN: Tip of forefinger of right **'BENT ONE'** hand, palm toward the body, is used to touch the chin. (Sign selection depends on the context. When a description of the chin is being given, the signer generally chooses an all-inclusive sign that conveys **chin**, *n.,* as well as its description.)

chip in: *v.* to contribute either help or money. *The team is going to* **chip in** *to buy the coach a gift.*

SIGN: **'FLAT O'** hands are held apart, fingers pointing toward each other and palms facing. The hands are then brought closer together as the thumbs slide across the fingers to form **'A'** hands.

chiropractor: *n.* someone who treats physical problems by manipulating various joints, especially the spine. *He sees a* **chiropractor** *regularly for help with his bad back.*

SIGN: **'SPREAD EXTENDED C'** hands are held parallel with palms down. The left hand remains fixed as the right wrist rotates to twist the hand two or three times so that the palm alternates between facing entirely downward and slanting leftward.

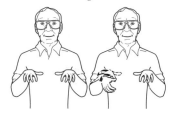

chocolate: *n.* a sweetened, flavoured product made from ground cacao nuts. *His favourite flavour is* **chocolate**.

SIGN: Vertical right **'C'** hand, palm facing away from the body, rests on the back of the left **'STANDARD BASE'** hand, and is moved in two small counter-clockwise circles. (**CHOCOLATE** is frequently fingerspelled in an abbreviated form: **CHOC**.)

choice: *n.* the act or privilege of making a selection; an option; something or someone selected. *My* **choice** *for dessert is apple pie with ice cream.*

SIGN: Left **'5'** hand is held in a fixed position with palm facing chest and fingers pointing upward/ rightward. Thumb and forefinger of right **'FLAT OPEN F'** hand pluck at tip of left forefinger, and close to form a **'FLAT F'** hand. (The left handshape for **choice** will vary depending on how many things there are to choose from. If there are two things to choose from, the left hand will take the shape of a **'BENT V'**.)

choke: *v.* to stop the breathing by obstructing the windpipe. *People can* **choke** *if they do not chew their food carefully.*

SIGN: Horizontal right **'C'** hand, palm facing the body, is firmly thrust toward the throat to encircle it.

choose: *v.* to select by preference or make a decision. *You must* **choose** *the best answer.*

SIGN: Right **'FLAT OPEN F'** hand, palm forward, is drawn back toward the chest as it changes to an **'F'** hand. ❖

chop: *v.* to cut up into small pieces. *I will* **chop** *the vegetables for the salad.*

SIGN: Left **'EXTENDED B'** hand is held in a fixed position with palm facing upward but slanted toward the body slightly while the fingers point rightward/forward. Edge of right **'EXTENDED B'** hand, palm facing left and fingers pointing forward, is used to simulate a chopping motion on the left palm.

chop down: *v.* to cut down a tree by strokes of a sharp tool. *George Washington decided to* **chop down** *a cherry tree.*

SIGN: Left **'5'** hand is held upright to represent a tree while the edge of the right **'EXTENDED B'** hand, palm up and fingers pointing leftward/forward, is used to strike repeatedly against the left forearm with a chopping motion.

chores: *n.* small routine tasks. *Every camper was given specific* **chores** *to do.*

SIGN: Wrist of right **'A'** (or **'S'**) hand, palm facing away from the body, strikes wrist of the left **'A'** (or **'S'**) hand, which is held in front of/below the right hand with palm facing downward. Motion is repeated. (**CHORES** is frequently fingerspelled.)

chow: See **food**.

Christ: *n.* Jesus of Nazareth; the son of God. *Christmas is a celebration of the birth of Christ.*

SIGN: Right **'C'** hand, palm facing left, is moved diagonally across the torso from the left shoulder to the right side of the waist. SAME SIGN—**Christian**, *n.*, Agent Ending (see p. LIV) may follow.

Christian name: *n.* a person's given or first name. *Although his Christian name is Edward, everyone calls him Ted.*

SIGN: Left **'EXTENDED A'** hand is held horizontally with thumb up and palm facing rightward but slanted slightly toward the body. Tip of forefinger of right **'ONE'** hand moves at a leftward/backward angle until making contact with tip of left thumb. Next, **'U'** hands are held horizontally with left palm facing right but angled slightly toward the body while right palm faces leftward at a slight angle toward the body. Right hand is positioned above the left at right angles to it. Right midfinger is then tapped twice on left forefinger. (ASL CONCEPT—**first - name**.)

Christmas: *n.* December 25th, observed by Christians as the date of Christ's birth. *Christmas is my favourite holiday.*

SIGN #1: Right **'C'** hand is held upright in front of left side of body with palm facing forward. The wrist then rotates to turn the hand around so that the palm faces backward as the hand is moved to a position in front of the right side of the body.

SIGN #2 [ATLANTIC]: Forefinger of right **'COVERED T'** hand, palm facing downward/rightward, is lowered from the forehead and circled in front of the mouth as if spooning food into it.

OR

SIGN #3 [ATLANTIC]: Fingertips of horizontal right **'C'** hand are placed on the forehead and then moved down to be placed on the chin.

OR

SIGN #4 [ATLANTIC/PRAIRIE]: Fingertips of horizontal right **'C'** hand are placed on the chin and then moved up to be placed on the forehead.

SIGN #5 [ONTARIO]: Right **'CROOKED 5'** hand is held upright with palm facing left and thumbtip on lower right jawbone. The wrist then rotates as the hand moves in an arc in front of the mouth so that the tip of the little finger eventually touches the lower left jawbone.

chronic: *adj.* continuing; prolonged; lasting a long time. *She has chronic bronchitis.*

SIGN: **'EXTENDED A'** hands are held side by side with palms down and right thumbtip pressing against left thumbnail as the hands are moved purposefully forward.

chubby: *adj.* having a plump or round form. *He is a healthy, chubby baby.*

SIGN: **'SPREAD C'** hands, palms toward the face, are placed upright near the cheeks which are slightly inflated as the hands are moved simultaneously outward. This sign may be formed at various locations on the body, such as the chest or hips to specify plumpness in that area.

chuckle: *v.* to laugh softly to oneself. *Your comments made me chuckle.*

SIGN: **'CLAWED 5'** hands, right palm down and left palm up, represent the upper and lower teeth as the right hand is held just above the left. The hands are then simultaneously shaken up and down.

---

chum: *n.* an intimate friend. *She was a chum of mine in Junior High School.*

SIGN: Left **'CROOKED ONE'** hand is held palm-up with forefinger pointing rightward/forward, while right **'CROOKED ONE'** hand is held palm-down with forefinger laid across left forefinger at right angles to it. The wrists then rotate so that the hands reverse positions. ALTERNATE SIGN—**(best) friend**

church: *n.* a building used for public worship. *They attend **church** every Sunday morning.*

SIGN: Right **'C'** hand is held upright with palm facing forward/leftward as it is tapped up and down on the back of the left **'STANDARD BASE'** hand which is held loosely in front of the chest.

cigar: *n.* a roll of tobacco leaves shaped and prepared for smoking. *He smokes a **cigar** occasionally after dinner.*

SIGN: Back of right **'BENT R'** hand, with palm facing forward/downward, and extended fingers pointing forward, is tapped against right side of chin twice. (Signs vary.)

cigarette: *n.* a small roll of finely cut tobacco in thin paper. *Smoking **cigarettes** is not allowed in this building.*

SIGN: Extended fingertips of right **'COMBINED I + ONE'** hand, held palm down, are tapped twice on forefinger of left **'ONE'** hand, which is held palm down with forefinger pointing rightward/forward.

cinema: See **movie.**

circle: *n.* a round or spherical shape. *The circumference of the **circle** is 32 cm.*

SIGN: Forefinger of right **'BENT ONE'** hand is used to inscribe an imaginary clockwise circle in front of the chest.
SAME SIGN—**circular,** *adj.*

circulate: *v.* to cause something to be passed from place to place or person to person. *Please **circulate** this memo to all staff members before our next meeting.*

SIGN: Right **'CONTRACTED B'** hand is held palm-up with fingers pointing forward/leftward in front of left side of body. The hand then makes a sweeping arc rightward as if passing something out. (As a modification, the hand may bounce slightly several times while completing the arc to indicate the giving of something to individual recipients.)

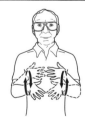

circulation: *n.* the movement of blood throughout the body. *Exercise increases your blood **circulation**.*

SIGN: **'CROOKED 5'** hands, palms toward the body, are held horizontally but slanted downward slightly, as they circle backward past one another. These are rather large movements. The cheeks are puffed.

circumcise: *v.* to surgically remove the fore-skin of the penis. *The doctor will **circumcise** the baby if the parents request it.*

SIGN: Left **'ONE'** hand is held in a fixed position with palm facing the body and forefinger pointing rightward. Right **'A'** hand is held with palm facing forward/downward and tip of thumb touching end of left forefinger. Right wrist then rotates clockwise as the thumb is circled forward around the left forefinger, the right palm eventually facing the body.
SAME SIGN—**circumcision,** *n.*

circumstance: *n.* situation; the conditions associated with a certain event. *What were the **circumstances** leading to his arrest?*

SIGN: **'ONE'** hands, palms facing each other and forefingers pointing forward, are held apart and then turned over so that the palms face down. (The ASL sentence is syntactically different than the English one. The sample sentence in ASL is: *HE ARREST...pause... BEFORE HAPPEN (questioning look?)* Signs vary considerably depending on the context.

circus: *n.* a public performance given by a travelling company of entertainers and involving a wide variety of acts. *Most children love the clown and animal acts in a **circus**.*

SIGN: **'CLAWED V'** hands, palms down, are held apart in front of the chest, one hand held higher than the other. The hands are then circled forward.
ALTERNATE SIGN—**clown**

cite: *v.* to quote or refer to for proof or support. *Will you please **cite** a few examples from the book?*

SIGN: Parallel horizontal **'V'** hands are held with the left hand slightly ahead of the right and the extended fingertips of both hands pointing leftward/forward. The forearms then move simultaneously rightward and slightly upward as the hands take on **'CLAWED V'** shapes, and finally resume the **'V'** shape as they continue moving rightward and slightly downward.

citizen: *n.* a registered member of a nation. *The immigrant was eager to become a Canadian citizen.*

SIGN: Fingerspell CITIZEN. (When using **citizen(s)** in a general sense to mean person/people, the sign for **person/people** may be used.)

city: *n.* a place inhabited by a large, permanent, organized community. *The highest official of an incorporated city is the mayor.*

SIGN: Vertical **'EXTENDED B'** hands, left palm facing right and right palm facing left, are held so that their fingertips can be tapped together twice. (When the word **'City'** is in the place name, as in **'Quebec City'** or **'Mexico City'**, CITY is fingerspelled.)

civil: *adj.* having to do with the ordinary life of citizens. *Some policies discriminate against the civil rights of people.*

SIGN: Fingerspell CIVIL.

civilization: *n.* a human society that has a complex cultural organization. *We are studying early Greek civilization.*

SIGN: Fingerspell CIVILIZATION.

claim: *v.* to assert ownership of or the right to take possession of. *Whoever lost a pair of black gloves can claim them at my office.*

SIGN #1: Fingerspell CLAIM.

claim: *v.* to assert or maintain; to state as truth. *He claims he was away when the crime took place.*

SIGN #2: Tip of forefinger of vertical right **'4'** hand, palm facing left, is tapped twice against the chin.

claim: *n.* a demand for something deserved. *He made an insurance claim after his home had been vandalized.*

SIGN #3: Right **'B'** (or **'EXTENDED B'**) hand, palm up, fingers pointing forward, is thrust forward as if presenting a bill.

claim responsibility: *v.* to admit fault or guilt. *He claimed responsibility for the terrorist act.*

SIGN #4: Vertical left **'EXTENDED B'** is raised above shoulder level as right **'EXTENDED B'** hand is held with palm against chest, and is brought forward so that the palm faces upward at a slight angle toward the body. This sign is accompanied by a 'sheepish' facial expression.

clam: *n.* a burrowing, hard-shelled mollusk. *While digging in the sand, he found a clam.*

SIGN: Fingerspell CLAM.

clap: *v.* to applaud by audibly putting the hands together several times. *The audience stood at the end of the performance and clapped loudly.*

SIGN: **'EXTENDED B'** hands, left palm facing upward and right palm facing downward, are brought together at least twice in a clapping motion.

clarify: *v.* to make something clearer or easier to understand. *Will you please clarify your purpose in writing this essay?*

SIGN: **'O'** (or **'FLAT O'**) hands are placed side by side, palms facing forward. Then they are moved apart and upward as the fingers spread to form **'5'** hands, palms still facing away from the body.

SAME SIGN—**clarification**, *n.*

clash: *v.* to conflict or be incompatible; to look inharmonious together (as with certain colour combinations). *That tie will clash with your shirt.*

SIGN #1: **'ONE'** hands, palms toward the chest and forefingers pointing toward each other at an upward angle, are held slightly apart and then thrust toward each other so the forefingers cross with the left one in front of the right.

clash: *v.* to disagree strongly or have a heated argument. *The teenager and his mother often clash over his bedtime on a school night.*

SIGN #2: Vertical **'MODIFIED O'** hands, palms facing, are held slightly apart and are changed to **'5'** hands as they are brought together to strike each other firmly.

class: *n.* a group of students being taught together. *The English class will meet in the library.*

SIGN: **'SPREAD C'** hands are held upright and slightly apart with palms facing each other. The wrists then rotate forward, bringing the hands to a horizontal position.

classify: *v.* to arrange in classes or categories. *Can you classify these movies into different types?*

SIGN: **'SPREAD C'** hands are held upright and slightly apart, palms facing each other. The wrists then rotate forward, bringing the hands to a horizontal position. The movement is repeated three times—to the left, in front of, and to the right of the body.

classy: *adj.* elegantly stylish. *Her clothes are always very classy.*

SIGN: Horizontal right **'S'** hand, palm toward the body, is held on the chin and the forefinger is thrust out to form a **'ONE'** handshape. (This sign is formed along with the release of a slight puff of air from between the lips as the forefinger is flicked out.)
ALTERNATE SIGN—**dressy**

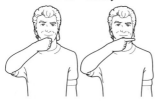

clatter: See **noise**.

clay: *n.* the earth of which bricks and pottery are made. *There is a deep layer of red clay under the topsoil.*

SIGN: Fingerspell **CLAY**.

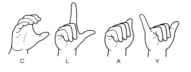

clean: *v.* to free from dirt or other foreign matter. *I will hire someone to clean my house on Saturday.*

SIGN: Hands are held at right angles to one another as downturned palm of right **'EXTENDED B'** hand is smoothed rightward/forward across upturned palm of left **'EXTENDED B'** hand. Motion is repeated a few times. (For **clean**, *adj.*, the motion is not repeated.)

clear: *adj.* distinct or bright, not dim or clouded. *The sky is clear and sunny.*

SIGN: **'O'** (or **'FLAT O'**) hands are placed side by side, palms facing forward. Then they are moved apart and upward as the fingers spread to form **'5'** hands, palms still facing away from the body.

clever: *adj.* bright, talented, ingenious. *He is a clever student.*

SIGN #1: Tip of middle finger of vertical right **'BENT MIDFINGER 5'** hand, palm toward the face, touches the forehead. Then the wrist is rotated so that the palm faces away from the body.

clever (cont.)

OR

SIGN #2: Tip of forefinger of vertical right **'ONE'** hand, palm facing left, touches the forehead. The forearm then moves forward.

client: *n.* a person using the services of a professional. *The defence attorney won the case for his* **client**.

SIGN: Fingerspell **CLIENT**.

climax: *n.* the most exciting or intense point in the action of a story. *Can you identify the* **climax** *in this story?*

SIGN #1: Middle fingers of horizontal **'BENT MIDFINGER 5'** hands, palms toward the body, are brushed up and off the chest in alternating circular motions. Next, left **'EXTENDED B'** hand is held in a fixed position in front of the upper chest with palm down and fingers pointing rightward, while right **'EXTENDED B'** hand is held in a lower position. The right hand is then brought up sharply so that the back of it hits the left palm at right angles to it. (ASL CONCEPT—**excite - maximum**.) **CLIMAX** in this context may be fingerspelled and its meaning explained.

climax: *n.* the high point of sexual pleasure. *An orgasm is the ultimate* **climax** *of the sexual act.*

SIGN #2: Fingerspell **CLIMAX**. (In this context, **climax** may be signed in a variety of ways.)

climb (a ladder): *v.* to ascend or move up. *The painter* **climbed the ladder** *to the roof.*

SIGN #1: Vertical right **'CROOKED C'** hand is held, palm forward, in front of the right side of the upper chest, or higher, and as it is moved in an upward/forward arc, it closes to form an **'S'** shape as if grabbing hold of the next rung of a ladder. At this point, the vertical left **'CROOKED C'** hand is held out in front of the left side of the body and repeats the same action that the right hand has just taken. The hands continue to alternate in this way to simulate the climbing of a ladder.

climb (an inclined surface): *v.* to ascend or walk up. *I will* **climb the stairs** *and go to bed.*

SIGN #2: Right **'CLAWED EXTENDED V'** hand is held palm down with fingers pointing downward and fluttering (to simulate two legs walking) as the hand moves upward/forward.

climb (something cylindrical and vertical): *v.* to go up. *The telephone lineman had to* **climb the pole**.

SIGN #3: Bent knuckles of right **'CLAWED V'** (or **'CLAWED EXTENDED V'**) hand, palm down, are placed in an inverted position against the side of the upright forefinger of the left **'ONE'** hand. Then the right hand is moved upward with the clawed fingers wiggling.

climb (the face of a mountain): *v.* to ascend. *They are planning to* **climb a mountain** *in Jasper National Park.*

SIGN #4: Vertical **'CROOKED 5'** hands, palms forward, are alternately circled upward and forward.

clinic: *n.* a centre that offers a service such as counselling or medical treatment. *Dr. Robinson and his associates work at the medical* **clinic**.

SIGN: Fingerspell **CLINIC**.

clip: *n.* a fastener used to hold things in a certain way. *He used a large **clip** to keep the invoices together.*

SIGN #1: Left **'EXTENDED B'** hand is held in a fixed position with palm facing the body and fingers pointing upward/rightward. The fingertips of the left hand are then clamped between the fingers and the palm of the right **'OPEN A'** hand.

SAME SIGN—**clipboard**, *n.*

(paper) clip: *n.* a fastener used to keep papers together. *The **paper clip** held the papers together.*

SIGN #2: Left **'EXTENDED B'** hand is held in a fixed position with palm facing the body and fingers pointing right as thumb and extended fingers of the right **'DOUBLE MODIFIED G'** hand, palm down, move downward to simulate a clipping motion on the left hand.

clip: *n.* a haircut for a dog. *The poodle will have a **clip** this afternoon.*

SIGN #3: Extended fingers of horizontal right hand alternate between a **'V'** and a **'U'** shape a few times as the hand moves upward along the left bicep to the shoulder.

clip: *v.* to cut or trim one's fingernails or toe-nails. *He **clips** his fingernails every two or three weeks.*

SIGN #4: Fingertips of left **'STANDARD BASE'** hand rest on side of crooked forefinger of horizontal **'A-INDEX'** hand, of which the palm faces left. The right hand then moves forward/leftward as the thumb moves up and down to simulate the use of nail clippers.

clipping: *n.* an article cut out of a newspaper. *He showed us a newspaper **clipping** about the accident.*

SIGN #1: Left **'EXTENDED B'** hand is held in a fixed position with palm up and fingers pointing rightward/forward. Right **'CLAWED EXTENDED V'** hand, with palm facing leftward, is placed on left palm and curled slightly so that while the palm continues to face leftward, it is now slanted a little toward the body and the clawed fingers are further retracted.

OR

SIGN #2: Thumb and forefinger of right **'C-INDEX'** hand, palm facing left, are stroked downward across the right-facing palm of the left **'EXTENDED B'** hand.

ALTERNATE SIGN—**column** #3

clock: *n.* an instrument for measuring and indicating time. *The kitchen **clock** is five minutes fast.*

SIGN: Tip of forefinger of right **'CROOKED ONE'** hand, palm facing downward, is tapped on the back of the wrist of the left **'STANDARD BASE'** hand. Then vertical **'CROOKED L'** hands are firmly positioned at above face level with palms facing forward. (ASL CONCEPT—**time - clock-on-wall**.) The second part of this sign varies depending on the size, shape and location of the clock.

ALTERNATE SIGN—**time** #1

close (a book): *v.* to shut a book. *You will now **close** your books in readiness for the test.*

SIGN #1: **'EXTENDED B'** hands are held side by side with palms up and fingers pointing forward. The wrists then rotate inward until the palms come together.

close (a business): *v.* to shut a business. *All banks will **close** on Monday.*

SIGN #2: Vertical **'B'** hands are held apart with palms facing forward at a slight downward angle. The hands are then drawn together.

close (a door): *v.* to shut a door. *Will you please **close** the door?*

SIGN #3: Vertical left **'B'** hand is held in a fixed position with palm facing forward/rightward while vertical right **'B'** hand is held just to the right of it with palm facing leftward but angled backward slightly. The right wrist then rotates, turning the hand so that its palm faces forward/leftward and its forefinger comes to rest against the forefinger of the left hand, resulting in the creation of a **'V'** formation.

close (one's eyes): *v.* to shut one's eyes. *You will have to* **close your eyes** *before we can give you a present.*

SIGN #4: Thumbtips of vertical **'CONTRACTED L'** hands, palms facing, are held by each eye. Then thumbs and forefingers simultaneously close to form **'CLOSED G'** handshapes.

close (a gate): *v.* to shut a gate. *You must* **close the gate** *or the horse will get out.*

SIGN #5: Horizontal left **'BENT EXTENDED B'** hand is held in a fixed position with palm facing right while horizontal right **'EXTENDED B'** hand is held just to the right of it with palm facing that of the left hand and fingers pointing forward. The right hand then becomes a **'BENT EXTENDED B'** as the fingers move backward so that the fingertips touch those of the left hand.

close (a window): *v.* to shut a window. *Will you please* **close the window?**

SIGN #6: Horizontal **'BENT EXTENDED B'** hands, left palm facing right and right palm facing left, are held with the right some distance above the left. The right hand is then lowered until it rests on the edge of the left hand. (Signs vary according to the type of window being closed.)

close to: *adv.* near in space or time. *I live* **close to** *the airport.*

SIGN: Horizontal **'BENT EXTENDED B'** hands are held right in front of left with right palm facing leftward and left palm facing rightward. Right hand is then moved backward so that fingers of right hand touch fingers of left hand to indicate nearness.

closed-captioned: *adj.* the subtitles added to a movie or television program. *Most movies and television programs are now* **closed-captioned.**

SIGN: Fingerspell **CC**. (See also **caption**.)

closet: *n.* a small room used for storage. *Her* **closet** *is full of expensive, designer clothes.*

SIGN: Fingerspell **CLOSET**.

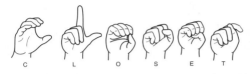

clot: *n.* a soft, thick lump or mass. *The doctor found a blood* **clot** *in her leg.*

SIGN: Fingerspell **CLOT**.

cloth: *n.* a piece of fabric used for a specific purpose. *There was enough* **cloth** *left to make a belt for the dress.*

SIGN: Fingerspell **CLOTH**.

clothes [*or* **clothing**]: *n.* the garments worn by humans. *She wears inexpensive but stylish* **clothes.**

SIGN: Thumbs of **'5'** hands, with palms toward the body, are held at either side of upper chest and brushed downward a couple of times.

cloud: *n.* a white or grey mass of vapor floating in the atmosphere. *He gazed skyward for a long time studying a cumulus* **cloud.**

SIGN: **'SPREAD C'** hands are held upright and slightly apart above face level, palms facing each other. The wrists then rotate forward, bringing the hands to a horizontal position. To indicate plurality, motion may be repeated as arms move rightward.

cloudy: *adj.* covered with clouds. *The sky was* **cloudy** *so we thought it might rain.*

SIGN: Vertical **'CROOKED 5'** hands are held apart above face level, with palms facing forward. They are then moved in circles, the left turning clockwise while the right turns counter-clockwise. The hands do not move symmetrically, but are offset as they circle.

clout: *n.* political, social or judicial influence and power. *Her opinions carry a lot of clout in the community.*

SIGN #1: Fingertips of right **'SPREAD C'** hand are brought forcefully against left bicep.

clout: *v.* to strike with a heavy blow. *If he tries to escape, the policeman will clout him with his baton.*

SIGN #2: Right **'S'** hand is held upright with palm facing left, and is moved forward/downward so that it is almost horizontal. Motion may be repeated to simulate a 'clubbing' action.

clown: *n.* a professional buffoon; someone who entertains by appearing silly. *The clown was doing stunts at the circus.*

SIGN: Vertical right **'OPEN SPREAD O'** hand, palm toward the body, encloses the tip of the nose and wobbles.

clown around: *v.* to behave foolishly or to play jokes or tricks. *The students always clown around when the teacher leaves the room.*

SIGN: **'Y'** hands are held upright, left ahead of right, in front of the face with left palm facing right and right palm facing left. The forearms then move simultaneously in small, continuous circles. From the signer's perspective, the right hand moves in a counter-clockwise direction while the left hand moves clockwise.

club: *n.* an organization of persons with a common purpose. *The bridge club meets every Wednesday evening.*

SIGN #1: Fingerspell **CLUB**.

(Deaf) Club: *n.* a place were the Deaf Community traditionally gathers, primarily for social purposes. *I will see you at the Deaf Club on Saturday night.*

SIGN #2: Fingerspell **CLUB**.

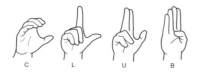

club: *n.* the black clover leaf on a playing card, or a suit of cards marked with these shapes. *Her bridge partner bid one club.*

SIGN #3: Crooked fingertips of right **'CLAWED V'** hand, palm down, are tapped twice on the back of the left **'STANDARD BASE'** hand.

club: *v.* to hit someone with a stout stick. *He clubbed the intruder with a baseball bat.*

SIGN #4: Right **'S'** hand is held upright with palm facing left, and is moved forward/downward so that it is almost horizontal. Motion may be repeated to simulate a 'clubbing' action. (For **club** *n.*, meaning a stout stick which is suitable for use as a weapon, sign choice depends entirely on the size and shape of the club.)

clue: *n.* a hint or piece of information that helps to solve a problem or mystery. *The detective discovered a very important clue.*

SIGN: Fingerspell **CLUE**.

clumsy: *adj.* lacking ability, physical coordination, or grace. *A toddler is usually clumsy on his feet.*

SIGN: **'3'** hands, held slightly apart with the palms down, are alternately raised and lowered.

clutter: *v.* to litter or create disorder. *Do not clutter the room with junk.*

SIGN: The arms gradually move forward as the hands, which are held apart with palms down, alternately change from **'S'** to **'CONTRACTED 5'** shapes several times as if dropping things on the floor.

coach: *n.* sports trainer and director. *He is a good hockey coach.*

SIGN: Fingertips of palm-down right **'SPREAD C'** hand are tapped twice on right shoulder. Alternatively, this sign may be made using both hands, one on each shoulder. (**COACH** is frequently fingerspelled.)

coal: *n.* a black mineral used as fuel. *At one time, many people used* **coal** *to heat their homes.*

SIGN: Fingerspell **COAL**.

coast: *n.* the land next to the sea. *She gathered many shells along the* **coast**.

SIGN: Fingerspell **COAST**.

coat: *n.* a heavy outer garment that opens down the front. *It is too warm today to wear a* **coat**.

SIGN #1: Vertical **'EXTENDED A'** hands are held parallel close to the upper chest with palms facing each other. They are then simultaneously lowered a short distance as palms turn downward.

coat: *n.* a layer of something spread over a surface. *This chair needs another* **coat** *of paint.*

SIGN #2: Fingerspell **COAT**. (In certain contexts, the left hand assumes an appropriate handshape to represent a given object while the right **'MODIFIED G'** hand is held close to it, or moved across or around it to represent a *coat* or *coating* of some kind.)

coax: *v.* to try to persuade. *She tried to* **coax** *them to join us.*

SIGN: Horizontal **'X'** hands, are held apart with palms facing each other and the right hand slightly ahead of the left hand. The hands are then simultaneously moved forward and back at least twice with short deliberate movements as though prodding a reluctant individual.

cocaine: *n.* a white, crystalline substance used as a narcotic. *Cocaine can be a very harmful drug.*

SIGN: Thumb of vertical right **'EXTENDED A'** hand, palm facing left, is raised to each nostril, to simulate the sniffing of cocaine. (Alternatively, the tip of the thumb may simply move back and forth under the nostrils a couple of times as if passing something under the nose to be smelled.)

cochlear implant: *n.* a surgical procedure that involves the implantation of electrical impulses into the cochlea. *The introduction of* **cochlear implants** *created a lot of controversy.*

SIGN: Extended fingertips of right **'CLAWED V'** hand are tapped behind the right ear.

cock: *n.* a full-grown male of domestic fowl; a rooster. *We must arise when the* **cock** *crows.*

SIGN: Thumb of vertical right **'3'** hand, with palm facing left, is tapped against middle of forehead to represent rooster's comb.

cocktail: *n.* any mixed drink with an alcohol base. *My favourite* **cocktail** *is a gin and tonic.*

SIGN: Right **'CLAWED L'** hand is held in a horizontal position near the mouth with palm facing left. The wrist then rotates backward slightly to tip the hand upward so that it is in vertical position. Motion is repeated.

cocky: *adj.* very sure of oneself; too proud of oneself; conceited. *He has been very* **cocky** *since his promotion.*

SIGN: Horizontal **'CLAWED L'** hands are held with forefingers resting on either side of the forehead. The hands are then simultaneously thrust outward to indicate 'big-headness'.

code: *n.* a system of letters, figures, or words with arbitrary meanings. *This message is written in* **code** *so it will be hard to decipher.*

SIGN: Fingerspell **CODE**.

coerce: *v.* to force or to exert excessive pressure on someone to do or think something. *He was coerced to sign the document.*

SIGN: Vertical right **'C'** hand, palm facing forward/leftward, is placed on the back of the left **'STANDARD BASE'** hand and is thrust forward/leftward across the left hand as the wrist bends causing the right hand to hang palm-down over the left hand. (Alternatively, this sign may be formed without the use of the left hand.) ❖ SAME SIGN—**coercion**, *n.*

coffee: *n.* a hot beverage made from ground roasted coffee beans. *Bring me a cup of black coffee, please.*

SIGN #1: Horizontal right **'S'** hand, palm facing leftward but angled toward the body, is held on top of the horizontal left **'S'** hand, of which the palm faces right. The right hand then makes small, circular, counter-clockwise motions, as if grinding coffee beans.

OR

SIGN #2: Right **'C'** hand is held upright with palm facing forward/leftward, and is wobbled slightly.

cognition: See **knowledge** under **know** #1.

coherent: *adj.* logical, consistent, orderly or intelligible. *It is very difficult for profoundly Deaf children to develop coherent speech.*

SIGN: Vertical **'O'** (or **'FLAT O'**) hands are placed side by side, palms facing forward. Then they are moved apart and slightly upward as the fingers spread to form **'5'** hands.

coil: *n.* something that is wound in a connected series of loops. *We carry a coil of rope in our boat for emergencies.*

SIGN: Horizontal **'C'** hands, palms facing each other, are held apart and are simultaneously lowered firmly to indicate the circumference of the coil. Then the right **'BENT ONE'** hand, forefinger pointing down, is held above the left **'EXTENDED C'** hand and is circled clockwise several times. Signs vary according to 'what' is actually coiled, *e.g.*, snake, vine, wire, etc.

coin: *n.* a piece of metal stamped by government authority, to be used as money. *Do you have any coins in your pocket?*

SIGN: Thumb and forefinger of right **'F'** hand, palm left, represent a coin lying flat in the upturned palm of the left hand. To indicate plurality, the 'coin' rises and touches down at various places on the left palm. (**COIN** is frequently fingerspelled.)

coincide: *v.* to happen to occur at the same time. *Our workshop in Quebec City coincides with the Quebec Winter Carnival.*

SIGN #1: Left **'ONE'** hand is held at chest level with palm facing right, and forefinger pointing forward. Right **'ONE'** hand is held slightly higher with palm facing left, and is then turned downward to match the simultaneously downward turning left hand. Next, horizontal **'CROOKED 5'** hands, palms facing the body, are held just in front of the shoulders and are then moved toward each other until the fingers interlock. (ASL CONCEPT—**happen - match same time**.)
ALTERNATE SIGN—**coincidence**

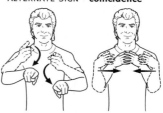

coincide: *v.* to agree or to be of the same opinion. *His views coincide with mine.*

SIGN #2: Left **'ONE'** hand is held at shoulder or face level with palm facing the body and forefinger pointing rightward while right **'ONE'** hand is held at the same level but off to the right of the body with palm facing left and forefinger pointing forward. The wrists then rotate inward to turn the palms down. Next, the hands stay where they are but assume horizontal **'CROOKED 5'** shapes with palms facing backward. The hands then move toward each other until the fingers interlock.
(ASL CONCEPT—**agree - match**.)

103

coincidence: *n.* an unexpected or unplanned sequence of events which appear to be related. *It was a **coincidence** that both of the lottery winners were from Moncton, New Brunswick.*

SIGN: Horizontal right **'S'** hand, palm facing left, moves forward to strike upright forefinger of left **'ONE'** hand, which is held with palm facing right.

Coke: *n.* trademark and abbreviation for Coca-Cola. *Coke is a popular carbonated drink.*

SIGN #1: Fingerspell **COKE**. (Alternatively, **Coke** in this context is sometimes signed. See **coke** #3.)

coke: *n.* a white, crystalline substance used as a narcotic. *Coke is an abbreviation for cocaine.*

SIGN #2: Thumb of vertical right **'EXTENDED A'** hand, palm facing left, is raised to each nostril, to simulate the sniffing of cocaine. (Alternatively, the tip of the thumb may simply move back and forth under the nostrils a couple of times as if passing something under the nose to be smelled.) **COKE** may be fingerspelled.

coke: *n.* cocaine taken by injection. *Using needles is a common practice among coke addicts.*

SIGN #3: Tip of forefinger of right **'FLAT L'** hand is poked into left upper arm to simulate a hypodermic syringe. Movement is repeated.

cold: *adj.* having no warmth. *It is cold and windy outside today.*

SIGN #1: **'A'** (or **'S'**) hands are held apart, palms facing each other, and are shaken, along with the shoulders, as if the signer is shivering.

cold: *n.* an acute viral infection of the upper respiratory passages. *She stayed home from work because she had a bad cold.*

SIGN #2: Thumb and forefinger of right **'A-INDEX'** (or **'G'**) hand are used to cover the nostrils and close slightly toward the tip of the nose as the hand is brought downward/forward a short way. The movement is repeated to simulate the wiping of the nose with a handkerchief.

collapse: *v.* to break down or cave in suddenly. *The floor of the burning building collapsed.*

SIGN #1: Fingers of **'CROOKED 5'** hands, palms down, interlock slightly and then drop down so that backs of fingers are almost touching.

collapse: *v.* (for a human) to fall down due to exhaustion, lack of strength, lack of oxygen, or trauma of some kind. *Having inhaled the toxic fumes in an unventilated room, he collapsed.*

SIGN #2: **'S'** hands are crossed at the wrists, left hand ahead of right hand, with left palm facing rightward/downward and right palm facing leftward/downward. As the head tilts rightward and the eyes close, the hands are drawn apart and the palms turned downward. ALTERNATE SIGN—**faint** #1

OR

SIGN #3: Left **'EXTENDED B'** hand is held in a fixed position with palm up and fingers pointing forward/rightward. Vertical right **'ONE'** hand is held above/behind left hand with palm facing forward/leftward. The head falls forward as the right forearm then drops forward/downward so that the right hand comes to rest palm-down in the palm of the left hand. (In this context, the right **'ONE'** hand represents a *person* who is *originally standing* and then falls over. Signs vary depending on whether or not someone is standing or sitting or whether the reference is to a person or an animal.)

collar: *n.* the part of a garment that fits around the neck and shoulders. *He was wearing a blue and white striped shirt with a plain white collar.*

SIGN: Thumb and forefinger of right **'C-INDEX'** hand are placed at the right shoulder and the hand is moved down along the collarbone with the palm facing the chest. (Signs vary according to the type of collar.)

colleague: *n.* a fellow worker, staff member, or a member of the same profession. *Dr. Banting and his colleague, Dr. Best, discovered insulin.*

SIGN: Fingerspell **COLLEAGUE**. (ASL users tend to sign rather than fingerspell **colleague**, but sign choice can vary considerably and often takes the form of an ASL phrase rather than just one sign.)

C O L L E A G U E

collect: *v.* to gather together or accumulate. *Caroline collects stamps.*

SIGN: Horizontal right **'SPREAD EXTENDED C'** hand is moved across upturned palm of left **'EXTENDED B'** hand in a circular, counter-clockwise 'gathering' motion, with the palm toward the body.
SAME SIGN—**collection**, *n.*

college: *n.* an institution providing higher or specialized education; an institution offering post-secondary education. *Several colleges in Canada offer sign language programs.*

SIGN: Horizontal left **'EXTENDED B'** hand is held in a fixed position with palm up and fingers pointing rightward/forward. Right **'EXTENDED B'** hand is placed palm down on left palm at right angles to it. The right hand then slides rightward across the left palm and spirals upward in a counter-clockwise direction until it is directly above the left hand, palm still down with fingers pointing leftward/forward.

collide: *v.* to crash against with a violent impact. *My car collided with a truck.*

SIGN: Horizontal **'S'** hands, palms facing the body, are brought together with force. (The handshapes for this sign vary.)
SAME SIGN—**collision**, *n.*

cologne: *n.* a liquid made of alcohol and various scented oils. *I like the smell of his cologne.*

SIGN: Fingers of right **'EXTENDED B'** hand are used to pat each cheek alternately. (This sign applies to cologne worn by *men* only. For that worn by *women*, see **perfume**.)

colon: *n.* a mark of punctuation used for a variety of specific purposes. *A colon (:) usually precedes a list.*

SIGN: Wrist of vertical right **'CLOSED X'** hand, palm forward, bends to thrust the hand forward in a pecking manner as it simulates the making of two dots, one below the other.

colour [*also spelled* **color**]: *n.* a visual perception resulting from the reflection of light. *The colours of the Canadian flag are red and white.*

SIGN #1: Fingertips of right **'5'** hand, with palm toward the body, are fluttered on the lips (or chin).

SIGN #2 [ATLANTIC]: Extended fingers of horizontal **'U'** hand, palm down, are placed on the upturned palm of the left **'EXTENDED B'** hand and are rubbed back and forth.

colourful: *adj.* vivid, rich and distinctive in colour. *She always wears colourful, flamboyant clothes.*

SIGN: **'5'** hands, palms facing backward and fingers fluttering, are brought toward the lips several times so that the fingertips lightly touch the mouth/chin with each movement.

column: *n.* an upright pillar, usually having a cylindrical shape. *We examined the intricate design around the base of the white marble column.*

SIGN #1: Horizontal **'C'** hands are held apart with palms facing each other. Then they are moved upward simultaneously. (The distance between the hands depends on the diameter of the column.)

column: *n.* a regular feature in a newspaper. *Have you read Ann Landers's column in today's newspaper?*

SIGN #2: Thumb and forefinger of right **'C-INDEX'** hand, palm facing left, are stroked downward across the right-facing palm of the left **'EXTENDED B'** hand.

column: *adj.* a narrow vertical section of print. *The accountant put the figures into one column.*

SIGN #3: Horizontal right **'CLAWED L'** hand with the palm facing away from the body, is brought down firmly in front of the chest.

coma: *n.* a state of unconsciousness from which a person cannot be aroused and which generally has a medical cause. *She has been in a coma since the car accident.*

SIGN: Fingerspell **COMA**.

comb: *v.* to use a toothed device to arrange or disentangle the hair. *Comb your hair before you have your picture taken.*

SIGN: Right **'SPREAD EXTENDED C'** hand, palm toward the head, is held at the right side of the head at an upright/forward angle, and is moved backward/downward twice as if combing the hair.

SAME SIGN—**comb**, *n.*

combat: *n.* an action fought between two forces. *The soldier was killed in combat.*

SIGN: **'BENT 4'** hands, are held slightly apart, palms facing downward, with right fingers pointing left and left fingers pointing right. Hands are then moved simultaneously to right and left twice.

ALTERNATE SIGN—**battle** #3

combine: *v.* to join or blend together. *If you combine red and yellow you will produce an orange shade.*

SIGN: **'CLAWED 5'** hands are held apart in front of the chest in an almost upright position but slanted slightly toward each other with palms facing the body. The forearms then move downward toward each other until the fingers mesh.

SAME SIGN—**combination**, *n.*

come: *v.* to move toward a specified place. *She will come early.*

SIGN #1: Right forearm is extended to the right with the **'ONE'** (or **'CROOKED ONE'**) hand palm up but slanted slightly toward the body and forefinger pointing rightward/forward. The forearm then moves toward the chest as the wrist bends, causing the forefinger to arc so that it eventually points to the body.

come: *v.* (to tell someone) to move toward a specified place. *Come and join the fun.*

SIGN #2: Right forearm is extended to the right with the **'EXTENDED B'** hand palm up but slanted slightly toward the body and fingers pointing rightward/forward. The forearm then moves toward the chest as the wrist bends.

come over: *v.* to come to someone's home or place of business for a visit or other specific purpose. *Come over tonight and we will discuss our plans for the holidays.*

SIGN: Right forearm is extended to the right with the **'BENT EXTENDED B'** hand held palm up. The forearm then moves toward the chest as the wrist bends, causing the palm to eventually face the body at a downward angle. (Two hands may be used for this sign.)

come to: *v.* to regain consciousness after fainting or passing out. *The robbers hurried because the guard, whom they had hit on the head, might come to any minute.*

SIGN: Thumbs of forefingers of **'CLOSED MODIFIED G'** (or **'CLOSED X'**) hands are placed at either cheek, and opened to form **'L'** (or **'CONTRACTED L'**) hands as they move outward a short distance from the face.

comedy: *n.* a light, amusing dramatic work. *Shakespeare's A Midsummer Night's Dream is a well-known comedy.*

SIGN: The two extended fingers of the vertical **'BENT EXTENDED U'** hand, palm toward the face, stroke the nose at least twice in a downward motion.

ALTERNATE SIGN—**clown around**

comet: *n.* a celestial body that orbits the sun and has a starlike nucleus and long, bright tail. *Seeing the comet through the telescope was very exciting.*

SIGN: Fingerspell **COMET**.

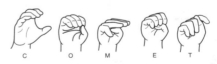

comfortable: *adj.* relaxed and at ease. *This chair is very* **comfortable.**

SIGN: Left **'CROOKED EXTENDED B'** hand is held palm down with fingers pointing rightward/forward at a downward angle while right **'CROOKED EXTENDED B'** hand is held palm down on left hand at right angles to it. The right hand is drawn rightward/backward across the back of the left hand, which moves out from under the right hand to take up a position on top of it so that the positioning of the hands is the reverse of their original position. The left hand is then drawn leftward/backward across the back of the right hand, which moves out from under the left hand to take up a position on top of it.
SAME SIGN—**comfort**, *n.*

comic: *adj.* characterized by wit or humour. *I enjoy the* **comic** *elements of the drama.*

SIGN: The two extended fingers of the vertical **'BENT EXTENDED U'** hand, palm toward the face, stroke the nose at least twice in a downward motion.
SAME SIGN—**comical**, *adj.*

comics: *n.* book, newspaper, or magazine sections featuring comic strips. *Do you read the* **comics** *in your daily newspaper?*

SIGN #1: Fingerspell **COMICS**.

SIGN #2 [ONTARIO]: Right **'Y'** hand is placed palm down on the back of the left **'STANDARD BASE'** hand and is moved back and forth as if rubbing the left hand.

comma: *n.* a mark of punctuation used to indicate a slight pause. *A* **comma** *is used to separate two ideas in a sentence.*

SIGN: Forefinger of vertical right **'CROOKED ONE'** (or **'BENT ONE'**) hand makes a quarter turn twist to the right to trace the outline of an imaginary apostrophe.

command: *v.* to give an order. *The general* **commanded** *his troops to open fire.*

SIGN #1: Tip of forefinger of vertical right **'ONE'** hand, palm forward, is placed on the lips and the hand is thrust forward. ❖

command: *v.* to be in control or authority over. *He* **commands** *a large army.*

SIGN #2: Horizontal **'X'** hands are held slightly apart with left palm facing right and right palm facing left. Then they are alternately moved backward and forward.

Commandments: *n.* the divine commands of the Old Testament. *Are you familiar with the Ten* **Commandments?**

SIGN: Left forearm is held at a semi-upright angle in front of the chest as the vertical right **'C'** hand, palm facing left, is placed against the outer edge of the left wrist and is lowered to the elbow.

commence: *v.* to start or cause to begin. *Graduation exercises will* **commence** *at 2:00 p.m. sharp.*

SIGN: Left **'5'** hand is held with palm facing right while forefinger of right **'ONE'** hand is inserted between first two fingers of left hand and twisted 180 degrees to the right.

commend: *v.* to praise or recommend. *You are to be* **commended** *for your remarkable achievements.*

SIGN: **'EXTENDED B'** hands, left palm facing upward and right palm facing downward, are brought together twice in a clapping motion.

commensurate: *adj.* corresponding in degree, amount, size, or proportion. *Your salary will be* **commensurate** *with your qualifications and experience.*

SIGN: **'CLAWED 5'** hands are held apart in front of the chest in an almost upright position but slanted slightly toward each other with palms facing the body. The forearms then move downward toward each other until the fingers mesh.

comment: *v.* to make a remark or express an opinion. *He would not comment on the outcome of the trial.*

SIGN: Tip of forefinger of vertical right **'4'** hand, palm facing left, is tapped twice against the chin. (**COMMENT** is frequently fingerspelled, particularly when using the expression **no comment**.)

commercial: *n.* an advertisement on radio or TV. *The TV program was interrupted by a commercial for dog food.*

SIGN #1: **'S'** hands, palms facing downward, are held slightly apart, with right in front of left. Right hand then strikes left hand and moves forward and back to strike it a second time.

commercial: *adj.* related to business or trade; done for profit. *He is looking for a new commercial enterprise.*

SIGN #2: Wrist of vertical right **'B'** hand, palm facing forward/leftward, is brushed back and forth against wrist of left **'STANDARD BASE'** hand.
ALTERNATE SIGN—**business** #2

commit: *v.* to perform or perpetrate (an error, misdemeanour or crime). *He promised never to commit another crime.*

SIGN #1: Fingerspell **COMMIT**. (This term is uncommon in ASL.)

commit: *v.* to pledge or ally oneself to an individual or a cause. *After careful considera-tion, he committed himself to the project.*

SIGN #2: Tip of forefinger of vertical right **'ONE'** hand, palm facing left, is held just under the lower lip. The hand is then moved at a forward/downward angle as the wrist rotates and the hand changes to an **'EXTENDED B'** shape, the palm firmly striking the left **'S'** hand which is held in a fixed position in front of the body with the palm facing rightward/downward. (Facial expression is important.)

commitment: *n.* an obligation, pledge, or promise. *He made a commitment to remain with the company for five years.*

SIGN: Tip of forefinger of vertical right **'ONE'** hand, palm facing left, is held just under the lower lip. The hand is then moved at a forward/downward angle as the wrist rotates and the hand changes to an **'EXTENDED B'** shape, the palm firmly striking the left **'S'** hand which is held in a fixed position in front of the body with the palm facing rightward/downward. (Facial expression is important.)

committee: *n.* a group of people appointed to perform a specified function. *She is a member of the nominating committee.*

SIGN #1: Thumbtip of vertical right **'EXTENDED C'** hand, palm facing left, is placed against the left shoulder. The hand is then moved in an arc to take up the same position at the right shoulder.
ALTERNATE SIGN—**group** #1

SIGN #2 [PACIFIC]: Left **'CROOKED 5'** hand is held in front of the chest with palm up but slanted toward the body slightly while tip of forefinger of vertical **'CROOKED 5'** hand, palm facing left, is held just in front of the mouth. The hands are then brought together as they close to form **'A'** hands with the right on top of the left, and palms facing.

common: *adj.* average, usual, or ordinary. *It is common for teenagers to defy their parents.*

SIGN #1: Right **'BENT U'** hand, palm down, is circled clockwise over the left **'STANDARD BASE'**, and the extended fingers are brought down to rest on it. (**COMMON** is frequently fingerspelled.)

common: *adj.* prevailing or widespread. *This is a common problem throughout the world.*

SIGN #2: **'Y'** hands, with palms facing down, are held apart in front of the chest and moved simultaneously in a wide counter-clockwise circle. (**COMMON** is frequently fingerspelled.)

common-law: *adj.* a term that denotes a marriage that is deemed to exist after a couple has lived together for some time. *His common-law wife inherited his estate.*

SIGN #1: Right horizontal **'EXTENDED C'** hand, palm toward the body, is tapped on the upper left arm once or twice. (**Common-law** is frequently fingerspelled **CL**.)

OR

SIGN #2: Horizontal **'S'** hands are held side by side with palms down. Forefingers and mid-fingers are flipped forward simultaneously to form horizontal **'BENT U'** hands. Motion is repeated.

common sense: *n.* sound and practical thinking. *Common sense tells us that very few things in life are free.*

SIGN: Right vertical **'EXTENDED C'** hand, palm toward the face, is held with fingertips touching the right side of the forehead. The hand is then quickly drawn forward/rightward as the fingers close to form an **'S'** handshape.

communicate: *v.* to exchange thoughts by speech, writing, or signing. *It is important for parents to communicate with their children.*

SIGN: Vertical **'C'** hands, with left palm facing right and right palm facing left, are moved back and forth simultaneously but in opposite directions, in front of the neck/chin area.
SAME SIGN—**communication**, *n.*

communism: *n.* a political movement based on the philosophy of Karl Marx. *Communism has been replaced by democracy in Russia.*

SIGN: Forefinger of right **'CROOKED ONE'** hand, palm facing forward/leftward but slanted downward, is tapped a few times on the upper edge of the thumb of the left **'C'** hand, which is held upright with palm facing rightward/forward.

community: *n.* a group of people brought together by common interests. *He is a highly respected member of the community.*

SIGN #1: **'SPREAD C'** hands are held upright and slightly apart with palms facing each other. The wrists then rotate forward, bringing the hands to a horizontal position.

community: *n.* the locality in which a group of people lives. *This community is made up largely of senior citizens.*

SIGN #2: Horizontal left **'S'** hand is held in a fixed position with palm rightward/backward. Right **'EXTENDED B'** hand, fingers pointing forward and palm down, rubs the top of the left hand as it moves in several counter-clockwise circles.
ALTERNATE SIGN—**area** #1

(Deaf) Community: *n.* a group of predominantly Deaf people who are drawn together by common needs, interests, and goals; a respect for each other's Deafness; and an inherent need/desire to communicate in ASL. *Deaf people become members of the Deaf Community by virtue of their attitude rather than because they are Deaf.*

SIGN #3: Vertical right **'ONE'** hand is held with tip of forefinger just in front of the right ear. The hand is then lowered so that the tip of the forefinger touches the right side of the mouth. Next, vertical **'EXTENDED B'** hands, left palm facing right and right palm facing left, are held so that their fingertips can be tapped together twice.

OR

SIGN #4: Vertical right **'ONE'** hand is held with tip of forefinger just in front of the right ear. The hand is then lowered so that the tip of the forefinger touches the right side of the mouth. Next, vertical **'EXTENDED B'** hands, left palm facing backward/rightward and right palm facing forward/leftward, are held with fingertips touching. The fingertips then move apart momentarily as the wrists rotate a quarter turn so that the left palm eventually faces forward/rightward while the right palm faces backward/leftward and the fingertips are reunited.

(Deaf) Community *(cont.)*

OR

SIGN #5: Vertical right **'ONE'** hand is held with tip of forefinger just in front of the right ear. The hand is then lowered so that the tip of the forefinger touches the right side of the mouth. Next, horizontal left **'W'** hand is held with palm facing right. Vertical right **'W'** hand is held above the left hand with palm facing left. The right hand then drops to a horizontal position so that it is resting on the left hand. (ASL CONCEPT—**Deaf - world**.)

commute: *v.* to travel regularly back and forth. *Caroline* **commutes** *to work by bus.*

SIGN: Horizontal right **'EXTENDED A'** hand is moved back and forth either from left to right with palm facing left, or forward and back with palm facing body. ❖

compact: *adj.* small. *We see more* **compact** *cars in North America now than we used to.*

SIGN: Horizontal **'EXTENDED B'** hands are held apart with palms facing each other and fingers pointing forward. They are then moved toward each other slightly a couple of times.

compact disc: *n.* a small disc on which sounds and/or images are recorded in a series of small metallic indentations enclosed in a synthetic thermoplastic material and read by an optical laser system. *She has every song he has recorded on* **compact disc**.

SIGN: Fingerspell **CD**.

companion: *n.* a comrade, associate, or someone who provides another with company. *She is looking for a* **companion** *for her housebound father.*

SIGN: **'A'** hands are held together, palms facing each other, and knuckles touching. Together, they are shaken or moved back and forth slightly.

ALTERNATE SIGNS—**friend** or **partner**

companionship: *n.* being with someone; fellowship. ***Companionship*** *can help to relieve loneliness.*

SIGN: **'A'** hands are held together, palms facing each other, and knuckles touching. Together, they are shaken or moved back and forth slightly.

company: *n.* a guest, or a number of guests. *I expect to have* **company** *for dinner tonight.*

SIGN #1: **'BENT V'** hands, palms toward the body and extended fingers pointing upward, are alternately circled forward. (Alternatively, **COMPANY** may be fingerspelled. See also **group** #1.)

company: *n.* a business enterprise. *He has his own construction* **company**.

SIGN #2: Fingerspell **CO**.

compare: *v.* to examine in order to note the similarities and differences of. *Many people* **compare** *him with his father.*

SIGN: Right **'BENT EXTENDED B'** hand is held close to the body in a virtually upright position, palm forward/leftward but slanted slightly downward while the left **'BENT EXTENDED B'** hand takes up a lower position farther forward than the right hand with palm facing that of the right hand. The wrists then simultaneously rotate a quarter turn to the right as the left hand moves closer to the body with palm facing forward/rightward but slanted slightly downward while the right hand moves to a lower position farther forward than the left hand with the palm facing that of the left hand. Motion is repeated.

SAME SIGN—**comparison**, *n.*

compass: *n.* an instrument used for determining direction. *It is important to carry a* **compass** *when you are hiking in wilderness areas.*

SIGN: Horizontal left **'EXTENDED B'** hand is held in a fixed position with palm up but angled toward the body and fingers pointing rightward/forward. Right **'ONE'** hand, palm facing left, is placed on the left palm with forefinger pointing forward/rightward but slanted upward. The right wrist then bends up and down, causing the hand to pivot so that the forefinger moves back and forth to simulate the action of a compass needle.

compassion: *n.* a feeling of pity for the misfortune of others. *A nurse must have compassion for her patients.*

SIGN: Right **'BENT MIDFINGER 5'** hand is held upright with palm facing forward but slanted downward slightly. It is then moved forward with circular motions to simulate the stroking of an imaginary person with the middle finger. Appropriate facial expression is important. (Alternatively, this sign may be made with two hands.)
SAME SIGN—**compassionate**, *adj.*

compatible: *adj.* capable of being used together without modification; well suited or matched; able to live together harmoniously. *Make sure the disks are compatible with that computer.*

SIGN: **'SPREAD EXTENDED C'** hands are held slightly apart in front of the chest, palms facing the body, and are brought together so that the fingers mesh.
SAME SIGN—**compatibility**, *n.*

compel: *v.* to force. *By using torture, the captors compelled their prisoner to tell the truth.*

SIGN: Vertical right **'C'** hand, palm facing forward/leftward, is placed on the back of the left **'STANDARD BASE'** hand and is thrust forward/leftward across the left hand as the wrist bends causing the right hand to hang palm-down over the left hand. (Alternatively, this sign may be formed without the use of the left hand.) ❖

compensate: *v.* to make amends for, or to counterbalance the effects of. *The company will compensate you for your efforts by giving you time off.*

SIGN #1: Horizontal **'F'** (or **'COVERED T'**) hands, left palm facing right and right palm facing left, are held so that the left is further from the chest than the right. Then their positions are simultaneously switched as the left hand moves back toward the body in an arc over the right hand while the right hand moves away from the body in an arc under the left hand.
SAME SIGN—**compensation**, *n.*, in this context.

compensate: *v.* to reimburse or to pay for. *The company will compensate you for your time and expenses.*

SIGN #2: Horizontal right **'FLAT O'** hand is held out in front of right shoulder with palm left. The forearm then moves downward/forward as the thumb slides along the fingertips to form an **'A'** hand. ❖
SAME SIGN—**compensation**, *n.*, in this context.

compete: *v.* to contend against for victory, profit or reward. *The teams are competing for the NHL championship.*

SIGN: **'A'** hands, palms facing, are held close to one another and moved alternately back and forth. This is a wrist movement.
SAME SIGN—**competition**, *n.*

competent: *adj.* having sufficient skill or knowledge for a specific purpose. *Alan is a competent artist.*

SIGN: Left **'EXTENDED B'** hand, palm facing right and fingers up, is grasped by right **'OPEN A'** hand. Then right hand is pulled forward sharply and closed to form an **'A'** hand.
SAME SIGN—**competence**, *n.*
ALTERNATE SIGN—**capable**

complain: *v.* to express dissatisfaction. *I will complain to the manager about the clerk's rudeness.*

SIGN: Right **'SPREAD C'** hand is held in a horizontal position as thumb and fingertips thump against chest. Thumping is sometimes repeated for emphasis or to indicate 'constant complaining'. Facial expression is important.
SAME SIGN—**complaint**, *n.*, but the movement is repeated.

complete: *v.* to finish. *He should complete his report soon.*

SIGN #1: Left horizontal **'BENT EXTENDED B'** hand is held in a fixed position with palm facing the body and fingers pointing rightward. Right horizontal **'EXTENDED B'** hand, palm facing left and fingers pointing forward, makes a chopping motion near the fingertips of the left hand.

OR

SIGN #2: Vertical **'5'** hands, palms facing the body, are held at chest level, and swung around, away from the body so that palms face down.

complete: *adj.* whole; having every necessary part. *He has a complete set of mechanic's tools.*

SIGN #3: Right **'EXTENDED B'** hand, palm down with fingers pointing forward/leftward, grazes top of horizontal left **'S'** hand as the right hand is firmly swept leftward.
ALTERNATE SIGN—**everything** #2

complex: *adj.* made up of many interconnected parts. *The Civil Service is a complex bureaucratic network.*

SIGN #1: **'CROOKED 5'** hands are held apart and almost upright with left palm facing rightward/downward and right palm facing leftward/downward. Crooked forefingers wiggle up and down as the hands move toward one another in front of the face, coming to rest when they have crossed slightly.

OR

SIGN #2: **'X'** hands are held apart and almost upright with left palm facing rightward/downward and right palm facing leftward/downward. The crooked forefingers wiggle up and down as the hands move toward one another in front of the face, coming to rest when they make contact in front of the nose with right hand directly behind left so that the hands appear to be crossed.
SAME SIGN—**complexity**, *n.*

complicate: *v.* to make something complex or perplexing. *Having two different versions of the story complicates the police investigation.*

SIGN: Horizontal **'SPREAD EXTENDED C'** hands are held, right above left, with palms facing each other. Then right hand moves in a counter-clockwise direction while left hand moves in the opposite direction.

complicated: *adj.* difficult to understand or analyze. *Computer instructions are often very complicated.*

SIGN: **'CROOKED 5'** hands are held apart and almost upright with left palm facing rightward/downward and right palm facing leftward/downward. Crooked forefingers wiggle up and down as the hands move toward one another in front of the face, coming to rest when they have crossed slightly.
ALTERNATE SIGN—**complex** #2

compliment: *v.* to express respect and admiration. *I would like to compliment you on your recent promotion.*

SIGN: **'EXTENDED B'** hands, palms facing each other, are clapped together.
SAME SIGN—**complimentary**, *adj.*, in this context.

complimentary: *adj.* given free, as a courtesy or for advertising purposes. *I received complimentary tickets for the hockey game.*

SIGN: **'F'** hands, left palm facing right and right palm facing left, are held upright with right hand directly behind left hand. Then they are simultaneously drawn apart as wrists rotate outward so that left palm faces rightward/forward while right palm faces leftward/forward.

comply [*or* **comply with**]: *v.* to act in accordance with rules or wishes. *We must comply with school policy.*

SIGN: Horizontal **'EXTENDED A'** hands, left palm facing right and right palm facing left, are held with the right hand behind and slightly above the left. The hands are then moved forward/downward together.

component: *n.* a constituent part of something more complex. *A component of the microphone will need to be replaced.*

SIGN: Horizontal left **'EXTENDED B'** hand is held in a fixed position with palm up but angled toward the body and fingers pointing rightward/forward while edge of horizontal right **'EXTENDED B'** hand, palm facing left, is placed on left palm and is drawn back toward the body.

compose: *v.* to make up or create. *He composed a short story for his creative writing class.*

SIGN: Tip of forefinger of vertical right **'4'** hand, palm facing left, is placed against the forehead and the hand is then pushed upward and forward slightly.

(be) composed of: *v.* to be made up of. *The team is composed of players with a lot of talent.*

SIGN #1: Right **'CONTRACTED 5'** hand, palm facing down, is circled in a clockwise direction over the opening of the horizontal left **'C'** hand whose palm faces right. Right hand is then closed to form a **'FLAT O'** hand of which the fingertips are inserted into the opening of the left hand.

composed: *adj.* calm, self-controlled. *She thought she would be nervous speaking in public, but she was quite composed.*

SIGN #2: **'5'** (or **'EXTENDED B'**) hands are held parallel with palms down and fingers pointing forward. The hands are then simultaneously moved a short distance up and down a couple of times.

composition: *n.* a story. *He wrote a composition about his dog.*

SIGN: Left **'CONTRACTED C'** (or **'OPEN 8'**) hand is held horizontally with palm facing right while right **'CONTRACTED C'** (or **'OPEN 8'**) hand is held upright with palm facing left. The hands are held close enough together to be loosely interlocked. They are then drawn apart, closed and returned several times, thus alternating between **'CONTRACTED C'** (or **'OPEN 8'**) and **'FLAT O'** (or **'8'**) shapes with each movement.

compound: *adj.* consisting of two or more parts. *"Baseball" is a compound word.*

SIGN #1: **'OPEN F'** hands are brought together so that the thumbs and forefingers are linked to form **'F'** hands.
ALTERNATE SIGN—**combine**

compound: *v.* to add to or to increase; to make worse. *His driving without a licence compounded the problem.*

SIGN #2: Vertical left **'BENT U'** hand is held in a fixed position with palm down and extended fingers pointing rightward/forward. Right **'U'** hand is held to the right of the left hand with palm left and extended fingers pointing forward. The right hand then moves in an upward/leftward arc as the wrist rotates leftward causing the palm to turn downward and the extended fingertips to come to rest on the backs of the extended fingers of the left hand.
ALTERNATE SIGN—**worse** #1

comprehend: *v.* to understand. *Sometimes it is hard to comprehend legal terms.*

SIGN: Vertical right **'S'** hand, with knuckles near right side of forehead, is changed to a **'ONE'** hand as the forefinger is flicked upward.
SAME SIGN—**comprehension**, *n.,* but the movement is repeated.

comprehensive: *adj.* having a broad scope or content. *His book is a comprehensive history of the oil industry in Alberta.*

SIGN: Right **'CONTRACTED 5'** hand, palm facing down, is circled widely in a clockwise direction over the opening of the horizontal left **'C'** hand whose palm faces right. Right hand is then closed to form a **'FLAT O'** hand of which the fingertips are inserted into the opening of the left hand.

compress: *v.* to press or squeeze together into a smaller space. *This machine will compress the body of a car into a small block of metal.*

SIGN: **'SPREAD EXTENDED C'** hands are held, palms facing, with the right above the left at right angles and the right is then slowly pressed downward toward the left.

comprised of: *v.* to consist of, or be made up of. *The executive committee is comprised of the president, vice-president, secretary and treasurer.*

SIGN: Right **'CONTRACTED 5'** hand is held palm down above horizontal left **'C'** hand of which the palm faces rightward/backward. The right hand is then closed to form a **'FLAT O'** hand as it plunges fingers first into the opening at the top of the left hand.

compromise: *v.* to reach an agreement by making concessions. *We can compromise and each pay for half of the damage.*

SIGN: Left **'ONE'** hand is held at chest level with palm facing right and forefinger pointing away from body. Right **'ONE'** hand, palm facing left, is held slightly higher and then turned downward to match the simultaneously downward-turning left hand.

compulsory: *adj.* absolutely essential or required by law. *Most civilized nations provide compulsory education for all children between the ages of 6 and 16.*

SIGN: Tip of forefinger of right **'X'** hand is placed in right-facing palm of left **'EXTENDED B'** hand. Together the hands are moved firmly toward the chest, giving the impression that the left hand is being tugged by the right forefinger.
ALTERNATE SIGN—**must**

compute: See **calculate**.

computer: *n.* an electronic device that processes data according to a set of instructions. *Do you own a home computer?*

SIGN #1: Vertical right **'C'** hand, palm facing forward/leftward slides back and forth along left forearm.

OR

SIGN #2: Thumb of vertical right **'EXTENDED C'** hand, palm facing left, is held at right side of forehead, and the forearm is moved very slightly back and forth a couple of times.

comrade: See **friend** #1 & #2.

con: *v.* to swindle, defraud, or fool. *He was able to con several people out of their life savings.*

SIGN #1: Vertical right **'A'** hand, with palm forward and slightly leftward, is knocked against forefinger of vertical left **'ONE'** hand whose palm faces right. ❖
ALTERNATE SIGN—**cheat**

con: *adv.* against. *The issue of mainstreaming was debated pro and con.*

SIGN #2: Left **'BENT EXTENDED B'** hand is held horizontally with fingers pointing to the right and palm facing the body but angled slightly rightward. Right **'EXTENDED B'** hand is held upright very close to the chest with palm facing left. The right hand then drops from the wrist until it is horizontal with fingertips forcefully striking left hand between the palm and the fingers.

conceal: *v.* to hide something from view; to prevent others from discovering something. *She was concealing a weapon under her coat.*

SIGN #1: Thumbnail of right **'A'** hand, palm facing left, is placed against the lips and the hand is then lowered and concealed under the downturned palm of the left **'CROOKED EXTENDED B'** hand.

conceal information: *v.* to hide information; to keep something secret. *The police believed that the man they had arrested was concealing information.*

SIGN #2: Vertical **'C'** hands are held together, left ahead of right, in front of the mouth with left palm facing rightward and right palm facing leftward. The hands are then simultaneously closed to form **'S'** hands.

concede [*or* **make a concession**]: *v.* to admit or acknowledge as true; to give up something, such as a right or privilege. *Finally she conceded that she had lied.*

SIGN: Right **'EXTENDED B'** hand is held with palm against chest, and is brought forward so that the palm faces upward at a slight angle toward the body. Alternatively, this sign may be made with two hands, beginning with one at either side of the chest.

conceited: *adj.* having an exaggerated opinion of oneself. *The conceited fellow thinks he is the best hockey player on the team.*

SIGN: Horizontal **'CLAWED L'** hands are held with forefingers resting on either side of the forehead. The hands are then simultaneously thrust outward to indicate 'big-headedness'.
SAME SIGN—**conceit**, *n.*

conceive: *v.* to think up or develop an idea. *The device known as the TTY was conceived by a Deaf man.*

SIGN #1: Tip of little finger of right **'I'** hand, palm toward the face, is placed on the right side of the forehead and is drawn forward/upward a brief distance.
ALTERNATE SIGN—**invent**

conceive: *v.* to imagine or to form a mental picture. *It is hard to conceive what the earth will be like in 100 years.*

SIGN #2: Tip of forefinger of right **'ONE'** hand touches centre of forehead. Then vertical **'S'** hands are held together, left in front of right, at centre of forehead with left palm facing right and right palm facing left. As the hands move apart, they open to form **'CROOKED 5'** hands.
ALTERNATE SIGN—**conceive** #1

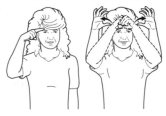

conceive: *v.* to become pregnant. *She and her husband want children very much but she is unable to conceive.*

SIGN #3: Horizontal **'5'** hands, with palms facing the body, are brought together in front of the abdomen so that the fingers of each hand interlock.

concentrate: *v.* to think very carefully. *It was hard to concentrate with all the distractions in the room.*

SIGN: Vertical **'EXTENDED B'** hands are held one at either side of the face, and are brought forward simultaneously.

SAME SIGN—**concentration**, *n.*, but the movement is repeated.

concept: *n.* a general idea. *The scientist explained the concept of nuclear fusion.*

SIGN: Tip of little finger of right **'I'** hand, palm toward the face, is placed on the right side of the forehead and is drawn forward/upward a brief distance. (Sometimes this sign is made with a **'C'** hand rather than an **'I'** hand, in which case the sign begins with the thumb of the **'C'** hand, palm facing left, placed on the right side of the forehead.)

conception: *n.* a notion, idea or plan. *He has a strange conception of Canadian winters.*

SIGN #1: Tip of forefinger of right **'ONE'** hand touches centre of forehead. Then vertical **'S'** hands are held together, left in front of right, at centre of forehead with left palm facing right and right palm facing left. As the hands move apart, they open to form **'CROOKED 5'** hands.

conception: *n.* the point at which an ovum is fertilized by a sperm in the womb. *It is about 40 weeks from conception to birth.*

SIGN #2: Horizontal **'5'** hands, with palms facing the body, are brought together in front of the abdomen so that the fingers of each hand interlock. Then, left **'5'** hand is held with palm facing right while forefinger of right **'ONE'** hand is inserted between first two fingers of left hand and twisted 180 degrees to the right. (ASL CONCEPT—**pregnant - start**.)

concern: *v.* to relate to or affect. *Please pay attention because this concerns you.*

SIGN #1: Horizontal left **'FLAT C'** hand is held in a fixed position with palm facing right. Right **'CONTRACTED C'** hand is held above left hand and slightly closer to the body with palm down and fingers pointing forward. As the right hand is thrust forward/downward, the fingers come together to form a **'FLAT O'** shape which is inserted into the opening at the top of the left hand.

ALTERNATE SIGNS—**about** #1, #2 & #3

concern: *n.* business; something that affects a person. *This is none of your concern so please stay out of it.*

SIGN #2: Wrist of right upright **'B'** hand, palm facing forward/leftward, is brushed back and forth against wrist of left **'STANDARD BASE'** hand.

concerned: *adj.* worried or anxious. *People were concerned about the high rate of unemployment.*

SIGN #1: Tips of midfingers of horizontal **'BENT MIDFINGER 5'** hands, palms toward the body, are tapped alternately on either side of the chest. This sign is accompanied by a concerned facial expression.

ALTERNATE SIGN—**anxious** #1

OR

SIGN #2: Vertical **'ONE'** hands are held, one at either side of the face with palms facing backward, and are alternately circled in front of the face. From the signer's perspective, the left hand appears to move clockwise while the right hand moves counter-clockwise. This sign is accompanied by a concerned facial expression.

concerning: *prep.* about or regarding. *They are discussing problems concerning the safety of children.*

SIGN: Left **'BENT ONE'** hand, palm facing right and forefinger pointing right, remains fixed while forefinger of right **'BENT ONE'** hand circles the left forefinger in a clockwise direction.

REGIONAL VARIATION—**about** #2 & #3

concert: *n.* a live musical performance. *The concert will feature several jazz musicians.*

SIGN: Horizontal right **'EXTENDED B'** hand is positioned above left forearm with palm facing leftward/backward. The right wrist makes slight back and forth rotations so that the palm alternates between being angled slightly upward and being angled slightly downward. (**CONCERT** is frequently fingerspelled.) See **drama** to refer to a staged theatrical performance as connoted by **concert** in the following sentence: *The school Christmas concert will begin at 7:30 p.m.*

concession: *n.* a small business allowed to operate in a certain place. *He bought a hot dog at a small concession in the park.*

SIGN: Vertical **'MODIFIED O'** hand, palm facing the body, is brought toward the mouth so that the fingertips touch the lips. Next, **'CONTRACTED B'** hands are held parallel with palms down as the wrists bend simultaneously to move the hands back and forth a couple of times. (ASL CONCEPT—**food - sell**.) Signs vary depending on the nature of the product being sold. (For **concession** meaning something given up or conceded, see **concede**.)

concise: *adj.* brief and to the point. *He gave an excellent, concise report.*

SIGN: **'SPREAD C'** hands are held horizontally and slightly apart, right above left, with left palm facing right and right palm facing left. Then both are closed to form **'S'** hands as they move toward one another and the right hand is brought down to rest on top of the left.
ALTERNATE SIGN—**short** #1

conclude: *v.* to come to an end. *Many speakers conclude their speeches with jokes.*

SIGN #1: Horizontal left **'EXTENDED B'** hand is held in a fixed position with palm facing the body. Right **'EXTENDED B'** hand is held at right angles to left hand with palm down as it moves rightward along the top edge of the left hand until it reaches the fingertips, whereupon the right wrist rotates clockwise, thus turning the palm leftward as the right hand is lowered straight down.

conclude: *v.* to deduce or decide by reasoning. *What did you conclude from the leadership debate?*

SIGN #2: **'F'** hands, with palms facing each other, are held apart in front of chest and are simultaneously lowered.

conclusion: *n.* the end; the close; the last part. *She enjoyed reading the book but was disappointed with the conclusion.*

SIGN: Horizontal left **'I'** hand is held with palm facing the body at a rightward angle and little finger pointing forward/rightward. Vertical right **'I'** hand, with palm facing leftward/backward, is held to the right of and above the left hand. The right hand is then lowered so that the tip of the little finger strikes the tip of the little finger of the left hand.

concrete: *n.* construction material that hardens into a solid, stone-like mass. *They poured the concrete for their new driveway.*

SIGN #1: Tip of forefinger of right **'CROOKED ONE'** hand, palm toward the body, is tapped against the upper front teeth.

concrete: *adj.* pertaining to something that is real and easy to understand, as opposed to something abstract. *Young children like to play with concrete objects that can be physically manipulated.*

SIGN #2: Forefinger of vertical right **'ONE'** hand, palm facing left, is held against the lips and the hand is moved sharply forward. (**CONCRETE** may be fingerspelled.)

concur: *v.* to agree; to be of the same opinion. *Researchers concur that ASL is a complex language.*

SIGN: Left **'ONE'** hand is held at chest level with palm facing right and forefinger pointing away from body. Right **'ONE'** hand, palm facing left, is held slightly higher and then turned downward to match the simultaneously downward-turning left hand.

condense: *v.* to reduce in volume or size. *Please condense this information into one paragraph.*

SIGN: **'SPREAD C'** hands are held horizontally and slightly apart, right above left, with left palm facing right and right palm facing left. Then both are closed to form **'S'** hands as the right is brought down to rest on top of the left.

condescend: See **look down on**.

condition: *n.* situation; circumstances. *Under no condition are you to leave the house without permission.*

SIGN #1: Fingerspell **CONDITION**. (A simple word for sign translation is not possible in this case. The concept of **condition** in this context is generally expressed in ASL by using a phrase rather than a single sign.)

condition: *n.* state of health or physical fitness. *Olympic athletes need to be in top condition.*

SIGN #2: **'BENT 5'** hands, with fingertips on either side of chest and palms facing the body, are drawn forward to form **'S'** hands. (Sign choice depends largely on the object whose condition is being referred to. This sign would not be appropriate when referring to the condition of an inanimate object. **CONDITION** is frequently fingerspelled.)

condolence: *n.* expression of sympathy. *We did not attend the funeral, but we sent our condolences.*

SIGN: Right **'A'** (or **'EXTENDED A'**) hand, palm facing the body, is rubbed on the chest with a circular motion which, in the eyes of onlookers, appears clockwise.
ALTERNATE SIGN—**sympathy** #2

condom: *n.* a rubber sheath worn on the penis during sexual intercourse to prevent conception and/or infection. *It is wise to use a condom to avoid sexually transmitted diseases.*

SIGN: Side of crooked forefinger of vertical right **'X'** hand is tapped a couple of times against right side of chin with palm facing leftward/forward. The wrist then rotates forward as the hand drops, bringing the crooked forefinger down so that it hooks the tip of the forefinger of the vertical left **'ONE'** hand. The right crooked forefinger then slides down the length of the left forefinger. (ASL CONCEPT— **rubber - sheath**.) Alternatively, only the second part of this sign may be used. **CONDOM** is frequently fingerspelled.

condominium: *n.* a residential complex in which apartments or houses are individually owned but common areas are cooperatively maintained. *She owns a three-bedroom condominium with an ocean view.*

SIGN: Fingerspell **CONDO**.

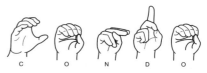

conduct: *n.* behaviour. *Her conduct during the interview was inappropriate.*

SIGN #1: **'SPREAD C'** hands are held parallel with palms down and are simultaneously swung from side to side.

conduct: *v.* to direct or handle. *In the president's absence, the vice president will conduct the meetings.*

SIGN #2: Horizontal **'X'** hands are held slightly apart with left palm facing right and right palm facing left. Then they are alternately moved backward and forward.

cone: *n.* anything that tapers from a circular section to a point. *She prefers ice cream in a cone rather than in a dish.*

SIGN: Fingerspell **CONE**. (Sometimes **cone** is signed, but sign selection depends on the size and shape of the cone.)

confederation: *n.* an alliance of political units, provinces, states, etc. *Confederation in 1867 united Upper and Lower Canada.*

SIGN: **'F'** hands with thumbs and forefingers interlocked, and palms facing each other, are moved in a complete circle in front of the body using a counter-clockwise motion.

confer: *v.* to consult together or discuss. *The executive will confer and will reach a decision by Monday.*

SIGN: Forefinger of horizontal right **'ONE'** hand, palm toward the body, is tapped several times on the upturned palm of the left **'EXTENDED B'** hand, of which the fingers are pointing rightward/forward.

conference: *n.* a meeting with a planned agenda. *He reserved the boardroom for our conference.*

SIGN: **'CONTRACTED 5'** hands are held virtually upright at a slight forward angle with palms facing each other. The fingers then come together to form **'FLAT O'** hands with fingertips of each hand touching those of the other. Motion is repeated.

ALTERNATE SIGN—**convention**

confess: *v.* to admit or concede to be true. *He finally confessed his guilt.*

SIGN #1: Right **'EXTENDED B'** hand is held with palm against chest, and is brought forward so that the palm faces upward at a slight angle toward the body. Alternatively, this sign may be made with two hands, beginning with one at either side of the chest.

OR

SIGN #2: Horizontal **'S'** hands, palms toward the body, are held together with the left hand against the chest and the right hand on top of the left but farther forward than the left hand as if the hands were holding onto a pole at a forward/upward angle. The hands are then flung forward as they open to form **'CROOKED 5'** hands with the palms facing upward, but still slanted toward the body slightly.

SAME SIGN—**confession**, *n.*

confidence: *n.* trust in a person or thing; belief in someone's abilities. *I have great confidence in my supervisor.*

SIGN #1: **'SPREAD EXTENDED C'** hands are held with palms toward the body at an upward angle, the left hand close to the chest and the right hand just above/ahead of the left. The hands are then thrust forward as they are snapped shut to form **'S'** hands.

SAME SIGN—**confident**, *adj.*

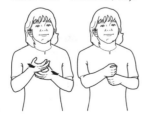

(in) confidence: *adv.* secretly; with the expectation that information shared will not be passed on to anyone else. *He told her about the problem in confidence.*

SIGN #2: Vertical **'C'** hands are held together, left ahead of right, in front of the mouth with left palm facing rightward and right palm facing leftward. The hands are then simultaneously closed to form **'S'** hands.

ALTERNATE SIGN—**confidential**

confidential: *adj.* private; to be kept secret. *All the letters in this file are confidential.*

SIGN: Right **'A'** hand is brought to the lips with the thumb pointed upward and the palm facing left. Then the lips are touched twice with the thumbnail.

ALTERNATE SIGN—**in confidence**

confine: *v.* to keep within limitations; to restrict. *She was confined to a liquid diet.*

SIGN #1: **'BENT EXTENDED B'** hands are held apart, right above left, with palms facing the body, but the left palm slanted slightly rightward while the right palm is slanted slightly leftward. The wrists then rotate to swing the hands into a position whereby the left palm faces forward at a rightward angle while the right hand faces forward at a leftward angle.

confine: *v.* to keep within a certain limited space. *He was confined to his bedroom for the rest of the evening.*

SIGN #2: Vertical right **'Y'**, palm facing forward/rightward is thrust forward at a rightward angle. (Sign choice depends entirely on context.)

confirm: *v.* to make sure of certain arrangements; to prove to be correct or valid. *Always call and confirm your international flights.*

SIGN: Tip of forefinger of vertical right **'ONE'** hand, palm facing left, is held just under the lower lip. The hand is then moved at a forward/downward angle as the wrist rotates and the hand changes to an **'EXTENDED B'** shape, the palm firmly striking the left **'S'** hand which is held in a fixed position in front of the body with the palm facing rightward/downward.

SAME SIGN—**confirmation**, *n.*

ALTERNATE SIGN—**check** #1

confiscate: *v.* to seize by way of a penalty. *The government confiscated his property.*

SIGN: Right **'SPREAD C'** hand is held palm down at chest level and is then closed to form an **'S'** hand as it is thrust forward. Alternatively, this sign may be made with two hands held apart in front of the chest.

conflict: *n.* opposition between ideas, interests, etc.; clash; controversy. *The conflict between French and English speaking Canadians needs to be resolved.*

SIGN: **'ONE'** hands, palms toward the chest and forefingers pointing toward each other at an upward angle, are held slightly apart and then thrust toward each other so the forefingers cross with the left one in front of the right.

conform: *v.* to comply in behaviour. *The committee members will conform to the new by-laws.*

SIGN: Both **'CONTRACTED 5'** hands, palms down, are brought toward the chest while they are being closed to form **'FLAT O'** hands, with fingertips touching the body.
ALTERNATE SIGN—**comply**

---

confound: See **confuse**.

confront: *v.* to face boldly. *He confronted his employer about a raise.*

SIGN: Vertical left **'EXTENDED B'** hand is held in a fixed position with palm toward face. Vertical right **'EXTENDED B'** hand, palm forward, is moved forward to stop near, but not touching the left hand. ❖

confuse: *v.* to perplex, mix up, or make things unclear. *Please do not confuse me.*

SIGN #1: Horizontal **'SPREAD EXTENDED C'** hands are held, right above left, with palms facing each other. Then right hand moves in a counter-clockwise direction while left hand moves in the opposite direction. This sign is accompanied by a look of confusion.
SAME SIGN—**confused**, *adj.*, or **confusion**, *n.*

OR

SIGN #2: Vertical right **'CROOKED 5'** hand is held against right side of forehead with palm facing left while left **'CROOKED 5'** hand is held palm-up in front of left side of chest. The arms are then simultaneously moved rightward/ upward as both wrists rotate rightward a quarter turn so that the right palm faces the body at a slight downward angle while the left palm faces rightward/forward. This sign is accompanied by a look of confusion.
SAME SIGN—**confused**, *adj.*, or **confusion**, *n.*

congenial: *adj.* pleasant and agreeable. *They are a very congenial couple so we enjoy their company.*

SIGN: **'5'** hands, palms facing backward, move backward with fingers fluttering until they come to rest close to either side of the face.

congenitally: *adv.* describing a condition of birth. *Angela is congenitally Deaf.*

SIGN: Horizontal **'EXTENDED B'** hands are held in front of the abdomen, palms facing the body, with the back of the right hand resting against the left palm. Then the right hand is curved down and under the left until its palm faces downward.

congratulate: *v.* to praise or express pleasure toward someone for his/her achievement(s) or good fortune. *We congratulated the members of the graduating class.*

SIGN: The hands are clasped together and shaken back and forth in an upright position in front of the chest.
SAME SIGN—**congratulations**, *n.*

connect: *v.* to join or be linked with. *The wires should be connected to the battery.*

SIGN: **'OPEN F'** hands are brought together so that the thumbs and forefingers are linked to form **'F'** hands. ❖
SAME SIGN—**connection**, *n.*

connote: *v.* to imply an idea other than the literal meaning. *'Mother' means a female parent but it also **connotes** love, care and tenderness.*

SIGN: Horizontal left **'EXTENDED B'** hand is held in a fixed position with palm facing right while tip of forefinger of right palm-down **'BENT V'** hand is jabbed into the left palm. The right hand then moves away from the left hand as the right wrist rotates a quarter turn clockwise, and the middle fingertip is jabbed into the left palm.

SAME SIGN—**connotation,** *n.*

conquer: *v.* to overcome or surmount an obstacle; to beat or defeat. *The Allies were able to **conquer** Germany in 1945.*

SIGN: Vertical right **'S'** hand, palm facing forward, is curved downward from the wrist across the extended finger of the left **'ONE'** hand, which is held horizontally with the palm facing downward. ❖

cons: *n.* negative considerations about a specific matter. *We listed the pros and **cons** of the decision.*

SIGN: Edge of forefinger of horizontal right **'BENT ONE'** hand is rested against the forward-facing palm of the vertical left **'EXTENDED B'** hand and both hands are simultaneously lowered.

conscience: *n.* the sense of right and wrong that governs a person's thoughts or actions. *Her **conscience** forced her to reveal the truth.*

SIGN: Side of forefinger of right **'ONE'** hand, palm facing downward, is tapped twice against left side of chest.

conscious: *adj.* awake. *He was fully **conscious** during the surgery.*

SIGN: Vertical **'C'** hands, with palms facing each other, are brought up so tips of thumbs touch either side of face at the cheekbones.

conscious of: *adj.* aware of. *She was **conscious of** the fact that someone was following her.*

SIGN: Right **'BENT EXTENDED B'** hand, palm toward the face, is brought toward the head so that the fingertips touch the forehead.

consecutive: *adj.* following a chronological sequence without interruption. *The streets and avenues are numbered in **consecutive** order.*

SIGN: Left **'5'** hand is held with palm facing the body and fingers pointing rightward/upward. Right **'DOUBLE CONTRACTED L'** hand is held with back against left thumb and palm facing the body. Right hand then moves rightward in an arc across fingertips of left hand while opening and closing several times, thus alternating between a **'DOUBLE CONTRACTED L'** shape and a **'CLOSED DOUBLE MODIFIED G'**. (Spatial positioning of this sign varies a great deal. The right hand is often used alone, and while the handshape and movement remain generally the same, the position and direction vary depending on precisely what it is that is consecutive.)

ALTERNATE SIGN—**(put) in order**

consent: *v.* to give approval or permission. *His father **consented** to his sister's marriage.*

SIGN: **'K'** hands, palms down, are held apart, extended fingers pointing downward, and are then flicked upward from the wrist so that the hands are held in either a horizontal or upright position.

SAME SIGN—**consent,** *n.*

ALTERNATE SIGN—**allow** #2

consequence: *n.* a conclusion, result, or effect. *What was the **consequence** of your protest?*

SIGN: **'ONE'** hands, palms facing each other, are held slightly apart, fingers pointing away from the body, and are turned over so that the palms face down. (ASL users think of a 'consequence' as something that happens afterward; the sample sentence is syntactically different than it would appear in ASL: *PROTEST, WHAT HAPPEN?* There would be only two signs: **protest + happen**. Facial expression would signal that the sentence is a question.)

consequently: *adv.* hence; thus; so. *He has been working a lot of overtime; consequently, he does not have much free time.*

SIGN: **'5'** hands are held apart with palms toward the body and fingertips of each hand pointing toward those of the other hand, yet angled slightly upward as well. Then as the head tilts to one side, the hands are simultaneously curved forward/downward from the wrists so the palms are facing up. This sign is often held as the signer pauses between thoughts.

conserve: *v.* to save or protect from harm or loss. *We must conserve our natural resources.*

SIGN: Left **'V'** hand is held in a fixed position with palm facing chest and extended fingers pointing upward/rightward. Right **'V'** hand is held just ahead of left hand with palm facing chest and extended fingers pointing upward/leftward while tapping a couple of times against the fingers of the left hand.
SAME SIGN—**conservation**, *n.*

consider: *v.* to think carefully about something. *One should consider the consequences before dropping out of school.*

SIGN: Vertical **'ONE'** hands are held, one at either side of the face with palms facing backward, and are alternately circled in front of the face. From the signer's perspective, the left hand appears to move clockwise while the right hand moves counter-clockwise.

considerate: *adj.* kind and thoughtful toward others. *It was very considerate of you to visit me in the hospital.*

SIGN: Horizontal **'BENT EXTENDED B'** hands, palms facing each other, are alternately circled forward around each other.
ALTERNATE SIGN—**thoughtful** #2

consist of: *v.* to be composed of. *Most cities consist of many ethnic communities.*

SIGN: Right **'CONTRACTED 5'** hand, palm facing down, is circled widely in a clockwise direction over the opening of the horizontal left **'C'** hand whose palm faces right. Right hand is then closed to form a **'FLAT O'** hand of which the fingertips are inserted into the opening of the left hand.

consistency: *n.* the texture of a given substance; firmness; degree to which a substance holds or sticks together. *When the mixture is the right consistency, put it in the refrigerator.*

SIGN: Horizontal right **'CROOKED L'** hand is held, palm toward the body, with tips of forefinger and thumb at either side of the mouth. The wrist then bends slowly, causing the hand to move forward so that the palm is slanted upward. (For **consistency**, meaning steadiness or the continuation of a certain course of action, see **consistent**.)

consistent: *adj.* showing steadiness; continuing to follow the same course of action. *Parents should be consistent in disciplining their children.*

SIGN: **'EXTENDED A'** hands are held side by side with palms facing forward/downward and right thumbtip pressing against left thumbnail as the hands are purposefully and repeatedly moved forward and back a short distance.

consistent with: *adj.* in harmony with. *You should choose furniture that is consistent with the style of your house.*

SIGN: **'CLAWED 5'** hands are held apart in front of the chest in an almost upright position but slanted slightly toward each other with palms facing the body. The forearms then move downward toward each other until the fingers mesh.

console: *v.* to comfort (someone). *She consoled the injured boy.*

SIGN: Left **'CROOKED EXTENDED B'** hand is held palm down with fingers pointing rightward/forward at a downward angle while right **'CROOKED EXTENDED B'** hand is held palm down on left hand at right angles to it. The right hand is drawn rightward/backward across the back of the left hand, which moves out from under the right hand to take up a position on top of it so that the positioning of the hands is the reverse of their original position. The left hand is then drawn leftward/backward across the back of the right hand, which moves out from under the left hand to take up a position on top of it.

consonant: *n.* any letter of the alphabet other than a vowel. *There are 21 consonants in the English alphabet.*

SIGN: Fingerspell **CONSONANT**.

C O N S O N A N T

conspiracy: *n.* a plot to do something evil or illegal. *There was a conspiracy to assassinate the president.*

SIGN: Right **'A'** hand is brought to the lips with the thumb pointed upward and the palm facing left. Then the lips are touched twice with the thumbnail. Next, horizontal **'EXTENDED B'** hands, palms facing each other, are held parallel in front of the left side of the body and are simultaneously moved rightward. (ASL CONCEPT—**secret - plan**.)

constant: *adj.* incessant; continual. *He lives in constant fear of the Mafia.*

SIGN #1: **'EXTENDED A'** hands are held side by side with palms facing forward/downward and right thumbtip pressing against left thumbnail as the hands are purposefully and repeatedly moved forward and back a short distance.

constant: *n.* something that is invariable or unchanging. *Monthly visits from his grandmother were the only constants in his life.*

SIGN #2: **'Y'** hands are held parallel with palms forward and are moved very slightly but firmly forward.

constipation: *n.* infrequent or difficult evacuation of the bowels. *Drinking fruit juice may help to relieve constipation.*

SIGN: **'ONE'** hands are held in front of chest with the right higher than the left, and both palms facing down. Then the right forefinger is brought down vigorously to strike the left forefinger at right angles to it. Next, horizontal left **'S'** hand is held in a fixed position with palm facing right and enclosing thumb of horizontal right **'5'** (or **'EXTENDED A'**) hand, of which the palm faces left. Then the right hand is pulled down sharply. (ASL CONCEPT—**can't - bowel movement**.)

constituency: *n.* an area represented by an elected legislator. *The voters in his constituency were very supportive during the election campaign.*

SIGN: Right **'5'** hand, palm down, is circled in a counter-clockwise motion.

ALTERNATE SIGN—**region**

constituent: *n.* a citizen represented by an elected legislator; someone, especially a voter, living in a specific constituency. *She has the support of constituents in her riding.*

SIGN: Joined thumb and forefinger of horizontal right **'F'** hand, palm down, appear to peck at the top of the horizontal left **'S'** hand, whose palm faces right. Agent Ending (see p. LIV) may follow.

ALTERNATE SIGN—**people**

For **constituent** meaning component or part, see **component**.

constitute: *v.* to comprise; to take the form of. *Armed robbery constitutes a very serious crime.*

SIGN: Horizontal left **'EXTENDED B'** hand is held in a fixed position with palm facing right while tip of forefinger of right palm-down **'BENT V'** hand is jabbed into the left palm. The right hand then moves away from the left hand as the right wrist rotates a quarter turn clockwise, and the middle fingertip is jabbed into the left palm. (Signs vary according to context.)

constitution: *n.* the fundamental principles of a society or state. *Organizations usually have* **constitutions** *and by-laws.*

SIGN: Left forearm is held at a semi-upright angle in front of the chest as the vertical right **'C'** hand, palm facing left, is placed against the outer edge of the left wrist and is lowered to the elbow.

construct: *v.* to build or assemble. *They will* **construct** *a new bridge across the Fraser River.*

SIGN: Fingers of **'BENT EXTENDED B'** (or **'BENT EXTENDED U'** or **'U'**) hands, palms facing each other, are alternately slid up from under to be placed on top of one another.
SAME SIGN—**construction**, *n.*

consult: *v.* to seek information (from a book). *You may* **consult** *the reference books for an answer to the question.*

SIGN #1: Left **'EXTENDED B'** hand is held in a fixed position with fingers pointing forward and palm facing rightward but slanted upward. Thumb of right **'EXTENDED A'** hand, palm down, is jabbed backward into left palm a few times as right forearm moves in small clockwise circles.

consult: *v.* to seek professional advice from. *You should* **consult** *a lawyer before you buy that house.*

SIGN #2: Vertical right **'ONE'** hand, palm facing forward is moved firmly forward and slightly downward as the forefinger retracts to form an **'X'** hand. Next, fingertips of right **'FLAT O'** hand rest on back of left **'STANDARD BASE'** hand. Right hand is then thrust forward as it opens slightly to form a **'CONTRACTED 5'** hand. (ASL CONCEPT—**ask - advice**.)

consult: *v.* to exchange views or deliberate. *The architect* **consulted** *with the builder.*

SIGN #3: Forefinger of horizontal right **'ONE'** hand, palm toward the body, is tapped several times on the upturned palm of the left **'EXTENDED B'** hand, of which the fingers are pointing rightward/forward.

consume: *v.* to eat or drink. *The children* **consume** *two loaves of bread every day.*

SIGN #1: Vertical right **'MODIFIED O'** hand, palm facing the body, is brought toward the mouth so that the fingertips touch the lips.

consume: *v.* to use up. *Canadians* **consume** *more fuel than people who live in warmer climates.*

SIGN #2: Vertical right **'U'** hand, palm facing forward/leftward, is circled clockwise just above left **'STANDARD BASE'** hand two or three times with the heel of its palm striking the back of the left hand each time. This sign may be made without the left hand.

consume: *v.* to destroy. *The entire house was* **consumed** *by fire.*

SIGN #3: Left **'CLAWED 5'** hand is held palm-up while right **'CLAWED 5'** hand is held palm-down to the right and above/ahead of left hand. The hands close to form **'A'** hands as they are brought together and just past each other, the knuckles of the right hand grazing those of the left. The knuckles brush against each other again as the left hand moves firmly backward/leftward and the right hand moves firmly rightward/forward.

consumer: *n.* a person who pays to use a product or service. *All videotapes should be captioned for the benefit of the Deaf* **consumer**.

SIGN: Fingerspell **CONSUMER**.

(time-)consuming: See **time-consuming**.

contact: *v.* to get in touch with. *How can I* **contact** *him?*

SIGN #1: Vertical **'BENT MIDFINGER 5'** hands are held with palms facing each other. Then tips of middle fingers are tapped against one another a couple of times.

(be in) contact with: *v.* in association with. *If you have* **been in contact with** *a contagious disease, you should inform your doctor.*

SIGN #2: Vertical **'BENT MIDFINGER 5'** hands are held with palms facing each other. Then tips of middle fingers are tapped against one another a couple of times.

contact lens: *n.* a lens that is placed directly on the surface of the eye to correct vision defects. *Sometimes it is uncomfortable to wear contact lenses.*

SIGN: Right **'BENT MIDFINGER 5'** hand is brought close to each eye alternately with the palm toward the face. (The fingerspelled abbreviation **CL** is frequently used rather than a sign.)

contagious: *adj.* capable of being passed on or spread by direct contact. *Influenza is a highly contagious disease.*

SIGN: Thumbs and forefingers of **'F'** hands are interlocked, palms facing each other, as the hands are moved directly forward from the chest.
ALTERNATE SIGN—**widespread**

contain: *v.* to hold or include. *This book contains a lot of useful information.*

SIGN: Right **'CONTRACTED 5'** hand, palm facing down, is circled widely in a clockwise direction over the opening of the horizontal left **'C'** hand whose palm faces right. Right hand is then closed to form a **'FLAT O'** hand of which the fingertips are inserted into the opening of the left hand.

container: *n.* a square or rectangular shaped object capable of holding or storing. *Please bring me a container for these leftovers.*

SIGN #1: With a slight but deliberate downward thrust horizontal **'EXTENDED B'** hands are held parallel, with palms facing each other and fingers pointing forward. Then the hands take on a **'BENT EXTENDED B'** shape as they are swung inward with a slight downward thrust again, and the right hand positioned ahead of the left, both palms facing the body.

container: *n.* a cylindrical object capable of holding or storing. *Please fill this container with juice.*

SIGN #2: Horizontal right **'C'** hand, palm facing left, is placed on upturned palm of left **'EXTENDED B'** hand. Right hand is then moved upward.

contaminate: *v.* to pollute or make impure. *Factory smoke contaminates the atmosphere.*

SIGN: Right **'MODIFIED 4'** hand is held under chin with palm down, as the fingers flutter. Facial expression must convey displeasure.
SAME SIGN—**contamination**, *n.*

contemplate: *v.* to think about intently; to consider. *She contemplated the question before she answered it.*

SIGN: Vertical **'FLAT O'** hands are held just in front of either side of the forehead with palms facing backward and fingers rapidly fluttering as the hands move in small circles. From the signer's perspective, the left hand moves clockwise while the right hand moves counterclockwise. (Alternatively, this sign may be made with one hand only.)
SAME SIGN—**contemplation**, *n.*

contempt: *n.* disrespect; scorn; willful disregard or disobedience. *She shows contempt for people who have less ability than she has.*

SIGN: Vertical **'MODIFIED O'** hands are held apart with left palm facing forward/rightward and right palm facing forward/leftward. The hands are then thrust downward and outward to a horizontal position with palms facing. Next, vertical right **'R'** hand is held in front of the face with palm facing forward/leftward while vertical left **'R'** hand is held just below in front of the right hand with palm facing forward/rightward. Both hands are then moved forward at a slight downward angle. Facial expression is important.
(ASL CONCEPT—**no - respect.**)

contend: *v.* to struggle or strive against. *Pioneers had to contend with hunger and severe hardships.*

SIGN #1: Horizontal left **'BENT ONE'** hand is held out in front of the body with palm toward the body and forefinger pointing at an upward/rightward angle toward the body. Horizontal right **'BENT ONE'** hand, palm left, is held higher and closer to the body with forefinger pointing directly at tip of left forefinger. The hands then circle forward simultaneously a couple of times. This is a slow, painstaking movement, which is accompanied by an appropriate facial expression.

OR

SIGN #2: Thumb of right **'A'** hand, palm facing left, is pressed against the chin and the hand is twisted from the wrist several times. Facial expression must clearly convey suffering.

contend: *v.* to compete. *The boxers will contend for the heavyweight title.*

SIGN #3: **'A'** hands, palms facing, are held close to one another and moved alternately back and forth. This is a wrist movement.

content: *adj.* satisfied or comfortable with things as they are. *Some people are content to stay at home rather than join the work force.*

SIGN #1: **'BENT B'** hands, right above left, with left palm facing right and right palm facing left, are placed firmly against the chest.

content: *n.* the significance or meaning, as opposed to the form, of something communicated through any form of expression. *This book has a lot of historical content.*

SIGN #2: Left **'MODIFIED O'** hand is held at about shoulder level with palm facing upward but angled slightly toward the body while right **'MODIFIED O'** hand is held upright just in front of the forehead with palm toward the face. The forearms then move simultaneously forward/downward as the hands open to assume **'MODIFIED 4'** shapes with palms facing upward.

contents: *n.* all that is contained or held within something. *She described the contents of the missing jewelry box.*

SIGN: Horizontal left **'FLAT C'** hand is held with palm facing the body but angled rightward slightly. Right **'FLAT O'** hand is held palm down just above the left hand. Then the bunched fingers of the right hand are brought down and inserted into the opening at the top of the left hand. Movement is repeated. (For **table of contents**, use the sign for **list** #1.)

contest: *n.* a competition. *A drawing contest was held last week.*

SIGN: **'A'** hands, palms facing, are held close to one another and moved alternately back and forth. This is a wrist movement.

context: *n.* circumstances that specify meaning in conversation or writing. *Both ASL signs and English words can vary in meaning, depending on context.*

SIGN: Fingerspell **CONTEXT**.

continue: *v.* to carry on with a certain action; to stay in the same position. *She will continue to volunteer her services with organizations that promote Deaf sports.*

SIGN: **'EXTENDED A'** hands are held side by side with palms down and right thumbtip pressing against left thumbnail as the hands are moved purposefully forward.

contraceptive: *n.* a device or medication used for the intentional prevention of pregnancy. *The birth-control pill is a widely used contraceptive.*

SIGN: **'EXTENDED B'** hands are held at right angles to one another, the left hand in front of the right, with fingers of left hand pointing upward to the right and fingers of right hand pointing upward to the left. The hands are then pushed firmly forward. Next, horizontal **'5'** hands, palms toward body, are brought together in front of abdomen with fingers interlocked. (ASL CONCEPT—**prevent - pregnant**.) SAME SIGN—**contraception**, *n.*

contract: *n.* a legal agreement. *My lawyer will draw up the contract.*

SIGN: Right **'U'** hand, palm facing left and extended fingers pointing forward, is twisted from the wrist as it moves in a leftward arc so that the palm faces down and extended fingers come to rest in upturned palm of left **'EXTENDED B'** hand.

contradict: *v.* to declare to be false or incorrect; to state the opposite. *These statistics contradict your theory.*

SIGN: **'ONE'** hands, palms toward the chest and forefingers pointing toward each other at an upward angle, are held slightly apart and then thrust toward each other so the forefingers cross with the left one in front of the right.
SAME SIGN—**contradiction**, *n.*

contrary: *adj.* opposed. *His opinion is always contrary to that of everyone else.*

SIGN #1: Horizontal **'BENT ONE'** hands are held together, palms facing the body, and tips of forefingers almost touching. Then they are pulled apart with a short, firm motion.

contrary: *adj.* stubborn; obstinate. *He is too contrary to ask for help.*

SIGN #2: Thumb of vertical right **'EXTENDED B'** hand, palm forward, is placed near the right temple and the fingers are firmly lowered to form a **'BENT EXTENDED B'** hand. A look of fierce determination accompanies this sign. (Alternatively, this sign may be made in the same location and with the same movement, but with a **'B'** handshape.)

contrast: *n.* a distinctive or striking dissimilarity. *There is an effective contrast between the black and white in the painting.*

SIGN: Horizontal **'BENT ONE'** hands are held together, palms facing the body, and tips of forefingers almost touching. Then they are pulled apart with a short, firm motion.

contribute: *v.* to donate for a common purpose or fund. *She contributes to the Canadian Cancer Society.*

SIGN: Vertical **'X'** hands, palms facing each other, are held slightly apart, and thrust forward and downward simultaneously. (This sign is often made with one hand slightly ahead of the other.) ❖
SAME SIGN—**contribution**, *n.*

control: *v.* to be in charge; to rule or direct; to hold in check or restraint. *Kim is trying to control her spending.*

SIGN: Horizontal **'X'** hands are held slightly apart with left palm facing right and right palm facing left. Then they are alternately moved backward and forward.

controversy: *n.* a debate concerning matters about which there is strong disagreement. *There has always been a great controversy over the methods of educating the Deaf.*

SIGN: Horizontal **'BENT ONE'** hands are held parallel in front of the left side of the body with palms facing. The forearms are then simultaneously moved to the right and then back to the left.
SAME SIGN—**controversial**, *adj.*

convene: *v.* to come together for a meeting or for some official purpose. *We will convene after lunch to discuss that issue.*

SIGN: **'CONTRACTED 5'** hands are held virtually upright at a slight forward angle with palms facing each other. The fingers then come together to form **'FLAT O'** hands with fingertips of each hand touching those of the other.

convenient: *adj.* close by, handy, or easy to use. *The library is arranged to provide convenient access to information.*

SIGN: Left **'BENT EXTENDED B'** hand is held in a fixed position with palm up. Palm of horizontal right **'EXTENDED B'** (or **'BENT EXTENDED B'**) hand faces left but is slanted slightly upward and toward the body as the fingers are brushed upward against the backs of the fingers of the left hand at least twice. (Signs vary a great deal, depending on context.)

convention: *n.* a large, formal assembly of a group having common interests. *We will attend the annual convention.*

SIGN: Thumb and forefinger of right **'C-INDEX'** hand, palm facing the body, are stroked downward twice on right side of chest.
ALTERNATE SIGN—**conference**

converge: See **merge**.

conversation: *n.* an exchange of ideas or information; communication. *He had an interesting conversation with his friend.*

SIGN: Vertical **'ONE'** hands are held apart with right palm facing left and left palm facing right. The hands are positioned so that tips of forefingers are about level with the mouth or chin as forearms move alternately back and forth.

SAME SIGN—**converse**, *v.*
ALTERNATE SIGN—**chat**

convert: *v.* to change in opinion or belief. *Due to the influence of the missionaries, many of the villagers converted to Christianity.*

SIGN: **'X'** hands (or **'A'** hands), palms facing, simultaneously rotate 180 degrees so that their positions are reversed.

SAME SIGN—**conversion**, *n.*

convey: *v.* to communicate a message; to express. *The president conveyed warm wishes to everyone attending the conference.*

SIGN: #1 Horizontal **'S'** hands, palms toward the body, are held together with the left hand against the chest and the right hand on top of the left but farther forward than the left hand as if the hands were holding onto a pole at a forward/upward angle. The hands are then flung forward as they open to form **'CROOKED 5'** hands with the palms facing upward, but still slanted toward the body slightly.

ALTERNATE SIGN—**inform**

convey: *v.* to carry from one location to another. *The pipeline conveys natural gas to Eastern Canada.*

SIGN: #2 **'EXTENDED B'** hands are held parallel with palms up in front of right side of body. Then they are simultaneously moved in a slight arc to the left.

convict: *n.* someone serving a sentence in prison. *Police are on the lookout for an escaped convict.*

SIGN: **'4'** (or **'5'**) hands are held with palms facing the body. Back of right hand, whose fingers point slightly upward to the left, is positioned behind palm of left hand at right angles, and is thrust against it. (For **convict** *v.*, meaning to pronounce someone guilty in a court of law, see **conviction** #1.)

conviction: *n.* the act of being declared guilty. *After his conviction of manslaughter, he was held for sentencing.*

SIGN #1: **'ONE'** hands, palms down, tips of forefingers touching either side of the mouth, are swung outward so that forefingers point upward and palms face away from the body. Then sides of thumb and forefinger of right **'MODIFIED G'** hand, palm facing leftward/downward, are firmly placed against the left side of the chest just below the shoulder. (ASL CONCEPT—**announce - guilty**.)

conviction: *n.* a firmly held belief or opinion. *His political convictions are very radical.*

SIGN #2: Vertical right **'MODIFIED O'** hand is held just in front of mid-forehead with palm facing left, and is bobbed slightly.

convince: *v.* to persuade firmly to agree with something or to see the truth or validity of something. *His speech finally convinced us to vote for him.*

SIGN: Horizontal **'EXTENDED B'** hands are held apart at about shoulder level with palms facing upward but slanted so that they are facing each other slightly as well. The forearms then move firmly downward/inward a short distance. ❖

127

cook: *v.* to prepare food using heat. *She prefers to cook simple meals.*

SIGN: Right **'EXTENDED B'** (or **'K'**) hand is held palm down with fingers pointing forward/leftward as they are placed on the upturned palm of the left **'EXTENDED B'** hand, of which the fingers point slightly forward and to the right. Right hand is then flipped over so that palm faces up.
SAME SIGN—**cook**, *n.*, meaning one who prepares food for eating.

cookie: *n.* a small, flat sweet cake. *Many people like chocolate chip cookies.*

SIGN #1: Fingertips of right **'SPREAD C'** hand are placed against right-facing palm of left **'EXTENDED B'** hand. The right hand then separates momentarily from the left hand as the right wrist rotates a quarter turn forward. The fingertips re-establish contact with the left palm, then separate once again as the wrist rotates back to its original position and the fingertips make contact once more. While the right wrist is making its rotations, the left wrist is rotating in the opposite direction. It is as if the right hand is imprinting a cookie cutter into the left hand.

SIGN #2 [ATLANTIC]: Vertical right **'CLAWED 5'** hand, palm toward the body, is waved from side to side a few times in front of the mouth. (This sign involves movement of the forearm, not just the hand.)

cool: *adj.* comfortably free of heat. *This room feels cool.*

SIGN #1: **'BENT EXTENDED B'** hands are held in front of either shoulder, with palms facing backward, and the fingers are simultaneously waved up and down in a fanning motion. (**COOL** is frequently fingerspelled.)

cool: *adj.* not easily rattled or upset; having an accepting, almost indifferent nature. *All the girls liked him because he was so cool.*

SIGN #2: Fingerspell **COOL**.

cooperate: *v.* to work or act together toward the same end. *The employees should cooperate to get the job done.*

SIGN: **'F'** hands with thumbs and forefingers interlocked, and palms facing each other, are moved in a complete circle in front of the body using a counter-clockwise motion.
SAME SIGN—**cooperation**, *n.*

coordinate: *v.* to organize or arrange in a harmonious order. *She will coordinate the plans for the conference.*

SIGN: **'F'** hands with thumbs and forefingers interlocked, and palms facing each other, are moved in a complete circle in front of the body using a counter-clockwise motion.
ALTERNATE SIGN—**arrange**

cope: *v.* to handle or manage well; to deal successfully with. *The intern had to cope with a heavy workload.*

SIGN: Horizontal **'X'** hands are held slightly apart with left palm facing right and right palm facing left. Then they are alternately moved backward and forward. (**COPE** may be fingerspelled.)

copy: *v.* to imitate. *Children usually copy the behaviour of their elders.*

SIGN #1: Left **'EXTENDED B'** hand is held in a fixed position with palm up and fingers pointing forward/rightward. Right **'CONTRACTED 5'** hand is positioned at the end of the left hand with palm facing forward. As the right hand is drawn backward toward the palm or heel of the left hand, it closes to form a **'FLAT O'** shape. ❖

SIGN #2 [ATLANTIC]: As right **'CONTRACTED 5'** hand, with palm forward, moves backward/upward to the centre of the forehead, the fingers come together to form a **'FLAT O'** shape.

copy [or **make a copy**]: *v.* to photocopy; to duplicate or make a reproduction of. *Please make a copy of the membership list.*

SIGN #3: Left **'EXTENDED B'** hand is held in a fixed position with palm down and fingers pointing forward/rightward while right **'MODIFIED O'** hand is held palm up beneath the left hand. The right hand then moves in a forward/rightward direction beyond the left hand. As it does so, the fingers open to form a **'CONTRACTED 5'** shape. The right hand then returns to its original position as the fingers close to resume the **'MODIFIED O'** shape. ALTERNATE SIGN—**copy** #4

copy: *n.* a photocopy; a page of text and/or illustrations that has been duplicated or reproduced on a photocopy machine. *Please give me a copy of the membership list.*

SIGN #4: Left **'EXTENDED B'** hand is held in a fixed position with palm down and fingers pointing forward/rightward while right **'CONTRACTED 5'** hand is held palm up with fingers touching left palm. The right hand is then drawn downward as it closes to form a **'FLAT O'** hand. ALTERNATE SIGN—**duplicate** #2

copyright: *n.* the exclusive right to produce copies of an original work of literature, music or art. *Researchers should always observe the laws related to copyright.*

SIGN: Left **'EXTENDED B'** hand is held in a fixed position with fingers pointing forward and palm facing right but slanted slightly downward. Thumb and fingertips of horizontal right **'CONTRACTED 5'** hand are placed against the left palm and are then drawn rightward and slightly downward as the fingers and thumb come together to form a **'FLAT O'** shape. Next, the edge of the right **'EXTENDED B'** hand is placed on the upturned palm of the left **'EXTENDED B'** hand, and is pushed forward in a short, upward curving motion so that the fingers point upward. (**COPYRIGHT** is frequently fingerspelled.)

cord: *n.* a length of electrical cable. *The cord on his block heater is bright orange.*

SIGN: Horizontal **'I'** hands are held with tips of little fingers touching each other and palms facing the body. The hands are then drawn apart. (For a *thicker cord*, this sign is made with **'F'** hands held together in the initial position with palms down and extended fingers pointing forward. For an even thicker cord, the signer uses **'C'** hands held together in the initial position with palms down.)

cordial: *adj.* warm and friendly. *The hostess gave each guest a cordial greeting.*

SIGN: **'5'** hands, palms facing backward, move backward with fingers fluttering until they come to rest close to either side of the face. ALTERNATE SIGN—**warm**

core: *n.* the central or essential part of something. *They launched a massive cleanup campaign in the downtown core.*

SIGN: With palm down, horizontal right **'BENT MIDFINGER 5'** hand is circled clockwise from the wrist above upturned left palm, tip of right midfinger falling in the centre of the left palm.

cork: *n.* a piece of cork used as a stopper for a bottle. *You need a corkscrew to take the cork out of this bottle.*

SIGN: Fingerspell **CORK**.

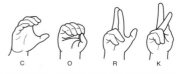

corn: *n.* a cereal plant of which the yellow seeds are eaten as a vegetable. *My favourite vegetable is creamed corn.*

SIGN: Fingerspell **CORN**.

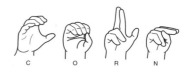

corn on the cob: *n.* an ear of corn. *Corn on the cob is delicious when served with butter and salt.*

SIGN: **'S'** hands are held at either side of the mouth, the palms alternating between facing forward and downward as the hands twist up and down a few times from the wrists. (Handshapes for this sign vary while the movement remains basically the same.)

corner: *n.* the place where two converging lines or surfaces meet. *I will meet you at the corner of Main Street and Third Avenue at noon.*

SIGN #1: Tips of forefingers of horizontal **'ONE'** hands (or fingertips of horizontal **'EXTENDED B'** hands) are tapped together a couple of times to create a **'V'** formation with palms facing each other but slanted slightly toward the body.

corner: *v.* to place in a position from which escape is difficult. *The detectives cornered the suspect in a blind alley.*

SIGN #2: Left **'ONE'** hand is held upright in a fixed position while right **'CLAWED V'** hand is held palm down behind it. The right hand is then thrust forward so that the left forefinger is inserted between the clawed right forefinger and middle finger. ❖

(just around the) corner: *adv.* very near at hand; very close. *The school is just around the corner from our house.*

SIGN #1: Tip of joined thumb and forefinger of horizontal right **'F'** hand (or tip of thumb of **'EXTENDED K'** hand), palm toward the face, is held at the end of the nose. The wrist then twists to turn the hand palm-downward. Motion may be repeated once or twice.

SIGN #2 [ONTARIO]: Thumbnail of horizontal right **'CONTRACTED 3'** hand, palm left, is held at the tip of the nose and the extended fingers are snapped back to form a **'CLOSED DOUBLE MODIFIED G'** hand.

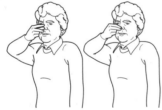

(just around the) corner: *adv.* soon to come. *Christmas is just around the corner.*

SIGN #3: Horizontal left **'BENT EXTENDED B'** hand is held in a fixed position with palm facing right and fingers pointing right. Horizontal right **'BENT EXTENDED B'** hand is held closer to the body and slightly higher than the left hand with palm facing left and fingers pointing left. The right hand then moves forward/downward haltingly toward the left hand. The signer winces, with eyes squinting and teeth visible as if saying 'ee'.

SIGN #4: Thumb of right **'EXTENDED B'** (or **'5'**) hand, palm facing left, is stroked forward a few times against right cheek. The signer winces, with eyes squinting and teeth visible as if saying 'ee'.

corpse: *n.* a dead body. *The police are still trying to identify the corpse.*

SIGN: **'EXTENDED B'** hands are held with fingers pointing forward, left palm facing up and right palm facing down. Then they are flipped over simultaneously so that the palm positions are reversed. Next, horizontal **'EXTENDED B'** hands, palms toward body, fingertips touching either side of the chest, are moved down and placed at the waist. (ASL CONCEPT—**dead - body**.)

correct: *adj.* right or accurate. *This is the correct answer.*

SIGN #1: **'ONE'** hands are held right above left with forefingers pointing forward and the left palm facing right while the right palm faces left. Right hand is brought down firmly to rest on top of left.

correct: *v.* to remove errors. *Please correct the mistakes on your test paper.*

SIGN #2: Vertical **'X'** hands are held slightly apart with palms facing. The hands are then simultaneously lowered as rotations of the wrists cause the hands to alternately fall forward and back several times.
SAME SIGN—**corrections**, *n.*

correction fluid: *n.* a substance used to paint over errors in typewritten work so they can be corrected. *The typist used correction fluid to delete a comma.*

SIGN: Fingertips of right **'CONTRACTED 5'** hand, palm toward the body, are placed against the middle of the chest and the hand is then drawn forward as it closes to form a **'FLAT O'** hand. Next, tips of extended fingers of right **'BENT EXTENDED U'** hand, palm down, are brushed back and forth on palm of left **'EXTENDED B'** hand which is held with palm facing upward, but angled toward the body. (ASL CONCEPT—**white - paint-on-hand**.)

correspond with: *v.* to communicate by letter. *She always corresponds with her relatives in Ontario.*

SIGN #1: Vertical right **'S'** hand is held just in front of the upper chest, or a little higher, with palm forward while vertical left **'S'** hand is held farther forward with palm facing that of the right hand. The hands then bend toward each other from the wrists as the forefingers are simultaneously flicked out toward each other to form **'BENT ONE'** hands. Motion is repeated a few times. ❖

correspond with: *v.* to be consistent or compatible with. *The accountant checked to make sure the figures in the first column correspond with those in the second column.*

SIGN #2: **'CLAWED 5'** hands are held apart in front of the chest in an almost upright position but slanted slightly toward each other with palms facing the body. The forearms then move downward toward each other until the fingers mesh. ❖
ALTERNATE SIGN—**according to**

corridor: *n.* a hallway; a narrow passageway. *The nurse suggested that the patient walk up and down the corridor to get some exercise.*

SIGN: Vertical **'EXTENDED B'** hands are held apart with palms facing each other, and are simultaneously moved forward to indicate a long, narrow space.

corrode: *v.* to wear away or to rust. *The metal barrel was corroded from having been exposed to the weather for so many years.*

SIGN: Vertical left **'EXTENDED B'** (or **'5'**) hand is held in a fixed position with palm facing right while vertical right **'SPREAD EXTENDED C'** hand, palm facing left, is held with fingertips against heel of left hand. The right hand then moves upward with fingers wiggling as if nibbling at the left hand. (Signs vary depending on the nature of the object being corroded.)

corrupt: *adj.* depraved or dishonest. *The corrupt politician was voted out of office.*

SIGN: Right **'EXTENDED A'** hand, palm facing left, thumb under chin, is thrust forward. Next, left **'EXTENDED B'** hand is held in a fixed position with palm facing left but slanted upward slightly and fingers pointing forward as right **'U'** hand is held with palm facing left and tip of middle finger placed at heel of left hand. The right hand is then moved straight forward along the left palm until the tip of the right middle finger reaches the tip of the left middle finger. (ASL CONCEPT—**not - honest**.)

corruption: *n.* immorality; dishonesty. *Corruption in society can have an undesirable influence on our children.*

SIGN: Right **'MODIFIED 5'** hand is held under chin with palm down, as the fingers flutter. Then wrist of right **'S'** hand, palm facing forward/leftward, is brushed back and forth against wrist of left **'STANDARD BASE'** hand. Facial expression must convey displeasure. (ASL CONCEPT—**dirty - business**.)

cosmetics: *n.* preparations applied to the face or body for beautification purposes. *Some cosmetics are hypoallergenic.*

SIGN: Fingertips of **'FLAT O'** hands are placed on either cheek and the hands are moved in circles as if rubbing in cream.

cost: *v.* to require a payment of; to be obtainable in exchange for. *This car costs over $20,000 dollars.*

SIGN #1: Forefinger of horizontal right **'x'** hand, palm toward the body at a leftward-facing angle, is brought down smartly across the palm of the horizontal left **'EXTENDED B'** hand, which is facing rightward but angled toward the body.
SAME SIGN—**cost**, *n.*

OR

SIGN #2: Vertical **'F'** hands, palms facing forward, are brought together so the joined thumbs and forefingers touch each other twice.
SAME SIGN—**cost**, *n.*

costly: *adj.* expensive. *Many assistive devices for the Deaf are very costly.*

SIGN: Left **'EXTENDED B'** hand is held in a fixed position with palm up and fingers pointing rightward/forward. Back of fingers of right **'FLAT O'** hand are placed on the palm of the left hand. The right hand is then lifted, moved rightward, and dropped firmly downward as it opens to form a **'CONTRACTED 5'** hand with palm facing down.

costume: *n.* a certain style of clothing, such as that worn in a specific country, or during a certain period in history, or by an established character. *He wore a jester's costume in his role as the Court Fool.*

SIGN: Thumbs of **'5'** hands, with palms toward the body, are held at either side of upper chest and brushed downward a couple of times.

cot: *n.* a narrow bed, especially one with a collapsible frame for easy storage. *The hotel staff brought us a cot so our family could stay in one room.*

SIGN: Fingerspell **COT**.

cottage: *n.* a small, simple house, often in a rural area. *We spend most of the summer at our lake-front cottage.*

SIGN: Fingerspell **COTTAGE**.

cotton: *n.* cloth or thread made from the fibres of the cotton plant. *Denim jeans are made of heavy, hard-wearing cotton.*

SIGN: Fingerspell **COTTON**.

couch: *n.* a piece of upholstered furniture used to seat more than one person. *We sat on the couch to watch TV.*

SIGN: Fingerspell **COUCH**.

cough: *v.* to expel air from the lungs explosively. *He had a bad cough with his cold.*

SIGN: Tips of thumb and fingers of horizontal right **'SPREAD C'** hand are held against the centre of the chest, and maintain contact with the chest as the forearm moves up and down several times.

council: *n.* a group of people elected or appointed to serve in a certain capacity. *He is a member of the town council.*

SIGN: Thumbtip of vertical right **'EXTENDED C'** hand, palm facing left, is placed against the left shoulder. The hand is then moved in an arc to take up the same position at the right shoulder. **COUNCIL** is frequently fingerspelled.
ALTERNATE SIGN—**group** #1

counsel: *n.* advice or guidance. *You should seek counsel from a financial advisor before investing in the stock market.*

SIGN #1: Fingertips of right **'FLAT O'** hand rest on back of left **'STANDARD BASE'** hand. Right hand is then thrust forward as it opens slightly to form a **'CONTRACTED 5'** hand.
SAME SIGNS—**counsellor**, *n.*, Agent Ending (see p. LIV) may follow, and **counsel**, *v.*, but the movement is repeated.

counsel: *n.* a person whose advice is sought. *On the advice of* ***counsel****, they settled the matter out of court.*

SIGN #2: Right **'L'** hand, palm facing left, is placed against the upright fingers of the left **'EXTENDED B'** hand, of which the palm faces right, and is then moved down to the base of the left hand. Agent Ending (see p. LIV) may follow.

ALTERNATE SIGN—**attorney** #2

count: *v.* to determine the total of. *The cashier* ***counts*** *the money before she deposits it.*

SIGN: Thumb and forefinger of right **'F'** hand, palm down, are stroked forward once or twice across upturned palm of left **'EXTENDED B'** hand.

count on: *v.* to reply or depend upon. *We can* ***count on*** *them to help.*

SIGN: Tips of forefingers of **'ONE'** hands are crossed slightly with the right on top of the left, and both palms facing down. Together, the hands are lowered as if the right forefinger is exerting downward pressure on the left forefinger. ❖

country: *n.* a nation; a geographical territory which is within specified boundaries and has its own government. *Canada is a very large country.*

SIGN #1: Right **'Y'** hand, with palm facing the body, is placed near the elbow of the bent left forearm, and is circled in a direction that appears to the onlooker to be clockwise.

country: *n.* a rural area. *We drove out to the country.*

SIGN #2: Right **'EXTENDED B'** hand, with palm toward the body, is placed near the elbow of the bent left forearm, and is circled in a direction that appears to the onlooker to be clockwise.

county: *n.* one of several types of administrative subdivisions in many English-speaking countries. *In some Canadian provinces, each county has its own school board.*

SIGN: Fingerspell **COUNTY**.

coup [*abbreviation for* **coup d'etat**]: *n.* a sudden overthrow or illegal seizure of a government. *After the* ***coup****, the country was under military control.*

SIGN: Left **'CROOKED 5'** hand is held palm-up with fingers pointing forward while right **'CROOKED 5'** hand is held apart and slightly higher with palm down and fingers pointing forward. The arms are then simultaneously moved upward/rightward as the hands are purposefully twisted rightward from the wrist so that the left palm faces right and the right palm faces left.

couple: *n.* two people who are together regularly or united for some reason. *The engaged* ***couple*** *will be married in the spring.*

SIGN #1: Vertical left **'V'** hand is held in a fixed position with palm facing rightward. Right **'BENT V'** hand is held beside left hand with palm facing left and extended fingertips tapping alternately a few times on the extended fingertips of the left hand. (**COUPLE**, in this context, is frequently fingerspelled.)

(a) couple of: *adj.* two of something; colloquially used to mean a few. *He needs* ***a couple*** *of new parts for his truck.*

SIGN #2: Right **'V'** hand is held upright with palm facing the body to indicate 'two'.

ALTERNATE SIGN—**a few**

(a) couple of days ago: *adv.* the day before yesterday. *It snowed* ***a couple of days ago****.*

SIGN #3: Vertical right **'SLANTED V'** hand is held with palm facing backward and middle finger resting against the right cheek. The wrist then twists to rotate the hand so that the tip of the forefinger is held against the cheek and the palm is facing forward/leftward.

(in a) couple of days: *adv.* two days from now. *I will see him in a couple of days.*

SIGN #4: Vertical right **'SLANTED V'** hand is held with palm facing backward and middle finger resting against the right cheek. The hand is then flicked forward from the wrist so that the palm is at an upward/backward facing angle.

(in a) couple of minutes: *adv.* two minutes from now. *She will be with you in a couple of minutes.*

SIGN #5: Left **'ONE'** hand is held palm down with tip of forefinger touching wrist of vertical right **'V'** hand, of which the palm faces left. The right hand then drops from the wrist so that the fingers point forward at an upward angle.

coupon: *n.* a voucher which is exchangeable for certain goods. *The store offered a 50 cent coupon for canned tomatoes.*

SIGN: Tips of forefingers and thumbs touch as **'CONTRACTED L'** hands are held together with palms facing forward/downward. The arms are then drawn apart and each forefinger and thumb come together to form **'CLOSED MODIFIED G'** shapes. (**COUPON** is frequently fingerspelled.)

courage: *n.* bravery; the power to face fear or danger. *Do you have the courage to tell your parents what you have done?*

SIGN: **'BENT 5'** hands, with fingertips on either side of chest and palms facing the body, are drawn forward to form **'S'** hands.
SAME SIGN—**courageous**, *adj.*
REGIONAL VARIATION—**brave** #2

courier: *n.* a messenger; an individual or company hired to deliver something official or urgently needed. *He sent the documents by airmail courier.*

SIGN: Fingerspell **COURIER**.

C O U R I E R

course: *n.* a number of lessons which make up a section of a curriculum. *ASL courses are offered at that university by the foreign languages department.*

SIGN: Left **'EXTENDED B'** hand is held in a fixed position with palm up and fingers pointing rightward/forward. Horizontal right **'BENT EXTENDED B'** hand, with palm facing left, is placed on the fingers of the left hand, then raised, moved backward, and placed on the heel of the left hand.

(of) course: *adv.* as is to be expected, or naturally. *Of course we will attend the wedding if we are invited.*

SIGN: Right **'U'** hand is held above left **'STANDARD BASE'** hand with extended fingers pointing forward/upward at a leftward angle. Right hand is then brought down from the wrist so the fingertips lightly slap the back of the left hand. (**OF COURSE** may be fingerspelled.)

court: *n.* the place where a trial is held. *The alleged murderer will appear in court tomorrow.*

SIGN #1: Horizontal **'F'** hands, palms facing each other, are alternately raised and lowered a few times.

SIGN #2 [ATLANTIC]: **'Y'** hands, palms down, are held slightly apart and are alternately moved forward and back a few times.

court: *n.* a marked, enclosed area where certain games such as tennis or basketball are played. *We have a badminton court in our backyard.*

SIGN #3: **'BENT ONE'** hands, palms down, are held with downward-pointing forefingers side by side. The hands are drawn apart, then moved back toward the body, and finally brought together again as if outlining a rectangle on a horizontal surface. (**COURT** is frequently fingerspelled.)

courteous: *adj.* polite and considerate in manner. *I received a courteous reply to my letter.*

SIGN: Thumb of vertical right **'EXTENDED B'** hand, palm facing left, is tapped a few times against centre of chest.
SAME SIGN—**courtesy**, *n.*

cousin *(female)*: *n.* the daughter of one's uncle or aunt. *She introduced her cousin, Mary Jones, to all her friends.*

SIGN #1: Side of forefinger of vertical right **'C'** hand, palm facing leftward/forward, is brushed downward a couple of times against right side of chin. (Alternatively, vertical right **'C'** hand, palm facing leftward/forward, is held near the right side of the chin and is shaken with slight twists of the wrist.) If the sex of the cousin is not specified, the same sign is used but the hand is held by the right cheek. To indicate plurality, including both male and female cousins, the sign for **cousin** *(male)* is used; then the hand is lowered to the **cousin** *(female)* position.

cousin *(male)*: *n.* the son of one's uncle or aunt. *She introduced her cousin, Mike Jones, to all her friends.*

SIGN #2: Side of forefinger of vertical right **'C'** hand, palm facing leftward/forward, is brushed downward a couple of times against right side of forehead. (Alternatively, vertical right **'C'** hand, palm facing leftward/forward, is held near the right temple and is shaken with slight twists of the wrist.) If the sex of the cousin is not specified, the same sign is used but the hand is held by the right cheek. To indicate plurality, including both male and female cousins, the sign for **cousin** *(male)* is used; then the hand is lowered to the **cousin** *(female)* position.

cover: *v.* to place or spread something over for protection. *I will cover my plants tonight to protect them from frost.*

SIGN #1: **'CROOKED 5'** hands are held out from the body at about chest level with palms down. The hands are then drawn apart and curved downward so that the palms face each other. (This sign is used to refer to the covering of objects that are in an *upright* as opposed to a horizontal position.)

cover: *v.* to place or spread something over for protection. *The police covered the body of the accident victim.*

SIGN #2: **'CLOSED A-INDEX'** (or **'F'**) hands are held palms down, the left hand positioned ahead of and to the left of the right hand. The hands are then simultaneously moved leftward/backward in an arc. (This sign is used to refer to the covering of *horizontal* objects only.)

cover: *v.* to deal with or include. *The course covers several interesting topics.*

SIGN #3: Right **'CONTRACTED 5'** hand, palm facing down, is circled widely in a clockwise direction over the opening of the horizontal left **'C'** hand whose palm faces right. Right hand is then closed to form a **'FLAT O'** hand of which the fingertips are inserted into the opening of the left hand.

cover: *v.* to take over for someone in his absence or to justify his absence if discovered by someone who demands reasons for it. *I will cover for you while you dash home to let the dog out.*

SIGN #4: Right **'EXTENDED B'** hand is held palm down with fingers pointing forward/leftward as it moves in a complete counter-clockwise circle above the left **'STANDARD BASE'** hand.

cover: *v.* to stand guard in order to protect someone. *The soldier was ordered to cover the other soldiers as they moved toward enemy lines.*

SIGN #5: Horizontal **'S'** hands are held, the left just in front of the right, with palms down in front of the centre of the chest. The hands are then simultaneously moved emphatically forward a short distance.

cover: *v.* to defend or act as a back-up, especially in sports. *The coach told the left fielder to cover third base.*

SIGN #6: Vertical left **'ONE'** hand is held in a fixed position with palm facing forward while vertical right **'ONE'** hand is moved leftward to fall into alignment behind the left hand.

cover: *n.* anything that spreads over to protect or conceal. *This book has a leather cover.*

SIGN #7: Left **'EXTENDED B'** hand is held in a fixed position with palm down and fingers pointing rightward/forward while the leftward/forward-pointing fingers of the palm down right **'EXTENDED B'** hand are placed on the end of the left hand at right angles to are moved leftward/backward along the left hand as if petting it. (Signs vary depending on the location, shape and size of the object.)

cover: *n.* a blanket used to keep warm in bed. *How many **covers** do you have on your bed in the winter time?*

SIGN #8: '**BENT EXTENDED B**' hands are held apart just in front of the upper chest with palms down and fingers pointing forward but toward each other slightly. The hands are then turned inward from the wrists so that the fingertips touch the chest. Alternatively, this sign may be made with one hand only.

cover up: *v.* to attempt concealment; to hide the truth about something such as a crime. *He tried to **cover up** his mistakes.*

SIGN: Left '**EXTENDED B**' hand is held in a fixed position with palm facing the body and fingers pointing upward/rightward. Vertical right '**EXTENDED B**' hand is held just to the right of the left hand with palm facing forward. The right hand is then firmly thrust leftward so that the palm brushes across that of the left hand. (This sign is accompanied by a look of suspicion.)

covert: *adj.* concealed or secret. *The police investigation was a **covert** operation.*

SIGN: Thumbnail of right '**A**' hand, palm facing left, is placed against the lips and the hand is then lowered and concealed under the downturned palm of the left '**CROOKED EXTENDED B**' hand.
ALTERNATE SIGN—**secret**

covet: See **envy**.

cow: *n.* the mature female of the cattle species. *The veterinarian treated the **cow** for milk fever.*

SIGN: Thumb of right '**Y**' hand, palm facing downward, is placed on right temple and is twisted counter-clockwise until palm faces forward and little finger points upward.

coward: *n.* a person who shrinks from anything dangerous or painful. *Only a **coward** would run from the enemy during a battle.*

SIGN: Right '**MODIFIED G**' hand is held at chin, palm facing forward, while thumb and forefinger are opened and closed at least twice to simulate the movement of a chicken's beak. **COWARD** is frequently fingerspelled.
SAME SIGN—**cowardice**, *n.*
ALTERNATE SIGNS—**afraid** #1 & #2

cowboy/cowgirl: *n.* one who herds or tends cattle; someone who performs at a rodeo. *The best **cowboy/cowgirl** at the town's rodeo will win a saddle.*

SIGN: Horizontal '**L**' hands are held apart with palms facing each other, and are alternately circled forward as if shooting with hand pistols.

cozy: *adj.* snug, comfortable, intimate, and friendly. *My apartment was **cozy** and warm during the blizzard.*

SIGN: Left '**CROOKED EXTENDED B**' hand is held palm down with fingers pointing rightward/forward at a downward angle while right '**CROOKED EXTENDED B**' hand is held palm down on left hand at right angles to it. The right hand is drawn rightward/backward across the back of the left hand, which moves out from under the right hand to take up a position on top of it so that the positioning of the hands is the reverse of their original position. The left hand is then drawn leftward/backward across the back of the right hand, which moves out from under the left hand to take up a position on top of it. Movement is repeated. (**COZY** is frequently fingerspelled.)

crab: *n.* a shellfish with five pairs of legs, the front pair having pincers. *The science teacher explained that the **crab** is a crustacean.*

SIGN: Horizontal '**V**' hands are held parallel with palms down and extended fingers pointing forward. The hands remain stationary as the fingers rapidly open and close, thus alternating between '**V**' and '**U**' shapes. (**CRAB** is frequently fingerspelled, especially when referring to the edible meat of the crab.)

crabby: *adj.* irritable, surly, grouchy or cranky. *He is always crabby if his team loses.*

SIGN: Right vertical **'CROOKED 5'** hand is held with palm toward the face as the fingers rapidly alternate between a relaxed state (**'CROOKED 5'**) and a clawed state (**'CLAWED SPREAD C'**). This sign is accompanied by an appropriate facial expression.

crack: *v.* to break partially or split. *My plates cracked during the move.*

SIGN #1: Left **'EXTENDED B'** hand is held in a fixed position with palm up and fingers pointing rightward/forward. Right **'EXTENDED B'** hand, palm facing left, is held on the left palm with fingers pointing forward. The right hand then moves backward in a zigzag pattern across the palm of the left hand. (Signs vary slightly with regard to positioning of the right hand, often depending on the actual location of the crack and whether or not it is a vertical or horizontal crack.)

crack: *v.* to solve. *His client was overjoyed when he cracked the case.*

SIGN #2: **'FLAT O'** hands are held parallel with palms up and slanted slightly toward the body. As the hands are drawn apart the thumbs slide across the fingertips, causing the hands to assume **'A'** shapes.

cracker: *n.* a dry, thin, crisp biscuit. *I always put crackers in my soup.*

SIGN #1: Right **'A'** (or **'CROOKED 5'**) hand, with palm facing backward, thumps elbow of left arm.

OR

SIGN #2: Left **'EXTENDED B'** hand is held in a fixed position with palm facing the body at a rightward angle while thumb and forefinger of right **'CROOKED L'** hand are used to outline a cross on the left palm.

SIGN #3 [ATLANTIC]: Right **'BENT EXTENDED B'** hand is held palm down with the side of the forefinger against the chin. While maintaining contact with the chin, the hand wobbles as the wrist twists back and forth a few times.

craft: *n.* skill; proficiency. *Everyone admires his craft in woodwork.*

SIGN #1: Left **'EXTENDED B'** hand, palm facing right and fingers pointing upward, is grasped by right **'OPEN A'** hand. Then right hand is pulled forward sharply and closed to form and **'A'** hand.

craft: *n.* an occupation or hobby, usually requiring manual dexterity. *Rug-hooking can be an expensive craft.*

SIGN #2: Fingerspell **CRAFT**.

crafty: *adj.* sly; cunning; skilled in deception. *He is very crafty in his business dealings.*

SIGN: Thumb and forefinger of the right **'FLAT OPEN F'** hand are laid flat against the left cheek with the palm facing leftward/backward. The forefinger moves rapidly up and down several times so that the hand alternates between a **'FLAT OPEN F'** shape and a **'FLAT F'**.

cramp *(usually plural):* *n.* a painful, involuntary muscular contraction. *She had stomach cramps after eating at that restaurant.*

SIGN: **'SPREAD C'** hands are held parallel in front of the stomach with palms down, and are closed slowly with a wringing motion to form **'S'** hands, as the left wrist bends backward to raise the fist and the right wrist bends forward to turn the fist downward/inward. (The positioning of this sign varies depending on the location of the cramp.)

cranky: See **crabby**.

crash: *v.* to collide violently. *Please slow down or you will crash.*

SIGN #1: Left **'EXTENDED B'** hand is held with palm facing the body at a rightward angle and fingers pointing rightward/forward while horizontal right **'S'** hand is held closer to the chest with palm facing leftward and slanted slightly toward the body. The hands then come together with force. (This sign may be used to refer to the crashing of any ground vehicle.) ❖ ALTERNATE SIGN—**accident** #1

(plane) crash: *n.* the sudden, violent and destructive landing of an airplane. *The plane crash claimed many lives.*

SIGN #2: Left **'EXTENDED B'** hand is held with palm facing upward at a rightward/backward angle and fingers pointing rightward/forward while horizontal right **'COMBINED LY'** hand is held further to the right, higher, and closer to the body with palm down and extended fingers pointing forward/leftward. The hands then come together with force, causing the extended fingers of the right hand to crumple as they make contact with the left palm.

crave: *v.* to long for or desire intensely. *Julie craved licorice during her pregnancy.*

SIGN: Tip of forefinger of right **'ONE'** hand is placed just under the chin and moves downward along the throat. Facial expression is important.
SAME SIGN—**craving**, *n.*
ALTERNATE SIGN—**wish**

crawl: *v.* to move very slowly, usually on one's hands and knees. *The baby is learning to crawl.*

SIGN #1: Left **'EXTENDED B'** hand is held in a fixed position with palm up and fingers pointing rightward/forward. Horizontal right **'CLAWED V'** hand, palm facing the body, is placed on the left palm and drawn rightward/forward along the left hand with clawed fingers wiggling.

OR

SIGN #2: **'CROOKED 5'** hands are held with palms down and are alternately moved forward several times to simulate the act of crawling.

crayon: *n.* a small pencil of coloured wax. *He used a red crayon to colour the valentine.*

SIGN: Fingertips of right **'5'** hand, with palm toward the body, are fluttered on the lips (or chin). Next, left **'EXTENDED B'** hand is held in a fixed position with palm up and fingers pointing rightward/forward while thumb and forefinger of right **'CLOSED X'** hand, palm down, are placed on the left palm. The right hand moves back and forth as if colouring. (ASL CONCEPT—**colour - write back and forth.**)

crazy: *adj.* insane; not sensible. *Canadians have to be crazy to live in such a cold climate.*

SIGN #1: Vertical right **'CROOKED 5'** (or **'SPREAD C'**) hand is held near the right side of the head with the palm toward the body, and is twisted back and forth several times from the wrist.

OR

SIGN #2: Right **'ONE'** hand is held palm down with forefinger pointing toward the right side of the head, and is spun in a clockwise direction from the wrist.

crazy: *adj.* excessively fond of. *I am not crazy about turnip.*

SIGN #3: Vertical right **'CROOKED SLANTED 5'** hand is held just to the right of the forehead with palm facing leftward/backward. As the wrist bends, the hand drops down so that the palm faces downward and the fingers are dangling in front of the face.

OR

SIGN #4: Tips of extended fingers of vertical right **'V'** hand, palm toward the head, are placed on the right side of the forehead. The hand then moves away from the head slightly as the fingers retract to form a **'CLAWED V'** shape.

cream: *n.* the fatty part of whole milk. *Fresh cream tastes good in coffee or on cereal.*

SIGN: Left **'EXTENDED B'** hand is held in a fixed position with palm up and fingers pointing forward/rightward. Horizontal right **'EXTENDED C'** hand, palm leftward/backward, is placed on the left hand and makes a gathering motion across the left hand to form a small leftward/backward arc. (**CREAM** is frequently fingerspelled.)

create: *v.* to devise or to make something original. *He will create a children's story that takes place on another planet.*

SIGN #1: Tip of forefinger of vertical right **'4'** hand, palm facing left, is placed against the forehead and the hand is then pushed upward and forward slightly.

create: *v.* to cause something to exist; to make. *According to the* Bible, *God* **created** *the universe in seven days.*

SIGN #2: Horizontal right **'s'** hand is placed on top of horizontal left **'s'** hand as both palms face the body. The right hand is then raised slightly and both wrists are bent causing the hands to turn so that the right palm faces left and the left palm faces right as the right hand re-establishes contact with the left hand.

create: *v.* to produce or give rise to; to cause a certain result. *She* **created** *a lot of distrust by keeping secrets from her husband.*

SIGN #3: Horizontal **'s'** (or **'a'**) hands are held slightly apart with palms facing upward, the left hand slightly ahead of the right hand. The hands are then thrust forward slightly as the fingers open to form **'5'** hands.

creative: *adj.* showing originality and imagination. *She teaches* **creative** *writing at the university.*

SIGN: Vertical **'4'** hands are held in front of either side of the forehead with palms facing each other, and are alternately circled forward a few times.
SAME SIGN—**creativity,** *n.*

credit: *n.* recognition; praise; commendation. *He deserves some* **credit** *for a job well done.*

SIGN: Tip of forefinger of right **'CROOKED ONE'** hand is positioned at corner of right eye and is brought down to rest on upturned palm of left **'EXTENDED B'** hand. **CREDIT** may be fingerspelled.
ALTERNATE SIGN—**praise**

credit card: *n.* a card issued by a bank or business, permitting the holder to obtain goods or services on credit. *She used her* **credit card** *to pay for a new television.*

SIGN: Horizontal right **'s'** hand, palm toward body at a leftward-facing angle, lies on the upturned palm of the left **'EXTENDED B'** hand, and is pressed back and forth along the length of the left hand as if imprinting a credit card. Next, tips of forefingers and thumbs touch as **'CONTRACTED L'** hands are held together with palms facing forward/downward. The arms are then drawn apart and each forefinger and thumb come together to form **'CLOSED MODIFIED G'** shapes. (ASL CONCEPT—**charge - card**.) **CREDIT CARD** may be fingerspelled.

credits: *n.* acknowledgments listed at the end of a film. *I saw his name in the* **credits** *following the movie.*

SIGN #1: **'4'** hands are held right above left with palms facing the body and fingers of right hand pointing leftward as fingers of left hand point rightward. Holding this position, the arms are raised directly upward. (For acknowledgments of the type found in a book, see **list** #1.)

credits: *n.* official recognition that certain educational requirements have been met. *She received four* **credits** *for a course she completed at another school.*

SIGN #2: Fingerspell **CREDITS**.

cremation: *n.* the burning of a corpse to reduce it to ashes. *Cremation will follow the memorial service, and the ashes will be placed in the family vault.*

SIGN: Horizontal **'EXTENDED B'** hands are placed slightly apart, fingertips opposite, with palms on upper chest. Then they are moved simultaneously down to waist level. Next, right **'BENT 5'** hand, with palm facing upward but slanted slightly toward the body, is moved forward and back with fingers fluttering under the left **'STANDARD BASE'** hand. (ASL CONCEPT—**body - burn**.) CREMATION is frequently fingerspelled.

crime: *n.* an unlawful act. *Murder is a crime punishable by life imprisonment.*

SIGN: Fingerspell **CRIME**.

crimson: *adj.* a deep red colour. *His face turned crimson with embarrassment.*

SIGN: Vertical right **'ONE'** hand is held with palm facing the body and tip of forefinger touching the lower lip. As the hand is then drawn very firmly forward at a downward angle, the forefinger crooks to form an **'x'** shape.

crippled: *adj.* lame. *The crippled woman walked with a cane.*

SIGN: **'BENT ONE'** hands, held apart with palms down and forefingers pointing downward, are alternately raised and lowered.

crisis: *n.* a period of serious trouble or danger. *The War Measures Act was put into effect during the crisis.*

SIGN: Left **'CROOKED 5'** hand is held palm-up with fingers pointing forward while right **'CROOKED 5'** hand is held apart and slightly higher with palm down and fingers pointing forward. The arms are then simultaneously moved upward/rightward as the hands are purposefully twisted rightward from the wrist so that the left palm faces right and the right palm faces left. (**CRISIS** is frequently fingerspelled.)

critical: *adj.* making severe or negative judgements. *She is critical of all government programs.*

SIGN #1: Tip of forefinger of right **'ONE'** hand draws an **'x'** across palm of horizontal left **'EXTENDED B'** hand which faces the body at a slight rightward angle.

critical: *adj.* extremely important or urgently required. *They have reached a critical stage in their plans for the future.*

SIGN #2: Vertical **'F'** hands are held apart with palms facing forward. The hands are then brought purposefully together.
ALTERNATE SIGN—**important** #2

critical: *adj.* used in reference to a serious medical condition. *The hospital kept him on the critical list for a week.*

SIGN #3: Vertical right **'BENT ONE'** hand is held with tip of forefinger touching chin and palm facing leftward but slanted toward the body. The wrist then rotates, turning the hand so that the palm fully faces the body. (**CRITICAL** is frequently fingerspelled.)
ALTERNATE SIGNS—**serious** #2 & #3

criticize: *v.* to judge with disapproval; to find fault. *The teacher criticized my illegible handwriting.*

SIGN: Tip of forefinger of right **'ONE'** hand draws an **'x'** across palm of horizontal left **'EXTENDED B'** hand which faces the body at a slight rightward angle.
SAME SIGN—**criticism**, *n.*

crochet: *v.* to create by looping and inter-twining thread with a hooked needle. *This pattern of afghan is simple to crochet.*

SIGN: Left **'x'** hand is held in a fixed position with palm facing the body and forefinger pointing rightward. Forefinger of horizontal right **'CROOKED ONE'** hand, palm toward the body, is placed on the left forefinger and retracts to assume an **'x'** shape as it is drawn rightward. Motion is repeated.

crocodile: *n.* a large reptile with thick skin and long, tapering jaws. *A full grown crocodile is larger than an alligator.*

SIGN: **'SPREAD C'** hands are held, right above left, palms facing each other, with fingertips touching. They are then moved apart and back together again to simulate the opening and closing of a crocodile's jaws.

crop: *n.* the yield of a field's produce during a particular season. *The farmer will harvest his crop in September.*

SIGN: Fingerspell **CROP**.

cross: *adj.* ill-tempered and disagreeable. *She was cross with her son for being rude to their guests.*

SIGN #1: As the vertical right **'5'** (or **'SPREAD C'**) hand, palm backward, is brought purposefully toward the face, the fingers retract to create a **'CLAWED SPREAD C'** hand. Facial expression is important.

cross: *v.* to move or go across. *Look both ways before you cross the street.*

SIGN #2: Horizontal **'EXTENDED B'** hand, palm facing left, is placed on the back of the left **'STANDARD BASE'** hand at right angles to it and is moved forward across it.
ALTERNATE SIGN—**walk** #2

cross: *v.* to traverse or intersect. *The new highway should not cross the migration path of the elk herd.*

SIGN #3: Horizontal **'ONE'** hands are held apart with palms facing the body but slanted toward each other slightly and the left fore-finger pointing rightward/forward while the right forefinger points leftward/forward. The hands then move toward each other, causing the right forefinger to cross over the left fore-finger in a converging motion.

cross: *n.* a structure consisting of two pieces intersecting at right angles to one another. *Their family purchased a cross to mark the grave.*

SIGN #4: Right **'EXTENDED C'** hand, palm facing away from the body, is used to outline the shape of a cross, beginning at the top of the vertical line and ending with the right end of the horizontal line.

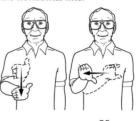

OR

SIGN #5: Left **'ONE'** hand is held in a fixed position with palm down and forefinger pointing rightward. Right **'ONE'** hand is held behind the left hand with palm facing left and forefinger pointing upward. The right hand then moves forward so that the forefinger strikes the forefinger of the left hand at right angles to it.

cross: *n.* any mark or shape consisting of two intersecting lines. *Put a cross in each appropriate box when you answer the question-naire.*

SIGN #6: Left **'ONE'** hand is held with palm facing the body at a rightward angle and fore-finger pointing rightward/forward. Right **'ONE'** hand is held slightly above and to the right of the left hand with palm facing the body at a leftward angle and forefinger point-ing leftward/forward. The right hand is then lowered so that the forefinger is placed firmly on the forefinger of the left hand at right angles to it. (This sign is used for **cross**, *n.*, in the sample sentence only if a separate sign is used for **put**, *v.* See also **(put a) cross**.)

(put a) cross: *v.* to mark an 'X' on some-thing. *Put a cross in each appropriate box when you answer the questionnaire.*

SIGN #7: Left **'EXTENDED B'** hand is held in a fixed position with palm up and fingers point-ing leftward/forward as forefinger and thumb of right palm down **'CLOSED X'** hand inscribe an **'x'** on the palm of the left hand.

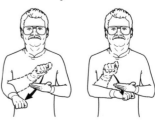

141

cross-country running: *n.* a sport in which participants run long distances over open ground. *Cross-country running requires a lot of training.*

SIGN #8: Vertical right **'C'** hand is held with palm facing forward. The wrist then bends so that the hand falls forward making the palm face downward. The hand then moves in a rightward arc. (It is as if the signer is finger-spelling **CC** to someone on the floor rather than someone directly in front of him/her.) Next, horizontal **'CLAWED L'** hands are held, left in front of right, with left thumb and right forefinger linked, and right palm facing left while left palm faces right. Together, the hands are moved firmly forward a short distance.

cross-country skiing: *n.* a sport in which participants ski over open ground. *Cross-country skiing is a great form of exercise.*

SIGN #9: Vertical right **'C'** hand is held with palm facing forward. The wrist then bends so that the hand falls forward making the palm face downward. The hand then moves in a rightward arc. (It is as if the signer is finger-spelling **CC** to someone on the floor rather than someone directly in front of him/her.) Next, horizontal **'S'** hands are held apart with right palm facing left and left palm facing right, and are alternately moved back and forth to simulate the arm movement involved in cross-country skiing.

cross-examine: *v.* to question carefully; to question a witness who has already been questioned by the opposing side in a court-room. *The defence attorney will now cross-examine the witness.*

SIGN #10: Vertical **'ONE'** hands, palms forward, are held apart, one at a slightly higher level than the other. The hands then alternately move forward and slightly downward in repeated circular motions. As the hands move forward, they take on the **'X'** handshape, and as they circle back toward the chest, they resume the **'ONE'** shape.

cross off: *v.* to strike off, remove, or delete something that is printed or written by putting a line through it. *He will cross off the names of those who withdraw from the program.*

SIGN #11: Right **'CLOSED X'** hand, palm down, is placed on the upturned palm of the left **'EXTENDED B'** hand and is then firmly stricken across it from left to right.

cross out: *v.* to strike out, remove, or delete something that is printed or written by putting a cross through it. *I will cross out the names of those who cannot attend the banquet.*

SIGN #12: Tip of forefinger of right **'ONE'** hand draws an **'X'** across palm of horizontal left **'EXTENDED B'** hand which faces the body at a slight rightward angle.

crouch: *v.* to squat with legs bent. (In the case of certain animals, to **crouch** indicates a readiness to pounce on prey). *The bank teller crouched behind the counter when the robber demanded money.*

SIGN: Right **'V'** hand is positioned with palm down and tips of forefinger and midfinger on upturned palm of left **'EXTENDED B'** hand. Then the right hand collapses to form a **'CLAWED V'** handshape.

crowd: *n.* a large number of things or people gathered together. *It is easy for a person to get lost in a crowd.*

SIGN #1: **'SPREAD C'** hands are held upright and slightly apart with palms facing each other. The wrists then rotate forward, bringing the hands to a horizontal position. (**CROWD** may be fingerspelled.)

(large) crowd: *n.* a very large number of things or people gathered together. *There was a large crowd in the streets waiting for the parade to begin.*

SIGN #2: **'SPREAD EXTENDED C'** hands are held one just in front of each shoulder, with palms down. The hands are then simultaneously moved forward.

crowded: *adj.* a large number of things or people pressed together in a confined space. *It was crowded in the stores with all the Christmas shoppers.*

SIGN: Vertical **'S'** hands are held one just in front of each shoulder, with palms facing each other at a slight forward angle, and are moved a bit closer together as the forearms are squeezed against the sides of the chest and the wrists rotate to turn the palms to face the body.

crown: *n.* an ornamental headdress symbolizing sovereignty. *The king wore a crown of gold and rubies.*

SIGN: **'CLAWED L'** hands are held slightly apart in a horizontal position just above the head, with palms facing each other. Then they are lowered simultaneously as if setting something down on the head.

crucial: *adj.* critical or very important. *Funding is a crucial factor in educational programming.*

SIGN: Vertical **'F'** hands are held apart with palms facing forward. The hands are then brought purposefully together.
ALTERNATE SIGN—**important** #2

cruel: *adj.* causing pain or suffering without any pity. *It is cruel to keep a large animal confined in a small cage.*

SIGN: Right **'CROOKED 5'** hand is held with palm facing left and tip of forefinger touching or near end of nose while left **'CROOKED 5'** hand, palm facing right, is held just in front of/below right hand. The hands eventually assume **'A'** shapes as they brush past one another, the right hand moving downward/forward and the left hand moving upward/backward. Appropriate facial expression is important.
SAME SIGN—**cruelty**, *n.*

cruise: *n.* a trip by sea. *They went on a cruise for their honeymoon.*

SIGN: **'CROOKED EXTENDED B'** hands, palms facing each other at a slight angle, are cupped together to form the hull of a boat. Together, the hands are moved forward. (**CRUISE** is frequently fingerspelled.)

crush: *v.* to damage by pressing against. *He crushed the tomato between his hands.*

SIGN #1: **'CROOKED 5'** hands are held, heels together but the hands themselves offset, with left palm facing right and right palm facing left. As the hands maintain contact at the heels, the right wrist rotates forward and the left wrist rotates backward, bringing the fingers of each hand closer together. A look of determination accompanies this sign. (Signs vary.)

crush: *n.* an infatuation; a usually short-lived passion or attraction, as in the case of 'puppy love'. *She had a **crush** on the new boy at school.*

SIGN #2: Left **'EXTENDED B'** hand is held in a fixed position with palm up and fingers pointing forward/rightward. Right **'ONE'** hand is held, palm forward/downward, with forefinger just in front of the nose and pointing forward/upward. The right hand then falls forward, coming to rest heavily on the left palm. (**CRUSH** in this context may be fingerspelled.)

crutches: *n.* devices used to support the weight of the body and enable mobility. *You will need to use **crutches** while your leg is in a cast.*

SIGN: **'S'** hands, with elbows bent, are held at either side of the waist with the palms toward the body, and are simultaneously circled forward a few times to simulate the use of crutches. (To refer to the singular form **crutch**, the same sign may be made with one hand only.)

cry: *v.* to weep or sob. *He **cried** at his brother's funeral.*

SIGN #1: Vertical **'L'** hands are held so that the tips of the forefingers are just below each eye and the palms are toward the face. The forefingers are then simultaneously stroked downward on the cheeks, thus taking on **'BENT L'** shapes. Motion is repeated. (Signs vary a great deal, often depending on the duration of the crying and whether or not it is quiet sobbing or convulsive crying.)

cry: *v.* to scream or shout in pain or terror. *I heard her **cry out** in pain.*

SIGN #2: Right vertical **'SPREAD C'** hand, palm toward the body, is held near the mouth and is forcefully drawn forward at an upward angle.

cult: *n.* a group of people who share an intense devotion to a specific religious leader or set of beliefs. *The leader of the **cult** demanded strict obedience from his followers.*

SIGN: Fingerspell **CULT**.

culture: *n.* the shared customs, beliefs, and values of a people. *A person's **culture** is often a source of pride.*

SIGN #1: Left **'ONE'** hand is held in a fixed position with palm facing rightward/forward at a downward angle while vertical right **'EXTENDED C'** hand, with palm facing leftward/forward is held just to the right of the left forefinger. The right wrist then rotates 180 degrees forward until the palm is facing the body at an upward angle.
SAME SIGN—**cultural**, *adj.*

(Deaf) Culture: *n.* all those things which set the Deaf Community apart from other groups, *e.g.,* a common set of objectives, beliefs, values, heritage, and a unique language known as ASL; distinctive behavioural characteristics resulting from a need to have a clear field of vision; a sense of pride in being Deaf; a sense of humour that is characteristically 'Deaf'; and a shared sense of what is important to Deaf people collectively. (Whereas 'Deaf Culture' exists worldwide, signed languages vary considerably just as spoken languages do. In Canada, the languages of the Deaf are ASL and LSQ.) ***Deaf Culture*** *may be one of the most distinctive cultures that the world has ever known.*

SIGN #2: Vertical right **'ONE'** hand is held with tip of forefinger just in front of the right ear. The hand is then lowered so that the tip of the forefinger touches the right side of the mouth. Next, left **'ONE'** hand is held in a fixed position with palm facing rightward/forward at a downward angle while vertical right **'EXTENDED C'** hand, with palm facing leftward/forward is held just to the right of the left forefinger. The right wrist then rotates 180 degrees forward until the palm is facing the body at an upward angle.

cunning: *adj.* crafty and shrewd in a deceitful way; sly. *The fox is a **cunning** animal.*

SIGN: Thumb and forefinger of the right **'FLAT OPEN F'** hand are laid flat against the left cheek with the palm facing leftward/backward. The forefinger moves rapidly up and down several times so that the hand alternates between a **'FLAT OPEN F'** shape and a **'FLAT F'**.

cup: *n.* a small, open container usually having a handle, and used for drinking. *Your coffee cup is empty now.*

SIGN #1: Left **'EXTENDED B'** hand is held in a fixed position with palm up and fingers pointing forward/rightward. Right **'C'** hand, palm facing left but angled toward the body slightly, is placed on the left palm and is raised and lowered twice.

cup: *n.* a trophy resembling a cup. *The Toronto Maple Leafs won the Stanley Cup that year.*

SIGN #2: Fingerspell **CUP**. (When referring to a **cup** of this kind, the sign for **trophy** may be used. When the cup is named, as in the case of 'Stanley Cup' or 'Grey Cup', the word **CUP** is always fingerspelled.)

cure: *n.* a remedy. *Researchers are trying to find a cure for that medical condition.*

SIGN: Fingerspell **CURE**.

curious: *adj.* inquisitive, or desirous of learning and knowing. *People have always been curious about how the universe was created.*

SIGN #1: Thumb and forefinger of right **'F'** hand are held at the throat, as the hand wobbles due to a slight twisting of the wrist.

SIGN #2 [PRAIRIE]: Fingertips of vertical right **'SPREAD EXTENDED C'** hand are placed near right side of forehead and are flexed so that they repeatedly touch the forehead.
SAME SIGN—**curiosity**, *n.*

curling: *n.* a game played on ice with heavy stones and brooms or brushes. *Curling is a popular winter sport in Canada.*

SIGN: Right **'S'** hand is held near right side of body with palm facing down, and is then moved forward as the wrist twists rightward and the hand opens into a **'SLANTED 5'** hand with the palm facing left and fingers pointing forward.

curly hair: *adj.* hair which tends to curl or be wavy. *She thinks that curly hair is easier to care for than straight hair.*

SIGN: **'SPREAD C'** hands, with palms facing each other, are held near either side of the head and are alternately moved in small circles, the right hand moving clockwise and the left hand moving counter-clockwise. Both hands are circled in a forward direction.

currency: *n.* any form of money used as exchange. *The basic unit of currency in our country is the Canadian dollar.*

SIGN: Back of right **'CONTRACTED B'** (or **'BENT EXTENDED B'**) hand, palm up, is tapped two or three times on upturned palm of left **'EXTENDED B'** hand.

current: *adj.* pertaining to the immediate present. *The students discuss current world events in their Social Studies class.*

SIGN: **'Y'** hands, palms up, are held slightly apart and are simultaneously lowered.
ALTERNATE SIGN—**now** #2

curriculum: *n.* a specific course of study in one school subject. *A new ASL curriculum is being developed by the committee.*

SIGN: Left **'EXTENDED B'** hand is held in a fixed position with palm facing the body and fingers pointing upward/rightward. Right **'C'** hand, palm facing left, is placed against the palm of the left hand, and is transformed to a **'FLAT M'** shape as it is moved up and over the fingers of the left hand coming to rest against the back of the left hand.

curse: *v.* to damn or to wish someone misfortune. *He cursed his father for embarrassing him in front of his friends.*

SIGN #1: Vertical right **'SPREAD C'** hand with palm toward the face, is firmly brought forward from in front of the mouth, and is closed to form an **'S'** hand. This sign is accompanied by a very angry facial expression.

curse: *v.* to use a profane or obscene expression; to swear. *He cursed at the other driver for changing lanes suddenly without signalling.*

SIGN #2: Left **'ONE'** hand is held in a fixed position with palm down and forefinger pointing forward/rightward. Right **'Y'** hand, with palm down, is moved forward/rightward along the length of the left forefinger.

cursor: *n.* a movable point. *The computer cursor flashes on the display unit while you type on the keyboard.*

SIGN: Vertical right **'FLAT O'** hand is held with the palm toward the body. The fingers are rapidly opened and closed several times, thus alternating between a **'FLAT O'** and **'CONTRACTED 5'** shape.

curtain: *n.* the drapery that is hung on windows or across the front of a stage. *The curtains in the living room were custom-made to fit the windows.*

SIGN: Vertical **'4'** hands, palms forward, are held apart above shoulder level. The wrists then simultaneously bend forward so that the hands drop to a palms down position.

custody: *n.* legal care or guardianship. *The court granted him custody of his son.*

SIGN: Fingerspell **CUSTODY**.

custom: *n.* a practice that is habitual. *Gathering for a large dinner at Thanksgiving is a family custom.*

SIGN: Vertical right **'S'** hand, palm facing leftward/downward, is held with wrist against back of left **'S'** hand, which is held with palm down. Together, the hands are lowered.

customer: *n.* a person who purchases goods or services. *The cashier is trained to be courteous to every customer.*

SIGN: Fingerspell **CUSTOMER**.

customs: *n.* a government department responsible for duties and tariffs on imported goods. *We declared all our purchases when we went through Canada Customs.*

SIGN: Fingerspell **CUSTOMS**.

cut: *n.* an incision or an opening in the skin caused by a sharp instrument. *He has a bad cut from a knife.*

SIGN #1: Tip of forefinger of right **'ONE'** hand, with palm facing leftward/backward, is drawn firmly backward across back of left **'STANDARD BASE'** hand. (The location of this sign will vary according to which part of the body has been affected.)

cut: *v.* to separate something into parts by using scissors. *He cut the paper in half.*

SIGN #2: Right **'3'** hand, palm facing left and extended fingers pointing forward is held beside the left **'STANDARD BASE'** hand and is moved directly forward as the extended fingers close and open several times, the hand thus alternating between a **'3'** and an **'EXTENDED U'** shape to simulate the use of a pair of scissors. ❖

cut (cake): *v.* to divide a cake into pieces using a knife. *You may cut the cake now.*

SIGN #3: Right **'EXTENDED B'** hand is held well out in front of the body with palm facing left and fingers pointing forward/downward. The hand is then drawn straight backward toward the body. (Signs will vary depending on the shape of the cake and the pattern of cutting.)

cut (class): *v.* to absent oneself without permission. *She missed a lot of important information when she cut class yesterday.*

SIGN #4: Left **'BENT MIDFINGER 5'** hand is held in a fixed position with palm down while the forefinger of the right **'ONE'** hand is used to strike the midfinger of the left hand at a backward/leftward/downward angle.

cut (meat): *v.* to separate meat into pieces using a knife and fork. *You will need a sharp knife to cut the meat.*

SIGN #5: Left **'CLOSED A-INDEX'** hand is held in a fixed position with palm down. Right **'CLOSED A-INDEX'** hand is held palm down beside the left hand and is moved forward and back a few times to simulate the action of cutting with a knife and fork. (Signs vary.)

cut down (a tree): *v.* to fell a tree. *It will take a lot of time and energy to cut this tree down.*

SIGN: Left **'5'** hand is held upright to represent a tree while the edge of the right **'EXTENDED B'** hand, palm up and fingers pointing leftward/forward, is used to strike against the left forearm with a chopping motion.

cut it out: *v.* a command insisting that a person stop doing something undesirable. *When our father entered the room and saw us fighting, he told us to* **cut it out**.

SIGN: Horizontal right **'5'** hand, palm left, is firmly thrust forward a short distance as the wrist turns slightly but firmly leftward so that the palm, though still facing leftward, is now angled downward. An angry facial expression generally accompanies this sign.

cut off: *v.* to remove by cutting or to discontinue a supply of something. *If you do not pay your bill, your electricity will be* **cut off**.

SIGN: Vertical left **'BENT B'** hand is held in a fixed position with palm facing rightward/forward. Horizontal right **'SLANTED V'** (or **'EXTENDED K'**) hand is held just behind and to the right of the left hand with palm facing downward/leftward. The right hand then moves forward/leftward, the extended fingers grazing the fingertips of the left hand and closing as if simulating the action of scissors in the process of snipping the fingernails of the left hand.

cut out: *v.* to remove or extract by using scissors. *The teacher* **cut out** *several newspaper articles to discuss for current events.*

SIGN: Left **'EXTENDED B'** hand is held in a fixed position with palm up and fingers pointing rightward/forward. Right **'CLAWED EXTENDED V'** hand, with palm facing leftward but angled toward the body, is placed on left palm and circled counter-clockwise several times with extended fingers continually flexing.

cute: *adj.* attractive or pretty, often in a dainty or precious sort of way. *She has a lot of* **cute** *clothes for her baby.*

SIGN: Tips of extended fingers of right **'EXTENDED U'** hand, palm facing the body, are brushed downward on chin. This movement involves only the extended fingers, which bend in the process. The hand itself does not move.

cycle: *n.* one execution or occurrence of a regularly repeated action or phenomenon. *The dishwasher is now on the "rinse"* **cycle**.

SIGN #1: Forefinger of right **'BENT ONE'** hand is used to inscribe an imaginary clockwise circle in front of the chest. (Motion may be repeated.)

cycle: *v.* to travel by bicycle. *I plan to* **cycle** *to Banff this summer.*

SIGN #2: **'S'** hands are held palms down, and moved forward alternately in small circles to simulate the pedaling of a bicycle.
ALTERNATE REGIONAL VARIATION—**bicycle** #2.

cynical: See **negative** #1.

cyst: *n.* an abnormal membranous sac or pouch filled with fluid or semisolid matter. *The* **cyst** *was surgically removed from her abdomen.*

SIGN: Fingerspell **CYST**.

D

dad: *n.* informal word for father. *Dad does the shopping and the cooking.*

SIGN: Tip of forefinger of right **'ONE'** hand taps twice against the right side of the forehead. ALTERNATE SIGNS—**father** #2 & #3

daily: *adv.* every day. *We check daily to see if we have any e-mail messages.*

SIGN: Knuckles of right **'A'** hand, with palm toward face, are brushed forward across the right cheek twice.

dairy: *adj.* related to milk and milk products. *You can get calcium from dairy products.*

SIGN: Horizontal right **'S'** hand is squeezed and relaxed several times, thus alternating between a tight and more loosely held fist. (**DAIRY** may be fingerspelled.)

dam: *n.* a barrier built across a river to control the flow or level of water. *Building a dam requires careful planning.*

SIGN: Fingerspell **DAM**.

damage: *v.* to do injury or harm. *Severe frostbite can permanently damage your skin.*

SIGN #1: Left **'CLAWED 5'** hand is held palm-up while right **'CLAWED 5'** hand is held palm-down to the right and above/ahead of left hand. The hands close to form **'A'** hands as they are brought together and just past each other, the knuckles of the right hand grazing those of the left. The knuckles brush against each other again as the left hand moves firmly backward/leftward and the right hand moves firmly rightward/forward.

SIGN #2 [ATLANTIC]: Right horizontal **'I'** hand, palm left but angled toward the body, is placed on upturned palm of left **'EXTENDED B'** hand and is then firmly pushed forward/rightward across it, the right wrist rotating so that the palm eventually faces downward.

damn: *inter.* an informal expression of anger, annoyance or disappointment. *Damn! Why didn't you tell me?*

SIGN: Vertical right **'D'** hand, with palm facing leftward/forward, is held in front of the chest and is firmly moved downward/forward at a rightward angle. Facial expression must clearly convey the mood of the signer.

damp: *adj.* slightly wet. *Her clothes are still damp from the rain.*

SIGN: The hands are held apart with palms up and they simultaneously alternate between **'FLAT C'** and **'FLAT O'** shapes as they open slightly and close a few times.

dance: *v.* to move the feet and body rhythmically to keep time to music. *They are learning how to dance the polka.*

SIGN: Right **'BENT V'** hand, palm facing downward, is held above upturned palm of left **'EXTENDED B'** hand. Extended fingers of right hand are brushed back and forth lightly across left palm.

dandruff: *n.* loose bits of dead skin that are shed from the scalp. *Certain types of shampoo can be used to control dandruff.*

SIGN: Fingerspell **DANDRUFF**.

dangerous: *adj.* having the potential to result in injury or pain. *Auto racing can be a dangerous sport.*

SIGN #1: Left **'A'** hand is held in a fixed position with palm facing downward but slanted toward the chest. Right **'A'** hand is held just in front of the left hand with palm facing left and is circled forward a couple of times so that the thumb firmly brushes upward against the back of the left hand with each revolution.
SAME SIGN—**danger**, *n.*

SIGN #2 [ATLANTIC/ONTARIO]: **'EXTENDED B'** hands are held with palms facing each other and fingers pointing forward at a slight upward angle. The hands are firmly clapped together and move in an upward/outward arc as they come apart. Movement is repeated. Facial expression is important.
SAME SIGN—**danger**, *n.*

SIGN #3 [ONTARIO]: Tip of forefinger of vertical right **'V'** hand, palm facing left, brushes tip of nose as the hand moves leftward/downward a couple of times in front of the face. Facial expression is important.
SAME SIGN—**danger**, *n.*

SIGN #4 [PRAIRIE]: Vertical **'CLAWED V'** hand, palm facing left, is held with side of forefinger against the nose. The hand moves abruptly forward, and then the wrist bends to turn the palm downward. Facial expression is important.
SAME SIGN—**danger**, *n.*

dare: *v.* to challenge a person to do something to prove his courage. *He dared me to jump.*

SIGN #1: Left horizontal **'EXTENDED A'** hand is held, palm facing the body, just ahead of right **'EXTENDED A'** hand, which is held with palm facing leftward but angled slightly toward the body. Then the wrists are simultaneously twisted so that the thumbs point more emphatically upward as the hands are moved closer together. They may even touch.

dare: *v.* to be brave enough to do something. *I was surprised that she would dare to ask her boss for more time off.*

SIGN #2: Fingerspell **DARE**.
(**DARE** is fingerspelled slowly for emphasis in this context and is accompanied by a look of astonishment.)
ALTERNATE SIGN—**daring**

D A R E

daring: *adj.* bold; adventurous; not afraid to take a risk. *He was very daring to talk to his boss like that.*

SIGN: Horizontal right **'S'** hand, palm facing the body at an upward angle, is placed against the upper right part of the chest and is brushed downward twice in a circular motion. Facial expression is important.

dark: *adj.* without much or any light. *The night is very dark.*

SIGN #1: **'EXTENDED B'** hands are held near either side of the face with palms facing backward. The hands then move toward and past each other so that the forearms appear to be crossed.

dark: *adj.* not light in colour. *She wears dark colours, especially black or brown.*

SIGN #2: **'CROOKED 5'** hands are held parallel with palms down. They then jerk slightly forward/downward as the fingers retract to form **'CLAWED SPREAD C'** hands.

darn it: *inter.* a euphemism for 'damn it'. *I tried to hit the bull's eye, but darn it, I missed!*

SIGN: Right **'BENT D'** hand, palm facing left, is twisted briskly from the wrist as it changes to an **'A'** handshape.

dart: *n.* a narrow, pointed object that is thrown in a game of darts. *His first dart missed the target.*

SIGN: Right vertical **'CLOSED X'** hand, palm forward, is thrust forward from the wrist as it changes to a **'CONTRACTED L'** handshape.

data: *n.* information; a set of observations, measurements, or facts. *Researchers need to use good methods for collecting data.*

SIGN: Left **'MODIFIED O'** hand is held at about shoulder level with palm facing upward but angled slightly toward the body while right **'MODIFIED O'** hand is held upright just in front of the forehead with palm toward the face. The forearms then move simultaneously forward/downward as the hands open to assume **'MODIFIED 5'** shapes with palms facing upward.

data base: *n.* a collection of one or more computer files treated as a whole unit. *The data base of the museum's collection was very useful.*

SIGN: Fingerspell **DB**.

date: *n.* a specific day of a month, a year, or an event. *They have set their wedding date for June 15th next year.*

SIGN #1: Fingerspell **DATE**.

date: *n.* an appointment for a specific time and usually for an arranged event, especially with a member of the opposite sex. *On their first date, they went to a movie.*

SIGN #2: Fingerspell **DATE**.

daughter: *n.* a female offspring. *They are the proud parents of a new daughter.*

SIGN #1: Right **'B'** hand is held with tip of forefinger touching chin and palm facing leftward/downward. The right forearm then drops downward as the wrist rotates forward causing the palm to turn upward as the hand comes to rest on the left forearm.

SIGN #2 [ATLANTIC]: Outer edge of right **'BENT EXTENDED B'** hand, palm angled slightly upward/rightward, is tapped against centre of chest at least twice.

dawdle: *v.* to be slow, lag behind, or waste time. *You had better not dawdle or you will miss the bus.*

SIGN: **'5'** hands are held parallel with palms down in front of the left side of the body and are simultaneously moved rightward in arc formation so that they are in front of the right side of the body. They are then moved leftward in arc formation to their original position. (Appropriate facial expression must accompany this sign. Cheeks are puffed and the face shows a clear lack of concern.)

dawn: *n.* the time of morning when daylight begins to appear; daybreak. *The rooster crowed at dawn.*

SIGN: Left **'STANDARD BASE'** hand represents the horizon and right **'C'** (or **'O'** or **'F'**) hand, palm leftward/downward, represents the rising sun as it is held just ahead of/below the left hand and then raised to a level above the left hand.

day: *n.* the period of sunlight between sunrise and sunset. [See TIME CONCEPTS, p. LXXI.] *The longest day of the year is in late June.*

SIGN: Right **'ONE'** hand is held upright as right elbow rests on back of left **'EXTENDED B'** hand. Then the right arm is lowered until the hand rests on the left arm near the elbow.

day after tomorrow: *adv.* two days from now. *I will see you the day after tomorrow.*

SIGN: Right **'SLANTED V'** hand is held with palm facing backward and tip of middle finger touching right cheek. The hand then moves slightly forward.

day before yesterday: *adv.* two days ago. *We planned to go on a picnic the day before yesterday, but it rained.*

SIGN: Vertical right **'SLANTED V'** hand is held with palm facing backward and middle finger resting against the right cheek. The wrist then twists to rotate the hand so that the tip of the forefinger is held against the cheek and the palm is facing forward/leftward.

daydream: *v.* to indulge in a pleasant fantasy while awake. *He just sits and daydreams all day.*

SIGN: Tip of the forefinger of the right **'ONE'** hand is placed at the right side of the forehead, with palm toward the face. The hand then moves forward/rightward/upward as the forefinger alternates from a **'ONE'** to an **'X'** position in a series of rapid movements. (When **daydream** is used to mean 'to allow one's mind to wander instead of paying attention to matters at hand', the same basic sign is used but, instead of one fluid motion, it is a repeated, almost staccato movement with the forefinger repeatedly flexing and extending as it appears to peck at the forehead.)

dead: *adj.* no longer alive. *The accident victim was dead on arrival at the hospital.*

SIGN: **'EXTENDED B'** hands are held with fingers pointing forward, left palm facing up and right palm facing down. Then they are flipped over simultaneously so that the palm positions are reversed.

deadline: *n.* a time limit or due date for an activity or the completion of an assignment. *The deadline for the submission of applications is next Friday.*

SIGN: Horizontal left **'I'** hand is held with palm facing the body at a rightward angle and little finger pointing forward/rightward. Vertical right **'I'** hand, with palm facing leftward/backward, is held to the right of and above the left hand. The right hand is then lowered so that the tip of the little finger strikes the tip of the little finger of the left hand. (Sign will only make sense when placed within the correct ASL syntactic framework. The sample sentence in ASL is: *APPLICATION GIVE-BACK LAST NEXT WEEK FRIDAY.*)

Deaf: *adj.* partially or totally unable to hear. *Deaf people communicate as effectively in ASL as hearing people do in spoken English.*

SIGN: Vertical right **'ONE'** hand is held with tip of forefinger just in front of the right ear. The hand is then lowered so that the tip of the forefinger touches the right side of the mouth. Alternatively, this sign may progress from the mouth to the ear. See also **profoundly Deaf**.

Deaf Community: See **(Deaf) Community**.

Deaf Culture: See **(Deaf) Culture**.

deafened: *v.* having become Deaf either temporarily or permanently. *Industrial noise has deafened many workers.*

SIGN: Tip of forefinger of right **'ONE'** hand touches the right ear. Then **'EXTENDED A'** hands are held parallel near either ear with palms facing, and are simultaneously moved downward.

Deaflympics: See **Olympic**.

deal: *n.* an agreement. *The deal fell through because they could not raise enough money.*

SIGN #1: Left **'ONE'** hand is held at chest level with palm facing right and forefinger pointing away from body. Right **'ONE'** hand, palm facing left, is held slightly higher and then turned downward to match the simultaneously downward-turning left hand. (**DEAL** is frequently fingerspelled, especially in informal conversation, *e.g.,* 'It's a deal!' or 'I bought a new car and I got a good deal.')

deal: *v.* to distribute cards to the players in a card game. *I dealt the last round, so you can deal now.*

SIGN #2: Horizontal left **'CLOSED A-INDEX'** hand is held in a fixed position with palm toward the body at a slight rightward angle. While the right hand moves back and forth several times in front of the left hand, the handshape alternates between an **'A-INDEX'** and a **'CLOSED A-INDEX'** as the thumb and forefinger repeatedly open and close.

dean: *n.* an administrative official of a college or university faculty. *The Dean of Education was interviewed by the journalist.*

SIGN: Fingerspell **DEAN**.

dear: *adj.* beloved or precious. *My dog is very dear to me.*

SIGN #1: Knuckles of vertical right **'OPEN SPREAD O'** hand, palm toward the body, are placed on the chin and are firmly drawn downward, closing to form an **'S'** hand. (For **dear** in the 'birthday song', i.e., *Happy birthday dear John*, see **beloved**.)

dear: *adj.* used in a form of address such as 'Dear Sir'. *Letters often begin with 'Dear Sir or Madam'.*

SIGN #2: Fingerspell **DEAR**.

death: *n.* the permanent end of life. *After the death of a loved one, people show their grief in different ways.*

SIGN: **'EXTENDED B'** hands are held with fingers pointing forward, left palm facing up and right palm facing down. Then they are flipped over simultaneously so that the palm positions are reversed.

debate: *v.* to have a formal discussion in which opposing arguments are put forward. *The M.P.s debated the bill for several weeks before it became law.*

SIGN: Leftward-pointing forefinger of horizontal right **'ONE'** hand, palm toward the body, is tapped several times on the upturned palm of the left **'EXTENDED B'** hand, of which the fingers are pointing rightward/forward. (There are variations; sometimes the right forefinger points forward.)

debit: *n.* a sum that is owed and is entered on the left side of an account. *Expenses are always recorded as debits.*

SIGN: Right **'CROOKED 5'** hand, palm down, is held so the wrist is directly below the left **'STANDARD BASE'** hand. Then the right hand is drawn back toward the chest as it closes to form an **'S'** hand.

ALTERNATE SIGN—**deduct**

debt: *n.* something owed, such as money, goods or services. *He is working hard to pay off his debt.*

SIGN: Tip of forefinger of right **'ONE'** hand, palm toward body, is tapped twice against right-facing palm of horizontal left **'EXTENDED B'** hand.

decade: *n.* a time period of ten years. *The 1990s constituted the final decade of the 20th century.*

SIGN: Right **'EXTENDED A'** hand, palm left and thumb pointing upward, is shaken slightly. Next, horizontal **'S'** hands, palms toward the body, are held so the right is slightly above the left. Then the right is circled forward around the left, coming to rest on top of it. (ASL CONCEPT—**ten - year**.)

decay: *n.* deterioration; rot. *Good oral hygiene helps to prevent tooth decay.*

SIGN: **'A'** hands are held together with palms facing the chest. The hands then gradually rotate forward with fingers spreading until they take on a **'CROOKED 5'** shape with palms facing upward.

deceased: *adj.* dead. *She removed his name from the company files because he is now deceased.*

SIGN: **'EXTENDED B'** hands are held with fingers pointing forward, left palm facing up and right palm facing down. Then they are flipped over simultaneously so that the palm positions are reversed.

deceive: *v.* to mislead or deliberately misrepresent. *I deceived him by pretending I was rich and famous.*

SIGN: Vertical right **'A'** hand, with palm forward and slightly leftward, is knocked against forefinger of vertical left **'ONE'** hand whose palm faces right. ❖

SAME SIGN—**deceit**, *n.*

ALTERNATE SIGN—**lie** #1

December: *n.* the twelfth month of the year, consisting of 31 days. *We celebrate Christmas on December 25th.*

SIGN: Fingerspell **DEC**.

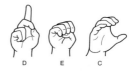

decent: *adj.* proper; acceptable; suitable. *You will have to change into decent clothes to go to that restaurant.*

SIGN #1: Right **'ONE'** hand, palm facing left, is held above left **'ONE'** hand, palm facing right, with forefingers pointing forward. Then right hand is tapped at least twice on left hand. (Signs in this context vary.)

decent: *adj.* good; law-abiding. *He is considered a decent person.*

SIGN #2: Fingertips of right **'BENT EXTENDED B'** hand are placed on the lips so that the palm is toward the body. The hand then moves a short distance forward and back a few times so that the fingertips tap repeatedly against the lips.

decibel: *n.* a unit for measuring the intensity of sound. *If a person has a hearing loss of 90 decibels, he/she is profoundly Deaf.*

SIGN: Fingerspell **DB**.

decide: *v.* to reach a decision; to conclude. *I need to think about your offer before I can decide whether or not I will accept it.*

SIGN: **'F'** hands, with palms facing each other, are held apart in front of chest and are simultaneously lowered.
SAME SIGN—**decision**, *n.*

decimal point: *n.* a dot or period placed between integers to show the fractional part that follows it. *In the amount $10.50, the decimal point is placed between the zero and the five.*

SIGN: Right **'BENT ONE'** hand, palm forward, is stabbed forward firmly from the wrist.

deck: *n.* a surface or platform; the floor of a ship. *We built a deck at the back of our house.*

SIGN #1: Fingerspell **DECK**.

deck of cards: *n.* a pack of playing cards. *Do you have a new deck of cards for this game?*

SIGN #2: Horizontal right **'C'** hand, palm facing left but angled slightly toward the body, is held just above the upturned palm of the left **'EXTENDED B'** hand, which is held with fingers pointing forward/rightward. The right hand is then lowered into the left palm, raised, and lowered once again.

OR

SIGN #3: Left **'BENT EXTENDED B'** hand is held with palm up as horizontal right **'EXTENDED C'** hand is held against the backs of the fingers on the left hand and moved up and down a couple of times.

declare: *v.* to announce officially or make a formal statement. *On returning to Canada you must use this form to declare goods you bought during your trip abroad.*

SIGN: Left **'MODIFIED O'** hand is held at about shoulder level with palm facing upward but angled slightly toward the body while right **'MODIFIED O'** hand is held upright just in front of the forehead with palm toward the face. The forearms then move simultaneously forward/downward as the hands open to assume **'MODIFIED 5'** shapes with palms facing upward.

decline: *v.* to deteriorate gradually; to enter a downward trend. *The economy has declined as a result of the new trading policies.*

SIGN #1: Right **'BENT EXTENDED B'** hand is held with palm facing down and fingers pointing forward/downward. The forearm is then thrust downward/forward.

decline: *v.* to deteriorate gradually in terms of health. *His health has declined since he underwent surgery.*

SIGN #2: Edge of right **'EXTENDED B'** hand is placed in the crook between the left bicep and forearm. The right hand is then moved downward to the left wrist.
ALTERNATE SIGN—**deteriorate** #1

decline: *v.* to refuse politely (used in more formal settings). *She will decline the nomination.*

SIGN #3: Forefinger of right **'ONE'** hand is placed on the lips. Then the right hand is changed to an **'EXTENDED B'** hand as it is brought down to be placed on the upturned palm of the left **'EXTENDED B'** hand. When the two palms meet, the right is brushed forward firmly across the left.

decline: *v.* to refuse politely (used in informal situations). *She declined the invitation to join our club.*

SIGN #4: Vertical right **'5'** hand, palm forward, is waved back and forth lightly from the wrist. A head shake and an appropriate facial expression should accompany this sign.

decode: *v.* to translate from a code into ordinary language. *Were you able to decode the scrambled message?*

SIGN: **'X'** (or **'A'**) hands, palms facing each other, are twisted 180 degrees.
ALTERNATE SIGN—**translate**

decoder: *n.* a device used to display captioning on TV or videotape. *A closed caption* ***decoder*** *displays a printed message on the television screen.*

SIGN: Horizontal **'F'** hands, palms facing other, thumbs and forefingers touching, are moved apart with a slight rotation of the wrists so that palms face downward/forward. Movement is repeated.

decompose: *v.* to break down by bacterial or fungal action; decay; rot. *Materials that do not* ***decompose*** *readily are environmental hazards.*

SIGN: **'A'** hands are held together with palms facing the chest. The hands then gradually rotate forward with fingers spreading until they take on a **'CROOKED 5'** shape with palms facing upward.

decorate: *v.* to ornament; adorn. *How will you* ***decorate*** *the hall for your Hallowe'en party?*

SIGN: Vertical **'SPREAD C'** hands are held apart with palms forward and are simultaneously circled outward in opposite directions, the right hand moving clockwise and the left hand moving counter-clockwise.
SAME SIGN—**decoration,** *n.*

decrease: *v.* to diminish in size, value, strength or mass. *Your weight has* ***decreased*** *slightly.*

SIGN #1: Left **'BENT U'** hand is held in a fixed position with palm rightward/forward and extended fingers pointing rightward/forward. Right **'BENT U'** hand is held with palm leftward/forward and tips of extended fingers resting on those of the left hand at right angles. The right wrist then rotates rightward causing the hand to turn palm upward as it drops slightly. (If the weight loss is progressive, the movement is repeated.)

decrease: *v.* to diminish in size, value, or strength. *The boss will* ***decrease*** *your workload next month.*

SIGN #2: Horizontal **'BENT EXTENDED B'** (or **'ONE'**) hands are held right above left with left palm up and right palm forward/downward. The right hand is then lowered toward the left hand.

decrease: *v.* to diminish in size, value, or strength. *Stock values* ***decrease*** *sharply during a market crash.*

SIGN #3: Right **'BENT EXTENDED B'** hand is held with palm facing down and fingers pointing forward/downward. The forearm is then thrust downward/forward.

decree: *n.* an order or law established by someone in authority. *The President issued the* ***decree*** *that all hostages were to be released at once.*

SIGN: **'F'** hands, with palms facing each other, are held apart in front of chest and are simultaneously lowered.

decrepit: *adj.* weakened by old age, or broken down by long use. *That* ***decrepit*** *house will be demolished.*

SIGN: Right **'S'** hand, slightly open, palm facing left, is brought down firmly from the chin as it closes. Next, fingertips of right **'5'** hand, palm toward the body, are placed on upturned palm of left **'EXTENDED B'** hand. Then the fingers buckle so that the hand is transformed into a **'CLAWED 5'** shape.
(ASL CONCEPT—**old - weak.**)

dedicate: *v.* to address a book or performance to someone as a token of affection and/or respect. *He will* ***dedicate*** *his new book to his parents.*

SIGN: Right **'U'** hand, palm facing left, is held in a vertical position so that the side of the forefinger touches the middle of the forehead. Then the hand is moved forward away from the head.

dedicated: *adj.* totally involved in a special project, career, or cause. *He is our most* ***dedicated*** *employee.*

SIGN: Fingerspell **DEDICATED**.

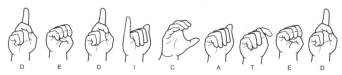

D E D I C A T E D

deduce: *v.* to conclude or infer by logical reasoning. *We were able to deduce from his note that he was pleading for help.*

SIGN: Right **'CROOKED OPEN C'** hand is held near right temple, palm facing left, and is moved leftward as it closes to form an **'S'** hand.
SAME SIGN—**deduction,** *n.,* in this context.
ALTERNATE SIGN—**figure out**

deduct: *v.* to subtract or take away. *Sometimes you can deduct the cost of medicine as an exemption from your income tax.*

SIGN: Horizontal left **'EXTENDED B'** hand is held in a fixed position with palm rightward/backward and fingers pointing forward/rightward. Fingertips of right **'SPREAD C'** hand are placed against the palm of the left hand. Then the right hand is pulled down and closed to form an **'S'** hand.
SAME SIGN—**deduction,** *n.,* in this context.

deed: *n.* an act; something that is done. *A Boy Scout is expected to do a good deed every day.*

SIGN #1: Wrist of right **'A'** (or **'S'**) hand, palm facing away from the body, strikes wrist of left **'A'** (or **'S'**) hand, which is held in front of/below the right hand with palm facing downward. Motion is repeated. Next, horizontal left **'A'** (or **'EXTENDED A'**) hand, palm facing the body but turned slightly rightward, is positioned on the upturned fingers of the right **'EXTENDED B'** hand and the hands are tapped together a couple of times.
(ASL CONCEPT—**work - help.**)

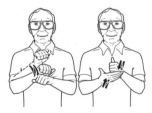

deed: *n.* a legal document, usually pertaining to ownership or transfer of property. *He signed the deed to the ranch.*

SIGN #2: Fingerspell **DEED**.

D E E D

deep: *adj.* extending far below the surface. *There is a deep hole in the back yard.*

SIGN: Edge of downward-pointing forefinger of right **'BENT ONE'** hand is placed against right-facing palm of the left **'EXTENDED B'** hand. Then the right hand is pushed firmly downward.

deer: *n.* a hoofed, ruminant mammal, having antlers in the male. *The deer scraped at the snow to find grass.*

SIGN: Vertical **'5'** hands, palms forward but facing slightly, are placed at either side of the head, thumbs on the forehead. The arms are then moved slightly so that the thumbs tap gently against the forehead.

deface: *v.* to spoil the appearance of. *He was arrested for defacing the building.*

SIGN: **'CLAWED 5'** hand is held palm-up while right **'CLAWED 5'** hand is held palm-down to the right and above/ahead of left hand. The hands close to form **'A'** hands as they are brought together and just past each other, the knuckles of the right hand grazing those of the left. The knuckles brush against each other again as the left hand moves firmly backward/leftward and the right hand moves firmly rightward/forward.

defeat: *v.* to beat; to win a victory over. *We can defeat our opponents if we just use the right tactics.*

SIGN: Vertical right **'S'** hand, palm facing forward, is curved downward from the wrist across the extended finger of the left **'ONE'** hand, which is held horizontally with the palm facing downward. ❖

defecate: *v.* to excrete solid body waste through the anus. *Dog owners should clean up after pets that defecate in public areas.*

SIGN: Horizontal left **'S'** (or **'A'**) hand is held in a fixed position with palm facing right and enclosing thumb of horizontal right **'5'** (or **'EXTENDED A'**) hand, of which the palm faces left. Then the right hand is pulled down sharply.

defect: *n.* an imperfection; flaw. *The shirt is on sale because it has a small defect.*

SIGN: Vertical right **'Y'** hand, palm toward the body, is firmly tapped on the chin.

defence [*also spelled* **defense**]: *n.* the players who are responsible for preventing the opposing team from scoring. *The Vancouver Canucks had a strong defence that year.*

SIGN #1: Vertical right **'D'** hand, palm forward, is shaken back and forth slightly from the wrist.

OR

SIGN #2: Horizontal left **'EXTENDED B'** hand is held in a fixed position with palm up and fingers pointing forward/rightward. Outside edge of horizontal right **'EXTENDED B'** hand, palm toward the body but slanted leftward slightly, is placed in palm of left hand. The right hand is then moved forward/rightward a couple of times as if pushing something off the left hand.

defend: *v.* to protect from harm or danger. *Do not worry, we will defend you.*

SIGN: Horizontal **'S'** hands are held, the left just in front of the right, with palms down in front of the centre of the chest. The hands are then simultaneously moved emphatically forward a short distance.

SAME SIGN—**defence**, *n.*, in this context.

defer: *v.* to postpone. *You may defer payment until next month.*

SIGN: Horizontal **'F'** hands, palms facing each other, are held with joined tips of thumb and forefinger of each hand touching those of the other hand. The left hand remains fixed as the right hand moves forward in an arc formation.

ALTERNATE SIGN—**postpone**

defiant: *adj.* boldly resistant to authority. *Teenagers are sometimes defiant of their parents' rules.*

SIGN: Vertical right **'S'** hand, palm facing backward, is held at or above shoulder level and is forcefully twisted a half turn so that palm faces forward. Alternatively, this sign may be made with two hands.

SAME SIGN—**defiance**, *n.*

deficient: *adj.* having a lack or shortage of. *The doctor told her she was deficient in calcium.*

SIGN: Thumb of right **'EXTENDED A'** hand, palm facing left, is placed under the chin and is flicked forward firmly. Next, horizontal left **'S'** hand is held in a fixed position with palm facing right. Horizontal right **'EXTENDED B'** hand is held palm down with fingers pointing forward/leftward and is brushed forward/rightward a couple of times across the top of the left hand. (ASL CONCEPT—**not - enough**.)

deficit: *n.* the amount that a sum of money is less than that which is required or expected. *The federal deficit has become an issue.*

SIGN: Edge of downward-pointing forefinger of right **'BENT ONE'** hand is placed against right-facing palm of the left **'EXTENDED B'** hand. Then the right hand is pushed firmly downward.

define: *v.* to state the exact meaning of. *It is a difficult term to define.*

SIGN: **'F'** hands are held horizontally with palms facing each other, and are alternately moved backward and forward a few times.

definite: *adj.* exact; clearly defined; known for certain. *Attending university is a definite goal he has in mind.*

SIGN: Forefinger of vertical right **'ONE'** hand, palm facing left, is held against the lips and the hand is moved sharply forward.

definition: *n.* a precise explanation of the meaning of a word. *We hope you find the* ***definitions*** *in this dictionary helpful.*

SIGN: Horizontal left **'EXTENDED B'** hand is held in a fixed position with palm facing right while tip of forefinger of right palm-down **'BENT V'** hand is jabbed into the left palm. The right hand then moves away from the left hand as the right wrist rotates a quarter turn clockwise, and the middle fingertip is jabbed into the left palm.
ALTERNATE SIGN—**define**

deflate: *v.* to collapse through the removal of air or gas. *That punctured tire will* ***deflate***.

SIGN: Thumb of vertical right **'CONTRACTED C'** hand, palm forward/leftward, rests on left **'STANDARD BASE'** hand. The fingers of the right hand then close down to form a **'FLAT O'** shape. (Signs vary according to 'what' specifically is being deflated.)

deflect: *v.* to swerve. *The puck* ***deflected*** *off the boards.*

SIGN: Horizontal left **'EXTENDED B'** hand is held in a fixed position with palm right and fingers pointing forward. Right **'ONE'** hand, palm down, approaches the left hand from behind/right, stabs the left palm and careens forward/rightward. (Handshapes vary depending on the size and shape of both the object being deflected and the one being deflected against. The movement remains constant however.)

deformed: *adj.* misshapen; disfigured. *He was left* ***deformed*** *after the car accident.*

SIGN: Horizontal **'CLAWED SPREAD C'** hands are held apart in front of the upper chest with left palm facing the body and right palm facing down. The left wrist then rotates backward to turn the hand palm-downward while the right wrist rotates forward to turn the hand so that the palm is toward the body. Facial expression is important. (Signs vary considerably depending on the nature and location of the deformity.) **DEFORMED** may be fingerspelled.

defraud: *v.* to take something such as money away from someone through fraud; swindle; cheat. *He was jailed for* ***defrauding*** *the company of thousands of dollars.*

SIGN: Signs vary from region to region. See **cheat**.

defrost: *v.* to thaw; remove frost or ice from. *It is safer to* ***defrost*** *a turkey in the refrigerator than at room temperature.*

SIGN: **'FLAT O'** hands are held parallel with palms up and slanted slightly toward the body. As the hands are drawn apart the thumbs slide across the fingertips, causing the hands to assume **'A'** shapes. (**DEFROST** may be fingerspelled.)

deft: *adj.* skillful; nimble; dexterous. *She is becoming very* ***deft*** *at signing ASL.*

SIGN: Left **'EXTENDED B'** hand, palm facing right and fingers up, is grasped by right **'OPEN A'** hand. Then right hand is pulled forward sharply and closed to form an **'A'** hand.
ALTERNATE SIGN—**adept** #2

defy: *v.* to boldly resist. *Many teenagers* ***defy*** *their parents' and society's rules.*

SIGN #1: Vertical right **'S'** hand, palm facing backward, is held at or above shoulder level and is forcefully twisted a half turn so that palm faces forward. Alternatively, this sign may be made with two hands.
SAME SIGNS—**defiant**, *adj.*, and **defiance**, *n.*

defy: *v.* to be in opposition to or in conflict with. *Superman's flights through the sky* ***defy*** *the law of gravity.*

SIGN #2: **'ONE'** hands, palms toward the chest and forefingers pointing toward each other at an upward angle, are held slightly apart and then thrust toward each other so the forefingers cross with the left one in front of the right.

degenerate: *v.* to deteriorate to a lower mental or physical level. *His memory has* ***degenerated*** *since he had brain surgery.*

SIGN: **'EXTENDED A'** hands are held slightly apart in front of the chest with the palms facing each other, and are lowered slowly but simultaneously to waist level.

degrade: *v.* to reduce in worth, character or status. *The scandal is bound to degrade the government's credibility.*

SIGN: **'BENT EXTENDED B'** hands are held apart in front of upper chest with palms facing each other. The hands are then simultaneously moved downward in a slight arc toward the body.

degree: *n.* a qualification earned upon successful completion of a program of studies at a university or college. *She completed her BA degree at Gallaudet University.*

SIGN #1: Horizontal **'F'** hands are held side by side, palms down and extended fingers pointing forward, and are drawn apart.

degree: *n.* the seriousness of a burn or a crime, especially murder. *He was convicted of murder in the first degree.*

SIGN #2: Fingerspell **DEGREE**.

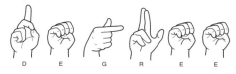

D E G R E E

degree: *n.* a unit of temperature. *It is 30 degrees Celsius today, even in the shade.*

SIGN #3: Vertical left **'ONE'** hand is held in a fixed position with palm facing rightward/forward. Horizontal right **'ONE'** hand is held palm down and moves up and down as forefinger slides up and down against back of left forefinger.

degree: *n.* a unit of measure for angles. *This angle measures 45 degrees.*

SIGN #4: With palm facing left, vertical **'O'** hand wobbles. (Sometimes the degree of an angle is shown by positioning the hands in such a way that they clearly form an angle of a specified measurement.)

dehydrated: *adj.* having lost necessary moisture. *If you have a high fever, your body will become dehydrated.*

SIGN: Side of crooked forefinger of right **'X'** hand, palm facing down, is placed on left side of chin and firmly drawn across to the right side.

SAME SIGN—**dehydration**, *n.*

dejected: *adj.* downhearted; sad; depressed. *She felt lonely and dejected after her parents separated.*

SIGN: Tips of middle fingers of **'BENT MID-FINGER 5'** hands are held at either side of upper chest and are simultaneously lowered.
ALTERNATE SIGN—**depressed** #2

delay: *v.* to postpone; put off to a later time. *The storm will probably delay our flight.*

SIGN: Horizontal **'F'** hands, palms facing each other, are held with joined tips of thumb and forefinger of each hand touching those of the other hand. The left hand remains fixed as the right hand moves forward in an arc formation.
ALTERNATE SIGN—**postpone**

delectable: See **delicious**.

delegate: *n.* a representative; someone chosen to act for others, especially at a conference or meeting. *He is our official convention delegate.*

SIGN #1: Tip of forefinger of horizontal right **'BENT ONE'** hand is placed against right facing palm of left **'EXTENDED B'** hand. Together, the hands are moved slightly forward and back a few times.

OR

SIGN #2: Horizontal right **'D'** hand is held at upper left side of chest with palm toward the body and forefinger pointing leftward. The wrist then rotates quickly toward the body a couple of times causing tips of joined thumb and forefinger to brush downward against the upper left chest.

delegate: *v.* to give duty or authority to someone else. *I will delegate that responsibility to you.*

SIGN #3: Right **'X'** hand is held upright with palm facing left, and is thrust forward and downward to a horizontal position. ❖

delete: *v.* to remove something printed or written. *Delete that file from the computer.*

SIGN: Left **'ONE'** hand is held in a fixed position with palm rightward at a slight downward angle and forefinger pointing forward/rightward. Right **'COVERED T'** hand is held to the right of the left hand with palm up and forefinger touching tip of left forefinger. The right hand then moves rightward/upward as the thumb is flicked out to form an **'EXTENDED A'** hand.

deliberate: *v.* to think carefully; to consider deeply. *He deliberated for a long time before making his decision.*

SIGN #1: Vertical **'FLAT O'** hands are held just in front of either side of the forehead with palms facing backward and fingers rapidly fluttering as the hands move in small circles. From the signer's perspective, the left hand moves clockwise while the right hand moves counter-clockwise.

deliberate: *adj.* carefully thought out beforehand; intentional. *They made a deliberate effort to discredit our organization.*

SIGN #2: Tip of forefinger of vertical right **'ONE'** hand, palm toward the face, is used to touch right side of forehead. Then the hand-shape is changed to a **'BENT V'** and the extended fingertips are placed against the right-facing palm of the horizontal left **'EXTENDED B'** hand. Next, the fingertips of the right hand are separated from the left hand as the right wrist makes a quarter turn clockwise, and the fingertips re-establish contact with the left palm.

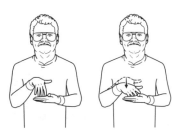

delicate: *adj.* fragile; weak, especially in terms of health. *His delicate health prevents him from participating in physical activities.*

SIGN #1: Fingertips of right **'5'** hand, palm toward the body, are placed on upturned palm of left **'EXTENDED B'** hand. Then the fingers buckle so that the hand is transformed into a **'CLAWED 5'** shape.

delicate: *adj.* pleasantly light; subtle. *The artist's delicate brush strokes give the painting a very soft effect.*

SIGN #2: **'BENT MIDFINGER 5'** hands are held apart, the left palm facing downward/ rightward and the right palm facing downward/ leftward. The wrists then rotate outward causing the hands to turn so that the left palm faces rightward/upward while the right palm faces leftward/upward.

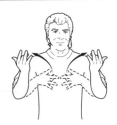

delicate: *adj.* sensitive. *It is a delicate matter so be careful what you say to her about it.*

SIGN #3: **'OPEN 8'** hands are held parallel with palms up as tips of middle fingers and thumbs tap together several times to form **'8'** shapes.

delicatessen: *n.* a shop where specialty foods are prepared and sold. *I bought some cold cuts at the delicatessen.*

SIGN: Fingerspell **DELI**.

delicious: *adj.* tasting very good. *Maple syrup is delicious on pancakes.*

SIGN #1: Thumb and midfinger of right **'8'** hand are placed at the lips, with the palm toward the face and are then snapped apart to form an **'A'** hand. Facial expression is important. (Signs vary.)
ALTERNATE SIGN—**lucky** #2

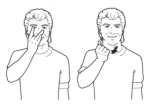

SIGN #2 [ATLANTIC]: Right **'5'** hand, palm down and fingers pointing leftward, is held with thumb touching the chin as the hand moves rightward with fingers fluttering. Facial expression is important.

SIGN #3 [ATLANTIC]: Horizontal right **'L'** hand, palm facing backward, is held with forefinger against chin and pointing leftward. The hand is then drawn rightward, as it closes to form an **'EXTENDED A'** hand. Facial expression is important.

delighted: *adj.* very happy. *I was delighted to hear the good news.*

SIGN: Horizontal right **'EXTENDED B'** hand, palm toward the body, is brushed up and off the chest twice in a circular motion.

delirious: *adj.* in a state of wild excitement and mental confusion. *The child was delirious due to a high fever.*

SIGN: **'CROOKED 5'** hands, palms facing backward, are circled slowly in opposite directions in front of the face, the left hand appearing to the signer to move clockwise while the right hand moves counter-clockwise. (The eyes and tongue are an important feature of this sign—the eyes appearing glazed and the tongue relaxed but showing slightly between the teeth. The head may also loll from side to side.)

deliver: *v.* to distribute or bring to a specific destination. *They will deliver the furniture tomorrow.*

SIGN: **'EXTENDED B'** hands are held parallel with palms up in front of left side of body. Then they are simultaneously moved in a slight arc to the right.

SAME SIGN—**delivery**, *n.*, in this context.

deliver a speech [*or* **lecture**]: *v.* to give a talk to a group of people. *The visiting professor will deliver the lecture tonight.*

SIGN: Right arm is raised and the vertical **'EXTENDED B'** hand, palm facing left, is brought forward sharply from the wrist a couple of times.

delude: See **deceive**.

demand: *v.* to ask for urgently. *You can demand immediate attention in an emergency.*

SIGN: Tip of forefinger of right **'X'** hand is placed in right-facing palm of left **'EXTENDED B'** hand. Together the hands are moved firmly toward the chest, giving the impression that the left hand is being tugged by the right forefinger.

demean: See **degrade**.

demeanour (demeanor): See **behaviour** under **behave**.

demented: See **insane**.

democracy: *n.* a form of government in which the people exercise political power. *The Prime Minister is devoted to the principles of democracy.*

SIGN: Vertical right **'D'** hand, palm forward, is shaken back and forth slightly from the wrist.

demolish: *v.* to tear down; wreck; destroy. *It is a shame to demolish any building of historic significance.*

SIGN: **'CROOKED 5'** hands are held with fingers touching and palms facing downward. The forearms then simultaneously fall inward so that the hands fall downward.

ALTERNATE SIGN—**destroy**

demon: *n.* a devil or an evil spirit. *They read a mystery story about an ancient demon.*

SIGN: Thumb of vertical right **'CROOKED EXTENDED V'** hand is placed against the right side of the forehead, palm facing forward, and the two bent fingers are simultaneously wiggled up and down. Alternatively, this sign may be made with two hands, one at either side of the forehead.

demonstrate: *v.* to explain by example or by showing. *The Deaf artist will demonstrate her techniques at the workshop.*

SIGN: Tip of forefinger of horizontal right **'BENT ONE'** hand is placed against right facing palm of left **'EXTENDED B'** hand. Together, the hands are moved forward in a short arc. (The sign for **demonstration**, *n.*, begins in the same position, but the hands move straight forward rather than in an arc, and the movement is repeated.)

demote: *v.* to move to a lower position, grade or rank. *The executive wanted to demote the worker for his poor performance.*

SIGN #1: Left **'5'** hand is held in a fixed position with palm facing the body and fingers pointing rightward. Vertical right **'CLAWED V'** hand, palm forward, is held just behind/above the left hand and is then lowered so that it is directly behind the left hand.

OR

SIGN #2: **'BENT EXTENDED B'** hands are held apart in front of upper chest with palms facing each other. The hands are then simultaneously moved downward in a slight arc toward the body.

SAME SIGN—**demotion**, *n.*

den: *n.* a small room, usually used for various forms of relaxation such as reading or television viewing. *Your den is such a cozy room.*

SIGN #1: Fingerspell **DEN**.

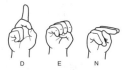

den: *n.* the shelter or home of a wild animal; lair. *The hunters had great difficulty finding the lion's den.*

SIGN #2: Fingerspell **DEN**.
ALTERNATE SIGN—**home**

denote: *v.* to indicate or be a sign of; to clearly mean. *That particular facial expression denotes the signer's disappointment.*

SIGN: Horizontal left **'EXTENDED B'** hand is held in a fixed position with palm facing right while tip of forefinger of right palm-down **'BENT V'** hand is jabbed into the left palm. The right hand then moves away from the left hand as the right wrist rotates a quarter turn clockwise, and the middle fingertip is jabbed into the left palm.

denounce: *v.* to make an official accusation against something; to openly criticize. *Many taxpayers denounce the government's cuts to health and education programs.*

SIGN: Horizontal left **'BENT EXTENDED B'** hand is held with palm facing rightward/backward and fingers pointing to the right. Right **'EXTENDED B'** (or **'B'**) hand is held upright very close to the chest with palm facing left. The right hand then drops from the wrist until it is horizontal with fingertips forcefully striking left hand between the palm and the fingers. Facial expression is important.

dent: *n.* a hollow in a surface, usually from being hit. *There is a big dent in the passenger door of our new car.*

SIGN: Horizontal **'BENT EXTENDED B'** hands are held with palms facing each other and fingertips of each hand touching those of the other hand. The fingers then buckle inward toward the body.

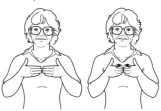

dentist: *n.* a person who is qualified to treat disorders of the teeth and gums. *Yearly visits to the dentist will help prevent tooth decay.*

SIGN #1: Tip of crooked forefinger of right **'X'** hand is tapped in the area of the right side of the lower lip.

OR

SIGN #2: Edge of right **'EXTENDED A'** hand, palm facing backward, is tapped twice against lower right jaw.

OR

SIGN #3: Right **'BENT THUMB L'** hand is held with tip of forefinger touching the face near the right corner of the mouth while the thumb repeatedly moves up and down slightly as if depressing the plunger of a syringe. (Signs vary considerably.)

dentures: *n.* a set of artificial teeth. *The dentist will fit my grandmother with a new set of dentures.*

SIGN: Side of forefinger of right **'ONE'** hand, palm facing leftward/forward, is lightly brushed forward/downward twice on the right cheek, forefinger either remaining upright or bending slightly to become a **'BENT ONE'**. Next, tip of forefinger of vertical right **'X'** hand, palm toward the face, is drawn back and forth in front of the upper front teeth. (ASL CONCEPT—**false - teeth**.)

deny: *v.* to reject as false. *He tried to **deny** his involvement in the crime.*

SIGN #1: Thumbs of **'EXTENDED 'A'** hands, palms facing each other at a slight forward angle, are placed under either side of the chin. The hands are then simultaneously thrust forward/outward.
SAME SIGN—**denial**, *n.*

deny: *v.* to refuse to give or allow. *The judge **denied** the defendant bail.*

SIGN #2: Horizontal right **'EXTENDED A'** hand, with palm facing leftward, is raised abruptly to an upright position so that the thumb points over the right shoulder. Next, **'K'** hands, palms down, are held apart, extended fingers pointing downward, and are then flicked upward from the wrists so that the hands are held in either a horizontal or upright position. (ASL CONCEPT—**won't - allow**.)

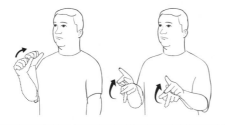

deodorant: *n.* a substance used to destroy or suppress offensive body odours. *There are many new **underarm deodorants** on the market.*

SIGN: Horizontal right **'S'** hand brushes downward at least twice against the left underarm as if applying a stick or roll-on deodorant. (An **'X'** handshape is held near the underarm to simulate the spraying on of deodorant. If the deodorant is for 'other than underarm use', signs vary according to context.)

depart: *v.* to leave. *The train will **depart** in five minutes.*

SIGN: **'EXTENDED B'** hands are held parallel with palms down and fingers pointing forward/rightward. The hands are then drawn simultaneously leftward/backward as they close to form **'A'** (or **'EXTENDED A'**) hands.
SAME SIGN—**departure**, *n.*

department: *n.* a subdivision of the administration of a government, business, or institution; a specialized area of skill or responsibility. *He is the manager of the sales department.*

SIGN: Fingerspell **DEPT**.

D   E   P   T

depend: *v.* to rely (on). *Her children **depend** on her too much.*

SIGN: Tips of forefingers of **'ONE'** hands are crossed slightly with the right on top of the left, and both palms facing down. Together, the hands are lowered as if the right forefinger is exerting downward pressure on the left forefinger. ❖

dependable: *adj.* reliable. *He is a very **dependable** employee.*

SIGN: **'BENT EXTENDED B'** hands, palms facing the body, are tapped against the right shoulder a couple of times with the fingertips.

dependent: *adj.* unable to get along without relying on others. *He is **dependent** on his parents for financial support.*

SIGN: Tips of forefingers of **'ONE'** hands are crossed slightly with the right on top of the left, and both palms facing down. Together, the hands are lowered a few times as if the right forefinger is exerting downward pressure on the left forefinger.

depict: *v.* to represent by drawing or to describe in words. *His painting attempts to **depict** pioneer life on the prairies.*

SIGN: Tip of forefinger of horizontal right **'BENT ONE'** hand is placed against right facing palm of left **'EXTENDED B'** hand. Together, the hands are moved forward in a short arc.

deplete: *v.* to use up; to empty partially or entirely. *Our wasteful habits continue to **deplete** Canada's natural resources.*

SIGN: Thumb of vertical right **'CONTRACTED C'** hand, palm forward/leftward, rests on left **'STANDARD BASE'** hand. The fingers of the right hand then close down to form a **'FLAT O'** shape.
SAME SIGN—**depletion**, *n.*
ALTERNATE SIGN—**run out of**

deport: *v.* to expel or remove someone from a country by force. *Canadian authorities have the right to **deport** an illegal alien to his original country.*

SIGN: Fingertips of right **'BENT EXTENDED B'** hand, palm down, are placed on upturned palm of left **'EXTENDED B'** hand and brushed forward to form a straight **'EXTENDED B'** hand. ❖ SAME SIGN—**deportation**, *n.*

depose: *v.* to remove from office or a position of power. *The revolutionary army plans to **depose** the President.*

SIGN: Horizontal **'S'** hands are held slightly apart with left palm down and right palm up. The arms then move simultaneously rightward as the hands open to form **'CROOKED 5'** shapes.

deposit: *v.* to put money into a bank account. *She is going to **deposit** her cheque now.*

SIGN #1: Vertical left **'C'** hand is held with palm facing right. Then the forward-pointing fingertips of the right **'FLAT O'** hand are inserted into the opening in the left hand.

deposit: *n.* money given in partial payment or as a security. *We must pay a **deposit** for a hotel reservation.*

SIGN #2: **'EXTENDED A'** hands are held with thumbtips touching and palms down but facing each other slightly. Then the wrists are rotated inward as the hands are moved apart and turned so that the palms are fully downward.

depot: *n.* a bus or railway station. *The last bus will leave the **depot** at midnight.*

SIGN: Fingerspell **DEPOT.**

D   E   P   O   T

depressed: *adj.* sad; downcast; low in spirits. *After her visitors left, our neighbour was **depressed** and lonely.*

SIGN #1: Tips of middle fingers of **'BENT MIDFINGER 5'** hands are held at either side of upper chest and are simultaneously lowered. SAME SIGN—**depression**, *n.*, in this context.

OR

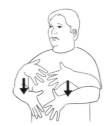

SIGN #2: Palms of both **'5'** hands, fingers pointing down, are held against either side of upper chest and are simultaneously pushed downward.
SAME SIGN—**depression**, *n.*, in this context.

depression: *n.* a slump in a nation's economy. *Low interest rates and a high rate of unemployment are signs of an economic **depression**.*

SIGN: Right **'BENT EXTENDED B'** hand is held with palm facing down and fingers pointing forward/downward. The forearm is then thrust downward/forward.

deprive: *v.* to take something away from or to prevent the enjoyment of something. *The captor would **deprive** the prisoner of meals if he did not give him information.*

SIGN: Horizontal right **'SPREAD C'** hand, palm facing left, is pulled backward as it closes to form an **'S'** hand. (If someone is depriving *me*, the horizontal right **'SPREAD C'** hand is held under the horizontal left **'EXTENDED B'** hand, which is held palm-down just in front of the chest with fingers pointing rightward. The right hand then moves forward as the fingers close to form an **'S'** shape.) ❖

(be) deprived of *(passive voice):* *v.* to be without something important. *He **was deprived of** love as a boy.*

SIGN: **'O'** hands are held upright with palms facing forward. They are then simultaneously thrust downward/forward as the wrists rotate, turning the left palm upward/rightward and the right palm upward/leftward.

depth: *n.* the distance down or through. *Do not dive into a swimming pool unless you know the **depth** of the water.*

SIGN: Edge of downward-pointing forefinger of right **'BENT ONE'** hand is placed against right-facing palm of the left **'EXTENDED B'** hand. Then the right hand is pushed firmly downward.

deputy: *adj.* appointed to represent someone else. *He will act as **deputy** chairperson while she is absent.*

SIGN: Horizontal left **'EXTENDED A'** hand is held in a fixed position with palm toward the body. Horizontal right **'L'** (or **'EXTENDED A'**) hand is positioned so that the thumbtip taps at least twice against the underside of the left hand.

derail: *v.* to cause a train to go off the rails. *Careless maintenance of railroad tracks may cause a train to **derail**.*

SIGN: **'B'** hands, palms down, are positioned so that the fingertips of the right are near the inside edge of the left wrist and all fingers are pointing forward. Then both hands are simultaneously flipped slightly to the right to simulate the appearance of a train going off the tracks.

deride: *v.* to ridicule; treat with contempt; make fun of. *It is discriminatory to **deride** other races or cultures.*

SIGN: Horizontal **'BENT COMBINED I + ONE'** hands, palms down, are held slightly apart, with the right hand nearer the chest, and simultaneously make small jabbing motions. This sign is accompanied by a scornful facial expression. ❖
SAME SIGN—**derision**, *n.*

dermatologist: *n.* a medical specialist qualified to treat skin disorders. *If your skin condition does not improve you should consult a **dermatologist**.*

SIGN: Right cheek is pinched with thumb and forefinger of right **'A-INDEX'** hand. Next, fingertips of palm-down right **'BENT EXTENDED B'** (or **'FLAT M'** or **'SPREAD EXTENDED C'**) hand are tapped a couple of times against the inside of the left wrist. (ASL CONCEPT—**skin - doctor**.)

descend: *v.* to move downward. *The plane is beginning to **descend**.*

SIGN: Left **'EXTENDED B'** hand is held in a fixed position with palm up and fingers pointing forward/rightward. Right **'COMBINED LY'** hand is held with palm forward/leftward at a downward angle. The right forearm is then lowered in a forward/leftward direction, so that it lands palm-down on the left palm. (Sign choice varies considerably, depending on the 'size and shape' of the object and the 'manner' in which it is descending.)

descendant: *n.* the progeny of an earlier individual or race. *She is a **descendant** of Louis Riel.*

SIGN: Fingertips of horizontal right **'BENT EXTENDED B'** hand, palm toward the body, are placed against the right shoulder while horizontal left **'BENT EXTENDED B'** hand, palm toward the body, is held a short distance in front of it. Then both hands are circled forward around one another several times.

describe: *v.* to give the details of in words. *He **described** the beauty of the Northern Lights.*

SIGN: **'F'** hands are held horizontally with palms facing each other, and are alternately moved backward and forward a few times.
SAME SIGN—**description**, *n.*

desert: *n.* an area that has little or no vegetation due to low rainfall. *Camels are used in the **desert** because they can survive on very little water.*

SIGN #1: Edge of forefinger of right **'ONE'** hand, palm down, is drawn across the chin from left to right as it changes to an **'X'** hand. Then **'FLAT O'** hands are held slightly apart with palms up and the fingers are slid across the thumbs, thus creating **'OFFSET O'** hands. Next, horizontal right **'5'** hand is held with palm down and fingers pointing forward. The hand then makes a wide arc leftward as it inscribes a circle in front of the body. (ASL CONCEPT—**dry - land - vast**.) DESERT may be fingerspelled.

desert: *v.* to leave a person or place with no intention of returning, usually contrary to one's responsibility. *When did their father desert the family?*

SIGN #2: **'5'** hands are thrust forward to the left and down from shoulder level, palms facing each other. ❖

deserve: *v.* to be worthy of. *He deserves the award for his bravery.*

SIGN: Right **'SPREAD EXTENDED C'** hand is moved across upturned palm of left **'EXTENDED B'** hand in a circular, counter-clockwise 'gathering' motion, with the palm toward the body. (**DESERVE** is frequently fingerspelled.)

design: *v.* to create or invent. *He will design a computer program to make his work easier.*

SIGN #1: Tip of forefinger of vertical right **'4'** hand, palm facing left, is placed against the forehead and the hand is then pushed upward and forward slightly. (Signs for **design**, *v.*, vary according to context.)

design: *n.* pattern; arrangement of features. *The advertising department created some interesting designs to present at the meeting.*

SIGN #2: Left **'EXTENDED B'** hand is held in a fixed position with palm toward the body and fingers pointing upward/rightward. Right **'BENT U'** hand, with palm toward the body, is held against left palm and zigzagged downward.

OR

SIGN #3: Left **'EXTENDED B'** hand is held in a fixed position with palm toward the body and fingers pointing upward/rightward. Right **'I'** hand, with palm left, is held against left palm and zigzagged downward.

desire: *v.* to want; wish. *The native people desire to preserve their culture and history.*

SIGN: **'CROOKED 5'** hands, palms up, are held slightly apart in front of the body. Then they retract to form **'CLAWED 5'** hands as they are simultaneously drawn toward the chest. ALTERNATE SIGN—**wish**

desk: *n.* a writing table. *She has a large desk in her office.*

SIGN: Forearms are bent so that they are held parallel to and very close to the chest with the right arm directly above the left. Then the right arm is tapped down on the left forearm a couple of times. (**DESK** is frequently fingerspelled.)

despair: *n.* a total loss of hope. *The parents were in despair when their lost child could not be found.*

SIGN: Tips of middle fingers of **'BENT MIDFINGER 5'** hands are held at either side of upper chest and are simultaneously lowered. ALTERNATE SIGN—**depressed** #2

desperate: *adj.* in an unbearable situation because of great need or anxiety. *He was desperate for a loan.*

SIGN: Tip of forefinger of right **'ONE'** hand is placed just under the chin and moved downward along the throat. Facial expression shows strain and the teeth must be clenched as if articulating an 'EE' sound. (Signs vary. The sign for **need** is often used, particularly when someone is 'desperate' for *money* or *food*. The facial expression remains constant however.)

despise: *v.* to look down on with contempt; loathe; hate. *I despise him for his cruel treatment of the workers.*

SIGN: Horizontal **'ONE'** hands are held with the left hand ahead of/to the left of the right hand. Left palm faces rightward at a slight forward angle while right palm faces leftward at a slight angle toward the body. Forefingers point forward/leftward as the hands are simultaneously jabbed in that direction. Facial expression is important. ALTERNATE SIGNS—**abhor** or **hate**

despite: *prep.* in spite of. *The airplane passengers survived despite the sub-zero weather.*

SIGN: Fingers of horizontal **'BENT EXTENDED B'** hands, palms facing the chest, are alternately brushed back and forth against each other.

despondent: See **depressed**.

dessert: *n.* food, especially something sweet, which is served at the end of a meal. *Apple pie is my favourite dessert.*

SIGN: Fingertips of right **'SPREAD EXTENDED C'** hand, palm facing down, are tapped against the back of the left **'STANDARD BASE'** hand in a series of very short arcs moving in a forward/rightward/downward direction along the left hand. (**DESSERT** may be fingerspelled.)

(reach a) destination: *v.* to arrive at the expected end of a journey. *We should reach our destination in an hour or so.*

SIGN: Right **'BENT EXTENDED B'** hand, with palm facing the body, is brought down and laid palm-up on the upturned palm of the left **'EXTENDED B'** hand.
REGIONAL VARIATION—**arrive**

destroy: *v.* to demolish; ruin. *Angry mobs often destroy property during a riot.*

SIGN: Left **'CLAWED 5'** hand is held palm-up while right **'CLAWED 5'** hand is held palm-down to the right and above/ahead of left hand. The hands close to form **'A'** hands as they are brought together and just past each other, the knuckles of the right hand grazing those of the left. The knuckles brush against each other again as the left hand moves firmly backward/leftward and the right hand moves firmly rightward/forward.
SAME SIGN—**destruction**, *n.*, is often used.

destructible: *adj.* capable of being destroyed. *People who believed the "Titanic" was not destructible were proved to be wrong.*

SIGN: **'A'** hands, palms down, are held slightly apart, and are brought down firmly in front of the chest. Next, left **'CLAWED 5'** hand is held palm-up while right **'CLAWED 5'** hand is held palm-down to the right and above/ahead of left hand. The hands close to form **'A'** hands as they are brought together and just past each other, the knuckles of the right hand grazing those of the left. The knuckles brush against each other again as the left hand moves firmly backward/leftward and the right hand moves firmly rightward/forward. (ASL CONCEPT—**can - destroy**.)

detach: *v.* to disconnect or unfasten. *The trailer hitch became detached from the car.*

SIGN: Thumbs and forefingers of **'F'** hands, palms facing each other, are interlocked. The hands are then drawn apart to form **'OPEN F'** hands. ❖

detail: *n.* a small segment or part of the whole; an item. *You forgot one important detail.*

SIGN: Vertical left **'ONE'** hand is held in a fixed position with palm facing rightward/forward. Horizontal right **'ONE'** hand is held behind left hand with palm facing left. The right hand then makes a slight but firm bounce as if intending to strike the tip of the left forefinger with that of the right forefinger but not quite touching it. (**DETAIL** is frequently fingerspelled.) See *plural* **details**.

detailed: *adj.* containing a lot of specific information. *His report is very detailed.*

SIGN: Vertical left **'ONE'** hand is held in a fixed position with palm facing rightward/forward. Horizontal right **'ONE'** hand is held behind left hand with palm facing left. The hands then move simultaneously downward. (Signs vary. Sometimes a variation of the sign for **explain** may be used. The eyes are squinted, the lips are pursed, and the movement is repeated several times within a very small signing space.)
ALTERNATE SIGN—**deep**

details: *n.* small segments or parts of the whole; items. *For further details, see Christine.*

SIGN: Vertical left **'ONE'** hand is held in a fixed position with palm facing rightward/forward. Horizontal right **'ONE'** hand is held behind left hand with palm facing left. The hands then move simultaneously downward. **DETAILS** is frequently fingerspelled. See *singular* **detail**.
ALTERNATE SIGN—**information** under **inform**

detect: *v.* to perceive or notice. *I detect some bitterness in his manner.*

SIGN: Tip of forefinger of right **'CROOKED ONE'** hand is positioned at corner of right eye and brought down to rest on upturned palm of left **'EXTENDED B'** hand. (Various signs may be used, depending on which of the senses is involved.)

detective: *n.* a person, usually a police officer who investigates crimes. *The police assigned two detectives to investigate the murder.*

SIGN: Joined midfinger and thumb of right **'D'** hand are placed against the upper left side of the chest and the hand is moved in a small, clockwise (from the onlooker's perspective) circle.

deteriorate: *v.* to worsen (in terms of one's state of health). *The patient's condition is beginning to deteriorate.*

SIGN #1: **'EXTENDED A'** hands are held parallel at about shoulder level with palms facing each other. Then they are lowered simultaneously to waist level.

SAME SIGN—**deterioration**, *n.*, in this context.

ALTERNATE SIGNS—**decline** #1 & #2

deteriorate: *v.* to worsen or depreciate. *The appearance of this neighbourhood is beginning to deteriorate.*

SIGN #2: **'EXTENDED A'** hands are held parallel at about shoulder level with palms facing each other. Then they are lowered simultaneously to waist level.

SAME SIGN—**deterioration**, *n.*, in this context.

determine: *v.* to decide conclusively. *We should determine what the problem is first.*

SIGN: **'F'** hands, with palms facing each other, are held apart in front of chest and are simultaneously lowered.

determined: *adj.* unwavering; resolute; firm. *He was determined to succeed.*

SIGN: Thumb of vertical right **'EXTENDED B'** hand, palm forward, is placed near the right temple and the fingers are firmly lowered to form a **'BENT EXTENDED B'** hand. A look of fierce determination accompanies this sign.

ALTERNATE SIGN—**determine**

detest: *v.* to dislike very much; loathe; hate. *I detest my boss.*

SIGN: Horizontal **'ONE'** hands are held with the left hand ahead of/to the left of the right hand. Left palm faces rightward at a slight forward angle while right palm faces leftward at a slight angle toward the body. Forefingers point forward/leftward as the hands are simultaneously jabbed in that direction. Facial expression is important.

ALTERNATE SIGNS—**abhor** or **hate**

detour: *n.* a deviation from the direct route. *The highway was under construction so we took a detour.*

SIGN: **'ONE'** hands are held together with palms down and forefingers pointing forward. The left hand remains fixed while the right hand curves forward/rightward in a fairly wide arc.

devastated: *adj.* feeling crushed or deeply hurt emotionally. *He was devastated when his application was rejected.*

SIGN #1: Right **'SPREAD C'** hand, palm up, is held against the chest and is drawn slightly downward as it closes to form an **'S'** hand. Facial expression is important.

ALTERNATE SIGN—**depressed** #2. For contexts in which an inanimate object is devastated, see **destroy**.

OR

SIGN #2: Vertical right **'CONTRACTED C'** hand is held close to the chest with palm facing left. The hand then closes to form a **'FLAT O'** hand. Facial expression is important.

develop: *v.* to create, expand or grow gradually. *The secretary will develop a new application form.*

SIGN #1: Left **'EXTENDED B'** hand is held in a fixed position with palm right and fingers pointing forward/upward. Right **'B'** hand, palm forward/downward and fingers pointing forward/upward, is held with side of forefinger against palm of left hand. The right hand is then moved firmly forward/upward.

SAME SIGN—**development**, *n.*

develop: *v.* to put camera film into a chemical solution to produce a visible image. *The photographer likes to develop his own film.*

SIGN #2: **'CONTRACTED B'** hands are held slightly apart with palms facing each other and fingers of left hand pointing rightward while fingers of right hand point leftward. The hands are then simultaneously moved from side to side a few times.

deviate: *v.* to stray from what is considered usual or normal. *They were happy to deviate from the normal routine.*

SIGN: **'ONE'** hands are held together with palms down and forefingers pointing forward. The left hand remains fixed while the right hand curves forward/rightward in a fairly wide arc.

device: *n.* a tool or machine designed for a specific use. *The TTY is a valuable communication device used by Deaf people.*

SIGN: Right **'EXTENDED B'** hand, palm facing up, fingertips pointing forward, is moved from left to right in an arc. (**DEVICE** may be fingerspelled.)

devil: *n.* the main spirit of evil. *The devil is often depicted as a human figure with horns and a tail.*

SIGN: Thumb of vertical right **'CROOKED EXTENDED V'** hand is placed against the right side of the forehead, palm facing forward, and the two bent fingers are simultaneously wiggled up and down. Alternatively, this sign may be made with two hands, one at either side of the forehead.

devise: *v.* to work out mentally or plan; create. *He tried to devise a plan for getting rid of the wasps in the attic.*

SIGN: Tip of forefinger of vertical right **'4'** hand, palm facing left, is placed against the forehead and the hand is then pushed upward and forward slightly.

(be) devoid of: *v.* to be lacking in or totally without. *He is devoid of guilt.*

SIGN: Vertical **'O'** hands are held with palms facing each other. They are then thrust downward/forward as the wrists rotate outward to turn the hands so that the palms face upward but are slanted toward one another slightly.

devotion: *n.* affection characterized by dedicated loyalty. *The couple's devotion to each other was obvious.*

SIGN: Vertical **'EXTENDED B'** hands, one at either side of the face with palms facing each other, are simultaneously moved forward a few times.

devour: *v.* to eat greedily. *He was so hungry that he had devoured the huge sandwich before I knew it.*

SIGN: Vertical right **'BENT EXTENDED B'** hand is held with palm backward and is then moved firmly to a position just above the right shoulder as the mouth closes.

diabetes: *n.* a disorder caused by a deficiency of insulin. *A person who has diabetes must follow a strict diet.*

SIGN: Fingertips of right **'BENT EXTENDED B'** hand, palm toward the body, are brushed downward twice on the chin.

diagnose: *v.* to examine symptoms of something for the purpose of identifying a problem. *Doctors use modern technology to diagnose most ailments.*

SIGN: **'V'** hands, palms down, extended fingers of one hand pointing toward those of the other hand, are simultaneously moved apart at least twice while the extended fingers retract to take on **'CLAWED V'** handshapes. Then **'F'** hands, with palms facing each other, are held apart in front of chest and are simultaneously lowered. (ASL CONCEPT—**analyze - decide**.) SAME SIGN—**diagnosis**, *n.*

diagonal: *adj.* slanting or oblique; a line that extends at a slant between opposite corners of a four-sided figure. *She drew a diagonal line through the rectangle.*

SIGN: Right **'EXTENDED B'** hand, palm angled leftward/upward, is drawn down from right to left in a slanting manner.

diagram: *n.* a sketch or drawing which shows how something is formed or how it works. *To assemble the weightlifting equipment, follow the diagram carefully.*

SIGN: Left **'EXTENDED B'** hand is held in a fixed and relatively fixed position with palm facing the body. The tip of the little finger of the right **'I'** hand is stroked downward twice along the middle of the left palm.

ALTERNATE SIGN—**picture**

dial (phone): *v.* to initiate a telephone connection by pushing a specific set of numbers (or turning a dial to select a specific set of numbers). *Be sure to dial the correct number.*

SIGN #1: Forefinger of right **'BENT ONE'** hand points either forward or downward (depending on whether the telephone is mounted on a wall or resting on a horizontal surface) and jabs in the air to simulate the pushing of a set of numbers on a telephone. (When referring to the dialing of a telephone with a round disk dial, right **'BENT ONE'** (or **'CROOKED ONE'**) hand is curved rightward from the wrist two or three times to simulate the dialing of a telephone.)

dial (knob): *n.* the control on a radio or television set for changing the station, channel or volume. *The volume dial on this radio is broken.*

SIGN #2: Vertical right **'SPREAD C'** hand, palm forward, is twisted back and forth from the wrist. (Handshapes vary depending on the size and shape of the dial.)

dial: *n.* a meter with a pointer which indicates direction, measurement, etc. *There were many light indicators and dials on the instrument panel in the cockpit.*

SIGN #3: Horizontal left **'EXTENDED B'** hand is held in a fixed position with palm up but angled toward the body and fingers pointing rightward/forward. Right **'ONE'** hand, palm facing left, is placed on the left palm with forefinger pointing forward/leftward but slanted upward. The hand then pivots (from the wrist) so that the forefinger moves back and forth to simulate the action of a compass needle.

dialogue: *n.* a conversation between two or more people. *The drama was a series of dialogues between the two main characters.*

SIGN: Vertical **'ONE'** hands are held apart with right palm facing left and left palm facing right. The hands are positioned so that tips of forefingers are about level with the mouth or chin as forearms move alternately back and forth.

diamond: *n.* a hard, crystalline form of carbon used as a precious stone. *She had an engagement ring with a beautiful diamond.*

SIGN #1: Joined thumb and midfinger of right **'D'** hand brush downward a couple of times against base of ring finger of left **'STANDARD BASE'** hand.

ALTERNATE SIGN—**diamond** #3

SIGN #2 [ATLANTIC]: Tip of midfinger of right **'BENT MIDFINGER 5'** hand, palm down, taps down a couple of times against base of ring finger of left **'STANDARD BASE'** hand.

diamond: *n.* a playing card which bears one or more red, diamond-shaped symbols. *I only had one diamond in my hand when my partner bid three diamonds.*

SIGN #3: Vertical right **'D'** hand, palm forward, is shaken back and forth slightly from the wrist.

ALTERNATE SIGN—**diamond** #2

diamond: *n.* the playing field for a game of baseball. *I am going to the ball diamond now.*

SIGN #4: **'BENT ONE'** hands are held a considerable distance in front of the chest with palms down and tips of forefingers held together. The hands trace the shape of a diamond as they move backward/outward and then backward/inward, coming together again near the chest.

diaper: *n.* the soft, protective material that is wrapped around a baby to absorb its excrement. *The baby is crying because she needs her diaper changed.*

SIGN: **'CONTRACTED 3'** hands, palms toward the body and extended fingers pointing downward but angled toward each other, are held just below either side of the waist, and are simultaneously snapped shut to form **'CLOSED DOUBLE MODIFIED G'** hands. The motion may be repeated and is intended to simulate the fastening of a diaper.

diarrhea: *n.* frequent and abnormally liquid bowel movements. *If you have diarrhea, it is important to drink lots of liquids.*

SIGN: Left **'EXTENDED C'** hand is held in a fixed position with palm at a rightward/backward angle and fingers pointing forward/rightward/upward. Horizontal right **'5'** hand is positioned just to the right of the left hand, and as the right wrist rotates leftward several times, the thumbtip is repeatedly brushed downward against the left palm.

diary: *n.* a daily record of personal experiences. *She writes in her diary every night before she goes to bed.*

SIGN: Horizontal left **'EXTENDED B'** hand is held in a fixed position with palm facing rightward/backward. Thumb and forefinger of right **'CLOSED X'** hand move forward/rightward twice along the palm of the left hand. (**DIARY** may be fingerspelled.)

dice: *n.* two small cubes used in games of chance. *You need a pair of dice to play Monopoly.*

SIGN: Right **'S'** hand is held with palm up at a leftward angle and is shaken back and forth. As it stops shaking, it is thrust forward and opened to form a **'5'** hand as if throwing dice.

---

dicker: See **bargain** #1.

dictionary: *n.* a book consisting of alphabetically arranged words and their meanings. *Every home should have a good dictionary.*

SIGN: Left **'EXTENDED B'** hand is held in a fixed position with fingers pointing forward and palm facing upward/rightward. Joined thumb and midfinger of right **'D'** hand are placed against heel of left hand. Then the right hand is circled at least twice in a clockwise direction, brushing upward and off the heel of the left hand with each revolution.

die: *v.* to stop living. *Many people die in traffic accidents.*

SIGN: Right **'EXTENDED B'** hand is held palm down with fingers pointing forward. The wrist then rotates rightward, turning the hand palm upward.

diet: *n.* the food and drink that a person consumes regularly. *Exercise and a healthy diet will speed your recovery.*

SIGN #1: Fingertips of vertical right **'MODIFIED O'** hand, palm facing backwards, are tapped against the mouth twice.

diet: *n.* a specific allowance of food and drink designed for weight loss. *I am going on a diet to lose at least 10 pounds.*

SIGN #2: Fingerspell **DIET**.

D   I   E   T

different: *adj.* not the same; unlike. *His personality is very different from his brother's.*

SIGN: Forefingers of **'ONE'** hands are crossed. The hands are then turned outward so that they become vertical with palms facing forward. SAME SIGN—**difference**, *n.*

difficult: *adj.* not easy to do. *It was a difficult task to decide which vocabulary should be included in this dictionary.*

SIGN: **'CLAWED V'** hands are held, right above left, at an angle somewhere between vertical and horizontal, with left palm facing right and right palm facing left. The hands then come together and strike each other with force.

difficulty: *n.* the condition of not being easy; problem. *He experienced great difficulty trying to budget his money on such a small salary.*

SIGN: Horizontal **'CLAWED V'** hands are held with palms facing the body and knuckles knocking against each other as the hands are alternately moved up and down.

dig: *v.* to turn over or remove earth, sand, etc., with a shovel. *He will dig for earthworms in the garden before he goes fishing.*

SIGN #1: **'A'** (or **'S'**) hands are positioned in front of the body as if they are holding a spade. Then they are moved downward and flung to the right of the body to simulate the scooping up of soil and tossing it. (Signs vary.)

dig: *v.* to make a hole in the ground with claws. *Groundhogs dig holes in farmers' fields.*

SIGN #2: **'SPREAD EXTENDED C'** hands are held apart with palms down and are alternately and rapidly circled forward several times.

digest: *n.* a magazine or periodical containing condensed or summarized articles. *He enjoys reading the Sports Digest.*

SIGN: **'SPREAD C'** hands are held horizontally and slightly apart, right above left. Then both are closed to form **'S'** hands as the right is brought down to rest on top of the left. (For **digest**, *v.*, meaning to process food in the body, see **digestion**.)

digestion: *n.* the process of food absorption in the body. *The action of enzymes is important in the digestion of food.*

SIGN: Fingertips of vertical right **'MODIFIED O'** hand, palm facing backwards, are tapped against the mouth twice. Next, horizontal **'A'** hands are held, right on top of left, with palms facing each other and knuckles of each hand touching those of the other. Then they are circled counter-clockwise in offset rotations as if grinding something between them. (ASL CONCEPT—**food - chew in stomach.**)

dignified: *adj.* characterized by a stately, noble manner or appearance. *She dresses in a dignified and elegant manner.*

SIGN: Thumb of vertical right **'5'** hand, palm facing left, is placed at the middle of the chest and the hand is circled forward twice so that the thumb brushes the up and off chest with each revolution.

dignity: *n.* the quality of being worthy of honour. *She performs her duties with grace and dignity.*

SIGN: **'EXTENDED A'** hand, with thumb pointing downward, is moved upward from stomach to chest. (**DIGNITY** is frequently fingerspelled.)

digress: *v.* to stray from the subject about which one is writing or speaking. *He has an unfortunate tendency to digress during his lectures.*

SIGN: Left **'ONE'** hand, palm facing rightward/forward, is held upright and remains fixed as tip of forefinger of right **'BENT ONE'** hand flicks leftward/backward off tip of left forefinger.

dilate: *v.* to enlarge or widen. *The doctor will put drops in your eyes to dilate your pupils.*

SIGN: Vertical **'S'** hands are held one in front of each eye with palms facing each other at a forward angle. The hands gradually open to form **'F'** hands. (The formation and location of this sign varies according to 'what' is dilating.)

dilemma: *n.* a situation requiring a choice between equally undesirable alternatives. *He is in a dilemma about whether or not to withdraw from the course.*

SIGN: Tips of index and middle fingers of right **'BENT EXTENDED U'** hand, palm down, rest on forefinger of horizontal left **'B'** (or **'ONE'**) hand, whose palm is facing right. Right hand then sways from side to side several times as though trying to balance on left forefinger.
ALTERNATE SIGN—**uncertain #1**

diligent: *adj.* giving great care and attention to one's tasks or duties; hard-working; industrious. *He is the most diligent worker in our office.*

SIGN: Wrist of right **'S'** (or **'A'**) hand, palm facing away from the body, strikes wrist of left **'S'** (or **'A'**) hand, which is held in front of/below right hand with palm facing downward. Motion is repeated several times with slow, exaggerated emphasis so that the right hand appears to be moving in circles.
SAME SIGN—**diligence,** *n.*

dill: *n.* a plant of which the leaves and/or seeds are used for flavouring food. *These pickles need more dill and less garlic.*

SIGN: Fingerspell **DILL**.

dim: *v.* to cause a light to become less bright. *Most restaurants dim the lights after 6:00 p.m.*

SIGN: **'CONTRACTED 5'** hands, which are held parallel above shoulder level with palms down, are slowly contracted further.

dime: *n.* a ten cent coin. *A dime is equal to one-tenth of a dollar.*

SIGN: Tip of forefinger of right **'L'** hand touches right side of forehead. The hand is then drawn rightward/downward as it changes to a wobbling **'EXTENDED A'** hand with palm facing left.

dimension: *n.* the measurement of a certain space, especially that of length, width or height. *What are the dimensions of this room?*

SIGN: **'Y'** hands are held parallel with palms forward/downward, and tips of thumbs are tapped together at least twice.

diminish: *v.* to become or to make smaller, fewer, or less. *He thinks that drinking lots of water will **diminish** his appetite.*

SIGN: Horizontal **'BENT EXTENDED B'** (or **'ONE'**) hands are held right above left with left palm up and right palm forward/downward. The right hand is then lowered toward the left hand.

dimple: *n.* a small natural depression, usually in the cheek(s) or chin. *When she smiles, there is a **dimple** in her right cheek.*

SIGN: Tip of forefinger of right **'BENT ONE'** hand touches the right cheek and the wrist is twisted forward slightly. (The positioning of this sign depends entirely on the location of the dimple.)

din: *n.* a loud, confusing noise. *The children were creating such a **din** in the playroom that nobody heard the doorbell ringing.*

SIGN: Thumbtips of vertical **'MODIFIED 5'** hands are held near either ear, palms facing forward but angled slightly toward each other, as forearms are simultaneously thrust outward/forward and back at least twice.

dine: *v.* to eat dinner. *We **dine** at a local restaurant every Sunday.*

SIGN: Fingertips of vertical right **'MODIFIED O'** hand, palm facing backwards, are tapped against the mouth twice.

dinner: *n.* the main meal of the day, either at noon or in the early evening. *We usually have our **dinner** around seven o'clock.*

SIGN: Fingertips of vertical right **'MODIFIED O'** hand, palm facing backwards, are tapped against the mouth twice.

dinosaur: *n.* an extinct reptile of gigantic size. *Bones from **dinosaurs** are found in the Drumheller area in southern Alberta.*

SIGN: Heels of **'CLAWED V'** hands are tucked into either side of chest with left palm facing right and right palm facing left. The arms remain fixed as the hands are alternately moved up and down from the wrists.

dip: *n.* a creamy, usually savoury mixture into which finger foods can be dipped before they are eaten. *They had several kinds of **dip** for the raw vegetables.*

SIGN: Fingerspell **DIP**.
(Many signs are applicable for **dip**, *v.*)

diploma: *n.* a document conferring a qualification such as a university degree. *He will receive his **diploma** at the spring convocation.*

SIGN: Horizontal **'F'** hands are held side by side, palms down and extended fingers pointing forward, and are drawn apart. (**DIPLOMA** may be fingerspelled.)

dire: *adj.* urgent; ominous; foreboding disaster. *The United Nations issued a **dire** warning to the Palestinian and Israeli warriors.*

SIGN: Vertical right **'BENT ONE'** hand is held with tip of forefinger touching chin and palm facing leftward but slanted toward the body. The wrist then rotates, turning the hand so that the palm fully faces the body.

ALTERNATE SIGN—**terrible**

direct: *v.* to control the affairs of; manage. *Mr. Kelly will **direct** the activities at the Community Centre.*

SIGN #1: Horizontal **'X'** hands are held slightly apart with left palm facing right and right palm facing left. Then they are alternately moved backward and forward.
SAME SIGN—**director**, *n.*, and may be followed by the Agent Ending (see p. LIV).

direct: *v.* to order or command. *The chairperson **directed** the board members to pay close attention.*

SIGN #2: Tip of forefinger of vertical right **'ONE'** hand, palm forward, is placed on the lips and the hand is thrust forward so that the palm faces downward. ❖

direct: *v.* to tell or show the way to a place or person. *Could you please direct me to the manager's office?*

SIGN #3: Tip of forefinger of horizontal right **'BENT ONE'** hand is placed against right facing palm of left **'EXTENDED B'** hand. Then both hands are moved backward simultaneously toward the chest. Next, vertical right **'ONE'** hand, palm forward, is shaken. ❖ (ASL CONCEPT—**show-me - where**.)

direct: *adj.* straightforward. *Most politicians avoid giving direct answers to the questions of reporters.*

SIGN #4: Vertical right **'B'** hand, palm facing left, is held directly in front of the face and thrust forward and slightly downward.

direction: *n.* guidance. *Teenagers often need direction from adults when it comes to making important decisions.*

SIGN: Fingertips of right **'FLAT O'** hand rest on back of left **'STANDARD BASE'** hand. Right hand is then thrust forward as it opens slightly to form a **'CONTRACTED 5'** hand. Motion is repeated.

ALTERNATE SIGN—**guide**

directions: *n.* instructions which explain how to do something. *You should read the directions before building the toy.*

SIGN #1: **'F'** hands are held horizontally with palms facing each other, and are alternately moved backward and forward a few times.

directions: *n.* instructions that explain how to find a place. *Could you give me directions to the post office?*

SIGN #2: Vertical right **'ONE'** hand, palm forward, is held near the right shoulder and is waved from side to side a few times. The movement is from the wrist. Then horizontal right **'ONE'** hand is held with forefinger pointing forward and the hand is snaked forward. (ASL CONCEPT—**where - go-forward?**) This sign appears at the *end* of the ASL sentence. The sample sentence in ASL is: *P-O, **WHERE GO?***

dirt: *n.* soil; mud. *The cat tracked dirt all over the clean rug.*

SIGN: **'FLAT O'** hands are held slightly apart with palms up. Then the fingers are slid across the thumbs a few times, thus alternating between **'FLAT O'** and **'OFFSET O'** hands.

dirty: *adj.* unclean; grimy. *The boy had dirty hands after he played in the mud.*

SIGN: Right **'MODIFIED 5'** hand is held under chin with palm down as the fingers flutter.

dis-: *prefix* indicates negation or reversal. *People distrust him because he has not been very honest in the past.*

SIGN: Right **'EXTENDED A'** hand, palm facing left, thumb under chin, is thrust forward. (The prefix **DIS** is often fingerspelled for emphasis.) This prefix is frequently not signed separately but rather is incorporated in the sign for the root or base word as in the words 'disconnect' or 'disrupt'. This happens when **'dis-'** cannot be translated as 'not' or 'do not'.

disability: *n.* an inability or incapacity to do certain things. *Deafness is not considered a disability.*

SIGN: Fingerspell **DA**.

disadvantage: *n.* something that is detrimental or unfavourable. *It is a disadvantage to have no plans in case of an emergency.*

SIGN: Horizontal **'CLAWED V'** hands are held with palms facing the body and knuckles knocking against each other as the hands are alternately moved up and down.

disagree: *v.* to have a different opinion; not agree. *I disagree with what you just said.*

SIGN: Left **'ONE'** hand is held in a fixed position in front of the upper chest with palm right and forefinger pointing forward. Right **'BENT ONE'** hand is positioned with tip of forefinger touching the centre of the forehead and is then brought downward and forward, the tip of its forefinger brushing against the tip of the left forefinger on its way past. Facial expression is important.

SAME SIGN—**disagreement**, *n.*

disappear: *v.* to vanish from sight. *The magician made the rabbit disappear.*

SIGN #1: Left **'EXTENDED B'** hand is held in a fixed position with palm down and fingers pointing rightward. Forefinger of right **'ONE'** hand is protruded upward between forefinger and midfinger of the left hand. Then the right hand is pulled down firmly.

OR

SIGN #2: **'FLAT O'** hands are held parallel with palms up and slanted slightly toward the body. As the hands are drawn apart the thumbs slide across the fingertips, causing the hands to assume **'A'** shapes. (**Disappear #1** would be more appropriate for referring to the disappearance of a 'person'.)

ALTERNATE SIGN—**missing**

disappointed: *adj.* feeling unhappy or let down because certain hopes or expectations have not been met. *Your parents are disappointed because you have dropped out of high school.*

SIGN: Tip of forefinger of right **'ONE'** hand is pressed firmly against the chin. Facial expression is important.

SAME SIGN—**disappointment**, *n.*

disaster: *n.* a happening that causes great distress or destruction. *The tornado created a disaster wherever it struck.*

SIGN: Right **'COVERED 8'** hand, palm facing left, is held upright at about shoulder level. The hand is then thrust backward as the middle finger and thumb flick apart to form a **'MODIFIED 5'** hand.

ALTERNATE SIGN—**catastrophe** #2

disbelief: *n.* difficulty believing; refusal to believe. *His face showed his shock and disbelief.*

SIGN: Vertical **'CLAWED V'** hand is held with palm toward the face and the clawed fingers wiggling in front of the eyes as the head is shaken back and forth. Facial expression is important.

disbursement: *n.* a payout of funds. *The annual financial statement will show our revenues and disbursements.*

SIGN: **'FLAT O'** hands are held with palms up, the left hand slightly ahead of the right hand. The hands move simultaneously forward while the hands close to form **'A'** hands.

discard: *v.* to throw away; get rid of. *Where can I discard this old battery?*

SIGN #1: Vertical right **'S'** hand, palm facing left, is thrust forward/downward as it is transformed with a flicking motion into a **'U'** hand. (Signs vary considerably. See also **dispose of** and **oust**.)

discard: *v.* to get rid of (a playing card). *I think you should discard your queen of diamonds.*

SIGN #2: Left **'CONTRACTED B'** hand is held with palm facing the body at an upward angle as the fingers point upward/rightward. Right **'COVERED T'** hand is held beside left hand with palm facing left. The right hand then arches forward/downward as if placing a card on the table.

discharge: *v.* to release or dismiss from duty. *The army discharged the soldier after he was wounded.*

SIGN #1: Fingers of right **'B'** hand, palm-down, are placed on and at right angles to fingers of upturned palm of left **'EXTENDED B'** hand. Right hand is then slid at a forward/rightward angle across and off the left hand.

discharge: *v.* to shoot or fire (a weapon). *The police officer discharged his gun in the line of duty.*

SIGN #2: Horizontal right **'L'** hand represents a gun as it is held with palm left and forefinger pointing forward. The forearm then jerks backward slightly so that the forefinger points forward/upward as the thumb bends to form a **'BENT THUMB L'** hand. ❖

discharge: *n.* emission; the pouring forth of a fluid. *The gynecologist noted that the patient had an abnormal discharge.*

SIGN #3: Horizontal left **'4'** hand is held in a fixed position with palm toward the body and fingers pointing right. Horizontal right **'4'** hand, palm toward the body, is held with leftward-pointing fingers in front of those of the left hand. Right hand then drops downward from the wrist so that the fingers point downward/leftward. Motion is repeated.

discipline: *n.* a system of rules for behaviour. *It is a common belief that young children need discipline.*

SIGN: Horizontal **'X'** hands are held slightly apart with left palm facing right and right palm facing left. Then they are alternately moved backward and forward.

disclose: *v.* to reveal knowledge. *Did you disclose any confidential information?*

SIGN #1: Tip of forefinger of right **'BENT ONE'** hand, palm toward the body, is held just under the chin and flicked forward, thus creating a **'ONE'** hand. (This sign is appropriate when information is being *disclosed to one person only.*)

disclose: *v.* to reveal knowledge. *Did you disclose any confidential information?*

SIGN #2: Right **'FLAT O'** hand is held with the fingertips touching the forehead while left **'FLAT O'** hand is held in front of left shoulder with palm facing upward/backward. The forearms are then simultaneously swung outward and slightly downward/forward as the hands open to assume **'MODIFIED 5'** shapes with palms facing upward. (This sign is appropriate only when information is being *disclosed to more than one person.*)
ALTERNATE SIGN—**announce**

disconnect: *v.* to unfasten or break a connection. *The computer will not work if you disconnect the keyboard.*

SIGN: Thumbs and forefingers of **'F'** hands, palms facing each other, are interlocked. The hands are then drawn apart to form **'OPEN F'** hands. ❖
SAME SIGN—**disconnection**, *n.*

discontinue: *v.* to bring to an end; stop. *The government will discontinue several of its programs for seniors.*

SIGN: Right **'EXTENDED B'** hand, palm facing left, is brought down sharply from a semi-vertical position to strike the upward/backward facing palm of the rigidly held left **'EXTENDED B'** hand, whose fingers point rightward/forward.

discount: *n.* a deduction from the regular price. *Senior citizens are given a discount on their meals at that restaurant.*

SIGN: Horizontal **'BENT EXTENDED B'** (or **'ONE'**) hands are held right above left with left palm up and right palm forward/downward. The right hand is then lowered toward the left hand.

discourage: *v.* to advise against. *She wanted to quit her job but I discouraged her.*

SIGN: Vertical right **'5'** hand, palm forward, is waved back and forth lightly from the wrist as the head is shaken. An appropriate facial expression should accompany this sign. (This sign may be used at the end of a sentence or as a sentence substitute but is never used at the beginning of a sentence that has a lot of information following. It would *not* be used in this sentence: *I discouraged her from quitting her job because she needed the money.*)

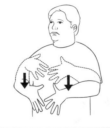

discouraged/discouraging: *adj.* disheartened/disheartening. *He felt very discouraged after failing the exam. It was a very discouraging experience for him.*

SIGN: Palms of both **'5'** hands, fingers pointing down, are held against either side of upper chest and are simultaneously pushed downward.

discover: *v.* to find or find out; to be the first to find out. *Researchers hope to discover a cure for cancer.*

SIGN: Right **'OPEN F'** hand is held palm down. The hand then moves upward as the thumb and forefinger close to form an **'F'** hand with palm facing forward.
SAME SIGN—**discovery**, *n.*

discreet: *adj.* tactful and unobtrusive; very careful, especially in keeping secrets confidential. *We were discreet about our relationship as we did not want people to know about it.*

SIGN: Right **'EXTENDED B'** hand is held with palm toward the face and fingers pointing upward/leftward, and the forearm is moved from side to side slightly a few times.

discriminate against: *v.* to treat unfairly and with prejudice. *It is cruel to **discriminate against** people for any reason.*

SIGN #1: Horizontal left **'BENT EXTENDED B'** hand is held with palm facing rightward/backward and fingers pointing to the right. Right **'EXTENDED B'** (or **'B'**) hand is held upright very close to the chest with palm facing left. The right hand then drops from the wrist until it is horizontal with fingertips forcefully striking left hand between the palm and the fingers. SAME SIGN—**discrimination,** *n.*

OR

SIGN #2: Left **'EXTENDED B'** hand is held in a fixed position with palm down and fingers pointing rightward/forward. Right **'V'** hand is held under left hand with extended fingers pointing downward at a leftward/forward angle. The right hand is then raised up from the wrist so that the extended fingers strike the left palm. Motion is repeated. SAME SIGN—**discrimination,** *n.*

discriminate between: *v.* to differentiate; distinguish; show or recognize a distinct difference between two things. *Can you **discriminate between** a native and a near-native signer?*

SIGN: Fingertips of right **'EXTENDED B'** (or **'BENT EXTENDED B'**) hand, with palm facing body, are tapped against right side of forehead. Next, horizontal **'ONE'** hands are held parallel with palms facing forward. The forefingers, first the right and then the left, make slight jabbing motions forward as if pointing at two objects/people in front of the signer. Finally the forefingers are crossed, then turned outward and swept apart so that they are parallel and both forefingers point straight up. (ASL CONCEPT—**know - that - that - different.**)

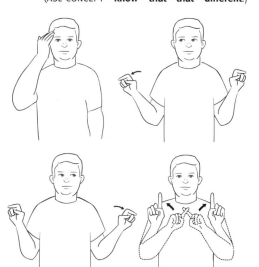

discus: *n.* a disc-shaped object used in throwing competitions by athletes. *Ancient Greeks originally hurled a circular stone instead of a **discus**.*

SIGN: Right horizontal **'OPEN A'** hand, palm downward, is held near the right side of the body and is flung forward as it changes to a **'5'** hand, thus simulating the hurling of a discus.

discuss: *v.* to talk about. *We can **discuss** our travel plans at another time.*

SIGN: Forefinger of horizontal right **'ONE'** hand, palm toward the body, is tapped several times on the upturned palm of the left **'EXTENDED B'** hand, of which the fingers are pointing rightward/forward. SAME SIGN—**discussion,** *n.*

disease: *n.* an impairment that produces certain symptoms of ill health. *AIDS is a serious **disease**.*

SIGN: Midfinger of each **'BENT MIDFINGER 5'** hand is placed on the body—the right against the forehead, and the left against the stomach. The hands are then simultaneously moved slightly back and forth twice. (**DISEASE** is frequently fingerspelled.)

disgrace: *n.* dishonour; shame or loss of reputation. *It was a **disgrace** how he cheated the company out of so much money.*

SIGN: The backs of the fingers of the right **'BENT EXTENDED B'** hand, palm facing right shoulder, are brushed forward against right cheek as palm faces up. A look of disgust accompanies this sign.

disgusted: *adj.* sickened; filled with loathing. *Many viewers are **disgusted** by violence on television.*

SIGN: Right **'CLAWED C'** hand, palm toward the body, is circled in a clockwise direction (from the onlooker's perspective) in front of the stomach. Facial expression is very important in conveying this concept. (This sign is used only in a passive voice situation or as an adjective to describe someone's feelings. It would *not* be possible to use this sign in an active voice situation such as: *Violence on television **disgusts** many viewers*.)

dish: *n.* an open, shallow container used for holding and serving food. *We need one more dish to put vegetables in.*

SIGN: Horizontal **'C-INDEX'** hands are held parallel with palms facing each other.

(satellite) dish: *n.* a large circular reflector used in satellite broadcasting. *They installed a satellite dish to increase the number of TV stations available.*

SIGN: Left horizontal **'ONE'** hand is held steady, palm down, with forefinger pointing at right wrist. Right **'MODIFIED 5'** hand, palm forward, is held beside and slightly in front of left hand and is drawn toward it and away from it a few times, intermittently touching the tip of the left forefinger.

dishwasher: *n.* a machine used for washing dishes. *It is your job to load the dishwasher after our meals.*

SIGN: Fingerspell **DISH**. Then **'SPREAD C'** hands, palms facing, are held apart with the right above the left and are simultaneously twisted back and forth (from the wrists) in opposite directions. (**DISHWASHER** is frequently finger-spelled.)

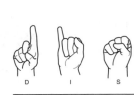

disintegrate: *v.* to break into fragments. *This metal will disintegrate if submerged in an acid solution.*

SIGN: **'FLAT O'** hands are held parallel with palms up and slanted slightly toward the body. As the hands are drawn apart the thumbs slide across the fingertips, causing the hands to assume **'A'** shapes.

disk: *n.* a direct-access computer storage device. *It is wise to back up your data on a second disk.*

SIGN: Vertical left **'EXTENDED B'** hand is held in a fixed position with palm facing right. Joined thumb and midfinger of vertical right **'D'** hand, palm left, are placed against the left palm and the right hand moves in a clockwise direction as if inscribing a circle on the left palm. (**DISK** is frequently fingerspelled.)

dislike: *v.* to consider unpleasant or disagreeable. *I dislike selfish people.*

SIGN: Tips of thumb and middle finger of horizontal right **'OPEN 8'** hand are placed in the centre of the chest. As the hand moves away from the chest, the tips of thumb and middle finger come together to form an **'8'** hand. The hand then turns palm-downward as it takes on a **'MODIFIED 5'** shape. Facial expression is important.

dismiss: *v.* to discontinue consideration of; to allow or direct to leave. *The judge will dismiss the case due to lack of evidence.*

SIGN: Fingers of right **'B'** hand, palm-down, are placed on and at right angles to fingers of upturned palm of left **'EXTENDED B'** hand. Right hand is then slid at a forward/rightward angle across and off the left hand.
SAME SIGN—**dismissal,** *n.*

disobey: *v.* to refuse to follow an order or rule. *A soldier who disobeys an order can be in serious trouble.*

SIGN: Vertical right **'S'** hand, palm facing backward, is held at or above shoulder level and is forcefully twisted a half turn so that palm faces forward.
SAME SIGNS—**disobedience,** *n.,* and **disobedient,** *adj.*

ALTERNATE SIGN—**not + obey**

disorder: *n.* a confusion or disturbance of public order. *The traffic on city streets was in disorder during the blizzard.*

SIGN #1: Left **'CROOKED 5'** hand is held palm-up with fingers pointing forward while right **'CROOKED 5'** hand is held apart and slightly higher with palm down and fingers pointing forward. The arms are then simultaneously moved upward/rightward as the hands are purposefully twisted rightward from the wrist so that the left palm faces right and the right palm faces left.

disorder: *n.* a problem, especially health-related, which prevents normal functioning. *Bulimia is an eating disorder.*

SIGN #2: Horizontal **'CLAWED V'** hands are held with palms facing the body and knuckles knocking against each other as the hands are alternately moved up and down.

disorganized: *adj.* not systematic or orderly in doing things. *His boss is not satisfied with his work because he is so disorganized.*

SIGN #1: Right **'EXTENDED A'** hand, palm facing left, thumb under chin, is thrust forward. Next, horizontal **'EXTENDED B'** hands, palms facing each other and fingers pointing forward, are held slightly apart at the left side of the body and are moved simultaneously toward the right.

disorganized: *adj.* not orderly; not in a systematic arrangement. *His desk is always disorganized.*

SIGN #2: **'5'** hands are held offset with palms down and fingers pointing forward. They are then alternately moved backward and forward.

disown: *v.* to refuse to acknowledge any kinship or connection with. *In some religions, if a person marries outside his faith, his family might disown him.*

SIGN: Thumbs and forefingers of **'F'** hands, palms facing each other, are interlocked. The hands are then drawn apart to form **'OPEN F'** hands. (**DISOWN** is frequently fingerspelled.) ❖

dispatch [*also spelled* **despatch**]: *v.* to send off promptly. *The central office will dispatch a taxi for you.*

SIGN: Fingertips of horizontal right **'BENT EXTENDED B'** hand are placed on the back of the left **'STANDARD BASE'** hand. The right hand then moves forward as the fingers straighten to form an **'EXTENDED B'** hand.

disperse: *v.* to scatter or distribute over a wide area; to go away or cause to go away in various directions from a gathering. *The police asked the crowd to disperse.*

SIGN: Horizontal **'S'** hands are held side by side with palms down. The hands are then thrust forward/outward as the fingers open to form **'MODIFIED 5'** shapes.

display: *v.* to show; exhibit. *They will display native arts at the museum.*

SIGN: Tip of forefinger of horizontal right **'BENT ONE'** hand is placed against right facing palm of left **'EXTENDED B'** hand. Together, the hands are moved forward in a short arc. (The sign for **display**, *n.,* begins in the same position, but the hands move straight forward rather than in an arc, and the movement is repeated.)

dispose of: *v.* to throw away or get rid of. *You can dispose of your garbage at the dumpsite on the outskirts of town.*

SIGN: Vertical right **'S'** hand, palm forward, is flung downward from the wrist as it opens to form a **'CROOKED 5'** shape. Alternatively, this sign may be made with both hands.

disposition: See **personality**.

disprove: *v.* to establish the incorrectness of a claim, assertion or allegation. *The lawyer will attempt to disprove the witness's testimony.*

SIGN: Vertical left **'ONE'** hand is held with palm facing right while right **'CROOKED 5'** hand is held with palm facing forward and resting on the tip of the left forefinger. The right hand then bends forward from the wrist, thus turning itself palm-downward and forcing the left forefinger downward/forward somewhat.

dispute: *n.* an argument, debate, or quarrel. *Their long dispute ended after they understood each other's views.*

SIGN: **'BENT ONE'** hands, palms toward the chest, forefingers pointing toward each other, are either simultaneously or alternately moved up and down from the wrist.

disqualify: *v.* to make or become ineligible for something. *The officials had to disqualify the skater when she fell during her performance.*

SIGN: Fingerspell **DISQ**.

D · I · S · Q

disregard: *v.* to ignore; pay no attention to. *He lost the respect of his friends when he continued to disregard their feelings.*

SIGN: Tip of forefinger of horizontal right **'4'** hand, palm facing downward, is placed on the nose and the hand is curved rightward from the wrist away from the face.

disrupt: *v.* to throw into turmoil or disorder. *I am sorry to disrupt your meeting.*

SIGN: Left **'CROOKED 5'** hand is held palm-up with fingers pointing forward while right **'CROOKED 5'** hand is held apart and slightly higher with palm down and fingers pointing forward. The arms are then simultaneously moved upward/rightward as the hands are purposefully twisted rightward from the wrist so that the left palm faces right and the right palm faces left.

ALTERNATE SIGN—**interrupt**

dissect: *v.* to cut open a plant or animal for critical examination. *We dissected a frog in biology class today.*

SIGN: Thumbnail of horizontal right **'EXTENDED A'** (or **'Y'**) hand, palm down, is placed on the rightward facing palm of the left **'EXTENDED B'** hand. Then the right thumb is drawn downward across the left palm. Next, **'V'** hands, palms down, extended fingers of one hand pointing toward extended fingers of the other hand, are simultaneously moved apart at least twice while the extended fingers retract to take on **'CLAWED V'** handshapes. (ASL CONCEPT—**operate - analyze**.)

disseminate: *v.* to distribute; disperse. *To make our project successful we must disseminate information to the public.*

SIGN: Horizontal **'CONTRACTED B'** hands are held with palms up and fingertips almost touching. The hands then move forward in an outward arc as the fingers spread to assume a **'SLANTED 5'** shape.

ALTERNATE SIGN—**circulate**

dissent: *n.* a strong difference of opinion or rejection of policies and practices; disagreement. *The workers marched in dissent due to the layoffs and budget cuts.*

SIGN: Left **'ONE'** hand is held in a fixed position in front of the upper chest with palm right and forefinger pointing forward. Right **'BENT ONE'** hand is positioned with tip of forefinger touching the centre of the forehead and is then brought downward and forward, the tip of the forefinger brushing against the tip of the forefinger of the left hand on its way past. Facial expression is important.

SAME SIGN—**dissident**, *n.*, and may be followed by the Agent Ending (see p. LIV).

ALTERNATE SIGNS—**boycott** or **oppose**, depending on the context, might be used.

dissolve: *v.* to melt; become liquid. *The mixture should be stirred over low heat until the chocolate dissolves.*

SIGN: **'FLAT O'** hands are held parallel with palms up and slanted slightly toward the body. As the hands are drawn apart the thumbs slide across the fingertips, causing the hands to assume **'A'** shapes.

distance: *n.* the space between two points. *Distance is sometimes measured in kilometres.*

SIGN: Left **'BENT ONE'** hand is held in a fixed position with palm down and forefinger pointing downward at a slight forward angle. Right **'BENT ONE'** hand is held with palm down and tip of downward-pointing forefinger touching tip of left forefinger. The right hand is then moved directly forward.

distant: *adj.* far. *Although mountains appear to be near, they are quite distant.*

SIGN #1: Horizontal **'EXTENDED A'** hands are held together with palms facing each other. Then the right hand is moved forward in a small arc. (Alternatively, this sign may be made without the left hand.)

distant: *adj.* cool or aloof in one's manner. *She has been rather **distant** toward us lately.*

SIGN #2: Thumbs and forefingers of **'F'** hands, palms facing each other, are interlocked. The hands are then drawn apart to form **'OPEN F'** hands.

(in the) distant future: *adv.* far away in terms of time; a long way off (in the future). ***In the distant future** perhaps the study of ASL will be required in all Canadian schools.*

SIGN: Right **'EXTENDED B'** hand, palm facing left, is held in a vertical position near the right side of the head. The forearm is then thrust firmly forward a considerable distance so that the fingers eventually point forward. The cheeks are puffed.

(in the) distant past: *adv.* a long time ago. ***In the distant past** only aboriginal people inhabited Canada.*

SIGN: Cheeks are puffed as right **'5'** hand is held in front of right shoulder with palm facing left and is slowly but deliberately moved backward in a wide arc toward the shoulder.

distinguish between: *v.* to differentiate; to show or recognize a distinct difference between two things. *It is hard to **distinguish between** Ron and his identical twin, Rick.*

SIGN: Fingertips of right **'EXTENDED B'** (or **'BENT EXTENDED B'**) hand, with palm facing body, are tapped against right side of forehead. Next, horizontal **'ONE'** hands are held parallel with palms facing forward. The forefingers, first the right and then the left, make slight jabbing motions forward as if pointing at two objects/people in front of the signer. Finally the forefingers are crossed, then turned outward and swept apart so that they are parallel and both forefingers point straight up. (ASL CONCEPT—**know - that - that - different**.)

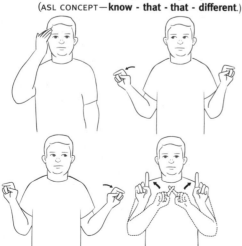

distinguished: *adj.* famous; honourable. *He received the award for his **distinguished** service during the Persian Gulf War.*

SIGN: Right **'U'** hand, palm facing left, is held in a vertical position so that the side of the forefinger touches the middle of the forehead. The hand is curved downward slightly and moved forward. (Alternatively, this sign may be made with two hands, in which case the vertical left **'U'** hand, palm facing right, is held below the right hand and follows its movement.)

(be) distracted: *v.* to have one's attention diverted from something. *If the classroom door is open, the children will **be distracted** from their work.*

SIGN: Right **'BENT V'** hand is held with palm forward and extended fingers pointing forward. The head turns abruptly rightward as the right wrist twists, causing the extended fingers to point rightward/forward.

distribute: *v.* to give out; dispense. *Be sure to **distribute** the information to everyone at the rally.*

SIGN #1: Horizontal **'CONTRACTED B'** hands are held with palms up and fingertips almost touching. The hands then move forward in an outward arc as the fingers spread to assume a **'SLANTED 5'** shape.

OR

SIGN #2: Horizontal left **'CLOSED A-INDEX'** hand is held in a fixed position with palm toward the body at a slight rightward angle. While the right hand moves back and forth several times in front of the left hand, the handshape alternates between an **'A-INDEX'** and a **'CLOSED A-INDEX'** as the thumb and forefinger repeatedly open and close.

OR

SIGN #3: Right **'CONTRACTED B'** hand is held palm-up with fingers pointing forward/leftward in front of left side of body. The hand then makes a sweeping arc rightward as if passing something out. (As a modification, the hand may bounce slightly several times while completing the arc to indicate the giving of something to individual recipients.)

district: *n.* a specific locality, territory or region. *We have always lived in the downtown **district**.*

SIGN: Right **'5'** hand, palm down, is circled in a counter-clockwise motion.
ALTERNATE SIGN—**region**

disturb: *v.* to interrupt. *Please do not disturb my nap.*

SIGN: Edge of right **'EXTENDED B'** hand is brought down with a chopping motion between index and middle finger of left **'5'** hand. ❖ SAME SIGN—**disturbance**, *n.*, but the movement is repeated.

ditch: *n.* a channel dug in the earth, sometimes as a boundary marker or for the purpose of drainage or irrigation. *There is a lot of water in the ditch.*

SIGN: Right horizontal **'EXTENDED B'** hand is initially held with fingers pointing forward and palm facing left. It is then curved downward, rightward, and up, so that the palm eventually faces rightward. (**DITCH** is frequently finger-spelled.)

dive: *v.* to plunge headfirst into the water. *The children like to dive into the pool.*

SIGN: Vertical left **'BENT U'** hand is held in a fixed position with palm facing right and extended fingers, which represent a diving board, pointing rightward. Horizontal right **'BENT U'** hand is held with palm down and tips of extended fingers balanced on the ends of the extended fingers of the left hand. The right hand then moves upward, the wrist rotates rightward, and the hand drops forward to simulate a diving motion.

diverse: *adj.* assorted; varied. *They were a diverse group of people with several common interests.*

SIGN: **'ONE'** hands, palms forward/downward, are held so that the right forefinger is crossed over the left. The fingers then uncross and move apart. This movement is repeated several times as the hands simultaneously move from left to right. Head may turn rightward as the eyes follow the progression of the hands. SAME SIGN—**diversity**, *n.* ALTERNATE SIGN—**vary**

divert: *v.* to turn aside or deflect. *Traffic was diverted due to road construction.*

SIGN: **'ONE'** hands are held together with palms down and forefingers pointing forward. The left hand remains fixed while the right hand curves forward/rightward in a fairly wide arc.

divide: *v.* to separate into parts or groups. *She will divide the candy equally between the two children.*

SIGN: Edge of right **'EXTENDED B'** hand is placed within the space between the thumb and forefinger of the left **'EXTENDED B'** hand, both palms facing the chest at a slight angle. Then they are separated with a downward curve so that both palms face down. (When the division is between more than two groups the hands move a number of times while repeating the sign. Sometimes this movement takes a clockwise path in a horizontal plane in front of the signer, or it could be a straight left to right progression, depending on the situation.)

dividend: *n.* a portion of the net profits received by a shareholder of a company. *Stockholders receive their dividends annually.*

SIGN: Thumb and forefinger of right **'F'** hand, palm facing down, are brought slightly downward to be inserted into an imaginary pocket at waist level. Alternatively, the imaginary pocket is sometimes located at the left side of the chest.

division: *n.* a mathematical process whereby one finds the number of times a given number is contained within another number. *Division is a difficult mathematical process for some students.*

SIGN: Edge of right **'EXTENDED B'** hand is placed within the space between the thumb and forefinger of the left **'EXTENDED B'** hand, both palms facing the chest at a slight angle. Then they are separated with a downward curve so that both palms face down.

divorce: *v.* to dissolve a marriage legally. *They decided to divorce and go their separate ways.*

SIGN: Horizontal **'OPEN A'** hands are held with palms facing and backs of fingers touching. The hands are then drawn apart as they close to form **'EXTENDED A'** shapes. (Handshapes may vary.)

dizzy: *adj.* affected by a whirling sensation. *The children felt dizzy when the merry-go-round stopped.*

SIGN: Right **'SPREAD EXTENDED C'** hand is held near the head with the palm toward the face, and is moved in clockwise (from the onlooker's perspective) circles as the head lolls and the eyes are rolled slightly.

do: *v.* to perform a deed or action. *The police-man will do his duty.*

SIGN #1: Fingerspell **DO**.
(When **do** is used as an auxiliary verb in English, it has no direct translation in ASL because it is incorporated in the main verb. In English: *Do you like turnip?* In ASL: *YOU LIKE T-U-R-N-I-P?*)

don't/doesn't: *v.* contraction of 'do not'/ 'does not'. *I don't think it's a good idea.*

SIGN #2: Head shaking, right **'EXTENDED A'** hand, palm facing left, thumb under chin, is thrust forward. [**Doesn't** and **don't** are some-times incorporated within the sign for the main verb rather than signed as separate entities. See **(don't) know, (don't) like, (don't) want**.] Alternatively, **DON'T** may be fingerspelled when giving an emphatic command. The fingerspelling in this case does not move rightward, however, but moves slightly yet forcefully forward and is accompanied by a stern facial expression; **doesn't**, however, is never fingerspelled.

(have too much to) do: *v.* to be stressfully busy. *I have too much to do today.*

SIGN #3: Horizontal **'BENT D'** hands, palms upward, are held slightly apart and are simul-taneously circled counter-clockwise as they alternate from **'BENT D'** to **'CLOSED BENT D'** handshapes very rapidly. (An appropriate facial expression must accompany this sign.)

(what to) do: *s.s.* This sign may be used as a direct translation of the phrase 'what to do', *e.g., You can not tell me what to do.* It is most often used to ask what someone 'did, 'was doing', 'does', 'is doing', or 'will do'. *e.g., What were you doing? or What will you do?*)

SIGN #4: Right **'BENT D'** hand is held with palm facing upward, but angled slightly toward the body. Tip of forefinger is then rapidly and repeatedly tapped against thumbtip, thus alternating between a **'BENT D'** and a **'CLOSED BENT D'**. (Two hands may be used for this sign.)

do up: *v.* to fasten. *It is cold out there so do up your coat.*

SIGN: **'COVERED T'** hands, palms toward the body, are held at mid-waist so that the right is above the left. Then the right is drawn upward to simulate the zipping of a garment. (Signs vary according to 'what' is being done up and 'how' it is being done up.)

docile: *adj.* easily-managed or disciplined. *The horse became docile after being given the injection.*

SIGN: **'B'** (or **'EXTENDED B'**) hands are crossed in front of the mouth, left palm facing right-ward/downward and right palm facing leftward/downward with the right hand just behind the left hand. Then they are drawn apart until the palms face completely downward.

dock: *n.* a pier; wharf. *We are building a new dock at the cottage.*

SIGN: Fingerspell **DOCK**. (Various signs may be used. For **dock**, *v.*, **arrive** is sometimes used.)

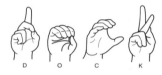

doctor: *n.* a person licensed to practice medi-cine. *The doctor treated the injured woman.*

SIGN: Fingertips of palm-down right **'SPREAD EXTENDED C'** (or **'BENT EXTENDED B'** or **'FLAT M'**) hand are tapped a couple of times against the inside of the left wrist. (The abbre-viation **DR** is frequently fingerspelled. When **doctor** refers to a person who holds a Ph.D., the highest level of education in a field other than the medical profession, the abbreviation **DR** is always fingerspelled.)

document: *n.* a paper or booklet of an official nature. *This document provides proof of my age.*

SIGN #1: Horizontal **'CROOKED 5'** hands, right palm down and left palm up, are positioned so that the right hand is slightly above the left. Then the right hand moves leftward/backward and the left hand moves rightward as the heels of each hand strike against each other at least twice. (**DOCUMENT** may be fingerspelled.)

document: *v.* to record the details of. *Police officers are required to document every detail of their investigations.*

SIGN #2: Right **'O'** hand is held palm-down with fingertips touching upturned palm of left **'EXTENDED B'** hand. Fingers of right hand then open to form an **'EXTENDED B'** hand with fingers coming to rest on left palm at right angles to it.

dog: *n.* a domesticated canine mammal related to the wolf and fox. *My dog has fleas.*

SIGN #1: Palm of right **'EXTENDED B'** hand, with fingers pointing downward, is tapped against upper part of right thigh a couple of times.

OR

SIGN #2: Right **'D'** hand is held with palm up but slanted slightly leftward. End of middle finger slides up and down several times against left side of thumb. (**DOG** is frequently fingerspelled.)

doll: *n.* a small toy replica of a human. *Many children enjoy playing with dolls.*

SIGN #1: Side of crooked forefinger of right **'X'** hand is stroked downward from the tip of the nose twice. (Signs vary considerably.)

OR

SIGN #2: Side of forefinger of vertical right **'ONE'** hand, palm left, is stroked leftward twice across the lips.

OR

SIGN #3: With elbow resting on left **'STANDARD BASE'** hand, vertical right **'X'** hand is held with palm facing backward as the right forearm moves in small counter-clockwise circles.

dollar: *n.* the standard monetary unit of Canada, equivalent to 100 cents. *How many dollars have you saved?*

SIGN #1: Left **'EXTENDED B'** hand is held in a fixed position with palm toward the body at a rightward angle and fingers pointing right. Right **'C'** hand is held with fingertips resting along the top of the left hand and thumbtip touching the bottom edge of the left hand. The right hand then slides along the length of the left hand and off. (When the *number* of dollars is specified, there is no separate sign accorded **dollar**; instead, the concept is incorporated in the sign for the number which is twisted toward the body. *One* dollar would be expressed with the right **'ONE'** hand which is twisted toward the body to show that the unit, of which there is 'one', is a monetary unit.)

OR

SIGN #2: Left **'EXTENDED B'** hand is held in a fixed position with palm toward the body and fingers pointing right. Fingers of horizontal right **'FLAT C'** hand grasp fingers of left hand and slide rightward off the end of it as the fingers of the right hand close to form a **'FLAT O'**. (As a slight variation, the end of the left hand is grasped by the right **'OPEN A'** hand which slides rightward and closes to become an **'A'** hand.)

ALTERNATE SIGN—**bill** #3. See also comments under **dollar** #1.

dome: *n.* an arched roof. *We could see the dome of the cathedral above the treetops.*

SIGN: Right **'EXTENDED B'** (or **'BENT EXTENDED B'**) hand, palm down and fingers pointing forward, is used to inscribe an arch from left to right. (**DOME** may be fingerspelled.)

dominant: *adj.* having the most influence or control. *For most signers, the right hand is the dominant hand.*

SIGN: **'S'** hands are held parallel with palms facing the chest. The forearms are then simultaneously and purposefully lowered so that the palms, which still face the body, are slanted slightly upward.

dominate: *v.* to control or rule. *She always tries to dominate our committee.*

SIGN: Horizontal **'x'** hands are held slightly apart with left palm facing right and right palm facing left. Then they are alternately moved backward and forward.
SAME SIGNS—**domineering**, *adj.*, and **dominance**, *n.*, in this context.

donate: *v.* to give money, especially to a charity. *Will you donate to our fund?*

SIGN: Right **'x'** hand, palm facing left, is held upright and thrust forward and down into a horizontal position.
SAME SIGNS—**donor**, *n.*, and **donation**, *n.* For **donor**, the Agent Ending (see p. LIV) may follow. For **donations**, *pl.*, both hands are used and are alternately thrust forward a number of times.

done: *adj.* to be ended or finished. *The project will be done by Friday.*

SIGN #1: Vertical **'5'** hands, palms facing the body, are held at chest level, and swung outward, away from the body so that the palms face down. (When describing 'how' something has been done, **job** is used. 'Well done' is translated **good job**.)

done: *adj.* cooked long enough. *The cake will be done soon.*

SIGN #2: Vertical **'5'** hands, palms facing the body, are held at chest level, and swung outward, away from the body so that the palms face down. Next, fingers of right **'EXTENDED B'** hand are placed palm down on, and at right angles to upturned palm of left **'EXTENDED B'** hand, of which the fingers point slightly forward and to the right. Right hand is then flipped over so that palm faces up. (ASL CONCEPT— **finish - cook**.) To indicate that 'meat' is **done**, see **full + cook**. When referring to the degree to which something is cooked, as in 'well done', **DONE** is fingerspelled.

donkey: *n.* a long-eared member of the horse family. *A donkey is smaller than a horse and is more sure-footed on mountain trails.*

SIGN: **'B'** (or **'BENT EXTENDED B'**) hands are placed at either side of the head with palms forward and fingers simultaneously moving up and down to represent flapping ears.

door: *n.* a movable barrier to open and close an entrance. *Please leave through the front door.*

SIGN #1: Vertical **'B'** hands are held together with palms forward. The left hand remains fixed while the right wrist twists rightward to turn the hand so that the palm faces leftward/backward. Motion is repeated.

OR

SIGN #2: Right **'EXTENDED B'** hand, palm facing the body and fingers pointing leftward, is tapped twice against the left forearm which is folded in front of the chest.
See also **close (a door)** and **open (a door)**.

doorbell: *n.* a bell or buzzer used to signal that someone is at the door. *Our doorbell is connected to a flashing light.*

SIGN: Right **'EXTENDED A'** hand is brought leftward, and thumb is pressed at least twice against right-facing palm of vertical left **'EXTENDED B'** hand.

dope: *n.* an illegal drug, usually marijuana. *Young people must be taught the hazards of using dope.*

SIGN: Joined thumb and forefinger of vertical right **'CLOSED X'** hand, palm left, are tapped against the right side of the mouth several times. (**DOPE** may be fingerspelled)

dope: See **imbecile**.

dormitory: *n.* a large room containing several beds. *Many Deaf people live in dormitories when attending school.*

SIGN: Right **'D'** hand, palm toward the face, is placed on the chin and then moved to the right cheek. (Alternatively, the abbreviation **DORM** may be fingerspelled.)

double: *v.* to make or become twice as much in terms of size, strength, or number. *We will double our order next year.*

SIGN #1: Left **'EXTENDED B'** hand is held in a fixed position with fingers pointing forward and palm facing right while tip of midfinger of horizontal right **'K'** hand is held against the left palm. As the wrist of the right hand rotates rightward, the tip of the midfinger of the right hand is flicked upward off the left palm.

OR

SIGN #2: **'EXTENDED B'** hands, fingers pointing forward and palms facing but angled slightly upward, are held apart and then brought together with a curved motion so the palms meet.

double-date: *v.* to go out on a date with another couple. *We have all been friends since high school when we double-dated.*

SIGN: Vertical **'V'** hands, palms facing, are held quite close together and the tips of the extended fingers are lightly tapped together.

doubles: *n.* a game such as tennis in which there are two players on each side. *We watched a game of doubles being played at Wimbledon.*

SIGN: Vertical **'V'** hands, palms facing, are held quite close together and the tips of the extended fingers are lightly tapped together.

doubt: *v.* to disbelieve. *I doubt that your story is factual.*

SIGN: Vertical **'V'** hand is held with palm toward the face and tips of extended fingers in front of the eyes. The hand is then moved slightly but firmly forward/downward as the fingers retract to form a **'CLAWED V'** hand and the head is shaken back and forth. Facial expression is important. For **doubtful,** *adj.,* and **doubt,** *n.,* the vertical **'CLAWED V'** hand is held with palm toward the face and the clawed fingers wiggling in front of the eyes as the head is shaken back and forth.
ALTERNATE SIGN—**uncertain** #1

doughnut [*also spelled* **donut**]: *n.* a small sweet cake that is ring-shaped and cooked in hot fat. *The bakery sells a variety of doughnuts.*

SIGN #1: **'F'** hands are held side by side with palms down and extended fingers pointing forward. The wrists then rotate outward causing the hands to curve outward/downward and to come together once again with palms up. (Signs vary considerably.)

OR

SIGN #2: **'R'** hands are held with the extended fingertips placed together and the palms down. The hands are then curved outward/backward toward the chest and the fingertips come together once again.

SIGN #3 [ATLANTIC]: Joined thumb and forefinger of right **'F'** hand encircle right eye as the hand taps against this area of the face a couple of times.

down: *adv.* at or to a lower level. *He works down on the first floor.*

SIGN #1: Forefinger of right **'BENT ONE'** hand points downward. (The use of a separate sign for **down** is rather uncommon as the concept of 'down' is often incorporated with a verb such as **fall (down), get (down), lie (down), look (down), put (down),** etc.)

down [*or* **downcast** *or* **downhearted**]: *adj.* depressed; dejected. *Whenever I am feeling down, I pamper myself with a hot bath.*

SIGN #2: Tips of middle fingers of **'BENT MIDFINGER 5'** hands are held at either side of upper chest and are simultaneously lowered.
ALTERNATE SIGNS—**depressed** #2 or **sad**

down payment: *n.* a deposit paid on a mortgage or some item that is being purchased or rented. *To purchase a house, you will need a down payment.*

SIGN: **'EXTENDED A'** hands are held with thumbtips touching and palms down but facing each other slightly. Then the wrists are rotated inward as the hands are moved apart and turned so that the palms are fully downward.

downsize: *v.* to reduce in size (especially as used in relation to departments of government or business in times of financial restraint). *The research department was **downsized** when the company experienced financial difficulties.*

SIGN: **'CROOKED L'** hands, palms facing, are held apart just above shoulder level and are then moved purposefully downward/inward toward each other.

downstairs: *adv.* on or to a lower floor. *He works **downstairs**.*

SIGN: Forefinger of right **'BENT ONE'** hand points downward twice.

downtown: *adv.* the central or main commercial area of a city or town. *He went **downtown** to pick up a few supplies.*

SIGN #1: Vertical **'EXTENDED B'** hands, left palm facing right and right palm facing left, are held so that their fingertips can be tapped together twice.

SIGN #2 [ATLANTIC]: Horizontal left **'S'** hand is held in a fixed position while extended fingertips of horizontal right **'BENT EXTENDED U'** hand, palm down, are used to stroke firmly backward across the top of the left hand a few times.

SIGN #3 [ONTARIO]: Vertical left **'EXTENDED B'** hand is held in a fixed position with palm facing right. Fingertips of vertical right **'BENT EXTENDED B'** hand slap downward against the left palm and then the right hand moves rightward while the fingers simultaneously move up and down slightly a few times as if waving.

doze: *v.* to sleep lightly or intermittently. *Do not **doze** off while you are driving.*

SIGN: Right **'CONTRACTED 5'** hand is held with palm toward the face. Then it is moved downward as it closes to form a **'FLAT O'** hand and the eyes gradually close.

dozen: *n.* a group of twelve. *Please pick up a **dozen** dinner rolls on your way home.*

SIGN: Fingerspell **DOZ** or **DOZEN**.

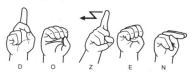

D O Z E N

draft: *n.* a preliminary or rough piece of writing. *This is the first **draft** of the president's speech.*

SIGN #1: Left **'EXTENDED B'** hand is held in a fixed position with fingers pointing forward/rightward and palm facing rightward but slanted toward the body and slightly upward. Fingertips of right **'SPREAD EXTENDED C'** hand, palm down, are brushed forward/rightward a few times along the left palm. This sign is accompanied by a lip pattern such that the upper teeth are resting on the lower lip as if articulating an **'F'**.

draft: *n.* a current of air. *Is there a **draft** in this room?*

SIGN #2: **'5'** hands are held parallel with fingers pointing forward and palms facing each other. The hands are then simultaneously moved leftward a few times. This is a small, gentle movement. (Alternatively, one hand may be used. Signs vary according to the location and intensity of the draft.)

draft (draught) beer: *n.* beer that is drawn from a cask or keg. *We ordered a large pitcher of **draft beer** for our table.*

SIGN: Left hand lightly steadies right forearm as it is drawn toward the chest a couple of times, the right **'S'** hand, with palm facing left, simulating the pulling of a lever to extract draft beer.

drafting: *n.* the preparation of plans or designs for structures; mechanical drawing. *Many Deaf people take up **drafting** as a career.*

SIGN: **'Y'** hands, which are held with palms down and thumbtips touching, alternately wobble slightly.

drag: *v.* to pull along the ground with force. *They tried to **drag** the fallen tree off the road.*

SIGN: Horizontal **'S'** hands are held in front of the left side of the body, the left hand ahead of and to the left of the right. Then both hands are drawn simultaneously toward the chest as if pulling something.

drag: *n.* a colloquial expression meaning a dull or boring person or thing. *His lectures are such a drag that they put me to sleep.*

SIGN: With fingers pointing leftward, side of forefinger of right palm-down **'MODIFIED 5'** hand is held at left side of chin. As it is drawn rightward across the chin, it becomes a **'CLAWED 5'** hand, which is then flung forward/downward and becomes a **'5'** hand with palm down. Facial expression must clearly convey 'boredom'.
ALTERNATE SIGN—**bored/boring** #1

drama: *n.* a play; a work to be performed by actors. *Most children like to participate in a drama.*

SIGN: **'EXTENDED A'** hands, palms facing each other, are rotated alternately in small circles which are brought down against the chest.

drapes: *n.* curtains. *My mother made all the drapes for our new house.*

SIGN: Vertical **'4'** hands, palms forward, are held apart above shoulder level. The wrists then simultaneously bend forward so that the hands drop to a palms down position.

draw: *v.* to sketch with pencil, pen, charcoal, etc. *I will draw a picture for you.*

SIGN #1: Left **'EXTENDED B'** hand is held in a fixed and relatively fixed position with palm facing the body. The tip of the little finger of the right **'I'** hand is stroked downward twice along the middle of the left palm.

draw: *v.* to attract. *His lecture is sure to draw a large crowd.*

SIGN #2: Horizontal **'CLAWED L'** hands are held apart with palms up, and forearms are moved sharply back toward the body as hands take on **'A'** shapes.

draw: *n.* a raffle; lottery. *Have you entered the draw for the grand prize?*

SIGN #3: Right **'FLAT OPEN F'** hand is held palm down with thumb and forefinger within the opening formed by the thumb and forefinger of the horizontal left **'EXTENDED C'** hand. Then the right hand is drawn upward as the thumb and forefinger close to form an **'F'** hand.

draw: *n.* a game or contest that ends in a tie. *The game ended in a draw.*

SIGN #4: **'COVERED T'** hands, palms facing body, are held close together, circled forward around one another, and then drawn firmly apart as though tying something.

drawback: *n.* a disadvantage. *The only drawback to my new job is that I have to work Saturdays.*

SIGN: Horizontal **'CLAWED V'** hands are held with palms facing the body and knuckles knocking against each other as the hands are alternately moved up and down.

drawer: *n.* a sliding, box-like compartment in a chest, desk, or table. *The keys are in the top drawer.*

SIGN: **'S'** hands are held parallel with palms up at about face level with arms extended away from the body. The hands then move simultaneously toward the body as if opening a drawer. Motion is repeated.

drawn out: *adj.* taking up too much time; prolonged; dragged out. *The trial has been such a long, drawn out affair.*

SIGN: Left **'S'** hand is held with palm facing rightward/downward. Right **'S'** hand is held just in front of the left hand with palm facing leftward/downward. The right hand is then wobbled forward/rightward.

(be) drawn to: *v.* attracted to. *When considering career options he was drawn to the notion of becoming a draftsman.*

SIGN: **'SPREAD C'** (or **'MODIFIED 5'**) hands are held with the right hand directly in front of the face, palm facing left, while the left hand is a little lower and farther forward, palm facing right. As the forearms move forward/downward, the fingers close to form **'S'** hands. (Alternatively, the right hand only may be used.)

dread: *v.* to anticipate with reluctance. *I **dread** my mother's visit because she always wants to control my life.*

SIGN #1: Vertical right **'BENT MIDFINGER 5'** hand is held with palm left and tip of middle finger touching forehead. The wrist then rotates to turn the palm toward the face. Facial expression is important.

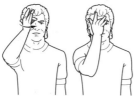

dread: *v.* to fear greatly. *I **dread** having to drive on icy streets.*

SIGN #2: Horizontal **'5'** hands, palms toward the body, are held out from either side of the chest, and are moved vigorously toward each other, stopping abruptly in front of the chest. Facial expression is important.

dreadful: *adj.* very unpleasant; terrible. *The earthquake was a **dreadful** disaster that left hundreds of people dead.*

SIGN: Thumb and forefinger of right **'COVERED 8'** hand, which is held near right side of face with palm facing left, are snapped open as the hand is thrust slightly forward to form a **'MODIFIED 5'** hand. This sign can be made with either one or two hands, one at either side of the face. Appropriate facial expression is important.

dream: *n.* a series of events imagined during sleep. *Do you remember the details of your **dream**?*

SIGN: Tip of the forefinger of the right **'ONE'** hand is placed at the right side of the forehead, with palm toward the face. The hand then moves forward/rightward/upward as the forefinger alternates from a **'ONE'** to an **'X'** position in a series of rapid movements.

dress: *n.* a one-piece article of clothing worn mainly by women and girls and consisting of a skirt and bodice. *That is a lovely **dress** you are wearing.*

SIGN #1: Thumbs of **'5'** hands, with palms toward the body, are held at either side of upper chest and brushed downward a couple of times.

dress: *v.* to attire oneself; to put on clothes. *You must **dress** for school now.*

SIGN #2: Thumbs of **'MODIFIED 5'** hands, with palms toward the body and fingertips opposite, are placed at either side of upper chest. The wrists then rotate simultaneously to turn the hands so that the palms face away from the body and fingers point forward/upward. (See also **put on clothes**.)

dress up: *v.* to put on one's best or formal clothes. *Let us get **dressed up** and go dancing.*

SIGN: Thumbs of **'MODIFIED 5'** hands, with palms toward the body and fingertips opposite, are placed at either side of upper chest. The wrists then rotate simultaneously to turn the hands so that the palms face away from the body and fingers point forward/upward.

dresser: *n.* a storage chest having drawers and usually a mirror on top. *The bedroom suite includes a large **dresser**.*

SIGN: **'EXTENDED B'** (or **'B'**) hands are held together at about shoulder level with palms down and fingers pointing forward. The arms move apart to indicate the top of the chest, and as the wrists rotate so that the palms face each other, the hands move straight down to outline the sides of the chest. Next, **'S'** hands are held parallel with palms up at about face level with arms extended away from the body. The hands then move simultaneously toward the body as if opening a drawer. Motion is repeated once or twice, each time at a lower level.

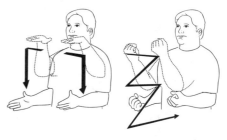

dressing: *n.* stuffing for poultry. *We usually make sage and onion **dressing** for our Thanksgiving turkey.*

SIGN #1: Vertical left **'C'** hand is held with palm facing right. Then the forward-pointing fingertips of the right **'FLAT O'** hand are inserted into the opening in the left hand. (**DRESSING** is frequently fingerspelled.)

dressing: *n.* a sauce used especially for salads. *I prefer an oil and vinegar **dressing** on a tossed salad.*

SIGN #2: Horizontal right **'Y'** hand, with thumb pointing downward and palm facing away from the body, is circled in a counter-clockwise direction. (**DRESSING** is frequently fingerspelled.)

dressing: *n.* a bandage; covering for a wound. *The nurse wrapped the injured hand with a sterile **dressing.***

SIGN #3: Right **'BENT B'** (or **'B'**) hand, fingers pointing left and palm facing body, is rotated continuously forward around left **'BENT B'** (or **'B'**) hand, whose fingers point right and palm faces the body.

dressy: *adj.* elegant and stylish in reference to clothing. *This pantsuit is **dressy** enough for formal wear.*

SIGN: Thumbs of **'MODIFIED 5'** hands, with palms toward the body and fingertips opposite, are placed at either side of upper chest. The wrists then rotate simultaneously to turn the hands so that the palms face away from the body and fingers point forward/upward.
ALTERNATE SIGN—**classy**

dribble: *v.* to bounce a ball by tapping it repeatedly with the hand. *Can you **dribble** the basketball from here to that wall?*

SIGN: Right **'EXTENDED B'** hand, palm down and fingers pointing forward, is moved up and down with a bouncing motion.

drill: *v.* to bore a hole. *He **drilled** a hole in the board.*

SIGN #1: Forefinger of right **'ONE'** (or **'L'**) hand is jabbed between forefinger and middle finger of vertical left **'EXTENDED B'** hand which is held with palm facing right.

drill: *v.* to train or give repeated instruction. *The coach will **drill** the basketball team in dribbling techniques.*

SIGN #2: Vertical **'O'** hands are held parallel with palms facing each other and are simultaneously moved in deliberate circles which move forward over and over again in place. ❖

drill: *n.* repeated practice. *We had a fire **drill** this morning.*

SIGN #3: Left **'ONE'** hand is held in a fixed position with palm down and forefinger pointing forward/rightward. With palm facing downward at a slight leftward/forward angle and knuckles lying along the left forefinger, the right **'A'** hand slides back and forth.

drink: *v.* to swallow (something liquid). *He **drinks** a glass of orange juice every morning for breakfast.*

SIGN: Right **'C'** hand is held in a horizontal position near the mouth with palm facing left. The hand is then tipped upward slightly.

drip: *v.* to fall in drops. *Your bathroom tap **dripped** all night.*

SIGN: **'S'** hand is held with palm down. Forefinger then flicks downward repeatedly to form a **'BENT ONE'** hand.

drive: *v.* to operate (a vehicle). *You can **drive** my car while yours is being repaired.*

SIGN #1: **'S'** hands are held parallel with palms facing the body and are simultaneously moved forward. ❖

drive: *v.* to strike the ball with a driver when playing golf. *The instructor demonstrated how to **drive** the ball without slicing.*

SIGN #2: Left **'COVERED T'** hand is held horizontally with palm facing right while right **'COVERED T'** hand is held upright with palm facing forward. The signer then simulates a golf swing by moving the right forearm in a downward/leftward arc as both wrists rotate rightward so that the left palm is turned downward while the right palm eventually faces leftward/upward.

drive: *n.* high motivation; ambition. *Individual **drive** enabled him to achieve all his goals.*

SIGN #3: **'A'** hands are held in front of either side of the chest with palms facing each other and are alternately circled forward, the thumbs brushing upward and forward off the chest with each revolution.

drool: *v.* to dribble from the mouth. *Babies seem to drool a lot.*

SIGN: Vertical right **'4'** hand, with palm left and tip of forefinger positioned at right side of mouth, is drawn downward.

drop: *n.* a globule or very small quantity of liquid. *I think I saw a drop of rain.*

SIGN #1: **'S'** hand is held with palm down. Forefinger then flicks downward to form a **'BENT ONE'**.

drop: *n.* a sudden decrease in amount or value. *There has been a recent drop in interest rates.*

SIGN #2: Left **'BENT U'** hand is held in a fixed position with palm rightward/forward and extended fingers pointing rightward/forward. Right **'BENT U'** hand is held with palm leftward/forward and tips of extended fingers resting on those of the left hand at right angles. The right wrist then rotates rightward causing the hand to turn palm upward as it drops slightly.

drop: *v.* to let fall. *Did you drop your keys?*

SIGN #3: Right **'S'** hand is held palm down. The hand then bends downward from the wrist as the fingers open to form a **'MODIFIED 5'** hand.

drop: *v.* to discontinue. *They agreed to drop their plans for renovations.*

SIGN #4: **'S'** hands are held parallel with palms down. Then they are simultaneously lowered slightly as the fingers open to form **'CROOKED 5'** hands.

drop out: *v.* to withdraw or stop participating; to quit a course before it is completed. *He was worried that his daughter might drop out of school.*

SIGN: Extended fingers of horizontal right **'U'** hand are inserted into an opening created in the left horizontal **'S'** hand. Then the extended fingers of the right hand are withdrawn from the left hand, becoming more upright as they move back toward the chest. ❖

drought: *n.* a prolonged period without rain. *Drought on the Prairies will affect the price of grain.*

SIGN: Side of crooked forefinger of right **'X'** hand, palm facing down, is placed on left side of chin and firmly drawn across to the right side.

drown: *v.* to die or be killed by immersion in water or another liquid. *Every summer people drown in boating accidents.*

SIGN #1: Horizontal **'CROOKED 5'** hands are held, one above each shoulder, with fingers pointing to neck. The arms are then simultaneously moved upward so that the hands are closer to the top of the head.

OR

SIGN #2: Thumb of right **'EXTENDED A'** hand, palm facing left, is placed between midfinger and forefinger of left **'STANDARD BASE'** hand. Then the right hand is drawn downward.

drowsy: *adj.* sleepy. *She felt drowsy in the stuffy room.*

SIGN: Right **'CONTRACTED 5'** hand is held with palm toward the face. Then it is moved downward as it closes to form a **'FLAT O'** hand. Motion is repeated as the head tilts downward to the right and the eyes gradually close.

drug: *n.* a chemical substance used in medical treatment. *Every drug has potential side effects.*

SIGN #1: Tip of middle finger of right **'BENT MIDFINGER 5'** hand is placed on the upturned left palm, and maintains contact with the left palm as the right hand teeters back and forth a few times. (**DRUG** in this context may be fingerspelled. For **drugstore**, fingerspell **DRUG** and sign **store** #1.)

drug: *n.* a chemical substance taken for the effects it produces on the user. *Many parents are unaware that their children are using drugs.*

SIGN #2: Right horizontal **'S'** hand, palm toward the body, is used to tap firmly on the inside of the bent elbow of the left arm which also has an **'S'** handshape, palm facing upward.

drum: *n.* a percussion instrument sounded by striking. *Can you feel the drum vibrate?*

SIGN #1: Bass drum only—Left **'A'** hand is held in a fixed position with palm facing downward. Horizontal right **'CLOSED A-INDEX'** hand is held slightly lower and to the right of the left hand with palm facing left. The right hand firmly moves a short distance leftward several times as if striking a drum.

OR

SIGN #2: Drum played with drumsticks— **'CLOSED A-INDEX'** hands are held apart with palms facing the body and are alternately raised and lowered from the wrists as if drumming on a snare drum. Signs vary according to how the drum is played.

drunk: *adj.* intoxicated with alcohol. *He was too drunk to drive home safely.*

SIGN #1: Right **'EXTENDED A'** hand is held in front of the mouth with palm facing left. The forearm is then tipped firmly downward/leftward causing the palm to face downward.

OR

SIGN #2: Back of right **'B'** hand is placed under the chin with fingers pointing leftward, and the hand is pulled firmly to the right.

dry: *adj.* not wet; lacking moisture. *The air in the prairie provinces is dry compared to that of maritime regions.*

SIGN: Side of crooked forefinger of right **'X'** hand, palm facing down, is placed on left side of chin and firmly drawn across to the right side. (Various signs are used for **dry**, *v.,* depending on the context. Natural gestures are often used to simulate the act of drying.)

dry cleaner: *n.* a business that cleans fabrics with a solvent other than water. *I took my silk shirts to the dry cleaner.*

SIGN: **'S'** hands are held parallel with palms down as the forearms are simultaneously moved up and down at least twice.

dual: *adj.* double or twofold. *This instrument serves a dual purpose.*

SIGN: Left **'EXTENDED B'** hand is held in a fixed position with fingers pointing forward and palm facing right while tip of midfinger of horizontal right **'K'** hand is held against the left palm. As the wrist of the right hand rotates rightward, the tip of the midfinger of the right hand is flicked upward off the left palm. Alternatively, the right **'V'** hand may be held upright with palm facing the body to indicate 'two'. (Signs vary according to context. In the case of **dual citizenship**, DUAL is fingerspelled.)

dubious: *adj.* doubtful; uncertain; disbelieving; skeptical. *The members of the jury were dubious about his claim to innocence.*

SIGN: Vertical **'CLAWED V'** hand is held with palm toward the face and the clawed fingers wiggling in front of the eyes as the head is shaken back and forth. Facial expression is important.

duck: *n.* an aquatic bird with short legs, webbed feet and a broad, flat, rounded bill. *We watched the ducks in the pond.*

SIGN #1: Back of right **'CONTRACTED 3'** hand is placed against the chin with the palm down. The thumb and extended fingers are closed and opened a couple of times, thus alternating between a **'CONTRACTED 3'** and a **'CLOSED DOUBLE MODIFIED G'** shape to simulate the opening and closing of a duck's bill.

duck: *v.* to lower (one's head or body) to avoid something. *The little boy ducked so that his mother would not find him.*

SIGN #2: Left **'B'** (or **'EXTENDED B'**) hand is held palm-down with fingers pointing right. Vertical right **'S'** hand represents a person's head as it is held above/behind the left hand and is then quickly lowered so that it is below the level of the left hand. The signer's head follows the movement of the right hand and appears to 'duck'.

due: *adj.* owed as a debt. *The rent is due on the last day of each month.*

SIGN #1: Tip of forefinger of right **'ONE'** hand, palm toward body, is tapped twice against right-facing palm of horizontal left **'EXTENDED B'** hand. (**DUE** is frequently fingerspelled.)

due: *adj.* expected to show up or arrive; required by or expected to be ready or finished by (a specified time). *Your homework is due next Wednesday.*

SIGN #2: Fingerspell **DUE**.

due to: *conj.* because of; caused by. *She missed several weeks of work due to illness.*

SIGN: Vertical right **'BENT MIDFINGER 5'** hand is held with palm facing right side of forehead and middle finger repeatedly tapping gently in mid-air. (The sign shown here is *rarely* used in this context. In ASL, it is more common to see *no sign* for word translation for **due to**. Instead, the signer will convey the meaning by pausing and using an appropriate facial expression before continuing.)

dull: *adj.* not bright; not sharp. *Rainy days are usually dull and cloudy.*

SIGN #1: Fingerspell **DULL**.

dull: *adj.* uninteresting; unexciting; boring. *The lecture was so dull that a few students fell asleep.*

SIGN #2: Tip of forefinger of right **'ONE'** hand is placed against right side of nose, and is twisted half a turn clockwise. Facial expression must clearly convey 'boredom'.
ALTERNATE SIGN—**bored/boring** #2

dumb: *adj.* a slang expression for dim-witted or stupid. *He felt dumb after making such a mistake.*

SIGN: Right **'A'** hand, palm facing backward, is thumped against the forehead.
ALTERNATE SIGN—**ignorant**

dumbfounded [also spelled **dumfounded**]: *adj.* astonished; speechless with amazement. *The students were dumbfounded when the teacher told them the news.*

SIGN: **'BENT 5'** hands are held apart, fingertips pointing downward, and are moved sharply downward.

dump: *v.* to dispose of; to drop heavily. *Dump the garbage into the chute.*

SIGN: Right **'S'** hand is held palm down. The hand then bends downward from the wrist as the fingers open to form a **'MODIFIED 5'** hand. Alternatively, two hands may be used. (For **dump**, *n.*, meaning an area where waste materials are disposed of, fingerspell **DUMP**.)

dupe: See **deceive**.

duplicate: *v.* to copy. *We will duplicate their system of filing.*

SIGN #1: Left **'EXTENDED B'** hand is held in a fixed position with palm up and fingers pointing forward/rightward. Right **'CONTRACTED 5'** hand is positioned at the end of the left hand with palm facing forward. As the right hand is drawn backward toward the palm or heel of the left hand, it closes to form a **'FLAT O'** shape.

duplicate: *n.* an exact copy of an original. *A duplicate of the document is in our files.*

SIGN #2: Left **'EXTENDED B'** hand is held in a fixed position with palm right and fingers pointing forward. Horizontal right **'CONTRACTED 5'** hand, palm left, is held with fingertips touching left palm. The right hand then moves rightward as the fingers close to form a **'FLAT O'** hand.

durable: *adj.* tough; long-lasting. *Army tents are made of very durable canvas.*

SIGN: **'S'** hands are held parallel with palms facing the body at an upward angle and are simultaneously jerked backward so that the palms fully face the body. Next, **'EXTENDED A'** hands are held side by side with palms down and right thumbtip pressing against left thumbnail as the hands are moved purposefully forward. (ASL CONCEPT—**strong - continue**.)

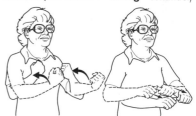

duration: *n.* the period of time from now until something ends. *The candidate was asked to leave for the duration of the meeting.*

SIGN: Horizontal **'BENT EXTENDED B'** hands, palms facing each other, are positioned so that the fingers of the right hand are just in front of the fingers of the left hand. The right hand is then moved forward briskly.

during: *prep.* within the limit of a specific period of time. *We were excited to be in Australia during the Olympics.*

SIGN: **'ONE'** hands are held apart close to the chest with palms down and forefingers pointing forward. The hands are then moved forward from the body in parallel lines.

dust: *n.* a dry, fine, powdery substance. *Are you allergic to house dust?*

SIGN #1: Fingerspell **DUST**.

D　U　S　T

dust: *v.* to wipe to remove dust. *You dust and I will vacuum.*

SIGN #2: Right **'EXTENDED B'** (or **'A'**) hand is held palm forward/downward and appears to wipe as it moves in a wide counter-clockwise circle.

dusty: *adj.* covered with dust. *The furniture was very dusty.*

SIGN: Right **'5'** hand is placed under the chin, palm down, and the fingers are wiggled up and down. Next, right **'MODIFIED G'** hand, palm downward/forward, is placed on the back of the left **'STANDARD BASE'** hand and moved rightward toward the fingertips. (ASL CONCEPT—**dirty - layer**.)

duty: *n.* a legal or moral responsibility; obligation. *It is my duty to supervise the children during their morning recess.*

SIGN: Joined thumb and midfinger of right **'D'** hand are tapped down on the back of the left **'STANDARD BASE'** hand at least twice.

dwarf: *n.* an abnormally short person. *"Snow White and the Seven Dwarfs" is a classic fairytale.*

SIGN: Right **'EXTENDED B'** hand is held out to the right side of the body with palm down and is moved up and down to indicate the shortness of stature. (**DWARF** may be fingerspelled.)

dwell: *v.* to live as a resident. *They dwell in a brightly painted house by the sea.*

SIGN: Horizontal **'L'** hands are placed at either side, somewhere above the waist, with palms toward the body and forefingers pointing toward each other. They are then raised to a higher position on the chest.

dwell on: *v.* to think about too long or too much. *You must stop dwelling on that problem.*

SIGN: Tip of middle finger of right **'BENT MIDFINGER 5'** hand touches centre of forehead and moves downward to rest on back of left **'STANDARD BASE'** hand. Together the two hands then circle forward at least twice. (ASL CONCEPT—**think - touch-long-time**.)

dwelling: *n.* residence; home; abode. *They live in a small dwelling by the sea.*

SIGN: Fingertips of **'EXTENDED B'** hands, palms facing each other, are placed together at an angle in 'tent' fashion. The hands are then drawn apart, straightened to a more vertical posture, and lowered simultaneously. ALTERNATE SIGN—**home**

dwindle: *v.* to become less in size, intensity or number. *When his funds began to dwindle he decided to get a job.*

SIGN: **'CROOKED L'** hands, palms facing, are held apart and are then wobbled from the wrists as they are drawn slightly downward toward each other.

dye: *v.* to change the colour of fabric, hair, etc., by saturating it in a colour solution. *I will dye the shirt blue.*

SIGN: **'F'** hands are held slightly apart with palms down and are simultaneously moved up and down to simulate dipping an article into a dye-bath.

dying: *v.* approaching death. *The family were at her bedside when she was **dying**.*

SIGN: Horizontal left **'BENT EXTENDED B'** hand is held in a fixed position with palm facing right while horizontal right **'BENT EXTENDED B'** hand is held a little higher and much closer to the body with palm facing left. The right hand then moves forward toward the left hand in a series of short arcs. Next, **'EXTENDED B'** hands are held with fingers pointing forward, left palm facing up and right palm facing down. Then they are flipped over simultaneously so that the palm positions are reversed. (ASL CONCEPT—**near near near - death**.) **DYING** is frequently fingerspelled.

dynamic: *adj.* pertaining to something that changes or moves. *Fashion is a **dynamic** concept; what is stylish this year may be out-of-fashion the next year.*

SIGN #1: Horizontal **'COVERED T'** hands are held apart with palms toward the chest. They are then alternately circled backward several times. This is a wrist action.

dynamic: *adj.* energetic; forceful. *People enjoyed listening to the **dynamic** speaker.*

SIGN #2: Fingertips of right **'SPREAD C'** hand are brought forcefully against left bicep. (Signs vary according to context.)

dynamics: *n.* the psychological behaviour characteristic of an interpersonal relationship. *It was interesting to observe the group **dynamics** in the classroom.*

SIGN: **'CROOKED 5'** hands are held with palms facing the body, the fingers of the right hand pointing downward while those of the left point upward. The hands then revolve around each other in a counter-clockwise direction as the fingers flutter.

dyslexia: *n.* a reading disability. *People with **dyslexia** have a hard time learning to read.*

SIGN: Left **'EXTENDED B'** hand is held in a fixed position with palm facing the body and fingers pointing rightward while horizontal right **'V'** hand is held behind the left hand with palm down and extended fingers pointing forward. Right wrist then bends downward so that the tips of the extended fingers strike downward against the left palm. Next, **'CLAWED V'** hands are held horizontally with palms facing the body and knuckles knocking against each other as the hands are alternately moved up and down. (ASL CONCEPT—**reading - problem**.) **DYSLEXIA** may be fingerspelled.

E

each: *adj.* every one of two or more (things or people) considered individually. *Each person will have an important role to play.*

SIGN: With palm facing right, left **'EXTENDED A'** hand is held in front of right **'EXTENDED A'** hand, of which the palm faces left. The right hand is then drawn downward along the length of the left thumb.

each other: *pron.* one another. *The members of the group support each other in every way.*

SIGN: Right **'EXTENDED A'** hand is held thumb-down above left **'EXTENDED A'** hand which is held thumb-up. The hands then revolve around each other in a counter-clockwise direction.

eager: *adj.* very desirous; anxious. *He was eager to begin his holiday.*

SIGN: Horizontal **'EXTENDED B'** hands are held with palms together and fingers pointing forward. The hands are alternately rubbed back and forth against each other.

ALTERNATE SIGN—**excited**
The sign for **excited** may either be used alone or followed by the sign above.

eagle: *n.* a large bird of prey. *Our school's mascot is the golden eagle.*

SIGN: Vertical right **'X'** hand is held in front of the face with palm forward/leftward, and the back of the crooked forefinger is tapped a couple of times against the nose.

ear: *n.* the organ of hearing. *He has an infection in his right ear.*

SIGN: Tip of forefinger of right **'ONE'** hand, palm left, is tapped against right ear.

earache: *n.* pain in the ear. *If you have an earache you should see your doctor.*

SIGN: Horizontal **'BENT ONE'** hands are held by the ear with palms facing and forefingers simultaneously stabbed toward each other a few times.

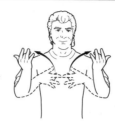

early: *adv.* before the expected or usual time; near the beginning. *The flight was due at 10:15 a.m., but it arrived early.*

SIGN #1: Tips of midfingers of **'BENT MIDFINGER 5'** hands, palms toward the body, are placed slightly apart on the chest. The wrists then rotate forward as the hands move forward so that, while the palms still face the body, they are now angled upward slightly. (**EARLY** may be fingerspelled and is often fingerspelled in a small clockwise circle for emphasis to mean *'very early'*.)

OR

SIGN #2: Right **'BENT MIDFINGER 5'** hand is held palm down with tip of middle finger on the wrist of the left **'STANDARD BASE'** hand and is moved forward at a leftward angle.

SIGN #3 [ATLANTIC]: **'CROOKED 5'** hands are held with palms up, the right wrist resting on the left palm. The left hand remains fixed as the right hand slides backward/rightward toward the body across the left palm.

SIGN #4 [ONTARIO]: Horizontal right **'S'** hand, palm facing left, is placed on the back of the left **'STANDARD BASE'** hand. The left hand remains fixed while the right hand is opened to form a **'MODIFIED 5'** hand as it is drawn back toward the body.

earn: *v.* to be paid in return for work or service. *I work hard to earn money.*

SIGN: Horizontal right **'SPREAD EXTENDED C'** hand is moved across upturned palm of left **'EXTENDED B'** hand in a circular, counter-clockwise 'gathering' motion, with the palm toward the body.

earnest: *adj.* having sincere or serious intentions; determined; eager. *She is an earnest author whose work is highly respected.*

SIGN: Vertical right **'BENT ONE'** hand is held with tip of forefinger touching chin and palm facing leftward but slanted toward the body. The wrist then rotates, turning the hand so that the palm fully faces the body.
ALTERNATE SIGNS—**serious** #2 & #3

earphones: *n.* a device worn over the ears to receive sound waves. *The new earphones were comfortable to wear.*

SIGN: Vertical **'SPREAD C'** hands are cupped over the ears and the fingertips are tapped against the head.

earrings: *n.* ornaments for the ears. *She likes silver earrings better than gold.*

SIGN: **'OPEN O-INDEX'** hands are held at either cheek with thumbs touching the back of the ear lobes. Tips of forefingers are then tapped a couple of times against the front of the ear lobes. (Signs vary, depending on the size, shape, type and number of earrings.)

Earth: *n.* the planet on which we live. *The Earth is the third planet from the sun in our solar system.*

SIGN #1: Right **'OPEN 8'** hand is held palm-down and thumb and midfinger are used to grasp either side of the back of the left **'STANDARD BASE'** hand near the wrist. Left hand remains fixed while right hand rocks back and forth without losing its hold on the left hand.

earth: *n.* loose, soft material on the ground; soil. *The earth in the flowerpot will absorb the moisture.*

SIGN #2: **'FLAT O'** hands are held slightly apart with palms up. Then the fingers are slid across the thumbs a few times, thus alternating between **'FLAT O'** and **'OFFSET O'** hands.

earthquake: *n.* a series of vibrations in the earth's surface. *The earthquake caused several buildings to collapse.*

SIGN: Right **'OPEN 8'** hand is held palm-down and thumb and midfinger are used to grasp either side of the back of the left **'STANDARD BASE'** hand near the wrist. Left hand remains fixed while right hand rocks back and forth without losing its hold on the left hand. Next, **'S'** hands are held parallel with palms down, and are simultaneously slid from side to side a few times.

(at) ease: *adj.* relaxed; comfortable. *I feel at ease with people of any age.*

SIGN: Left **'CROOKED EXTENDED B'** hand is held palm down with fingers pointing rightward/forward at a downward angle while right **'CROOKED EXTENDED B'** hand is held palm down on left hand at right angles to it. The right hand is drawn rightward/backward across the back of the left hand, which moves out from under the right hand to take up a position on top of it so that the positioning of the hands is the reverse of their original position. The left hand is then drawn leftward/backward across the back of the right hand, which moves out from under the left hand to take up a position on top of it. Movement is repeated.

east: *n.* the direction of the earth's rotation. *The sun rises in the east.*

SIGN: Vertical right **'E'** hand is held near the right shoulder with palm forward. Then it is moved sharply to the right. (While the positioning and movement of this sign may vary, the handshape remains the same.)

Easter: *n.* a Christian festival commemorating the Resurrection of Christ. *Easter is a time that we associate with coloured eggs.*

SIGN: Vertical **'E'** hands are held parallel with palms forward. Then they are simultaneously circled, the right hand moving clockwise (from the signer's perspective), and the left hand moving counter-clockwise. (This sign may vary in terms of movement but the handshape remains constant.)

ALTERNATE SIGNS—**egg** and **rabbit**

easy: *adj.* not difficult. *He said that the work was too easy.*

SIGN #1: Left **'BENT EXTENDED B'** hand is held in a fixed position with palm up. Palm of horizontal right **'EXTENDED B'** (or **'BENT EXTENDED B'**) hand faces left but is slanted slightly upward and toward the body as the fingers are brushed upward against the backs of the fingers of the left hand at least twice.

SIGN #2 [ATLANTIC/PRAIRIE]: Tip of forefinger of **'CROOKED ONE'** hand taps right cheek twice.

easygoing: *adj.* relaxed in manner and attitude. *People who are easygoing appear to be less susceptible to stress.*

SIGN: **'EXTENDED B'** hands are held parallel with palms down and fingers pointing forward. The forearms are simultaneously lowered a short distance, then moved rightward in an arc formation, and back to their original position in a leftward arc.

eat: *v.* to take food into the mouth, chew it and swallow it. *Eat your breakfast before you leave.*

SIGN: Vertical right **'MODIFIED O'** hand, palm facing the body, is brought toward the mouth so that the fingertips touch the lips.

eavesdrop: *v.* to listen secretly to the private conversations of others. *It is extremely rude to eavesdrop.*

SIGN: Right **'CROOKED EXTENDED V'** hand is held with thumb at right ear and palm facing left as extended fingers are repeatedly retracted and relaxed. (This sign refers to something which is done by hearing individuals only and would be an inappropriate sign choice when referring to a Deaf individual who is trying to glean information from a private conversation visually.)

eccentric: *adj.* odd or irregular. *He has some rather eccentric habits.*

SIGN: Vertical right **'C'** hand, palm facing left, is held near the face and is abruptly dropped downward from the wrist so the palm faces down.

REGIONAL VARIATION—**odd** #2

echo: *n.* a reflected sound. *There was a loud echo in the tunnel when we drove through it.*

SIGN: Fingerspell **ECHO**.

economic: *adj.* relating to finance. *We bought a small car for economic reasons.*

SIGN: Back of right **'CONTRACTED B'** (or **'BENT EXTENDED B'**) hand, palm up, is tapped two or three times on upturned palm of left **'EXTENDED B'** hand.

SAME SIGN—**economy,** *n.*

economize: *v.* to manage one's money carefully to reduce expenses. *During this recession, we need to economize.*

SIGN: **'CONTRACTED B'** hands, palms up, are circled backward around one another's fingertips.

ecstatic: *adj.* extremely happy; delighted; rapturous. *We were ecstatic when we heard the good news.*

SIGN: Left **'EXTENDED B'** hand is held in a fixed position with palm up and fingers pointing forward/rightward. Right **'CROOKED V'** is held palm down with tips of extended fingers resting on the left palm. The right hand then rises with extended fingers wiggling and falls back to its original position. Facial expression is important.

SAME SIGN—**ecstasy,** *n.*

ALTERNATE SIGN—**excited**

edge: *n.* the part of something that is farthest from the centre. *This piece of metal has a sharp edge.*

SIGN: Right **'BENT EXTENDED B'** hand is held above left **'STANDARD BASE'** hand with palm down and inside of fingers held against outside edge of left hand near the wrist. The right hand then slides along the edge of the left hand to the end of the little finger.

edible: *adj.* fit to be eaten. *Some mushrooms are poisonous but most species are edible.*

SIGN: **'A'** hands, palms down, are held slightly apart, and are then firmly pushed a very short distance downward. Then vertical **'MODIFIED O'** hand, palm facing the body, is brought toward the mouth so that the fingertips touch the lips. (ASL CONCEPT—**can - eat**.)

edit: *v.* to prepare material for publication by checking for accuracy and/or rearranging the material. *The publisher will appoint someone to edit your novel.*

SIGN #1: Vertical **'X'** hands are held slightly apart with palms facing. The hands are then simultaneously lowered as rotations of the wrists cause the hands to alternately fall forward and back several times. (**EDITOR**, *n.*, is always fingerspelled.)

edit: *v.* to remove or delete information or details. *I think we should edit these pages to make the report more concise.*

SIGN #2: **'COVERED T'** hands are held apart with palms upward but slanted toward the body. The hands alternately move upward/outward several times as the thumbs flick out.

edit: *v.* to prepare a film for presentation by cutting, splicing, etc. *They will edit the film by cutting some scenes.*

SIGN #3: Horizontal **'SLANTED V'** hands are held parallel with palms facing each other and extended fingers pointing forward. They are then moved very slightly but firmly forward/downward a couple of times as the extended fingers close, open and reclose as if they were blades of scissors in the process of snipping.

educate: *v.* to impart knowledge through formal instruction; teach. *This videotape will help to educate the public.*

SIGN: Vertical **'MODIFIED O'** hands are held parallel with palms facing each other and are moved slightly but firmly forward. ❖

education: *n.* the process of acquiring knowledge or training. *A good education is one of the most important gifts parents can give a child.*

SIGN: Left **'EXTENDED B'** hand is held in a fixed position with palm up and fingers pointing forward/rightward. Fingertips of right **'CONTRACTED 5'** hand, palm down, are placed on the left palm. Then the right hand is changed to a **'FLAT O'** handshape as it is raised. (The abbreviation **ED** is frequently fingerspelled.)
ALTERNATE SIGN—**educate**

eek: *s.s.* a colloquial expression which indicates adamant disapproval or that someone has been unpleasantly surprised. *Eek! What is this mouse doing in here?*

SIGN: Vertical **'E'** hands are held against either side of the chin with palms facing forward but angled toward each other slightly. The hands are then simultaneously thrust forward/outward as they change to **'K'** shapes. The mouth is open as if actually articulating 'EEK!'

eel: *n.* a fish with a long snake-like body and smooth slippery skin. *Some people consider eel a gourmet treat so it is often on the menu in fine restaurants.*

SIGN: Fingerspell **EEL**.

E   E   L

effect: *n.* something produced by a cause. *The effect of praise is always positive.*

SIGN: Fingertips of right **'FLAT O'** hand rest on back of left **'STANDARD BASE'** hand. Right hand is then thrust forward as it opens slightly to form a **'CONTRACTED 5'** hand.

effective: *adj.* capable of producing a positive result. *The new sales program has been very effective.*

SIGN #1: 'ONE' hands, palms down, forefingers almost touching either side of forehead, are raised so that fingers point upward and palms face away from the body.

effective: *adj.* operative (from a certain time onward); enforceable. *The new by-law becomes effective on January 1st.*

SIGN #2: Left '5' hand is held with palm facing right while forefinger of right 'ONE' hand is inserted between first two fingers of left hand and twisted 180 degrees either to the right or left. Next, 'BENT EXTENDED B' hands, palms facing each other, are positioned so that the fingers of the right hand are just in front of the fingers of the left hand. The right hand is then moved forward briskly.

(ASL CONCEPT—**start - from now on**.)

efficiently: *adv.* competently; smoothly; with a minimum of expense, effort and time. *She ran the meeting very efficiently.*

SIGN: 'FLAT O' hands are held with palms up, the left hand slightly ahead of the right hand. The hands move simultaneously forward while the hands close to form 'A' hands.

effort: *n.* a determined attempt. *The group effort resulted in success.*

SIGN: Horizontal 'EXTENDED A' (or 'S') hands are held apart with palms facing the chest. The wrists then rotate toward the chest, causing the palms to turn downward as the hands curve downward and forward.

egg: *n.* an oval reproductive body laid by a domestic bird and often used as food. *I would like a scrambled egg and some bacon for breakfast.*

SIGN #1: 'BENT U' hands, palms toward the body, are held in a horizontal position in front of the chest so that the side of the right midfinger lies across the side of the left forefinger. Then the hands are curved downward away from each other so that the extended fingers point downward.

SIGN #2 [ATLANTIC]: Horizontal left 'S' hand is held in a fixed position with palm facing rightward/backward. Extended fingertips of right 'BENT EXTENDED U' hand, palm down, are brushed backward/rightward a couple of times against the top of the left hand.

ego: *n.* a person's self-concept. *Losing the race was a hard on his ego.*

SIGN: Fingerspell **EGO**.

E   G   O

egotistic [*or* **egotistical** *or* **egocentric**]: *adj.* self-centred; concentrating too much on oneself. *Egotistic people usually are not very popular with their peers.*

SIGN: Vertical right 'I' hand, palm facing left, is thumped against the centre of the chest. Alternatively, two 'I' hands may thump alternately and repeatedly against either side of the chest. An arrogant facial expression accompanies this sign.

eight: *n.* See NUMBERS, p. LX.

eighteen: *n.* See NUMBERS, p. LXI.

eighty: *n.* See NUMBERS, p. LXII.

either: *conj.* one or the other of two. *You can either make your own choices or accept someone else's.*

SIGN #1: Right hand alternates between 'FLAT OPEN F' and 'F' as thumb and forefinger pluck first at tip of forefinger of vertical left 'V' hand (palm facing the body) and then at tip of middle finger.

ALTERNATE SIGN—**whether**

OR

SIGN #2: Vertical left 'V' hand is held in a fixed position with palm facing rightward. Right 'BENT V' hand is held beside left hand with palm facing left and extended fingertips tapping alternately a few times on the extended fingertips of the left hand.

either: *adv.* also, likewise. *If you are not going, I will not go either.*

SIGN #3: Vertical right **'Y'** hand is held with palm forward and appears to wobble from side to side as the wrist twists. (ESL USERS: **Either** is used in a *negative* sentence as in the sample sentence. In a *positive* sentence, **too** is used: *If you go, I will go too.*)

ejaculation: *n.* the act of discharging semen during orgasm. *Sperm is released through ejaculation.*

SIGN: Horizontal left **'ONE'** hand is held in a fixed position with palm right and tip of forefinger touching heel of horizontal right **'S'** hand, of which the palm faces left. Fingers of the right hand then suddenly open to form a **'MODIFIED 5'** hand.

eke out a living [*or* **eke out an existence**]: *v.* to make do by being very thrifty. *They were able to eke out a living from their small farm.*

SIGN: **'BENT MIDFINGER 5'** hands, palms toward the body, are alternately circled backward so that the tips of the middle fingers brush downward on either side of the chin with each revolution.

elaborate: *adj.* carefully planned; complex; detailed; highly ornamented or decorative. *Sir Christopher Wren is noted for his elaborate architecture.*

SIGN #1: Vertical **'SPREAD C'** hands are held apart with palms forward and are simultaneously circled outward in opposite directions, the right hand moving clockwise and the left hand moving counter-clockwise. (Signs vary according to context.)

elaborate: *v.* to explain in detail. *The author will elaborate on that topic in later chapters of the book.*

SIGN #2: **'F'** hands are held horizontally with palms facing each other, and are alternately moved backward and forward a few times. Next, edge of downward-pointing forefinger of right **'BENT ONE'** hand is placed against right-facing palm of left **'EXTENDED B'** hand. Then the right hand is pushed firmly downward. (ASL CONCEPT—explain - deep.)

elastic: *adj.* able to return to its original size and shape after stretching. *This skirt has an elastic waistband.*

SIGN: Horizontal **'CLAWED V'** hands, palms toward the body, are knocked together and drawn apart at least twice.

elated: *adj.* filled with happiness and/or pride; joyful. *We were elated when our daughter won the award.*

SIGN: Tips of middle fingers of horizontal **'BENT MIDFINGER 5'** hands are placed slightly apart on the chest. The wrists then rotate forward as the hands move forward so that, while the palms still face the body, they are now angled upward slightly. (Signs vary depending on the context. If there is *no feeling of pride* involved, one might choose the sign for **ecstatic** or **excited**.)

elbow: *n.* the joint between the forearm and the upper arm. *My elbow is sore.*

SIGN: Left forearm is folded across in front of the chest as the fingers of the right **'EXTENDED B'** hand tap the left elbow a couple of times.

elderly: *adj.* quite old (used to describe *people only*). *My elderly grandmother lives in Fredericton, New Brunswick.*

SIGN: Right **'S'** hand, slightly open, palm facing left, is brought down firmly from the chin as it closes.

elect: *v.* to select by voting. *In Canada we elect a government every four or five years.*

SIGN: The joined thumb and forefinger of the horizontal right **'F'** hand, palm down, are used to move in and out of the opening of the horizontal left **'F'** hand of which the palm is facing right. Motion is repeated.
SAME SIGN—**election**, *n.*

electric: *adj.* charged with electricity. *The burner on the electric stove was red hot.*

SIGN #1: Crooked forefingers of horizontal **'X'** hands, palms facing body, are tapped together at least twice.
SAME SIGN—**electricity**, *n.*

electric *(cont.)*

SIGN #2 [ATLANTIC]: Tip of crooked forefinger of right **'CROOKED ONE'** hand, is tapped against an upper front tooth. Then horizontal **'X'** hands, palms facing the chest, are tapped together a couple of times. Alternatively, the **'X'** hands are held farther apart and simultaneously moved inward and outward very slightly a couple of times.
SAME SIGN—**electricity**, *n.*

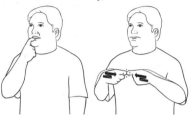

elegant: *adj.* fine and/or graceful in dress, style, or design. *She looks **elegant** in formal evening attire.*

SIGN: Vertical **'5'** hands are held at either side of chest with palms facing each other and are alternately circled forward a few times, the thumbs brushing upward and off the chest with each revolution.
ALTERNATE SIGN—**posh**

element: *n.* one of the basic parts of something. *Conflict is an important **element** in the plot of a story.*

SIGN: Horizontal left **'EXTENDED B'** hand is held in a fixed position with palm up but angled toward the body and fingers pointing rightward/forward while edge of horizontal right **'EXTENDED B'** hand, palm facing left, is placed on left palm and is drawn back toward the body. (When referring to a substance included in a chemist's periodic table of elements, **ELEMENT** is fingerspelled. For **element**, meaning the burner on a stove, see **dish**, followed by the circling of the right forefinger as it points to the palm of the left hand. For the plural **elements**, see **weather**.)

elementary: *adj.* introductory or fundamental; basic; not difficult. *She teaches an **elementary** ASL course at the community college.*

SIGN: Right **'EXTENDED B'** hand, palm down, fingers pointing slightly forward and to the left, is circled counter-clockwise beneath left **'STANDARD BASE'** hand.

elementary school: *n.* the early years of schooling (generally, grades one to six or eight). *She teaches in an **elementary school**.*

SIGN: Horizontal **'EXTENDED B'** hands, palms down and fingers pointing forward, are held almost side by side except that right hand is raised slightly so that the right thumb is just above the left. The hands are then drawn apart. (The accompanying lip pattern is such that the signer appears to be articulating *'mall'*.)

elephant: *n.* a very large, thick-skinned mammal with a prehensile trunk, and usually having two ivory tusks. *Elephants are sometimes trained for circus acts.*

SIGN: Vertical right **'C'** hand with the palm facing left, is positioned in front of the nose and is curved downward and forward.

elevate: *v.* to lift up; raise. *They will **elevate** the stage for the final act of the drama.*

SIGN: **'EXTENDED B'** hands are held parallel with palms down and fingers pointing forward. The hands are then raised simultaneously to a higher level. (Sign selection depends on 'what' is being elevated and 'how' it is being elevated.)

elevator: *n.* a mechanical hoist or lift. *A hospital **elevator** is usually crowded.*

SIGN: Left **'EXTENDED B'** hand is held in a fixed position with palm up and fingers pointing forward/rightward. Right **'BENT V'** hand is held in an inverted position with palm down and tips of extended fingers resting on left palm. Together, the hands are moved up and down a couple of times.

eleven: *n.* See NUMBERS, p. LX.

eligible: *adj.* qualified; worthy. *Only those whose names appear on the electors' list are **eligible** to vote.*

SIGN: **'K'** hands, palms down, are held apart, extended fingers pointing downward, and are then flicked upward from the wrists so that the hands are held in either a horizontal or upright position.
ALTERNATE SIGN—**can** #1

eliminate: *v.* to remove; get rid of; take out. *He was eliminated from the team after testing positive for steroid use.*

SIGN: Left **'ONE'** hand is held in a fixed position with palm leftward at a slight downward angle and forefinger pointing forward/ rightward. Right **'COVERED T'** hand is held to the right of the left hand with palm up and forefinger touching tip of left forefinger. The right hand then moves rightward/upward as the thumb is flicked out to form an **'EXTENDED A'** hand.
ALTERNATE SIGN—**dismiss**

elk: *n.* a large deer which is sometimes called a 'wapiti'. *Large herds of elk can be seen around the Jasper townsite.*

SIGN: **'5'** hands, palms forward but facing slightly, are placed at either side of the head, thumbs on the forehead. To show the span of the elk's antlers, the arms are then moved outward as the wrists twist slightly to turn the palms fully forward. (**ELK** is often fingerspelled following this sign in order to be more specific.)

elm: *n.* a deciduous shade tree found in the northern hemisphere. *We sat under a tall elm to eat our picnic lunch.*

SIGN: Fingerspell **ELM**.

else: *adj.* other; different; in addition; more. *What else did the speaker have to say?*

SIGN: Right **'EXTENDED A'** hand is held palm down, and the wrist rotates rightward so that the palm faces left and the thumb is pointing upward. (**ELSE** may be fingerspelled.)

e-mail: *v.* to send a message electronically through the Internet. *I will e-mail you tomorrow.*

SIGN: **E-MAIL** is fingerspelled in the direction of the person receiving the message. (For **E-MAIL**, *n.*, the hand remains in one place as the word is fingerspelled.)

embargo: *n.* a government ban on commercial ships entering or leaving a port. *The government ordered an embargo on all shipments from the offending country.*

SIGN: **'CLAWED L'** hands, palms forward, are held slightly apart and are simultaneously thrust ahead with a short, firm, abrupt movement.
ALTERNATE SIGN—**ban**

embark: *v.* to begin a journey, adventure or new project. *After graduation, most students are eager to embark on their careers.*

SIGN: Left **'5'** hand is held with palm facing right while forefinger of right **'ONE'** hand is inserted between first two fingers of left hand and twisted 180 degrees to either the right or left.
ALTERNATE SIGN—**go ahead**

embarrassed: *adj.* self-conscious. *He was embarrassed when someone complimented him on his performance.*

SIGN #1: Vertical right **'SPREAD C'** hand is held with fingertips touching right side of the neck. The hand then appears to be tugged downward slightly as the fingers close to form an **'S'** hand.

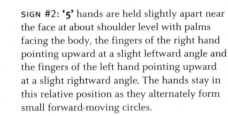

OR

SIGN #2: **'5'** hands are held slightly apart near the face at about shoulder level with palms facing the body, the fingers of the right hand pointing upward at a slight leftward angle and the fingers of the left hand pointing upward at a slight rightward angle. The hands stay in this relative position as they alternately form small forward-moving circles.

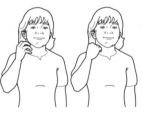

embezzle: *v.* to defraud by taking money or property belonging to someone else. *The clerk embezzled company funds to purchase a home on Lakeshore Drive.*

SIGN: Left arm is folded across in front of the chest. Horizontal right **'V'** hand is held with thumb against left forearm near the elbow and palm facing the arm. The right hand is then drawn rightward at a slight upward angle along the left forearm as the extended fingers retract to form a **'CLAWED V'** hand.
SAME SIGN—**embezzlement**, *n.*

embrace: *v.* to clasp each other in affection or greeting; hug. *The two sisters embraced warmly when they met at the airport.*

SIGN #1: **'S'** hands, palms toward the body, are crossed at the wrists and are placed against the chest. Then they are pressed firmly against the body while the shoulders are hunched.

embrace: *v.* to include; encompass. *His lecture about ASL embraced many interesting features which make this language unique.*

SIGN #2: Right **'CONTRACTED 5'** hand is held palm down above horizontal left **'C'** hand of which the palm faces rightward/backward. The right hand is then closed to form a **'FLAT O'** hand as it plunges finger first into the opening at the top of the left hand. (In situations where **embrace** means 'to eagerly accept or take up', a more appropriate sign choice might be **accept**, **take** #2 or **like** #1.)

embryo: *n.* an animal, human or plant in the early stages of development. *The fetus is an embryo at this stage.*

SIGN: Fingerspell **EMBRYO**.

emerge: *v.* to become apparent or come into view. *Some interesting theories might emerge from their discussion.*

SIGN: Left **'EXTENDED B'** hand is held, palm down, in a fixed position. Right **'ONE'** hand, palm forward, is brought up underneath the left hand and the extended forefinger is thrust upward between the forefinger and middle finger of the left hand.

emergency: *n.* an unexpected or sudden occurrence demanding immediate action. *In an emergency, call 911 for help.*

SIGN #1: Right **'E'** hand, palm forward, is held upright near the right shoulder, and is shaken from side to side.

OR

SIGN #2: **'E'** hands, palms facing each other, come together forcefully so that the knuckles of one hand knock against those of the other. The hands then arc upward and apart in circular formation before colliding and moving upward and outward once again.

emotion: *n.* any strong feeling such as joy, sorrow, love, fear, etc. *Jealousy can be a destructive emotion.*

SIGN: **'E'** hands, palms toward the body, are alternately circled so that they brush upward and off the chest with each circular motion. SAME SIGN—**emotional**, *adj.*

emperor: *n.* a monarch who rules over an empire. *Napoleon became the emperor of France in 1804.*

SIGN: Horizontal right **'EXTENDED A'** hand, palm facing the body at a slight leftward angle, is raised purposefully upward. Next, **'X'** hands are held slightly apart in a horizontal position, palms facing each other. Then they are moved backward and forward alternately. (ASL CONCEPT—**chief - control**.)

emphasize: *v.* to give special importance to; stress. *The dietitian's presentation will emphasize the need for good nutrition.*

SIGN: Left **'EXTENDED B'** hand is held in a fixed position with palm right and fingers pointing forward/upward. Right **'EXTENDED A'** hand is held with palm down and thumbtip touching left palm. The right wrist then rotates forward, thus turning the hand so that the palm faces the body at a downward angle. SAME SIGN—**emphasis**, *n.*

employ: *v.* to hire a person to do a job. *The company cannot afford to employ another labourer.*

SIGN: Horizontal right **'SPREAD C'** hand is held well out in front of the body with palm facing leftward. As the hand is then brought backward toward the body, the hand closes to assume an **'S'** shape. ❖

(be) employed: *v.* to work; to have a job. *He is employed as an ASL instructor.*

SIGN: Wrist of right **'S'** (or **'A'**) hand, palm facing away from the body, strikes wrist of the left **'S'** (or **'A'**) hand, which is held in front of/below the right hand with palm facing downward. Motion is repeated.

employee: *n.* a person who is hired to work in return for payment. *He is an employee of the federal government.*

SIGN: Wrist of right **'S'** (or **'A'**) hand, palm facing away from the body, strikes wrist of the left **'S'** (or **'A'**) hand, which is held in front of/below the right hand with palm facing downward. Motion is repeated. Agent Ending (see p. LIV) may follow.

employer: *n.* a person or firm that employs workers. *My employer is very kind and generous to his staff.*

SIGN: Vertical right **'ONE'** hand is held near the right side of the forehead with palm forward and slightly leftward. The wrist then rotates forward to turn the hand as the forefinger tucks into a **'BENT ONE'** position with the fingertip coming to rest on the right side of the forehead.

employment: *n.* a person's work or occupation. *She is seeking employment as a nurse.*

SIGN: Wrist of right **'S'** (or **'A'**) hand, palm facing away from the body, strikes wrist of the left **'S'** (or **'A'**) hand, which is held in front of/below the right hand with palm facing downward. Motion is repeated.

empower: *v.* to authorize, enable or permit someone to exercise power. *Legal recognition of ASL as an official language in Canada would empower Deaf people both educationally and politically.*

SIGN: Right **'X'** hand is held upright with palm facing left, and is thrust forward and downward to a horizontal position. ❖ Then fingertips of right **'SPREAD C'** hand are brought forcefully against left bicep. (ASL CONCEPT—**give - power**.)

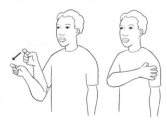

empty: *adj.* having nothing or no one inside. *The room is empty.*

SIGN #1: Tip of middle finger of right **'BENT MIDFINGER 5'** hand strokes forward/rightward across back of left **'STANDARD BASE'** hand. (This sign is used to mean 'devoid of individual people or things'.)

empty: *adj.* having nothing inside. *The gas tank is empty.*

SIGN #2: Right **'BENT EXTENDED B'** hand, fingertips pointing backward, strikes right side of neck sharply. (This sign is used for **empty** when the signer is referring to *volume*.)

enable: *v.* to make possible; to give (someone) the means to do something. *The inheritance will enable them to pay off their mortgage.*

SIGN: Horizontal left **'A'** (or **'EXTENDED A'**) hand, palm facing the body but turned slightly rightward, rests on the upturned palm of the right **'EXTENDED B'** hand. Both hands are lifted upward in one motion toward the person receiving help. ❖

enclose: *v.* to put inside (an envelope especially). *I have enclosed a cheque to cover your expenses.*

SIGN: Horizontal left **'FLAT C'** hand is held with palm facing the body but angled rightward slightly. Right **'FLAT O'** hand is held palm down just above the left hand. Then the bunched fingers of the right hand are brought down and inserted into the opening at the top of the left hand.

encode: *v.* to convert a message into code. *The spy will encode the secret information before transmitting it.*

SIGN: **'X'** (or **'A'**) hands, palms facing, simultaneously rotate 180 degrees so that their positions are reversed.

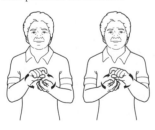

encore: *n.* extra entertainment provided in response to applause from an audience. *The crowd called for an encore.*

SIGN: Right **'BENT EXTENDED B'** hand, palm up, is overturned and brought downward so that the fingertips touch the upturned palm of the left **'EXTENDED B'** hand.
ALTERNATE SIGNS—**more** #1 & #2

encounter: *v.* to be faced with or meet unexpectedly. *You may encounter many problems throughout your life.*

SIGN: Vertical left **'EXTENDED B'** hand is held in a fixed position with palm toward face. Vertical right **'EXTENDED B'** hand, palm forward, is moved forward to stop near, but not touching the left hand. (To refer to the encountering of a *person*, see **meet** #1.)

encourage: *v.* to inspire with confidence (to do something); foster. *It is better to encourage good behaviour than to criticize bad behaviour.*

SIGN: Horizontal **'EXTENDED B'** hands are held apart with palms angled so that they partly face each other while partly facing forward. The hands then simultaneously make several small circles outward.
SAME SIGN—**encouragement**, *n.*

encyclopedia: *n.* a set of books dealing with the whole range of human knowledge. *The Canadian Encyclopedia was originally published by Hurtig.*

SIGN: Horizontal right **'E'** hand, palm down, is brushed across the upturned palm of the left **'EXTENDED B'** hand in a clockwise circular motion at least twice.

end: *v.* to finish or bring to a conclusion; to be over. *The tournament will end in one week.*

SIGN #1: Vertical **'5'** hands, palms facing the body, are held at chest level, and swung outward, away from the body so that palms face down.

OR

SIGN #2: Left horizontal **'EXTENDED B'** hand is held in a fixed position with palm facing the body and fingers pointing rightward. Right horizontal **'EXTENDED B'** hand, palm facing left and fingers pointing forward, makes a chopping motion near the fingertips of the left hand.

end: *v.* to conclude or bring to a finish; stop. *We hope the new treaty will end the war.*

SIGN #3: Right **'EXTENDED B'** hand, palm facing left, is brought down sharply from a semi-vertical position to strike the upward/backward facing palm of the rigidly held left **'EXTENDED B'** hand, whose fingers point rightward/forward.

end: *n.* the last part. *The hero always dies at the end of a Shakespearean tragedy.*

SIGN #4: Horizontal left **'I'** hand is held with palm facing the body at a rightward angle and little finger pointing forward/rightward. Vertical right **'I'** hand, with palm facing leftward/backward, is held to the right of and above the left hand. The right hand is then lowered so that the tip of the little finger strikes the tip of the little finger of the left hand.

endeavour [*also spelled* **endeavor**]: *v.* to make an effort (to do something); try. *They will endeavour to finish the construction before winter.*

SIGN: Horizontal **'EXTENDED A'** (or **'S'**) hands are held apart with palms facing the chest. The wrists then rotate toward the chest, causing the palms to turn downward as the hands curve downward and forward.

endorse: *v.* to sign one's name (*i.e.*, on the back of a cheque). *You must endorse this cheque before we can deposit it.*

SIGN #1: Right **'U'** hand, palm facing left and extended fingers pointing forward, is twisted from the wrist as it moves in a leftward arc so that the palm faces down and extended fingers come to rest in upturned palm of left **'EXTENDED B'** hand.

endorse: *v.* to give approval or sanction to. *Management endorsed the employee's proposal for a more efficient operation of the business.*

SIGN #2: Horizontal right **'S'** hand, palm toward the body and facing left slightly, is brought down firmly to rest on the upturned palm of the left **'EXTENDED B'** hand.

endorse: *v.* to support; recommend a product. *Athletes often endorse products related to their sport.*

SIGN #3: **'S'** hands, palms toward the body, are held at chest level with the left slightly above the right. Then the right is brought upward to strike the left.
ALTERNATE SIGN—**advertise**

endowment: *n.* funds donated or bequeathed to an individual or institution. *The hospital received an endowment of $1,000,000.*

SIGN: **'X'** hands, right palm facing left and left palm facing right, are alternately held upright and thrust forward and down into a horizontal position.

endure: *v.* to bear; tolerate. *He could not endure another crisis.*

SIGN #1: Right **'A'** hand, with thumbnail touching closed lips and palm facing left, is moved slowly down chin.

endure: *v.* to continue. *They vowed their love would endure forever.*

SIGN #2: **'EXTENDED A'** hands are held side by side with palms down and right thumbtip pressing against left thumbnail as the hands are moved purposefully forward.

enemy: *n.* someone who is hostile toward another person; foe; adversary. *He is a fierce enemy.*

SIGN: Horizontal **'BENT ONE'** hands are held together, palms facing the body, and tips of forefingers almost touching. Then they are pulled apart with a short, firm motion.

energy: *n.* capacity for intense activity; vitality. *If you do not eat you will not have enough energy to go skiing.*

SIGN: Right **'E'** (or **'CROOKED EXTENDED B'**) hand, palm down, is placed at left shoulder. As the right wrist then rotates in a clockwise direction, an arc is formed as the hand moves forward and downward, coming to rest on the left bicep with palm upward at a slight backward angle. (Signs vary according to context. For **electrical energy**, see **electric**.)

enforce: *v.* to demand or impose obedience to rules or laws. *The responsibility of the RCMP is to enforce the laws of the country.*

SIGN: Tip of forefinger of right **'X'** hand is placed in right-facing palm of left **'EXTENDED B'** hand. Together the hands are moved firmly toward the chest, giving the impression that the left hand is being tugged by the right forefinger. Next, the right forefinger moves in a wide counter-clockwise arc as if pointing at a group of people in front of the signer. Finally, horizontal **'EXTENDED A'** hands, left palm facing right and right palm facing left, are held with the right hand behind/above the left. The hands are then moved forward/downward together. Facial expression is firm.
(ASL CONCEPT—**require - you all - follow**.)

engaged: *adj.* pledged to be married. *Carolyn and Jim are engaged to be married.*

SIGN #1: Right **'E'** hand, palm down, is circled clockwise above the left **'STANDARD BASE'** hand and placed on the ring finger of the left hand. (**Engaged** has a variety of meanings in English and has a variety of translations in ASL.)

SIGN #2 [ATLANTIC]: Horizontal left **'EXTENDED A'** hand is held in a fixed position with palm facing the chest at a rightward angle. Extended fingertips of horizontal right **'BENT EXTENDED U'** hand, palm left, are brushed backward on the ring finger of the left hand, closing to form an **'EXTENDED A'** hand which then moves backward/leftward to come together with the left hand.

engine: *n.* a motor. *My car has a small engine.*

SIGN: Fingers of horizontal **'CLAWED 5'** hands, palms toward the body, are interlocked and remain so as they are shaken up and down. This is a wrist action.

English: *n.* the official language of Britain, the U.S.A., and many other countries, especially those belonging to the Commonwealth. *The two official languages of Canada are English and French.*

SIGN: Right **'CROOKED EXTENDED B'** hand, palm down, clamps down on left **'STANDARD BASE'** hand at a right angles to it.

engrave: *v.* to inscribe by carving or etching. *The jeweller offered to engrave my name on the bracelet.*

SIGN: Thumb of right **'EXTENDED A'** hand, palm down, is used to jab twice in an upward/backward direction at the fixed palm of the left **'EXTENDED B'** hand, which is held with fingers pointing forward/rightward, and palm facing rightward, but slanted slightly toward the body.

engrossed: *adj.* having one's attention fully occupied. *He was engrossed in a mystery novel.*

SIGN: **'SPREAD C'** (or **'MODIFIED 5'**) hands are held with the right hand directly in front of the face, palm facing left, while the left hand is a little lower and farther forward, palm facing right. As the forearms move forward/downward, the fingers close to form **'S'** hands. Alternatively, the right hand only may be used.
ALTERNATE SIGN—**absorbed**

enhance: *v.* to increase in quality, power, value, popularity, appearance, etc.; make better; improve. *The politician's opinions about capital punishment will enhance his popularity among certain voters.*

SIGN: Edge of right **'EXTENDED B'** hand is placed on wrist of left forearm and moved upward in a small arc toward the elbow.

enigma: See **mystery** #2.

enjoy: *v.* to get pleasure from. *I enjoy reading.*

SIGN: Horizontal right **'EXTENDED B'** hand is held with palm against upper chest and fingers pointing left. Horizontal left **'EXTENDED B'** hand is held with palm against the body below the right hand and fingers pointing rightward. The hands then move in circles, the right hand appearing to the onlooker to be moving clockwise while the left hand moves counter-clockwise, palm on the chest, is moved in a circular motion, which appears to onlookers to be clockwise. The hands may not quite touch the body. (Alternatively, one hand only may be used.)
SAME SIGN—**enjoyment**, *n.*

enlarge: *v.* to increase or expand in size. *The farmer will enlarge his herd of cattle.*

SIGN #1: Horizontal **'SPREAD C'** hands are held with palms facing each other and fingertips either close together or touching. The hands are then drawn apart. (Signs vary depending on what is being enlarged.)

enlarge: *v.* to increase (something such as a photograph) in size. *The photographer bought some new equipment to enlarge photographs.*

SIGN #2: Horizontal **'S'** hands are held, right on top of left, with right palm facing leftward/backward and left palm facing rightward/backward. The hands are then drawn apart as the fingers open to form **'SPREAD C'** hands.

enlist: *v.* to get someone's help or cooperation. *I will enlist the services of my friends to help us with fundraising.*

SIGN #1: Vertical **'BENT EXTENDED B'** hands are held parallel at about shoulder level or above with palms facing backward. They are then waved back and forth limply from the wrist as if motioning people to come toward you. (When enlisting the help of only one person, this sign may be made with one hand only.)

enlist: *v.* to enter the armed forces. *We will enlist in the army.*

SIGN #2: Right **'EXTENDED B'** hand, palm down, is curved under left **'EXTENDED B'** palm to simulate 'entrance'. (Sometimes **enlist** means to 'persuade someone to enter the armed forces', in which case the sign illustrated here would be inappropriate.)

enormous: *adj.* extremely large. *Dinosaurs were enormous animals.*

SIGN: Horizontal **'CLAWED L'** hands, with palms facing, are held slightly apart and then simultaneously moved farther apart. Facial expression is important and the syllable 'CHA' is formed on the lips. (Signs vary depending on the shape and specific size of what is being described.)

enough: *adj.* sufficient. *I do not have enough money to buy that car.*

SIGN: Horizontal right **'EXTENDED B'** hand is held palm down with fingers pointing forward/leftward and is brushed forward/rightward across the top of the left hand. (This movement is repeated, especially when this sign appears as the *last word* in the ASL sentence.)

enraged: *adj.* greatly angered; incensed. *The enraged child stamped her feet to get attention.*

SIGN: **'CLAWED 5'** hands, palms toward body, fingertips touching chest, are swept vigorously upward/outward. Facial expression must clearly convey 'anger'.

enrol [*also spelled* **enroll**]: *v.* to register or become a member. *You should enrol in a sign language class.*

SIGN: Right **'U'** hand, palm facing left and extended fingers pointing forward, is twisted from the wrist as it moves in a leftward arc so that the palm faces down and extended fingers come to rest in upturned palm of left **'EXTENDED B'** hand.

en route: *adv.* on or along the way. *They encountered a severe storm in the Kootenay area en route to Vancouver.*

SIGN: Vertical **'ONE'** hands, palms forward, are staggered so that the right hand is held slightly closer to the chest than the left. The wrists then bend, causing the hands to fall forward so that the palms face downward. (The sign for **drive** #1 could be used for 'en route' in the sample sentence.)

ensure: *v.* to guarantee; to make certain. *Due to budget cuts, hospital administrators could not ensure that the quality of services would be maintained.*

SIGN: Tip of forefinger of vertical right **'ONE'** hand, palm facing left, is placed just under the lower lip. As the right hand is then brought purposefully forward/downward, it takes on a **'B'** handshape and is pressed against the left **'STANDARD BASE'** hand. (The handshapes for this sign may vary.)

entail: *v.* to necessitate; require. *The project will entail some very careful planning.*

SIGN: Right **'CONTRACTED 5'** hand is held palm down above horizontal left **'C'** hand of which the palm faces rightward/backward. The right hand is then closed to from a **'FLAT O'** hand as it plunges fingers first into the opening at the top of the left hand.

ALTERNATE SIGN—**require**

enter: *v.* to go into. *Please stand when the bride enters the church.*

SIGN: Right **'EXTENDED B'** hand, palm down, is curved under left **'EXTENDED B'** palm to simulate 'entrance'. ❖

SAME SIGNS—**entrance**, *n.*, and **entry**, *n.*

enterprise: *n.* project; something undertaken, such as a business. *This seems to be a very profitable enterprise.*

SIGN: Wrist of vertical right **'B'** hand, palm facing forward/leftward, is brushed back and forth against wrist of left **'STANDARD BASE'** hand. (In certain situations, the sign for **challenge** might provide a more appropriate translation for **enterprise**.)

enterprising: *adj.* having lots of energy and initiative. *Only an enterprising individual would come up with an idea like that.*

SIGN: **'A'** hands are held in front of either side of the chest with palms facing each other and are alternately circled forward, the thumbs brushing upward and forward off the chest with each revolution.

entertainment: *n.* an activity which gives pleasure or amuses. *They will provide some kind of after-dinner entertainment.*

SIGN: Horizontal right **'EXTENDED B'** hand is held with palm against upper chest and fingers pointing left. Horizontal left **'EXTENDED B'** hand is held with palm against the body below the right hand and fingers pointing rightward. The hands then move in circles, the right hand appearing to the onlooker to be moving clockwise while the left hand moves counter-clockwise. (Alternatively, the hands may not quite touch the body and sometimes only the right hand is used.)

enthusiastic: *adj.* eager; very interested. *He was a very enthusiastic ASL student.*

SIGN #1: **'A'** hands are held in front of either side of the chest with palms facing each other and are alternately circled forward, the thumbs brushing upward and forward off the chest with each revolution.

SAME SIGN—**enthusiasm**, *n.*, in this context. While **enthusiastic** #1 and #2 may appear to be synonymous in English, there is a slight difference in the meaning of the two signs. **Enthusiastic** #2 means 'eager or intensely interested' while **enthusiastic** #1 also means 'eager or intensely interested', but further implies an excitement about performing well or excelling.

enthusiastic: *adj.* eager; very interested. *I am very enthusiastic about going to Vancouver for my holiday.*

SIGN #2: Tips of middle fingers of **'BENT MIDFINGER 5'** hands, palms toward the body, are brushed up and off the chest in alternating circular motions.

SAME SIGN—**enthusiasm**, *n.*, in this context.

entice: *v.* to attract; lure; tempt. *We are try-ing to **entice** members to attend the meeting by offering free refreshments.*

SIGN: Horizontal **'CLAWED L'** hands are held apart with palms up, and forearms are moved sharply back toward the body as hands take on **'A'** shapes. (Signs vary according to context.)

entire: *adj.* whole or complete. *The **entire** student body went to watch the Olympic torch being carried into the stadium.*

SIGN: Left **'EXTENDED B'** hand is held with palm facing body and fingertips pointing to the right. Right **'EXTENDED B'** hand is circled around the left hand with the back of the right hand coming to rest in the palm of the left hand.

(be) entitled: *v.* to have the right to do or have something. *You **are entitled** to a day off because of all your hard work.*

SIGN: **'A'** hands, palms down, are held slightly apart, and are then firmly pushed a very short distance downward. (In ASL, the clauses in the sample sentence are reversed: *YOU WORK WORK* - pause - *D-A-Y O-F-F CAN*.)
ALTERNATE SIGN—**allow** #1

envelope: *n.* a flat paper covering used to enclose a letter. *She put the letter in the **envelope** and sealed it.*

SIGN: Tips of forefingers and thumbs touch as **'CONTRACTED L'** hands are held together with palms facing forward/downward. The arms are then drawn apart and each forefinger and thumb come together to form **'CLOSED G'** shapes. (This sign is used for a variety of flat, rectangular objects. In contexts where the specific nature of the object is understood, as in the sample sentence, the sign described above is sufficient. Otherwise, the concept of **envelope** can be specified by preceding this sign with the sign for **letter** #1 or by following this sign with the sign for **seal** #3.)

environment: *n.* surroundings. *We should take greater care of the **environment**.*

SIGN: Left **'ONE'** hand is held in a fixed position with palm facing rightward/forward while vertical right **'E'** hand, with palm facing left-ward/forward is held just to the right of the left forefinger. The right wrist then rotates 180 degrees forward until the palm is facing the body at an upward angle. (Signs vary according to context.)

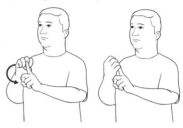

envision: *v.* to imagine; form a picture in the mind. *We tried to **envision** what the baby would look like in ten years.*

SIGN: Tip of forefinger of right **'ONE'** hand touches centre of forehead. Then vertical **'S'** hands are held together, left in front of right, at centre of forehead with left palm facing right and right palm facing left. As the hands move apart, they open to form **'CROOKED 5'** hands.

envy: *v.* to view with jealousy; a wish to have something that someone else has. *She has undertaken a difficult task so I do not **envy** her.*

SIGN: Vertical right **'4'** hand, with palm left and tip of forefinger positioned at right side of mouth, is drawn downward.
SAME SIGN—**envious**, *adj.*
ALTERNATE SIGN—**jealous**

epidemic: *n.* a widespread disease. *Without sufficient vaccine another typhoid epidemic could occur.*

SIGN: Midfinger of each **'BENT MIDFINGER 5'** hand is placed on the body—the right against the forehead, and the left against the abdomen. Next, **'FLAT O'** hands are held with the palms down and sides of tips of forefingers touching. The hands are then opened to form **'5'** hands as they are moved apart in an outward/ forward direction.
(ASL CONCEPT—**sick - spread**.)

epilepsy: *n.* a nervous disorder that sometimes causes convulsions and and/or unconsciousness. *He controls his epilepsy with medication.*

SIGN: Edge of forefinger of right horizontal **'B'** hand, palm down, is placed between the lips as the wrist makes small twisting movements back and forth to rock the hand rapidly. (Signs vary and **EPILEPSY** is frequently fingerspelled.)

episode: *n.* one event in a series. *The final episode of that TV series will be shown next week.*

SIGN: Left **'CONTRACTED C'** (or **'OPEN 8'**) hand is held horizontally with palm facing right while right **'CONTRACTED C'** (or **'OPEN 8'**) hand is held upright with palm facing left. The hands are held close enough together to be loosely interlocked. They are then drawn apart, closed and returned several times, thus alternating between **'CONTRACTED C'** (or **'OPEN 8'**) and **'FLAT O'** (or **'8'**) shapes with each movement. (Signs vary considerably. In this context, the signs **story + happen** could be used. In other contexts, **happen** or **event** might be better sign choices.)

equal: *adj.* of the same size, quantity, degree, status, etc. *All citizens have equal rights under the law.*

SIGN: Vertical **'BENT EXTENDED B'** hands are held slightly apart with palms facing each other, and are then brought together so that the fingertips meet. Motion is repeated.
SAME SIGN—**equality**, *n.*

equilibrium: *n.* balance. *The control centre for one's physical equilibrium is located in the inner ear.*

SIGN: **'EXTENDED B'** hands, palms down and fingers pointing forward, are held apart and alternately raised and lowered.

equine: *adj.* related to or resembling a horse. *The zebra is a member of the equine family.*

SIGN: Thumbtip of right **'BENT EXTENDED U'** hand is placed on the right temple and the two extended fingers are simultaneously fluttered.

equipment: *n.* a set of items designed for a specific purpose. *You must take good care of your sports equipment or it will not last.*

SIGN: Right **'EXTENDED B'** (or **'E'**) hand, palm facing up, fingers pointing forward, is moved from left to right in a series of successive short arcs. (In English, **equipment** may be either singular or plural. There is never an "s" added to this word.)

equitable: *adj.* fair; just. *He did an equitable share of the work.*

SIGN: Vertical **'BENT EXTENDED B'** hands are held slightly apart with palms facing each other, and are then brought together so that the fingertips meet. Motion is repeated.

equivalent: *adj.* equal in value, quantity, meaning, etc. *One metre and 100 centimetres are equivalent measurements.*

SIGN: Vertical **'BENT EXTENDED B'** hands are held slightly apart with palms facing each other, and are then brought together so that the fingertips meet. Motion is repeated.

eradicate: *v.* to get rid of; obliterate. *The government will eradicate the deficit within five years.*

SIGN: Horizontal right **'A'** hand, palm facing left, is held against right-facing palm of horizontal left **'EXTENDED B'** hand, and is then moved rightward and downward as it opens to become a **'CROOKED 5'** hand with the palm facing down.

erase (pencil marks): *v.* to rub out; remove. *I will **erase** the errors in my essay.*

SIGN #1: Horizontal left **'EXTENDED B'** hand is held in a fixed position with palm upward at a rightward/backward angle. Forefinger of right **'CLOSED A-INDEX'** hand, palm down, is placed against the left palm and rubbed back and forth. Alternatively, this sign may be made with the horizontal right **'S'** hand, palm facing the body at a leftward angle, rubbing back and forth on the left palm. Another variation is to rub the left palm with the palm-down right **'A'** hand. (For **eraser,** *n.,* see **rubber** #1 or #2 + **erase** #1.)

erase (board): *v.* to wipe; to remove what is on (a chalkboard). *I will **erase the board** for you.*

SIGN #2: Right elbow is raised as the **'A'** hand, palm forward, is waved up and down several times to simulate the act of using a chalkboard eraser.

erection: *n.* the state of an erect penis during sexual intercourse. *Some males have difficulty achieving an **erection**.*

SIGN: Tip of forefinger of horizontal left **'ONE'** hand is held against the wrist of the right **'ONE'** hand which is held with palm facing left and forefinger pointing downward/forward. The right forearm then moves upward so that the forefinger eventually points upward/forward.

erosion: *n.* the wearing away of rocks and soil. *Due to many centuries of natural **erosion** of the coastline, the island has gradually become smaller.*

SIGN #1: In the sample sentence, the left **'EXTENDED B'** hand represents the coastline as it is held with palm down and fingers pointing forward. It is jostled as it is slapped repeatedly by the palm of the right **'EXTENDED B'** hand of which the palm faces leftward/downward and the fingers point leftward/upward. The motion is like that of waves crashing against the shoreline. (Signs vary considerably, depending on 'what' is being eroded and 'how' it is being eroded.)

erosion: *n.* the gradual wearing away or discontinuance of something. *Church officials met to discuss how to deal with the perceived **erosion** of family values.*

SIGN #2: **'FLAT O'** hands are held parallel with palms up and slanted slightly toward the body. As the hands are drawn apart the thumbs slide across the fingertips, causing the hands to assume **'A'** shapes.

error: *n.* a mistake; inaccuracy. *I did not find any **errors** in the calculation.*

SIGN: Vertical **'Y'** hand, palm toward the face, is firmly tapped on the chin.

erupt: *v.* to burst forth suddenly. *The volcano is extinct so it will not **erupt** again.*

SIGN: Right **'FLAT O'** hand is thrust upward through horizontal left **'C'** hand, as fingers open into a **'CONTRACTED 5'** hand. SAME SIGN—**eruption,** *n.*

escalator: *n.* a moving staircase. *Use the **escalator** if you are too tired to climb the stairs.*

SIGN: Tips of extended fingers of right **'BENT U'** hand, palm down, are placed on the back of the left **'STANDARD BASE'** hand. Together, the hands rise at a forward angle.

escape: *v.* to break free; flee. *The prisoner tried to **escape** but was apprehended by the guards.*

SIGN: Forefinger of right **'ONE'** hand, palm facing leftward/forward, is placed upright between the first two fingers of the left **'EXTENDED B'** hand which is held palm down with fingers pointing rightward/forward. Then the right forefinger is vigorously thrust forward/rightward.

escort: *v.* to accompany; go with. *He will **escort** her to the graduation dance.*

SIGN: **'A'** hands are held together, palms facing each other, and knuckles touching. Then they are thrust forward/downward together from chest level. ❖ (**ESCORT,** *n.,* is fingerspelled.)

Eskimo: *n.* a person who is native to northern Canada, Greenland, Alaska and Siberia (more properly known as the **Inuit**). *The **Eskimos** are noted for their beautiful soapstone carvings.*

SIGN: Vertical **'SPREAD C'** hands, palms facing, are held side by side just above the forehead. The hands then move apart and arch downward to ear level as the wrists rotate to turn the palms upward.

especially: *adv.* particularly. *They have a lot of animals on the farm, especially sheep.*

SIGN #1: Horizontal left **'EXTENDED A'** hand is held in a fixed position with palm facing right. Horizontal right **'EXTENDED A'** hand is held at a lower level with palm facing left. The right hand then moves upward causing the knuckles to brush against those of the left hand on its way up. (While **especially** is a simple, straight-forward concept in English, it is more complex in ASL.)

especially: *adv.* particularly. *I like sports, especially rugby and soccer.*

SIGN #2: Right **'BENT EXTENDED B'** hand, fingers on lips and pointing leftward, palm backward, is drawn upward to the right of the face as the fingers bend to form an **'EXTENDED A'** hand with thumb pointing upward. Appropriate facial expression is essential. (This sign is used exclusively in positive contexts.)

especially: *adv.* particularly. *I find him hard to deal with, especially since we had that argument.*

SIGN #3: Vertical **'K'** (or **'V'**) hands, palms facing each other but angled slightly toward the body, are held apart and are simultaneously thrust toward each other, ending with the wrists crossed. (This sign is generally used in negative contexts.)

especially: *adv.* particularly. *I was not especially happy about the news.*

SIGN #4: Forefinger of vertical right **'ONE'** hand, palm facing left, is held against the lips and the hand is moved sharply forward. (This sign is used for **especially** when it connotes 'really' or 'very'.)

especially: *adv.* particularly; specifically. *The book is designed especially for children.*

SIGN #5: Vertical left **'ONE'** hand is held in a fixed position with palm facing rightward/forward. Horizontal right **'ONE'** hand is held behind left hand with palm facing left. The right hand then makes a slight but firm bounce as if intending to strike the tip of the left forefinger with that of the right forefinger but not quite touching it.

essay: *n.* a short literary composition. *Have you finished writing your essay on "Pollution"?*

SIGN: Left **'CONTRACTED C'** (or **'OPEN 8'**) hand is held horizontally with palm facing right while right **'CONTRACTED C'** (or **'OPEN 8'**) hand is held upright with palm facing left. The hands are held close enough together to be loosely interlocked. They are then drawn apart, closed and returned several times, thus alternating between **'CONTRACTED C'** (or **'OPEN 8'**) and **'FLAT O'** (or **'8'**) shapes with each movement. (**ESSAY** is frequently fingerspelled.) In 'essay question', **essay**, *adj.*, could be signed as **paragraph**.

essential: *adj.* absolutely necessary; a 'must'. *A good knowledge of physics is essential for this job.*

SIGN: Horizontal right **'X'** hand is held palm down and shaken up and down from the wrist at least twice.

ALTERNATE SIGNS—**require** and **important**

establish: *v.* to set up. *I hope to establish good rapport with the students.*

SIGN: Right **'EXTENDED A'** hand is held palm down over left **'STANDARD BASE'** hand, then twisted so that it comes to rest on the back of the left hand with thumb pointing upward and palm facing leftward.

esteem: *n.* a favourable opinion; respect. *He is held in high esteem by his colleagues.*

SIGN: Vertical right **'R'** hand is held in front of the face with palm facing forward/leftward while vertical left **'R'** hand is held just below/in front of the right hand with palm facing forward/rightward. Both hands are then moved forward at a slight downward angle. Alternatively, the right hand only may be used.

estimate: *v.* to make an approximate calculation. *We will estimate the total cost.*

SIGN #1: **'K'** hands are held, right above left, somewhere between horizontally and vertically with extended fingers pointing more or less forward, left palm facing right and right palm facing left yet both palms are angled slightly toward the body. The two hands brush against one another a few times as the right hand repeatedly moves leftward slightly, and the left hand moves rightward.

estimate: *v.* to form an approximate idea of; guess. *She will **estimate** the amount of fabric needed for the dress.*

SIGN #2: Vertical right **'SPREAD C'** hand is held in front of right side of forehead with palm facing left, and is moved leftward as it closes to form an **'S'** hand.

estimation: *n.* opinion; judgment. *In my **estimation**, he is the right man for the job.*

SIGN: Vertical right **'MODIFIED O'** hand is held just in front of mid-forehead with palm facing left, and is bobbed slightly.

estranged: *adj.* having lost affection; alienated. *The **estranged** couple decided to file for divorce.*

SIGN: Horizontal **'BENT EXTENDED B'** hands, palms facing chest and knuckles almost touching each other, are drawn apart.

etc.: *abbrev.* for et cetera, meaning 'and others'; and so forth. *His job involves typing, photocopying, filing, **etc.***

SIGN: **'BENT L'** hands are positioned with palms either downward or facing the body, and tips of forefingers touching each other, the right finger pointing leftward as the left finger points rightward. The hands are then moved apart with forefingers fluttering.

eternal: *adj.* lasting forever. *He believes in **eternal** life and reincarnation.*

SIGN: Vertical right **'ONE'** hand, palm facing backward, is held just in front of the right shoulder and is circled counter-clockwise. The hand is then changed to a **'Y'** shape with palm forward at a slight downward slant and the arm is extended in a forward/rightward direction.

ethic [*or* **ethics**]: *n.* a set of principles or values; an idea of what is right or proper conduct. *He has a very strong work **ethic** and has never missed a day's work.*

SIGN: Tip of forefinger of right **'ONE'** hand is placed on forehead. The hand is then brought down as it changes to a **'CROOKED EXTENDED B'** hand and is placed palm down on the upturned palm of the left **'CROOKED EXTENDED B'** hand so that the two hands clasp.
ALTERNATE SIGNS—**believe** #2 and #3.
(Alternatively, **ETHIC(S)** may be fingerspelled.)

ethical: *adj.* in accordance with rules for acceptable and/or professional conduct. *It is not **ethical** for a lawyer to discuss his clients' cases with friends.*

SIGN: Right **'ONE'** hand, palm left, is held above left **'ONE'** hand, of which the palm faces right. Forefingers point forward. Right hand is then brought down firmly to rest on top of left hand.

ethnic: *adj.* relating to a human group having such traits in common as race, religion, language, etc. *In our multicultural society, there are many different **ethnic** groups.*

SIGN: Left **'ONE'** hand is held in a fixed position with palm facing rightward/forward at a downward angle while vertical right **'EXTENDED C'** hand, with palm facing leftward/forward is held just to the right of the left forefinger. The right wrist then rotates 180 degrees forward until the palm is facing the body at an upward angle.

etiquette: *n.* the customs or rules that govern correct social behaviours; socially acceptable manners. *Etiquette differs according to whether an event is formal or casual.*

SIGN: Thumb of vertical right **'EXTENDED B'** hand, palm facing left, is tapped a few times against centre of chest.

evacuate: *v.* to leave a place (often because of danger). *The police asked us to **evacuate** the building.*

SIGN: **'EXTENDED B'** hands are held parallel with palms down and fingers pointing forward/rightward. The hands are then drawn simultaneously leftward/backward as they close to form **'A'** (or **'EXTENDED A'**) hands. (Signs vary according to circumstances.)

evade: *v.* to avoid, shirk, or dodge. *It is risky to **evade** income tax payment.*

SIGN: Horizontal right **'EXTENDED A'** hand, palm facing left, is held directly behind horizontal left **'EXTENDED A'** hand, of which the palm faces right. Left hand remains fixed as right hand zigzags backward toward the chest.
SAME SIGN—**evasion,** *n.*

evaluate: *v.* to judge or assess the ability, value, or worth of. *Canadian sign language instructors will be evaluated every two years.*

SIGN #1: Horizontal **'BENT V'** hands are held slightly apart with fingers pointing forward and are circled in opposite directions (the left hand clockwise and the right hand counter-clockwise). Next, **'CROOKED ONE'** hands are held parallel with palms forward/downward and forefingers pointing upward/forward. The arms are simultaneously lowered as fore-fingers retract to form **'X'** hands. Motion is repeated. (ASL CONCEPT—**observe - test**.)

OR

SIGN #2: Vertical **'E'** hands, palms forward, are held slightly apart and are alternately moved up and down. ❖

evaporate: *v.* to change from a liquid or solid state to a gas or vapour. *Ground water will evaporate quickly in very hot weather.*

SIGN: **'BENT 5'** hands are held parallel with palms down and fingers pointing downward. The fingers flutter as the hands are simul-taneously raised and finally closed to form **'MODIFIED O'** (or **'S'**) shapes. At the **'BENT 5'** stage of this sign, the mouth is rather square-shaped. As the hands are raised, the signer sucks in air and finally closes the lips abruptly as the hands take on the **'MODIFIED O'** shape. (Signs vary considerably, depending on the context.)

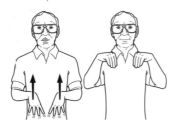

evasive: *adj.* not straightforward; intention-ally vague. *The suspect was very evasive about where he had been while the crime was being committed.*

SIGN: Vertical left **'ONE'** hand is held in a fixed position with palm rightward/forward. Hori-zontal right **'BENT ONE'** hand, palm alternating between leftward and downward as the wrist twists back and forth, weaves from side to side between the left hand and the body.
ALTERNATE SIGN—**vague**

eve: *n.* the night (or day) before a special day. *We attended a candlelight service on Christmas Eve.*

SIGN: Fingerspell **EVE**. (The archaic meaning of *eve* is 'evening' and appears occasionally in poetry. In this case, see **evening**.)

even: *adj.* equally balanced. *The two teams are an even match.*

SIGN #1: Vertical **'BENT EXTENDED B'** hands are held slightly apart with palms facing each other, and are then brought together so that the fingertips meet. Motion is repeated.

even: *adj.* on the same level or elevation. *The ground is very even here.*

SIGN #2: **'BENT EXTENDED B'** hands are held upright, the right just ahead of the left, with right palm facing left and left palm facing right. The right hand is then moved straight forward. (Signs vary depending on context.)

even: *adj.* without any variation or fluctuation. *He is a very even-tempered individual.*

SIGN #3: Vertical right **'BENT EXTENDED B'** hand is held just in front of the body with palm forward. The hand is then moved directly forward.

even: *adv.* in spite of any expectation to the contrary; despite the fact that it seems unlikely. *We even dressed up for the occasion.*

SIGN #4: Fingerspell **EVEN**.

even: *adj.* a number that is evenly divisible by two. *The even-numbered houses are on this side of the street.*

SIGN #5: Fingerspell **EVEN**.

(get) even: *v.* to get revenge. *I will get even with you for hurting me like that.*

SIGN #6: Vertical **'BENT EXTENDED B'** hands are positioned so that the right hand is held close to the chest with palm facing forward/leftward while the left hand is held to the left and farther forward with the palm facing that of the right hand. The fingertips of one hand make contact with those of the other as the hands come forcefully together and then rebound. Facial expression is important. ❖
ALTERNATE SIGN—**revenge**

even so: *conj.* nevertheless; though it seems unlikely. *He worked hard and did his best; even so, he was not accepted into the Faculty of Medicine.*

SIGN: Forefingers of **'ONE'** hands are crossed. The hands are then turned outward so that they become vertical with palms facing forward. Next, horizontal **'Y'** hands are held apart with palms facing chest, and are twisted smoothly from the wrists so that the palms face downward/forward. Sometimes only the right hand is used for this part of the sign. (ASL CONCEPT—**but - still**.)
ALTERNATE SIGN—**nevertheless**

even though: *conj.* despite the fact that. *He worked hard and did his best even though he was not accepted into the Faculty of Medicine.*

SIGN: (To translate the sample sentence into ASL, two signs are required, one at the beginning of the sentence and one in the middle to join the two clauses. The sample sentence in ASL is: **NO MATTER WORK HARD, STILL FACULTY MEDICINE NOT ACCEPT.**)
no matter: Fingers of horizontal **'BENT B'** hands, palms facing the chest, are alternately brushed back and forth against each other.
still: Horizontal **'Y'** hands are held apart with palms facing chest, and are twisted smoothly from the wrists so that the palms face downward/forward. Sometimes only the right hand is used for this part of the sign.

evening: *n.* the end of the day between afternoon and nightfall. *It is a beautiful evening so let us go for a walk.*

SIGN: Wrist of right **'BENT EXTENDED B'** hand, palm leftward/forward/downward, is tapped a couple of times against the back of the wrist of the left **'STANDARD BASE'** hand.

event: *n.* a special occasion. *The festival will be a big event.*

SIGN #1: Tips of midfingers of **'BENT MIDFINGER 5'** hands, palms toward the body, are placed slightly apart on the chest. The wrists then rotate forward as the hands move forward so that, while the palms still face the body, they are now angled upward slightly.

event: *n.* an incident; occurrence. *His accidental death was a tragic event for his family.*

SIGN #2: **'ONE'** hands, palms facing each other and forefingers pointing forward, are held slightly apart and then turned over so that the palms face down.

(in any) event: *adv.* no matter what happens. *I might be a bit late, but in any event, I plan to be there.*

SIGN: Fingers of horizontal **'BENT EXTENDED B'** hands, palms facing the chest, are alternately brushed back and forth against each other.

eventually: *adv.* finally; after a long time. *Newcomers to Edmonton eventually get used to the weather.*

SIGN: Horizontal left **'I'** hand is held with palm facing left and little finger pointing forward/rightward. Vertical right **'I'** hand, with palm facing leftward/backward, is held to the right of and above the left hand. The right hand is then lowered so that the tip of the little finger strikes the tip of the little finger of the left hand. (In contexts where there has been a long, slow struggle preceding a given eventuality, **finally** #2 may be used for **eventually**.)

ever: *adv.* at any time. *Can you ever forgive me for my thoughtlessness?*

SIGN: Right **'ONE'** hand, palm facing mainly upward but angled toward the body, makes a couple of counter-clockwise circles. (**EVER** may be fingerspelled.)

everlasting: *adj.* continuing forever or for a very long time. *The bride and groom pledged their everlasting love.*

SIGN: **'EXTENDED A'** hands are held side by side with palms down and right thumbtip pressing against left thumbnail as the hands are moved purposefully forward. Next, vertical right **'ONE'** hand, palm facing backward, is held just in front of the right shoulder and is circled counter-clockwise. The hand is then changed to a **'Y'** shape with palm forward at a slight downward slant and the arm is extended in a forward/rightward direction. (ASL CONCEPT— **continue - forever**.) This sign only appears at the *end* of an ASL sentence. In translating the sample sentence, **love**, *n.*, would be signed first, followed by **everlasting**, *adj.*

every: *adj.* each one, without exception. *He knows every person in the room.*

SIGN: With palm facing right, left **'EXTENDED A'** hand is held in front of right **'EXTENDED A'** hand, of which the palm faces left. The right hand is then drawn downward along the length of the left thumb.

everybody: *pron.* every person or everyone. [See also PRONOUNS, p. LXIII.] *Everybody was invited to the party.*

SIGN: Vertical **'A'** hands are held parallel at about shoulder level with palms facing each other. The hands are then simultaneously thrust forward as they take on **'L'** shapes. (This sign is derived from the fingerspelled word **ALL**.)
ALTERNATE SIGN—**all** #2

everyday: *adj.* commonplace, or happening each day. *Cooking is an everyday job in a family.*

SIGN: Knuckles of the right **'A'** hand, with palm toward face, are brushed forward across the right cheek twice.

everyone: *pron.* every person. [See also PRONOUNS, p. LXIII.] *Everyone was invited to the party.*

SIGN: Vertical **'A'** hands are held parallel at about shoulder level with palms facing each other. The hands are then simultaneously thrust forward as they take on **'L'** shapes. (This sign is derived from the fingerspelled word **ALL**.)
ALTERNATE SIGN—**all** #2

everything: *pron.* all things. [See also PRONOUNS, p. LXIII.] *Do not worry, we will take care of everything.*

SIGN #1: **'A'** hands are held slightly apart with the right a little higher than the left and both palms up. The hands move toward one another so that the right just grazes the left as the wrists cross. Then the hands are flung apart as they open to form **'5'** hands.

everything: *pron.* all that pertains to a specific subject. [See also PRONOUNS, p. LXIII.] *His new car has everything on it.*

SIGN #2: Right **'CONTRACTED 5'** hand, palm facing down, is circled widely in a clockwise direction over the opening of the horizontal left **'C'** hand whose palm faces right. Right hand is then closed to form a **'FLAT O'** hand of which the fingertips are inserted into the opening of the left hand.
ALTERNATE SIGN—**everything** #1. However, **everything** #1 and #2 are not always interchangeable. **Everything** #2 would not be appropriate in: *'How is everything?'*

everywhere: *adv.* in all parts or places. *We searched everywhere but could not find the kitten.*

SIGN: Horizontal right **'5'** hand is held with palm down and fingers pointing forward. The hand then makes a wide arc leftward as it inscribes a circle in front of the body. (**Everywhere** is a concept that is generally incorporated in the verb. In the sample sentence, the sign for **search** becomes wider and much slower than usual.)

evict: *v.* to legally expel from property; force out. *The landlord has the right to evict noisy, destructive tenants.*

SIGN: Horizontal **'S'** hands are held slightly apart with left palm down and right palm up. The arms then move simultaneously rightward as the hands open to form **'CROOKED 5'** (or **'V'**) shapes. (Alternatively, this sign may be made with **'EXTENDED A'** handshapes in both the initial and final positions.)

evidence: *n.* data on which to base proof or determine truth. *The judge considered all the evidence before he reached a decision.*

SIGN: Horizontal left **'EXTENDED B'** hand is held in a fixed position with palm up and fingers pointing forward/rightward. Horizontal right **'EXTENDED B'** hand is held palm up with fingers pointing forward/leftward and is brought down sharply onto the left palm.

evident: *adj.* clear; obvious. *It is evident that he is not telling the truth.*

SIGN: **'O'** (or **'FLAT O'**) hands are placed side by side, palms facing forward. Then they are moved apart and upward as the fingers spread to form **'5'** hands, palms still facing away from the body.

evil: *adj.* morally wrong; bad; wicked; sinful. *Shakespeare characterized Richard III as an evil king.*

SIGN: Right **'EXTENDED B'** hand, with fingertips on chin and palm facing body, is turned away, so that palm is facing down.
ALTERNATE SIGN—**bad** #2

exact: *adj.* precise; correct in every detail. *You will need the exact change for bus fare after 9 p.m.*

SIGN: **'CLOSED X'** hands are held, right above left, with palms facing. The hands are then brought together sharply so that the joined thumbs and forefingers touch. Alternatively, the right hand sometimes moves in a small clockwise circle before making contact with the left hand.

exaggerate: *v.* to represent as greater, more successful or more important than is true. *Fishermen tend to exaggerate the size of a fish that gets away.*

SIGN: Left **'S'** hand is held with palm facing rightward/downward. Right **'S'** hand is held just in front of the left hand with palm facing leftward/downward. The right hand is then wobbled forward/rightward.
SAME SIGN—**exaggeration,** *n.*

examination [*or* **exam**]: *n.* a set of questions or exercises designed to test one's knowledge and/or skills. *The comprehensive examination lasted four hours.*

SIGN: **'ONE'** hands are held parallel with palms down and forefingers pointing forward/upward. The hands are then simultaneously lowered somewhat as the forefingers are retracted to form **'S'** hands which are flung open to form **'MODIFIED 5'** hands with palms down. (For **medical examination**, see **examine** #2.) **EXAM** is frequently fingerspelled.
REGIONAL VARIATION—**test**

examine: *v.* to analyze in detail. *The scientist will examine the fragments of the meteorite.*

SIGN #1: **'V'** hands, palms down, extended fingers of one hand pointing toward those of the other hand, are simultaneously moved apart at least twice while the extended fingers retract to take on **'CLAWED V'** handshapes. (This sign is used when the examination is of a very detailed nature.)
SAME SIGN—**examination,** *n.*, in this context.

examine: *v.* to inspect; check. *The doctor will examine you now.*

SIGN #2: Left **'EXTENDED B'** hand is held in a fixed position with palm turned upward but slanted slightly rightward and toward the body while fingers point rightward/forward. Right **'ONE'** hand is held palm down as tip of forefinger brushes forward several times against palm of left hand.

SAME SIGN—**examination,** *n.*, in this context.

example: *n.* a model that is typical of a group or set; sample. *Being considerate sets a good example for the children.*

SIGN: Tip of forefinger of horizontal right **'BENT ONE'** hand is placed against right facing palm of left **'EXTENDED B'** hand. Together, the hands are moved forward in a short arc.

exasperated: *adj.* aggravated; provoked. *They were exasperated by their son's behaviour.*

SIGN: Right **'B'** hand, palm down, is held limp-wristed in front of the chest and is flicked upward from the wrist so that it strikes the underside of the chin with fingers pointing left.

ALTERNATE SIGN—**frustrated**

excavate: *v.* to make a hole or tunnel by removing earth, usually with heavy mechanical equipment. *The construction crew began to excavate a basement for the new highrise apartment building.*

SIGN: Right **'SPREAD EXTENDED C'** hand is inverted and circled forward and downward at least twice, the fingers representing the teeth of a large mechanical device as it scoops out large quantities of soil.

SAME SIGN—**excavation,** *n.*

exceed: *v.* to go beyond certain limits; surpass. *I will not exceed my budget allowance.*

SIGN: Right **'EXTENDED B'** hand is held just in front of the right shoulder with palm left and fingers pointing forward/upward. The arm is then extended as the hand is thrust forward in a large arc formation, ending up with the fingers pointing forward.

excel: *v.* to do better than most people; to be outstanding. *He excels at most sports.*

SIGN: Left **'EXTENDED B'** hand, palm facing right and fingers pointing upward/forward, is grasped by right **'OPEN A'** hand. Then right hand is pulled forward sharply and closed to form an **'A'** hand.

ALTERNATE SIGN—**adept** #2

excellent: *adj.* extremely good; of high quality. *I think that is an excellent idea.*

SIGN #1: Vertical **'EXTENDED B'** hands, palms facing forward, are held apart near the face. Forearms are pushed purposefully forward a short distance. (This sign is used to refer to things, qualities, actions, etc., but not to describe a person's abilities.)

excellent: *adj.* extremely good. *Caroline Waldo is an excellent synchronized swimmer.*

SIGN #2: Tips of joined forefinger and thumb of horizontal right **'F'** hand, palm toward the body, are brought purposefully up to strike the chin. (This sign is used specifically to describe a person's abilities.)

except: *prep.* other than; apart from; excluding. *Everyone may go except John and Bob.*

SIGN: Thumb and forefinger of right **'OPEN F'** hand, palm facing down, grasp tip of forefinger of left **'ONE'** (or **'5'**) hand, which is held with palm toward body. Then right hand is used to pull left hand upward.

excerpt: *n.* an extract or passage taken from a book, speech, etc. *This passage is an excerpt from Margaret Laurence's The Stone Angel.*

SIGN: Parallel horizontal **'V'** hands are held with the left hand slightly ahead of the right and the extended fingertips of both hands pointing leftward/forward. The forearms then move simultaneously rightward and slightly upward as the hands take on **'CLAWED V'** shapes, and finally resume the **'V'** shape as they continue moving rightward and slightly downward.

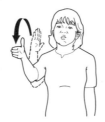

excess: *n.* more than or above the normal amount or quantity. *If you earn in excess of $100,000 your taxes will greatly increase.*

SIGN: Right **'EXTENDED B'** hand is held just in front of the right shoulder with palm left and fingers pointing forward/upward. The arm is then extended as the hand is thrust forward in a large arc formation, ending up with the fingers pointing forward. (Signs vary. See also **too much**.)

exchange: *v.* to replace with something else. *If you are not satisfied with this item, you may exchange it.*

SIGN: Horizontal **'F'** (or **'COVERED T'**) hands, left palm facing right and right palm facing left, are held so that the left is further from the chest than the right. Then their positions are simultaneously switched as the left hand moves back toward the body in an arc over the right hand while the right hand moves away from the body in an arc under the left hand.

excise: *v.* to remove surgically. *The doctor will excise the tumor.*

SIGN: Thumbnail of horizontal right **'EXTENDED A'** (or **'Y'**) hand, palm down, is placed on the rightward/upward facing palm of the left **'EXTENDED B'** hand. then the right thumb is drawn downward across the left palm. (The positioning of this part of the sign will vary according to which part of the body is undergoing surgery.) Left hand remains fixed as right **'A'** hand is placed palm down on left palm, moved rightward, and lowered slightly as the fingers open to form a **'CROOKED 5'** hand with palm down. (ASL CONCEPT—operate - remove.) For **excise**, *n.*, fingerspell **TAX**.

excited: *adj.* thrilled; aroused. *The fans are always excited when their team scores.*

SIGN: Tips of middle fingers of **'BENT MIDFINGER 5'** hands, palms toward the body, are brushed up and off the chest in alternating circular motions.
SAME SIGN—**excitement**, *n.*

exclaim: *v.* to speak out suddenly and excitedly. *"I'm innocent!" exclaimed the defendant.*

SIGN: Vertical right **'MODIFIED 5'** hand, palm left, is held with tip of forefinger at chin. The hand is then thrust forward at an upward angle. (This sign is used to refer to the way in which a user of spoken language says something but may not be used to refer to the way in which an ASL user signs something.)

exclude: *v.* to keep out; prevent from entering. *She was excluded from participating in the competition because she did not meet all the requirements.*

SIGN: Left **'ONE'** hand is held in a fixed position with palm rightward at a slight downward angle and forefinger pointing forward/rightward. Right **'COVERED T'** hand is held to the right of the left hand with palm up and forefinger touching tip of left forefinger. The right hand then moves rightward/upward as the thumb is flicked out to form an **'EXTENDED A'** hand. (Sign choice for **exclude** varies according to context. See also **not + allow**.)

excursion: *n.* a short return trip. *Last weekend we took an excursion to the capital city.*

SIGN: Horizontal left **'BENT ONE'** hand is held with forefinger pointing rightward. Horizontal right **'BENT ONE'** hand is held beside the left hand with forefinger pointing leftward so that the tips of the forefingers touch. The right arm then moves forward/ rightward and back so that the tips of the forefingers are reunited. (Signs vary, depending particularly on the mode of transportation used.)

excuse: *v.* to pardon; forgive. *The teacher excused the boy for being late.*

SIGN #1: Fingers of right **'B'** hand, palm-down, are placed on and at right angles to fingers of upturned palm of left **'EXTENDED B'** hand. Right hand is then slid at a forward/rightward angle across and off the left hand.

excuse: *n.* an explanation given to defend or justify one's actions. *She said she did not feel well but that was just an excuse to miss work.*

SIGN #2: Left **'BENT EXTENDED B'** hand is held upright with palm facing right. Right **'BENT EXTENDED B'** hand is held upright with palm facing left and fingers resting on those of the left hand. The right hand then slides forward, off and under the left hand as the left hand slides forward, off and under the right hand. The motion is repeated.

(be) executed (by electrocution): *v.* to be put to death as punishment for a crime. *She will be executed tomorrow.*

SIGN #1: **'CROOKED ONE'** hands, palms toward the head, are held at either side of the head and the fingertips are simultaneously tapped against the temples. The ASL sentence is syntactically different than the sample sentence, e.g., *TOMORROW DIE WILL...ELECTRIC* or *TOMORROW DIE WILL...HOW? ELECTRIC*. ALTERNATE SIGN—**electric**

(be) executed (by gas): *v.* to be put to death as punishment for a crime. *She will* ***be executed*** *tomorrow.*

SIGN #2: Fingerspell **GAS**. (The ASL sentence is syntactically different than the sample sentence, *e.g.*, *TOMORROW DIE WILL...GAS* or *TOMORROW DIE WILL...HOW? GAS.*)

(be) executed (by guillotine): *v.* to be put to death as punishment for a crime. *She will be executed tomorrow.*

SIGN #3: Horizontal right **'EXTENDED B'** hand represents the blade of a guillotine as it is held palm down just above the right shoulder with fingers pointing backwards. As the hand swivels clockwise from the wrist, the fingertips brush against the neck and the fingertips eventually point forward/leftward. (The ASL sentence is syntactically different than the sample sentence, *e.g.*, *TOMORROW DIE WILL... OFF HEAD* or *TOMORROW DIE WILL...HOW? OFF HEAD.*)

(be) executed (by hanging): *v.* to be put to death as punishment for a crime. *She will be executed tomorrow.*

SIGN #4: Right **'S'** hand, palm facing forward, is held in a horizontal position at the right side of the neck and is forcefully drawn upward/rightward to simulate the tightening of a noose. (The ASL sentence is syntactically different than the sample sentence, *e.g.*, *TOMORROW DIE WILL...HANG* or *TOMORROW DIE WILL...HOW? HANG.*)

(be) executed (by lethal injection): *v.* to be put to death as punishment for a crime. *She will be executed tomorrow.*

SIGN #5: Tip of forefinger of right **'BENT L'** hand is poked into the crook of the extended left arm between the bicep and forearm. (The ASL sentence is syntactically different than the sample sentence, *e.g.*, *TOMORROW DIE WILL...NEEDLE (SHOT)* or *TOMORROW DIE WILL...HOW? NEEDLE (SHOT).*)

exempt: *adj.* excused from a certain obligation. *In some provinces, seniors are* ***exempt*** *from paying health care premiums.*

SIGN: Fingers of right **'B'** hand, palm-down, are placed on and at right angles to fingers of upturned palm of left **'EXTENDED B'** hand. Right hand is then slid at a forward/rightward angle across and off the left hand.

exercise: *v.* to perform a physical activity. *The ladies* ***exercise*** *daily during their lunch hour.*

SIGN #1: **'S'** hands, palms forward, are held just above either shoulder and are simultaneously raised and lowered several times.

exercise: *n.* a task that is designed to give practice or training in a specific skill. *The teacher assigned an* ***exercise*** *in problem solving for homework.*

SIGN #2: Left **'ONE'** hand is held in a fixed position with palm down and forefinger pointing forward/rightward. With palm facing downward at a slight leftward/forward angle and knuckles lying along the left forefinger, the right **'A'** hand slides back and forth.

exert: *v.* to put into action; apply; bring to bear. *The detective* ***tried to exert pressure on*** *the suspect to get him to talk.*

SIGN #1: Left **'S'** hand is held with palm rightward/downward. Right **'EXTENDED B'** hand is held with fingers pointing forward/leftward/upward and palm forward/leftward/downward. With the palm of the right hand held against the top of the left hand, the right hand very firmly pushes the left hand forward/downward at a slight leftward angle. Facial expression is firm. (Whereas **exert** is used as a *verb* in English, it is used as an *adverb* in ASL and conveyed through a firm facial expression and a very deliberate signing of the action. Sign choice for **exert** is totally dependent on the specific action. The sample sentence in ASL is: *DETECTIVE PRESSURE-HARD COME-ON CONFESS.*) ❖

exert oneself: *v.* to put forth great effort. *He always* ***exerts himself*** *when he exercises.*

SIGN #2: Facial expression is strained as **'S'** hands, palms forward, are held just above either shoulder and are simultaneously raised and lowered several times with great effort. (Whereas **exert** is used as a *verb* in English, it is used as an *adverb* in ASL and conveyed through a strained facial expression and a slow, drawn out signing of the action. Sign choice for **exert** is totally dependent on the specific action. The sample sentence in ASL is: *HE TEND EXERCISE-HARD.*)

exhale: *v.* to breathe out. *When we exhale in the wintertime, we can see our own breath.*

SIGN: Right **'O'** hand, palm forward, is placed just to the right of the mouth and is thrust forward as the fingers open to form a **'CONTRACTED 5'** hand.
ALTERNATE SIGN—**breathe**

exhausted: *adj.* very tired; drained of energy; worn out. *Alex Baumann was exhausted when he finished the race.*

SIGN: Horizontal right **'V'** hand, palm up, is laid across upturned palm of left **'EXTENDED B'** hand and is then drawn backward toward the body.
SAME SIGN—**exhaustion**, *n.*
ALTERNATE SIGN—**tired**

exhibit: *v.* to display; show. *They will exhibit Eskimo carvings at the museum.*

SIGN: Tip of forefinger of horizontal right **'BENT ONE'** hand is placed against right facing palm of left **'EXTENDED B'** hand. Together, the hands are moved forward in a short arc. (The sign for **exhibit**, *n.*, and **exhibition**, *n.*, begins in the same position, but the hands move straight forward rather than in an arc, and the movement is repeated.)

exhume: *v.* to remove (a body) from a grave; disinter. *The body will be exhumed for further analysis.*

SIGN: **'CROOKED SLANTED 5'** hands, palms facing each other, are inverted as if with fingertips under something which then appears to be lifted as the hands simultaneously rise and the fingers close to form **'S'** hands.

exile: *v.* to officially expel or banish someone from his/her homeland. *At one time, convicted criminals in England were exiled to Australia.*

SIGN: Fingertips of right **'BENT EXTENDED B'** hand, palm down, are placed on upturned palm of left **'EXTENDED B'** hand and brushed forward to form a straight **'EXTENDED B'** hand.

exit: *n.* a way out. *In case of fire, everyone should go to the nearest exit.*

SIGN #1: Right **'CONTRACTED 5'** hand is held palm down with fingers pointing downward and enclosed in the left **'C'** hand, which is held horizontally with palm facing the body but angled slightly rightward. The right hand then closes to form a **'FLAT O'** as it is withdrawn from the left hand with an upward/rightward motion.

OR

SIGN #2: **'ONE'** hands are held with palms forward and forefingers pointing upward/forward, the tips touching. The hands are then drawn apart, moved downward, and back together to outline the shape of a small, rectangular sign. Next, **EXIT** is fingerspelled.

E   X   I   T

exit: *v.* to leave; go out. *All cars in the right lane must exit.*

SIGN #3: Horizontal right **'3'** hand, palm left, represents a car leaving a freeway as it curves forward/rightward. (Handshape depends on 'what'/'who' is exiting. When referring to an actor making an exit from the stage, the vertical right forefinger represents that person. Direction and speed of the movement similarly depends on the actual movement. Sometimes the sign for **leave** may be used as in: *I will make my exit soon.*)

exonerate: *v.* to prove or declare not guilty; to release from obligation or free from a criminal charge. *The lawyer's client was exonerated when someone else confessed to the crime.*

SIGN: Right **'OPEN F'** hand is held palm down. The hand then moves upward as the thumb and forefinger close to form an **'F'** hand with palm facing forward. Next, right **'EXTENDED A'** hand, palm facing left, thumb under chin, is thrust forward. Then sides of thumb and forefinger of right **'MODIFIED G'** hand (or side of forefinger of right **'ONE'** hand), palm facing leftward/downward, are (is) firmly placed against the left side of the chest just below the shoulder. Finally, fingers of right **'B'** hand, palm-down, are placed on and at right angles to fingers of upturned palm of left **'EXTENDED B'** hand. Right hand is then slid at a forward/rightward angle across and off the left hand. (ASL CONCEPT—**find - not - guilty - excuse**.)

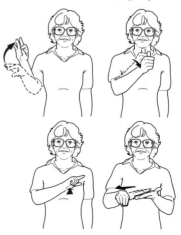

expand: *v.* to make or become greater in size, volume, extent, or scope; enlarge. *We will expand the business next year.*

SIGN: Horizontal **'SPREAD C'** hands are held with palms facing each other and fingertips either close together or touching. The hands are then drawn apart.
SAME SIGN—**expansion**, *n.*

expect: *v.* to think of as likely to happen. *We expect another cold winter.*

SIGN: Tip of forefinger of right **'ONE'** hand touches forehead and then, staying in the same place, the hand assumes a vertical **'BENT EXTENDED B'** shape, palm facing left. Vertical left **'BENT EXTENDED B'** hand, palm facing right, is held just in front of left shoulder. Fingers of both hands are then simultaneously moved up and down once or twice.
(ASL CONCEPT—**think - expect**.)
SAME SIGN—**expectation**, *n.*

expel: *v.* to officially dismiss from school or college. *The boy was expelled from school.*

SIGN: Horizontal **'S'** hands are held slightly apart with left palm down and right palm up. The arms then move simultaneously rightward as the hands open to form **'CROOKED 5'** shapes.
SAME SIGN—**expulsion**, *n.*
ALTERNATE SIGN—**banish**

expense: *n.* money spent for a specific purpose; cost. *His car payments are his biggest expense each month.*

SIGN: **'FLAT O'** hands are held with palms up, the left hand slightly ahead of the right hand. The hands move simultaneously forward while the hands close to form **'A'** hands.

expensive: *adj.* costly. *Hockey equipment can be very expensive.*

SIGN: Left **'EXTENDED B'** hand is held in a fixed position with palm up and fingers pointing rightward/forward. Back of fingers of right **'FLAT O'** hand are placed on the palm of the left hand. The right hand is then is then lifted, moved rightward, and dropped firmly downward as it opens to form a **'CONTRACTED 5'** hand with palm facing down.

experience: *n.* direct personal participation or observation. *Living in a dormitory is an experience shared by many Deaf people.*

SIGN: Fingertips of right **'CONTRACTED 5'** hand are placed near the right temple and as the hand is drawn downward, the fingers are closed to form a **'FLAT O'** hand. Motion is repeated.

experienced: *adj.* having accumulated a lot of skill or knowledge. *She is an experienced interpreter.*

SIGN: Fingertips of right **'CONTRACTED 5'** hand touch the right temple and as the hand is drawn downward, the fingers are closed to form a **'FLAT O'** hand. Motion is repeated. Facial expression is important. (This sign is basically the same as that used for **experience** but the movement is more drawn out and emphatic.)

experiment: *v.* to test the validity of a hypothesis. *Scientists are experimenting to determine the effects of acid rain.*

SIGN #1: **'ONE'** hands are held parallel with palms forward/downward. As the forearms simultaneously move downward/forward, the forefingers retract to form **'X'** hands. Movement is repeated.

OR

SIGN #2: **'E'** hands are held parallel with palms forward/downward and are alternately rotated backwards several times.

expert: *n.* someone who is very knowledgeable in a particular field. *He is an expert in Canadian history.*

SIGN #1: Horizontal **'C'** hands, which are held with the left directly in front of the right, are pulled backward in a short jerking motion toward the forehead.

expert: *adj.* highly skilled in a particular field. *He is an expert carpenter.*

SIGN #2: Tips of joined forefinger and thumb of horizontal right **'F'** hand, palm toward the body, are brought purposefully up to strike the chin.
ALTERNATE SIGN—**adept** #1

expire: *v.* to come to an end. *Her driver's licence will **expire** this month.*

SIGN: Vertical '**5**' hands, palms facing the body, are held at chest level, and swung outward, away from the body so that palms face down. (Context is very important when choosing signs. In situations where **expire** means 'to die', use the sign for **die**. When it means 'to breathe out', use the sign for **exhale**.)

explain: *v.* to make something understandable. *Brian Mulroney tried to **explain** the terms of the Meech Lake Accord.*

SIGN: '**F**' hands are held horizontally with palms facing each other, and are alternately moved backward and forward a few times.
SAME SIGN—**explanation**, *n.*

explicit: *adj.* precisely or clearly expressed; specific. *The teacher gave the class **explicit** instructions regarding the assignment.*

SIGN #1: '**CLOSED X**' hands are held, right above left, with palms facing. The hands are then brought together sharply so that the joined thumbs and forefingers touch. Alternatively, the right hand moves in a small clockwise circle before making contact with the left hand.
ALTERNATE SIGN—**clear**

explicit: *adj.* very clear; graphically detailed. *The movie about family violence was quite **explicit**.*

SIGN #2: Signer's cheeks are puffed as right '**BENT EXTENDED B**' (or '**CROOKED 5**') hand is held palm down in front of the right side of the body and is shaken back and forth from the wrist several times. Next, tip of forefinger of horizontal right '**BENT ONE**' hand is placed against right facing palm of left '**EXTENDED B**' hand. Together, the hands are moved forward in a short arc. (ASL CONCEPT—**too much - show**.)

explode: *v.* to burst noisily. *Lighting a match could cause the gas to **explode**.*

SIGN: '**S**' hands are held with wrists crossed and palms down, the right hand nearest the body. Then both hands are thrust upward forcefully so that the palms face each other.
SAME SIGN—**explosion**, *n.*

exploit: *v.* to take advantage of a person or situation for one's own benefit. *Some large corporations **exploit** their employees.*

SIGN: Middle finger of right '**BENT MIDFINGER 5**' hand is placed on the upturned palm of the left '**EXTENDED B**' hand, whose fingers point forward/rightward, and is then retracted as it is brought back smartly toward the body. (In situations where **exploit**, *n.*, means 'a daring or noteworthy act', this sign would not be appropriate.)

explore: *v.* to investigate for a specific purpose; examine; study. *The students will **explore** a variety of career options.*

SIGN #1: Left '**EXTENDED B**' hand is held in a fixed position with palm turned upward but slanted slightly rightward and toward the body while the fingers point rightward/forward. Right '**ONE**' hand is held palm down as tip of forefinger brushes forward several times against palm of left hand.
SAME SIGN—**exploration**, *n.*, in this context.

explore: *v.* to search in order to discover. *We **explored** the island looking for hidden treasure.*

SIGN #2: Vertical right '**C**' hand, palm facing left, is circled counter-clockwise (from the signer's perspective) in front of the face or upper chest.
SAME SIGN—**exploration**, *n.*, in this context.

export: *v.* to ship goods for sale to foreign countries. *Canada will **export** most of its grain to eastern Europe.*

SIGN: Fingertips of horizontal right '**BENT EXTENDED B**' hand are placed on the back of the left '**STANDARD BASE**' hand. The right hand then moves forward as the fingers straighten to form an '**EXTENDED B**' hand. (**EXPORT**, *n.*, is fingerspelled.)

exposure: *n.* the act of being influenced or affected by conditions or experience. *Having grown up on a remote farm, he has had very little **exposure** to urban life.*

SIGN #1: Fingertips of right '**CONTRACTED 5**' hand are placed near the right temple and as the hand is drawn downward, the fingers are closed to form a '**FLAT O**' hand. Motion is repeated.

exposure: *n.* the act of being influenced or affected through repeated or continual involvement with something. *To learn a language, you need lots of **exposure** to it.*

SIGN #2: Vertical left **'ONE'** hand is held with palm facing rightward/forward. Horizontal right **'COVERED O'** hand is held to the right of/behind the left hand and is opened to form a **'MODIFIED 5'** hand with fingertips pointing at the left forefinger. Movement is repeated.

exposure: *n.* the bringing of information to public notice. ***Exposure** of the scandal on national television caused great embarrassment.*

SIGN #3: **'MODIFIED O'** hands are held just in front of the forehead, left hand in front of right, with palms facing upward but slanted toward the forehead. The forearms are then simultaneously swung outward and slightly downward/forward as the hands open to assume **'MODIFIED 5'** shapes with palms facing upward.

exposure: *n.* the act of crudely exposing one's genitals or other body parts to public view. *The police arrested the man and charged him with indecent **exposure.***

SIGN #4: **'S'** hands, palms toward the body, are held side by side at the centre of the chest and are simultaneously flung outward as if opening a coat. (Sign choice in this context depends on what part of the body is being exposed and how it is being exposed.)

exposure: *n.* a frame on a photographic film. *This film has 24 **exposures.***

SIGN #5: Left **'EXTENDED B'** hand is held in a fixed position with palm facing right and fingers pointing forward/upward as vertical right **'C'** hand is held against the right cheek with palm forward at a slight leftward angle. Right hand is then moved forward/downward and placed firmly against the left palm.
ALTERNATE SIGN—**picture** #2
When **exposure** connotes 'the effects of extreme *weather* conditions', sign choice depends on what type of weather is involved. The signs for **cold** and/or **freeze** might be used as a translation for 'exposure' in this sentence: *The climber died of **exposure** on the snowy mountain top.* When **exposure** connotes 'a position relative to the direction faced', the signer might use the sign for the specific direction. The sign for **east** might be used to mean 'eastern exposure' in: *The kitchen has an eastern **exposure.***

express: *v.* to communicate one's thoughts or feelings. *You must learn to **express** your feelings.*

SIGN #1: Horizontal **'S'** hands, palms toward the body, are held together with the left hand against the chest and the right hand on top of the left but farther forward than the left hand as if the hands were holding onto a pole at a forward/upward angle. The hands are then flung forward as they open to form **'CROOKED 5'** hands with the palms facing upward, but still slanted toward the body slightly.
SAME SIGN—**expression**, *n.*, meaning the general communication of one's thoughts or feelings.

express: *adj.* fast and direct, said especially of a bus that travels straight through to its destination without stopping. *He is waiting for the next **express** bus to the shopping mall.*

SIGN #2: Right **'EXTENDED B'** hand is held just in front of the right shoulder with palm left and fingers pointing forward/upward. The arm is then extended as the hand is thrust forward in a large arc formation, ending up with the fingers pointing forward. (**EXPRESS** in this context may be fingerspelled.)

expression: *n.* a phrase used conventionally to communicate an idea. *Many famous expressions come from the works of Shakespeare.*

SIGN: Vertical **'V'** hands, palms facing forward, are held apart just above shoulder level, and are curved outward slightly from the wrists as they become **'CLAWED V'** hands.

(facial) expression: *n.* a look on a person's face that shows emotion. *Facial expression is an essential component of American Sign Language.*

SIGN: Vertical **'X'** hands, palms facing each other, are held slightly apart and alternately raised and lowered in front of the face.

exquisite: *adj.* exceptional in appearance; unusually beautiful. *She has exquisite taste in clothes.*

SIGN: Right **'CONTRACTED 5'** hand is circled counter-clockwise (from the signer's perspective) around the face as the fingers close to form a **'FLAT O'** hand, with palm and fingers toward the chin.

extend: *v.* to stretch out to make longer. *He wants to extend the warranty on his car.*

SIGN #1: Left **'S'** hand is held with palm facing rightward/downward. Right **'S'** hand is held just in front of the left hand with palm facing leftward/downward. The left hand remains fixed while the right hand is firmly moved directly forward. (Sign choice always depends upon context. In situations where **extend** means 'to broaden, expand or enlarge', sign choice depends in part on 'what' is being extended.)

extend: *v.* to offer; give. *He extended an invitation to everyone to come to his home for refreshments.*

SIGN #2: Right **'BENT EXTENDED B'** hand is held out in front of the body with fingers pointing leftward and palm facing the body but angled upward slightly. The hand is then drawn in toward the chest. (A separate sign is not accorded **extend** in this context. Instead the concept is incorporated in the sign for the object of the verb **extend**. '*To extend an invitation*' is simply translated **invite**.) ❖

extensive: *adj.* comprehensive; a lot of. *He has had extensive training in his field.*

SIGN: Right **'CONTRACTED 5'** hand is held palm down above horizontal left **'C'** hand of which the palm faces rightward/backward. The right hand is then closed to form a **'FLAT O'** hand as it plunges fingers first into the opening at the top of the left hand. (Signs vary. See also **complete** #3, **intensive**, and **much**.)

exterior: *adj.* outward or on the outside. *This paint is to be used on exterior surfaces only.*

SIGN: Right **'CONTRACTED 5'** hand is held palm down with fingers pointing forward and enclosed in the left **'C'** hand which is held upright with palm facing right. The right hand then closes to form a **'FLAT O'** as it is withdrawn from the left hand and moved toward the body. (Sign choice depends on the object whose exterior is under discussion.)

external: *adj.* referring to medicine which is applied to the outside of the body. *This medication is for external use only, and is to be applied to the rash.*

SIGN: Fingertips of **'CROOKED EXTENDED B'** (or **'EXTENDED B'**) hands are moved back and forth in a rubbing motion on various parts of the body. Natural gestures are used rather than a specific sign, depending on what sort of application is intended. (Sometimes **outside** #2 is used for **external** when it simply means exterior.)

extinct: *adj.* having died out; no longer in existence. *The passenger pigeon is an extinct species.*

SIGN: **'FLAT O'** hands are held parallel with palms up and slanted slightly toward the body. As the hands are drawn apart the thumbs slide across the fingertips, causing the hands to assume **'A'** shapes.

extinguish: *v.* to put out. *I hope the firefighters are able to extinguish the fire.*

SIGN: **'CLAWED L'** hands are held with palms up, the left hand in front of the right, as if holding a hose, and are simultaneously moved from side to side. Handshapes for this sign may vary. (Sign choice varies according to context.)

extra: *adj.* more than what is usual, needed or expected. *I bought some extra groceries in case they come to visit this weekend.*

SIGN: Horizontal left **'FLAT O'** hand is held in a fixed position with palm toward the body while the right **'CONTRACTED 5'** hand is held palm-down to the right of and at a lower level than the left hand. The right wrist then rotates rightward/forward as the fingers close to form a **'FLAT O'** hand which is swung upward to touch the underside of the left hand. (**EXTRA** is frequently fingerspelled.)

extract: *v.* to pull out (often with considerable effort). *My mouth is frozen because I had a tooth extracted this morning.*

SIGN #1: Vertical **'S'** hand is held by the right side of the open mouth with palm facing leftward/forward. The hand is then pulled forward/rightward at an upward angle. (Sign choice varies according to 'what' is being extracted and 'how' it is being extracted.)

extract: *n.* a passage taken from a longer piece of writing. *The students read an extract from a lengthy report.*

SIGN #2: Parallel horizontal **'V'** hands are held with the left hand slightly ahead of the right and the extended fingertips of both hands pointing leftward/forward. The forearms then move simultaneously rightward and slightly upward as the hands take on **'CLAWED V'** shapes, and finally resume the **'V'** shape as they continue moving rightward and slightly downward.

extravagant: *adj.* spending money excessively. *His extravagant lifestyle led to his bankruptcy.*

SIGN: **'S'** hands are held, one at either hip, with palms up. The hands are then flung simultaneously upward/outward as they open to form **'CROOKED 5'** hands. Movement is repeated. (Alternatively, the hands may be flung alternately and repeatedly.)

SAME SIGN—**extravagance,** *n.*

extreme: *n.* one of two things or conditions that are very opposite or different from one another. *The mountain climber brought light-weight and warm clothing because of the temperature extremes he would experience.*

SIGN: **'BENT ONE'** hands are held, right above left, with right palm down and left palm up while tips of forefingers touch or almost touch. The hands are then drawn apart with a short, firm motion. (In contexts where **extreme** means 'of a high degree or intensity', the concept is often conveyed by placing emphasis on the noun being described rather using a separate sign for **extreme**. The translation for 'extreme heat' is **heat**, signed in a rather drawn out manner with the addition of a pained facial expression. If 'extreme' carries the connotation of being 'drastic', see **severe**.)

extremely: *adv.* very. *He was extremely disappointed that he did not get the job.*

SIGN: Vertical **'V'** hands are held with palms facing and fingertips of left hand touching those of right hand. The hands are then drawn apart. (Rather than being accorded a separate sign, the concept of **extremely** is often incorporated in the sign for the adjective it describes by giving greater emphasis to the sign itself as well as the facial expression.)

eye: *n.* the organ of sight. *My right eye is bothering me.*

SIGN: Forefinger of right **'BENT ONE'** hand touches face just under right eye. (Sign selection for **eye** depends on the context, and when a description of the eye is being given, the signer often chooses an all-inclusive sign that conveys **eye,** *n.,* as well as its description.)

eyesore: *n.* something bothersome to look at. *That run-down, old shed in the back yard is an eyesore.*

SIGN #1: Signer winces and turns face to the left somewhat as left **'5'** hand is held with palm facing the body at a downward/rightward angle, and the edge of the right **'EXTENDED B'** (or **'BENT EXTENDED B'**) hand, palm toward the body, is inserted between the left forefinger and middle finger and makes a couple of chopping motions. (Signs vary.)

OR

SIGN #2: Vertical **'F'** hands, left palm facing forward/rightward and right palm facing forward/leftward, are alternately circled backward. Facial expression is important.

F

fable: *n.* a short story with a moral. *The characters in this **fable** are all animals.*

SIGN: Left **'CONTRACTED C'** (or **'OPEN 8'**) hand is held horizontally with palm facing right while right **'CONTRACTED C'** (or **'OPEN 8'**) hand is held upright with palm facing left. The hands are held close enough together to be loosely interlocked. They are then drawn apart, closed and returned several times, thus alternating between **'CONTRACTED C'** (or **'OPEN 8'**) and **'FLAT O'** (or **'8'**) shapes with each movement.

fabric: *n.* any cloth made from fibres by weaving, knitting, etc. *She bought enough **fabric** to make her costume.*

SIGN: Horizontal **'F'** hands, palms facing downward, are held so the joined thumbs and forefingers are touching. The hands are then simultaneously drawn apart in slight arc formation. Motion is repeated.
ALTERNATE SIGN—**material** #1

fabricate: *v.* to manufacture; build; construct. *We **fabricate** blades for figure skates.*

SIGN #1: Horizontal right **'S'** hand is placed on top of horizontal left **'S'** hand as both palms face the body. The right hand is then raised slightly and both wrists are bent causing the hands to turn so that the right palm faces left and the left palm faces right as the right hand re-establishes contact with the left hand.

fabricate: *v.* to devise; make up (as in lie). *Joe can always **fabricate** an excuse for his lateness.*

SIGN #2: Right **'4'** hand is held upright in front of forehead with palm facing leftward. The hand is then moved forward (at a slight downward angle) in short jerky motions until the fingers are pointing forward.

fabulous: *adj.* extremely good; wonderful; incredible. *He is a **fabulous** Deaf storyteller.*

SIGN: Vertical **'EXTENDED B'** hands, palms facing forward, are held apart near the face. Forearms are purposefully pushed forward a short distance.

face: *n.* the front of the head from forehead to lower jaw. *She has a pretty **face**.*

SIGN #1: Forefinger of right **'ONE'** hand, palm toward the face, is used to outline the face in a counter-clockwise direction (from the signer's perspective).

face: *v.* to confront; to deal with in a brave way. *He had to **face** many difficult situations.*

SIGN #2: Vertical left **'EXTENDED B'** hand is held in a fixed position with palm toward face. Vertical right **'EXTENDED B'** hand, palm forward, is moved forward to stop near, but not touching the left hand. ❖

face to face: *adv.* opposite one another in confrontation. *The detective finally came **face to face** with the suspect.*

SIGN: Vertical left **'EXTENDED B'** hand is held in a fixed position with palm toward face. Vertical right **'EXTENDED B'** hand, palm forward, is moved forward to stop near but not touching the left hand.

(make) faces: *v.* to distort the face; grimace; assume an unusual or silly facial expression. *I cannot concentrate while you **make faces** at me.*

SIGN: The head is cocked from side to side as vertical **'X'** hands, palms facing each other, are held slightly apart and alternately raised and lowered in front of the face. (Appropriate facial expression is essential.)

facetious: *adj.* flippant; joking, especially at inappropriate times. *The heckler made **facetious** remarks at the town meeting.*

SIGN: **'BENT COMBINED I + ONE'** hands, left palm facing right and right palm facing left, are positioned so the tip of the right forefinger is at the end of the nose and the left hand is held slightly lower and to the left of the right hand. Then the right hand is curved forward/leftward, making contact with the left hand which is moving rightward so that the hands are eventually crossed at the wrists.

facial expression: See (facial) expression.

facilitate: *v.* to assist; make easier. *They will facilitate communication by providing an interpreter.*

SIGN: Horizontal left **'A'** (or **'EXTENDED A'**) hand, palm facing the body but turned slightly rightward, rests on the upturned palm of the right **'EXTENDED B'** hand. Both hands are moved forward in one motion toward the person receiving help. ❖

facsimile: *n.* an exact copy. *This picture is a facsimile of the original.*

SIGN: Left **'EXTENDED B'** hand is held in a fixed position with palm down and fingers pointing forward/rightward while right **'CONTRACTED 5'** hand is held palm up with fingers touching left palm. The right hand is then drawn downward as it closes to form a **'FLAT O'** hand. (For **facsimile**, meaning 'a message or document sent by a telegraphic facsimile system', see **fax**.)

fact: *n.* something that is known for certain to have happened or to be true; a verifiable truth. *Is this your opinion or is it a fact?*

SIGN: Forefinger of vertical right **'ONE'** hand, palm facing left, is held against the lips and the hand is moved sharply forward. (**FACT** is frequently fingerspelled.)

factory: *n.* building(s) where things are manufactured. *My father worked in a steel factory.*

SIGN #1: Fingers of horizontal **'SPREAD EXTENDED C'** hands, palms toward the body, are interlocked and remain so as they are shaken up and down. This is a wrist action.

SIGN #2 [ATLANTIC]: Horizontal **'CLAWED L'** hands are held slightly apart with palms facing each other and are then drawn apart.

faculty: *n.* the staff of a university or college department. *The professor joined the faculty of Gallaudet University.*

SIGN: Fingerspell **FACULTY** or **FAC**.

fad: *n.* a fashion with a short-lived popularity. *It is expensive to keep up with every fad.*

SIGN: Fingerspell **FAD**.

(become a) fad: *v.* to catch on for a while; to become a fashion with a short-lived popularity. *Shaving one's head has become a fad for teenagers.*

SIGN: **'FLAT O'** hands are held with tips of forefingers touching and palms forward/downward but slanted toward each other slightly. The hands are then flung forward/outward as the fingers spread to form **'5'** hands with the palms down.

fade: *v.* to lose colour or brightness. *Bright sunlight will cause the colour of your rugs to fade.*

SIGN: **'FLAT O'** hands are held parallel with palms up and slanted slightly toward the body. As the hands are drawn apart the thumbs slide across the fingertips, causing the hands to assume **'A'** shapes.

fade out: *v.* to gradually disappear (said of the image on a television or movie screen). *When you videotape the play, fade out as the curtain closes.*

SIGN: Vertical **'SPREAD C'** hands, right palm facing left and left palm facing right, are held apart with the right closer to the chest than the left. The hands then move toward a central point in front of the chest so that the right hand is directly behind the left as the fingers close to form **'S'** hands.

Fahrenheit: *adj.* related to a temperature scale which was invented by a German physicist named Fahrenheit and is symbolized by the letter 'F'. *Americans use the Fahrenheit scale to measure the temperature.*

SIGN: Right **'F'** hand is held upright with palm facing forward and is wobbled slightly.

fail: *v.* to be unsuccessful in trying (to do something). *He will fail two courses this semester.*

SIGN: Left **'EXTENDED B'** hand is held in a fixed position with palm up and fingers pointing forward/rightward. Horizontal right **'K'** hand is held with palm toward the body and extended fingers lying in the left palm pointing leftward. The right hand then slides firmly forward/rightward off the left hand so that the palm eventually faces left and fingers point forward. SAME SIGN—**failure**, *n.*

faint: *v.* to lose consciousness. *She fainted while waiting for the bus on a hot day.*

SIGN #1: Tip of forefinger of right **'ONE'** hand is placed on forehead. The head then drops as the hand assumes an **'A'** shape and is lowered to chest level where it is held parallel to the left **'A'** hand, palms down. Finally, the hands drop further as they open to take on **'5'** shapes with fingers pointing downward. While this sign actually consists of three parts, it is made in one fluid motion. (Signs in this context may vary considerably.)

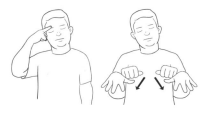

faint: *adj.* difficult to discern; lacking clarity. *There was faint writing on the wall but I could not decipher the message.*

SIGN #2: **'BENT MIDFINGER 5'** hands are held apart, the left palm facing downward/rightward and the right palm facing downward/leftward. The wrists then rotate outward causing the hands to turn so that the left palm faces rightward/upward while the right palm faces leftward/upward. (This sign would not be appropriate when referring to a sound or a pulse that is faint.)

fair: *adj.* free from discrimination or dishonesty; just. *The Human Rights Commission was created in an effort to be fair to all people.*

SIGN #1: Vertical **'BENT EXTENDED B'** hands are held slightly apart with palms facing each other, and are then brought together so that the fingertips meet. Motion is repeated. (For **not fair**, see **unfair**.)

fair: *adj.* average. *With only fair grades he will be unable to pursue a medical career.*

SIGN #2: Right **'5'** hand, palm down, is held with fingers pointing forward and is rocked as the wrist twists from side to side a few times. Facial expression is important.

fair: *adj.* light in colour (as in pale-skinned or blond-haired). *He sunburns easily because of his fair complexion.*

SIGN #3: Fingerspell **FAIR**.

fair: *adj.* pretty; lovely. *The prince fell in love with the fair maiden.*

SIGN #4: Right **'CONTRACTED 5'** hand is circled counter-clockwise (from the signer's perspective) around the face as the fingers close to form a **'FLAT O'** hand, with palm and fingers toward the chin.

fair: *n.* a gathering at which people exhibit things for competition and enjoy amusements such as midway rides; carnival. *He showed his calf at the county fair.*

SIGN #5: **'CLAWED V'** hands, palms down, are held apart in front of the chest, one hand held higher than the other. The hands are then circled forward.

fairy: *n.* a tiny, imaginary supernatural being. *Young children often believe in the tooth fairy.*

SIGN: **'BENT EXTENDED B'** hands, fingertips touching either shoulder, palms down, are swung outward and are then moved up and down slightly as though they were wings.

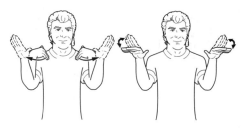

faith: *n.* a strong belief in the value or capabilities of a person or thing; complete confidence or trust. *I have faith in my supervisor.*

SIGN #1: **'SPREAD EXTENDED C'** hands are held with palms toward the body at an upward angle, the left hand close to the chest and the right hand just above/ahead of the left. The hands are then thrust forward as they are snapped shut to form **'S'** hands. (Signs for **faithful** *adj.*, depend on the context.)

faith: *n.* a strong belief in an idea or concept. *I have faith in the criminal justice system.*

SIGN #2: Tip of forefinger of right **'ONE'** hand is placed on forehead. The hand is then brought down as it changes to a **'CROOKED EXTENDED B'** hand and is placed palm down on the upturned palm of the left **'CROOKED EXTENDED B'** hand so that the two hands clasp.

faith: *n.* a specific religion. *Many Canadians belong to the Roman Catholic faith.*

SIGN #3: The right wrist rotates toward the chest as the crossed fingertips of the horizontal **'R'** hand are brushed off the left shoulder in a slight downward arc.

fake: *adj.* not real or genuine. *This is a fake diamond ring.*

SIGN #1: Side of forefinger of right **'ONE'** hand, palm facing leftward/forward, is lightly brushed forward/downward twice on the right cheek, forefinger either remaining upright or bending slightly to become a **'BENT ONE'**.

fake: *v.* to pretend; feign. *If you want to leave the party early, you can always fake a headache.*

SIGN #2: Outer edge of forefinger of vertical right **'ONE'** hand, palm forward, is brushed forward twice across the bump formed by placing the tongue in the right cheek.

fake: *n.* a person who misleads people. *You can never believe him because he is such a fake.*

SIGN #3: Vertical right **'BENT B'** hand, palm left, is brushed leftward twice across the chin. ALTERNATE SIGN—**hypocrite**

fall: *n.* autumn. *In the fall, the leaves on the maple trees are very colourful.*

SIGN #1: Side of forefinger of right **'B'** hand, palm down, is brushed downward against bent elbow of the left arm.

fall: *n.* demise; collapse; loss of power. *This term in history, we are learning about the fall of the Roman Empire.*

SIGN #2: Left forearm is folded across in front of the chest so that the right elbow rests on the back of the left hand. Right **'S'** hand, palm facing backward, then falls so that the right forearm ends up lying along the left forearm.

fall: *v.* to drop as a result of gravity. *Do not fall and hurt yourself.*

SIGN #3: Horizontal left **'EXTENDED B'** hand is held in a fixed position with palm up and fingers pointing forward/rightward. Extended fingers of right **'V'** hand represent legs as the hand is held palm down with tips of extended fingers resting in the left palm. The right hand then rises as the wrist twists, turning the palm to face the body and the extended fingers to point leftward. As the wrist continues to rotate rightward, the hand falls landing on its back with a thud in the left palm.

fall: *v.* to drop; decrease; become lower in number. *The price of gas will likely fall if the tax is decreased.*

SIGN #4: Left **'BENT U'** hand is held in a fixed position with palm rightward/forward and extended fingers pointing rightward/forward. Right **'BENT U'** hand is held with palm leftward/forward and tips of extended fingers resting on those of the left hand at right angles. The right wrist then rotates rightward causing the hand to turn palm upward as it drops slightly.

fall: *v.* to take on a look of disappointment. *Losing the contest caused his face to fall.*

SIGN #5: The signer smiles while **'FLAT C'** hands are held palms down by either side of the mouth. The facial expression then suddenly changes to one of disappointment as the elbows and shoulders drop and the wrists bend so that the palms are facing each other. (ASL CONCEPT—**happy - sad**.) Used when referring to *facial expression* only. Signs for this concept may vary.

fall: *v.* to drop (leaves). *Soon the leaves will fall from the trees.*

SIGN #6: Horizontal right **'EXTENDED B'** hand is held aloft with palm down and fingers pointing forward. The hand then gently flutters downward as the wrist rocks slightly. (This sign is used when referring to *leaves* only.)

fall apart: *v.* to become disassembled. *If you do not assemble the model ship carefully, it might fall apart.*

SIGN: Horizontal **'CROOKED 5'** hands are held with palms facing the body and the fingers of the right hand against the backs of the fingers of the left hand. The wrists then simultaneously rotate outward to draw the hands apart so that the palms are facing upward but slanted slightly toward each other. Meanwhile, the tongue visibly lies limply between the teeth.

fall asleep: *v.* to pass into the condition of sleep. *If the lecture is boring, I might fall asleep.*

SIGN #1: Right **'CONTRACTED 5'** hand, palm toward face, is held in front of the eyes and is drawn downward to about chin level as the fingers close to form a **'MODIFIED O'** hand, the eyes close and the head drops.

OR

SIGN #2: Horizontal left **'BENT EXTENDED B'** hand is held in a fixed position in front of the chest with palm right. Vertical right **'BENT EXTENDED B'** hand is held against the forehead with palm facing left. The right hand then drops downward as the wrist twists to turn the palm toward the body. The right hand eventually comes to rest on the upper edge of the left hand. As the right hand is being lowered, the eyes close and the head drops.

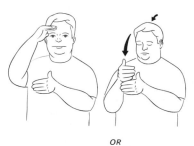

OR

SIGN #3: Left **'A'** hand is held in a fixed position in front of the chest with palm up. Right **'CONTRACTED 5'** hand, palm toward face, is held in front of the eyes and is drawn downward as the fingers close to form an **'A'** hand and the wrist twists, turning the hand palm down as it comes to rest on the left hand. As the right hand is being lowered, the eyes close and the head drops.

fall down: *v.* to collapse; to drop suddenly. *If the tent is not pitched properly it might fall down.*

SIGN: Fingers of **'CROOKED 5'** hands, palms down, interlock slightly and then drop down so that backs of fingers are almost touching. (When referring to a *person* who is **falling down**, you might use the sign for **fall** #3.)

fall in love: *v.* to become enamoured of another person and wish to be romantically involved. *Suzanne might fall in love with Peter.*

SIGN: Left **'EXTENDED B'** hand is held in a fixed position with palm up and fingers pointing forward/rightward. Right **'ONE'** hand is held, palm forward/downward, with forefinger just in front of the nose and pointing forward/upward. The right hand then falls forward, coming to rest heavily on the left palm.

fall over: *v.* to move from a vertical position to a horizontal one. *Be careful not to **fall over** that log on the path.*

SIGN: Right **'SLANTED V'** hand is held behind left **'STANDARD BASE'** hand with extended fingers pointing downward. It then moves forward, colliding with the left hand, and bouncing forward over it in arc formation while the wrist twists causing the fingers to point leftward and the palm to face backward/leftward as the hand comes to rest firmly in front of the left hand. (Sign choice varies according to context.)

false: *adj.* not true. *Is the statement true or false?*

SIGN: Vertical right **'ONE'** hand, palm facing left, is held with forefinger just to the right of the mouth. The wrist bends, causing the forefinger to brush lightly leftward/downward against the lips with the palm eventually facing downward/leftward.

fame: *n.* the state of being widely known or recognized. *Charlie Chaplin achieved **fame** in silent movies.*

SIGN: **'BENT ONE'** hands, palms toward the body but slanted slightly toward each other, are positioned with tips of forefingers touching either side of chin. The arms then move forward/upward/outward simultaneously in two arcs.

familiar: *adj.* well-known. *This place seems familiar to me.*

SIGN: Fingertips of right **'BENT EXTENDED B'** hand, with palm toward the face, are tapped against right side of forehead.

family: *n.* a social group consisting of parents and children. *I am grateful to my **family** for their support.*

SIGN: Tips of the joined thumbs and forefingers of vertical **'F'** hands, palms facing each other at a forward angle, are placed together. The wrists then rotate outward, causing the hands to move apart and turn so that the tips of the little fingers come together and the palms are facing the body.

famine: *n.* a serious shortage of food. *If the crops fail, many people will die of **famine**.*

SIGN: Fingertips of horizontal right **'EXTENDED C'** hand, palm toward the body, are placed against middle of upper chest and the hand is drawn firmly downward.
REGIONAL VARIATION—**hungry** #2

famished: *adj.* very hungry or weak due to lack of food. *The **famished** refugees were given their food rations.*

SIGN: Fingertips of horizontal right **'EXTENDED C'** hand, palm toward the body, are placed against middle of upper chest and the hand is drawn firmly downward.
REGIONAL VARIATION—**hungry** #2

famous: *adj.* well-known; recognized by many people. *Farley Mowat is a **famous** Canadian writer.*

SIGN: **'BENT ONE'** (or **'CROOKED ONE'**) hands, palms toward the body but slanted slightly toward each other, are positioned with tips of forefingers touching either side of chin. The arms then move forward/upward/outward simultaneously in two arcs.

fan: *n.* a device with blades that rotate to create a current of air. *The heater **fan** in my car is not working properly.*

SIGN #1: Horizontal right **'ONE'** hand, palm down and forefinger pointing forward, is rapidly rotated clockwise several times from the wrist.

(ceiling) fan: *n.* a device suspended from the ceiling with blades that rotate to create a current of air. *The motel room had a **ceiling fan** to cool us off.*

SIGN #2: Vertical right **'ONE'** hand is held above shoulder level as the forearm makes several small counter-clockwise rotations.

fan: *n.* a hand-held object waved near the face to cool oneself off. *They brought me a lovely hand-painted **fan** from Japan.*

SIGN #3: Right **'FLAT O'** hand, with fingers pointing toward the face, is waved back and forth from the wrist as if fanning the face.

fan: *n.* an enthusiastic admirer. *He is a devoted **fan** of his hometown football team.*

SIGN #4: Fingerspell **FAN**.

fancy: *adj.* very decorative; elaborate. *That is a very fancy cake design.*

SIGN #1: Vertical **'SPREAD C'** hands are held apart with palms forward and are simultaneously circled outward in opposite directions, the right hand moving clockwise and the left hand moving counter-clockwise.

fancy: *adj.* elegant (clothing); dressy. *That is a fancy dress you are wearing.*

SIGN #2: Thumb of vertical right **'5'** hand, palm facing left, is placed on the middle of the chest and the hand is circled forward twice so that the thumb brushes up and off the chest with each revolution. (Alternatively, two hands may be used to circle alternately at either side of the chest.)

fantastic: *adj.* (informal) very good; excellent; wonderful. *This restaurant has fantastic service.*

SIGN: Vertical **'EXTENDED B'** hands, palms facing forward, are held apart near the face. Forearms are pushed purposefully forward a short distance.

fantasy: *n.* a far-fetched mental image. *She had a fantasy about being swept off her feet by a knight in shining armour.*

SIGN #1: Vertical **'I'** hands are held at about eye level or above with palms facing backward and are alternately circled forward.

fantasy: *n.* a dreamlike scenario within the realm of possibility. *Joanne's fantasy is to win the lottery.*

SIGN #2: Tip of the forefinger of the right **'ONE'** hand is placed at the right side of the forehead, with palm toward the face. The hand then moves forward/rightward/upward as the forefinger alternates from a **'ONE'** to an **'X'** shape several times.

fantasy: *n.* absolute fiction. *What he says is pure fantasy.*

SIGN #3: Right **'4'** hand is held upright in front of forehead with palm facing leftward. The hand is then moved forward (at a slight downward angle) in short jerky motions until the fingers are pointing forward.

far: *adv.* at, to, or from a great distance. *My home is far from here.*

SIGN #1: Horizontal **'EXTENDED A'** hands are held together with palms facing each other. Then the right hand is moved forward in arc formation. Alternatively, this sign may be made without the left hand. The more slowly the sign is produced, the greater is the distance implied. (See also **far** #2.)

far: *adv.* at, to, or from a great distance. *My home is very far from here.*

SIGN #2: Right horizontal **'ONE'** hand, palm left, is pointed forward and is jerked back slightly. (This sign is used for *very* great distances. The actual extent of the distance is indicated by the facial expression.)

far: *adv.* very much. *I feel far better today than I did yesterday.*

SIGN #3: Right **'BENT EXTENDED B'** hand, fingers on lips and pointing leftward, palm backward, is drawn rightward as the fingers bend to form an **'EXTENDED A'** hand with thumb pointing upward. (There is no pat sign for **far** when it means very much; instead it is often incorporated in the sign for the adjective it modifies through a slower and/or larger than usual rendering of that sign and an appropriate facial expression. Alternatively, the adjective might be preceded by the sign **more** #1.) (ASL CONCEPT—**more better**.)

far-fetched: *adj.* unlikely; improbable; unrealistic. *His story about the aliens is far-fetched.*

SIGN: Right **'4'** hand is held upright in front of forehead with palm facing leftward. The hand is then moved forward (at a slight downward angle) in short jerky motions until the fingers are pointing forward.

far out: *adj.* a colloquial expression meaning fantastic or incredible. *Her clothes and accessories are always far out.*

SIGN: Left **'ONE'** hand is held palm down with forefinger pointing forward/rightward. Base of thumb of right **'SPREAD C'** hand, palm facing forward/leftward, slides forward/rightward along back of left hand and off to form an **'S'** hand. Fingers of right hand may flutter while sliding along left hand. Facial expression is important.

fare: *n.* the amount of money charged for public transportation in a taxi, bus, train, etc. *Cab fare increases during peak hours.*

SIGN: Vertical **'F'** hands, palms facing forward, are brought together so the joined thumbs and forefingers touch each other twice. (**FARE** may be fingerspelled.)

farewell: *n.* goodbye. *The family bid farewell to the relatives.*

SIGN: Vertical right **'BENT EXTENDED B'** hand is held with palm forward as the fingers are fluttered in unison.

farm: *n.* an area of land used for agricultural purposes. *There are many wheat farms in southern Saskatchewan.*

SIGN #1: Right **'EXTENDED B'** hand, with palm toward the body, is placed near the elbow of the bent left forearm, and is circled in a direction that appears to the onlooker to be clockwise. SAME SIGN—**farmer**, *n.*, and may be followed by the Agent Ending (see p. LIV).

OR

SIGN #2: Vertical **'MODIFIED 5'** hand, palm left, is positioned with thumbtip touching the left side of the chin. The thumbtip slides across the chin as the hand is moved rightward a couple of times. SAME SIGN—**farmer**, *n.*, and may be followed by the Agent Ending (see p. LIV).

SIGN #3 [ONTARIO]: Horizontal left **'EXTENDED B'** hand is held in a fixed position with palm up and fingers pointing forward/rightward. Outside edge of horizontal right **'EXTENDED B'** hand, palm toward the body but slanted leftward slightly, is placed in palm of left hand. The right hand is then moved forward/rightward a couple of times as if pushing something off the left hand. SAME SIGN—**farmer**, *n.*, and may be followed by the Agent Ending (see p. LIV).

fart: *v.* a vulgar equivalent of the term 'to break wind'. *It is impolite to fart in public.*

SIGN: Back of right **'FLAT O'** hand, palm down, is grasped by the left **'C'** hand, also with palm down. Then fingers and thumb of right hand open to form a **'CONTRACTED 5'** and close to resume a **'FLAT O'** shape. (Signs may vary.)

farther: *adv.* at a greater distance. *He lives farther from the university than I do.*

SIGN: Vertical **'MODIFIED O'** hands, palms facing each other, are tapped together. Then right horizontal **'ONE'** hand, palm left, is pointed forward and is jerked back slightly. (ASL CONCEPT—more - far.)

fascinated: *adj.* greatly interested. *I am fascinated with this new computer program.*

SIGN: **'SPREAD C'** (or **'MODIFIED 5'**) hands are held with the right hand directly in front of the face, palm facing left, while the left hand is a little lower and farther forward, palm facing right. As the forearms move forward/downward, the fingers close to form **'S'** hands. (Alternatively, the right hand only may be used.) SAME SIGN—**fascination**, *n.*

fashion: *adj.* pertaining to clothing styles. *He enjoys reading fashion magazines.*

SIGN: **'MODIFIED 5'** hands are held apart just in front of the upper chest and are alternately circled backward a few times so that the thumbs brush downward and off the chest with each rotation.

fashion show: *n.* an event which features people modelling the latest clothing styles. *We attended a fashion show in Toronto.*

SIGN: **'MODIFIED 5'** hands are held apart just in front of the upper chest and are alternately circled backward a few times so that the thumbs brush downward and off the chest with each rotation. Vertical left **'EXTENDED B'** is then held in front of the right shoulder with palm rightward but slanted forward slightly. Horizontal right **'BENT ONE'** hand is held with tip of forefinger touching the left palm. Together, the hands make a wide arc forward/leftward ending up in front of the left shoulder. (Signs vary.)

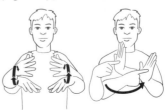

fast: *adj.* capable of moving quickly; rapid; swift. *He is a very fast runner.*

SIGN #1: Thumb and midfinger of vertical right **'COVERED 8'** hand are placed near the forehead. Then they are flicked apart to form a **'MODIFIED 5'** shape as the hand is thrust forward a short distance.

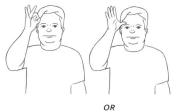

OR

SIGN #2: Left horizontal **'L'** hand, palm facing right, is held apart from and slightly ahead of right horizontal **'L'** hand, whose palm faces left. The hands are then simultaneously jerked upward toward the body as they are changed to **'CLAWED L'** hands.

fast: *v.* to abstain from eating. *Moslems fast during Ramadan.*

SIGN #3: Right **'EXTENDED A'** hand, palm facing left, thumb under chin, is thrust forward. Next, horizontal **'EXTENDED B'** hands are held with palms facing and fingers pointing forward. The hands are then swept upward simultaneously from the wrists so that the fingers point upward. Finally, vertical right **'MODIFIED O'** hand, palm facing the body, is brought toward the mouth so that the fingertips touch the lips. (ASL CONCEPT—**not - allow - eat**.)
See **won't + eat** if the fasting is being done as a form of protest.

fasten: *v.* to close by locking, buttoning, etc. *Make sure you fasten the lid securely.*

SIGN: Sign selection for **fasten** depends entirely on *what* is being fastened and *how* it is being fastened.

fasten a seatbelt: *v.* to do up a belt around oneself to hold one securely in place for protection in case of accident or sudden stops. *The flight attendant asked the passenger to fasten his seatbelt.*

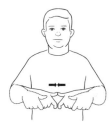

SIGN: **'CLAWED L'** hands are held at either side of waist, palms toward body, and are moved together to simulate the fastening of a belt buckle. (Signs may vary depending on the type of seatbelt and how it is fastened.)

fat: *adj.* very plump. *Santa Claus is a fat man with a big white beard and a red suit.*

SIGN #1: The signer's cheeks are puffed out as horizontal **'CROOKED 5'** hands, palms toward the body, are held apart in front of the chest and are simultaneously moved apart. (**FAT** may also be fingerspelled.) (This sign and the sign shown for **chubby** are used in positive contexts to imply that there is 'something endearing about the fatness'. For a less complimentary sign, see **fat** #2.)
ALTERNATE SIGN—**chubby**

fat [*or* **to get fat**]: *adj./v.* overweight (or to gain weight). *Some people get fat during the Christmas holidays.*

SIGN #2: Horizontal **'CROOKED 5'** hands are held apart in front of the chest with palms toward the body. The hands then simultaneously fall forward/downward.

fat: *n.* solidified animal or vegetable oil; lard. *You should avoid having too much fat in your diet.*

SIGN #3: Fingerspell **FAT**.

fatal: *adj.* resulting in death. *The man suffered a fatal heart attack.*

SIGN: **'EXTENDED B'** hands are held with fingers pointing forward, left palm facing up and right palm facing down. Then they are flipped over simultaneously so that the palm positions are reversed. (Word order in ASL is often very different than in English. The sample sentence in ASL is: *MAN HEART-ATTACK FATAL*.)
SAME SIGN—**fatality**, *n.*

fate: *n.* the inevitable circumstances of someone's future. *It seems to be his **fate** to suffer.*

SIGN: Fingerspell **FATE**.

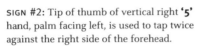

father: *n.* a male parent. *My **father** bought presents for us at Christmas.*

SIGN #1: Tip of forefinger of right **'ONE'** hand taps twice against the right side of the forehead.

OR

SIGN #2: Tip of thumb of vertical right **'5'** hand, palm facing left, is used to tap twice against the right side of the forehead.

SIGN #3 [ATLANTIC] : Left **'U'** hand is held palm down with extended fingers pointing forward/rightward. Right **'U'** (or **'CROOKED U'**) hand is held palm down just above the left hand and at right angles to it. The extended fingers of the right hand are then tapped a couple of times on those of the left.

fatigue: *n.* tiredness; weariness; exhaustion. *The patient was suffering from **fatigue**.*

SIGN: Fingertips of **'BENT EXTENDED B'** hands are placed against either side of upper chest with palms facing the body. The wrists then rotate forward, causing the hands to drop while the fingertips maintain contact with the chest. Head may tilt to one side.
ALTERNATE SIGN—**exhausted**

fault: *n.* responsibility for a mistake or problem. *It is your **fault** that we missed the bus.*

SIGN #1: Fingertips of right **'BENT EXTENDED B'** hand, palm toward body, are placed against right shoulder. The wrist then rotates forward, causing the hand to drop while the fingertips maintain contact with the body.

fault: *n.* a flaw or defect. *One of his **faults** as a father is that he does not spend enough time with the children.*

SIGN #2: Vertical right **'Y'** hand, palm toward the body, is firmly tapped on the chin.

fault: *n.* a crack in the earth's surface resulting in displacement of the surrounding area. *If the stress along the **fault** is too great, an earthquake might occur.*

SIGN #3: Horizontal **'B'** (or **'EXTENDED B'**) hand is extended out in front of the body with fingers pointing forward and palm facing left. The hand is then snaked backward as if outlining a crack in the earth's surface. (Signs in this context may vary.)

favour [*also spelled* **favor**]: *v.* to prefer; like. *Many Canadians **favour** a place with a warm climate for winter vacations.*

SIGN #1: Tip of middle finger of right **'BENT MIDFINGER 5'** hand, palm toward the body, makes contact with the chin.

favour [*or* **be in favour of**]: *v.* to support; advocate. *He **favours** the liberal candidate in this election.*

SIGN #2: **'S'** hands, palms toward the body, are held at chest level with the left slightly above the right. Then the right is brought upward to strike the left.

(do someone a) favour: *v.* to perform an act out of kindness. *Do me a **favour** and water my plants while I am away.*

SIGN #3: Right **'ONE'** hand is held with tip of forefinger touching tip of nose. The wrist then twists counter-clockwise as the hand moves downward/forward and the forefinger ends up pointing downward/forward at a leftward angle.

favourite [*also spelled* **favorite**]: *adj.* regarded with special preference or liking. *Ice cream is my **favourite** dessert.*

SIGN #1: Tip of bent midfinger of right **'BENT MIDFINGER 5'** hand, palm toward the body, is tapped lightly against the chin.

OR

SIGN #2: Back of right **'S'** hand is brought up toward the mouth, kissed, and moved downward at a forward angle.

SIGN #3 [PRAIRIE]: Left arm is folded in front of the chest while right **'S'** hand, palm down, is brought back to strike the left arm firmly near the elbow.

fax: *v.* to send a message or document by a telegraphic facsimile system. *I will fax you about our change in plans.*

SIGN: **FAX** is fingerspelled in a forward direction. This is a fluid motion ending up with the **'x'** in a horizontal position with palm left. (**FAX**, *n.,* is fingerspelled with the hand in a fixed position.)

fear: *n.* fright caused by real or potential danger or pain. *Many children have a great fear of darkness.*

SIGN #1: Horizontal **'5'** hands, palms toward the body, are held out from either side of the chest, and are moved vigorously toward each other, stopping abruptly in front of the chest as the face registers an expression of fear.
SAME SIGN—**fearful**, *adj.*

fear: *n.* fright caused by real or potential danger or pain. *I have a great fear of what might happen if we do that.*

SIGN #2: Vertical **'5'** hands are held parallel in front of the chest with palms facing forward and are simultaneously waved slightly outward and downward as the face registers an expression of fear. (This sign is used specifically to indicate fear of God or an authority figure, fear of someone perceived as strict or rough, or fear of something that might happen in the future.)
SAME SIGN—**fearful** *adj.,* in this context.

feasible: See **possible.**

feast: *n.* a large, sumptuous meal. *The cook prepared a great feast for the guests.*

SIGN: **'FLAT O'** hands, palms facing the body, are circled alternately toward the mouth.

feather: *n.* a single unit of a bird's plumage. *He added a feather to his native costume.*

SIGN: Fingerspell **FEATHER**.

feature: *n.* a characteristic; prominent or distinctive part of something. *Facial expression is an important feature of ASL.*

NOTE—Because the syntax of ASL is so different from that of English, the concept **feature** can be conveyed in a multitude of ways in ASL depending on the specific context. Often the actual feature(s) of something will be discussed without any need for a general sign meaning **feature**. The sample sentence in ASL is: *ASL...FACIAL-EXPRESSION IMPORTANT.*

February: *n.* the second month of the year. *February is the shortest month of the year.*

SIGN: Fingerspell **FEB**.

feces: *n.* solid bodily waste that is discharged from the bowels through the anus; excrement. *The doctors analyzed the feces in the lab.*

SIGN: Horizontal left **'A'** (or **'EXTENDED A'**) hand is held in a fixed position with palm facing backward/rightward. Thumb of horizontal right **'EXTENDED A'** hand is inserted in the base of the left hand. The right hand is then lowered from this position. Motion is repeated.

fed up: *adj.* having reached the end of one's patience; having had enough; annoyed. *I am fed up with your constant complaining.*

SIGN: Right **'B'** hand, palm down, is held limp-wristed in front of the chest and is flicked upward from the wrist so that it strikes the underside of the chin with fingers pointing left.

federal: *adj.* pertaining to the central government of a federation. *The Post Office is controlled by the federal government in Ottawa.*

SIGN: Vertical right **'F'** hand is held very close to the right side of the forehead with palm facing forward. The wrist then rotates so that the palm faces the head and the joined tips of the thumb and forefinger touch the forehead.

fee: *n.* a payment for services rendered. *Interpreters are paid a fee for their services.*

SIGN: Fingerspell **FEE**.

feeble: *adj.* lacking physical strength; weak. *The elderly man is becoming more **feeble** each year.*

SIGN: Fingertips of right **'5'** hand, palm toward the body, are placed on upturned palm of left **'EXTENDED B'** hand. Then the fingers buckle so that the hand is transformed into a **'CLAWED 5'** shape.

feeble-minded: *adj.* mentally deficient; lacking in intelligence. *He laughed at her **feeble-minded** excuse.*

SIGN: Fingertips of right vertical **'CROOKED 5'** hand, palm toward the face, remain on the forehead as the fingers buckle to form a **'CLAWED 5'** shape. Motion is repeated.

feed: *v.* to give food to. *I have to **feed** my cat his dinner.*

SIGN #1: Left **'CONTRACTED B'** hand is held palm-up in front of the left side of the upper chest. Right **'CONTRACTED B'** hand is held with palm toward the body and fingertips on the lips. The right hand then drops forward/downward to a position slightly closer to the chest than the left hand. The hands then simultaneously bounce forward/downward a couple of times. ❖

OR

SIGN #2: Vertical right **'FLAT O'** hand, palm forward and slightly leftward, is held behind the left **'STANDARD BASE'** hand and the heel of the right hand strikes the left hand a couple of times as the hands briskly move together and apart twice. ❖

feedback: *n.* information given in response to an inquiry or survey. *Have you received any **feedback** regarding the new working hours?*

SIGN #1: Tip of little finger of right **'I'** hand, palm toward the face, is placed on the right side of the forehead and is drawn forward/upward a brief distance. ALTERNATE SIGN—**inform**

feedback: *n.* a high-pitched squeal from the sound component of a microphone/amplifier system. *We are receiving **feedback** from this microphone.*

SIGN #2: Thumbtips of vertical **'MODIFIED 5'** hands are held near either ear, palms facing forward but angled slightly toward each other, as forearms are simultaneously thrust outward/forward and back at least twice. (To indicate that there is feedback coming from a hearing-aid specifically, vertical right **'E'** hand is held by the right ear with palm facing forward, and is wobbled rightward.)

feel: *v.* to have a physical sensation. *I can **feel** the vibration from the music.*

SIGN #1: Tip of middle finger of right **'BENT MIDFINGER 5'** hand, palm toward the body, is brushed upward and off the chest at least twice. (This sign may also be used for **feel** *v.*, when it means to **sense, have a hunch** or **suspect**.) SAME SIGNS—**feeling**, *n.*, and **feelings**, *n.*

feel: *v.* to have an emotional sensation. *I **feel** hurt when you insult me.*

SIGN #2: Tip of middle finger of right **'BENT MIDFINGER 5'** hand, palm toward the body, is brushed upward and off the chest.

feel: *v.* to touch; examine by touching or handling. *I want you to **feel** this fabric.*

SIGN #3: **'FLAT O'** hands are held slightly apart with palms up. Then the fingers are slid across the thumbs a few times, thus alternating between **'FLAT O'** and **'OFFSET O'** hands.

feel like: *v.* to have an inclination toward doing something. *I **feel like** watching TV.*

SIGN: Tip of middle finger of right **'BENT MIDFINGER 5'** hand, palm toward the body, touches the chest. The wrist then rotates to turn the palm forward/leftward as the hand takes on a **'Y'** shape and wobbles from side to side.

feet: *n.* the parts of the legs below the ankle joints. *My **feet** are cold!*

SIGN #1: Fingerspell **FEET**.

feet: *n.* the plural of **foot** in reference to a measurement of 12 inches. *How many feet of cord will you need to tie up this bundle?*

SIGN #2: Fingerspell **FEET**.

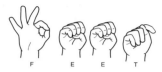

feign: *v.* to pretend. *Do not feign innocence; we all know you're guilty.*

SIGN: Side of forefinger of right **'ONE'** hand, palm facing leftward/forward, is lightly brushed forward/downward twice on the right cheek, forefinger either remaining upright or bending slightly to become a **'BENT ONE'**.

feline: *adj.* related to or belonging to the cat family. *All feline species are predators.*

SIGN: Right **'FLAT F'** hand, palm facing left, is held upright with thumb and forefinger near the right corner of the mouth. Then the hand is drawn backwards several times.

fellow: *n.* a man or boy. *Who is that fellow in the red shirt and blue jeans?*

NOTE—For **fellow** meaning a *young male*, see **boy**; for **fellow** meaning an *adult male*, see **man**. (Whereas in English **fellow** may have the connotation of someone in the same position or at the same level, this is not the case in ASL.)

fellowship: *n.* a sharing of the same interests and activities. *We enjoy the fellowship that exists within the Deaf Community.*

SIGN: **'F'** hands with thumbs and forefingers interlocked, and palms facing each other, are moved in a complete circle in front of the body using a counter-clockwise motion. (When **FELLOWSHIP** means a scholarship or a sum of money awarded for advanced study, the word is fingerspelled.)

felony: *n.* a serious crime. *Arson is a felony, punishable by lengthy imprisonment.*

SIGN: Fingerspell **FELONY**.

female: *adj.* characteristic of a woman. *Is the cat male or female?*

SIGN: Thumbtip of right **'EXTENDED A'** hand, palm left, is placed on the right cheek and is stroked forward/downward. Motion may be repeated. (This sign is used for animals and for young female persons. For *adult female persons*, see **woman**.)

fence: *n.* a post and rail or wire barrier that encloses an area. *I built a fence around my yard.*

SIGN: Horizontal **'4'** hands are held with palms facing the body and tips of fingertips very close, perhaps touching. The hands are then drawn apart.

fencing: *n.* the sport of fighting with swords. *During the 18th century, fencing was a common method of dueling.*

SIGN: Horizontal right **'COVERED A-INDEX'** hand, palm facing left, is twisted clockwise from the wrist with a flourish, then jabbed forward as if brandishing a sword.

Ferris wheel: *n.* a large wheel from which seats are freely suspended for passengers to ride in for their amusement. *County fairs usually have a Ferris wheel.*

SIGN: **'CLAWED V'** hands, palms down, are held apart in front of the chest, one hand held higher than the other. The hands are then circled forward.

ferry: *n.* a vessel used to transport vehicles and passengers across a body of water as a regular service. *We took the earliest ferry from Sydney to Port aux Basques.*

SIGN: **'CROOKED EXTENDED B'** hands, palms facing each other at a slight angle, are cupped together to form the hull of a boat. Then they are moved up and down in a bobbing motion. (**FERRY** is frequently fingerspelled.)

(be) fertile: *v.* to have the nutrients necessary for abundant plant growth (said of soil). *The soil in that part of the country is fertile.*

SIGN #1: Left **'BENT EXTENDED B'** hand is held in a fixed position with palm up. Palm of horizontal right **'EXTENDED B'** (or **'BENT EXTENDED B'**) hand faces left but is slanted slightly upward and toward the body as the fingers are brushed upward against the backs of the fingers of the left hand at least twice. Next, right **'FLAT O'** hand is thrust upward through left **'C'** hand as fingers open into a **'CONTRACTED 5'** hand. (ASL CONCEPT—**easy - grow**.) ALTERNATE REGIONAL SIGN—**easy** #2, for the first part of this sign.

(be) fertile: *v.* to be capable of becoming pregnant. *The fact that she had ten children would indicate that she was fertile.*

SIGN #2: **'A'** hands, palms down, are held slightly apart, and are brought down firmly in front of the chest. Next, horizontal **'5'** hands are held apart with palms facing each other but slanted slightly toward the body. The hands are then moved together so that the fingers interlock. (ASL CONCEPT—**can - pregnant**.)

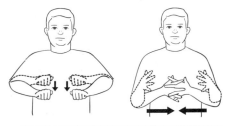

festival: *n.* an occasion for celebrating and/or feasting. *We enjoyed ourselves at the festival.*

SIGN: Vertical **'COVERED T'** hands are held at either side of the head, palms facing each other, and are swung in small circles above the shoulders.

fetch: *v.* to go after and bring back. *Please fetch my slippers for me.*

SIGN: **'EXTENDED B'** hands are held parallel with palms up in front of the left side of body. Then they are simultaneously moved to the right.

fetus [*also spelled* **foetus**]: *n.* the embryo of a mammal in the later stages of development prior to birth. *The ultrasound showed the fetus was normal.*

SIGN: Horizontal left **'FLAT C'** hand is held just in front of the abdomen with palm facing the body but angled rightward slightly. Right **'FLAT O'** hand is held palm down just above the left hand. Then the bunched fingers of the right hand are brought down and inserted into the opening at the top of the left hand. Next, fingers of palm-up right **'BENT EXTENDED B'** hand point leftward as they rest on rightward-pointing fingers of palm-up left **'BENT EXTENDED B'** hand. The arms are simultaneously moved from side to side as if rocking a baby in one's arms. (ASL CONCEPT—**inside-abdomen - baby**.) **FETUS** may be fingerspelled.

feud: *n.* long and bitter hostility between two individuals or groups; a long-standing quarrel. *The feud between the two families lasted for ten years.*

SIGN: Horizontal **'BENT ONE'** hands, palms toward each other and forefingers pointing toward each other, are drawn firmly apart as the head turns slightly but abruptly to the right and the face appears obstinate.

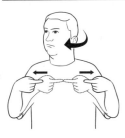

fever: *n.* an abnormally high body temperature. *I was sick yesterday with a fever and nausea.*

SIGN: Fingerspell **FEVER**.

(a) few: *adj.* a small number. *He has won a few awards for his ASL poetry.*

SIGN #1: Right **'A'** hand, palm up, is moved slightly forward/rightward as each fingertip gradually slides forward off the thumbtip to create a **'4'** hand.

few: *adj.* hardly any; not many. *He has won few awards for his ASL poetry.*

SIGN #2: Tip of forefinger of the right **'COVERED T'** hand, palm toward the face, is held in front of the nose and the thumb is flicked out, thus forming an **'A-INDEX'** hand.

fiancé (male)/**fiancée** (female): *n.* a person who is engaged to be married. *She and her fiancé will set a wedding date soon.*

SIGN: Right **'E'** hand, palm down, is circled clockwise above the left **'STANDARD BASE'** hand and placed on the ring finger of the left hand.
REGIONAL VARIATION—**engaged** #2

fiasco: *n.* complete chaos; humiliating failure. *The wedding ceremony was a fiasco because so many things went wrong.*

SIGN: Left **'V'** hand is held with palm up and extended fingers pointing forward at a slight rightward angle while right **'V'** hand is held just above the left hand with palm facing leftward at a downward/forward angle and extended fingers pointing leftward/upward at a slightly forward angle. Right hand is brought down to strike left hand, then bounces forward in arc formation as it takes on a **'K'** shape and the wrist rotates to turn the palm leftward at a downward angle.
ALTERNATE SIGN—**chaos**

fib: *v.* to tell an unimportant, harmless lie. *He fibs when he says he is only 39 years old.*

SIGN: Vertical right **'B'** hand, palm left, slides firmly leftward across the chin.

fibre [*also spelled* **fiber**]: *n.* a substance such as bran which is essential in one's daily diet. *A healthy diet should be low in fat and high in fibre.*

SIGN #1: Fingerspell **FIBRE** or **FIBER**.

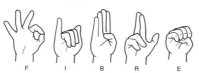

fibre [*also spelled* **fiber**]: *n.* a strand of material such as cotton or nylon. *This fabric consists of a blend of silk and wool fibres.*

SIGN #2: **'I'** hands are held with tips of little fingers touching each other and palms facing the body. The hands are then drawn apart twice.

fickle: *adj.* very changeable in one's affections. *She has so many boyfriends that most people consider her very fickle.*

SIGN: Left **'V'** hand is held with palm facing upward and angled toward the body while tip of forefinger of vertical right **'V'** hand, palm forward at a leftward-facing angle, touches the centre of the forehead. The right hand is lowered to make contact with the left hand so that the heels of the hands are touching. The right wrist then rotates 180 degrees forward while the left wrist rotates 180 degrees backward so that the right hand ends up with palm facing upward and the palm of the left hand faces downward/rightward, the hands still held together at the heels. Movement is repeated several times.

fiction: *n.* literary works of the imagination; not factual. *Robertson Davies was a master of fiction.*

SIGN #1: Side of forefinger of right **'ONE'** hand, palm facing leftward/forward, is lightly brushed forward/downward twice on the right cheek, forefinger either remaining upright or bending slightly to become a **'BENT ONE'**.

OR

SIGN #2: Right **'4'** hand is held upright in front of forehead with palm facing leftward. The hand is then moved forward (at a slight downward angle) in short jerky motions until the fingers are pointing forward.

field: *n.* an area of open land. *The farmer expects his grain field to produce a bumper crop.*

SIGN #1: **'FLAT O'** hands are held slightly apart with palms up. Then the fingers are slid across the thumbs a few times, thus alternating between **'FLAT O'** and **'OFFSET O'** hands. Next, horizontal right **'5'** hand is held with palm down and fingers pointing forward. The hand then makes a wide arc leftward as it inscribes a circle in front of the body.
(ASL CONCEPT—**land - area**.)

field: *n.* a specialized area of human activity or knowledge. *Linguistics is a fascinating field.*

SIGN #2: Left **'B'** hand is held in a fixed position with palm facing right and fingers pointing forward. Right **'B'** hand, palm facing left, and fingers pointing forward, is positioned on top of the left hand and firmly moved forward.

fierce: *adj.* violent; savage. *They have several fierce dogs guarding their property.*

SIGN #1: Horizontal **'CLAWED 5'** hands are held with the right slightly above the left and palms facing. The sign is accompanied by a fierce facial expression with the teeth bared. (This sign is appropriate only when referring to a *dog*. For a sign with a more general application, see **fierce** #2.)

fierce: *adj.* wild; terrible; severe. *There was a fierce storm last night.*

SIGN #2: Right **'COVERED 8'** hand, palm facing left, is held upright at about shoulder level. The hand is then thrust backward as the middle finger and thumb flick apart to form a **'MODIFIED 5'** hand.

fierce: *adj.* intense. *The competition was fierce.*

SIGN #3: Right **'CLAWED 5'** hand is held with fingertips touching or close to the lips. The wrist then rotates briskly causing the palm to face leftward/downward.

fifteen: *n.* See NUMBERS, p. LXI.

fifty: *n.* See NUMBERS, p. LXII.

fight: *v.* to struggle physically against someone. *Go outside if you want to fight.*

SIGN #1: Vertical **'S'** hands, palms originally facing each other, are moved vigorously downward so that they come to rest side by side with palms facing down.

fight: *v.* [PRAIRIE]: Vertical **'I'** hands, palms facing the body, are tapped briskly against one another at least twice so that the little fingers meet with each movement.

SIGN #2 [PRAIRIE]: Vertical **'I'** hands, palms facing the body, are tapped briskly against one another at least twice so that the little fingers meet with each movement.

fight: *v.* to struggle for a cause. *Deaf people all over the world are determined to fight for their rights.*

SIGN #3: Vertical **'S'** hands, palms originally facing each other, are moved vigorously downward so that they come to rest side by side with palms facing down.

fight: *v.* to argue; quarrel. *They fight about the silliest things.*

SIGN #4: **'BENT ONE'** hands, palms toward the chest, forefingers pointing toward each other, are simultaneously moved up and down from the wrists.

figure: *n.* the human form, especially the *female* body shape. *She has a nice figure.*

SIGN #1: **'A'** hands, palms facing each other, are held parallel just above shoulder level. Then they are simultaneously curved downward to outline the shape of an hourglass.

figure: *n.* a person who is thought of in a certain way, especially a well-known individual. *Pierre Trudeau is an interesting figure in Canadian history.*

SIGN #2: **'K'** hands are held parallel at about shoulder level with palms down and are simultaneously lowered.

figure: *n.* a number. *He has a good memory for facts and figures.*

SIGN #3: **'MODIFIED O'** hands are positioned so that the bunched fingertips of each hand are touching those of the other hand. Initially, left palm faces upward but is angled slightly toward the body while right palm faces downward but is angled forward slightly. Fingertips maintain contact as the hands then twist, thus reversing the palm orientations.

figure: *n.* a diagram. *Please look at Figure #2 on page 94 of your text book.*

SIGN #4: Left **'EXTENDED B'** hand is held in a fixed position with palm facing right and fingers pointing forward/upward as vertical right **'C'** hand is held against the right cheek with palm forward at a slight leftward angle. Right hand is then moved forward/downward and placed firmly against the left palm. (This sign may be followed by another sign which specifies exactly what kind of **figure** is being referred to, *i.e.*, a **bar graph**.)

figure: *v.* a colloquial term meaning to conclude; predict; believe. *I figure he will ask her to marry him tonight.*

SIGN #5: Tip of middle finger of right **'BENT MIDFINGER 5'** hand, palm toward the body, is brushed upward and off the chest at least twice as the hand makes small circular-like movements in a clockwise direction.

figure out: *v.* to calculate; solve; come to understand. *Can you figure out approximately how much the trip will cost?*

SIGN: **'K'** hands are held, right above left, somewhere between horizontally and vertically, left palm facing right and right palm facing left yet both palms are angled slightly toward the body. The two hands brush against one another a few times as the right hand repeatedly moves leftward slightly, and the left hand moves rightward.

figure skating: *n.* a form of skating in which the skater performs intricate patterns and difficult maneuvers. *Canada has produced several world champions in figure skating.*

SIGN: **'BENT MIDFINGER 5'** hands, left palm up and right palm down, are positioned so the right is above the left with midfingers pointing toward each other. Then the hands are simultaneously moved forward/rightward with the midfinger of the right hand jiggling rapidly as the signer's lips are pursed to allow a thin stream of air to be released between them.

file: *v.* to put papers in order. *My secretary will file all my business letters.*

SIGN #1: Horizontal left **'EXTENDED B'** hand is held in a fixed position with palm facing the body and fingers pointing rightward. Right **'BENT EXTENDED B'** hand, palm down, is held with fingers just in front of the left hand and pointing downward. The right hand is then moved forward in a series of small arcs. Alternatively, the right hand may move straight forward.

OR

SIGN #2: Vertical left **'EXTENDED B'** hand is held in a fixed position with palm facing right while the edge of the right **'EXTENDED B'** hand, palm toward the body, is inserted firmly between the left forefinger and middle finger.

file: *v.* to apply (for a legal judgment). *He plans to file for divorce.*

SIGN #3: Extended fingers of right **'V'** hand are brought downward on either side of forefinger of left **'ONE'** hand, which is held upright and fixed, palm facing right.

file: *v.* to complete and submit a legal document. *My accountant will file my income tax return for me.*

SIGN #4: Fingertips of right **'FLAT O'** hand are slid from fingertips to heel of upturned left **'EXTENDED B'** hand. Next, fingertips of horizontal right **'BENT EXTENDED B'** hand are placed on the back of the left **'STANDARD BASE'** hand. The right hand then moves forward as the fingers straighten to form an **'EXTENDED B'** hand. (ASL CONCEPT—**fill out - send**.)

file: *n.* a document or a unit of information kept on paper, film or on a computer disk. *Please bring me the file on Deaf Culture.*

SIGN #5: Fingerspell **FILE**. (After a particular file has been introduced through fingerspelling, it may thereafter be signed as in **file #2**.) When **FILE** means an organized *collection* of files, it is fingerspelled, e.g., *I will look through the F-I-L-E to see if I can find the folder on Deaf Culture.*

F I L E

file: *n.* a hand tool with a ridged surface used for shaping and smoothing (often metal) objects. *She used a file to remove the small bumps from the metal rod.*

SIGN #6: **'MODIFIED G'** hands are held close together with palms forward and tips of fore-fingers and thumbs of one hand touching those of the other. The hands are then drawn apart. Next, the object being filed is repre-sented by the left **'STANDARD BASE'** hand as the extended fingers of the horizontal right **'U'** hand, palm left, move back and forth against the fingertips of the left hand. (ASL CONCEPT—**bar - rub**.)

(nail) file: *n.* a hand tool used for shaping and smoothing the fingernails. *The manicurist uses a nail file to shape fingernails.*

SIGN #7: Left **'OPEN A'** is held in a fixed position with palm right. The right hand may take on one of a variety of shapes as it moves back and forward several times beside the left hand as if filing the fingernails of the left hand.

fill: *v.* to make (something) full. *The service station attendant will fill my tank.*

SIGN #1: Left **'S'** hand is held, not in a tight fist but loosely, with palm down but slanted slightly rightward. Right **'EXTENDED A'** hand, palm down but slanted rightward as well, is positioned above and to the right of the left hand. The right hand then moves downward/leftward so that the extended thumb is inserted into the opening at the top of the left hand. (Signs vary according to 'what' is being filled and 'how' it is being filled.)

fill: *v.* to make (something) full. *I will fill the bathtub with warm water.*

SIGN #2: **'EXTENDED B'** hands are held parallel with palms down and fingers pointing forward. The hands are then raised simultaneously to a higher level. (This sign is used for relatively *large* surfaces.)

fill out: *v.* to complete a form. *Did you fill out the evaluation form?*

SIGN #1: Fingertips of right **'FLAT O'** hand are slid from fingertips to heel of upturned horizontal left **'EXTENDED B'** hand.

fill out: *v.* to become larger, rounder or fuller. *Joe is very thin but he will fill out when he regains his health.*

SIGN #2: The signer's cheeks are puffed out as horizontal **'CROOKED 5'** hands, palms toward the body, are held apart in front of the chest and are simultaneously moved apart.

filling: *n.* a substance inserted into the prepared cavity of a tooth. *The dentist told me that I needed one new filling.*

SIGN: The tip of the middle finger of the right **'BENT MIDFINGER 5'** hand, palm down, is inserted into the opening in the top of the horizontal left **'S'** hand. The right hand is then raised, changed to a **'5'** hand, and slapped palm-downward on the top of the left hand.

film: *v.* to use a camera in the photographing of a movie or videotape. *The crew will **film** the performance.*

SIGN #1: Horizontal right **'3'** hand, palm facing left, is moved back and forth a couple of times from the wrist. ❖

film: *n.* a motion picture; movie. *We are making a **film** about Deaf Culture in Canada.*

SIGN #2: Horizontal left **'5'** hand is held with fingers pointing forward/rightward and palm facing rightward/backward. Vertical right **'5'** hand is held with heel in palm of left hand and is shaken back and forth. This is a wrist movement.

ALTERNATE SIGN—**movie** #2

film: *n.* a strip of cellulose used to make photographic negatives or movies. *We bought several rolls of **film** to take pictures at the party.*

SIGN #3: Fingerspell **FILM**.

filthy: *adj.* very dirty. *I fell in the mud and now my clothes are **filthy**.*

SIGN: Right **'S'** hand is held under chin with palm down. The fingers then flick out forcefully, forming a **'CONTRACTED 5'** hand with the fingers pointing leftward. Facial expression must convey displeasure.

ALTERNATE SIGN—**dirty**

final: *adj.* occurring at the end; last. *Are you ready for **final** exams?*

SIGN: Little finger of right horizontal **'I'** hand, palm facing the body and angled leftward slightly, is used to strike downward against little finger of left horizontal **'I'** hand, of which the palm faces the body at a rightward angle.

finally: *adv.* lastly, at the end; in conclusion. *Finally, her report gave details of the club's expenditures.*

SIGN #1: Little finger of right horizontal **'I'** hand, palm facing the body and angled leftward slightly, is used to strike downward against little finger of left horizontal **'I'** hand, of which the palm faces the body at a rightward angle.

finally: *adv.* at last; eventually; after a long time. *They **finally** settled the free trade agreement.*

SIGN #2: Tips of forefingers of **'ONE'** hands touch either side of the forehead. The hands then move outward/forward as the wrists rotate to turn the hands so that the palms face forward and the forefingers point upward.

finance: *n.* money management. *It might be helpful to take a course in **finance** before incorporating our business.*

SIGN #1: Back of right **'CONTRACTED B'** (or **'BENT EXTENDED B'**) hand, palm up, is tapped two or three times on upturned palm of left **'EXTENDED B'** hand.

SAME SIGN—**financial**, *adj.*

finance: *v.* to provide funds for; pay for. *How will you **finance** your new car?*

SIGN #2: Horizontal left **'EXTENDED B'** hand is held with palm facing upward/rightward. Right **'ONE'** hand is held with tip of forefinger on left palm. The right forefinger is then flicked forward. ❖

find: *v.* to discover by chance. *Did you **find** the wallet you lost?*

SIGN #1: Right **'OPEN F'** hand is held. The hand then moves upward as the thumb and forefinger are closed to form an **'F'** hand with palm facing forward.

find: *v.* to conclude after due consideration. *Do you think the jury will **find** her guilty as charged?*

SIGN #2: **'F'** hands, with palms facing each other, are held apart in front of chest and are simultaneously lowered.

fine: *adj.* very good; quite well. *I feel **fine** now that my fever is gone.*

SIGN #1: The head nods while the tip of the thumb of the vertical right **'5'** hand, palm facing left, is tapped a couple of times against the chest. (Alternatively, the right hand may move forward in a slight arc formation.)

fine: *adj.* very thin; slender. *The wire is so **fine** that we can hardly see it.*

SIGN #2: Joined thumb and forefinger of right **'CLOSED X'** (or **'F'**) hand, palm toward the body, are held against the mouth and the hand is drawn downward as if drawing a straight line down the chin.

fine: *n.* an amount of money ordered to be paid as a penalty. *I got caught speeding and now I have to pay a $75.00 **fine**.*

SIGN #3: Forefinger of horizontal right **'X'** hand, palm toward the body at a leftward-facing angle, is brought down smartly across the palm of the horizontal left **'EXTENDED B'** hand, which is facing rightward but angled toward the body.

finger: *n.* one of the digits of the human hand, excluding the thumb. *What happened to your **finger**?*

SIGN: Tip of forefinger of horizontal right **'ONE'** hand, palm down, is used to tap on whichever digit is being referred to in the context. (A separate sign is not always accorded **finger**. In certain contexts, it is incorporated in the sign for the verb and/or another noun in the sentence, e.g., for the sample sentence: *ME CUT-ON-THIRD-**FINGER**-OF-LEFT-HAND*. Not only is the ASL sentence shorter, consisting as it does of only two signs, it also contains more information as it specifies precisely which finger is cut.)

fingernail: *n.* the hard plate covering the end joint of the finger. *My **fingernail** turned black after I shut the car door on it.*

SIGN: Left **'BENT ONE'** hand is held in a fixed position with palm down and forefinger pointing rightward/forward. Tip of forefinger of right **'BENT ONE'** hand, palm down, is tapped down a couple of times on the fingernail of the left forefinger. (A separate sign is not always accorded **fingernail**. In certain contexts, it is incorporated in the sign for the verb or an adjective which describes it.)

fingerprints: *n.* an inked impression of a person's fingerprints. *The suspect's **fingerprints** matched those on the murder weapon.*

SIGN: Fingertips of right **'5'** hand, palm down, touch down one at a time on the upturned palm of the left **'5'** hand, beginning with the little finger and ending with the forefinger.

fingerspell: *v.* to use a manual alphabet. *Can you **fingerspell** that long word?*

SIGN: **'BENT 5'** hand, palm downward/forward and fingers pointing forward, is moved rightward with fingers fluttering.

finish: *v.* to complete; bring to an end. *The project is scheduled to **finish** in five years.*

SIGN: Vertical **'5'** hands, palms facing the body, are held at chest level, and swung outward, away from the body so that the palms face down.
ALTERNATE SIGN—**complete** #1

fire: *n.* a burning mass. *The **fire** destroyed the house.*

SIGN #1: Vertical **'5'** hands with palms facing body, are simultaneously moved upward with fingers fluttering.

fire: *v.* to dismiss from a job. *The foreman had to **fire** two workers.*

SIGN #2: Horizontal left **'S'** hand is held in a fixed position with palm facing the body at a slight rightward angle. Back of right **'BENT EXTENDED B'** hand, palm up, grazes the top of the left hand as it is firmly brought backward/leftward. (Handshapes for the left hand may vary.)

fire: *v.* to shoot a firearm. *When the woman began to shoot at innocent people, the police officer **fired** at her.*

SIGN #3: Horizontal right **'L'** hand represents a gun as it is held with palm left and forefinger pointing forward. The forearm then jerks backward slightly so that the forefinger points forward/upward as the thumb bends to form a **'BENT THUMB L'** hand. (Signs in this context may vary depending on what kind of firearm is being discharged. A different sign would be used for the firing of a rifle than the firing of a handgun.)

fire extinguisher: *n.* a portable canister with a nozzle used to put out a fire. *Every kitchen should have a **fire extinguisher** for use in an emergency.*

SIGN: Horizontal **'c'** hands are held, right on top of left, with the left palm facing right and the right palm facing left. The right hand is then raised straight upward. Next, the right hand changes to a **'CLOSED X'** shape as it is lowered to a horizontal position in front of the chest with palm facing leftward and wrist cupped in the left hand. As the right wrist bends, the hand swerves from side to side to give the impression of using a hose. (ASL CONCEPT—**canister - hose**.)

firefighter: *n.* a person who fights fires. *When Joey grows up, he wants to be a **firefighter**.*

SIGN #1: Vertical right **'C-INDEX'** hand, palm facing left, is tapped a couple of times against the middle of the forehead.

SIGN #2 [ATLANTIC/ONTARIO]: Vertical right **'F'** hand, palm facing left, is tapped a couple of times against the middle of the forehead.

fireplace: *n.* a recessed area at the bottom of a chimney used for making a fire; a hearth. *On a cold night I love to sit in front of the **fireplace**.*

SIGN: Fingers continually flutter as **'5'** hands, palms facing the body, are alternately circled upward and backward towards the body.

fireworks: *n.* a spectacle in which combustible materials are ignited to produce colourful showers of sparks. *On Canada Day, we have wonderful displays of **fireworks** all across the nation.*

SIGN: The signer looks skyward as **'S'** hands are held high, the right behind but touching the left, and the right palm facing downward at a leftward angle as the left palm faces downward at a rightward angle. The hands are then drawn apart to vertical positions. The sign is repeated several times. (Signs vary.)

firm: *adj.* not soft-hearted or indecisive. *They practice **firm** discipline with their children.*

SIGN #1: Vertical right **'CLAWED V'** hand, palm left, is raised abruptly so the crooked forefinger strikes the nose.
ALTERNATE SIGN—**strict** #2

(stand) firm: *adj.* determined; definite; resolute; unyielding. *Despite all the opposition to his plan, he **stood firm** in his decision to increase taxes.*

SIGN #2: Elbows are stuck out to the sides as **'S'** hands are held palms down, the right hand slightly to the right of and higher than the left hand. As the teeth clench, the hand moves downward, striking the left hand with force on the way down.
ALTERNATE SIGN—**strong**

firm: *adj.* solid; hard. *The ice on the river is not **firm** enough to skate on.*

SIGN #3: **'A'** hands are held palms down, right hand directly above the left. As the teeth clench, the right hands is lowered and strikes the back of the left hand with force. (Signs vary.)

firm: *n.* a company; business partnership. *He works for a legal **firm** in St. John's.*

SIGN #4: Wrist of vertical right **'B'** hand, palm facing forward/leftward, is brushed back and forth against wrist of left **'STANDARD BASE'** hand.
ALTERNATE SIGNS—**business** #2 or fingerspell **CO** as an abbreviation for **company**.

first: *adj.* coming before anyone/anything else. *I was first in line at the movie.*

SIGN #1: Left **'EXTENDED A'** hand is held horizontally with thumb up and palm facing rightward but slanted slightly toward the body. Tip of forefinger of right **'ONE'** hand moves at a leftward/backward angle until making contact with tip of left thumb. (Alternatively, the right hand takes the form of a **'BENT EXTENDED B'** hand and moves backward until the palm makes contact with the thumb of the left horizontal **'EXTENDED A'** hand.)
ALTERNATE SIGN—**first** #2

first: *adj.* before others in order. [For an explanation of ordinals, see NUMBERS, p. LIX.] *The first thing we have to do is clean this place.*

SIGN #2: Vertical **'ONE'** hand is held with palm forward and slanted leftward slightly. As the wrist twists, the hand turns so that the palm faces the chest.
ALTERNATE SIGN—**first** #1

first: *n.* in the winning position. *Hilda placed first in the track and field event last Saturday.*

SIGN #3: Horizontal right **'ONE'** hand, palm facing left, is drawn back sharply toward the body.

fish: *n.* an aquatic vertebrate. *He caught a fish.*

SIGN: Horizontal **'B'** hands are held with the left directly behind the right. Left palm faces right and right palm faces left. The fingers of the left hand rest against the pulse in the right wrist. The right wrist then bends to make the hand wave from side to side. Alternatively, the right hand only may be used.

fisherman: *n.* a person who fishes for a livelihood or for sport. *In P.E.I., many people work as fishermen.*

SIGN: **'COVERED T'** hands, left palm facing right and right palm facing left, are positioned with the right hand slightly above and to the right of the left as if they were holding onto a fishing rod. Then both hands are shaken forward a few times, thus alternating between vertical and horizontal positions.

fishing: *n.* the activity of catching fish. *Fishing is a popular pastime in Canada.*

SIGN: **'COVERED T'** hands, left palm facing right and right palm facing left, are positioned with the right hand slightly above and to the right of the left as if they were holding onto a fishing rod. Then both hands are shaken forward a few times, thus alternating between vertical and horizontal positions.
SAME SIGN—**fish**, *v.*

fishy: *adj.* suspicious; questionable; odd. *There is something fishy about his business.*

SIGN: Right **'CROOKED ONE'** hand, palm toward the head, is held with tip of forefinger stroking downward slightly against the right temple, then bouncing away a short distance as the finger retracts to form an **'X'** hand. Movement is repeated at least once. A look of suspicion accompanies this sign. (**FISHY** may be finger-spelled.)

fist: *n.* a hand with the fingers clenched into the palm. *He waved his fist at me.*

SIGN: Right vertical **'S'** hand is held with the palm toward the body. In the context of the sentence featured here, the fist is shaken and the facial expression is probably menacing.

fit: *v.* to be of the right size and shape. *These jeans fit me perfectly.*

SIGN #1: Fingerspell **FIT**.
(**Fit** has a great variety of connotations in English.)

fit: *v.* to belong; be suited for. *Melissa does not really fit in this group.*

SIGN #2: **'CLAWED 5'** hands are held apart in front of the chest in an almost upright position but slanted slightly toward each other with palms facing the body. The forearms then move downward toward each other until the fingers mesh. ❖

fit: *n.* a sudden attack; seizure; convulsion. *His fits can be controlled with medication.*

SIGN #3: The signer's head jerks to one side repeatedly as if involuntarily while horizontal right **'CROOKED V'** hand, palm left but slanted toward the body, appears to flounder on the upturned palm of the left **'CROOKED 5'** hand. (Alternatively, **FIT**, in this context, may be fingerpelled. For **epileptic fit**, see **epilepsy**.)

fitting: *adj.* appropriate; proper; suitable. *It is very fitting that we should honour Dr. Mason this evening.*

SIGN: Right **'ONE'** hand, palm facing left, is held above left **'ONE'** hand, palm facing right, with forefingers pointing relatively forward. Then right hand is tapped at least twice on left hand.

five: *n.* See NUMBERS, p. LX.

fix: *v.* to repair. *Will you help me fix my car?*

SIGN #1: Left **'S'** hand is held in a fixed position with palm down. Right **'S'** hand is held just above the left hand with palm upward/toward the body. The right hand is moved in very small clockwise (from the signer's perspective) circles so that the back of it touches the back of the left hand with each rotation. (Signs may vary considerably.)

OR

SIGN #2: **'F'** hands, palms facing each other at a forward angle, are placed together with tips of thumbs and forefingers of each hand touching. The left hand remains steady while the right hand wobbles as the wrist twists back and forth slightly a few times.

OR

SIGN #3: Tip of forefinger of horizontal right **'CROOKED ONE'** hand is placed on the up-turned palm of the left **'EXTENDED B'** hand. The right hand then makes several small movements from side to side without dislodging the forefinger from its original position on the left palm.

fix: *v.* to adjust; rectify; solve (a problem). *Do not worry about that problem; I will fix it for you.*

SIGN #4: **FIX** is fingerspelled in a forward direction. This is a fluid motion ending up with the **'X'** in a horizontal position with palm left.

flabbergasted: *adj.* overcome with surprise and bewilderment. *He was flabbergasted when he heard the strange story.*

SIGN #1: Right **'S'** hand, palm facing left, is placed on the chin and is abruptly sprung open to form a **'CLAWED 3'** hand while the face registers an expression of shock. (Signs may vary considerably.)

OR

SIGN #2: **'S'** hands, palms facing each other, are placed in front of the eyes. As the hands move forward, they open to form **'C'** hands. Then they move back to their original positions as they close to form **'S'** shapes again. This sign is accompanied by a look of 'astonishment' or 'bewilderment'.

OR

SIGN #3: Tips of extended fingers of vertical right **'CLAWED V'** hand touch the mouth. The forearm then drops forward abruptly so that the palm is facing upward. This sign is accompanied by a look of 'astonishment' or 'bewilderment'.

OR

SIGN #4: Left **'CLAWED V'** hand is held palm down on the right **'CLAWED V'** hand which is held palm up. As the signer's lower jaw drops in amazement, the right hand also drops.

flag: *n.* a piece of cloth decorated with a design and used as an emblem or symbol. *The Canadian flag is red and white and depicts a maple leaf.*

SIGN: Right horizontally held **'EXTENDED B'** hand is waved left and right from the wrist while tip of forefinger of left **'ONE'** hand is held against right forearm.

flair: *n.* natural talent; ability. *She has a **flair** for drama.*

SIGN: Tips of joined forefinger and thumb of horizontal right **'F'** hand, palm toward the body. are brought purposefully up to strike the chin.

flame: *n.* burning gas which flickers from ignited combustible material. *The **flames** of the forest fire lit the night sky.*

SIGN: Fingers continually flutter as **'5'** hands, palms facing the body, are alternately circled upward and backward towards the body. (To refer to a 'single' flame, see **candle**.)

flammable: *adj.* easily set on fire. *Gasoline is a highly **flammable** substance.*

SIGN: Left **'BENT EXTENDED B'** hand is held in a fixed position with palm up. Palm of horizontal right **'EXTENDED B'** (or **'BENT EXTENDED B'**) hand faces left but is slanted slightly upward and toward the body as the fingers are brushed upward against the backs of the fingers of the left hand at least twice in a small circular motion. Next, vertical **'5'** hands with palms facing body, are simultaneously moved upward with fingers fluttering. (ASL CONCEPT—**easy - burn**.)

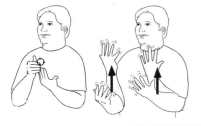

flash: *n.* a small bulb (in a camera) which produces a bright flash of light when being used indoors or in darkened areas. *Sometimes the **flash** on this camera does not work.*

SIGN #1: Right **'FLAT O'** hand is held upright, palm forward, and is opened to form a **'CONTRACTED 5'** hand, then returned to its original **'FLAT O'** handshape.

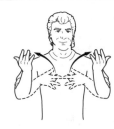

(news) flash: *n.* a short announcement about a recent news event. *I have a **news flash** for you!*

SIGN #2: Tips of midfingers of **'BENT MIDFINGER 5'** hands, palms toward the body, are placed slightly apart on the chest. The wrists then rotate forward as the hands move forward so that, while the palms still face the body, they are now angled upward slightly.

flashback: *n.* a transition to an earlier event. *The **flashback** in the film provided important information about the main character's past.*

SIGN: Right **'BENT V'** hand is held with palm backward and tip of middle finger just under/ to the right of the right eye. The hand is then moved to the right and back so that it is just above the right shoulder.

flashing light(s): *n.* sudden, repeating bursts of light (such as those that alert a Deaf person to the phone ringing or someone at the door). *The **flashing lights** told me that someone was at my front door.*

SIGN #1: With palm facing the body, the right hand is held upright as it rapidly opens and closes several times, thus alternating between a **'FLAT O'** and a **'CONTRACTED 5'** hand. (This sign may be made with palm facing upward if it is a table lamp that is flashing.)

flashing light(s): *n.* sudden, repeated bursts of coloured light (such as those emitted from an emergency vehicle). *I could see the **flashing lights** of the police cruiser.*

SIGN #2: Left hand grasps wrist of right **'CONTRACTED 5'** hand. Then right hand is twisted around to the left from the wrist several times to simulate the action of a flashing light.

flashlight: *n.* a portable, cylindrical, battery-powered lamp. *You should have a **flashlight** in case the power goes off.*

SIGN: Wrist of right **'CONTRACTED 5'** hand, palm down, is firmly grasped by the left hand. Then the right hand is moved from side to side several times. (Signs vary.)

flat: *adj.* having a horizontal, smooth, level, even surface. *Manitoba and Saskatchewan have a lot of **flat** land.*

SIGN #1: Vertical **'BENT EXTENDED B'** hands are held together, right in front of left, close to the chest with the right palm facing left and the left palm facing right. The left hand remains fixed while the right hand moves directly forward.

OR

SIGN #2: **'B'** hands are held side by side with palms down and fingers pointing forward. The hands are then drawn apart.

flat: *adj.* not bubbly due to exposure to the air. *This soft drink tastes flat.*

SIGN #3: Right **'EXTENDED B'** hand is held with fingertips just to the left of the mouth and pointing leftward/upward while the palm faces the body. The hand then moves quickly rightward past the mouth which is expelling air as if blowing the dust off of something. Next, tip of middle finger of right **'BENT MIDFINGER 5'** hand, palm toward the body, is tapped lightly against the chin a couple of times. (ASL CONCEPT—**no - flavour**.) FLAT in this context may be fingerspelled.

flat: *adj.* dull; not shiny or glossy. *This room needs a fresh coat of flat paint.*

SIGN #4: Fingerspell **FLAT**.

flat: *adj.* dull; boring; uninteresting. *His boring lecture on fish scales was rather flat.*

SIGN #5: Tip of forefinger of right **'ONE'** hand is placed against right side of nose, and is twisted half a turn clockwise. Facial expression must clearly convey boredom.
ALTERNATE SIGN—**bored/boring** #2

flat: *adv.* exactly; no more and no less. *He can walk from his house to mine in ten minutes flat.*

SIGN #6: Right **'EXTENDED B'** hand is held in front of the left side of the body with palm down and fingers pointing forward. The hand then firmly swivels rightward.

OR

SIGN #7: **'CLOSED X'** hands are held, right above left, with palms facing. The hands are then brought together sharply so that the joined thumbs and forefingers touch. Alternatively, the right hand sometimes moves in a small clockwise circle before making contact with the left hand.

flat rate: *n.* a set price. *The taxi driver charges a flat rate from the hotel to the airport.*

SIGN #8: Vertical **'F'** hands, palms facing forward, are brought together so the joined thumbs and forefingers touch each other. Next, **'Y'** hands are held parallel with palms down but slanted slightly forward. The hands are then firmly pushed a very short distance downward. Finally, right **'EXTENDED B'** hand is held in front of the left side of the body with palm down and fingers pointing forward and slightly leftward. The hand then firmly swivels rightward. (ASL CONCEPT—**price - stay - same**.)

flat shoes: *n.* footwear without raised heels. *I always wear flat shoes because I am on my feet all day.*

SIGN #9: Left **'EXTENDED B'** hand is held in a fixed position with palm down and fingers pointing forward and slightly rightward. Fingers of right **'EXTENDED B'** hand, palm up, point leftward as they are placed under the left palm and slid forward/rightward along the underside of the left hand and off.

flat tire: *n.* a deflated tire. *I had a flat tire on my way home from work yesterday.*

SIGN #10: Thumb of vertical right **'CONTRACTED C'** hand, palm forward/leftward, rests on left **'STANDARD BASE'** hand. The fingers of the right hand then close down to form a **'FLAT O'** shape.

flat-chested: *adj.* having a flat chest or very small breasts. *The model was flat-chested.*

SIGN #11: Right **'EXTENDED B'** hand is held with palm against upper right chest and fingers pointing leftward. The hand is then slid straight down the chest.

flatter: *v.* to praise insincerely, especially for the purpose of getting something in return. *The salesman tried to flatter the customer.*

SIGN: Fingertips of horizontal right **'EXTENDED B'** hand, palm facing left, brush back and forth a few times against the forefinger of the vertical left **'ONE'** hand which is held with palm forward/rightward. ❖

flavour [*also spelled* **flavor**]: *n.* a taste perceived in food or drink. *The shop sells ice cream in a variety of flavours.*

SIGN: Tip of middle finger of right **'BENT MIDFINGER 5'** hand, palm toward the body, is tapped lightly against the chin a couple of times.

flaw: *n.* an imperfection; defect. *The bridge collapsed because of flaws in its structural design.*

SIGN: Vertical right **'Y'** hand, palm toward the body, is firmly tapped on the chin.
REGIONAL VARIATION—**wrong** #2

flawless: *adj.* perfect. *The figure skater's performance was flawless.*

SIGN: Right **'F'** hand is held above and slightly to the right of the left **'F'** hand with palms facing. The hands then come together so that the joined thumb and forefinger of one hand strikes those of the other hand. (Alternatively, this sign may be made with **'K'** hands, the tips of the middle fingers coming together.)

flea: *n.* a very small, parasitic insect which lives on the skin of warm-blooded animals. *Can you see this flea on the dog's coat?*

SIGN: Fingerspell **FLEA**.

F   L   E   A

flee: *v.* to escape; run away from. *The criminal tried to flee to another country.*

SIGN: Forefinger of right **'ONE'** hand, palm facing leftward/forward, is placed upright between the first two fingers of the left **'EXTENDED B'** hand which is held palm down with fingers pointing rightward/forward. Then the right forefinger is vigorously thrust forward/rightward.

flesh: *n.* the soft part of the body of an animal or human. *The flesh of a deer is called venison.*

SIGN: Right **'OPEN F'** hand, palm facing away from the body, is brought down to grasp the skin between thumb and forefinger of horizontal left **'EXTENDED B'** hand whose palm faces body. Hands then make small back and forth movements together.

flexible: *adj.* adaptable; variable; easily bent. *My work schedule is very flexible.*

SIGN: Horizontal **'CONTRACTED B'** hands, palms toward the body, are held slightly apart with the fingers of one hand pointing toward those of the other. Then they are alternately moved back and forth several times from the wrists.

flight: *n.* a trip on an aircraft. *Airline personnel called to tell us the flight had been cancelled due to the storm.*

SIGN: Right **'COMBINED LY'** hand, palm downward and slightly forward, is moved a short distance forward twice. (Note that when referring to a scheduled airline flight with an assigned number, the word **FLIGHT** is fingerspelled. For **flight**, as it pertains to a flying animal, see **fly** #2.)

flight attendant: *n.* a person who manages the food services and other arrangements for passengers on an aircraft. *The flight attendant told us we would be landing in twenty minutes.*

SIGN: Right **'COMBINED LY'** hand, palm downward and slightly forward, is moved a short distance forward twice. Next, horizontal **'EXTENDED B'** hands are held apart at about shoulder level with palms up and fingers pointing outward, and are alternately moved from side to side. (ASL CONCEPT—**fly - serve**.) If the location has previously been specified as being on an aircraft, the first part of this sign is omitted.

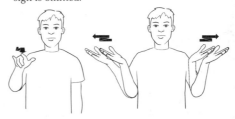

flippant: *adj.* impertinent; saucy; showing disrespect. *The accused teenager gave flippant replies to the questions he was asked in court.*

SIGN: Vertical right **'A-INDEX'** hand, palm facing left, quivers as thumb and forefinger are used to grasp skin of right cheek. Facial expression is an important feature of this sign.

flirt: *v.* to behave amorously without serious intentions. *She flirts with every man in the office.*

SIGN: **'5'** hands are held with palms down, thumbtips touching and fingers pointing forward as they flutter.

float: *v.* to rest on the surface without sinking. *The wooden plank floated on the river.*

SIGN: Right **'EXTENDED B'** hand is held with palm down and fingers pointing forward as it bobs forward. (Signs for **float** vary depending on 'who' or 'what' is floating.)

flock: *n.* a group of animals of one kind such as sheep or birds. *A flock of geese is flying south.*

SIGN #1: Horizontal **'5'** hands are held aloft in a staggered formation with the right slightly ahead of/to the right of the left, palms down and forefingers pointing forward/rightward. Together the hands move in a forward/rightward direction as the fingers flutter. (The same sign may be used for a *flock of sheep* but would be lowered so that it is formed just in front of the chest.)

flock: *v.* to come together; assemble. *Deaf people from all over the city flocked to the meeting.*

SIGN #2: Both **'BENT 5'** hands, palms facing forward, are moved forward and slightly downward from shoulder level, fingers wiggling. ❖

flood: *n.* the overflowing of a body of water. *The mountain streams create a flood every spring.*

SIGN: Forefinger of vertical right **'W'** hand, palm facing left, is tapped against the chin. Next, **'5'** hands, are held parallel with palms down and fingers pointing forward. The hands then rise simultaneously. (ASL CONCEPT— **water - rise.**) For **flood,** *v.,* only the second part of this sign is used.

floor: *n.* the lower surface of a room. *I washed and waxed the kitchen floor.*

SIGN: **'B'** hands are held side by side with palms down and fingers pointing forward. The hands are then drawn apart.

flop: *n.* a failure. *The movie was a flop.*

SIGN #1: Vertical right **'3'** hand is held with palm facing left and tip of thumb touching the nose. The hand then moves forward/downward in an arc formation as the wrist rotates to turn the hand to a horizontal position. A look of displeasure accompanies this sign. (**FLOP** may be fingerspelled).

flop: *v.* to fall loosely or heavily. *I was so tired that I just flopped on the bed and fell asleep immediately.*

SIGN #2: Left **'EXTENDED B'** hand is held in a fixed position with palm up and fingers pointing forward/rightward. Vertical right **'V'** hand is held with palm facing the upper chest. The right forearm then drops forward so that the hand lands palm up with a thud in the left palm. (Signs vary considerably depending on context.)

floss: *v.* to clean between one's teeth with a special silky thread. *You should floss several times daily.*

SIGN: Vertical **'CLOSED A-INDEX'** hands, palms facing each other, are alternatively moved back and forth as if using a length of dental floss to clean between the signer's teeth.

flour: *n.* finely ground, powdery grain. *How much flour do you need for this cake?*

SIGN: Fingerspell **FLOUR**.

flow: *v.* to move freely in a continuous stream. *The river flows through the valley.*

SIGN #1: **'5'** hands are held with palms down and fingers pointing forward, the left hand slightly ahead of the right. The hands then move simultaneously forward while the fingers flutter. ❖

flow: *n.* a smooth, natural way of expressing oneself. *His ASL vocabulary is pretty good but he needs to improve the **flow** of his finger-spelling.*

SIGN #2: **'FLAT O'** hands are held with palms up, the left hand slightly ahead of the right. The hands move simultaneously forward while the fingers slide across the thumbs to form **'A'** hands.

flower: *n.* the blossom of a plant. *My favourite **flower** is the Alberta wild rose.*

SIGN: Fingertips of right **'FLAT O'** hand are placed at right side of nose and then moved around to left side.

fluctuate: *v.* to vary in an irregular way; rise and fall like waves. *The price of gas **fluctuated** a lot this year.*

SIGN: Vertical right **'EXTENDED B'** hand, palm forward, dips as it takes on a **'BENT EXTENDED B'** shape with palm down and then rises to its original position. The hand continues to move up and down in a wavy pattern to show fluctuation.
ALTERNATE SIGN—**vary**

fluent: *adj.* able to communicate in a language with ease. *These students are **fluent** in both French and Spanish.*

SIGN: Left **'EXTENDED B'** hand, palm facing right and fingers pointing upward/forward, is grasped by right **'OPEN A'** hand. Then right hand is pulled forward sharply and closed to form an **'A'** hand.
SAME SIGN—**fluency,** *n.*

fluid: *n.* any substance that has the capacity to flow, such as a liquid. *Sound waves set the **fluid** in the inner ear in motion.*

SIGN: Fingerspell **FLUID**.

F L U I D

flunk: *v.* a colloquial term meaning to fail (in one's school work). *If you do not study, you will **flunk** your exam.*

SIGN: Vertical left **'EXTENDED B'** hand is held in a fixed position with palm forward/rightward as vertical right **'F'** hand, with palm forward/leftward, is brought firmly backward/leftward against the palm of the left hand.

flurry: *n.* a light snowfall. *Snow **flurries** are forecast for tonight.*

SIGN: **'5'** hands are held parallel with palms forward at a slight downward/leftward angle. The arms move up and down a few times at a slight leftward angle as the fingers flutter.

flush: *v.* to show a rosy colour. *When the boys teased her, her face **flushed**.*

SIGN #1: Tip of forefinger of right **'ONE'** hand is stroked downward from lips to form an **'X'** hand, palm facing the body. Next, **'CROOKED L'** hands are brought upward to frame the eyes and cheeks. (ASL CONCEPT—**red - face.**)
ALTERNATE SIGN—**blush**

flush: *v.* to wash or rinse out with a sudden rush of water. *Several litres of water are required to **flush** a toilet.*

SIGN #2: Right **'S'** hand is held palm down. As the wrist rotates clockwise, the hand is turned so that the palm faces leftward. (Signs vary according to 'what' is being flushed and 'how' it is being flushed.)

fly: *v.* to travel in an airplane. *Steve often **flies** from Edmonton to Toronto.*

SIGN #1: Right **'COMBINED LY'** hand, palm downward and forward slightly, is thrust forward/upward. ❖

fly: *v.* to move through the air by flapping the wings (said of an animal). *Most birds can **fly**.*

SIGN #2: Horizontal **'EXTENDED B'** hands, palms down, are held parallel at about shoulder level as the arms flap to simulate the movement of wings in flight.

fly: *n.* a flying insect. *The fly came in through a hole in the screen door.*

SIGN #3: Fingerspell **FLY**.

fly: *n.* a flap at the front of a pair of pants concealing a zipper. *These jeans need a new fly.*

SIGN #4: **'COVERED T'** hands, palms toward the body, are held near the lower abdomen so that the right is above the left. Then the right is drawn upward to the waist to simulate the zipping of a fly. (**FLY** may be fingerspelled.) This sign can also mean 'TO *DO UP* A FLY'. For '*UNDO* A FLY', the action is reversed, that is, begun at waist level and lowered. To indicate that someone's fly is undone, the signer may just point to that individual's fly. For a fly which is buttoned or has other means of fastening, the sign shown here is inappropriate.

flyer [*also spelled* **flier**]: *n.* a pamphlet distributed (usually for advertising purposes). *We sent out flyers to let people know about our fundraising banquet.*

SIGN: **'ONE'** hands, palms down and fingers pointing forward, are placed side by side and are drawn apart, moved down, and brought together again to outline the printed page. Next, **'S'** hands, palms facing downward, are held slightly apart, with right in front of left. Right hand then strikes left hand and moves forward and back to strike it a second time. (ASL CONCEPT—**paper - advertise**.) FLYER may be fingerspelled.

foal: *n.* a young horse. *The foal was born last week.*

SIGN: Fingers of palm-up right **'BENT EXTENDED B'** hand point leftward as they rest on rightward-pointing fingers of palm-up left **'BENT EXTENDED B'** hand. The arms are simultaneously moved from side to side as if rocking a baby in one's arms. Next, thumbtip of right **'BENT EXTENDED U'** hand is placed on the right temple and the two extended fingers are simultaneously fluttered. (ASL CONCEPT—**baby - horse**.)

foam: *n.* a mass of froth, bubbles or suds on the surface of a liquid. *The beer has a lot of foam on it.*

SIGN #1: Horizontal left **'SPREAD C'**, palm right, appears to be holding onto a glass as the right **'SPREAD C'** is held palm down above the left hand and circled several times in a counter-clockwise direction as the fingers flutter. The signer's cheeks are puffed. (If the foam covers a larger surface as it might on an ocean wave, both hands are held palm down with fingers fluttering. The movement and amount of foam can be specified by varying the direction/speed of the sign as well as the size of the signing space, but the handshape generally remains constant.) FOAM may be fingerspelled.

foam: *n.* solid, spongy material used as insulation or to pad a hard surface. *I will put a sheet of foam under my sleeping bag.*

SIGN #2: Vertical **'FLAT C'** hands, palms forward, are held side by side and are drawn apart. (Signs vary depending on the size, shape, texture, location and use of the foam.) FOAM may be fingerspelled.

focus: *v.* to adjust an instrument producing an image so that the object being viewed is distinct and clearly defined. *A photographer will usually focus before taking a picture.*

SIGN #1: Vertical **'C'** hands are held together in front of the face, right hand in front of left, left palm facing right and right palm facing left. The left hand generally remains fixed as the right wrist alternately bends and straightens a couple of times to turn the palm downward, then leftward again.

focus on: *v.* to concentrate on. *The workshop will focus on bilingualism and biculturalism.*

SIGN #2: **'EXTENDED B'** hands are held to either side of the face with palms facing each other at a downward angle, thumbtips close to the cheekbones, and fingers pointing forward/upward. Wrists then bend to turn palms to face one another fully as the hands simultaneously move forward/downward to a point where they almost converge.
SAME SIGN—**focus**, *n.*, meaning **focal point** or **centre of attention**.

foe: *n.* an enemy or rival. *The warrior fought very hard against his foe.*

SIGN: Horizontal **'BENT ONE'** hands are held together, palms facing the body, and tips of forefingers almost touching. Then they are pulled apart with a short, firm motion.

fog: *n.* a cloud of mist or any substance that reduces visibility. *The fog made driving difficult.*

SIGN: Fingerspell **FOG**.

fold: *v.* to bend so that one part covers another. *I will help you fold the laundry.*

SIGN #1: **'EXTENDED B'** hands are held slightly apart with palms up and fingers pointing forward. The hands are then alternately turned inward so that the palms face downward as if actually folding clothing. Motion is repeated. (Signs vary considerably depending on 'what' is being folded and 'how' it is being folded.)

fold: *v.* a colloquial term meaning to fail or collapse. *The company will fold if business does not improve.*

SIGN #2: Fingers of **'CROOKED 5'** hands, palms down, interlock slightly and then drop down so that backs of fingers are almost touching.

folder: *n.* a file or case for holding loose documents. *The lawyer put the papers back into the folder.*

SIGN: Right horizontal **'EXTENDED B'** hand, palm up, is inserted, into the opening of the left **'FLAT C'** hand of which the palm is facing up. The motion is repeated.

folk: *n.* people of a particular group or class. *Our ancestors were all country folk.*

SIGN: Vertical **'K'** hands are held apart with palms forward but facing each other slightly, and are alternately circled backward.

folklore: *n.* traditional, unwritten stories about a particular group or region. *Native folklore has many beautiful legends.*

SIGN: Left **'CONTRACTED C'** (or **'OPEN 8'**) hand is held horizontally with palm facing right while right **'CONTRACTED C'** (or **'OPEN 8'**) hand is held upright with palm facing left. The hands are held close enough together to be loosely interlocked. They are then drawn apart, closed and returned several times, thus alternating between **'CONTRACTED C'** (or **'OPEN 8'**) and **'FLAT O'** (or **'8'**) shapes with each movement. Next, horizontal **'CONTRACTED B'** hands, right palm facing left and left palm facing right, are held up high to the right with the right hand extended so that it is higher and farther forward than the left. The hands are then simultaneously moved in a series of small arcs toward the chest.
(ASL CONCEPT—**stories - pass down**.)

folks *(informal):* *n.* the members of a family, especially parents. *Where do your folks live now?*

SIGN: Tips of the joined thumbs and forefingers of vertical **'F'** hands, palms facing each other at a forward angle, are placed together. The wrists then rotate outward, causing the hands to move apart and turn so that the tips of the little fingers come together and the palms are facing the body.

follow: *v.* to come/go after in the same direction. *Follow your leader to the campsite.*

SIGN #1: Horizontal left **'EXTENDED A'** hand is held with palm facing right while horizontal right **'EXTENDED A'** hand is held directly behind the left hand with palm facing right. Together, the hands are moved purposefully forward.

follow: *v.* to go by; to obey. *If you follow the manual, you should not have a problem.*

SIGN #2: Horizontal left **'EXTENDED A'** hand is held with palm facing right while horizontal right **'EXTENDED A'** hand is held directly behind the left hand with palm facing left. Together, the hands are moved purposefully forward/downward.

follow: *v.* to understand. *She found the lecture very difficult to follow.*

SIGN #3: Vertical right **'S'** hand, with knuckles near right side of forehead, is changed to a **'ONE'** hand as the forefinger is flicked upward.

(be) fond of: *v.* to have a liking for (someone). *They are fond of their daughter's boyfriend.*

SIGN #1: Horizontal right **'OPEN 8'** hand is held with palm toward the chest and tips of thumb and middle finger touching the centre of the chest. The hand then moves forward as the thumb and middle finger close to form an **'8'** hand.

ALTERNATE SIGN—**(be) fond of** #2

(be) fond of: *v.* to have a liking for (something). *I am fond of Italian food.*

SIGN #2: Back of right **'S'** hand is brought up toward the mouth, kissed, and moved downward at a forward angle. (Facial expression and duration of the 'kiss' indicates the extent of one's fondness.)

ALTERNATE SIGNS—**(be) fond of** #1 or **crazy** #3

fondle: *v.* to touch or stroke; caress. *The man fondled his wife.*

SIGN: Tip of middle finger of right **'BENT MIDFINGER 5'** hand, palm down, touches down on the back of the left **'STANDARD BASE'** hand. Then **'CROOKED 5'** hands are held parallel in front of the body with palms forward but slanted toward each other. The hands move downward in a waving motion as if fondling someone's body. (ASL CONCEPT—**touch - touch body.**) Sign choice depends on which part of the body is being fondled and how it is being done. It also depends on whether or not the fondling is desirable or forced upon a person.

font: *n.* style of type. *This font is very clear and easy to read.*

SIGN: Fingerspell **FONT**.

food: *n.* anything edible that provides nourishment. *What is your favourite food?*

SIGN: Right **'MODIFIED O'** hand, palm toward body, is brought upward to the mouth, and fingertips are tapped against lips.

fool: *n.* a stupid person; someone who does not have good judgement. *Only a fool puts aluminum in the microwave oven.*

SIGN #1: Fingerspell **FOOL**. (See also **stupid**.)

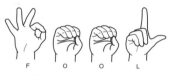

fool: *v.* to trick; deceive. *A magician tries to fool his audience.*

SIGN #2: Vertical right **'A'** hand, with palm forward and slightly leftward, is knocked against forefinger of vertical left **'ONE'** hand whose palm faces right. (Signs may vary considerably.) ❖

OR

SIGN #3: Vertical right **'X'** hand, palm facing left, is held with side of crooked forefinger against the nose. The right hand then tugs downward slightly. (**FOOL** is frequently fingerspelled.)

fool: *v.* to joke; jest. *Do not believe him; he is just fooling.*

SIGN #4: With palm facing left, horizontal right **'X'** hand is stroked forward at least twice across the top of horizontal left **'X'** hand, which is held with palm facing right.

fool around: *v.* to act foolish deliberately. *He likes to fool around when he is supposed to be working.*

SIGN: **'Y'** hands are held upright, left ahead of right, in front of the face with left palm facing right and right palm facing left. The forearms then move simultaneously in small, continuous circles. From the signer's perspective, the right hand moves in a counter-clockwise direction while the left hand moves clockwise.

foolish: *adj.* silly; ridiculous; absurd; unwise. *It was **foolish** of him to go outside without his coat*

SIGN: Vertical right **'Y'** hand, palm toward the nose, is twisted forward so that the palm faces left.

foot: *n.* the part of the leg below the ankle joint. *He is limping because he injured his **foot**.*

SIGN #1: Fingerspell **FOOT**. (The plural **FEET** is also fingerspelled.)

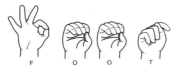

foot: *n.* a unit of measurement equal to 12 inches. *She bought one **foot** of ribbon.*

SIGN #2: Fingerspell **FOOT**. (The plural **FEET** is also fingerspelled.)

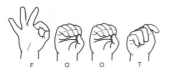

football: *n.* a team sport played on a large field with an oval ball. ***Football** is one of Canada's most popular sports.*

SIGN #1: **'5'** (or **'4'**) hands are held apart in semi-vertical positions with palms down but facing each other slightly as the fingers of the left hand point rightward/upward and the fingers of the right hand point leftward/upward. The hands then come together a couple of times so that the fingers mesh with each other. (Signs vary considerably.)

OR

SIGN #2: **'C'** hands are held side by side with palms down. The hands are then drawn apart as they take on **'S'** shapes.

OR

SIGN #3: Vertical left **'EXTENDED B'** hand is held with palm facing forward while right **'BENT EXTENDED B'** hand, palm facing backward, is tucked and tapped a couple of times against the right side of the torso under the right armpit.

for: *prep.* directed to; with regard to. (There are a great many possible meanings for this word.) *He works **for** the federal government.*

SIGN: Tip of forefinger of right **'ONE'** hand touches right side of forehead. As the hand moves forward slightly, the wrist rotates so that the hand is turned palm-forward.

forbid: *v.* to prohibit in an authoritative way; to order (someone) not (to do something). *There are laws that **forbid** you to do certain things.*

SIGN: Right **'L'** hand, palm facing left, is tapped smartly against right-facing palm of vertical left **'EXTENDED B'** hand. (Alternatively, this sign may be made with a vertical right **'ONE'** hand, palm facing forward.)

force: *v.* to use exertion against someone or something that resists; compel. *Nobody can **force** you to agree.*

SIGN #1: Vertical right **'C'** hand, palm facing forward/leftward, is placed on the back of the left **'STANDARD BASE'** hand and is thrust forward/leftward across the left hand as the wrist bends causing the right hand to hang palm-down over the left hand. (Alternatively, this sign may be formed without the use of the left hand.) ❖

force: *n.* a group of individuals organized for military functions. *Canada's peacekeeping **force** is highly respected internationally.*

SIGN #2: **'A'** hands are placed on the left side of the chest, palms facing the body, with the right hand above the left. Then they are simultaneously moved forward and back to tap twice against the body.

fore-: *prefix* before (in time). *I suggest you give this decision some **forethought**.*

SIGN #1: Back of fingers of horizontal right **'BENT EXTENDED B'** hand are held against fingers of horizontal left **'BENT EXTENDED B'** hand, palms facing each other. Right hand is then moved toward the body. (ASL and English word order are frequently different. The sample sentence in ASL is: *THIS DECISION BETTER THINK BEFORE*.) The prefix **fore-**, meaning 'before' is often conveyed by an all-inclusive sign that expresses the root or base word as well as the prefix, as is the case with **forecast**.

fore-: *prefix* the front part. *He has very strong forearms.*

NOTE—There is no specific sign for the prefix **fore-** meaning 'the front part'; instead, an all-inclusive sign is used to convey the root or base word as well as the prefix.

forecast: *v.* to predict; figure out in advance. *The weatherman has forecast snow for tomorrow.*

SIGN: Right **'BENT V'** hand, palm facing backward, is held with tip of midfinger under the right eye and is then swung forward under the left **'STANDARD BASE'** hand which is held loosely in front of the body below eye level.

foreign: *adj.* of or from another land. *Many people from foreign countries emigrate to Canada.*

SIGN: Joined thumb and forefinger of right **'F'** hand, palm down, are placed near the bent elbow of the left forearm which is held loosely in front of the chest. The right hand is then circled in small rotations against the left forearm. This is not just a wrist movement, but the entire right arm moves, however slightly. (When referring to **foreign (matter)**, for example, the signer might choose the signs **not + normal**.)

foremost: *adv.* first in time, place, rank or position. *Completing this project is foremost in my mind.*

SIGN: Horizontal left **'5'** hand is held stationary with palm rightward but angled slightly toward the body and fingers pointing forward/rightward. Right **'5'** hand, with palm down and fingers pointing forward/leftward, is used to tap several times on the thumbtip of the left hand.

forest: *n.* a large wooded area. *British Columbia is well known for its forests.*

SIGN: Both arms drift rightward as right elbow rests on left **'STANDARD BASE'** hand, and vertical right **'5'** hand shimmies or repeatedly twists back and forth in short, jerky movements.

foretell: *v.* to predict; tell beforehand; prophesy. *It is impossible to foretell accurately the outcome of an election.*

SIGN: Right **'BENT V'** hand, palm facing backward, is held with tip of midfinger under the right eye and is then swung forward under the left **'STANDARD BASE'** hand which is held loosely in front of the body below eye level.

forever: *adv.* without end; for always; everlastingly. *Romeo and Juliet vowed their love would last forever.*

SIGN: Vertical right **'ONE'** hand, palm facing backward, is held just in front of the right shoulder and is circled counter-clockwise. The hand is then changed to a **'Y'** shape with palm forward at a slight downward slant and the arm is extended in a forward/rightward direction.

forfeit: *v.* to give up as a penalty. *I had to forfeit certain rights while I was in prison.*

SIGN #1: **'OPEN A'** hands, held slightly apart at waist level, palms down, are thrust upward to form **'EXTENDED B'** hands with palms facing forward.

forfeit: *v.* to award (as a penalty to oneself or one's team) an automatic 'win' to one's opponent. *Injury forced me to forfeit the tennis match.*

SIGN #2: Right **'X'** hand is held upright with palm facing left, and is thrust forward and downward to a horizontal position. ❖ (This sign is used for **forfeit** only in a *sports* context.)

forget: *v.* to fail to remember. *Please remind me in case I forget.*

SIGN #1: Fingertips of horizontal right **'BENT EXTENDED B'** hand, palm toward the face, are placed in the centre or at the right of the forehead. The hand is then drawn downward/outward as it closes to form an **'EXTENDED A'** hand. (For **forgetful**, *adj.*, the sign is made with the hands moving alternately downward/outward from either side of the forehead a few times.)

forget: *v.* to fail to remember. *I forgot my friend's birthday!*

SIGN #2: Tip of middle finger of right **'BENT MIDFINGER 5'** hand, palm toward the face, is placed on the left side of the forehead, and is firmly drawn across to the right side of the forehead. (This sign tends to be used specifically when some feeling of guilt is involved.)

forget what one was going to say: *v.*
to fail to remember what one had planned to
say. *I forgot what I was going to say!*

SIGN #3: Tip of forefinger of vertical right
'ONE' hand, palm forward/leftward, touches
centre of forehead. Then the hand drops so
that the forefinger slips down between the
forefinger and middle finger of the left
'EXTENDED B' hand which is held palm down.
(ASL CONCEPT—**think - disappear**)
ALTERNATE SIGN—**disappear** #1

forgive: *v.* to pardon. *We will forgive him for
breaking the rules if he promises never to do so
again.*

SIGN: Fingers of right **'B'** hand, palm-down,
are placed on and at right angles to fingers of
upturned palm of left **'EXTENDED B'** hand.
Right hand is then slid at a forward/rightward
angle across and off the left hand. Motion is
repeated at least once.

fork: *n.* a pronged implement used for lifting
food to the mouth. *The fork is usually placed
at the left side of the plate in a table setting.*

SIGN: Extended fingertips of horizontal right
'BENT V' hand are placed against right-facing
palm of horizontal left **'EXTENDED B'** hand.
The fingertips of the right hand are then
separated from the left hand as the right wrist
makes a quarter turn clockwise, the left hand
turns slightly upward so that the fingers now
point forward/upward, and the fingertips of
the right hand re-establish contact with the
left palm.

forklift: *n.* a vehicle with two power-operated
horizontal prongs that can be raised or lowered
for lifting and carrying heavy things. *They need
a forklift to load the crates onto the truck.*

SIGN: Horizontal **'V'** hands are held parallel
with palms up and extended fingers pointing
forward. The hands are then simultaneously
raised as if lifting something.

form: *v.* to establish; set up. *We will form a
new committee immediately.*

SIGN #1: Right **'EXTENDED A'** hand is held
palm down over left **'STANDARD BASE'** hand,
then twisted so that it comes to rest on the
back of the left hand with thumb pointing
upward and palm facing leftward. (**Form** has
many different meanings.)

form: *n.* a printed document with spaces in
which to put information. *Would you please
fill out this form?*

SIGN #2: **'ONE'** hands, palms down and fingers
pointing forward, are placed side by side and
are drawn apart, moved down, and brought
together again to outline the printed page.

formal: *adj.* following established ways or
rules; ceremonial. *A black tie event is considered
formal.*

SIGN: Thumb of vertical right **'5'** hand, palm
facing left, is placed on the middle of the
chest and the hand is circled forward twice so
that the thumb brushes up and off the chest
with each revolution.

format: *n.* the style or arrangement of a TV
program, publication or computer program.
*Beginning on March 1st, CBC newscasts will
have a different format.*

SIGN: Fingerspell **FORMAT**.

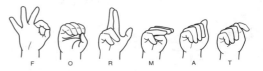

former: *adj.* past; previous. *Pierre Trudeau is
a former Prime Minister of Canada.*

SIGN #1: Vertical right **'5'** hand, palm facing
forward/leftward, is circled backwards just in
front of the right shoulder.

former: *adj.* the first of two things mentioned. *Baseball and hockey have little in
common. The former is a summer sport while
the latter is a winter sport.*

SIGN #2: Vertical **'ONE'** hand is held with
palm forward and slanted leftward slightly.
As the wrist twists, the hand turns so that the
palm faces the chest.

formidable: *adj.* difficult to defeat, overcome or manage due to great size, excellence, etc. *Napoleon was a formidable general.*

SIGN: '**S**' hands, palms down, are held slightly apart with the right higher than the left. Then the right is brought down sharply so that its knuckles strike across those of the left. Sign choice varies according to context.
ALTERNATE SIGN—**tough**

forsake: *v.* to give up something that has been valued or enjoyed; abandon. *He would never forsake his wife and children.*

SIGN: '**5**' hands are thrust forward to the left and down from shoulder level, palms facing each other. ❖
ALTERNATE SIGN—**ignore**

fort: *n.* an enclosure that is fortified for defence against enemies. *Early fur-traders built a fort where Edmonton now stands.*

SIGN: Fingerspell **FORT**.

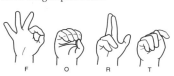

fortitude: *n.* strength and firmness of mind; courage to endure hardships. *He has shown great fortitude during the family crisis.*

SIGN: Right '**A**' hand, with thumbnail touching closed lips and palm facing left, is moved slowly down chin. Next, vertical left '**5**' hand is held with palm facing the body as the horizontal right '**EXTENDED B**' hand with palm facing left is thrust forward between the forefinger and middle finger of the left hand. (ASL CONCEPT—**patient - through**.) In the sample sentence, 'during' would not be accorded a separate sign because its meaning would already be incorporated in the sign for **fortitude**.

fortunate: *adj.* having good luck. *He is fortunate to have a supportive family.*

SIGN: Tips of extended fingers of right '**U**' hand, palm toward the body, are placed on the chin. The hand then swivels forward and downward from the wrist.
SAME SIGN—**fortune**, *n.*, when it means **luck**.
ALTERNATE SIGN—**lucky** #2

fortune: *n.* wealth. *He left his entire fortune to his only grandchild.*

SIGN: Left '**CROOKED 5**' hand is held with palm up while right '**CROOKED 5**' hand is held just above it with palm down. The hands are then moved apart, the right hand moving upward and back toward the body while the left hand is lowered slightly. (In contexts where **fortune** means *luck*, fingerspell **LUCK**.)

forty: *n.* See NUMBERS, p. LXII.

forward: *v.* to redirect one's mail or to send by mail. *I will forward the mail to your new address.*

SIGN #1: Vertical right '**S**' hand, palm forward, is thrust ahead as it opens to form a '**CONTRACTED 5**' hand. ❖
ALTERNATE SIGN—**send** #1

forward: *adj.* bold; presumptuous; impudent. *He was forward enough to ask the most popular girl for a date.*

SIGN #2: '**A**' hands are held in front of either side of the chest with palms facing each other and are alternately circled forward, the thumbs brushing upward and forward off the chest with each revolution.

forward: *n.* an attacking (or offensive) player in various sports such as hockey, football, etc. *He is a forward on our college soccer team.*

SIGN #3: Right '**F**' hand is held upright with palm facing forward and is wobbled slightly.

(look) forward to: See **look forward to**.

(move) forward: *v.* to move ahead. *Move forward please.*

SIGN #5: Horizontal '**BENT EXTENDED B**' hands are held parallel with palms facing, and are simultaneously moved forward. (Signs vary according to *the number of people* moving forward and *how* they are moving.)

foster: *v.* to promote; encourage. *The organization tries to* **foster** *equality between the sexes.*

SIGN #1: Horizontal **'EXTENDED B'** hands are held apart with palms angled so that they partly face each other while partly facing forward. The hands then simultaneously make several small circles outward.

foster: *adj.* part of a family, but not related by blood. *They act as* **foster** *parents to dozens of children.*

SIGN #2: Side of forefinger of right **'ONE'** hand, palm facing left, is brushed lightly downward twice on the right cheek, forefinger either remaining upright or bending slightly to become a **'BENT ONE'**. (**FOSTER** is frequently fingerspelled.)

foul: *adj.* offensive; profane; dirty. *The movie was full of* **foul** *language.*

SIGN #1: Back of right **'5'** hand is placed under the chin, palm down, and the fingers are wiggled up and down. (Signs vary considerably depending on context.)

foul: *n.* a violation of the rules in a sport. *A good player avoids committing* **fouls.**

SIGN #2: Right **'ONE'** hand, palm facing forward, is held just behind the right ear and the tip of the forefinger is used to strike forward against the right ear.

foul smell: *n.* an offensive or repulsive odour. *There was a* **foul smell** *emanating from the science lab.*

SIGN #3: Right **'5'** hand is held with palm facing leftward/downward and thumbtip touching or close to the tip of the nose. The hand is then firmly thrust a short distance forward at a slight downward angle. Meanwhile, a grimace appears on the signer's face and the lips appear to be articulating the syllable 'PO'.

found: *v.* to establish; set up; create. *Forrest C. Nickerson* **founded** *the Canadian Cultural Society of the Deaf.*

SIGN: Right **'EXTENDED A'** hand is held palm down over left **'STANDARD BASE'** hand, then twisted so that it comes to rest on the back of the left hand with thumb pointing upward and palm facing leftward. (For **found**, meaning the past tense of **find**, *v.*, see **find** #1.)

foundation: *n.* the base on which something stands. *The* **foundation** *of the building is solid.*

SIGN #1: Left arm is folded in front of the body with the hand in a horizontal **'S'** position with palm down. Vertical right **'S'** hand, palm facing left, is brought upward firmly to strike the underside of the left forearm near the wrist. The right hand is then lowered, moved leftward, and raised again to strike the underside of the left forearm near the elbow.

foundation: *n.* basis. *A good* **foundation** *of general knowledge is important for an interpreter.*

SIGN #2: Right **'EXTENDED B'** hand, palm down, fingers pointing slightly forward and to the left, is circled counter-clockwise beneath left **'STANDARD BASE'** hand.

fountain: *n.* a spray of water. *A* **fountain** *is a lovely addition to a park.*

SIGN #1: Forefinger of vertical right **'W'** hand, palm facing left, is tapped against the chin. Next, vertical **'O'** (or **'FLAT O'**) hands are placed side by side, palms facing forward. Then they are moved apart and slightly upward as the fingers spread to form **'5'** hands. (ASL CONCEPT—**water - spray**.) Signs for **fountain** may vary.

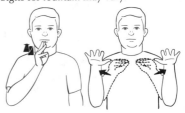

(drinking) fountain: *n.* a device that provides drinking water. *We use the* **drinking fountain** *after every squash game.*

SIGN #2: Forefinger of vertical right **'W'** hand, palm facing left, is tapped against the chin. Next, the head is bowed while the right **'A-INDEX'** hand rotates forward as if turning the handle on a drinking fountain. This is a wrist movement. (ASL CONCEPT—**water - turn handle**.)

four: *n.* See NUMBERS, p. LX.

fourteen: *n.* See NUMBERS, p. LX.

fowl: *n.* a large edible bird. *Turkey is the fowl most commonly served at banquets.*

SIGN: Right **'MODIFIED G'** hand is held at chin, palm facing forward, while extended fingers are opened and closed at least twice to simulate the movement of a bird's beak.

fox: *n.* a predatory, bushy-tailed canine mammal, usually reddish-brown or grey in colour. *A fox killed several of the farmer's hens.*

SIGN: Joined thumb and forefinger of vertical right **'F'** hand, palm facing left, are held against the nose and the wrist is twisted back and forth slightly making the hand appear to wobble.

foxy: *adj.* sly; crafty. *Do not trust him; he is very foxy.*

SIGN: Thumb and forefinger of the right **'FLAT OPEN F'** hand are laid flat against the left cheek with the palm facing leftward/backward. The forefinger moves rapidly up and down several times so that the hand alternates between a **'FLAT OPEN F'** shape and a **'FLAT F'**. A look of suspicion accompanies this sign.

fraction: *n.* one or more parts of a whole, expressed in mathematical terms as one number over another. *The students are learning about fractions in math class.*

SIGN #1: Horizontal left **'BENT ONE'** hand is held in a fixed position with palm facing down and forefinger pointing right. Vertical right **'F'** hand, palm forward, then makes a pecking motion, once above the left forefinger and then once below the left forefinger. (This sign tends to be used primarily in the math classroom. In other situations, the concept is expressed by signing actual fractions like 1/2, 1/3, etc., rather than using a generic sign.)

fraction: *n.* a small piece or part. *Only a fraction of the membership attended the meeting.*

SIGN #2: Left **'EXTENDED B'** hand is held in a fixed position with palm up and fingers pointing forward/rightward. Side of horizontal right **'EXTENDED B'** hand, palm leftward/backward, rests on the fingertips of the left hand and moves rightward/backward in a slight arc formation. (To say that something has been purchased at a **fraction** of the cost, use **cheap**.)

fracture: *v.* to break. *When Tom fell from the tree, he fractured his leg.*

SIGN: **'S'** hands are placed side by side, palms down. Then they are wrenched apart so that palms face one another.

fragile: *adj.* weak; frail; delicate. *This rope is too fragile to hold the anchor.*

SIGN #1: Fingertips of right **'5'** hand, palm toward the body, are placed on upturned palm of left **'EXTENDED B'** hand. Then the fingers buckle so that the hand is transformed into a **'CLAWED 5'** shape.

fragile: *adj.* apt to break easily. *The vase is fragile so please wrap it carefully.*

SIGN #2: Left **'BENT EXTENDED B'** hand is held in a fixed position with palm up. Palm of horizontal right **'EXTENDED B'** (or **'BENT EXTENDED B'**) hand faces left but is slanted slightly upward and toward the body as the fingers are brushed upward against the backs of the fingers of the left hand at least twice. Next, **'S'** hands are placed side by side, palms down. Then they are wrenched apart so that palms face one another.
(ASL CONCEPT—**easy - break**.)

fragrance: *n.* a sweet or pleasant smell. *He could recognize the fragrance of the wild rose as he walked along.*

SIGN: Right **'CONTRACTED 5'** hand is circled counter-clockwise (from the signer's perspective) around the face as the fingers close to form a **'FLAT O'** hand, with palm and fingers toward the chin. Next, right **'EXTENDED B'** hand is held with palm facing the body, and fingertips just in front of the nose and pointing leftward/upward. The hand is then circled forward a few times in small clockwise circles.
(ASL CONCEPT—**pretty - smell**.)
SAME SIGN—**fragrant**, *adj.* When **fragrance** means a kind of perfume, cologne, etc., see **perfume**.

frail: *adj.* physically weak and delicate. *The old woman appeared frail.*

SIGN: Fingertips of right **'5'** hand, palm toward the body, are placed on upturned palm of left **'EXTENDED B'** hand. Then the fingers buckle so that the hand is transformed into a **'CLAWED 5'** shape.

frame: *n.* the enclosing border of a picture. *A nice frame complements any painting.*

SIGN #1: Thumbs and forefingers of **'MODIFIED G'** hands, palms forward, are placed side by side in front of the chest, then drawn apart, moved downward, and brought together again as they outline the rectangular shape of a picture. (The size and geometric outline of this sign varies according to the size and shape of the picture.)

frame: *v.* to plant evidence to make an innocent person appear guilty. *He insisted that his co-workers were trying to frame him.*

SIGN #2: Horizontal **'EXTENDED B'** hands, palms facing each other and fingers pointing forward, are held slightly apart at the left side of the body and are moved simultaneously toward the right. Next, horizontal right **'EXTENDED A'** hand, palm facing left, is thrust forward twice across the back of the left **'A'** hand of which the palm faces downward. Facial expression must be accusatory. (ASL CONCEPT—**plan - blame**.) The past tense **FRAMED** is generally fingerspelled. ❖

(eyeglass) frames: *n.* the outer structure into which the lenses of glasses are fitted. *I need to go to the optometrist to get new frames.*

SIGN: **'CROOKED L'** hands, palms facing each other, are held in a vertical position beside each eye. The forearms then move outward and inward slightly a few times so that the thumbtips tap against the cheeks. (Alternatively, the right hand only is frequently used.)

framework: *n.* the structural basis for a plan or project. *We developed a framework for the proposal.*

SIGN #1: Left **'EXTENDED B'** hand is held in a fixed position with fingers pointing forward/rightward and palm facing rightward but slanted toward the body and slightly upward. Fingertips of right **'SPREAD EXTENDED C'** hand, palm down, are brushed forward/rightward a few times along the left palm. This sign is accompanied by a lip pattern such that the upper teeth are resting on the lower lip as if articulating an **'F'**.

framework: *n.* the structure or frame which supports a building. *The construction workers have completed the framework of the new house.*

SIGN #2: Vertical **'4'** hands, palms facing, are held a slight distance apart and are simultaneously moved upward, then angled toward each other so that the fingers mesh to indicate the shape of a roof. (Signs vary.)

frank: *adj.* honest; straightforward; blunt. *Sally was frank about her problem.*

SIGN: Left **'EXTENDED B'** hand is held in a fixed position with palm facing right but slanted upward slightly and fingers pointing forward as right **'U'** hand is held with palm facing left and tip of middle finger placed at heel of left hand. The right hand is then moved straight forward along the left palm until the tip of the right middle finger reaches the tip of the left middle finger.

ALTERNATE SIGNS—**honest** #2 or **blunt** #1

frankfurters: *n.* small smoked sausages. *Roasting frankfurters over an open fire is great fun.*

SIGN: Vertical **'CONTRACTED L'** hands are held very close together with palms facing. Then they are moved apart as they alternate between **'CLOSED MODIFIED G'** hands and the original **'CONTRACTED L'** hands.

fraternity: *n.* a group of people united in interests and goals. *They belong to the local chapter of a national Deaf fraternity.*

SIGN: Fingerspell **FRAT**. (When the fraternity refers to a club made up of *male college or university students only*, it is still spelled **FRAT**.)

fraud: *n.* a hoax; swindle; deliberate deception. *Fraud is a criminal offense.*

NOTE—See regional variations for **cheat**.

freckles: *n.* small brownish-yellow spots on the skin. *The little red-haired boy has freckles all over his face.*

SIGN: Fingertips of right **'SPREAD EXTENDED C'** hand are tapped against that (those) part(s) of the body which is (are) freckled. (Two hands may be used.)

free: *v.* to liberate; release from captivity. *The president's aim was to free the slaves.*

SIGN #1: **'S'** (or **'F'**) hands, left palm facing rightward/downward and right palm facing leftward/downward, are crossed at the wrists with the right hand nearer the body. Then they break apart so that they are held parallel with palms facing forward.
SAME SIGNS—**free**, *adj.*, (meaning unrestricted) and **freedom**, *n.*

free: *adj.* without charge; at no cost. *The store was giving away free balloons.*

SIGN #2: **'F'** hands, left palm facing right and right palm facing left, are held upright with right hand directly behind left hand. Then they are drawn apart as wrists rotate outward so that left palm faces rightward/forward while right palm faces leftward/forward. (**FREE** is frequently fingerspelled.)

freeway: *n.* an expressway. *The accident occurred on the freeway.*

SIGN: **'V'** hands are held fairly close together with left palm toward the body and right palm forward. The wrists simultaneously bend up and down a few times causing the extended fingers to alternate between upright and semi-horizontal positions as they represent the flow of traffic in opposite directions.
ALTERNATE SIGN—**highway** #2

freeze: *v.* to feel the effects of extreme cold; to solidify due to the lowering of the temperature. *Exposed skin will freeze quickly in frigid temperatures.*

SIGN: **'CROOKED 5'** hands are held parallel with palms down. They then jerk slightly forward/downward as the fingers retract to form **'CLAWED SPREAD C'** hands.

freezer: *n.* a cabinet used for storing frozen foods. *When the power failed, the meat in the freezer was spoiled.*

SIGN: The hands, held parallel with palms down, alternate between **'CROOKED 5'** and **'CLAWED 5'** shapes as the fingers are retracted and relaxed a few times.

French: *n.* the official language of France. *The two official languages of Canada are English and French.*

SIGN: Right **'F'** hand is held palm down. The wrist then rotates rightward, turning the palm to face left. (Alternatively, the vertical right **'F'** hand is held with palm toward the head and joined thumb and forefinger touching the right side of the head. The wrist then rotates to turn the hand so that the palm faces forward. As yet another variation, the right **'F'** hand may be held palm down in front of the right side of the body as the wrist twists back and forth several times.)

french fries: *n.* deep-fried potato strips. *We ordered french fries with our hamburgers.*

SIGN: Right **'F'** hand is held palm-down. The wrist bends to bounce the hand downward slightly, and then move it rightward in an arc formation before bouncing it downward slightly once again. The movement is virtually that of fingerspelling **F-F** but the palm is downward rather than forward.

frequent/frequently: *adj./adv.* recurring at short intervals; taking place or appearing often. *His visits are frequent.*

SIGN #1: Left **'EXTENDED B'** hand is held in a fixed position with fingers pointing forward and palm facing upward but angled rightward slightly. Fingertips of horizontal right **'BENT EXTENDED B'** hand, palm down, are used to strike palm of left hand. Right hand then moves forward in a small arc with fingertips coming to rest at the end of the left hand. (The concept of **frequency** is often incorporated in the sign for the verb through repetitions of the basic sign movement.)

OR

SIGN #2: Horizontal right **'BENT EXTENDED B'** hand, palm left, is moved forward quickly in a series of small arcs. (This sign is not appropriate in all situations.)

frequent: *v.* to go to often or on a regular basis. *He frequents a bar on the west side of town.*

SIGN #3: Vertical left **'ONE'** hand is held in a fixed position with palm forward/rightward while horizontal right **'B'** hand is held just behind the left hand with palm left and fingers pointing forward. The fingertips of the right hand make contact with the left forefinger as the right hand is jabbed toward it several times. (The signer's lips protrude when making this sign.)

fresh: *adj.* newly grown, harvested or made (often used to describe food). *Prince Edward Island is known for its fresh fish and other seafood.*

SIGN #1: Fingerspell **FRESH**.

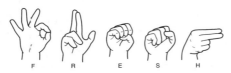

fresh: *adj.* new; original. *We need some fresh ideas for fundraising.*

SIGN #2: Horizontal left **'EXTENDED B'** hand remains stationary with palm up and fingers pointing forward/rightward while back of right **'BENT EXTENDED B'** hand is brought leftward with palm up across left palm with a scooping motion. (**FRESH** in this context is frequently fingerspelled.)

fresh air: *n.* air that is revitalizing and originates outside as opposed to air that exists in an enclosed area. *Let us go outside for some fresh air.*

SIGN #3: **'5'** hands are held basically upright at about shoulder level with palms facing backwards. The wrists simultaneously bend backwards several times to draw the fingertips toward the shoulders.

freshman: *adj.* designating the first year of study at Gallaudet University. (This sign is not used to mean the freshman year at any other university, only at Gallaudet.) *Christine is in her freshman year at Gallaudet University.*

SIGN: Tip of forefinger of right **'ONE'** hand, palm facing left, taps the end of the ringfinger of the horizontal left **'5'** hand, which is held with palm facing right but angled slightly toward the body.

fret: *v.* to be distressed; worry. *When Pat lost her keys, she began to fret.*

SIGN: **'B'** (or **'EXTENDED B'**) hands are held apart in front of the face at such an angle that the palms face each other but slant downward while the fingers of the left hand point upward/rightward and the fingers of the right hand point upward/leftward. The hands are then alternately circled toward each other a few times. Facial expression must clearly convey 'anxiety'.

Friday: *n.* the sixth day of the week. [See TIME CONCEPTS, p. LXX.] *Friday is usually the last working day of the week.*

SIGN: Right **'F'** hand is held upright with palm toward the chest and the forearm moves in small counter-clockwise circles.

friend: *n.* a person whom one knows well, likes, and trusts. *They have been friends since childhood.*

SIGN #1: Left **'CROOKED ONE'** hand is held palm-up with forefinger pointing rightward/forward, while right **'CROOKED ONE'** hand is held palm-down with forefinger laid across left forefinger at right angles to it. The wrists then rotate so that the hands reverse positions. SAME SIGN—**friendship**, *n.*

SIGN #2 [ATLANTIC]: Horizontal **'ONE'** hands, palms down, are held with right forefinger pointing forward/leftward and left forefinger pointing forward/rightward, and are alternately moved up and down as the extended forefingers strike down against each other.

(best *or* **close) friend:** *n.* a person whom one knows very well and is very fond of. *She has been my best friend since we were in kindergarten.*

SIGN #1: Crooked fingers of **'X'** hands are interlocked so that palm of left hand, which is closest to the body, faces up while right palm faces down. Holding this position, the hands are simultaneously and firmly moved forward/downward slightly as interlocked fingers tighten.

OR

SIGN #2: Vertical right **'EXTENDED R'** (or **'R'**) hand, palm toward the body, is firmly thrust forward a short distance.

friendly: *adj.* amicable; warm. *Canadians are considered **friendly** people.*

SIGN: **'5'** hands, palms facing backward, move backward with fingers fluttering until they come to rest close to either side of the face.

fright: *n.* sudden fear. *They ran away in **fright** when they heard the shots.*

SIGN: Horizontal **'5'** hands, palms toward the body, are held out from either side of the chest, and are moved vigorously toward each other, stopping abruptly in front of the chest. SAME SIGN—**frighten,** *v.*

frigid: *adj.* very cold. *With the furnace out of order the house was **frigid**.*

SIGN: **'S'** (or **'A'**) hands are held apart, palms facing each other, and are shaken, along with the shoulders, as if the signer is shivering.

frisk: *v.* to search someone's body for something hidden, especially a weapon, by passing the hands quickly over his/her clothing. *Expecting to find a knife, the police officer **frisked** the suspect.*

SIGN: Vertical **'CROOKED 5'** hands are extended from the body and held parallel with palms facing but slanted forward slightly. They then move downward simultaneously in a waving motion as if actually frisking someone.

frisky: *adj.* lively; energetic; playful. *Kittens are usually much more **frisky** than adult cats.*

SIGN: Horizontal **'Y'** hands, palms toward the body, are held parallel and wobble as they are simultaneously circled clockwise several times.

frivolous: *adj.* trivial; insignificant; not sensible; silly. *She spends her money on **frivolous** things.*

SIGN: Vertical right **'Y'** hand, palm toward the nose, is twisted forward so that the palm faces left.

frog: *n.* a short, squat, tailless amphibian with webbed feet and long hind legs for hopping. *The tadpole will become a **frog**.*

SIGN: Right **'CLOSED V'** hand is held at the chin with palm down. Then the forefinger and middle finger are flicked forward/leftward to form a **'V'** hand. Movement is repeated.

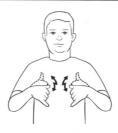

frolic: *n.* a happy, carefree, lively time. *Summer is a time for fun and **frolic**.*

SIGN: Horizontal **'Y'** hands are held parallel with palms facing each other but slanted slightly toward the body. The hands are then simultaneously bounced up and down twice. This is a wrist action.

from: *prep.* originating with; starting with. *I received a letter **from** her.*

SIGN: Vertical left **'ONE'** hand, palm forward/rightward, is held in a fixed position in front of horizontal right **'ONE'** hand which is held with palm facing left and tip of forefinger touching the middle of the left forefinger. The right hand is then flicked backward/rightward to assume a vertical position as the forefinger retracts to take on an **'X'** shape. (Alternatively, this sign may be made with both hands beginning and ending with **'X'** shapes.)

from now on: *adv.* from this time onward; henceforth. *From now on the cars must be parked in front of this building.*

SIGN: Horizontal **'BENT EXTENDED B'** hands, palms facing each other, are positioned so that the fingers of the right hand are just in front of the fingers of the left hand. The right hand is then moved forward briskly.

front: *n.* the forward part of something. *The children wanted to sit at the **front** of the bus.*

SIGN: Horizontal right **'EXTENDED B'** hand, palm toward the face, is held in front of the forehead and is moved down toward the chin a couple of times.

frost: *n.* white ice crystals formed by temperatures below freezing. *There was **frost** on my car window this morning.*

SIGN: **'CROOKED 5'** hands are held parallel with palms down. They then jerk slightly forward/downward as the fingers retract to form **'CLAWED SPREAD C'** hands. (**FROST** may be fingerspelled.)

frown: *v.* to wrinkle the forehead, usually as a sign of displeasure. *The teacher frowned when she tried to read my sloppy writing.*

SIGN: **'ONE'** hands are held with palms down and forefingers above each eye and pointing to each other. The hands then move slightly toward each other as the forefingers curl to take on **'CROOKED ONE'** shapes. Facial expression is important.

frozen: *adj.* having become ice or ice-covered; having stiffened due to extremely cold temperatures. *The river is still frozen despite the warm weather.*

SIGN: **'CROOKED 5'** hands are held parallel with palms down. They then jerk slightly forward/downward as the fingers retract to form **'CLAWED SPREAD C'** hands.

frugal: See **thrifty**.

fruit: *n.* a fleshy, edible plant that contains seeds. *Fruit is grown in the Okanagan Valley.*

SIGN: Fingerspell **FRUIT**.

frustrated: *adj.* upset; agitated; discouraged. *He was frustrated by the difficult puzzle.*

SIGN #1: **'B'** hands, palms forward, are alternately circled backward so that the backs of the fingers strike the lower part of the face with each revolution. (This sign tends to be used for **frustrated** when the frustration is a result of one's own inadequacy.)
SAME SIGN—**frustration**, *n.,* in this context.

frustrated: *adj.* thwarted; upset; disappointed. *He felt frustrated when he failed to get the job.*

SIGN #2: Right **'B'** hand, palm forward, is brought upward/backward to a vertical position so that the back of the hand strikes the face. (This sign tends to be used for **frustrated** when the cause of the frustration is beyond one's control.)
SAME SIGN—**frustration**, *n.,* in this context.

fry: *v.* to cook in fat or oil over direct heat. *The chef will fry the mushrooms in butter.*

SIGN: Right **'EXTENDED B'** hand is held palm down with fingers pointing forward/leftward as they are placed on the upturned palm of the left **'EXTENDED B'** hand, of which the fingers point slightly forward and to the right. Right hand is then flipped over so that palm faces up.

fuel: *n.* a substance burned as a source of power. *Most cars burn unleaded fuel only.*

SIGN: Left **'S'** hand is held, not in a tight fist but loosely, with palm down but slanted slightly rightward. Right **'EXTENDED A'** hand, palm down but slanted rightward as well, is positioned above and to the right of the left hand. The right hand then moves downward/leftward so that the extended thumb is inserted into the opening at the top of the left hand. The motion is repeated.

full: *adj.* containing as much as possible. *The gas tank was full when we left for Montreal.*

SIGN #1: Right **'EXTENDED B'** hand, palm down with fingers pointing forward/leftward, grazes top of horizontal left **'S'** hand as the right hand is firmly swept leftward.

full: *adj.* having consumed enough food and/or drink. *After the seven-course dinner, I was full.*

SIGN #2: Right **'B'** hand, palm down, is held limp-wristed in front of the chest and is flicked upward from the wrist so that it strikes the underside of the chin with fingers pointing left. The cheeks are puffed.

full: *adj.* having consumed *more than enough* food and/or drink. *I was so full after dessert that I could hardly move.*

SIGN #3: Left **'CROOKED EXTENDED B'** hand is held out in front of the body with palm facing the stomach and fingers pointing rightward. Horizontal right **'S'** hand is held close to the stomach with palm facing left and is thrust forward to punch the left palm. The cheeks are puffed.

fumble: *v.* to drop a football which is in play. *He **fumbled** the ball in yesterday's Grey Cup game.*

SIGN: Horizontal left **'CROOKED EXTENDED B'** hand is held with palm facing the stomach and fingers pointing rightward. Horizontal right **'S'** hand, palm facing left, is held against the left palm and dropped straight downward. (Signs vary according to the situation.)

fume: *n.* a usually toxic, often unpleasant smelling gas, vapour or smoke (often plural). *The steel workers wore face masks to protect them from the toxic **fumes**.*

SIGN #1: Right **'EXTENDED B'** hand is held with palm facing the body, and fingertips just in front of the nose and pointing leftward/upward. The hand is then circled forward a few times in small clockwise circles. This sign is accompanied by a grimace to show irritation. (This sign may be followed by the fingerspelled word **GAS**.)

fume: *v.* to become angry. *She was **fuming** when she discovered that someone had slashed her tires.*

SIGN #2: Right **'BENT 5'** hand is held palm up and fingers fluttering under left **'STANDARD BASE'** hand. Facial expression must clearly show 'anger'.

fun: *n.* a source of enjoyment; a good time. *The children had **fun** playing tag at recess.*

SIGN: Fingerspell **FUN**. (This word is often fingerspelled quite briskly so that the **U** is barely discernible.)

F   U   N

function: *n.* the purpose of a person or thing in a specific role. *An interpreter's **function** is to facilitate communication.*

SIGN #1: Wrist of right **'S'** (or **'A'**) hand, palm facing away from the body, strikes wrist of left **'S'** (or **'A'**) hand, which is held in front of/below right hand with palm facing downward. Motion is repeated.

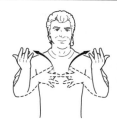

function: *n.* an official or formal social occasion. *The Canadian Association of the Deaf is hosting a **function** next month to raise funds for a special project.*

SIGN #2: Tips of midfingers of **'BENT MIDFINGER 5'** hands, palms toward the body, are placed slightly apart on the chest. The wrists then rotate forward as the hands move forward so that, while the palms still face the body, they are now angled upward slightly.

fund: *n.* a reserve of money set aside for a specific purpose. *The Canadian government should allocate **funds** for social services.*

SIGN: Back of right **'CONTRACTED B'** (or **'BENT EXTENDED B'**) hand, palm up, is tapped two or three times on upturned palm of left **'EXTENDED B'** hand. (**FUND** is frequently fingerspelled.)

fundamental: *adj.* basic; primary. *I have only a **fundamental** knowledge of how the system works.*

SIGN: Right **'EXTENDED B'** hand, palm down, fingers pointing slightly forward and to the left, is circled counter-clockwise beneath left **'STANDARD BASE'** hand.

fundraising: *n.* the gathering of money for a specific purpose or cause. ***Fundraising** is an ongoing activity for most charitable organizations.*

SIGN: Back of right **'CONTRACTED B'** (or **'BENT EXTENDED B'**) hand, palm up, is tapped two or three times on upturned palm of left **'EXTENDED B'** hand. Next, horizontal right **'EXTENDED C'** hand, palm toward the body, is held on the upturned palm of the left **'EXTENDED B'** hand. The right hand then closes into an **'EXTENDED A'** shape as it is drawn across the left palm in a leftward arc toward the body. (ASL CONCEPT—**money - earn**.)

funeral: *n.* a burial ceremony. *The **funeral** will be held in the chapel.*

SIGN #1: Vertical **'V'** hands are held so the left is slightly ahead of the right with palms forward. The hands then simultaneously move forward, pause, and move forward once again.

funeral (cont.)

OR

SIGN #2: **'BENT EXTENDED B'** hands are held with palms toward the shoulders and fingertips brushing backward against either side of the neck at least twice.

funny: *adj.* amusing; humorous; comical; causing laughter. *The audience laughed at the comedian's funny stories.*

SIGN #1: The two extended fingers of the **'BENT EXTENDED U'** hand, palm toward the face, stroke the nose at least twice in a downward motion.

SIGN #2 [ONTARIO]: Right **'EXTENDED C'** hand, palm facing downward/backward, is brought backward so that the thumbtip pokes the chin.

funny: *adj.* strange; odd. *It is funny that Tom is not here yet.*

SIGN #3: Vertical right **'C'** hand, palm facing left, is held near the face and is abruptly dropped downward from the wrist so the palm faces down.

fur: *n.* the hairy coat of certain mammals. *The kitten has soft, silky fur.*

SIGN: Fingerspell **FUR**.

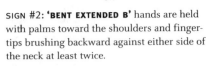

F   U   R

furious: *adj.* very angry; enraged. *When Pat made fun of him, Lee was furious.*

SIGN: **'CLAWED 5'** hands, palms toward body, fingertips touching chest, are swept vigorously upward/outward. Facial expression must clearly convey 'anger'.

ALTERNATE SIGN—**mad** #1

furniture: *n.* the moveable things in a room which are necessary for living or working. *The only furniture in the room was a narrow bed.*

SIGN: Vertical right **'F'** hand, palm facing forward, is shaken several times from the wrist. (In English, **furniture** may be either singular or plural. There is never an 's' added to this word.)

further: *adv.* at a greater distance; farther. *The Carters live a block further down the street.*

SIGN #1: Right **'BENT ONE'** hand, palm forward, is held close to the chest. The head then tilts backward a little as the signer looks into the distance and the forearm moves forward in a slight arc formation, ending with the palm down.

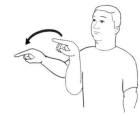

further: *adv.* in addition. *Further to our discussion, I suggest that someone prepare a written report.*

SIGN #2: Horizontal left **'FLAT O'** hand is held in a fixed position with palm toward the body while the right **'CONTRACTED 5'** hand is held palm-down to the right of and at a lower level than the left hand. The right wrist then rotates rightward/forward as the fingers close to form a **'FLAT O'** hand which is swung upward to touch the underside of the left hand.

further: *adj.* additional; more. *If you have any further questions, we can continue our discussion tomorrow.*

SIGN #3: Right **'EXTENDED A'** hand is held palm down. As the wrist rotates rightward, the hand is turned so that the palm faces left.

ALTERNATE SIGNS—**more** #1 & #2

furthermore: *adv.* in addition; besides. *Furthermore, the applicant does not have the right qualifications.*

SIGN: Horizontal right **'CONTRACTED 5'** hand, palm facing the body, is drawn from left to right as it closes to form a **'FLAT O'** hand.

fury: *n.* violent anger or rage. *In his fury, he smashed his fist against the wall.*

SIGN: **'CLAWED 5'** hands, palms toward body, fingertips touching chest, are swept vigorously upward/outward. Facial expression must clearly convey 'anger'.

fussy: *adj.* inclined to be overly particular about minor details. *She is very fussy about her house and yard.*

SIGN: Vertical right **'COMBINED U + Y'** hand, palm forward, is held in front of the right shoulder and the forearm is drawn firmly backward a short distance. This is essentially a jerking motion. (**FUSSY** is frequently fingerspelled.)

future: *n.* the time yet to come. *With his skills, he should have a successful future as a fashion designer.*

SIGN: Right **'EXTENDED B'** hand, palm facing left, is held in a vertical position near the right side of the head. The forearm is then moved forward a short distance so that the fingers eventually point forward/upward.

G

ga: See **go ahead**.

gab: *v.* to chatter excessively. *The students like to **gab** about what they did on the weekend.*

SIGN: Vertical **'CONTRACTED C'** hands are held with palms facing. The fingers of each hand repeatedly close down on the thumb, thus alternating between **'CONTRACTED C'** and **'FLAT O'** shapes. (In order to produce this sign naturally, the signer should not hold his hands rigidly in a fixed position. The arms should move up and down slightly.)

gaiety: *n.* festivity or merrymaking; cheerfulness; joyousness. *There was much **gaiety** at the staff party.*

SIGN: Horizontal right **'EXTENDED B'** hand, palm toward the body, is brushed up and off the chest twice in a circular motion.

gain: *v.* to increase, improve, or advance. *If you increase your calorie intake, you are likely to **gain** weight.*

SIGN #1: Left **'U'** hand is held in a fixed position with palm down and extended fingers pointing rightward/forward. Beside it is the right **'U'** hand, which is held with palm facing left and extended fingers pointing forward/leftward. The right wrist then rotates to turn the hand palm down as the extended fingers come to rest on those of the left hand at right angles to them.

gain: *v.* to acquire or obtain. *A summer job will help you **gain** experience.*

SIGN #2: Horizontal **'SPREAD C'** hands, right on top of left, are closed to form **'S'** hands as they are brought toward the chest.

gale: *n.* a strong wind. *A **gale** prevented the ship from reaching the port.*

SIGN: **'5'** hands, palms facing each other, are waved from side to side with great force. Facial expression is an important feature of this sign.

Gallaudet University: *n.* a liberal arts university in Washington, D.C. especially for Deaf students. *Gary Malkowski, the first Deaf Member of Ontario's Provincial Parliament, graduated from **Gallaudet University**.*

SIGN: Right **'MODIFIED G'** hand is held by the right temple with palm forward and thumb and forefinger pointing forward/leftward. The hand then moves backward as the thumb and forefinger close to assume a **'CLOSED G'** shape.

gallery: *n.* a building in which artistic work is displayed. *He enjoyed the tour of the art **gallery**.*

SIGN: Fingerspell **GALLERY**.

gallop: *n.* the rapid movement of a horse in which all four legs are off the ground simultaneously. *The riders raced across the meadow at a **gallop**.*

SIGN: **'V'** hands are held with palms down and extended fingers pointing forward, the right hand just to the right of and slightly above the left hand. The extended fingers retract to form **'CLAWED V'** shapes as the hands are drawn downward and backward toward the body. This is a fluid motion in which the hands simultaneously circle forward several times, alternating between **'V'** and **'CLAWED V'** shapes.

gamble: *v.* to bet on the outcome of an event. *He likes to **gamble** on the horse races.*

SIGN: Right **'S'** hand is held with palm up at a leftward angle, and is shaken back and forth. As it stops shaking, it is thrust forward and opened to form a **'5'** hand as if throwing dice.

game: *n.* amusement; pastime; contest; sporting event. *Chess is a challenging **game**.*

SIGN: Horizontal **'EXTENDED A'** hands are held slightly apart with palms toward the body. The hands are then brought together so that the knuckles strike against each other a couple of times.

gang: *n.* a group of people who normally associate with one another. *Most of the old gang attended the reunion.*

SIGN #1: **'SPREAD C'** hands are held upright and slightly apart with palms facing each other. The wrists then rotate forward, bringing the hands to a horizontal position.

gang: *n.* an organized body of people who carry out illegal or criminal activities. *He belongs to a motorcycle gang that has a history of criminal activity.*

SIGN #2: Horizontal right **'S'** hand, palm facing the body at an upward angle, is placed against the upper right part of the chest and is brushed downward twice in a circular motion. This sign is accompanied by a grimace.

gang up on: *v.* to attack in a group. *It is cruel to gang up on someone.*

SIGN: Vertical left **'ONE'** hand is held in a fixed position with palm facing left and tip of forefinger touching palm of right **'CROOKED 5'** hand which is held with palm facing forward and fingers pointing upward/forward. With a bend of the wrist, the right hand then falls forward so that the palm faces downward. ❖

gangster: *n.* a member of an organized group of criminals. The Godfather *was a movie about a notorious gangster.*

SIGN: Horizontal right **'S'** hand, palm facing the body at an upward angle, is placed against the upper right part of the chest and is brushed downward twice in a circular motion. This sign is accompanied by a grimace.

garage: *n.* a building used to house motor vehicles. *I will clean the garage this weekend.*

SIGN: Right **'3'** hand, palm facing left, is held in a horizontal position and is moved forward a short distance under left **'STANDARD BASE'** hand. Motion is repeated. (**GARAGE** is frequently fingerspelled.)

garbage: *n.* trash or rubbish. *It is your turn to take out the garbage.*

SIGN #1: Forefinger of right **'ONE'** hand, palm facing forward/left, is moved in an arc in front of left arm from about mid-forearm to elbow. As the hand moves, it twists from the wrist so that the palm eventually faces the body.

SIGN #2 [ONTARIO]: Right **'MODIFIED 5'** hand is held under chin with palm down, as the fingers flutter.

garbled: *adj.* unintentionally scrambled or jumbled so as to be unintelligible. *Your TTY message was garbled so please repeat it.*

SIGN: Vertical **'X'** hands, left palm facing right and right palm facing left at a slightly downward angle, are held together with the left hand in front of the right. Then the hands are simultaneously moved from left to right with the forefingers rapidly flexing as they represent the moving print on a TTY screen.

garden: *n.* a piece of ground where fruits, vegetables or flowers are grown. *These roses are from our garden.*

SIGN: Fingerspell **GARDEN**.

garlic: *n.* a bulbous plant which has a strong taste and odour, and is used in cooking. *The shrimp was flavoured with garlic.*

SIGN: Fingerspell **GARLIC**.

garment: *n.* an article of clothing. *The ancient Romans wore a loose garment called a toga.*

SIGN: Thumbs of **'5'** hands, with palms toward the body, are held at either side of upper chest and brushed downward a couple of times.

garnish: *v.* to decorate or improve the appearance to make it more appealing (especially food). *He will garnish the pudding with coconut.*

SIGN: Right **'O'** hand is held with palm down. Fingers flutter as the hand moves in a counter-clockwise circle.

gas: *n.* a vaporous substance. *Helium is a gas often used in balloons.*

SIGN #1: Fingerspell **GAS**.

gas [abbreviation for **gasoline**]: *n.* a liquid fuel used in motor vehicles. *We started on our trip with a full tank of gas.*

SIGN #2: Left **'S'** hand is held, not in a tight fist but loosely, with palm down but slanted slightly rightward. Right **'EXTENDED A'** hand, palm down but slanted rightward as well, is positioned above and to the right of the left hand. The right hand then moves downward/leftward so that the extended thumb is inserted into the opening at the top of the left hand. The motion is repeated. (**GAS** is frequently fingerspelled.)

gate: *n.* a moveable barrier that closes an opening in a fence. *The gate needs a new coat of paint.*

SIGN: **'BENT EXTENDED B'** hands are held with palms facing each other. The right hand straightens to form an **'EXTENDED B'** hand, and then returns to its original handshape as it resumes its original position. (**GATE** may also be fingerspelled.) See also **close (a gate)** and **open (a gate)**.

gather: *v.* to collect. *He gathers statistics for his report.*

SIGN #1: Horizontal left **'EXTENDED B'** hand is held in a fixed position with palm up and fingers pointing rightward/forward. Horizontal right **'SPREAD C'** hand, palm facing leftward/backward, is swept across left palm in a counter-clockwise semicircle as it closes to form an **'S'** shape with palm toward the body.

gather: *v.* to assemble. *Deaf people gather at the Community Centre for meetings and social events.*

SIGN #2: Both **'BENT 5'** hands, palms facing forward, are moved forward and slightly downward from shoulder level, fingers wiggling. ❖
ALTERNATE SIGN—**gathering**

gather: *v.* to understand; figure out; conclude. *I gather from his absence that he is not feeling well today.*

SIGN #3: Vertical right **'S'** hand, with knuckles near right side of forehead, is changed to a **'ONE'** hand as the forefinger is flicked upward.
ALTERNATE SIGN—**guess**

gathering: *n.* get-together; assembly of people. *There will be a small gathering at the Deaf Community Centre on Friday evening.*

SIGN: Horizontal **'SPREAD C'** hands are held apart with palms facing. Then hands are then moved purposefully toward one another.

gaudy: *adj.* tastelessly bright and colourful. *He hopes to attract attention by wearing gaudy shirts.*

SIGN: Vertical left **'ONE'** hand is held to the left of the body with palm facing forward while vertical right **'ONE'** hand is held with palm forward and tip of forefinger touching the face just in front of the right ear. The hands both take on **'S'** shapes then as they simultaneously move from side to side a few times. Meanwhile the signer grimaces and forms the word 'POW' on his lips.

gauge: *n.* meter; device used for measuring. *The gas gauge indicated that his car was low on fuel.*

SIGN: Horizontal left **'EXTENDED B'** hand is held in a fixed position with palm up but angled toward the body and fingers pointing rightward/forward. Right **'ONE'** hand, palm facing left, is placed on the left palm with forefinger pointing forward/rightward but slanted upward. The right wrist then bends up and down, causing the hand to pivot so that the forefinger moves back and forth to simulate the action of a compass needle.

gaunt: *adj.* thin, bony, emaciated in appearance. *The woman looked gaunt after not eating for several days.*

SIGN: Right **'MODIFIED G'** (or **'OPEN F'**) hand, palm toward the face, is held in a horizontal position with tips of thumb and forefinger touching either side of the mouth. The hand is then drawn downward to the bottom of the face.
ALTERNATE SIGN—**skinny**

gay: *adj.* carefree and merry. *The crowd at the party was happy and gay.*

SIGN #1: Horizontal right **'EXTENDED B'** hand, palm toward the body, is brushed up and off the chest twice in a circular motion.

gay: *adj.* homosexual. *He is a member of the gay community.*

SIGN #2: Fingerspell **GAY**.

G   A   Y

gaze: *v.* to stare or look at for a long time. *She gazed longingly at the photograph.*

SIGN: Right **'BENT V'** hand, palm facing forward, is positioned near the right shoulder with extended fingers pointing forward, and the hand is circled forward several times. ❖

general: *adj.* common or widespread. *General elections are often held in November.*

SIGN #1: Horizontal **'EXTENDED B'** hands are held with palms together and fingers pointing forward. The hands are then swung apart so that the palms face mainly forward.

general: *n.* a senior-ranking officer who commands a large military formation. *The general gave the order to attack.*

SIGN #2: Fingertips of palm-down right **'SPREAD C'** hand are tapped twice on right shoulder.

generate: *v.* to create, produce. *Water can be used to generate electricity.*

SIGN: Horizontal right **'S'** hand is placed on top of horizontal left **'S'** hand as both palms face the body. The right hand is then raised slightly and both wrists are bent causing the hands to turn so that the right palm faces left and the left palm faces right as the right hand re-establishes contact with the left hand.

generation: *n.* a successive stage in the natural descent of people. *A mother, a daughter and a granddaughter represent three generations.*

SIGN: Fingertips of right **'BENT EXTENDED B'** hand, palm toward the body, are placed against the right shoulder while the left **'BENT EXTENDED B'** hand, palm toward the body, is held a short distance in front of it. Then both hands are circled forward around one another several times.

generous: *adj.* liberal with one's time or money; very giving. *It was a generous act to give him the funds he needed.*

SIGN: Horizontal **'BENT EXTENDED B'** hands, palms facing each other, are alternately circled forward around each other.

SAME SIGN—**generosity**, *n.*

genial: See **congenial**.

genius: *n.* someone with outstanding intellect or ability. *He is a genius at mathematics.*

SIGN: Tip of forefinger of right **'CONTRACTED L'** hand, palm facing left, is held at right side of forehead. Hand then moves forward at an upward angle as thumb and forefinger come together and rub against each other smoothly to eventually become an **'A'** hand. (**GENIUS** may be fingerspelled.)

gentle: *adj.* soft, temperate, mild or moderate. *He is a very gentle boy, especially around the family dog.*

SIGN: **'CONTRACTED 5'** hands are held slightly apart with palms up and are drawn downward a few times as they are changed to **'FLAT O'** hands.

gentleman: *n.* a polite term for 'man'. *The painting was sold to the gentleman in the grey suit.*

SIGN #1: Right **'5'** hand is held with palm facing leftward/downward, fingers pointing upward/leftward, and tip of thumb touching the middle of the forehead. The hand is then lowered so that the tip of the thumb comes to rest at about mid-chest.

gentleman: *n.* a refined, well-mannered man. *He always behaves like a gentleman.*

SIGN #2: Vertical right **'FLAT O'** hand is held just in front of the centre of the forehead with palm facing left. The hand is then transformed to a **'5'** hand as it is lowered, the tip of the thumb coming to rest at about mid-chest.

genuine: *adj.* real or authentic. *That is a genuine diamond.*

SIGN: Forefinger of vertical right **'ONE'** hand, palm facing left, is held against the lips and the hand is moved sharply forward.

geography: *n.* the study of the earth's surface features. *They are studying Canadian geography.*

SIGN: Right **'OPEN 8'** hand is held palm-down and thumb and midfinger are used to grasp either side of the back of the left **'STANDARD BASE'** hand near the wrist. Left hand remains fixed while right hand rocks back and forth without losing its hold on the left hand.

geometry: *n.* the area of mathematics involving points, lines, angles and surfaces. *You will need a set of measuring instruments for this assignment in geometry.*

SIGN: **'MODIFIED G'** hands are held, left in front of right, with left palm facing right and left forefinger pointing right while right palm faces left and right forefinger points left. The hands brush against each other repeatedly as the right hand moves leftward a short distance and the left hand simultaneously moves rightward a few times.

germ: *n.* a microscopic organism, especially one which causes disease. *She studied the germ under the microscope.*

SIGN: Fingerspell **GERM**.

gesture: *n.* a motion of the hands, head, or body to express an idea or emotion. *He used gestures to get his point across.*

SIGN: Horizontal **'5'** hands, palms facing, are held apart and are alternately circled forward.

get: *v.* to obtain or receive. *You can get a copy of that book from the library.*

SIGN #1: Horizontal **'SPREAD C'** hands, right on top of left, are closed to form **'S'** hands as they are brought toward the chest. (In cases where **get** means 'become', as in 'to get tired', there is no equivalent sign for the word **get**. Instead, the concept of **get** or **become** is incorporated in the sign for the adjective which follows. In this case, the sign for **tired** is used to express 'to get tired'.) ❖

get: *v.* to arrive. *At what time did they get here?*

SIGN #2: Right **'BENT EXTENDED B'** hand, with palm facing the body, is brought down and laid palm-up on the upturned palm of the left **'EXTENDED B'** hand.

REGIONAL VARIATION—**arrive** #2

get along: *v.* to progress. *How are you getting along with the project?*

SIGN #1: Horizontal **'BENT EXTENDED B'** hands are held parallel with palms facing, and are simultaneously moved forward.

get along: *v.* to interact harmoniously; to have a compatible relationship. *He and his sister get along so well together.*

SIGN #2: Horizontal **'BENT EXTENDED B'** hands are held parallel with palms facing, and are simultaneously moved forward.

get dressed: *v.* to clothe oneself. *I will get dressed and go to work now.*

SIGN: Thumbs of **'MODIFIED 5'** hands, with palms toward the body and fingertips opposite, are placed at either side of upper chest. The wrists then rotate simultaneously to turn the hands so that the palms face away from the body and fingers point forward/upward. (See also **put on clothes**.)

get in: *v.* to enter; to be permitted to enter. *At this club, only members can get in free of charge.*

SIGN #1: Right **'EXTENDED B'** hand, palm down and fingers pointing forward, is curved forward under downward-facing palm of left **'EXTENDED B'** hand to simulate 'entrance'. ❖

get in: *v.* to enter a car, train, airplane, etc. *When his cab arrived, he got in and told the driver to hurry.*

SIGN #2: Side of forefinger of palm-down right **'CROOKED V'** hand is thrust against right-facing palm of left **'EXTENDED B'** hand, of which the fingers point forward.

get it: *v.* to comprehend or understand. *He explained the procedure but most of us did not get it.*

SIGN: Vertical right **'S'** hand, with knuckles near right side of forehead, is changed to a **'ONE'** hand as the forefinger is flicked upward.

get off: *v.* to leave or to descend from a bus, train, plane, etc. *She will get off the train at the next station.*

SIGN: Left **'EXTENDED B'** hand is held in a fixed position with palm facing right and fingers pointing forward. Side of forefinger of right palm-down **'CLAWED V'** hand is held against the left palm. The right forearm then moves rightward in an arc formation.

get off a horse: *v.* to dismount from a horse. *He often has stiff legs after he gets off a horse.*

SIGN: Left **'B'** hand is held in a fixed position with palm right and fingers pointing forward. Extended fingers of right **'CROOKED V'** hand straddle the left hand. The right hand then rises from the left hand and moves rightward in an arc formation.

get on: *v.* to go aboard. *It will soon be time to get on the bus.*

SIGN: Side of forefinger of palm-down right **'CROOKED V'** hand is thrust against right-facing palm of left **'EXTENDED B'** hand, of which the fingers point forward.

get on a horse: *v.* to mount a horse. *It is not easy to get on this horse.*

SIGN: Left **'B'** hand is held in a fixed position with palm right and fingers pointing forward. Right **'V'** hand is held to the right of the left hand with palm toward the body and extended fingers pointing left at an upward angle. The right hand then moves leftward in an arc formation, coming to rest with the extended fingers straddling the left hand.

get out: *v.* a command meaning 'vacate or leave the premises'. *Get out of my house!*

SIGN: Right **'EXTENDED A'** hand, palm toward the chest, is firmly thrust to the right at an angle which results in the thumb pointing over the right shoulder.

get out of: *v.* to depart from a vehicle. *He thanked the driver when he got out of the car.*

SIGN: Left **'EXTENDED B'** hand is held in a fixed position with palm facing right and fingers pointing forward. Side of forefinger of right palm-down **'CLAWED V'** hand is held against the left palm. The right forearm then moves rightward in an arc formation.

get out of the way: *v.* a command meaning 'move away from a specific place'. *You are blocking the traffic, so get out of the way!*

SIGN: Horizontal right **'BENT EXTENDED B'** hand, palm facing left, is alternated several times with an **'EXTENDED B'** handshape as the wrist bends quickly back and forth.

get the point across: See **(get the) point across**.

get up: *v.* to rise from one's bed. *We get up at 6:30 every morning.*

SIGN: Right **'CROOKED V'** hand, palm upward, is raised and overturned as it is brought downward, extended fingertips coming to rest on upturned palm of left **'EXTENDED B'** hand.

ghastly: See **horrible**.

ghetto: *n.* an area populated by a minority group, especially a disadvantaged one; an area where residents are segregated from the rest of society; a slum. *He feels more accepted in the ghetto than anywhere else.*

SIGN: Fingerspell **GHETTO**.

ghost: *n.* the disembodied spirit of someone who has died. *Some people believe the former owner's ghost still haunts the mansion.*

SIGN: Horizontal left **'F'** (or **'S'**) hand is held in a fixed position with palm facing the body at a rightward angle. Thumb and forefinger of right **'F'** hand, palm down, are inserted in the opening at the top of the left hand. Then the right hand is drawn upward with a wavy motion.

giant: *n.* a mythical character who is unusually large (often appearing in fairy tales). *Jack was frightened when he saw the giant.*

SIGN: Vertical right **'BENT EXTENDED B'** hand is held at about shoulder level with palm facing left. The hand is then emphatically raised high in the air in an upward/backward arc. For added emphasis, an 'SH' formation appears on the signer's lips. (For the purposes of storytelling, when a giant is first introduced, this sign is often preceded by the sign for **man**. Thereafter this sign only will suffice.)

gift: *n.* a present. *I received a lovely **gift** from my parents when I graduated.*

SIGN: Fingerspell **GIFT**. (Alternatively, the phrase 'to give a gift' may be expressed by using the sign for **give** #2. The phrase 'to receive a gift' may be expressed by using the reverse of the sign for **give** #2. That is, the same basic sign is used except that the movement is in the opposite direction.)

gifted: *adj.* having extraordinary ability or intelligence. *He attended a special school for **gifted** children.*

SIGN: Tip of middle finger of right **'BENT MIDFINGER 5'** hand, palm toward face, touches right side of forehead, then shimmies outward at an upward angle, giving the impression of a shimmering light. **GIFTED** may be fingerspelled.

ALTERNATE SIGNS—**genius** or **brilliant** #2

gigantic: *adj.* extraordinarily large. *Vegreville, Alberta is well known for its **gigantic** Ukrainian egg.*

SIGN: **'CLAWED L'** (or **'EXTENDED B'**) hands, with palms facing, are held slightly apart and then simultaneously moved farther apart.

giggle: *v.* to titter; to laugh nervously. *Some people **giggle** to cover their embarrassment.*

SIGN #1: **'CLAWED 5'** hands, right palm down and left palm up, represent the upper and lower teeth as the right hand is held just above the left. The hands are then simultaneously shaken up and down. The shoulders are raised for this sign and merriment is visible on the face.

OR

SIGN #2: Side of crooked forefinger of vertical right **'X'** hand is tapped lightly a few times against the throat. The shoulders are raised for this sign and merriment is visible on the face.

gin: *n.* an alcoholic drink made from a grain such as rye and flavoured with juniper berries. *Gin and tonic is a popular drink.*

SIGN: Fingerspell **GIN**.

giraffe: *n.* a long-necked mammal found in tropical Africa. *The **giraffe** is the tallest mammal in existence.*

SIGN: Horizontal right **'C'** (or **'EXTENDED C'**) hand, palm toward the body, is held in front of the neck. Then it is drawn upward/forward to indicate the length of a giraffe's neck.

girl: *n.* a young female person. *I was the only **girl** in my family.*

SIGN: Thumbtip of right **'EXTENDED A'** hand, palm left, is placed on the right cheek and is stroked forward/downward. Motion may be repeated.

girl guide: *n.* a girl who is a member of a world-wide organization founded in 1908 by Lord Baden-Powell. *A **girl guide** learns to be self-sufficient and to help others.*

SIGN: Vertical right **'CLOSED W'** hand, palm forward, is tapped against right side of forehead a couple of times.

give: *v.* to place in the possession of another. *I will **give** you some money.*

SIGN #1: Horizontal right **'CONTRACTED B'** hand is held with palm facing leftward/upward and fingers pointing left. The hand then moves forward in a slight arc formation as if giving something to someone. (Handshapes for this sign vary according to the size and shape of the object being given; however, the basic movement remains the same.) ❖

give: *v.* to place in the possession of another. *I will **give** you one million dollars if you help me.*

SIGN #2: Right **'X'** hand is held upright with palm facing left, and is thrust forward and downward to a horizontal position. (This sign is used instead of **give** #1 when what is being given is a gift, reward or something either surprising or large in size or amount.) ❖

give out: *v.* to hand out or distribute. *Will you please **give out** the application forms?*

SIGN: Horizontal **'CONTRACTED B'** hands are held with palms up and fingertips almost touching. The hands then move forward in an outward arc as the fingers spread to assume a **'SLANTED 5'** shape.

ALTERNATE SIGN—**circulate**

give up: *v.* to surrender or abandon hope. *Despite several setbacks he refused to **give up** his dream of becoming a doctor.*

SIGN: **'OPEN A'** hands, held slightly apart at waist level, palms down, are thrust upward to form **'EXTENDED B'** hands with palms facing forward. (Signs vary.)

glad: *adj.* happy; pleased. *I am **glad** to see you again.*

SIGN: Horizontal right **'EXTENDED B'** hand, palm toward the body, is brushed up and off the chest twice in a circular motion.

glance: *v.* to look briefly. *The driver **glanced** at the hitchhiker and kept on driving.*

SIGN: Right **'BENT V'** hand is held with palm forward and extended fingers pointing forward. The signer's head and gaze turn rightward as the right wrist twists, causing the extended fingers to point rightward/forward.

glass: *n.* a container used for drinking. *Do you want a **glass** of water?*

SIGN #1: Horizontal right **'C'** hand, palm facing left but angled slightly toward the body, is held just above the upturned palm of the left **'EXTENDED B'** hand, which is held with fingers pointing forward/rightward. The right hand is then lowered into the left palm, raised, and lowered once again. (Signs may vary depending on the size and shape of the glass.)

glass: *n.* a hard, brittle, transparent solid. *Window panes are made of **glass**.*

SIGN #2: Tip of forefinger of right **'CROOKED ONE'** hand, palm toward the body, is tapped against the upper front teeth. (**GLASS** in this context may be fingerspelled.)

glasses: *n.* a pair of lenses for correcting faulty vision. *Do you wear **glasses** when you read?*

SIGN: **'CROOKED L'** hands, palms facing each other, are held in a vertical position beside each eye. The forearms then move outward and inward slightly a few times so that the thumbtips tap against the cheeks. (Alternatively, the right hand only is frequently used.)

glimpse [*or* **catch a glimpse of**]: *v.* to get a short or incomplete look at. *I caught a **glimpse** of the celebrity as he made his way through the cheering crowd.*

SIGN: Right **'BENT V'** hand is held with palm forward and extended fingers pointing forward. The head turns abruptly rightward as the right wrist twists, causing the extended fingers to point rightward/forward. This sign is generally accompanied by an open-mouthed look of surprise.

ALTERNATE SIGN—**spot** #3

glisten: *v.* to shine with a sparkling gleam. *The gold **glistened** as the light shone on it.*

SIGN: Tip of middle finger of right **'BENT MIDFINGER 5'** hand, palm down, is placed on back of left **'STANDARD BASE'** hand. The right hand wobbles as it moves upward/rightward. (Sometimes this sign is made without the left hand; instead the middle finger of the right hand is placed on the actual object or on the place where the object is imagined to be. Handshapes for the right hand may vary as well.)

globe: *n.* a sphere that represents the earth. *The teacher used the **globe** in her geography lesson.*

SIGN: Right **'OPEN 8'** hand is held palm-down and thumb and midfinger are used to grasp either side of the back of the left **'STANDARD BASE'** near the wrist. Left hand remains fixed while right hand rocks back and forth without losing its hold on the left hand. Next, **'CROOKED 5'** hands are held side by side with palms down and fingers pointing forward. The hands are then moved away from each other in a downward/outward arc, coming together again with palms facing upward. **GLOBE** is frequently fingerspelled. (ASL CONCEPT—**earth - sphere**.)

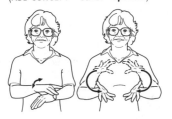

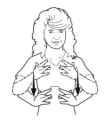

gloom: *n.* a state of sadness or depression. *The grey skies create a feeling of **gloom**.*

SIGN: Tips of middle fingers of **'BENT MIDFINGER 5'** hands are held at either side of upper chest and are simultaneously lowered.

ALTERNATE SIGN—**depressed** #2

SAME SIGN—**gloomy**, *adj.*, in this context.

glory: *n.* praise or honour. *The Romans wanted fame and glory.*

SIGN: Tip of middle finger of right **'BENT MIDFINGER 5'** hand, palm down, is placed on back of left **'STANDARD BASE'** hand. The right hand wobbles as it moves upward/rightward.

glove: *n.* a covering for the hand with individual coverings for the fingers and thumb. *You should wear gloves when you go out in cold weather.*

SIGN #1: Forefinger of horizontal right **'ONE'** hand, palm toward the body at a leftward angle, is used to trace the fingers of the horizontal left **'5'** hand which is held with palm facing right but slanted toward the body.

OR

SIGN #2: Fingertips of right **'BENT 5'** hand, palm down, are used to stroke the back of the left **'STANDARD BASE'** hand. The movement of the right hand is directed toward the chest. (Signs may vary.)

glue: *n.* a sticky adhesive substance. *The teacher gave the children some glue to make Valentines.*

SIGN: Right **'MODIFIED G'** hand, palm facing left, is held in a vertical position at the left side of the chin and the thumb and forefinger are opened and closed rapidly several times as the hand is drawn to the right.

glum: See **sad**.

gluttony: *n.* the practice of eating or drinking too much. *Gluttony may result in obesity or other health problems.*

SIGN: **'FLAT O'** hands, palms toward the body, are held slightly apart and circled alternately toward the mouth. The cheeks are puffed out.

gnaw: *v.* to bite (at), gradually wearing away with the teeth. *The beaver gnawed at the fallen log.*

SIGN: Left **'ONE'** hand is held in a fixed position with palm down and forefinger pointing rightward/forward. The left forefinger is positioned between the tips of the extended fingers and thumb of the right **'CLAWED 3'** hand, of which the palm faces leftward/forward, and the fingers and thumb act as teeth as they clamp down several times on the left forefinger. (Signs vary according to what is being gnawed, how it is being gnawed, and what sort of animal is doing the gnawing.)

go [*or* **go to**]: *v.* to proceed from one place to another. *We will go to a movie tonight.*

SIGN #1: Vertical right **'ONE'** hand is held with palm facing forward. The wrist then bends, causing the hand to fall forward so that the palm faces down. (Alternatively, this sign may be made with two hands.)

OR

SIGN #2: Right **'CONTRACTED 5'** hand, palm toward the body, is drawn forward at a slight rightward angle as the fingers close to form a **'FLAT O'** handshape.

go [*or* **go to**] **very happily:** *v.* to proceed from one place to another (with great pleasure). *I will go to Paris next week!*

SIGN #3: Vertical right **'SLANTED 5'** hand is held with palm forward/leftward. The hand then moves firmly rightward/forward as it closes to form an **'S'** (or **'A'**) hand. (This sign is generally used when someone is *looking forward to* or *excited about* going somewhere.)

go [*or* **get going**]: *v.* to leave, or to be on one's way. *I am already late for my appointment so I have to get going.*

SIGN #4: Left **'EXTENDED B'** hand is held with palm basically downward but slanted rightward/forward while fingers point upward at a rightward/forward angle. Right **'EXTENDED B'** hand, with palm basically upward but slanted backward/leftward and fingers pointing leftward at a forward angle, is held with fingers against left palm. The right hand then glides rapidly along the length of the left hand and off at an upward/rightward/forward angle. (This sign generally implies a sense of urgency or a sudden decision to leave.)

go ahead: *v.* to proceed. *The letters GA on a TTY screen mean "go ahead".*

SIGN: Horizontal **'BENT EXTENDED B'** hands are held parallel with palms facing, and are simultaneously moved forward. (The TTY abbreviation **GA** is frequently fingerspelled.)

go away: *v.* to remove oneself from a given place. *I told him to go away and stop bothering me.*

SIGN: Right **'BENT EXTENDED B'** hand is held with palm down and fingers pointing down. The fingers then straighten so that they point forward/rightward as the hand moves slightly but quickly forward/rightward.

go by: *v.* to pass by, via, or by way of. *We go by Red Deer when we drive to Calgary.*

SIGN #1: Vertical **'A'** hands are held with knuckles together and palms facing each other. Then the right hand is moved forward/downward.

go by: *v.* to act according to. *If we go by the instructions in the manual, the equipment should be easy to operate.*

SIGN #2: Horizontal left **'EXTENDED A'** hand is held with palm facing right while horizontal right **'EXTENDED A'** hand is held directly behind the left hand with palm facing left. Together, the hands are moved purposefully forward/downward.

go on: *v.* to move or proceed from one point to another. *We cannot go on with our work until we get his approval.*

SIGN: Horizontal **'BENT EXTENDED B'** hands are held parallel with palms facing, and are simultaneously moved forward.

go out: *v.* to engage in activities away from a certain place such as one's home. *We should go out for lunch today.*

SIGN #1: Right **'CONTRACTED 5'** hand, palm toward the body, is drawn forward at a slight rightward angle as the fingers close to form a **'FLAT O'** handshape.

go out: *v.* in the case of a fire, to stop burning. *The flame will go out if you leave the candle in the open window.*

SIGN #2: Right **'CONTRACTED 5'** hand is held with palm facing upward. The wrist then bends back causing the hand to drop down as the fingers come together to form a **'MODIFIED O'** hand. (Two hands are used to refer to the extinction of a fire which is larger than a single flame.)

go out with: *v.* to engage in activities outside the home in the company of another person. *I go out with Ryan every Friday evening.*

SIGN: **'A'** hands are held together, palms facing each other, and knuckles touching. Then they are thrust forward/downward together from chest level.

go over: *v.* to proceed from one point to another. *Did you go over to their house last night?*

SIGN #1: Right **'BENT EXTENDED B'** hand is held to the right of and slightly ahead of the left **'BENT EXTENDED B'** hand. Palms face downward/forward and fingers point forward/rightward. The hands then move simultaneously forward/rightward in an arc formation. (Alternatively, this sign may be made with one hand only.) ❖

go over: *v.* to check or inspect. *Our mechanic will go over your car to see if any repairs are necessary.*

SIGN #2: Left **'EXTENDED B'** hand is held in a fixed position with palm turned upward but slanted slightly rightward and toward the body while fingers point rightward/forward. Right **'ONE'** hand is held palm down as tip of forefinger brushes forward several times against palm of left hand.

OR

SIGN #3: Horizontal **'BENT V'** hands are held slightly apart with fingers pointing forward and are circled in opposite directions (the left hand clockwise and the right hand counterclockwise). Depending on the situation, the sign for **examine** is sometimes used to mean **go over**.

go over: *v.* to review. *I plan to go over my notes once more before the exam.*

SIGN #4: Left **'EXTENDED B'** hand is held in a fixed position with palm toward the body at an upward angle and fingers pointing rightward. Right **'V'** hand is held behind and slightly above the left hand with palm down and extended fingers pointing forward. The right hand then moves rightward in a series of small arcs as the wrist bends up and down several times.

go over: *v.* to discuss. *We should go over the contract briefly.*

SIGN #5: Forefinger of horizontal right **'ONE'** hand, palm toward the body, is tapped several times on the upturned palm of the left **'EXTENDED B'** hand, of which the fingers are pointing rightward/forward.

go to bed: *v.* to get under the covers. *He will go to bed early and get a good night's sleep.*

SIGN: Left '**S**' hand is held loosely without actually forming a fist while the palm faces downward. Right '**U**' hand is held to the right of the left hand and closer to the body with palm facing upward but slanted leftward and toward the body while the extended fingers point forward/leftward. As the hands then move toward each other, the extended fingers of the right hand, which are meant to represent someone's legs, are inserted into the opening in the left hand. When making this sign, the signer generally closes her eyes as her head tilts rightward.

go under: *v.* to fail (in business) or go bankrupt. *She was worried that her business might go under.*

SIGN: Extended fingers of right '**BENT V**' hand are thrust downward against right-facing palm of vertical left '**EXTENDED B**' hand, and beyond.

ALTERNATE SIGN—**broke**

goal: *n.* the aim or object towards which one's efforts are directed. *My goal in life is to become rich and famous.*

SIGN #1: Vertical '**ONE**' hands, left palm facing right and right palm facing left, are held out in front of the face, with the left hand directly ahead of the right. The hands are then simultaneously moved forward.

goal: *n.* a successful scoring attempt in hockey or soccer. *Our team needs one more goal to win the game.*

SIGN #2: Forefinger of horizontal right '**ONE**' hand, palm left, falls forward/downward until it lies between forefinger and midfinger of vertical left '**5**' hand, of which the palm is facing the body.

OR

SIGN #3: Vertical left '**5**' hand is held in a fixed position with palm facing the body while right '**EXTENDED B**' hand, palm facing left, is brought down firmly and thrust between forefinger and middle finger of left hand.

goalie [*or* **goalkeeper** *or* **goaltender**]: *n.* the player on a hockey or soccer team who protects his/her team's goal against scoring by the opposing team. *The goalie made an impressive save.*

SIGN #1: '**EXTENDED B**' hands are held out to either side of the body with wrists bent back, palms forward and fingers basically pointing outward. The wrists then twist, causing the hands to alternately wave up and down.

OR

SIGN #2: Right '**S**' hand, palm leftward/downward, is held just in front of the left forearm and pounds the left arm a couple of times near the elbow.

goat: *n.* a sure-footed, agile mammal with hollow horns. *Mountain goats inhabit many areas of the Rockies.*

SIGN: Vertical right '**S**' hand, palm facing backward, touches the chin. The forefinger and middle finger flick out to form a '**CROOKED V**' hand. The hand then moves up to the forehead and goes through the transition from '**S**' to '**CROOKED V**' shape again with fingers pointing upward. (Signs vary.)

gobble: *v.* to eat hastily in large mouthfuls. *The children will gobble up the birthday cake.*

SIGN: '**FLAT O**' hands, palms toward the body, are held slightly apart and circled alternately toward the mouth. The cheeks are puffed out.

God: *n.* a supreme being worshipped in most religions. *Christians believe in a benevolent God.*

SIGN: Right '**EXTENDED B**' hand, palm facing left, is held horizontally with fingers pointing forward. The hand is then raised to a vertical position.

gold: *n.* a precious yellow metal used as a monetary standard. *Gold is mined in British Columbia and the Yukon.*

SIGN: Tip of forefinger of right '**COMBINED LY**' hand, palm facing left, is placed just in front of the right ear. The forearm then moves forward and slightly downward as the hand is transformed to a '**Y**' shape and the wrist twists back and forth to make the hand wobble. (This sign is generally accompanied by an 'O' lip pattern.)
SAME SIGNS—**gold**, *adj.* (colour) and **golden**, *adj.*

golf: *n.* a game played on a large open course using clubs and a small ball. *Many people play golf for exercise and relaxation.*

SIGN: Left **'CLOSED T'** hand is held horizontally with palm facing left while right **'CLOSED T'** hand is held upright with palm facing forward. The signer then simulates a golf swing by moving the right forearm in a downward/leftward arc as both wrists rotate rightward so that the left palm is turned downward while the right palm eventually faces leftward/upward.

gone: *adj.* lost or missing. *My house had been broken into and my television set was gone.*

SIGN #1: Right **'CONTRACTED 5'** hand, palm up, becomes a **'FLAT O'** hand as it is drawn downward behind the horizontal left **'CROOKED 5'** hand of which the palm is facing the body.

gone: *adj.* used up or consumed. *When we arrived, all the food was gone.*

SIGN #2: Right horizontal **'SPREAD C'** hand, palm toward the chest, is placed on the upturned palm of the left **'EXTENDED B'** hand. Then the right hand is drawn forward as it changes to an **'S'** handshape.

SIGN #3 [ONTARIO]: Left **'A'** hand is held in a relatively fixed position with palm toward the body at an upward angle. Right **'A'** hand is held above and slightly to the right of the left hand with the palm facing that of the left hand. The right hand then moves purposefully downward/rightward, the knuckles striking against those of the left hand on the way past.

(be) gone: *v.* to be away. *Our neighbours are gone for two weeks.*

SIGN #4: Right **'BENT EXTENDED B'** hand is held with palm down and fingers pointing down. The fingers then straighten so that they point forward/rightward as the hand moves slightly but quickly forward/rightward.

ALTERNATE SIGN—**go out** #1

gonorrhea: *n.* an infectious venereal disease that causes a discharge of mucous from the genitals. *Gonorrhea is highly contagious and can be readily passed on to sex partners.*

SIGN: Fingerspell **GONORRHEA**. (Alternatively, the abbreviation **VD** meaning 'venereal disease' is fingerspelled.)

G O N O R R H E A

good: *adj.* having positive qualities. *The meal was good.*

SIGN #1: Fingertips of right **'BENT EXTENDED B'** hand are placed on the lips so that the palm is toward the body. Then the hand is moved purposefully forward a brief distance.

(very) good: *adj.* having extremely positive qualities. *That meal was very good.*

SIGN #2: Right **'EXTENDED A'** hand is held in a relatively horizontal position with palm facing left. The forearm then firmly moves a short distance forward.

(no) good: *adj.* bad or of no practical use. *The broken tennis racquet is no good.*

SIGN: Right **'N'** hand is held upright with palm forward/leftward. The hand then moves quickly upward/rightward as the wrist rotates rightward and the hand takes on a **'BENT L'** shape.

goodbye: *n.* farewell. *Saying goodbye is not always easy to do.*

SIGN: Fingertips of right **'BENT EXTENDED B'** hand are placed on the lips. The hand then moves forward/rightward as the wrist rotates to turn the palm forward and the fingers flutter in unison. (When **goodbye** is used as a sentence substitute, as is the case when a signer simply says, "Goodbye", only the latter half of the sign is used.)

good-hearted: See **kind** #1 & #2.

goods: *n.* merchandise. *The people are taxed for buying goods and services.*

SIGN: Right **'EXTENDED B'** hand, palm facing up, fingertips pointing forward, is moved from left to right in a series of successive short arcs.

goose: *n.* a large, long-necked, web-footed bird. *The national bird of Canada is the Canada Goose.*

SIGN: Right **'CONTRACTED 3'** hand, palm facing away from the body, is placed on left shoulder. The right hand then moves along the slightly bent left arm as the thumb and extended fingers open and close several times, thus alternating between **'CONTRACTED 3'** and **'CLOSED DOUBLE MODIFIED G'** shapes. GOOSE may be fingerspelled.
ALTERNATE SIGN—**duck** #1

gorgeous: *adj.* very beautiful or magnificent. *The bride wore a gorgeous gown.*

SIGN: Right **'CONTRACTED 5'** hand is circled clockwise (to the onlooker) around the face as the fingers close to form a **'FLAT O'** hand, with palm and fingers toward the chin.

gorilla: *n.* the largest species of ape. *The gorilla is a stocky animal covered with coarse, dark hair.*

SIGN: Horizontal **'A'** hands, palms toward the body, are thumped alternately on either side of the chest.

gossip: *n.* idle chatter, often involving rumours about people. *Have you heard any gossip lately?*

SIGN: Vertical **'MODIFIED G'** hands, palms facing each other, are held apart in front of the mouth or upper chest and are rapidly alternated with **'CLOSED MODIFIED G'** handshapes as they are being moved simultaneously in a semicircular direction.

(have) got to: *v.* must; have to. *We have got to hurry or we will be late.*

SIGN: Right **'X'** hand, palm facing away from the body, is held in a vertical position in front of the chest and is sharply thrust downward from the wrist so that the palm faces down.

govern: *v.* to control or rule over. *The Prime Minister and the Cabinet govern Canada.*

SIGN: Horizontal **'X'** hands are held slightly apart with left palm facing right and right palm facing left. Then they are alternately moved backward and forward.

government: *n.* a unit empowered to exercise political authority. *The Progressive Conservative party formed Canada's government after the election.*

SIGN #1: Vertical right **'ONE'** hand is held near the right side of the forehead with palm forward and slightly leftward. The wrist then rotates forward to turn the hand as the forefinger tucks into a **'BENT ONE'** position with the fingertip coming to rest on the right side of the forehead.

OR

SIGN #2: Right **'G'** hand, palm facing left, is moved a short distance rightward in a rightward/upward arc formation.

gown: *n.* a woman's evening dress or a loose robe. *The women wore fashionable gowns to the ball.*

SIGN: Right **'BENT EXTENDED B'** hand is held with palm facing the body and fingers pointing to right upper chest. The hand is then lowered straight down the length of the torso to about waist level. Next, thumbs of **'MODIFIED 5'** hands, with palms toward the body and fingertips opposite, are placed at either side of upper chest. The wrists then rotate simultaneously to turn the hands so that the palms face away from the body and fingers point forward/upward. Alternatively, GOWN may be fingerspelled.
(ASL CONCEPT—**long - dress**.)

grab: *v.* to seize hold of. *He grabbed his homework and left the house.*

SIGN: Sign choice depends on what is being grabbed and where the grabbing is taking place. In each case, the sign takes the form of a natural gesture, beginning with the hand open and fingers spread, and ending with a closed fist. ❖

grace: *n.* a mealtime prayer, giving thanks for the food. *Who will say grace before the meal?*

SIGN: **'EXTENDED B'** hands, palms together, are held in a vertical position in front of the chest and the head is bowed in an attitude of prayer.

gracious: *adj.* characterized by kindness and courtesy. *It was gracious of you to invite me to your house for dinner.*

SIGN: Horizontal **'BENT EXTENDED B'** hands, palms facing each other, are alternately circled forward around each other.

grade: *n.* a division within a school curriculum by years of achievement. *In the tenth grade we studied Romeo and Juliet.*

SIGN: Fingerspell **GRADE**.

gradual: *adj.* happening in small, slow stages. *His recovery since the accident has been gradual.*

SIGN: Right **'CROOKED 5'** hand is held palm down with fingertips touching the end of the left **'STANDARD BASE'** hand. The right hand is then drawn backward leftward along the back of the left hand as though petting it. Next, horizontal **'BENT EXTENDED B'** hands, left palm facing right and right palm facing left, are held with the right above the left. The hands then pass over and under each other as the forearms are simultaneously and plodingly circled forward a few times. (ASL CONCEPT— **slow - process.**) Signs vary and are often incorporated in other signs within the sentence such as the verb.

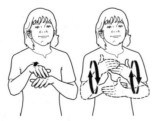

graduate: *v.* to successfully complete a course of studies. *Many Canadians have graduated from Gallaudet University.*

SIGN: Left **'EXTENDED B'** hand is held in a fixed position with palm up and fingers pointing forward/rightward. Vertical right **'MODIFIED G'** hand, palm facing leftward/forward, is held above the left hand. The right hand is then lowered as the wrist rotates clockwise with a flourish, twisting the hand a quarter turn so that the palm now faces leftward as the hand comes to rest on the left palm.
SAME SIGN—**graduation**, *n.*

graduate school: *n.* an educational institution where a student may work toward a degree beyond the bachelor's level. *Paul is at graduate school working on a Master of Science degree.*

SIGN: Forearms are crossed at the wrists with left arm in front of right and both palms facing the body. The back of the wrist of the right **'V'** hand taps twice against the inside of the wrist of the left **'5'** hand.

grain: *n.* the seeds of cereal grasses, or other small, seedlike particles. *Farmers in Canada grow a variety of grain.*

SIGN: Fingerspell **GRAIN**.

gram: *n.* a metric unit of weight. *A gram is one thousandth of a kilogram.*

SIGN: Fingerspell **GRAM**.

grammar: *n.* the structure and syntax of a language. *It is important to understand the grammar of American Sign Language.*

SIGN: Horizontal **'MODIFIED G'** hands, palms facing each other, are held close together and wobble slightly as they are then drawn apart.

grand: *adj.* wonderful. *They had a grand time at the fair.*

SIGN #1: Vertical **'EXTENDED B'** hands, palms facing forward, are held apart near the face. Forearms are pushed purposefully forward a short distance.

grand: *adj.* elaborate; impressive. *The banquet was a grand affair.*

SIGN #2: Vertical right '**5**' hand is held very close to or touching the chest with palm facing left. The hand is then moved slightly upward and off the chest a few times in small circles. The body is held erect. (When used as part of a proper noun such as *Grand* Canyon or *Grand* Banks, **GRAND** is fingerspelled.)

granddaughter: *n.* the daughter of one's son or daughter. *My granddaughter bears a strong resemblance to her mother.*

SIGN: Fingerspell **GRAND**. Then right '**B**' hand is held with tip of forefinger touching chin and palm facing leftward/downward. The right forearm then drops downward as the wrist rotates forward causing the palm to turn upward as the hand comes to rest on the left forearm.

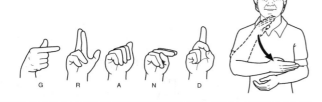

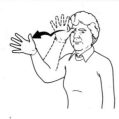

grandfather: *n.* one's father's or mother's male parent. *My grandfather was born in Italy.*

SIGN #1: Thumb of vertical right '**5**' hand, palm facing left, is placed in centre of forehead. As the hand is then moved forward in two successive short arcs, it becomes horizontal with fingers pointing forward.

SIGN #2 [ATLANTIC]: Right '**S**' hand, slightly open, palm facing left, is brought down firmly from the chin as it closes. Next, left '**U**' hand is held palm down with extended fingers pointing forward/rightward. Right '**U**' (or '**CROOKED U**') hand is held palm down just above the left hand and at right angles to it. The extended fingers of the right hand are then tapped a couple of times on those of the left.
(ASL CONCEPT—**old - father**.)

SIGN #3 [ONTARIO]: Vertical right '**M**' hand, palm facing leftward/forward, is placed to the right of the forehead and the three uncovered fingers are moved up and down a few times as the fingertips brush downward against the right side of the forehead.

SIGN #4 [PRAIRIE]: Vertical '**BENT EXTENDED B**' hand is held with palm toward the face at a slight leftward angle and fingertips touching the right side of the forehead. The hand is then moved forward in two successive short arcs.

grandmother: *n.* one's father's or mother's female parent. *My grandmother is now in a nursing home.*

SIGN #1: Thumb of vertical right '**5**' hand, palm facing left, is placed at chin. As the hand is then moved forward in two successive short arcs, it becomes horizontal with fingers pointing forward.

SIGN #2 [ATLANTIC]: Right '**S**' hand, slightly open, palm facing left, is brought down firmly from the chin as it closes. Next, left '**EXTENDED B**' hand is held in a fixed position with palm up and fingers pointing forward/rightward. Right '**M**' (or '**EXTENDED B**') hand is held palm down with fingers pointing forward/leftward as they are tapped once or twice on the palm of the left hand.
(ASL CONCEPT—**old - mother**.)

SIGN #3 [ONTARIO]: Vertical right '**M**' hand, palm facing leftward/forward, is held near lower right jaw and the three uncovered fingers are moved up and down a few times as the fingertips brush downward against the lower right cheek.

SIGN #4 [PRAIRIE]: Vertical '**BENT EXTENDED B**' hand is held with palm facing the body at a slight leftward angle and fingertips touching the lower right jaw. The hand is then moved forward in two successive short arcs.

grandson: *n.* the son of one's son or daughter. *He likes to take his grandson fishing.*

SIGN: Fingerspell **GRAND**. Then right **'B'** hand is held with side of forefinger touching forehead and palm facing leftward/downward. The right forearm then drops downward as the wrist rotates forward causing the palm to turn upward as the hand comes to rest on the left forearm.

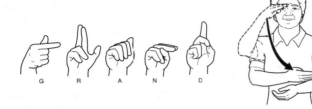

grant: *n.* a sum of money provided by a public fund for a specific purpose. *She received a government grant for further research in linguistics.*

SIGN #1: Right **'X'** hand is held upright with palm facing left, and is thrust forward and downward to a horizontal position. (**GRANT** in this context is frequently fingerspelled.)

grant: *v.* to permit as a favour. *I will grant you that request.*

SIGN #2: Horizontal **'EXTENDED B'** hands are held with palms facing and fingers pointing forward. The hands are then swept upward simultaneously from the wrists so that the fingers point upward.
ALTERNATE SIGN—**allow** #1

grapefruit: *n.* a large citrus fruit with a yellow rind and juicy flesh. *I often eat a grapefruit for breakfast.*

SIGN: Fingerspell **GRAPEFRUIT**.

grapes: *n.* the edible fruit of a grapevine. *Grapes are used to make juice, wine and raisins.*

SIGN #1: Fingertips of right **'SPREAD EXTENDED C'** hand, palm facing down, are tapped against the back of the left **'STANDARD BASE'** hand in a series of very short arcs moving in a forward/rightward/downward direction along the left hand. (**GRAPES** is frequently fingerspelled.)

SIGN #2 [ATLANTIC]: Left **'ONE'** hand is held in a fixed position with palm facing the body and forefinger pointing rightward. Fingers and thumb of right **'OPEN SPREAD O'** hand, palm facing left, are used to grasp the tip of the left forefinger. Then the right hand is twisted back and forth several times.

grapevine: *n.* an unofficial means of relaying information from person to person. *We heard through the grapevine that he got the job.*

SIGN: Vertical **'MODIFIED G'** hands, palms facing each other, are held apart in front of the mouth or upper chest and are rapidly alternated with **'CLOSED MODIFIED G'** handshapes as they are being moved simultaneously in a semicircular direction.

graph: *n.* a diagram depicting a certain set of relationships. *Will you please plot these intercepts on the graph?*

SIGN: Fingertips of right **'5'** hand, palm down, are stroked downward across palm of horizontal left **'5'** hand which is facing the chest, but angled rightward. Then the right wrist rotates forward a quarter turn so that the palm is turned toward the body at a leftward-facing angle as the fingertips are stroked across the left palm from left to right.

graphics: *n.* the process of drawing to mathematical scale. *She is studying graphics as part of her computer science program.*

SIGN: **'Y'** hands, which are held with palms down and thumbtips touching, alternately wobble slightly.
ALTERNATE SIGN—**art**

grasp: *v.* to seize hold of and grip with the hands. *He grasped the pole.*

SIGN #1: Sign choice for **grasp** depends on what is being grasped and where the grasping is taking place. In each case, the sign takes the form of a natural gesture, beginning with the hand(s) open and fingers spread, and ending with (a) closed fist(s). ❖

grasp: *v.* to understand or catch on. *She grasped the object of the game very quickly.*

SIGN #2: Vertical right **'SPREAD C'** hand, with palm facing forward, is held just above horizontal left **'SPREAD C'** hand, of which the palm faces downward. Then both hands are closed simultaneously to form **'S'** hands as the right hand is brought down to rest on the back of the left hand. A look of realization accompanies this sign.

ALTERNATE SIGN—**understand**

grass: *n.* a family of green plants, such as those which make up a lawn. *The grass needs to be watered often during dry spells.*

SIGN #1: Back of right **'CROOKED 4'** hand, palm down, is held under the chin and the hand is moved briskly in small circular motions, brushing backward against the underside of the chin with each cycle.

OR

SIGN #2: Heel of right **'SPREAD EXTENDED C'** hand, palm upward, is placed under the chin and the hand is moved briskly in small circular motions, brushing forward/upward against the underside of the chin with each cycle.

grate: *v.* to scrape or shred. *I will grate the cheese for our pizza.*

SIGN: Right **'A'** hand is placed palm-down on the upturned palm of the left **'EXTENDED B'** hand and is moved rightward/forward a few times as if scraping repeatedly against the left palm. (Signs vary.)

grateful: *adj.* appreciative or thankful. *I am grateful for your support.*

SIGN: Fingertips of vertical **'BENT EXTENDED B'** hands, palms toward the body, are placed on or just in front of the lips. The hands are then moved purposefully forward a brief distance. (Alternatively, this sign may be made with one hand only.)

gratifying: *adj.* pleasing; satisfying. *It was gratifying to see our donation put to such good use.*

SIGN: Palms of horizontal **'EXTENDED B'** hands are held right above left against the chest. Then the hands are circled simultaneously in opposite directions.

ALTERNATE SIGN—**satisfy**

grave: *n.* an underground place for the burial of a corpse. *She wept when they lowered her husband into his grave.*

SIGN #1: **'BENT EXTENDED B'** hands are held parallel with palms down and fingers pointing down. The hands are then drawn upward and back toward the body with a curving motion, to form **'EXTENDED B'** hands with palms facing forward/downward.

grave: *adj.* solemn; serious; important; suggesting danger. *I have some grave concerns about this situation.*

SIGN #2: Vertical right **'BENT ONE'** hand is held with tip of forefinger touching chin and palm facing leftward but slanted toward the body. The wrist then rotates, turning the hand so that the palm fully faces the body.

gravel: *n.* a mixture of rock fragments and small stones. *The truck spread gravel on the country road.*

SIGN: Fingerspell **GRAVEL**.

gravity: *n.* the force of attraction that governs certain scientific principles. *Weightlessness in outer space results from a lack of gravity.*

SIGN: Fingerspell **GRAVITY**.

gravy: *n.* thickened, flavoured sauce made from meat juices. *Do you want gravy or ketchup on your french fries?*

SIGN #1: Thumb and midfinger of right **'OPEN 8'** hand grasp edge of left **'EXTENDED B'** (or **'5'**) hand, which is held with palm facing rightward but angled slightly toward the body while the fingers point forward/rightward at a slight upward angle. The right hand is then drawn downward at least twice, forming an **'8'** shape with each downward movement.

OR

SIGN #2: Horizontal right **'Y'** hand, with thumb pointing downward and palm facing away from the body, is circled in a counter-clockwise direction.

greasy: *adj.* coated with grease. *The french fries are very greasy.*

SIGN: Thumb and midfinger of right **'OPEN 8'** hand grasp edge of left **'EXTENDED B'** (or **'5'**) hand, which is held with palm facing right-ward but angled slightly toward the body while the fingers point forward/rightward at a slight upward angle. The right hand is then drawn downward at least twice, forming an '8' shape with each downward movement. (This sign is generally accompanied by a grimace. Sometimes the signer uses his/her facial expression without signing to indicate that something is greasy.)

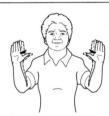

great: *adj.* remarkable, excellent or fantastic. *Thomas Hopkins Gallaudet was a great man in the history of Deaf education.*

SIGN #1: Vertical **'EXTENDED B'** hands, palms facing forward, are held apart near the face. Forearms are pushed purposefully forward a short distance.

great: *adj.* very big. *We sat in the shade of a great oak tree to eat our lunch.*

SIGN #2: **'CLAWED L'** (or **'EXTENDED B'**) hands, with palms facing, are held slightly apart and then simultaneously moved farther apart. (When used as part of a proper noun such as *Great* Lakes or *Great* Britain, **GREAT** is finger-spelled.)

great-: *adj.* a generation removed. *Her great-grandfather founded the company.*

SIGN #3: Fingerspell **GREAT**.

greedy: *adj.* too desirous of food, money, etc. *Do not be greedy with your possessions.*

SIGN: Right **'S'** hand, palm downward/leftward, makes counter-clockwise (from the signer's perspective) circles as it is rubbed on the chin.

SAME SIGN—**greed**, *n.*
ALTERNATE SIGN—**mean** #3

green: *adj.* of a shade of colour that lies between blue and yellow in the spectrum. *A Canadian twenty-dollar bill is green in colour.*

SIGN: Vertical right **'MODIFIED G'** hand, palm facing left, is shaken from slight but quick twists of the wrist.

greet: *v.* to address in a friendly way. *He always greets me when we meet on the street.*

SIGN #1: Side of forefinger of vertical right **'B'** hand, palm facing left, is placed against right side of forehead. The forearm is then moved forward/rightward as the hand tips forward/rightward from the wrist so that the fingers point in the same direction as if the signer is saluting someone. (If more than one person is being greeted, the hands salute alternately several times.)

greet: *v.* to welcome. *He will greet the guests as they arrive.*

SIGN #2: Right **'EXTENDED B'** hand is held out in front of the body with fingers pointing left-ward and palm facing the body but angled upward slightly. The hand is then drawn in toward the body.

grey [*also spelled* **gray**]: *adj.* of a neutral tone between white and black. *The sky is grey today.*

SIGN: Right **'R'** (or **'EXTENDED R'**) hand is held with palm facing left and extended fingers pointing forward/upward. The hand then twists a few times from the wrist as if turning a key back and forth in a lock.

grief: *n.* deep sadness, especially after someone dies. *She went through a long period of grief after her father died.*

SIGN #1: Vertical **'CROOKED 5'** hands are held slightly apart with palms toward the face. The hands are then simultaneously lowered somewhat and the head tilts to the right. Facial expression is important.

OR

SIGN #2: **'S'** hands are held side by side with palms down in front of (often at the left side of) the chest. The wrists then simultaneously twist in opposite directions, the left wrist twisting backward so that the palm faces forward/rightward and the right wrist twisting forward so that the palm faces the body. The movement resembles that of wringing out a damp cloth. Facial expression is important.

grief: *n.* anxiety; deep mental anguish. *The rebellious teenager caused her parents a lot of grief.*

SIGN #3: **'B'** (or **'EXTENDED B'**) hands are held apart in front of the face at such an angle that the palms face each other but slant downward while the fingers of the left hand point upward/rightward and the fingers of the right hand point upward/leftward. The hands are then alternately circled toward each other a few times. Facial expression must clearly convey 'anxiety'.

grievance: *n.* a complaint prompted by what is perceived to be an unjust situation. *The labour union investigates every grievance against the employers.*

SIGN: Right **'SPREAD C'** hand is held in a horizontal position as thumb and fingertips thump against chest once.

grieve: *v.* to mourn a loss; to feel deep sadness over someone's death. *It is natural to grieve when someone dies.*

SIGN: Vertical **'CROOKED 5'** hands are held slightly apart with palms toward the face. The hands are then simultaneously lowered somewhat and the head tilts to the right. Facial expression is an important feature of this sign.
ALTERNATE SIGN—**grief** #2

grim: *adj.* not pleasant; harsh; severe. *Conditions are grim for survivors of the hurricane.*

SIGN: Vertical **'CROOKED 5'** hands are held slightly apart with palms toward the face. The hands are then simultaneously lowered somewhat and the head tilts to the right. Facial expression is important. (Signs may vary considerably. Other signs that might be used are: **depressed**; **not - good**; **serious**; **terrible**.)

grimace: *v.* to contort one's facial expression suddenly to indicate pain, disapproval or disgust. *The painful injection made him grimace.*

SIGN: This concept is expressed through the face.

grimy: *adj.* coated with dirt and filth. *These grimy walls should be washed and painted.*

SIGN: Back of right **'5'** hand is placed under the chin, palm down, and the fingers are wiggled up and down.

grin: *v.* to smile. *We saw him grin when he accepted the award.*

SIGN: **'ONE'** hands, palms downward, are positioned so that the tips of the forefingers are touching either side of the chin and are curved upward slightly.

grind: *v.* to crush into small particles, usually by cranking the handle on a small grinding mill. *If you grind these peppercorns, you will have fresh pepper.*

SIGN #1: Horizontal left **'S'** hand is held in a fixed position with palm facing rightward. Horizontal right **'S'** hand is held above left hand with palm facing leftward but slanted slightly toward the body. The right forearm then moves in a counter-clockwise direction, completing a least two revolutions. (Signs in this context vary according to the size and shape of the grinding apparatus, as well as the nature of the action required to operate it.)

grind: *v.* to crush into small particles, usually with a rubbing or grinding action. *She will grind the corn into a fine powder.*

SIGN #2: Right **'A'** hand is held palm-down at a leftward/forward angle against left **'A'** hand, of which the palm faces upward at a rightward/backward angle. The hands are rubbed against each other with circular motions in opposite directions.

grind: *n.* a colloquial term meaning an excessively hard or laborious task. *The course was a grind for the students.*

SIGN #3: Left **'S'** (or **'A'**) hand is held in a fixed position with palm down. Heel of right **'S'** (or **'A'**) hand, palm facing leftward/forward, strikes repeatedly against right side (or 'thumb' side) of left hand in a rightward/forward direction. The motion is laboured and appears as a series of counter-clockwise circles. Cheeks are puffed.

gripe: *v.* to complain in a nagging way. *Some students gripe about the amount of homework they are given.*

SIGN: Right **'SPREAD C'** hand is held in a horizontal position as thumb and fingertips thump against chest. This motion may be repeated to indicate persistence. Facial expression is important.

groceries: *n.* food items sold by a grocer. *Every Monday she goes to the store to buy groceries.*

SIGN: Vertical **'MODIFIED O'** hand, palm facing the body, is brought toward the mouth so that the fingertips are tapped against the lips.

groom: *n.* a man who is about to be married. *The ushers at the wedding were friends of the groom.*

SIGN: Fingerspell **GROOM**.

G　R　O　O　M

gross: *adj.* pertaining to total money earned prior to deductions. *His gross earnings were relatively high.*

SIGN #1: Fingerspell **GROSS**.

G　R　O　S　S

gross: *v.* to earn money as a total income prior to deductions. *He will gross $65,000 this year.*

SIGN #2: Left **'EXTENDED B'** hand is held in a fixed position with palm up and fingers pointing rightward/forward while horizontal right **'SPREAD EXTENDED C'** hand is held out in front of the right side of the body at a considerable distance. As the right hand then moves in a wide counter-clockwise arc, it closes to take on an **'S'** shape with palm facing the body and ends up sliding across the palm of the left hand.

gross: *adj.* a colloquial term meaning disgusting; repugnant; offensive to one's taste or morality. *The horror movie contained many gross scenes.*

SIGN #3: This concept is generally expressed through the face. (**GROSS** may be fingerspelled.)

ALTERNATE SIGNS—**awful** or **disgusted**

grotesque: *adj.* strangely distorted or misshapen. *Gargoyles are grotesque creatures.*

SIGN: Forefingers of **'ONE'** hands are crossed, left in front of right, in front of the nose. Palms are down, but the left palm is angled slightly rightward while the right palm is angled slightly leftward. The left forefinger points upward/rightward; the right forefinger points upward/leftward. The hands are then drawn apart as the forefingers curl to form **'X'** hands. (Facial expression is important.)

grouchy: *adj.* grumbling and complaining. *The old man is grouchy when the children play on his property.*

SIGN: Vertical right **'CROOKED 5'** hand is held with palm toward the face as the fingers rapidly alternate between a relaxed state (**'CROOKED 5'**) and a clawed state (**'CLAWED SPREAD C'**). This sign is accompanied by an appropriate facial expression.

ground: *n.* soil. *He prepared the ground for tree planting.*

SIGN #1: **'FLAT O'** hands are held slightly apart with palms up. Then the fingers are slid across the thumbs a few times, thus alternating between **'FLAT O'** and **'OFFSET O'** hands.

ground: *n.* the earth's surface. *The ground looks very white after last night's snowfall.*

SIGN #2: **'FLAT O'** hands are held slightly apart with palms up. Then the fingers are slid across the thumbs to form **'OFFSET O'** hands. Next, horizontal right **'EXTENDED B'** hand is held with palm down and fingers pointing forward. The hand then makes a wide arc leftward as it inscribes a circle in front of the body.

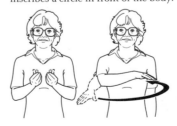

(be) grounded: *v.* an informal term meaning to be confined to one's room or home for a period of time and not permitted to attend social activities. *John was grounded by his parents for staying out late.*

SIGN: Right **'EXTENDED A'** hand, palm facing left, thumb under chin, is thrust forward. Next, **'K'** hands, palms down, are held apart, extended fingers pointing downward, and are then flicked upward from the wrists so that the hands are held in either a horizontal or upright position. Finally, right **'CONTRACTED 5'** hand, palm toward the body, is drawn forward at a slight rightward angle as the fingers close to form a **'FLAT O'** handshape. (ASL CONCEPT—**not - allow - out**.)
ALTERNATE SIGN—**punish**

group: *n.* a number of persons or things forming a collective unit. *The group will hold a panel discussion.*

SIGN #1: **'SPREAD C'** hands are held upright and slightly apart with palms facing each other. The wrists then rotate forward, bringing the hands to a horizontal position.

OR

SIGN #2: **'MODIFIED G'** hands are held with palms facing each other and tips of forefingers touching or at least held close to each other. Then the wrists rotate as the hands are simultaneously circled away from each other and brought together (or close to each other) again so that the thumbs and forefingers are pointed toward the body at an upward angle.

grow: *v.* to expand in size. *This plant grows well in indirect sunlight.*

SIGN: Right **'FLAT O'** hand is thrust upward through horizontal left **'C'** hand, as fingers open into a **'CONTRACTED 5'** hand.

grow up: *v.* to grow to adulthood; to reach maturity. *What does your daughter want to be when she grows up?*

SIGN: Right **'EXTENDED B'** hand is held palm-down with fingers pointing forward near right side of body. The hand is then moved directly upward.
ALTERNATE SIGN—**grow**

grownup: *n.* an adult. *When you are a grownup, you can make all your own decisions.*

SIGN: Vertical right **'BENT EXTENDED B'** hand, palm facing left, is held just above shoulder at chin level and moved up level with top of head. (For the plural 'grownups', see **adults**.)

grumble: *v.* to mutter discontentedly or complain in a nagging way. *Everyone grumbles about paying taxes.*

SIGN: Right **'SPREAD C'** hand is held in a horizontal position as thumb and fingertips thump repeatedly against chest. Facial expression is important feature.

guarantee: *v.* to give formal assurance. *I guarantee this product will work.*

SIGN: Tip of forefinger of vertical right **'ONE'** hand, palm facing left, is held just under the lower lip. The hand is then moved at a forward/downward angle as the wrist rotates and the hand changes to an **'EXTENDED B'** shape, the palm firmly striking the left **'S'** hand which is held in a fixed position in front of the body with the palm facing rightward/downward. (Facial expression is important.)

guard: *v.* to shield or protect from harm. *These drapes will guard against cold drafts.*

SIGN: Horizontal **'S'** hands are held, the left just in front of the right, with palms down in front of the centre of the chest. The hands are then simultaneously moved emphatically forward a short distance. (The sign for **guard**, *n.*, is similar except that the movement is not emphatically forward but is a very slight, repeated forward and back motion.)

guardian: *n.* someone who looks after and protects. *The child was placed with a guardian after his parents died.*

SIGN: Fingerspell **GUARDIAN**.

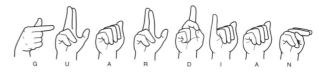

guess: *v.* to express an uncertain estimate or conclusion. *Can you guess the answer?*

SIGN: Vertical right **'SPREAD C'** hand is held in front of right side of forehead with palm facing left, and is moved leftward as it closes to form an **'S'** hand.

guest: *n.* a person who receives hospitality from another; a visitor. *He will be our guest for the weekend.*

SIGN: Right arm is extended so that **'BENT EXTENDED B'** hand is held out in front of the body and to the right at a considerable distance with palm facing forward/leftward at an upward angle. The hand is then drawn in toward the body. **GUEST** is frequently fingerspelled, especially when used as an adjective, as in 'guest speaker'.
ALTERNATE SIGN—**visit**

guidance: *n.* advice; counsel. *I will give you some guidance in making your decision.*

SIGN: Fingertips of right **'FLAT O'** hand rest on back of left **'STANDARD BASE'** hand. Right hand is then thrust forward as it opens slightly to form a **'CONTRACTED 5'** hand. Movement is repeated.

guide: *v.* to lead; to show the way. *I need someone to guide me out of this maze.*

SIGN: Left **'EXTENDED B'** hand is held with fingers pointing forward/rightward and palm facing right but angled toward the body. The fingertips of the left hand are grasped between the fingers and the heel of the right **'OPEN A'** hand. Then the right hand draws the left hand forward/rightward.

guilty: *adj.* having committed an offense or misdeed. *Is he guilty or innocent of the alleged assault?*

SIGN: Sides of thumb and forefinger of right **'MODIFIED G'** hand (or side of forefinger of right **'ONE'** hand), palm facing leftward/downward, are (is) firmly placed against the left side of the chest just below the shoulder. When referring to guilt as a 'feeling', the same basic sign is used but the right hand is tapped several times against the left shoulder.
SAME SIGN—**guilt**, *n.*

guitar: *n.* an instrument, usually having six strings, which are either plucked or strummed to create music. *Deaf people can feel vibrations from an electric guitar.*

SIGN: Left **'OPEN A'** hand, palm up but slanted toward the body, appears to be grasping the fingerboard of a guitar while right **'CLAWED 5'** hand, palm toward the body, moves up and down as if strumming the strings that are stretched across the sounding board.

gullible: *adj.* easily deceived, cheated or tricked. *He is so gullible that he believes everything he is told.*

SIGN #1: Left **'BENT EXTENDED B'** hand is held in a fixed position with palm toward the chest and fingers pointing rightward. Tongue protrudes as right **'ONE'** hand is placed at right angles on left hand with palm facing left and forefinger pointing forward. Tongue disappears into the mouth as the mouth closes and the right hand slides backward/downward behind the left hand so that the right forefinger eventually points upward.

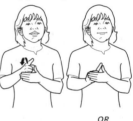

OR

SIGN #2: Tongue protrudes as vertical right **'BENT EXTENDED B'** hand, palm facing backward, is placed near the right cheek and is briskly shoved back toward the shoulder, the tongue disappearing into a closing mouth.

gum: *n.* a flavoured, sticky substance used for chewing. *The students are not allowed to chew gum in class.*

SIGN #1: Fingertips of vertical right **'CROOKED V'** (or **'CROOKED EXTENDED V'**) hand are placed on lower right cheek and the extended fingers buckle a few times so that the hand alternates between **'CROOKED V'** and **'CLAWED V'** shapes. (Handshapes for this sign may vary.)

gum *(cont.)*

SIGN #2 [ATLANTIC]: Thumbtip of right **'CROOKED L'** (or **'CROOKED EXTENDED V'**) hand is placed on the right cheek so that the palm faces forward/leftward at a downward angle. While the thumb maintains contact with the cheek, the wrist bends a few times as the hand appears to make forward rotations.

SIGN #3 [ONTARIO]: Side of forefinger of vertical right **'X'** hand, palm facing leftward, is brushed downward/leftward against the chin at least twice.

SIGN #4 [PRAIRIE]: Tip of forefinger of right **'ONE'** hand is placed on right cheek and the finger buckles a couple of times so that it alternates between a **'ONE'** and a **'CROOKED ONE'** shape.

gun: *n.* a weapon with a barrel from which a bullet is discharged. *My grandfather owns a gun for hunting.*

SIGN: Right **'L'** hand, palm facing left, is held in a horizontal position in front of the chest and the thumb is bent and straightened a few times as if repeatedly cocking (the hammer of) a gun. (**GUN** is frequently fingerspelled.)

gym [abbreviation for **gymnasium**]: *n.* a large room equipped for physical training. *The aerobics classes are held in the gymnasium.*

SIGN #1: Fingertips of **'BENT EXTENDED B'** hands, palms facing the body, are simultaneously tapped on the shoulders several times. (Signs for **gym** may vary; however, although the handshape and movement vary, the sign is generally formed in the area of the shoulders as illustrated here. Alternatively, **GYM** may be fingerspelled.)

SIGN #2 [ONTARIO]: **'EXTENDED B'** hands are held apart in front of the left side of the body with palms down and fingers pointing forward. The forearms then move rightward in an arc formation, coming to rest on the same plane in front of the right side of the body.

gymnastics: *n.* exercises intended to develop physical strength and agility. *She practices her gymnastics every day.*

SIGN: Left **'BENT U'** hand is held in a fixed position with palm down and extended fingers pointing rightward. Right **'U'** hand is held above left hand with palm forward and extended fingers pointing upward at a leftward angle. The right wrist then rotates 360 degrees in a clockwise direction, so that the right hand encircles the left hand and ends up with its palm toward the body and its back resting against the left hand.

gynecologist: *n.* a doctor who specializes in female reproductive organs and their functions. *She saw her gynecologist because her menstrual periods were very irregular.*

SIGN: Fingertips of palm-down right **'SPREAD EXTENDED C'** (or **'BENT EXTENDED B'** or **'FLAT M'**) hand are tapped a couple of times against the inside of the left wrist. Then right **'B'** hand, palm facing left and fingers pointing forward, slides along top of left **'B'** hand, of which the palm faces right and the fingers point forward. (Alternatively, the forefinger of the right **'ONE'** hand slides along the forefinger of the left **'ONE'** hand.) Next, thumbtip of vertical right **'5'** hand, palm left, is placed on chin and is lowered to mid-chest. (ASL CONCEPT—**doctor - specialize - woman.**)

H

habit: *n.* a tendency to behave in a fixed way; something that is done often. *Biting your fingernails is a bad habit.*

SIGN: Vertical right **'S'** hand, palm facing leftward/downward, is held with wrist against back of left **'S'** hand, which is held with palm down. Together, the hands are lowered.

ha-ha: *s.s.* an expression of amusement or scorn. *Ha-ha. I won.*

SIGN: Right **'BENT EXTENDED U'** hand is held with palm leftward but slanted toward the body. The extended fingers then move back and forth a few times.

haggle: See **bargain** #1.

hail: *n.* small pellets of frozen rain. *The hail seriously damaged the crops.*

SIGN: Horizontal **'F'** hands, palms facing each other, are held apart and alternately moved up and down to simulate the falling of hailstones. (When **hail** first appears in a conversation, it is frequently signed and then fingerspelled for greater clarity. Thereafter it is simply signed.)

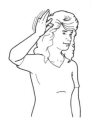

hair: *n.* any threadlike growth from follicles beneath the skin of mammals. *He has nice hair.*

SIGN: Thumb and forefinger of right **'F'** hand, palm facing left, grasp a small amount of hair on the right side of the head, and tug a few times. (**Hair** is sometimes not signed, but is incorporated in the sign for an adjective that describes the hair. There would just be one sign for **curly hair** and not separate signs for **curly** and **hair**. See also **long hair** and **short hair**.) **HAIR** is frequently fingerspelled.

haircut: *n.* the cutting of the hair. *My hair is so long that I will need a haircut soon.*

SIGN: Vertical **'V'** hands are held just in front of either side of the head with palms facing each other. The hands are then simultaneously moved backward toward the area of the ears as the extended fingers close to form **'U'** hands. Motion is repeated.

hairdresser: *n.* a hairstylist. *I will phone my hairdresser to make an appointment.*

SIGN: Vertical **'V'** hands are held just in front of either side of the head with palms facing each other. The hands are then simultaneously moved backward toward the area of the ears as the extended fingers close to form **'U'** hands. Motion is repeated. (Signs vary.)

half: *n.* one of two equal parts. *The recipe calls for half a cup of sugar.*

SIGN #1: Right **'ONE'** hand is held with palm facing the body at a leftward angle and forefinger pointing leftward/forward/upward. The hand is then lowered slightly as the middle finger is flicked out to form a **'V'** hand.

half: *n.* a part that approximately equals the remainder of something. *Half of her family is Deaf.*

SIGN #2: Left **'ONE'** hand is held in a fixed position with palm down and forefinger pointing rightward. Right **'ONE'** hand, palm facing left, is held with forefinger pointing forward/upward and laid at right angles across forefinger of left hand. The right hand then slides downward toward the body.
ALTERNATE SIGN—**half** #1

half hour: *n.* thirty minutes. *Classes will begin in a half hour.*

SIGN: Right **'D'** hand is initially held with palm left and forefinger pointing forward/upward. As the hand drops downward slightly, it is transformed to a **'SLANTED V'** shape and then moves rightward, taking on an **'R'** shape with the palm down and the extended fingers pointing forward at a slight rightward angle. This sign is made quickly so that the medial stage may not even be discernible to the onlooker.

hall: *n.* a passageway or corridor. *Students are discouraged from loitering in the hall.*

SIGN #1: Vertical **'EXTENDED B'** hands are held apart with palms facing each other, and are simultaneously moved forward to indicate a long, narrow space. (**HALL** is frequently fingerspelled.)

hall: *n.* a building used for public gatherings. *They will rent a **hall** for their wedding reception.*

SIGN #2: Fingerspell **HALL**.

Hallowe'en: *n.* the evening of October 31, when children celebrate by wearing costumes and going door to door asking for treats or playing pranks. *Children enjoy wearing costumes for **Hallowe'en**.*

SIGN #1: Back of right **'SPREAD C'** hand, palm facing downward/leftward, is held against lower left jaw and is drawn across the chin to the right cheek as it changes to an **'S'** hand. (Handshapes for the initial position may vary.)

SIGN #2: **'CROOKED EXTENDED B'** hands, palms toward the face, are held upright so that the fingertips are near the eyes. The wrists are then simultaneously rotated back and forth twice causing the palms to alternate between facing the face, thus hiding it, and facing each other, thus revealing the face.

SIGN #3 [ATLANTIC]: Back of right **'S'** hand is placed at left side of chin and abruptly opened to form a **'CONTRACTED 5'** hand, palm downward at a forward/leftward angle. Then the same procedure is repeated at the right side of the chin.

SIGN #4 [ONTARIO]: Back of right **'EXTENDED B'** hand is tapped against left cheek a couple of times. This is a wrist action which results in the palm alternating between facing downward and facing leftward.

SIGN #5 [PACIFIC]: Right **'MODIFIED 5'** hand is held stationary in front of the mouth with palm down and left-pointing fingers fluttering. (Alternatively, this sign may be made as the hand moves rightward in front of the mouth.)

hallucination: *n.* a delusion or fantasy. *He has a high fever and is having **hallucinations**.*

SIGN: Vertical **'I'** hands are held apart in front of/above the head with palms facing backward but slanted toward each other slightly and one hand positioned a little higher than the other. The hands are then alternately rotated upward/forward in several wide circles.
SAME SIGN—**hallucinatory**, *adj.*, and **hallucinate**, *v.*

hallway: *n.* a passageway or corridor. *The bellboy left the suitcases in the **hallway**.*

SIGN: Vertical **'EXTENDED B'** hands are held apart with palms facing each other, and are simultaneously moved forward to indicate a long, narrow space.

halt: *v.* to interrupt; stop; put an end to. *The policeman shouted to **halt** the thief.*

SIGN: Right **'EXTENDED B'** hand, palm facing left, is brought down sharply from a semi-vertical position to strike the upward/backward facing palm of the rigidly held left **'EXTENDED B'** hand, whose fingers point rightward/forward.

ham: *n.* smoked meat from the hindquarters of a pig. *I like **ham** and eggs for breakfast.*

SIGN: Fingerspell **HAM**.

hamburger: *n.* a patty of ground beef in a bun. *This restaurant makes good **hamburgers**.*

SIGN: **'EXTENDED C'** hands are loosely clasped with the right hand on top of the left. The hands are then drawn apart slightly as their positions are reversed, and then they are clasped again.

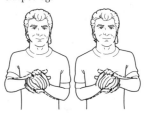

hammer: *n.* a hand tool used to drive nails. *Every carpenter needs a good **hammer**.*

SIGN: Left **'CLOSED A-INDEX'** hand is held upright with palm facing right while right **'CLOSED A-INDEX'** hand is held just behind the left hand with palm facing left. Then the right hand makes a tapping motion toward the left hand to simulate the pounding action of a hammer. (This sign may be made with the right hand only, in which case the hand may take the form of either a **'CLOSED A-INDEX'** (or an **'S'** shape).)

hamster: *n.* a burrowing, short-tailed, pouchy-cheeked rodent which is popular as a pet. *I need someone to feed my pet hamster while I am away.*

SIGN: Fingerspell **HAMSTER**.

hand [#1]: See **hands**.

hand: *n.* one round of cards dealt to a player. *My bridge hand was so poor I could not bid.*

SIGN #2: **'4'** hands, palms toward the chest, are held with fingers of right hand against those of the left hand at right angles so that the fingers of the left hand point rightward/upward and the fingers of the right hand point leftward/upward. The wrists then bend outward and as they come together, the hands eventually end up side by side in a completely upright position.

(on the other) hand: *conj.* from the opposite point of view. *The rumour might be true; on the other hand, it is doubtful.*

SIGN: Forefingers of **'ONE'** hands are crossed. The hands are then turned outward so that they become vertical with palms facing forward.

hand in: *v.* to give (something) to another person for consideration. *The teacher expects us to hand in our essays today.*

SIGN: Right **'EXTENDED B'** hand, palm up and fingers pointing forward, is moved forward in an arc.

hand out: *v.* to give out or distribute something by hand. *She will hand out copies of the information after the lecture.*

SIGN: Horizontal **'CONTRACTED B'** hands are held with palms up and fingertips almost touching. The hands then move forward in an outward arc as the fingers spread to assume a **'SLANTED 5'** shape.

ALTERNATE SIGN—**circulate**

hand to: *v.* to give or pass something on to someone else. *When you finish reading this, please hand it to him.*

SIGN: Horizontal right **'CONTRACTED B'** hand is held with palm facing leftward/upward and fingers pointing left. The hand then moves forward in a slight arc formation as if giving something to someone. (Handshapes vary according to the size and shape of the object being given; however, the basic movement remains the same.) ❖

handcuffs: *n.* a pair of locking metal rings which fit around the wrists and are used to secure prisoners or persons under arrest. *The police put handcuffs on the suspect.*

SIGN: Horizontal **'A'** hands, palms facing, are held so that the wrists are touching each other to simulate the concept of being handcuffed.

handicapped: *adj.* mentally or physically disabled (or may be used as a noun, usually preceded by 'the', in reference to a collective group of handicapped persons). *Deaf people do not consider themselves handicapped; rather, they are culturally unique.*

SIGN: Fingerspell **HC**.

handkerchief: *n.* a piece of absorbent material used to wipe the nose or cover a sneeze. *My grandfather always has a handkerchief.*

SIGN: Thumb and forefinger of right **'A-INDEX'** (or **'G'**) hand are used to cover the nostrils and close slightly toward the tip of the nose as the hand is brought downward/forward a short way. The movement is repeated to simulate the wiping of the nose with a handkerchief.

handle: *v.* to control, manage or deal with in a specific way. *The committee will handle the publicity for the event.*

SIGN #1: Horizontal **'X'** hands are held slightly apart with left palm facing right and right palm facing left. Then they are alternately moved backward and forward.

handle: *n.* the part of an object that is held in one's hand while the object is being used, moved, opened, etc. *We cannot open the fridge because the handle is broken.*

SIGN #2: Sign choice depends entirely on the size and shape of the handle.

hands: *n.* the part of the body at the end of each arm, having a thumb, four fingers and a palm. *Signers use their hands, face and body to communicate.*

SIGN: **'EXTENDED B'** hands are crossed with the right hand behind the left. The palms face the body and the fingers point basically upward although the fingers of the left hand are angled slightly rightward while the fingers of the right hand are angled slightly leftward. The right hand slides downward/rightward, then moves out in front of the left hand which slides downward/leftward. (When referring to *one hand only*, the signer might fingerspell **HAND** or hold up a vertical **'5'** hand with the palm facing the body. Alternatively, the signer might simply point to one of his hands.)

handshake: *n.* the grasping and shaking of another person's hand as a form of greeting, leave-taking, agreeing, congratulating, etc. *They concluded their business deal with a handshake.*

SIGN: Hands are clasped close to chest and shaken.
ALTERNATE SIGN—**shake** #2

handshape: *n.* the form or configuration assumed by the hand. *Even a slight error in handshape can create confusion in ASL.*

SIGN: **'EXTENDED B'** hands are crossed with the right hand behind the left. The palms face the body and the fingers point basically upward although the fingers of the left hand are angled slightly rightward while the fingers of the right hand are angled slightly leftward. The right hand slides downward/rightward, then moves out in front of the left hand which slides downward/leftward. **SHAPE** is then fingerspelled.

handsome: *adj.* good-looking. *He is a very handsome man.*

SIGN #1: Right **'EXTENDED B'** hand is held virtually upright with fingers pointing upward at a slight leftward angle, fingertips just in front of the mouth, and palm facing the body. The hand is moved firmly forward a short distance and then brought upward/backward slightly and moved from side to side at least twice in front of the face. (ASL CONCEPT—**good - looking**.)

SIGN #2 [ATLANTIC]: Right **'EXTENDED C'** hand, palm facing backward, is held upright and is then twisted from the wrist to cross in front of the face until the palm is turned downward. (Signs in the Atlantic provinces vary.)

SIGN #3 [PRAIRIE]: As right **'CONTRACTED 5'** hand, palm toward the face, moves downward in front of the face, the wrist rotates leftward to turn the hand palm downward. The hand then moves back upward in front of the face as the fingers close to form a **'MODIFIED O'** hand in front of the forehead with palm left.

handy: *adj.* skilful with the hands. *The boxer was very handy with his fists.*

SIGN #1: Left **'EXTENDED B'** hand, palm facing right and fingers up, is grasped by right **'OPEN A'** hand. Then right hand is pulled forward sharply and closed to form an **'A'** hand.
ALTERNATE SIGN—**adept** #2

handy: *adj.* convenient or easily accessible. *It is handy to live within walking distance of my job.*

SIGN #2: Fingerspell **HANDY**.

hang [or **hung**]: *v.* [*p.t.*] to suspend from a hook or hanger. *Please **hang** up your coat.*

SIGN #1: Crooked forefinger of right **'X'** hand is placed on the forefinger of the horizontal left **'ONE'** hand, whose palm faces downward. Then they are lowered slightly. (Signs vary depending on what is being hung as well as where and how it is being hung.)

hang [or **hanged**]: *v.* [*p.t.*] to die or be put to death by being suspended from the neck. *He will **hang** for his crimes.*

SIGN #2: Right **'S'** hand, palm facing forward, is held in a horizontal position at the right side of the neck and is forcefully drawn upward/rightward to simulate the tightening of a noose.

hang around [or **hang out**]: *v.* a colloquial term meaning to loiter or to spend relatively aimless time somewhere. *He often **hangs** around at the shopping mall with his friends.*

SIGN: **'BENT MIDFINGER 5'** hands are held right above left with left palm facing upward and right palm facing downward. The right hand wobbles as both hands move in a sweeping counter-clockwise arc.

hang in: *v.* to persist with patience. *Hang in there and you will eventually succeed.*

SIGN: Right **'A'** hand, with thumbnail touching closed lips and palm facing left, is moved slowly down chin.

hang on: *v.* to persist with patience; to persevere. *Just **hang on** and someone will be there to help you soon.*

SIGN #1: Right **'A'** hand, with thumbnail touching closed lips and palm facing left, is moved slowly down chin.

hang on: *v.* a colloquial term meaning to wait. *Hang on, I am busy just now.*

SIGN #2: Forefinger of right **'ONE'** hand, palm forward, is held upright and very firmly moved forward a short distance. Appropriate facial expression is essential.

hang on: *v.* to hold on or cling to. *He lifted his son onto his shoulders and told him to hang on.*

SIGN #3: Natural gestures are used to convey this concept and vary according to the specific context.

hang out: *v.* a colloquial term meaning to frequent or to spend a lot of time somewhere. *He **hangs** out at the bar with his friends.*

SIGN: Vertical left **'ONE'** hand is held in a fixed position with palm forward/rightward while horizontal right **'B'** hand is held just behind the left hand with palm left and fingers pointing forward. The fingertips of the right hand make contact with the left forefinger as the right hand is jabbed toward it several times. (The signer's lips protrude when making this sign.)

hang up: *v.* to return the telephone receiver to its cradle at the end of a conversation. *She said "goodbye" and **hung up**.*

SIGN: Horizontal right **'Y'** hand is held with palm facing left. The wrist then rotates leftward to turn the palm downward.

hang up on: *v.* to return the telephone receiver to its cradle in the middle of a telephone conversation. *He was rude to me so I **hung up on** him.*

SIGN: Horizontal right **'Y'** hand is held with palm facing left. The hand then moves purposefully leftward in arc formation as the wrist rotates leftward to turn the palm downward. Facial expression must clearly convey annoyance or anger.

hanger: *n.* a wire, wooden or plastic device on which a garment may be hung. *I need a **hanger** for my jacket.*

SIGN: Crooked forefinger of right **'CROOKED ONE'** hand, palm facing away from the body, is brought slightly downward/forward and hooked onto the forefinger of the left **'ONE'** hand which is held palm down. Motion is repeated.

hangover: *n.* the unpleasant aftereffects of drinking too much alcohol. *He had a **hangover** in the morning.*

SIGN: Fingerspell **HANGOVER**. (Various signs may be used depending on the specific context. Alternatively, the concept might be expressed in the form of a phrase such as 'DRINK-LIQUOR' - 'NEXT-MORNING' - 'HEADACHE' or 'DIZZY'.)

hang-up: *n.* a colloquial term meaning psychological or emotional problem or preoccupation. *He was referred for counseling because of his emotional hang-ups.*

SIGN: **'CLAWED V'** hands are held horizontally with palms facing the body and knuckles knocking against each other as the hands are alternately moved up and down.

happen: *v.* to take place or occur. *The accident happened on Tuesday.*

SIGN: **'ONE'** hands, palms facing each other and forefingers pointing forward, are held apart and then turned over so that the palms face down.

happy: *adj.* feeling or expressing pleasure or joy. *Martha was happy to find a job.*

SIGN: Horizontal right **'EXTENDED B'** hand, palm toward the body, is brushed up and off the chest twice in a circular motion. SAME SIGN—**happiness**, *n.*

harassment: *n.* persistent torment. *He accused the police department of harassment.*

SIGN #1: Joined thumb and forefinger of right **'CLOSED X'** hand, palm forward, are used to pick at the upright forefinger of the left **'ONE'** hand in an aggressive manner. **HARASSMENT** is frequently fingerspelled.
SAME SIGN—**harass**, *v.*, in this context.
ALTERNATE SIGNS—**bother** #1 & #2

(sexual) harassment: *n.* persistent torment of an overtly or subtly sexual nature. *She accused her boss of sexual harassment.*

SIGN #2: Fingerspell **HARASSMENT**. (Various signs such as **bother**, **tease** or **touch** may be used depending on the specific nature of the sexual harassment.)

harbour [*also spelled* **harbor**]: *n.* a sheltered port or place of safety. *Halifax is a major Canadian harbour.*

SIGN: Fingerspell **HARBOUR** or **HARBOR**.

hard: *adj.* difficult to understand or accomplish; not easy. *This test is hard.*

SIGN #1: **'CLAWED V'** hands are held, right above left, at an angle somewhere between vertical and horizontal, with left palm facing right and right palm facing left. The hands then come together and strike each other with force.

hard: *adj.* firm, rigid; not soft. *Diamonds are hard precious stones.*

SIGN #2: **'A'** hands are held palms down, right hand directly above the left. As the teeth clench, the hands come together and strike each other with force.

Hard of Hearing: *adj.* partially Deaf. *She belongs to an organization for Hard of Hearing people.*

SIGN: Horizontal right **'U'** hand, palm facing left, is brought down sharply and then moved rightward in an arc formation. (It is the hand which moves, and not the entire arm.)

hardly: *adv.* scarcely or barely; with difficulty. *He was so nervous he could hardly speak.*

SIGN: Both **'BENT EXTENDED B'** hands are held with palms toward the body. The left hand remains steady, while the fingertips of the right hand are brushed upward from the knuckles of the left. Next, the left **'ONE'** hand is held palm-down with forefinger pointing forward/rightward. The forefinger of the right **'ONE'** hand is held above the left, then brought down sharply to strike the left forefinger. (ASL CONCEPT—**almost - cannot**.)

hardly ever: *adv.* almost never. *She is hardly ever home.*

SIGN: Both **'BENT EXTENDED B'** hands are held with palms toward the body. The left hand remains steady, while the fingertips of the right hand are brushed upward from the knuckles of the left. Next, right **'B'** (or **'EXTENDED B'**) hand, palm facing left, is held upright near the face and is vigorously curved downward. (ASL CONCEPT—**almost - never**.)

hardship: *n.* something that makes life very difficult to endure. *Losing your job can certainly be a hardship.*

SIGN: Horizontal **'CLAWED V'** hands are held with palms facing the body and knuckles knocking against each other as the hands are alternately moved up and down. (Signs vary according to context. To indicate *extreme hardship,* **suffer** could be used.)

hardware: *n.* metal implements, tools, screws, nails, hinges, etc. *The store mainly sells hardware.*

SIGN #1: Fingerspell **HARDWARE**.

hardware: *n.* the physical equipment that comprises a computer system (as opposed to 'software' which comprises the programs used with the system). *The hardware for the company's new computer system is now in place.*

SIGN #2: Fingerspell **HW**.

hare: *n.* a large rabbit-like mammal. *The hunter followed the tracks of a hare in the snow.*

SIGN: **'CONTRACTED U'** hands are held together in an almost vertical position, the right hand behind/above the left, with the left palm facing right and the right palm facing left. The extended fingers of each hand simultaneously flutter, thus alternating several times between **'CONTRACTED U'** and **'BENT U'** shapes.
ALTERNATE SIGN—**rabbit** #2

harm: *v.* to cause injury or damage. *Too much cholesterol can harm your heart.*

SIGN: Horizontal left **'X'** hand is held in a fixed position with palm rightward but slanted toward the body slightly while horizontal right **'X'** hand is held above/behind left hand with palm leftward. The right hand then slides briskly along the top of the left hand and continues to move in a forward/rightward direction.
SAME SIGN—**harmful**, *adj.*

harmony: *n.* pleasant interaction; agreement in action, feeling, opinion, sound, etc. *They work in harmony because their characters are similar.*

SIGN: With palms facing the body, **'CLAWED 5'** hands are held together so that little fingers interlock. As the hands are simultaneously lowered from the wrists, the corresponding fingers of each hand interlock to simulate the meshing of gears.

harsh: *adj.* stern, severe, cruel or grating on one's senses. *His treatment of the prisoners was harsh.*

SIGN: Horizontal left **'CLAWED V'** hand is held in a fixed position with palm toward the body while right **'CLAWED V'** hand is held above/to the right of the left hand with palm facing the body. The right hand is then thrust downward so that the knuckles of the forefinger and middle finger rap those of the left hand on the way past. Appropriate facial expression is essential. (Sign choice depends on the specific context.)
ALTERNATE SIGNS—**cruel**, **rough** #1 & #2, **severe**, **strict**

harvest: *n.* ripened crops; the gathering of ripened crops. *In southern Saskatchewan the harvest usually begins in August.*

SIGN: Fingerspell **HARVEST**.

hassle: *n.* a great deal of trouble. *We abandoned the idea because it was not worth the hassle.*

SIGN: **'B'** (or **'EXTENDED B'**) hands are held apart in front of the face at such an angle that the palms face each other but slant downward while the fingers of the left hand point upward/rightward and the fingers of the right hand point upward/leftward. The hands are then alternately circled toward each other a few times. Facial expression is important.

haste: *n.* the act of hurrying, often in a careless way. *The form was incomplete because he wrote it in haste.*

SIGN: Horizontal **'U'** hands are held apart with left palm facing right and right palm facing left, and the forearms are alternately circled forward repeatedly.

hat: *n.* a head covering, usually with a brim and a shaped crown. *A milliner makes or sells hats.*

SIGN: Right **'EXTENDED B'** hand, palm down, is patted on the top of the head. (Signs vary depending on the size and shape of the hat.)

hat trick: *n.* the scoring of three goals by the same player in any one game of ice hockey. *Wayne Gretzky was famous for his **hat tricks.***

SIGN: Vertical right **'3'** hand is held with palm facing left. Then forefinger of horizontal right **'ONE'** hand, palm left, falls forward/downward until it lies between forefinger and midfinger of vertical left **'5'** hand, of which the palm is facing the body. (ASL CONCEPT—**three - goal.**) Alternatively, see **goal** #3 for the first part of this sign.

hatch: *v.* to cause the young of various species to emerge from an egg. *After the eggs hatch, the mother bird must feed her hungry brood.*

SIGN: Horizontal **'SPREAD C'** hands are held with palms facing and fingertips of one hand almost touching those of the other. The wrists then rotate outward causing the palms to face upward at such an angle that they also face each other slightly.

hate: *v.* to loathe or detest. *I hate you!*

SIGN #1: Horizontal **'COVERED 8'** hands, left palm facing right and right palm facing left, are held with one hand slightly ahead of the other. Then both midfingers are snapped forward simultaneously to form **'MODIFIED 5'** hands. Facial expression is important. ❖ ALTERNATE SIGN—**abhor**

SIGN #2 [ONTARIO]: Vertical left **'ONE'** hand is held in a fixed position with palm forward/rightward. Horizontal right **'B'** hand, which is held behind left hand with palm facing leftward but angled backward slightly, is thrust forward so that the fingertips strike the forefinger of the left **'ONE'** hand. Facial expression is important.

have: *v.* to own or be in possession of. *I have a new car.*

SIGN #1: Horizontal right **'BENT EXTENDED B'** hand is brought back firmly so that fingertips make contact with upper right chest. At the same time, the signer's upper front teeth are resting on the lower lip.

have: *v.* used as an auxiliary verb to express completion of an action. *I have eaten.*

SIGN #2: Vertical **'5'** hands, palms facing the body, are held at chest level, and swung outward, away from the body so that palms face down.

have to: *v.* must. *I have to finish my homework.*

SIGN: Right **'X'** hand, palm facing away from the body, is held in a vertical position in front of the chest and is sharply thrust downward from the wrist so that the palm faces down.

havoc: *n.* confusion or destruction. *The tornado caused great havoc.*

SIGN: Vertical right **'CROOKED 5'** hand is held against right side of forehead with palm facing left while left **'CROOKED 5'** hand is held palm-up in front of left side of chest. The arms are then simultaneously moved rightward/upward as both wrists rotate rightward a quarter turn so that the right palm faces the body at a slight downward angle while the left palm faces rightward/forward.

hawk: *n.* a bird of prey that resembles an eagle but is smaller in size. *A hawk's diet consists mainly of small rodents.*

SIGN: Vertical right **'X'** hand is held in front of the face with palm forward/leftward, and the back of the crooked forefinger is tapped a couple of times against the nose. **HAWK** may also be fingerspelled.

hay: *n.* grass that is cut and dried to feed livestock. *The hay in the north meadow is ready to harvest.*

SIGN: Back of right **'CROOKED 4'** hand, palm down, is held under the chin and the hand is moved briskly in small circular motions, brushing backward against the underside of the chin with each cycle. **HAY** is frequently fingerspelled. ALTERNATE SIGN—**grass** #2

hazard: *n.* risk; danger; something that is likely to cause injury or damage. *Older drivers are sometimes a **hazard** on the highways.*

SIGN: Left **'A'** hand is held in a fixed position with palm facing downward but slanted toward the chest. Right **'A'** hand is held just in front of the left hand with palm facing left and is circled forward a couple of times so that the thumb firmly brushes upward against the back of the left hand with each revolution.
SAME SIGN—**hazardous**, *adj.*
REGIONAL VARIATION—**dangerous**

he: *pron.* used to refer to a male previously named or whose identity is clear. [See PRONOUNS, p. LXIV.] *He is well-known in the Deaf Community.*

SIGN: Horizontal right **'BENT ONE'** hand is held with palm facing forward/rightward as the forefinger points at the person or animal being referred to.
SAME SIGN—**him**, *obj. pron.*

head: *n.* the upper part of the body containing the brain, eyes, ears, nose and mouth. *I hurt my **head** when I fell.*

SIGN #1: Fingertips of vertical right **'BENT EXTENDED B'** hand, palm toward the head, are tapped first against right side of forehead. The hand is then lowered and tapped against lower right cheek.

head: *n.* the person in charge or in command. *She is the **head** of a big company.*

SIGN #2: Horizontal right **'EXTENDED A'** hand, palm facing left, is raised purposefully from shoulder level upward.

headache: *n.* a continuous pain in the head. *Drinking too much alcohol can cause a **headache**.*

SIGN: **'BENT ONE'** hands are held slightly apart in front of the forehead with palms facing each other at a downward angle and forefingers pointing toward each other. The hands are then sharply stabbed toward each other at least twice.

headlights: *n.* lights on the front of a vehicle. *The driver asked the gas station attendant to wash his **headlights**.*

SIGN: Vertical **'FLAT O'** hands are held parallel with palms forward. The fingers then open to form **'MODIFIED 5'** hands. (Only one hand is used to indicate singularity, the left hand to represent the left headlight and the right hand to represent the right headlight.)

headline: *n.* the large, bold-type title of a newspaper or magazine article, thought to be important or interesting news. *The **headline** drew my attention to the article.*

SIGN: Left **'EXTENDED B'** hand is held in a fixed position with palm toward the body and fingers pointing rightward. Vertical right **'C-INDEX'** hand is held just above the wrist of the left hand with palm facing forward and then moves directly rightward. (The positioning of this sign may vary and it is sometimes made without the left hand; however, the movement is generally the same.)

headquarters: *n.* a centre from which certain operations are directed. *The company's **headquarters** are in Toronto.*

SIGN: Fingerspell **HQ**.

H   Q

headstrong: *adj.* stubborn, rash or defiantly self-willed. *Many teenagers are **headstrong** and rebellious.*

SIGN: Thumb of vertical right **'EXTENDED B'** hand, palm forward, is placed near the right temple and the fingers are firmly lowered to form a **'BENT EXTENDED B'** hand. A look of fierce determination accompanies this sign.

heal: *v.* to cure or restore to normal health or condition. *It took several weeks for his wounds to heal.*

SIGN: **'BENT 5'** hands, with fingertips on either side of chest and palms facing the body, are drawn forward to form **'S'** hands. (**HEAL** is frequently fingerspelled.)

health: *n.* condition of body and/or mind; well-being. *Good nutrition is vital to maintaining good **health**.*

SIGN: Horizontal **'BENT EXTENDED B'** hands are held apart with fingertips touching either side of upper chest. The hands are then simultaneously drawn forward slightly and downward in an arc formation, re-establishing contact with the body at a somewhat lower level.

healthy: *adj.* having good health; conducive to good health. *The aerobics instructor is **healthy**.*

SIGN: **'BENT 5'** hands, with fingertips on either side of chest and palms facing the body, are drawn forward to form **'S'** hands.

heap: *n.* a collection of things in a pile. *There was a heap of laundry on the floor.*

SIGN #1: Right **'BENT EXTENDED B'** hand, palm forward, is used to outline an arch representative of the size of the heap. (Other signs may be used if the heap is small or inordinately large.)

heap: *n.* a large number, amount or quantity. *I have a heap of homework to do tonight.*

SIGN #2: Left **'BENT EXTENDED B'** hand is held in a fixed position with palm up. Vertical right **'BENT EXTENDED B'** hand, palm left and fingers pointing left, is held above left hand at a distance which indicates the height of the object under discussion. The hands are then simultaneously moved firmly forward a very short distance. The signer's lips appear to be articulating the syllable 'CHA'.

hear: *v.* to perceive sound through the sense of hearing; to be informed about something. *It is hard to hear from the back of the theatre.*

SIGN: Tip of forefinger of right **'ONE'** hand, palm left, is tapped against right ear.

hearing: *adj.* having an intact sense of hearing. *It is often difficult for hearing people to learn ASL.*

SIGN #1: Side of forefinger of right **'ONE'** hand, palm down, is brushed upward against the lips several times with small forward circular motions.

hearing: *n.* an investigation by a court of law. *There will be a preliminary hearing of the case on April 5th.*

SIGN #2: Horizontal **'F'** hands, palms facing each other, are alternately raised and lowered a few times.

hearing aid: *n.* an assistive, battery-powered hearing device. *My hearing aid needs a new battery.*

SIGN: Side of crooked forefinger of right **'X'** hand, palm facing forward, is tapped a couple of times against right ear. (Signs vary depending on the type of hearing aid.)

heart: *n.* the organ that propels blood through the circulatory system. *He has a weak heart.*

SIGN #1: Tip of midfinger of right **'BENT MIDFINGER 5'** hand is tapped a couple of times against the left side of the chest in the vicinity of the heart.

SAME SIGN—**heart**, *n.*, a suit in playing cards.

heart: *n.* courage, tenderness, kindness or spirit. *He was well known for his big heart and good deeds.*

SIGN #2: Tips of midfingers of **'BENT MIDFINGER 5'** hands (or tips of forefingers of **'BENT ONE'** hands), palms toward the chest, are placed together just below the left shoulder and are drawn apart to trace the outline of a heart, coming together again at a lower point.

heart attack: *n.* a case of sudden, severe heart failure. *High blood pressure can lead to a heart attack.*

SIGN: Tip of midfinger of right **'BENT MIDFINGER 5'** hand pokes left side of chest in the vicinity of the heart. Then the right hand changes to an **'S'** shape and strikes vigorously against the palm of the horizontal left **'EXTENDED B'** hand which is positioned directly in front of it.

heartbeat: *n.* a throbbing or pulsating of the heart. *The doctor checked to see if the patient's heartbeat was regular.*

SIGN: Right **'S'** hand, with palm facing the body, is thumped repeatedly between left horizontally-held **'EXTENDED B'** hand and left side of chest in the area of the heart.

heartbreak: *n.* intense feeling of disappointment usually due to lost love. *The couple's decision to divorce caused much heartbreak for their children.*

SIGN: **'S'** hands are held side by side with palms down close to the left side of the chest. The wrists then simultaneously twist in opposite directions, the left wrist twisting backward so that the palm faces forward/rightward and the right wrist twisting forward so that the palm faces the body. The movement resembles that of wringing out a damp cloth. Facial expression is important.

heartwarming: *adj.* emotionally moving or pleasing. *It was heartwarming to see the family reunited.*

SIGN: Right **'5'** hand is held with palm on chest and fingertips pointing leftward/upward. The hand is then pushed purposefully upward. Alternatively, this sign may be made with two hands, one on either side of chest, especially for emphasis. Facial expression is important.
ALTERNATE SIGN—**touching**

heat: *n.* a high degree of warmth. *Plants need heat, light and water.*

SIGN: Right **'CLAWED 5'** hand is held with fingertips touching or close to the lips. The wrist then rotates briskly causing the palm to face leftward/downward. (**HEAT** is frequently fingerspelled.)

heaven: *n.* a pleasant place where God and the angels are thought to exist. *Some people believe in everlasting life in **heaven** after death.*

SIGN: **'BENT EXTENDED B'** hands are held up high with palms facing and are circled forward so that the fingers of each hand revolve around those of the other hand. The hands are then drawn apart. (Movement for this sign may vary slightly.)

heavy: *adj.* of relatively great weight. *The television set is heavy.*

SIGN: Horizontal **'BENT EXTENDED B'** (or **'CROOKED 5'**) hands are held apart with palms upward but facing each other slightly, and are simultaneously lowered as if they are bearing a heavy weight.

hectic: *adj.* characterized by extreme excitement or feverish activity and confusion. *Running a small business can be hectic at times.*

SIGN: Vertical **'BENT EXTENDED B'** hands are held with palms facing each other and fingertips touching either side of forehead. Fingertips maintain contact with the forehead while the wrists rapidly twist back and forth several times in opposite directions.

heed: *v.* to give careful or thoughtful attention to something. *You should heed your parents' advice and not drop out of school.*

SIGN: Horizontal **'EXTENDED A'** hands, left palm facing right and right palm facing left, are held with the right hand directly behind the left. The hands are then moved forward together.
ALTERNATE SIGN—**pay attention**

heedless: *adj.* careless, neglectful or thoughtless. *He is heedless of danger.*

SIGN: Extended fingers of right **'V'** hand are waved up and down in front of the forehead with palm alternately facing leftward and downward. Facial expression is important.
ALTERNATE SIGN—**neglect**.

height: *n.* the distance from the bottom of something to the top. *He measured the height of the plant with a ruler.*

SIGN #1: Horizontal **'Y'** hands are held, right just above left, with left palm facing the body and right palm facing forward. Then the right thumbtip is tapped on the left thumbtip several times.

height: *n.* the distance from the floor to the top of a person's head. *His height is 140 cm.*

SIGN #2: Side of forefinger of right **'ONE'** hand, palm facing left, is raised and used to tap on the top of the head.
ALTERNATE SIGN—**height** #1

heir: *n.* a person who legally inherits money, property, titles or traditions from a deceased relative or other forerunner. *In a monarchy, the eldest son is usually the heir to the throne.*

SIGN: Fingerspell **HEIR**.

helicopter: *n.* an aircraft that can hover or move horizontally or vertically in any direction. *A helicopter flew over the house today.*

SIGN: Right **'5'** hand is held palm down on tip of forefinger of vertical left **'ONE'** hand. Then the right wrist twists back and forth slightly but rapidly, causing the hand to wobble briskly.

hell: *n.* a place for the eternal punishment of sinners and disbelievers after death. *Followers of certain religions believe in hell and eternal damnation.*

SIGN: Horizontal right **'U'** hand is held with palm facing left but angled toward the body slightly and is thrust vigorously rightward/downward. (**HELL** is frequently fingerspelled.)

hello: *s.s.* an expression used to greet someone. *He signed 'hello' to his Deaf friend as they met on the street.*

SIGN: Side of forefinger of vertical right **'B'** hand, palm facing left, is placed against right side of forehead. The forearm is then moved forward/rightward as the hand tips forward/rightward from the wrist so that the fingers point in the same direction, as if the signer is saluting someone.

helmet: *n.* protective headgear. *All cyclists should wear helmets.*

SIGN: Vertical **'CROOKED 5'** hands, palms facing, are held at either side of the head and are simultaneously lowered slightly to simulate the putting on of a helmet.

help: *v.* to assist or give aid by sharing work or cost. *I will help you finish this project.*

SIGN #1: (current) Horizontal left **'A'** (or **'EXTENDED A'**) hand, palm facing the body but turned slightly rightward, rests on the upturned palm of the right **'EXTENDED B'** hand. Both hands are moved forward in one motion toward the person receiving help. (For **help**, *n.,* and **helpful**, *adj.,* the left **'A'** (or **'EXTENDED A'**) hand, palm facing the body but turned slightly rightward, may be positioned on the upturned fingers of the right **'EXTENDED B'** hand. The hands both move as they are tapped together twice in a fixed location.) ❖

OR

SIGN #2: (used occasionally) Upturned palm of right **'EXTENDED B'** hand is placed under the bent elbow of the left arm. Together, the arms are raised slightly.

hem: *v.* to add a finished edge to a piece of cloth, especially an article of clothing, by folding the raw edge under and sewing it down. *I will hem your skirt for you.*

SIGN: **'EXTENDED B'** hands are held parallel with palms down and fingers pointing forward. The hands then bounce very slightly as the fingers curl to assume **'OPEN A'** shapes. (Alternatively, **HEM** may be fingerspelled, particularly when used as a noun.)

hemorrhage: *n.* profuse bleeding from ruptured blood vessels. *She died of a brain hemorrhage.*

SIGN: Fingertips of horizontal right **'5'** hand are placed against back of left **'EXTENDED B'** (or **'5'**) hand, which is held with palm toward body and fingertips pointing to the right. Then right hand, with fingers fluttering, is then lowered to a point below left hand.

hemorrhoids: *n.* swollen or twisted veins near the anus from which blood is sometimes discharged. *Hemorrhoids can be painful and often require surgery.*

SIGN: Fingerspell **HEMORRHOIDS**.

hen: *n.* a female bird (used especially when referring to domestic fowl). *The mother hen protected her brood of chicks.*

SIGN #1: Right **'MODIFIED G'** hand is held at chin, palm facing forward, while extended fingers are opened and closed at least twice to simulate the movement of a chicken's beak. (**HEN** is frequently fingerspelled.)

REGIONAL VARIATION—**chicken** #2

SIGN #2 [ONTARIO]: Tip of thumb of right **'3'** hand, palm left, is tapped against the middle of the chin.

hence: *adv.* therefore; for this reason. *The cost of tuition increased; hence, enrolment decreased.*

SIGN: Vertical right **'CLOSED X'** hand, palm forward, is used to make three imaginary dots which form a triangle, beginning at the apex, then moving leftward/downward and finally rightward. (The signer might mouth 'therefore' while making this sign, but would never mouth 'hence' as this would confuse most ASL users.)

ALTERNATE SIGN—**consequently**

henceforth: *adv.* from now on; from this time forward. *I hope you have learned a lesson and henceforth will never drink and drive again.*

SIGN: Horizontal **'BENT EXTENDED B'** hands, palms facing each other, are positioned so that the fingers of the right hand are just in front of the fingers of the left hand. The right hand is then moved forward briskly.

her: *pron.* used to refer to a female whose identity is already known. [See PRONOUNS, pp. LXIV.] *The teacher barely recognized her after the summer.*

SIGN #1: Horizontal right **'BENT ONE'** hand is held with palm facing forward/rightward as the forefinger points at the person or animal being referred to.

her/hers: *pron.* used to refer to something belonging to or related to a female whose identity is already known. [See PRONOUNS, p. LXVI.] *She was in a panic when her car stalled on the freeway.*

SIGN #2: Vertical right **'EXTENDED B'** hand, palm facing forward/rightward, is held in front of the right shoulder and moved slightly in the direction of the person or animal being referred to.

herb: *n.* an aromatic plant used to season, flavour or garnish food when cooking. *Thyme is a commonly used herb.*

SIGN: Fingerspell **HERB**.

here: *adv.* in, at or to this place. *She was here but had to go home.*

SIGN: **'EXTENDED B'** hands are held parallel with palms up and are simultaneously circled outward.

hereditary: *adj.* pertaining to the transmission of genetic factors from one generation to another. *Deafness can be hereditary.*

SIGN: Fingertips of the right **'BENT EXTENDED B'** hand, palm toward the body, are placed against the right shoulder while the left **'BENT EXTENDED B'** hand, palm toward the body, is held a short distance in front of it. Then both hands are circled forward around one another several times.

heritage: *n.* a tradition or legacy that has been handed down from the past. *She enjoyed reading about her heritage.*

SIGN: Fingertips of horizontal right **'BENT EXTENDED B'** hand, palm toward the body, are placed against the right shoulder while horizontal left **'BENT EXTENDED B'** hand, palm toward the body, is held a short distance in front of it. Then both hands are circled forward around one another several times.

hernia: *n.* the pushing of a body part through the wall that ordinarily contains it; a rupture. *He has a hernia that needs surgery.*

SIGN: Fingerspell **HERNIA**.

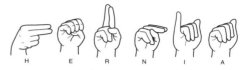

heroin: *n.* a white, odorless bitter-tasting drug which is very addictive. *The police found a large quantity of heroin in his suitcase.*

SIGN: Horizontal right **'S'** hand, palm toward the body, is tapped firmly against the crook of the left arm. (This sign is also used for the adjectival form, as in 'heroin addict'.)

herpes: *n.* an inflammatory disease caused by a virus that produces clusters of watery blisters. *Some strains of herpes are sexually transmitted.*

SIGN: Fingerspell **HERPES**.

herself: *pron.* used to emphasize the subject she. [See PRONOUNS, p. LXVI.] *She looked at herself in the mirror.*

SIGN: Horizontal right **'EXTENDED A'** hand, thumb pointing upward and palm facing leftward/forward, is jabbed a couple of times in the direction of the person or animal being referred to.

hesitate: *v.* to pause or to be slow and uncertain. *Do not hesitate to ask any questions about Deaf Culture.*

SIGN: Horizontal **'5'** hands, palms toward the body, are held out from either side of the chest, and are moved toward each other. (This sign is appropriate only in situations where there is a feeling of nervousness, uncertainty or fear implicit in **hesitate**. Depending on the context, other signs such as **pause** or **resist** might be used.)

hey: *s.s.* an expression used to get the attention of an individual or group. *Hey! Where have you been?*

SIGN: Right **'CROOKED 5'** hand is waved up and down rapidly from the wrist in the direction of the person(s) whose attention the signer is trying to get.

hi: *s.s.* an informal word for 'hello'. *Hi Jane. How are you?*

SIGN: Side of forefinger of vertical right **'B'** hand, palm facing left, is placed against right side of forehead. The forearm is then moved forward/rightward as the hand tips forward/rightward from the wrist so that the fingers point in the same direction, as if the signer is saluting someone. (**HI** is frequently finger-spelled.)

hiccups: *n.* spasms of the diaphragm which cause the glottis to close during inhalation resulting in an unusual sound. *There are many popular cures for hiccups.*

SIGN: Right **'B'** hand is held palm-down with fingers pointing leftward and side of forefinger positioned against the chest. The signer's torso, seemingly involuntarily, moves slightly but abruptly up and down as the right hand moves up and down against the chest. Facial expression is important.

hide: *v.* to put something/someone out of sight and keep the whereabouts a secret. *We should hide the cake before he arrives.*

SIGN #1: Thumbnail of right **'A'** hand, palm facing left, is placed against the lips and the hand is then lowered and concealed under the downturned palm of the left **'CROOKED EXTENDED B'** hand.

SIGN #2 [ATLANTIC]: **VERTICAL 'B'** hands touch as they are held left in front of right directly in front of the face, the left palm facing right and the right palm facing left as the head moves slightly rightward as if peeking out from behind the hands.

hide-and-seek: *n.* a children's game in which one child tries to find others who are hiding. *Playing hide-and-seek has been enjoyed by children for centuries.*

SIGN: Vertical **'EXTENDED B'** hands are held with palms toward the face and are moved backward and forward slightly a few times with fingers covering the eyes. (Signs vary.)

hideous: *adj.* very ugly; repulsive. *He wore a hideous mask with his Hallowe'en costume.*

SIGN: Forefingers of **'ONE'** hands are crossed, left in front of right, in front of the nose. Palms are down, but the left palm is angled slightly rightward while the right palm is angled slightly leftward. The left forefinger points upward/rightward; the right forefinger points upward/leftward. The hands are then drawn apart as the forefingers curl to form **'X'** hands. Facial expression is important.

hierarchy: *n.* a body of persons or things arranged according to rank. *In Canada's governing hierarchy, the Prime Minister ranks highest.*

SIGN: **'S'** hands, palms down, are held side by side and fanned outward and slightly downward as the fingers open to form **'CROOKED 5'** handshapes. (Signs vary.)

high: *adj.* far above the average. *The figure skater received high scores for her performance.*

SIGN #1: Horizontal right **'U'** hand, palm facing the body and extended fingers pointing leftward is raised directly upward.

high: *adj.* far above the bottom. *The water level in the river is high at the moment.*

SIGN #2: **'EXTENDED B'** hands are held parallel with palms down and fingers pointing forward. The hands are then simultaneously moved upward.

high: *adj.* a colloquial term meaning intoxicated by drugs or alcohol. *Laughing gas makes dental patients feel high.*

SIGN #3: Vertical right **'SPREAD EXTENDED C'** hand is held near the head with the palm toward the face, and is moved in clockwise (from the onlooker's perspective) circles as the head lolls and the eyes are rolled slightly. (Signs in this context vary.)

high school: *n.* a secondary school. *She graduated from high school in 2000.*

SIGN: Right **'U'** hand is held with palm facing the body and extended fingers pointing leftward at a slight upward angle. The hand is then firmly drawn rightward as the extended fingers are retracted so that the hand takes on an **'S'** shape with palm facing leftward.

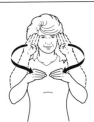

highlight: *v.* to emphasize or focus on. *The teachers' conference will highlight the education of Deaf children.*

SIGN #1: **'B'** (or **'EXTENDED B'**) hands are held upright with sides of tips of forefingers touching either temple and palms facing basically forward but slightly toward each other at a slight downward angle. The wrists then rotate forward as the hands simultaneously move away from the head and drop to a horizontal position as they take on **'BENT B'** (or **'BENT EXTENDED B'**) shapes with palms facing each other and fingertips coming almost together to create a **'V'** formation.

ALTERNATE SIGN—**emphasize**

highlight: *n.* the most exciting or memorable part of an event. *Winning the trophy was the **highlight** of my athletic career.*

SIGN #2: Vertical **'F'** hands are held apart with palms facing forward. The hands are then brought purposefully together.
ALTERNATE SIGN—**important** #2

highly: *adv.* very. *He is **highly** qualified for the job.*

SIGN: Vertical **'V'** hands are held with palms facing and fingertips of left hand touching those of right hand. The hands are then drawn apart.

highway: *n.* a main public roadway. *The Trans-Canada **highway** was completed in the early 1950s.*

SIGN #1: **'V'** hands are held fairly close together with left palm toward the body and right palm forward. The wrists simultaneously bend up and down a few times causing the extended fingers to alternate between upright and semi-horizontal positions as they represent the flow of traffic in opposite directions.

OR

SIGN #2: Vertical **'BENT EXTENDED B'** hands, palms facing, are held apart at shoulder level and the forearms are moved a short distance forward. Motion is repeated.

hijacker: *n.* a person who seizes or diverts a vehicle, airplane or other craft while it is in transit. *The **hijacker** demanded that he be flown to a neutral country.*

SIGN: Fingerspell **HIJACKER**.

hike: *v.* to take a long walk, usually for pleasure. *We **hiked** through the woods this morning.*

SIGN: Tip of forefinger of right **'ONE'** hand, palm down, is used to stroke upward from the wrist along the left arm. Next, **'EXTENDED B'** hands, palms down and fingers pointing forward, are alternately moved so that the right hand moves forward/rightward while the left hand moves backward/rightward. The left hand then moves forward/leftward while the right hand moves backward/leftward. The movement is repeated several times to simulate the act of walking. This is often done with a flourish so that the palms slant slightly forward as the hands move forward, and the palms slant toward the body as the hands move backward. (ASL CONCEPT—**long - walk**.) The first part of this sign may be omitted and the concept of 'long' conveyed through increased repetition and/or greater length of stride indicated in the sign for 'walk'. **HIKE** is frequently fingerspelled.

hill: *n.* a raised area of land. *A mountain is higher and more rugged than a **hill**.*

SIGN: Right **'EXTENDED B'** hand, palm down and fingers pointing forward, is curved upward to the right and downward as it outlines the shape of a hill. (For **hilly**, *adj.*, the sign progresses rightward as it outlines the shape of two or three hills.) **HILL** is frequently fingerspelled.

him: *pron.* used to refer to a male whose identity is already known. [See PRONOUNS, p. LXIV.] *The teacher barely recognized **him** after the summer.*

SIGN: Horizontal right **'BENT ONE'** hand is held with the palm facing forward/rightward as the forefinger points at the person or animal being referred to.

himself: *pron.* used to emphasize the subject he. [See PRONOUNS, p. LXVI.] *He looked at **himself** in the mirror.*

SIGN: Horizontal right **'EXTENDED A'** hand, thumb pointing upward and palm facing leftward/forward, is jabbed a couple of times in the direction of the person or animal being referred to.

311

hinder: *v.* to get in the way of something; to obstruct. *Accidents on the roads hinder the flow of traffic.*

SIGN: **'EXTENDED B'** hands are held at right angles to one another, the left hand in front of the right, with fingers of left hand pointing upward to the right and fingers of right hand pointing upward to the left. The hands are then pushed firmly forward. ❖
SAME SIGN—**hindrance**, *n.*

hinge: *n.* a device used to hold two parts together so that one or both of them can swing freely. *The door has a squeaky hinge.*

SIGN: Horizontal **'SPREAD EXTENDED C'** hands, palms toward the chest, are held so that the fingers are meshed. Then the hands are simultaneously moved back and forth from the wrists without unhinging the fingers. (Handshapes may vary. Alternatively, **HINGE** may be fingerspelled.)

hint: *n.* a helpful piece of advice or information given in a subtle manner. *If you cannot guess the answer I will give you a hint.*

SIGN: Fingerspell **HINT**.

hip: *n.* the area around the bone and joint that connects the leg to the body's trunk. *Elderly people often break a hip when they fall.*

SIGN: Right **'EXTENDED B'** hand, palm toward the body and fingers pointing downward, is used to pat the right hip. (**HIP** may also be fingerspelled.)

hippopotamus: *n.* a very large, heavy animal living in or near the rivers of tropical Africa. *The hippopotamus is the second-largest land mammal.*

SIGN: **'CROOKED EXTENDED B'** hands are placed upright near the cheeks with palms facing each other and are drawn forward to outline the shape of the snout of a hippopotamus, ending with the little fingers side by side. Next, **'SPREAD C'** hands are held, right above left, palms facing each other, with fingertips touching. The hands are then moved apart and back together again to simulate the opening and closing of jaws.

hire: *v.* to acquire the services of a person in return for payment. *He hired a nanny to look after his children.*

SIGN: Horizontal right **'SPREAD C'** hand is held well out in front of the body with palm facing leftward. As the hand is then brought backward toward the body, the hand closes to assume an **'S'** shape. ❖
ALTERNATE SIGN—**invite**

his: *pron.* used to refer to something belonging to or related to a male whose identity is already known. [See PRONOUNS, p. LXVI.] *He was in a panic when his car stalled on the freeway.*

SIGN: Vertical right **'EXTENDED B'** hand, palm facing forward/rightward, is held in front of the right shoulder and moved slightly in the direction of the person or animal being referred to.

history: *n.* record of what has happened in the past. *The book, Deaf Heritage in Canada, is a collection of stories about Deaf history.*

SIGN: Right **'U'** hand is held with palm facing left and extended fingers pointing forward/upward. The hand is moved up and down at least twice from the wrist.
SAME SIGN—**historical**, *adj.*

hit: *v.* to strike. *He was punished because he hit another student.*

SIGN: Right **'S'** hand, palm facing left, is moved forward forcefully to strike the forefinger of the left **'ONE'** hand which is held upright with palm facing rightward/forward. (Signs vary according to context. Use natural gestures if the connotation specifies 'slapping', 'punching', 'pounding', etc.) ❖

hitch: *v.* to connect or fasten. *He will hitch the team of horses to the sleigh.*

SIGN: **'OPEN F'** hands are held slightly apart, palms facing each other, and are then brought together to form **'F'** hands, with thumbs and forefingers linked. (Signs vary according to context.)

hitchhike: *v.* to travel by getting free rides in passing vehicles. *He hitchhiked from British Columbia to Ontario.*

SIGN: Vertical right **'EXTENDED A'** hand is held in front of right shoulder with palm facing backward and is moved rightward a few times.

HIV: *n.* the abbreviation for 'human immuno-deficiency virus'. *Infection with HIV can weaken the immune system.*

SIGN: Fingerspell **HIV**.

hive: *n.* a colony of social bees or the structure in which they live. *Every hive has a queen, workers and drones.*

SIGN: Fingerspell **HIVE**.

hoax: *n.* a deception or practical joke. *They think his story is a hoax.*

SIGN: Side of forefinger of right **'ONE'** hand, palm facing leftward/forward, is lightly brushed forward/downward twice on the right cheek. This sign is made with tongue in cheek and a facial expression showing suspicion.
ALTERNATE SIGNS—**bluff** & **nonsense** #2

hobby: *n.* an activity taken up for enjoyment and/or relaxation in one's spare time. *His favourite hobby is woodworking.*

SIGN: Fingerspell **HOBBY**.

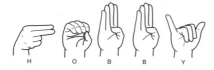

hockey: *n.* a sport played on ice by two teams whose object is to propel a puck into their opponents' goal. *Hockey is a popular sport in Canada.*

SIGN: Left **'EXTENDED B'** hand is held in a fixed position with palm right but slanted toward the body and fingers pointing forward/rightward at a slight upward angle. Knuckle of crooked forefinger of right **'X'** hand, palm facing the body at an upward angle, is stroked backward toward the body at least twice against the palm of the left hand.

hoe: *n.* a long-handled garden tool used for weeding and loosening the soil around plants. *He digs out weeds with a hoe.*

SIGN: Left **'EXTENDED B'** hand is held in a fixed position with palm up and fingers pointing rightward/forward. Fingertips of right **'BENT EXTENDED B'** hand, palm facing down, are used to scrape lightly across the left **'EXTENDED B'** hand toward the body a few times. The motion is intended to simulate the action of a hoe.
ALTERNATE SIGN—**rake** #1

hog: *n.* a domesticated pig. *He took the hog to market.*

SIGN: Right **'BENT EXTENDED B'** hand, palm left, is positioned with fingers under the chin. The fingers then flap up and down a few times.
REGIONAL VARIATION—**pig** #2 & #3

hold: *v.* to have in one's hands or to clasp. *He was holding the money in his hand.*

SIGN #1: Right **'S'** hand is clenched with palm upward but slanted toward the body and is moved in what appear from the signer's perspective to be small counter-clockwise circles. (When held up toward someone's face, this sign connotes 'HOLD THAT THOUGHT'.) Signs vary greatly depending on what is being held and how it is being held. This sign would be totally inappropriate for the *holding of a baby* which could not be held in one's hand in the way that a small object might be.

hold: *v.* to reserve or keep (for). *Please hold two tickets for me.*

SIGN #2: Right **'S'** hand is clenched with palm upward but slanted toward the body and is moved in a what appear from the signer's perspective to be small clockwise circles.

hold: *v.* to keep, reserve or set aside seats. *Hold these two seats, please.*

SIGN #3: **'SPREAD C'** hands are held slightly apart with palms down at chest level and are then closed to form **'S'** hands as they are thrust forward.

hold: *v.* to be kept waiting on a telephone line for any of a variety of reasons. *The secretary asked me to hold until she could put her boss on the line.*

SIGN #4: **'ONE'** hands, palms down, are held so that the forefingers are crossed at right angles to one another, the right on top of the left. As the forefingers then retract to form **'x'** hands, the forefinger of the right hand hooks around the forefinger of the left hand, lifting it firmly upward. (When the word **HOLD** is used in the context of TTY use, it may be fingerspelled.)

hold on: *v.* to persist with patience; to persevere. *Hold on and someone will help you soon.*

SIGN #1: Right **'A'** hand, with thumbnail touching closed lips and palm facing left, is moved slowly down chin.

hold on: *v.* a colloquial term meaning to wait. *Hold on, I am busy just now.*

SIGN #2: Forefinger of right **'ONE'** hand, palm forward, is held upright and very firmly moved forward a short distance. Appropriate facial expression is essential.

hold on: *v.* to hang on or cling to. *He lifted his son onto his shoulders and told him to hold on.*

SIGN #3: Natural gestures are used to convey this concept and will vary according to the specific context.

holdup: *n.* an armed robbery. *There was a holdup at the local store last night.*

SIGN: **'L'** (or **'EXTENDED U'**) hands are held parallel with palms facing and extended fingers pointing forward/upward. The forearms are then simultaneously thrust downward to a horizontal position so that extended fingers point directly forward.

hole: *n.* an opening in something. *The boys watched the game through a hole in the fence.*

SIGN: Fingerspell **HOLE**.

holiday: *n.* a period during which a break is taken from work. *July 1st is Canada's national holiday.*

SIGN #1: **'5'** hands are held with thumbtips touching either side of the upper chest, palms facing each other, and the fingers fluttering and pointing basically upward, although those of the left hand point slightly rightward while those of the right hand point slightly leftward.

SIGN #2 [ATLANTIC]: **'EXTENDED B'** hands are held with palms facing backwards and fingers of left hand pointing upward/rightward while fingers of right hand point upward/leftward. In one fluid motion, the hands drop inward to a horizontal position in front of the face, and are then swept apart as they assume **'EXTENDED A'** shapes. (This sign may be made with the right hand only.)

holier-than-thou: *adj.* showing a sanctimonious, self-righteous attitude that is offensive to others. *We are all sick of her holier-than-thou opinions.*

SIGN: Vertical right **'COMBINED U + Y'** hand, palm forward, is held in front of the right shoulder and the forearm is drawn firmly backward a short distance. This is essentially a jerking motion.

hollow: *adj.* not solid; having empty space inside. *The pipe is hollow.*

SIGN: Right **'BENT MIDFINGER 5'** hand, palm forward, is drawn firmly rightward/forward. (Signs vary according to the length, size, shape and location of the hollow object. Movement and location of the sign varies but the handshape generally remains the same.)

holy: *adj.* sacred, or associated with a deity. *Good Friday is a holy day in the Christian religion.*

SIGN: Hands are held at right angles to one another as downturned palm of right **'EXTENDED B'** hand is smoothed rightward/forward across upturned palm of left **'EXTENDED B'** hand.

home: *n.* the house or dwelling where one lives. *The children go home after school.*

SIGN: Fingertips of right **'MODIFIED O'** hand are placed against right cheek near the mouth, and the hand is then moved back to a position on the cheek that is nearer the right ear.

home economics: *n.* the study of all topics concerned with running a home efficiently. *We learned about nutrition and child care in our home economics class.*

SIGN: Place fingertips of right **'MODIFIED O'** hand against right cheek near the mouth, and then move the hand back to a position on the cheek that is nearer the right ear. Then fingerspell **EC**.

homely: *adj.* unattractive; not good-looking. *Cinderella was much more beautiful than her homely sisters.*

SIGN: Forefinger of right **'ONE'** hand, palm facing down, points leftward as it is held either under or in front of the nose. The hand is then drawn rightward as the forefinger curls into an **'x'** hand. Alternatively, this sign may be formed with two hands, beginning with the forefingers of the **'ONE'** hands crossed in front of the nose. The two-handed version is generally used for emphasis.

homework: *n.* school assignments that are done at home. *She does her homework between 6 and 7 p.m.*

SIGN: Bunched fingertips of vertical right **'MODIFIED O'** hand are placed against right cheek. The hand then takes on an **'S'** shape with palm facing forward/leftward, and is lowered to a position where the heel of the hand is used to strike once or twice against the left **'S'** hand which is held with palm downward but slanted slightly toward the body.

homicide: *n.* the killing of one human by another. *The police are treating his death as a homicide.*

SIGN: Vertical left **'EXTENDED B'** hand is held in a fixed position with palm facing rightward and slightly forward. Right **'ONE'** (or **'K'**) hand is held palm down as it moves forward/downward at a slight leftward angle, the forefinger firmly grazing the left palm.

homosexual: *adj.* sexually attracted to members of the same sex. *She announced to her family that she was homosexual.*

SIGN: Fingerspell **HOMOSEXUAL** or **GAY**.

honest: *adj.* trustworthy; not inclined to lie, cheat or steal. *The jury believed that the witness's testimony was honest.*

SIGN #1: Left **'EXTENDED B'** hand is held in a fixed position with palm facing right but slanted upward slightly and fingers pointing forward as right **'U'** hand is held with palm facing left and tip of middle finger placed at heel of left hand. The right hand is then moved straight forward along the left palm until the tip of the right middle finger reaches the tip of the left middle finger.

OR

SIGN #2: Left **'EXTENDED B'** hand is held in a fixed position with palm basically downward at a rightward/forward angle and fingers pointing basically upward at a rightward/forward angle. Right **'CONTRACTED U'** hand is held with palm toward the body and fingertips of forefinger and middle finger touching heel of left hand. The wrist of the right hand rotates clockwise as the extended fingers stroke the left hand in a straight line from the heel, along the palm and fingers and onward in an upward/rightward/forward direction. SAME SIGN—**honesty**, *n.*

honey: *n.* a sweet substance made from nectar by bees and used as food by humans. *Most people love honey.*

SIGN: Tip of middle finger of vertical right **'BENT MIDFINGER 5'** hand is placed on right cheek and the handshape is quickly changed to an **'EXTENDED B'** as it slaps lightly against the cheek. (Various signs may be used.)

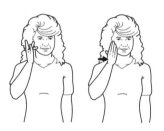

honeymoon: *n.* a holiday trip taken by a newly married couple. *They plan to go on a Mediterranean cruise for their honeymoon.*

SIGN: Tip of middle finger of vertical right **'BENT MIDFINGER 5'** hand is placed on right cheek and the handshape is quickly changed to an **'EXTENDED B'** as it slaps lightly against the cheek. (**HONEYMOON** is frequently fingerspelled. Alternatively, various signs may be used.)

honour [*also spelled* **honor**]: *v.* to give an outward sign of great respect and esteem. *On Remembrance Day we honour the veterans of war.*

SIGN: Right **'U'** hand, palm facing left, is held in a vertical position so that the side of the forefinger touches the middle of the forehead. The hand is curved downward slightly and moved forward. (Alternatively, this sign may be made with two hands, in which case the vertical left **'U'** hand, palm facing right, is held below the right hand and follows its movement.)

hood: *n.* a loose head covering usually attached to a coat. *My new ski jacket has a warm hood.*

SIGN #1: **'CLOSED A-INDEX'** hands are held palm downward at either shoulder and are simultaneously flipped upward so that the palms face backward. The motion resembles that of flipping a hood over one's head.

hood: *n.* a hinged part of an automobile that lifts up to give access to the engine. *To meet safety requirements, all cars must have a hood.*

SIGN #2: Left **'EXTENDED B'** hand is held in a fixed position with palm down and fingers pointing forward. The wrist of the right **'SPREAD EXTENDED C'** hand rests on the back of the left hand as the right hand, which represents the 'hood', moves up and down so that the palm alternates between facing forward and downward.

hook: *n.* a curved device, generally made of metal, used to suspend, hold or pull something. *You will need a good hook to catch a salmon.*

SIGN: Right **'X'** hand is inverted with palm backward/rightward at a slight downward angle, and is tugged upward slightly. (Signs vary but the **'X'** handshape generally remains constant.)

hooked: *adj.* a slang term meaning addicted to something such as a drug. *Many people are hooked on caffeine and nicotine.*

SIGN: Tip of forefinger of right **'CROOKED ONE'** hand is held at right corner of mouth, and pulled slightly to the right. The head turns rightward at the same time.

hooker: *n.* a prostitute. *The social worker helped the hooker get off the street.*

SIGN: Vertical right **'OPEN A'** hand is held with palm toward the face and backs of fingers (up to the second joint) touching the right cheek. The hand is then brushed forward off the cheek a couple of times.

hooray [*also spelled* **hurrah**]: *s.s.* an exclamation indicating great pleasure. *"Hooray!" shouted the fans when the winner was announced.*

SIGN: Vertical **'S'** hands, palms forward but angled slightly toward each other, are held apart at about shoulder height and are pushed forcefully and simultaneously upward. (Appropriate facial expression and body language are important.)

hop: *v.* to move forward or upward in short jumps. *The teacher asked the children to hop like kangaroos.*

SIGN: Tips of extended fingers of right **'V'** hand, are placed on upturned left palm, then raised quickly and retracted to form a **'CROOKED V'**. Motion is repeated. (For one-footed hopping, the same basic sign is used but instead of a **'V'** hand, a **'BENT ONE'** hand is used to move up and down on the left palm. Alternatively, the middle finger may be used, but only to specify the use of the *right* foot.)

hope: *v.* to desire or wish for something to be or to happen. *I hope to go to Prince Edward Island for my summer vacation.*

SIGN #1: Vertical left **'BENT EXTENDED B'** hand is held in front of the left shoulder with palm facing right but slanted toward the body slightly while vertical **'BENT EXTENDED B'** hand is held apart and somewhat higher with palm facing that of the left hand. Bent fingers of each hand are then simultaneously flapped up and down once or twice as if the hands are waving to each other. (The flapping is definitely repeated for **hopeful**, *adj.*)

SIGN #2 [ATLANTIC]: Fingertips of right **'BENT EXTENDED B'** hand, palm toward the chest, bend as they are brushed rightward/downward across the chin once or twice.

horizontal: *adj.* parallel to the horizon; flat; level. *The opposite of horizontal is vertical.*

SIGN: Right **'EXTENDED B'** hand, palm down and fingers pointing forward, is held in front of the left side of the chest and is drawn straight across to the right side.

hormone: *n.* a chemical substance produced by an endocrine gland (or any synthetic substance which can produce the same effects). *The hormone secreted by the thyroid gland can influence a child's rate of growth and development.*

SIGN: Fingerspell **HORMONE**.

horn: *n.* a musical wind instrument. *He plays a horn in the school band.*

SIGN #1: Vertical **'SPREAD C'** hands are held in front of the mouth or chin, the right hand just in front of the left, with the left palm facing right and the right palm facing left while the fingers flutter as if tapping on keys. (Signs vary depending on the 'type' of horn and 'how it is played'.)

horn: *n.* a device which is pushed to produce a warning sound. *I used the horn to warn the driver about the oncoming truck.*

SIGN #2: Right **'SPREAD EXTENDED C'** hand is held upright with wrist bent and palm forward. The hand is pressed forward a couple of times as if applying pressure to the horn on the steering wheel of a vehicle.

horns: *n.* a pair of bony growths on the heads of certain mammals. *Look at the horns on that bull.*

SIGN: Vertical **'SPREAD C'** hands are held at the temples with palms forward. The wrists then rotate as the hands curve outward/forward from the head with palms eventually facing the head at a slight angle toward each other as the fingers close to form **'S'** hands. (Signs vary according to the size, shape and specific location.)

horny: *adj.* a slang expression meaning sexually aroused. *He feels horny whenever he sees a pretty woman.*

SIGN: Vertical **'CLAWED EXTENDED V'** hands are held with palms facing each other at either side of the upper part of the chest and the clawed fingers are rapidly retracted and relaxed several times as the hands move downward a short distance.

horrendous: *adj.* dreadful; horrible; causing one to shudder, tremble or show fear. *We heard a horrendous crash before the tanker exploded.*

SIGN: Right **'COVERED 8'** hand, palm facing left, is held upright at about shoulder level. The hand is then thrust backward as the middle finger and thumb flick apart to form a **'MODIFIED 5'** hand. Facial expression is important feature. See also **horrible**.
ALTERNATE SIGN—**awful**

horrible/horrid: *adj.* terrible; dreadful; creating horror or serious unpleasantness. *We witnessed a horrible accident downtown.*

SIGN: Thumb and forefinger of vertical right **'COVERED 8'** hand, which is held near right side of face with palm facing left, are snapped open and thrust slightly forward to form a **'MODIFIED 5'** hand. This sign can be made with either one or two hands, one at either side of the face. Facial expression is important.

horror: *n.* intense fear, dread, disgust or loathing. *It is hard to imagine the horror experienced by victims of violent crimes.*

SIGN #1: Thumbs and forefingers of **'COVERED 8'** hands, which are held near either side of face with palms facing each other, are snapped open and thrust slightly forward to form **'MODIFIED 5'** hands. Facial expression is important.

horror: *adj.* causing intense fear, dread, disgust or loathing. *We watched a horror movie last night.*

SIGN #2: **'SPREAD C'** hands are held palm-down at about shoulder level and are shaken. Facial expression is important.

horse: *n.* a member of the equine species, used for riding or pulling loads. *There are many horses at the Calgary Stampede.*

SIGN: Thumbtip of right **'BENT EXTENDED U'** hand is placed on the right temple and the two extended fingers are simultaneously fluttered.

horseback riding: *n.* travelling while sitting astride a horse. *Horseback riding is a popular pastime in the mountains.*

SIGN: Extended fingers of right **'EXTENDED K'** hand, palm down, are used to straddle the top of the left **'EXTENDED B'** hand which is held in a horizontal position with palm facing right. Together the hands move up and down in a circular fashion to simulate the gait of a horse.

hose: *n.* a flexible rubber or plastic tube that carries liquid from one place to another. *I use a hose to water the garden.*

SIGN #1: Forefinger of vertical right **'W'** hand, palm facing left, is tapped against the lips or chin. The right hand then changes to a **'CLOSED X'** shape as it is lowered to a horizontal position in front of the chest with palm facing leftward and wrist cupped in the left hand. As the right wrist bends, the hand swerves from side to side to give the impression of using a hose. **HOSE** may also be fingerspelled. (ASL CONCEPT—**water - spray**.)

hose: *n.* stockings or pantyhose. *I usually buy nylon hose with reinforced toes.*

SIGN #2: Forefingers of **'ONE'** hands, palms down, are held side by side and alternately moved back and forth so that the sides of the forefingers brush each other with each movement. (**HOSE** may also be fingerspelled.)

SIGN #3 [ONTARIO]: Joined thumb and forefinger of right **'F'** hand, palm toward the body, are used to brush downward on the chin several times.

hospitable: *adj.* friendly and welcoming toward guests. *She is hospitable with her dinner guests.*

SIGN: **'5'** hands, palms facing backward, move backward with fingers fluttering until they come to rest close to either side of the face.

hospital: *n.* a place where sick or injured people are treated medically. *The accident victims were taken to the nearest hospital.*

SIGN #1: Tips of extended fingers of right **'BENT U'** hand, palm toward the body, are used to outline a small cross on the upper left arm.

SIGN #2 [ATLANTIC]: Side of forefinger of right vertical **'U'** (or **'B'**) hand, palm facing left, touches left side of forehead and then right side.

OR

SIGN #3 [ATLANTIC]: Left **'EXTENDED B'** hand is held in a fixed position with palm up and fingers pointing rightward/forward while vertical right **'BENT MIDFINGER 5'** hand is held with palm toward the face and tip of middle finger touching the centre of the forehead. The right hand then turns palm-downward as it is lowered and the middle finger glides along the length of the left hand, continuing on in a rightward/ forward direction.

OR

SIGN #4 [ATLANTIC]: Joined thumb and forefinger of right **'F'** hand, palm facing the body, are tapped against the throat a couple of times.

SIGN #5 [ONTARIO]: Fingertips of vertical right **'SPREAD EXTENDED C'** hand, palm toward the face, are placed first against the forehead, and then moved down to the chin.

SIGN #6 [PACIFIC/PRAIRIE/ATLANTIC]: Left **'BENT MIDFINGER 5'** hand is held upright with palm facing right while vertical right **'BENT MIDFINGER 5'** hand is held with palm toward the face and tip of middle finger touching middle of forehead. The right wrist then twists to turn the palm leftward as the hand is lowered to the level of the left hand where the tips of the middle fingers come together before the hands are drawn apart sideways so that the palms eventually face forward at a slight inward angle.

hospitality: *n.* warmth and kindness in welcoming guests. *The couple extends warm hospitality to all their guests.*

SIGN: Fingerspell **HOSPITALITY**. (ASL users recount specific hospitable acts rather than refer to them in a general sense by using **hospitality**.)

host: *v.* to act as the host of a social event. *The CCSD will host a party to thank its volunteers.*

SIGN #1: **'SPREAD C'** hands, palms down, are held apart and are simultaneously raised as they change to **'S'** hands.

host: *n.* someone who entertains guests, usually in his/her own home, but sometimes also at public functions or on television/radio programs. *He is always a gracious host.*

SIGN #2: Fingerspell **HOST**

hostage: *n.* a person being held by someone as a security for having certain demands met. *The revolutionaries allowed one hostage to speak to the journalist.*

SIGN: Fingerspell **HOSTAGE**.

hostess: *n.* a woman who receives and entertains guests in her home; a woman who welcomes customers to a restaurant, club, etc. *She is always a gracious hostess.*

SIGN: Fingerspell **HOSTESS**.

hostile: *adj.* antagonistic or opposed; unfriendly. *He was hostile toward people in positions of authority.*

SIGN: Horizontal left **'BENT EXTENDED B'** hand is held with palm facing rightward/backward and fingers pointing to the right. Right **'EXTENDED B'** (or **'B'**) hand is held upright very close to the chest with palm facing left. The right hand then drops from the wrist until it is horizontal with fingertips forcefully striking left hand between the palm and the fingers. Facial expression is important.
SAME SIGN—**hostility**, *n.*
ALTERNATE SIGNS—**disagree** & **enemy**

hot: *adj.* very warm. *Canadian summers are hot but pleasant.*

SIGN #1: Right **'CLAWED 5'** hand is held with fingertips touching or close to the lips. The wrist then rotates briskly causing the palm to face leftward/downward.

OR

SIGN #2: Tip of middle finger of right **'BENT MIDFINGER 5'** hand is used to touch the chin. The wrist then rotates briskly causing the palm to face leftward.

hot: *adj.* spicy. *She likes hot Mexican food.*

SIGN #3: Vertical **'SPREAD C'** hand is held with palm facing backward and fingertips touching the open mouth. The mouth remains open as the hand moves forward, fingers fluttering and finally closing to form an **'S'** handshape. (Signs in this context vary.)

hot dog: *n.* a frankfurter served in a long roll. *Children love to eat hot dogs at picnics.*

SIGN: **'EXTENDED C'** hand is held in a fixed position with palm up but slanted toward the body slightly. Extended fingers of right **'U'** hand, palm facing the body, are tapped into the palm of the left hand so that the ends of the fingers lay in the crook between left thumb and forefinger.

hotel: *n.* a business establishment that provides sleeping accommodation for paying guests. *The businessman checked into a five-star hotel.*

SIGN: Bunched fingertips of vertical right **'MODIFIED O'** hand, palm facing left, touch right cheek. Then the handshape changes to an **'EXTENDED B'** with the fingers held flat against the right cheek. (**HOTEL** is frequently fingerspelled.)

OR

SIGN #2: Vertical right **'ONE'** hand, palm facing forward, is held against the right-facing palm of the vertical left **'EXTENDED B'** hand. Then the right wrist rotates, turning the hand in a clockwise direction so that the movement of the forefinger resembles that of the hand of a clock which eventually returns to the twelve o'clock position, the palm facing the body.

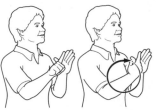

hot-tempered: *adj.* easily angered. *It is not easy to calm down a hot-tempered person.*

SIGN: Right **'CLAWED 5'** hand is held with fingertips touching or close to the lips. The wrist then rotates briskly causing the palm to face leftward/downward. Next, the tip of the forefinger of the right **'CROOKED ONE'** hand, palm toward the head, is tapped a couple of times against the right side of the forehead. (ASL CONCEPT—**hot - brain**.)

house: *n.* a building used as a place where people live. *They are building a house in a suburb of Halifax.*

SIGN: Fingertips of **'EXTENDED B'** hands, palms facing each other, are placed together at an angle in 'tent' fashion. The hands are then drawn apart, straightened to a more vertical posture, and lowered simultaneously.

how: *adv.* in what way; by what means; in what condition; to what extent. *How does the coffee maker work?*

SIGN #1: **'OPEN A'** hands are held side by side with backs of fingers touching and palms facing each other at a downward angle. The right wrist then moves rapidly back and forth so that the right hand appears to wobble while maintaining contact with the left hand. (Signs vary. This sign is sometimes made using **'Y'** handshapes.)

OR

SIGN #2: **'OPEN A'** hands are held side by side with backs of fingers touching and palms facing each other at a downward angle. The wrists then rotate forward, thus turning the hands so that the palms face the body at an upward angle while the hands maintain contact at about the second joint. (This sign is most commonly used when asking: *How are you?*)

hour: *n.* a period of time equal to sixty minutes. *He was gone for about an hour.*

SIGN #1: Vertical right **'ONE'** hand, palm facing left, is held against the right-facing palm of the vertical left **'EXTENDED B'** hand. The right hand then makes a complete clockwise circle on the left palm. (In order to specify the number of hours, the same sign is used but the shape of the right hand takes the form of a number sign with the palm facing the left hand. [See also NUMBERS, p. LIX.] This applies only to the numbers 1 to 9. To specify the number of hours above 9, the number sign is used first and then the sign above.)

how *(cont.)*

OR

SIGN #3: Horizontal left **'EXTENDED B'** hand is held in a fixed position with palm facing right but slanted slightly toward the body while right **'OPEN A'** hand is held with palm facing left and the backs of the fingers up to the second joint held against the left palm. The right wrist then rotates rapidly back and forth so that the hand appears to wobble while maintaining contact with the left hand.

how many: *adv.* what number of. *She needs to know how many people will attend the banquet.*

SIGN #1: Horizontal **'S'** hands are held apart with palms facing up. Then they are thrust upward simultaneously as they are opened to form **'CONTRACTED 5'** hands.

SIGN #2 [ATLANTIC]: Vertical **'5'** hands, palms facing backwards at a slight upward angle, are held parallel with the fingers wiggling.

how much: *adv.* what amount or quantity. *He wants to know how much seasoning to add to the casserole.*

SIGN #1: Horizontal **'SPREAD C'** hands are held close together with palms facing. They are then moved apart as they are simultaneously moved slightly upward and then outward in arc formation.

how much: *adv.* what cost or price. *She asked how much the dealer was asking for the new car.*

SIGN #2: Vertical **'F'** hands, palms facing forward, are brought together so the joined thumbs and forefingers touch each other twice.

however: *adv.* but; still; nevertheless. *She cannot come; however, she will be here next week.*

SIGN: Forefingers of **'ONE'** hands are crossed. The hands are then turned outward so that they become vertical with palms facing forward.

howl: *v.* to cry out in pain, sadness or anger. *The little girl howled when her brother pulled her hair.*

SIGN #1: Right vertical **'SPREAD C'** hand, palm toward the body, is held near the mouth and is forcefully drawn forward at an upward angle.

howl: *v.* to burst into loud, prolonged laughter. *The audience howled at the skit presented by the Deaf actors.*

SIGN #2: **'SPREAD EXTENDED C'** hands are held with right palm down and left palm up. The right hand is held slightly higher than the left, but the hands are offset as they alternately move back and forth several times. Great merriment appears on the face.

howl: *n.* the long, plaintive cry of a wolf or certain breed of dog. *The howl of a farm dog broke the stillness of the night.*

SIGN #3: **'EXTENDED B'** hands are positioned near the face, right above left, palms facing, and fingers pointing forward. Then they are simultaneously dipped and pointed upward with the fingers of the right hand fluttering. The mouth is rounded.

howl: *n.* the sound of a violent wind. *The howl of the wind indicated the severity of the storm.*

SIGN #4: **'5'** hands, palms facing each other, are simultaneously waved from side to side with great force. The mouth is rounded and the cheeks puffed out.

hue: *n.* the shade or tint of a colour. *There are many different hues of blue.*

SIGN: Fingertips of right **'5'** hand, with palm toward the body, are fluttered on the lips (or chin).
REGIONAL VARIATION—colour #2

hug: *v.* to embrace or clasp tightly with affection. *The little boy hugged his mother after the searchers found him.*

SIGN: **'S'** hands, palms toward the body, are crossed at the wrists and are placed against the chest. Then they are pressed firmly against the body while the shoulders are hunched.

huge: *adj.* extremely large. *Whistler has a huge ski resort.*

SIGN: Horizontal **'CLAWED L'** hands, which are held slightly apart with palms facing, are simultaneously moved farther apart as the wrists rotate to turn the palms down. Facial expression is important and the syllable 'CHA' is formed on the lips. (Signs vary depending on the shape and specific size of what is being described.)

human: *adj.* pertaining to people or mankind. *The ancient Greeks gave their gods human characteristics.*

SIGN: Fingerspell **HUMAN**.

humble: *adj.* modest or conscious of one's faults. *A humble woman never boasts about her achievements.*

SIGN: Horizontal left **'BENT EXTENDED B'** hand is held in a fixed position in front of the chest with palm facing the body at a rightward angle. Vertical right **'B'** hand, with palm left and fingertips just under the mouth, is lowered so that the side of the hand slides straight down along the left hand between its palm and fingers.
SAME SIGN—**humility**, *n.*

humid: *adj.* moist or damp. *On hot summer days, the air is often humid.*

SIGN: The hands are held apart with palms up and they simultaneously alternate between **'FLAT C'** and **'FLAT O'** shapes as they open slightly and close a few times. **HUMID** is frequently fingerspelled.
SAME SIGN—**humidity**, *n.*

humiliated: *adj.* degraded; hurt due to a loss of pride and dignity. *She was humiliated when her boss criticized her publicly.*

SIGN: Vertical right **'S'** hand represents a person's head as it is held with palm forward/leftward. Horizontal left **'C'** hand remains stationary as it loosely encircles the middle of the right forearm, which is lowered so that the left hand is encircling the right wrist.
ALTERNATE SIGN—**embarrassed**

humorous: *adj.* funny; amusing; comical. *He writes humorous material for the CAD Newsletter.*

SIGN: The two extended fingers of the right **'BENT EXTENDED U'** hand, palm toward the face, stroke the nose at least twice in a downward motion.
SAME SIGN—**humour**, *n.* (also spelled **humor**)

hunch [*or* **to have a hunch**]: *n.* [*or v.*] an intuition or feeling created by guessing or assuming. *I have a hunch that our jobs will be terminated.*

SIGN: Tip of middle finger of right **'BENT MIDFINGER 5'** hand, palm toward the body, is brushed upward and off the chest at least twice as the hand makes small circular-like movements in a clockwise direction.

hundred: *n.* one hundred; 100. [See NUMBERS, p. LXII.] *The child learned to count from one to one hundred.*

SIGN: Vertical right **'ONE'** hand, palm facing left, is held upright and is rapidly changed to a **'C'** hand as it is moved slightly forward/downward. (Signs for the numbers 200, 300, 400, and 500 are derived from the signs for the numbers 2, 3, 4 and 5 respectively with the modification that the extended fingers in each case are crooked rather than straight and retracted and extended a few times. For multitudes of a hundred above 500, the base number is used followed by a **'C'**. For example, 600 is signed by using the sign for **'6'** and then a fingerspelled **C**.)

hungry: *adj.* feeling the need for food. *He was so hungry that he ate three servings of meat and potatoes.*

SIGN #1: Fingertips of horizontal right **'EXTENDED C'** hand, palm toward the body, are placed against middle of upper chest and the hand is drawn firmly downward.

SIGN #2 [ATLANTIC]: Fingertips of **'BENT EXTENDED B'** hands, palms toward the body, are placed on either side of the stomach. The fingertips maintain contact as the hands drop downward so that the palms face up.
SAME SIGN—**hunger**, *n.*

hunt: *v.* to search for. *The children will hunt for Easter eggs on Sunday morning.*

SIGN #1: Vertical right **'C'** hand, palm facing left, is circled in front of the face several times in what appears to the signer as a counter-clockwise direction.

hunt: *v.* to search for and kill animals for food and/or sport. *In the fall, the men hunt deer and moose.*

SIGN #2: **'L'** hands are held, right slightly ahead of/above the left, pointing forward/upward and right palm facing left while the left palm faces right. The forearms are then simultaneously moved slightly but firmly up and down a couple of times.

hurdle: *n.* one of a number of obstacles over which runners must leap in certain athletic events. *He won the bronze medal for the 110 metre hurdles.*

SIGN: Right **'EXTENDED K'** hand, palm down and forefinger pointing forward, is held above the left **'STANDARD BASE'** hand. The hands move back and forth several times in opposite directions, the right hand moving forward while the left hand moves backward, the right midfinger flicking it lightly during each movement.

hurricane: *n.* a storm with extremely strong winds. *The hurricane destroyed everything in its path.*

SIGN: **'5'** hands, palms facing each other, are simultaneously waved from side to side with great force. Facial expression is important. (**HURRICANE** is frequently fingerspelled. If named, as in 'Hurricane Andrew', **HURRICANE** is always fingerspelled.)

hurry: *v.* to rush; to move quickly. *Every morning he must hurry to school.*

SIGN #1: Horizontal **'U'** hands are held apart with left palm facing right and right palm facing left, and the forearms are alternately circled forward repeatedly.

hurry [*or* **hurry up**]: *v.* (often used as a command to urge someone) to move quickly. *Hurry, or you will miss the bus!*

SIGN #2: Horizontal **'U'** hands are held parallel with palms facing and are slightly but firmly and rapidly moved up and down simultaneously as they move forward.

hurt: *v.* to become or cause to become physically or mentally injured. *He hurt himself when he fell off the bicycle.*

SIGN #1: Horizontal **'BENT ONE'** hands are held slightly apart, then moved toward one another as the right hand twists slightly forward and the left hand twists slightly backward. This sign is generally made near the afflicted area of the body. (**HURT** may be fingerspelled.)

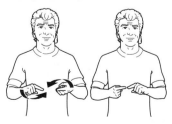

OR

SIGN #2: Thumb of right **'A'** hand, palm facing left, is pressed against the chin as the wrist rotates to twist the hand so that the palm is toward the body.

SIGN #3 [ATLANTIC]: Edge of forefinger of horizontal right **'BENT ONE'** hand, palm angled downward/leftward, is placed at the bottom of the right side of the chin and is then pushed across to the left side. (This sign may vary slightly in that it could be made either 'on' or just 'under' the chin. In addition, the leftward movement may be straight or curved in either a slight upward or downward arc.)

SIGN #4 [ONTARIO]: Thumb of right horizontal **'MODIFIED Y'** hand, palm toward the body, is drawn across the chin from the left side to the right.

OR

SIGN #5 [ONTARIO]: Tip of forefinger of vertical right **'SLANTED V'** hand, palm left, brushes the tip of the nose as the hand is moved leftward past it two or three times.

husband: *n.* a male partner in marriage. *He is my husband and the father of our children.*

SIGN: Thumbtip of right **'EXTENDED C'** hand, palm down, is positioned at the centre of the forehead and the hand is brought downward to clasp left **'EXTENDED C'** hand, of which the palm faces upward.

hush: *v.* to make or become quiet. *Please hush or the librarian will ask you to leave.*

SIGN: Side of forefinger of vertical right **'ONE'** hand, palm facing left, is placed against the lips which have taken on an 'SH' formation.

hustle: *v.* to move or shove roughly, or to hurry furtively. *The security guards hustled him out of the legislature when he became unruly.*

SIGN: **'5'** hands are held parallel with palms down and fingers pointing downward. The forearms move forward as the hands move up and down simultaneously from the wrists as if shooing someone out of a place. (Sign choice varies according to context.)

hygiene: *n.* clean and healthy practices used in maintaining good health. *Oral hygiene is an important factor in preventing tooth decay.*

SIGN: Hands are held at right angles to one another as downturned palm of right **'EXTENDED B'** hand is smoothed rightward across upturned palm of left **'EXTENDED B'** hand.

hymn: *n.* a song praising God. *The congregation stood to sing the closing hymn.*

SIGN: Horizontal right **'EXTENDED B'** hand is positioned above left forearm with palm facing leftward/backward. The right wrist makes slight back and forth rotations so that the palm alternates between being angled slightly upward and being angled slightly downward.

hypnosis: *n.* an induced condition in which specific parts of the brain are more susceptible to access by a hypnotist. *Hypnosis is used sometimes to treat patients with psychological problems.*

SIGN: **'BENT 5'** hands, palms downward/forward and fingers pointing forward, are positioned with the left hand to the left of and a little farther forward than the right hand. The hands then simultaneously move forward with fingers fluttering. Hands return to the original position and movement is repeated.
SAME SIGN—**hypnotism**, *n.*

hypocrite: *n.* a person who pretends to be something he is not. *The hypocrite pretended to support the motion and then voted against it.*

SIGN: **'EXTENDED B'** hands are held, right on top of left, with palms down and fingers pointing forward. The fingers of both hands then bend so that they point downward.
SAME SIGN—**hypocrisy**, *n.*

hypodermic syringe: *n.* a cylinder with a tightly fitting piston and a needle, used to give injections or to withdraw blood samples from the body. *The nurse used a hypodermic syringe to immunize the child.*

SIGN: Tip of forefinger of right **'BENT L'** hand is jabbed into upper left arm and thumb is repeatedly bent and extended as though depressing a plunger into a syringe.

hysterectomy: *n.* surgical removal of the uterus. *The doctors advised the woman to have a complete hysterectomy.*

SIGN: Right **'EXTENDED A'** hand, palm down but slanted toward the body, is held with tip of thumb touching left side of abdomen. The arm then moves rightward as the thumb traces an imaginary line across the abdomen. Next, the left **'EXTENDED B'** hand is held in a fixed position in front of the abdomen with palm upward/rightward and fingers pointing rightward/downward. Right **'SPREAD C'** hand is held palm-down with fingertips resting in the left palm. In one fluid movement, the right hand rises from the left hand as the fingers close to form an **'S'** shape, and then hand drops downward as the fingers open to form a **'5'** hand with fingers pointing downward.
(ASL CONCEPT—**operate - abdomen - remove**.)
HYSTERECTOMY is frequently fingerspelled.

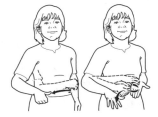

I

I: *pron.* used by the signer when referring to himself/herself. [See Pronouns, p. LXIV.] *I promised to help you, so please trust me.*

SIGN: Horizontal right **'BENT ONE'** hand is held with tip of forefinger touching the chest.

ice: *n.* frozen water. *Do you want some ice for your drink?*

SIGN: Fingerspell **ICE**.

ice cream: *n.* a sweet, frozen dessert made from flavoured milk or cream. *Vanilla is my favourite flavour of ice cream.*

SIGN: Right **'S'** hand, palm facing left, is held in a vertical position near the mouth as if holding an ice cream cone and is twisted from the wrist toward the chin at least twice.

ice hockey: See **hockey**.

ice skating: *n.* gliding on ice while wearing boots fitted with steel blades on the soles. *Ice skating is one of the most popular forms of winter recreation in Canada.*

SIGN: Horizontal **'X'** hands, are held apart with palms up and are alternately drawn back and forth, the left hand moving backward/rightward while the right hand moves forward/rightward, then the left hand moving forward/leftward while the right hand moves backward/leftward.

icing: *n.* a frosting or coating that decorates baked goods. *The best part of the cake was the icing.*

SIGN: Right **'MODIFIED G'** hand, palm forward/leftward, is placed on the back of the left **'STANDARD BASE'** hand near the wrist. Then the right hand is drawn rightward/forward to the end of the left hand. (**ICING** is frequently fingerspelled.)

icy: *adj.* frozen; full of or covered with ice; slippery. *The roads were icy after the storm.*

SIGN: Fingerspell **ICY**. (This fingerspelled word is often followed by a sign that indicates the degree and/or effect of the 'iciness'. See **catastrophe** #1.)

idea: *n.* a concept formulated in the mind. *It was Chris's idea to go camping on the weekend.*

SIGN: Tip of little finger of right **'I'** hand, palm toward the face, is placed on the right side of the forehead and is drawn forward/upward a brief distance.

ideal: *adj.* considered to be perfect. *The weather is ideal for a picnic.*

SIGN: Right **'F'** hand is held above and slightly to the right of the left **'F'** hand with palms facing. The hands then come together so that the joined thumb and forefinger of one hand strikes those of the other hand. (Alternatively, this sign may be made with **'K'** hands, the tips of the middle fingers coming together.)

identical: *adj.* exactly alike or the very same. *Their shirts are identical.*

SIGN: Vertical right **'Y'** hand is held with palm forward and appears to wobble from side to side as the wrist twists.

identification: *n.* documentation which proves a person is who he says he is. *We need two pieces of identification before we can accept your cheque.*

SIGN: Fingerspell **ID**. (For a more generic connotation of **identification**, *n.*, **identity** is generally used.)

identify: *v.* to prove or recognize as being a certain thing or person. *The police have not been able to **identify** the body of the murder victim.*

SIGN: Tip of forefinger of right **'CROOKED ONE'** hand is positioned at corner of right eye and brought down to rest on upturned palm of left **'EXTENDED B'** hand. Then fingertips of right **'EXTENDED B'** hand, with palm facing body, are tapped against right side of forehead. (ASL CONCEPT—**notice - know**.)
ALTERNATE SIGN—**identity**

identity: *n.* the fact of being a certain person or thing. *The **identity** of the woman leaving the scene of the crime has not been determined.*

SIGN: Vertical left **'EXTENDED B'** hand is held in a fixed position with palm right but slanted slightly forward. Vertical right **'I'** hand, palm forward at a slight leftward angle, is held to the right of the left hand and is moved briskly leftward to make contact with the palm of the left hand.

idiom: *n.* linguistic usage that is characteristic of native speakers and cannot be understood on the basis of the usual meanings of the individual words. *"It is raining cats and dogs" is an **idiom**.*

SIGN: Fingerspell **IDIOM**.

idiot: *n.* a very stupid or foolish person. *He feels like an **idiot** because he has made so many mistakes.*

SIGN: Back of right **'V'** hand is thrust briskly against the middle of the forehead. For emphasis, **IDIOT** may be fingerspelled.
ALTERNATE SIGNS—**blockhead** or **stupid**

idle: *adj.* unoccupied; inactive; not working; lazy. *A business cannot succeed if the employees are **idle**.*

SIGN: **'CROOKED 5'** hands are held apart with palms toward the chest, fingers pointing basically downward, and wrists limp. A vacant or disinterested facial expression accompanies this sign. (Signs vary.)
ALTERNATE SIGN—**lazy**

idol: *n.* the image of a god or a person who is greatly admired and loved. *Elvis Presley was an **idol** to millions of fans.*

SIGN: Fingerspell **IDOL**.

idolize: *v.* to admire greatly; revere. *Young people often **idolize** well-known athletes.*

SIGN: **'V'** hands are held apart with one slightly ahead of the other and palms down. The hands then curve forward/upward so that the palms face forward and the extended fingers point upward at a slightly forward angle. ❖

if: *conj.* supposing that; on condition that; in case that (with the assumption that there are *definite consequences*). *If you want to see him, you will have to make an appointment first.*

SIGN #1: Fingerspell **IF**. (**If** in this context is fingerspelled firmly for emphasis, and the signer's upper teeth are clearly visible on the lower lip as if forming an 'F'.)

if: *conj.* supposing that; on condition that; in case that (with the assumption that a *realistic possibility* exists that the condition will be met). *If he does not arrive, we should go ahead without him.*

SIGN #2: Vertical right **'OFFSET F'** hand is held with palm forward and extended fingers fluttering. The signer's upper teeth are clearly visible on the lower lip as if forming an 'F'. (This is an ASL conjunction which appears only at the beginning of a sentence and never in the middle.)

if: *conj.* supposing that; on condition that; in case that (with the understanding that it is just a *hypothetical notion*). *If you had grown up on a farm, your interests would be different now.*

SIGN #3: Tip of little finger of right **'I'** hand, palm facing backward, is tapped lightly against the right cheek. (This is an ASL conjunction which appears only at the beginning of a sentence and never in the middle.)

ignite: *v.* to cause fire or combustion. *The arsonist used gasoline and a lighter to **ignite** the blaze.*

SIGN: Left **'5'** hand is held with palm facing right while forefinger of right **'ONE'** hand is inserted between first two fingers of left hand and twisted 180 degrees to the right.

ignorant: *adj.* without knowledge, education or understanding. *It was an **ignorant** remark from someone who claims to be an expert.*

SIGN: Back of right **'V'** hand is thrust briskly against the middle of the forehead. A look of disgust generally accompanies this sign. SAME SIGN—**ignorance**, *n.*

ignore: *v.* to disregard or refuse to notice. *You should not **ignore** his warnings.*

SIGN: Tip of forefinger of horizontal right **'4'** hand, palm facing downward, is placed on the nose and the hand is curved rightward from the wrist away from the face.

ill: *adj.* sick; in a state of poor health. *Seriously **ill** patients stay in the hospital.*

SIGN #1: **'BENT MIDFINGER 5'** hands are then positioned so that the tip of the right middle finger is in the middle of the forehead and the tip of the left middle finger is on the stomach. Sometimes this sign is made with the right hand only. SAME SIGN—**illness**, *n.*

ill: *adj.* bad; suggesting evil; lacking in kindness; harsh. *The incident created **ill** feeling among the staff members.*

SIGN #2: Right **'EXTENDED B'** hand, with fingertips on chin and palm facing body, is turned away, so that palm is facing down. ALTERNATE SIGN—**bad** #2

ill at ease: *adj.* uncomfortable; unable to relax. *His crude jokes make most people feel **ill at ease**.*

SIGN: Right **'EXTENDED A'** hand, palm facing left, thumb under chin, is thrust forward. Next, left **'CROOKED EXTENDED B'** hand is held palm down with fingers pointing rightward/forward at a downward angle while right **'CROOKED EXTENDED B'** hand is held palm down on left hand at right angles to it. The right hand is drawn rightward/backward across the back of the left hand, which moves out from under the right hand to take up a position on top of it so that the positioning of the hands is the reverse of their original position. The left hand is then drawn leftward/backward across the back of the right hand, which moves out from under the left hand to take up a position on top of it. Movement is repeated. (ASL CONCEPT—**not - comfortable**.)

illegal: *adj.* forbidden by law. *It is **illegal** to park your car in front of a fire hydrant.*

SIGN: Right **'L'** hand, palm facing left, is tapped smartly against right-facing palm of left **'EXTENDED B'** hand. (**ILLEGAL** is frequently fingerspelled.)

illicit: *adj.* illegal. *I hope they are not involved in the **illicit** sale of drugs.*

SIGN: Right **'L'** hand, palm facing left, is tapped smartly against right-facing palm of left **'EXTENDED B'** hand.

illiterate: *adj.* unable to read and write. *The library's reading program helps illiterate adults.*

SIGN: Left **'ONE'** hand is held palm-down with forefinger pointing forward/rightward. The forefinger of the right **'ONE'** hand is held above the left, then brought down sharply to strike the left forefinger. Next, horizontal left **'EXTENDED B'** hand is held in a fixed position with palm rightward but slanted slightly toward the body while the fingers point rightward/forward. Right **'V'** hand, palm forward, bends from the wrist, causing the tips of the extended fingers to brush downward against the left palm. Then the right hand changes to a **'CLOSED X'** hand which strikes rightward/forward along the length of the left hand.
(ASL CONCEPT—**can't - read - write**.)

illustrate: *v.* to clarify or explain by using pictures, diagrams, maps, etc. *The children illustrate their stories with simple drawings.*

SIGN: Left **'EXTENDED B'** hand is held in a fixed and relatively fixed position with palm facing the body. The tip of the little finger of the right **'I'** hand is stroked downward twice along the middle of the left palm.

image: *n.* a concept held by people in general. *The politician is trying to change hi public image.*

SIGN: Fingerspell **IMAGE**. (Signs vary depending on the context.)

imagery: *n.* clearly descriptive language in literature. *The teacher asked the student to comment on the imagery in the poem.*

SIGN: Tip of forefinger of right **'ONE'** hand touches centre of forehead. Then vertical **'S'** hands are held together, left in front of right, at centre of forehead with left palm facing right and right palm facing left. As the hands move apart, they open to form **'CROOKED 5'** hands.
ALTERNATE SIGN—**describe**

imaginary: *adj.* fictitious or existing only in the mind; not real. *All her fears are imaginary.*

SIGN: Right **'4'** hand is held upright in front of forehead with palm facing leftward. The hand is then moved forward (at a slight downward angle) in short jerky motions until the fingers are pointing forward.
ALTERNATE SIGN—**artificial**

imaginative: *adj.* very creative in one's thinking. *He is an imaginative writer.*

SIGN: Vertical **'I'** hands are held at about eye level or above with palms facing backward and are alternately circled forward.
SAME SIGN—**imagination**, *n.*

imagine: *v.* to form a picture in one's mind. *Can you imagine being a millionaire and having everything?*

SIGN: Tip of little finger of right **'I'** hand, palm toward the face, is placed on the right side of the forehead and is drawn forward/upward a brief distance.

imbecile: *n.* an extremely stupid or foolish person. *Although he should know better, he often behaves like an imbecile.*

SIGN: Thumb and forefinger of right **'MODIFIED G'** hand are pointed at forehead, with palm facing left. Then wrist is twisted, thus rotating **'MODIFIED G'** hand a quarter turn so that palm is toward face. For greater emphasis, this sign may be made with a **'FLAT C'** handshape.
ALTERNATE SIGN—**stupid**

imitate: *v.* to copy the actions of another. *It is natural for children to **imitate** adults.*

SIGN: Left **'EXTENDED B'** hand is held in a fixed position with palm up and fingers pointing forward/rightward. Right **'CONTRACTED 5'** hand is positioned at the end of the left hand with palm facing forward. As the right hand is drawn backward toward the palm or heel of the left hand, it closes to form a **'FLAT O'** shape. ❖
REGIONAL VARIATION—**copy** #2

imitation: *adj.* not real or genuine. *The purse is made of **imitation** leather.*

SIGN: Side of forefinger of right **'ONE'** hand, palm facing left, is brushed lightly downward twice on the right cheek, forefinger either remaining upright or bending slightly to become a **'BENT ONE'**.

immaculate: *adj.* extremely clean; spotless. *He always looks **immaculate**, even when he is wearing blue jeans.*

SIGN: Horizontal **'EXTENDED B'** hands are held, right on top of left, left palm facing upward and right palm facing downward, the fingers pointing basically forward. Together, the hands appear to jerk backward a short distance although the hands do not move any real distance at all. This is a twitchlike movement.

immature: *adj.* not fully grown or developed; childish. *He has some **immature** ideas about life.*

SIGN: Side of forefinger of right **'COMBINED I + ONE'** hand is placed, palm down, under the nose, and the hand is wiggled by twisting the wrist. Alternatively, the hand may be moved slightly leftward a couple of times rather than wiggled. A look of disapproval accompanies this sign. (**IMMATURE** may be fingerspelled with emphasis on the 'IM' at the beginning.)

immediate: *adj.* taking place or requiring attention at once, or without delay. *This letter needs an **immediate** response.*

SIGN: Vertical **'COVERED T'** hands are held apart with palms facing, and are jerked forward as thumbs flick upward, resulting in horizontal **'CLAWED L'** hands, palms still facing. Sign choice varies according to context.
ALTERNATE SIGN—**quick** #2

immense: *adj.* extremely large; huge; vast. *Lake Superior is an **immense** body of water.*

SIGN: Horizontal **'CLAWED L'** (or **'EXTENDED B'**) hands, with palms facing, are held slightly apart and then simultaneously moved farther apart.

immerse: *v.* to dip or plunge into a liquid. *The garment should be **immersed** in the dye for at least 20 minutes.*

SIGN: **'MODIFIED O'** hands, which are held parallel with palms down, are simultaneously lowered and then raised as if dipping something into a liquid.

immersion: *n.* a complete, deep involvement. *Total **immersion** in Deaf Culture provides the best opportunity for learning ASL.*

SIGN: Vertical right **'CLAWED V'** hand, palm facing backward, is thrust forward and slightly downward so that the back of the hand makes contact with the palm of the horizontal left **'SPREAD C'** hand which is held with the palm facing the body. The right hand then slides downward slightly but purposefully.

immigrant: *n.* a person who legally settles in a country other than his native land. *He is one **immigrant** among many in Canada.*

SIGN: Fingerspell **IMMIGRANT**.

I M M I G R A N T

imminent: *adj.* probably about to happen soon; impending. *The dark sky indicates that a thunderstorm is **imminent**.*

SIGN: Horizontal left **'BENT EXTENDED B'** hand is held in a fixed position with palm facing right while horizontal right **'BENT EXTENDED B'** hand is held a little higher and much closer to the body with palm facing left. The right hand then moves forward toward the left hand in a series of short arcs.

immodest: *adj.* improper; indecent; shameless; bold. *It is **immodest** to wear such a revealing bikini.*

SIGN #1: Tips of joined forefinger and thumb of horizontal right **'F'** hand, palm toward the body, are brought purposefully up to strike the chin.

immodest *(cont.)*

OR

SIGN #2: Knuckles of right vertical **'CLAWED V'** hand, palm toward the face, are placed against the right cheek and the hand is twisted a quarter turn forward.

immoral: *adj.* corrupt, unethical or unscrupulous. *Although his actions were not illegal, they were certainly immoral.*

SIGN: Right **'EXTENDED B'** hand, with fingertips on chin and palm facing body, is turned away, so that palm is facing down. ALTERNATE SIGN—**bad** #2

immortal: *adj.* having everlasting life; living forever. *The ancient Greeks believed their gods were immortal.*

SIGN #1: Right **'B'** (or **'EXTENDED B'**) hand, palm facing left, is held upright near the face and is vigorously curved downward. Next, **'EXTENDED B'** hands are held with fingers pointing forward, left palm facing up and right palm facing down. Then they are flipped over simultaneously so that the palm positions are reversed. (ASL CONCEPT—**never - die.**)

OR

SIGN #2: Horizontal **'L'** hands are placed at either side, somewhere above the waist, with palms toward the body and forefingers pointing toward each other. They are then raised to a higher position on the chest. Next, vertical right **'ONE'** hand, palm facing backward, is held just in front of the right shoulder and is circled counter-clockwise. The hand is then changed to a **'Y'** shape with palm forward at a slight downward slant and the arm is extended in a forward/rightward direction. (ASL CONCEPT—**live - forever.**)

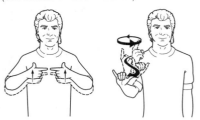

immortal: *adj.* remembered eternally; having everlasting fame or value in people's minds. *Shakespeare's love story, Romeo and Juliet is immortal.*

SIGN #3: Right **'B'** (or **'EXTENDED B'**) hand, palm facing left, is held upright near the face and is vigorously curved downward. Next, **'FLAT O'** hands are held parallel with palms up and slanted slightly toward the body. As the hands are drawn apart the thumbs slide across the fingertips, causing the hand to assume **'A'** shapes. (ASL CONCEPT—**never - fade.**)

immune: *adj.* having either a natural or acquired resistance to specific diseases. *This inoculation will make the infant immune to certain diseases.*

SIGN: **'EXTENDED B'** hands are held at right angles to one another, the left hand in front of the right, with fingers of left hand pointing upward to the right and fingers of right hand pointing upward to the left. The hands are then pushed firmly forward. (**IMMUNE** is frequently fingerspelled.) ALTERNATE SIGN—**protect**

immunization: *n.* the act of protecting a person from disease by inoculation. *It is important that all children receive immunization against communicable diseases.*

SIGN: Tip of forefinger of right **'BENT L'** hand is jabbed into upper left arm and thumb is repeatedly bent and extended as though depressing a plunger into a syringe.

impact: *n.* the effect that something has on someone or something else. *The movie had a profound impact on the viewers.*

SIGN: Horizontal right **'S'** hand, palm facing left, is moved forward forcefully to strike the forefinger of the vertical left **'ONE'** hand which is held with palm facing right.

impair: *v.* to weaken or reduce in strength or quality. *Excessive use of alcohol can impair one's judgment.*

SIGN: Horizontal left **'x'** hand is held in a fixed position with palm rightward but slanted toward the body slightly while horizontal right **'x'** hand is held above/behind left hand with palm leftward. The right hand then slides briskly along the top of the left hand and continues to move in a forward/rightward direction. Sign choice depends entirely on the context. Many Deaf people find **impair** offensive when used in reference to the sense of hearing. They do not consider themselves 'hearing impaired', a term which suggests deficiency.

ALTERNATE SIGN—**deteriorate**

impaired driving: *n.* the operation of a motor vehicle after drinking too much alcohol. *He was charged with impaired driving.*

SIGN: Right **'EXTENDED A'** hand is held in front of the mouth with palm facing left. The forearm is then tipped firmly downward/leftward causing the palm to face downward. Next, **'s'** hands are held parallel with palms facing the body and are simultaneously moved forward. (ASL CONCEPT—**drunk - drive**.)

impartial: *adj.* not biased or prejudiced toward or against any particular side. *A judge must be impartial.*

SIGN: Right **'BENT U'** hand is held upright with palm forward and is moved slightly but rapidly from side to side. This is a wrist movement.

ALTERNATE SIGN—**fair** #1

impatient: *adj.* intolerant or easily irritated by others. *Children may become impatient if expected to wait too long.*

SIGN: Right **'A'** hand, palm facing left, is positioned with the thumb against the lips and is slowly drawn downward and off the chin. Then right **'o'** hand is held upright with palm facing left, and is thrust downward/forward so that the palm faces upward/leftward. Alternatively two **'o'** hands may be used. (ASL CONCEPT—**patient - no** or **no - patient**.) SAME SIGN—**impatience**, *n.*

impeach: *v.* to bring a criminal charge against a high-ranking official, bringing his/her honesty and integrity into question, and usually resulting in removal from office. *Many Americans wanted to impeach President Nixon for the Watergate scandal, but he resigned before they could.*

SIGN: Horizontal **'s'** hands are held slightly apart with left palm down and right palm up. The arms then move simultaneously rightward as the hands open to form **'CROOKED 5'** shapes.

impeccable: *adj.* completely without fault, flaw or error. *He has an impeccable record as a 25-year employee of the company.*

SIGN: Left **'F'** hand is held with palm upward but slanted toward the body slightly. Right **'F'** hand is held closer to the body and higher than the left hand with palm downward but slanted forward slightly. The hands then simultaneously move very slightly but firmly upward/backward and then equally slightly downward/forward for emphasis. Facial expression is important.

ALTERNATE SIGN—**neat**

impede: *v.* to obstruct or restrict in progress or action; to block. *The storm will impede the climber's ascent of Mt. Everest.*

SIGN: **'EXTENDED B'** hands are held at right angles to one another, the left hand in front of the right, with fingers of left hand pointing upward to the right and fingers of right hand pointing upward to the left. The hands are then pushed firmly forward.

imperative: *adj.* essential; necessary; mandatory. *It is **imperative** that we hold a meeting tomorrow.*

SIGN: Vertical right **'X'** hand, palm facing forward, is bent forward smartly from the wrist so that the palm faces downward. Facial expression is important.

impertinent: *adj.* rude; impolite; disrespectful. *It is **impertinent** to interrupt the class for no reason.*

SIGN: Vertical right **'A-INDEX'** hand, palm facing left, quivers as thumb and forefinger are used to grasp skin of right cheek. Facial expression is important.
SAME SIGN—**impertinence**, *n.*

impish: *adj.* full of mischief. *The child's **impish** grin endeared him to everyone.*

SIGN: Thumbs of **'CROOKED EXTENDED V'** hands, palms facing each other at a forward angle, are placed just in front of either side of the forehead and the crooked fingers retract still further several times as the forearms simultaneously move up and down slightly.

implant: *v.* to surgically insert or embed. *The surgeon will **implant** new corneas in the patient's eyes.*

SIGN: **'FLAT O'** hands are held parallel with palms forward/downward and are moved forward in a slight arc formation. Alternatively, one hand only may be used. (To specify that it is a cochlear implant being inserted, the vertical right **'CLAWED V'** hand, palm forward, is bent downward from the wrist so that the palm faces downward.) **IMPLANT**, *n.*, is generally fingerspelled. See also **cochlear implant**. ❖

implement: *n.* a tool, utensil or piece of equipment. *A hoe is an essential garden **implement**.*

SIGN #1: Right **'EXTENDED B'** hand, palm upward and fingers pointing forward, is moved rightward in an arc formation.

implement: *v.* to put into action. *They will **implement** the new policy immediately.*

SIGN #2: Left **'5'** hand is held with palm facing right while forefinger of right **'ONE'** hand is inserted between first two fingers of left hand and twisted 180 degrees either to the left or to the right.
ALTERNATE SIGN—**use**

implore: *v.* to beg; to plead with. *The principal **implored** her staff to help enforce the new discipline policy.*

SIGN: Horizontal **'X'** hands, are held apart with palms facing each other and the right hand slightly ahead of the left hand. The hands are then simultaneously moved forward and back at least twice with short deliberate movements as though prodding a reluctant individual. ❖

imply: *v.* to express or suggest by hinting. *The doctor's serious facial expression **implied** that something was wrong.*

SIGN: Horizontal left **'EXTENDED B'** hand is held in a fixed position with palm facing right while tip of forefinger of right palm-down **'BENT V'** hand is jabbed into the left palm. The right hand then moves away from the left hand as the right wrist rotates a quarter turn clockwise, and the middle fingertip is jabbed into the left palm.

import: *v.* to bring in goods and/or services from another country. *Canada continues to **import** foreign cars.*

SIGN: **'EXTENDED B'** hands, palms toward the body but angled slightly upward, are held a short distance apart with the right ahead of the left, and are simultaneously brought toward the body. (**IMPORT**, *n.*, is fingerspelled.)

important: *adj.* having great value or significance. *It is **important** to learn about Deaf Culture.*

SIGN #1: Vertical **'F'** hands are held apart with palms facing forward. The hands are then brought purposefully together.

OR

SIGN #2: Horizontal **'I'** hands are held right on top of left with right palm facing leftward and left palm facing rightward. Together, they are tipped back toward the chest, thus assuming an upright position.
SAME SIGN—**importance**, *n.*

impose: *v.* to establish as compulsory; enforce. *The government imposes taxes on gasoline.*

SIGN #1: Vertical right **'C'** hand, palm facing forward/leftward, is placed on the back of the left **'STANDARD BASE'** hand and is thrust forward/leftward across the left hand as the wrist bends causing the right hand to hang palm-down over the left hand. Alternatively, this sign may be formed without the use of the left hand.

ALTERNATE SIGNS—**establish** or **start**

impose: *v.* to interfere or interrupt by forcing oneself (or one's presence) on others. *I do not mean to impose, but our bus is leaving immediately.*

SIGN #2: Left **'5'** hand is held in a fixed position with palm facing the body while right horizontal **'EXTENDED B'** hand is inserted forcefully between forefinger and middle finger of left hand.

impose on: *v.* to take advantage of. *Her family tends to impose on her kindness.*

SIGN: Middle finger of right **'BENT MIDFINGER 5'** hand is placed on the upturned palm of the left **'EXTENDED B'** hand, whose fingers point forward/rightward, and is then retracted as it is brought back smartly toward the body.

impossible: *adj.* not capable of being or happening. *It is impossible to sign ASL and speak the English version at the same time.*

SIGN: Right **'Y'** hand, palm down, is tapped smartly on the upturned left palm.

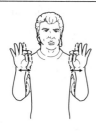

impotent: *adj.* powerless; not having enough strength. *A minority government is often impotent if there is a strong opposition.*

SIGN #1: Vertical **'F'** hands, palms forward, are held slightly apart and simultaneously shaken from the wrists. (Appropriate facial expression is important.)

impotent: *adj.* unable to perform sexual intercourse (referring to males). *He was worried about being impotent, so he consulted a doctor.*

SIGN #2: Left **'ONE'** hand is held palm-down with forefinger pointing forward/rightward. The forefinger of the right **'ONE'** hand is held above the left, then brought down sharply to strike the left forefinger. Next, tip of fore-finger of horizontal left **'ONE'** hand is held against the wrist of the right **'ONE'** hand which is held with palm facing left and fore-finger pointing downward/forward. The right forearm then moves upward so that the fore-finger eventually points upward/forward. (ASL CONCEPT—**can't - erect.**) The signs may be reversed, i.e., **erect - can't. IMPOTENT** is frequently fingerspelled.

impoverished: *adj.* living in poor, deprived conditions. *Canada provides assistance to many impoverished nations.*

SIGN: Thumb and fingertips of right **'CONTRACTED 5'** hand grasp left elbow and close to form a **'FLAT O'** as they slide down-ward off the elbow. Motion is repeated.

impregnate: *v.* to make pregnant. *The woman was impregnated through artificial insemination.*

SIGN: Horizontal **'4'** (or **'5'**) hands are held apart with palms facing each other and fingers pointing forward. The hands are then brought together so that the fingers mesh and the palms face the body.

impress: *v.* to have a strong, favourable effect upon. *I want to impress the boss at my job interview.*

SIGN: Left **'EXTENDED B'** hand is held in a fixed position with palm right and fingers pointing forward/upward. Right **'EXTENDED A'** hand is held with palm down and thumbtip touching left palm. The right wrist then rotates forward, thus turning the hand so that the palm faces the body at a downward angle.

(be) impressed: *v.* to be favourably affected. *I was impressed with his lecture.*

SIGN: Left **'EXTENDED B'** hand is held in a fixed position with palm right and fingers pointing forward/upward. Right **'EXTENDED A'** hand is held with palm down and thumbtip touching left palm. Together, the hands are moved firmly back toward the chest.

imprison: *v.* to confine, incarcerate or put in jail. *The bank robbers will be imprisoned for 20 years.*

SIGN: **'4'** (or **'5'**) hands are held with palms facing the body. Back of right hand, whose fingers point slightly upward to the left, is positioned behind palm of left hand at right angles, and is thrust against it.
SAME SIGN—**imprisonment**, *n.*

improve: *v.* to make or become better. *You can improve your signing skills through practice.*

SIGN: Edge of right **'EXTENDED B'** hand is tapped on wrist of left forearm and brought upward to the elbow.
SAME SIGN—**improvement**, *n.*

impudent: *adj.* rude, impolite; disrespectful. *The defendant's impudent remarks placed him in contempt of court.*

SIGN: Vertical right **'A-INDEX'** hand, palm facing left, quivers as thumb and forefinger are used to grasp skin of right cheek. Facial expression is important.
SAME SIGN—**impudence**, *n.*

impure: *adj.* combined with unclear or tainted material; not pure; unclean. *Drinking impure water can cause dysentery.*

SIGN: Right **'MODIFIED 5'** hand is held under chin with palm down, as the fingers flutter.
SAME SIGN—**impurity**, *n.*

in: *prep.* within; inside of. *The children played in the house.*

SIGN: Horizontal left **'FLAT C'** hand is held with palm facing the body but angled rightward slightly. Right **'FLAT O'** hand is held palm down just above the left hand. Then the bunched fingers of the right hand are brought down and inserted into the opening at the top of the left hand.

in-: *prefix* not. *She is incapable of running that fast.*

SIGN: Right **'EXTENDED A'** hand, palm facing left, thumb under chin, is thrust forward. Sometimes, particularly for emphasis, the prefix **IN-** is fingerspelled.

NOTE—Many words beginning with the prefix **'in-'** do not appear in this dictionary as they simply mean and are signed either **'can't'** or **'not'** + root word.

inaccessible: *adj.* not accessible or approachable. *The roof is inaccessible to the public.*

SIGN: Left **'ONE'** hand is held palm-down with forefinger pointing forward/rightward. The forefinger of the right **'ONE'** hand is held above the left, then brought down sharply to strike the left forefinger. Next, right **'EXTENDED B'** hand, palm down, is curved under downturned palm of left **'EXTENDED B'** hand to simulate 'entrance'. (ASL CONCEPT—**can't - enter.**)

incensed: *adj.* enraged; infuriated; angry. *The workers were incensed when they were laid off.*

SIGN: **'CLAWED 5'** hands, palms toward body, fingertips touching chest, are swept vigorously upward/outward. Facial expression must clearly convey 'anger'.

incentive: *n.* an influence that stimulates or motivates. *Profit-sharing is an important job incentive offered by the company.*

SIGN: **'A-INDEX'** hands are held apart with palms up and one hand slightly ahead of the other. As the hands are jerked backward toward the body, they close to form **'CLOSED A-INDEX'** hands.

incest: *n.* sexual intercourse between people who are closely related. *Incest is socially taboo in many cultures.*

SIGN: Fingerspell **INCEST**.

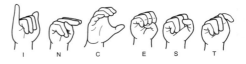

inch: *n.* a unit of measurement equal to 1/12 of a foot. *There are twelve **inches** in a foot.*

SIGN: **'Y'** hands are held parallel with palms forward/downward, and tips of thumbs are tapped together at least twice. (**INCH** may be fingerspelled.)

incident: *n.* an occurrence; event. *The FLQ Crisis was an unfortunate **incident** in Canadian history.*

SIGN: **'ONE'** hands, palms facing each other, are held slightly apart, fingers pointing away from the body, and are turned over so that the palms face down.

incision: *n.* a cut made with the scalpel during a surgical operation. *The **incision** will leave a scar.*

SIGN: Thumbnail of right horizontal **'EXTENDED A'** (or **'Y'**) hand, palm down, is placed on the rightward/upward facing palm of the left **'EXTENDED B'** hand. Then the right thumb is drawn downward across the left palm. (This sign may be made with the right hand only, the thumb being drawn across the actual location of the incision on the body.)

inclination: *n.* a feeling of being disposed towards something. *I have no **inclination** to work this morning.*

SIGN: Tip of middle finger of right **'BENT MIDFINGER 5'** hand, palm toward the body, touches the chest. The wrist then rotates to turn the palm forward/leftward as the hand takes on a **'Y'** shape and wobbles from side to side. (ASL CONCEPT—**feel - like**.)

inclined: *adj.* to have a tendency toward something. *He is **inclined** to procrastinate.*

SIGN: Tip of middle finger of right **'BENT MIDFINGER 5'** hand, palm toward the body, is placed on the right side of the chest and the hand is drawn away abruptly. An essential feature of this sign is the release of a puff of air from the lips as if whispering a 'P'. (Two hands may be used for this sign, with the left hand just below that of the right.)

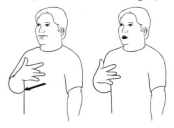

include: *v.* to cause to become part(s) of a whole. *You should **include** facial expression as an important component of ASL.*

SIGN: Right **'CONTRACTED 5'** hand is held palm down above horizontal left **'C'** hand of which the palm faces rightward/backward. The right hand is then closed to form a **'FLAT O'** hand as it plunges, fingers first, into the opening at the top of the left hand.

(all-)inclusive: *adj.* everything considered together; comprehensive. *His **all-inclusive** report covered every issue.*

SIGN: Right **'CONTRACTED 5'** hand, palm facing down, is circled widely in a clockwise direction over the opening of the horizontal left **'C'** hand whose palm faces right. Right hand is then closed to form a **'FLAT O'** hand of which the fingertips are inserted into the opening of the left hand.

income: *n.* salary or money that is received. *He has an annual **income** of $40,000.*

SIGN: Horizontal left **'EXTENDED B'** hand is held in a fixed position with palm up and fingers pointing rightward/forward. Horizontal right **'SPREAD C'** hand, palm facing leftward/backward, is swept across left palm in a counter-clockwise semicircle as it closes to form an **'S'** shape with palm toward the body. Movement is repeated.

income tax: *n.* a personal tax levied on one's annual income. *The new budget will likely increase my **income tax** next year.*

SIGN: Fingerspell **INCOME TAX**.

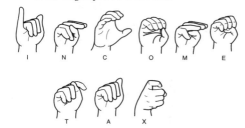

incomparable: *adj.* something without equal; the very best; of the highest standard. *She is known for her **incomparable** knowledge of computer technology.*

SIGN: Right **'BENT EXTENDED B'** hand, fingers on lips and pointing leftward, palm backward, is drawn upward to the right of the face as the fingers bend to form an **'EXTENDED A'** hand with thumb pointing upward. Appropriate facial expression is essential.

incompatible: *adj.* opposite in nature or not in harmony with each other. *Roommates sometimes find they are incompatible.*

SIGN: Horizontal **'CLAWED 5'** hands, palms toward the chest, are held so the knuckles are almost touching and are then alternately moved up and down to convey the impression that they do not quite mesh or fit together. SAME SIGN—**incompatibility**, *n.*

incompetent: *adj.* lacking in ability, skills or knowledge for a specific purpose. *He is incompetent in the kitchen.*

SIGN: Right **'EXTENDED A'** hand, palm facing left, thumb under chin, is thrust forward. Next, left **'EXTENDED B'** hand, palm facing right and fingers pointing upward/forward, is grasped by right **'OPEN A'** hand. Then right hand is pulled forward sharply and closed to form an **'A'** hand. (ASL CONCEPT—**not - skilled**.) SAME SIGN—**incompetence**, *n.*
ALTERNATE SIGN—**inept**

inconsiderate: *adj.* thoughtless; uncaring. *It was inconsiderate of you to forget my birthday.*

SIGN: Vertical right **'A-INDEX'** hand, palm facing left, quivers as thumb and forefinger are used to grasp skin of right cheek. Facial expression is important.

inconsistent: *adj.* irregular; not constant. *Sometimes his work is excellent, but it is inconsistent.*

SIGN: Right hand is initially held palm down with fingers pointing forward. As the hand moves forward, dipping and rising several times as if forming waves, it alternates between an **'EXTENDED B'** and **'BENT EXTENDED B'** shape.

incorporate: *v.* to include as part of a whole. *The author incorporated several ideas into his essay.*

SIGN #1: Right **'CONTRACTED 5'** hand, palm facing down, is circled widely in a clockwise direction over the opening of the horizontal left **'C'** hand whose palm faces right. Right hand is then closed to form a **'FLAT O'** hand of which the fingertips are inserted into the opening of the left hand.

incorporate: *v.* to set up as a legally recognized business or organization. *When you incorporate next year, you will have to buy a licence.*

SIGN #2: Right **'EXTENDED A'** hand is held palm down over left **'STANDARD BASE'** hand, then twisted so that it comes to rest on the back of the left hand with thumb pointing upward and palm facing leftward but slanted toward the body. Next, wrist of vertical right **'B'** hand, palm facing forward/leftward, is brushed back and forth against wrist of left **'STANDARD BASE'** hand. (ASL CONCEPT—**set up - business**.)

incorrigible: *adj.* impossible to control, correct or reform. *Young offenders are often placed in detention centres because they are considered incorrigible.*

SIGN: Left **'ONE'** hand is held palm-down with forefinger pointing forward/rightward. The forefinger of the right **'ONE'** hand is held above the left, then brought down sharply to strike the left forefinger. Next, **'X'** hands are held slightly apart in a horizontal position, palms facing each other. Then they are moved backward and forward alternately.
(ASL CONCEPT—**can't - control**.)

increase: *v.* to make or to become greater in size, amount, extent, frequency, etc. *The club membership has increased 50% in the last 5 years.*

SIGN: Vertical left **'BENT U'** hand is held in a fixed position with palm down and extended fingers pointing rightward/forward. Right **'U'** hand is held to the right of the left hand with palm left and extended fingers pointing forward. The right hand then moves in an upward/leftward arc as the wrist rotates leftward causing the palm to turn downward and the extended fingertips to come to rest on the backs of the extended fingers of the left hand.

incredible: *adj.* unbelievable; amazing. *The feats performed by the stunt man were incredible.*

SIGN #1: Right **'CROOKED 5'** hand, palm toward face, is held upright and tilted slightly leftward as it is waved leftward, then rightward in front of the face. Motion is repeated. Facial expression is important. (Signs vary. See **WOW** #1.)

OR

SIGN #2: **'CLAWED V'** hands are held, right above left, at an angle somewhere between vertical and horizontal, with left palm facing right and right palm facing left. The hands then come together and strike each other with force. Next, edge of forefinger of right **'CROOKED EXTENDED B'** hand is held at forehead and lowered into upturned palm of left **'CROOKED EXTENDED B'** hand so that the two hands clasp. (ASL CONCEPT—**hard - believe**.)

increment: *n.* an increase. *All employees of this company receive an annual increment in salary.*

SIGN: Vertical left **'BENT U'** hand is held in a fixed position with extended fingers pointing rightward/forward. Right **'U'** hand is held to the right of the left hand with palm left and extended fingers pointing forward. The right hand then moves in an upward/leftward arc as the wrist rotates leftward causing the palm to turn downward and the extended fingertips to come to rest on the backs of the extended fingers of the left hand. Movement is repeated.

incurable: *adj.* (most commonly used in reference to disease) does not respond to any known forms of treatment or therapy; cannot be healed. *At one time, tuberculosis was considered incurable.*

SIGN: Left **'ONE'** hand is held palm-down with forefinger pointing forward/rightward. The forefinger of the right **'ONE'** hand is held above the left, then brought down sharply to strike the left forefinger. Next, **CURE** is fingerspelled. (ASL CONCEPT—**can't - cure**.)

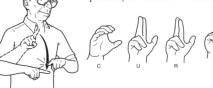

indecision: *n.* the state of being unable to make up one's mind. *Her indecision was hindering the completion of the project.*

SIGN: **'S'** (or **'A'**) hands are held apart with palms down and are alternately raised and lowered.
ALTERNATE SIGN—**uncertain** #2

indeed: *adv.* truly; certainly; in fact. *The doctors were indeed amazed at the child's recovery.*

SIGN: Forefinger of vertical right **'ONE'** hand, palm facing left, is held against the lips and the hand is moved sharply forward.

indefinite: *adj.* unsettled; uncertain. *Their plans are still indefinite.*

SIGN: Right **'EXTENDED B'** hand is held to the right side of the body with fingers pointing downward and palm facing backward. Fingers simultaneously move back and forth. This movement is accompanied by a protruding tongue. Next, the horizontal right **'OPEN F'** hand is held by the right temple with palm facing leftward/downward while the horizontal left **'OPEN F'** hand is held in front of the left shoulder with palm facing rightward/downward. As the forefingers and thumbs close to form **'F'** shapes, the hands are simultaneously and purposefully lowered. (ASL CONCEPT—**not yet - decide**.)
ALTERNATE SIGN—**uncertain** #1

independence: *n.* the state of being free from control; self-governing. *It is natural for a teenager to want independence.*

SIGN: Vertical **'I'** hands are held together, left in front of right, with left palm facing right and right palm facing left. The hands are then drawn apart as the wrists twist to turn the hands palm forward.
SAME SIGN—**independent**, *adj.*

index: *n.* an alphabetically arranged list of persons, places and subjects along with the page numbers on which they can be found in a publication. *I can not find the scientist's name in the index.*

SIGN: Fingerspell **INDEX**. (See also **list** #1.) **Index** has a variety of meanings, particularly when used as an adjective as it is in 'index finger', 'index number', 'indexed pension'. In these instances, it is fingerspelled.

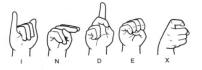

Indian: *n.* a native or aboriginal North American. *His great-grandfather was an Algonquin Indian.*

SIGN: Joined thumb and forefinger of vertical right **'F'** hand, palm facing left, are placed just to the right of the mouth and then moved backward and set down once again in front of the ear. Alternatively, this sign may progress from either the tip of the nose to just in front of the right ear, or from the tip of the nose to the centre of the forehead. (For **Indian** from **India**, see GEOGRAPHIC PLACE NAMES, p. LXXXI.)

indicate: *v.* to show; point out. *Indicate your support by signing the petition.*

SIGN #1: Tip of forefinger of right **'ONE'** hand, palm down, is held against right-facing palm of vertical left **'EXTENDED B'** hand, and the hands are moved forward together.

indicate: *v.* to imply; signify. *His disruptive behaviour indicates that there is an underlying problem.*

SIGN #2: Horizontal left **'EXTENDED B'** hand is held in a fixed position with palm facing right while tip of forefinger of right palm-down **'BENT V'** hand is jabbed into the left palm. The right hand then moves away from the left hand as the right wrist rotates a quarter turn clockwise, and the middle fingertip is jabbed into the left palm.

(feel) indifferent: *v.* to feel no interest or concern; to be apathetic. *She abstained from voting because she felt indifferent about the issue.*

SIGN: Right **'MODIFIED O'** hand, palm toward the face, is held at the tip of the nose and is turned from the wrist as it is thrust forward/rightward and changed to a **'CONTRACTED 5'** handshaped with palm facing downward. SAME SIGN—**indifference**, *n.*

indignant: *adj.* displeased or angry about something unfair or unkind. *Deaf people become indignant when anyone says ASL is not a language.*

SIGN: Right **'5'** hand is held palm down with tip of thumb touching centre of chest. The wrist then rotates rightward as the hand moves away from the chest and turns so that the palm faces leftward at a slight angle toward the body. Facial expression is important and must clearly convey a feeling that something is unjust.

indistinct: *adj.* unclear. *Her licence plate was so muddy that the numbers were indistinct.*

SIGN: Vertical **'5'** hands are held with palms either touching or at least close together. Left hand, palm facing body, is held steady while right hand faces forward and is circled counter-clockwise.

individual: *n.* a person as considered separately from others. *Each individual on a team must make a contribution.*

SIGN #1: Horizontal **'EXTENDED B'** hands are held parallel with palms facing each other and fingers pointing forward. Then they are simultaneously lowered with a decisive movement. (Sign choices for **individual** vary when it refers to a person with a mind of her/his own or when it is used as an adjective to refer to 'things' as opposed to people.)

OR

SIGN #2: Horizontal **'I'** hands are held parallel with palms facing each other. Then they are simultaneously lowered with a decisive movement.

indolent: *adj.* lazy; idle; not inclined to work or put forth any effort. *His **indolent** ways make him a poor employee.*

SIGN: Right **'L'** hand, palm toward the body, is tapped against the left side of the chest, near the shoulder. Next, **'CROOKED 5'** hands are held parallel with fingers pointing downward and palms facing downward but slanted toward the body. The hands simultaneously move in a slow counter-clockwise circle while the face appears lifeless and the tongue protrudes slightly. (ASL CONCEPT—**lazy - no energy**.)

indoors: *adv.* inside a house or other building. *When the weather is rainy the children play **indoors**.*

SIGN: Horizontal left **'FLAT C'** hand is held with palm facing the body but angled rightward slightly. Right **'FLAT O'** hand is held palm down just above the left hand. Then the bunched fingers of the right hand are brought down and inserted into the opening at the top of the left hand. Movement is repeated.

induce: *v.* to persuade. *The hypnotist **induced** his subject to bark like a dog.*

SIGN #1: Horizontal **'X'** hands, are held apart with palms facing each other and the right hand slightly ahead of the left hand. The hands are then simultaneously moved forward and back at least twice with short deliberate movements as though prodding a reluctant individual.

induce: *v.* to hasten labour during the birth process by using drugs to stimulate uterine contractions. *When a birth is overdue, doctors will sometimes **induce** labour.*

SIGN #2: Vertical right **'C'** hand, palm facing forward/leftward, is placed on the back of the left **'STANDARD BASE'** hand and is thrust forward/leftward across the left hand as the wrist bends causing the right hand to hang palm-down over the left hand. (Alternatively, this sign may be formed without the use of the left hand.) ❖

industrious: *adj.* diligent; hard-working. *He has always been an **industrious** student.*

SIGN: Left **'S'** (or **'A'**) hand is held in a fixed position with palm down. Heel of right (**'S'** or **'A'**) hand, palm facing leftward/forward, strikes repeatedly against right side (or 'thumb' side) of left hand in a rightward/forward direction. The motion is laboured and appears as a series of counter-clockwise circles. Cheeks are puffed.

industry: *n.* a branch of commercial enterprise resulting in a specific product or service. *My father was in the construction **industry** all his life.*

SIGN: Wrist of right upright **'B'** hand, palm facing forward/leftward, is brushed back and forth against wrist of left **'STANDARD BASE'** hand.

inebriated: *adj.* intoxicated as a result of excessive alcohol consumption; drunk. *Driving while **inebriated** can have devastating results.*

SIGN: Right **'EXTENDED A'** hand is held in front of the mouth with palm facing left. The forearm is then tipped firmly downward/leftward causing the palm to face downward.
ALTERNATE SIGN—**drunk** #2

inept: *adj.* incompetent; awkward; clumsy. *She is an **inept** housekeeper.*

SIGN: Thumb of right **'SPREAD EXTENDED C'** hand, palm toward the body at a downward angle, is inserted into the opening at the right side of the left **'S'** hand which is held loosely in a fixed position with palm down. The right hand is then twisted upward from the wrist so that the palm faces directly downward.

inevitable: *adj.* certain to happen; unavoidable. *Accidents are **inevitable** if you do not drive carefully.*

SIGN: Right **'EXTENDED B'** hand, palm facing left, is held in a vertical position near the right side of the head. The forearm is then moved forward a short distance so that the fingers eventually point forward/upward. This movement is emphatic and accompanied by an appropriate facial expression. (This sign always appears at the *end* of the sentence. The sample sentence in ASL is: *NOT DRIVE CAREFULLY [head shaking], ACCIDENT **WILL**.*)

inexpensive: *adj.* cheap. *My new T-shirt was inexpensive.*

SIGN: Side of forefinger of right palm-down **'B'** hand is brushed downward against right-facing palm of left **'EXTENDED B'** hand.

inexplicable: *adj.* impossible to explain or clarify. *His strange behaviour is inexplicable.*

SIGN: Left **'ONE'** hand is held palm-down with forefinger pointing forward/rightward. The forefinger of the right **'ONE'** hand is held above the left, then brought down sharply to strike the left forefinger. Next, **'F'** hands are held horizontally with palms facing each other, and are alternately moved backward and forward. Motion is repeated.
(ASL CONCEPT—**can't - explain**.)

infant: *n.* a baby. *The infant cried all night.*

SIGN: Fingers of palm-up right **'BENT EXTENDED B'** hand point leftward as they rest on rightward-pointing fingers of palm-up left **'BENT EXTENDED B'** hand. The arms are simultaneously moved from side to side as if rocking a baby in one's arms.

infatuation: *n.* the state of being filled with foolish or unreasonable affection or passion. *Mature love is different from puppy love or infatuation.*

SIGN: Left **'EXTENDED B'** hand is held in a fixed position with palm up and fingers pointing forward/rightward. Right **'ONE'** hand is held, palm forward/downward, with forefinger just in front of the nose and pointing forward/upward. The right hand then falls forward, coming to rest heavily on the left palm. (Signs vary.)

infection: *n.* a medical condition caused by microorganisms which damage body tissue. *Infection in a wound can have serious consequences.*

SIGN: Fingerspell **INFECTION**. (Alternatively, a fingerspelled **'I'** is wobbled a bit from side to side. This is a wrist action.)

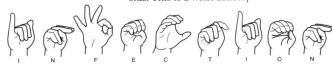

I N F E C T I O N

infectious: *adj.* transmittable; capable of being passed on to another person without direct contact. *I hope it is not an infectious disease.*

SIGN: Thumbs and forefingers of **'F'** hands are interlocked, palms facing each other, as the hands are moved directly forward from the chest.
ALTERNATE SIGN—**spread** #1

infer: *v.* to deduce or assume information as a logical consequence. *From your letter, I infer that you are dissatisfied with our decision.*

SIGN: Vertical right **'SPREAD C'** hand is held in front of right side of forehead with palm facing left, and is moved leftward as it closes to form an **'S'** hand.

inferior: *adj.* lower in ability or value. *He feels inferior to his classmates.*

SIGN #1: Vertical right **'I'** hand, palm toward the body, is held under the left **'STANDARD BASE'** hand and is moved counter-clockwise in small circles. (This sign is only appropriate when referring to *someone's perception of himself as somehow inadequate*. It would not be suitable for describing a substance or material as substandard in quality.)

OR

SIGN #2: **'BENT EXTENDED B'** hands are held apart in front of the upper chest with palms facing each other. The hands are then simultaneously lowered in a slight arc toward the body.

inferior: *adj.* not of good quality. *He sells inferior merchandise.*

SIGN #3: Side of forefinger of right palm-down **'B'** hand is brushed downward against right-facing palm of left **'EXTENDED B'** hand.

infinite: *adj.* a great deal of; a vast amount of. *Learning to ski requires infinite patience.*

SIGN #1: Horizontal **'CROOKED 5'** hands are held with palms facing and fingertips touching. The hands are then simultaneously drawn apart.

infinite: *adj.* endless or without limits in time, space, extent or magnitude. *The amount of space in the universe is infinite.*

SIGN #2: **'EXTENDED A'** hands are held side by side with palms down and right thumbtip pressing against left thumbnail as the hands are purposefully and repeatedly moved forward and back a short distance. Then, right **'O'** hand is held upright with palm facing left, and is thrust downward/forward so that the palm faces upward/leftward. (Alternatively, two hands may be used for this part of the sign.) Next, right **'EXTENDED B'** hand, palm facing left, is brought down sharply from a semi-vertical position to strike the upward/backward facing palm of the rigidly held right **'EXTENDED B'** hand, whose fingers point forward/rightward.
(ASL CONCEPT—**continue - no - stop**.)

infinite: *adj.* neverending; without limits. *The process of counting numbers is infinite.*

SIGN #3: **'EXTENDED A'** hands are held side by side with palms down and right thumbtip pressing against left thumbnail as the hands are purposefully and repeatedly moved forward and back a short distance. Then right **'B'** (or **'EXTENDED B'**) hand, palm facing left, is held upright near the face and is vigorously curved downward. Next, right **'EXTENDED B'** hand, palm facing left, is brought down sharply from a semi-vertical position to strike the upward/backward facing palm of the rigidly held right **'EXTENDED B'** hand, whose fingers point forward/rightward.
(ASL CONCEPT—**continue - never - stop**.)

infirmary: *n.* a place such as a hospital where sick or injured people are treated. *When I sprained my ankle, I went to the infirmary.*

SIGN: Tips of extended fingers of right **'BENT U'** hand, palm down, tap at least twice on the upturned wrist of the horizontal left **'CROOKED EXTENDED B'** hand.
ALTERNATE SIGN—**hospital**

inflammable: *adj.* apt to catch fire easily. *Certain fabrics are highly inflammable and should not be used in children's clothing.*

SIGN: Left **'BENT EXTENDED B'** hand is held in a fixed position with palm up. Palm of horizontal right **'EXTENDED B'** (or **'BENT EXTENDED B'**) hand faces left but is slanted slightly upward and toward the body as the fingers are brushed upward against the backs of the fingers of the left hand at least twice. Then both vertical **'5'** hands with palms facing body, are simultaneously moved upward with fingers fluttering.
(ASL CONCEPT—**easy - fire**.)

inflate: *v.* to cause expansion by filling with gas or air. *We need someone to inflate balloons for the party.*

SIGN: **'S'** hands are held at the mouth, one behind the other. They are then moved outward and opened to form **'SPREAD C'** hands with right palm facing left and left palm facing right. Cheeks are puffed out. (Signs vary according to context.)

inflation: *n.* a progressive increase in the general level of prices due to a combination of economic factors. *Inflation has greatly affected the value of the Canadian dollar.*

SIGN: Fingerspell **INFLATION**.

influence: *n.* an effect on something or someone. *He is a good influence on his little brother.*

SIGN: Right **'FLAT O'** hand is held, palm down, so that the fingertips are resting on the back of the left **'STANDARD BASE'** hand. Then the right hand moves forward as the fingers spread to form a **'5'** hand.

inform: *v.* to tell; give information to. *The police must inform suspects of their legal rights.*

SIGN: Left **'MODIFIED O'** hand is held at about shoulder level with palm facing upward but angled slightly toward the body while right **'MODIFIED O'** hand is held upright just in front of the forehead with palm toward the face. The forearms then move simultaneously forward/downward as the hands open to assume **'MODIFIED 5'** shapes with palms facing upward. ❖
SAME SIGN—**information**, *n.*

ingenious: *adj.* having or showing great talent and/or cleverness. *They came up with an ingenious plan.*

SIGN: Tip of middle finger of right **'BENT MIDFINGER 5'** hand, palm toward face, touches right side of forehead, then shimmies outward on an upward angle, giving the impression of a shimmering light.

ingredient: *n.* something added as part of a mixture, especially in cooking. *Be sure you have all the ingredients you will need for that recipe.*

SIGN: Sign choice depends entirely on context.

inhabit: *v.* to live in; reside in; dwell in. *Very few wild animals inhabit this region.*

SIGN: Horizontal **'EXTENDED A'** hands are placed at either side, somewhere above the waist, with palms toward the body. They are then raised to a higher position on the chest.
ALTERNATE SIGN—**alive** #2

inhale: *v.* to breathe in. *He tried not to inhale when he smoked the cigarette.*

SIGN: Right **'CONTRACTED 5'** hand, palm down, is held a short distance from the face and is drawn toward the mouth as it closes to form an **'O'** hand. Meanwhile, the mouth appears to be sucking in air. (The same basic sign is used to mean 'inhale through the nose' but the hand is held palm down and drawn upward toward the nose.)

inherit: *v.* to receive money, property, etc., as an heir. *My children will inherit my money when I die.*

SIGN: Horizontal **'SPREAD C'** hands, right on top of left, are closed to form **'S'** hands as they are brought toward the chest.

inhumane: *adj.* having no sympathy; cruel; brutal. *The soldier was court-martialled for his inhumane actions toward civilians in Somalia.*

SIGN: Right **'CROOKED 5'** hand is held with palm facing left and tip of forefinger touching or near end of nose while left **'CROOKED 5'** hand, palm facing right, is held just in front of/below right hand. The hands eventually assume **'A'** shapes as they brush past one another, the right hand moving downward/forward and the left hand moving upward/backward. Appropriate facial expression is important.

initiate: *v.* to begin; originate. *He will initiate divorce proceedings very soon.*

SIGN: Left **'5'** hand is held with palm facing right while forefinger of right **'ONE'** hand is inserted between first two fingers of left hand and twisted 180 degrees to the right.

initiative: *n.* a tendency to make the first move or to be active in creating and following through on new ideas. *She has the initiative we look for in our employees.*

SIGN: **'A'** hands, thumbs up, palms facing each other, are brought alternately up against the chest and circled outward.

injection: *n.* a fluid that is introduced into the body with a hypodermic syringe. *The doctor gave me an injection of cortisone.*

SIGN: Tip of forefinger of right **'BENT L'** hand is jabbed into upper left arm and thumb is repeatedly bent and extended as though depressing a plunger into a syringe.

injure: *v.* to hurt or wound. *He will injure himself if he falls.*

SIGN: Horizontal **'BENT ONE'** hands are held slightly apart, then moved toward one another as the right hand twists slightly forward and the left hand twists slightly backward. This sign is generally made near the afflicted area of the body.
SAME SIGN—**injury**, *n.*
ALTERNATE SIGN—**hurt**

ink: *n.* a colored writing fluid. *Editors often make corrections in red ink.*

SIGN: Fingerspell **INK**.

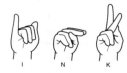

in-law: *adj.* a relative by marriage. *My mother-in-law works for the police department.*

SIGN: With left arm bent at the elbow, the right **'L'** hand is placed first at the wrist, then at the elbow of the left forearm.
ALTERNATE SIGN—**attorney** #1

inline skating: See **roller blading**.

inmate: *n.* someone confined to an institution, especially a prison. *He has spent over half of his life as an inmate at Kingston Penitentiary.*

SIGN: **'4'** (or **'5'**) hands are held with palms facing the body. Back of right hand, whose fingers point slightly upward to the left, is positioned behind palm of left hand at right angles, and is thrust against it twice.

innocent: *adj.* blameless or not guilty of a crime. *The accused claimed he was innocent of any wrongdoing.*

SIGN: Tips of extended fingers of **'U'** hands, palms toward the body, are placed at either side of the mouth and the hands are simultaneously thrust forward/downward so that palms face upward.
SAME SIGN—**innocence**, *n.*

inoculation: *n.* a shot given to make the body immune to a certain disease. *The baby will receive an inoculation against diphtheria.*

SIGN: Tip of forefinger of right **'BENT L'** hand is jabbed into upper left arm and thumb is repeatedly bent and extended as though depressing a plunger into a syringe.

input: *n.* data that is entered into a computer. *When the input is complete, we can run a statistical analysis on the data.*

SIGN #1: Horizontal left **'FLAT C'** hand is held with palm facing the body but angled rightward slightly. Right **'FLAT O'** hand is held palm down just above the left hand. Then the bunched fingers of the right hand are brought down and inserted into the opening at the top of the left hand.

input: *n.* ideas; information; suggestions; opinions put forward. *The executive wanted input from the members before making a decision.*

SIGN #2: Tip of little finger of right **'I'** hand, palm toward the face, is placed on the right side of the forehead and is drawn forward/upward a brief distance. Next, left **'MODIFIED O'** hand is held at about shoulder level with palm facing upward but angled slightly toward the body while right **'MODIFIED O'** hand is held upright just in front of the forehead with palm toward the face. The forearms then move simultaneously forward/downward as the hands open to assume **'MODIFIED 5'** shapes with palms facing upward. Next, **'EXTENDED B'** hands, palms up, are held slightly apart with the right just ahead of the left, and are simultaneously thrust forward in an arc. (ASL CONCEPT —**idea - information - suggest**.) Any of these three words may be used alone or in any combination to mean **input**.) Alternatively, **INPUT** is frequently fingerspelled.

inquire: *v.* to ask for information. *I want to inquire about your educational programs.*

SIGN: Vertical right **'ONE'** hand, palm facing forward is moved firmly forward and slightly downward as the forefinger retracts to form an **'X'** hand. ❖
ALTERNATE SIGN—**ask**

insane: *adj.* mentally deranged; not sane. *The murderer was declared insane.*

SIGN #1: Vertical right **'SPREAD EXTENDED C'** hand, palm toward the head, is positioned with fingertips touching right side of forehead. The fingers buckle a few times while the fingertips maintain contact with the forehead.

OR

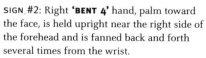

SIGN #2: Right **'BENT 4'** hand, palm toward the face, is held upright near the right side of the forehead and is fanned back and forth several times from the wrist.

OR

SIGN #3: Left **'EXTENDED B'** hand is held in a fixed position with palm up and fingers pointing rightward/forward. Horizontal right **'EXTENDED B'** hand, palm facing left, slides forward along the left hand as the fingers bend to form a **'BENT EXTENDED B'** shape.
SAME SIGN—**insanity**, *n.*

inscribe: *v.* to write or engrave words on something (such as wood, stone, metal, paper, etc.). *The sculptor will* **inscribe** *the details on the plaque at the foot of the statue.*

SIGN: Thumb of right **'EXTENDED A'** hand, palm down, is used to jab twice in an upward/backward direction at the fixed palm of the left **'EXTENDED B'** hand, which is held with fingers pointing forward/rightward, and palm facing rightward, but slanted slightly toward the body.
SAME SIGN—**inscription**, *n.*

insect: *n.* a very small animal usually having three pairs of legs and two pairs of wings; a bug. *Tiger beetles are fascinating* **insects**.

SIGN #1: **'SPREAD C'** hands are held with palms down and wrists crossed, as the fingers wiggle. (**INSECT** may be fingerspelled.)\

OR

SIGN #2: Thumb of right **'3'** hand is placed on nose, palm facing left, and the two extended fingers are drawn in and out toward the nose.

insecure: *adj.* apprehensive; not confident. *Too much criticism can make a child feel* **insecure**.

SIGN: Right **'O'** hand is held upright with palm facing left, and is thrust downward/forward so that the palm faces upward/leftward. Alternatively, two hands may be used. Next, **'SPREAD EXTENDED C'** hands are held with palms toward the body at an upward angle, the left hand close to the chest and the right hand just above/ahead of the left. The hands are then thrust forward as they are snapped shut to form **'S'** hands. (ASL CONCEPT—**no - confidence**.)
ALTERNATE SIGN—**inferior** #1

insert: *v.* to place something in or between. *Please* **insert** *this page in the appropriate section of the binder.*

SIGN: Left **'FLAT C'** hand is held palm up with fingers pointing rightward/forward. Right **'EXTENDED B'** hand is held just to the right of the left hand with palm up and fingers pointing forward at a slight leftward angle. The hands then move toward each other as the right hand is firmly inserted between the thumb and palm of the left hand. (Sign choice varies according to the kind, size, shape and location of the object being inserted as well as the kind, size, shape and location of the object into which it is being placed.)

inside: *n.* the inner or interior part of something. *The* **inside** *of the drawer is lined with paper.*

SIGN: Horizontal left **'FLAT C'** hand is held with palm facing the body but angled rightward slightly. Right **'FLAT O'** hand is held palm down just above the left hand. Then the bunched fingers of the right hand are brought down and inserted into the opening at the top of the left hand. Movement is repeated.

insignificant: *adj.* trivial; meaningless; of little or no importance. *Please do not waste time discussing* **insignificant** *details.*

SIGN: Horizontal **'F'** hands, left palm facing right and right palm facing left, are held so the joined thumb and forefinger of the right hand are near the nose, and the left hand is slightly lower. Then the right hand is brought down firmly so the joined thumbs and forefingers strike each other and the right hand moves downward/rightward away from the left.
SAME SIGN—**insignificance**, *n.*

insist: *v.* to demand strongly. *The employees* **insisted** *that they be given a morning coffee break.*

SIGN: Tip of forefinger of right **'X'** hand is placed in right-facing palm of left **'EXTENDED B'** hand. Together, the hands are moved firmly toward the chest, giving the impression that the left hand is being tugged by the right forefinger.

insolent: *adj.* impudent; disrespectful; insulting. *The hockey player was* **insolent** *to the referee.*

SIGN: Vertical right **'A-INDEX'** hand, palm facing left, quivers as thumb and forefinger are used to grasp skin of right cheek.
SAME SIGN—**insolence**, *n.*

insomnia: *n.* a chronic inability to fall asleep or to maintain uninterrupted sleep. *My friend suffers from insomnia so she is always tired.*

SIGN: Left **'ONE'** hand is held palm-down with forefinger pointing forward/rightward. The forefinger of the right **'ONE'** hand is held above the left, then brought down sharply to strike the left forefinger. Next, right **'CONTRACTED 5'** hand is held with palm toward the face. The hand is then drawn downward as the fingers close to form a **'FLAT O'** hand just in front of the chin or neck. Finally, left **'EXTENDED B'** hand is held in a fixed position with palm up and fingers pointing rightward/forward. Right **'CROOKED V'** hand is placed palm-downward on the left palm. The right wrist then twists rightward and leftward a few times so that the palm alternates between facing upward and facing downward. (ASL CONCEPT—**can't - sleep - restless** or **sleep - can't - restless**.) ALTERNATE SIGN—**alert**

inspect: *v.* to examine or look over carefully for faults or errors. *Security staff at the airport will inspect your luggage.*

SIGN #1: Left **'EXTENDED B'** hand is held in a fixed position with palm turned upward but slanted slightly rightward and toward the body while fingers point rightward/forward. Right **'ONE'** hand is held palm down as tip of forefinger brushes forward several times against palm of left hand.

SIGN #2 [ATLANTIC]: Right **'Y'** hand is held palm down with tip of thumb just in front of the nose. The hand then wobbles as it moves forward away from the face along the upturned palm of the left **'EXTENDED B'** hand which is held with fingers pointing forward. (Alternatively, this sign may be made without the left hand.) SAME SIGN—**inspection**, *n.*

inspired: *adj.* uplifted; beneficially affected; moved. *We were greatly inspired by his lecture.*

SIGN: Right **'5'** hand is held with palm on chest and fingertips pointing leftward/upward. The hand is then pushed purposefully upward. Alternatively, this sign may be made with two hands, one on either side of chest, especially for emphasis. SAME SIGNS—**inspiration**, *n.*, and **inspirational**, *adj.*

install: *v.* to put equipment in place and adjust it for use. *The mechanic will install the new motor in my car tomorrow.*

SIGN: Vertical **'FLAT O'** hands are held parallel with palms forward and are simultaneously moved forward in arc formation. SAME SIGN—**installation**, *n.*

(for) instance: *conj.* for example. *There are many ways to invest money; for instance, you could buy savings bonds.*

SIGN: Tip of little finger of right **'I'** hand, palm facing backward, is tapped lightly against the right cheek. (This sign may only be used to introduce a thought and is never used at the end of a sentence.)

instant: *adj.* designed to allow for very quick and easy preparation (of foods especially). *I will make us some instant coffee.*

SIGN #1: Fingerspell **INSTANT**. (There is frequently no 'sign for word' translation for **instant**. Instead, the concept is conveyed through faster than usual signing.)

instant: *n.* a specific point in time; moment. *Let me know the instant he arrives.*

SIGN #2: There is no 'sign for word' translation for **instant** in this context. To translate the sample sentence into ASL, the clauses would have to be reversed: *HE ARRIVE (eyebrows raised; next part signed quickly) INFORM-ME.*

(this) instant: *adv.* at this very moment; right now. *I do not know where Susanna is this instant.*

SIGN: **'Y'** hands, palms up, are held slightly apart and are simultaneously lowered. ALTERNATE SIGN—**now** #2

instantly: *adv.* immediately; quickly; at once. *He died instantly in the collision.*

SIGN: Right vertical **'COVERED T'** hand, palm facing left, is jerked forward as thumb flicks upward, resulting in horizontal **'CLAWED L'** hand. (There is frequently no 'sign for word' translation for **instantly**. Instead, the concept is conveyed through faster than usual signing.)

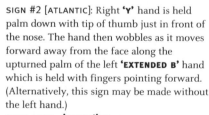

instead [*or* **instead of**]: *adv./prep.* as a replacement or substitute; in the place of. *Instead of flowers, the family prefers we make a charitable donation.*

SIGN: Horizontal '**F**' hands, left palm facing right and right palm facing, are held so that the left is further from the chest than the right. Then their positions are simultaneously switched as the left hand moves back toward the body in arc over the right hand while the right hand moves away from the body in an arc under the left hand.

instinct: *n.* intuition; innate sensitivity. *My instinct tells me that I made an unwise decision.*

SIGN: Tip of middle finger of horizontal right '**BENT MIDFINGER 5**' hand, palm toward the body, is placed on the chest and the hand is circled clockwise so that the fingertip brushes upward against the chest with each rotation.

institute: *v.* to initiate; start; establish; set up. *We will institute the changes you recommended next month.*

SIGN #1: Left '**5**' hand is held with palm facing right while forefinger of right '**ONE**' hand is inserted between first two fingers of left hand and twisted 180 degrees to the right.
ALTERNATE SIGN—**establish**

institute: *n.* an organization founded for specific work in education, art, science, etc. *WCCSD is an institute for Deaf studies at the University of Alberta.*

SIGN #2: '**SPREAD C**' hands are held upright and slightly apart with palms facing each other. The wrists then rotate forward, bringing the hands to a horizontal position. This concept frequently appears as part of an acronym such as CNIB (Canadian National *Institute* for the Blind) which is simply fingerspelled **CNIB**.
ALTERNATE SIGN—**organization** #1

institution: *n.* a building such as a college or hospital; a building which houses a specific organization. *The institution is situated on beautifully landscaped grounds.*

SIGN: Fingers of '**BENT EXTENDED B**' (or '**BENT EXTENDED U**' or '**U**') hands, palms facing each other, are alternately slid up from under to be placed on top of one another. (**Institution** has multiple meanings, and context must be considered. For a 'hospital', a sign for **hospital** would be used. In certain instances, **custom** or **tradition** might be more appropriate sign choices.)

instruct: *v.* to teach someone how to do something. *If you cannot swim, perhaps I can instruct you.*

SIGN: Vertical '**MODIFIED O**' hands are held parallel with palms facing each other and are moved slightly but firmly forward. ❖ SAME SIGN—**instruction**, *n.*, in this context. For **instructor**, *n.*, the Agent Ending (see p. LIV) may follow.

instructions: *n.* directions; orders; an explanation of how to do something. *Read the instructions carefully.*

SIGN: '**F**' hands are held horizontally with palms facing each other, and are alternately moved backward and forward a few times.

instrument: *n.* a tool used for a specific purpose. *The wound indicated the victim had been beaten with a blunt instrument.*

SIGN: Right '**EXTENDED B**' hand, palm upward and fingers pointing forward, is moved rightward in an arc formation. (Signs vary according to context. When referring to a musical instrument, the signer generally imitates the playing of a particular instrument.)

instrumental: *adj.* influential; helpful. *He was instrumental in getting the law changed.*

SIGN: Vertical '**F**' hands are held apart with palms facing forward. The hands are then brought purposefully together.
ALTERNATE SIGN—**important** #2

insubordinate: *adj.* disobedient; not submissive to authority. *The soldier was insubordinate to his superior officer.*

SIGN: Vertical right '**S**' hand, palm facing backward, is held at or above shoulder level and is forcefully twisted a half turn so that palm faces forward.
SAME SIGN—**insubordination**, *n.*

insulation: *n.* material used to prevent the transmission of heat, electricity or sound. *The roof leaks because the builder used too little insulation.*

SIGN: Fingerspell **INSULATION**.

insult: *v.* to behave or speak rudely and contemptuously toward someone. *I am sorry if I insulted you.*

SIGN: Right **'ONE'** hand, palm facing left, is held in a horizontal position in front of the chest and is then curved upward from the wrist as it moves forward with a stabbing motion. Alternatively, this sign may be made with two hands alternately stabbing, either with or without the curving motion. ❖

insurance: *n.* financial protection against death, loss or damage. *The hurricane victim had no insurance on his home.*

SIGN: Vertical right **'I'** hand, palm facing forward, moves slightly from side to side several times.

intact: *adj.* still complete or whole and functional; unaffected; unimpaired. *She had a partial hysterectomy but her ovaries remained intact.*

SIGN: Horizontal **'Y'** hands, palms toward the body, are held apart and are simultaneously brought toward the abdomen to be placed firmly against the general area of the ovaries. (Sign choice varies depending on the context. The sign often represents an English phrase such as **remained intact** rather than the single word **intact**.)

integer: See **number**.

integral: *adj.* necessary to make something complete; essential. *A practicum is an integral part of the teacher training program.*

SIGN: Vertical **'F'** hands are held apart with palms facing forward. The hands are then brought purposefully together.
ALTERNATE SIGN—**important** #2

integrate: *v.* to bring all the parts together to make a whole. *We will integrate our ideas into one proposal.*

SIGN #1: With palms facing the body, **'CLAWED 5'** hands are held together so that little fingers interlock. As the hands are simultaneously lowered from the wrists, the corresponding fingers of each hand interlock to simulate the meshing of gears.
SAME SIGN—**integration**, *n.*, in this context.

integrate: *v.* to mainstream or desegregate. *Mainstreaming is an attempt to integrate Deaf and hearing students in public schools.*

SIGN #2: **'5'** hands are held slightly apart with palms downward but slanted toward the body, and fingers of each hand pointing toward those of the other hand. The wrists then turn, causing the hands to dovetail so that the fingers point directly forward, the palms are down, and the right hand is on top of the left.
SAME SIGN—**integration**, *n.*, in this context.

integrity: *n.* the quality of having high moral principles; honesty. *Some politicians are not noted for their integrity.*

SIGN: Left **'EXTENDED B'** hand is held in a fixed position with palm facing right but slanted upward slightly and fingers pointing forward as right **'U'** hand is held with palm facing left and tip of middle finger placed at heel of left hand. The right hand is then moved straight forward along the left palm until the tip of the right middle finger reaches the tip of the left middle finger.
ALTERNATE SIGN—**honest** #2

intelligent: *adj.* clever; wise. *The child's progress in school shows that she is very intelligent.*

SIGN: Tip of middle finger of right **'BENT MIDFINGER 5'** hand touches forehead and the hand is flung outward so that the palm faces away from face.
SAME SIGN—**intelligence**, *n.*

intelligible: *adj.* easily understood; comprehensible. *With a poor phone connection, the conversation is not always intelligible.*

SIGN: Vertical **'O'** (or **'FLAT O'**) hands are placed side by side, palms facing forward. Then they are moved apart and slightly upward as the fingers spread to form **'5'** hands.

intend: *v.* to propose; plan; have in mind. *I did not* **intend** *to drop the bowl.*

SIGN: Tip of forefinger of vertical right **'ONE'** hand, palm toward the face, is used to touch right side of forehead. Then the handshape is changed to a **'BENT V'** and the extended fingertips are placed against the right-facing palm of the horizontal left **'EXTENDED B'** hand. Next, the fingertips of the right hand are separated from the left hand as the right wrist makes a quarter turn clockwise, the right hand turns slightly upward so that the fingers now point forward/upward and the fingertips of the right hand re-establish contact with the left palm.

SAME SIGNS — **intention**, *n.,* and **intentional**, *adj.*

intense: *adj.* an extreme degree, amount or strength. *Exposure to* **intense** *sunlight can lead to the development of skin cancer.*

SIGN #1: **'O'** (or **'FLAT O'**) hands are placed side by side, palms facing forward. Then they are moved apart and upward as the fingers spread to form **'5'** hands, palms still facing away from the body. (Sign choice varies according to the noun it modifies.)

intense: *adj.* characterized by strong emotions or passionate feelings. *Ryan Smyth is an* **intense** *hockey player.*

SIGN #1: Vertical right **'BENT ONE'** hand is held with tip of forefinger touching chin and palm facing leftward but slanted toward the body. The wrist then rotates, turning the hand so that the palm fully faces the body.

ALTERNATE SIGN — **serious**

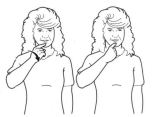

intensity: *n.* an extreme degree of magnitude or power. *The* **intensity** *of the light can be increased with a bulb of higher wattage.*

SIGN: Fingertips of right **'SPREAD C'** hand are brought forcefully against left bicep.

ALTERNATE SIGN — **strong**

intensive: *adj.* characterized by greater than average length or depth. *The court recommended* **intensive** *psychological counseling for the young offender.*

SIGN: Edge of downward-pointing forefinger of right **'BENT ONE'** hand is placed against right-facing palm of the left **'EXTENDED B'** hand. Then the right hand is pushed firmly downward.

inter: See **bury.**

interact: *v.* to act on or in close relation with each other. *If you want to learn ASL, you must* **interact** *with proficient users of the language.*

SIGN: Right **'EXTENDED A'** hand is held thumb-down above left **'EXTENDED A'** hand which is held thumb-up. The hands then revolve around each other in a counter-clockwise direction.

intercept: *v.* to prevent something from proceeding or arriving. *The halfback* **intercepted** *the pass.*

SIGN: Right horizontal **'V'** hand, palm left, is abruptly drawn back/upward as it changes to a **'CLAWED V'** hand in a more or less vertical position. (While this sign is appropriate in a *football* context to mean the interception of a pass by a player on the opposing team, it may not be appropriate in other contexts. Sign choice varies according to context.)

intercourse: *n.* the sexual act between two individuals. *Some cultures do not condone premarital* **intercourse.**

SIGN: Left **'V'** hand is held with palm up and extended fingers pointing forward at a slight rightward angle while right **'V'** hand is held just above the left hand with palm facing leftward at a downward/forward angle and extended fingers pointing leftward/upward at a slightly forward angle. The hands are brought together a few times so that the heels of the hands repeatedly collide.

interest: *n.* a charge for borrowing money or using credit. *The interest on my mortgage is quite reasonable.*

SIGN: Horizontal right **'I'** hand, with palm facing left but angled toward the body, is placed on the back of the left **'STANDARD BASE'** hand and is circled counter-clockwise.

interesting: *adj.* arousing curiosity or holding one's attention. *This is an interesting book.*

SIGN #1: Horizontal **'OPEN 8'** hands, palms toward the body, are placed on the chest with the right slightly above the left, and are drawn forward as the thumbs and middle fingers join to form **'8'** hands. Alternatively, this sign may be made with one hand only. Facial expression is important. (Signs #1, #2 & #3 may also be used for **interested**, *adj.*)

OR

SIGN #2: Horizontal **'EXTENDED B'** hands are held with palms together and fingers pointing forward. The hands are alternately rubbed back and forth against each other. Facial expression is important.

OR

SIGN #3: **'CLAWED L'** hands, palms facing backward, are held so that the right is just in front of the nose and mouth and the left is just below/ahead of the right hand. They are then simultaneously drawn forward as they close to form **'A'** hands. Alternatively, this sign may be made with the right hand only. Facial expression is important.

interface: *v.* to be interactive with. *Word processing software can often interface with electronic mail.*

SIGN: Horizontal **'CLAWED 5'** hands are held apart with palms facing the chest. The hands then move toward each other until the fingers of one hand mesh with those of the other.

interfere: *v.* to hinder; get in the way or intrude in someone else's business. *The police interfered with the criminal's plans.*

SIGN: Vertical left **'5'** hand is held in a fixed position with palm facing the body while right **'EXTENDED B'** hand, palm facing left, is brought down firmly and thrust between forefinger and middle finger of left hand. ❖ SAME SIGN—**interference**, *n.*, but the movement is repeated.

interior: *n.* the inside surface or area of something. *The interior of the house is tastefully decorated.*

SIGN: Horizontal left **'FLAT C'** hand is held with palm facing the body but angled rightward slightly. Right **'FLAT O'** hand is held palm down just above the left hand. Then the bunched fingers of the right hand are brought down and inserted into the opening at the top of the left hand. Movement is repeated.

intermediate: *adj.* in between two points, occurrences, places, levels, stages, etc. *She is in an intermediate class in swimming.*

SIGN: Right **'EXTENDED B'** hand, with palm facing left and fingers pointing forward, slides from side to side a few times along forefinger of horizontally held left **'EXTENDED B'** hand, whose palm is facing the body.

intermission: *n.* a pause or interval between parts of a production, performance, conference, etc. *There will be a 15-minute intermission after the third act.*

SIGN: Left horizontal **'5'** hand is held with palm facing body while fingers of right palm-down **'EXTENDED B'** hand are inserted between forefinger and middle finger of left hand.

internal: *adj.* inner; inside; interior. *He does not understand the internal workings of machines.*

SIGN: Horizontal left **'FLAT C'** hand is held with palm facing the body but angled rightward slightly. Right **'FLAT O'** hand is held palm down just above the left hand. Then the bunched fingers of the right hand are brought down and inserted into the opening at the top of the left hand. Movement is repeated.

international: *adj.* pertaining to two or more nations. *An international conference will be held in Paris.*

SIGN: Right **'I'** hand is held just above left **'I'** hand, right palm facing downward/leftward and left palm facing downward/rightward. Then the hands each complete a 360 degree forward revolution around one another, ending up with the right hand resting on the left.

Internet: *n.* a worldwide exchange of information accessible through a computer. *There is so much information available through the Internet.*

SIGN: **'BENT MIDFINGER 5'** hands are held upright with palms facing each other. Tips of midfingers touch and maintain contact as the hands alternately pivot back and forth from the wrist.

interpret: *v.* to translate, either orally or in sign. *She will interpret the lecture for me.*

SIGN: **'F'** hands, palms facing each other at a forward angle, are placed together with tips of thumbs and forefingers of each hand touching. The left hand remains steady while the right hand wobbles as the wrist twists back and forth slightly a few times.
SAME SIGN—**interpreter**, *n.*, and may be followed by the Agent Ending (see p. LIV).

interrogate: *v.* to question closely. *The policeman interrogated the suspect.*

SIGN: Vertical **'ONE'** hands, palms facing forward, are held apart, one at a slightly higher level than the other. The hands then alternately move forward and slightly downward in repeated circular motions. As the hands move forward, they take on the **'x'** handshape, and as they circle back toward the chest, they resume the **'ONE'** shape. ❖
SAME SIGN—**interrogation**, *n.*

interrupt: *v.* to hinder by intruding. *I am sorry to interrupt you while you are working.*

SIGN: Left **'5'** hand is held in a fixed position with palm facing the body while right horizontal **'EXTENDED B'** hand is inserted forcefully between forefinger and middle finger of left hand. ❖
SAME SIGN—**interruption**, *n.*, but the movement is repeated.

intersect: *v.* to pass through or across. *101 Avenue and 50 Street intersect near a mall.*

SIGN: Horizontal **'ONE'** hands are held apart with palms facing the body but slanted toward each other slightly and the left forefinger pointing rightward/forward while the right forefinger points leftward/forward. The hands then move toward each other, causing the right forefinger to cross over the left forefinger in a converging motion.

intersection: *n.* a road or street junction. *The accident occurred at a busy intersection.*

SIGN: Horizontal **'ONE'** hands, palms facing mainly toward the chest, are positioned so the left is stationary and the forefinger of the right is used to tap down across the forefinger of the left in such a way as to form an **'x'** with each tap.

intervene: *v.* to interfere in the affairs of others. *If the fighting continues, the United Nations may have to intervene.*

SIGN: Vertical left **'5'** hand is held in a fixed position with palm facing the body while right **'EXTENDED B'** hand, palm facing left, is brought down firmly and thrust between forefinger and middle finger of left hand. Next, left **'A'** (or **'EXTENDED A'**) hand, palm facing the body but turned slightly rightward, rests on the upturned palm of the right **'EXTENDED B'** hand. Both hands are lifted slightly upward and extended directly forward. (ASL CONCEPT—**interfere - help**.)
SAME SIGN—**intervention**, *n.*

interview: *v.* to conduct a conversation through asking questions. *The boss must interview you before he can hire you.*

SIGN: Vertical **'I'** hands, left palm facing right and right palm facing left, are held apart so that tips of little fingers are about level with the chin or mouth. The hands are then alternately moved straight back and forth.

into: *prep.* toward the inside. *The boys ran into the clubhouse.*

SIGN: Right **'EXTENDED B'** hand, palm down, is curved under left **'EXTENDED B'** palm to simulate 'entrance'. (In ASL the meaning of **into** is frequently incorporated in an all-inclusive sign which conveys the *subject, verb* and *object of the preposition* rather than expressed through a separate sign such as that shown here. The sentence "The car ran into a wall" is expressed in ASL as one sign, the left hand representing the wall and the right hand representing the car as it makes contact with the wall.)

intoxicated: *v.* drunk; inebriated. *He could not walk in a straight line because he was intoxicated.*

SIGN: Right **'EXTENDED A'** hand is held in front of the mouth with palm facing left. The forearm is then tipped firmly downward/leftward causing the palm to face downward.
ALTERNATE SIGN—**drunk** #2

intrepid: See **brave**.

intricate: *adj.* complex; difficult to understand. *Most people cannot comprehend the intricate details of the legislation.*

SIGN: **'X'** hands are held apart and almost upright with left palm facing rightward/downward and right palm facing leftward/downward. The crooked forefingers wiggle up and down as the hands move toward one another in front of the face, coming to rest when they make contact in front of the nose with right hand directly behind left so that the hands appear to be crossed.
SAME SIGN—**intricacy**, *n.*
ALTERNATE SIGN—**complex** #1

intrigued: *adj.* fascinated; full of curiosity and interest. *The children were intrigued with the magician's tricks.*

SIGN: Vertical **'SPREAD C'** hands are positioned so that the right hand is just in front of the nose and mouth with palm facing left while the left hand is just ahead of/below the right hand with palm facing right. The hands are then moved forward/downward as they close to form **'S'** hands.

introduce: *v.* to present someone to another person. *I will introduce you to my boss.*

SIGN: **'BENT EXTENDED B'** hands are held apart with palms facing each other and fingers of each hand pointing toward those of the other hand. The hands are then drawn closer together.

introduction: *n.* the beginning of a book, play, etc. *The introduction was so interesting that I could not put the book down.*

SIGN: **'B'** hands are placed side by side with palms forward but slanted downward slightly. The wrists then rotate outward as the hands move apart resulting in the palms facing each other.
ALTERNATE SIGN—**introduce**

introspective: *adj.* being inclined to examine one's own thoughts and feelings. *Being introspective helps me to recognize my faults.*

SIGN: **'BENT V'** hands are held with palms facing each other and tips of forefingers by either eye. The hands then move directly forward, then downward as the wrists rotate, causing the hands to turn inward so that the extended fingers are pointing at the chest. Next, **'V'** hands, palms down, extended fingers of one hand pointing toward extended fingers of the other hand, are simultaneously moved apart at least twice while the extended fingers retract to take on **'CLAWED V'** handshapes. (ASL CONCEPT—**look into myself - analyze**.)
SAME SIGN—**introspection**, *n.*

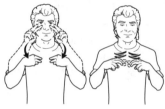

intrude: *v.* to involve oneself or offer one's views without being invited to do so. *Please do not intrude in my business affairs.*

SIGN: Left **'5'** hand is held in a fixed position with palm facing the body while right horizontal **'EXTENDED B'** hand is inserted forcefully between forefinger and middle finger of left hand. ❖
SAME SIGN—**intrusion**, *n.*, but the movement is repeated.

Inuit [*also spelled* **Innuit**]**:** *n.* an aboriginal of Arctic North America or Greenland. *The life of an Inuit is often much different than that of a southern Canadian.*

SIGN: Fingerspell **INUIT**.

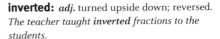

invade: *v.* to enter by force. *The troops will* **invade** *the enemy camp at dawn.*

SIGN: Right **'EXTENDED B'** hand, palm down and fingers pointing forward/leftward, is thrust under left **'STANDARD BASE'** hand to simulate forceful entry.
SAME SIGN—**invasion**, *n.*

invalid: *n.* a person who is ill, recovering from illness or in chronic ill health. *Her elderly mother is an* **invalid.**

SIGN #1: **'BENT MIDFINGER 5'** hands are positioned so that the tip of the right middle finger is in the middle of the forehead and the tip of the left middle finger is on the stomach. Sometimes this sign is made with the right hand only.

invalid: *adj.* void; legally ineffective or unacceptable. *This cheque is* **invalid** *because there is no signature on it.*

SIGN #2: Right **'N'** hand is held upright with palm forward/leftward. The hand then moves quickly upward/rightward as the wrist rotates rightward and the hand takes on a **'BENT L'** shape.

invaluable: *adj.* of great worth. *Your help on this project has been* **invaluable.**

SIGN: Vertical **'F'** hands, palms facing forward, are brought together so the joined thumbs and forefingers touch each other twice.

invent: *v.* to create; devise first; originate. *Basketball was* **invented** *by a Canadian, James Naismith.*

SIGN #1: Tip of forefinger of vertical right **'4'** hand, palm facing left, is placed against the forehead and the hand is then pushed upward and forward slightly.
SAME SIGN—**invention**, *n.*
For **inventor**, *n.*, the Agent Ending (see p. LIV) may follow.

invent: *v.* to make up; fabricate. *He* **invented** *an alibi for his whereabouts on the night of the murder.*

SIGN #2: Right **'4'** hand is held upright in front of forehead with palm facing leftward. The hand is then moved forward (at a slight downward angle) in short jerky motions until the fingers are pointing forward.

inverted: *adj.* turned upside down; reversed. *The teacher taught* **inverted** *fractions to the students.*

SIGN: Right **'V'** hand is held with palm down and extended fingers pointing left. The wrist then rotates forward, causing the hand to turn slightly toward the body as it takes on a **'K'** form.
SAME SIGN—**inversion**, *n.*

invest: *v.* to put (money) into a business, stocks, bonds, property, etc., with the expectation of making a profit. *He will* **invest** *in a new company.*

SIGN #1: Vertical left **'C'** hand is held with palm facing right. Then the forward-pointing fingertips of the right **'FLAT O'** hand are inserted into the opening in the left hand.

OR

SIGN #2: Vertical right **'DOUBLE C-INDEX'** hand is held with palm forward and is moved firmly forward a short distance.

investigate: *v.* to inquire into a problem or situation carefully; to check out. *The police will* **investigate** *the murder.*

SIGN: Left **'EXTENDED B'** hand is held in a fixed position with palm turned upward but slanted slightly rightward and toward the body while fingers point rightward/forward. Right **'ONE'** hand is held palm down as tip of forefinger brushes forward several times against palm of left hand.
SAME SIGN—**investigation**, *n.*
For **investigator**, *n.*, the Agent Ending (see p. LIV) may follow.
REGIONAL VARIATION—**probe** #2

investment: *n.* the act of putting (money) into a business, stocks, bonds, property, etc., with the expectation of making a profit. *Putting money into mutual funds is often a good* **investment.**

SIGN: **'DOUBLE C-INDEX'** hands are held apart with palms forward/downward and are alternately thrust forward with circular movements.

invincible: *adj.* impossible to conquer or defeat. *The 1984–85 Edmonton Oilers were invincible.*

SIGN: Left **'ONE'** hand is held palm-down with forefinger pointing forward/rightward. The forefinger of the right **'ONE'** hand is held above the left, then brought down sharply to strike the left forefinger. Next, right **'S'** hand, palm facing forward, is curved downward from the wrist across the extended finger of the left **'ONE'** hand. (ASL CONCEPT—**can't-beat**.) Alternatively, the ASL compound **hard-beat** may be used.

invisible: *adj.* not able to be seen; not easily noticed. *The magician made the woman invisible.*

SIGN: **'CONTRACTED 5'** hands are held, right above left, with palms facing. The fingers of each hand then snap closed against the thumbs to create **'MODIFIED O'** shapes.

invite: *v.* to welcome or request the presence of. *I will invite you to my wedding.*

SIGN: Right **'BENT EXTENDED B'** hand is held out in front of the body with fingers pointing leftward and palm facing the body but angled upward slightly. The hand is then drawn in toward the chest. ❖
SAME SIGN—**invitation**, *n.*

invoice: See **bill** #1.

involve: *v.* to include as a part. *You should try to involve yourself in Deaf activities.*

SIGN: Horizontal left **'FLAT C'** hand is held in a fixed position with palm facing right. Right **'CONTRACTED C'** hand is held above left hand and slightly closer to the body with palm down and fingers pointing forward. As the right hand is thrust forward/downward, the fingers come together to form a **'FLAT O'** shape which is inserted into the opening at the top of the left hand.
SAME SIGN—**involvement**, *n.*

involved: *adj.* absorbed; engrossed. *He is too involved in his studies to think about anything else.*

SIGN #1: Vertical right **'CLAWED V'** hand, palm facing backward, is thrust forward and slightly downward so that the back of the hand makes contact with the palm of the horizontal left **'SPREAD C'** hand which is held with the palm facing the body. The right hand then slides downward slightly but purposefully.

involved: *adj.* complex; intricate. *This needlework pattern is very involved.*

SIGN #2: **'X'** hands are held apart and almost upright with left palm facing rightward/downward and right palm facing leftward/downward. The crooked forefingers wiggle up and down as the hands move toward one another in front of the face, coming to rest when they make contact in front of the nose with right hand directly behind left so that the hands appear to be crossed.
ALTERNATE SIGN—**complex** #1

irate: *adj.* angry; enraged; furious. *The boy's parents were irate when they saw his report card.*

SIGN: **'CLAWED 5'** hands, palms toward body, fingertips touching chest, are swept vigorously upward/outward. Facial expression must clearly convey 'anger'.

iron: *adj.* made of a certain strong metal. *He put up an iron railing on either side of the steps leading up to his front door.*

SIGN #1: Tip of forefinger of right **'CROOKED ONE'** hand, palm toward the body, is tapped against the upper front teeth. (**IRON** may be fingerspelled.)

iron: *n.* a small appliance used for pressing fabrics. *You will need a very hot iron to press this linen blouse.*

SIGN #2: Left **'EXTENDED B'** hand is held in a fixed position with fingers pointing rightward and palm upward but slanted toward the body. Right **'S'** (or **'EXTENDED A'**) hand is inverted with palm toward the body at a downward slant and is moved from side to side across the left palm.

iron: *n.* a dietary requirement sometimes taken in pill form as a supplement but usually obtained in sufficient quantities from eating certain foods. *Dark green leafy vegetables, such as spinach, are rich in iron.*

SIGN #3: Fingerspell **IRON**.

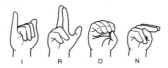

irony: *n.* a situation or statement in which reality is opposite to what it seems or is expected to be. *Can you see any irony in the fact that the mail carrier, who said he needed a break from all the walking, went off on a hiking holiday?*

SIGN: **'BENT COMBINED I + ONE'** hands, left palm facing right and right palm facing left, are positioned so the tip of the right forefinger is at the end of the nose and the left hand is held slightly lower and to the left of the right hand. Then the right hand is curved forward/leftward, making contact with the left hand which is moving rightward so that the hands are eventually crossed at the wrists. SAME SIGN—**ironic,** *adj.*

irregular: *adj.* not following the usual custom. *The judge allowed the witness to bring her dog into the courtroom even though the situation was highly irregular.*

SIGN #1: Right **'EXTENDED A'** hand, palm facing left, thumb under chin, is thrust forward. Next, right **'BENT U'** hand, palm down, is circled clockwise over the left **'STANDARD BASE'** hand, and the extended fingers are brought down to rest on it. (ASL CONCEPT—**not - normal**.)

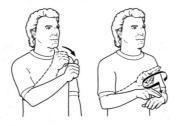

irregular: *adj.* not happening at the usual or expected times. *Due to medical problems, his attendance at meetings has been irregular lately.*

SIGN #2: Right **'EXTENDED A'** hand, palm facing left, thumb under chin, is thrust forward. Next, **'ONE'** hands are held right on top of left, with left palm facing rightward/backward and right palm facing leftward/backward while left forefinger points forward/rightward and right forefinger points leftward/forward at an upward angle. Together, the hands are lowered. (ASL CONCEPT—**not - regular**.) Various signs may be used, particularly if the irregularity refers to the *shape* of something.

irrelevant: *adj.* not related to the matter being discussed; off the point. *The heckler's comments were irrelevant to the topic under discussion.*

SIGN #1: Left **'ONE'** hand, palm facing rightward/forward, is held upright and remains fixed as tip of forefinger of right **'BENT ONE'** hand flicks leftward/backward off tip of left forefinger.

OR

SIGN #2: Right **'EXTENDED A'** hand, palm facing left, thumb under chin, is thrust forward. Next, thumbs and forefingers of **'F'** hands are linked, left palm facing rightward/backward and right palm facing leftward/forward. Together, the hands make a couple of short, quick movements forward and backward. (ASL CONCEPT—**not - related**.)

irrelevant: *adj.* having no significance in a given situation. *Qualifications are important, but gender and age are **irrelevant** for this job.*

SIGN #3: Right **'EXTENDED A'** hand, palm facing left, thumb under chin, is thrust forward. Next, vertical **'F'** hands are held apart with palms facing forward. The hands are then brought purposefully together.
(ASL CONCEPT—**not - important**.)

irreplaceable: *adj.* impossible to replace. *The fire in Windsor Castle destroyed many national treasures which are **irreplaceable**.*

SIGN: Left **'ONE'** hand is held palm-down with forefinger pointing forward/rightward. The forefinger of the right **'ONE'** hand is held above the left, then brought down sharply to strike the left forefinger. Next, horizontal **'F'** hands, left palm facing right and right palm facing, are held so that the left is further from the chest than the right. Then their positions are simultaneously switched as the left hand moves back toward the body in arc over the right hand while the right hand moves away from the body in an arc under the left hand.
(ASL CONCEPT—**can't - replace**.)

irresponsible: *adj.* not dependable; not reliable; not caring about the consequences of one's actions. *He is too **irresponsible** to hold down a job.*

SIGN: Right **'EXTENDED B'** hand is held just to the left of the lower part of the face with palm facing backward and fingers pointing leftward upward. The signer then blows on the hand as it moves rightward past the mouth, coming to rest in a vertical position to the right of the face. Next, fingertips of **'BENT EXTENDED B'** hands, palms facing the body, are tapped simultaneously against the right shoulder.
(ASL CONCEPT—**no - responsible**.)
SAME SIGN—**irresponsibility**, *n.*

irritable: *adj.* crabby; easily annoyed. *I feel **irritable** when I have a cold.*

SIGN: Right vertical **'CROOKED 5'** hand is held with palm toward the face as the fingers rapidly alternate between a relaxed state (**'CROOKED 5'**) and a clawed state (**'CLAWED SPREAD C'**).
SAME SIGN—**irritability**, *n.*

island: *n.* a land mass that is completely surrounded by water. *Victoria, the capital of British Columbia, is situated on an **island**.*

SIGN: Horizontal right **'I'** hand, with palm facing left but angled toward the body, is placed on the back of the left **'STANDARD BASE'** hand and is circled counter-clockwise.

isolated: *v.* to set apart; to cause to be alone. *He feels **isolated** since he moved out to the country.*

SIGN: Vertical right **'ONE'** hand, palm facing the body, is moved in a small counter-clockwise circle.
SAME SIGN—**isolation**, *n.*

issue: *n.* an important topic or subject usually requiring an official decision. *Most politicians avoid discussion of moral **issues** such as abortion and euthanasia.*

SIGN #1: Vertical **'V'** hands, palms facing forward, are held apart just above shoulder level, and are curved outward slightly from the wrists as they become **'CLAWED V'** hands. (Signs vary considerably depending on context.)

issue: *v.* to supply; give out; distribute. *The police department* **issues** *a uniform and a handgun to each new officer.*

SIGN #2: Horizontal right **'CONTRACTED B'** hand is held with palm facing leftward/upward and fingers pointing left. The hand then moves forward in a slight arc formation as if giving something to someone. (See **give out** if several people are being issued with something.)

it: *pron.* referring to a place, object, animal, or something abstract that has already been mentioned. [See PRONOUNS, p. LXIV.] *Ottawa is a beautiful city; it has many points of interest.*

SIGN: Horizontal right **'BENT ONE'** hand is held with palm facing forward/rightward as the forefinger points at the thing being referred to.

italics: *n.* a form of print or type that sets specific words, phrases or paragraphs apart from the rest of the text by putting them on a rightward slant. *All references to race and religion were printed in* **italics** *in the article.*

SIGN: Vertical **'4'** hands are held slightly apart with palms facing. The wrists then bend to slant the hands rightward so that the fingers eventually point rightward/upward.

itch: *v.* to have or create a feeling which causes a desire to scratch. *Poison ivy causes the skin to* **itch**.

SIGN: Fingertips of right **'SPREAD EXTENDED C'** hand, palm down, are used to scratch the back of the left forearm. (This sign is positioned according to the specific location of the itch.)
SAME SIGN—**itchy**, *adj.*

item: *n.* a thing or unit, especially in a list or collection. *I have an interesting* **item** *to show you.*

SIGN: Right **'EXTENDED B'** hand, palm facing up, fingertips pointing forward, is moved from left to right in an arc. To indicate plurality, the hand continues to move rightward in a series of small arcs. (**ITEM** may be finger-spelled.)

itemize: *v.* to make a list. *We need to* **itemize** *all our valuables for the insurance company.*

SIGN: Vertical left **'EXTENDED B'** hand is held in a fixed position with palm facing right. Right **'FLAT O'** hand is positioned with bunched fingertips against the fingers of the left hand and is then slid downward to the heel of the left hand. (Sometimes this downward movement is made in small successive arcs.)

its: *pron.* used to refer to something belonging to or related to an object or animal. [See PRONOUNS, p. LXVI.] *The plant is shedding* **its** *leaves.*

SIGN: Vertical right **'EXTENDED B'** hand, palm facing forward/rightward, is held in front of the right shoulder and moved slightly in the direction of the thing being referred to.

itself: *pron.* used to emphasize the (understood) subject 'it' in reference to a place, object, or animal. [See PRONOUNS, p. LXVI.] *Gallaudet University has made a name for* **itself**.

SIGN: Horizontal right **'EXTENDED A'** hand, thumb pointing upward and palm facing leftward/forward, is jabbed a couple of times in the direction of the thing being referred to.

J

jacket: *n.* an outer garment for the upper part of the body; a short coat. *Put on your jacket before you go outside.*

SIGN: Vertical **'EXTENDED A'** hands are held parallel close to the upper chest with palms facing each other. They are then simultaneously lowered as palms turn downward.

jail: *n.* a place of confinement for criminals; a prison. *The thief was convicted and sent to jail.*

SIGN: **'4'** (or **'5'**) hands are held with palms facing the body. Back of right hand, whose fingers point slightly upward to the left, is positioned behind palm of left hand at right angles, and is thrust against it.

jam: *n.* a preserve containing fruit and sugar. *My mother makes delicious peach jam.*

SIGN: Fingerspell **JAM**.

janitor: *n.* a person hired to clean and generally take care of a building. *The floors have been spotless since that janitor was hired.*

SIGN #1: **'CLOSED A-INDEX'** hands are positioned left in front of right, with palms at a slight upward-facing angle, to simulate the holding of a mop handle and are drawn back and forth as if mopping a floor.

OR

SIGN #2: Forefinger and thumb of right **'CONTRACTED L'** hand, palm toward the body, are placed one on either side of the chin and are drawn downward to form a **'CLOSED MODIFIED G'** hand. Motion is repeated.

January: *n.* the first month of the year. *January is usually the coldest month of the year in most parts of Canada.*

SIGN: Fingerspell **JAN**.

jaundice: *n.* a condition that causes a yellowing of the skin. *Jaundice is very common among newborn infants.*

SIGN: Thumb and forefinger of right **'A-INDEX'** hand are used to grasp a small fold of skin on the right cheek. Right hand is then changed to a **'Y'** hand, with palm facing left, and is twisted slightly from the wrist several times. (ASL CONCEPT—**skin - yellow**.)

javelin: *n.* a long, pointed spear that is thrown forward in competitive field events. *Throwing a javelin requires training.*

SIGN: Vertical right **'S'** hand, palm facing left, is thrust forward as it opens to form a **'MODIFIED 5'** hand.

jealous: *adj.* suspicious or afraid of being replaced by a rival; resentful (of) or vindictive (towards). *The girl was jealous of her new baby brother.*

SIGN #1: Tip of forefinger of right **'CROOKED ONE'** hand, palm leftward, is placed at right side of chin and hand is twisted clockwise a quarter turn from the wrist. This sign is accompanied by a lip pattern such as that used to produce a 'SH' sound.

OR

SIGN #2: Tip of little finger of right **'I'** hand, palm facing left, is placed at right side of chin, and the hand is twisted clockwise a quarter turn from the wrist. This sign is accompanied by a lip pattern such as that used to produce a 'SH' sound.

SAME SIGN—**jealousy**, *n.*

jeans: *n.* trousers for casual wear, made of denim or corduroy. *Everyone wore* ***jeans*** *to the barbecue.*

SIGN #1: Fingerspell **JEANS**.

SIGN #2 [ONTARIO]: Thumb-tip of horizontal right **'MODIFIED 5'** hand, palm facing backward, is placed at left side of chin and is then moved across in front of the chin to the right side as it changes to a **'CLAWED SPREAD C'** hand.

---

jeer: See **deride**.

---

jelly: *n.* a fruit-flavoured dessert or preserve. *My mother makes delicious crabapple jelly.*

SIGN: Fingerspell **JELLY**.

---

jeopardy: *n.* danger; risk. *Driving under the influence of alcohol puts lives in jeopardy.*

SIGN: Left **'A'** hand is held in a fixed position with palm facing downward but slanted toward the chest. Right **'A'** hand is held just in front of the left hand with palm facing left and is circled in a clockwise direction a couple of times so that the thumb firmly brushes upward against the back of the left hand with each revolution.

REGIONAL VARIATION—**dangerous**

Jesus: *n.* the founder of Christianity. *Have you seen the drawing of Jesus done by Forrest Nickerson?*

SIGN: **'BENT MIDFINGER 5'** hands, palms facing, are held slightly apart, fingers pointing forward. Tip of left middle finger is used to tap right palm and vice versa.

---

jet: *n.* a large, jet-propelled airplane. *The company has its own jet to transport executives to business meetings.*

SIGN: Fingerspell **JET**.
ALTERNATE SIGN—**airplane**

---

jet lag: *n.* tiredness caused by crossing time zones in an airplane. *We suffered from jet lag after our long flight.*

SIGN: Fingerspell **JET LAG**.

---

jewellery [*also spelled* **jewelry**]: *n.* objects such as rings, necklaces, bracelets, etc. that are worn for personal adornment. *She had her jewellery insured.*

SIGN: Fingerspell **JEWELLERY** or **JEWELRY**. (Various signs may be used.)

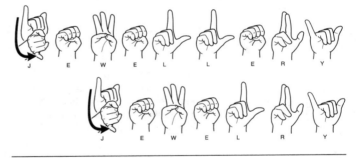

---

jigsaw: *n.* a mechanical saw used to cut intricate curves in a sheet of material. *The man used his jigsaw to make wooden toys.*

SIGN: Forefinger of right **'BENT ONE'** (or **'BENT L'**) hand is moved downward in jabbing motions between forefinger and middle finger of left **'STANDARD BASE'** hand.

---

jigsaw puzzle: *n.* a puzzle involving the reassembling of a picture that has been cut into irregularly shaped pieces. *He is working on a difficult jigsaw puzzle containing 1,500 pieces.*

SIGN #1: Vertical **'BENT U'** hands, palms facing each other and extended fingers of one hand pointing toward those of the other, are tapped together several times.

jigsaw puzzle *(cont.)*

SIGN #2: **'EXTENDED A'** hands, with palms down and thumbs appearing to press down on something, are alternately raised and lowered.

---

jinx: *n.* a thing, person, or force that brings bad luck to someone. *There seemed to be a jinx on our entire vacation.*

SIGN: Fingerspell **JINX**.

jittery: *adj.* characterized by nervousness and anxiety. *He was jittery before he took his driving test.*

SIGN: Horizontal **'5'** hands are held parallel with fingers pointing forward and palms facing each other at a downward angle. The hands are then shaken as the wrists rapidly twist back and forth slightly.

job: *n.* work; occupation. *It is not easy to find a job if you have no qualifications.*

SIGN #1: **JOB** is either fingerspelled in the usual way or, after making the **J**, the right hand misses the **O** as it is twisted around to make the **B** with the palm toward the body.

OR

SIGN #2: Wrist of right **'S'** (or **'A'**) hand, palm facing away from the body, strikes wrist of the left **'S'** (or **'A'**) hand, which is held in front of/below the right hand with palm facing downward. Motion is repeated.

jog: *v.* to run slowly for physical exercise. *She jogs every morning before she goes to work.*

SIGN #1: Forefinger of horizontal right **'CLAWED L'** hand is hooked around upright thumb of horizontal left **'CLAWED L'** hand. Maintaining this position, the hands are thrust forward together a couple times.

OR

SIGN #2: Horizontal **'S'** hands are held at the sides of the body with palms facing and are alternately circled forward as the shoulders move up and down.

join: *v.* to connect or bring together. *The Siamese twins were joined at the hip.*

SIGN #1: **'OPEN F'** hands are held slightly apart, palms facing each other, and are then brought together to form **'F'** hands, with thumbs and forefingers linked. ❖

join: *v.* to become a part of or associated with. *I would like to join this club.*

SIGN #2: Extended fingers of right **'U'** hand, palm left, are inserted into the slightly open left **'S'** hand. ❖

joint: *n.* the junction between two or more bones. *My knee joint is very sore.*

SIGN: **'S'** hands are positioned with knuckles together and palms down. Then they are simultaneously moved up and down slightly from the wrist a few times while maintaining contact between the knuckles at the bottom.

---

joke: *n.* a funny anecdote or something that is done for fun. *He always has a joke to tell.*

SIGN #1: Fingerspell **JOKE**.

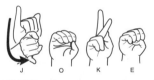

joke: *v.* to behave in a teasing manner. *I was only joking and did not mean to insult you.*

SIGN #2: With palm facing left, horizontal right **'X'** hand is stroked forward at least twice across the top of horizontal left **'X'** hand, which is held with palm facing right. ❖

jolly: *adj.* full of good humour. *Santa Claus is portrayed as a jolly man.*

SIGN: Horizontal right **'EXTENDED B'** hand, palm toward the body, is brushed up and off the chest twice in a circular motion.

jolt: *n.* a surprise; shock. *The news of his sudden death was a jolt to all of us.*

SIGN: Tip of forefinger of right **'ONE'** hand touches right side of forehead. **'BENT 5'** hands, palms facing down and fingertips pointing down, are then held parallel to one another and simultaneously thrust downward. (ASL CONCEPT—**think - shock**.)

jot down: *v.* to make a brief note. *I will jot down his phone number.*

SIGN: Bunched fingertips of right **'O'** hand, palm down, are placed on the upturned left palm. Right hand opens to form an **'EXTENDED B'** hand and is then tapped down smartly on the left palm.

journal: *n.* a periodical publication. *Medical journals are kept in this section of the library.*

SIGN #1: Thumb and forefinger of right **'A-INDEX'** (or **'MODIFIED G'**) hand are slid up and down outer edge of left **'EXTENDED B'** hand, which is held with palm facing body. Motion is repeated.

journal: *n.* a book in which a daily record is kept. *I keep a journal of my activities.*

SIGN #2: Horizontal left **'EXTENDED B'** hand is held in a fixed position with palm facing rightward/backward. Thumb and forefinger of right **'CLOSED X'** hand move forward/ rightward twice along the palm of the left hand.

journey: *n.* a trip from one place to another. *Our trip around the world was an incredible journey.*

SIGN: Right **'CROOKED V'** hand, palm down, is snaked forward.

joy: *n.* much happiness. *Their grandchildren bring them an abundance of joy.*

SIGN: Horizontal right **'EXTENDED B'** hand, palm toward the body, is brushed up and off the chest twice in a circular motion. SAME SIGN—**joyful**, *adj.*

joystick: *n.* a lever for controlling the movement of an object on a computer screen. *You need a joystick to play certain computer games.*

SIGN: Horizontal right **'S'** hand, palm facing left, is placed on upturned left palm and twisted left and right.

jubilant: *adj.* joyful; very happy. *They were jubilant after winning their first game of the season.*

SIGN: Horizontal right **'EXTENDED B'** hand, palm toward the body, is brushed up and off the chest twice in a circular motion.

jubilee: *n.* a special anniversary or time for rejoicing. *The pageant was performed in honour of the queen's silver jubilee.*

SIGN: Vertical **'COVERED T'** hands are held at either side of the head, palms facing each other, and are swung in small circles above the shoulders.

judge: *n.* a person with the authority to preside over court cases and pronounce judgement. *The judge sentenced the accused to five years in prison.*

SIGN: Horizontal **'F'** hands, palms facing each other, are alternately raised and lowered a few times.

judo: *n.* a kind of jujitsu (martial arts). *He has a black belt in judo.*

SIGN: Fingerspell **JUDO**.

jug: *n.* a container used for holding and pouring liquids, usually having a handle and a spout. *Mother made us a jug of lemonade for our picnic.*

SIGN: Horizontal right **'S'** hand, palm facing leftward/backward, is tipped leftward from the wrist to simulate the act of pouring from a jug.

juggle: *v.* to toss and catch objects with a continuous motion. *Children love to watch the clowns juggle Indian clubs.*

SIGN: **'CROOKED 5'** hands are held apart with palms up and are alternately moved up and down to simulate the act of tossing and catching.

juice: *n.* a drink made from fruit. *She started the day with a glass of juice and a bowl of cereal.*

SIGN: Fingerspell **JUICE**.

July: *n.* the seventh month of the year. *Canada Day is celebrated on the first of July.*

SIGN: Fingerspell **JULY**.

jump: *v.* to leap or spring clear of the ground. *The children jump in gym.*

SIGN: Tips of extended fingers of right **'V'** hand, are placed on upturned left palm, then raised quickly and retracted to form a **'CROOKED V'**. Motion is repeated.

June: *n.* the sixth month of the year. *Many brides choose June for their weddings.*

SIGN: Fingerspell **JUNE**.

jungle: *n.* a tropical forest. *Do not venture into the jungle without a guide.*

SIGN: Both arms drift rightward as right elbow rests on left **'STANDARD BASE'** hand, and vertical right **'5'** hand shimmies or repeatedly twists back and forth in short, jerky movements. (**JUNGLE** is frequently fingerspelled.)

junior: *adj.* younger in years. *She is five years my junior.*

SIGN #1: Vertical **'MODIFIED O'** hands, palms facing each other, are tapped together. Then, fingertips of both **'BENT EXTENDED B'** hands, palms facing the body, are brushed upward against the chest.

(ASL CONCEPT—**more - young**.)

ASL users generally tend to expand in cases like this by giving the actual ages of the two people for further clarification.

junior [*more frequently abbreviated* **jr.**]: *adj.* the younger of two people, usually a son as distinguished from his father. *Frank Smith Jr. is now attending Gallaudet University.*

SIGN #2: Fingerspell **JR**.

junior: *adj.* designating the third year of study at Gallaudet University. (This sign is not used to mean the junior year at any other university—only at Gallaudet.) *Frank is in his junior year at Gallaudet University.*

SIGN #3: Tip of forefinger of right **'ONE'** hand, palm facing left, taps the very end of forefinger of horizontal left **'5'** hand, which is held with palm facing right and angled slightly toward the body.

junk: *n.* a collection of discarded objects or rubbish. *This junk should be thrown out.*

SIGN: Fingerspell **JUNK**.

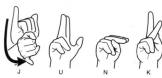

jurisdiction: *n.* control or authority; the extent of such authority; the territory under one's control; the authority to enforce the law. *The college operates under the jurisdiction of a board of governors.*

SIGN: Horizontal **'X'** hands are held slightly apart with left palm facing right and right palm facing left. Then they are alternately moved backward and forward. (Sign selection depends on the context.)

jury: *n.* a group of twelve people appointed to hear trial evidence and deliver a verdict as to the guilt or innocence of the accused. *The jury found him guilty of manslaughter.*

SIGN: Fingerspell **JURY**.

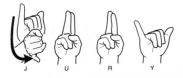

just: *adj.* fair; equitable. *Some people think life imprisonment is a just penalty for murder.*

SIGN #1: Vertical **'BENT EXTENDED B'** hands are held slightly apart with palms facing each other, and are then brought together so that the fingertips meet. Motion is repeated. (To translate the sample sentence into ASL, the adjective 'just' *follows* rather than precedes the noun 'penalty'.)

just: *adv.* only; merely. *He is just a child and does not know any better.*

SIGN #2: Vertical right **'ONE'** hand is held with palm facing forward. Then it is twisted from the wrist so that the palm faces backward.

just: *adv.* recently; a brief time ago. *Bob was just here five minutes ago.*

SIGN #3: Side of crooked forefinger of right **'X'** hand, palm facing right shoulder, is pressed into right cheek.

ALTERNATE SIGN—**recent** #2

just: *adv.* by a narrow margin. *He just managed to place second in the race.*

SIGN #4: Tips of thumb and forefinger of right **'F'** (or **'CLOSED X'**) hand, palm toward the face, are held against forehead over right eyebrow as right hand moves sharply forward as if plucking the eyebrow.

just in case: *adv.* in the event that. *I brought an extra pen just in case you need one.*

SIGN: Tips of thumbs of horizontal **'MODIFIED 5'** hands, held with palms facing down but slightly tilted toward the body, are poked twice into either side of upper chest near shoulders. This movement is accompanied by a protruding tongue.

justice: *n.* the administration of law according to accepted principles. *The Attorney General oversees the Department of Justice.*

SIGN #1: Horizontal **'F'** hands, palms facing each other, are alternately raised and lowered a few times.

justice: *n.* fair treatment or judgment. *In the name of justice, all Canadians should be equal before the law.*

SIGN #2: Vertical **'BENT EXTENDED B'** hands are held slightly apart with palms facing each other, and are then brought together so that the fingertips meet. Motion is repeated.

justified: *adj.* warranted; proven to be right, fair, valid or necessary. *He was justified in being upset over spending ten years in prison for a crime he did not commit.*

SIGN: Right **'ONE'** hand, palm facing left, is held above left **'ONE'** hand, palm facing right, with forefingers pointing relatively forward. Then right hand is tapped at least twice on left hand.

justify: *v.* to account for; explain the need for. *Can you justify spending so much money on a dress when you already have a wardrobe full of clothing?*

SIGN #1: Horizontal **'F'** hands are held with palms facing each other, and are alternately moved backward and forward. Vertical right **'BENT MIDFINGER 5'** hand is then held with palm facing right side of forehead and middle finger repeatedly tapping gently in mid-air. (ASL CONCEPT—**explain - why**.)

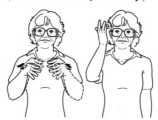

OR

SIGN #2: Horizontal **'F'** hands are held with palms facing each other, and are alternately moved backward and forward. Then vertical right **'EXTENDED R'** (or **'R'**) hand, palm toward face, makes small circles (clockwise in the eyes of the onlooker) at right side of forehead. (ASL CONCEPT—**explain - reason**.)

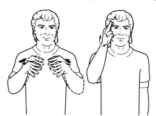

justify: *v.* to prove to be fair, reasonable or valid. *Can you justify your suspicions with solid evidence?*

SIGN #3: Horizontal left **'EXTENDED B'** hand is held in a fixed position with palm up and fingers pointing forward/rightward. Horizontal right **'EXTENDED B'** hand is held palm up with fingers pointing forward/leftward and is brought down sharply onto the left palm.

justify: *v.* to adjust lines of print (using a word processing system) in order to make them equidistant from the edge of the page. *Can you justify your right margin?*

SIGN #4: Right **'EXTENDED B'** hand is held on a forward/upward angle with the palm facing left. The forearm is then lowered so that the hand becomes horizontal with the fingers pointing forward.

juvenile: *adj.* youthful or immature; pertaining to young people. *This court deals with juvenile offenders.*

SIGN: **'BENT EXTENDED B'** hands, held parallel with palms facing backward and fingertips touching the chest, are brushed upward against the chest a couple times.

K

kangaroo: *n.* a large marsupial of Australia having powerful hind legs for leaping. *Like other marsupials, the kangaroo carries her young in a pouch.*

SIGN: **'BENT EXTENDED B'** hands, palms facing down, are held slightly apart and moved vigorously up and down simultaneously to simulate a kangaroo's leaping.

---

karate: *n.* a traditional Japanese system of unarmed combat. *Many women are learning karate as a means of self-defence.*

SIGN: Fingerspell **KARATE.**

K A R A T E

keep: *v.* to have or retain possession of. *I keep all my letters from home.*

SIGN: Horizontal right **'K'** hand, with palm facing left, is held above horizontal left hand, which is held with palm facing right. Then right hand is brought purposefully down to strike left hand.

(I will) keep it for myself: *s.s.* This sentence is always used in a positive sense. There is no implication of selfishness. Its meaning is self-explanatory. *I will keep it for myself.*

SIGN: Vertical right **'MODIFIED Y'** hand, palm facing left, is moved backward in a small circular pattern to repeatedly make contact with the chest.

---

ketchup: *n.* a sauce made from tomatoes, vinegar and spices. *I prefer hot dogs with ketchup.*

SIGN: Vertical right **'ONE'** hand is held with palm facing the body and tip of forefinger touching the lower lip. As the hand is then drawn very firmly forward at a downward angle, the forefinger crooks to form an **'X'** shape. Next, right **'C'** hand is held with palm forward as if clutching a ketchup bottle and is shaken from side to side as if trying to get the ketchup to come out of the bottle.

(ASL CONCEPT—**red - shake bottle**.) Signs vary.

---

kettle: *n.* a metal container with a handle and spout for boiling water. *When the kettle boils, I will make some tea.*

SIGN: Fingerspell **KETTLE.**

K E T T L E

key: *n.* a metal object used to operate the mechanism of a lock. *I often misplace my car key.*

SIGN #1: Forefinger of right **'COVERED T'** hand, palm down, is twisted back and forth slightly against right-facing horizontal left palm.

key: *n.* a small square or rectangular-shaped surface bearing a letter, number, symbol or word, such as those found on a typewriter, computer keyboard or telephone device for the Deaf. *The 'shift' key is used for upper case letters.*

SIGN #2: Right **'BENT ONE'** hand, palm down, makes a pecking motion as though tapping a key on a keyboard.

key: *adj.* important; essential. *Salary was the key issue in the negotiation.*

SIGN #3: Vertical **'F'** hands are held apart with palms facing forward. The hands are then brought purposefully together.

ALTERNATE SIGN—**important** #2

365

keyboard: *n.* a row of keys that are usually hand-operated as on a piano, typewriter, etc. *I want to buy a* **keyboard** *for my computer today.*

SIGN: **'SPREAD C'** hands, palms facing down, are held parallel with fingers wiggling up and down to simulate the action of typing. Next, **'BENT ONE'** hands, palms down, are held side by side, then moved apart, drawn simultaneously toward chest, and brought together again as they trace the outline of a keyboard.

keynote address [*or* **keynote speech**]: *n.* an opening speech that generally outlines issues to be addressed. *The president of the Canadian Association of the Deaf gave the* **keynote address** *at the convention.*

SIGN: Fingerspell **KEYNOTE**. Right arm is then raised and the vertical **'EXTENDED B'** hand, palm facing left, is brought forward sharply from the wrist a couple of times.

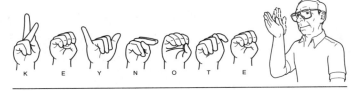

kick: *v.* to strike with one's foot. *Jim will* **kick** *the first ball.*

SIGN: Right **'B'** hand, fingers pointing down and palm facing left, is swung upward from the wrist to strike the underside of the left **'STANDARD BASE'** hand. ❖

kid: *n.* a colloquial term meaning a child. *The* **kid** *with the curly hair is from a place called Eyebrow, Saskatchewan.*

SIGN #1: Vertical right **'BENT EXTENDED B'** hand is held with palm facing forward and fingers pointing forward. It is then lowered slightly to indicate the relatively low physical stature of a child.

kid: *v.* to tease in a good-natured way. *I just* **kid** *you because I like to see you laugh.*

SIGN #2: With palm facing left, horizontal right **'X'** hand is stroked forward at least twice across the top of horizontal left **'X'** hand, which is held with palm facing right. ❖

kidnap: *v.* to carry off and hold another person, usually for ransom. *The terrorist* **kidnapped** *the diplomat.*

SIGN: Horizontal right **'SPREAD C'** hand, palm facing left, is pulled backward as it closes to form an **'S'** hand. ❖

kill: *v.* to cause the death of. *Hunters sometimes* **kill** *animals for food.*

SIGN: Vertical left **'EXTENDED B'** hand is held in a fixed position with palm facing rightward and slightly forward. Right **'ONE'** (or **'K'**) hand is held palm down as it moves forward/downward at a slight leftward angle, the forefinger firmly grazing the left palm. ❖

(be) killed: *v.* to lose (one's) life; die. *He was* **killed** *in a car accident last night.*

SIGN: Vertical right **'K'** hand, palm facing left, moves forward as it changes to an **'I'** shape and then to an **'L'**, which appears to vibrate before the hand continues to move forward, taking on an **'E'** and finally a **'D'** shape. (This sign tends to be used when the death is *accidental*.)

kilogram: *n.* a metric unit of weight measurement. *The meat will require 25 minutes of cooking time per* **kilogram**.

SIGN: Fingerspell **KG**.

kilometre: *n.* a metric unit of distance measurement. *The distance around the track is one* **kilometre**.

SIGN: Fingerspell **KM**.

kin: *n.* a person's relatives collectively. *Most of my kin will gather for a family reunion.*

SIGN: Fingerspell **KIN**.

kind: *adj.* having a friendly, warmhearted, generous nature. *I admire him because he is such a kind person.*

SIGN #1: Horizontal **'BENT EXTENDED B'** hands, left palm facing right and right palm facing left, are alternately circled forward around each other.
SAME SIGN—**kindness**, *n.*

OR

SIGN #2: Forefingers of right **'BENT EXTENDED B'** hand, palm toward the body, are brushed downward twice on the chin.

kind: *n.* variety, class, group or sort. *What kind of gum do you prefer to chew?*

SIGN #3: Right **'K'** hand, palm facing left and slightly toward the body, is held just above left **'K'** hand, which is held with palm facing right and slightly toward the body. Hands are then circled forward around one another one full turn, stopping with right hand resting on top of left. (**KIND** may be fingerspelled.)
ALTERNATE SIGN—**assorted**

kindergarten: *n.* a school for young children aged 4 to 6. *My son will be old enough to attend kindergarten next fall.*

SIGN: The vertical right **'K'** hand, palm forward, is shaken from side to side slightly a couple of times. (Signs vary.)

king: *n.* a male monarch. *Henry VIII was a famous English king.*

SIGN: Right **'K'** hand, palm toward body, is placed upright against left shoulder, and then moved diagonally down across chest and placed at right side of waist.

kiss: *n.* a touch or caress with the lips to show affection or respect, or to greet someone. *A kiss might make me feel better.*

SIGN #1: Fingertips of right **'BENT EXTENDED B'** hand, palm toward the body, touch the chin first, and then the right cheek.

OR

SIGN #2: Vertical **'FLAT O'** hands, palms facing each other, are brought together so that the bunched fingertips touch and then the hands are drawn apart. Movement is accompanied by a simultaneous puckering of the lips.

kitchen: *n.* a room equipped for preparing and cooking food. *He cooked a gourmet meal in his tiny kitchen.*

SIGN: Right **'EXTENDED B'** (or **'K'**) hand is held palm down with fingers pointing forward/leftward as they are placed on the upturned palm of the left **'EXTENDED B'** hand, of which the fingers point slightly forward and to the right. Right hand is then flipped over so that palm faces up.

kite: *n.* a light paper or cloth-covered frame, which can be flown on a windy day while holding on to the string attached. *The kite became lodged in the branches of a tree.*

SIGN: Tip of forefinger of right **'ONE'** hand, palm facing left, touches wrist just under forward/rightward-facing palm of vertical left **'EXTENDED B'** hand. Hands are moved up and down together twice. (Movement for this sign may vary slightly. Alternatively, **KITE** may be fingerspelled.)

kitten: *n.* a young cat. *We have had our Siamese cat since she was a kitten.*

SIGN: Fingers of palm-up right **'BENT EXTENDED B'** hand point leftward as they rest on rightward-pointing fingers of palm-up left **'BENT EXTENDED B'** hand. The arms are simultaneously moved from side to side as if rocking a baby in one's arms. Next, vertical right **'FLAT F'** hand, palm facing left, is held near the right corner of the mouth and is drawn backward/rightward several times.
(ASL CONCEPT—**baby - cat**.)

knapsack: See **backpack**.

kneel: *v.* to rest on one's knees. *The bride and groom will kneel at the altar.*

SIGN: Right **'CROOKED V'** hand is inverted and placed on upturned palm of left **'EXTENDED B'** hand to give the appearance of two legs bent in a kneeling position.

knife: *n.* a cutting instrument consisting of a blade and a handle. *You will need a knife to shred the cabbage.*

SIGN: Horizontal right **'U'** hand, with palm facing left, is held above and at right angles to horizontal left **'U'** hand, of which fingers are angled forward/rightward. Extended fingers of right hand are then brushed forward/rightward twice off the end of extended fingers of left hand.

knit: *v.* to create a garment by looping wool over long eyeless needles. *She will knit a sweater to sell at the bazaar.*

SIGN: Forefingers of horizontal **'ONE'** hands, palms facing each other, are crossed with the right forefinger resting on the left. Then both hands are moved back and forth to simulate the action of a pair of knitting needles.

knob: *n.* the rounded handle of a door, drawer, etc. *The knob on the back door is loose.*

SIGN: Vertical right **'SPREAD C'** hand, palm forward, is twisted back and forth from the wrist.

knock: *v.* to rap sharply with the knuckles. *Please knock before you enter the room.*

SIGN: Knuckles of right **'A'** hand, palm facing left, rap against right-facing palm of vertical left **'EXTENDED B'** hand.

knockout: *n.* a blow that renders someone unconscious. *The boxer suffered six knockouts.*

SIGN #1: Right horizontal **'K'** hand is held with palm facing left. The hand is then quickly transformed into a horizontal **'O'** hand with palm still facing left as the hand firmly moves forward a short distance.

knockout: *n.* a very attractive or impressive person or thing. *The winner of the beauty pageant was a real knockout.*

SIGN #2: Right **'CONTRACTED 5'** hand is circled clockwise (to the onlooker) around face as fingers close at chin to form a **'FLAT O'** hand.

knot: *n.* a fastening formed by looping and tying a rope, cord, etc. *I have a knot in my shoelace.*

SIGN: Horizontal **'COVERED T'** hands, palms facing body, are held close together, circled forward around one another, and then drawn firmly apart as though tying something.

know: *v.* to be aware of or familiar with; to be well-informed or certain about something. *Did you know that Beethoven was Deaf?*

SIGN #1: Fingertips of right **'EXTENDED B'** (or **'BENT EXTENDED B'**) hand, with palm facing body, are tapped against right side of forehead. SAME SIGN—**knowledge**, *n.*

(don't/doesn't/didn't) know: *v.* having no opinion or knowledge about something. *I don't know what will happen to the victims.*

SIGN #2: The fingertips of the right **'EXTENDED B'** (or **'BENT EXTENDED B'**) hand, palm toward the face, are placed on the forehead or in the area of the right cheekbone, and the hand is then curved to the right with the palm facing down.

know nothing: *v.* to be unaware of or unfamiliar with. *Many people know nothing about Deaf Culture.*

SIGN: Side of right **'O'** (or **'F'**) hand, with palm facing left, is placed against middle of forehead.

knuckles: *n.* the joints of the fingers. *I hurt my knuckles in a fist fight.*

SIGN: Tip of extended finger of right **'ONE'** hand touches each knuckle of left **'S'** hand which is held with the palm down.

L

label: *n.* a tag, card or other material attached to something to identify it or give specific instructions/details. *The instructions are on the label.*

SIGN #1: Tips of forefingers and thumbs touch as **'MODIFIED G'** hands are held together with palms facing forward/downward. The arms are then drawn apart and each forefinger and thumb come together to form **'CLOSED MODIFIED G'** shapes. (Signs for **label**, *n.*, vary considerably depending on the *size, shape* and *location* of the label.)

label: *v.* to put a label on something. *Please label each envelope for me.*

SIGN #2: Left **'EXTENDED B'** hand is held in a fixed position with fingers pointing rightward and palm upward but slanted toward the chest. Tips of extended fingers of horizontal right **'U'** hand, palm downward, is brushed rightward across the left palm. (Signs for **label**, *v.*, may vary.)

label: *v.* to classify (often negatively) in a word or phrase. *I did not like being labelled a slow learner when I was a child.*

SIGN #3: Vertical left **'EXTENDED B'** hand is held in a fixed position with palm facing forward/rightward while tips of extended fingers of horizontal right **'CONTRACTED U'** hand, palm leftward/backward, are brushed backward/rightward across the left palm. ❖

laboratory: *n.* an area used for scientific research or for teaching the sciences. *The instructor conducted the experiment in the high school science laboratory.*

SIGN: Fingerspell **LAB**.

labour [*also spelled* **labor**]: *v.* to work hard. *He laboured to succeed.*

SIGN #1: Left **'S'** (or **'A'**) hand is held in a fixed position with palm down. Heel of right **'S'** (or **'A'**) hand, palm facing leftward/forward, strikes repeatedly against right side (or 'thumb' side) of left hand in a rightward/ forward direction. The motion is laboured and appears as a series of counter-clockwise circles. Cheeks are puffed and head may move up and down with each strike of the hand.

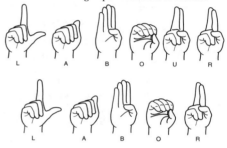

labour [*also spelled* **labor**]: *n.* work. *He is well paid for his labour.*

SIGN #2: Wrist of right **'A'** (or **'S'**) hand, palm facing away from the body, strikes wrist of left **'A'** (or **'S'**) hand, which is held in front of/below the right hand with palm facing downward. Motion is repeated.

labour [*also spelled* **labor**]: *n.* the process of childbirth and the physical effort involved. *She went into labour at ten o'clock last night.*

SIGN #3: Fingerspell **LABOUR** or **LABOR**.

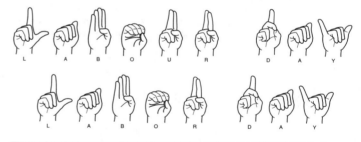

Labour [*or* **Labor**] **Day:** *n.* a public holiday in many countries in honour of workers. In Canada it is celebrated in September. *Labour Day is a holiday to honour the working people in Canada and U.S.A.*

SIGN: Fingerspell **LABOUR** [*or* **LABOR**] **DAY**.

lace: *n.* a delicate, ornamental fabric. *The bride's gown was made of white satin and lace.*

SIGN #1: Fingerspell **LACE**. (Alternatively, **'ONE'** (or **'4'**) hands may be positioned in such a way as to indicate lace at the neck or the wrists or wherever there might be lace on a given garment.)

lace: *n.* a cord drawn through eyelets or around hooks to fasten shoes, boots or other garments. *I need a new lace for one of my gym shoes.*

SIGN #2: **'COVERED T'** hands, palms facing body, are held close together, circled forward around one another, and then drawn firmly apart as though tying something.
ALTERNATE SIGN—**string**

laceration: *n.* a rough, jagged tear in the flesh. *The laceration on my hand was deep.*

SIGN: Tip of forefinger of right **'ONE'** hand, with palm facing leftward/backward, is drawn firmly backward across back of left **'STANDARD BASE'** hand. (The location of this sign will vary according to which part of the body has been affected.)

(a) lack of: *n.* a shortage of (something that is required or desired); not enough. *Due to a lack of funds, he had to withdraw from Gallaudet University.*

SIGN: Thumb of right **'EXTENDED A'** hand, palm facing left, is placed under the chin and is flicked forward firmly. Next, horizontal left **'S'** hand is held in a fixed position with palm facing right. Horizontal right **'EXTENDED B'** hand is held palm down with fingers pointing forward/leftward and is brushed forward/rightward a couple of times across the top of the left hand. (ASL CONCEPT—**not - enough.**)

lad: *n.* a boy; young man. *The lad is only ten years old.*

SIGN: Right **'FLAT C'** hand is held in front of forehead, with palm facing left, and is closed twice into a **'FLAT O'** hand.
REGIONAL VARIATION—**boy** #2

ladder: *n.* a device with rungs for climbing up or down. *He fell off the ladder and broke his leg.*

SIGN: Vertical right **'CROOKED C'** hand is held, palm forward, in front of the right side of the upper chest, or higher, and as it is moved in an upward/forward arc, it closes to form an **'S'** shape as if grabbing hold of the next rung of a ladder. At this point, the vertical left **'CROOKED C'** hand is held out in front of the left side of the body and repeats the same action that the right hand has just taken. The hands continue to alternate in this way to simulate the climbing of a ladder.

lady: *n.* a woman, especially one who is considered refined. *I sat by the lady on the bench.*

SIGN: Thumbtip of vertical right **'A'** hand, palm left, is placed on chin and as it is lowered to mid-chest, the hand opens out to assume a **'5'** shape.
ALTERNATE SIGN—**woman** #1

lag: *v.* to fall behind. *Sometimes an interpreter lags behind the speaker.*

SIGN: Horizontal **'EXTENDED A'** hands are held together and palms facing each other. Right hand is then moved backward in a slight arc. (See also **jet lag.**)

laid-back: *adj.* relaxed; easy-going. *He will not mind because he is a laid-back person.*

SIGN: **'EXTENDED B'** hands are held parallel with palms down and fingers pointing forward. The forearms are simultaneously lowered a short distance, then moved rightward in an arc formation, and back to their original position in a leftward arc.

(be) laid up: *v.* a colloquial expression meaning to be incapacitated due to illness or injury. *He has been laid up for several weeks with a sore back.*

SIGN: **'V'** hands are held, left in front of right, in a semi-vertical position with extended fingers pointing forward/upward at a slight leftward angle as left palm faces right and right palm faces left. As the head turns to the right, the hands are simultaneously jerked backward/rightward to an entirely upright position and the extended fingers retract to form **'CLAWED V'** hands. (This sign may begin and end with **'CLAWED V'** hands; alternatively, it may begin and end with **'V'** hands.)

lake: *n.* a large inland body of water. *We went to the lake for our summer vacation.*

SIGN: Fingerspell **LAKE**.

lamb: *n.* a young sheep. *The ewe and her lamb are in the shed.*

SIGN: Fingers of palm-up right **'BENT EXTENDED B'** hand point leftward as they rest on rightward-pointing fingers of palm-up left **'BENT EXTENDED B'** hand. The arms are simultaneously moved from side to side as if rocking a baby in one's arms. Next, right **'K'** hand, palm facing the body, is held in the crook of the left arm and circled twice in a clockwise direction. (ASL CONCEPT—**baby - sheep.**) Alternatively, **LAMB** may be fingerspelled, and is always fingerspelled when it refers to a kind of *meat*.

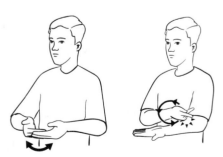

lame: *adj.* disabled or crippled in the legs or feet causing one to limp. *People who are lame often use canes.*

SIGN: **'BENT ONE'** hands, held apart with palms down and forefingers pointing downward, are alternately raised and lowered.

lamp: *n.* a device that produces light. *That lamp needs a new bulb.*

SIGN: Right **'MODIFIED O'** hand is held out to the right side of the body with palm down. The fingers then open to form a **'CONTRACTED 5'** hand. (**LAMP** is frequently fingerspelled.)

land: *n.* ground. *With the increase in the price of land, fewer people are attracted to farming.*

SIGN #1: **'FLAT O'** hands are held slightly apart with palms up. Then the fingers are slid across the thumbs a few times, thus alternating between **'FLAT O'** and **'OFFSET O'** hands.

land: *v.* to come down to earth after a flight. *We stood on the observation deck and watched his plane land.*

SIGN #2: Left **'EXTENDED B'** hand is held in a fixed position with palm up and fingers pointing forward/rightward. Right **'COMBINED LY'** hand is held with palm forward/leftward at a downward angle. The right forearm is then lowered in a forward/leftward direction, so that it lands palm-down on the left palm. (Signs vary according to 'what/who' is landing and 'how' they are landing.) When the emphasis is on the 'arrival of an airplane' rather than the 'descent and landing', **arrive** may be used: *My father's plane will land at 9:15 this evening.*

landing strip: *n.* a hard, level roadway where aircraft take off and land. *Every Arctic community has a landing strip for planes and helicopters.*

SIGN: **'EXTENDED B'** hands, held parallel with palms facing one another and fingers pointing forward, are simultaneously moved forward.

landlord *(male)***/landlady** *(female)*: *n.* a person who owns and rents houses, property, etc. to someone else. *The landlady decided to increase our rent after painting our apartment.*

SIGN: Horizontal **'L'** hand appears to bounce as it is placed palm down with forefinger pointing forward and then moved upward/rightward in a slight arc. (It is as if the signer is fingerspelling **LL** to someone on the floor rather than someone directly in front of him/her.)

language: *n.* a system for communicating one's thoughts and/or feelings. *ASL is the native* **language** *of Deaf people.*

SIGN: **'L'** hands are held palms down with forefingers pointing forward and thumbtips touching each other. The hands are then drawn apart.
ALTERNATE SIGN—**sentence** #1

lantern: *n.* a light enclosed in a transparent case. *Do not forget to pack the* **lantern** *for our camping trip.*

SIGN: Left **'S'** hand is held palm down while the right **'CONTRACTED 5'** hand, palm down, is held beneath it and swung back and forth a few times. (**LANTERN** may be fingerspelled.)

lap: *n.* the area formed by the front of the thighs of a seated person. *The little girl likes to sit on her grandmother's* **lap.**

SIGN #1: **'EXTENDED B'** hands, palms down and fingers pointing forward, are tapped against the thighs a couple of times.

lap: *n.* one complete circuit of a racetrack. *The runners were on the last* **lap** *of the race.*

SIGN #2: Vertical right **'ONE'** hand, palm facing the body, is moved in an oval circuit in what appears to the signer to be a counter-clockwise direction.

lap: *v.* to take a drink by dipping the tongue into a liquid and scooping it into the mouth. *The dog always gets the floor wet when he* **laps** *up water from his dish after a long walk.*

SIGN #3: Left **'EXTENDED B'** hand is held in a fixed position with palm up and fingers pointing rightward/forward. The extended fingers of the right **'BENT EXTENDED U'** hand, palm down, represent a 'lapping' tongue as they brush forward several times against the left palm. Meanwhile, the signer's tongue is visible as it appears to be 'lapping' too.

lapse: *v.* to be discontinued or expire due to failure or negligence. *My newspaper subscription has* **lapsed.**

SIGN: Vertical **'5'** hands, palms facing the body, are held at chest level, and swung outward, away from the body so that the palms face down. (**Lapse** can have various meanings.)

laptop: *n.* a small portable computer. *He works on his* **laptop** *when travelling for his business.*

SIGN: Left **'EXTENDED B'** hand is held in a fixed position with palm facing the body at an upward angle and fingers pointing rightward while the right **'EXTENDED B'** hand is held directly on top of the left hand with palm down and fingers pointing leftward. The two hands appear to be hinged at the front as the right wrist rotates forward to flip the right hand up so that the palm faces the body but the front edge of the hand maintains contact with the front edge of the left hand. Motion is repeated. (**LAPTOP** may be fingerspelled.)

large: *adj.* big. *The new community centre is* **large.**

SIGN #1: Horizontal **'CLAWED L'** hands, which are held slightly apart with palms facing, are simultaneously moved farther apart as the wrists rotate to turn the palms down. The signer's lips appear to be articulating the syllable 'CHA'.

large: *adj.* big in terms of the height (of something such as a drink). *I will have a hamburger and a* **large** *root beer.*

SIGN #2: Left **'BENT EXTENDED B'** hand is held in a fixed position with palm up. Vertical right **'BENT EXTENDED B'** hand, palm left and fingers pointing left, is held above left hand at a distance which indicates the height of the object under discussion. The hands are then simultaneously moved firmly forward a very short distance. The signer's lips appear to be articulating the syllable 'CHA'.

large: *adj.* big in terms of clothing size. *He asked the sales clerk for this shirt in* **large.**

SIGN #3: Vertical right **'L'** hand, palm facing forward, appears to wobble slightly. This is a wrist movement. For **extra large**, fingerspell **XL**.

lash: *v.* to strike with a whip or rope. *In most countries it is now forbidden to* **lash** *prisoners.*

SIGN: Right **'CLOSED A-INDEX'** hand is forcefully drawn diagonally downward to the left, then up and diagonally downward to the right in an **'X'** pattern as if actually lashing someone.

last: *adj.* final; with no others coming afterward. *This will be your **last** warning before you are punished.*

SIGN #1: Horizontal left **'I'** (or **'ONE'**) hand is held with palm facing the body at a rightward angle and little finger pointing forward/rightward. Vertical right **'I'** hand, with palm facing leftward/backward, is held to the right of and above the left hand. The right hand is then lowered so that the tip of the little finger strikes the tip of the little finger of the left hand.

last: *v.* to continue; go on. *I wish that summer would **last** forever.*

SIGN #2: **'EXTENDED A'** hands are held side by side with palms down and right thumbtip pressing against left thumbnail as the hands are moved purposefully forward.
SAME SIGN—**lasting,** *adj.*

late: *adv.* happening or arriving after the correct time. *Some people have a habit of arriving **late** for their appointments.*

SIGN #1: Right **'EXTENDED B'** hand is held to the right side of the body with fingertips pointing downward and palm facing backward. Fingers simultaneously move back and forth. (**LATE** is frequently fingerspelled.)

(too) late: *adj.* happening or arriving after something unfortunate has occurred, or an opportunity has been missed. *The doctors tried to save the accident victim but it was **too late**.*

SIGN #2: Right **'EXTENDED B'** hand is held to the right side of the body with fingertips pointing forward and palm down. The wrist then bends firmly downward so that the fingers point down and the palm faces backward.

late: *adj.* referring to someone who has died, especially recently. *A memorial service was held for the **late** president.*

SIGN #3: **'EXTENDED B'** hands are held with fingers pointing forward, left palm facing up and right palm facing down. Then they are flipped over simultaneously so that the palm positions are reversed.

lately: *adv.* recently. *The new parents have not been to the movies **lately**.*

SIGN: Tips of forefingers of **'BENT ONE'** hands, palms facing the body, are placed slightly apart on the right shoulder. The hands then drop forward/downward from the wrists so that the palms are facing upward and the forefingers are pointing forward/upward.
ALTERNATE SIGN—**recent**

later: *adv.* afterward; after a while; subsequently. *We will go shopping **later**.*

SIGN #1: Vertical right **'L'** hand, palm facing left, is held at about shoulder height. The hand then drops so that the forefinger points forward.

later: *adv.* the comparative form of **late**, but indicating a lengthy period of time in subsequent weeks, months or years. *This project will begin **later** in our 5-year plan.*

SIGN #2: Horizontal right **'BENT EXTENDED B'** hand, palm left, is held just in front of the right shoulder and is moved forward. The distance of the movement indicates the length of time involved.

Latin: *n.* the language of ancient Rome. *Many words in the English language originally come from **Latin**.*

SIGN: Tips of extended fingers of right **'N'** hand, palm toward the face, are placed in the middle of the forehead and are drawn down to the nose. (**LATIN** may be fingerspelled.)

latitude: *n.* the distance of a certain place from the equator. *We learned about the imaginary lines of **latitude** today in social studies class.*

SIGN: Horizontal right **'4'** hand, palm facing the body is held out in front of the left side of the body and is moved rightward in an arc formation (bowing forward slightly). Alternatively, this sign may be preceded by the sign for **globe**. When referring to one specific latitudinal line, the sign shown here is made using a **'BENT ONE'** hand. To point out a certain place along that line, the signer might first draw the line with the forefinger of the **'BENT ONE'** hand and then point to the exact location along the line.

latter: *adj.* the second of two things mentioned. *Baseball and hockey have little in common. The former is essentially a summer sport while the **latter** is a winter sport.*

SIGN: Left **'V'** hand is held with palm facing the body and extended fingers pointing rightward/upward while the tip of the forefinger of the right **'ONE'** hand is tapped a couple of times against the tip of the left midfinger. (Sometimes **latter** means 'more recent' or 'nearer the end', in which case this sign would be inappropriate.)

375

laugh: *v.* to express amusement through facial expression and short bursts of voiced noise. *The clown made the children* **laugh**.

SIGN #1: **'L'** hands are held with palms backwards and tips of forefingers at either side of the mouth. The forefingers are then simultaneously stroked backward/downward so that the hands alternate between **'L'** and **'BENT L'** shapes. A look of merriment accompanies this sign. Signs may vary considerably. See also **rolling in the aisles**.
SAME SIGN—**laughter**, *n.*

OR

SIGN #2: Vertical right **'CLAWED 5'** hand, palm toward the body, is waved from side to side a few times in front of the mouth. (This sign involves movement of the forearm, not just the hand.) Alternatively, both hands may be used, the left in front of the right.

launch: *v.* to start off; set in motion. *We are ready to* **launch** *our annual fundraising drive.*

SIGN #1: Left **'5'** hand is held with palm facing right while forefinger of right **'ONE'** hand is inserted between first two fingers of left hand and twisted 180 degrees either to the right or left.
ALTERNATE SIGN—**go ahead**

launch: *v.* to set a missile or spacecraft into motion. *They will* **launch** *the rocket tomorrow.*

SIGN #2: Heel of vertical right **'R'** hand, palm forward, rests on the back of the left **'STANDARD BASE'** hand. Then the right hand is pushed upward firmly. (Signs vary according to 'what' is being launched and 'how' it is being launched.)

launder: *v.* to wash clothes and/or household linens. *I should* **launder** *my gym clothes before I wear them again.*

SIGN: **'SPREAD C'** hands, palms facing, are held apart with the right above the left and are simultaneously twisted back and forth (from the wrists) in opposite directions. To specify that the laundering is done by hand, **'A'** hands, left palm facing up and right palm facing down, are rubbed together.
SAME SIGN—**laundry**, *n.*

lavatory: *n.* a room with toilet facilities. *A public* **lavatory** *is often hard to find in Europe.*

SIGN: Vertical right **'T'** hand is held with palm forward and is jiggled from side to side.

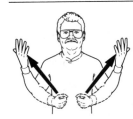

lavish: *adj.* extravagantly generous; wasteful. *Many politicians are eligible for* **lavish** *pensions when they retire from government.*

SIGN: **'S'** hands are held, one at either hip, with palms up. The hands are then flung simultaneously upward/outward as they open to form **'CROOKED 5'** hands.

law: *n.* an enforceable rule or set of rules established by authority. *The* **law** *clearly states that seatbelts must be worn.*

SIGN: Vertical left **'EXTENDED B'** hand is held in a fixed position with palm facing right. Right **'L'** hand, palm facing left, is placed against the fingers of the left hand and then lowered to the heel of the left hand. **LAW** may be fingerspelled for emphasis.
SAME SIGN—**lawyer**, *n.*, and may be followed by the Agent Ending (see p. LIV).

lawn: *n.* an area of mown grass, especially around a house. *We had a picnic on the* **lawn**.

SIGN: Back of right **'CROOKED 4'** hand, palm down, is held under the chin and the hand is moved briskly in small circular motions, brushing backward against the underside of the chin with each cycle.
ALTERNATE SIGN—**grass** #2
GRASS may be fingerspelled.

lawn mower: *n.* a machine for cutting grass. *The* **lawn mower** *has run out of gas.*

SIGN: **'S'** hands are held parallel with palms down and are simultaneously pushed forward a couple of times. (To refer to a **riding mower**, the signer would use **'S'** hands to grip and steer an imaginary steering wheel.)

laxative: *n.* medication that relieves constipation. *If you are constipated, perhaps you should take a* **laxative**.

SIGN: Tip of middle finger of right **'BENT MIDFINGER 5'** hand is placed on the upturned left palm, and maintains contact with the left palm as the right hand teeters back and forth a few times. Next, horizontal left **'S'** hand is held in a fixed position with palm facing right and enclosing thumb of horizontal right **'5'** (or **'EXTENDED A'**) hand, of which the palm faces left. Then the right hand is pulled down sharply. (ASL CONCEPT—**medicine - constipation**.)

lay: *v.* to set (something) down. *Lay the baby on the bed and I will change his diaper.*

SIGN: **'BENT EXTENDED B'** hands are held parallel with palms up in front of the right side of the body and are simultaneously moved leftward/downward as if setting something down. (Signs vary according to *what* is being laid and *how* it is being laid.) ❖

lay eggs: *v.* to produce and set down eggs. *The mother bird will lay her eggs in this nest.*

SIGN: **'BENT U'** hands, palms toward the body, are held in a horizontal position in front of the chest so that the side of the right mid-finger lies across the side of the left forefinger. Then the hands are curved downward away from each other so that the extended fingers point downward. Motion is repeated.

layer: *n.* a single thickness or coating of a substance on a surface. *There was a thick layer of dust on all the furniture.*

SIGN: Right **'MODIFIED G'** hand, palm downward/forward, is placed on the back of the left **'STANDARD BASE'** hand and moved rightward toward the fingertips.

lay off: *v.* to impose a period of unemployment. *The company will lay off several workers because business has been so slow.*

SIGN: Left **'EXTENDED B'** hand is held in a fixed position with palm up and fingers pointing forward/rightward. Right **'EXTENDED B'** hand is held on the left palm with fingers pointing forward/leftward and palm facing backward/leftward. The right wrist then rotates in a counter-clockwise direction, thus turning the palm downward as the hand moves forward/rightward off the end of the left hand.

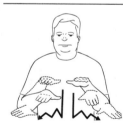

layout: *n.* the way that pictures and text are arranged on a page. *He works on the layout of the newspaper.*

SIGN: **'EXTENDED B'** hands are held apart with palms down and fingers pointing forward. The hands move about as they are alternately raised and lowered a few times.

lazy: *adj.* sluggish; not eager or willing to work. *I feel lazy today.*

SIGN: Right **'L'** hand, palm toward the body, is tapped a couple of times against the left side of the chest, near the shoulder.
SAME SIGN—**laziness**, *n.*

lead: *v.* to guide; show the way. *He will lead us to the farm.*

SIGN #1: Left **'EXTENDED B'** hand is held with fingers pointing forward/rightward and palm facing right but angled toward the body. The fingertips of the left hand are grasped between the fingers and the heel of the right **'OPEN A'** (or **'F'**) hand. Then the right hand draws the left hand forward/rightward.
SAME SIGN—**leader**, *n.*, and may be followed by the Agent Ending (see p. LIV).

lead: *n.* a metallic element. *Lead is a very heavy, dense metal.*

SIGN #2: Fingerspell **LEAD**.

L E A D

leaf: *n.* one unit of a plant's foliage. *The students collected some leaves and identified them for their science projects.*

SIGN: Right **'5'** hand, bent at the wrist with the palm facing down, is waved from side to side as the tip of the forefinger of the left **'ONE'** hand touches the right wrist. (**LEAF** may be fingerspelled.)

leaflet: *n.* a printed page (usually folded) for distribution; flyer. *We distributed leaflets about the upcoming event.*

SIGN: Thumb and forefinger of right **'A-INDEX'** (or **'MODIFIED G'**) hand are slid up the edge of the left **'EXTENDED B'** hand, which is held with palm facing body. Motion is repeated.

league: *n.* a group united to promote the interests of its members; an association of sports clubs which compete mainly against each other. *He joined the soccer league last summer.*

SIGN: Fingerspell **LEAGUE**.

L E A G U E

leak: *v.* to get out through a small space (said of a liquid substance). *My car is leaking oil.*

SIGN: Horizontal right **'4'** hand, palm left and fingers pointing forward, is held just under left **'STANDARD BASE'** hand near the fingertips and moves downward several times. This is a wrist movement. **LEAK** may also be finger-spelled.
ALTERNATE SIGN—**drip**

lean: *adj.* having no extra fat. *Regular exercise will keep you lean and fit.*

SIGN: Vertical **'EXTENDED B'** hands are held against the upper chest with palms facing and are simultaneously lowered. The signer's mouth is opened ever so slightly to allow a stream of air to escape. (**LEAN** is fingerspelled when it refers to a cut of *meat*.)

lean against: *v.* to rest against (something), often in an inclined position. *After running two laps, I had to lean against the wall until I caught my breath.*

SIGN: Vertical left **'EXTENDED B'** is held in a fixed position with palm facing right. Right **'BENT U'** hand, palm down, is propped against the left palm. (Signs for **lean** vary according to 'what/who' is leaning against 'what/whom' and at 'what' angle.)

leap: *v.* to jump forward. *The actor will leap off the stage at the end of Act One.*

SIGN: Right **'CLAWED V'** hand is held palm down on the back of the left **'STANDARD BASE'** hand and is then arched upward and forward off the left hand. (See **jump** for **leap** meaning to jump *straight upward*.)

learn: *v.* to gain knowledge; acquire skills. *To learn ASL, you should practise with Deaf friends.*

SIGN #1: Left **'EXTENDED B'** hand is held in a fixed position with palm up and fingers pointing forward/rightward. Fingertips of right **'CONTRACTED 5'** hand, palm down, are placed on the left palm. Then the right hand is changed to a **'FLAT O'** handshape as it is raised.

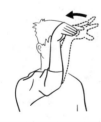

SIGN #2 [ATLANTIC]: Right **'CONTRACTED 5'** hand is held palm down a short distance from the middle of the forehead and is drawn back toward the forehead as the fingers close to form a **'FLAT O'** handshape.

lease: *n.* a contract that provides rental privileges for a period of time. *Most tenants are required to sign a one-year lease.*

SIGN: Fingerspell **LEASE**. (When used as a verb, **LEASE** is fingerspelled also.)

leash: *n.* a cord or chain used to control a dog or other animal. *A city by-law requires that every dog in any city park must be kept on a leash.*

SIGN: Right **'CLOSED A-INDEX'** hand is held palm down by the right side of the neck and is drawn straight rightward/upward.

least: *adj.* the smallest amount, number or quantity. *Which beaker contains the least liquid?*

SIGN #1: Horizontal **'BENT EXTENDED B'** (or **'ONE'**) hands are held right above left with left palm up and right palm forward/downward. The right hand is then lowered toward the left hand. (Signs may vary considerably.)

least: *adj.* the smallest in importance; slightest. *She gets upset over the least thing.*

SIGN #2: Tip of forefinger of the right **'COVERED T'** hand, palm toward the face, is held in front of the nose and the thumb is flicked out, thus forming an **'A-INDEX'** hand. ALTERNATE SIGN—**nothing** #2

(at) least: *adv.* a minimum of; this much or more. *You will earn at least $20 per hour at this job.*

SIGN #3: Left **'EXTENDED B'** hand is held palm-down, with fingertips pointing right. Fingertips of right palm-down **'EXTENDED B'** hand rest on and at right angles to back of left hand and are then moved upward from the wrist.

(at) least: *adv.* in any case. *I know we failed, but at least we tried.*

SIGN #4: Vertical **'F'** hands, palms facing forward, are held apart, then brought together so the joined thumbs and forefingers touch each other.

leather: *n.* the skin of an animal made smooth by tanning. *His jacket was made of leather.*

SIGN: Vertical right **'A-INDEX'** hand, palm facing left, quivers as thumb and forefinger are used to grasp skin of right cheek. (**LEATHER** is frequently fingerspelled.)

leave: *v.* to depart from; go out of; go away from. *We will be leaving Windsor at noon.*

SIGN #1: **'EXTENDED B'** hands are held parallel with palms down and fingers pointing forward/rightward. The hands are then drawn simultaneously leftward/backward as they change to **'A'** (or **'EXTENDED A'**) hands.

leave: *v.* to cause to remain behind; to go away without taking; abandon. *Leave your books on your desk when you are finished.*

SIGN #2: **'5'** hands are thrust forward to the left and down from shoulder level, palms facing each other.

leave out: *v.* to omit; exclude. *Please check this list to make sure I did not leave out anyone's name.*

SIGN: Right **'CONTRACTED 5'** hand, palm up, becomes a **'FLAT O'** hand as it is drawn downward behind the horizontal left **'CROOKED 5'** hand of which the palm is facing the body. ALTERNATE SIGNS—**miss** #2 & #3

lecture: *n.* an informative talk given to an audience on a particular subject. *The lecture was about Deaf Culture.*

SIGN: Right arm is raised and the vertical **'EXTENDED B'** hand, palm facing left, is brought forward sharply from the wrist a couple of times. (This sign is also used for **lecture**, *v.,* or **to give a lecture**.) For **lecture**, meaning 'a lengthy scolding', see **preach**.

leech: *n.* a worm that sucks blood and tissues from other animals. *Long ago, doctors would use a leech to draw blood from a patient.*

SIGN #1: Fingerspell **LEECH**.

leech: *n.* a person who clings to or takes advantage of another. *Because he habitually depends on me to lend him money, he is becoming a real leech.*

SIGN #2: Left **'BENT U'** hand is held in a fixed position with palm down and extended fingers pointing rightward/forward. Vertical right **'CONTRACTED 3'** hand is held above the level of the right shoulder with palm forward and is purposefully lowered so that the extended fingers and thumb snap shut on the extended fingers of the left hand.

left: *adj.* opposite to right. *I need to replace my left headlight.*

SIGN #1: Vertical left **'L'** hand, palm forward, is held out to the left and shaken lightly. (This sign is also used for the adverbial phrase 'on the left'.) For **left** meaning the past tense of **leave**, see **leave** #1 & #2.

(turn) left: *v.* to move in a direction that is opposite to rightward. *Turn left at the next set of traffic lights.*

SIGN #2: Vertical left **'EXTENDED B'** (or **'L'**) hand is held with palm facing right. The wrist then rotates to turn the palm forward as the hand curves leftward.

left-handed: *adj.* able to use the left hand with more ease and skill than the right hand. *Left-handed people are sometimes called "southpaws".*

SIGN: Vertical left **'L'** hand, palm forward, is held out to the left and shaken lightly.

leftover: *adj.* left unused. *I will use the leftover roast to make a shepherd's pie.*

SIGN: Horizontal **'5'** hands are held apart with palms facing each other. The forearms are then simultaneously lowered.

leg: *n.* one of the lower limbs of the body. *He broke his leg in a skiing mishap.*

SIGN: Fingerspell **LEG**.

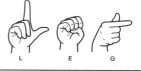

legal: *adj.* relating to the law profession. *The lawyer will take care of all legal matters.*

SIGN #1: Vertical left **'EXTENDED B'** hand is held in a fixed position with palm facing right. Right **'L'** hand, palm facing left, is placed against the fingers of the left hand and then lowered to the heel of the left hand. **LEGAL** may also be fingerspelled. ALTERNATE SIGN—**attorney** #2

legal: *adj.* permitted by law. *It is legal to ride a motorcycle without a helmet in some U.S. states.*

SIGN #2: **'K'** hands, palms down, are held apart, extended fingers pointing downward, and are then flicked upward from the wrists so that the hands are held in either a horizontal or upright position.

legend: *n.* a popular story handed down from earlier times. *Nobody knows where the legend originated, but it has been retold by many generations of the tribe.*

SIGN: Left **'CONTRACTED C'** (or **'OPEN 8'**) hand is held horizontally with palm facing right while right **'CONTRACTED C'** (or **'OPEN 8'**) hand is held upright with palm facing left. The hands are held close enough together to be loosely interlocked. They are then drawn apart, closed and returned several times, thus alternating between **'CONTRACTED C'** (or **'OPEN 8'**) and **'FLAT O'** (or **'8'**) shapes with each movement. (**LEGEND** is frequently finger-spelled.) For **legendary**, *adj.*, see **famous**.

legible: *adj.* easy to read. *Her handwriting is always very legible.*

SIGN: Left **'BENT EXTENDED B'** hand is held in a fixed position with palm up. Palm of horizontal right **'EXTENDED B'** (or **'BENT EXTENDED B'**) hand faces left but is slanted slightly upward and toward the body as the fingers are brushed upward against the backs of the fingers of the left hand at least twice in a small circular motion. Next, horizontal left **'EXTENDED B'** hand is held in a fixed position with palm rightward but slanted slightly toward the body while the fingers point rightward/forward. Right **'V'** hand, palm forward, bends from the wrist, causing the tips of the extended fingers to brush downward against the left palm. (ASL CONCEPT—**easy - read**.)

legislature: *n.* a group of persons with the power to make laws. *The members of the legislature voted unanimously to repeal the law.*

SIGN: Vertical right **'L'** hand is held with palm facing left and thumbtip touching the upper chest just under the left shoulder. The forearm then moves forward/rightward in a slight arc formation ending up with the thumbtip just under the right shoulder.

legitimate: *adj.* genuine; authentic; conforming to established standards of usage and acceptable principles of reasoning; legal; authorized by law. *ASL is accepted as a legitimate language.*

SIGN: Forefinger of vertical right **'ONE'** hand, palm facing left, is held against the lips and the hand is moved sharply forward.

leisure: *adj.* related to free time for rest and relaxation. *He likes to garden during his leisure time.*

SIGN: **'EXTENDED B'** hands, palms toward the body, are crossed at the wrists and are then placed on the chest.
ALTERNATE SIGN—**enjoy**

lemon: *n.* the yellowish citrus fruit of a small tree grown in tropical regions. *The recipe calls for the juice and rind of one lemon.*

SIGN #1: Thumbtip of vertical right **'L'** hand, palm facing left, is tapped at least twice against the middle of the chin.

OR

SIGN #2: Vertical right **'MODIFIED Y'** hand, palm facing left, is positioned with thumbtip in the centre of the chin as the hand wobbles slightly. This is a wrist movement.

lend: *v.* to permit the use of something with the expectation that it will be returned. *Do not worry, I will lend you my notes.*

SIGN: Vertical **'K'** (or **'V'**) hands are held close to the chest, the left directly in front of the right, left palm facing right and right palm facing left. Together the hands drop forward to a horizontal position. ❖

length: *n.* the measurement of something from end to end. *The length of our front walk is about 20 metres.*

SIGN: Left **'BENT ONE'** hand is held in a fixed position with palm down and forefinger pointing downward at a slight forward angle. Right **'BENT ONE'** hand is held with palm down and tip of downward-pointing forefinger touching tip of left forefinger. The right hand is then moved directly forward.
ALTERNATE SIGN—**long** #1, especially when referring to the duration of time.

lenient: *adj.* not strict; merciful. *He is a lenient father but his wife is a strong disciplinarian.*

SIGN #1: Right **'EXTENDED A'** hand, palm facing left, thumb under chin, is thrust forward. The hand then assumes a **'CLAWED V'** shape and is brought upward to an upright position with palm facing left and side of forefinger held against the bridge of the nose.
(ASL CONCEPT—**not - strict**.)

OR

SIGN #2: Vertical **'F'** hands, palms forward, are held slightly apart and simultaneously shaken from the wrists. (Appropriate facial expression is important.)

lens: *n.* a piece of glass that allows light to enter a camera. *The photographer needs a special lens for his new camera.*

SIGN #1: Vertical **'C'** hands are held together in front of the face, right hand in front of left, left palm facing right and right palm facing left. The left hand generally remains fixed as the right wrist alternately bends and straightens a couple of times to turn the palm downward, then leftward again.

lens: *n.* the glass or plastic part of a pair of glasses through which the wearer looks. *I need a new lens for my glasses.*

SIGN #2: Fingerspell **LENS**.

L E N S

lesbian: *n.* a female homosexual. *Some of history's most creative women have been lesbians.*

SIGN: Tip of forefinger of horizontal right **'L'** hand, palm backward, is tapped on the chin.

less: *adv.* a comparative form of little; not so much. *If you ate less, maybe you would lose some weight.*

SIGN #1: Horizontal **'BENT EXTENDED B'** hands are held right above left with left palm up and right palm forward/downward. The right hand is then lowered toward the left hand.

less than: *adv.* not as much as. *He earns less than $40,000 per year.*

SIGN #2: Left **'EXTENDED B'** hand, palm down and fingers pointing rightward, is placed on the fingers of the right **'EXTENDED B'** hand of which the palm faces downward and the fingers point forward. The right hand is then moved sharply downward from the wrist.

-less: *suffix* without; having no; unable to. *I have had many sleepless nights since my husband has been on the racing circuit.*

SIGN #3: Sign choice for the suffix **-less** depends entirely on context. For two possibilities, see **no** #2 and **cannot**. Sometimes there is no specific sign accorded this suffix. Instead it is incorporated in the base or root word to which it is attached, as in **careless**.

lesson: *n.* a unit of instruction in a subject. *Our lesson for today is based on Chapter Two.*

SIGN: Left **'EXTENDED B'** hand is held in a fixed position with palm up and fingers pointing rightward/forward. Horizontal right **'BENT EXTENDED B'** hand, with palm facing left, is placed on the fingers of the left hand, then raised, moved backward, and placed on the heel of the left hand.

lest: *conj.* to prevent the possibility that. *Lest we forget, we set aside a day each year to honour the soldiers who fought in World Wars I and II.*

SIGN: Tips of thumbs of horizontal **'MODIFIED 5'** hands, held with palms facing down but slightly tilted toward the body, are poked twice into either side of upper chest near shoulders.

let: *v.* to allow; give permission to. *The doctor will not let her leave the hospital until Thursday.* (ESL USERS: Although **allow**, *v.*, and **permit**, *v.*, are often followed by the word **to**, **let**, *v.*, may not be followed by **to**; e.g., *Allow me to help you. Permit me to help you. Let me help you.*)

SIGN: Horizontal **'EXTENDED B'** hands are held with palms facing and fingers pointing forward. The hands are then swept upward simultaneously from the wrists so that the fingers point upward.
ALTERNATE SIGN—**permit** #1

let go: *v.* to release; set free. *I hope they will let the falcon go today.*

SIGN: **'CROOKED 5'** hands are held parallel with palms toward the body and fingers pointing downward. The hands are then flipped up so that the palms face downward. This is a wrist action. (**Let go** can have various connotations in English and sign choice depends on the context.)

lethal: *adj.* capable of causing death. *Taking an overdose of that medication could be lethal.*

SIGN: **'A'** hands, palms down, are held slightly apart, and are then firmly pushed downward. Next, **'EXTENDED B'** hands are held with fingers pointing forward, left palm facing up and right palm facing down. Then they are flipped over simultaneously so that the palm positions are reversed. (ASL CONCEPT—can - die.) The sample sentence in ASL is: *MEDICINE TOO-MUCH CAN DIE.* When referring to a **lethal** weapon, the sign **dangerous** is used.

lethargic: *adj.* sluggish; lacking in energy. *He was lethargic after taking the medicine.*

SIGN: Right **'L'** hand, palm toward the body, is tapped against the left side of the chest, near the shoulder. Next, **'CROOKED 5'** hands are held parallel with fingers pointing downward and palms facing downward but slanted toward the body. The hands simultaneously move in a slow counter-clockwise circle while the face appears lifeless and the tongue protrudes slightly. (ASL CONCEPT—lazy - no energy.)
SAME SIGN—**lethargy**, *n.*

letter: *n.* a written or printed message, usually sent through the mail. *A copy of this letter will be sent to your employer.*

SIGN #1: Left **'EXTENDED B'** hand is held in a fixed position with palm facing backward/rightward and fingers pointing rightward/forward. Right **'EXTENDED A'** hand begins with palm toward the body and thumbtip on the lips, and is then lowered as the wrist twists to turn the palm down and the thumbtip is pressed into the left palm.

SIGN #2 [ONTARIO]: **'L'** hands, palms forward, are tapped together a couple of times so that the thumbtips touch.

letter: *n.* a character of the alphabet. *K is the 11th letter of the alphabet.*

SIGN #3: Fingerspell **LETTER**. (**Letter** in this context may be signed, but is generally signed as an ASL phrase rather than a single sign. See **alphabet**.)

(lower case) letter: *n.* a small letter as opposed to a capital letter. *This word should begin with a lower case letter.*

SIGN #4: Right **'MODIFIED G'** hand, palm forward, is moved very slightly forward. The signer's lips are pursed. (To indicate that all the letters are lower case, the sign is moved rightward.)

(upper case) letter: *n.* a capital letter. *The name of a city always begins with an upper case letter.*

SIGN #5: Right **'C-INDEX'** hand is held upright with palm facing forward at a slight leftward angle, and is moved very slightly forward. (To indicate that all the letters are capitalized, vertical right **'C-INDEX'** hand is held in front of the left side of the body with palm forward at a slight leftward angle, and is moved straight rightward.)

lettuce: *n.* a plant grown for its large, edible leaves. *Romaine is the best type of lettuce to use in a Caesar salad.*

SIGN: Fingerspell **LETTUCE**.

level: *n.* stage; degree of progress. *I am now taking the beginners' level.*

SIGN #1: Vertical **'BENT EXTENDED B'** hands, palms facing each other and fingertips touching, are drawn apart.

level: *adj.* flat; on a horizontal plane. *The ground is quite level here.*

SIGN #2: Vertical **'BENT EXTENDED B'** hands are held together, right in front of left, close to the chest with the right palm facing left and the left palm facing right. The left hand remains fixed while the right hand moves directly forward.

level with: *v.* to be frank and straightforward. *If you have any doubts about my plan, please level with me.*

SIGN: Vertical right **'B'** hand, palm facing left, is held directly in front of the face and thrust forward and slightly downward.

liable: *adj.* legally responsible. *You will be held liable for all the damages.*

SIGN: Fingertips of both **'BENT EXTENDED B'** hands, palms facing the body, are placed on right shoulder. Shoulder is pushed slightly downward to signify the bearing of a burden. SAME SIGN—**liability**, *n.*

liaison: *n.* communication or close contact between groups. *Liaison between provincial and national organizations is important.*

SIGN: **'F'** hands, with thumbs and forefingers linked, are moved from side to side a couple of times.

liberal: *adj.* broad-minded. *I admire my grandfather because he is so liberal compared with others of his generation.*

SIGN: Fingertips of **'B'** (or **'EXTENDED B'**) hands come together in front of forehead and are swung outward so that the palms face mainly forward. (**Liberal** has a variety of meanings in English.)

liberate: *v.* to set free; release. *I hope they will liberate the hostages soon.*

SIGN: **'CROOKED 5'** hands are held parallel with palms toward the body and fingers pointing downward. The hands are then flipped up so that the palms face downward. This is a wrist action. Next, **'F'** hands, left palm facing right and right palm facing left, are held upright with right hand directly behind left hand. Then they are drawn apart as wrists rotate outward so that left palm faces rightward/forward while right palm faces leftward/forward. (ASL CONCEPT—**let go - free**.)

liberty: *n.* freedom. *We value our liberty very highly.*

SIGN: **'F'** hands, left palm facing right and right palm facing left, are held upright with right hand directly behind left hand. Then they are drawn apart as wrists rotate outward so that left palm faces rightward/forward while right palm faces leftward/forward.

library: *n.* a place where a collection of literary materials is kept for loan and reference. *The books must be returned to the library by Friday.*

SIGN: Vertical right **'L'** hand, palm forward/leftward, is held in front of the right shoulder and is circled clockwise.

licence [*also spelled* **license**]: *n.* a document giving official permission to do something. *My driver's licence will expire this year.*

SIGN: **'L'** hands, palms forward, are tapped together a couple of times so that the thumb-tips touch.

lick: *v.* to pass the tongue over something. *My dog likes to lick my face.*

SIGN: Tips of extended fingers of right **'BENT EXTENDED U'** hand, palm toward the body, are stroked upward against the right cheek at least twice. The signer's tongue visibly moves up and down in the mouth. (Alternatively, a **'BENT EXTENDED B'** handshape may be used, and the location of the sign is determined by the context. This sign is generally reserved for animals.)

lid: *n.* a cover for a receptacle. *A vegetable steamer should have a tight-fitting lid.*

SIGN: Left **'S'** hand is held in a fixed position with palm rightward/backward and left **'CROOKED EXTENDED B'** hand is held palm down on top of the left hand. (Various signs may be used, depending on the type of lid and shape of the receptacle.)

lie: *v.* to speak untruthfully with the purpose of deceiving. *He lied about the mileage on the car he sold.*

SIGN #1: Vertical right **'BENT B'** (or **'BENT ONE'**) hand, palm left, is brushed leftward across the chin.

SAME SIGN—**liar**, *n.*, and may be followed by the Agent Ending (see p. LIV).

lie [*or* **lie down**]: *v.* to place oneself in a horizontal position. *I will lie down and rest for a while.*

SIGN #2: Left **'EXTENDED B'** hand is held in a fixed position with palm up and fingers pointing forward at a slight rightward angle. Right **'V'** hand is laid on the left palm with palm up and extended fingers pointing forward.

OR

SIGN #2: Vertical right **'ONE'** hand, palm facing left, is brushed upward/forward off the chin a couple of times.

(in) lieu of: *conj.* instead of; in place of. *We were given new merchandise in lieu of a cash refund.*

SIGN: Horizontal **'F'** (or **'COVERED T'**) hands, left palm facing right and right palm facing left, are held so that the left is further from the chest than the right. Then their positions are simultaneously switched as the left hand moves back toward the body in an arc over the right hand while the right hand moves away from the body in an arc under the left hand.

light: *adj.* not heavy. *This is a very light briefcase.*

SIGN #3: Horizontal **'BENT MIDFINGER 5'** hands are held apart with palms down. The wrists are then rotated outward a quarter turn, causing the hands to turn so that the palms face each other.

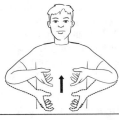

life: *n.* the time between birth and death. *A biography details the events in a person's life.*

SIGN: Horizontal **'L'** hands are placed at either side, somewhere above the waist, with palms toward the body and forefingers pointing toward each other. They are then raised to a higher position on the chest. (Fingerspell LIFE to mean the 'rest of one's life' as in: *He will be on this medication for life* or *She got life for murdering her husband.*)

light: *adj.* not great in degree or intensity. *The shirt is light blue.*

SIGN #4: Horizontal **'BENT MIDFINGER 5'** hands are held apart with palms down. The wrists are then rotated outward a quarter turn, causing the hands to turn so that the palms face each other. (Rather than using **light** #4, the intensity of colour is shown through variations in the sign for the actual colour. *Bright blue* would be expressed using the sign for **blue**, but the sign is made with a flourish and in a larger space than what is usual for the sign **blue**. The eyes are wide open. *Light blue* would be expressed using the sign for **blue** but in a subtle, understated way so that the movement is minimal and the signer's eyes are almost squinting.)

lift: *v.* to raise; to move (something) upward. *This box is too heavy for us to lift.*

SIGN #1: **'CROOKED SLANTED 5'** hands, palms facing each other, are inverted as if with fingertips under something which then appears to be lifted as the hands simultaneously rise. (Signs vary depending on what is being lifted.)

light: *v.* to set fire to; ignite. *You light a fire and I will get the hot dogs.*

SIGN #5: Left **'EXTENDED B'** hand is held in a fixed position with palm right and fingers pointing forward/upward. Right **'COVERED T'** hand, palm down, is held with forefinger against left palm. The right wrist then rotates clockwise as the forefinger resembles a match being struck against the left palm. The palm of the right hand eventually faces the body as the right hand moves away from the left.

lift: *v.* a slang expression meaning to steal. *He was able to lift funds from the company's vault for months before the theft was discovered.*

SIGN #2: Left arm is folded across in front of the chest. Horizontal right **'V'** hand is held with thumb against left forearm near the elbow and palm facing the arm. The right hand is then drawn rightward at a slight upward angle along the left forearm as the extended fingers retract to form a **'CLAWED V'** hand.

light-headed: See **dizzy.**

light-hearted: See **happy.**

light: *n.* illumination which makes it possible to see. *Good light is essential for communication in sign language.*

SIGN #1: Right **'COVERED 8'** hand is held upright, palm facing body, as middle finger flicks off thumb and strikes chin.

lightning: *n.* a flash of light in the sky caused by a discharge of electricity. *The old elm tree was struck by lightning.*

SIGN: Upright forefinger of right **'ONE'** hand, palm facing forward, is used to trace a zigzag pattern from in front of the face downward, to simulate a flash of lightning.

like: *v.* to find (something/someone) pleasant or enjoyable. *I **like** movies with lots of action.*

SIGN #1: Horizontal right **'OPEN 8'** hand is held with palm toward the chest and tips of thumb and middle finger touching the centre of the chest. The hand then moves forward as the thumb and middle finger close to form an **'8'** hand.

OR

SIGN #2: Horizontal right **'EXTENDED B'** hand, palm on the chest, is moved in a circular motion, which appears to onlookers to be clockwise.

SIGN #3 [ONTARIO]: Tip of middle finger of right **'BENT MIDFINGER 5'** hand, palm facing backwards, is used to tap against the chin a couple of times.

like: *adj.* having similar characteristics. *Ringette is a little **like** hockey.*

SIGN #4: Vertical right **'Y'** hand is held with palm forward and appears to wobble from side to side as the wrist twists.

(don't) like: *v.* to consider unpleasant or disagreeable. *I don't **like** your suggestion.*

SIGN #1: Horizontal right **'EXTENDED B'** hand is held with the palm against the chest. The hand is then flung forward as the palm is turned downward and the fingers point forward. Facial expression must clearly convey displeasure.

OR

SIGN #2: Tips of joined thumb and forefinger of horizontal right **'8'** hand are placed in the centre of the chest. As the wrist rotates in a counter-clockwise direction, the hand is flung forward and assumes a **'MODIFIED 5'** shape with palm down. Facial expression must clearly convey displeasure.

limb: *n.* an arm or a leg. *A plaster cast is usually applied to a broken **limb** until it heals.*

SIGN: Right **'CROOKED 5'** hand grasps the upper left arm and moves downward to the wrist of the left **'STANDARD BASE'** hand. (Signs vary according to which limb is being discussed. For **limb** meaning a part of a tree, see **branch** #1.)

limit: *v.* to restrict; confine. *You will have to **limit** your activities or you will have a breakdown.*

SIGN #1: **'BENT EXTENDED B'** hands are held apart, right above left, with palms facing the body, but the left palm slanted slightly rightward while the right palm is slanted slightly leftward. The wrists then rotate to swing the hands into a position whereby the left palm faces forward at a rightward angle while the right hand faces forward at a leftward angle.

limit: *n.* the maximum extent, degree or amount. *There is a daily **limit** to the amount of money you may withdraw from a banking machine.*

SIGN #2: Left **'EXTENDED B'** hand is held in a fixed position with palm down and fingers pointing rightward/forward. Right **'EXTENDED B'** hand is held below the left hand with palm down and fingers pointing downward. The right hand is then flipped upward from the wrist to strike the underside of the left hand at right angles to it.

limousine: *n.* a large, luxurious car. *The **limousine** has a glass division between the driver and the passengers.*

SIGN: Fingerspell **LIMO**.

limp: *v.* to walk with uneven steps due to weakness or injury to a leg or foot. *After the surgery, he **limped** for several months.*

SIGN: **'BENT ONE'** hands, held apart with palms down and forefingers pointing downward, are alternately raised and lowered.

line: *n.* a narrow, continuous mark. *Do not step across the **line** when you serve the ball.*

SIGN: Horizontal **'I'** hands are held with tips of little fingers touching each other and palms facing the body. The hands are then moved apart. (The positioning of this sign indicates that the line is *horizontal*. To indicate that a line is *vertical*, simply rotate this sign a quarter turn so that the left hand is above the right hand in the initial position before the hands are drawn apart. By the same token, the sign may be rotated an eighth of a turn to indicate that a line is *diagonal*. For **draw a line**, see **underline** #2, bearing in mind that the positioning and movement of the sign may vary according to what kind of line is being drawn.)

line up: *v.* to form a line of people (queue). *People will line up at the box office for hours, hoping to get tickets for the rock concert.*

SIGN: Vertical **'4'** hands, left palm facing forward/rightward and right palm facing backward/leftward, are held so that the right is slightly behind the left. Then the right hand is drawn back toward the right shoulder. (Signs vary depending on which way the people are facing.)

linger: *v.* to stay longer than what is usual or expected. *The smell of boiled cabbage lingers long after it has been cooked.*

SIGN: **'Y'** hands are held parallel with palms down and are slowly circled forward and downward several times.

linguistics: *n.* the scientific study of language. *She is doing research in the field of linguistics.*

SIGN #1: **'L'** hands are held palms down with forefingers pointing forward and thumbtips touching each other. The hands are then drawn apart. Next, left **'EXTENDED B'** hand is held in a fixed position with fingers pointing rightward and palm toward the body at a slight upward angle. Right **'BENT 5'** hand is held a little higher and closer to the chest with the palm down and the fingers fluttering as they point toward the left palm. (ASL CONCEPT—**language - study**.)

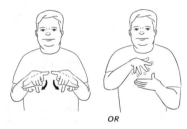

OR

SIGN #2: **'L'** hands are held with palms down, thumbtips touching and forefingers pointing forward. The hands are then drawn apart as they change to **'S'** hands.

link: *v.* to unite; connect. *His fingerprints on the weapon link him with the crime.*

SIGN: **'OPEN F'** hands are held slightly apart, palms facing each other, and are then brought together to form **'F'** hands, with thumbs and forefingers linked.

linoleum: *n.* a type of floor covering installed in large sheets. *Most older houses once had linoleum on the kitchen floor.*

SIGN: Fingerspell **LINO**.

lion: *n.* a large predatory feline mammal. *A male lion can be distinguished by its shaggy mane.*

SIGN: Right **'CROOKED SLANTED 5'** hand is suspended just above the head with palm down and fingers overhanging the forehead. The hand is then curved backward across the top of the head.

lipreading: See **speechreading**.

lips: *n.* the two fleshy folds surrounding the mouth. *His lips are always chapped in the winter because of the cold, dry weather.*

SIGN: Tip of forefinger of right **'ONE'** hand touches the lips as it outlines them by moving in a clockwise (to the onlooker) direction. (If the signer is referring to a particular place on the lips, he/she might just point to that specific place.)

lipstick: *n.* a cosmetic stick used to colour one's lips. *Her lipstick is bright red.*

SIGN: Vertical right **'CLOSED X'** hand, palm toward the body, is held with joined thumb and forefinger against the upper lip and moved back and forth from the wrist a couple of times tracing an arc as it outlines the upper lip.

liquid: *adj.* able to flow; fluid. *The patient will be kept on a liquid diet for 24 hours.*

SIGN: Fingerspell **LIQUID**.

liquidate: *v.* to terminate the operations of a business. *The company is in receivership and must liquidate.*

SIGN: Vertical **'B'** hands are held apart with palms facing forward at a slight downward angle. The hands are then drawn together. Next, the wrist of the vertical right **'B'** hand, palm facing forward/leftward, is brushed back and forth against wrist of left **'STANDARD BASE'** hand. (ASL CONCEPT—**close - business**.)

liquor: *n.* an alcoholic drink. *There will be no liquor provided at the wedding reception.*

SIGN: Horizontal right **'COMBINED I + ONE'** hand is held above and at right angles to horizontal left **'COMBINED I + ONE'** hand, whose palm faces slightly to the right and slightly toward the body. The two hands are then tapped together twice.

list: *n.* an item-by-item written record. *The Deaf Club has a membership list.*

SIGN #1: Left **'EXTENDED B'** hand is held in a fixed position with palm toward the body at a rightward and slightly upward angle. Right **'BENT EXTENDED B'** hand, palm leftward/backward, is placed against the fingers of the left hand and then slid down to the heel of the left hand. (Sometimes this downward movement is made in small successive arcs.)

list: *v.* to itemize; make a list. *I will list the names of those who qualify for assistance.*

SIGN #2: Vertical left **'EXTENDED B'** hand is held in a fixed position with palm facing right. Right **'FLAT O'** hand is positioned with bunched fingertips against the fingers of the left hand and is then slid downward to the heel of the left hand. (Sometimes this downward movement is made in small successive arcs.)

listen: *v.* to concentrate on hearing. *The judge will now listen to your testimony.*

SIGN: Vertical right **'CROOKED EXTENDED B'**, palm facing forward, is used to cup the right ear.

listless: *adj.* showing no interest or energy. *This hot, humid weather makes me feel listless.*

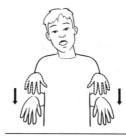

SIGN: **'CROOKED 5'** hands are held parallel with fingers pointing downward and are simultaneously dropped downward as the body slumps, the face appears lifeless and the tongue protrudes slightly.

literacy: *n.* the ability to read and write. *Literacy is considered an important objective in most schools.*

SIGN: Horizontal left **'EXTENDED B'** hand is held in a fixed position with palm rightward but slanted slightly toward the body while the fingers point rightward/forward. Right **'V'** hand, palm forward, bends from the wrist, causing the tips of the extended fingers to brush downward against the left palm. Then the right hand changes to a **'CLOSED X'** hand which strikes rightward/forward along the length of the left hand. (ASL CONCEPT—**read - write**.)

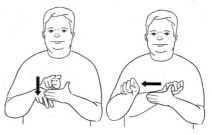

(ASL) literacy: *n.* the ability to express oneself and to comprehend messages expressed in ASL. *ASL literacy is an important objective in many schools for the Deaf.*

SIGN: Fingerspell **LITERACY**.

literate: *adj.* capable of reading and writing. *Free and compulsory education was intended to make all children equally **literate**.*

SIGN: **'A'** hands, palms down, are held slightly apart, and are brought down firmly in front of the chest. Next, horizontal left **'EXTENDED B'** hand is held in a fixed position with palm rightward but slanted slightly toward the body while the fingers point rightward/forward. Right **'V'** hand, palm forward, bends from the wrist, causing the tips of the extended fingers to brush downward against the left palm. Then the right hand changes to a **'CLOSED X'** hand which strikes rightward/forward along the length of the left hand. (ASL CONCEPT—**can - read - write**.)

literature: *n.* written work such as poetry, novels, etc. *The British have produced a lot of popular **literature**.*

SIGN #1: Left **'CONTRACTED C'** (or **'OPEN 8'**) hand is held horizontally with palm facing right while right **'CONTRACTED C'** (or **'OPEN 8'**) hand is held upright with palm facing left. The hands are held close enough together to be loosely interlocked. They are then drawn apart, closed and returned several times, thus alternating between **'CONTRACTED C'** (or **'OPEN 8'**) and **'FLAT O'** (or **'8'**) shapes with each movement. (**Literature** is often finger-spelled **L-I-T**, especially when it refers to the title of an academic course.)

literature: *n.* any printed material. *I will go to the travel agency and gather all the literature they have on cruises.*

SIGN #2: Left **'MODIFIED O'** hand is held at about shoulder level with palm facing upward but angled slightly toward the body while right **'MODIFIED O'** hand is held upright just in front of the forehead with palm toward the face. The forearms then move simultaneously forward/downward as the hands open to assume **'MODIFIED 5'** shapes with palms facing upward.

literature: *n.* written material produced by scholars in a certain field. *The **literature** shows that fluency in one language helps a person to learn a second language.*

SIGN #3: Left **'EXTENDED B'** hand is held in a fixed position with palm turned upward but slanted slightly rightward and toward the body while fingers point rightward/forward. Right **'ONE'** hand is held palm down as tip of forefinger brushes forward several times against palm of left hand.

litre [*also spelled* **liter**]: *n.* a metric unit of volume equal to about 1.056 liquid quarts. *The price of gas went up to 75 cents per **litre**.*

SIGN: Vertical right **'L'** hand, palm facing forward, appears to wobble slightly. This is a wrist movement.

litter: *v.* to make a place untidy by strewing unwanted objects around. *Responsible campers do not **litter** public campgrounds with their garbage.*

SIGN #1: The arms gradually move forward as the hands, which are held apart with palms down, alternately change from **'S'** to **'CONTRACTED 5'** shapes several times as if dropping things on the floor. (For **litter**, *n.*, see **garbage**.)

(have a) litter: *v.* to give birth to a group of (more than two) baby mammals (not humans) at one birth. *My dog **had a litter** of puppies yesterday.*

SIGN #2: Horizontal **'EXTENDED B'** hands, palms facing the body, are positioned with the back of the right hand resting against the left palm. Then the right hand is curved down and under the left until its palm faces downward. Movement is repeated several times.

little: *adj.* small or less than average in size. *He is just a **little** dog.*

SIGN #1: Horizontal **'EXTENDED B'** hands are held apart with palms facing each other and fingers pointing forward. They are then moved toward each other slightly a couple of times.

little: *adj.* small or less than average in stature. *His **little** girl looks just like him.*

SIGN #2: Vertical right **'BENT EXTENDED B'** hand is held with palm forward and is firmly moved downward a very short distance.

(a) little: *adv.* a small quantity. *I will have a little mayonnaise on my sandwich please.*

SIGN #3: Right **'x'** hand is held palm-up with forefinger tightly crooked and tip of thumb repeatedly scraping downward against tip of forefinger.

little: *adv.* not much. *I have little faith in him; he has let me down too many times.*

SIGN #4: Tip of forefinger of the right **'COVERED T'** hand, palm toward the face, is held in front of the nose and the thumb is flicked out, thus forming an **'A-INDEX'** hand.

live: *v.* to reside; dwell. *I grew up in Ontario, but I now live in British Columbia.*

SIGN: Horizontal **'L'** hands are placed at either side, somewhere above the waist, with palms toward the body and forefingers pointing toward each other. They are then raised to a higher position on the chest.
ALTERNATE SIGN—**alive** #1

liver: *n.* an abdominal organ that secretes bile and plays a part in metabolism. *Excessive use of alcohol may cause damage to the liver.*

SIGN: Fingerspell **LIVER**.

livid: See **furious**.

living room: *n.* a room in one's home used for relaxation and entertainment. *The family is watching television in the living room.*

SIGN: Vertical **'EXTENDED B'** hand, palm left, is tapped a couple of times against the centre of the chest.

load: *v.* to transfer a program to the memory system of a computer. *I will load this program into my computer.*

SIGN #1: Vertical left **'C'** hand is held with palm facing right. Then the forward-pointing fingertips of the right **'FLAT O'** hand are inserted into the opening in the left hand.

load: *v.* to place goods on a means of conveyance such as a truck, ship, etc. *They will begin to load the baggage when the passengers enter the aircraft.*

SIGN #2: Vertical **'S'** hands, palms forward and left slightly ahead of the right, are opened and closed several times with the fingers spreading and flicking forward simultaneously. (Signs vary according to 'what' is being loaded and 'how' it is being loaded.)

load: *n.* a certain weight or quantity of goods being conveyed. *The truck is carrying a load of dangerous goods.*

SIGN #3: Vertical right **'BENT EXTENDED B'** hand, palm left, is held near the chest and arched forward to simulate the concept of a large rounded mass.

load: *n.* a burden; heavy responsibility. *She has a heavy load now that she has a full time job and six children at home to look after.*

SIGN #4: Fingertips of both **'BENT EXTENDED B'** hands, are placed on right shoulder. Shoulder is pushed slightly downward to signify the bearing of a burden.

loaf: *n.* a shaped mass of food. *Please buy me a loaf of bread and a dozen rolls while you are at the store.*

SIGN #1: **'C'** hands, palms down, are held side by side and drawn apart.

loaf: *v.* to be idle or lazy. *During my vacation, I did nothing but loaf.*

SIGN #2: Right **'L'** hand, palm toward the body, is tapped a couple of times against the left side of the chest, near the shoulder.

loan: *v.* to lend. *I will loan you my car this evening.*

SIGN #1: Vertical **'K'** (or **'V'**) hands are held close to the chest, the left directly in front of the right, left palm facing right and right palm facing left. Together the hands drop forward to a horizontal position. ❖

loan: *n.* a sum of money lent, usually at a certain interest rate. *If I decide to buy a new boat, I will need to get a bank loan.*

SIGN #2: Right **'V'** (or **'K'**) hand, palm facing left, is placed on left **'V'** (or **'K'**) which is held with palm facing right. The hands are initially positioned horizontally and then tilted back to an upright position.

loathe: *v.* to feel strong hatred or disgust for; abhor. *I loathe violence in any form.*

SIGN: Thumb of right **'MODIFIED 5'** hand is held at the chin, with palm facing left. Then the hand is thrust forward firmly. Alternatively, this sign may be made two-handed with the left **'MODIFIED 5'** hand in front of the right **'MODIFIED 5'** hand. Facial expression must clearly convey 'abhorrence'.
ALTERNATE SIGN—**hate**

lobby: *n.* an entrance hall; vestibule; foyer. *We met our friends in the hotel lobby.*

SIGN #1: Fingerspell **LOBBY**.

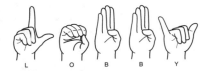

lobby: *v.* to attempt to influence legislators in the forming of policies. *They will lobby for better captioning services for the Deaf and Hard of Hearing.*

SIGN #2: Vertical left **'S'** hand is held with palm right while the vertical right **'EXTENDED B'** hand, palm forward, comes from behind to push the left hand forward twice. A look of determination accompanies this sign.

lobster: *n.* a salt water crustacean with large pincers. *She ordered a lobster for dinner.*

SIGN: **'CONTRACTED C'** hands are held parallel with palms toward each other at a forward/downward angle. The extended fingers of both hands represent pincers as they are opened and closed repeatedly to alternate between **'CONTRACTED C'** and **'FLAT O'** shapes.
ALTERNATE SIGN—**crab**

local: *adj.* associated with a particular area or region. *She works at the local supermarket.*

SIGN: Horizontal left **'S'** hand is held in a fixed position with palm rightward/backward. Right **'EXTENDED B'** hand, fingers pointing forward and palm down, rubs the top of the left hand as it moves in several counter-clockwise circles.
ALTERNATE SIGNS—**area** #1 and **near**

locale: *n.* a place or area where certain events take place. *While the stadium is being renovated all sports events will be moved to a different locale.*

SIGN: Right **'5'** hand, palm down, is circled in a counter-clockwise motion.
ALTERNATE SIGN—**place** #1

locate: *v.* to find. *I have not been able to locate the file we need.*

SIGN #1: Right **'OPEN F'** hand is held palm down. The hand then moves upward as the thumb and forefinger close to form an **'F'** hand with palm facing forward.

locate: *v.* to situate in a certain place. *The new company will locate in Toronto.*

SIGN #2: Right **'EXTENDED A'** hand is held palm down over left **'STANDARD BASE'** hand, then twisted so that it comes to rest on the back of the left hand with thumb pointing upward and palm facing leftward but slanted toward the body.

location: *n.* a site; position; place. *The exact location of the new arena is still being debated.*

SIGN: Right **'5'** hand, palm down, is circled in a counter-clockwise motion.
ALTERNATE SIGN—**place** #1

lock: *v.* to fasten with a lock or bolt for security purposes. *Be sure to lock the door before you leave.*

SIGN #1: **'V'** hands, palms toward the body, are held semi-upright with the right hand directly behind the left. Then the right hand is thrust forward against the left so that the extended fingers are crossed over those of the left hand.

OR

SIGN #2: Left **'EXTENDED B'** hand is held in a fixed position with palm rightward/backward and fingers pointing forward/rightward. Right **'COVERED T'** hand is held with the palm down and the forefinger against the left palm. Then the right wrist rotates a quarter turn clockwise to turn the palm toward the body as the forefinger grinds into the left palm.

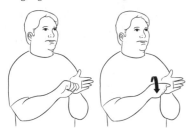

lock *(cont.)*

OR

SIGN #3: Left **'S'** hand is held in a fixed position with palm down. Right **'S'** hand is held palm down above the left hand. The right wrist then sharply rotates 180 degrees in a clockwise direction to turn the palm upward as the hand drops down onto the back of the left hand.

SIGN #4 [ATLANTIC]: Tips of extended fingers of right **'BENT V'** hand are thrust toward the throat.

locker: *n.* a lockable compartment for storing things. *His locker smells awful because his gym shoes have been shut up in there all year.*

SIGN: **'V'** hands, palms toward the body, are held semi-upright with the right hand directly behind the left. Then the right hand is thrust forward against the left so that the extended fingers are crossed over those of the left hand. (**LOCKER** may be fingerspelled.)

log: *n.* a length of tree trunk with the branches removed. *Matthew has ordered many logs for the building of his house.*

SIGN: Horizontal right **'EXTENDED B'** hand, fingertips pointing forward/leftward and palm facing left, is placed on the left **'STANDARD BASE'** hand. Both hands then move back and forth in a sawing motion. Alternatively, the left hand may take the shape of a horizontal **'EXTENDED B'** with fingertips pointing forward/rightward and palm facing right. (REGIONAL VARIATION—**wood** #2 for this part of the sign.) Next, **'C'** hands, palms down, are held side by side and drawn apart. (ASL CONCEPT—**wood - round long**.)

logic: *n.* reasoned thought; effectiveness in argument or dispute. *There is much logic in what he says.*

SIGN: Fingerspell **LOGIC**.

loiter: *v.* to stand around idly or aimlessly. *The principal told the students not to loiter in the halls.*

SIGN: **'BENT MIDFINGER 5'** hands are held right above left with left palm facing upward and right palm facing downward. The right hand wobbles as both hands move in a sweeping counter-clockwise arc.

lollipop: *n.* candy on a stick. *The children were each given a lollipop at the circus.*

SIGN: Vertical right **'COVERED T'** hand, palm facing left, is moved a short distance forward/downward and back several times while the lips smack as if licking a lollipop.

lone: *adj.* alone; unaccompanied. *A lone rider was approaching at a gallop.*

SIGN: Vertical right **'ONE'** hand, palm facing the body, is moved in a small counter-clockwise circle.

lonely: *adj.* unhappy because of being alone; lonesome. *She is often lonely because her husband is a workaholic.*

SIGN: Side of forefinger of vertical right **'ONE'** hand, palm facing left, is drawn downward a couple of times over the lips and chin.

lonesome: *adj.* unhappy because of being alone; lonely. *The child was sent to a summer camp where he was lonesome.*

SIGN: Side of forefinger of vertical right **'ONE'** hand, palm facing left, is drawn downward a couple of times over the lips and chin.

long: *adj.* of a relatively great extent in terms of distance, duration of time, etc. *You will have a long wait for the next bus.*

SIGN #1: Tip of forefinger of right **'ONE'** hand, palm down, is used to stroke upward from the wrist along the left arm.

long: *adj.* having an unusually great length. *That's a long hot dog!*

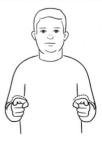

SIGN #2: Horizontal **'ONE'** hands, palms facing and forefingers pointing forward, are positioned a considerable distance apart and are lowered with a very short but firm movement.

long: *v.* to have a strong desire for; yearn. *The soldiers **long** to be home for Christmas.*

SIGN #3: Fingertips of horizontal right **'SPREAD EXTENDED C'** hand, palm toward the body, are placed against middle of upper chest and the hand is drawn firmly downward.

long hair: *n.* hair which is not short. *He prefers girls with **long hair**.*

SIGN: **'BENT EXTENDED B'** hands are held against either side of the neck just under the ears with palms facing backward and fingers pointing backward as well. The hands are then simultaneously lowered so that the fingertips come to rest on the shoulders.

long-winded: *adj.* having a tendency to speak or write for too long at a time, making people feel bored. *He is so **long-winded** that he puts me to sleep at every meeting.*

SIGN: Horizontal left **'BENT ONE'** hand is held with palm downward/backward and forefinger pointing rightward toward the mouth. Horizontal right **'BENT ONE'** hand is held with palm facing backward, forefinger pointing toward the mouth, the tip of the forefinger almost touching that of the left hand. The right hand is then drawn straight forward/rightward at a slight downward angle as the tongue visibly moves up and down in the mouth.
ALTERNATE SIGN—**drawn out**

longitude: *n.* the distance in degrees east or west of the prime meridian, which is located at Greenwich, England. *Time zones are basically determined by meridians of **longitude**.*

SIGN: Right **'4'** hand is held with palm forward/downward. It is then drawn downward, the wrist bending to turn the palm fully forward. Alternatively, this sign may be preceded by the sign for **globe**. When referring to one specific longitudinal line, the sign shown here is made using a **'BENT ONE'** hand. To point out a certain place along that line, the signer might first draw the line with the forefinger of the **'BENT ONE'** hand and then point to the exact location along the line.

look [*or* **look at**]: *v.* to use one's eyes to see. *Look in the fridge to see if there is any milk left.*

SIGN #1: Right **'BENT V'** hand, palm forward, is held at shoulder level or above and is moved forward a short distance. ❖

look: *v.* to have a certain appearance. *He **looks** very tired.*

SIGN #2: Forefinger of right **'ONE'** hand, palm toward the face, is used to outline the face in a counter-clockwise direction (from the signer's perspective).

look after: *v.* to take care of or be responsible for. *They will **look after** the children while we finish this project.*

SIGN: Vertical right **'BENT V'** hand, palm forward and slightly leftward, is held behind the left **'S'** hand which is held palm down. The heel of the right hand strikes the left hand a couple of times as the hands briskly move together and apart twice.
ALTERNATE SIGN—**care for** [*or* **take care of**]

look back: *v.* to think about something that happened in the past. *When I **look back**, I miss my old school days.*

SIGN: Right **'BENT V'** hand is held with palm backward and tip of middle finger just under/to the right of the right eye. The hand is then moved to the right and back so that it is just above the right shoulder.

look down on: *v.* to show contempt for. *They **look down on** you because you never tell the truth.*

SIGN: **'V'** hands are held apart with one slightly ahead of the other, palms down and extended fingers pointing forward. The wrists then bend to drop the hands so that the extended fingers point downward and slightly forward. ❖

look for: *v.* to search for; try to find. *She asked the teacher to help her **look for** her book.*

SIGN: Vertical right **'C'** hand, palm facing left, is circled in front of the face several times in what appears to the signer as a counter-clockwise direction.

look forward to: *v.* to await something with pleasure. *I **look forward to** receiving your letter.*

SIGN: **'V'** hands are held apart with one slightly ahead of the other, palms forward/downward and extended fingers pointing forward and slightly upward. The hands are simultaneously jabbed forward twice.

look into: *v.* to investigate; check into. *I will look into the matter for you and see what I can find out.*

SIGN: Left **'EXTENDED B'** hand is held in a fixed position with palm turned upward but slanted slightly rightward and toward the body while fingers point rightward/forward. Right **'ONE'** hand is held palm down as tip of forefinger brushes forward several times against palm of left hand.

look like: *v.* to resemble; have the appearance of. *You look like your father.*

SIGN: Tip of forefinger of right **'ONE'** hand touches cheekbone near right eye. The forearm then moves quickly forward a short distance as the wrist rotates and the hand takes on a vertical **'Y'** shape, the palm forward/leftward, and teeters from side to side several times. This is a wrist action.

look out: *v.* to be careful; watch out. *Look out for falling rock in the mountain pass.*

SIGN: Horizontal **'K'** (or **'V'**) hands are held, right above left, with extended fingers pointing forward, the left palm facing rightward and the right palm facing leftward. The hands are brought together to strike each other a couple of times. Next, vertical right **'BENT V'** hand is held palm forward in front of the right shoulder and is jabbed forward. Facial expression is important. (ASL CONCEPT—**be careful - watch out**.) The second part of this sign may vary slightly depending on the location of the object of concern.

look over: *v.* to inspect. *The insurance adjuster will look over your car to assess the damage from your accident.*

SIGN: Left **'EXTENDED B'** hand is held in a fixed position with palm turned upward but slanted slightly rightward and toward the body while fingers point rightward/forward. Right **'ONE'** hand is held palm down as tip of forefinger brushes forward several times against palm of left hand.

look (someone) up: *v.* to visit; make contact (with someone). *If you still live in Antigonish when I am here next time, I will certainly look you up.*

SIGN: **'BENT V'** hands, palms toward the body and extended fingers pointing upward, are alternately circled forward. As a variation on this sign, the **'BENT V'** hands may be held with the right slightly ahead of the left. Both hands are then moved purposefully forward/rightward a short distance.

look up: *v.* to search in a reference book for information. *If you are not sure, you can look up the answer in the encyclopedia.*

SIGN: Left **'EXTENDED B'** hand is held in a fixed position with fingers pointing forward and palm facing rightward but slanted upward. Thumb of right **'EXTENDED A'** hand, palm down, is jabbed backward into left palm a few times as right forearm moves in small clockwise circles.

look up to: *v.* to have admiration and respect for. *The students look up to her.*

SIGN: **'V'** hands are held apart with one slightly ahead of the other and palms down. The hands then curve forward/upward so that the palms face forward and the extended fingers point upward at a slightly forward angle. ❖

loonie: *n.* colloquial term meaning the Canadian coin that has a one dollar value. *This vending machine will only take a loonie and no other coins.*

SIGN: Right **'ONE'** hand is held horizontally with palm facing left and forefinger pointing forward at a slight upward angle as the forearm wobbles slightly.

loose: *adj.* free from confinement or restraint, or not fitting closely. *I prefer to wear loose sweaters and T-shirts.*

SIGN: Fingerspell **LOOSE**. (This word is frequently signed rather than fingerspelled or signed as well as fingerspelled. Signs vary considerably depending on the specific object that is loose and where it is located. Signs for **loose** require limp wrists and repeated movement. This aspect of the sign could not be conveyed with enough clarity through a drawing so, we have not included a sign illustration.)

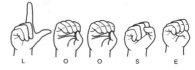

loquacious: See talkative.

Lord: *n.* God. *His faith in the Lord has helped him through many hard times.*

SIGN: Thumbtip of right **'L'** hand, palm leftward/downward is placed against the left shoulder. The hand is then moved diagonally across the torso so that the thumbtip touches the right side of the waist and the palm is now downward.

lose: *v.* to cease to have or possess. *Please do not lose your ticket.*

SIGN #1: Horizontal **'OPEN A'** hands, palms facing the body, are held together so that the knuckles of the bunched fingers are touching each other. The fingers are then unfurled so that the hands are swept apart, becoming horizontal **'CROOKED 5'** hands with palms facing each other and fingers pointing forward. SAME SIGN—**loss**, *n.*, when it refers to something which has been misplaced.

lose: *v.* to fail to win. *I hope they will not lose all their games this year.*

SIGN #2: Left **'EXTENDED B'** hand is held in a fixed position with palm up and fingers pointing forward/rightward. Right **'V'** hand is brought downward to strike the left palm. SAME SIGN—**loss**, *n.*, when it refers to something which has not been won.

lot: *n.* an area of land. *They cleared the lot on which they will build a log cabin.*

SIGN: Tips of forefingers of **'BENT ONE'** hands, palms down, are placed together out in front of the chest. The hands are drawn apart, then moved toward the chest, and finally come together again closer to the chest as the forefingers outline the shape of a square or rectangle. **LOT** is frequently fingerspelled. ALTERNATE SIGN—**property**

(a) lot of [*or* **lots of**]: *adj.* a great number or quantity of. *I eat a lot of fresh fruit and vegetables.*

SIGN: Horizontal **'CROOKED 5'** hands are held with palms facing and fingertips touching. The hands are then simultaneously drawn apart. ALTERNATE SIGN—**abundance** #2

lottery: *n.* a game in which tickets are sold and the winner is determined in a chance drawing. *Everyone dreams of winning a million dollar lottery.*

SIGN: Fingerspell **LOTTERY**.

loud: *adj.* related to sound that is great in volume. *The music at the dance was very loud.*

SIGN #1: Thumbtips of vertical **'MODIFIED 5'** hands are held near either ear, palms facing forward but angled slightly toward each other, as forearms are simultaneously thrust outward/forward and back at least twice. (This sign is accompanied by a grimace.)

OR

SIGN #2: Vertical left **'ONE'** hand is held to the left of the body with palm facing forward while vertical right **'ONE'** hand is held with palm forward and tip of forefinger touching the face just in front of the right ear. The hands take on **'S'** shapes then as they simultaneously move from side to side a few times. Meanwhile the signer grimaces and forms the word 'POW' on his lips.

lousy: *adj.* a slang expression meaning bad, inferior or poor. *I am a lousy cook!*

SIGN: Vertical right **'3'** hand is held with palm facing left and tip of thumb touching the nose. The hand then moves forward/downward in an arc formation as the wrist rotates to turn the hand to a horizontal position. A look of displeasure accompanies this sign.

love: *v.* to have great affection for. *I love all my aunts, uncles and cousins.*

SIGN: **'A'** hands, palms facing the body, the right resting on the back of the left, are pressed to the chest and held snugly. (See also **fall in love**.)

(I) love you: *s.s.* an expression of affection. *This is an international hand symbol for 'I Love You'.*

SIGN: Vertical right **'COMBINED LY'** hand is held with palm forward.

lovely: *adj.* beautiful; very attractive. *She looks lovely in the blue gown.*

SIGN: Right **'CONTRACTED 5'** hand is circled clockwise (to the onlooker) around the face as the fingers close to form a **'FLAT O'** hand, with palm and fingers toward the chin. (**LOVELY** is frequently fingerspelled.)

lover: *n.* someone who is very fond of something or someone. *He is a devoted lover of classical music.*

SIGN #1: Back of right **'s'** hand is brought up toward the mouth, kissed, and moved downward at a forward angle.

lover: *n.* someone who has a sexual relationship with another person, especially one that is extra-marital. *The prosecutor asked the witness if he and the defendant were lovers.*

SIGN #2: Horizontal **'s'** hands are held side by side with palms down. Forefingers and midfingers are flipped forward simultaneously to form horizontal **'BENT U'** hands. Motion is repeated.

lover: *n.* someone who has a loving relationship with another person. *Pat lives with his lover, Chris, in a bungalow on the north side of town.*

SIGN #3: **'A'** hands, palms facing the body, the right resting on the back of the left, are pressed to the chest and held snugly. Agent Ending (see p. LIV) follows. (**LOVER** in this context may be fingerspelled.)

low: *adj.* not high. *He always gets low grades in math.*

SIGN #1: Right **'EXTENDED B'** hand is held in front of the right side of the chest with palm down and fingers pointing forward. It is the purposefully lowered. (Signs vary depending on context.)

low: *adj.* depressed. *I have been feeling low all week.*

SIGN #2: Tips of middle fingers of **'BENT MIDFINGER 5'** hands are held at either side of upper chest and are simultaneously lowered.
ALTERNATE SIGN—**depressed** #2

low class: *adj.* inferior in social status or prestige. *When they went bankrupt, they had to move into a low class area of the city.*

SIGN: **'BENT EXTENDED B'** hands are held apart in front of upper chest with palms facing each other. The hands are then simultaneously moved downward in a slight arc toward the body.

loyal: *adj.* faithful. *He is very loyal to the Deaf Community.*

SIGN: **'S'** hands, palms toward the body, are held at chest level with the left slightly above the right. Then the right is brought upward to strike the left. Signs vary.
SAME SIGN—**loyalty**, *n.*, in this context.

luck: *n.* success which has come about due to chance or good fortune. *It was our luck that we bought the winning tickets.*

SIGN: Fingerspell **LUCK**.

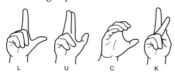

lucky: *adj.* having or bringing good fortune. *Susan was lucky to win the lottery.*

SIGN #1: Tips of extended fingers of right **'U'** hand, palm toward the body, are placed on the chin. The hand then swivels forward and downward from the wrist.

OR

SIGN #2: Right **'BENT MIDFINGER 5'** hand is held with palm toward the body and tip of middle finger on the chin. The wrist is then rotated to turn the hand so that the palm faces downward.

ludicrous: See **absurd**.

luggage: *n.* baggage; suitcases. *She had too much luggage for only a weekend in Toronto.*

SIGN: Right **'s'** hand is held at one's side, with palm toward body, and the arm is moved up and down to simulate the carrying of a suitcase.
REGIONAL VARIATION—**baggage** #2.

lumber: *n.* wood that has been sawed into boards. *We will need a lot of lumber to build a house that size.*

SIGN: Horizontal right **'EXTENDED B'** hand, fingertips pointing forward/leftward and palm facing left, is placed on the left **'STANDARD BASE'** hand at right angles to it. Both hands then move back and forth in a sawing motion. (Alternatively, the left hand may take the shape of a horizontal **'EXTENDED B'** with fingertips pointing forward/rightward and palm facing right.)
REGIONAL VARIATION—**wood** #2.

lump: *n.* a small solid mass; swelling. *She went to see the doctor about the lump on the back of her left hand.*

SIGN: Forefinger of right **'ONE'** hand, palm down, defines a small arc on back of left **'STANDARD BASE'** hand, or anywhere else on the body.

lunch: *n.* a midday meal eaten between breakfast and supper. *We are having soup and sandwiches for **lunch** tomorrow.*

SIGN: Right **'MODIFIED O'** hand, palm toward the body, is brought upward to the mouth, and the fingertips are tapped against the lips. Next, right **'EXTENDED B'** hand is held upright with palm facing left as elbow rests on back of left **'EXTENDED B'** hand which is held palm down in front of right side of body. (ASL CONCEPT—**eat - noon**.) Alternatively, this sign may be made with the first part only, particularly if it is already understood that the meal being referred to is a 'noon' meal.

lungs: *n.* a pair of spongy, saclike respiratory organs within the chest cavity. *Smoking is harmful to the **lungs**.*

SIGN: Fingertips of **'BENT EXTENDED B'** hands, palms facing body, are positioned at either side of chest and simultaneously slid up and down. (Alternatively, **LUNGS** may be finger-spelled.)

lure: *v.* to try to tempt or attract by promising some kind of reward. *The company is trying to **lure** foreign investors with their advertising.*

SIGN: Horizontal **'CLAWED L'** hands are held apart with palms up, and forearms are moved sharply back toward the body as hands take on **'A'** shapes.

lust: *n.* a strong desire for sex. *Every time he sees a beautiful woman he has difficulty controlling his **lust**.*

SIGN: Tip of forefinger of right **'ONE'** hand is placed under the chin and is drawn down-ward slowly over the throat while the lips appear to be articulating an 'SH' sound.

luxury: *n.* an extravagant, sumptuous indul-gence which is not a necessity. *A new car is an expensive **luxury**.*

SIGN: Fingerspell **LUXURY**.

M

machine: *n.* a mechanical device that performs useful work. *The machine needs to be repaired.*

SIGN: Fingers of horizontal **'CLAWED 5'** hands, palms toward the body, are interlocked and remain so as they are shaken up and down. This is a wrist action. (For washing machine, see **wash** #1. For sewing machine, see **sew** #2.)

machine gun: *n.* a rapid-firing automatic gun. *The gun-control lobbyists hope to make an individual's possession of a machine gun illegal.*

SIGN: Horizontal **'S'** hands, left palm facing right and right palm facing left, are held left ahead of right as if holding and aiming a machine gun. Then they are vigorously shaken to simulate the vibration caused by the firing of the gun.

macho: *adj.* strongly and often exaggeratedly masculine. *The team admires him because he is macho.*

SIGN: Fingerspell **MACHO**.

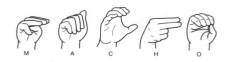

mad: *adj.* (informal) angry; resentful. *Quick-tempered people get mad easily.*

SIGN #1: As the vertical right **'5'** (or **'SPREAD C'**) hand, palm backward, is brought purposefully toward the face, the fingers retract to create a **'CLAWED SPREAD C'** hand. Facial expression is important.
ALTERNATE SIGN—**angry**

mad: *adj.* mentally deranged; insane. *She was placed in a psychiatric hospital for treatment because she was thought to be mad.*

SIGN #2: Vertical right **'CROOKED 5'** (or **'SPREAD C'**) hand is held near the right side of the head with the palm toward the body, and is twisted back and forth several times from the wrist.
SAME SIGN—**madness**, *n.*

mad: *adj.* extremely fond of; crazy about. *I am mad about cheese; I could eat it five times a day.*

SIGN #3: Vertical right **'CROOKED SLANTED 5'** hand is held just to the right of the forehead with palm facing leftward/backward. As the wrist bends, the hand drops down so that the palm faces downward and the fingers are dangling in front of the face.

made up of: *v.* constituted of a number of parts or elements. *The government is made up of many departments.*

SIGN: Horizontal left **'FLAT C'** hand is held in a fixed position with palm facing right. Right **'CONTRACTED C'** hand is held above left hand and slightly closer to the body with palm down and fingers pointing forward. As the right hand is thrust forward/downward, the fingers come together to form a **'FLAT O'** shape which is inserted into the opening at the top of the left hand.

magazine: *n.* a periodic paperback publication containing articles, photographs, etc. *Maclean's is considered to be Canada's national news magazine.*

SIGN: Thumb and forefinger of right **'A-INDEX'** (or **'MODIFIED G'**) hand are slid up the edge of the left **'EXTENDED B'** hand, which is held with palm facing body. Motion is repeated.

magic: *n.* the practice of illusory tricks that entertain. *He is a magician who thrills his audience with incredible feats of magic.*

SIGN: Vertical **'S'** hands, palms forward, are held slightly apart and are simultaneously thrust forward, as they open into **'CONTRACTED 5'** handshapes with palms down.

magnet: *n.* something that can attract certain substances such as iron or steel. *To make a simple compass, you will need a magnet.*

SIGN: Vertical left **'EXTENDED B'** hand is held in a fixed position with palm forward at a rightward angle. Right **'CONTRACTED 5'** hand, with palm down, is drawn backward and closes to take on a **'FLAT O'** shape as it makes contact with the left palm. The signer's lips start out in a tight 'O' formation and appear to be sucking in air before closing completely as the right hand makes contact with the left.
SAME SIGN—**magnetic**, *adj.*

magnificent: *adj.* splendid; impressive. *Canada has some of the most **magnificent** scenery in the world.*

SIGN: Vertical **'EXTENDED B'** hands, palms facing forward, are held apart near the face. Forearms are pushed purposefully forward a short distance.

magnify: *v.* to increase or enlarge in apparent size, usually with some type of lens. *You will need a strong lens to **magnify** this print to make it readable.*

SIGN: Horizontal right **'MODIFIED G'** hand is held with palm facing left. The thumb and forefinger are then drawn apart as the hand assumes a **'C-INDEX'** shape.

magnifying glass: *n.* a convex lens that has the capacity to enlarge images. *He needs to use a **magnifying glass** to read fine print.*

SIGN: Right **'CLOSED A-INDEX'** hand, palm leftward, is held near the squinting right eye and is moved downward (toward an imaginary book or document) and back.

magnitude: *n.* importance; significance. *The politicians underestimated the **magnitude** of voter dissatisfaction.*

SIGN: Vertical **'F'** hands are held apart with palms facing forward. The hands are then brought purposefully together.

maid: *n.* a female servant. *The **maid** will clean your room while you enjoy your breakfast.*

SIGN: Fingerspell **MAID**. (For archaic contexts in which **maid** refers to a young, unmarried woman, see **girl**.)

maiden name: *n.* a woman's surname before marriage. *Many married women keep their **maiden names**.*

SIGN: Little finger of right horizontal **'I'** hand, palm facing the body and angled leftward slightly, is used to strike downward against little finger of left horizontal **'I'** hand, of which the palm faces the body at a rightward angle. Next, back of fingers of right **'BENT EXTENDED B'** hand are held against fingers of left **'BENT EXTENDED B'** hand, which is held horizontally with palm facing the body. Right hand is then moved toward the body. Lastly, **'EXTENDED C'** hands are held apart with palms facing and the right hand slightly above the left. The hands are then clasped together. (ASL CONCEPT—**last - before - marry**.) Alternatively, the ASL compound **last - name - before - marry** or simply **name - before - marry** may be used for **maiden name**.

mail: *n.* letters and packages that are delivered by the post office. *I did not get any **mail** last Friday.*

SIGN #1: Left **'EXTENDED B'** hand is held in a fixed position with palm facing backward/rightward and fingers pointing rightward/forward. Right **'EXTENDED A'** hand begins with palm toward the body and thumbtip on the lips, and is then lowered as the wrist twists to turn the palm down and the thumbtip is pressed into the left palm. REGIONAL VARIATION—**letter** #2

mail: *v.* to send by post. *She will **mail** the letter to City Hall today.*

SIGN #2: Vertical right **'S'** hand, palm forward, is thrust ahead as it changes to a **'CONTRACTED 5'** handshape. ❖ ALTERNATE SIGN—**send** #1

main: *adj.* most important; chief; principal; major. *The teacher explained the **main** idea in the paragraph.*

SIGN: Vertical **'F'** hands are held apart with palms facing forward. The hands are then brought purposefully together. (**MAIN** may be fingerspelled, especially if referring to a busy street in the town centre.)

mainly: *adv.* for the most part. *The living room has several colour accents but it is mainly grey.*

SIGN: Horizontal left **'EXTENDED A'** hand is held in a fixed position with palm facing right. Horizontal right **'EXTENDED A'** hand is held at a lower level with palm facing left. The right hand then moves upward causing the knuckles to brush against those of the left hand on its way up.

mainstream: *v.* to integrate into the main society. *Whether or not to mainstream Deaf children has been a controversial issue in Deaf education.*

SIGN: **'5'** hands are held slightly apart with palms downward but slanted toward the body, and fingers of each hand pointing toward those of the other hand. The wrists then turn, causing the hands to dovetail so that the fingers point directly forward, the palms are down, and the right hand is on top of the left. (This sign is generally used in the context of **Deaf education** specifically.)

maintain: *v.* to retain; keep up; continue to have. *You will have to study in order to maintain your grades.*

SIGN #1: Horizontal right **'K'** hand, with palm facing left, is held just above horizontal left **'K'** hand, which is held with palm facing right. Then hands are tapped together several times as the hands move forward and upward slightly.
ALTERNATE SIGN—**continue**
SAME SIGN—**maintenance**, *n.*, in this context.

maintain: *v.* to provide with money and the necessities of life. *He does not earn enough to maintain his large family.*

SIGN #2: **'S'** hands, palms toward the body, are held at chest level with the left slightly above the right. Then the right is brought upward to strike the left.
ALTERNATE SIGN—**take care of**
SAME SIGN—**maintenance**, *n.*, in this context.

maintain: *v.* to keep in good working order; make repairs to. *The municipal government maintains our city streets.*

SIGN #3: Tip of forefinger of horizontal right **'CROOKED ONE'** hand is placed on the upturned palm of the left **'EXTENDED B'** hand. The right hand then makes several small movements from side to side without dislodging the forefinger from its original position on the left palm.
ALTERNATE SIGN—**take care of**
SAME SIGN—**maintenance**, *n.*, in this context.

maintain: *v.* to state; assert. *He maintains that his research results are reliable.*

SIGN #4: Vertical **'4'** hand, with palm facing left, is brought back firmly so that the tip of the forefinger touches the chin.

majestic: *adj.* grand; magnificent. *The view of the mountains from our hotel window was truly majestic.*

SIGN: Right **'CONTRACTED 5'** hand is circled clockwise (to the onlooker) around face as fingers close at chin to form a **'FLAT O'** hand.
SAME SIGN—**majesty**, *n.*, in this context.

majesty: *n.* a title used to refer to a queen or king. *A large crowd had gathered to watch Her Majesty inspect the troops.*

SIGN: Fingerspell **MAJESTY**.

M   A   J   E   S   T   Y

major: *adj.* of great importance. *Cuts in government spending are a major political issue at this time.*

SIGN #1: Vertical **'F'** hands are held apart with palms facing forward. The hands are then brought purposefully together.
ALTERNATE SIGN—**big** #1

major: *adj.* serious. *He is having major surgery tomorrow.*

SIGN #2: Vertical right **'BENT ONE'** hand is held with tip of forefinger touching chin and palm facing leftward but slanted toward the body. The wrist then rotates, turning the hand so that the palm fully faces the body. **MAJOR** in this context is frequently fingerspelled. ALTERNATE SIGNS—**serious** #2 & #3

major: *n.* a student's main field of study at a college or university. *My major at Gallaudet University was drama.*

SIGN #3: Left **'B'** hand is held in a fixed position with palm facing right and fingers pointing forward. Right **'B'** hand, palm facing left, and fingers pointing forward, is positioned on top of the left hand and firmly moved forward.

majority: *n.* the greater part or number (of something); most. *The majority of Canadians are law-abiding citizens.*

SIGN: Horizontal left **'EXTENDED A'** hand is held in a fixed position with palm facing right. Horizontal right **'EXTENDED A'** hand is held at a lower level with palm facing left. The right hand then moves upward causing the knuckles to brush against those of the left hand on its way up. (**Majority** is frequently fingerspelled **MAJ.**) ALTERNATE SIGN—**huge**

make: *v.* to create; produce something by putting different things together. *She will make a cake for her son's birthday.*

SIGN #1: Horizontal right **'S'** hand is placed on top of horizontal left **'S'** hand as both palms face the body. The right hand is then raised slightly and both wrists are bent causing the hands to turn so that the right palm faces left and the left palm faces right as the right hand re-establishes contact with the left hand.

make: *v.* to earn (money). *They should make some money from the garage sale.*

SIGN #2: Horizontal right **'SPREAD EXTENDED C'** hand is moved across upturned palm of left **'EXTENDED B'** hand in a circular, counter-clockwise 'gathering' motion, with the palm toward the body. ALTERNATE SIGN—**profit**

make: *v.* to equal; amount to. *Three plus five makes eight.*

SIGN #3: **'BENT EXTENDED B'** hands, palms facing each other, are held upright and slightly apart, then brought together so that the fingertips tap against each other. Motion is repeated.

make: *v.* to appoint. *They will make him captain of the ship.*

SIGN #4: Thumb and forefinger of right **'OPEN F'** hand are closed to form an **'F'** shape as the hand is brought toward the chest. Alternatively, vertical left **'EXTENDED B'** hand is held with palm facing forward/rightward while thumb and forefinger of right **'OPEN F'** hand are closed to form an **'F'** shape as the hand is brought back against the left palm.

make: *v.* to compel; force, usually against one's will. *I know you want to keep it a secret, but I will make you tell me.*

SIGN #5: Vertical right **'C'** hand, palm facing forward/leftward, is placed on the back of the left **'STANDARD BASE'** hand and is thrust forward/leftward across the left hand as the wrist bends causing the right hand to hang palm-down over the left hand. (Alternatively, this sign may be formed without the use of the left hand.) ❖

make a bed: *v.* to tidy a bed and arrange its covers. *She has to make the bed every morning.*

SIGN: Head tilts slightly to the right, supported by right **'EXTENDED B'** hand, which is held against right side of face. Next, hands are held at right angles to one another as downturned palm of right **'EXTENDED B'** hand is smoothed rightward/forward across upturned palm of left **'EXTENDED B'** hand. Motion is repeated a few times. (ASL CONCEPT—**bed - clean.**)

make a pig of oneself: See **(make a) pig of oneself**.

make believe: *v.* to pretend; fantasize. *When the temperature is -40 degrees, I like to make believe I am in Hawaii.*

SIGN: Vertical **'I'** hands are held at about eye level or above with palms facing backward and are alternately circled forward. (For **make-believe**, *n.*, see **creative**.)

make do: *v.* to manage with whatever is available. *I have been laid off from my job but we will make do.*

SIGN: **'BENT MIDFINGER 5'** hands, palms toward the body, are alternately circled backward so that the tips of the middle fingers brush downward on either side of the chin with each revolution.

make eyes at: *v.* to look at in a flirtatious manner; ogle. *She makes eyes at every handsome man.*

SIGN: Vertical **'MODIFIED G'** hands, palms forward, are held near each eye and are rapidly alternated with **'CLOSED MODIFIED G'** hands several times while the eyes are blinking coyly. The head may move back and forth.

make faces: See **(make) faces**.

make fun of: *v.* to deride; mock; ridicule. *All his classmates make fun of his clothes.*

SIGN: Horizontal **'BENT COMBINED I + ONE'** hands, palms down, are held slightly apart, with the right hand nearer the chest, and simultaneously make small jabbing motions. This sign is accompanied by a mocking facial expression. ❖

make it: *v.* to succeed in accomplishing something. *I hope to make it through medical school.*

SIGN #1: **'ONE'** hands, palms down, forefingers almost touching either side of forehead, are raised so that fingers point upward and palms face away from the body.

make it: *v.* to be able to attend. *I could not go to the last meeting but can make it tonight.*

SIGN #2: Vertical **'ONE'** hands, palms forward, are staggered so that the right hand is held slightly closer to the chest than the left. The wrists then bend, causing the hands to fall forward so that the palms face downward. ❖

make love: *v.* to have sexual intercourse with someone. *They make love often.*

SIGN: Left **'V'** hand is held with palm up and extended fingers pointing forward at a slight rightward angle while right **'V'** hand is held just above the left hand with palm facing leftward at a downward/forward angle and extended fingers pointing leftward/upward at a slightly forward angle. The hands are brought together a few times so that the heels of the hands repeatedly collide.

make out: *v.* an informal reference to making love or leading up to sexual intercourse. *They often make out in the back of the car.*

SIGN #1: With right palm facing left and left palm facing right, vertical **'S'** hands are crossed at the wrists with the left hand in front of the right. The hands maintain contact as they simultaneously bend downward and upward a few times from the wrist.

make out: *v.* to manage, with difficulty, to understand something. *She could barely make out what he was trying to say.*

SIGN #2: Vertical right **'S'** hand, with knuckles near right side of forehead, is changed to a **'ONE'** hand as the forefinger is flicked upward. (Other possibilities in this situation might be **see** or **hear**.)

make out: *v.* to be reasonably successful in one's life or work. *He will make out okay in the future.*

SIGN #3: **'ONE'** hands, palms down, forefingers almost touching either side of forehead, are raised so that fingers point upward and palms face forward.

make out: *v.* to purposely give the wrong impression; pretend. *Do not* **make out** *that you are innocent!*

SIGN #4: Outer edge of forefinger of vertical right **'ONE'** hand, palm forward, is brushed forward twice across the bump formed by placing the tongue in the right cheek.

make out: *v.* to write all the required information on a blank cheque. *Please* **make out** *a cheque in this amount.*

SIGN #5: Horizontal left **'EXTENDED B'** hand is held in a fixed position with palm facing rightward/backward. Thumb and forefinger of right **'CLOSED X'** hand move forward/rightward along the palm of the left hand.

make out: *v.* to complete the details of a standard form to be used for a specific purpose. *You will need to* **make out** *an application.*

SIGN #6: Fingertips of right **'FLAT O'** hand are slid from fingertips to heel of upturned left **'EXTENDED B'** hand.

make the most of: *v.* to produce maximum results or gains from one's efforts or advantages. *They decided to* **make the most of** *the fine weather by painting the fence.*

SIGN: Horizontal right **'SPREAD C'** hand moves in small circles as it brushes against the upturned palm of the left **'EXTENDED B'** hand and is rapidly opened and closed several times to alternate between **'SPREAD C'** and **'S'** handshapes.

make up: *v.* to create (a fantasy or pretense). *Most children like to* **make up** *stories.*

SIGN #1: Vertical **'4'** hands are held in front of either side of the forehead with palms facing each other, and are alternately circled forward a few times.

make up: *v.* to become friendly again after an argument. *They often have loud disagreements but they always kiss and* **make up.**

SIGN #2: Right **'A'** (or **'EXTENDED A'**) hand, palm facing the body, is rubbed on the chest with a circular motion which, in the eyes of onlookers, appears clockwise.

ALTERNATE SIGN—**forgive**

make up: *v.* to work at a time not usually required in order to compensate for time missed. *You may leave now but you must* **make up** *the time later.*

SIGN #3: Tip of forefinger of right **'ONE'** hand, palm toward body, is tapped twice against right-facing palm of horizontal left **'EXTENDED B'** hand.

make up for: *v.* to take the place of or be a substitute for. *Money can not* **make up for** *love in a child's life.*

SIGN #4: Horizontal **'F'** (or **'COVERED T'**) hands, left palm facing right and right palm facing left, are held so that the left is further from the chest than the right. Then their positions are simultaneously switched as the left hand moves back toward the body in an arc over the right hand while the right hand moves away from the body in an arc under the left hand.

make up one's mind: *v.* to decide. *I can not* **make up my mind** *what to do with all this money.*

SIGN #5: **'F'** hands, with palms facing each other, are held apart in front of chest and are simultaneously lowered.

make-up: *n.* cosmetics, especially those which are applied to the face. *She is beautiful although she uses very little* **make-up.**

SIGN #1: Fingertips of **'FLAT O'** hands are placed on either cheek and the hands are moved in circles as if rubbing in cream.

make-up: *adj.* referring to a substitute for something that was missed. *She missed the final exam but was able to take a* **make-up** *test.*

SIGN #2: Right **'EXTENDED A'** hand is held palm down. As the wrist rotates rightward, the hand is turned so that the palm faces left.

malady: See **disease.**

male: *adj.* characteristic of men or boys. *The veterinarian explained that the cat was* **male.**

SIGN: Right **'FLAT C'** hand is held in front of forehead, with palm facing left, and is closed twice into a **'FLAT O'** hand. (This sign is used for *animals* and for *young male persons.* For *adult male persons,* see **man.**)

malice: *n.* an evil intention to do harm. *There is always **malice** in his behaviour toward his classmates.*

SIGN: Right **'CROOKED 5'** hand is held with palm facing left and tip of forefinger touching or near end of nose while left **'CROOKED 5'** hand, palm facing right, is held just in front of/below right hand. The hands eventually assume **'A'** shapes as they brush past one another, the right hand moving downward/forward and the left hand moving upward/backward. Appropriate facial expression is important.
SAME SIGN—**malicious**, *adj.*

malignant: *adj.* (used in a pathological sense) resistant to therapy; uncontrollable; life-threatening. *The tumour proved to be **malignant**.*

SIGN: Fingerspell **MALIGNANT**.

mall: *n.* an enclosed complex of shops and services, also featuring large parking areas and public walkways. *We went shopping at the **mall**.*

SIGN: Fingerspell **MALL**.

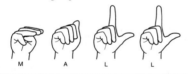

man: *n.* an adult male human being. *A **man** takes care of our yard for us.*

SIGN: Right **'5'** hand is held with palm facing leftward/downward, fingers pointing upward/leftward, and tip of thumb touching the middle of the forehead. The hand is then lowered so that the tip of the thumb comes to rest at about mid-chest. (For **man** meaning 'people in general', see **mankind**.)

manage: *v.* to control; direct. *Some students are hard to **manage**.*

SIGN: Horizontal **'X'** hands are held slightly apart with left palm facing right and right palm facing left. Then they are alternately moved backward and forward.
SAME SIGN—**management**, *n.*
(For **manager**, *n.*, the Agent Ending (see p. LIV) may follow.)

mandate: *n.* an official requirement. *The federal government has a **mandate** to treat all Canadians equally.*

SIGN: Tip of forefinger of right **'X'** hand is placed in right-facing palm of left **'EXTENDED B'** hand. Together the hands are moved firmly toward the chest, giving the impression that the left hand is being tugged by the right forefinger.

mandatory: *adj.* compulsory; obligatory. *Wearing seatbelts in motor vehicles is **mandatory**.*

SIGN: Tip of forefinger of right **'X'** hand is placed in right-facing palm of left **'EXTENDED B'** hand. Together the hands are moved firmly toward the chest, giving the impression that the left hand is being tugged by the right forefinger.
ALTERNATE SIGN—**must**

maneuver [*also spelled* **manoeuvre**]: *v.* to skillfully make things happen the way you want them to. *He manages to **maneuver** through rush hour traffic without much trouble.*

SIGN: Tips of joined forefinger and thumb of horizontal right **'F'** hand, palm toward the body, are brought purposefully up to strike the chin. Then the right **'ONE'** hand, palm left and forefinger pointing forward, zigzags forward. (ASL CONCEPT—**skilled - go through**.) Signs vary according to context.

manicure: *v.* to care for the fingernails. *The esthetician is qualified to **manicure** your nails.*

SIGN: Fingertips of left **'STANDARD BASE'** hand rest on side of crooked forefinger of horizontal **'A-INDEX'** hand, of which the palm faces left. The right hand then moves forward/leftward as the thumb moves up and down to simulate the use of nail clippers. (Signs vary.)

manifesto: *n.* a public declaration issued by a government or a political party. *The Separatists issued a manifesto regarding their intent to hold a referendum.*

SIGN: **'ONE'** hands, palms down, tips of forefingers touching either side of the mouth, are swung outward so that forefingers point upward and palms face away from the body.

manipulate: *v.* to control or influence cleverly and skillfully (sometimes in a devious way). *He gets everything he wants because he knows how to manipulate his parents.*

SIGN: Horizontal **'X'** hands are held slightly apart with left palm facing right and right palm facing left. Then they are alternately moved backward and forward.
SAME SIGN—**manipulation**, *n.*

mankind: *n.* the human race; all human beings. *Some environmentalists suggest that mankind is in danger of extinction.*

SIGN: Vertical **'K'** hands are held apart with palms forward but facing each other slightly, and are alternately circled backward.

manner: *n.* a way of doing something. *I do not like the manner in which she has completed the project.*

SIGN: **'EXTENDED B'** hands, held parallel with palms facing one another and fingers pointing forward, are simultaneously moved forward.

mannerly: See **polite**.

manners: *n.* a socially acceptable way of behaving. *It is important to teach children good manners.*

SIGN: Thumb of vertical right **'EXTENDED B'** hand, palm facing left, is tapped a few times against centre of chest.

manual: *n.* a guidebook; book of instructions or information. *We have several manuals on Deaf Culture.*

SIGN #1: Thumb and forefinger of right **'A-INDEX'** (or **'MODIFIED G'**) hand are slid up the edge of the left **'EXTENDED B'** hand, which is held with palm facing body. Motion is repeated. (This sign is appropriate only for small, flat publications. For more comprehensive publications, see **book** #1. Alternatively, **MANUAL** may be fingerspelled.)

manual: *adj.* related to the hands. *He prefers to do manual work rather than sit in an office all day.*

SIGN #2: **'EXTENDED B'** hands are crossed with the right hand behind the left. The palms face the body and the fingers point basically upward although the fingers of the left hand are angled slightly rightward while the fingers of the right hand are angled slightly leftward. The right hand slides downward/rightward, then moves out in front of the left hand which slides downward/leftward.

manual: *adj.* related to the use of ASL as opposed to spoken English. (ASL is *not*, strictly speaking, a 'manual' language. Rather, it is a 'visual' language, including a wide variety of facial expression, lip patterns, body posture, as well as hand movements.) *An oral versus manual controversy has historically existed in Deaf education.*

SIGN #3: Horizontal **'ONE'** hands are held slightly apart with palms facing the chest at a downward angle. As the wrists rotate backward toward the chest, the forefingers revolve around one another.

manual alphabet: *n.* the hand alphabet used by people who sign. *The American manual alphabet is one-handed whereas the British is a two-handed system.*

SIGN: Right hand, palm facing forward, spells **'ABC'**, and then forms a **'BENT 5'** hand which moves from left to right, fingers fluttering. (ASL CONCEPT—**A-B-C - spell**.)

manufacture: *v.* to make a product from raw materials. *Our new company will manufacture educational toys.*

SIGN: Horizontal right **'S'** hand is placed on top of horizontal left **'S'** hand as both palms face the body. The right hand is then raised slightly and both wrists are bent causing the hands to turn so that the right palm faces left and the left palm faces right as the right hand re-establishes contact with the left hand.

manure: *n.* animal excrement sometimes mixed with chemicals and used as fertilizer. *They bought a load of **manure** to fertilize their lawn.*

SIGN: Without lifting the fingertips of the **'BENT EXTENDED B'** hands from their positions at either side of the chest, the forearms move inward and outward. Next, horizontal left **'A'** (or **'EXTENDED A'**) hand is held in a fixed position with palm facing backward/rightward. Thumb of horizontal right **'EXTENDED A'** hand is inserted in the base of the left hand. The right hand is then lowered from this position. Motion is repeated. (ASL CONCEPT—**animal - feces.**) **MANURE** may be fingerspelled.

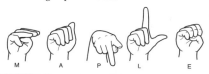

many: *adj.* a large number of. ***Many** of our relatives live in the city of Montreal.*

SIGN: **'S'** hands are held parallel with palms up and are thrust forward simultaneously as they are opened to form **'CROOKED 5'** hands. (Each repetition of this sign indicates an even greater number.)

map: *n.* a diagrammatic representation of an area. *Every tourist should have a **map** of the city.*

SIGN: Fingerspell **MAP**.

maple: *adj.* related to a tree with winged seeds and lobed leaves. *The leaf of the **maple** tree is Canada's national symbol.*

SIGN: Fingerspell **MAPLE**.

mar: *v.* to spoil; damage. *Do not use that harsh cleanser on the coffee table; it will **mar** the surface.*

SIGN: Horizontal left **'X'** hand is held in a fixed position with palm rightward but slanted toward the body slightly while horizontal right **'X'** hand is held above/behind left hand with palm leftward. The right hand then slides briskly along the top of the left hand and continues to move in a forward/rightward direction.

marathon: *n.* a long footrace (usually 42 kilometres). *He participates in the **marathon** every year.*

SIGN: Tip of forefinger of right **'ONE'** hand, palm down, is used to stroke upward from the wrist along the left arm. Next, horizontal **'CLAWED L'** hands are held, left in front of right, with left thumb and right forefinger linked, and right palm facing left while left palm faces right. Together, the hands are moved firmly forward a short distance. The motion is repeated several times. (ASL CONCEPT—**long - run run.**) The second part of the sign may vary depending on the type of marathon being discussed. It could be a **dance** marathon or a **swimming** marathon. (**MARATHON** may be fingerspelled, especially if the marathon is named, *e.g.,* the Vancouver Marathon.)

marble: *n.* a small, hard ball of glass used in a children's game. *He won every **marble** in the game.*

SIGN #1: Horizontal **'COVERED T'** hand is held with palm facing left, as the thumb is repeatedly flicked upward to form an **'A-INDEX'** hand.

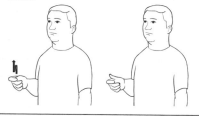

marble: *n.* a hard type of rock that can be polished to make it more pleasing to look at. *The steps leading up to the museum were made of **marble**.*

SIGN #2: Fingerspell **MARBLE**.

march: *v.* to walk with regular steps in a procession, as practised by the military. *The veterans will **march** at the head of the parade.*

SIGN #1: **'BENT 4'** hands are held left in front of right with palms down and are lightly swept forward a couple of times.

March: *n.* the third month of the year. *St. Patrick's Day is celebrated on March 17th.*

SIGN #2: Fingerspell **MARCH**.

margarine: *n.* a butter substitute, usually made from vegetable oils. *This margarine is made of corn oil.*

SIGN: Tips of extended fingers of right **'BENT EXTENDED U'** hand, are brushed back twice against right-facing palm of left **'EXTENDED B'** hand. (**MARGARINE** may be fingerspelled to emphasize a distinction between margarine and butter.)

REGIONAL VARIATION—**butter** #2

margin: *n.* an edge; border. *The teacher wrote comments about my essay beside the margin.*

SIGN: Right **'EXTENDED B'** hand is held on a forward/upward angle with the palm facing left. The forearm is then lowered so that the hand becomes horizontal with the fingers pointing forward.

marijuana: *n.* dried leaves and flowers of the hemp plant used in cigarette form as a narcotic. *Use of marijuana is illegal in Canada.*

SIGN: Joined thumb and forefinger of vertical right **'F'** (or **'CLOSED X'** or **'CLOSED G'**) hand, palm left, are tapped a couple of times against the right side of the lips.

mark: *n.* a spot; scratch. *There is a mark on the table.*

SIGN #1: Left **'EXTENDED B'** hand is held in a fixed position with palm up and fingers pointing forward at a slight rightward angle. Tip of forefinger of right **'ONE'** hand is used to indicate the mark on the left palm. (Signs in this context vary considerably, depending on the type and location of the mark.)

mark: *v.* to grade or evaluate school work. *The teacher will mark our test papers immediately.*

SIGN #2: Left **'EXTENDED B'** hand is held out in front of the body with fingers pointing rightward and palm toward the body. Right **'ONE'** (or **'K'**) hand is held closer to the body with palm facing leftward and forefinger pointing toward the left palm. Both hands move downward as the right wrist twists back and forth several times. (For **mark**, *n.,* meaning academic grade, see **percent** or fingerspell **MARK**.)

mark a calendar: *v.* to make a note of a date or appointment on a calendar. *Please remember to mark your calendar for our meeting on Wednesday at 7:30 p.m.*

SIGN #3: Vertical left **'EXTENDED B'** hand is held in a fixed position with palm toward the body at a rightward angle. Bunched fingertips of vertical right **'O'** hand are placed on the left palm. Right hand opens to form an **'EXTENDED B'** hand and then comes together purposefully with the left palm.

market: *v.* to sell. *The farmer will market his crops through the Wheat Pool.*

SIGN #1: **'FLAT O'** hands, held parallel with palms down and fingers pointing down, are swung forward/upward from the wrists a couple of times.

market: *n.* a place where goods (often fresh fruits and vegetables) are offered for sale. *We go to a roadside market every Saturday to buy fresh produce.*

SIGN #2: Fingerspell **MARKET**. (Alternatively, see **farm** + **food**.)

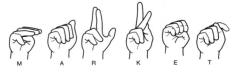

marriage: *n.* a legal union between two people. *Their marriage has lasted over 50 years.*

SIGN: Left **'EXTENDED C'** hand is held in a fixed position with palm facing the body but slanted slightly rightward. Right **'EXTENDED C'** hand, with palm facing that of the left hand is circled in a clockwise direction before it is brought down firmly to clasp the left hand.

marry: *v.* to unite in marriage. *He finally asked her to marry him.*

SIGN: **'EXTENDED C'** hands are held apart with palms facing and the right hand slightly above the left. The hands are then clasped together.

marvellous [*also spelled* **marvelous**]: *adj.* splendid; wonderful. *The actress looks marvellous in her costume.*

SIGN: Vertical **'EXTENDED B'** hands, palms facing forward, are held apart near the face. Forearms are pushed purposefully forward a short distance.

mash: *v.* to beat or crush into a soft mass. *You mash the potatoes while I make the gravy.*

SIGN: Left **'EXTENDED B'** hand is held in a fixed position with palm up and fingers pointing forward/rightward. Horizontal right **'S'** hand, palm facing the body, repeatedly pounds the left palm. (Sometimes this is a circular movement in a clockwise direction.)

mask: *n.* a covering that hides the face. *The robber wore a mask to disguise his identity.*

SIGN #1: Vertical right **'CROOKED 5'** hand, palm toward the face, is held just in front of the face.

OR

SIGN #2: **'CROOKED EXTENDED B'** hands, palms toward the face, are held upright so that the fingertips are near the eyes. The wrists are then simultaneously rotated, causing the hands to turn so that the palms face each other and the face is revealed.

mask: *v.* to cover up something you do not want people to know about. *He tries to mask his insecurity by bragging about himself.*

SIGN #3: Vertical right **'EXTENDED B'** hand is held just to the right and in front of the face with the palm facing backward. The forearm then swings sharply downward past the face so that the hand is eventually positioned in front of the chest with fingers pointing leftward.

mass: *n.* the amount of physical matter contained in an object; bulk. *In science class, we calculated the mass of various objects.*

SIGN #1: **'Y'** hands are held parallel with palms down, and tips of thumbs are tapped together at least twice.

mass: *n.* an abnormal growth such as a lump or tumor in a person's body. *The surgeon removed a large mass from the patient's abdomen.*

SIGN #2: Vertical **'SPREAD C'** hands, palms facing, are held close so that fingertips of one hand are almost touching those of the other. The hands are then simultaneously moved very purposefully a short distance forward. This sign may be made near any part of the body where the mass is said to exist. Cheeks are puffed out.

Mass: *n.* a religious ceremony, in the Roman Catholic and some Protestant churches, during which Communion is a part of the ritual. *The priest chanted during certain parts of the Mass.*

SIGN #3: Horizontal **'F'** hands, palms facing each other, are held apart, then drawn together and moved upward. (**MASS** may be fingerspelled.)

massacre: *n.* the cruel, violent killing of a large number of people. *The sculpture commemorates the massacre at Seven Oaks.*

SIGN: Left **'EXTENDED B'** hand is held in a fixed position in front of the left side of the body with palm facing rightward and slightly forward. Right **'ONE'** (or **'K'**) hand is held palm down as it moves forward/downward at a slight leftward angle, the forefinger firmly grazing the left palm. The sign is repeated a few times as the hands move rightward.

massage: *v.* to rub a person's body by pressing against the skin firmly to release tension and/or ease painful muscles. *Let me massage your stiff muscles for you.*

SIGN: **'SPREAD EXTENDED C'** hands are held parallel with palms down. The wrists then rotate outward to twist the hands two or three times so that the palms alternate between facing entirely downward and slanting toward each other. (Signs vary depending on which part of the body is being massaged.)

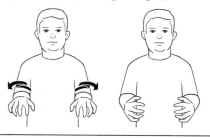

massive: *adj.* very large. *It is easy to get lost in that massive building.*

SIGN #1: Horizontal **'CLAWED L'** hands, which are held slightly apart with palms facing, are simultaneously moved farther apart as the wrists rotate to turn the palms down. Facial expression is important and the syllable 'CHA' is formed on the lips. (Sign selection for **massive** depends on the context.)

massive: *adj.* of grave seriousness or significance. *The patient died of a massive stroke.*

SIGN #2: Fingerspell **MASSIVE**. (Alternatively, see **serious**.)

mastectomy: *n.* the surgical removal of a breast. *A mastectomy is usually performed when breast cancer is found.*

SIGN: Horizontal right **'BENT EXTENDED B'** hand is held in front of the right side of the chest with palm facing the body and fingers pointing toward the body as well. The wrist then rotates in a counter-clockwise direction to firmly turn the hand palm-down. (This sign may be formed with either the left or the right hand, or both, depending on which breast is being removed.)

master: *n.* the owner of an animal. *The dog follows his master wherever he goes.*

SIGN #1: Fingerspell **MASTER**.

master: *n.* a person, especially a man, who is in a position of control. *He is the master of the household.*

SIGN #2: Vertical right **'ONE'** hand is held near the right side of the forehead with palm forward and slightly leftward. The wrist then rotates forward to turn the hand as the forefinger tucks into a **'BENT ONE'** position with the fingertip coming to rest on the right side of the forehead.

master: *v.* to become proficient at; learn to do (something) well. *He was able to master the use of a computer in just a few days.*

SIGN #3: Left **'EXTENDED B'** hand is held in a fixed position with palm up and fingers pointing forward/rightward. Fingertips of right **'CONTRACTED 5'** hand, palm down, are placed on the left palm. Then the right hand is changed to a **'FLAT O'** handshape as it is raised.

master: *adj.* expert; highly skilled. *He is a master carpenter.*

SIGN #4: Left **'EXTENDED B'** hand, palm facing right and fingers pointing upward/forward, is grasped by right **'OPEN A'** hand. Then right hand is pulled forward sharply and closed to form an **'A'** hand.

ALTERNATE SIGN—**experienced**

master (bedroom): *adj.* the largest or main (bedroom). *The master bedroom of the house overlooks the park.*

SIGN #5: Fingerspell **MASTER**.

master (key): *adj.* a passkey or one which opens all the locks of a specific set. *Anyone with a master key has access to all apartments in this building.*

SIGN #6: Fingerspell **MASTER**.

master/mistress of ceremonies [*also referred to informally as* **emcee**]: *n.* the man/woman who hosts a formal event, generally by welcoming people and introducing speakers or entertainers. *The master of ceremonies introduced the guest speaker at the banquet.*

SIGN: Fingerspell **MC**.

match: *v.* to harmonize with; go together well. *His blue shirt and grey tie match nicely.*

SIGN #1: **'SPREAD EXTENDED C'** hands are held slightly apart in front of the chest, palms facing the body, and are brought together so that the fingers mesh. ❖

match: *v.* to have the same qualities, strengths or abilities. *The Maple Leafs' defense can match that of the Canucks.*

SIGN #2: Vertical **'BENT EXTENDED B'** hands are positioned so that the right hand is held close to the chest with palm facing forward/leftward while the left hand is held to the left and farther forward with the palm facing that of the right hand. The fingertips of one hand make contact with those of the other as the hands come together, then move apart a short distance.

match: *n.* a strip of wood or cardboard tipped with a chemical that catches fire easily by friction. *I need a match to light the fire.*

SIGN #3: Left **'EXTENDED B'** hand is held in a fixed position with palm right and fingers pointing forward/upward. Right **'COVERED T'** hand, palm down, is held with forefinger against left palm. The right wrist then rotates clockwise as the forefinger resembles a match being struck against the left palm. The palm of the right hand eventually faces the body as the right hand moves away from the left. (Sometimes this is a small, repetitive movement rather than one fluid movement.)

match: *n.* a formal sports event; game. *We are going to the tennis match.*

SIGN #4: Horizontal **'EXTENDED A'** hands are held slightly apart with palms toward the body. The hands are then brought together so that the knuckles strike against each other a couple of times.

mate: *v.* to come together as a male and female for the purpose of sex. *Many zoo animals will not mate while in captivity.*

SIGN #1: Left **'V'** hand is held with palm up and extended fingers pointing forward at a slight rightward angle while right **'V'** hand is held just above the left hand with palm facing leftward at a downward/forward angle and extended fingers pointing leftward/upward at a slightly forward angle. The hands are brought together a few times so that the heels of the hands repeatedly collide.

mate: *n.* a person's husband or wife; spouse. *This invitation includes your mate.*

SIGN #2: Thumbtip of right **'EXTENDED C'** hand, palm down, is positioned at the centre of the forehead and the hand is brought downward to clasp left **'EXTENDED C'** hand, of which the palm faces upward. Then thumbtip of right **'EXTENDED C'** hand, palm down, is positioned at right cheek and the hand is brought downward to clasp left **'EXTENDED C'** hand, of which palm faces upward. (ASL CONCEPT—husband - wife.) When **mate** refers specifically to a 'husband', the first part of this sign is used only; when the word refers specifically to a 'wife', the second part of this sign is used only.

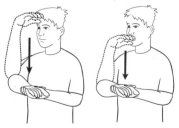

mate: *n.* an informal term used mainly in reference to men as chums or friends. (This term is more common in Great Britain.) *He was a mate of mine when we were at school.*

SIGN #3: Left **'CROOKED ONE'** hand is held palm-up with forefinger pointing rightward/forward, while right **'CROOKED ONE'** hand is held palm-down with forefinger laid across left forefinger at right angles to it. The wrists then rotate so that the hands reverse positions. (See also **friend**.)

(room)mate: *n.* a person who shares a room with someone. *He was my roommate at college.*

SIGN #4: **'SPREAD EXTENDED C'** hands are held slightly apart in front of the chest, palms facing the body, and are brought together so that the fingers mesh. Movement is repeated.

material: *n.* cloth; fabric. *You will need two metres of material for this pattern.*

SIGN #1: **'FLAT O'** hands are held slightly apart with palms up. Then the fingers are slid across the thumbs a few times, thus alternating between **'FLAT O'** and **'OFFSET O'** hands. ALTERNATE SIGN—**fabric**

material: *n.* the equipment necessary for a particular activity. *Before you begin your project, assemble all your materials.*

SIGN #2: Right **'EXTENDED B'** hand, palm facing up, fingers pointing forward, is moved from left to right in a series of successive short arcs. (Sign choice depends on context.)

maternal: *adj.* related to a mother. *My maternal relatives came from the Ukraine.*

SIGN: Tip of thumb of vertical right **'5'** hand, palm facing leftward, is tapped against the right side of the chin. The hand, still vertical, then assumes an **'EXTENDED B'** shape with palm forward/leftward, and is firmly pushed forward/leftward a very short distance. (ASL CONCEPT—**mother - her side**. Alternatively, the second part may be fingerspelled **SIDE** rather than signed.) When **maternal** means 'motherly,' only the first part of this sign is used.

mathematics: *n.* a science that deals with quantities, forms and their relationships and includes such things as algebra, geometry, trigonometry and calculus. *Addition, subtraction, multiplication and division are the four basic operations in* **mathematics.**

SIGN: **'M'** hands are held, left in front of right, with left palm facing right and right palm facing left. The hands brush against each other repeatedly as the right hand moves leftward a short distance and the left hand simultaneously moves rightward a few times.

matter: *n.* a substance that takes up space and has mass. *Waste vegetable* **matter** *is used to make fertilizer.*

SIGN #1: Right **'EXTENDED B'** hand, palm facing up, fingers pointing forward, is moved from left to right in a series of successive short arcs.

matter: *n.* a thing; affair; issue; concern. *We have some important* **matters** *to discuss now.*

SIGN #2: Right **'EXTENDED B'** hand, palm facing up, fingers pointing forward, is moved from left to right in a series of successive short arcs. (The English word **matters** in this context is often incorporated in the verb when expressed in ASL rather than accorded a separate sign. The sample sentence in ASL is: *YOU-ME* **DISCUSS** *IMPORTANT NOW.*)

(it doesn't) matter: *s.s.* regardless of; irrespective of. *It* **doesn't matter** *what else you have planned, you must attend the meeting tonight.*

SIGN #3: Fingers of horizontal **'BENT EXTENDED B'** hands, palms facing the chest, are alternately brushed back and forth against each other.

SAME SIGN—**no matter**

(what's the) matter?: *s.s.* What is the problem? or What is wrong? *What's the* **matter** *with you?*

SIGN #4: Vertical right **'Y'** hand, palm toward the body, is tapped a couple of times against the chin.

mattress: *n.* a large, flat pad which is placed on a bed frame. *Some people prefer a firm* **mattress** *while others like a softer one.*

SIGN: Head tilts slightly to the right, supported by right **'EXTENDED B'** hand, which is held against right side of face. Next, the signer's cheeks are puffed out as vertical **'CONTRACTED C'** hands are held apart with palms forward/ downward. The fingers and thumbs relax slightly to form **'FLAT C'** shapes, open to resume **'CONTRACTED C'** shapes and continue to alternate a few times. (ASL CONCEPT—**bed - soft**.) **MATTRESS** is frequently fingerspelled.

mature: *adj.* fully grown; fully developed. *Grey hair makes you look* **mature.**

SIGN: Fingerspell **MATURE**.

maximum: *adj.* related to the greatest possible amount. *Major highways have* **maximum** *speed limits posted at regular intervals.*

SIGN: Left **'EXTENDED B'** hand is held in a fixed position in front of the upper chest with palm down and fingers pointing rightward, while right **'EXTENDED B'** hand is held in a lower position with palm facing the body and fingers pointing downward. The right hand is then brought up sharply so that the back of it hits the left palm at right angles to it.

may: *v.* to have the possibility. *We* **may** *go to Europe next summer.*

SIGN #1: **'EXTENDED B'** hands, held apart with palms up and fingers pointing forward, are alternately raised and lowered at least twice.

may: *v.* to be allowed or permitted. *You* **may** *go if you have finished all your work.*

SIGN #2: **'A'** hands, palms down, are held slightly apart, and are brought down firmly in front of the chest.

May: *n.* the fifth month of the year. *Her birthday is in May.*

SIGN #3: Fingerspell **MAY**.

maybe: *adv.* perhaps; possibly. *Maybe you should ask your mother first.*

SIGN: **'EXTENDED B'** hands, held apart with palms up and fingers pointing forward, are alternately raised and lowered at least twice.

mayonnaise: *n.* a creamy sauce made with egg yolks, oil, vinegar and seasoning. *Some people like mayonnaise on their sandwiches.*

SIGN: Fingertips of right **'CONTRACTED 5'** hand, palm toward the body, are placed against the middle of the chest and the hand is then drawn forward as it closes to form a **'FLAT O'** hand. Next, left **'EXTENDED B'** hand is held in a fixed position with palm up and fingers pointing forward/rightward. Right **'EXTENDED B'** hand is held with palm down and fingers pointing forward/leftward as they are rubbed in a counter-clockwise direction on the left palm. (ASL CONCEPT—**white - spread on food**.) **Mayonnaise** is frequently fingerspelled in the abbreviated form **MAYO**.

mayor: *n.* the head of a town, city or municipal corporation. *The mayor will officially open the new City Hall next week.*

SIGN: Fingerspell **MAYOR**.

maze: *n.* a system of passages that is difficult or confusing to find one's way through. *We were lost in the maze and had to call for help to get out.*

SIGN: Fingerspell **MAZE**.

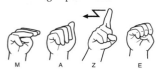

me: *pron.* used by the signer when referring to himself/herself. [See PRONOUNS, p. LXIV.] *I promised to help you, so please trust me.*

SIGN: Horizontal right **'BENT ONE'** hand is held with tip of forefinger touching the chest.

meadow: *n.* a grassy area often used for the grazing of livestock. *Several Jersey cows were grazing in the meadow.*

SIGN: Right **'CROOKED 4'** hand, palm down, and fingers pointing leftward, is held just in front of the chin and the hand is moved backward briskly in small circular motions, brushing against the underside of the chin with each cycle. Next, horizontal right **'5'** hand is held with palm down and fingers pointing forward. The hand then makes a wide arc leftward as it inscribes a circle in front of the body. (ASL CONCEPT—**grass - field**.)

meal: *n.* the food served and eaten at breakfast, lunch, dinner, etc. *After eating a hearty meal we were ready to start working.*

SIGN: Vertical **'MODIFIED O'** hand, palm facing the body, is brought toward the mouth so that the fingertips touch the lips.

mean: *v.* to intend; denote; connote; signify. *What does this word mean?*

SIGN #1: Horizontal left **'EXTENDED B'** hand is held in a fixed position with palm facing right while tip of forefinger of right palm-down **'BENT V'** hand is jabbed into the left palm. The right hand then moves away from the left hand as the right wrist rotates a quarter turn clockwise, and the middle fingertip is jabbed into the left palm.

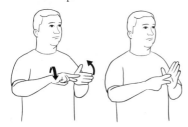

mean: *adj.* cruel; malicious. *Do not pull the puppy's tail; that is **mean!***

SIGN #2: Right **'CROOKED 5'** hand is held with palm facing left and tip of forefinger touching or near end of nose while left **'CROOKED 5'** hand, palm facing right, is held just in front of/below right hand. The hands eventually assume **'A'** shapes as they brush past one another, the right hand moving downward/forward and the left hand moving upward/backward. Appropriate facial expression is important.

mean: *adj.* stingy; miserly; ungenerous. (This connotation of **mean** is common in Great Britain but rare in Canada.) *Scrooge was wealthy but **mean.***

SIGN #3: Right **'SPREAD EXTENDED C'** hand is held palm down on the upturned palm of the left **'EXTENDED B'** hand and the fingertips scrape firmly backward toward the chest. (Facial expression is important.)

mean: *adj.* the middle point; average. *The **mean** temperature during January was minus 16 degrees.*

SIGN #4: Right **'EXTENDED B'** hand, with palm facing left and fingers pointing forward, slides from side to side a few times along forefinger of horizontally held left **'EXTENDED B'** hand, whose palm is facing the body.

meaningless: *adj.* having no importance or relevance. *Why do teachers ask students to memorize **meaningless** information?*

SIGN #1: Right **'EXTENDED A'** hand, palm facing left, thumb under chin, is thrust forward. Next, vertical **'F'** hands are held apart with palms facing forward. The hands are then brought purposefully together.
(ASL CONCEPT—**not - important**.)
Appropriate facial expression is important.
ALTERNATE SIGN—**trivial**

meaningless: *adj.* having no meaning due to a lack of knowledge or comprehension. *They spoke in Greek which was **meaningless** to me.*

SIGN #2: Vertical right **'S'** hand, with knuckles near right side of forehead, is changed to a **'ONE'** hand as the forefinger is flicked upward. Next, left **'EXTENDED B'** hand is held in a fixed position with palm facing upward but slanted slightly toward the body at a rightward angle. Vertical right **'O'** hand, palm facing left, is lowered so that it strikes the left palm.
(ASL CONCEPT—**understand - zero**.)

(in the) meantime [*or* **meanwhile**]: *adv.* during the intervening period of time; at the same time. *I will start the barbecue; **in the meantime**, you can prepare the salad.*

SIGN: Generally, there is no specific sign for this concept. It is conveyed by a pause between the two clauses. The sample sentence would be signed as: *B-B-Q, ME START* - pause - *SALAD, YOU MAKE.*

measles: *n.* a very contagious viral disease common among children. *A mother's exposure to German **measles** during the first trimester of her pregnancy can result in deafness for her baby.*

SIGN: Fingertips of **'SPREAD EXTENDED C'** hands, palms toward the body, are used to tap against the face, neck and chest in a series of small arcs.

measure: *v.* to calculate the exact size, amount, or extent. *Let us **measure** the length and width of our garden plot.*

SIGN: **'Y'** hands are held parallel with palms down, and tips of thumbs are tapped together at least twice.
SAME SIGN—**measurement**, *n.*

meat: *n.* the flesh of animals, especially mammals, used as food. *My favourite type of **meat** is veal.*

SIGN #1: Right **'OPEN F'** hand, palm facing away from the body, is brought down to grasp the skin between thumb and forefinger of horizontal left **'EXTENDED B'** hand whose palm faces body. Hands then make small back and forth movements together.

meat *(cont.)*

SIGN #2 [ATLANTIC]: Left **'U'** hand is held with extended fingers pointing forward/rightward and palm facing rightward/backward while extended fingers of right **'U'** hand are positioned on and at right angles to fingers of left hand. Then both hands make small back and forth movements as though cutting meat.

SIGN #3 [ONTARIO]: Left **'5'** hand is held palm down with fingers pointing slightly forward and to the right while right **'5'** hand is held palm down with fingers pointing slightly forward and to the left. Both hands are moved toward each other, until thumb and forefinger of each hand are inserted between thumb and forefinger of the other hand. Motion is repeated.

mechanic: *n.* a person skilled in maintaining machinery. *You must serve an apprenticeship in order to become a licensed mechanic.*

SIGN: Extended fingers of horizontal right **'V'** hand, palm facing left and angled toward the body, are used to grasp and rock on horizontal forefinger of left **'ONE'** hand, thus simulating the function of a wrench.

mechanical: *adj.* related to machinery. *A mechanical device was used to place the sign on the roof of the shop.*

SIGN: Fingers of horizontal **'CLAWED 5'** hands, palms toward the body, are interlocked and remain so as they are shaken up and down. This is a wrist action.

medal: *n.* a small, round, metal, inscribed award given in commemoration of an outstanding accomplishment. *Jo-Anne Robinson won four gold swimming medals in 1965.*

SIGN: Vertical right **'C-INDEX'** hand, palm facing left, is tapped repeatedly against the middle of the chest.

meddle: *v.* to interfere annoyingly; intrude. *You should never meddle in other people's affairs.*

SIGN: Tip of forefinger of right **'CROOKED ONE'** hand touches nose and is then dropped downward and inserted at least twice into the small opening at the top of the horizontal left **'S'** hand which is held with the palm facing right. ❖

ALTERNATE SIGN—**butt in** #2

media: *n.* those who report the news through such means as newspaper articles or television broadcasts. *The media did a good job of reporting the proceedings of the trial.*

SIGN: Fingerspell **MEDIA**.

median: *n.* a point in the middle. *The math teacher asked the students to locate the median point on a given line.*

SIGN: With palm down, horizontal right **'BENT MIDFINGER 5'** hand is circled clockwise from the wrist above upturned left palm, tip of right midfinger falling in the centre of the left palm. (Sometimes, **median** has the connotation of **average**.)

medicine: *n.* a remedy used to treat illness. *The doctor prescribed some medicine to relieve his pain.*

SIGN #1: Tip of middle finger of right **'BENT MIDFINGER 5'** hand is placed on the upturned left palm, and maintains contact with the left palm as the right hand teeters back and forth a few times.

SAME SIGN—**medical**, *adj.*

SIGN #2 [ATLANTIC]: Left **'S'** hand is held in a fixed position with palm down as the little finger of the right **'I'** hand, palm facing down, is inserted into the opening at the top of the left **'S'** hand and shaken.

mediocre: *adj.* average or ordinary in quality. *This method of training produced only mediocre results.*

SIGN: Right **'5'** hand, palm down, is held with fingers pointing forward and is rocked as the wrist twists from side to side a few times. Facial expression is important.

meditate: *v.* to think deeply, often about spiritual matters. *After you meditate, you will feel at peace with yourself.*

SIGN: Vertical **'FLAT O'** hands are held just in front of either side of the forehead with palms facing backward and fingers rapidly fluttering as the hands move in small circles. From the signer's perspective, the left hand moves clockwise while the right hand moves counterclockwise.

SAME SIGN—**meditation**, *n.*

medium: *adj.* midway between extremes; intermediate; average. *The waitress asked "Would you like your steak rare, **medium**, or well done?"*

SIGN #1: Left **'EXTENDED B'** hand is held in a fixed position with palm facing the body and fingers pointing right. Vertical right **'EXTENDED B'** hand, held just behind the left hand with palm facing left, is lowered from the wrist as it strikes the space between the thumb and forefinger of the left hand a couple of times.

medium: *adj.* average in terms of clothing size. *Do you have this shirt in **medium**?*

SIGN #2: Vertical right **'M'** hand, palm facing forward/leftward, is wobbled slightly. (Sign choice for **medium**, especially in noun form, depends on context.)

meek: *adj.* patient; humble; submissive. *A **meek** person is often referred to as mild-mannered.*

SIGN: **'B'** (or **'EXTENDED B'**) hands are crossed in front of the mouth, left palm facing rightward/downward and right palm facing leftward/downward with the right hand just behind the left hand. Then they are drawn apart until the palms face completely downward.

meet: *v.* to encounter; come together; make the acquaintance of. *I will **meet** you in front of the bank at two o'clock.*

SIGN #1: Vertical **'ONE'** hands are held slightly apart with palms facing and are then brought together so that they touch one another.

meet: *v.* to assemble or gather for a specific purpose. *The committee members will **meet** to plan the picnic.*

SIGN #2: **'CONTRACTED 5'** hands are held virtually upright at a slight forward angle with palms facing each other. The fingers then come together to form **'FLAT O'** hands with fingertips of each hand touching those of the other.

meet: *v.* to satisfy; fulfill. *It is difficult to **meet** the needs of all disabled persons.*

SIGN #3: **'BENT B'** hands, right above left, with left palm facing right and right palm facing left, are placed firmly against the chest.

meet: *n.* a sporting competition. *She entered the track and field **meet**.*

SIGN #4: Horizontal **'EXTENDED A'** hands are held slightly apart with palms toward the body. The hands are then brought together so that the knuckles strike against each other.

meeting: *n.* the assembly of a group for a specific purpose. *They will hold a special **meeting** tonight.*

SIGN: **'CONTRACTED 5'** hands are held virtually upright at a slight forward angle with palms facing each other. The fingers then come together to form **'FLAT O'** hands with fingertips of each hand touching those of the other. Motion is repeated.

melancholy: *adj.* gloomy; depressed; sad. *He has been in a **melancholy** state ever since his parents divorced.*

SIGN: Tips of middle fingers of **'BENT MIDFINGER 5'** hands are held at either side of upper chest and are simultaneously lowered. ALTERNATE SIGNS—**depressed** #2 or **sad**

melody: *n.* a piece of music that forms a distinctive tune. *The song has a pleasant **melody**.*

SIGN: Horizontal right **'EXTENDED B'** hand is positioned above left forearm with palm facing leftward/backward. The right wrist makes slight back and forth rotations so that the palm alternates between being angled slightly upward and being angled slightly downward.

melon: *n.* a large fruit with a hard rind and juicy flesh. *It is hard to tell if a **melon** is ripe enough to eat.*

SIGN: Right horizontal **'COVERED 8'** hand is held with palm down just above left **'STANDARD BASE'** hand. Then tip of middle finger of left hand is flicked against back of left hand, thus becoming an **'OPEN 8'** hand. Motion is repeated.

melt: *v.* to dissolve; change from a solid to liquid form; gradually disappear. *The snow will **melt** when the sun comes out.*

SIGN: **'FLAT O'** hands are held parallel with palms up and slanted slightly toward the body. As the hands are drawn apart the thumbs slide across the fingertips, causing the hands to assume **'A'** shapes.

member: *n.* a person who belongs to an organized group. *He is a **member** of the Canadian Cultural Society of the Deaf.*

SIGN #1: Horizontal right **'BENT EXTENDED B'** hand, palm toward the body, is placed first against the left side of the chest below the shoulder, and then moved across to a parallel position on the right side.

OR

SIGN #2: **'OPEN F'** hands are held slightly apart, palms facing each other, and are then brought together to form **'F'** hands, with thumbs and forefingers linked.

Member of the Legislative Assembly: *n.* an elected representative of a provincial government. *He was a **Member of the Legislative Assembly** in Manitoba before he became a Member of Parliament in Ottawa.*

SIGN: Fingerspell **MLA**.

M   L   A

Member of Parliament: *n.* an elected member of the federal government, representing Canadians in the House of Commons. *He is a highly respected **Member of Parliament** in Ottawa.*

SIGN: Fingerspell **MP**.

M   P

Member of the Provincial Parliament: *n.* an elected representative of a provincial government. *As a **Member of the Provincial Parliament** in Ontario, she leads a busy life.*

SIGN: Fingerspell **MPP**.

M   P   P

memorize: *v.* to study in an effort to remember; learn by heart. *The actor **memorized** his lines.*

SIGN: Right **'SPREAD C'** hand is held with fingertips on the forehead and is drawn forward as the hand closes to form an **'S'** hand.

memory: *n.* the ability of the mind to store and recall knowledge. *The teacher used a variety of exercises and activities to try to improve the child's **memory**.*

SIGN #1: Right **'SPREAD C'** hand is held with fingertips on the forehead and is drawn forward as the hand closes to form an **'S'** hand.

memory: *n.* a specific recollection of an event or person. *Attending the annual fair with my family is my favourite childhood **memory**.*

SIGN #2: Right **'BENT V'** hand is held with palm backward and tip of middle finger just under/to the right of the right eye. The hand is then moved to the right and back so that it is just above the right shoulder.

(in) memory of: *adv. phr.* in remembrance or commemoration of (after death). *A wreath was placed on the Cenotaph **in memory of** those who died in the war.*

SIGN #3: Horizontal left **'EXTENDED A'** hand is held in a fixed position in front of the chest with palm toward the body. Right **'EXTENDED A'** hand is held palm down with thumbtip touching the centre of the forehead. Then the right hand is lowered and the thumbtip placed on that of the left hand.

mend: *v.* to heal; recover; improve. *Her broken arm will take time to **mend**.*

SIGN #1: Edge of right **'EXTENDED B'** hand is placed on wrist of left forearm and moved upward in a small arc toward the elbow.

mend: *v.* to repair; fix. *He is very good at **mending** broken things.*

SIGN #2: **'F'** hands, palms facing each other at a forward angle, are placed together with tips of thumbs and forefingers of each hand touching. The left hand remains steady while the right hand wobbles as the wrist twists back and forth slightly a few times.

mend: *v.* to repair something that is torn. *The housekeeper will try to **mend** these torn sheets.*

SIGN #3: Horizontal **'F'** hands are held slightly apart with palms facing each other. The left hand remains in a fixed position as the right hand is rotated clockwise at least twice so that the thumb and forefinger make contact with those of the left hand each time they brush past.

meningitis: *n.* an illness caused by inflammation of the membranes around the brain or spinal cord. *Meningitis in very young children sometimes results in deafness.*

SIGN: Fingerspell **MENINGITIS**.

menopause: *n.* the period during which a woman's menstrual cycle stops (usually during her late forties or early fifties). *Hot flushes are a common symptom of menopause.*

SIGN: Vertical right **'A'** hand, palm toward the face, is tapped lightly against the right cheek. Then the right **'EXTENDED B'** hand, palm facing left, is brought down sharply from a semi-vertical position to strike the upturned left palm which is held in a rigid manner in front of the chest. (ASL CONCEPT—**period - stop**.) **MENOPAUSE** is frequently fingerspelled.

menstruate: *v.* to discharge blood and other debris from the uterus cyclically. *Most women of child-bearing age who are not pregnant menstruate monthly.*

SIGN: Vertical right **'A'** hand, palm toward the face. is tapped lightly against the right cheek twice.

SAME SIGN—**menstruation**, *n.*

mental: *adj.* involving the mind. *Thinking is a mental process.*

SIGN: Tip of forefinger of right **'CROOKED ONE'** hand, palm toward the head, is tapped against right side of forehead.

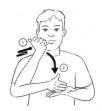

mention: *v.* to refer to or talk about briefly or incidentally. *He asked if the teacher mentioned anything about the exam next week.*

SIGN: Tip of forefinger of vertical right **'4'** hand, palm facing left, is tapped twice against the chin. (Signs vary. **Tell** is sometimes used. For **mention someone's name**, use **name** followed by the person's name or appropriate pronoun.)

menu: *n.* a list of items that can be ordered at a restaurant. *The main dining room at the hotel has an extensive menu.*

SIGN #1: Vertical **'MODIFIED O'** hand, palm facing the body, is brought toward the mouth so that the fingertips touch the lips. Next, left **'EXTENDED B'** hand is held in a fixed position with palm toward the body at a rightward and slightly upward angle. **'BENT EXTENDED B'** hand, palm leftward/backward, is placed against the fingers of the left hand and then slid down to the heel of the left hand. Sometimes this downward movement is made in small successive arcs.
(ASL CONCEPT—**food - list**.)
MENU in this context may be fingerspelled.

menu: *n.* a list of options from which a computer operator can select an action to be carried out. *This menu has functions related to editing.*

SIGN #2: Horizontal left **'CONTRACTED B'** hand is held in a fixed position with palm facing the body. Horizontal right **'4'** hand, palm facing the body, is held just under the left hand with side of forefinger touching that of the little finger of the left hand. The right hand is then lowered. To indicate plurality, the motion is repeated. (**MENU** in this context may be fingerspelled.)

merchandise: *n.* goods offered for sale. *The merchandise in that store is very expensive.*

SIGN: Right **'EXTENDED B'** hand, palm facing up, fingers pointing forward, is moved from left to right in a series of successive short arcs.

merchant: *n.* a person who buys and sells for profit. *He is a diamond merchant for a chain of jewellery stores.*

SIGN: **'FLAT O'** hands, held parallel with palms down and fingers pointing down, are swung forward/upward from the wrists a couple of times.

mercy: *n.* a compassionate attitude toward an offender; pity. *The lawyer pleaded for mercy on behalf of her client.*

SIGN: Right **'BENT MIDFINGER 5'** hand is held upright with palm facing forward but slanted downward slightly. It is then moved forward with circular motions to simulate the stroking of an imaginary person with the middle finger. Appropriate facial expression is important. (Alternatively, this sign may be made with two hands.)
SAME SIGN—**merciful,** *adj.*

merge: *v.* to blend. *Because their interests merge, they spend a great deal of time together.*

SIGN #1: **'SPREAD EXTENDED C'** hands are held slightly apart in front of the chest, palms facing the body, and are brought together so that the fingers mesh. ❖

merge: *v.* to come together; join. *The two companies will merge under a new name.*

SIGN #2: **'OPEN F'** hands are brought together so that the thumbs and forefingers are linked to form **'F'** hands. ❖ (This sign is used when it refers specifically to *companies or corporations.*)

merge: *v.* to come together; join. *The two highways will merge up ahead.*

SIGN #3: **'ONE'** hands are held apart with palms down and forefingers pointing forward. As the hands come together, they are moved forward together. (This sign is used when it refers specifically to *two paths, routes or channels which run parallel and then come together to form one path.*)

merge: *v.* to come together; join. *Traffic must merge now.*

SIGN #4: Horizontal **'3'** hands are held parallel with palms facing each other but angled toward the body. As the hands move forward, the palms directly face each other and the extended fingers point forward. (This sign is used for **merge** when it refers specifically to *two lanes of traffic that come together to form one lane.*)

merit: *n.* value; excellence; superior quality. *Her work in the field of medicine is of great merit.*

SIGN: Vertical **'F'** hands are held apart with palms facing forward. The hands are then brought purposefully together. **MERIT** may be fingerspelled.
ALTERNATE SIGN—**important** #2

merry: *adj.* jolly; full of fun and happiness. *We wished them a merry Christmas.*

SIGN: Horizontal right **'EXTENDED B'** hand, palm toward the body, is brushed up and off the chest twice in a circular motion.

mesh: *v.* to combine with; fit together well. *All planned events must mesh with our time schedule.*

SIGN #1: **'SPREAD EXTENDED C'** hands are held slightly apart in front of the chest, palms facing the body, and are brought together so that the fingers mesh. ❖

mesh: *n.* a net-like material. *The butterfly struggled to free itself from the mesh.*

SIGN #2: Fingers of right **'4'** hand, palm facing the body, point leftward/upward and are laid against rightward/upward pointing fingers of left **'4'** hand, of which the palm faces the body too. The hands are then drawn apart at a downward angle.

mess: *n.* a state of confusion; untidiness; clutter. *The babysitter left the kitchen in a mess.*

SIGN #1: Right **'MODIFIED 5'** hand is held under chin with palm down as the fingers flutter.

OR

SIGN #2: **'5'** hands are held offset with palms down and fingers pointing forward. They are then alternately moved backward and forward. (**MESS** is frequently fingerspelled.)

message: *n.* a brief communication. *She left a message on the answering machine.*

SIGN: Left **'MODIFIED O'** hand is held at about shoulder level with palm facing upward but angled slightly toward the body while right **'MODIFIED O'** hand is held upright just in front of the forehead with palm toward the face. The forearms then move simultaneously forward/downward as the hands open to assume **'MODIFIED 5'** shapes with palms facing upward. (**MESSAGE** is frequently fingerspelled.)

messy: *adj.* dirty; cluttered; untidy. *Her desk is always messy.*

SIGN: **'5'** hands are held offset with palms down and fingers pointing forward. They are then alternately moved backward and forward.

metal: *n.* a material made of chemical elements such as iron, silver, copper, etc. *The body of the car is made of metal.*

SIGN: Tip of forefinger of right **'CROOKED ONE'** hand, palm toward the body, is tapped against the upper front teeth.

metaphor: *n.* a figure of speech implying a comparison, *e.g.,* 'the autumn of his life' (based on the concept that spring is a time of birth; summer represents youth; autumn connotes middle age; and winter symbolizes old age, leading eventually to death). *The use of metaphor in someone's writing can create a more vivid mental picture for the reader.*

SIGN: Fingerspell **METAPHOR**.

M　E　T　A　P　H　O　R

meter: *n.* a device that measures and records a quantity of whatever has passed through it during a certain period of time. *The man came to our house to read our water, gas and electricity meters.*

SIGN: Horizontal left **'EXTENDED B'** hand is held in a fixed position with palm up but angled toward the body and fingers pointing rightward/forward. Right **'ONE'** hand, palm facing left, is placed on the left palm with forefinger pointing forward/rightward but slanted upward. The right wrist then bends up and down, causing the hand to pivot so that the forefinger moves back and forth to simulate the action of a compass needle.

method: *n.* a way (of doing something). *Her method of doing things is always different from mine.*

SIGN: **'EXTENDED B'** hands, held parallel with palms facing one another and fingers pointing forward, are simultaneously moved forward.

methodical: *adj.* very organized and systematic in doing things; orderly. *A research scientist needs to be methodical.*

SIGN: Tip of forefinger of right **'ONE'** hand touches forehead. Then horizontal **'BENT EXTENDED B'** hands, with palms facing each other, are deliberately moved up and forward over each other in leapfrog fashion. (ASL CONCEPT—**think - step by step**.)

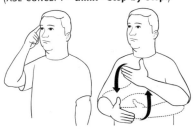

meticulous: *adj.* extremely careful (perhaps too careful) about details; very precise. *His meticulous nature makes him a good bookkeeper.*

SIGN #1: Vertical right **'COMBINED U + Y'** hand, palm forward, is held in front of the right shoulder and the forearm is drawn firmly backward a short distance. This is essentially a jerking motion.

OR

SIGN #2: The hands are very firmly set in place with right **'CLOSED X'** hand held above and slightly to the right of the left **'CLOSED X'** hand, palms facing.

metre [*also spelled* **meter**]: *n.* a metric unit of length equal to 100 centimetres or about 1.1 yards. *You will need one metre of fabric to make the blouse.*

SIGN: Vertical right **'M'** hand, palm facing forward/leftward, is wobbled slightly.

metric: *adj.* related to a specific system of measurement. *Canada adopted the metric system during the 1970s.*

SIGN: Fingerspell **METRIC**.

M　E　T　R　I　C

microphone: *n.* a device that converts sound waves into electrical energy. *The speaker will test the* **microphone** *before beginning his lecture.*

SIGN: Right **'s'** hand, palm facing left, is held in front of the mouth or chin while the lips move rapidly as if speaking.

microscope: *n.* an instrument used to magnify the image of small objects. *A* **microscope** *is required to observe the development of bacteria.*

SIGN: Horizontal **'c'** hands are held, right above left, with left palm facing right and right palm facing left. The right eye appears to squint as it looks down into the space created by the hands which are twisted inward slightly from the wrists a couple of times to simulate the focusing of the lens.

microscopic: *adj.* tiny; too small to see without a microscope. *We studied* **microscopic** *organisms in biology class.*

SIGN: Vertical right **'MODIFIED G'** hand is set firmly in place with palm forward/leftward. The signer's lips appear to be articulating the syllable 'MO'.

microwave: *n.* an abbreviation for 'microwave oven', a device in which food is cooked by electromagnetic radiation. *I use the* **microwave** *to heat leftovers.*

SIGN: Horizontal **'s'** hands are held slightly apart with palms facing each other and are simultaneously thrust open to form **'CONTRACTED 5'** handshapes. The hands then close to resume their original shapes.

mid: *adj.* related to the middle part of something. *His birthday is in* **mid**-*March.*

SIGN: With palm down, horizontal right **'BENT MIDFINGER 5'** hand is circled clockwise from the wrist above upturned left palm, tip of right midfinger falling in the centre of the left palm.
ALTERNATE SIGN—centre #2

midday: *n.* the middle of the day; noon. *Lunch will be served at* **midday**.

SIGN: Right **'EXTENDED B'** hand is held upright with palm facing left as elbow rests on back of left **'EXTENDED B'** hand which is held palm down in front of right side of body.

middle: *n.* centre. *Draw the diagram in the* **middle** *of the page.*

SIGN: With palm down, horizontal right **'BENT MIDFINGER 5'** hand is circled clockwise from the wrist above upturned left palm, tip of right midfinger falling in the centre of the left palm.
ALTERNATE SIGN—centre #2

midget: *n.* a dwarf whose features and body structure are of normal proportions. *A* **midget** *played the leading role in the play.*

SIGN: Right **'EXTENDED B'** hand is held out to the right side of the body with palm down and is moved up and down slightly to indicate the shortness of stature.

midnight: *n.* 12 o'clock at night. [See TIME CONCEPTS, p. LXXIII.] *At* **midnight**, *the sky was very dark.*

SIGN: Fingertips of left **'EXTENDED B'** hand, palm toward the body, are placed on the inside of the crook in the right arm which is extended forward and slightly downward. The right hand is positioned with palm facing left and fingers pointing forward and slightly downward as the arm moves from side to side slightly.

midst: *n.* the middle. *The log cabin stood in the* **midst** *of the tall pines.*

SIGN: With palm down, horizontal right **'BENT MIDFINGER 5'** hand is circled clockwise from the wrist above upturned left palm, tip of right midfinger falling in the centre of the left palm.

might: *v.* to have a possibility. *The weather forecaster said it* **might** *rain this afternoon.*

SIGN: **'EXTENDED B'** hands, held apart with palms up and fingers pointing forward, are alternately raised and lowered at least twice.

mighty: *adj.* powerful; strong. *Hercules was a* **mighty** *hero in Greek mythology.*

SIGN: **'s'** hands are held parallel with palms facing the chest. The forearms are then simultaneously and purposefully lowered so that the palms, which still face the body, are slanted slightly upward.

migraine: *n.* a throbbing headache usually affecting only one side of the head. *She often suffers from a migraine when she is under stress.*

SIGN: Fingerspell **MIGRAINE**. (The finger-spelling of this word is frequently followed by the sign for **headache** accompanied by obvious and severe pain and discomfort.)

migrant: *adj.* having the tendency to move from place to place. *Native Canadians were once migrant people.*

SIGN: **'CONTRACTED B'** hands are held parallel with palms down and are moved forward simultaneously in a swerving pattern.

migrate: *v.* to travel between different habitats at specific times of the year. *Many birds migrate south every winter.*

SIGN: Horizontal **'5'** hands are held aloft in a staggered formation with the right slightly ahead of/to the right of the left, palms down and forefingers pointing forward/rightward. Together the hands move in a forward/right-ward direction as the fingers flutter.

SAME SIGN—**migration**, *n.*

mild: *adj.* gentle; moderate; not extreme. *My wife likes sharp-flavoured cheddar but I prefer mild cheese.*

SIGN: Left **'EXTENDED B'** hand is held in a fixed position with palm facing the body and fingers pointing right. Vertical right **'EXTENDED B'** hand, held just behind the left hand with palm facing left, is lowered from the wrist as it strikes the space between the thumb and forefinger of the left hand a couple of times.

mile: *n.* a unit of length that is equal to 1.6c934 kilometres. *We were only one mile from home when we ran out of gas.*

SIGN: Fingerspell **MILE**.

militant: *adj.* involved in vigorous, aggressive support of a cause; showing a fighting spirit. *Women became more militant in their demands for equality during that period of time.*

SIGN: Vertical right **'S'** hand, palm facing backward, is held at or above shoulder level and is forcefully twisted a half turn so that palm faces forward. Alternatively, this sign may be made with two hands. (Signs vary.)

military: *n.* the armed forces. *The military took over Manitoba School for the Deaf from 1940 to 1943.*

SIGN: Horizontal **'A'** hands are placed on the left side of the chest, palms facing the body, with the right hand above the left. Then they are simultaneously moved forward and back to tap twice against the body.

milk: *n.* a white liquid secreted by the mammary glands of mature female mammals and used as food. *Milk is used in the production of butter, cheese and ice-cream.*

SIGN: Horizontal right **'S'** hand is squeezed and relaxed several times, thus alternating between a tight and more loosely held fist.

milligram: *n.* a measure equal to one thousandth of a gram. *The recipe calls for 15 milligrams of cinnamon.*

SIGN: Fingerspell **MG**.

million: *adj.* one thousand thousand; 1,000,000. [See NUMBERS, p. LXII.] *She won a million dollars in a lottery.*

SIGN: Left **'EXTENDED B'** hand is held in a fixed position with palm facing right at a slight upward angle and fingers pointing forward. Right **'BENT EXTENDED B'** hand is held with palm facing left and fingertips on the heel of the left hand. The right hand then moves rightward slightly and then forward in as small arc, re-establishing contact with the left hand between the palm and fingers. [The same basic sign is used for **millions** except that the fingertips of the right hand slide straight forward repeatedly (to indicate plurality) along the left palm.]

millilitre: *n.* one thousandth of a litre. *The recipe calls for 25 millilitres of lemon juice.*

SIGN: Fingerspell **ML**.

mime: *n.* a dramatic presentation done entirely by gesture, facial expression and body language without the use of words or ASL signs. *Many Deaf people excel at mime.*

SIGN: Vertical **'M'** hands, palms facing each other, are rotated alternately in small circles which are brought backward and down against the chest.

mimic: *v.* to imitate a person or manner, sometimes in a mocking way. *The students like to mimic that teacher.*

SIGN: Horizontal **'V'** hands are held in staggered formation, the left ahead of/to the left of the right, with left palm facing mainly rightward and right palm facing mainly leftward, the extended fingers pointing forward at a slight leftward angle. The hands then assume **'CLAWED V'** shapes as they are simultaneously jerked toward the chest. Movement may be repeated.

ALTERNATE SIGN—**copy** #1

mind: *n.* the human intellect. *He has a keen mind.*

SIGN #1: Tip of forefinger of right **'CROOKED ONE'** hand, palm toward the head, is tapped against right side of forehead.

mind: *v.* to look after; take care of. *Will you please mind the children while I go to the store?*

SIGN #2: **'K'** (or **'V'**) hands are positioned horizontally with the right one resting on top of the left one. The hands are then moved together in a counter-clockwise motion.

mind: *v.* to object; take offence. *Do you mind if I turn down the heat?*

SIGN #3: Right **'SPREAD C'** hand is held in a horizontal position as thumb and fingertips thump against chest. Eyebrows are raised to indicate that a question is being asked.

OR

SIGN #4: Right **'ONE'** hand is held with tip of forefinger touching tip of nose. The wrist then twists counter-clockwise as the hand moves downward/forward and the forefinger ends up pointing downward/forward at a leftward angle. (ESL USERS: When asked the sample question: To answer *'No, I don't mind'* indicates that you agree to that person's action; it is fine with you. To answer *'Yes, I do mind'* indicates that you are against the person's action; you would not like it. In ASL, the opposite applies: a 'no' reply to this sign means that you would not like it whereas a 'yes' reply means that it is fine with you.)

SAME SIGN—**don't mind**

(change one's) mind #5: See **change one's mind.**

(make up one's) mind #6: See **make up (one's mind).**

(never) mind: *s.s.* do not worry; forget about it. *Never mind; it is not important.*

SIGN #7: Fingers of horizontal **'BENT EXTENDED B'** hands, palms facing the chest, are alternately brushed back and forth against each other.

(out of one's) mind: *adj.* not in a sound mental state. *You are out of your mind if you think I will accept this.*

SIGN #8: Vertical right **'CROOKED 5'** (or **'SPREAD C'**) hand is held near the right side of the head with the palm toward the body, and is twisted back and forth several times from the wrist.

ALTERNATE SIGN—**crazy** #2

mine: *n.* an excavation in the ground for extracting ore, precious stones, etc. *Many old mines in the Northwest Territories have been closed.*

SIGN #1: Left **'EXTENDED B'** hand is held in a fixed position with palm upward at a slight rightward angle and fingers pointing forward. Right **'CROOKED ONE'** hand, palm down, uses the tip of the forefinger to scrape the left palm backward toward the body a couple of times.

mine: *pron.* used to indicate something belonging to or related to the signer. [See PRONOUNS, p. LXVI.] *This is not my book. Mine has my name on it.*

SIGN #2: Right **'EXTENDED B'** hand, palm facing the body, is laid against the middle of the chest.

mingle: *v.* to mix; come into close association with. *You should go to the party and mingle with people.*

SIGN #1: **'BENT 5'** hands are held right above left with palms facing each other, the fingers of the right hand pointing downward while the fingers of the left hand point upward. As all the fingers flutter, the hands are circled around one another in a direction which appears to the signer to be counter-clockwise.

OR

SIGN #2: **'ONE'** hands are held basically upright but slanted forward slightly with left palm facing the body while right palm faces away from the body. The two hands then brush against each other as they move from side to side a few times in opposite directions. (This sign is used only when the people involved are unfamiliar.)

miniature: *n.* a very small scale model or copy. *There is a miniature of the first railway system at the museum.*

SIGN Horizontal **'EXTENDED B'** hands are held apart with palms facing each other and fingers pointing forward. They are then moved toward each other slightly a couple of times.

minimal: *adj.* a little; an insignificant amount. *Only minimal damage was done to our vehicle.*

SIGN: Right **'X'** hand is held palm-up with forefinger tightly crooked and tip of thumb repeatedly scraping downward against tip of forefinger.

ALTERNATE SIGNS—**little** #1, #4 & **insignificant**

minimum: *n.* the smallest possible number, amount or degree. *We need a minimum of eight people for our board.*

SIGN: Left **'EXTENDED B'** hand is held palm-down, with fingertips pointing right. Fingertips of right palm-down **'EXTENDED B'** hand rest on and at right angles to back of left hand and are then moved upward from the wrist.

minister: *n.* a member of the clergy. *Our minister gives very interesting sermons.*

SIGN #1: Horizontal **'EXTENDED U'** hands, palms facing backward, are held with tips of extended fingers on the throat. The fingers are then brushed backward to create **'BENT EXTENDED U'** shapes.

minister: *n.* the head of a government department. *The Minister of Education will attend our meeting.*

SIGN #2: Horizontal right **'EXTENDED A'** hand, palm facing left, is raised purposefully from shoulder level upward. (Signs vary. Alternatively, **MINISTER** in this context may be fingerspelled.)

minor: *adj.* of lesser importance. *I would like to talk to you about a minor problem.*

SIGN #1: Right **'X'** hand is held palm-up with forefinger tightly crooked and tip of thumb repeatedly scraping downward against tip of forefinger.

ALTERNATE SIGN—**small** #1

minor: *n.* a secondary field of study in post-secondary education. *His major is English and his minor is Physics.*

SIGN #2: Horizontal **'B'** hands are positioned so the left rests on the right, palms facing left and right and fingers pointed forward. Then the right hand is firmly pushed forward.

minor: *n.* a person who is below the age of legal majority. (This age varies from province to province or territory.) *He was refused service in the bar because he was a minor.*

SIGN #3: **'EXTENDED B'** hands are held, palms down, left on top of and at right angles to right. Right hand is then moved sharply downward. (This sign is followed by the number representing the legal age.)

minority: *n.* a small group that is in some way different from the larger group of which it is a part. *ASL users are a visible minority.*

SIGN: Horizontal **'EXTENDED B'** hands are held apart with palms facing each other and fingers pointing forward. They are then moved toward each other. Next, **'SPREAD C'** hands are held upright and slightly apart with palms facing each other. The wrists then rotate forward, bringing the hands to a horizontal position. (ASL CONCEPT—**small - group.**)

mint: *adj.* related to the leaves of a plant used to flavour certain foods. *I love **mint** sauce with lamb.*

SIGN #1: Fingerspell **MINT**.

mint: *n.* a place where money is manufactured by government authority. *We visited the **Mint** in Ottawa where security was very tight.*

SIGN #2: Fingerspell **MINT**.

minus: *prep.* designating an amount less than zero. *In the winter, the temperature sometimes drops to **minus** 20 degrees Celsius.*

SIGN #1: Edge of extended forefinger of right horizontal **'BENT ONE'** hand, palm down, is tapped against forward-facing palm of vertical left **'EXTENDED B'** hand.

minus: *prep.* subtract or reduce by. *Five **minus** two equals three.*

SIGN #2: Left **'EXTENDED B'** hand is held in a fixed position with palm facing the body and fingers pointing right while right **'SPREAD C'** hand is held just behind the left hand with palm forward/downward. The right hand then moves downward, the fingertips scraping down against the left palm as the right hand closes to take on an **'S'** shape.

minute: *n.* a unit of time equal to 60 seconds. *We warmed the buns in the microwave for less than a **minute**.*

SIGN #1: Vertical left **'EXTENDED B'** hand is held with palm right and vertical right **'ONE'** hand is placed against the left hand. Then the right hand is twisted forward from the wrist so that the forefinger points forward at an upward angle.

minute: *adj.* tiny; very small; insignificant. *I am not interested in the **minute** details of your surgery.*

SIGN #2: Right **'EXTENDED A'** hand, palm facing left, thumb under chin, is thrust forward. Next, horizontal **'F'** hands are held parallel, with palms facing. Palms are then overturned and eventually face downward as the two hands are brought purposefully together. (ASL CONCEPT— **not - important**.) ASL syntax differs considerably from that of English. The sample sentence in ASL is: *YOU EXPLAIN-EXPLAIN-EXPLAIN SURGERY NOT-IMPORTANT.* (For contexts in which **minute** means 'very small', but not necessarily insignificant, see **minimal**.)

(last) minute [or **at the last minute**]: *adj.* [*adv. phr.*] occurring at the very end, usually abruptly, with no time left for further discussion or change. *His run for the presidency was a **last minute** decision.*

SIGN #3: Horizontal left **'I'** hand is held with palm facing the body at a rightward angle and little finger pointing forward/rightward. Vertical right **'I'** hand, with palm facing leftward/ backward, is held to the right of and above the left hand. The right hand is then lowered so that the tip of the little finger strikes the tip of the little finger of the left hand. Next, vertical left **'EXTENDED B'** hand is held with palm facing right. Right **'ONE'** hand, palm facing left and forefinger pointing forward, brushes against left palm as the right wrist bends to bring the hand into an upright position.

(ASL CONCEPT— **last - minute backward**.)

miracle: *n.* a wonderful or amazing event. *That nobody was injured in the accident is a **miracle**.*

SIGN: Vertical **'EXTENDED B'** hands, palms facing forward, are held apart near the face. Forearms are pushed purposefully forward a short distance. **MIRACLE** is frequently fingerspelled.
SAME SIGN—**miraculous**, *adj.*

mirror: *n.* a surface that reflects images. *There is a full-length mirror in the dressing room.*

SIGN: Vertical right **'EXTENDED B'** hand is held with palm toward the face and is rapidly twisted back and forth from the wrist several times.

misbehave: *v.* to behave badly or inappropriately. *Children often misbehave when they are left with a babysitter.*

SIGN: Right **'EXTENDED B'** hand, with fingertips on chin and palm facing body, is turned away, so that palm is facing down. Then, **'SPREAD C'** (or **'B'**) hands, palms down, are simultaneously swung from side to side. (ASL CONCEPT—**bad - behave.**) SAME SIGN—**misbehaviour**, *n.*

miscalculate: *v.* to figure incorrectly; misjudge. *The figures used in our bid must be accurate so be sure not to miscalculate.*

SIGN: Vertical right **'Y'** hand, palm toward the body, is firmly tapped on the chin. Next, **'K'** hands are held, right above left, somewhere between horizontally and vertically with extended fingers pointing more or less forward, left palm facing right and right palm facing left yet both palms are angled slightly toward the body. The two hands brush against one another a few times as the right hand repeatedly moves leftward slightly, and the left hand moves rightward. (ASL CONCEPT—**wrong - figure.**) SAME SIGN—**miscalculation**, *n.*

miscarriage: *n.* the giving of birth to a fetus before it can survive outside the womb. *All her pregnancies have resulted in miscarriage.*

SIGN #1: Fingers of palm-up right **'BENT EXTENDED B'** hand point leftward as they rest on rightward-pointing fingers of palm-up left **'BENT EXTENDED B'** hand. The arms are simultaneously moved from side to side as if rocking a baby in one's arms. Next, horizontal **'OPEN A'** hands, palms facing either upward or backward, are held close, perhaps even touching. The fingers are then unfurled so that the hands are swept apart, becoming horizontal **'CROOKED 5'** hands with palms facing each other and fingers pointing forward. (ASL CONCEPT—**baby - lose.**) MISCARRIAGE is frequently fingerspelled.

miscarriage: *n.* a failure to achieve what is desired or right. *Imprisoning that innocent man is a miscarriage of justice.*

SIGN #2: Vertical right **'Y'** hand, palm toward the body, is firmly tapped on the chin.

miscellaneous: *adj.* composed of a mixture or variety of things. *Everyone has a kitchen drawer for miscellaneous articles.*

SIGN: **'BENT L'** hands are positioned palms-down with tips of forefingers touching each other, the right finger pointing leftward and the left finger pointing rightward. Then they are moved apart with forefingers fluttering.

mischievous: *adj.* a tendency to play tricks on people or behave in a way that will annoy someone; impish. *The mischievous boys were playing in a mud puddle.*

SIGN: Thumbs of **'CROOKED EXTENDED V'** hands, palms facing each other at a forward angle, are placed just in front of either side of the forehead and the crooked fingers retract still further several times as the forearms simultaneously move up and down slightly. (**Mischievous** has various connotations, *i.e.*, 'public mischief' and 'malicious mischief'. Signs must be selected according to context.) SAME SIGN—**mischief**, *n.*

misconception: *n.* a false or mistaken opinion. *Some people have **misconceptions** about deafness.*

SIGN: Vertical right **'Y'** hand, palm toward the body, is firmly tapped on the chin. Then tip of little finger of right **'I'** hand, palm toward the face, is placed on the right side of the forehead and is drawn forward/upward a brief distance. (ASL CONCEPT—**wrong - idea**.) ALTERNATE SIGN—**misunderstand**

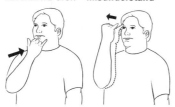

misconduct: *n.* behaviour that is considered immoral, unethical or professionally negligent. *The psychiatrist was charged with **misconduct** and had his licence revoked.*

SIGN: Vertical right **'Y'** hand, palm toward the body, is firmly tapped on the chin. Then **'SPREAD C'** (or **'B'**) hands, palms down, are simultaneously swung from side to side. (ASL CONCEPT—**wrong - behave**.) **MISCONDUCT** may be fingerspelled.

miser: *n.* someone who hoards money or possessions often while living in poor conditions. *His neighbours were astonished to find out the old **miser** was a millionaire.*

SIGN: Back of right **'CONTRACTED B'** (or **'BENT EXTENDED B'**) hand, palm up, is tapped two or three times on upturned palm of left **'EXTENDED B'** hand. Next, right **'SPREAD EXTENDED C'** hand is held palm down on the upturned palm of the left **'EXTENDED B'** hand and the fingertips scrape firmly backward toward the chest. (ASL CONCEPT—**money - greedy**.) Facial expression is important.

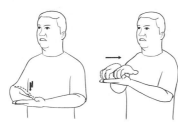

miserable: *adj.* very unpleasant. *We have had **miserable** weather for over a month.*

SIGN #1: Thumb and forefinger of vertical right **'COVERED 8'** hand, which is held near right side of face with palm facing left, are snapped open and thrust slightly forward to form a **'MODIFIED 5'** hand. This sign can be made with either one or two hands, one at either side of the face.

miserable: *adj.* unhappy; depressed; not in a good mood. *She has been **miserable** since she lost her job.*

SIGN #2: Tips of middle fingers of **'BENT MIDFINGER 5'** hands are held at either side of upper chest and are simultaneously lowered. (**Miserable** has various connotations in English and signs vary according to context.)

mishap: *n.* an unfortunate or accidental occurrence. *It was an unfortunate **mishap**, but we will get over it.*

SIGN: **'ONE'** hands, palms facing each other and forefingers pointing forward, are held apart and then turned over so that the palms face down. (For a **mishap** that refers specifically to an automobile accident, see **accident**.)

misinterpret: *v.* to get the wrong idea. *Please do not **misinterpret** what I am saying.*

SIGN: Right **'V'** hand is held with palm leftward/forward and the tip of the forefinger touching the right side of the forehead. The hand then comes away from the forehead as short distance as the wrist twists so that the palm faces backward and the tip of the middle finger comes to rest on the right side of the forehead. (Sometimes **misinterpret** means 'to incorrectly convey what someone has said', in which case, see **wrong + explain**.)

misleading: *adj.* false; confusing; guiding in the wrong direction. *We were given misleading instructions by our boss.*

SIGN: Vertical right **'CROOKED 5'** hand is held against right side of forehead with palm facing forward while left **'CROOKED 5'** hand is held palm-up in front of left side of chest. The arms are then simultaneously moved rightward/upward as both wrists rotate rightward a quarter turn so that the right palm faces the body at a slight downward angle while the left palm faces rightward/forward. This sign is accompanied by a look of confusion.

misplace: *v.* to put something in the wrong place; lose. *She misplaced the car keys again.*

SIGN: Horizontal **'OPEN A'** hands, palms facing the body, are held together so that the knuckles of the bunched fingers are touching each other. The fingers are then unfurled so that the hands are swept apart, becoming horizontal **'CROOKED 5'** hands with palms facing each other and fingers pointing forward.

misprint: *n.* a printing error. *There are always many misprints in our local newspaper.*

SIGN: Vertical right **'Y'** hand, palm toward the body, is firmly tapped on the chin. Then, **'SPREAD C'** hands, palms facing down, are held parallel with fingers wiggling up and down to simulate the action of typing. (ASL CONCEPT—**wrong - type**.)

Miss: *n.* the title given to an unmarried woman. *The secretary of our club is Miss Smith.*

SIGN #1: Fingerspell **MISS**.

miss: *v.* to fail to hear, see, understand or achieve (something). *If you do not pay attention you will miss the point of the lecture.*

SIGN #2: Vertical right **'C'** hand, palm facing left, is held in front of the face and is closed to form an **'S'** hand as it is purposefully curved to the left.

OR

SIGN #3: Vertical right **'F'** hand, palm facing left, is held in front of the nose and is purposefully curved downward/leftward in front of the face.

miss: *v.* to feel the absence or loss of. *I miss my home in Manitoba.*

SIGN #4: Tip of forefinger of right **'ONE'** hand is pressed firmly against the chin. Facial expression is important.

miss [*or* **miss out**]: *v.* to lose out; not have an opportunity. *If you do not attend, you will miss out on all the fun.*

SIGN #5: Horizontal **'OPEN A'** hands, palms facing the body, are held together so that the knuckles of the bunched fingers are touching each other. The fingers are then unfurled so that the hands are swept apart, becoming horizontal **'CROOKED 5'** hands with palms facing each other and fingers pointing forward.

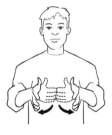

missile: *n.* a weapon, especially one which is fired or launched at a certain target. *The U.S.A. tested its cruise missile in Alberta.*

SIGN: Right **'ONE'** hand is held out from the body with palm facing left, forefinger pointing forward/upward and forearm resting on left **'STANDARD BASE'** hand. Right forearm jerks downward/backward, then jerks back to its original position to show the recoil action of something being launched into space with tremendous power.

missing: *adj.* absent; lost. *Several important papers are missing from the file.*

SIGN: Right **'CONTRACTED 5'** hand, palm up, becomes a **'FLAT O'** hand as it is drawn downward behind the horizontal left **'CROOKED 5'** hand of which the palm is facing the body.

missionary: *n.* a member of a religious mission. *He is a medical **missionary** in Ethiopia.*

SIGN: Vertical right **'M'** hand, palm facing left, is placed just below the left shoulder and the hand is circled in a direction that appears to onlookers to be clockwise.

mistake: *n.* an error. *There is a spelling **mistake** in your essay.*

SIGN: Vertical **'Y'** hand, palm toward the body, is tapped a couple of times against the chin. REGIONAL VARIATION—**wrong** #2

mister: See **Mr.**

mistress: *n.* a woman who has a long-term extramarital sexual relationship with a man. *His wife does not know he has a **mistress**.*

SIGN: Fingerspell **MISTRESS**.

misunderstand: *v.* to get the wrong meaning. *I hope I did not **misunderstand** your message.*

SIGN: Right **'V'** hand is held with palm leftward/forward and the tip of the forefinger touching the right side of the forehead. The hand then comes away from the forehead as short distance as the wrist twists so that the palm faces backward and the tip of the middle finger comes to rest on the right side of the forehead.
SAME SIGN—**misunderstanding**, *n.*

mitt [*or* **mitten**]: *n.* a hand covering that encloses the four fingers in a single unit and the thumb separately. *The child lost a **mitt** on the school playground.*

SIGN #1: Left **'EXTENDED B'** hand is held with palm toward the body and fingers pointing upward/rightward. Then the forefinger of the right **'ONE'** hand, palm down, is used to outline the shape of a mitt around the thumb and fingers of the left hand.

SIGN #2: Fingertips of right **'BENT 5'** hand, palm down, are used to stroke the back of the left **'STANDARD BASE'** hand. The movement of the right hand is directed toward the chest.

mix: *v.* to blend together. *If you **mix** red and blue dye you will create a shade of purple.*

SIGN: Horizontal **'SPREAD EXTENDED C'** hands are held, right above left, with palms facing each other. Then right hand moves in a counter-clockwise direction while left hand moves in the opposite direction. (If it is specifically *people* who are mixing, see **mix with**.)

mix with: *v.* to mingle or fraternize with. *The officers never **mix with** the soldiers.*

SIGN: Right **'EXTENDED A'** hand is held thumb-down above left **'EXTENDED A'** hand which is held thumb-up. The hands then revolve around each other in a counter-clockwise direction. ALTERNATE SIGN—**mingle** #1

moan: *v.* to utter a low sound that may express suffering, pleading or sometimes pleasure. *When he regained consciousness, he began to **moan** in pain.*

SIGN #1: **'SPREAD EXTENDED C'** hands, palms toward the face, are held near the mouth, fingers close to the lips, and are alternately rotated forward. (Facial expression accompanying this sign must clearly signify pain or pleasure according to context.)

moan: *v.* a colloquial expression meaning to grumble or complain. *He always seems to have something to **moan** about.*

SIGN #2: Right **'SPREAD EXTENDED C'** hand is held in a horizontal position as thumb and fingertips thump repeatedly against chest. Facial expression is important.

mobile: *adj.* movable; able to move or be moved easily. *I will need a **mobile** blackboard.*

SIGN: **'CONTRACTED B'** hands are held parallel with palms down and are moved forward simultaneously in a swerving pattern. (Signs vary considerably, depending on the size and shape of the object being described as mobile.)

mock: *v.* to treat with scorn or contempt; ridicule. *He was afraid she might mock his marriage proposal.*

SIGN #1: Horizontal **'BENT COMBINED I + ONE'** hands, palms down, are held slightly apart, with the right hand nearer the chest, and simultaneously make small jabbing motions. This sign is accompanied by a mocking facial expression. ❖

mock: *adj.* counterfeit, not real; serving as a substitute for the real thing. *The teacher arranged for the drama class to hold a mock trial.*

SIGN #2: Side of forefinger of right **'ONE'** hand, palm facing leftward/forward, is lightly brushed forward/downward twice on the right cheek, forefinger either remaining upright or bending slightly to become a **'BENT ONE'**.

mode: *n.* a way of doing something. *The professor's mode of lecturing is interesting.*

SIGN: **'EXTENDED B'** hands, held parallel with palms facing one another and fingers pointing forward, are simultaneously moved forward.

model: *n.* a design, style or type of a particular product. *He bought a 2002 model Porsche.*

SIGN #1: Fingerspell **MODEL**.

model: *n.* a standard of excellence; someone/something to be imitated. *A Deaf child needs an adult Deaf role model.*

SIGN #2: Fingerspell **MODEL**.

model: *n.* someone who wears certain products in order to encourage others to buy them. *The model wore all the latest fashions.*

SIGN #3: Fingerspell **MODEL**. (Signs for **model**, *v.*, in this context vary considerably.)

model: *n.* a small representation of a larger object. *For his birthday, his parents gave him a model of a Corvette Stingray to assemble.*

SIGN #4: Fingerspell **MODEL**.

model: *adj.* serving as a standard of excellence; ideal. *We were proud to hear the teacher say that our son was a model student.*

SIGN #5: Vertical **'EXTENDED B'** hands, palms facing forward, are held apart near the face. Forearms are pushed purposefully forward a short distance. (**MODEL** in this context may be fingerspelled.)

modem: *n.* a device that translates typed computer signals into a comprehensible form for transmission over telephone lines. *The computer I bought has a built-in modem.*

SIGN: Fingerspell **MODEM**.

modern: *adj.* contemporary; involving the recent or present time. *She is a collector of modern art.*

SIGN: Horizontal left **'EXTENDED B'** hand remains stationary with palm up and fingers pointing forward/rightward while right **'BENT EXTENDED B'** hand, palm facing upward, is brought leftward across left palm using a scooping motion. (**MODERN** is frequently fingerspelled.)

modest: *adj.* humble; not boastful. *He is very modest about winning the award.*

SIGN: Horizontal left **'BENT EXTENDED B'** hand is held in a fixed position in front of the chest with palm facing the body at a rightward angle. Vertical right **'B'** hand, with palm left and fingertips just under the mouth, is lowered so that the side of the hand slides straight down along the left hand between its palm and fingers.

SAME SIGN—**modesty**, *n.*

modify: *v.* to change the structure, character, etc; alter. *We will **modify** the architectural plans for the new school.*

SIGN: **'A'** hands, palms facing each other, are twisted 180 degrees.

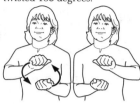

moist: *adj.* slightly damp or wet. *The cake from the bakery is **moist** and fresh.*

SIGN: Left **'CONTRACTED 5'** hand is held palm-up in front of chest while vertical right **'CONTRACTED 5'** hand is held with palm toward the body, and tip of middle finger touching the chin. Right hand is then lowered to a position parallel to the left hand as both hands are simultaneously closed to form **'FLAT O'** hands. The hands may then be simultaneously opened and closed a number of times, thus alternating between **'CONTRACTED 5'** and **'FLAT O'** shapes. (Alternatively, this sign may be made with the hands beginning in a parallel position rather than with the right hand beginning at the chin.)

SAME SIGN—**moisture**, *n.*

molest: *v.* to assault with sexual intentions. *She claimed that an acquaintance had **molested** her.*

SIGN: Tip of middle finger of right **'BENT MIDFINGER 5'** hand, palm down, touches down on the back of the left **'STANDARD BASE'** hand. Then **'CROOKED 5'** hands are held parallel in front of the body with palms forward but slanted toward each other. The hands move downward in a waving motion as if fondling someone's body. (ASL CONCEPT—**touch - touch on body**.)

mom: *n.* an informal word for mother. *Ask your **mom** if she will make cookies for our bake sale.*

SIGN: Tip of forefinger of right **'ONE'** hand taps twice against the right side of the chin. ALTERNATE SIGNS—**mother** #2 & #3

moment: *n.* a short indefinite period of time. *He had to wait a **moment** while she got her coat.*

SIGN: Vertical left **'EXTENDED B'** hand is held with palm right and vertical right **'ONE'** hand is placed against the left hand. Then the right hand is twisted forward from the wrist so that the forefinger points forward at an upward angle.

momentous: *adj.* very important. *Graduation is a **momentous** occasion.*

SIGN #1: Vertical **'F'** hands are held apart with palms facing forward. The hands are then brought purposefully together.

OR

SIGN #2: Horizontal **'I'** hands are held right on top of left with right palm facing leftward and left palm facing rightward. Together, they are tipped back toward the chest, thus assuming an upright position.

monarch: *n.* a king, queen or emperor who rules, usually by hereditary right. *A **monarch** usually lives in a palatial home.*

SIGN: Sides of extended fingers of right **'MODIFIED G'** hand, palm down, are placed at the left shoulder. Then the hand is moved diagonally downward so the fingers come to rest at the right side of the waist. Next, right **'K'** hand, palm toward body, is placed upright against left shoulder, and then moved diagonally down across chest and placed at right side of waist. (ASL CONCEPT—**queen - king**.) Only the first part of this sign is used when referring specifically to a 'female monarch'; only the second part is used when referring specifically to a 'male monarch'.

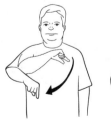

Monday: *n.* the 2nd day of the week. [See TIME CONCEPTS, p. LXIX.] *I will see you on Monday.*

SIGN: Right **'M'** hand, palm up, is circled in a direction which appears to the signer to be counter-clockwise.

money: *n.* currency used in exchange for goods or services. *He often borrows money from the bank.*

SIGN #1: Back of right **'CONTRACTED B'** (or **'BENT EXTENDED B'**) hand, palm up, is tapped two or three times on upturned palm of left **'EXTENDED B'** hand.

OR

SIGN #2: Right **'OFFSET O'** hand is held palm up as the fingers move back and forth so that the side of the forefinger rubs against the thumb several times.

monitor: *v.* to check and record the quality of. *The doctor will continue to monitor the patient's condition.*

SIGN #1: Vertical **'BENT V'** hands are positioned so that the left is a little closer to the chest than the right with extended fingers of the left hand pointing forward at a slight rightward angle while those of the right hand point forward at a slight leftward angle. The hands are simultaneously jabbed forward a few times. A look of intense concentration accompanies this sign.

monitor: *n.* a screen (such as a television or computer screen) that displays information. *The patient is in Intensive Care attached to a heart monitor.*

SIGN #2: **'ONE'** hands are held with palms forward/downward and forefingers pointing forward at a slight upward angle, the tips touching. The hands are then drawn apart, moved downward, and back together to outline the shape of the monitor.

monkey: *n.* any primate with the exception of man. *The organ grinder has a trained monkey.*

SIGN: Fingertips of both **'CLAWED 5'** hands, one on either side of the rib-cage, palms toward the body, are brushed upward with a scratching motion.

monotonous: *adj.* tedious; repetitious; without variety. *Driving across the prairies can be monotonous.*

SIGN: Horizontal **'Y'** hands are held slightly apart with palms down and are simultaneously circled slowly in opposite directions, the right hand appearing to the signer to be moving in a clockwise direction while the right hand is moving counter-clockwise. Facial expression must clearly convey 'boredom'.
SAME SIGN—**monotony**, *n.*
ALTERNATE SIGN—**bored/boring**

monster: *n.* an imaginary frightening creature. *The child imagined there was a monster under her bed.*

SIGN: **'SPREAD C'** hands are held with palms down at about shoulder level and are shaken. Facial expression is important.

monstrous: *adj.* hideous; horrible; outrageous; shocking. *Murder is a monstrous crime.*

SIGN #1: Vertical **'COVERED 8'** hands are held, one at either side of face, with palms facing each other at a slight forward angle. As the hands are thrust forward a short distance, thumbs and forefingers are snapped open to form **'MODIFIED 5'** hands. Facial expression is important.

monstrous: *adj.* huge; enormous. *They are building another monstrous shopping mall in the area.*

SIGN #2: Horizontal **'CLAWED L'** hands, which are held slightly apart with palms facing, are simultaneously moved farther apart as the wrists rotate to turn the palms down. Facial expression is important and the syllable 'CHA' is formed on the lips.

month: *n.* one of the twelve divisions of a calendar year. [See TIME CONCEPTS, p. LXXII.] *February is the shortest month of the year.*

SIGN: Vertical left **'ONE'** hand is held in a fixed position with palm forward/rightward. Horizontal right **'ONE'** hand, palm toward the body and forefinger pointing leftward, is positioned so that the first joint of the forefinger is held against the left forefinger and drawn downward along it.

monthly: *adv.* once every month. *Mortgage payments are usually paid monthly.*

SIGN: Vertical left **'ONE'** hand is held in a fixed position with palm forward/rightward. Horizontal right **'ONE'** hand, palm toward the body and forefinger pointing leftward, is positioned so that the first joint of the forefinger is held against the left forefinger and drawn downward along it. The movement is repeated several times.

mooch: *v.* a colloquial term meaning to obtain something at someone else's expense. *He often mooches food from his friends.*

SIGN: Left **'BENT U'** hand is held in a fixed position with palm down and extended fingers pointing rightward/forward. Vertical right **'CONTRACTED 3'** hand is held above the level of the right shoulder with palm forward and is purposefully lowered so that the extended fingers and thumb snap shut on the extended fingers of the left hand.

mood: *n.* a state of mind or feeling; overall feeling. *She is always in a bad mood.*

SIGN: Fingerspell **MOOD**.

M O O D

moody: *adj.* changeable in terms of moods; often in a gloomy mood; temperamental. *She is a very moody person.*

SIGN: Vertical right **'EXTENDED B'** hand, palm forward, dips as it takes on a **'BENT EXTENDED B'** shape with palm down and then rises to its original position. The hand continues to move up and down in a wavy pattern to show fluctuation. **MOODY** is frequently fingerspelled.

moon: *n.* a satellite of the earth. *Neil Armstrong was the first human to walk on the moon.*

SIGN: Thumbtip of vertical right **'C'** (or **'CLAWED L'**) hand, palm leftward but angled slightly forward, is tapped against the right side of the head near the eye.

moose: *n.* a large North American deer with large, flat antlers. *We saw a moose in the national park.*

SIGN: **'5'** hands, palms forward but facing slightly, are placed at either side of the head, thumbs on the forehead. To show the span of the moose's antlers, the arms are then moved outward as the wrists twist slightly to turn the palms fully forward. (**MOOSE** is often finger-spelled following this sign in order to be more specific.)

mop: *n.* a cleaning implement with a wooden handle and a head often made of cotton strands. *I bought a mop to keep the kitchen floor clean.*

SIGN: **'CLOSED A-INDEX'** hands are positioned left in front of right, with palms at a slight upward-facing angle, to simulate the holding of a mop handle and are drawn back and forth as if mopping a floor.

morbid: *adj.* gruesome; fixated on death or unpleasant things. *I do not want to hear any more morbid details of the accident.*

SIGN: Vertical **'COVERED 8'** hands are held, one at either side of face, with palms facing each other at a slight forward angle. As the hands are thrust forward a short distance, thumbs and forefingers are snapped open to form **'MODIFIED 5'** hands. Facial expression is important.

more: *adj.* a greater number, quantity, extent or degree. *We need more ASL instructors.*

SIGN #1: Vertical **'MODIFIED O'** hands, palms facing each other, are tapped together.

SIGN #2 [ATLANTIC]: Left **'EXTENDED B'** hand is held in a fixed position with palm up and fingers pointing rightward/forward. Right **'EXTENDED B'** hand, palm facing the body at a slight leftward angle and fingers pointing leftward/forward, is placed on the heel of the left hand and slides forward/rightward across the palm to the end of the fingers.

more [*or* **even more**]: *adv.* to a greater extent or degree. *She was upset yesterday, but she is even more upset today.*

SIGN #3: Vertical **'K'** (or **'V'**) hands, palms facing each other but angled slightly toward the body, are held apart and are simultaneously thrust toward each other, ending with the wrists crossed. This sign is used only *with reference to degree*, and not number or quantity. It could not be used to mean 'more milk'.)

more than: *adv.* a greater height, length, extent or degree. *No building in this area can be more than ten stories high.*

SIGN #4: Left **'EXTENDED B'** hand is held palm-down, with fingertips pointing right. Fingertips of right palm-down **'EXTENDED B'** hand rest on and at right angles to back of left hand and are then moved upward from the wrist.

(what's) more: *conj.* not only that, but; in addition; as if that were not enough. *She screamed and hollered at him in front of everyone in the restaurant; what's more, she poured a glass of wine on him!*

SIGN #5: Vertical **'K'** (or **'V'**) hands, palms facing each other but angled slightly toward the body, are held apart and are simultaneously thrust toward each other, ending with the wrists crossed. (This sign is used for emphasis and is generally followed by a pause.)

431

morgue: *n.* a building where dead bodies are kept before cremation or burial. *We were asked by the police to go to the morgue to identify the body.*

SIGN: Fingerspell **MORGUE**.

morning: *n.* the early part of the day ending at noon. [See TIME CONCEPTS, p. LXXII.] *The sun rises in the morning.*

SIGN #1: The edge of the left **'EXTENDED B'** hand rests in the crook of the right arm, of which the hand faces palm up and fingers point forward. Sometimes the right forearm is raised slightly so that the fingers point forward at an upward angle.

SIGN #2 [ATLANTIC]: **'S'** hands are crossed at the wrists, right above left, with palms facing upward. The wrists are then tapped against each other a couple of times.

SIGN #3 [ONTARIO]: Left **'EXTENDED B'** hand is positioned with palm up and fingers pointing forward/rightward. Horizontal right **'BENT EXTENDED B'** hand, palm facing leftward/backward, is tapped against the left palm a couple of times.

moron: *n.* a stupid person. *What a moron I was to miss such a wonderful career opportunity.*

SIGN: Thumb and forefinger of right **'MODIFIED G'** hand are pointed at forehead, with palm facing left. Then wrist is twisted, thus rotating **'MODIFIED G'** hand a quarter turn so that palm is toward face. For greater emphasis, this sign may be made with a **'FLAT C'** handshape.

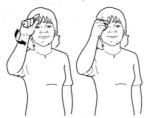

morose: *adj.* gloomy; sad. *I would describe the mood of the poem as morose.*

SIGN: Tips of middle fingers of **'BENT MIDFINGER 5'** hands are held at either side of upper chest and are simultaneously lowered.
ALTERNATE SIGN—**depressed** #2

morphine: *n.* a drug extracted from opium and used as an anesthetic or sedative. *The doctor prescribed morphine to relieve the patient's pain.*

SIGN: Fingerspell **MORPHINE**.

mortgage: *n.* a contract that ensures that property is secured during the period of time in which a loan is being repaid. *They have taken out a second mortgage on their home.*

SIGN: Fingerspell **MORTGAGE**.

mortified: *adj.* humiliated. *The mathematics professor was mortified to discover a mistake in his calculations.*

SIGN: **'5'** hands are held slightly apart near the face at about shoulder level with palms facing the body, the fingers of the right hand pointing upward at a slight leftward angle and the fingers of the left hand pointing upward at a slight rightward angle. The hands stay in this relative position as they alternately form small forward-moving circles.
ALTERNATE SIGN—**embarrassed** #1

mosquito: *n.* a stinging, bloodsucking, flying insect. *The mosquito is an insect that breeds in stagnant water.*

SIGN: Forefinger and thumb of right **'F'** hand are placed against right cheek. **'F'** hand is then changed to a **'B'** hand which lightly slaps right cheek.

most: *adj.* the largest number or quantity of; almost all of. *Whoever gets the most points will win the game.*

SIGN: Horizontal left **'EXTENDED A'** hand is held in a fixed position with palm facing right. Horizontal right **'EXTENDED A'** hand is held at a lower level with palm facing left. The right hand then moves upward causing the knuckles to brush against those of the left hand on its way up.

motel: *n.* a hotel used mainly by motorists. *We found a motel that is clean and quiet.*

SIGN: Fingerspell **MOTEL**.

moth: *n.* a nocturnal, winged insect with a stout body. *A beautiful moth emerged from the cocoon.*

SIGN: Fingerspell **MOTH**.

mother: *n.* a female parent. *My mother always cooks good nutritious meals for the family.*

SIGN #1: Tip of forefinger of right **'ONE'** hand taps twice against the right side of the chin.

OR

SIGN #2: Tip of thumb of vertical right **'5'** hand, palm facing leftward, is tapped against the right side of the chin.

SIGN #3 [ATLANTIC]: Left **'EXTENDED B'** is held in a fixed position with palm up and fingers pointing rightward/forward. Right **'M'** hand is held with palm down and fingers pointing leftward/forward as they are tapped a couple of times on the left palm.

motion: *n.* a formal proposal to be discussed and put to a vote. *The motion was passed at the executive meeting.*

SIGN #1: **'EXTENDED B'** hands, palms up and fingers pointing forward, are held slightly apart with the right just ahead of the left, and are simultaneously thrust forward in an arc.

motion: *n.* movement or change in physical position. *In physics class, we are studying motion.*

SIGN #2: **'CONTRACTED B'** hands are held parallel with palms down and are moved forward simultaneously in a swerving pattern. (Signs vary considerably, depending 'what' is in motion and in 'what way'.)

motivate: *v.* to give incentive to. *The prospect of a high paying job will motivate him to complete the course.*

SIGN: Horizontal **'EXTENDED B'** hands are held apart with palms angled so that they partly face each other while partly facing forward. The hands then simultaneously make several small circles outward.

motivated: *adj.* having incentive or interest. *He is a highly motivated student.*

SIGN: Horizontal **'EXTENDED B'** hands are held with palms together and fingers pointing forward. The hands are alternately rubbed back and forth against each other. (This sign is used only in a passive voice situation or as an adjective to describe someone's feelings. It would *not* be possible to use this sign in an active voice situation such as: *The teacher motivated the student.*)

motive: *n.* the reason for someone's action. *The prosecuting attorney tried to explain the defendant's motive for committing the crime.*

SIGN: Vertical right **'EXTENDED R'** (or **'R'**) hand, palm toward face, makes small circles (clockwise in the eyes of the onlooker) at right side of forehead.

motor: *n.* the engine of a vehicle. *This boat has a new motor.*

SIGN: Fingers of horizontal **'CLAWED 5'** hands, palms toward the body, are interlocked and remain so as they are shaken up and down. This is a wrist action.

motorcycle: *n.* a two-wheeled vehicle driven by a gasoline engine. *He always wore a helmet when he rode his motorcycle.*

SIGN: Horizontal **'S'** hands, with palms down, are placed so that they appear to be holding onto the handlebars of a motorcycle. Then the right hand is moved up and down several times from the wrist as if accelerating. (See also **vehicle** for explanatory notes.)

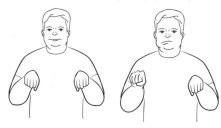

motto: *n.* a saying that expresses an ideal or a guiding principle. *The motto of the Boy Scouts is "Be Prepared".*

SIGN: Vertical **'V'** hands, palms facing forward, are held apart just above shoulder level, and are curved outward slightly from the wrists as they become **'CLAWED V'** hands.

mount: *v.* to get up on a horse. *At the Riding Academy, we learned how to mount correctly.*

SIGN: Left **'B'** hand is held in a fixed position with palm right and fingers pointing forward. Right **'V'** hand is held to the right of the left hand with palm toward the body and extended fingers pointing left at an upward angle. The right hand then moves leftward in an arc formation, coming to rest with the extended fingers straddling the left hand. (Sign choice depends on context.)

mountain: *n.* a part of the earth's surface that is higher and steeper than a hill. *Everest is the highest mountain on earth.*

SIGN: Left **'A'** hand is held in a fixed position with palm down. Right **'A'** hand is tapped palm-down on the back of the left hand. (Sometimes the right hand will then move in an arc formation and touch down again on the left forearm.) Next, **'EXTENDED B'** hands, the right closer to the body than the left, are held with palms down and fingers pointing leftward/forward. The hands then indicate the slope of the mountain as they are raised so that the palms face leftward at a slight downward/forward angle. (Signs vary considerably.)

mourn: *v.* to feel sad about someone's death. *It is natural to mourn the death of a family member.*

SIGN: Vertical **'CROOKED 5'** hands are held slightly apart with palms toward the face. The hands are then simultaneously lowered somewhat and the head tilts to the right.
SAME SIGN—**mournful**, *adj.*

mouse: *n.* a small, long-tailed rodent similar to a rat. *The mouse was eating the cheese on the trap.*

SIGN #1: Side of forefinger of right **'ONE'** hand, palm facing leftward at a slight downward angle, is brushed leftward across the nose twice.

mouse: *n.* a hand-held computer device that controls the cursor on a computer screen. *Your mouse will last longer if you use a mouse pad.*

SIGN #2: Right **'CLAWED L'** hand is held palm down and circled counter-clockwise at least twice. (Signs vary considerably, depending on the type of **mouse** being used, its location with respect to the computer, and the type of movement required.)

mouth: *n.* the opening in the head through which food is taken and vocal sounds are issued. *His mouth was sore after the oral surgery.*

SIGN: Tip of forefinger of right **'ONE'** hand touches the lips as it outlines them by moving in a clockwise (to the onlooker) direction. (If the signer is referring to a particular place on the mouth, he/she might just point to that specific place. In addition, **mouth** is often incorporated in the sign for the verb rather than having a specific sign accorded it. See **shut up** [or **shut your mouth**].)

movable: *adj.* able to be moved. *He told the rug cleaners that the piano was movable.*

SIGN: **'CONTRACTED B'** hands are held parallel with palms down and are moved forward simultaneously in a swerving pattern. (Signs vary considerably, depending on the size and shape of the object being described as movable.)

move: *v.* to change one's place of residence or business. *I will move to a new apartment next month.*

SIGN #1: **'FLAT O'** hands are held parallel with palms down and are simultaneously flung forward/rightward/upward as they open to form **'MODIFIED 5'** hands. (This sign is used exclusively for 'moving *to a different residence or business location'*. Signs for **move** in a general sense vary depending on the context, and natural gestures are often used.)

move: *v.* to propose or suggest as part of parliamentary procedure. *I move that we accept the nominations for president.*

SIGN #2: **'EXTENDED B'** hands, palms up and fingers pointing forward, are held slightly apart with the right just ahead of the left, and are simultaneously thrust forward in an arc.

move in: *v.* to begin to occupy (a home). *The landlord said we could **move in** tomorrow.*

SIGN: Vertical right **'FLAT O'** hand is held just in front of the right shoulder with palm facing forward/leftward. Vertical left **'FLAT O'** hand is held a little further forward in front of the left side of the chest with palm facing the same way as the right hand. The hands are then firmly moved forward/leftward.

movie: *n.* a film. *"Children of a Lesser God" is a popular **movie**.*

SIGN #1: Horizontal left **'5'** hand is held with fingers pointing forward/rightward and palm facing rightward/backward. Vertical right **'5'** hand is held with heel in palm of left hand and is shaken back and forth. This is a wrist movement.

OR

SIGN #2: **'EXTENDED B'** hands, with palms down and fingers spread slightly, are positioned so that the fingers of the right are resting on the back of the left at right angles to it. The right hand then rubs back and forth along the back of the left hand.

moving: *adj.* emotionally touching; inspiring. *Her signing of the National Anthem was a **moving** performance.*

SIGN: Right **'5'** hand is held with palm on chest and fingertips pointing leftward/upward. The hand is then pushed purposefully upward. Alternatively, this sign may be made with two hands, one on either side of chest, especially for emphasis. Facial expression is important.

mow: *v.* to cut (grass). *My son helps me **mow** the lawn every weekend.*

SIGN: **'S'** hands are held parallel with palms down and are simultaneously pushed forward.

Mr.: *n.* a title used before the surname of a man (an abbreviation of **mister**). *Mr. Chapman manages a restaurant in Bedford, Nova Scotia.*

SIGN: Fingerspell **MR**.

Mrs.: *n.* a title used before the surname of a married woman (an abbreviation of **mistress**). *Mrs. Alex MacPherson is visiting her parents in Scotland.*

SIGN: Fingerspell **MRS**.

Ms. [*or* **Ms**]: *n.* a title used before any woman's surname whether she is married or not (an abbreviation of **mistress** and a substitute for either Mrs. or Miss). *The letter was addressed to Ms. G.G. Burns.*

SIGN: Fingerspell **MS**.

much: *adv.* a great quantity or degree of. *My stomach hurts because I ate too **much**.*

SIGN: Horizontal **'CROOKED 5'** hands are held with palms facing and fingertips touching. The hands are then simultaneously drawn apart.

mud: *n.* a soft, wet earth found on the ground after rain or at the bottom of ponds, etc. *My car was covered with **mud** after driving on a wet country road.*

SIGN #1: Fingerspell **MUD**.

SIGN #2 [ONTARIO]: Heel of right **'SPREAD EXTENDED C'** hand, palm upward, is placed under the chin and the hand is moved briskly in small circular motions, brushing forward/upward against the underside of the chin with each cycle.

muddle: *v.* to mix up; confuse. *Do not* ***muddle*** *these papers because they are arranged in numerical order.*

SIGN: Vertical right **'CROOKED 5'** hand is held against right side of forehead with palm facing forward while left **'CROOKED 5'** hand is held palm-up in front of left side of chest. The arms are then simultaneously moved rightward/upward as both wrists rotate rightward a quarter turn so that the right palm faces the body at a slight downward angle while the left palm faces rightward/forward. This sign is accompanied by a look of confusion.

muffin: *n.* a small cup-shaped sweet roll. *My breakfast consists of a* ***muffin*** *and a cup of coffee.*

SIGN: Left **'EXTENDED B'** hand is held in a fixed position with palm up and fingers pointing forward/rightward. Right **'SPREAD C'** hand, palm down, bounces slightly a few times on the left palm. (**MUFFIN** is frequently fingerspelled.)

muffler: *n.* a silencing device on the exhaust system of a motor vehicle. *The* ***muffler*** *on my car is faulty so it makes a loud noise.*

SIGN: Left hand grasps wrist of vertical right **'COVERED O'** hand which is held with palm facing the right shoulder. Then the right hand is opened and closed several times as it alternates between **'COVERED O'** and **'CONTRACTED 5'** shapes.

mug: *n.* a cup with a handle. *Everyone must bring his own coffee* ***mug*** *to the meeting.*

SIGN: Left **'EXTENDED B'** hand is held in a fixed position with palm up and fingers pointing forward/rightward. Right **'C'** hand, palm facing left but angled toward the body slightly, is placed on the left palm and is raised and lowered twice. (**MUG** may also be fingerspelled.)

mule: *n.* the sterile offspring of a male donkey and a female horse. *A* ***mule*** *is a good pack animal for mountaineers.*

SIGN: **'B'** (or **'BENT EXTENDED B'**) hands are placed at either side of the head with palms forward and fingers simultaneously moving up and down to represent flapping ears.

mull over: *v.* to contemplate; ponder; consider carefully. *I will* ***mull over*** *your ideas before I make a final decision.*

SIGN: Vertical **'FLAT O'** hands are held just in front of either side of the forehead with palms facing backward and fingers rapidly fluttering as the hands move in small circles. From the signer's perspective, the left hand moves clockwise while the right hand moves counter-clockwise. (Alternatively, this sign may be made with one hand only.)

multicultural: *adj.* made up of more than two cultures. *Canada constitutes a* ***multicultural*** *society.*

SIGN: **'ONE'** hands, palms forward/downward, are held so that the right forefinger is crossed over the left. The fingers then uncross and move apart. This movement is repeated several times as the hands simultaneously move from left to right. Next, left **'ONE'** hand is held in a fixed position with palm facing rightward/forward at a downward angle while vertical right **'EXTENDED C'** hand, with palm facing leftward/forward is held just to the right of the left forefinger. The right wrist then rotates 180 degrees forward until the palm is facing the body at an upward angle.

(ASL CONCEPT—**different - culture**.)

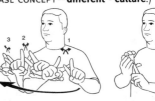

multilingual: *adj.* able to speak more than two languages. *Many people who live in Switzerland are* ***multilingual***.

SIGN: Fingertips of right **'EXTENDED B'** (or **'BENT EXTENDED B'**) hand, with palm facing body, are tapped against right side of forehead. Then, right **'A'** hand, palm up, is moved slightly forward/rightward as each fingertip gradually slides forward off the thumbtip to create a **'4'** hand. Next, **'L'** hands are held palms down with forefingers pointing forward and thumbtips touching each other. The hands are then drawn apart.

(ASL CONCEPT—**know - several - language**.)

multiple: *adj.* having many parts. *He sustained **multiple** wounds in the car accident.*

SIGN: **'s'** hands are held parallel with palms up and are thrust forward simultaneously as they are opened to form **'CROOKED 5'** hands.

multiple sclerosis: *n.* a progressive disease of the central nervous system. *Multiple Sclerosis can impair speech, vision, and muscular coordination.*

SIGN: Fingerspell **MS**.

M   S

multiplication: *n.* a mathematical process whereby a product is found by repeating a given number a specific number of times. *Multiplication of large numbers can be done more quickly on a calculator.*

SIGN: Left **'ONE'** hand is held with palm rightward at a slight forward/downward angle and forefinger pointing upward to the right. Right **'ONE'** hand moves forward with forefinger at right angles to left forefinger and taps against it twice.

multiply: *v.* to find a product by using the mathematical process of multiplication. *If you **multiply** two by three, you will end up with six.*

SIGN #1: Vertical **'V'** hands, palms facing each other but angled slightly toward the body, are held apart and are simultaneously thrust toward each other, ending with the wrists crossed.

multiply: *v.* to increase in quantity or number. *Our problems seem to **multiply** whenever he is around.*

SIGN #2: Left **'U'** hand is held in a fixed position with palm down and extended fingers pointing rightward/forward. Beside it is the right **'U'** hand, which is held with palm facing left and extended fingers pointing forward/leftward. The right wrist then rotates to turn the hand palm down as the extended fingers come to rest on those of the left hand at right angles to them. Motion is repeated as the hands simultaneously move upward.
ALTERNATE SIGN—**multiply** #1

multitude: *n.* a large number. *We have had a **multitude** of problems since we bought this used car.*

SIGN #1: **'s'** hands are held parallel with palms up and are thrust forward simultaneously as they are opened to form **'CROOKED 5'** hands. (Each repetition of this sign indicates an even greater number.)

multitude: *n.* a large gathering of people. *There is never enough food for the starving **multitude** in many parts of the world.*

SIGN #2: **'SPREAD EXTENDED C'** hands are held one just in front of each shoulder, with palms down. The hands are then simultaneously moved forward.

mumps: *n.* an acute, contagious, viral disease. *Two common symptoms of the **mumps** are swollen glands and fever.*

SIGN: Vertical **'SPREAD C'** hands, palms facing each other, are tapped a couple of times against the sides of the neck.

municipal: *adj.* relating to a city or town, and/or the local government. *The maintenance of local roads is a **municipal** responsibility.*

SIGN: Vertical **'EXTENDED B'** hands, left palm facing right and right palm facing left, are held so that their fingertips can be tapped together twice.

murder: *n.* the illegal, premeditated killing of a person. *The convict is serving a life sentence for first degree **murder**.*

SIGN: Vertical left **'EXTENDED B'** hand is held in a fixed position with palm facing rightward and slightly forward. Right **'ONE'** (or **'K'**) hand is held palm down as it moves forward/downward at a slight leftward angle, the forefinger firmly grazing the left palm.

muscle: *n.* bundles of tissue that contract and relax to enable movement of body parts. *Weightlifting helps to tone one's **muscles**.*

SIGN: Fingertips of right **'BENT EXTENDED B'** hand tap against the biceps in the left forearm. The location of this sign may vary depending on which part of the body is under discussion. (**MUSCLE** is frequently fingerspelled.)

museum: *n.* a building in which items are displayed for their historical, artistic, or scientific value. *The Tyrrell Museum at Drumheller, Alberta is a world-class facility displaying dinosaur artifacts.*

SIGN: Fingerspell **MUSEUM**.

mushroom: *n.* a fleshy fungus, usually having a rounded cap and a stem. *Some mushrooms are poisonous but there are also many edible varieties.*

SIGN: Left **'ONE'** hand is held with palm facing the body and finger pointing rightward/upward. Right **'SPREAD EXTENDED C'** hand is tapped palm-down on the tip of the left forefinger at least twice. (**MUSHROOM** is frequently fingerspelled.)

music: *n.* a melodious sequence of sounds. *Deaf people often enjoy music with a strong bass component because of the vibrations created.*

SIGN: Horizontal right **'EXTENDED B'** hand is positioned above left forearm with palm facing leftward/backward. The right wrist makes slight back and forth rotations so that the palm alternates between being angled slightly upward and being angled slightly downward.

must: *v.* to be obliged, required or compelled. *I must stay at home to study tonight.*

SIGN: Vertical right **'X'** hand, palm facing forward, is bent forward smartly from the wrist so that the palm faces downward. Facial expression is important.

mustard: *n.* a brownish-yellow coloured condiment made from the seeds of the mustard plant. *I like lots of mustard on my hot dog.*

SIGN: Right **'Y'** hand, palm left, is wiggled back and forth from the wrist several times. Next, left **'EXTENDED B'** hand is held in a fixed position with palm up and fingers pointing forward/rightward. Right **'EXTENDED B'** hand is held with palm down and fingers pointing forward/leftward as they are rubbed in a counterclockwise direction on the left palm. (ASL CONCEPT—**yellow - spread on food**.) **MUSTARD** is frequently fingerspelled.

mute: *adj.* making no sound; unable to speak. *I have never met a Deaf person who is truly mute.*

SIGN #1: Fingerspell **MUTE**. (A word of caution: Deaf people generally do not appreciate being referred to as **mute**. While learning to speak is very challenging for Deaf people, we are not without voice.)

mute: *adj.* making no sound; choosing not to speak. *Knowing they were guilty, the children remained mute, with their heads down, throughout their father's scolding.*

SIGN #2: **'B'** (or **'EXTENDED B'**) hands are crossed in front of the mouth, left palm facing rightward/downward and right palm facing leftward/downward with the right hand just behind the left hand. Then they are drawn apart until the palms face completely downward.

muted: *adj.* soft (in terms of either sound or colour). *The colours of a Yorkshire landscape are generally muted.*

SIGN: **'CONTRACTED 5'** hands are held slightly apart with palms up and are drawn downward a few times as they are changed to **'FLAT O'** hands.

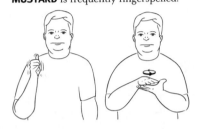

mutual: *adj.* common; shared by both. *She and I have many **mutual** friends.*

SIGN #1: Vertical right **'Y'** hand is held at shoulder level with palm forward. The forearm then moves from side to side several times so that the hand appears to move in an arc. (If there is something mutual between 'you' and 'me', the sign is made with the palm facing left and the movement backward and forward.)

mutual: *adj.* related to a corporation which invests in various businesses on behalf of it shareholders. *I have some money invested in **mutual** funds.*

SIGN #2: Fingerspell **MUTUAL**.

M   U   T   U   A   L

muzzle: *n.* a guard placed over an animal's jaws and nose to prevent it from biting. *The veterinarian had to put a **muzzle** on the dog while he removed the thorns from his paws.*

SIGN: Right **'SPREAD C'** hand, palm toward the face, is brought upward to cover the nose and mouth.

my: *pron.* used to indicate something belonging to or related to the signer. [See PRONOUNS, p. LXVI.] *This is not **my** book. Mine has **my** name on it.*

SIGN: Right **'EXTENDED B'** hand, palm facing the body, is laid against the middle of the chest.

myself: *pron.* used by the signer to emphasize the subject "I". [See PRONOUNS, p. LXVI.] *I want to complete the project **myself**.*

SIGN: Horizontal right **'EXTENDED A'** hand, thumb pointing upward and palm facing the body, is tapped a couple of times against the chest.

mystery: *n.* a story or movie that arouses suspense because of concealed facts. *I am reading an Agatha Christie **mystery** right now and finding it hard to put down.*

SIGN #1: Right **'CROOKED ONE'** hand, palm toward the head, is held with tip of forefinger stroking downward slightly against the right temple, then bouncing away a short distance as the finger retracts to form an **'x'** hand. Movement is repeated at least once. A look of suspicion accompanies this sign. Next, left **'CONTRACTED C'** (or **'OPEN 8'**) hand is held horizontally with palm facing right while right **'CONTRACTED C'** (or **'OPEN 8'**) hand is held upright with palm facing left. The hands are held close enough together to be loosely interlocked. They are then drawn apart, closed and returned several times, thus alternating between **'CONTRACTED C'** (or **'OPEN 8'**) and **'FLAT O'** (or **'8'**) shapes with each movement. (ASL CONCEPT—**suspicious - story**.) **MYSTERY** is frequently fingerspelled.

mystery: *n.* an unexplained event; something unknown or puzzling. *It is a **mystery** to me how a two-year-old child could break his father's arm!*

SIGN #2: Back of the right **'ONE'** hand, palm forward and forefinger pointing upward, is placed just in front of the middle of the forehead and is drawn backward while the forefinger is crooked to form an **'x'** handshape. (A look of 'bewilderment' accompanies this sign.)

myth: *n.* a fictional tale about supernatural beings of an earlier age. *My favourite myth is a Greek one about a young man called Narcissus who was turned into a flower because he was so fascinated with his own image.*

SIGN #1: Right **'4'** hand is held upright in front of forehead with palm facing leftward. The hand is then moved forward (at a slight downward angle) in short jerky motions until the fingers are pointing forward. Next, left **'CONTRACTED C'** (or **'OPEN 8'**) hand is held horizontally with palm facing right while right **'CONTRACTED C'** (or **'OPEN 8'**) hand is held upright with palm facing left. The hands are held close enough together to be loosely interlocked. They are then drawn apart, closed and returned several times, thus alternating between **'CONTRACTED C'** (or **'OPEN 8'**) and **'FLAT O'** (or **'8'**) shapes with each movement. (ASL CONCEPT—**fantasy - story**.) **MYTH** is frequently fingerspelled.

myth: *n.* an idea that is fictional or unproven. *It is a myth that, with practice, anyone can become an expert speechreader.*

SIGN #2: Right **'EXTENDED A'** hand, palm facing left, thumb under chin, is thrust forward. Next, forefinger of vertical right **'ONE'** hand, palm facing left, is held against the lips and the hand is moved sharply forward. This sign is accompanied by a look of 'disbelief'. (ASL CONCEPT—**not - true**.) **MYTH** is frequently fingerspelled.

OR

SIGN #3: Vertical right **'4'** hand is held in front of forehead with palm facing leftward. The hand is then moved firmly forward at a slight downward angle. This sign is accompanied by a look of 'disbelief'.

N

nab: *v.* to seize suddenly or to arrest. *The police hope to **nab** the culprits.*

SIGN: Right **'SPREAD C'** hand, palm facing left, is moved left and becomes an **'S'** hand as it grabs the forefinger of the vertical left **'ONE'** hand whose palm faces right. Alternatively, this sign may be made with two hands held apart in front of the chest. ❖
ALTERNATE SIGNS—**arrest** #1 & #3

nag: *v.* to annoy by constantly complaining, scolding or criticizing. *He did not want his wife to **nag** him about his chores.*

SIGN: Thumb and forefinger of right **'CLOSED X'** hand, palm forward, are used to peck repeatedly against upright forefinger of left **'ONE'** hand. ❖

nail: *n.* a metal fastening device with a point at one end and a head at the other. *He needed a **nail** to hang the picture.*

SIGN: Fingerspell **NAIL**. (For **nail**, *v.*, see **hammer**.)

naive: *adj.* lacking a fully developed power of reasoning or criticism. *She was so **naive** that she believed the salesman.*

SIGN: Tips of extended fingers of **'U'** hands, palms toward the body, are placed at either side of the mouth and the hands are simultaneously thrust forward/downward so that palms face upward. This sign is accompanied by a rather blank facial expression. (**NAIVE** is frequently fingerspelled.)

naked: *adj.* undressed or having no covering. *They sketched a **naked** man in art class.*

SIGN: Tip of middle finger of right **'BENT MIDFINGER 5'** hand strokes forward/rightward across back of left **'STANDARD BASE'** hand.

name: *n.* a word or phrase by which a person or thing is known. *Please sign your **name** at the bottom of the page.*

SIGN: **'U'** hands are held horizontally with left palm facing right but angled slightly toward the body while right palm faces leftward at a slight angle toward the body. Right hand is positioned above the left at right angles to it. Right midfinger is then tapped twice on left forefinger. (For **name**, *v.*, see **call** #2.)

nap: *n.* a short, light sleep. *He always takes a **nap** in the afternoon.*

SIGN: Fingerspell **NAP**.

napkin: *n.* a piece of cloth or paper used while eating to protect the clothes, wipe the mouth, etc. *She unfolded the table **napkin** and placed it on her lap.*

SIGN: Right **'EXTENDED B'** hand, palm toward the body and fingertips in front of the mouth, is circled in what appears to the signer to be a counter-clockwise direction.

narcotics: *n.* drugs such as opium and morphine that produce numbness, a dreamlike condition or sleepiness. Continued use of such drugs can lead to addiction. *Heroin and cocaine are **narcotics**.*

SIGN: Right horizontal **'S'** hand, palm toward the body, is used to tap firmly on the inside of the bent elbow of the left arm which also has an **'S'** handshape, palm facing upward.

narrate: *v.* to tell a story. *He will **narrate** the story while the children watch the film.*

SIGN: Left **'CONTRACTED C'** (or **'OPEN 8'**) hand is held horizontally with palm facing right while right **'CONTRACTED C'** (or **'OPEN 8'**) hand is held upright with palm facing left. The hands are held close enough together to be loosely interlocked. They are then drawn apart, closed and returned several times, thus alternating between **'CONTRACTED C'** (or **'OPEN 8'**) and **'FLAT O'** (or **'8'**) shapes with each movement.

narrator: *n.* a person who tells a story. *Please pay attention to the narrator.*

SIGN: Left **'CONTRACTED C'** (or **'OPEN 8'**) hand is held horizontally with palm facing right while right **'CONTRACTED C'** (or **'OPEN 8'**) hand is held upright with palm facing left. The hands are held close enough together to be loosely interlocked. They are then drawn apart, closed and returned several times, thus alternating between **'CONTRACTED C'** (or **'OPEN 8'**) and **'FLAT O'** (or **'8'**) shapes with each movement. Next, tip of forefinger of right **'BENT ONE'** hand, palm toward the body, is held just under the chin and flicked forward. Agent Ending (see p. LIV) may follow. (ASL CONCEPT—**story - teller**.)

narrow: *adj.* not wide. *The bridge is very narrow.*

SIGN: Horizontal **'EXTENDED B'** hands are held close together with palms facing one another and are pushed forward simultaneously.

narrow-minded: *adj.* having a limited outlook; prejudiced; bigoted. *He is so narrow-minded that he will not consider any alternatives.*

SIGN: Tip of forefinger of right **'ONE'** hand, palm toward face, touches right side of forehead. Then tips of horizontal **'B'** hands are brought together at about chest level to form a **'V'** shape with the apex pointing forward. (ASL CONCEPT—**think - close**.)

nasal: *adj.* related to the nose. *Certain English speech sounds are produced in the nasal cavity.*

SIGN: Fingerspell **NASAL**.

N A S A L

nasty: *adj.* mean; cruel. *Pulling a dog's tail is a nasty thing to do.*

SIGN #1: Right **'CROOKED 5'** hand is held with palm facing left and tip of forefinger touching or near end of nose while left **'CROOKED 5'** hand, palm facing right, is held just in front of/below right hand. The hands eventually assume **'A'** shapes as they brush past one another, the right hand moving downward/forward and the left hand moving upward/backward. Appropriate facial expression is important.

nasty: *adj.* rude; inconsiderate. *He is always saying nasty things about his former wife.*

SIGN #2: Thumb and forefinger of right **'A-INDEX'** hand, palm left, grasp skin of right cheek. Appropriate facial expression is important.

nasty: *adj.* unpleasant; awful. *He has a nasty wound where the arrow struck him.*

SIGN #3: Thumb and forefinger of vertical right **'COVERED 8'** hand, which is held near right side of face with palm facing left, are snapped open and thrust slightly forward to form a **'MODIFIED 5'** hand. This sign can be made with either one or two hands, one at either side of the face. Appropriate facial expression is important. (Sign selection depends on the context.)

natal: *adj.* relating to birth. *Natal information can be obtained from an obstetrician.*

SIGN: Horizontal **'EXTENDED B'** hands are held in front of the abdomen, palms facing the body, with the back of the right hand resting against the left palm. Then the right hand is curved down and under the left until its palm faces downward. (Alternatively, **NATAL** may be fingerspelled.)

nation: *n.* a community of people bound by common descent, language, customs, and history. *Canadians are fortunate to live in a prosperous nation.*

SIGN: Right **'BENT U'** hand, palm down, is circled clockwise from the wrist and brought down so that the extended fingertips come to rest on the back of the left **'STANDARD BASE'** hand.
SAME SIGN—**national**, *adj.*
ALTERNATE SIGN—**country**

Native: *adj.* aboriginal; of or pertaining to a group of people who originated in a particular place. *There are many different Native reserves across Canada.*

SIGN #1: Joined thumb and forefinger of vertical right **'FLAT F'** hand, palm facing left, are placed just to the right of the mouth and then moved backward and set down once again in front of the ear. (This sign is used to refer to Natives of North America only. To refer to a native of any other continent, fingerspell **NATIVE**.)

native: *adj.* acquired as a result of the circumstances of someone's birth or early life. *ASL is his native language.*

SIGN #2: Fingerspell **NATIVE**.

natural: *adj.* normal or to be expected. *It is natural for little children to be curious about their environment.*

SIGN: Right **'BENT U'** hand, palm down, is circled clockwise from the wrist and brought down so that the extended fingertips come to rest on the back of the left **'STANDARD BASE'** hand.

nature: *n.* the physical world of plant and animal life (usually outdoors). *As a nature lover, he enjoys long walks along the river.*

SIGN #1: Right **'BENT U'** hand, palm down, is circled clockwise from the wrist and brought down so that the extended fingertips come to rest on the back of the left **'STANDARD BASE'** hand.

nature: *n.* the fundamental qualities or essential character of a person. *It is not my nature to complain.*

SIGN #2: Horizontal right **'C'** hand, palm facing the body, is twisted in a circular motion from the wrist so that it becomes upright with palm facing leftward as it is brought back against the left shoulder.

naughty: *adj.* mischievous or disobedient; badly behaved. *He was sent to his room because he was naughty.*

SIGN: Right **'EXTENDED B'** hand, with fingertips on chin and palm facing body, is turned away, so that palm is facing down.

nausea: *n.* the sensation that precedes vomiting. *Seasickness creates a feeling of nausea.*

SIGN: Right **'CLAWED C'** hand, palm toward the body, is circled in a clockwise direction (from the onlooker's perspective) in front of the stomach. Facial expression is very important. SAME SIGN—**nauseous**, *adj.*

navy: *n.* a country's seafaring military defence organization. *He joined the navy to see the world.*

SIGN #1: Fingerspell **NAVY**.

navy: *adj.* having a dark blue colour. *He wore a navy blue suit to the banquet.*

SIGN #2: Fingerspell **NAVY**.

near: *adv.* close to, close by; just a short distance from. *He lives near the airport.*

SIGN: Horizontal **'BENT EXTENDED B'** hands are held right in front of left with right palm facing leftward and left palm facing rightward. Right hand is then moved backward so that fingers of right hand touch fingers of left hand to indicate nearness. Motion may be repeated. (If you wish to indicate that something/someone is *very* near, see **(just around the) corner**.)

nearly: *adv.* not exactly, but almost. *He nearly finished first in the race.*

SIGN: Both **'BENT EXTENDED B'** hands are held with palms toward the body. The left hand remains steady, while the fingertips of the right hand are brushed upward from the knuckles of the left.

neat: *adj.* orderly, clean or tidy. *Their house and yard are always neat.*

SIGN: Hands are held at right angles to one another as downturned palm of right **'EXTENDED B'** hand is smoothed rightward/forward across upturned palm of left **'EXTENDED B'** hand.

nebulous: See **vague**.

necessary: *adj.* required, needed or inevitable. *Food is necessary for human survival.*

SIGN: Horizontal right **'x'** hand is held palm down and shaken up and down from the wrist at least twice.
SAME SIGN—**necessity,** *n.*

neck: *n.* the part of the body that connects the head with the torso. *She hurt her neck in an automobile accident.*

SIGN #1: Fingertips of right **'BENT EXTENDED B'** hand, palm toward the body, are tapped against right side of neck. Alternatively, a **'BENT ONE'** hand may be used with forefinger tapping against neck. (Sign selection depends on context. When a description of the neck is being given, the signer often chooses an all-inclusive sign which conveys **neck,** *n.,* as well as its description.)

neck: *v.* a colloquial expression meaning to kiss and caress passionately. *The couple was necking in the back seat of the car.*

SIGN #2: With right palm facing left and left palm facing right, vertical **'s'** hands are crossed at the wrists with the left hand in front of the right. The hands maintain contact as they simultaneously bend downward and upward a few times from the wrist.

necklace: *n.* jewelry worn around the neck. *She received a gold necklace for her birthday.*

SIGN: Fingertips of both **'BENT ONE'** hands, palms toward the chest, are placed near each other in the centre of the upper chest and are drawn apart and upward to outline where a necklace is worn.

nee: *adj.* indicating the maiden name of a married woman. *The speaker is Mrs. Bloggs, nee Harriet Blandish.*

SIGN: Little finger of right horizontal **'I'** hand, palm facing the body and angled leftward slightly, is used to strike downward against little finger of left horizontal **'I'** hand, of which the palm faces the body at a rightward angle. Next, back of fingers of right **'BENT EXTENDED B'** hand are held against fingers of left **'BENT EXTENDED B'** hand, which is held horizontally with palm facing the body. Right hand is then moved toward the body. Lastly, **'EXTENDED C'** hands are held apart with palms facing and the right hand slightly above the left. The hands are then clasped together. (ASL CONCEPT—**last - before - marry.**) Alternatively, the ASL compound **last - name - before - marry** or simply **name - before - marry** may be used for **nee.**

need: *v.* to require or to want something that is lacking. *You will need an assistant to complete this project.*

SIGN: Horizontal right **'x'** hand is held palm down and moved purposefully downward a short distance from the wrist.
SAME SIGN—**need,** *n.,* but the motion is repeated.

needle: *n.* a pointed, slender piece of metal with a hole at one end through which thread is passed for sewing. *There is a needle in my sewing basket.*

SIGN #1: Fingerspell **NEEDLE.**

needle: *n.* a slender, hollow, metal tube with a sharp point at one end and a hypodermic syringe at the other (used for injections). *The nurse jabbed the needle into the patient's left arm.*

SIGN #2: Tip of forefinger of right **'BENT L'** hand is jabbed into upper left arm and thumb is repeatedly bent and extended as though depressing a plunger into a syringe. (The location of this sign depends on which part of the body is receiving the injection.)

needy: *adj.* very poor. *'Santas Anonymous' was established for the benefit of **needy** children.*

SIGN: Thumb and fingertips of right **'CONTRACTED 5'** hand grasp left elbow and close to form a **'FLAT O'** as they slide downward off the elbow. Motion is repeated.

negative: *adj.* the opposite of positive. *She has a **negative** attitude toward the medical profession.*

SIGN #1: Edge of extended forefinger of right horizontal **'BENT ONE'** hand, palm down, is tapped against forward-facing palm of vertical left **'EXTENDED B'** hand.

negative: *adj.* indicative that there is no disease present. *The patient was relieved that his test results were **negative**.*

SIGN #2: Vertical **'O'** hands are held apart with palms facing each other and are simultaneously thrust downward/forward as the wrists rotate outward so that the palms face each other at an upward angle. (This sign is used when the type of test is already understood. Signs in this context vary.)

negative: *n.* photographic film previously exposed and developed, showing a black and white image in reversed tones. *I will give you the **negative** of this photograph so you can make a copy.*

SIGN #3: Fingerspell **NEG**. (Alternatively, the whole word **NEGATIVE** may be fingerspelled.)

neglect: *v.* to fail to look after properly or give enough time to; to ignore. *She did not want to **neglect** her responsibilities.*

SIGN: Tip of forefinger of horizontal right **'4'** hand, palm facing downward, is placed on the nose and the hand is curved rightward from the wrist away from the face.

negotiate: *v.* to try to reach an agreement through discussion. *Management will meet with union representatives to **negotiate** a pay settlement.*

SIGN: Vertical **'O'** hands are held with palms facing, thumbs touching and fingertips touching intermittently as they wiggle up and down. At the same time, both hands are repeatedly moved backward and forward.
SAME SIGN—**negotiation**, *n.*

neighbour [*also spelled* **neighbor**]: *n.* a person who lives near another. *My **neighbour** likes to cut his lawn early in the morning.*

SIGN: Underside of fingers of right horizontal **'EXTENDED B'** hand, palm facing left, are placed against the back of those of the left horizontal **'BENT EXTENDED B'** hand, of which the palm faces the body. Then the right hand is moved rightward in an upward arc. Agent Ending (see p. LIV) may follow.

neighbourhood: *n.* a district where one lives. *I live in a very quiet **neighbourhood**.*

SIGN: Underside of fingers of right horizontal **'EXTENDED B'** hand, palm facing left, are placed against the back of those of the left horizontal **'BENT EXTENDED B'** hand, of which the palm faces the body. Then the right hand is moved rightward in an upward arc. Next, right **'5'** hand is circled palm-down in a counter-clockwise motion.

neon: *adj.* very bright, glowing color. *Children wearing **neon** colors are very visible on the ski slopes.*

SIGN: Horizontal right **'V'** hand, palm toward the face, is held in front of the eyes and is snapped to the right as it changes to an upright **'CLAWED V'**.
ALTERNATE SIGN—**gaudy**

nephew: *n.* son of one's brother or sister. *My **nephew** and my son are the same age.*

SIGN: Fingertips of right vertical **'BENT U'** hand point leftward and are held close to right side of forehead. The hand then wobbles slightly from the wrist.

nerd: *n.* a slang expression for someone who is looked upon with contempt or derision because s/he is dressed oddly or behaves differently. *Everyone considers him a **nerd** because his clothes are always out of style and he has strange hobbies.*

SIGN: Back of right **'Y'** hand, palm forward, is placed against the forehead and the three fingers between the thumb and pinkie are fluttered up and down. The tongue is visible and the signer appears to be articulating a 'TH' sound. (Alternatively, **NERD** may be fingerspelled.)

nerve: *n.* a fibre that conducts impulses between the brain and another part of the body. *Damage to the optic nerve can cause blindness.*

SIGN #1: Fingerspell **NERVE**.

nerve: *n.* brazenness or boldness. *He had a lot of nerve to attend the party uninvited.*

SIGN #2: Knuckles of right vertical **'CLAWED V'** hand, palm forward, are placed against the right cheek and the hand is twisted a quarter turn forward so that the palm faces downward.

nervous: *adj.* very excitable or sensitive. *I was nervous when I presented my first lecture.*

SIGN #1: Horizontal **'5'** hands are held parallel with fingers pointing forward and palms facing each other at a downward angle. The hands are then shaken as the wrists rapidly twist back and forth slightly.

OR

SIGN #2: Extended fingertips of horizontal **'CROOKED V'** hand, palm down, are placed on the back of the left **'STANDARD BASE'** hand and are jiggled.

nervy: *adj.* bold or cheeky. *It is nervy of him to blame others for his foolishness.*

SIGN: Knuckles of right vertical **'CLAWED V'** hand, palm toward the face, are placed against the right cheek and the hand is twisted a quarter turn forward.

nest: *n.* a structure in which birds lay their eggs. *The robins built their nest in our tree.*

SIGN: Right **'MODIFIED G'** hand is held at chin, palm facing forward, while thumb and forefinger are opened and closed at least twice to simulate the movement of a bird's beak. Next, **'CROOKED EXTENDED B'** hands are held side by side with palms up. Then they are moved apart and upward to outline the shape of a bowl. (ASL CONCEPT—**bird - nest**.) **NEST** is frequently fingerspelled.

net: *n.* a device made of meshy fabric used to catch or enclose fish. *Fishermen spend many hours mending their nets.*

SIGN #1: Fingers of right **'4'** hand, palm facing the body, point leftward/upward and are laid against rightward/upward pointing fingers of left **'4'** hand, of which the palm faces the body too. The hands are then drawn apart at a downward angle. (**NET** is frequently fingerspelled.)

net: *adj.* pertaining to final income after all required deductions are made. *There is a big difference between my gross and net earnings.*

SIGN #2: Thumb and forefinger of right **'F'** hand, palm facing down, are brought slightly downward to be inserted into an imaginary pocket at waist level. Alternatively, the imaginary pocket is sometimes located at the left side of the chest. (Sign selection depends on context. **NET** is frequently fingerspelled.)

network: *n.* contacts formed through social interaction. *He communicates with a wide network of people through his computer modem.*

SIGN #1: **'BENT MIDFINGER 5'** hands are held upright with palms facing each other. Tips of midfingers touch and maintain contact as the hands alternately pivot back and forth from the wrist.

network: *n.* a group of radio or television stations broadcasting the same programs simultaneously. *Spencer Caldwell founded the CTV network in 1961.*

SIGN #2: Left **'MODIFIED O'** hand is held at about shoulder level with palm facing upward but angled slightly toward the body while right **'MODIFIED O'** hand is held upright just in front of the forehead with palm toward the face. The forearms then move simultaneously forward/downward as the hands open to assume **'MODIFIED 5'** shapes with palms facing upward.

neutral: *adj.* supporting neither side in a war or dispute. *Switzerland was a neutral nation during World War II.*

SIGN: Right **'BENT U'** hand is held upright with palm forward and is moved slightly but rapidly from side to side. This is a wrist movement.

never: *adv.* not ever or at no time. *I have never seen a more beautiful sunset.*

SIGN: Right **'B'** (or **'EXTENDED B'**) hand, palm facing left, is held upright near the face and is vigorously curved downward.

never mind: See (never) mind.

nevertheless: *adv.* however, yet, or in spite of that. *He is a charming fellow; **nevertheless**, I do not quite trust him.*

SIGN: Fingers of horizontal **'BENT EXTENDED B'** hands, palms facing the chest, are alternately brushed back and forth against each other.

new: *adj.* recently made or discovered. *They bought a house in a **new** subdivision.*

SIGN: Horizontal left **'EXTENDED B'** hand remains stationary with palm up and fingers pointing forward/rightward while right **'BENT EXTENDED B'** hand, palm facing upward, is brought leftward across left palm using a scooping motion.

news: *n.* important recent occurrences. *I watch the CBC closed-captioned **news** every evening.*

SIGN: Fingerspell **NEWS**.

N E W S

newspaper: *n.* a weekly or daily publication consisting of folded sheets of newsprint. *Most Canadian cities have at least one daily **newspaper**.*

SIGN #1: Thumbnail of right **'MODIFIED G'** hand, palm forward/downward, is placed on upturned palm of left **'EXTENDED B'** hand. Right forefinger then moves up and down several times, thus alternately creating **'MODIFIED G'** and **'CLOSED MODIFIED G'** handshapes.

SIGN #2 [ATLANTIC]: With left palm facing upward and right palm facing forward/downward, right horizontal **'A'** hand is held slightly above and to the right of left horizontal **'A'** hand. As the right hand moves leftward/backward and the left hand moves rightward/forward, the wrists brush quickly past each other. The hands brush past each other yet again as they then move quickly in the opposite direction and open, thus becoming **'5'** hands.

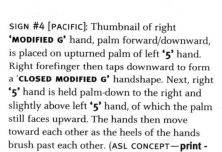

SIGN #3 [ONTARIO]: Horizontal right **'S'** hand is held palm-down above upturned palm of horizontal left **'EXTENDED B'** hand. The right wrist then rotates forward as the hand is brought down firmly to rest with palm toward the body on the left palm.

SIGN #4 [PACIFIC]: Thumbnail of right **'MODIFIED G'** hand, palm forward/downward, is placed on upturned palm of left **'5'** hand. Right forefinger then taps downward to form a **'CLOSED MODIFIED G'** handshape. Next, right **'5'** hand is held palm-down to the right and slightly above left **'5'** hand, of which the palm still faces upward. The hands then move toward each other as the heels of the hands brush past each other. (ASL CONCEPT—**print - paper**.)

SIGN #5 [PRAIRIE]: **'EXTENDED A'** hands are held upright with right thumbtip touching the nose and palm facing leftward, while left hand is positioned just in front of and slightly lower than right hand with palm facing rightward. The hands are then simultaneously curved downward and outward as they take on **'3'** shapes with extended fingertips pointing forward and palms facing each other but angled downward slightly.

next: *adv.* coming directly after in terms of time. *What will we do next?*

SIGN #1: With left palm facing right and right palm facing left, **'BENT EXTENDED B'** hands are held horizontally, the left hand just ahead of the right hand. The hands may even be touching. The right hand is then curved upward and forward over the left hand to take up a position in front of it. Alternatively, this sign may be formed without the left hand. (Sign selection depends on context. This sign would never be used to mean 'next to' in the sense that things or people are positioned side by side. Sign selection for 'next to' would depend entirely on what/whom was next to what/whom.)

next: *adv.* a word used to convey whose turn is to follow immediately after another's. *I hope the doctor will see me next.*

SIGN #2: Horizontal right **'CONTRACTED 3'** hand is held with palm facing left. The hand is then brought backward against the chest as the wrist rotates to turn the palm downward and extended fingers and thumb close to form a **'CLOSED DOUBLE MODIFIED G'** hand with extended fingers pointing downward. (This sign always moves in a direction from the person whose turn it is now to the person whose turn it will be next.)

OR

SIGN #3: Horizontal right **'L'** hand is held with palm facing left but angled slightly toward the body. The hand is then brought backward against the chest as the wrist rotates to turn the hand upright with palm facing leftward. (This sign always moves in a direction from the person whose turn it is now to the person whose turn it will be next.)

next door: in or at an adjacent house, apartment or other facility. *We live next door to the bank.*

SIGN: Underside of fingers of right horizontal **'EXTENDED B'** hand, palm facing left, are placed against the back of those of the left horizontal **'BENT EXTENDED B'** hand, of which the palm faces the body and fingers point toward the chest. Then the right hand is moved rightward in an upward arc.

nice: *adj.* pleasing, friendly, good or satisfactory. *Our neighbours are nice people.*

SIGN: Hands are held at right angles to one another as downturned palm of right **'EXTENDED B'** hand is smoothed rightward/forward across upturned palm of left **'EXTENDED B'** hand.

nickel: *n.* a coin worth five cents. *It only cost a nickel.*

SIGN: Tip of little finger of vertical right **'SLANTED 5'** hand, palm facing backwards, is brushed backward several times against right side of forehead. This is not a wrist movement, but a slight movement of the entire forearm.

niece: *n.* a daughter of one's sister or brother. *I have four nephews but only one niece.*

SIGN: Fingertips of right vertical **'BENT U'** hand point leftward and are held close to lower right cheek. The hand then wobbles slightly from the wrist.

night: *n.* the period of darkness that occurs each 24 hours. [See TIME CONCEPTS, p. LXXIII.] *I will see you Friday night.*

SIGN: Heel of right **'BENT EXTENDED B'** hand, palm forward/downward, makes contact with back of left **'STANDARD BASE'** hand near the wrist on the side closest to the body.

nightmare: *n.* a deeply distressing dream. *I had a terrible nightmare last night.*

SIGN: Right **'EXTENDED B'** hand, with fingertips on mouth or chin and palm facing body, is turned away, so that palm is facing down. Next, tip of forefinger of right **'ONE'** hand touches right side of forehead. The forearm then moves quickly away from the head at a rightward/upward angle as the forefinger retracts to form an **'X'** shape. (ASL CONCEPT— **bad - dream.**) NIGHTMARE is frequently fingerspelled.

nine: *n.* See NUMBERS, p. LX.

nineteen: *n.* See NUMBERS, p. LXI.

ninety: *n.* See NUMBERS, p. LXII.

nipple: *n.* the small conical projection in the centre of each breast. *The nipple contains the outlet of a mother's milk ducts.*

SIGN: Vertical right **'F'** hand, palm facing left, is placed against right breast. Two hands are used to indicate plurality.

no: *adv.* a word used to convey denial, refusal or disagreement. *No, you may not go to the dance.*

SIGN #1: Right **'DOUBLE CONTRACTED L'** hand is held upright with palm forward. Thumb and extended fingers are then snapped together to form a **'CLOSED DOUBLE MODIFIED G'**. Motion may be repeated. The sign is usually accompanied by the shaking of the head from side to side. (**NO** is frequently fingerspelled.)

no: *adj.* not any; none. *He has no relatives living in Canada.*

SIGN #2: Right **'O'** hand is held upright with palm facing left, and is thrust downward/forward as the wrist rotates rightward to turn the hand so that the palm faces upward/leftward. Two hands may be used.

SIGN #3 [COLLOQUIAL]: The signer blows on the upturned palm of the right **'EXTENDED B'** which is held in front of the chin with the fingers pointing forward. (This sign is used for emphasis.)

no: *adj.* a colloquial term meaning not any left; none left. *By the time I arrived there was no food left.*

SIGN #4: Right **'EXTENDED B'** hand is held with fingertips just to the left of the mouth and pointing leftward/upward while the palm faces the body. The hand then moves quickly rightward past the mouth which is expelling air as if blowing the dust off of something. (The use of this sign is very context specific.)

no more: *adv.* discontinued; no longer the case. *We used to be able to buy stamps there, but no more.*

SIGN: **'CROOKED 5'** hands are held apart limply with fingers pointing downward. The wrists then simultaneously rotate outward, flinging the hands into a position in which the palms are facing upward at a backward angle. At the same time, the signer, with eyes wide, clearly articulates the words 'no more' and shakes his head.

nobody/no one: *pron.* not one person. [See also PRONOUNS, p. LXIII.] *They scheduled a meeting but due to the weather, nobody came.*

SIGN: Vertical **'O'** hands are held parallel with palms forward but angled toward each other slightly, as the forearms are simultaneously shaken.

nod: *v.* to lower and raise one's head briefly. *Nod your head if you agree with me.*

SIGN: Vertical right **'S'** hand, palm forward, represents the head as it is moved forward and back from the wrist. The signer's head may actually nod. ❖

noise: *n.* a sound, usually loud and disturbing. *Constant exposure to industrial noise may result in hearing loss.*

SIGN: Thumbtips of vertical **'MODIFIED 5'** hands are held near either ear, palms facing forward but angled slightly toward each other, as forearms are simultaneously thrust outward/forward and back at least twice. SAME SIGN—**noisy**, *adj.*, but facial expression is important.

nominate: *v.* to name someone as a candidate for an office or position. *She will nominate him for the vice-presidency.*

SIGN: **'EXTENDED B'** hands, palms up and fingers pointing forward, are held slightly apart with the right just ahead of the left, and are simultaneously thrust forward in an arc. SAME SIGN—**nomination**, *n. sing.* See **nominations** for the plural form.

nominations: *n.* the act of proposing or naming people as candidates for certain offices or positions. *The meeting will open with nominations for officers.*

SIGN: **'EXTENDED B'** hands are held slightly apart with palms up and fingers pointing forward. The hands are alternately circled forward. (The sign illustrated here is used for the plural form of the noun only. For the singular form, see **nomination**.)

non-: *prefix* not. *The Canadian Cultural Society of the Deaf is a nonprofit organization.*

SIGN: Right **'EXTENDED A'** hand, palm facing left, thumb under chin, is thrust forward. (Alternatively, the prefix **NON-** may be fingerspelled for emphasis.)

nonalcoholic: *adj.* containing no alcohol. *Nonalcoholic cocktails were served before the banquet.*

SIGN: Right **'COMBINED I + ONE'** hand is held above and at right angles to left **'COMBINED I + ONE'** hand, whose palm faces slightly to the right and slightly toward the body. The two hands are then tapped together twice. Next, horizontal right **'BENT EXTENDED B'** hand is brought back firmly so that fingertips make contact with upper right chest. At the same time, the signer's upper front teeth are resting on the lower lip. Finally, the right **'O'** hand is held upright with palm facing left, and is thrust downward/forward so that the palm faces upward/leftward. Alternatively, two hands may be used for this part of the sign. (ASL CONCEPT—**alcohol - have - no**.)

none: *pron.* not any. *The apples are all gone; there are none left.*

SIGN: Right **'O'** hand is held upright with palm facing left, and is thrust downward/forward as the wrist rotates rightward to turn the hand so that the palm faces upward/leftward. Two hands may be used.

nonetheless: *adv.* in spite of that; however; nevertheless. *The weather turned very cold but our meeting was nonetheless well attended.*

SIGN: Fingers of horizontal **'BENT EXTENDED B'** hands, palms facing the chest, are alternately brushed back and forth against each other.

nonfiction: *n.* a written work that is based on reality or true events. *The curriculum requires that students study both fiction and nonfiction.*

SIGN: Right **'ONE'** hand is held upright with palm facing left as tip of forefinger touches the lips, then moves forward sharply. Next, left **'CONTRACTED C'** hand is held horizontally with palm facing right while right **'CONTRACTED C'** hand is held upright with palm facing left. The hands are held close enough together to be loosely interlocked. They are then drawn apart, closed and returned several times, thus alternating between **'CONTRACTED C'** and **'FLAT O'** shapes with each movement. (ASL CONCEPT—**true - story**.)

nonsense: *n.* foolishness. *I refuse to accept that nonsense.*

SIGN #1: Right **'Y'** hand, palm facing leftward, is held upright in front of the centre of the forehead, and is rapidly twisted back and forth from the wrist.
ALTERNATE SIGN—**silly**

nonsense: *int.* an exclamation of disagreement or doubt. *You believe in ghosts? Nonsense!*

SIGN #2: Right **'4'** hand is held upright in front of forehead with palm facing leftward. The hand is then moved forward (at a slight downward angle) in short jerky motions until the fingers are pointing forward.

nonsense: *int.* an *emphatic* exclamation of disagreement or doubt. *You won ten million dollars? Nonsense!*

SIGN #3: Vertical right **'B'** hand is held with palm facing the body. It then drops forward/downward as it closes to form an **'S'** hand with the palm facing upward. A look of sheer incredulity or skepticism accompanies this sign.

noon: *n.* 12 o'clock or mid-day. [See TIME CONCEPTS, p. LXXIII.] *We will hold the meeting at noon during our lunch hour.*

SIGN: Right **'EXTENDED B'** hand is held upright with palm facing left as elbow rests on back of left **'EXTENDED B'** hand which is held palm down in front of right side of body.

norm: *n.* an average level of achievement or performance. *Her marks are always well above the class norm.*

SIGN: Edge of right **'EXTENDED B'** hand, with palm facing left, slides from left to right in the space between thumb and forefinger of left **'EXTENDED B'** hand, whose palm is facing the body.

ALTERNATE SIGN—**average** #2

normal: *adj.* usual, regular, common or typical. *The child's development is normal for his age.*

SIGN: Right **'BENT U'** hand, palm down, is circled clockwise over left **'STANDARD BASE'** hand, and the extended fingers are brought down to rest on it.

north: *n.* a region to the left of where the sun rises or to the right of where the sun sets. *Canada is north of the United States.*

SIGN: Right **'BENT U'** hand is held upright at about shoulder level with palm facing left and is raised directly upward to a level near the top of the head. (While the positioning and movement of this sign may vary, the hand-shape remains the same.)

nose: *n.* the organ of smell as well as the entrance to the respiratory tract. *He uses his nose to identify perfumes.*

SIGN: Right vertical **'ONE'** hand is held with palm toward body, as tip of forefinger touches nose. (Sign selection depends on context. When a description of the nose is given, the signer often chooses an all-inclusive sign that conveys **nose**, *n.*, as well as its description. This sign may also be used for **nose** when it refers to the front of certain vehicles such as an airplane or car.)

nosy [*also spelled* **nosey**]: *adj.* prying or unduly inquisitive. *The landlady in my building is very nosy.*

SIGN #1: Tip of vertical forefinger of right **'ONE'** hand, palm toward the body, is tapped on the end of the nose at least twice. (Facial expression is important.)

OR

SIGN #2: Side of forefinger of horizontal right **'BENT ONE'** hand, palm down, is held against bridge of nose and circled forward around the nose so that it is eventually positioned between the nose and upper lip. (Facial expression is important.)

not: *adv.* a term to signify negation. *I am not going away during my summer vacation.*

SIGN: Right **'EXTENDED A'** hand, palm facing left, thumb under chin, is thrust forward.

note: *n.* a brief, informal letter or jotting. *I will leave a note for you.*

SIGN #1: Fingerspell **NOTE**.

N O T E

note: *v.* to take notice or observe carefully. *Please note that facial expression is an important component of ASL.*

SIGN #2: Tip of forefinger of right **'CROOKED ONE'** hand is positioned at corner of right eye and brought down to rest on upturned palm of left **'EXTENDED B'** hand.

note: *v.* to put down in writing; to make a note of. *I will note that information in my appointment book.*

SIGN #3: Right **'O'** hand is held palm-down with fingertips touching upturned palm of left **'EXTENDED B'** hand. Fingers of right hand then open to form an **'EXTENDED B'** hand with fingers coming to rest on left palm at right angles to it.

nothing: *n.* the absence of anything percep-tible. *There is nothing to eat in the house.*

SIGN #1: Vertical **'O'** hands are held parallel with palms forward but angled toward each other slightly, as the forearms are simultane-ously shaken.

ALTERNATE SIGN—**no** #2

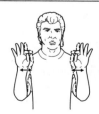

nothing: *n.* a matter of little relative signifi-cance or difficulty. *The storm was nothing compared with last year's tornado.*

SIGN #2: Vertical **'F'** hands, palms forward, are held slightly apart and simultaneously shaken from the wrists. (Appropriate facial expression is important.)

nothing: *n.* a word used to convey outrage over 'nothing' having been said or done; a word used to protest one's innocence. *Do not blame me! I did nothing!*

SIGN #3: Vertical right **'S'** hand, with palm facing left, is placed under the chin and is then thrust forward as the fingers open to form a **'5'** hand. (Appropriate facial expression is important.)

notice: *v.* to perceive, see or pay attention to. *She did not notice his unusual behaviour.*

SIGN: Tip of forefinger of right **'CROOKED ONE'** hand is positioned at corner of right eye and brought down to rest on upturned palm of left **'EXTENDED B'** hand.

notify: *v.* to inform. *Please notify the Board of your intention to resign.*

SIGN: Left **'MODIFIED O'** hand is held at about shoulder level with palm facing upward but angled slightly toward the body while right **'MODIFIED O'** hand is held upright just in front of the forehead with palm toward the face. The forearms then move simultaneously forward/downward as the hands open to assume **'MODIFIED 5'** shapes with palms facing upward. ❖
SAME SIGN—**notification**, *n.*

notion: *n.* a vague idea or impression. *Some people have an odd notion about Deafness.*

SIGN: Tip of little finger of right **'I'** hand, palm toward the face, is placed on the right side of the forehead and is drawn forward/upward a brief distance.

novel: *n.* a relatively long fictional work of prose. *Charlotte's Web is a novel that has been read and enjoyed by many young people.*

SIGN #1: Fingerspell **NOVEL**. (For **novelist**, *n.*, see **author**.)

novel: *adj.* the quality of being new and interesting. *That is a novel idea.*

SIGN #2: Horizontal **'EXTENDED B'** hand remains stationary with palm up and fingers pointing forward/rightward while back of right **'BENT EXTENDED B'** hand is brought left-ward with palm up across left palm with a scooping motion. (**NOVELTY**, *n.*, is generally fingerspelled.)

November: *n.* the eleventh month of the year. *November 11th is Remembrance Day.*

SIGN: Fingerspell **NOV**.

now: *adv.* at the present time. *The class is now studying Deaf Culture.*

SIGN #1: **'Y'** hands, palms up, are held slightly apart and are simultaneously lowered.

OR

SIGN #2: Both **'BENT EXTENDED B'** hands, palms up, are held slightly apart and are simultaneously lowered.

noxious: *adj.* poisonous or harmful. *The exhaust pipe of a car emits noxious fumes.*

SIGN: **'S'** (or **'CLAWED V'**) hands, palms facing chest, are crossed at the wrists, with the right hand nearest the body. Back of right wrist is tapped twice against left wrist.
ALTERNATE SIGN—**danger**

nuclear: *adj.* involving atomic bombs, energy or power. *The U.S.A. has a large supply of nuclear weapons.*

SIGN: Fingerspell **NUCLEAR**.

nucleus: *n.* a centre around which other things are grouped. *The Deaf Club forms the nucleus of the Deaf Community.*

SIGN: With palm down, horizontal right **'BENT MIDFINGER 5'** hand is circled clockwise from the wrist above upturned left palm, tip of right midfinger falling in the centre of the left palm.

nude: *adj.* completely undressed. *She was surprised to see so many nude sun-bathers on the beach.*

SIGN: Tip of middle finger of right **'BENT MIDFINGER 5'** hand strokes forward/rightward across back of left **'STANDARD BASE'** hand.

nuisance: *n.* anything that causes annoyance or bother. *Having to do all this paperwork is a real nuisance.*

SIGN: Vertical right **'BENT MIDFINGER 5'** hand is held with palm left and tip of middle finger touching forehead. The wrist then rotates to turn the palm toward the face. Facial expression must clearly convey 'annoyance'.

numb: *adj.* deprived of feeling through cold or shock. *Her hands were numb from the cold.*

SIGN: **'CROOKED 5'** hands are held parallel with palms down, and are jerked slightly toward the body as the fingers retract to form **'CLAWED 5'** hands. (**NUMB** is frequently fingerspelled.)

number: *n.* a unit used in counting; a quantity. *Do you have the local phone number for the Message Relay Service?*

SIGN: **'MODIFIED O'** hands are positioned so that the bunched fingertips of each hand are touching those of the other hand. Initially, left palm faces upward but is angled slightly toward the body while right palm faces downward but is angled forward slightly. Fingertips maintain contact as the hands then twist, thus reversing the palm orientations. (This sign is not used to express **number** in phrases such as 'a number of', which conceptually might mean **some** or **lots of**.)

numerous: *adj.* many. *Canada has numerous natural resources.*

SIGN: **'EXTENDED A'** hands, palms slightly facing the body and slightly facing upward, are simultaneously circled outward in opposite directions. The cheeks are puffed out.
ALTERNATE SIGN—**many**

numskull [*also spelled* **numbskull**]: *n.* blockhead; idiot; stupid person. *Stop behaving like a numskull!*

SIGN: Thumb and forefinger of right **'MODIFIED G'** hand are pointed at forehead, with palm facing left. Then wrist is twisted, thus rotating **'MODIFIED G'** hand a quarter turn so that palm is toward face. For greater emphasis, this sign may be made with a **'FLAT C'** handshape.

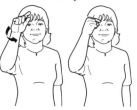

nun: *n.* a female member of a religious order. *A nun devotes her life to serving God.*

SIGN: **'BENT U'** (or **'BENT EXTENDED B'**) hands, palms facing each other are positioned in front of forehead so that extended fingertips are touching each other. Then the hands are simultaneously drawn apart and down so that extended fingertips touch either side of upper chest (or each shoulder).

nurse: *n.* a person who is trained to take care of the sick. *The nurse worked extra shifts at the hospital.*

SIGN: Tips of extended fingers of right **'BENT U'** hand, palm down, tap at least twice on the upturned wrist of the horizontal left **'CROOKED EXTENDED B'** hand.
ALTERNATE SIGN—**hospital** #1

nut: *n.* a dry, one-seeded fruit with a hard, woody shell. *If you plant this nut, a tree might grow.*

SIGN #1: Thumb of right **'EXTENDED A'** hand, palm facing left, wiggles against the upper front teeth.

nut: *n.* an idiot or fool. *He must be a nut to be out in this stormy weather.*

SIGN #2: Thumb and forefinger of right **'MODIFIED G'** hand are pointed at forehead, with palm facing left. Then wrist is twisted, thus rotating **'MODIFIED G'** hand a quarter turn so that palm is toward face. For greater emphasis, this sign may be made with a **'FLAT C'** handshape.

ALTERNATE SIGN—**crazy**

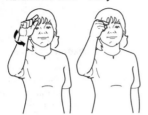

nut: *n.* a metal fastener that screws onto a bolt. *You can find the kind of nut you need in the hardware department.*

SIGN #3: Thumb and forefinger of right **'MODIFIED G'** hand represent a nut as they rotate clockwise half a turn around right-pointing forefinger of left **'BENT ONE'** hand. Motion is repeated.
(**NUT** is frequently fingerspelled.)

nutrition: *n.* a process that involves eating and assimilating the nourishing ingredients in food. *Fitness and good nutrition are the keys to good health.*

SIGN: Fingerspell **NUTRITION**.

O

oak: *n.* a deciduous, acorn-bearing tree. *We sat in the shade of a big oak to eat our lunch.*

SIGN: Fingerspell **OAK**.

oath: *n.* a solemn pledge. *The President took the oath of office.*

SIGN: Hands are positioned as they would be when one is swearing an oath in a courtroom with horizontal left **'EXTENDED B'** hand palm-down as if on a bible with fingers pointing forward, and right **'EXTENDED B'** hand held upright with palm facing forward.

oatmeal: *n.* ground oats (used in cooking). *Oatmeal is a good source of dietary fibre.*

SIGN: Fingerspell **OATMEAL**.

oats: *n.* a certain type of grass or the seeds from this grass. *We have a good crop of oats this year.*

SIGN: Fingerspell **OATS**.

obese: *adj.* excessively fat. *Obese children should be encouraged to diet and exercise.*

SIGN: **'SPREAD C'** hands are held one in front of either side of upper chest with palms toward the body but angled upward slightly. The forearms are then simultaneously and firmly moved a short distance forward at a slight downward angle. Cheeks are puffed out.
SAME SIGN—**obesity**, *n.*

obey: *v.* to comply with rules or demands. *Drivers are expected to obey all posted instructions.*

SIGN: Left **'MODIFIED O'** hand is held at about shoulder level with palm facing upward but angled slightly toward the body while right **'MODIFIED O'** hand is held upright just in front of the forehead with palm toward the face. The forearms then move simultaneously forward/downward as the hands open to assume **'MODIFIED 5'** shapes with palms facing upward.
SAME SIGNS—**obedience**, *n.*, and **obedient**, *adj.*

obituary: *n.* a published announcement of a death. *The obituary included a brief biography of the deceased man.*

SIGN: **'EXTENDED B'** hands are held with fingers pointing forward, left palm facing up and right palm facing down. Then they are flipped over simultaneously so that the palm positions are reversed. Next, thumb and forefinger of horizontal right **'C-INDEX'** hand, palm facing left, are stroked downward across right-facing palm of left **'EXTENDED B'** hand.
(ASL CONCEPT—**dead - article**.)

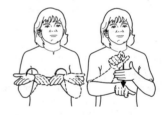

object: *n.* a visible and tangible thing. *This object has historical value and should be placed in the museum.*

SIGN #1: Right **'EXTENDED B'** hand, palm upward and finger pointing forward, is moved rightward in an arc formation.
SAME SIGN—**objection**, *n.*, in this context.

object: *v.* to express opposition or disagreement with a certain action. *I object to your using the car tonight.*

SIGN #2: Right **'SPREAD C'** hand is held in a horizontal position as thumb and fingertips thump against chest. Facial expression is important.
SAME SIGN—**objection**, *n.*, in this context.

object: *v.* to express opposition or disagreement with a certain idea or issue. *I object to the concept of indiscriminate mainstream education for all Deaf children.*

SIGN #3: Left **'BENT EXTENDED B'** hand is held horizontally with fingers pointing to the right and palm facing the body but angled slightly rightward. Right **'EXTENDED B'** hand is held upright very close to the chest with palm facing left. The right hand then drops from the wrist until it is horizontal with fingertips forcefully striking left hand between the palm and the fingers. Facial expression is important.
ALTERNATE SIGN—**object** #2

objective: *n.* a goal or aim. *The main objective of the course is to provide a basic understanding of Deaf Culture.*

SIGN: Vertical **'ONE'** hands, left palm facing right and right palm facing left, are held out in front of the face, with the left hand directly ahead of the right. Both hands are then simultaneously moved forward.

obligation: *n.* a moral or legal requirement; duty. *You are under no obligation to help.*

SIGN: Joined thumb and midfinger of right **'D'** hand are positioned on the back of the left **'STANDARD BASE'** hand, and the hands are lowered together.
ALTERNATE SIGN—**burden**

obligatory: *adj.* absolutely required, compulsory. *Saluting superior officers is obligatory among military personnel.*

SIGN: Tip of forefinger of right **'X'** hand is placed in right-facing palm of left **'EXTENDED B'** hand. Together the hands are moved firmly toward the chest, giving the impression that the left hand is being tugged by the right forefinger.
ALTERNATE SIGN—**must**

obnoxious: *adj.* extremely unpleasant or offensive. *Obnoxious people usually have few friends.*

SIGN: Thumb and forefinger of right **'A-INDEX'** hand, palm left, grasp skin of right cheek. Facial expression must clearly convey 'disgust'.

obscene: *adj.* extremely offensive; lewd. *Using obscene language is a violation of the school's rules of behaviour.*

SIGN: Right **'MODIFIED 5'** hand is held palm-down under the chin with fingers fluttering and pointing leftward. Facial expression is important.
ALTERNATE SIGN—**rude**

obscure: *adj.* vague, unclear or indistinct. *The point of the lecture was obscure.*

SIGN: Vertical **'5'** hands are held with palms either touching or at least close together. Left hand, palm facing body, is held steady while right hand faces forward and is circled counter-clockwise. A look of confusion accompanies this sign.

observe: *v.* to watch carefully. *The interns will observe the surgeon's technique.*

SIGN: Horizontal **'BENT V'** hands are held slightly apart with fingers pointing forward and are circled in opposite directions (the left hand clockwise and the right hand counter-clockwise).
SAME SIGNS—**observation**, *n.*, and **observant**, *adj.*

obsession: *n.* a persistent idea, feeling or preoccupation. *To become a millionaire is his latest obsession.*

SIGN: Tip of middle finger of right **'BENT MIDFINGER 5'** hand touches centre of forehead and moves downward to rest on back of left **'STANDARD BASE'** hand. Together the two hands then circle forward at least twice.
(ASL CONCEPT— **think - touch**.)

obsolete: *adj.* not current; out of use or practice. *Computers have made typewriters almost obsolete.*

SIGN: Right **'S'** hand, slightly open, palm facing left, is brought down firmly from the chin as it closes. Then right **'F'** hand, palm down, is moved in an arc from left to right in front of chest.

obstacle: *n.* something that opposes or hinders. *I can see no obstacle that might prevent your acceptance into our program.*

SIGN: **'EXTENDED B'** hands are held at right angles to one another, the left hand in front of the right, with fingers of left hand pointing upward to the right and fingers of right hand pointing upward to the left. The hands are then pushed firmly forward.

obstetrician: *n.* a doctor who specializes in the branch of medicine concerned with childbirth. *She saw her obstetrician regularly before and after her child was born.*

SIGN: Fingertips of palm-down right **'SPREAD EXTENDED C'** (or **'BENT EXTENDED B'** or **'FLAT M'**) hand are tapped a couple of times against the inside of the left wrist. Then right **'B'** hand, palm facing left and fingers pointing forward, slides along top of left **'B'** hand, of which the palm faces right and the fingers point forward. (Alternatively, the forefinger of the right **'ONE'** hand slides along the forefinger of the left **'ONE'** hand.) Next, fingers of palm-up right **'BENT EXTENDED B'** hand point leftward as they rest on rightward-pointing fingers of palm-up left **'BENT EXTENDED B'** hand. The arms are simultaneously moved from side to side as if rocking a baby in one's arms. Finally, the right hand is curved down and under the left hand until the right palm faces downward. (ASL CONCEPT—**doctor - specialize - baby - birth**.)

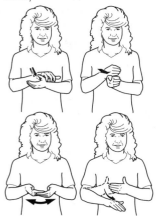

obstinate: *adj.* stubborn; self-willed; headstrong. *Despite the flood dangers, the man was too obstinate to evacuate his home.*

SIGN: Thumb of vertical right **'EXTENDED B'** hand, palm forward, is placed near the right temple and the fingers are firmly lowered to form a **'BENT EXTENDED B'** hand. A look of fierce determination accompanies this sign. SAME SIGN—**obstinacy**, *n.*

obstruct: *v.* to block off with a barrier. *A motor vehicle accident generally obstructs the flow of traffic.*

SIGN: **'EXTENDED B'** hands are held at right angles to one another, the left hand in front of the right, with fingers of left hand pointing upward to the right and fingers of right hand pointing upward to the left. The hands are then pushed firmly forward. ❖ SAME SIGN—**obstruction**, *n.* ALTERNATE SIGN—**stuck**

obtain: *v.* to acquire or get. *You can obtain useful information from the book, Deaf Heritage in Canada.*

SIGN: Horizontal **'SPREAD C'** hands, right on top of left, are closed to form **'S'** hands as they are brought toward the chest.

obvious: *adj.* easily seen or understood. *It is obvious that you know all the answers.*

SIGN: **'O'** (or **'FLAT O'**) hands are placed side by side, palms facing forward. Then they are moved apart and upward as the fingers spread to form **'5'** hands, palms still facing away from the body.

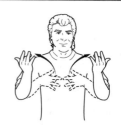

occasion: *n.* the time of a particular happening or event. *Christmas is always a happy occasion in our home.*

SIGN: Tips of midfingers of **'BENT MIDFINGER 5'** hands, palms toward the body, are placed slightly apart on the chest. The wrists then rotate forward as the hands move forward so that, while the palms still face the body, they are now angled upward slightly.

occasionally: *adv.* sometimes; once in a while. *I enjoy a big dessert occasionally.*

SIGN: As right forearm slowly circles clockwise, tip of forefinger of horizontal right **'ONE'** hand strikes upward/rightward facing palm of horizontal left **'EXTENDED B'** hand each time it goes past. (The speed of movement and height of the arcs depends on the *frequency* implied. The *more frequent*, the smaller and faster the arcs; the less *frequent*, the higher and slower the arcs.)

occupation: *n.* a person's regular work or profession. *List your present occupation first on your resume.*

SIGN: Wrist of right **'S'** (or **'A'**) hand, palm facing away from the body, strikes wrist of left **'S'** (or **'A'**) hand, which is held in front of/below the right hand with palm facing downward. Motion is repeated.

occupy: *v.* to take and maintain possession of. *Peacekeeping troops will occupy the country until a treaty can be negotiated.*

SIGN: **'SPREAD C'** hands are held parallel with palms down and are then closed to form **'S'** hands as they are simultaneously thrust forward. (Signs for **occupy** vary according to context.)

occur: *v.* to happen; take place. *The police asked, "When did the accident occur?"*

SIGN #1: **'ONE'** hands, palms facing each other, are held slightly apart, fingers pointing away from the body, and are turned over so that the palms face down.

occur: *v.* to appear or come into being. *The next leap year will occur in four years.*

SIGN #2: Left **'EXTENDED B'** hand is held, palm down, in a fixed position. Right **'ONE'** hand, palm forward, is brought up underneath the left hand and the extended forefinger is thrust upward between the index and middle finger of the left hand.

occur: *v.* to suggest itself or come to mind. *It did not occur to us that we ought to keep a record of our discussions.*

SIGN #3: Tip of forefinger of right **'ONE'** hand, palm toward the face, is used to touch right side of forehead. Then left **'EXTENDED B'** hand is held, palm down, in a fixed position. Right **'ONE'** hand, palm forward, is brought up underneath the left hand and the extended forefinger is thrust upward between the index and middle finger of the left hand.
(ASL CONCEPT—**think - appear**.)

OR

SIGN #4: Tip of forefinger of right **'ONE'** hand, palm toward the face, is moved purposefully upward/backward to touch centre of forehead.

ocean: *n.* a very large stretch of sea. *Three main oceans border Canada.*

SIGN: Forefinger of vertical right **'W'** hand, palm facing left, is tapped against the chin. Next, **'5'** hands are held slightly apart with palms down and fingers pointing forward/leftward. The hands are then moved simultaneously forward/leftward with a wave-like motion. (ASL CONCEPT—**water - wave**.) OCEAN is frequently fingerspelled. When the ocean is specified, both **OCEAN** and the name of the ocean are fingerspelled.

October: *n.* the tenth month of the year. *Hallowe'en is celebrated on October 31st.*

SIGN: Fingerspell **OCT**.

octopus: *n.* a sea creature with a soft body and eight suckered tentacles. *A team of divers will observe the habits of the octopus for scientific research.*

SIGN: Fingertips of right **'OPEN SPREAD O'** hand, palm down, are placed on the back of the left horizontal **'CONTRACTED 5'** hand, of which the palm faces downward and the dangling fingers wiggle. (Various signs may be used for **octopus**.)

odd: *adj.* strange, peculiar or unusual. *There was an odd cloud in the sky before the tornado struck.*

SIGN #1: Vertical right **'C'** hand, palm facing left, is held near the face and is abruptly dropped downward from the wrist so the palm faces down.

SIGN #2 [ATLANTIC]: Tip of forefinger of right **'BENT ONE'** hand is placed on the nose, and then dropped downward, palm still facing the body, and curved upward to the right, as if inscribing a check mark in the air.

odd: *adj.* a number not evenly divisible by two. *Odd numbers end with 1, 3, 5, 7 or 9.*

SIGN #3: Fingerspell **ODD**.

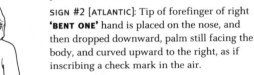

odometer: *n.* a device that records the number of kilometres a vehicle has travelled. *Tampering with the odometer of a car is illegal.*

SIGN: Left **'BENT ONE'** hand, palm facing right and forefinger pointing right, remains fixed while forefinger of right **'BENT ONE'** hand circles the left forefinger in a clockwise direction.

odour [*also spelled* **odor**]: *n.* scent or smell. *He could detect the odour of stale smoke.*

SIGN: Right **'EXTENDED B'** hand is held with palm facing the body, and fingertips just in front of the nose and pointing leftward/upward. The hand is then circled forward a few times in small clockwise circles. (Generally, this sign is used when referring to a mild odour, but a variety of signs may be used to refer to a strong odour.)

of: *prep.* a word that serves various purposes in English grammar, such as the introduction of phrases, the linking of nouns, the indication of periods of time, etc. Usage will vary according to purpose.

SIGN: Fingerspell **OF**.

off: used as a *preposition, particle* or *adverb* in a variety of ways to mean a variety of things.

SIGN: **OFF** is fingerspelled as the hand is sharply moved to the right; however, as **off** is often conceptually involved with other words in English, it frequently becomes incorporated in the sign for an accompanying word.

off and on: *adv.* occasionally or intermittently. *She yawned off and on throughout the lecture.*

SIGN: As right forearm slowly circles clockwise, tip of forefinger of horizontal right **'ONE'** hand strikes upward/rightward facing palm of horizontal left **'EXTENDED B'** hand each time it goes past.

off the point: *adj.* off-topic; unrelated to the topic under discussion. *Your arguments are off the point.*

SIGN: Left **'ONE'** hand, palm facing rightward/forward, is held upright and remains fixed as tip of forefinger of right **'BENT ONE'** hand flicks leftward/backward off tip of left forefinger.

off-colour: *adj.* in poor taste (as in a **dirty joke**). *He did not find her off-colour jokes the least bit funny.*

SIGN: Right **'MODIFIED 5'** hand is held palm-down under the chin with fingers fluttering and pointing leftward.

offence [*also spelled* **offense**]: *n.* a violation of the rules or laws. *First degree murder is the most serious criminal offence.*

SIGN #1: Right **'L'** hand, palm facing left, is tapped smartly against palm of left **'EXTENDED B'** hand, which is held with palm facing right and fingers pointing upward/forward. (**OFFENCE** is frequently fingerspelled in this context.)

offence [*also spelled* **offense**]: *n.* in team sports, the strategy of attacking or assaulting the opponents. *Our football team has the best offence in the league.*

SIGN #2: Right **'O'** hand, palm facing leftward/forward, is held upright and wobbled slightly.

offend: *v.* to hurt another person's feelings. *Racial slurs offend most people.*

SIGN: Right **'ONE'** hand, palm facing left, is held in a horizontal position in front of the chest and is then curved upward from the wrist as it moves forward with a stabbing motion. Alternatively, this sign may be made with two hands alternately stabbing, either with or without the curving motion. (**OFFEND** is frequently fingerspelled.) ❖

offer: *v.* to put forward for acceptance or rejection. *They will offer him free room and board in exchange for his help with the building repairs.*

SIGN: **'EXTENDED B'** hands, palms up and fingers pointing forward, are held slightly apart with the right just ahead of the left, and are simultaneously thrust forward in an arc. ❖

office: *n.* a room in which business, clerical or professional work is done. *He is working late at the office tonight.*

SIGN: Horizontal **'O'** hands are held, right just ahead of left, with right palm facing left but angled toward the body and left palm facing right but angled toward the body as well. The hands are then swung outward from the wrists so that the left palm faces fully rightward while the right palm faces leftward. (**OFFICE** is frequently fingerspelled.)

officer: *n.* a person who holds a position of responsibility and authority. *He is the company's chief executive officer.*

SIGN: Fingertips of palm-down right **'SPREAD C'** hand are tapped twice on right shoulder. Alternatively, this sign may be made using both hands, one on each shoulder.

459

official: *adj.* recognized as coming from a position of authority. *The prime minister will make an official statement today.*

SIGN #1: Horizontal **'F'** hands, palms facing, are held slightly apart and are simultaneously and firmly lowered. (**OFFICIAL** in this context is frequently fingerspelled.)

official: *n.* a person who holds a position of responsibility but is usually subordinate to a higher authority. *United Nations officials kept a kept close watch on activities in the war-torn country.*

SIGN #2: Fingertips of palm-down right **'SPREAD C'** hand are tapped twice on right shoulder. Alternatively, this sign may be made using both hands, one on each shoulder. (For **official** in the sense of someone who officiates in a game, see **referee**.)

offside: *adj.* said of a player in certain sports when the player is illegally ahead of the ball or puck in an offensive zone. *The play was ruled offside when the player crossed the blue-line before the puck.*

SIGN: **'CONTRACTED C'** hands are held palms down and are tapped at least twice against either side of the waist.

offspring: *n.* immediate descendant(s); child(ren) born to a person or young born to an animal. *My youngest offspring looks just like his father.*

SIGN: Vertical right **'BENT EXTENDED B'** hand is held with palm facing forward and fingers pointing forward. It is then lowered slightly to indicate the relatively low physical stature of a child. (Sign choice depends entirely on the context.)

off-topic: *adj.* unrelated to the topic under discussion; off the point. *Your comments are off-topic.*

SIGN: Left **'ONE'** hand, palm facing rightward/forward, is held upright and remains fixed as tip of forefinger of right **'BENT ONE'** hand flicks leftward/backward off tip of left forefinger.

often: *adv.* frequently or repeatedly. *We often see them at the Deaf Club.*

SIGN #1: Left **'EXTENDED B'** hand is held in a fixed position with fingers pointing forward and palm facing upward but angled rightward slightly. Fingertips of horizontal right **'BENT EXTENDED B'** hand, palm down, are used to strike palm of left hand. Right hand then moves forward in a small arc with fingertips coming to rest at the end of the left hand.

OR

SIGN #2: Horizontal right **'BENT EXTENDED B'** hand, palm left, is moved forward quickly in a series of small arcs. (This sign is not appropriate in all situations.)

ogle: *v.* to stare at someone, especially in a flirtatious manner. *If you ogle your co-workers you might be charged with sexual harassment.*

SIGN: **'F'** hands are held upright and slightly apart, left palm facing right and right palm facing left. Forearms then move simultaneously forward/downward and then back to their original positions. Meanwhile the signer's eyes look down and up the length of the person being ogled. In that person's absence, his/her presence will be imagined. (Various signs may be used for **ogle**.)

oh, I see: *s.s.* an expression commonly used to indicate one's realization or comprehension of a fact or detail. *That's why he left? Oh, I see.*

SIGN: Right **'Y'** hand is held with palm forward but angled downward slightly. The forearm then moves up and down slightly several times. (A look of realization should accompany this sign, and sometimes a slight nod.)

oil: *n.* a flammable viscous liquid which is insoluble in water. *I prefer oil and vinegar on my salad.*

SIGN: Fingerspell **OIL**.

O   I   L

oily: *adj.* greasy; laden with oil. *She has a rather oily complexion.*

SIGN: Thumb and midfinger of right **'OPEN 8'** hand grasp edge of left **'EXTENDED B'** (or **'5'**) hand, which is held with palm facing rightward but angled slightly toward the body while the fingers point forward/rightward at a slight upward angle. The right hand is then drawn downward at least twice, forming an **'8'** shape with each downward movement. (**OILY** is frequently fingerspelled.)

okay: *s.s.* a word that signals agreement or approval; all right. *Okay, I will do it.*

SIGN: Fingerspell **O**, drop the wrist, and fingerspell **K**, which may resemble a **P** due to its unusual positioning.
ALTERNATE SIGN—**all right**

old: *adj.* having lived or existed for a long time. *Many old household items are preserved by the museum.*

SIGN: Right **'s'** hand, slightly open, palm facing left, is brought down firmly from the chin as it closes.

old-fashioned: *adj.* outdated or characteristic of former times. *She has some very old-fashioned ideas.*

SIGN: Right **'s'** hand, slightly open, palm facing left, is brought down firmly from the chin as it closes. Then right **'F'** hand, palm down, is moved in an arc from left to right in front of chest.
REGIONAL VARIATION—**antique** #2.

olive: *n.* an edible fruit that grows in Mediterranean countries and becomes black when ripe. *I would like an olive with my sandwich.*

SIGN #1: Fingerspell **OLIVE**.

olive: *adj.* having a yellowish-green colour which resembles that of an unripe olive. *His shirt was an olive shade.*

SIGN #2: Fingerspell **OLIVE**.

Olympic: *adj.* related to an international sporting or athletic festival held every four years. *The Deaflympics are similar to the international Olympic games.*

SIGN: Left **'F'** hand is held horizontally with palm facing right while right **'F'** hand is held upright with palm facing forward/leftward. The two hands are linked by thumbs and forefingers. They are then separated as the left wrist rotates backward bringing the hand to an upright position while the right hand rotates forward to a horizontal position. Thumbs and forefingers are rejoined. (In 2001, it was decided that the Olympic-like event traditionally known as the World Games for the Deaf would be called the Deaflympics. See **Deaf + Olympic**.)

omit: *v.* to happen to leave out or fail to include. *Be sure not to omit anyone's name from the list.*

SIGN #1: Right **'CONTRACTED 5'** hand, palm up, becomes a **'FLAT O'** hand as it is drawn downward behind the horizontal left **'CROOKED 5'** hand of which the palm is facing the body.
SAME SIGN—**omission**, *n.*

omit: *v.* to intentionally leave out or fail to include. *The teacher instructed the students to omit the fourth question.*

SIGN #2: Right **'4'** hand is held upright with palm facing left and tip of forefinger touching tip of nose. The hand is then thrust forward/downward so that the fingers point forward.

on: *prep.* at the upper surface of. *Put the book on the table, please.*

SIGN: Horizontal right **'EXTENDED B'** hand, palm down, is brought down at right angles onto the back of the left **'STANDARD BASE'** hand. (This sign is used when the signer wishes to be emphatic. Otherwise, it rarely appears in ASL, even in this context, as the concept of **on** is generally incorporated with another sign. In this case, only one sign would be used to convey the four English words: 'Put the book on'.)

once: *adv.* one time; on one occasion or in one case. *I have only been to California once.*

SIGN: Tip of forefinger of horizontal right **'ONE'** hand, palm down but angled leftward slightly, is pressed against the upturned palm of the left **'EXTENDED B'** hand. The right wrist then rotates clockwise causing the forefinger to flick upward/rightward and the palm to flip upward while still angled slightly leftward.

one: *n.* See NUMBERS, p. LX.

onion: *n.* an edible, bulbous vegetable with a pungent odour. *There is onion in this casserole.*

SIGN: Knuckle of crooked forefinger of right **'X'** hand is pressed against right temple while the hand is twisted back and forth from the wrist. (Alternatively, this sign may be formed with an **'S'** hand rather than an **'X'** hand.)

only: *adv.* just; merely. *I do not know why you are upset; I was only asking a simple question.*

SIGN #1: Vertical right **'ONE'** hand, palm facing the body, is moved in a small counter-clockwise circle.

only: *adj.* alone; without anyone or anything else being included. *Gallaudet is the only university in the world that was built especially for Deaf students.*

SIGN #2: Vertical right **'ONE'** hand is held with palm forward. The wrist then rotates rightward to turn the hand so that the palm faces backward.

onus: See **burden**.

open: *adj.* not closed. *The office is open on weekdays from 9 a.m. to 5 p.m.*

SIGN #1: **'B'** hands are placed side by side with palms forward but slanted downward slightly. The wrists then rotate outward as the hands move apart resulting in the palms facing each other.

open (book): *v.* to create access to the page of a book. *Please open your books to page 91.*

SIGN #2: Horizontal **'EXTENDED B'** hands, palms together, fingers pointing forward, are opened to the palms-up position.

open (door): *v.* to make entry possible through a door. *Please open the door for me.*

SIGN #3: Vertical **'B'** hands create a **'V'** formation as they are held together with palms facing forward but angled toward each other slightly. The left hand remains fixed; the right hand moves rightward as the wrist rotates outward, thus resulting in the palm facing leftward and angled backward slightly.

open (gate): *v.* to make entry possible through a gate. *Please open the gate and let me through.*

SIGN #4: **'BENT EXTENDED B'** hands are held horizontally with palms facing and fingertips touching. The right hand then straightens out to form an **'EXTENDED B'** shape with fingers pointing forward. To indicate the opening of two sides of a gate, both hands will be straightened.

open (window): *v.* to create an unobstructed space between a window and its sill. *I always open the window before I go to bed.*

SIGN #5: Horizontal **'BENT EXTENDED B'** hands, left palm facing right and right palm facing left, are held so that little finger of right hand is resting on forefinger of left hand. Then the right hand is moved upward. (Signs may vary according to the type of window being opened.)

open-minded: *adj.* receptive to new ideas. *My parents are very open-minded about my political beliefs.*

SIGN: Tip of forefinger of right **'CROOKED ONE'** hand, palm toward body, is tapped against right side of forehead. Next, horizontal **'B'** (or **'EXTENDED B'**) hands create a **'V'** formation as the fingertips touch and palms face each other while angled slightly toward the face. The hands then swing outward until the palms face each other but are angled forward slightly. (ASL CONCEPT—**brain - open**.)

operate: *v.* to perform surgery on an animal or person. *The doctors will operate immediately.*

SIGN #1: Thumbnail of horizontal right **'EXTENDED A'** (or **'Y'**) hand, palm down, is placed on the rightward/upward facing palm of the left **'EXTENDED B'** hand. Then the right thumb is drawn downward across the left palm. (The positioning of this sign will vary according to which part of the body is undergoing surgery.)
SAME SIGN—**operation**, *n.*, in this context.

operate: *v.* to manage, direct or run. *He has learned a lot about how to operate a business.*

SIGN #2: Horizontal **'X'** hands are held slightly apart with left palm facing right and right palm facing left. Then they are alternately moved backward and forward.
SAME SIGN—**operation**, *n.*, in this context. For **operator**, *n.*, the Agent Ending (see p. LIV) may follow.
ALTERNATE SIGN—**run** #2
Sign selection depends on the context. To **operate** a car is to drive it; therefore, **drive** should be used.

opinion: *n.* belief or judgment not founded on certainty or proof. *Public opinion caused the politician to withdraw his statements.*

SIGN: Vertical right **'MODIFIED O'** hand is held just in front of mid-forehead with palm facing left, and is bobbed slightly.

opponent: *n.* a person who opposes another in a fight, game, debate, etc. *The two men proved to be formidable opponents throughout the debate.*

SIGN: Horizontal **'BENT ONE'** hands are held together, palms facing the body, and tips of forefingers almost touching. Then they are pulled apart with a short, firm motion.

opportunity: *n.* an advantageous set of circumstances. *There is an opportunity for advancement in this job.*

SIGN #1: **'A'** hands, palms down, are held slightly apart, and are lowered and raised a couple of times as if knocking.

(make the most of an) opportunity: *v.* to maximize one's benefit from a situation. *We will make the most of this opportunity to spend time together before you leave for France.*

SIGN #2: Right **'SPREAD C'** hand, palm facing left and toward the body slightly, is transformed to an **'S'** hand, palm facing the body, as it is brushed left twice along the fixed, upturned palm of the left **'EXTENDED B'** hand and finally raised above it.

oppose: *v.* to resist strongly. *Many Deaf people oppose the idea of educational mainstreaming.*

SIGN: Horizontal left **'BENT EXTENDED B'** hand is held with palm facing rightward/backward and fingers pointing to the right. Right **'EXTENDED B'** (or **'B'**) hand is held upright very close to the chest with palm facing left. The right hand then drops from the wrist until it is horizontal with fingertips forcefully striking left hand between the palm and the fingers. Facial expression is important.
SAME SIGN—**opposition**, *n.*, in this context.

opposite: *adj.* diametrically different in character, tendency, belief, etc. *The two political parties have opposite views on capital punishment.*

SIGN: Horizontal **'BENT ONE'** hands are held together, palms facing the body, and tips of forefingers almost touching. Then they are pulled apart with a short, firm motion.
SAME SIGN—**opposition**, *n.*, when it refers to a political party in a parliamentary system.

oppress: *v.* to subject to force or cruelty. *Certain governments have been known to oppress their people.*

SIGN: Left **'S'** hand is held with palm rightward/downward. Right **'EXTENDED B'** hand is held with fingers pointing forward/leftward/upward and palm forward/leftward/downward. With the palm of the right hand held against the top of the left hand, the right hand very firmly pushes the left hand forward/downward at a slight leftward angle. Facial expression is firm. ❖
(For **oppression**, *n.*, see **pressure** #1.)

opt: *v.* to choose or show a preference for. *I think I will opt for fruit instead of the chocolate cake.*

SIGN: Thumb and forefinger of right **'FLAT OPEN F'** hand are closed as hand is brought back toward chest

opt out: *v.* to choose not to be involved in a project or plan. *If I disagree with their philosophy, I will opt out of the group.*

SIGN: Extended fingers of right **'CLAWED U'** hand, palm down, are inserted into an opening created in the left horizontal **'S'** hand. The right hand is then drawn back toward the body. ❖

optimistic: *adj.* having a tendency to expect or see the best in everything. *I am very optimistic about the future.*

SIGN: Forearm moves forward/downward as forefinger of right **'ONE'** hand, palm left, is tapped a few times at right angles against horizontal forefinger of left **'ONE'** hand. SAME SIGN—**optimism,** *n.*

option: *n.* the power or freedom to choose. *You have only one option in this case.*

SIGN: Right hand alternates between **'FLAT OPEN F'** and **'F'** as thumb and forefinger pluck first at tip of forefinger of vertical left **'V'** hand (palm facing the body). To refer to more than one option, thumb and forefinger of right hand plucks at tip of forefinger of left **'V'** hand and then at tip of midfinger as well.

optometrist: *n.* a person who tests for visual acuity and prescribes corrective lenses. *The optometrist advised me to wear contact lenses instead of glasses.*

SIGN: Fingertips of palm-down right **'BENT EXTENDED B'** hand are tapped a couple of times against wrist of palm-up left **'EXTENDED B'** hand. Then right **'B'** hand, palm facing left and fingers pointing forward, slides along top of left **'B'** hand, of which the palm faces right and the fingers point forward. (Alternatively, the forefinger of the right **'ONE'** hand slides along the forefinger of the left **'ONE'** hand.) Next, forefinger of right **'BENT ONE'** hand touches face just under right eye, then touches face just under left eye. (ASL CONCEPT—**doctor - specialize - eyes.**)

or: *conj.* a conjunction used to join alternatives. *Would you like apple pie or cherry cheesecake for dessert?*

SIGN: Fingerspell **OR.**

O   R

oral: *adj.* spoken or verbal, as opposed to manual. *In the mid 1900s the communication policy at most schools for the Deaf was oral.*

SIGN #1: Right **'CLAWED V'** hand, held upright with the palm toward the body, is circled counter-clockwise in front of the lips. (Sign choice depends entirely on context. **ORAL** is frequently fingerspelled.)

oral: *adj.* spoken or verbal, as opposed to written. *The chairperson of the fundraising committee gave an oral report on our progress to date.*

SIGN #2: Tip of forefinger of vertical right **'4'** hand, palm facing left, is tapped against the chin.

(take medication) orally: *v.* to take medicine through the mouth in capsule, tablet, or pill form. *Take two tablets with water after every meal.*

SIGN #1: Vertical right **'S'** hand, palm toward the body, is held in front of the mouth and the forefinger is flicked forward a couple of times toward the mouth, thus alternating between an **'S'** and a **'BENT ONE'** hand.

(take medication) orally: *v.* to take medicine through the mouth in liquid form. *Take a teaspoon of cough syrup before you go to bed.*

SIGN #2: Wrist bends to allow right **'CLOSED A-INDEX'** hand to be held horizontally in front of the mouth with palm facing right and thumb pointing toward the mouth. The hand then moves toward the face a couple of times as if spooning something into one's mouth. At the same time, mouth opens and closes to receive medicine. (Sign choice always depends on context. If the medicine is to be drunk from a glass, use the sign for **drink.**)

orange: *n.* a citrus fruit that grows in warm regions. *An early frost destroyed most of the oranges in Florida that year.*

SIGN #1: Right **'C'** hand, palm facing left, is held upright in front of the mouth and is closed to form an **'S'** handshape. Motion is repeated as the hand opens and closes once again.

ALTERNATE SIGN—**orange** #2

orange: *adj.* having a shade of colour that lies between red and yellow. *The orange flames of a bonfire were visible in the distance.*

SIGN #2: Horizontal **'I'** (or **'Y'**) hands, palms facing the body, are held slightly apart as the little fingers are circled forward around one another.

ALTERNATE SIGN—**orange** #1

orbit: *v.* to move around a celestial body on a specific pathway. *The earth orbits the sun each year.*

SIGN: Left **'O'** hand is held upright with palm facing right while right **'BENT ONE'** hand, with forefinger pointing downward, circles counter-clockwise around the left hand.

orchestra: *n.* a large group of musicians who play a variety of instruments, usually including percussion, brass, woodwinds, and strings. *He is a member of the Toronto Symphony Orchestra.*

SIGN: Horizontal right **'EXTENDED B'** hand is positioned above left forearm with palm facing leftward/backward. The right wrist makes slight back and forth rotations so that the palm alternates between being angled slightly upward and being angled slightly downward. **'SPREAD C'** hands are then held upright and slightly apart at chest level, palms facing each other, then turned downward as they are moved forward simultaneously to a horizontal position. (ASL CONCEPT—**music - group**.) Signs vary.

ordeal: *n.* a very difficult or painful experience. *I do not know how we ever lived through that ordeal.*

SIGN: Right **'EXTENDED B'** hand, with fingertips on chin and palm facing body, is turned away, so that palm is facing down. Then right **'CONTRACTED 5'** hand is held with palm facing right side of head and fingers pointing at head. The fingers close to form a **'FLAT O'** shape as the hand moves slightly away from the head at a slight downward angle. Motion is repeated. (ASL CONCEPT—**bad - experience**.)

order: *v.* to give a command or instruction; to request that something be supplied. *When the waitress comes, we can order our meal.*

SIGN #1: Tip of forefinger of vertical right **'ONE'** hand, palm forward, is placed on the lips and the hand is thrust forward. ❖

order: *n.* acceptable, peaceful, nondisruptive conduct. *The judge called for order in the court.*

SIGN #2: **'B'** (or **'EXTENDED B'**) hands are crossed in front of the mouth, left palm facing rightward/downward and right palm facing leftward/downward with the right hand just behind the left hand. Then they are firmly drawn apart until the palms face completely downward. A solemn facial expression accompanies this sign.

order: *n.* quietness; attentiveness; readiness to proceed. *The meeting was called to order.*

SIGN #3: Fingerspell **ORDER**.

    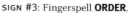

(in) order: *adj.* in a state which has been suitably arranged or put together. *Everything is in order.*

SIGN #1: With palms facing the body, **'CLAWED 5'** hands are held together so that little fingers interlock. As the hands are simultaneously lowered from the wrists, the corresponding fingers of each hand interlock to simulate the meshing of gears.

(in) order: *adj.* in sequence. *Please keep the pictures in this order.*

SIGN #2: Left **'5'** hand is held with palm facing the body and fingers pointing rightward/ upward. Right **'DOUBLE CONTRACTED L'** hand is held with back against left thumb and palm facing the body. Right hand then moves rightward in an arc across fingertips of left hand while opening and closing several times, thus alternating between a **'DOUBLE CONTRACTED L'** shape and a **'CLOSED DOUBLE MODIFIED G'**. (Spatial positioning of this sign varies a great deal. The right hand is often used alone, and while the handshape and movement remain generally the same, the position and direction varies depending on what/who is being arranged in what sort of sequence and in what particular place. Moreover, sometimes the verb is also incorporated in the sign, in which case an entirely different sign may be used). See **(put) in order**.

(put in) order: *v.* to arrange in sequence. *Put the recipe cards in order.*

SIGN: Horizontal left **'BENT EXTENDED B'** hand is held in a fixed position with palm facing right and fingers pointing rightward as well. Horizontal right **'BENT EXTENDED B'** hand is held with palm facing left and fingers positioned just in front of those of the left hand. Right hand then moves forward in a succession of small arcs. (The sign for **(put) in order** will vary considerably depending on *what* is being put in order and *where* it is taking place.)

ordinary: *adj.* commonplace or unexceptional. *The mayor lives in a very small, ordinary house in an inexpensive district.*

SIGN: Right **'BENT U'** hand, palm down, is circled clockwise over left **'STANDARD BASE'** hand, and the extended fingers are brought down to rest on it.
ALTERNATE SIGN—**daily**

organization: *n.* an official group or society with a united purpose. *The United Nations is an international organization whose purpose is to promote worldwide peace and cooperation.*

SIGN #1: Upright **'O'** hands, palms forward, are placed side by side and are curved apart and forward to create a circle with the wrists rotating so that the palms eventually face the body as the hands come together again.
ALTERNATE SIGN—**group** #1

organization: *n.* the act of organizing or arranging. *Hosting an international conference requires a lot of organization.*

SIGN #2: Horizontal **'EXTENDED B'** hands, palms facing each other and fingers pointing forward, are held slightly apart at the left side of the body and are moved simultaneously toward the right. Motion may be repeated.
SAME SIGN—**organize**, *v.*, but the motion is not repeated.

oriental: *adj.* relating to the Orient, an area in southeastern Asia. *Many oriental people attend Canadian universities.*

SIGN: Tip of forefinger of right **'BENT ONE'** hand, palm toward the face, is placed near the corner of the right eye and the hand is twisted back and forth from the wrist.

origin: *n.* the beginning or source of something. *Nobody knows the origin of that rumour.*

SIGN #1: Left **'5'** hand is held with palm facing right while forefinger of right **'ONE'** hand is inserted between first two fingers of left hand and twisted 180 degrees to the right.

origin: *n.* ancestry or parentage. *Canadians have a wide variety of ethnic origins.*

SIGN #2: Fingertips of horizontal right **'BENT EXTENDED B'** hand, palm toward the body, are placed against the right shoulder while horizontal left **'BENT EXTENDED B'** hand, palm toward the body, is held a short distance in front of it. Then both hands are circled forward around one another several times.

original: *adj.* the first genuine form of something, from which others are derived. *This dictionary contains numerous original signs used by our Deaf ancestors.*

SIGN #1: Left **'EXTENDED A'** hand is held horizontally with thumb up and palm facing rightward but slanted slightly toward the body. Tip of forefinger of right **'ONE'** hand moves at a leftward/backward angle until making contact with tip of left thumb. (Alternatively, the right hand takes the form of a **'BENT EXTENDED B'** hand and moves backward until the palm makes contact with the thumb of the left horizontal **'EXTENDED A'** hand.) Then tip of forefinger of right **'ONE'** hand, palm facing left, is placed on or at lips, and thrust forward. (ASL CONCEPT—**first - real**.)
ALTERNATE SIGN—**begin**

original: *adj.* fresh and unusual; new; creative. *The skits about Deaf Culture are original.*

SIGN #2: Tip of forefinger of vertical right **'4'** hand, palm facing left, is placed against the forehead and the hand is then pushed upward and forward slightly.

originate: *v.* to bring or come into being; to begin or come from. *The Canadian Cultural Society of the Deaf originated in Winnipeg in 1973.*

SIGN: Left **'5'** hand is held with palm facing right while forefinger of right **'ONE'** hand is inserted between first two fingers of left hand and twisted 180 degrees to the right.

other: *adj.* additional; further; different. *I will notify the other members of the society about our project.*

SIGN: Right **'EXTENDED A'** hand is held palm down. As the wrist rotates rightward, the hand is turned so that the palm faces left.

ought to: *v.* used to indicate obligation, expediency, expectation or desire; should. *You **ought to** find yourself a new partner.*

SIGN: Right **'X'** hand, palm facing away from the body, is held in a vertical position in front of the chest and is sharply thrust downward from the wrist so that the palm faces down.

our/ours: *pron.* used to refer to something belonging to the signer and one or more other person(s). [See PRONOUNS, p. LXVI.] *That new green car is **ours**.*

SIGN: Vertical right **'EXTENDED C'** hand, palm facing leftward/forward, is held with thumb-tip touching or just in front of the right shoulder. The arm then moves leftward as the wrist rotates so that the hand ends up against the left shoulder with the palm facing up.

ourselves: *pron.* used to emphasize the subject 'we'. [See PRONOUNS, p. LXVI.] *We did the work **ourselves**.*

SIGN: Vertical right **'EXTENDED A'** hand, palm facing left is held against the right shoulder and moved leftward so that it ends up against the left shoulder.

oust: *v.* to force an individual or group out of a position or place. *The political party decided to **oust** its leader.*

SIGN: Horizontal **'S'** hands are held slightly apart with left palm down and right palm up. The arms then move simultaneously rightward as the hands open to form **'CROOKED 5'** shapes.

out: *adv.* away from a certain place. *The opposite of 'in' is 'out'.*

SIGN #1: Right **'CONTRACTED 5'** hand is held palm down with fingers pointing downward and enclosed in the left **'C'** hand, which is held horizontally with palm facing the body but angled slightly rightward. The right hand then closes to form a **'FLAT O'** as it is withdrawn from the left hand with an upward/rightward motion. (This sign rarely appears in ASL to mean **out**. Sign choice depends entirely on the context and as **out** is often conceptually involved with other words in English, it frequently becomes incorporated in the sign for an accompanying word.)

out: *adv.* not at home or not in a particular place. *Your secretary said you were **out** when I called.*

SIGN #2: Right **'CONTRACTED 5'** hand, palm toward the body, is drawn forward at a slight rightward angle as the fingers close to form a **'FLAT O'** handshape.

out: *adj.* unable or ineligible to achieve something. *If we are required to write a provincial exam, that lets me **out**!*

SIGN #3: To express **OUT** in this context, the word is fingerspelled in such a way that the right hand moves rightward in an arc, lingering over the **U** which actually forms the arc while the **O** and **T** serve only as the beginning and end points of the arc.

out: *adj.* used to denote that a player in a specific sport must discontinue his/her role until summoned again. *The umpire declared that the batter was **out**.*

SIGN #4: Right **'EXTENDED A'** hand, palm toward the chest, is firmly thrust to the right at an angle which results in the thumb pointing over the right shoulder.

out of: *prep.* not having any left of a specific material or substance. *I could not make the dessert because we were **out of** eggs.*

SIGN: Right horizontal **'SPREAD C'** hand, palm toward the chest, is placed on the upturned palm of the left **'EXTENDED B'** hand. Then the right hand is drawn forward as it changes to an **'S'** handshape.

out of bounds: *adj.* outside certain prescribed limits; an area where entrance is not allowed. *The staff lounge is **out of bounds** to all students.*

SIGN: Right **'EXTENDED A'** hand, palm facing left, thumb under chin, is thrust forward. Then **'K'** hands, palms down, are held apart, extended fingers pointing downward, and are flicked upward from the wrist so that the hands are held in either a horizontal or upright position. (ASL CONCEPT—**not - allow**.)

out of order: *adj.* not working. *Please use the washroom on the next floor because this one is out of order.*

SIGN #1: Right **'EXTENDED A'** hand, palm facing left, thumb under chin, is thrust forward. Then wrist of right **'A'** (or **'S'**) hand, palm facing away from the body, strikes wrist of left **'A'** (or **'S'**) hand, which is held in front of/below right hand with palm facing downward. Motion is repeated. (ASL CONCEPT—**not - work**.) **OUT OF ORDER** is frequently fingerspelled. (If the piece of equipment not working is mechanical, **breakdown** is often used.)

out of order: *adj.* not following the usual rules or procedures. *His motion at the meeting was declared out of order.*

SIGN #2: Fingerspell **OUT OF ORDER**.

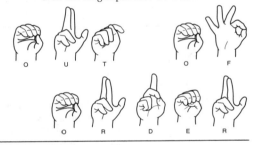

out of the way: *adv.* on an unusual or longer route. *He will have to go out of the way to pick me up.*

SIGN: **'ONE'** hands are held together with palms down and forefingers pointing forward. The left hand remains fixed while the right hand curves forward/rightward in a fairly wide arc.

outbreak: *n.* a sudden violent or spontaneous occurrence. *There has been an outbreak of influenza among the patients in the infirmary.*

SIGN: **'FLAT O'** hands are held with palms down and sides of tips of forefingers touching. The hands are then opened to form **'CONTRACTED 5'** hands as they are moved apart in an outward/forward direction.

outcome: *n.* result, consequence or action that followed a specific situation. *Please report the outcome of your investigation.*

SIGN: **'ONE'** hands, palms facing each other, are held slightly apart, fingers pointing away from the body, and are turned over so that the palms face down.

outdated [*or* **out of date**]: *adj.* no longer fashionable, widely accepted or used. *This computer is outdated and should be replaced.*

SIGN: Right **'S'** hand, slightly open, palm facing left, is brought down firmly from the chin as it closes. (**OUTDATED** may be fingerspelled.) ALTERNATE SIGN—**old-fashioned**

outdoors: *adv.* outside, or in the open air. *The children played outdoors during recess.*

SIGN #1: Right **'CONTRACTED 5'** hand is held palm down with fingers pointing downward and enclosed in the left **'C'** hand, which is held horizontally with palm facing the body but angled slightly rightward. The right hand then closes to form a **'FLAT O'** as it is withdrawn from the left hand with an upward/rightward motion. Motion is repeated.

OR

SIGN #2: Right **'FLAT C'** hand is held palm down with fingers inserted between thumb and fingers of horizontal left **'CONTRACTED C'** hand, of which the fingers point rightward and the palm faces right but is angled slightly toward the body. The right hand is then withdrawn from the left hand with an upward/rightward motion as it closes to form a **'FLAT O'**. Motion is repeated.

outgoing: *adj.* the quality of being friendly and sociable. *She is very shy but her twin sister is more outgoing.*

SIGN: **'A'** hands, thumbs up, palms facing each other, are brought alternately up against the chest and circled forward. Next, **'ONE'** hands are held basically upright but slanted forward slightly with left palm facing the body while right palm faces away from the body. The two hands then brush against each other as they move from side to side a few times in opposite directions. (ASL CONCEPT—**ambitious - meet**.) Alternatively, **OUTGOING** may be fingerspelled.

outline: *n.* a brief draft of the important features of a proposal, brief or other written work. *The government published an outline of the proposal.*

SIGN: **'SPREAD C'** hands are held horizontally and slightly apart, right above left. Then both are closed to form **'S'** hands as the right is brought down to rest on top of the left. Alternatively, **OUTLINE** may be fingerspelled. (If **outline** refers to the *shape* of something, the sign is entirely governed by the shape of the object or figure being referred to.)

outlook: *n.* a point of view or mental attitude. *His outlook toward the future is gloomy.*

SIGN: Tip of middle finger of right **'BENT V'** hand, palm toward the body, is held near the right eye. Then the hand is twisted clockwise from the wrist so that palm faces forward and extended fingers point at forefinger of vertical left **'ONE'** hand, whose palm faces rightward.

output: *n.* information made available by a computer. *The detective found the computer output very helpful in his investigation.*

SIGN: Right **'CONTRACTED 5'** hand is held palm down with fingers pointing downward and enclosed in the left **'C'** hand, which is held horizontally with palm facing the body but angled slightly rightward. The right hand then closes to form a **'FLAT O'** as it is withdrawn from the left hand with an upward/rightward motion.

outside: *adv.* outdoors. *All children are encouraged to play outside.*

SIGN #1: Right **'CONTRACTED 5'** hand is held palm down with fingers pointing downward and enclosed in the left **'C'** hand, which is held horizontally with palm facing the body but angled slightly rightward. The right hand then closes to form a **'FLAT O'** as it is withdrawn from the left hand with an upward/rightward motion. Motion is repeated.
ALTERNATE SIGN—**outdoors** #2

outside: *n.* the exterior surface of something. *The outside of the house needs painting.*

SIGN #2: Right **'CONTRACTED 5'** hand is held palm down with fingers pointing forward and enclosed in the left **'C'** hand which is held upright with palm facing right. The right hand then closes to form a **'FLAT O'** as it is withdrawn from the left hand and moved toward the body. (Sign choice depends on the object whose exterior is under discussion.)

outsmart: *v.* to outwit or get the better of someone. *The mischievous girl was able to outsmart her babysitter.*

SIGN: Vertical right **'U'** hand, palm facing left, is held just in front of the right shoulder. The wrist rotates clockwise a quarter turn as the hand is thrust ahead firmly ending with the palm forward. ❖

outspoken: *adj.* candid, blunt or bold in one's speech. *He is very outspoken on the subject of human rights.*

SIGN: Tip of forefinger of vertical right **'4'** hand, palm left, is placed on the lower lip. Then the hand is thrust forward rigidly. This sign is accompanied by a look of determination. (**OUTSPOKEN** may be fingerspelled.)

outstanding: *adj.* of prominent excellence; superior. *Forrest Nickerson was an outstanding illustrator.*

SIGN: Vertical **'EXTENDED B'** hands, palms facing forward, are held apart near the face. Forearms are pushed purposefully forward a short distance. Appropriate facial expression is essential.
ALTERNATE SIGNS—**best** #1 & #2

ovary: *n.* one of two female reproductive organs which produce ova and secrete estrogen. *She had a cyst removed from her ovary.*

SIGN: Joined thumb and forefinger of right **'F'** hand, palm toward the body, are tapped lightly against right side of lower abdomen. For **ovaries**, *pl.*, both **'F'** hands are used, one at either side of the abdomen. (**OVARY** is frequently fingerspelled.)

oven: *n.* the enclosed heated compartment of a stove. *Bread is baked in an oven.*

SIGN: Right **'EXTENDED B'** hand, palm up, with fingers pointing forward, slides under left palm-down **'EXTENDED B'** hand whose fingers point rightward. (**OVEN** is frequently fingerspelled.)

over: *prep.* on or to the other side of. *The horse jumped over the fence.*

SIGN #1: Left **'4'** hand is held with palm facing the body and fingers pointing rightward while horizontal right **'CLAWED V'** hand is held behind left hand with palm down. Right hand then moves forward in an arc over the left hand. (There is no 'all-purpose' sign for **over** meaning 'on or to the other side of'. This sign applies only in the case of an *animal going over a fence*. The shapes of both the left and right hands will vary depending on what/who is going over what.)

over: *prep.* more than. *Anyone over the age of 16 may compete in the tournament.*

SIGN #2: Left **'EXTENDED B'** hand is held palm-down, with fingertips pointing right. Fingertips of right palm-down **'EXTENDED B'** hand rest on and at right angles to back of left hand and are then moved upward from the wrist. (This sign tends to be used to mean **over** or **more than** in contexts where there is an implication that a certain age or number is *required or eligible*.)

over: *prep.* more than. *I am sure a car like that would cost over $60,000.*

SIGN #3: Right **'EXTENDED B'** hand is held just in front of the right shoulder with palm left and fingers pointing forward/upward. The arm is then extended as the hand is thrust forward in a large arc formation, ending up with the fingers pointing forward. Facial expression is important. (This sign tends to be used when **over** is expressed as a strong opinion or reaction to something.)

(all) over: *prep.* covering the extent of. *People all over the world have become concerned about environmental issues.*

SIGN #4: Horizontal right **'5'** hand is held with palm down and fingers pointing forward. The hand then makes a wide arc leftward as it inscribes a circle in front of the body.

over: *adj.* finished. *The class is over at noon.*

SIGN #5: Vertical **'5'** hands, palms facing the body, are held at chest level, and swung outward, away from the body so that palms face down.

OR

SIGN #6: Left horizontal **'BENT EXTENDED B'** hand is held in a fixed position with palm facing the body and fingers pointing rightward. Right horizontal **'EXTENDED B'** hand, palm facing left and fingers pointing forward, makes a chopping motion near the fingertips of the left hand.

over one's head: *adj.* beyond one's understanding. *The lecture material on nuclear physics was over his head.*

SIGN #7: **'BENT EXTENDED B'** hands are held upright just above and at either side of the head with palms facing backward. The arms are then swept backward past the head.

over: *adv.* again; once more. *The boy made many careless errors on his homework, so the teacher asked him to do it over.*

SIGN #8: Right **'BENT EXTENDED B'** hand, palm up, is overturned and brought downward so that the fingertips touch the upturned palm of the left **'EXTENDED B'** hand.

over-: *prefix* too (much); excessive(ly). *The meat is overcooked.*

SIGN #9: Left **'BENT EXTENDED B'** hand is held upright with palm facing right. Right **'BENT EXTENDED B'** hand is held upright with palm facing left and fingers resting on those of the left hand. The left hand remains stationary as the right hand moves firmly upward in a slight arc which curves toward the body and up to a position directly above the left hand. (The prefix **over-** is translated in a variety of ways, depending on the context, and is often incorporated in the sign for the root word rather than being expressed separately.)

overalls: *n.* trousers with a bib and shoulder straps. *The baby was dressed in red overalls.*

SIGN: Thumbnails of **'CONTRACTED 3'** hands, palms facing down, are placed on either side of the chest and the extended fingers are snapped back to form **'CLOSED DOUBLE MODIFIED G'** hands. Movement is repeated.

overcast: *adj.* covered, obscured, or darkened by clouds. *The sky was overcast and it looked like rain.*

SIGN: **'EXTENDED B'** hands are held high, palms facing backward, fingers of right hand pointing leftward/upward and fingers of left hand pointing rightward/upward. The forearms then bend gradually inward so that the hands are lowered in front of the face to a horizontal position whereby the left hand comes to rest just in front of the right hand.

overcome: *v.* to be victorious or to surmount obstacles. *I hope I can overcome my fear of spiders.*

SIGN #1: Vertical right **'S'** hand, palm facing forward, is curved downward from the wrist across the extended finger of the left **'ONE'** hand, which is held horizontally with the palm facing downward. ❖

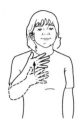

overcome: *adj.* overwhelmed with pleasure; deeply affected emotionally, especially when honoured. *He was overcome with joy at being named Deaf Citizen of the Year.*

SIGN #2: Right **'5'** hand is held with palm on chest and fingertips pointing leftward/upward. The hand is then pushed purposefully upward. Alternatively, this sign may be made with two hands, one on either side of chest, especially for emphasis. Facial expression is important. (Sign choice depends on context. This sign would be inappropriate when referring to someone who is 'overcome with *fear*'.)

overdue: *adj.* later than required or expected. *This library book is overdue.*

SIGN: Right **'EXTENDED B'** hand is held to the right side of the body with fingertips pointing downward and palm facing backward. Fingers simultaneously move back and forth. (Alternatively, **OVERDUE** is frequently fingerspelled.)

overflow: *v.* to run or spill over. *If you are not careful about pouring that coffee, the cup will overflow.*

SIGN: Right **'CROOKED 5'** hand is placed palm down on top of left horizontal **'C'** hand, of which the palm faces right but is angled slightly toward the body. The right hand then slides forward/downward, bending from the wrist, until fingers are pointing downward. (Signs vary, depending on the context. In particular, the shape of the left hand may vary in its representation of the shape of the object said to be overflowing.) ❖

overhead: *n.* a projector that throws an enlarged image on a surface above and behind the person using it. *She always uses transparencies on an overhead to illustrate her lectures.*

SIGN #1: Right vertical **'O'** hand, palm facing the right shoulder, is thrust backward and up as it opens to form a **'CONTRACTED 5'** hand.

overhead: *n.* a business's operating expenses, such as utilities, rent and taxes. *They moved their business to a location with a lower overhead.*

SIGN #2: Wrist of right vertical **'B'** hand, palm facing forward/leftward, is brushed back and forth against wrist of left **'STANDARD BASE'** hand. Then **'FLAT O'** hands are held with palms up, the left hand slightly ahead of the right hand. The hands move simultaneously forward while they close to form **'A'** hands. (ASL CONCEPT—**business - expense**.) Alternatively, **OVERHEAD** in this context may be fingerspelled.

overjoyed: *adj.* extremely happy; delighted. *We were overjoyed when we heard the news.*

SIGN: Left **'EXTENDED B'** hand is held in a fixed position with palm up and fingers pointing forward/rightward. Right **'CROOKED V'** is held palm down with tips of extended fingers resting on the left palm. The right hand then rises with extended fingers wiggling and falls back to its original position. Facial expression is important.

ALTERNATE SIGN—**excited**

overlap: *v.* to extend partly over something else or to coincide partly in terms of time or subject. *Our lecture topics may overlap slightly.*

SIGN: **'EXTENDED B'** hands are held slightly apart with palms down and fingers pointing forward. The hands then move toward each other and the right hand is laid on top of the left.

overlook: *v.* to fail to notice or take into account. *This is a serious mistake we cannot afford to overlook.*

SIGN: Vertical right **'EXTENDED B'** hand is held just to the right and in front of the face with the palm facing backward. The forearm then swings sharply downward past the face so that the hand is eventually positioned in front of the chest with fingers pointing leftward.

overnight: *adv.* for the duration of the night. [See TIME CONCEPTS, p. LXXIII.] *My friends are staying* **overnight**.

SIGN: Fingertips of left horizontal **'EXTENDED B'** hand make contact with crook of right elbow as right **'EXTENDED B'** hand is held out from the body with palm down and fingers pointing forward. The right forearm is then curved leftward as the wrist rotates to make the palm face the body.

overrule: *v.* to rule against. *The judge may* **overrule** *or sustain an objection.*

SIGN: Left **'ONE'** hand is held in a fixed position in front of the upper chest with palm right and forefinger pointing forward. Right **'BENT ONE'** hand is positioned with tip of forefinger touching the centre of the forehead and is then brought downward and forward, the tip of its forefinger brushing against the tip of the left forefinger on its way past. Facial expression is important.

oversee: *v.* to supervise; to watch over. *The company manager will* **oversee** *the day to day operation of the business.*

SIGN #1: **'K'** hands are positioned horizontally with the right one resting on top of the left one. The hands are then moved together in a counter-clockwise motion.

OR

SIGN #2: Right **'BENT V'** hand is held in front of left shoulder with palm facing left and extended fingers pointing left as well. The hand then makes a wide arc in a forward/rightward direction, coming to rest in front of the right side of the body with palm facing forward/rightward.

oversight: *n.* something overlooked; something missing or done wrong because of a failure to notice. *The error in the minutes was due to an* **oversight** *on the part of the secretary.*

SIGN: Vertical right **'EXTENDED B'** hand is held just to the right and in front of the face with the palm facing backward. The forearm then swings sharply downward past the face so that the hand is eventually positioned in front of the chest with fingers pointing leftward. (For **oversight** in the context of supervision, see **oversee** #1 & #2.)

oversleep: *v.* to sleep beyond the usual time. *The failure of my alarm clock's signal light caused me to* **oversleep**.

SIGN: Right **'CONTRACTED 5'** hand is held upright with the palm toward the face. As the hand then moves downward in front of the face, it closes to form a **'FLAT O'** shape. Gradually the right hand takes on an **'F'** shape as it dips, palm down, under the left **'STANDARD BASE'** hand, and subsequently rises in front of the left hand until the right **'F'** hand becomes upright with palm facing leftward. (ASL CONCEPT—**sleep - sunrise**.)

overtime: *n.* time in excess of a usual or set period. *The Montreal Canadiens beat the Toronto Maple Leafs during* **overtime**.

SIGN: Fingerspell **OT**.

overweight: *adj.* too heavy; weighing too much. *Sometimes* **overweight** *people have trouble finding clothes to fit them.*

SIGN: Horizontal **'CROOKED 5'** hands are held apart in front of the chest with palms toward the body. The hands then simultaneously fall forward/downward.

overwhelmed: *adj.* to be overpowered in one's thoughts, emotions or senses by an irresistible force. *We were* **overwhelmed** *by the kindness of the community after our home was destroyed by fire.*

SIGN #1: Right **'5'** hand is held with palm on chest and fingertips pointing leftward/upward. The hand is then pushed purposefully upward. Alternatively, this sign may be made with two hands, one on either side of chest, especially for emphasis. Facial expression is important. (Sign selection depends on the context.)

overwhelmed: *adj.* overcome, engulfed or buried (in work or responsibilities). *The young lawyer was* **overwhelmed** *by her case load.*

SIGN #2: Horizontal **'BENT EXTENDED B'** (or **'CROOKED 5'**) hands are held, one above each shoulder, with fingers pointing to neck. The arms are then moved upward so that the hands are level with the top of the head.

owe: *v.* to be in debt. *He owes me $5.00.*

SIGN: Tip of forefinger of right **'ONE'** hand, palm toward body, is tapped twice against right-facing palm of horizontal left **'EXTENDED B'** hand.

owl: *n.* a nocturnal bird of prey with a large head, front-facing eyes, and a short, hooked beak. *The owl is often used as a symbol of wisdom.*

SIGN #1: Vertical **'O'** hands, palms facing each other, are placed in front of the eyes. Then the wrists bend as the hands move toward each other a couple of times. (Alternatively, **OWL** may be fingerspelled.)

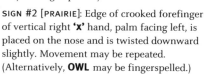

SIGN #2 [PRAIRIE]: Edge of crooked forefinger of vertical right **'X'** hand, palm facing left, is placed on the nose and is twisted downward slightly. Movement may be repeated. (Alternatively, **OWL** may be fingerspelled.)

own: *v.* to have as one's possession. *Do you own a car?*

SIGN: Horizontal right **'BENT EXTENDED B'** hand is brought back firmly so that fingertips make contact with upper right chest. At the same time, the signer's upper front teeth are resting on the lower lip. (**OWN** is frequently fingerspelled, particularly for emphasis in a sentence such as this: *Do you rent your home or do you own it?*) **OWNER**, *n.*, must be finger-spelled. In cases where **own** appears as an adjective following a possessive pronoun, the sign for the possessive pronoun is used to represent both the pronoun and **own**, *adj.* (See also PRONOUNS, p. LXIII.) In the following sentence, the sign for **your** would be used to mean **your own**: *Please tell us in your own words exactly what happened.*

oxygen: *n.* a gaseous element without colour, odour or taste. *Water is composed of two parts hydrogen and one part oxygen.*

SIGN: **'O'** hand, palm facing leftward/forward, is held upright and wobbled slightly. (**OXYGEN** is frequently fingerspelled.)

oyster: *n.* an edible mollusk with an irregularly shaped shell. *Divers sought a special pearl oyster in the warm coastal waters off southern Mexico.*

SIGN: Fingerspell **OYSTER**.

ozone: *n.* a gas that is present in the earth's atmosphere. *Environmentalists are worried about damage to the ozone which protects us from the sun's ultra violet rays.*

SIGN: Fingerspell **OZONE**.

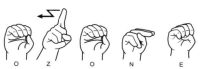

P

pace: *v.* to walk back and forth. *When he worries, he tends to pace.*

SIGN #1: Vertical right **'ONE'** hand, palm facing left, is moved across from right to left. The wrist then twists to turn the palm forward as the hand returns to its original position. The motion is repeated. (Alternatively, this sign may be made with a horizontal **'EXTENDED A'** hand.)

pace: *n.* the rate of proceeding; speed. *Each student is allowed to advance at his or her own pace.*

SIGN #2: Horizontal **'BENT EXTENDED B'** hands, left palm facing right and right palm facing left, are deliberately moved up and forward over each other a few times in leapfrog fashion. (The relative pace is indicated by the speed at which the hands rotate.)

pack: *v.* to arrange articles in a suitcase. *She has to pack before going home this weekend.*

SIGN: **'FLAT O'** hands are held apart with palms down and are alternately circled forward.

package: *n.* any wrapped or boxed article or group of articles; parcel. *We expect a package of brochures to be delivered this morning.*

SIGN: With a slight but deliberate downward thrust, horizontal **'EXTENDED B'** hands are held parallel with palms facing each other and fingers pointing forward. Then the hands take on a **'BENT EXTENDED B'** shape as they are swung inward with a slight downward thrust again, and the right hand positioned ahead of the left, both palms facing the body.

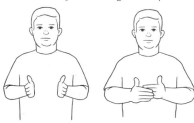

pad: *n.* a thick, often soft or cushiony, quantity (of something). *I need a new pad of paper.*

SIGN: Fingerspell **PAD**. (When referring to protective pads used in sports, **'EXTENDED C'** hands are used to cover the pertinent body parts, such as the shoulders, elbows or knees.)

paddle: *v.* to plunge an oar into the water to propel and/or steer a boat. *I will teach you how to paddle the canoe.*

SIGN: **'S'** hands are held, right above left, and are swept downward/backward simultaneously to simulate the paddling of a canoe. The motion is alternated from one side to the other.

page: *n.* one side of a leaf of a book or newspaper. *You will find the article on page 8 of Section D.*

SIGN #1: Fingerspell **PAGE**.

page: *v.* to call a person over a public address system or through an electronic device that beeps. *If I do not recognize him at the airport, I will have him paged.*

SIGN #2: Fingertips of right **'BENT EXTENDED B'** hand are placed on the back of the left **'STANDARD BASE'** hand. Then as the right hand is drawn slightly upward toward the body, the hand closes to form an **'EXTENDED A'** hand. ❖

pager: *n.* an electronic beeper worn to alert a person to incoming messages. *Most doctors use a pager when they are on call.*

SIGN: Right **'FLAT C'** hand, palm down, is placed on the right hip and is firmly pushed downward a short distance.

pail: *n.* a bucket. *We filled the pail with hot water.*

SIGN: Horizontal **'C'** hands are held apart with palms facing each other. The hands are then simultaneously raised to indicate the height of the pail.

ALTERNATE SIGN—**bucket**

pain: *n.* a feeling of acute physical hurt or discomfort. *A sudden intense pain in the chest may signal a heart attack.*

SIGN: Horizontal **'BENT ONE'** hands are held slightly apart, then moved toward one another as the right hand twists slightly forward and the left hand twists slightly backward. This sign is generally made near the afflicted area of the body.

SAME SIGN—**painful**, *adj.*

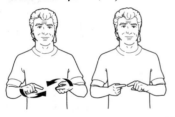

pain in the neck [*or* **pain in the ass** *or* **pain in the butt**]: *n.* an idiomatic expression meaning nuisance; pest. *I always try to avoid him because he is such a pain in the neck.*

SIGN: Vertical right **'BENT MIDFINGER 5'** hand is held with palm left and tip of middle finger touching forehead. The wrist then rotates to turn the palm toward the face. Facial expression must clearly convey 'annoyance'.

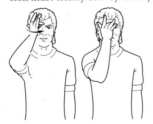

paint: *v.* to coat a surface with paint. *We decided to paint the kitchen white.*

SIGN #1: Vertical left **'EXTENDED B'** hand is held in a fixed position with palm facing right. Right **'EXTENDED B'** hand is held palm down with fingers pointing left as the fingertips are brushed up and down against the length of the left hand. This is a wrist action.

paint: *v.* to create a work of art by applying paint to a canvas or other surface. *The artist likes to paint landscapes and seascapes.*

SIGN #2: Vertical left **'EXTENDED B'** hand is held in a fixed position with palm facing right. Right **'BENT EXTENDED U'** hand is held with palm downward/leftward as the fingertips are brushed up and down against the left hand.

(a) pair of: *n.* two identical or similar things together. *They have a pair of Siamese cats.*

SIGN: Right **'V'** hand is held upright with palm facing the body to indicate 'two'. (When **pair** implies a single unit and is commonly part of a phrase, as in 'a pair of scissors' or 'a pair of pants', it has no distinct sign. In these cases, the sign for the actual object suffices, *e.g.*, **scissors** or **pants**.)

pal: *n.* a good friend; buddy; comrade. *She was my best pal when we were teenagers.*

SIGN: Crooked fingers of **'X'** hands are interlocked so that palm of left hand, which is closest to the body, faces up while right palm faces down. Holding this position, the hands are simultaneously and firmly moved forward/downward slightly as interlocked fingers tighten.

ALTERNATE SIGNS—**friend** & **best friend** #2

pale: *adj.* light in colour; not bright. *I bought some pale pink envelopes.*

SIGN #1: Horizontal **'BENT MIDFINGER 5'** hands are held apart with palms down. The wrists are then rotated outward a quarter turn, causing the hands to turn so that the palms face each other. (**PALE** may be fingerspelled.)

pale: *adj.* whitish; colourless; wan. *He looks pale and weak after his long illness.*

SIGN #2: Fingertips of right **'FLAT O'** hand, palm toward the body, are placed in the middle of the chest. The hand is then raised to a position in front of the face where it opens to become a **'CONTRACTED 5'** hand with the palm toward the face. (**PALE** may be fingerspelled.)

pamphlet: *n.* a thin publication or booklet with a paper cover. *This pamphlet may be used as a guide in completing the census forms.*

SIGN: Thumb and forefinger of right **'A-INDEX'** (or **'MODIFIED G'**) hand are slid up the edge of the left **'EXTENDED B'** hand, which is held with palm facing body. Motion is repeated.

pan: *n.* a shallow container used for cooking. *She burned a whole pan of cookies.*

SIGN: Fingerspell **PAN**.

pancake: *n.* a thin, flat cake which is fried on both sides. *We often have pancakes and sausages for breakfast on Sunday mornings.*

SIGN: Right **'EXTENDED B'** hand is held palm down with fingers pointing forward/leftward as they are placed on the upturned palm of the left **'EXTENDED B'** hand, of which the fingers point slightly forward and to the right. Right hand is then flipped over so that palm faces up. (**PANCAKE** is frequently fingerspelled.)

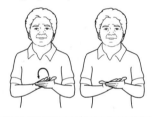

panic: *n.* a sudden, overwhelming fear, often affecting many people at the same time. *Everyone was in a panic when they heard the news about the flood.*

SIGN: Fingerspell **PANIC**.

pant: *v.* to breathe with deep noisy gasps. *We were panting after walking up six flights of steps.*

SIGN #1: Right **'5'** hand, palm toward the body, is used to pat the chest a couple of times while the tongue hangs loosely out of the mouth.

pant: *v.* to breathe with deep, noisy gasps and the tongue hanging loosely (said of dogs). *My dog pants a lot on hot days.*

SIGN #2: Right **'BENT EXTENDED U'** hand, palm down, is held near the chin and moved up and down slightly as the signer's tongue protrudes from the open mouth.

panties: *n.* a pair of women's or girl's underpants. *She wore white panties trimmed with lace.*

SIGN: Fingertips of **'BENT MIDFINGER 5'** hands are placed just below either hip, palms toward the body. The hands are then raised and repositioned at the waist. (Signs vary.)

pants: *n.* trousers; slacks. *I think you should wear your black pants with that shirt.*

SIGN #1: Fingertips of **'BENT 5'** hands, palms toward the body, are placed just below either hip and are stroked upward a couple of times.

OR

SIGN #2: **'EXTENDED B'** hands are held a thigh's width apart in front of the left side of the body at about hip level with palms facing each other and fingers pointed downward. The hands are simultaneously moved downward, then moved to the right side and moved downward once more.

Pap test: *n.* a medical procedure that allows cells taken from the uterus to be examined for abnormalities. *The doctor explained that her PAP test was clear.*

SIGN: Fingerspell **PAP**. Then **'ONE'** hands are held parallel with palms forward/downward. As the forearms simultaneously move downward/forward, the forefingers retract to form **'X'** hands. Movement is repeated.

paper: *n.* a thin sheet of material made from wood, rags, or other materials and used as a writing surface or for wrapping, decorating, etc. *Please write your name and address on this piece of paper.*

SIGN: Horizontal **'CROOKED 5'** hands, right palm down and left palm up, are positioned so that the right hand is slightly above the left. Then the right hand moves leftward/backward and the left hand moves rightward as the heels of each hand strike against each other at least twice.

paper clip: *n.* a wire that is bent into a certain shape for the purpose of holding sheets of paper together. *I need a paper clip to keep these pages together.*

SIGN: Horizontal **'CROOKED 5'** hands, right palm down and left palm up, are positioned so that the right hand is slightly above the left. Then the right hand moves leftward/backward and the left hand moves rightward as the heels of each hand strike against each other at least twice. Next, left **'EXTENDED B'** hand represents a piece of paper as it is held in a fixed position with palm toward the body and fingers pointing rightward. Right **'CLOSED DOUBLE MODIFIED G'** hand represents a paper clip as it is held palm down with the thumb and extended fingers grasping the left forefinger, then sliding downward.

paper cutter: *n.* a device with a blade used to cut paper. *The paper cutter is in the teachers' workroom.*

SIGN: Horizontal **'CROOKED 5'** hands, right palm down and left palm up, are positioned so that the right hand is slightly above the left. Then the right hand moves leftward/backward and the left hand moves rightward as the heels of each hand strike against each other at least twice. Next, right horizontal **'S'** hand, palm facing down, appears to be holding onto the handle which operates the blade of the paper cutter and is moved downward as if lowering the blade.

parachute: *n.* a large umbrella-shaped piece of cloth used to slow down a person's descent when jumping from an airplane. *The skydiver had a brightly coloured parachute.*

SIGN: Left **'CLAWED SPREAD C'** hand, palm down, is used to represent the open parachute while the right **'V'** hand, palm down, represents the legs of the person below it. The hands are simultaneously lowered and raised a couple of times. (For **parachute**, *v.*, see **skydive**.)

parade: *n.* an organized ceremonial march or procession. *We always watch the Grey Cup parade.*

SIGN: **'BENT 4'** hands are held left in front of right with palms down and are lightly swept forward a couple of times.

paragraph: *n.* a section of writing devoted to one idea. *The teacher asked us to write a descriptive paragraph.*

SIGN: Fingertips of vertical right **'C'** hand, palm facing left, are tapped a couple of times against the right-facing palm of the vertical left **'EXTENDED B'** hand.

parallel: *adj.* continuing in the same direction at the same distance apart. *The two lines are parallel.*

SIGN #1: **'ONE'** hands, held parallel with palms down and fingers pointing forward, are pushed forward simultaneously.

parallel: *v.* to be very similar; correspond in nature to. *The Deaflympics parallel the international Olympics.*

SIGN #2: Vertical right **'Y'** hand is held with palm forward and appears to wobble from side-to-side as the wrist twists.

paralyzed: *adj.* immobilized due to loss of voluntary muscle function. *Spinal cord injury can cause one's limbs to be paralyzed.*

SIGN: **'CROOKED 5'** hands are held parallel with palms down. They then jerk slightly forward/downward as they become **'SPREAD C'** hands. SAME SIGN—**paralysis**, *n.*

paranoid: *adj.* unreasonably suspicious or distrustful; tending to have delusions of being persecuted. *No one is talking about you; you are just being paranoid!*

SIGN: Vertical **'BENT EXTENDED B'** hands are held with palms facing each other and fingertips touching either side of forehead. Fingertips maintain contact with the forehead while the wrists rapidly twist back and forth several times in opposite directions. The eyes are narrowed as the face registers 'suspicion'.
SAME SIGN—**paranoia**, *n.*
ALTERNATE SIGN—**suspicious**

paraplegic: *n.* a person whose lower half of the body is immobilized due to paralysis. *Rick Hansen, a famous Canadian paraplegic, received international attention during his "Man in Motion" world tour.*

SIGN: **'CROOKED 5'** hands are held parallel with palms down. They then jerk slightly forward/downward as they become **'SPREAD C'** hands. Next, **'EXTENDED B'** hands are positioned at about waist level, the left resting on the right, with palms down. The right is then lowered while the left remains fixed.
(ASL CONCEPT—**paralyze - waist below**.)

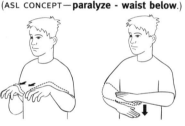

parasite: *n.* an animal that lives either in or on another from which it gets nourishment. *A tapeworm is a parasite passed on to humans through poorly cooked meat.*

SIGN #1: The edge of the forefinger of the right **'CROOKED ONE'** hand, palm down, is placed against the right-facing palm of the horizontal left **'EXTENDED B'** hand. Then the right hand is moved forward slowly with the crooked forefinger wiggling. (Sign choice depends on the context.)

parasite: *n.* a person who lives at the expense of others without giving anything in return. *He has been offered several jobs, but he prefers to be a parasite and depend on others to provide things for him.*

SIGN #2: Left **'BENT U'** hand is held in a fixed position with palm down and extended fingers pointing rightward/forward. Vertical right **'CONTRACTED 3'** hand is held above the level of the right shoulder with palm forward and is purposefully lowered so that the extended fingers and thumb snap shut on the extended fingers of the left hand.

parcel: *n.* a package that is usually wrapped up in paper. *I took the parcel to the post office and mailed it.*

SIGN: With a slight but deliberate downward thrust horizontal **'EXTENDED B'** hands are held parallel, with palms facing each other and fingers pointing forward. Then the hands take on a **'BENT EXTENDED B'** shape as they are swung inward with a slight downward thrust again, and the right hand positioned ahead of the left, both palms facing the body.

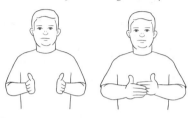

pardon: *v.* to free from punishment; excuse; forgive. *The judge pardoned the homeless man for stealing food because of his circumstances.*

SIGN: Fingers of right **'B'** hand, palm-down, are placed on and at right angles to fingers of upturned palm of left **'EXTENDED B'** hand. Right hand is then slid at a forward/rightward angle across and off the left hand.

pardon me: *s.s.* to ask to be excused or forgiven. *Please pardon me for being late.*

SIGN: Fingers of right **'B'** hand, palm-down, are placed on and at right angles to fingers of upturned palm of left **'EXTENDED B'** hand. Right hand is then slid at a forward/rightward angle across and off the left hand. Motion is repeated.

pare: *v.* to peel the outer layer from something. *It takes a long time to pare a bushel of apples.*

SIGN: Left **'CROOKED SLANTED 5'** hand is held in a fixed position with palm up. Right **'CLAWED L'** hand is held palm-down just above the left hand but a little further forward. Right hand then moves toward the body and the motion is repeated to simulate the peeling of something such as an apple or potato.

parentheses: *n.* a pair of brackets ( ) used to set off a phrase or explanatory note within a written or printed passage. *The explanation is enclosed in parentheses.*

SIGN: Horizontal **'CROOKED ONE'** hands are held parallel with palms down. The wrists then rotate outward, thus curving the hands so that the palms are facing each other.

parents: *n.* mothers and fathers. *The majority of Deaf children have hearing parents.*

SIGN: Tip of thumb of vertical right **'5'** hand, palm facing leftward, is tapped against the right side of the chin. The hand is then raised so that the thumb taps the right side of the forehead. (ASL CONCEPT—**mother - father**.)

parity: *n.* equality of rank, pay, etc. *The striking Alberta nurses are demanding wage parity with their B.C. counterparts.*

SIGN: Vertical **'BENT EXTENDED B'** hands are held slightly apart with palms facing each other, and are then brought together so that the fingertips meet. Motion is repeated.

park: *v.* to leave a vehicle (somewhere) temporarily. *We had to park our car three blocks away.*

SIGN #1: Horizontal right **'3'** hand, palm facing left, is thumped downward on the upturned palm of the left **'EXTENDED B'** hand.

park: *n.* an area used by the public for recreation. *People enjoy walking and cycling in Stanley Park.*

SIGN #2: Fingerspell **PARK**.

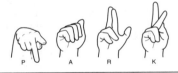

parka: *n.* a warm coat with a hood (originally worn by Inuits). *Most modern parkas are downfilled and trimmed with fake fur.*

SIGN: Vertical **'EXTENDED A'** hands are held parallel close to the upper chest with palms facing each other. They are then simultaneously lowered a few inches as palms turn downward. Next, **'CLOSED A-INDEX'** hands are held palm downward at either shoulder and are simultaneously flipped upward so that the palms face backward. The motion resembles that of flipping a hood over one's head. (ASL CONCEPT—**coat - hood**.)

parking lot: *n.* a car park. *The Community Centre has no parking lot.*

SIGN: Horizontal right **'3'** hand, palm facing left, is thumped downward a couple of times on the upturned palm of the left **'EXTENDED B'** hand.

parliamentary: *adj.* conforming to the procedures of parliament. *The president of our organization conducts all meetings according to parliamentary rules.*

SIGN: Left forearm is held parallel to the chest so that the hand is at about collarbone level. Right **'K'** hand, palm facing leftward/ downward, is brought back against the left wrist, is then moved downward in arc formation and placed near the left elbow. SAME SIGN—**parliament**, *n.*

parole: *n.* the early release of prisoners on the condition that their behaviour continues to be good. *She committed several crimes while on parole.*

SIGN: Fingerspell **PAROLE**.

part: *n.* a piece; portion. *They decided that part of the money would be used for research.*

SIGN #1: Horizontal left **'EXTENDED B'** hand is held in a fixed position with palm up but angled toward the body and fingers pointing rightward/forward while edge of horizontal right **'EXTENDED B'** hand, palm facing left, is placed on left palm and is drawn back toward the body. (When referring to **replacement parts**, the signer will fingerspell **PARTS**.)

part: *v.* to arrange a break or line in the hair where the scalp shows through. *He parts his hair on the left.*

SIGN #2: Right **'CROOKED ONE'** hand is held palm down with tip of forefinger pointing to a place near the crown of the head a little left of centre. The hand then moves forward in a straight line. Next, **'CLAWED 5'** hands are held with palms down on either side of the imaginary line just outlined on the left side of the head, and are moved apart slightly to draw attention to the 'part'. (The location of this sign varies according to the actual location of the 'part' being discussed.)

part: *v.* to separate; break up. *They decided to part and date other people for six months.*

SIGN #3: Horizontal **'BENT EXTENDED B'** hands, palms facing chest and knuckles almost touching each other, are drawn apart.

(play the) part of: *v.* to portray a certain character in a play. *He will play the part of Romeo in the film.*

SIGN #4: **'EXTENDED A'** hands, palms facing each other, are rotated alternately in small circles which are brought down against the chest.

(take) part: See **participate**.

participate: *v.* to take part; become actively involved in. *Students from many schools will participate in the tournament.*

SIGN: Extended fingers of right **'U'** hand are inserted into the slightly open left **'S'** hand. ❖
SAME SIGN—**participation**, *n.*

particular: *adj.* specific; certain. *The physiotherapist recommended a particular exercise that I can do to strengthen my knee.*

SIGN #1: Vertical left **'ONE'** hand is held in a fixed position with palm facing rightward/forward. Horizontal right **'ONE'** hand is held behind left hand with palm facing left. The right hand then makes a slight but firm bounce as if intending to strike the tip of the left forefinger with that of the right forefinger but not quite touching it. (For **particulars**, *pl.*, see **details**.)

particular: *adj.* fussy; hard to please. *She is very particular about how things should be done.*

SIGN #2: Vertical right **'COMBINED U + Y'** hand, palm forward, is held in front of the right shoulder and the forearm is drawn firmly backward a short distance. This is essentially a jerking motion.

particularly: *adv.* especially. *He enjoys learning languages and is particularly interested in ASL.*

SIGN: Vertical left **'ONE'** hand is held in a fixed position with palm facing rightward/forward. Horizontal right **'ONE'** hand is held behind left hand with palm facing left. The right hand then makes a slight but firm bounce as if intending to strike the tip of the left forefinger with that of the right forefinger but not quite touching it.
ALTERNATE SIGN—**most**

partner: *n.* one of two or more people who enter into a joint venture or activity such as business, dancing, card playing, etc. *I will need a partner to play bridge.*

SIGN: Right **'EXTENDED B'** hand, with palm facing left and fingers pointing forward, slides from side to side a few times along forefinger of horizontally held left **'EXTENDED B'** hand, whose palm is facing the body.

party: *n.* a social gathering for pleasure. *She plans on attending the staff Christmas party.*

SIGN #1: Vertical **'F'** hands, left palm facing right and right palm facing left, are alternately moved forward and back a couple of times so that the joined thumb and forefinger touch the side of the chin with each backward movement.

481

party (cont.)

OR

SIGN #2: Horizontal **'Y'** hands are held apart with palms facing each other and are simultaneously swung from side to side as the wrists rotate back and forth yet the palms continue to face in opposite directions.

OR

SIGN #3: **'K'** hands are held apart with palms down and are simultaneously swung from side to side. This is a wrist action. [See also **throw (a party)**.]

party: *n.* a group of people gathered for a certain purpose or activity. *They sent a rescue party out to the sinking ship.*

SIGN #4: **'SPREAD C'** hands are held upright and slightly apart with palms facing each other. The wrists then rotate forward, bringing the hands to a horizontal position.

party: *n.* a group of people who support a certain political ideology. *He is the leader of the Progressive Conservative party.*

SIGN #5: **'SPREAD C'** hands are held upright and slightly apart with palms facing each other. The wrists then rotate forward, bringing the hands to a horizontal position. (**PARTY** in this context may be fingerspelled.)

pass: *v.* to achieve an acceptable mark on an examination or for an assignment or course. *You will need a 75 percent average to pass the course.*

SIGN #1: Left **'A'** hand is held in a semi-vertical position with palm facing right while right **'A'** hand is held a little closer to the chest with palm facing left. The knuckles of the right hand brush past those of the left as the right forearm moves forward/downward.
SAME SIGN—**pass**, when referring to the approval of a bill or law by a legislative body.

pass: *v.* to go by; go beyond. *We will pass Belleville on the way to Kingston.*

SIGN #2: Left **'A'** hand is held in a semi-vertical position with palm facing right while right **'A'** hand is held a little closer to the chest with palm facing left. The knuckles of the right hand brush past those of the left as the right forearm moves forward/downward.

pass: *v.* to move past; overtake. *I had to pass the car so I could get to my appointment on time.*

SIGN #3: Horizontal right **'3'** hand is held in a fixed position with palm facing left. Horizontal left **'3'** hand is held directly behind the right hand with palm facing right. The left hand is then moved leftward and forward to a position directly in front of the right hand. (Handshapes will vary depending on who/what is passing whom/what.)

pass: *v.* to transfer something from the hand of one person to that of another. *Just be patient; I will pass you the butter in a minute.*

SIGN #4: Right **'FLAT O'** hand, palm up, is moved in arc formation from the vicinity of the person doing the passing to that of the person receiving the object. ❖

pass: *v.* to transfer the ball or puck to another player in such games as soccer, basketball or hockey. *You must learn how to pass if you want to become a good hockey player.*

SIGN #5: **'FLAT O'** hands are held close together with palms up and are rotated counter-clockwise, one hand just above the other. (To refer to a single pass from one player to another, the right **'FLAT O'** hand is held palm up and moved in arc formation from the vicinity of the passer to that of the player receiving the pass.) When referring to the game of football, the vertical right **'SPREAD C'** hand is held above the right shoulder and thrust forward to simulate the throwing of a football.

pass: *v.* to stop; disappear. *Your headache will pass if you lie down and rest.*

SIGN #6: **'FLAT O'** hands are held parallel with palms up and slanted slightly toward the body. As the hands are drawn apart the thumbs slide across the fingertips, causing the hands to assume **'A'** shapes.

(make a) pass at: *v.* to make sexual overtures toward someone you do not know very well. *He makes a pass at every pretty girl he sees.*

SIGN #7: **'5'** hands are held with palms down, thumbtips touching and fingers pointing forward as they flutter.

pass away: *v.* to die. *Her father passed away last year.*

SIGN: Right **'EXTENDED B'** hand is held palm down with fingers pointing forward. The wrist then rotates rightward, turning the hand palm upward.

pass down: *v.* to give (something) to someone younger. *Throughout the ages, people have tried to **pass down** ideas through storytelling.*

SIGN: Horizontal **'CONTRACTED B'** hands, right palm facing left and left palm facing right, are held up high to the right with the right hand extended so that it is higher and farther forward than the left. The hands are then simultaneously moved in a series of small arcs toward the chest. (This sign is used for something which has already been passed down. Future tense is indicated by beginning the sign in front of the chest and moving it forward/downward.)

pass out: *v.* to faint or become unconscious. *It was so hot in the room that people began to **pass out**.*

SIGN #1: Tip of forefinger of right **'ONE'** hand is placed on forehead. The head then drops as the hand assumes an **'A'** shape and is lowered to chest level where it is held parallel to the left **'A'** hand, palms down. Finally, the hands drop further as they open to take on **'5'** shapes with fingers pointing downward. While this sign actually consists of three parts, it is made in one fluid motion. (Signs in this context vary considerably.)

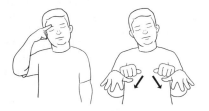

pass out: *v.* to distribute; hand out. *The teacher asked me to **pass out** the test booklets.*

SIGN #2: Right **'CONTRACTED B'** hand is held palm-up with fingers pointing forward/leftward in front of left side of body. The hand then makes a sweeping arc rightward as if passing something out. (As a modification of this sign, the hand may bounce slightly several times while completing the arc to indicate the giving of something to individual recipients.)
ALTERNATE SIGN—**distribute** #1

passage: *n.* a corridor or channel through which someone or something can pass. *The hikers found a **passage** through the mountains.*

SIGN #1: **'EXTENDED B'** hands, held parallel with palms facing one another and fingers pointing forward, are simultaneously moved forward.

passage: *n.* transportation for a journey or voyage. *We booked a **passage** to England on the Queen Elizabeth II.*

SIGN #2: Right **'CROOKED V'** hand, palm down, is snaked forward.

passage: *n.* a section of written work. *The minister began his sermon by reading a **passage** from the Book of Matthew.*

SIGN #3: Fingertips of vertical right **'C'** hand, palm facing left, are tapped a couple of times against the right-facing palm of the vertical left **'EXTENDED B'** hand.

passion: *n.* a very strongly felt emotion such as rage. *Shooting her husband's mistress was considered a crime of **passion**.*

SIGN #1: **'CLAWED 5'** hands, palms toward body, fingertips touching chest, are swept vigorously upward/outward. Facial expression must clearly convey 'anger'. (Sign choice depends on the specific emotion involved.)

(have a) passion for: *v.* to have an ardent love for. *She **has a passion for** downhill skiing.*

SIGN #2: Back of right **'S'** hand is brought up toward the mouth, kissed, and moved downward at a forward angle.
ALTERNATE SIGN—**adore** #1

passionate: *adj.* showing intense sexual feeling or desire. *She had a **passionate** lover.*

SIGN #1: Fingertips of horizontal right **'SPREAD EXTENDED C'** hand, palm toward the body, are placed against middle of upper chest and the hand is drawn downward a couple of times.
ALTERNATE SIGN—**horny**

passionate: *adj.* intensely emotional. *The lawyer made a **passionate** plea for mercy on behalf of his client.*

SIGN #2: **'E'** hands, palms toward the body, are alternately circled so that they brush upward and off the chest with each circular motion. (Signs vary depending on the context.)

passive: *adj.* not active; submissive; unresisting. *Everyone takes advantage of her because of her **passive** behaviour.*

SIGN: **'CROOKED 5'** hands are held parallel with fingers pointing downward and palms facing downward but slanted toward the body. The hands simultaneously move in a slow counter-clockwise circle while the face appears lifeless and the tongue protrudes slightly. (Signs vary according to context.)

passport: *n.* an official document identifying the holder and granting him/her permission to travel outside of the country. *He just renewed his Canadian **passport** so he can travel to Europe.*

SIGN: Horizontal right **'S'** hand, palm toward the body and facing left slightly, is brought down firmly to rest on the upturned palm of the left **'EXTENDED B'** hand. (**PASSPORT** is frequently fingerspelled.)

password: *n.* a secret word that ensures access by proving identity. *Before you can access the computer file, you must enter the **password**.*

SIGN: Right **'A'** hand is brought to the lips with the thumb pointed upward and the palm facing left. The lips are touched twice with the thumbnail. Next, tips of extended fingers of right **'MODIFIED G'** hand, palm facing left, are tapped against the forefinger of the horizontal left **'ONE'** hand of which the palm is facing right. (ASL CONCEPT—**secret - word**.) (**PASSWORD** is frequently fingerspelled.)

past: *n.* a time gone by. *My grandparents love to talk about the **past**.*

SIGN #1: Vertical right **'EXTENDED B'** hand, with palm toward right shoulder, becomes a **'BENT EXTENDED B'** hand as it bends toward the shoulder.

past: *prep.* beyond in time. *It is **past** midnight.*

SIGN #2: Right **'EXTENDED B'** hand is held with palm facing left and fingers pointing forward as it curves forward across the back of the left **'STANDARD BASE'** hand. ALTERNATE SIGN—**after**

past: *prep.* beyond (in terms of place). *The store is one block **past** the church.*

SIGN #3: **'A'** hands, palms facing each other, are held upright together with knuckles touching. Then the right hand is moved forward and slightly downward. (The ASL sentence is syntactically different than the sample sentence. In ASL: *CHURCH...PAST ONE BLOCK... STORE.*) One 'all-inclusive' ASL sign frequently conveys many English words. A vertical right forefinger moving from right to left in front of the body tells us many things, *i.e.*, that someone (a person, and not a thing) has gone past in front of (rather than at the side of) the signer (as opposed to anyone else) from right to left (rather than left to right) on foot (and not in a vehicle).

paste: *v.* to make something stick by using paste. *She helped the little girl **paste** pictures into her scrapbook.*

SIGN: **'EXTENDED A'** hands, palms facing downward and thumbtips almost touching, are drawn apart. Motion is repeated. (For **paste**, *n.*, see **glue**.)

pastel: *adj.* soft (in colour); pale. *They used **pastel** colours to decorate their living room.*

SIGN: **'CONTRACTED 5'** hands are held slightly apart with palms up and are drawn downward a few times as they are changed to **'FLAT O'** hands.

pastor: *n.* a clergyperson or minister in charge of a congregation. *He is a well known pastor for the Deaf in Toronto.*

SIGN: Vertical right **'F'** hand, palm facing forward, is poked forward a couple of times. This is a wrist movement. (This sign may be followed by a horizontal **'EXTENDED B'** hand, palm facing left, which is lowered slightly from the initial sign position.)

pasture: *n.* an area of grassy land. *The cattle are grazing in the south pasture.*

SIGN: Back of right **'CROOKED 4'** hand, palm down, is held under the chin and the hand is moved briskly in small circular motions, brushing backward against the underside of the chin with each cycle. Next, horizontal right **'5'** hand is held with palm down and fingers pointing forward. The hand then makes a wide arc leftward as it inscribes a circle in front of the body. (ASL CONCEPT— **grass - field**.)

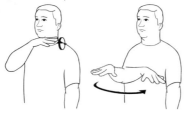

paternal: *adj.* relating to one's father. *My paternal grandparents are Deaf.*

SIGN: Tip of thumb of vertical right **'5'** hand, palm facing leftward, is tapped against the right side of the forehead. The hand, still vertical, then assumes an **'EXTENDED B'** shape with palm forward/leftward, and is firmly pushed forward/leftward a very short distance. (ASL CONCEPT—**father - his side**.) Alternatively, the second part may be fingerspelled **SIDE**.

paternalistic: *adj.* inclined to look after, do things for, and advise as a father would. *Some hearing people are very paternalistic toward Deaf people and are sometimes referred to in articles about the Deaf as 'audists'.*

SIGN: Right **'ONE'** hand is held with tip of forefinger touching right side of forehead while left **'ONE'** hand is held with palm toward the chest and forefinger pointing right. Both wrists then rotate to turn the hands so that the palms are downward and the forefingers point forward. Movement is rapidly repeated a few times.

path: *n.* a trail; road; way. *We followed the path through the woods.*

SIGN: Horizontal **'EXTENDED B'** hands, palms facing each other, are held slightly apart and are simultaneously moved forward in a meandering motion.

patient: *adj.* able to wait or put up with confusion without complaining; tolerant; even-tempered. *I am not telling you what I got you for your birthday; you will just have to be patient.*

SIGN #1: Right **'A'** hand, with thumbnail touching closed lips and palm facing left, is moved slowly down chin.
SAME SIGN—**patience**, *n.*

patient: *n.* a person who is receiving medical care. *He is a patient at the Toronto General Hospital.*

SIGN #2: Fingerspell **PATIENT**.

patronage: *n.* in politics, related to the granting of special favours to friends. *Governments have been known to make appointments on the basis of patronage.*

SIGN #1: Tip of bent midfinger of right **'BENT MIDFINGER 5'** hand, palm toward the body, is tapped lightly against the chin.
REGIONAL VARIATION—**favourite**

patronage: *n.* the support given to a certain company by doing regular business or shopping there. *The manager of the department store sent out a letter thanking customers for their loyal patronage.*

SIGN #2: Vertical left **'ONE'** hand is held in a fixed position with palm forward/rightward while horizontal right **'B'** hand is held just behind the left hand with palm left and fingers pointing forward. The fingertips of the right hand make contact with the left forefinger as the right hand is jabbed toward it several times. (The signer's lips protrude when making this sign.)

patronize: *v.* to go to regularly as a customer. *We* **patronize** *the finest restaurant in Victoria.*

SIGN #1: Vertical left **'ONE'** hand is held in a fixed position with palm forward/rightward while horizontal right **'B'** hand is held just behind the left hand with palm left and fingers pointing forward. The fingertips of the right hand make contact with the left forefinger as the right hand is jabbed toward it several times. (The signer's lips protrude when making this sign.)

OR

SIGN #2: Vertical **'ONE'** hands, palms forward, are staggered so that the right hand is held slightly closer to the chest than the left. The wrists then bend, causing the hands to fall forward so that the palms face downward. Movement is rapidly repeated a few times.

patronize: *v.* to treat in a condescending way. *I hate it when you* **patronize** *people!*

SIGN #3: Fingertips of horizontal right **'EXTENDED B'** hand, palm facing left, brush back and forth a few times against the forefinger of the vertical left **'ONE'** hand which is held with palm forward/rightward. ❖ SAME SIGN—**patronizing**, *adj.*

patterned: *adj.* something that is covered with a pattern or design. *He was wearing a brightly* **patterned** *Hawaiian shirt.*

SIGN: **'CLAWED SPREAD C'** hands, palms toward the body are circled in opposite directions on the chest.

pause: *v.* to stop for a short time. *We will* **pause** *for a few minutes before our next speaker.*

SIGN: **'ONE'** hands, palms down, are held so that the forefingers are crossed at right angles to one another, the right on top of the left. As the forefingers then retract to form **'X'** hands, the forefinger of the right hand hooks around the forefinger of the left hand, lifting it firmly upward.

ALTERNATE SIGN—**stop**

pay: *v.* to give money in return for goods or services. *I* **pay** *$800 a month in rent for my apartment.*

SIGN #1: Tip of forefinger of right **'ONE'** hand, palm down, is brushed forward across the upturned palm of the left **'EXTENDED B'** hand. This is a wrist movement; the right forearm does not move. ❖ (This sign tends to be used in situations involving 'regular' payments.)

OR

SIGN #2: Thumbtip of right **'EXTENDED A'** hand, palm down, is brushed forward across the upturned palm of the left **'EXTENDED B'** hand. ❖

pay: *v.* to give money for something. *I will* **pay** *for your lunch.*

SIGN #3: As the forearm is lowered slightly, the thumb of the horizontal right **'FLAT O'** hand, palm facing left, is slid across the bunched fingers until the handshape becomes an **'A'**. ❖ (This sign tends to be used in situations where payment is considered a 'treat' as opposed to a requirement.)

pay: *v.* to give money as required. *I have to* **pay** *for the broken window.*

SIGN #4: Right **'F'** hand is held with palm down at the right hip. As the forearm moves forward, the thumb and forefinger open to form a **'MODIFIED 5'** hand. (This sign tends to be used in situations where payment is required 'only once or unexpectedly'.)

pay: *v.* to be worthwhile. *It* **pays** *to have your house well insulated.*

SIGN #5: Vertical **'F'** hands are held apart with palms facing forward. The hands are then brought purposefully together.

pay attention [#6]: See **(pay) attention**.

pay (someone) back: *v.* to retaliate; get even. *I will* **pay** *you* **back** *for this.*

SIGN #7: Left **'CLOSED X'** hand is held in a fixed position with palm upward at a slight rightward angle. Right **'CLOSED X'** hand is held closer to the chest and at a higher level than the left hand. Palms are facing each other. The right hand then moves purposefully toward the left hand and strikes it. Facial expression is important. ❖ ALTERNATE SIGN—**get even**

pay cash [*or* **pay in cash**]: *v.* to give actual money rather than give a cheque or use a credit card. *I will pay cash for my new car.*

SIGN #8: Vertical right **'C'** hand, palm forward, slides forward along the upturned palm of the left **'EXTENDED B'** hand. ❖ (This sign is used for large sums of money only. When **CASH** is used in a general sense or to refer to smaller amounts of money, it is fingerspelled.)

pay off: *v.* to pay the complete amount owing. *He will pay off his student loan very soon.*

SIGN #1: Left **'EXTENDED B'** hand is held in a fixed position with palm up and fingers pointing forward/rightward. Tip of middle finger of right **'BENT MIDFINGER 5'** hand touches the middle of the left palm. The right hand is then transformed to an **'EXTENDED B'** hand with palm down and fingers pointing leftward/forward as it moves backward at a leftward angle and then reverses direction, smartly brushing forward/rightward across the left palm all in one decisive movement.

pay off: *v.* to be worthwhile or of benefit. *Do not worry, all our hard work will pay off.*

SIGN #2: Vertical **'F'** hands are held apart with palms facing forward. The hands are then brought purposefully together.

peace: *n.* a state of harmony between groups or nations; tranquillity; quiet; calm; without disturbance. *I believe the first priority of the United Nations should be to work toward world peace.*

SIGN: **'EXTENDED C'** hands are loosely clasped with the right hand on top of the left. The hands are then drawn apart slightly as their positions are reversed, and then they are clasped again. The hands are then opened to form **'EXTENDED B'** hands and are moved apart and downward, so that the palms eventually face downward and the fingers point forward.
SAME SIGN—**peaceful**, *adj.*

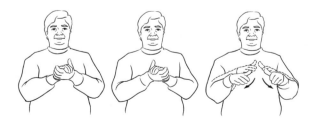

peach: *n.* a fruit with yellow flesh, fuzzy reddish-yellow skin, and an almond-shaped pit in the centre. *If you leave the peach on the counter, it will ripen in a few days.*

SIGN: Right **'CONTRACTED 5'** hand, palm toward the face, is positioned with fingertips on the right cheek. The fingers then close to form a **'FLAT O'** hand. Movement is repeated so that the hand alternates between a **'CONTRACTED 5'** and **'FLAT O'** shape. (Signs vary.)

peak: *n.* the point of greatest development or strength. *He is now at the peak of his career as a politician.*

SIGN #1: Left **'EXTENDED B'** hand is held in a semi-vertical position with palm facing right at a downward angle. Right **'EXTENDED B'** hand is held at a higher level in a semi-vertical position with palm facing left at a downward angle. The right forearm then moves downward so that the hand firmly strikes the fingertips of the left hand.

peak: *adj.* pertaining to the highest point of use or demand. *Bus fare is higher during peak hours.*

SIGN #2: Wrist of vertical right **'B'** hand, palm facing forward/leftward, is brushed back and forth against wrist of left **'STANDARD BASE'** hand.

peanut: *n.* the edible, nutlike seed of a leguminous plant. *Take the shell off the peanut before you eat it.*

SIGN: Thumb of right **'EXTENDED A'** hand, palm facing left, wiggles against the upper front teeth.

pear: *n.* a sweet, juicy, gritty-textured fruit that has a roundish base, is tapered toward the top and contains seeds much like those of an apple. *I think I will stop at the fruit stand and buy some pears.*

SIGN: Fingers of right **'CONTRACTED 5'** hand, palm facing left, are closed over the bunched fingers of the left **'FLAT O'** hand of which the palm is facing right. Then the right hand is drawn away as it forms a **'FLAT O'** hand. Movement is repeated. (**PEAR** is frequently fingerspelled.)

peas: *n.* vegetables in the form of small, round, green seeds that grow in pods on climbing vines. *Peas are my favourite vegetable.*

SIGN: Fingerspell **PEAS**.

peck: *v.* to strike with a beak or a pointed instrument. *Birds peck at seeds and insects.*

SIGN: Thumb and forefinger of right **'CLOSED X'** hand, palm forward, are used to peck repeatedly against upright forefinger of left **'ONE'** hand. ❖

peculiar: *adj.* strange; odd; unusual. *Some people have peculiar tastes.*

SIGN: Vertical right **'C'** hand, palm facing left, is held near the face and is abruptly dropped downward from the wrist so the palm faces down.

pedal: *n.* a foot-operated lever. *He asked the mechanic to check the gas pedal.*

SIGN #1: Right **'EXTENDED B'** hand is held with palm forward/downward. The wrist then bends to lower the hand to a palm down position to simulate the foot movement on the pedal of a car or machine. Motion is repeated. (For **brake pedal**, the right **'A'** hand, palm forward/downward, is moved slightly but firmly forward/downward a couple of times while the wrist remains rigid.)

pedal: *v.* to propel a cycle by operating the pedals. *The boy is learning to pedal his tricycle.*

SIGN #2: **'S'** hands are held palms down, and moved forward alternately in small circles to simulate the pedaling of a bicycle.

pedestrian: *n.* a person who is walking rather than riding in a vehicle. *Watch out for pedestrians!*

SIGN: Right **'BENT EXTENDED V'** hand is held palm down with fingers pointing downward and fluttering to simulate two legs walking as the arm moves from right to left in front of the chest. (Alternatively, vertical right **'ONE'** hand, palm facing left, is moved from right to left in front of the chest.) The location and direction of movement vary according to the actual location of the pedestrian and the direction in which she/he is walking.

pediatrician: *n.* a physician who specializes in the treatment of children. *The pediatrician detected the infant's deafness shortly after her birth.*

SIGN: Fingertips of palm-down right **'SPREAD EXTENDED C'** (or **'BENT EXTENDED B'** or **'FLAT M'**) hand are tapped a couple of times against the inside of the left wrist. Then right **'B'** hand, palm facing left and fingers pointing forward, slides along top of left **'B'** hand, of which the palm faces right and the fingers point forward. (Alternatively, the forefinger of the right **'ONE'** hand slides along the forefinger of the left **'ONE'** hand.) Next, right **'EXTENDED B'** hand is held palm down with fingers pointing forward. The hand then moves rightward in a couple of small arcs. (ASL CONCEPT—**doctor - specialize - children**.)

pee: *v.* an informal term meaning to urinate (used for humans). *I hope the movie is over soon because I have to pee.*

SIGN #1: Right **'A'** hand, with thumbnail on chin and palm facing left, is stroked downward twice. (This sign is used to refer to *women and girls only*.) Signs vary.

pee *(cont.)*

OR

SIGN #2: Right **'K'** hand, palm down at a slightly forward angle is held out in front of the body and is then tipped down from the wrist so that palm faces fully downward. (This sign is used to refer to *men and boys only*.)

OR

SIGN #3: Tip of middle finger of right **'K'** hand is used to touch the tip of the nose. (This sign is used to refer to *men and boys only*.)

pee: *v.* an informal term meaning to urinate (used for animals). *My dog likes to pee on every fire hydrant.*

SIGN #4: Left **'X'** hand is held palm down in front of the left side of the chest while the right elbow is raised so that the palm of the horizontal right **'X'** hand faces rightward. The hands are held motionless some distance apart to represent the legs of a *male dog* urinating. (If the *dog* is *female*, **'X'** hands are held parallel with palms down.) Sign choice with reference to other animals varies.

peek: *v.* to take a quick or furtive look at something. *If you peek around the corner, you will see something interesting.*

SIGN: Vertical left **'EXTENDED B'** hand is held in a fixed position with palm facing backward/rightward. Vertical right **'S'** hand, palm leftward/forward, represents a person's head as it is positioned against the left palm. The right wrist then rotates in a counter-clockwise direction to move the hand forward so that it is no longer hidden by the left hand. The right hand then returns to its original position. (The positioning and movement of the hands may vary. To indicate that someone is 'peeking *over*' something the left hand is held in a horizontal position with palm down while the right hand, held behind the left, is raised from a level below that of the left hand to a position above it.)

peel: *v.* to remove the skin, rind or shell of a fruit, vegetable, or egg, specifically with a knife. *The cook will peel the potatoes for dinner.*

SIGN #1: Left **'CROOKED SLANTED 5'** hand is held in a fixed position with palm up. Right **'CLAWED L'** hand is held palm-down just above the left hand but a little further forward. Right hand then moves toward the body and the motion is repeated to simulate the peeling of something such as an apple or potato.

peel: *v.* to remove the skin, rind or shell of a fruit, vegetable, or egg, specifically by hand. *I will peel the orange for you.*

SIGN #2: Horizontal left **'A'** hand is held with palm facing right while horizontal right **'EXTENDED A'** hand is held palm down beside and slightly above the left hand. The right wrist then rotates forward a couple of times to turn the palm to face the chest. Handshapes vary depending on the type of fruit being peeled. For a banana, the left hand assumes a **'ONE'** shape.

peel: *v.* to come off in flakes; shed (skin). *You have a very bad sunburn and your skin will probably peel.*

SIGN #3: Right **'V'** hand, palm down and extended fingers pointing leftward, is held against upper left arm and twisted forward from the wrist a couple of times so that the palm alternately faces downward and backward toward the arm. (The location of this sign varies according to context.)

peer: *n.* a person of equal status or age. *A teenager can often relate better to a peer than an adult.*

SIGN #1: Fingerspell **PEER**.

peer: *v.* to look intently as if trying to see more clearly. *We peered over the fence to see what they were doing.*

SIGN #2: Right **'BENT V'** hand, palm forward, is held at shoulder level or above and is moved forward a short distance. A look of intense concentration accompanies this sign. ❖

peeved: *adj.* irritated; annoyed. *The movie star was **peeved** when rumours about his private life appeared in the newspapers.*

SIGN: Vertical right **'BENT MIDFINGER 5'** hand is held with palm left and tip of middle finger touching forehead. The wrist then rotates to turn the palm toward the face. Facial expression must clearly convey 'annoyance'. (This sign is used only in a passive voice situation or as an adjective to describe someone's feelings. It would *not* be possible to use this sign in an active voice situation such as: *The rumours in the newspapers about the movie star's private life **peeved** him.*)

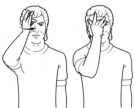

pen: *n.* an implement for writing or drawing with ink. *I prefer writing with a fine-point **pen.***

SIGN: Fingerspell **PEN**.

penalize: *v.* to impose a penalty on someone for breaking a rule or law. *The hockey player was **penalized** for roughing.*

SIGN: Forefinger of right **'ONE'** hand, palm down, is used to strike downward across the bent elbow of the left arm.
SAME SIGN—**penalty**, *n.*

pencil: *n.* a rod-shaped instrument made of wood with a graphite centre, sharpened for the purpose of writing or drawing. *The rough draft may be written in **pencil.***

SIGN #1: Right **'CLOSED X'** hand is held with joined tips of thumb and forefinger touching the mouth. The hand is then lowered and turned palm downward as it glides forward/ rightward along the upturned palm of the left **'EXTENDED B'** hand. (**PENCIL** is frequently fingerspelled.)

SIGN #2 [ONTARIO]: Horizontal left **'K'** hand is held in a fixed position in front of the left side of the chest with palm facing right while right **'K'** hand is held with tip of middle finger touching the mouth. The right hand is then lowered, the wrist twisting and the tip of the middle finger striking the tip of the middle finger on the left hand.

pending: *prep.* while waiting for. *The police will not release the names of the accident victims **pending** notification of next-of-kin.*

SIGN: **'BENT EXTENDED B'** hands are held apart with palms up and the right hand slightly ahead of the left while fingers simultaneously move back and forth. Motion may be repeated.
REGIONAL VARIATION—**wait** #2
Sign choices must be made on the basis of context.

penetrate: *v.* to enter into with force; pierce. *The bullet **penetrated** the wooden wall.*

SIGN: Extended forefinger of right **'ONE'** hand, palm facing left, is forcefully thrust forward between the forefinger and middle finger of the left **'5'** hand which is held with palm toward the body.
SAME SIGN—**penetration**, *n.,* in this context.

penguin: *n.* a flightless bird of the southern hemisphere, especially Antarctic regions. *Penguins are black and white birds with webbed feet and flippers instead of wings.*

SIGN: **'EXTENDED B'** hands are held at about waist level with palms down and are alternately moved up and down while the head and torso are bobbed from side to side.

penicillin: *n.* an antibiotic that is used to treat certain diseases. *The nurse gave him a series of shots of **penicillin** to combat pneumonia.*

SIGN: Fingerspell **PENICILLIN**.

penis: *n.* the male organ used for urination and sexual intercourse. *The **penis** is the external sexual organ in a male mammal.*

SIGN: Tip of middle finger of vertical right **'K'** hand, palm toward the body, taps the tip of the nose a couple of times. (**PENIS** may be fingerspelled.)

penitentiary: *n.* a prison for people who have committed serious crimes. *Hardened criminals are often sent to a **penitentiary**.*

SIGN: **'4'** (or **'5'**) hands are held with palms facing the body. Back of right hand, whose fingers point slightly upward to the left, is positioned behind palm of left hand at right angles, and is thrust against it.

penny: *n.* a bronze or copper coin worth 1/100 of a dollar. *The children collected pennies for UNICEF on Hallowe'en.*

SIGN: Vertical right **'ONE'** hand is held with palm toward the face as the tip of the forefinger strokes backward a couple of times on the right side of the forehead just above the temple.

pension: *n.* a regular payment made by government or former employer to certain persons or retired employees. *She is eligible to receive a widow's pension.*

SIGN: Right **'A-INDEX'** hand is held at an angle with palm facing partially upward and partially toward the body. The forearm is then brought smartly downward toward the body, with the hand taking on a **'CLOSED A-INDEX'** shape as the thumb and forefinger are retracted. Motion is repeated.

people: *n.* persons; human beings. *Deaf people share a unique culture.*

SIGN: Vertical **'K'** hands are held apart with palms forward but facing each other slightly, and are alternately circled backward.

pep: See **energy**.

pepper: *n.* a condiment having a sharp, hot, pungent taste. *Salt and pepper are used to season food.*

SIGN: Right **'F'** hand, palm forward, is shaken downward/leftward several times as if sprinkling pepper on food.

perceive: *v.* to recognize, observe, or become aware of something through the senses. *We soon perceived that there was a problem.*

SIGN: Tip of forefinger of right **'CROOKED ONE'** hand is positioned at corner of right eye and brought down to rest on upturned palm of left **'EXTENDED B'** hand.

percent: *n.* a number of parts out of 100. (The symbol % is used to show percentage.) *She graduated from college with an average of 90 percent.*

SIGN: Vertical right **'O'** hand, palm forward/leftward, moves rightward and then downward at a slight leftward angle as if tracing the number '7' in the air.

perception: *n.* an awareness created through one's senses, especially the sense of sight. *He explained his perception of the current economic situation.*

SIGN: Tip of middle finger of right **'BENT V'** hand, palm toward the body, is held near the right eye. Then the hand is twisted clockwise from the wrist so that palm faces forward and extended fingers point at forefinger of vertical left **'ONE'** hand, whose palm faces rightward.

perch: *v.* to rest on something above ground. *The bird perched on the branch of the tree.*

SIGN: Left **'ONE'** hand is held palm down with forefinger pointing forward/rightward while the right **'CLAWED V'** hand is held palm down with the tips of the clawed fingers resting on the left forefinger. (The location of this sign may vary though the shape of the right hand is likely to remain constant.)

perennial: *adj.* lasting throughout the year or for several years. *I think I will plant some perennial flowers at the side of the house.*

SIGN: Horizontal right **'S'** hand, palm facing left, is placed on top of horizontal left **'S'** hand whose palm faces right. Right forefinger is then flicked forward twice.
REGIONAL VARIATION—**annual** #2

perfect: *adj.* correct; precise; having no defects; excellent in every way. *The weather was perfect during our vacation.*

SIGN: Right **'F'** hand is held above and slightly to the right of the left **'F'** hand with palms facing. The hands then come together so that the joined thumb and forefinger of one hand strikes those of the other hand. (Alternatively, this sign may be made with **'K'** hands, the tips of the middle fingers coming together.)
SAME SIGN—**perfection**, *n.*

perform: *v.* to present a drama. *Our class will perform a skit after the banquet.*

SIGN: **'EXTENDED A'** hands, palms facing each other, are rotated alternately in small circles which are brought down against the chest.
SAME SIGN—**performance**, *n.*
In contexts where **perform** means to 'carry out an action', the concept is incorporated with other signs in the ASL sentence. In English: *The doctor will perform surgery soon.* In ASL: *DOCTOR OPERATE WILL SOON.*

perfume: *n.* a fragrance; pleasant scent. *Her fiance gave her a bottle of expensive perfume for Christmas.*

SIGN: Tip of forefinger of right **'ONE'** hand touches first the left side of the neck, then the right side. (Handshapes for this sign may vary.)

perhaps: *adv.* possibly; maybe. *Perhaps I will go shopping with you.*

SIGN: **'EXTENDED B'** hands, held apart with palms up and fingers pointing forward, are alternately raised and lowered at least twice.

peril: *n.* exposure to harm or danger; risk. *We must face the peril of being attacked by sharks if we swim in this area.*

SIGN: Left **'A'** hand is held in a fixed position with palm facing downward but slanted toward the chest. Right **'A'** hand is held just in front of the left hand with palm facing left and is circled forward a couple of times so that the thumb firmly brushes upward against the back of the left hand with each revolution.
SAME SIGN—**perilous**, *adj.*
REGIONAL VARIATION—**danger**

period: *n.* an interval of time. *The bus fare is $1.50 during the peak period.*

SIGN #1: Tip of forefinger of right **'CROOKED ONE'** hand, palm facing downward, is tapped on the back of the wrist of the left **'STANDARD BASE'** hand. Then vertical **'EXTENDED B'** hands are held apart with palms facing each other and are given a short but firm thrust forward. (ASL CONCEPT—**time - between (time)**.) Sign choice depends on context.

period: *n.* an occurrence of menstruation. *Her menstrual period usually lasts four or five days.*

SIGN #2: Vertical right **'A'** hand, palm toward the face, is tapped lightly against the right cheek twice.

period: *n.* a punctuation mark found at the end of a sentence. *Most declarative sentences end with a period.*

SIGN #3: Vertical right **'CLOSED X'** hand, palm facing forward, is firmly thrust forward a short distance as if putting a period on a vertical surface.

period: *inter.* an exclamation used for emphasis. *I do not trust you, period!*

SIGN #4: Vertical right **'CLOSED X'** hand is brought toward the mouth so that the tips of the joined thumb and forefinger touch the lips. The wrist then rotates to turn the hand palm-forward as it is vehemently thrust forward a short distance as if putting a period on a vertical surface. Facial expression is important.

periodical: *n.* a journal or newspaper, often academic, which deals with a specific subject and is published regularly. *Her article will appear in the periodical American Annals of the Deaf.*

SIGN: Thumb and forefinger of right **'A-INDEX'** (or **'MODIFIED G'**) hand are slid up the edge of the left **'EXTENDED B'** hand, which is held with palm facing body. Motion is repeated.

periodontist: *n.* a dentist with special qualifications to treat gum disease. *I have an appointment with a periodontist who will perform a gum graft.*

SIGN: Fingertips of palm-down right **'SPREAD EXTENDED C'** (or **'BENT EXTENDED B'** or **'FLAT M'**) hand are tapped a couple of times against the inside of the left wrist. Then right **'B'** hand, palm facing left and fingers pointing forward, slides along top of left **'B'** hand, of which the palm faces right and the fingers point forward. (Alternatively, the forefinger of the right **'ONE'** hand slides along the forefinger of the left **'ONE'** hand.) Next, the tip of the forefinger of the right **'CROOKED ONE'** hand slides along the upper gum from left to right. (ASL CONCEPT—**doctor - specialize - gum**.)

perish: *v.* to die in an untimely or violent manner. *Without food and water, they will perish quickly in the desert.*

SIGN: Right **'EXTENDED B'** hand is held palm down with fingers pointing forward. The wrist then rotates rightward, turning the hand palm upward.

perishable: *adj.* able to spoil or rot. *Fruit and vegetables are perishable so they can not be stored for very long.*

SIGN: **'A'** hands, palms down, are held slightly apart, and are then firmly pushed a very short distance downward. Next, left **'EXTENDED B'** hand is held in a fixed position with palm up and fingers pointing forward/rightward. Horizontal right **'I'** hand, palm facing the body at a slight leftward angle, is placed firmly on the left palm and slid forward/rightward along the left hand.
(ASL CONCEPT—**can - spoil**.)

permanent: *adj.* intended to continue to exist; not temporary. *She was lucky to find a permanent job.*

SIGN #1: **'EXTENDED A'** hands are held side by side with palms down and right thumbtip pressing against left thumbnail as the hands are moved purposefully forward.
SAME SIGN—**permanence**, *n.*

permanent: *n.* a hair treatment that produces long-lasting waves or curls. *My hair requires a permanent every three months.*

SIGN #2: Vertical **'S'** hands, palms forward, are held close to the temples and the fingers are repeatedly opened slightly and closed, the hands alternating between being tightly and loosely held fists as they move simultaneously toward the back of the head. (**Permanent** is frequently fingerspelled in the abbreviated form **PERM**.)

permit: *v.* to allow. *My mother permits me to sleep in as long as I want on weekends.*

SIGN #1: **'K'** hands, palms down, are held apart, extended fingers pointing downward, and are then flicked upward from the wrists so that the hands are held in either a horizontal or upright position.
SAME SIGN—**permission**, *n.*

permit: *n.* a document which gives permission to do something; licence. *He obtained a permit to build his house.*

SIGN #2: **'L'** hands, palms forward, are tapped together a couple of times so that the thumb-tips touch.

perpetual: *adj.* lasting forever or for a long time; eternal; continuous. *We seem to have a perpetual problem with mice.*

SIGN: **'EXTENDED A'** hands are held side by side with palms down and right thumbtip pressing against left thumbnail as the hands are circled forward a few times.

perplexed: *adj.* puzzled; bewildered. *He is perplexed by the judge's decision.*

SIGN: Back of the right **'ONE'** hand, palm forward and forefinger pointing upward, is placed just in front of the middle of the forehead and is drawn backward while the forefinger is crooked to form an **'X'** handshape. A look of 'bewilderment' accompanies this sign. (This sign is used only in a passive voice situation or as an adjective to describe someone's feelings. It would *not* be possible to use this sign in an active voice situation such as: *The judge's decision perplexes him.*)

persecute: *v.* to oppress, harass or mistreat persistently. *Sometimes people persecute those of a different race or religion.*

SIGN: Thumb and forefinger of right **'CLOSED X'** hand, palm forward, are used to peck repeatedly against upright forefinger of left **'ONE'** hand. ❖
SAME SIGN—**persecution**, *n.*

persevere: *v.* to continue with determination in a course of action and not give up. *They will persevere in their fight for freedom.*

SIGN: **'EXTENDED A'** hands are held side by side with palms down and right thumbtip pressing against left thumbnail as the hands are moved purposefully forward. Next, thumb of vertical right **'EXTENDED B'** hand, palm forward, is placed near the right temple and the fingers are firmly lowered to form a **'BENT EXTENDED B'** hand. A look of determination accompanies this sign. (ASL CONCEPT—**continue - stubborn**.)

persist: *v.* to continue without stopping; go on with determination despite opposition. *If your headache persists, you had better see your doctor.*

SIGN: **'EXTENDED A'** hands are held side by side with palms down and right thumbtip pressing against left thumbnail as the hands are moved purposefully forward.

person: *n.* a human being. *He is the only Deaf person that you have met.*

SIGN: **'K'** hands are held parallel at about shoulder level with palms down and are simultaneously lowered. (Alternatively, **'B'** hands are held parallel with palms facing each other and fingers pointing forward and are simultaneously lowered.)

personal: *adj.* relating to a person's private affairs. *This matter is too personal to discuss in public.*

SIGN #1: Right **'A'** hand is brought to the lips with the thumb pointed upward and the palm facing left. Then the lips are touched twice with the thumbnail.

personal: *adj.* belonging exclusively to one person and to no one else; relating to the body or physical appearance. *This telephone is here for my personal use.*

SIGN #2: Right **'EXTENDED B'** hand is held with palm firmly against the chest. (Signs in this context vary according to the person(s) to whom the signer is referring.) For possessive pronouns, see PRONOUNS, p. LXVI.

personality: *n.* the characteristics by which an individual is recognized as unique. *She has a very charming personality.*

SIGN: Right **'K'** hand, palm down, is held in front of the left shoulder. After being circled clockwise (from the onlooker's perspective), it is placed against the upper left side of the chest.

perspective: *n.* a way of looking at situations or facts; point of view. *I would like to hear your perspective on the new legislation being proposed by the government.*

SIGN: Tip of middle finger of right **'BENT V'** hand, palm toward the body, is held near the right eye. Then the hand is twisted clockwise from the wrist so that palm faces forward and extended fingers point at forefinger of vertical left **'ONE'** hand, whose palm faces rightward. (Sign choice must be made on the basis of context.)

perspire: *v.* to secrete sweat through the pores of one's skin. *People often perspire when they work or exercise vigorously.*

SIGN: **'SPREAD EXTENDED C'** hands, palms down, are held against either side of the face at about cheekbone level and are slowly and deliberately lowered. Teeth are visibly closed to show exertion.
SAME SIGN—**perspiration**, *n.*

persuade: *v.* to urge; try to convince. *I am trying to persuade my father to buy me a new car.*

SIGN: Horizontal **'X'** hands, are held apart with palms facing each other and the right hand slightly ahead of the left hand. The hands are then simultaneously moved forward and back at least twice with short deliberate movements as though prodding a reluctant individual. ❖
SAME SIGN—**persuasion**, *n.*

pertain to: *v.* to relate to; be associated with. *The explanation pertains to both English and ASL.*

SIGN: Thumbs and forefingers of both **'F'** hands interlock and are moved toward the person, place or thing to whom the situation pertains. Generally, the movement is forward from the chest. ❖

pessimistic: *adj.* having a tendency to be gloomy and expect the worst in everything. *She is so **pessimistic** that she makes us all feel depressed.*

SIGN: Edge of extended forefinger of right horizontal **'BENT ONE'** hand, palm down, is tapped against forward/rightward-facing palm of vertical left **'EXTENDED B'** hand several times. This is a circular motion in a counter-clockwise direction. Facial expression is important.
SAME SIGN—**pessimism**, *n.*

pest: *n.* a person or thing that annoys; nuisance. *She is such a **pest**; she phones me every evening!*

SIGN: Vertical right **'BENT MIDFINGER 5'** hand is held with palm left and tip of middle finger touching forehead. The wrist then rotates to turn the palm toward the face. Facial expression must clearly convey 'annoyance'.

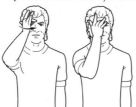

pester: *v.* to annoy; bother. *If you continue to **pester** him, he will never get his work done.*

SIGN: Right **'EXTENDED B'** hand, palm facing slightly left, is positioned above and at right angles to left **'EXTENDED B'** hand which faces slightly right. Then the right hand is brought down sharply between the thumb and forefinger of the left hand. Motion is repeated. ❖

pet: *v.* to stroke; pat gently. *The cat always purrs when someone **pets** her.*

SIGN: **'EXTENDED B'** hands, palms down, are positioned so that the right is held above and at right angles to the left and is stroked backward a couple of times along the back of the left hand. (**PET**, *n.,* is always fingerspelled.)

petition: *n.* a document signed by many people asking the government or another official body to bring about specific changes. *They presented a **petition** asking for a revision to the Labour Act.*

SIGN: Left **'EXTENDED B'** hand is held aloft with the palm toward the face at a rightward angle and the fingers pointing rightward/upward at a slight forward angle. Tips of extended fingers of right **'U'** hand, palm forward/leftward, are used to tap repeatedly against the left palm as the two hands are simultaneously lowered. (The tapping represents the actual listing of signatures on the document.) For **petition**, *v.,* see **propose**.

petty: *adj.* trivial; relatively unimportant. *I do not want to waste my time talking about **petty** things like that!*

SIGN: Horizontal left **'F'** hand is held in a fixed position with palm facing right. Horizontal right **'F'** hand is held slightly above the left hand with palm facing the body at a leftward angle. As the right wrist then rotates in a counter-clockwise direction, the joined thumb and forefinger strike the joined thumb and forefinger of the left hand on the way past. The right palm eventually faces downward.
ALTERNATE SIGN—**nothing** #2

petty cash: *n.* money that is kept aside from larger cash assets and is used to pay for small items that cost very little. *She took the money out of **petty cash** to buy a gift for the office manager who was in the hospital.*

SIGN: Fingerspell **PETTY CASH**.

pharmacy: *n.* a store where medicinal drugs are sold. *I took the doctor's prescription to the nearest pharmacy to be filled.*

SIGN: Tip of middle finger of right **'BENT MIDFINGER 5'** hand is placed on the upturned left palm, and maintains contact with the left palm as the right hand teeters back and forth a few times. Next, **'FLAT O'** hands, held parallel with palms down and fingers pointing down, are swung forward/upward from the wrists a couple of times. (ASL CONCEPT— **medicine - store**.)

phase: *n.* a distinct stage of development. *We are working on the last phase of the project now.*

SIGN #1: Horizontal left **'EXTENDED B'** hand is held in a fixed position with palm up but angled toward the body and fingers pointing rightward/forward while edge of horizontal right **'EXTENDED B'** hand, palm facing left, is placed on left palm and is drawn back toward the body.

phase: *n.* a noticeable change. *Some people think that the phases of the moon have an affect on people's behaviour.*

SIGN #2: **'X'** hands, palms facing, are twisted 180 degrees.

phase in: *v.* to introduce something new very gradually. *Modern farmers are beginning to phase in computer technology to improve agricultural methods.*

SIGN: Left **'5'** hand is held with palm facing right while forefinger of right **'ONE'** hand is inserted between first two fingers of left hand and twisted 180 degrees either to the right or left as the hands move very slowly forward.

phase out: *v.* to gradually withdraw something from use. *The federal government phased out the Family Allowance program.*

SIGN: **'FLAT O'** hands are held parallel with palms up and slanted slightly toward the body. As the hands are drawn apart the thumbs slide across the fingertips, causing the hands to assume **'A'** shapes.

philosophy: *n.* a personal outlook; viewpoint. *His philosophy is that if he is kind to others, they will be kind to him in return.*

SIGN: Right **'K'** hand, palm down, is held in front of the forehead and is repeatedly moves up and down from the wrist.
SAME SIGN—**philosophical**, *adj.*

phobia: *n.* a long-term, excessive, irrational fear that is often strong enough to restrict a person's life. *I have a phobia of snakes.*

SIGN: Horizontal **'5'** hands, palms toward the body, are held out from either side of the chest, and are moved vigorously toward each other, stopping abruptly in front of the chest. Facial expression is important.

phone: *v.* to call by telephone. *I will phone you when I have the information you need.*

SIGN #1: Forefinger of right **'X'** hand, palm facing leftward/forward, is moved in a straight line forward/rightward along the forefinger of the left palm-down **'ONE'** hand and beyond. ❖

OR

SIGN #2: Right **'Y'** hand, palm facing forward/leftward, is held upright near right side of face with thumb pointing to the area just to the right of the chin. Then the forearm is moved forward/rightward. ❖

phone: *n.* an abbreviation for telephone. *My phone does not seem to be working.*

SIGN #3: Right **'Y'** hand, with tip of little finger at the mouth and tip of thumb at the right ear, is tapped against the right jawline a couple of times.

phoney [also spelled **phony**]: *adj.* fake; not genuine. *He gave her a **phoney** diamond ring.*

SIGN: Side of forefinger of right **'ONE'** hand, palm facing leftward/forward, is lightly brushed forward/downward twice on the right cheek, forefinger either remaining upright or bending slightly to become a **'BENT ONE'**.

photocopy: *v.* to reproduce written, printed or graphic material by using a photocopier. *He asked the office clerk to **photocopy** all the documents related to the case.*

SIGN: Left **'EXTENDED B'** hand is held in a fixed position with palm down and fingers pointing forward/rightward while right **'CONTRACTED 5'** hand is held palm up with fingers touching left palm. The right hand is then drawn downward as it closes to form a **'FLAT O'** hand.

photograph: *n.* an image recorded by a camera. *This is our most recent family **photograph**.*

SIGN #1: Left **'EXTENDED B'** hand is held in a fixed position with palm facing right and fingers pointing forward/upward as vertical right **'C'** hand is held against the right cheek with palm forward at a slight leftward angle. Right hand is then moved forward/downward and placed firmly against the left palm.

OR

SIGN #2: Vertical right **'X'** hand is held with palm facing left and is moved downward a couple of times as the side of the crooked forefinger strokes the nose.

photograph: *v.* to take a picture with a camera. *A professional **photographed** her wedding.*

SIGN #3: Vertical **'CROOKED L'** (or **'C-INDEX'**) hands are held so as to frame the eyes with a thumb touching either side of face, and palms facing each other, but angled forward slightly. The forefinger of the right hand then makes small up and down movements as if clicking a camera.

OR

SIGN #4: Vertical left **'5'** hand is held in a fixed position with palm facing forward/rightward. Right **'CONTRACTED C'** hand is held against the left palm with palm forward/leftward and is opened and closed a couple of times, thus alternating between **'CONTRACTED C'** and **'FLAT O'** shapes.

phrase: *n.* a group of words that does not constitute a whole sentence. *The students were instructed to find an adverbial **phrase** in the paragraph.*

SIGN: Horizontal **'F'** hands are held with palms facing and joined tips of thumbs and forefingers touching. The hands are then drawn apart a short distance. (**PHRASE** may be fingerspelled.)

physical: *adj.* relating to the body. *He had a demanding **physical** job.*

SIGN: Horizontal **'BENT EXTENDED B'** hands are held apart with fingertips touching either side of upper chest. The hands are then simultaneously drawn forward slightly and downward in an arc formation, re-establishing contact with the body at a somewhat lower level.

physician: *n.* a doctor of medicine. *I go to my **physician** for annual checkups.*

SIGN: Fingertips of palm-down right **'SPREAD EXTENDED C'** (or **'BENT EXTENDED B'** or **'FLAT M'**) hand are tapped a couple of times against the inside of the left wrist. (**Doctor** is frequently fingerspelled in the abbreviated form **DR.**)

physics: *n.* a science involving interactions between matter and energy. *I studied **physics** in high school.*

SIGN: Crooked forefingers of horizontal **'CROOKED V'** hands, palms facing body, are tapped together at least twice.

piano: *n.* a musical instrument with keys which, when pressed, cause hammerlike devices to strike strings. *Although Beethoven was Deaf, he played the **piano** and composed music.*

SIGN: **'CROOKED 5'** hands, palms down, are held slightly apart and are simultaneously moved from side to side with the fingers wiggling to simulate the rapid depressing of piano keys.

pick: *v.* to choose; select. *You may **pick** the wallpaper for the living room.*

SIGN: Right **'FLAT OPEN F'** hand, palm forward, is drawn back toward the chest as it changes to an **'F'** hand. ❖

pick on: *v.* to persecute; tease. *Bullies usually pick on those who are weaker than they.*

SIGN: Thumb and forefinger of right **'CLOSED X'** hand, palm forward, are used to peck repeatedly against upright forefinger of left **'ONE'** hand. ❖

pick out: *v.* to select. *I picked out the best answer from the multiple choices.*

SIGN: Right **'FLAT OPEN F'** hand, palm forward, is drawn back toward the chest as it changes to an **'F'** hand. ❖

pick up: *v.* to stop to collect a passenger. *I picked up my friend and we went to the movie.*

SIGN #1: Fingers of the right **'CONTRACTED 5'** hand, palm down, are closed to form an **'S'** handshape as the hand is drawn upward.

pick up: *v.* to lift (something) up. *Please pick up that paper clip.*

SIGN #2: Right **'OPEN F'** hand is held palm down and is quickly raised (mainly from the wrist) as the thumb and forefinger close to form an **'F'** hand. (This sign is used for the picking up of *small objects*. To refer to the picking up of *larger objects*, see **pick up** #1.)

picket: *v.* to protest outside a place of business as part of a strike or demonstration. *The workers will picket the factory during the strike.*

SIGN: Horizontal **'S'** hands, palms toward the chest, are held so the right is resting on the left. Then they are moved back and forth at least twice. This sign is made purposefully along with a look of determination.

pickle: *n.* a vegetable, especially a cucumber, preserved in vinegar or brine. *I would like a dill pickle with my sandwich.*

SIGN: Fingerspell **PICKLE**.

picky: See **fussy**.

picnic: *n.* an excursion on which people bring food to be eaten outdoors. *Let us have a picnic in the park this afternoon.*

SIGN #1: **'BENT EXTENDED B'** hands are placed together, right on top of left, palms facing backwards and fingertips near the mouth. Then they are simultaneously moved back and forth slightly a few times.

OR

SIGN #2: **'EXTENDED B'** hands are held with palms together and fingertips near the mouth and pointing upward and slightly leftward. Together, the hands are moved from side to side slightly a few times. (Signs vary. Alternatively, **PICNIC** is frequently fingerspelled.)

picture: *n.* a visual representation of something made by drawing, painting or photographing. *The teacher asked me to draw a picture of my family.*

SIGN #1: Left **'EXTENDED B'** hand is held in a fixed position with palm facing right and fingers pointing forward/upward as vertical right **'C'** hand is held against the right cheek with palm forward at a slight leftward angle. Right hand is then moved forward/downward and placed firmly against the left palm.

OR

SIGN #2: Vertical right **'X'** hand is held with palm facing left and is moved downward a couple of times as the side of the crooked forefinger strokes the nose.

pidgin: *n.* a simple language created by combining basic elements from two other languages. *Communicating in a pidgin using ASL signs and English syntax can be confusing to native speakers of each language.*

SIGN: Fingerspell **PIDGIN**.

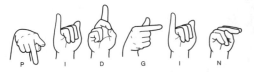

pie: *n.* a sweet or savory filling baked in a pastry crust. *My favourite dessert is lemon meringue pie.*

SIGN: Edge of the horizontal right **'EXTENDED B'** hand, palm facing left, is angled across the upturned left palm twice to indicate the shape of a wedge, the hand being drawn toward the chest with each movement.

piece: *n.* a portion forming part of a whole. *I like a piece of cheese for a snack.*

SIGN: Horizontal left **'EXTENDED B'** hand is held in a fixed position with palm up but angled toward the body and fingers pointing rightward/forward while edge of horizontal right **'EXTENDED B'** hand, palm facing left, is placed on left palm and is drawn back toward the body.

pierced: *adj.* having been thrust into with force, thus creating a hole. *He has one pierced ear.*

SIGN: Vertical right **'CROOKED ONE'** hand, palm facing backward, is held so that the tip of the forefinger is just in front of the right ear. The hand is then moved backward so that the tip of the forefinger taps the ear lobe. (Signs vary depending mainly on the location of the object of the piercing, but the sign generally involves the poking of the right forefinger into the relevant body part. For contexts in which things other than body parts are being pierced, see **penetrate**.)

pig: *n.* a domestic hog. *Her uncle raises pigs on his farm.*

SIGN #1: Right **'BENT EXTENDED B'** hand, palm left, is positioned with fingers under the chin. The fingers then flap up and down a few times.

SIGN #2 [ATLANTIC]: Right **'ONE'** hand is held with tip of forefinger touching the right side of the nose. The hand is then twisted back and forth several times from the wrist.

SIGN #3 [ONTARIO]: Vertical right **'S'** hand, palm facing left, is placed at the end of the nose and the fingers are repeatedly opened slightly and closed so that the hand alternates between being a tightly and loosely held fist.

(make a) pig of oneself: *v.* to eat greedily. *I always make a pig of myself at buffets.*

SIGN #4: Right **'B'** (or **'BENT EXTENDED B'**) hand is positioned palm down with fingers under the chin. The fingers then bend firmly downward while the signer's lips are squared as if articulating 'CH'.

---

pig-headed: See **stubborn**.

pigeon: *n.* a bird with a prominent chest that makes a cooing sound. *We often feed the pigeons in the park.*

SIGN #1 [ONTARIO]: Horizontal right **'C'** hand is held with palm facing the throat as the fingers are flexed and relaxed a couple of times.

SIGN #2 [PRAIRIE]: Tip of forefinger of right **'ONE'** hand, palm down, is placed on the right side of the neck and the hand is twisted back and forth from the wrist.

pile: *n.* a collection of items in a heap. *There was a pile of leaves on the ground.*

SIGN #1: Right **'BENT EXTENDED B'** hand, palm forward, is used to outline a large arch as it moves from left to right. (Signs for **pile**, *v.*, vary according to the size and shape of the items as well as the way in which they are being piled.)

pile: *n.* a large quantity; a stack. *I have done a pile of work today.*

SIGN #2: Left **'BENT EXTENDED B'** hand is held in a fixed position with palm up. Vertical right **'BENT EXTENDED B'** hand, palm left and fingers pointing left, is held above left hand at a distance which indicates the height of the object under discussion. The hands are then simultaneously moved firmly forward a very short distance. The signer's lips appear to be articulating the syllable 'CHA'. (This sign is used especially with reference to **paperwork**.)

pile: *n.* a large amount of money or profit. *He will need a **pile** of money if he hopes to set up his own company.*

SIGN #3: Back of right **'CONTRACTED B'** hand, palm up, is tapped a couple of times on upturned palm of left **'EXTENDED B'** hand. Then right hand is changed to a **'C'** shape with palm facing leftward/forward, and is placed upright on left palm. The hands are purposefully moved ever so slightly downward/forward together. (ASL CONCEPT—**money - pile**.) ALTERNATE SIGN—**wealth**

piles: *n.* swollen or twisted veins near the anus from which blood is sometimes discharged; hemorrhoids. *The doctor gave him medication to relieve the pain of his **piles**.*

SIGN: Fingerspell **PILES**.

pill: *n.* a small tablet of medicine to be swallowed whole. *Some people take **pills** to control their blood pressure.*

SIGN: Tip of middle finger of right **'BENT MIDFINGER 5'** hand is placed on the upturned left palm, and maintains contact with the left palm as the right hand teeters back and forth a few times.

pillow: *n.* a rectangular cushion on which one rests the head while sleeping. *I like to sleep on more than one **pillow**.*

SIGN: Head tilts slightly to the right, supported by right **'EXTENDED B'** hand, which is held against right side of face. Then vertical **'CONTRACTED C'** hands are held slightly apart with palms facing and are alternated with **'FLAT O'** handshapes as the fingers open and close a couple of times. (ASL CONCEPT—**bed - soft**.) Signs vary considerably. **PILLOW** is frequently fingerspelled.

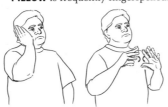

pilot: *n.* a person who operates an aircraft. *Edward ("Eddie") Thomas Payne was the first licensed Deaf **pilot** in Canada.*

SIGN: Right **'COMBINED LY'** hand, palm downward and slightly forward, is moved a short distance forward twice. Agent Ending (see p. LIV) may follow.

pimp: *n.* someone who controls prostitutes, getting clients for them and taking a large portion of their earnings. *He is a convicted **pimp** who is well-known to the police.*

SIGN: Fingerspell **PIMP**.

pimple: *n.* a small, inflamed swelling of the skin. *A teenager is often embarrassed about having a **pimple** on his face.*

SIGN: Tip of forefinger of right **'CROOKED ONE'** hand taps twice on the place where the blemish has appeared. (**PIMPLE** may be fingerspelled.)

pin: *n.* a stiff piece of wire used to fasten two or more parts or objects. *I need a **pin** to put this carnation on your lapel.*

SIGN: Fingerspell **PIN**. (Alternatively, various signs may be used depending on the type of pin.)

pinch: *v.* to squeeze something (usually human skin) quickly between the thumb and forefinger. *His mother told him not to **pinch** his little sister.*

SIGN: Right **'A-INDEX'** hand is placed on the left arm (or wherever the pinching takes place) and is twisted firmly. Alternatively, this sign may be made with the right hand only as it appears to pinch the air in front of the body. The signer's lips are squared as if articulating 'CH'.

pine: *n.* an evergreen tree with thin, sharp needles that have a pleasant, fresh smell. *The beautiful old **pine** had been struck by lightning.*

SIGN: Fingerspell **PINE**.

pineapple: *n.* a large, juicy oval fruit that is covered with a prickly woody skin. *You will need a fresh **pineapple** for this recipe.*

SIGN: Fingerspell **PINEAPPLE**.

ping-pong: *n.* table tennis. *Ping-Pong is popular in China.*

SIGN: Right **'CONTRACTED B'** hand, palm down and fingers pointing down, is held in front of the left side of the chest and is swung forward/upward from the wrist, then moved to a position in front of the right side of the chest and swung forward/upward again as if striking a ping-pong ball with a paddle.

pink: *adj.* having a pale reddish colour. *She wore **pink** lipstick.*

SIGN #1: Tip of middle finger of right **'K'** hand, palm toward the body, is brushed downward across the lips or chin at least twice.

SIGN #2 [ATLANTIC] : Vertical right **'8'** hand, palm forward/leftward, rapidly alternates with an **'OPEN 8'** a few times as the thumb and middle finger open and close.

SIGN #3 [ONTARIO]: Right **'K'** hand, palm facing left, is tapped twice against the chin.

SIGN #4 [PACIFIC/PRAIRIE]: Vertical right **'L'** hand, palm facing left, is brushed downward twice against the chin.

pinpoint: *v.* to locate or identify precisely. *They were able to **pinpoint** the exact time of his death.*

SIGN: Right **'OPEN F'** hand is held palm down. The hand then moves upward as the thumb and forefinger close to form an **'F'** hand with palm facing forward. Next, vertical left **'ONE'** hand is held in a fixed position with palm facing rightward/forward. Horizontal right **'ONE'** hand is held behind left hand with palm facing left. The right hand then makes a slight but firm bounce as if intending to strike the tip of the left forefinger with that of the right forefinger but not quite touching it. (ASL CONCEPT—**find - specific**.)

pioneer: *n.* one of the first people to be involved in something. *My great-grandfather was a **pioneer** who helped settle Western Canada.*

SIGN: Fingerspell **PIONEER**.

pipe: *n.* a device used to smoke tobacco or other substances. *My great-grandfather smoked a **pipe**.*

SIGN #1: Thumbnail of vertical right **'Y'** hand, palm facing leftward at a slight forward angle, is tapped against the lips several times.

pipe: *n.* a metal or plastic tube used to convey water, oil, gas, or other liquids. *The underground **pipe** is leaking.*

SIGN #2: **'C'** hands are held side by side with palms down and are then drawn apart. (Signs vary depending on size, shape and positioning. The **'F'** handshape is generally used for pipes which are relatively small in circumference.)

pipe down: *v.* an informal expression meaning be quiet or stop talking. *He told the children to **pipe down** because he could not sleep.*

SIGN: **'B'** hands are held semi-vertically with fingertips touching in front of the mouth and palms facing each other at a downward angle. As the wrists bend, the hands are simultaneously dropped so that the fingers point forward and the palms face downward.

pirate: *n.* a person who sails the seas and steals from the ships of others. *Captain Hook was a famous **pirate** in children's literature.*

SIGN: Right **'EXTENDED B'** hand, palm toward the face, covers the right eye, thus representing the black patch usually worn by pirates in illustrated fiction. (**Pirate** can also be used to denote the theft of information either through computer technology or from literary sources. In such cases this sign would be inappropriate.)

pissed off: *adj.* a vulgar term meaning annoyed; irritated. *He is **pissed off** with his parents for breaking their promise.*

SIGN: Middle finger of right **'K'** hand is brought up to touch the tip of the nose. The hand then turns forward and down as it forms an **'F'** hand. Facial expression must clearly convey 'annoyance'.

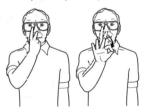

pistol: *n.* a handgun. *The man bought a **pistol** for protection.*

SIGN: Right **'L'** hand, palm facing left, is held in a horizontal position in front of the chest and the thumb is bent and straightened a few times as if repeatedly cocking (the hammer of) a gun.

pit: *n.* a large hole in the ground, often man-made for a specific purpose. *We need to dig a **pit** for our wiener roast.*

SIGN #1: Right horizontal **'EXTENDED B'** hand is initially held with fingers pointing forward and palm facing left. It is then curved downward, rightward, and up, so that the palm eventually faces rightward.

pit: *n.* a stone in the centre of a piece of fruit that contains a seed. *I think I broke my tooth on the **pit** in this plum.*

SIGN #2: Right **'COVERED F'** hand is held with palm facing left. (Sometimes an **'F'** is used rather than a **'COVERED F'** hand if the pit is 'larger'.)

pitch: *v.* to hurl or throw. *The baseball team needs a player who can **pitch**.*

SIGN: Vertical right **'CLAWED 3'** hand is held with palm forward. Then the wrist then bends forward to thrust the hand palm downward. (For **pitcher**, *n.*, in this context, the same basic sign is used but instead of the hand dropping to a palm-down position, it appears to jab forward a couple of times and the Agent Ending (see p. LIV) may follow.)

pitcher: *n.* a jug with a spout and a handle for pouring. *She passed me the **pitcher** of milk.*

SIGN: Horizontal right **'S'** hand, palm facing leftward/backward, is tipped leftward from the wrist to simulate the act of pouring from a pitcher.

pity: *n.* sympathy; sorrow felt for the suffering of others. *It is a **pity** that you can not attend the banquet.*

SIGN: Right **'BENT MIDFINGER 5'** hand is held upright with palm facing forward but slanted downward slightly. It is then moved forward with circular motions to simulate the stroking of an imaginary person with the middle finger. Appropriate facial expression is important (Alternatively, this sign may be made with two hands.)

pizza: *n.* an Italian dish consisting of a crust covered with cheese, tomatoes, and an assortment of toppings. *We ordered a large ham and pineapple **pizza**.*

SIGN: Fingerspell **PIZZA**. (In informal circumstances the fingerspelling of this word is often done quickly with a flourish, thus almost resembling a sign. In this case, the **P** and **I** are quickly fingerspelled, then the two **Z**'s are combined into a **'CLAWED V'** which zigzags in 'Z' formation so that the forefinger and middle finger simultaneously create the **Z**'s, and finally the **A** is fingerspelled.)

place: *n.* a particular space or geographical area. *Halifax is a place I want to visit.*

SIGN #1: Horizontal **'EXTENDED A'** hands are held out in front of the body with palms down and thumbtips touching. The hands then create a circle as they are drawn apart and brought toward the chest where they meet again.

OR

SIGN #2: Horizontal **'K'** hands are held out in front of the body with palms facing each other and tips of middle fingers touching. The hands then create a circle as they are drawn apart and brought toward the chest where they meet again.

place: *v.* to put or set in a particular spot. *You can place your things on the table.*

SIGN #3: Vertical **'FLAT O'** hands are held parallel with palms forward and are simultaneously moved forward in arc formation so that the palms eventually face down. (This sign is frequently made with the right hand only. Signs in this context vary considerably depending on the size and shape of the object and the manner in which it is being placed.)

place: *v.* to arrive at the finish line in a certain position (in a race); to be ranked in a certain order (in a contest or competition). *He placed third in the race.*

SIGN #4: Right **'3'** hand is held out from the body with palm facing left and extended fingers pointing forward. The forearm is then jerked straight backward toward the body. (Signs vary according to the actual number of the position or rank. To indicate that someone 'came in or placed first', the same sign is used but with a **'ONE'** handshape.)

place: *v.* to come in second in a (horse) race. *He bet on the horse to place.*

SIGN #5: Right **'V'** hand is held out from the body with palm facing left and extended fingers pointing forward. The forearm is then jerked straight backward toward the body.

placid: See **calm**.

plagiarize: *v.* to use someone else's work or ideas, claiming them as your own. *To plagiarize another author's work is highly unethical.*

SIGN: Parallel horizontal **'V'** hands are held with the left hand slightly ahead of the right and the extended fingertips of both hands pointing leftward/forward. The forearms then move simultaneously rightward and slightly upward as the hands take on **'CLAWED V'** shapes, and finally resume the **'V'** shape as they continue moving rightward and slightly downward. (ASL CONCEPT—**copy - cheat**) REGIONAL VARIATION—**cheat** SAME SIGN—**plagiarism**, *n.*

plague: *n.* a widespread epidemic of an infectious disease or pestilence. *Many Inuit died during a plague of smallpox.*

SIGN: **'BENT MIDFINGER 5'** hands are positioned so that the tip of the right middle finger is in the middle of the forehead and the tip of the left middle finger is on the stomach. Next, **'FLAT O'** hands are held with the palms down and sides of tips of forefingers touching. The hands are then opened to form **'5'** hands as they are moved apart in an outward/forward direction. (ASL CONCEPT—**sick - spread**)

plaid: *n.* a material with a tartan pattern. *The Balmoral plaid is worn by the royal family.*

SIGN: Horizontal right **'4'** hand, palm facing body and fingertips touching chest, is drawn rightward. Then the hand is turned over so that fingernails are on the chest and palm is upward. The hand is now drawn downward. (This sign may be formed in various places, such as on the left shoulder or on the back of the left **'STANDARD BASE'** hand.)

plain: *n.* an expanse of flat land. *It is often windy here on the plain.*

SIGN #1: Vertical **'BENT EXTENDED B'** hands are held together, right in front of left, close to the chest with the right palm facing left and the left palm facing right. The left hand remains fixed while the right hand moves directly forward.

plain: *adj.* common; ordinary; unpatterned. *She wanted to find a plain blouse to wear with her plaid skirt.*

SIGN #2: Tip of forefinger of vertical right **'ONE'** hand, palm facing left, is drawn downward from the lips. The hand is then changed to an **'EXTENDED B'** hand which is laid down at right angles onto the upturned palm of the left **'EXTENDED B'** hand and slid along the left hand in a forward/rightward direction. (**PLAIN** in this context may be fingerspelled.)

plain: *adj.* sheer; pure; utter. *At first I was annoyed, but now I am just plain angry!*

SIGN #3: Forefinger of vertical right **'ONE'** hand, palm facing left, is held against the lips and the hand is moved sharply forward.

plain: *adj.* clear; obvious. *It is plain to see that you are not happy.*

SIGN #4: Vertical **'O'** (or **'FLAT O'**) hands are placed side by side, palms facing forward. Then they are moved apart and slightly upward as the fingers spread to form **'5'** hands.

(in) plain English: *adv.* using straightforward language; in an outspoken way. *The police officer spoke to the young thief in plain English.*

SIGN #5: Vertical right **'B'** hand, palm facing left, is held directly in front of the face and thrust forward and slightly downward.

plan: *v.* to come up with ideas for doing something. *She helped me plan the party.*

SIGN: Horizontal **'EXTENDED B'** hands, palms facing each other and fingers pointing forward, are held slightly apart at the left side of the body and are moved simultaneously toward the right.

plane: *n.* abbreviation for **airplane**. *The plane needs refuelling.*

SIGN #1: Right **'COMBINED LY'** hand, palm downward and slightly forward, is moved a short distance forward twice.

plane: *n.* a tool with a steel blade used for smoothing wood. *He used a sharp plane to reduce the length of the door slightly so that it did not scrape the floor when opening and closing.*

SIGN #2: Horizontal **'S'** hands are held in a staggered formation, the left ahead of the right, with the left palm facing rightward at a forward angle and the right palm facing leftward at a slight backward angle. The hands are then moved forward/leftward a couple of times to simulate the action of planing wood.

planet: *n.* any one of the nine celestial bodies in the solar system. *Pluto is the most recently discovered planet.*

SIGN: Fingerspell **PLANET**.

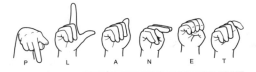

plant: *v.* to put *seeds* into the ground to grow. *I always plant my garden during the last May weekend.*

SIGN #1: Fingertips of right **'FLAT O'** hand, palm down, are repeatedly slid across the thumb to form an **'A'** shape as the hand moves forward a short distance.

plant: *v.* to put *plants* into the ground to grow. *I will plant some flowers there.*

SIGN #2: Right **'FLAT O'** hand, palm down, is moved forward in a series of arcs.

plant: *v.* to deceive by placing something somewhere. *The murderer planted evidence in order to frame his brother.*

SIGN #3: Vertical right **'FLAT O'** hand is held with palm facing forward. The wrist then bends to turn the hand so that the palm faces down.

plant: *n.* a living organism that takes root and grows. *A geranium is a nice plant for a kitchen window.*

SIGN #4: Right **'FLAT O'** hand is thrust upward through left **'C'** hand, as fingers open into a **'CONTRACTED 5'** hand.

plant: *n.* the buildings where an industry or business is carried out; factory. *Many jobs were created when the meat packing **plant** opened.*

SIGN #5: Fingers of horizontal **'CLAWED 5'** hands, palms toward the body, are interlocked and remain so as they are shaken up and down. This is a wrist action.

REGIONAL VARIATION—**factory** #2

plastic: *n.* a synthetic material that can be shaped when soft and then set. *Plastic is commonly used in most manufacturing industries.*

SIGN: Thumb and forefinger of right **'A-INDEX'** hand grasp tip of forefinger of left **'ONE'** hand with both palms both facing downward. Together, the hands are shaken a few times. (Signs vary. Alternatively, it may be finger-spelled.)

plate: *n.* a shallow dish on which food is served. *He passed his **plate** for another helping of turkey.*

SIGN #1: Horizontal **'C-INDEX'** hands are held parallel with palms facing each other.

OR

SIGN #2: **'ONE'** hands are held out from the body with palms down and tips of forefingers together. The hands are then curved apart in semicircles to be rejoined nearer the chest.

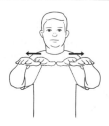

platform: *n.* a horizontal surface that is raised from the floor. *All the speakers were seated on the platform.*

SIGN: **'EXTENDED B'** hands, palms down, are positioned side by side and are simultaneously drawn apart. (If the term is used in reference to a political or an election 'platform', other sign choices would apply.)

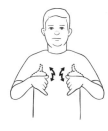

play: *v.* to take part in sports, games or amusements. *Children love to play outside in the summer.*

SIGN #1: Horizontal **'Y'** hands are held parallel with palms facing each other but slanted slightly toward the body. The hands are then simultaneously bounced up and down twice. This is a wrist action.

play: *n.* a dramatic production. *The Deaf students performed a play about Deaf people.*

SIGN #2: **'EXTENDED A'** hands, palms facing each other, are rotated alternately in small circles which are brought down against the chest.

playful: *adj.* full of fun; high-spirited. *The playful kittens were chasing their own tails.*

SIGN: Horizontal **'Y'** hands, palms toward the body, are held parallel and wobble as they are simultaneously circled clockwise several times.

playing cards: See **deck (of cards)** and **cards**.

(make a) plea: *v.* to make an earnest request. *The class made a plea to take their tests earlier.*

SIGN: Horizontal **'X'** hands, are held apart with palms facing each other and the right hand slightly ahead of the left hand. The hands are then simultaneously moved forward and back at least twice with short deliberate movements as though prodding a reluctant individual. ❖

plead: *v.* to beg earnestly. *The victim was trying to plead for mercy.*

SIGN #1: Horizontal **'X'** hands, are held apart with palms facing each other and the right hand slightly ahead of the left hand. The hands are then simultaneously moved forward and back at least twice with short deliberate movements as though prodding a reluctant individual. ❖

OR

SIGN #2: Palms of vertical **'EXTENDED B'** hands are placed together in prayer position. Facial expression is important.

OR

SIGN #3: Hands are clasped in an upright position, left **'A'** hand covered with right **'EXTENDED C'** hand, and they are moved forward purposefully.

plead: *v.* to give as an excuse. *You were informed by mail, so you can not **plead** ignorance of what was going on.*

SIGN #4: Left **'BENT EXTENDED B'** hand is held upright with palm facing right. Right **'BENT EXTENDED B'** hand is held upright with palm facing left and fingers resting on those of the left hand. The right hand then slides forward, off and under the left hand as the left hand slides forward, off and under the right hand. The motion is repeated.

plead: *v.* to argue (especially in a court of law). *He will **plead his case** in small claims court tomorrow.*

SIGN #5: Left **'EXTENDED B'** hand is held in a fixed position with palm up and fingers pointing forward/rightward while forward-pointing forefinger of right **'ONE'** hand, palm left, is tapped a few times on the left palm.

plead: *v.* to answer a charge in a court of law. *The lawyer advised his client to **plead** not guilty.*

SIGN #6: Tip of forefinger of right **'BENT ONE'** hand, palm toward the body, is held just under the chin and flicked forward, thus creating a **'ONE'** hand. (Alternatively, **admit** #2 may be used to mean **plead** in this sense but only when the plea is a *guilty* one.)

pleasant: *adj.* enjoyable; pleasing; agreeable. *The room has a **pleasant** decor.*

SIGN: Hands are held at right angles to one another as downturned palm of right **'EXTENDED B'** hand is smoothed rightward/forward across upturned palm of left **'EXTENDED B'** hand. (To refer to a person's nature as 'pleasant', see **amiable** for a more appropriate sign choice.)

please: *adv.* an expression used with a polite request. ***Please** help me with this.*

SIGN #1: Horizontal right **'EXTENDED B'** hand, palm on the chest, is moved in a circular motion, that appears to onlookers to be clockwise.

please: *v.* to give satisfaction, contentment or pleasure. *It would **please** me if you stopped smoking.*

SIGN #2: Horizontal right **'EXTENDED B'** hand, palm toward the body, is brushed up and off the chest twice in a circular motion. (The ASL sentence is syntactically different than the English one. The sample sentence in ASL is: *YOU STOP SMOKING...ME **HAPPY**.*)

pleased: *adj.* happy; satisfied. *I am **pleased** that you could come.*

SIGN: Horizontal right **'EXTENDED B'** hand, palm toward the body, is brushed up and off the chest twice in a circular motion.

pleasing: *adj.* giving pleasure; nice. *This dessert has a very **pleasing** taste.*

SIGN: Fingertips of right **'BENT EXTENDED B'** hand are placed on the lips so that the palm is toward the body. Then the hand is moved purposefully forward a brief distance.

pleasure: *n.* something that gives enjoyment. *It is my **pleasure** to make this presentation.*

SIGN: Palms of horizontal **'EXTENDED B'** hands are held right above left against the chest. Then the hands are circled simultaneously in opposite directions. (Alternatively, this sign may be made with one hand only.)

pledge: *v.* to promise. *Brownies **pledge** to do their best to help others.*

SIGN: Tip of forefinger of vertical right **'ONE'** hand, palm facing left, is placed just under the lower lip. As the right hand is then brought purposefully forward/downward, it takes on a **'B'** handshape and is pressed onto the top of the left **'STANDARD BASE'** hand. (Hand shapes vary.)

plenty: *n.* a large number, amount or quantity. *The hostess had **plenty** of food for all the guests.*

SIGN: Horizontal left **'S'** hand, palm facing right, is covered with palm of right **'EXTENDED B'** hand. Then the right hand is brushed firmly forward and slightly to the right. The cheeks are puffed out.
SAME SIGN—**plentiful**, *adj.*
ALTERNATE SIGN—**ample** #1

pliers: *n.* a gripping tool with pincers for picking up, turning, or cutting. *Mechanics need good **pliers** for their work.*

SIGN: Extended fingers of horizontal right **'V'** hand, palm facing left and angled toward the body, are used to grasp and rock on horizontal forefinger of left **'ONE'** hand, thus simulating the function of a wrench. (**PLIERS** may be fingerspelled.)

plot: *n.* the storyline of a play or novel. *The students must outline the **plot** of each novel they read.*

SIGN #1: Left **'CONTRACTED C'** (or **'OPEN 8'**) hand is held horizontally with palm facing right while right **'CONTRACTED C'** (or **'OPEN 8'**) hand is held upright with palm facing left. The hands are held close enough together to be loosely interlocked. They are then drawn apart, closed and returned several times, thus alternating between **'CONTRACTED C'** (or **'OPEN 8'**) and **'FLAT O'** (or **'8'**) shapes with each movement. (**PLOT** is frequently fingerspelled.)

plot: *n.* a small section of land. *They chose a suitable **plot** for their garden.*

SIGN #2: **'FLAT O'** hands are held slightly apart with palms up. Then the fingers are slid across the thumbs a few times, thus alternating between **'FLAT O'** and **'OFFSET O'** hands. Next, tips of forefingers of **'BENT ONE'** hands, palms down, are placed together out in front of the chest. The hands are drawn apart, then moved toward the chest, and finally come together again closer to the chest as the forefingers outline the shape of a square or rectangle. (ASL CONCEPT—**ground - square**.)

plot: *v.* to plan secretly to achieve a purpose, especially one which is underhanded or illegal. *The RCMP discovered their **plot** to steal the files.*

SIGN #3: Right **'A'** hand is brought to the lips with the thumb pointed upward and the palm facing left. Then the lips are touched twice with the thumbnail. Next, horizontal **'EXTENDED B'** hands, palms facing each other and fingers pointing forward, are held slightly apart at the left side of the body and are moved simultaneously toward the right. (ASL CONCEPT—**secret - plan**.)

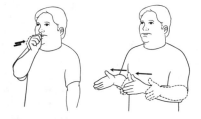

plot coordinates: *v.* to find a specific point on a graph by using a combination of numbers. *The teacher asked his students to **plot coordinates** on a graph.*

SIGN #4: Left **'ONE'** hand is held aloft with palm down and forefinger pointing right while vertical right **'ONE'** hand, palm forward, is held much lower and to the right of the left hand. The left hand then moves rightward as the right hand moves upward until the tips of the forefingers come together.

plough [*also spelled* **plow**]: *v.* to make furrows or grooves in a field by using an implement with sharp blades designed for this purpose. *My father will **plough** the north field tomorrow.*

SIGN #1: The left forearm is held parallel to the chest as the right **'SPREAD EXTENDED C'** hand, palm down, is scraped rightward along the left forearm.

plough [*also spelled* **plow**]: *v.* to clear away snow with a sharp-bladed implement. *The city crew will **plough** the snow from the streets when the blizzard is over.*

SIGN #2: Left **'EXTENDED B'** hand is held in a fixed position with palm up and fingers pointing rightward/forward. Right **'EXTENDED B'** hand, palm facing the body at a slight leftward angle and fingers pointing leftward/forward, is placed on the heel of the left hand and slides forward/rightward across the palm to the end of the fingers.

plug in: *v.* to connect something to an electrical power source. *You will need to **plug in** your car during the cold weather.*

SIGN: Horizontal **'V'** hands, palms facing each other but slanted a little toward the body, are held slightly apart. The right hand is then moved toward the left so that the forefinger of the right hand is thrust between the two extended fingers of the left hand. (Signs vary.)

plum: *n.* a roundish, edible fruit with a rather flat stone in the centre. *If a **plum** is left to dry out, it becomes a prune.*

SIGN: Fingerspell **PLUM**.

plumber: *n.* a person who installs and repairs water systems and heating equipment. *The **plumber** will fix the leaking faucet.*

SIGN: Extended fingers of horizontal right **'V'** hand, palm facing left and angled toward the body, are used to grasp and rock on horizontal forefinger of left **'ONE'** hand, thus simulating the function of a wrench.

plump: *adj.* chubby. *The **plump** baby was trying to take his first steps.*

SIGN: **'SPREAD C'** hands, palms toward the face, are placed upright near the cheeks which are slightly inflated as the hands are moved simultaneously outward. This sign may be formed at various locations on the body, such as the chest or hips to specify plumpness in that area.

plunge: *v.* to throw oneself downward (into something). *The first thing I am going to do when we arrive at the hotel is to **plunge** into the pool.*

SIGN #1: Vertical right **'CLAWED V'** hand, palm facing backward, is thrust forward and slightly downward so that the back of the hand makes contact with the palm of the horizontal left **'SPREAD C'** hand which is held with the palm facing the body. The right hand then slides downward.

plunge: *v.* to become deeply involved. *She will **plunge** into her work and try to forget about her personal problems.*

SIGN #2: Vertical right **'CLAWED V'** hand, palm facing backward, is thrust forward and slightly downward so that the back of the hand makes contact with the palm of the horizontal left **'SPREAD C'** hand which is held with the palm facing the body.

plunge: *v.* to thrust (something into something) with force. *He **plunged** a knife into the bear as it attacked him.*

SIGN #3: Vertical right **'S'** hand, palm facing left, is thrust forward/downward as if stabbing something. ❖

plunger: *n.* a device with a rubber suction cup at the end used for clearing a blocked toilet. *The toilet is not flushing very well so maybe we should buy a **plunger**.*

SIGN: Horizontal **'S'** hands are held right on top of left as if holding onto the handle of a plunger and are repeatedly moved up and down.

plural: *n.* the form of a word that indicates there is more than one of something. *In English, the **plural** of 'child' is 'children'.*

SIGN: **'S'** hands are held parallel with palms up and are thrust forward simultaneously as they are opened to form **'CROOKED 5'** hands. (**PLURAL** may be fingerspelled.)

plus: *prep.* increased by the addition of; in addition to. *Two **plus** two is four.*

SIGN: Forefinger of right **'ONE'** hand is dropped forward smartly to strike horizontal forefinger of left **'ONE'** hand at right angles.

pneumonia: *n.* an inflammation of the lungs. *The woman is in the hospital because she has **pneumonia**.*

SIGN: Fingertips of **'BENT EXTENDED B'** hands, palms facing body, are positioned at either side of chest and simultaneously slid up and down. (**Pneumonia** is frequently fingerspelled **PN**.)

pocket: *n.* a small pouch in a garment used for carrying small things. *My keys are in my pocket.*

SIGN: Inverted right **'EXTENDED B'** hand, palm toward the body and fingers pointed downward, is placed wherever one wishes to indicate the location of a pocket, and is pushed downward.

poem: *n.* a composition in verse. (This sign only refers to a poem that is expressed in ASL.) *Her **poems** delighted the Deaf audience.*

SIGN #1: Right **'S'** hand is held against the chest with the palm facing the body at an upward angle. The hand is then moved forward as the fingers open to form a **'MODIFIED 5'** hand.
SAME SIGN—**poetry**, *n.*, in this context.

poem: *n.* a composition in verse. (This sign only refers to a poem that is expressed in *spoken* or *written* form.) *The Canadian Cultural Society of the Deaf collects **poems** written by Deaf people.*

SIGN #2: Right **'K'** hand is positioned above left forearm with palm downward. The right wrist twists back and forth as the hand also moves back and forth above the right forearm.
SAME SIGN—**poetry**, *n.*, in this context.
POEM, *n.*, and **POETRY**, *n.*, are frequently fingerspelled.

point [or **point out**]: *v.* to indicate a specific person or thing among several. *Please point out the person who will be our interpreter.*

SIGN #1: Horizontal right **'ONE'** hand, palm facing left, is thrust forward in the direction of the item or person being identified. ❖

point: *n.* an essential element in a discussion. *The speaker made a good point.*

SIGN #2: Vertical left **'ONE'** hand is held in a fixed position with palm facing rightward/ forward. Horizontal right **'ONE'** hand is held behind left hand with palm facing left. The right hand then makes a slight but firm bounce as if intending to strike the tip of the left forefinger with that of the right forefinger but not quite touching it.

(at this) point: *adv.* at the present moment in time; right now. *At this point we do not know what might happen next.*

SIGN #3: **'Y'** hands, palms up, are held slightly apart and are simultaneously lowered. ALTERNATE SIGN—**now** #2

point of view [#4]: See **view** #3.

(get the) point across: *v.* to make oneself clearly understood. *He was able to get the point across by explaining the consequences of her behaviour.*

SIGN #5: Extended forefinger of right **'ONE'** hand, palm facing left, is forcefully thrust forward between the forefinger and middle finger of the left **'5'** hand that is held with palm toward the body. (This sign is used only when the signer is 'adamant'. Under other circumstances, **get the point across** might be expressed by using the signs for **explain + clear**.)

poison: *n.* a chemical substance that can cause sickness and/or death. *Arsenic is a deadly poison.*

SIGN #1: **'S'** hands, palms facing chest, are crossed at the wrists, with the right hand nearest the body. The back of the right wrist is tapped twice against the left wrist.

OR

SIGN #2: Tip of middle finger of right **'BENT MIDFINGER 5'** hand is placed on the upturned left palm, and maintains contact with the left palm as the right hand teeters back and forth a few times. SAME SIGN—**poisonous**, *adj.*

poke: *v.* to jab or prod with a finger, elbow or sharp object such as a stick. *I had to poke him when he fell asleep during the lecture.*

SIGN: Horizontal right **'ONE'** hand, palm facing left, is thrust forward in the direction of the person/thing being poked. ❖ (Signs vary according to what is being poked, what is being used to do the poking and how the poking is being done. If a hole is being poked into something the sign choice is different.)

poker face: *n.* a face that is totally without expression. *It is difficult to understand a person who signs with a poker face because facial expression is a key feature of ASL.*

SIGN: Horizontal right **'EXTENDED B'** hand, palm toward the face, is held in front of the forehead and is solemnly drawn downward. A blank facial expression accompanies this sign.

pokey [also spelled **poky**]: *adj.* slow or without energy. *He is always late because he is so pokey.*

SIGN: **'EXTENDED B'** hands are held parallel with palms down and fingers pointing forward. The forearms are simultaneously lowered a short distance, then moved rightward in an arc formation, and back to their original position in a leftward arc. This sign is made slowly and deliberately and the signer's cheeks are puffed out.

pole: *n.* a long slender piece of wood, metal or other material. *The car smashed into a telephone pole.*

SIGN #1: Horizontal **'C'** hands are held apart with palms facing each other. Then they are moved upward simultaneously. (The distance between the hands depends on the diameter of the pole. This sign is used for a pole that is relatively *large in diameter*.)

pole: *n.* a long slender piece of wood, metal or other material. *Can you make me a pole to set my bird feeder on?*

SIGN #2: If the pole is vertical, horizontal **'F'** hands are positioned right on top of left with the left palm facing right and the right palm facing left. The right hand then moves straight upward as the left hand moves downward. If the pole is horizontal, **'F'** hands are held side by side with palms down and are drawn apart. (This sign is used for a pole that is relatively *small in diameter*.)

police: *n.* a group of people responsible for maintaining law and order. *The police came to investigate the accident.*

SIGN: Vertical right **'C'** hand, palm facing left, is tapped twice against the left shoulder.
(**ESL USERS:** Police is a *plural* noun. In English, *one* person is referred to as 'police officer', 'policewoman', 'policeman', or 'constable'.)

policy: *n.* a plan of action adopted by an individual or group. *According to the company's policy, he is eligible to retire early.*

SIGN: Vertical left **'EXTENDED B'** hand is held in a fixed position with palm facing right while horizontal right **'K'** hand is placed palm down against the fingers of the left hand, and then lowered to a position nearer the heel of the left hand. (When it refers to a written contract such as an insurance policy, **POLICY** is fingerspelled.)

polish: *v.* to make glossy by rubbing. *He uses a soft cloth to polish his car.*

SIGN: Horizontal right **'A'** hand, palm down, is rubbed vigorously back and forth across the upturned palm of the left **'EXTENDED B'** hand.

polite: *adj.* courteous in manners, speech, etc. *I hope you will be polite to our visitors.*

SIGN: Thumb of vertical right **'EXTENDED B'** hand, palm facing left, is tapped a few times against centre of chest.

political: *adj.* relating to government or public administration. *Anyone can aspire to be a political leader.*

SIGN: Right **'K'** hand, palm left, is moved in a small clockwise circle, coming to rest with the tip of the middle finger touching the right temple. This is a wrist action.
SAME SIGN—**politics**, *n.*

poll: *n.* a survey conducted on a representative sample of people in order to determine a general opinion. *The poll indicates that most people are satisfied with the present government.*

SIGN: Left **'EXTENDED B'** hand is held in a fixed position with palm turned upward but slanted slightly rightward and toward the body while fingers point rightward/forward. Right **'ONE'** hand is held palm down as tip of forefinger brushes forward several times against palm of left hand.

(go to the) polls: *v.* to go to a voting station for the purpose of voting. *Canadians go to the polls when an election is called, usually every four or five years.*

SIGN: Joined thumb and forefinger of horizontal right **'F'** hand, palm down, appear to peck at the top of the horizontal left **'S'** hand, whose palm faces right.

pond: *n.* a pool of still water, often man-made. *The children were sailing their paper boats on the pond.*

SIGN: Fingerspell **POND**.

ponder: *v.* to consider carefully; think deeply about. *She needs more time to ponder the offer.*

SIGN: Vertical **'FLAT O'** hands are held just in front of either side of the forehead with palms facing backward and fingers rapidly fluttering as the hands move in small circles. From the signer's perspective, the left hand moves clockwise while the right hand moves counter-clockwise. (Alternatively, this sign may be made with one hand only.)
ALTERNATE SIGN—**concerned** #2

pool: *n.* a body of still water. *It is nice to have a swimming pool in one's backyard.*

SIGN #1: Fingerspell **POOL**.

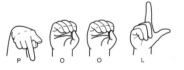

pool: *n.* a billiard game. *Joe enjoys playing pool.*

SIGN #2: Right **'S'** hand, palm toward body, is held near waist and used to simulate holding the handle of a billiard cue. Left **'S'** hand is extended in front of body, palm down, to simulate supporting the imaginary cue, and is held steady while right hand is moved back and forth twice.

pool: *v.* to combine funds or other resources into a communal reserve to be used for a joint enterprise. *If we pool our funds, we can purchase a bus for future field trips.*

SIGN #3: **'FLAT O'** hands are held apart, fingers pointing toward each other and palms facing. The hands are then brought closer together as the thumbs slide across the fingers to form **'A'** hands. (Signs vary according to what is being 'pooled'. The sample sign would be inappropriate in reference to a 'car pool' or a 'football pool', in which cases **POOL** would be fingerspelled.)

poor: *adj.* needy; without adequate financial resources. *Unemployment is often a contributing cause to people being poor.*

SIGN #1: Thumb and fingertips of right **'CONTRACTED 5'** hand grasp left elbow and close to form a **'FLAT O'** as they slide downward off the elbow. Motion is repeated.

OR

SIGN #2: Right **'FLAT OPEN F'** hand, palm downward/leftward, is held at the bent left elbow and is drawn downward/forward to form an **'F'** hand. Motion is repeated.

SIGN #3 [ONTARIO]: Left **'EXTENDED B'** hand is held in a fixed position with palm at a rightward/backward angle and fingers pointing upward/rightward at a forward angle. Right **'FLAT C'** hand is held under the left hand with palm up and fingers and thumb grasping the left palm. Then the right hand moves downward as the fingertips close against the thumbtip to form a **'FLAT O'** shape. Motion is repeated.

poor: *adj.* unfortunate; deserving pity or sympathy. *The poor kitten was stranded outside.*

SIGN #4: Right **'BENT MIDFINGER 5'** hand is held upright with palm facing forward but slanted downward slightly. It is then moved forward with circular motions to simulate the stroking of an imaginary person with the middle finger. Appropriate facial expression is important. (Alternatively, this sign may be made with two hands.)

poor: *adj.* inferior; below standard. *The quality of his work is poor.*

SIGN #5: Vertical right **'3'** hand is held with palm facing left and tip of thumb touching the nose. The hand then moves forward/downward in an arc formation as the wrist rotates to turn the hand to a horizontal position. A look of displeasure accompanies this sign.

pop: *n.* a flavoured, nonalcoholic, carbonated drink. *This is my favourite kind of pop.*

SIGN #1: The tip of the middle finger of the right **'BENT MIDFINGER 5'** hand, palm down, is inserted into the opening in the top of the horizontal left **'S'** hand. The right hand is then raised, changed to a **'5'** hand, and slapped palm-downward on the top of the left hand.

SIGN [ATLANTIC] #2: Horizontal **'COVERED T'** hand is held with palm facing left, as the thumb is repeatedly flicked upward to form an **'A-INDEX'** hand.

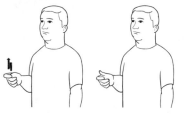

pop up: *v.* to appear; come up suddenly. *If no other questions pop up we can settle the debate.*

SIGN: Left **'EXTENDED B'** hand is held, palm down, in a fixed position. Right **'ONE'** hand, palm forward, is brought up underneath the left hand and the extended forefinger is thrust upward between the forefinger and middle finger of the left hand.

popcorn: *n.* corn kernels that puff up and burst when heated. *Many people like to eat popcorn while they watch movies.*

SIGN: **'S'** hands are held apart with palms up and are alternately and repeatedly thrust upward as they form **'ONE'** hands and then return to their original position and shape.

511

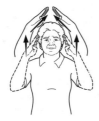

pope: *n.* the head of the Roman Catholic Church. *The Pope has an official residence in Rome.*

SIGN: Vertical **'B'** (or **'EXTENDED B'**) hands, palms facing each other, are placed at either side of head, and then moved upward until the fingertips meet to form the shape of a bishop's mitre. (**POPE** is frequently fingerspelled. It is *always* fingerspelled if it precedes the 'name' of a specific pope.)

poplar: *n.* a deciduous tree found in most regions of Canada. *A poplar has a tall, thin trunk and triangular-shaped leaves.*

SIGN: Fingerspell **POPLAR**.

popular: *adj.* widely favoured or admired; well liked. *He is a very popular teenager.*

SIGN #1: Left **'ONE'** hand is held palm down with forefinger pointing upward/rightward. Horizontal right **'CROOKED 5'** hand is held palm down as the wrist repetitively makes rapid forward movements so that the hand tilts forward slightly and the palm makes contact with the tip of the left forefinger with each movement. (**POPULAR** may be fingerspelled.) This sign generally applies to *people* but may also be used to describe things such as *sports*, *pastimes*, etc.

popular: *adj.* widely favoured; well attended. *Slo-pitch tournaments are very popular events.*

SIGN #2: Both **'BENT 5'** hands, palms facing forward, are moved forward and slightly downward from shoulder level, fingers wiggling. Movement is repeated. (This sign applies to *places* and *events*. The sample sentence in ASL is: *SLO-PITCH TOURNAMENT WOW POPULAR*.)

population: *n.* all of the people who live in a specific place. *Ontario has the largest population of all the Canadian provinces.*

SIGN: Vertical **'K'** hands are held apart with palms forward but facing each other slightly, and are alternately circled backward. (Note the differences between this English sentence and the ASL translation. In English: *What is the population of Kenora?* In ASL: *HOW MANY PEOPLE LIVE KENORA?*)

porch: *n.* a covered entrance leading into a main doorway of a house or other dwelling. *The house has both a front and a back porch.*

SIGN: Fingerspell **PORCH**.

porcupine: *n.* a large rodent with protective quills covering its body. *Our dog encountered a porcupine and came home with quills in his muzzle.*

SIGN: Right **'4'** hand, palm forward, is held upright at the forehead and is swept back across the top of the head, signifying the appearance of erect quills.

pore: *n.* a tiny opening in the skin. *A clogged pore can result in a blackhead.*

SIGN #1: Fingerspell **PORE**.

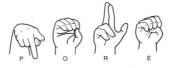

pore: *v.* to study very closely. *Lawyers must pore over many documents to prepare a case.*

SIGN #2: Left **'EXTENDED B'** hand is held in a fixed position with fingers pointing rightward and palm toward the body at a slight upward angle. Right **'BENT 5'** hand is held closer to the chest and circled in a counter-clockwise direction with palm down and fingers fluttering as they point toward the left palm.

pork: *n.* the meat of pigs used for food. *Our family eats pork at least once a week.*

SIGN: Fingerspell **PORK**.

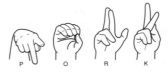

pornography: *n.* materials used to stimulate sexual excitement. *Certain literature, photographs and films can be classified as pornography.*

SIGN: Right **'MODIFIED 5'** hand is held under chin with palm down as the fingers flutter. Next, left **'EXTENDED B'** hand is held in a fixed position with palm facing right and fingers pointing forward/upward as vertical right **'C'** hand is held against the right cheek with palm forward at a slight leftward angle. Right hand is then moved forward/downward and placed firmly against the left palm. (ASL CONCEPT— **dirty - picture**.) Signs vary according to the type of pornography being referred to. Instead of **picture** the signer may choose **magazine, movie, book**, etc.

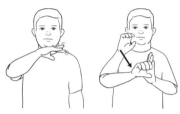

port: *n.* a town or city situated on a major waterway. *Vancouver is a major Canadian port.*

SIGN: Fingerspell **PORT**. (Signs vary depending on the intent of the sentence.)

portable: *adj.* designed in such a way that it can be easily carried or moved. *He bought a portable television.*

SIGN: **'A'** hands, palms down, are held slightly apart, and are then firmly pushed a very short distance downward. Next, right **'S'** hand is held at one's side, with palm toward body, and the arm is moved up and down as if carrying something. (ASL CONCEPT— **can - carry**.) ASL syntax differs from that of English and the adjective tends to follow rather than precede the noun. The sample sentence in ASL is: *HE BUY TV ITSELF PORTABLE.* (**PORTABLE** may be fingerspelled.)

portion: *n.* a part or piece of a whole. *The child asked for a big portion of apple pie.*

SIGN: Horizontal left **'EXTENDED B'** hand is held in a fixed position with palm up but angled toward the body and fingers pointing rightward/forward while edge of horizontal right **'EXTENDED B'** hand, palm facing left, is placed on left palm and is drawn back toward the body.

portrait: *n.* a painting or photograph of a person. *The artist was commissioned to paint a portrait of the queen.*

SIGN: Left **'EXTENDED B'** hand is held in a fixed position with palm facing right and fingers pointing forward/upward as vertical right **'C'** hand is held against the right cheek with palm forward at a slight leftward angle. Right hand is then moved forward/downward and placed firmly against the left palm.

portray: *v.* to show clearly. *The film portrays life in 17th century England.*

SIGN #1: Tip of forefinger of horizontal right **'BENT ONE'** hand is placed against right facing palm of left **'EXTENDED B'** hand. Together, the hands are moved forward in a short arc.

portray: *v.* to play the part of a certain character on stage or on film. *He likes to portray Shakespearean characters.*

SIGN #2: **'EXTENDED A'** hands, palms facing each other, are rotated alternately in small circles that are brought down against the chest.
ALTERNATE SIGN—**act** #1

pose: *v.* to assume a certain position for a painting or photograph. *The instructor brought in several models to pose so the students could paint them.*

SIGN #1: Right **'BENT V'** hand is held palm down with the tips of the two extended fingers resting on the upturned left palm. In addition, natural body language is used to convey the notion of striking a pose. (Sign choice generally depends on whether the individual posing is standing or sitting.)

pose a question: *v.* to put forward or ask a question. *The speaker posed a question that the audience found difficult to answer.*

SIGN #2: Vertical right **'S'** hand is held with palm facing forward. Then the right forefinger is flicked forward to form a **'ONE'** hand, palm facing down. ❖

pose as: *v.* to pretend you are someone or something you are not; assume a false identity. *The spy was able to pose as a security guard.*

SIGN #3: Side of forefinger of right **'ONE'** hand, palm facing leftward/forward, is lightly brushed forward/downward twice on the right cheek, forefinger either remaining upright or bending slightly to become a **'BENT ONE'**. Next, **'SPREAD C'** hands are held parallel with palms down and are simultaneously swung from side to side. Lastly, vertical right **'Y'** hand is held with palm forward and appears to wobble from side to side as the wrist twists. (ASL CONCEPT—**pretend - act - like**.)

posh: *adj.* elegant; fashionable. *That is a posh outfit you are wearing.*

SIGN #1: Tip of thumb of vertical right **'3'** hand, palm left, is placed on the chin. Then the hand is given a slight but firm lift. Facial expression is important.

OR

SIGN #2: Horizontal right **'S'** hand, palm toward the body, is held on the chin and the forefinger is thrust out to form a **'ONE'** handshape. (This sign is formed along with the release of a slight puff of air from between the lips as the forefinger is flicked out.)

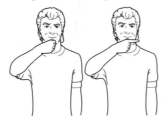

position: *n.* place; location. *My office is in a good position away from all the noise and activity of the shop floor.*

SIGN #1: Horizontal **'K'** hands are held out in front of the body with palms facing each other and tips of middle fingers touching. The hands then create a circle as they are drawn apart and brought toward the chest where they meet again. Sign choices must be made on the basis of context.
ALTERNATE SIGN—**place** #1

position: *n.* job; post (as in employment). *She applied for the new position in marketing.*

SIGN #2: Wrist of right **'A'** (or **'S'**) hand, palm facing away from the body, strikes wrist of the left **'A'** (or **'S'**) hand, which is held in front of/below the right hand with palm facing downward. Motion is repeated.
ALTERNATE SIGN—**position** #1

position: *n.* opinion; point of view. *He explained his position on the issue of disarmament.*

SIGN #3: Vertical right **'MODIFIED O'** hand is held just in front of mid-forehead with palm facing left, and is bobbed slightly.
ALTERNATE SIGN—**view** #3

(be in a) position to: *v.* to be able to. *I am in a position to help you; just tell me what you need.*

SIGN #4: **'A'** hands, palms down, are held slightly apart, and are then firmly pushed a very short distance downward.

positive: *adj.* tending to emphasize what is good or praiseworthy. *Positive thinking helps your self-image.*

SIGN #1: Forearm moves forward/downward as forefinger of right **'ONE'** hand, palm left, is tapped a few times at right angles against horizontal forefinger of left **'ONE'** hand.

positive: *adj.* indicative that there is disease present. *The patient became depressed after the doctor informed him that his test results were positive.*

SIGN #2: Horizontal right **'BENT EXTENDED B'** hand is brought back firmly so that fingertips make contact with upper right chest. At the same time, the signer's upper front teeth are resting on the lower lip. (The sample sentence in ASL is: *DOCTOR TEST...DIABETES* (or whatever the testing is for) *HAVE...TELL HIM/HER...DEPRESS.*) This sign is used when the type of test is already understood. Signs in this context vary. Sometimes **positive** #1 is used.

positive: *adj.* certain; sure. *He is positive that he knows that man.*

SIGN #3: Forefinger of vertical right **'ONE'** hand, palm facing left, is held against the lips and the hand is moved sharply forward.

positive: *adj.* expressing confidence or certainty about something. *I am positive we will finish on time.*

SIGN #4: **'SPREAD EXTENDED C'** hands are held with palms toward the body at an upward angle, the left hand close to the chest and the right hand just above/ahead of the left. The hands are then thrust forward as they are snapped shut to form **'S'** hands.

positive: *adj.* (Math) having a value greater than zero. *The answer to the problem will be a positive number.*

SIGN #5: Forefinger of right **'ONE'** hand is dropped forward smartly to strike horizontal forefinger of left **'ONE'** hand at right angles.

positive: *adj.* (Physics) related to the type of electrical charge created when there is one less electron in the outer electron ring of an atom. *The positive electrode on a battery is called an anode.*

SIGN #6: Forefinger of right **'ONE'** hand is dropped forward smartly to strike horizontal forefinger of left **'ONE'** hand at right angles.

possess: *v.* to own; have. *As a nurse, she must possess good interpersonal skills.*

SIGN: Horizontal right **'BENT EXTENDED B'** hand is brought back firmly so that fingertips make contact with upper right chest. At the same time, the signer's upper front teeth are resting on the lower lip.

possession: *n.* anything that is owned. *His most valued possession is his bicycle.*

SIGN: Right **'EXTENDED B'** hand, palm upward and fingers pointing forward, is moved rightward in an arc formation.

(take) possession of: *v.* to assume occupancy or ownership of real estate or other property. *We will take possession of our new home at the end of this month.*

SIGN: Vertical right **'FLAT O'** hand is held just in front of the right shoulder with palm facing forward/leftward. Vertical left **'FLAT O'** hand is held a little further forward in front of the left side of the chests with palm facing right. The hands are then firmly moved forward/leftward. (Signs vary depending upon what is being taken possession of. For items other than real estate, use **pick up** #1 or #2.)

possessive: *adj.* having an excessive desire to keep one's friends or property all to oneself and not to share. *The child is very possessive of all his toys.*

SIGN: Horizontal right **'EXTENDED B'** hand is firmly placed with palm against the chest while the left horizontal **'S'** hand, palm toward the body is held close to the chest in a possessive manner. (This sign is also used to mean 'possessive of a *person*' such as a friend or family member, but the left hand is held away from the body a short distance as if grasping the individual.)

possible: *adj.* capable of existing or happening. *It is possible to send 25 students to Youth Leadership Camp.*

SIGN: **'A'** hands, palms down, are held slightly apart, and are lowered and raised a couple of times as if knocking.
SAME SIGN—**possibility**, *n.*

post: *v.* to send by mail. *He will post his letter today.*

SIGN #1: Vertical right **'S'** hand, palm forward, is thrust ahead as it opens to form a **'CONTRACTED 5'** hand. ❖
ALTERNATE SIGN—**send** #1

post: *v.* to put up in a public place. *Please post the announcement of the meeting on the bulletin board.*

SIGN #2: Horizontal **'EXTENDED A'** hands, held apart with palms down, are pushed forward slightly, and then curved downward in arc formation (the arc bowing toward the body).

post: *n.* a length of wood, metal, or other material set upright in the ground to support or mark something. *The telephone post is broken.*

SIGN #3: Horizontal **'C'** hands are held apart with palms facing each other. Then they are moved upward simultaneously. (The distance between the hands depends on the diameter of the post.) If the post is relatively small in diameter, see **pole** #2.

post office: *n.* a place where stamps are sold and mail is received, sorted and sent out. *I will get the parcel weighed at the post office.*

SIGN: Fingerspell **PO**.

postage: *n.* the charge for having mail delivered. *You will need to have the parcel weighed to determine the cost of postage.*

SIGN: Left **'EXTENDED B'** hand is held with palm toward the body at an upward angle and fingers pointing rightward. Tips of extended fingers of right **'U'** hand touch the lips. The right wrist then rotates to turn the hand palm downward as it is lowered so that the tips of the extended fingers come to rest on the left palm.

postal code: *n.* a series of letters and numbers used in an address to help with the sorting and delivery of mail. *She had to look up the postal code for her apartment block.*

SIGN: Left **'EXTENDED B'** hand is held in a fixed position with palm facing backward/rightward and fingers pointing rightward/forward. Right **'EXTENDED A'** hand begins with palm toward the body and thumbtip on the lips, and is then lowered as the wrist twists to turn the palm down and the thumbtip is pressed into the left palm. Next, fingerspell **CODE**. (In contexts where the topic of 'mail' or 'addresses' is understood, **postal code** is frequently fingerspelled in the abbreviated form **PC**.)

postcard: *n.* a card, usually with a picture on the front and space for a written message, address and stamp on the back. *They sent us a postcard from Rome.*

SIGN: Fingerspell **POSTCARD**. (Alternatively, the abbreviated form **PC** may be fingerspelled.)

postdated: *adj.* having a future date (on a cheque) so that it will be cashed later than the present time. *Some rental agencies prefer that their tenants use a series of postdated cheques.*

SIGN: Fingerspell **POSTDATED**.

poster: *n.* a large advertisement, notice or picture that is posted. *She has a **poster** of her favourite actor on her bedroom wall.*

SIGN #1: Horizontal **'EXTENDED A'** hands are held apart with palms down, are pushed forward slightly, and then curved downward in arc formation (the arc bowing toward the body).

OR

SIGN #2: **'ONE'** hands, palms down and fingers pointing forward, are placed side by side and are drawn apart, moved down, and brought together again to outline the poster.

posthumous: *adj.* occurring after a person's death. *The soldier was given a **posthumous** award for his bravery.*

SIGN: Right **'EXTENDED B'** hand is held with palm facing left and fingers pointing forward as it curves forward across the back of the left **'STANDARD BASE'** hand. Next, **'EXTENDED B'** hands are held with fingers pointing forward, left palm facing up and right palm facing down. Then they are flipped over simultaneously so that the palm positions are reversed. (ASL CONCEPT—**after - death**.)

postmortem: *n.* the examination of a dead body to determine the cause of death. *A **postmortem** was conducted at the forensics laboratory.*

SIGN: **'EXTENDED B'** hands are held with fingers pointing forward, left palm facing up and right palm facing down. Then they are flipped over simultaneously so that the palm positions are reversed. Next, horizontal **'EXTENDED B'** hands, palms toward body, fingertips touching either side of the chest, are moved down and placed at the waist. Finally, **'V'** hands, palms down, extended fingers of one hand pointing toward extended fingers of the other hand, are simultaneously moved apart at least twice while the extended fingers retract to take on **'CLAWED V'** handshapes. (ASL CONCEPT—**dead - body - analyze**.)

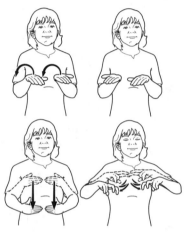

postpone: *v.* to put off; delay until a future time. *They decided to **postpone** the meeting.*

SIGN: Horizontal **'F'** hands are held parallel with palms facing each other and are simultaneously curved forward in a slight arc formation.
ALTERNATE SIGN—**delay**

postscript: *n.* a short message added after the signature at the end of a letter. *Her **postscript** informed us she would arrive on Friday.*

SIGN: Fingerspell **PS**.

posture: *n.* the position assumed by the body; the way in which the body is carried. *Appropriate exercise helps you to maintain good posture.*

SIGN: Fingerspell **POSTURE**.

pot: *n.* a heatproof container used for cooking food. *We will need a big pot to boil this many potatoes.*

SIGN #1: **'CROOKED EXTENDED B'** hands are held side by side with palms up. Then they are moved apart and upward to outline the shape of a bowl.

pot: *n.* a slang expression used for cannabis or marijuana. *Some of his friends smoked pot at parties.*

SIGN #2: Joined thumb and forefinger of vertical right **'F'** (or **'CLOSED X'** hand), palm left, are tapped a couple of times against the right side of the lips.

pot: *n.* the money or stakes in a game involving gambling. *Sometimes they play poker for a very large pot.*

SIGN #3: Back of right **'CONTRACTED B'** (or **'BENT EXTENDED B'**) hand, palm up, is tapped two or three times on upturned palm of left **'EXTENDED B'** hand.

pot belly: *n.* a protruded abdomen. *Santa Claus is noted for his pot belly.*

SIGN: Right **'EXTENDED B'** hand, palm down and fingers pointing forward, is held at mid waist and is curved forward and down as it changes to a **'BENT EXTENDED B'** handshape.

potato: *n.* a starchy oval tuber eaten as a vegetable. *My favourite vegetable is a baked potato.*

SIGN #1: Crooked fingertips of right **'CLAWED V'** hand, palm down, are tapped twice on the back of the left **'STANDARD BASE'** hand.

SIGN #2 [ATLANTIC]: Vertical left **'ONE'** hand is held in a fixed position with palm forward/rightward. Horizontal right **'ONE'** hand, palm toward the body and forefinger pointing leftward, is positioned so that the first joint of the forefinger is held against the left forefinger and drawn downward along it. The movement is repeated several times.

potent: *adj.* powerful; strong; persuasive. *The premier has a potent influence on his cabinet members.*

SIGN: **'S'** hands are held parallel with palms facing the chest. The forearms are then simultaneously and purposefully lowered so that the palms, which still face the body, are slanted slightly upward.

potential: *adj.* possible but not yet existing. *He suggested several potential ways to solve the problem.*

SIGN: **'A'** hands, palms down, are held slightly apart, and are lowered and raised a couple of times as if knocking.

pothole: *n.* a deep hole in a road or street surface resulting from weather conditions and continued use. *Every spring the city streets are full of potholes.*

SIGN: Horizontal **'C-INDEX'** hands are held parallel with palms facing each other. To indicate numerous potholes, the sign is repeatedly set down in various locations. (**POTHOLE** may be fingerspelled.)

potion: *n.* a drink of something medicinal, poisonous, or supposedly having magical properties. *The potion made her feel drowsy and weak.*

SIGN: Tip of middle finger of right **'BENT MIDFINGER 5'** hand is placed on the upturned left palm, and maintains contact with the left palm as the right hand teeters back and forth a few times. Next, right **'C'** hand is held in a horizontal position near the mouth with palm facing left. The hand is then tipped upward slightly. (ASL CONCEPT—**medicine** (or **poison** or **drug**, depending on the type of potion) - **drink**.)

potluck: *n.* a type of meal for which all partakers contribute food. *I am taking a casserole to the potluck at the church tomorrow.*

SIGN: Right **'MODIFIED O'** hand, palm toward body, is brought upward to the mouth, and fingertips are tapped against lips. Next, left **'EXTENDED B'** hand is held palm up in front of the left side of the upper chest while the right hand is held up high to the right with palm facing leftward/upward. As the right hand moves toward the chest, the left hand moves leftward to a higher position and the hands continue to alternate in this fashion. (ASL CONCEPT—**food - bring bring bring**.) **POTLUCK** is frequently fingerspelled.

potpourri: *n.* a mixture of various things. *The evening offered a potpourri of entertainment.*

SIGN #1: **'BENT L'** hands are positioned palms-down with tips of forefingers touching each other, the right finger pointing leftward and the left finger pointing rightward. Then they are moved apart with forefingers fluttering.

potpourri: *n.* a mixture of dried plants and flowers preserved to scent the air in a specific place, usually a drawer, closet, room, etc. *She has lavender potpourri in the bathroom.*

SIGN #2: Right **'EXTENDED B'** hand is held with palm facing the body, and fingertips just in front of the nose and pointing leftward/upward. The hand is then circled forward a few times in small clockwise circles.

pottery: *n.* articles made from clay and hardened by baking in a kiln. *She creates very distinctive pottery in her home studio.*

SIGN: Fingerspell **POTTERY**.

poultry: *n.* domestic fowl; chicken, turkey, duck, etc. *Most poultry are excellent sources of low-fat dietary protein.*

SIGN: Right **'MODIFIED G'** hand is held at chin, palm facing forward, while thumb and forefinger are opened and closed at least twice to simulate the movement of a bird's beak.

pounce on: *v.* to attack an unwitting person or idea; to spring or swoop down upon. *She is always ready to pounce on anyone who disagrees with her.*

SIGN: Right **'CLAWED V'** hand is used to strike forward/downward in whatever direction the target of the 'pouncing' happens to be located. (This sign is used specifically with *people*. For *animals*, two hands are used, one hand held slightly ahead of the other.) ❖

pound: *n.* a unit of weight equal to 16 ounces. *This bag of sugar weighs one pound.*

SIGN #1: Horizontal left **'U'** hand is held with palm facing rightward, but angled slightly toward the body while the fingers point forward/rightward. Extended fingers of horizontal right **'U'** hand are rested on extended fingers of left hand at right angles to them. The right hand then rocks up and down from the wrist a couple of times.

SIGN #2 [ONTARIO]: **'EXTENDED B'** hands, held apart with palms up and fingers pointing forward, are alternately raised and lowered at least twice.

pound: *n.* an enclosure where stray animals are kept until their owners claim them. *When our dog was lost we were relieved to find he had been taken to the pound.*

SIGN #3: Fingerspell **POUND**.

pound: *v.* to strike heavily and repeatedly. *The boxer* **pounded** *his opponent causing him to collapse.*

SIGN #4: Right **'S'** hand, palm facing left, is repeatedly moved forward forcefully to strike the forefinger of the left **'ONE'** hand which is held upright with palm facing rightward/ forward. (Signs vary considerably depending on what is being pounded and what is doing the pounding.)

pour: *v.* to cause to flow in a stream. *Please pour some milk on my cereal.*

SIGN: Horizontal right **'Y'** hand is held with palm facing left. The wrist then rotates to tilt the hand leftward so that the palm faces basically downward. (Handshapes vary according to the size and shape of the container that the liquid is being poured from. Movement also varies. Sometimes the hand is moved in small counter-clockwise circles.)

pout: *v.* to thrust out one's lips in a fit of sullenness; sulk. *A child might* **pout** *in order to get his own way.*

SIGN: Tips of forefingers of **'ONE'** hands are placed at either side of the mouth which is drawn downward in a pout. The face and arms then appear to slump slightly as one unit.

poverty: *n.* the condition of being without enough money, food, shelter and other necessities of life. *More than half of the people in the world live in* **poverty.**

SIGN: Thumb and fingertips of right **'CONTRACTED 5'** hand grasp left elbow and close to form a **'FLAT O'** as they slide down-ward off the elbow. Motion is repeated.
ALTERNATE SIGNS—**poor** #2 & #3

(face) powder: *n.* a preparation consisting of tiny loose particles that are patted on the face for cosmetic purposes. *Face powder is used to absorb excess stage makeup.*

SIGN #1: Left **'EXTENDED B'** hand is held palm up at upper chest level while the right **'EXTENDED B'** hand begins with palm down and fingers laid in the left palm at right angles. The right hand is raised as the fingers pat the right cheek. The right hand is then lowered to the left palm again and finally raised to pat the left cheek. (**POWDER** may be fingerspelled.)

powder: *n.* a preparation consisting of tiny loose particles. *I need to go to the drugstore to get some baby* **powder.**

SIGN #2: Right **'C'** hand is held with palm forward as if clutching a can or bottle and is shaken from side to side as if sprinkling powder.

(gun) powder: *n.* an explosive mixture such as that which is used in fireworks or shot from guns. *The jeep contained several crates of gun powder.*

SIGN #3: **'S'** hands are held with wrists crossed and palms down, the right hand nearest the body. Then both hands are thrust upward forcefully so that the palms face each other.

power: *n.* authority; influence. *American presidents have limited* **power** *to veto legislation.*

SIGN #1: Fingertips of right **'SPREAD C'** hand are brought forcefully against left bicep.
SAME SIGN—**powerful,** *adj.,* in this context.

power: *n.* strength; force. *The engine in this car has a lot of power.*

SIGN #2: **'S'** hands are held parallel with palms facing upward but angled toward the chest. The hands are then forcefully brought closer to the chest.

SAME SIGN—**powerful**, *adj.*, in this context.

power: *n.* electricity. *Power and water are included in the rent for this apartment.*

SIGN #3: Crooked forefingers of horizontal **'x'** hands, palms facing body, are tapped together at least twice.

(in) power: *adj.* in a position of control or authority. *Since Canadian Confederation in 1867, the Liberal party has been in power longer than any other.*

SIGN #4: Horizontal **'x'** hands are held slightly apart with left palm facing right and right palm facing left. Then they are alternately moved backward and forward.

practical: *adj.* level-headed; possessing common sense. *She is a very practical person.*

SIGN: Right vertical **'EXTENDED C'** hand, palm toward the face, is held with fingertips touching the right side of the forehead. The hand is then quickly drawn forward/rightward as the fingers close to form an **'S'** handshape. (The sample sentence in ASL is: *SHE COMMON SENSE (accompanied by nodding of the head and an approving facial expression).)* Sign choice depends on context.

practically: *adv.* virtually; almost. *We see each other practically everyday.*

SIGN: Both **'BENT EXTENDED B'** hands are held with palms toward the body. The left hand remains steady, while the fingertips of the right hand are brushed upward from the knuckles of the left.

practice: *n.* the repetition of an activity in order to improve one's skills. *The volleyball practice lasts for 2 hours every day.*

SIGN #1: Left **'ONE'** hand is held in a fixed position with palm down and forefinger pointing forward/rightward. With palm facing downward at a slight leftward/forward angle and knuckles lying along the left forefinger, the right **'A'** hand slides back and forth.

SAME SIGN—**practise**, *v.*, in this context, *e.g., We will practise our volleyball skills after school.*

practice: *n.* a business set up for a profession such as law or medicine. *She has a law practice in an office tower downtown.*

SIGN #2: Wrist of vertical right **'B'** hand, palm facing forward/leftward, is brushed back and forth against wrist of left **'STANDARD BASE'** hand.

ALTERNATE SIGN—**business** #2

Practise, *v.*, in this sense is not signed in this way. In English: *She practises law.* In ASL: *SHE LAWYER.*

practise [*also spelled* **practice**]: *v.* to do; follow a certain way of doing something. *You should practise what you preach.*

SIGN: Horizontal **'EXTENDED A'** hands, left palm facing right and right palm facing left, are held with the right hand behind/above the left. The hands are then moved forward/downward together.

pragmatic: *adj.* related to everyday, sensible, practical matters. *He takes a pragmatic approach to things.*

SIGN: Right vertical **'EXTENDED C'** hand, palm toward the face, is held with fingertips touching the right side of the forehead. The hand is then quickly drawn forward/rightward as the fingers close to form an **'S'** handshape.

SAME SIGN—**pragmatism**, *n.*

prairie: *adj.* pertaining to an expanse of flat or rolling grassland. *Alberta, Saskatchewan, and Manitoba are Canada's prairie provinces.*

SIGN: Vertical **'BENT EXTENDED B'** hands are held together, right in front of left, close to the chest with the right palm facing left and the left palm facing right. The left hand remains fixed while the right hand moves directly forward. (**PRAIRIE** is frequently fingerspelled.)

SAME SIGN—**prairie**, *n.*

praise: *v.* to applaud; commend. *Considerate employers praise their workers for their achievements.*

SIGN: Right **'EXTENDED B'** hand, palm down, fingers pointing forward and slightly to the left, is brought down twice on the upturned palm of the left **'EXTENDED B'** hand whose fingers point forward and slightly to the right.

(play a) prank on: *v.* to play a mischievous trick or practical joke on. *On April Fool's Day I always play a prank on my brother.*

SIGN #1: **'FLAT O'** hands, with palms up, are positioned so that the right hand is just in front of the mouth or chin while the left hand is a little lower and farther ahead. The thumbs slide across the fingers several times thus causing the handshapes to alternate between **'FLAT O'** and **'OFFSET O'**. Movement is repeated. Meanwhile, the signer's lips are protruded into a square shape with the closed teeth exposed. The facial expression must be a happy one or perhaps mischievous. Otherwise, it could be confused with **sadistic** which is similar except that it incorporates a menacing facial expression. ❖

OR

SIGN #2: With palm facing left, horizontal right **'X'** hand is stroked forward at least twice across the top of horizontal left **'X'** hand, which is held with palm facing right. ❖

pray: *v.* to make an earnest request of God. *They will pray for his recovery.*

SIGN: Palms of vertical **'EXTENDED B'** hands are placed together in prayer position.
SAME SIGN—**prayer**, *n.*, but there is a slight movement back and forth.

pre-: *prefix* prior to; before (something else). *The coach called the players in early for a pre-game warm-up.*

SIGN: Back of fingers of horizontal right **'BENT EXTENDED B'** hand are held against fingers of horizontal left **'BENT EXTENDED B'** hand, palms facing each other. Right hand is then moved toward the body.

preach: *v.* to give religious or moral instruction. *Most parents do not mean to preach at their children; they just want to give them some guidance.*

SIGN: Vertical right **'F'** hand, palm facing forward, is poked forward a few times. This is a wrist movement. ❖
SAME SIGN—**preacher**, *n.* (Alternatively, **preacher** may be followed by a horizontal **'EXTENDED B'** hand, palm facing left, which is lowered slightly from the initial sign position.)

precarious: *adj.* perilous; risky; subject to failure. *With more layoffs being announced and because she is a new employee, her position within the company is rather precarious.*

SIGN: As the signer slowly shakes his head with an expression of hopelessness on his face, the wrist of right **'S'** (or **'A'**) hand, palm facing away from the body, strikes wrist of the left **'S'** (or **'A'**) hand, which is held in front of/below the right hand with palm facing downward. Motion is repeated. (This sign applies specifically to this context. In other contexts, the head movement and facial expression remain the same but sign choice must reflect the specific object at risk. The sample sentence in ASL is: *LAYOFF MORE MORE...SHE RECENT HIRE...JOB (shake head hopelessly).*)

(as a) precaution: *adv.* taking care to avoid an undesirable or dangerous occurrence. *As a precaution, you should always have your computer data on a back-up disk.*

SIGN #1: Thumbtips of horizontal **'MODIFIED 5'** hands, palms facing down but slightly tilted toward the body, are poked twice into either side of upper chest near shoulders. This movement is accompanied by a protruding tongue.

(take) precaution: *v.* be careful to avoid problems. *We always take precaution to make certain all windows and doors are locked before we leave home.*

SIGN #2: Horizontal **'K'** (or **'V'**) hands are held, right above left, with extended fingers pointing forward, the left palm facing rightward and the right palm facing leftward. The hands are brought together to strike each other a couple of times. Facial expression is important.

precede: *v.* to go before in time or order. *The Great Depression preceded World War II.*

SIGN: Back of fingers of horizontal right **'BENT EXTENDED B'** hand are held against fingers of horizontal left **'BENT EXTENDED B'** hand, palms facing each other. Right hand is then moved toward the body.

precious: *adj.* cherished; beloved; dear. *They were very concerned when their precious child became ill.*

SIGN #1: Knuckles of vertical right **'OPEN SPREAD O'** hand, palm toward the body, are placed on the chin and are firmly drawn downward, closing to form an **'S'** hand.

precious: *adj.* very valuable or costly in reference to gemstones or metals. *Diamonds, rubies and opals are **precious** gems.*

SIGN #2: Vertical **'F'** hands, palms facing forward, are held apart, and then are simultaneously curved toward each other until the joined thumbs and forefingers come together.

precipitate: *v.* to cause something to happen. *The mayor thought the news might **precipitate** a riot.*

SIGN: Left **'5'** hand is held with palm facing right while forefinger of right **'ONE'** hand is inserted between first two fingers of left hand and twisted 180 degrees either to the right or left.

precipitation: *n.* rain, snow, hail, or sleet, falling to earth from overhead clouds. *It has been a very dry summer with little or no **precipitation.***

SIGN: **'SPREAD EXTENDED C'** hands are held parallel with palms down, and are bounced up and down slightly at least twice. This is a wrist action.

precise: *adj.* perfectly correct or accurate; exact. *The weatherman tries to be **precise** in his forecasting.*

SIGN: Right **'F'** hand is held above and slightly to the right of the left **'F'** hand with palms facing. The hands then come together so that the joined thumb and forefinger of one hand strikes those of the other hand. (Alternatively, this sign may be made with **'K'** hands, the tips of the middle fingers coming together.)
SAME SIGN—**precision**, *n.*

predict: *v.* to foretell; to say in advance (that something will happen). *It was hard to **predict** the outcome of the election.*

SIGN: Right **'BENT V'** hand, palm facing backward, is held with tip of midfinger under the right eye and is then swung forward under the left **'STANDARD BASE'** hand which is held loosely in front of the body below eye level.
SAME SIGN—**prediction**, *n.*

predominant: *adj.* superior in power and/or influence; most common. *French language and culture are **predominant** in Quebec.*

SIGN: **'S'** hands are held parallel with palms facing the chest. The forearms are then simultaneously and purposefully lowered so that the palms, which still face the body, are slanted slightly upward. (For **predominantly**, *adv.*, see **most**.)

preface: *v.* to say something beforehand. *The speaker **prefaced** her remarks with several brief anecdotes.*

SIGN #1: Left **'5'** hand is held with palm facing right while forefinger of right **'ONE'** hand is inserted between first two fingers of left hand and twisted 180 degrees either to the right or left.

preface: *n.* an introduction to a literary work; foreword. *The **preface** explained the author's purpose in writing the book.*

SIGN #2: **'BENT EXTENDED B'** hands are held apart with palms facing each other and fingers of each hand pointing toward those of the other hand. The hands are then drawn closer together.

prefer: *v.* to like better. *I **prefer** to stay at home rather than go to the hockey game.*

SIGN #1: Tip of middle finger of right **'BENT MIDFINGER 5'** hand, palm toward the body, is tapped lightly against the chin.

OR

SIGN #2: Palm of horizontal right **'EXTENDED B'** hand is placed on the chest, and as the hand is moved forward a little and slightly upward to the right, it is changed to an **'EXTENDED A'** shape with the thumb pointing upward.
SAME SIGN—**preference**, *n.*

pregnant: *adj.* carrying a fetus within the womb. *Her doctor confirmed that she was **pregnant.***

SIGN #1: Right **'CROOKED 5'** hand, fingers pointing downward and palm against the abdomen, is drawn forward.
SAME SIGN—**pregnancy**, *n.*

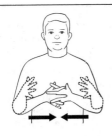

(get) pregnant: *v.* to become with child. *She has been trying to get pregnant for several years.*

SIGN #2: Horizontal **'5'** hands are held apart with palms facing each other but slanted slightly toward the body. The hands are then moved together so that the fingers interlock.

preheat: *v.* to bring an oven to the required temperature before placing food in it to be cooked. *The first step in making these cookies is to preheat the oven to 375°.*

SIGN: Right **'A-INDEX'** hand is held with palm downward and is twisted clockwise from the wrist.

prejudice: *n.* unfavourable judgement or discrimination based on inadequate facts; bias. *Hiring practices based on racial and sexual prejudice are forbidden by law.*

SIGN: Horizontal left **'BENT EXTENDED B'** hand is held with palm facing rightward/backward and fingers pointing to the right. Right **'EXTENDED B'** (or **'B'**) hand is held upright very close to the chest with palm facing left. The right hand then drops from the wrist until it is horizontal with fingertips forcefully striking left hand between the palm and the fingers. Facial expression is important.

preliminary: *adj.* occurring before or leading up to a scheduled event. *Preliminary trials are being held to see which skiers will join Team Canada.*

SIGN: Vertical left **'EXTENDED B'** hand is held in a fixed position with palm facing forward/rightward. Horizontal right **'EXTENDED B'** hand is held with palm facing left and the backs of the fingers against the back of the left hand. The right hand is then circled in a clockwise direction a couple of times making contact with the back of the left hand with each revolution. (Signs vary depending on context.)

premature: *adj.* before the usual or expected time. *Almost every year we have a premature snowfall in October.*

SIGN: Tips of midfingers of **'BENT MIDFINGER 5'** hands, palms toward the body, are placed slightly apart on the chest. The wrists then rotate forward as the hands move forward so that, while the palms still face the body, they are now angled upward slightly.

REGIONAL VARIATION—**early**

SAME SIGN—**premature**, when it refers to the birth of a baby prior to the expected due date. Alternatively in this case **PREMATURE** may be fingerspelled.

premeditated: *adj.* planned beforehand. *He was charged with premeditated murder.*

SIGN: Tip of forefinger of right **'CROOKED ONE'** hand, palm toward the head, is tapped against right side of forehead. Next, back of fingers of horizontal right **'BENT EXTENDED B'** hand are held against fingers of horizontal left **'BENT EXTENDED B'** hand, palms facing each other. Right hand is then moved toward the body. Finally, horizontal **'EXTENDED B'** hands, palms facing each other and fingers pointing forward, are held slightly apart at the left side of the body and are moved simultaneously toward the right. (ASL CONCEPT—**think - before - plan.**)

premier: *n.* the head of each provincial government in Canada. *The premier will call an election in November.*

SIGN: Fingerspell **PREMIER**.

premiere: *n.* the first public performance of a play, film, opera, etc. *We attended the premiere of Romeo and Juliet at the Shaw Festival in Stratford, Ontario.*

SIGN: **'B'** hands are placed side by side with palms forward but slanted downward slightly. The wrists then rotate outward as the hands move apart resulting in the palms facing each other.

premise: *n.* an idea on which an argument can be based or a conclusion drawn from. *Their decision to go into business was based on the premise that the economy would improve.*

SIGN: Tip of little finger of right **'I'** hand, palm toward the face, is placed on the right side of the forehead and is drawn forward/upward a brief distance.

premises: *n.* land and the buildings on it, especially a place of business. *The manager fired the employee and told him to leave the premises immediately.*

NOTE—When **premises** is already understood as in the sample sentence, no sign is necessary. The employee already knows that the manager means the 'worksite'. If there were any doubt about what constituted the premises, they would be specified in ASL by using the sign for **factory**, **store**, etc.

preoccupied: *adj.* engrossed or absorbed in one's own thoughts. *He was so preoccupied with the death of his dog that he could not do his work.*

SIGN: Tip of middle finger of right **'BENT MIDFINGER 5'** hand touches centre of forehead and moves downward to rest on back of left **'STANDARD BASE'** hand. Together the two hands then circle forward at least twice. (ASL CONCEPT—**think - touch long time**.) ALTERNATE SIGN—**absorbed**

prepaid: *adj.* paid for in advance. *The prepaid package was delivered yesterday.*

SIGN: Vertical **'5'** hands, palms facing the body, are held at chest level, and swung outward, away from the body so that the palms face down. Next, tip of forefinger of right **'ONE'** hand, palm down, is brushed forward across the upturned palm of the left **'EXTENDED B'** hand. This is a wrist movement; the right forearm does not move. (ASL CONCEPT—**finish - pay**.) PREPAID may be fingerspelled.

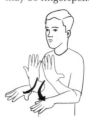

preparatory: *adj.* a preliminary year of study historically taken to raise basic academic skills to a level acceptable for entrance to Gallaudet University. *Ryan took a preparatory year at Gallaudet University in 2001.*

SIGN: Tip of forefinger of right **'ONE'** hand, palm facing left, taps the very end of little finger of left **'5'** hand, which is held horizontally with palm facing right and angled slightly toward the body.

prepare: *v.* to make ready in advance. *The hostess will need help to prepare the food.*

SIGN: Horizontal **'EXTENDED B'** hands, palms facing each other and fingers pointing forward, are held slightly apart at the left side of the body and are moved simultaneously toward the right. SAME SIGN—**preparation**, *n.*, but the movement is repeated.

prepared: *adj.* ready. *He was not prepared for the exam.*

SIGN: **'R'** hands are held apart with palms forward, the crossed fingers of the left hand pointing upward at a rightward angle while the crossed fingers of the right hand point upward at a leftward angle. The hands then fall outward so that the crossed fingers of the left hand point upward at a slight leftward angle and the crossed fingers of the right hand point upward at a slight rightward angle.

preposterous: *adj.* absurd; ridiculous. *He had the **preposterous** idea that he could pass the exam without studying.*

SIGN: Vertical right **'Y'** hand, palm toward the nose, is twisted forward so that the palm faces left.

prerequisite: *n.* something that is required as a prior condition. *An average of at least 70 percent is a **prerequisite** for entering most university programs.*

SIGN: Tip of forefinger of right **'X'** hand is placed in right-facing palm of left **'EXTENDED B'** hand. Together the hands are moved firmly toward the chest, giving the impression that the left hand is being tugged by the right forefinger.

prescription: *n.* written instructions from a doctor about medication to be dispensed. *The doctor gave me a **prescription** for a cough remedy.*

SIGN #1: Tip of middle finger of right **'BENT MIDFINGER 5'** hand is placed on the upturned left palm, and maintains contact with the left palm as the right hand teeters back and forth a few times. Next, left **'EXTENDED B'** hand is held in a fixed position with palm up and fingers pointing rightward/forward while thumb and forefinger of right **'CLOSED X'** hand, palm down, are placed on the left palm. The right hand moves back and forth as if colouring with a crayon. (ASL CONCEPT—**medicine - write on paper**.)

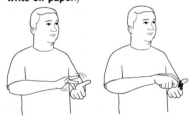

OR

SIGN #2: Vertical right **'R'** hand is held with palm facing forward. The wrist then rotates in a clockwise direction, thus turning the hand so that it is now held horizontally as the handshape is transformed to an **'X'** hand with palm facing left.

present: *n.* a gift. *She received a beautifully wrapped **present** from her friend.*

SIGN #1: Vertical **'X'** hands, with palms facing each other, are thrust forward simultaneously as they move to a horizontal position.

OR

SIGN #2: With a slight but deliberate downward thrust horizontal **'EXTENDED B'** hands are held parallel, with palms facing each other and fingers pointing forward. Then the hands take on a **'BENT EXTENDED B'** shape as they are swung inward with a slight downward thrust again, and the right hand positioned ahead of the left, both palms facing the body. (ASL users frequently fingerspell **GIFT** rather than use a sign for **present**.)

present: *v.* to give formally. *The mayor will **present** her with an award for bravery.*

SIGN #3: Vertical **'X'** hands, with palms facing each other, are thrust forward simultaneously as they move to a horizontal position. ❖ (Signs for **present** are often incorporated in the signs for objects of verbs as in '*present* a play' or '*present* a proposal', etc.)

present: *v.* to introduce someone, usually to an audience or group. *Ladies and gentlemen, I am here to **present** our guest speaker for tonight.*

SIGN #4: **'BENT EXTENDED B'** hands are held apart with palms facing each other and fingers of each hand pointing toward those of the other hand. The hands are then drawn closer together.

present a paper: *v.* to give (a lecture or formal speech). *The speaker will **present a paper** on Canadian architecture.*

SIGN #5: Right arm is raised and the vertical **'EXTENDED B'** hand, palm facing left, is brought forward sharply from the wrist a couple of times.

SAME SIGN—**to give a presentation**

present: *adj.* in a specific place, as opposed to being absent. *David is absent but the other students are present today.*

SIGN #6: **'CROOKED EXTENDED B'** hands are held parallel with palms up and are simultaneously circled outward. If **present** implies being somewhere other than in the immediate vicinity, this sign would be inappropriate. Instead the signer might use his right forefinger to point into space to indicate 'there' as opposed to 'here'. Alternatively, **show up** is used in certain contexts.

(at) present: *adv.* now; at this time. *At present, he is unemployed.*

SIGN #7: Both **'BENT EXTENDED B'** hands, palms up, are held slightly apart and are simultaneously lowered.
ALTERNATE SIGN—**now** #1

preserve: *v.* to protect; keep safe. *Deaf committee members will preserve the discussion by recording it on videotape.*

SIGN: Left **'V'** hand is held in a fixed position with palm facing chest and extended fingers pointing upward/rightward. Right **'V'** hand is held just ahead of left hand with palm facing chest and extended fingers pointing upward/leftward while tapping a couple of times against the fingers of the left hand.
SAME SIGN—**preservation**, *n.*
See **cherish** for a more appropriate sign choice when referring to the preservation of something of great value.

preside: *v.* to hold a position of control or authority. *The recently appointed judge will preside at the trial.*

SIGN: Horizontal **'X'** hands are held slightly apart with left palm facing right and right palm facing left. Then they are alternately moved backward and forward.

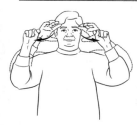

president: *n.* the head of state; head of a company or organization. *The president called the meeting to order.*

SIGN: Vertical **'MODIFIED 5'** hands, palms facing forward, are held near either temple and are simultaneously drawn outward as they close to become **'S'** hands.

press: *v.* to exert pressure on. *I will press the apples to extract the juice for making cider.*

SIGN #1: Horizontal **'EXTENDED C'** hands are held with the heels together, left palm facing up and right palm facing down. Together the hands are firmly moved downward as if the right hand is exerting pressure on the left. (Signs vary depending on what is being pressed. If it is a doorbell or an elevator button being pressed, the signer would use the right thumb to simulate the actual pressing action.)

press: *v.* to apply heat and pressure (to fabric) to smooth out creases; to iron. *I will press this skirt before I wear it.*

SIGN #2: Left **'EXTENDED B'** hand is held in a fixed position with fingers pointing rightward and palm upward but slanted toward the body. Right **'S'** (or **'EXTENDED A'**) hand is inverted with palm toward the body at a downward slant and is moved from side to side across the left palm.

press: *n.* the news media. *He was interviewed by the press.*

SIGN #3: Thumbnail of right **'MODIFIED G'** hand, palm forward/downward, is placed on upturned palm of left **'EXTENDED B'** hand. Right forefinger then moves up and down a couple of times, thus alternately creating **'MODIFIED G'** and **'CLOSED MODIFIED G'** handshapes.

press: *n.* a printing machine. *This press will print pictures on paper or on T-shirts.*

SIGN #4: **'S'** hands are held parallel with palms downward and are simultaneously lowered.

pressure: *n.* stress created by urgent demands; the force of something pressing against something else. *Deadlines create a lot of pressure for journalists.*

SIGN #1: Palm of horizontal right **'EXTENDED B'** hand is placed on top of horizontal left **'S'** hand of which the palm is facing right, but is angled slightly toward the body. Together, the hands are pressed very firmly downward a few times.

pressure: *v.* to make insistent demands; force through persuasion; compel. *Do not worry because I will not pressure you.*

SIGN #2: Left **'S'** hand is held with palm rightward/downward. Right **'EXTENDED B'** hand is held with fingers pointing forward/leftward/upward and palm forward/leftward/downward. With the palm of the right hand held against the top of the left hand, the right hand very firmly pushes the left hand forward/downward at a slight leftward angle. ❖

prestige: *n.* high status or reputation. *He bought a Jaguar thinking it would give him prestige.*

SIGN: Vertical **'BENT EXTENDED B'** hands, held at shoulder level with palms facing each other, are moved upward simultaneously and thrust forward very slightly.

presume: *v.* to assume; suppose. *I presume you will be free to attend our party.*

SIGN: Vertical right **'SPREAD C'** hand is held in front of right side of forehead with palm facing left, and is moved leftward as it closes to form an **'S'** hand.

presumptuous: *adj.* having too much confidence; too bold; arrogant. *It was presumptuous of you to agree to these expenses without approval from the members.*

SIGN: Horizontal **'CLAWED L'** hands are held with forefingers resting on either side of the forehead. The hands are then simultaneously thrust outward to indicate 'big-headedness'.

pretend: *v.* to make believe; to claim falsely or insincerely. *The children like to pretend they are cowboys.*

SIGN: Side of forefinger of right **'ONE'** hand, palm facing leftward/forward, is lightly brushed forward/downward twice on the right cheek, forefinger either remaining upright or bending slightly to become a **'BENT ONE'**.

pretentious: *adj.* pretending to be important; ostentatious. *I dislike the fact that she is so pretentious.*

SIGN: Tip of forefinger of right **'ONE'** hand touches forehead. Then vertical **'BENT EXTENDED B'** hands, held at shoulder level with palms facing each other, are moved upward simultaneously and thrust forward very slightly. This sign is accompanied by a haughty facial expression. (ASL CONCEPT— **think - high level**.) This sign is used specifically to describe *people*. When describing something such as a 'lifestyle' or a 'wardrobe' as pretentious, the first part of this sign is omitted.

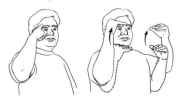

pretty: *adj.* pleasing to look at; attractive in a dainty or delicate way. *The girl has a pretty face.*

SIGN #1: Right **'CONTRACTED 5'** hand is circled counter-clockwise (from the signer's perspective) around the face as the fingers close to form a **'FLAT O'** hand, with palm and fingers toward the chin.

SIGN #2 [ATLANTIC]: Tip of forefinger of right **'L'** hand, palm facing backward, is stroked down the right cheek, thus causing the hand to assume an **'EXTENDED A'** shape.

pretzel: *n.* a brittle, salty snack food that comes either in sticks or knotted shapes. *A pretzel has a lower fat content than a potato chip.*

SIGN: Fingerspell **PRETZEL**.

prevail: *v.* to continue to be in use, in force or in control. *If current conditions prevail until December, our company will make a good profit.*

SIGN: **'EXTENDED A'** hands are held side by side with palms down and right thumbtip pressing against left thumbnail as the hands are moved purposefully forward. (Sign choices must be made on the basis of context.)

prevalent: *adj.* predominant; widespread; current. *Democratic governments are prevalent in the Western World.*

SIGN: Horizontal right **'5'** hand is held with palm down and fingers pointing forward. The hand then makes a wide arc leftward as it inscribes a circle in front of the body.

prevaricate: *v.* to speak falsely or evasively; to lie. *The jury must decide whether the witness was telling the truth or prevaricating.*

SIGN: Vertical right **'BENT B'** (or **'BENT ONE'**) hand, palm left, is brushed leftward across the chin.

prevent: *v.* to hinder; keep something from happening. *Snowstorms can prevent people from going to work.*

SIGN: **'EXTENDED B'** hands are held at right angles to one another, the left hand in front of the right, with fingers of left hand pointing upward to the right and fingers of right hand pointing upward to the left. The hands are then pushed firmly forward. ❖
SAME SIGN—**prevention**, *n.*

preview: *v.* to see a movie, art presentation or other event, before most people are invited to do so. *We were invited to preview her latest documentary film.*

SIGN #1: Right **'BENT V'** hand, palm forward, is held at shoulder level or above and is moved forward a short distance. (Alternatively, two hands may be used.)

preview: *n.* the showing of scenes from a movie for advertisement purposes. *I saw a preview of that movie last night.*

SIGN #2: **'SPREAD C'** hands are held horizontally and slightly apart, right above left. Then both are closed to form **'S'** hands as the right is brought down to rest on top of the left. Movement is repeated.

previous: *adj.* happening before; prior. *Have you had previous experience in this type of work?*

SIGN: Vertical right **'EXTENDED B'** hand, with palm toward right shoulder, becomes a **'BENT EXTENDED B'** hand as it bends toward the shoulder. Motion may be repeated.

prey on [*or* **prey upon**]: *v.* to seize (another animal) for food. *A hawk preys on field mice.*

SIGN #1: Right **'SPREAD C'** hand is held palm down at chest level and is then closed to form an **'S'** hand as it is thrust forward. Alternatively, this sign may be made with two hands held apart in front of the chest. ❖ (**PREY**, *n.,* is fingerspelled.)

prey on [*or* **prey upon**]: *v.* to make a victim of someone; to take unfair advantage of someone. *Thieves continue to prey upon careless homeowners.*

SIGN #2: Middle finger of right **'BENT MIDFINGER 5'** hand is placed on the upturned palm of the left **'EXTENDED B'** hand, whose fingers point forward/rightward, and is then retracted as it is brought back smartly toward the body. ❖

price: *n.* the amount of money asked in exchange for something being sold. *The price of a ticket to the hockey game is too high for me.*

SIGN: Vertical **'F'** hands, palms facing forward, are brought together so the joined thumbs and forefingers touch each other twice.

priceless: *adj.* very valuable. *She has a priceless art collection.*

SIGN: Vertical **'F'** hands, palms facing forward, are brought together so the joined thumbs and forefingers touch each other twice.

pride: *n.* satisfaction in oneself or one's accomplishments; self-respect. *Joe takes pride in his work.*

SIGN: **'EXTENDED A'** hand, with thumb pointing downward, is moved upward from stomach to chest. Facial expression must clearly convey 'pride'.

priest: *n.* an ordained member of the clergy. *He was the first Deaf priest in Canada.*

SIGN: Thumb and forefinger of vertical right **'MODIFIED G'** hand, palm leftward, are lightly brushed rightward several times across the throat.

primary: *adj.* first in importance. *His primary reason for attending university is to obtain a high-paying job.*

SIGN #1: Vertical **'F'** hands are held apart with palms facing forward. The hands are then brought purposefully together.
ALTERNATE SIGN—**important** #2

primary: *adj.* the first or elementary stage of a process. *Children are taught to read in the primary grades.*

SIGN #2: Horizontal **'EXTENDED B'** hands, palms down and fingers pointing forward, are held almost side by side except that right hand is raised slightly so that the right thumb is just above the left. The hands are then drawn apart. (The accompanying lip pattern is such that the signer appears to be articulating *'mall'*.)

primary colours: *n.* the three basic colours (red, yellow and blue) from which all other colours can be mixed. *You can create the colour green by mixing the primary colours yellow and blue.*

SIGN: Fingerspell **PRIMARY**. Then fingertips of right **'5'** hand, with palm toward the body, are fluttered on the lips (or chin).

prime minister: *n.* the head of government in certain countries, especially those with a parliamentary system of government. *Sir John A. Macdonald was Canada's first prime minister.*

SIGN: Fingerspell **PM**.

primitive: *adj.* crude; simple; basic; uncivilized. *They live in primitive conditions.*

SIGN: Vertical **'BENT EXTENDED B'** hands are held apart at chest level with palms facing each other. They then move a little closer to the body and downward.

prince: *n.* a son of a king or queen; the ruler of a certain region. *Prince Charles is very interested in environmental issues.*

SIGN: Right **'K'** hand, palm toward the body, is positioned with tip of middle finger touching the left shoulder. The hand is then moved diagonally across the chest to be placed at the right side of the waist.

princess: *n.* a daughter of a king or queen; the wife and consort of a prince. *Princess Anne is the only daughter of Queen Elizabeth II.*

SIGN: Right **'K'** hand, palm toward the body, is positioned with tip of middle finger touching the left shoulder. The hand is then moved diagonally across the chest to be placed at the right side of the waist.

principal: *n.* the head of a school. *The principal called a staff meeting to discuss the curriculum changes.*

SIGN: Horizontal **'K'** hand, palm down, is circled 180 degrees in a clockwise direction above the left **'STANDARD BASE'** hand and is then brought down so that the tip of the middle finger strikes the back of the left hand.

principle: *n.* a scientific law; basic truth. *The science instructor explained the principle of gravity.*

SIGN: Vertical left **'EXTENDED B'** hand is held in a fixed position with palm facing right while horizontal right **'K'** hand is placed palm down against the fingers of the left hand, and then lowered to a position nearer the heel of the left hand.

print: *v.* to write in the same style as printed or typewritten matter. *Most kindergarten students learn to **print** their own names.*

SIGN #1: Thumbnail of right **'MODIFIED G'** hand, palm forward/downward, is placed on upturned palm of left **'EXTENDED B'** hand. Right forefinger then moves down to create a **'CLOSED MODIFIED G'** shape. Next, vertical right **'CLOSED X'** hand, palm facing forward, moves up and down as it progresses rightward.

print: *v.* to reproduce in print. *The newspaper will **print** the story.*

SIGN #2: Thumbnail of right **'MODIFIED G'** hand, palm forward/downward, is placed on upturned palm of left **'EXTENDED B'** hand. Right forefinger then moves down to create a **'CLOSED MODIFIED G'** shape.
SAME SIGN—**printer**, *n.*, meaning 'a person whose job is printing', and may be followed by the Agent Ending (see p. LIV).

printer: *n.* a device that reproduces on paper information or graphics from a computer. *A laser **printer** produces the best copy.*

SIGN: Thumbnail of right **'MODIFIED G'** hand, palm forward/downward, is placed on upturned palm of left **'EXTENDED B'** hand. Right forefinger then moves up and down several times, thus alternately creating **'MODIFIED G'** and **'CLOSED MODIFIED G'** handshapes.

prior: *adj.* previous. *You must file your application **prior** to June 30th.*

SIGN: Vertical left **'EXTENDED B'** hand is held in a fixed position with palm facing forward/rightward. Horizontal right **'BENT EXTENDED B'** hand is held with palm facing left and the backs of the fingers against the back of the left hand. The left hand is then moved backward at a slight leftward angle a couple of times.

prioritize: *v.* to arrange in order of importance. *I think we should **prioritize** the items on the agenda.*

SIGN: Horizontal left **'5'** hand is held stationary with palm rightward but angled slightly toward the body and fingers pointing forward/rightward. Right **'5'** hand is held with the palm resting on the left thumbtip. The right hand is then curved forward/rightward and then downward as the palm touches each fingertip of the left hand.
SAME SIGN—**priorities**, *n., pl.*

priority: *n.* something being given special attention ahead of other things. *The completion of this project takes **priority** over all other assignments.*

SIGN: Horizontal left **'5'** hand is held stationary with palm rightward but angled slightly toward the body and fingers pointing forward/rightward. Right **'5'** hand, with palm down and fingers pointing forward/leftward, is used to tap several times on the thumbtip of the left hand.

prison: *n.* a jail. *If you break the law, you will be sent to **prison**.*

SIGN: **'4'** (or **'5'**) hands are held with palms facing the body. Back of right hand, whose fingers point slightly upward to the left, is positioned behind palm of left hand at right angles, and is thrust against it.

private: *adj.* pertaining to one person only; confidential. *It is difficult for Deaf people to have a **private** conversation.*

SIGN: Right **'A'** hand is brought to the lips with the thumb pointed upward and the palm facing left. Then the lips are touched twice with the thumbnail.
SAME SIGN—**privacy**, *n.*

privilege: *n.* a special right or benefit granted under certain conditions. *Inmates in the minimum security prison have several **privileges**.*

SIGN #1: **'K'** hands, palms down, are held apart, extended fingers pointing downward, and are then flicked upward from the wrists so that the hands are held in either a horizontal or upright position. Movement is repeated.

privilege: *n.* a special honour. *It is a privilege to be invited to the Lieutenant Governor's party.*

SIGN #2: Right **'U'** hand, palm facing left, is held in a vertical position so that the side of the forefinger touches the middle of the forehead. The hand is curved downward slightly and moved forward. (Alternatively, this sign may be made with two hands, in which case the vertical left **'U'** hand, palm facing right, is held below the right hand and follows its movement.)

privy to: *adj.* allowed to know certain information. *His secretary is privy to all of his business dealings.*

SIGN: **'K'** hands, palms down, are held apart, extended fingers pointing downward, and are then flicked upward from the wrists so that the hands are held in either a horizontal or upright position. Next, fingertips of right **'EXTENDED B'** (or **'BENT EXTENDED B'**) hand, with palm facing body, are tapped against right side of forehead. (ASL CONCEPT— **allow - know.**)

prize: *n.* something that is given to a winner. *His prize was a free trip to Ottawa.*

SIGN Fingerspell **PRIZE**.

pro: *n.* an abbreviation for 'professional' as applied to sporting activities. *The golf pro gave me a few pointers that helped me improve my game.*

SIGN #1: Fingerspell **PRO**.

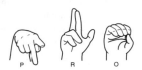

pro: *n.* for; in support of. *The issue of mainstreaming was debated pro and con.*

SIGN #2: Forefinger of right **'ONE'** hand is dropped forward smartly to strike horizontal forefinger of left **'ONE'** hand at right angles.

pro-: *prefix* in favour of; supportive of. *He became a member of a pro-Labour organization.*

SIGN #3: **'S'** hands, palms toward the body, are held at chest level with the left slightly above the right. Then the right is brought upward to strike the left.

probable: *adj.* likely to be or to happen, but not for certain. *The forecast is for probable rain in the afternoon.*

SIGN: **'A'** hands, palms down, are held slightly apart, and are lowered and raised a couple of times as if knocking.
SAME SIGN—**probability**, *n.*

probably: *adv.* most likely. *It will probably rain this afternoon.*

SIGN: **'EXTENDED B'** hands, held apart with palms up and fingers pointing forward, are alternately raised and lowered at least twice.

probation: *n.* a trial period during which prisoners are on temporary release into the community. *The convict was released on probation.*

SIGN #1: Vertical **'BENT V'** hands are positioned so that the left is a little closer to the chest than the right with extended fingers of the left hand pointing forward at a slight rightward angle while those of the right hand point forward at a slight leftward angle. The hands are simultaneously jabbed forward a few times. A look of intense concentration accompanies this sign. (**PROBATION** is frequently fingerspelled.)

probation: *n.* a trial period during which someone is given an opportunity to demonstrate his/her capabilities. *All new employees at this company are hired on six months' probation.*

SIGN #2: Vertical **'BENT V'** hands are positioned so that the left is a little closer to the chest than the right with extended fingers of the left hand pointing forward at a slight rightward angle while those of the right hand point forward at a slight leftward angle. The hands are simultaneously jabbed forward a few times. A look of intense concentration accompanies this sign. (**PROBATION** is frequently fingerspelled.)

probe: *v.* to examine closely; investigate. *Investigators will probe to find the cause of the airline disaster.*

SIGN #1: Left **'EXTENDED B'** hand is held in a fixed position with palm turned upward but slanted slightly rightward and toward the body while fingers point rightward/forward. Right **'ONE'** hand is held palm down as tip of forefinger brushes forward several times against palm of left hand.

SIGN #2 [ATLANTIC]: Right **'Y'** hand, palm down and tip of thumb positioned at the end of the nose, is moved downward and forward so that it slides across the upturned palm of the left **'EXTENDED B'** hand.

problem: *n.* something that is difficult to handle. *If you have a problem, come and see me.*

SIGN: Horizontal **'CLAWED V'** hands are held with palms facing the body and knuckles knocking against each other as the hands are alternately moved up and down.

procedure: *n.* an established method or course of action. *She explained the procedure for collecting social assistance.*

SIGN: Horizontal **'BENT EXTENDED B'** hands, left palm facing right and right palm facing left, are held with the right above the left. The hands then pass over and under each other as the forearms are simultaneously circled forward a few times.

proceed: *v.* to go ahead; advance; continue. *We could not proceed with our debate until all the candidates arrived.*

SIGN: Horizontal **'BENT EXTENDED B'** hands are held parallel with palms facing, and are simultaneously moved forward.

proceeds: *n.* profit. *Proceeds from this event will go to the Canadian Deaf Sports Association.*

SIGN: Back of right **'CONTRACTED B'** (or **'BENT EXTENDED B'**) hand, palm up, is tapped two or three times on upturned palm of left **'EXTENDED B'** hand.

process: *n.* a series of actions that produce a desired result. *The process of pasteurizing milk makes it completely safe to drink.*

SIGN: Horizontal **'BENT EXTENDED B'** hands, left palm facing right and right palm facing left, are held with the right above the left. The hands then pass over and under each other as the forearms are simultaneously circled forward a few times.

procession: *n.* a group of people moving forward in an orderly or ceremonial way. *The procession moved slowly along Bloor Street.*

SIGN: **'BENT 4'** hands are held left in front of right with palms down and are lightly swept forward a couple of times. (Sign choice depends on the type of procession being referred to and whether participants are walking or riding in a vehicle. This sign connotes 'people marching on foot'.)

proclaim: *v.* to announce publicly or officially. *Many Deaf Canadians would like to see ASL proclaimed an official language.*

SIGN: **'ONE'** hands, palms down, tips of forefingers touching either side of the mouth, are swung outward so that forefingers point upward and palms face away from the body. SAME SIGN—**proclamation,** *n.*

procrastinate: *v.* to delay needlessly; put off until later. *Sometimes I procrastinate when I am faced with tasks I dislike.*

SIGN: Horizontal **'F'** hands are held parallel with palms facing each other and are simultaneously moved forward in a series of small arcs. SAME SIGN—**procrastination,** *n.*

procure: *v.* to acquire; obtain; get. *His agent was able to procure the famous painting for him.*

SIGN: Horizontal **'SPREAD C'** hands, right on top of left, are closed to form **'S'** hands as they are brought toward the chest.

produce: *v.* to make; create; manufacture. *The Japanese produce a variety of electronics equipment.*

SIGN #1: Horizontal right **'S'** hand is placed on top of horizontal left **'S'** hand as both palms face the body. The right hand is then raised slightly and both wrists are bent causing the hands to turn so that the right palm faces left and the left palm faces right as the right hand re-establishes contact with the left hand.
SAME SIGN—**production,** *n.,* in this context.

produce: *n.* agricultural products collectively. *The produce always looks fresher at that store.*

SIGN #2: Fingerspell **FRUIT - VEG.**

profane: *adj.* coarse; disrespectful; blasphemous. *The use of profane language is forbidden in most schools.*

SIGN: Left **'ONE'** hand is held in a fixed position with palm down and forefinger pointing forward/rightward. Right **'Y'** hand, with palm down, is moved forward/rightward along the length of the left forefinger.
SAME SIGN—**profanity,** *n.*

profession: *n.* an occupation requiring special training in the arts or sciences. *Members of the medical profession require many years of training and internship.*

SIGN: Left **'B'** hand is held in a fixed position with palm facing right and fingers pointing forward. Right **'B'** hand, palm facing left, and fingers pointing forward, is positioned on top of the left hand and firmly moved forward.

professional: *adj.* related to any of the established professions such as law and medicine. *Professional ethics demand complete confidentiality between a doctor and his or her patients.*

SIGN: Left **'B'** hand is held in a fixed position with palm facing right and fingers pointing forward. Right **'B'** hand, palm facing left, and fingers pointing forward, is positioned on top of the left hand and firmly moved forward. (**Professional** is frequently fingerspelled **PRO** when it connotes 'having a great deal of skill or experience in a certain field'.)

professor: *n.* a high-ranking teacher such as one who teaches at a university. *She is the most popular professor in the Faculty of Law.*

SIGN: Vertical **'MODIFIED O'** hands are held parallel with palms facing each other and are moved slightly but firmly back and forth at least twice. (Agent Ending (see p. LIV) may follow.)

proficient: *adj.* having great skill, expertise or competence. *The award will be given to the most proficient skater in the competition.*

SIGN: Left **'EXTENDED B'** hand, palm facing right and fingers pointing upward/forward, is grasped by right **'OPEN A'** hand. Then right hand is pulled forward sharply and closed to form an **'A'** hand.
SAME SIGN—**proficiency,** *n.*

profile: *n.* a side view or outline of a human face. *The artist drew a profile of the wanted criminal.*

SIGN: Tip of forefinger of right horizontal **'ONE'** hand, palm toward the face, is used to trace the outline of the signer's features from forehead to chin. (Sign choices must be made on the basis of context.)

profit: *n.* money earned in a business after expenses are deducted. *The company made only a small profit this year.*

SIGN: Thumb and forefinger of right **'F'** hand, palm facing down, are brought slightly downward to be inserted into an imaginary pocket at waist level. Alternatively, the imaginary pocket is sometimes located at the left side of the chest.
SAME SIGN—**profitable,** *adj.*

profound: *adj.* showing or requiring much knowledge or depth of understanding. *A **profound** discussion of philosophical topics was led by the professor.*

SIGN: Edge of downward-pointing forefinger of right **'BENT ONE'** hand is placed against right-facing palm of the left **'EXTENDED B'** hand. Then the right hand is pushed firmly downward.

profoundly Deaf: *adj.* having no useful or functional hearing. ***Profoundly Deaf** people often prefer movies that have lots of action.*

SIGN: Tip of forefinger of vertical right **'ONE'** hand, palm forward, is placed just in front of the right ear. The hand is then very purpose-fully curved around the puffed right cheek, until the fingertip comes to rest at the mouth. Pursed lips and puffed cheeks are important features in conveying the concept of this sign. (This is a sign which is used with a great deal of pride and is used by Deaf users of ASL rather than hearing people unless a hearing person is referring to a Deaf person's degree of deafness with admiration.) Otherwise, one might sign **full + Deaf.**

prognosis: *n.* a prediction of the chance of recovery from a disease. *The doctors removed his malignant tumor and the **prognosis** for his complete recovery is excellent.*

SIGN: Right **'BENT V'** hand, palm facing backward, is held with tip of midfinger under the right eye and is then swung forward under the left **'STANDARD BASE'** hand which is held loosely in front of the body below eye level.

program: *n.* a plan; schedule; procedure. *The college offers a sign language **program**.*

SIGN #1: Left **'EXTENDED B'** hand is held in a fixed position with palm facing the body and fingers pointing forward/rightward. Horizontal **'K'** hand, palm down, is held just behind the left palm, then raised and lowered in front of the left hand.

program: *n.* a printed list of events in a public performance. *Please consult your **program** for details about the performance.*

SIGN #2: Left **'EXTENDED B'** hand is held in a fixed position with palm toward the body at a rightward and slightly upward angle. **'BENT EXTENDED B'** hand, palm leftward/backward, is placed against the fingers of the left hand and then slid down to the heel of the left hand.

program: *v.* to feed a program (into a computer). *I will **program** the computer using C++.*

SIGN #3: **'CONTRACTED B'** hands, palms forward, are held with the left slightly ahead of the right and are simultaneously jabbed forward a few times.

progress: *n.* satisfactory advancement. *Great **progress** has been made in technology for the Deaf.*

SIGN: Horizontal **'BENT EXTENDED B'** hands, left palm facing right and right palm facing left, are held with the right above the left. The hands then pass over and under each other as the forearms are simultaneously circled forward a few times.

progressive: *adj.* moving forward; favouring positive change. *The company has been very **progressive** in terms of adopting new technological advances.*

SIGN #1: Horizontal **'BENT EXTENDED B'** hands, left palm facing right and right palm facing left, are held with the right above the left. The hands then pass over and under each other as the forearms are simultaneously circled forward a few times.

progressive: *adj.* becoming more severe or worse (in terms of disease or a physical condition). *Multiple sclerosis is a **progressive** disease.*

SIGN #2: Horizontal **'K'** hands are held, right above left, with left palm facing right and right palm facing left yet both palms are angled slightly toward the body. The two hands brush against one another a few times as the right hand repeatedly moves leftward slightly, and the left hand moves rightward.

prohibit: *v.* to forbid by law or other author-ity. *At one time, many schools for the Deaf **prohibited** the use of ASL in the classroom.*

SIGN: Right **'L'** hand, palm facing left, is tapped smartly against right-facing palm of left **'EXTENDED B'** hand.

project: *n.* a proposal, plan or task requiring much effort. *The Canadian Cultural Society of the Deaf is working on a sign language* **project**.

SIGN: Vertical left **'EXTENDED B'** hand is held in a fixed position with palm toward the body. Horizontal right **'K'** hand, palm down, is held just behind the left hand, then is moved up and over the fingertips of the left hand. As it is lowered in front of the left hand, it takes on an **'I'** handshape and the wrist rotates in a clockwise direction to form a 'J'. (**PROJECT** is frequently fingerspelled.) This sign is used in educational settings. In other situations, the nature of the project is often specified, thus rendering the need for a sign for **project** unnecessary.

projector: *n.* a machine that projects an enlarged image on a screen. *She borrowed a* **projector** *and showed us the slides she had taken in the Orient.*

SIGN: Vertical right **'MODIFIED O'** hand, palm forward, is changed to a **'MODIFIED 5'** hand as it is thrust forward. (**PROJECTOR** may be fingerspelled.) See also **overhead** #1.

prologue: *n.* an explanatory introduction to a poem, play, speech or event. *The* **prologue** *gave the audience the historical background they needed before seeing the play.*

SIGN: **'BENT EXTENDED B'** hands are held apart with palms facing each other and fingers of each hand pointing toward those of the other hand. The hands are then drawn closer together.

prolong: *v.* to lengthen or extend beyond a normal time period. *Modern medicine allows doctors to* **prolong** *life.*

SIGN: **'EXTENDED A'** hands are held side by side with palms down and right thumbtip pressing against left thumbnail as the hands are moved purposefully forward. (See also **extend** #1.)

prom: *n.* a formal dance held at a high school or college. *She is buying an expensive dress to wear to the* **prom**.

SIGN: Right **'BENT V'** hand, palm facing downward, is held above upturned palm of left **'EXTENDED B'** hand. Extended fingers of right hand are brushed back and forth lightly across left palm. (**PROM** is frequently fingerspelled.)

promenade: *v.* to take a leisurely walk, especially in a public place as part of a special celebration. *Next Sunday, people wearing Victorian costumes will* **promenade** *in the park.*

SIGN: **'BENT 4'** hands are held left in front of right with palms down and are lightly swept forward a couple of times. (Sometimes **promenade** refers to a 'place where people walk', in which context this sign would be inappropriate.)

prominent: *adj.* eminent; widely known. *Chris Kenopic is a* **prominent** *Deaf leader in Canada.*

SIGN #1: **'BENT ONE'** hands, palms toward the body but slanted slightly toward each other, are positioned with tips of forefingers touching either side of chin. The arms then move forward/upward/outward simultaneously in two arcs.

prominent: *adj.* very noticeable; conspicuous; protruding; sticking out. *The CN Tower is a very* **prominent** *building on the Toronto skyline.*

SIGN #2: Vertical right **'CROOKED ONE'** hand is held with palm facing backward and tip of forefinger just under the right eye. As the hand moves forward, the wrist rotates to turn the hand so that the palm is eventually facing forward. Facial expression is important.
ALTERNATE SIGN—**notice**

promiscuous: *adj.* involving oneself in casual or indiscriminate sexual relationships. *Her* **promiscuous** *habits could result in her acquiring a sexually transmitted disease.*

SIGN: Vertical left **'5'** hand is held in a fixed position with palm facing right. Vertical right **'CLAWED V'** hand, palm facing left, is held against the left thumb and then drops forward to horizontal position. This is a wrist movement. (The reasoning behind this sign is that each finger of the left hand represents a different sexual partner as the right hand comes into contact with each one on the way past.)
SAME SIGN—**promiscuity**, *n.*

promise: *n.* an assurance given by one person to another. *It is important not to break your* ***promise*** *to the children.*

SIGN #1: Tip of forefinger of vertical right **'ONE'** hand, palm facing left, is placed just under the lower lip. As the right hand is then brought purposefully forward/downward, it takes on a **'B'** handshape and is pressed onto the top of the left **'STANDARD BASE'** hand. Handshapes vary.
SAME SIGN—**promise**, *v.*

SIGN #2 [ATLANTIC]: Right **'S'** hand is held with palm down, then twisted at the wrist so that the palm faces the body at a leftward angle as it is brought down emphatically to strike the upturned palm of the left **'EXTENDED B'** hand.

promising: *adj.* apt to have a positive outcome. *I can not say if your application will be accepted but it looks* ***promising***.

SIGN #1: Forearm moves forward/downward as forefinger of right **'ONE'** hand, palm left, is tapped a few times at right angles against horizontal forefinger of left **'ONE'** hand. (Signs vary depending on context.)

promising: *adj.* likely to have a successful future. *She is a very* ***promising*** *student.*

SIGN #2: **'ONE'** hands, palms more or less facing each other and forefingers touching (or almost touching) either side of forehead, are raised so that fingers point upward and palms face away from the body. Next, right **'EXTENDED B'** hand, palm facing left, is held in a vertical position near the right side of the head. The forearm is then moved forward a short distance so that the fingers eventually point forward/upward. (ASL CONCEPT—**success - will**.) The sample sentence in ASL is: *SHE STUDENT **SUCCESS WILL**.*

promote: *v.* to encourage the progress or existence of; further; foster. *The main objective of the Canadian Cultural Society of the Deaf is to* ***promote*** *Deaf Culture.*

SIGN #1: Horizontal **'EXTENDED B'** hands are held apart with palms angled so that they partly face each other while partly facing forward. The hands then simultaneously make several small circles outward.
SAME SIGN—**promotion**, *n.,* in this context.

promote: *v.* to advertise. *We will* ***promote*** *your product on this television station.*

SIGN #2: **'S'** hands, palms facing downward, are held slightly apart, with right in front of left. Right hand then strikes left hand and moves forward and back to strike it a second time.
SAME SIGN—**promotion**, *n.,* in this context.

promote: *v.* to raise to a higher rank or status. *The president of the company intends to* ***promote*** *her soon.*

SIGN #3: Vertical **'BENT EXTENDED B'** hands, palms facing each other, are held just above stomach level, then simultaneously moved upward and thrust forward very slightly.
SAME SIGN—**promotion**, *n.,* in this context.

OR

SIGN #4: Left **'5'** hand is held in a fixed position with palm facing the body and fingers pointing rightward. Vertical right **'CLAWED V'** hand, palm forward, is held just behind the left hand and then moved upward so that it is above the level of the left hand.
SAME SIGN—**promotion**, *n.,* in this context.

prompt: *adj.* done without delay. *She is very* ***prompt*** *at returning phone calls.*

SIGN #1: Left horizontal **'L'** hand, palm facing right, is held apart from and slightly ahead of right horizontal **'L'** hand, whose palm faces left. The hands are then simultaneously jerked upward toward the body as they are changed to **'CLAWED L'** hands.

prompt: *adj.* punctual; on time. *We have many important issues to discuss at the meeting so please be* ***prompt***.

SIGN #2: Right **'CROOKED ONE'** hand is brought down sharply so the tip of the forefinger touches the wrist of the left **'STANDARD BASE'** hand ever so briefly (as if touching the face of a wristwatch) before the hand is raised again.

prompt: *v.* to urge (someone to say or do something). *She prompted her son to complete his education before seeking employment.*

SIGN #3: Horizontal **'EXTENDED B'** hands are held apart with palms angled so that they partly face each other while partly facing forward. The hands then simultaneously make several small circles outward.

prone: *adj.* lying flat; face downwards. *Certain exercises are best when done in a prone position.*

SIGN #1: Left **'EXTENDED B'** hand is held in a fixed position with palm up and fingers pointing forward/rightward while the right **'V'** hand, palm facing relatively upward, rests in the left palm with extended fingers pointing leftward. The signer's head is also slumped forward and cocked slightly to the right.

prone: *adj.* tending; inclined (to). *He is prone to stretching the truth.*

SIGN #2: Tip of middle finger of right **'BENT MIDFINGER 5'** hand, palm toward the body, is placed on the right side of the chest and the hand is drawn away abruptly. An essential feature of this sign is the release of a puff of air from the lips as if whispering a 'P'. (Two hands may be used for this sign, with the left hand just below that of the right.)

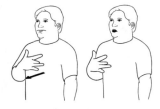

pronounce: *v.* to articulate; form spoken words. *She did not know how to pronounce the French word.*

SIGN #1: Right **'CLAWED V'** hand, held upright with the palm toward the body, is circled counter-clockwise (from this signer's perspective) in front of the lips.
SAME SIGN—**pronunciation**, *n.*

pronounce: *v.* to proclaim officially; declare. *At the end of the wedding ceremony, the minister will pronounce you husband and wife.*

SIGN #2: **'ONE'** hands, palms down, tips of forefingers touching either side of the mouth, are swung outward so that forefingers point upward and palms face away from the body.

pronounced: *adj.* clearly marked; noticeable. *He had a pronounced limp.*

SIGN: Tip of forefinger of right **'CROOKED ONE'** hand is positioned at corner of right eye and brought down to rest on upturned palm of left **'EXTENDED B'** hand.

proof: *n.* evidence that helps to establish the truth of a matter. *The police have no proof that he committed the crime.*

SIGN #1: Horizontal left **'EXTENDED B'** hand is held in a fixed position with palm up and fingers pointing forward/rightward. Horizontal right **'EXTENDED B'** hand is held palm up with fingers pointing forward/leftward and is brought down sharply onto the left palm.

proof: *n.* a trial photograph. *The photographer showed us proofs from our wedding.*

SIGN #2: Left **'EXTENDED B'** hand is held in a fixed position with palm facing right and fingers pointing forward/upward as vertical right **'C'** hand is held against the right cheek with palm forward at a slight leftward angle. Right hand is then moved forward/downward and placed firmly against the left palm.
ALTERNATE SIGN—**picture** #2

proof: *adj.* a term that applies to the potency of alcoholic fluids which has been standardized in most industrialized nations. *I do not know how anyone can drink whisky that is a hundred proof.*

SIGN #3: Vertical right **'O'** hand, palm forward/leftward, moves rightward and then downward at a slight leftward angle as if tracing the number '7' in the air.

-proof: *suffix* impervious to water, fire, ammunition, etc.; protected from. *Many well known people ride in bullet-proof cars.*

SIGN #4: **'EXTENDED B'** hands are held at right angles to one another, the left hand in front of the right, with fingers of left hand pointing upward to the right and fingers of right hand pointing upward to the left. The hands are then pushed firmly forward. (**PROOF** may be fingerspelled in this context.)

proofread: *v.* to read something written and mark errors to be corrected. *The editor* ***proofread*** *my manuscript before I sent it to the publisher.*

SIGN: Left **'EXTENDED B'** hand is held in a fixed position with palm facing rightward but slanted upward and toward the body slightly. Tip of forefinger of right **'ONE'** hand, palm down, is placed at the heel of the left hand, is stroked forward to the centre of the palm and deflected rightward/forward at an upward angle.

propaganda: *n.* the organized spreading of views or beliefs, especially those which hurt or offend other people. *That organization publishes racist* ***propaganda***.

SIGN: **'S'** hands, palms facing downward, are held slightly apart, with right in front of left. Right hand then strikes left hand and moves forward and back to strike it a second time.

proper: *adj.* appropriate; suitable. *It is important to use* ***proper*** *grammar when writing business letters.*

SIGN: Right **'ONE'** hand, palm left, is held above left hand, of which the palm faces right. Forefingers point forward. Right hand is then brought downward and tapped firmly on top of left hand a couple of times.

property: *n.* land; real estate. *They own some very expensive* ***property***.

SIGN: **'FLAT O'** hands are held slightly apart with palms up. Then the fingers are slid across the thumbs a few times, thus alternating between **'FLAT O'** and **'OFFSET O'** hands. (When the property referred to is anything other than land or real estate, sign choice varies according to context.)

prophecy: *n.* a prediction or guess about future events. *People believe that the Bible often reveals a divine message through a* ***prophecy***.

SIGN: Right **'BENT V'** hand, palm facing backward, is held with tip of midfinger under the right eye and is then swung forward under the left **'STANDARD BASE'** hand which is held loosely in front of the body below eye level.
SAME SIGN—**prophesy**, *v.*

(in) proportion to: *prep.* by comparison with the whole. *The Deaf Community is small in proportion to the general population.*

SIGN: Right **'BENT EXTENDED B'** hand is held close to the body in a virtually upright position, palm forward/leftward but slanted slightly downward while the left **'BENT EXTENDED B'** hand takes up a lower position farther forward than the right hand with palm facing that of the right hand. The wrists then simultaneously rotate a quarter turn to the right as the left hand moves closer to the body with palm facing forward/rightward but slanted slightly downward while the right hand moves to a lower position farther forward than the left hand with the palm facing that of the left hand. Motion is repeated.

propose: *v.* to offer for consideration; suggest. *I propose that we adjourn our meeting now.*

SIGN: **'EXTENDED B'** hands, palms up and fingers pointing forward, are held slightly apart with the right just ahead of the left, and are simultaneously thrust forward in an arc.
SAME SIGN—**proposal**, *n.*

pros: *n.* positive considerations about a specific matter. *We listed the* ***pros*** *and cons of the decision.*

SIGN: **'ONE'** hands, right palm facing left and left palm facing down, are positioned so the two forefingers form a cross. Then the hands are simultaneously lowered.

prose: *n.* continuous writing (not poetry). *The author is known for his exaggerated style of writing flowery* ***prose***.

SIGN: Left **'CONTRACTED C'** (or **'OPEN 8'**) hand is held horizontally with palm facing right while right **'CONTRACTED C'** (or **'OPEN 8'**) hand is held upright with palm facing left. The hands are held close enough together to be loosely interlocked. They are then drawn apart, closed and returned several times, thus alternating between **'CONTRACTED C'** (or **'OPEN 8'**) and **'FLAT O'** (or **'8'**) shapes with each movement.

prosecute: *v.* to bring legal action against (someone) in court. *Trespassers will be prosecuted.*

SIGN: Forefinger of horizontal right **'X'** hand, palm toward the body at a leftward-facing angle, is brought down smartly across the palm of the horizontal left **'EXTENDED B'** hand, which is facing rightward but angled toward the body.

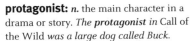

prospective: *adj.* expected; likely. *Choose your courses to suit your* ***prospective*** *career or profession.*

SIGN: Right **'EXTENDED B'** hand, palm facing left, is held in a vertical position near the right side of the head. The forearm is then moved forward a short distance so that the fingers eventually point forward/upward.

prosper: *v.* to thrive in a healthy way; succeed. *If you work hard, your business will likely* ***prosper***.

SIGN: **'ONE'** hands, palms down, forefingers almost touching either side of forehead, are raised so that fingers point upward and palms face forward.
SAME SIGNS—**prosperity**, *n.*, and **prosperous**, *adj.*

prostate [*also called* **prostate gland**]: *n.* a male gland surrounding the neck of the bladder. *Men sometimes have problems urinating as they get older because of the prostate.*

SIGN: Fingerspell **PROSTATE**.

prostitute: *n.* any male or female who engages in sexual activity for money. *The prostitute was often in danger on the street.*

SIGN: Vertical right **'OPEN A'** hand is held with palm toward the face and backs of fingers (up to the second joint) touching the right cheek. The hand is then brushed forward off the cheek a couple of times.
SAME SIGN—**prostitution**, *n.*

prostrate: *adj.* in a prone position; face down. *The police found the victim lying* ***prostrate*** *on the sidewalk.*

SIGN: Left **'EXTENDED B'** hand is held in a fixed position with palm up and fingers pointing forward/rightward while the right **'V'** hand is slumped in the left palm with wrist bent, palm facing relatively upward, and extended fingers pointing toward the chest. The signer's head is also slumped forward and cocked slightly to the right.

protagonist: *n.* the main character in a drama or story. *The* ***protagonist*** *in* Call of the Wild *was a large dog called Buck.*

SIGN: Vertical **'F'** hands are held apart with palms facing forward. The hands are then brought purposefully together. Next, horizontal right **'C'** hand, palm facing the body, is twisted in a circular motion from the wrist so that it becomes upright with palm facing leftward as it is brought back against the left shoulder. (ASL CONCEPT—**important - character**.)

protect: *v.* to defend from trouble or harm; guard. *A trained dog will* ***protect*** *your house.*

SIGN: Horizontal **'S'** hands are held, the left just in front of the right, with palms down in front of the centre of the chest. The hands are then simultaneously moved emphatically forward a short distance.
SAME SIGN—**protection**, *n.*

protest: *v.* to object, especially in a formal way. *Animal rights advocates will* ***protest*** *the sale of fur coats.*

SIGN: Vertical right **'S'** hand, palm facing backward, is held at or above shoulder level and is forcefully twisted a half turn so that palm faces forward. Alternatively, this sign may be made with two hands.
ALTERNATE SIGN—**object** #2
SAME SIGN—**protest**, *n.*

protocol: *n.* formal etiquette; procedures followed in diplomatic circles and at state events. *Protocol demands that dinner guests not be seated before the queen enters the room.*

SIGN: Thumb of vertical right **'EXTENDED B'** hand, palm facing left, is tapped a few times against centre of chest.

protrude: *v.* to stick out or thrust out from. *Certain signs are accompanied by the signer's tongue **protruding** between the teeth.*

SIGN: The tongue sticks out between the teeth as the vertical right **'BENT U'** hand is held against the chin with palm facing forward/leftward. (Sign choice depends entirely on what is protruding from what.)

proud: *adj.* pleased or satisfied with oneself. *Leaders in the Deaf Community are **proud** of their achievements.*

SIGN: **'EXTENDED A'** hand, with thumb pointing downward, is moved upward from stomach to chest. Facial expression must clearly convey 'pride'.

prove: *v.* to show to be true. *The DNA results will **prove** she was at the scene of the murder.*

SIGN: Horizontal left **'EXTENDED B'** hand is held in a fixed position with palm up and fingers pointing forward/rightward. Horizontal right **'EXTENDED B'** hand is held palm up with fingers pointing forward/leftward and is brought down sharply onto the left palm.

proverb: *n.* a short saying that expresses a well-known truth or fact. *My grandmother often quoted the **proverb** "A stitch in time saves nine".*

SIGN: Vertical **'V'** hands, palms facing forward, are held apart just above shoulder level, and are curved outward slightly from the wrists as they become **'CLAWED V'** hands.

provide: *v.* to supply; make available. *They needed a corporate sponsor to **provide** the funds for this project.*

SIGN: **'EXTENDED B'** hands, palms up and fingers pointing forward, are held slightly apart with one hand just ahead of the other, and are simultaneously thrust forward in an arc. ❖
SAME SIGN—**provision**, *n.*

province: *n.* a region of Canada that is governed as a special unit. *Each **province** of Canada will be represented at the conference.*

SIGN: Tip of middle finger of horizontal right **'K'** hand is used to mark a cross just below the left shoulder.
SAME SIGN—**provincial**, *adj.*

provoked: *adj.* angered; annoyed. *She is **provoked** because we did not include her in our plans.*

SIGN #1: Vertical right **'BENT MIDFINGER 5'** hand is held with palm left and tip of middle finger touching forehead. The wrist then rotates to turn the palm toward the face. Facial expression must clearly convey 'annoyance'.

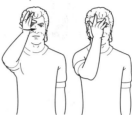

OR

SIGN #2: Right **'5'** hand is held palm down with tip of thumb touching centre of chest. The wrist then rotates rightward as the hand moves away from the chest and turns so that the palm faces the body. Facial expression is important and must clearly convey a feeling that something is unjust.

(These two signs are used only in passive voice situations or as adjectives to describe someone's feelings. It would *not* be possible to use these signs in an active voice situation such as: *We **provoked** her when we did not include her in our plans.*)

prowess: *n.* outstanding ability; bravery. *The athlete demonstrated his **prowess** in several sports.*

SIGN: Left **'EXTENDED B'** hand, palm facing right and fingers pointing upward/forward, is grasped by right **'OPEN A'** hand. Then right hand is pulled forward sharply and closed to form an **'A'** hand.
ALTERNATE SIGN—**adept** #2

proxy: *n.* a person authorized to act for someone else. *Anyone unable to attend the meeting will be allowed to vote by **proxy**.*

SIGN: Fingerspell **PROXY**.

prudent: *adj.* using good judgment; wise. *He is very prudent in managing his money.*

SIGN: Horizontal right **'X'** hand, palm down, is held in front of the mid-forehead and is shaken up and down from the wrist.
SAME SIGN—**prudence**, *n.*

prune: *n.* a purplish-black dried plum. *Although a prune may appear wrinkled and unappetizing, it is quite nutritious.*

SIGN #1: Fingerspell **PRUNE**.

SIGN #2 [PRAIRIE]: Tips of forefinger and thumb of vertical right **'MODIFIED G'** hand, palm toward the head, are placed on the right temple. As the hand is drawn slightly right-ward a couple of times, the thumb and forefinger close to form a **'CLOSED MODIFIED G'** shape.

pry: *v.* to ask impertinent questions (about someone's private matters); snoop. *I will try not to pry into your personal affairs.*

SIGN: Tip of forefinger of right **'CROOKED ONE'** hand touches nose and is then dropped down-ward and inserted at least twice into the small opening at the top of the horizontal left **'S'** hand which is held with the palm facing right. ❖

psalm: *n.* a sacred song from the Book of Psalms in the Old Testament. *The congregation said the Twenty-third Psalm.*

SIGN: Fingerspell **PSALM**.

pseudo: *adj.* not genuine or authentic. *They went through a pseudo marriage ceremony which was not legally binding.*

SIGN: Side of forefinger of right **'ONE'** hand, palm facing leftward/forward, is lightly brushed forward/downward twice on the right cheek. forefinger either remaining upright or bending slightly to become a **'BENT ONE'**.

psychiatry: *n.* a branch of medicine dealing with diagnosis and treatment of mental disorders. *One must have a medical degree before specializing in psychiatry.*

SIGN: Edge of right **'EXTENDED B'** hand, palm facing left, is tapped a couple of times between the thumb and forefinger of the vertical left **'CONTRACTED C'** hand of which the palm faces right.
SAME SIGN—**psychiatric**, *adj.*
For **psychiatrist**, *n.*, the Agent Ending (see p. LIV) may follow.

psychology: *n.* the study of human and animal behaviour. *Social work students need to take courses in psychology.*

SIGN: Edge of right **'EXTENDED B'** hand, palm facing left, is tapped a couple of times between the thumb and forefinger of the vertical left **'CONTRACTED C'** hand of which the palm faces right.
SAME SIGN—**psychological**, *adj.*
For **psychologist**, *n.*, the Agent Ending (see p. LIV) may follow.

psychotic: *adj.* having a very distorted view of reality. *Psychiatrists often treat psychotic patients with medication.*

SIGN: Left **'EXTENDED B'** hand is held in a fixed position with palm up and fingers pointing rightward/forward. Horizontal right **'EXTENDED B'** hand, palm facing left, slides forward along the left hand as the fingers bend to form a **'BENT EXTENDED B'** shape.

puberty: *n.* the period during adolescence when the sex glands become developed to a point where sexual reproduction is possible. *Some teenagers reach puberty earlier than others.*

SIGN: Fingerspell **PUBERTY**.

pubic: *adj.* relating to the lower part of the abdomen near the external genital organs. *Pubic hair starts to grow during adolescence.*

SIGN: Fingerspell **PUBIC**.

public: *n.* people in general. *This library is open to the **public** seven days a week.*

SIGN: Fingerspell **PUBLIC**. (ASL users rarely use this word as its meaning is already understood and not considered necessary. It is obvious that the library is intended for 'public' use unless otherwise stipulated.)

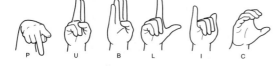

public school: *n.* any school that is part of a local free educational system. (This term usually connotes a school for hearing students as opposed to a school for the Deaf.) *The current trend is that **public schools** are mainstreaming Deaf children.*

SIGN: Side of forefinger of right **'ONE'** hand, palm down, is brushed upward against the lips several times with small forward circular motions. Next, right **'EXTENDED B'** hand, palm down, fingers pointing forward and slightly to the left, is brought down twice on the upturned palm of the left **'EXTENDED B'** hand whose fingers point forward and slightly to the right. (ASL CONCEPT—**hearing - school**.)

publicize: *v.* to make known to the general public; advertise. *The author was in Winnipeg to **publicize** his latest book.*

SIGN: **'S'** hands, palms facing downward, are held slightly apart, with right in front of left. Right hand then strikes left hand and moves forward and back to strike it a second time. SAME SIGN—**publicity**, *n.*

publish: *v.* to produce and distribute printed matter. *Our society will continue to **publish** a regular newsletter.*

SIGN: Thumbnail of right **'MODIFIED G'** hand, palm forward/downward, is placed on upturned palm of left **'EXTENDED B'** hand. Right forefinger then moves downward to form a **'CLOSED MODIFIED G'** shape. SAME SIGN—**publisher**, *n.*, and may be followed by the Agent Ending (see p. LIV).

puck: *n.* a small, black, hard rubber disk used in ice hockey. *The crowd rose and cheered as the **puck** went into the net.*

SIGN: Fingerspell **PUCK**.

pudding: *n.* a sweet dish, usually cooked and containing a variety of ingredients. *Mother always makes plum **pudding** for our Christmas dinner.*

SIGN: Fingertips of right **'SPREAD EXTENDED C'** hand, palm facing down, are tapped against the back of the left **'STANDARD BASE'** hand in a series of very short arcs moving in a forward/rightward/downward direction along the left hand. (**PUDDING** may be fingerspelled.)

puddle: *n.* a small pool of water. *Children love to play in the **puddles** after it rains.*

SIGN: Forefinger of vertical right **'W'** hand, palm facing left, is tapped against the chin. Next, horizontal **'C-INDEX'** hands are held parallel with palms facing each other. To indicate numerous puddles, the second part of this sign is repeatedly set down in various locations. (ASL CONCEPT—**water - hole**.)

puke: *v.* to vomit. *The smell of rancid meat made her **puke**.*

SIGN: Thumb of horizontal right **'MODIFIED 5'** hand, palm facing left, is held at chin while horizontal left **'MODIFIED 5'** hand is positioned just in front of right hand with palm facing right. The hands then move forward and downward in a slight arc.

pull: *v.* to move something by drawing it toward you. *He **pulled** the rope as hard as he could.*

SIGN: Horizontal **'S'** hands are held in front of the left side of the body, the left hand ahead of and to the left of the right. Then both hands are drawn simultaneously toward the chest as if pulling something. (Signs vary considerably depending on the size and shape of what is being pulled and how it is being pulled.)

pull off: *v.* to succeed in performing a difficult task or feat. *The gold medallist pulled off a perfect score.*

SIGN: **'ONE'** hands, palms down, forefingers almost touching either side of forehead, are raised so that fingers point upward and palms face forward. (When **pull off** means 'to physically remove or take something off', sign choice depends on what is being pulled off and from where. Often, natural gestures will suffice.)

pull over: *v.* to drive a motor vehicle to the side of the road and stop. *The police ordered the driver to pull over.*

SIGN: Horizontal right **'3'** hand, palm facing left, is moved firmly to the right and stopped abruptly.

pullover: *n.* a sweater that is pulled on over the head. *She is wearing a bright red pullover.*

SIGN: Horizontal **'A'** hands, palms facing the chest, are held against either side of upper chest near the shoulders and are simultaneously moved down in a slight arc formation to waist level.

pulse: *n.* the rhythmic throbbing of a heartbeat. *The rate of the average pulse is between 60 and 80 beats per minute.*

SIGN: Right **'FLAT C'** hand is used to clasp the wrist of the left hand of which the palm is facing up. (Signs vary according to where on the body the pulse is being taken, but the sign generally is formed by placing the fingers of the right hand on the pulse.)

pump: *n.* any device used to force the movement of a liquid or gas. *We need a pump to inflate this air mattress.*

SIGN: **'S'** hands are held slightly apart with palms down and are simultaneously pushed down and up several times. (Signs vary according to the type of pump and the actual movement required to activate it. Often, natural gestures will suffice.)

pumpkin: *n.* the large fruit of a creeping vine, having a thick orange rind, pulpy flesh and many seeds. *Each child has a pumpkin to make a jack-o-lantern.*

SIGN #1: Edge of forefinger of right horizontal **'B'** hand, palm down, is placed between the lips as the wrist makes small twisting movements back and forth to rock the hand rapidly. (Signs vary considerably.)

OR

SIGN #2: Right horizontal **'COVERED 8'** hand is held with palm down just above left **'STANDARD BASE'** hand. Then tip of middle finger of left hand is flicked against back of left hand, thus becoming an **'OPEN 8'** hand. Motion is repeated.

SIGN #3 [ONTARIO]: Vertical right **'SPREAD EXTENDED C'** hand is held with palm close to the right cheek as the heel of the hand pushes up against the lower right jaw a couple of times.

pun: *n.* the use of a word or words for humorous effect, often involving different senses of the same word or words that sound alike, e.g., "Before operating, the surgeon reassuringly informed his patient that he had never lost his 'patience' in the operating room." *A pun is a comical play on words.*

SIGN: Fingerspell **PUN**.

punch: *v.* to strike with a clenched fist. *Hockey players are penalized if they punch other players.*

SIGN #1: Right **'S'** hand, palm down, is driven forward with force. ❖

punch: *n.* a drink made from a mixture of fruit juices and sometimes alcohol in the form of wine or liquor. *He added sliced oranges to the punch.*

SIGN #2: Fingerspell **PUNCH**.

punctual: *adj.* always on time or within arranged time limits. *She picks me up every morning at 8 o'clock and is always punctual.*

SIGN: Right **'CROOKED ONE'** hand is brought down sharply so the tip of the forefinger touches the wrist of the left **'STANDARD BASE'** hand ever so briefly (as if touching the face of a wristwatch) before the hand is raised again.

punctuation: *n.* a system of symbols used in writing to convey pauses, intonations, and meanings, which are not otherwise conveyed in the written language. *The teacher corrected the punctuation in the students' essays.*

SIGN: Vertical right **'CLOSED X'** hand, palm facing forward, is firmly thrust forward a short distance as if putting a period on a vertical surface. Next, forefinger of vertical right **'CROOKED ONE'** (or **'BENT ONE'**) hand makes a quarter turn twist to the right to trace the outline of an imaginary apostrophe. (ASL CONCEPT—**period - comma**.) The series of punctuation marks may also include hyphens, parentheses, quotation marks, etc., according to the context.

puncture: *n.* a small hole made by a sharp object. *He is trying to mend the puncture in the bicycle tire.*

SIGN: Forefinger of vertical right **'ONE'** hand, palm facing left, is pushed upward between the forefinger and middle finger of the left **'EXTENDED B'** hand which is held palm down with fingers pointing rightward. (Signs vary according to context.)

pungent: *adj.* acrid; sharp. *A pungent odour told us there was a skunk near our campsite.*

SIGN: Right **'5'** hand is held with palm facing leftward/downward and thumbtip touching or close to the tip of the nose. The hand is then firmly thrust a short distance forward at a slight downward angle. Meanwhile, a grimace appears on the signer's face and the lips appear to be articulating the syllable 'PO'.
ALTERNATE SIGN—**strong + odour**
Pungent does not always describe a 'smell'. Sign choice depends on context.

punish: *v.* to impose a penalty on someone. *My parents will punish me for being late.*

SIGN: Forefinger of right **'ONE'** hand, palm down, is used to strike downward across the bent elbow of the left arm.
SAME SIGN—**punishment**, *n.*

punk: *n.* a young person who considers himself/herself tough and popular with a certain crowd. *Sometimes teenagers act like young punks.*

SIGN #1: Horizontal right **'S'** hand, palm facing the body at an upward angle, is placed against the upper right part of the chest and is brushed downward twice in a circular motion. This sign is accompanied by a grimace.

punk: *adj.* related to a late twentieth century movement that was characterized by unusual clothing and hairstyles as well as certain rock music. *Ragged jeans and spiked hair were part of the punk identity.*

SIGN #2: Fingerspell **PUNK**.

P   U   N   K

pupil: *n.* a student who is taught by a teacher. *He is the only pupil who has not completed his homework.*

SIGN #1: Right **'CONTRACTED 5'** hand is placed palm down on the upturned left palm and is closed to form a **'FLAT O'** shape as it is drawn upward, moved to the right, and flung open to resume a **'CONTRACTED 5'** shape.

pupil: *n.* the dark circular opening in the centre of the eye. *The opthamologist looked into my pupils.*

SIGN #2: Vertical **'COVERED F'** hands, palms facing each other, are held in front of the eyes and moved forward and back slightly a couple of times. (The sign for **pupil** is often incorporated with the verb. If the signer wishes to indicate that the 'pupils *have dilated*', s/he would begin with **'COVERED F'** hands which are gradually transformed to **'F'** shapes.)

puppet: *n.* a small doll or figure that can be manipulated by strings. *Children like to play with puppets.*

SIGN #1: **'F'** hands are held slightly apart with palms down and are alternately moved up and down.

(hand) puppet: *n.* a small doll or figure that can be fitted over and manipulated by the hand and forearm. *Children like to play with hand puppets.*

SIGN #2: Horizontal left **'C'** hand cups right forearm as right hand, held upright with palm facing forward, opens and closes a few times, alternating between **'CONTRACTED C'** and **'FLAT O'** shapes.

puppy: *n.* a young dog. *My father brought home a puppy and we were all very excited.*

SIGN: Fingerspell **PUPPY**.

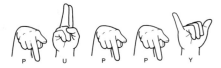

purchase: *v.* to buy. *They plan to purchase a new car.*

SIGN: Right **'BENT EXTENDED B'** hand is laid, palm up, on upturned palm of left **'EXTENDED B'** hand. Then right hand is moved upward and forward.

pure: *adj.* not mixed with any dissimilar things. *This is pure gold.*

SIGN: Left **'B'** hand is held in a fixed position with palm facing right and fingers pointing forward. Right **'B'** hand, palm facing left, and fingers pointing forward, is positioned on top of the left hand and firmly moved forward. (**PURE** may be fingerspelled for emphasis or when it means 'free from dirt or impurities' as in *pure water*. For contexts in which **pure** means 'complete' or 'utter' as in *pure genius*, see **real**.)

purebred: *adj.* a pure strain developed through many generations of controlled breeding. *The rancher raises purebred Charolais cattle.*

SIGN: Fingerspell **PUREBRED**.

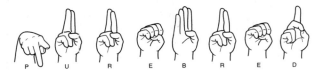

purge: *v.* to get rid of unwanted elements. *He must purge his files of incriminating evidence.*

SIGN: Fingertips of right **'BENT EXTENDED B'** hand, palm down, are placed on upturned palm of left **'EXTENDED B'** hand and brushed forward to form a straight **'EXTENDED B'** hand. ❖

purple: *adj.* having a reddish-blue colour. *She bought a purple dress to wear to the dance.*

SIGN: Inverted right **'K'** hand moves in small clockwise circles.

purpose: *n.* the reason for which something is done; aim. *The purpose of language is to enable humans to communicate.*

SIGN: Tip of forefinger of vertical right **'ONE'** hand, palm toward the face, is used to touch right side of forehead. Then the handshape is changed to a **'BENT V'** and the extended fingertips are placed against the right-facing palm of the horizontal left **'EXTENDED B'** hand. Next, the fingertips of the right hand are separated from the left hand as the right wrist makes a quarter turn clockwise, the right hand turns slightly toward so that the fingers now point forward/upward, and the fingertips of the right hand re-establish contact with the left palm.

purse: *n.* a small bag or pouch for carrying money and other small objects. *Put your money in your purse.*

SIGN: Horizontal right **'S'** hand, palm facing left and wrist bent, is held at the signer's side as if holding onto a purse and is moved up and down a couple of times. (Signs vary considerably depending on the size, shape and manner in which the purse is carried. **PURSE** is frequently fingerspelled.)

pursue: *v.* to follow in order to catch. *The police officer tried to pursue the robbers on foot.*

SIGN #1: Horizontal left '**A**' hand, palm facing right, is held ahead of and to the left of horizontal right '**EXTENDED A**' hand, of which the palm faces the body at a leftward angle. Then the right is moved forward in a series of small clockwise circles to approach the left hand.

pursue: *v.* to work toward a particular aim for which efforts must be made over a long period of time. *He wants to pursue a career in medicine.*

SIGN #2: Vertical '**ONE**' hands, left palm facing right and right palm facing left, are held out in front of the face, with the left hand directly ahead of the right. The hands are then simultaneously moved forward.

pus: *n.* a yellowish-white fluid produced by infection or inflammation. *The nurse cleaned the pus from the wound with an antiseptic.*

SIGN: Fingerspell **PUS**.

P   U   S

push: *v.* to thrust forward by applying force. *The teacher told the children not to push.*

SIGN: Vertical '**EXTENDED B**' hands, palms forward, are held slightly apart and are simultaneously shoved forward. ❖ (Signs vary considerably depending on the size and shape of what is being pushed and how it is being pushed.)

put: *v.* to cause something to be in a specific position or place. *Please put the meal on the table.*

SIGN: '**FLAT O**' hands are held parallel with palms relatively downward and are moved forward in arc formation so that the palms eventually face down. (This sign is frequently made with the right hand only. Signs vary considerably depending on the size and shape of the object and the manner in which it is being put somewhere.)

put down: *v.* to write down. *I must remember to put down his phone number so I can contact him later.*

SIGN #1: Bunched fingertips of right '**O**' hand, palm down, are placed on the upturned left palm. Right hand opens to form an '**EXTENDED B**' hand and is then tapped down smartly on the left palm. (For contexts in which *several* items or pieces of information are being put down, see **list** #1 or #2.)

put (an animal) down: *v.* to put an animal to death because of old age, illness or suffering. *We had to put down our dog because he was suffering from a terminal illness.*

SIGN #2: Tip of forefinger of right '**BENT L**' hand is jabbed into upper left arm and thumb is bent as though depressing a plunger into a syringe. Next, right '**EXTENDED B**' hand is held palm down with fingers pointing forward. The wrist then rotates rightward, turning the hand palm upward. (ASL CONCEPT—**inject - die**.) When the aspect of 'death' is already understood, the first part of this sign is used only.

put (someone) down: *v.* to make cruel, crushing remarks to someone as a form of rejection or humiliation. *His older brother put him down so often that he lost all his self-confidence.*

SIGN #3: Right '**ONE**' hand, palm facing left, is held in a horizontal position in front of the chest and is then curved upward from the wrist as it moves forward with a stabbing motion. Alternatively, this sign may be made with two hands alternately stabbing, either with or without the curving motion. ❖

put off: *v.* to postpone; delay. *Because it was raining, we had to put off our plans to paint the roof.*

SIGN: Horizontal **'F'** hands are held parallel with palms facing each other and are simultaneously curved forward in a slight arc formation.

ALTERNATE SIGN—**delay**

put on: *v.* to pretend; feign. *He did not really hurt his leg; he is just putting on that limp.*

SIGN #1: Side of forefinger of right **'ONE'** hand, palm facing leftward/forward, is lightly brushed forward/downward twice on the right cheek, forefinger either remaining upright or bending slightly to become a **'BENT ONE'**. (Sign choices must be made on the basis of context.)

put on: *v.* to place a bet. *He put $20.00 on the horse called Passing Fancy to win.*

SIGN #2: **'B'** (or **'EXTENDED B'**) hands are held slightly apart, fingers pointing forward and palms facing upward. They are then turned over simultaneously so that palms are facing down. Alternatively, this sign may be made with one hand only.

---

put on: *v.* to present or stage a form of entertainment. *They are planning to put on a fashion show.*

NOTE—There is no sign illustrated here as ASL users do not tend to use a sign meaning 'put on', 'present' or 'stage' in this context. Instead, they might use **have**, *v.*, or **take up**, *v.*

put (someone) on: *v.* to tease. *Do not worry, I am just putting you on.*

SIGN #4: With palm facing left, horizontal right **'X'** hand is stroked forward at least twice across the top of horizontal left **'X'** hand, which is held with palm facing right. ❖

put on clothes: *v.* to dress oneself. *She got up and put on her clothes.*

SIGN: Vertical left **'ONE'** hand represents the human body as it is held in a fixed position with palm facing forward/rightward. Right **'C'** hand, palm facing the body at a leftward angle, drops downward to envelop the left forefinger.

ALTERNATE SIGN—**get dressed**

put on weight: *v.* to gain weight. *He has put on weight since I saw him last.*

SIGN: Left **'U'** hand is held in a fixed position with palm down and extended fingers pointing rightward/forward. Beside it is the right **'U'** hand, which is held with palm facing left and extended fingers pointing forward/leftward. The right wrist then rotates to turn the hand palm down as the extended fingers come to rest on those of the left hand at right angles to them.

put one over on: *v.* to get someone to believe something preposterous; deceive; trick. *He will try to put one over on you, so be careful and do not let yourself be fooled.*

SIGN: Vertical right **'A'** hand, with palm forward and slightly leftward, is knocked against forefinger of vertical left **'ONE'** hand whose palm faces right. ❖

put out: *adj.* annoyed; angry; upset. *She was put out because she was not invited to the wedding.*

SIGN #1: Horizontal right **'EXTENDED B'** hand, palm on stomach and fingers pointing leftward, is turned 45° so the palm faces up. (Sign choices must be made on the basis of context.)

put out: *v.* to inconvenience; bother. *Will you be put out if I am late for dinner?*

SIGN #2: Left **'CROOKED 5'** hand is held palm-up with fingers pointing forward while right **'CROOKED 5'** hand is held apart and slightly higher with palm down and fingers pointing forward. The arms are then simultaneously moved upward/rightward as the hands are purposefully twisted rightward from the wrist so that the left palm faces right and the right palm faces left.

put out: *v.* to extinguish (a fire). *Be sure you put out the campfire before you go to bed.*

SIGN #3: **'EXTENDED C'** hands are positioned with the left ahead of the right, left palm up and right palm down, as if holding a jug or can of water. Then the hands are simultaneously thrust forward/leftward as if dousing a fire. (Signs vary depending on the size, location and type of fire.)

put out: *v.* to publish; distribute. *Our organization **puts out** a monthly newsletter.*

SIGN #4: **'FLAT O'** hands are held with the palms down and sides of tips of forefingers touching. The hands are then opened to form **'5'** hands as they are moved apart in an outward/forward direction.

put together: *v.* to assemble; fit together or join the parts of something. *Many children's toys need to be **put together** before they can be used.*

SIGN: **'FLAT O'** hands, palms facing down, are moved alternately up and down as if fitting components into a specific pattern. (In the following sentence, the sign for **plan** would be more appropriate: *We **put together** a farewell party for him.*)

put up with: *v.* to tolerate; endure. *I refuse to **put up with** her moodiness.*

SIGN: Right **'A'** hand, with thumbnail touching closed lips and palm facing left, is moved slowly down chin.

putty: *n.* a stiff paste used to fix glass into frames or to fill cracks and holes. *You need to get some **putty** to repair the walls before painting them.*

SIGN: **'EXTENDED A'** hand is held palm down with thumbtip resting against the backward/rightward-facing palm of the vertical left **'EXTENDED B'** hand and is repeatedly drawn downward.

puzzle: *n.* a picture created by fitting pieces together. *Working at a **puzzle** helps to relax me.*

SIGN #1: Vertical **'BENT U'** hands, palms facing each other and extended fingers of one hand pointing toward those of the other, are tapped together several times.

OR

SIGN #2: **'EXTENDED A'** hands, with palms down and thumbs appearing to press down on something, are alternately raised and lowered.

puzzled: *adj.* perplexed. *We were all **puzzled** over her absence.*

SIGN: Back of the right **'ONE'** hand, palm forward and forefinger pointing upward, is placed just in front of the middle of the forehead and is drawn backward while the forefinger is crooked to form an **'X'** handshape. A look of 'bewilderment' accompanies this sign. (This sign is used only in a passive voice situation or as an adjective to describe someone's feelings. It would *not* be possible to use this sign in an active voice situation such as: *Her absence **puzzled** us all.*)

pyjamas [*also spelled **pajamas**]: *n.* night clothes comprising a top and trousers. *Some Canadians wear flannelette **pyjamas** during the cold winter months.*

SIGN: Head tilts slightly to the right, supported by right **'EXTENDED B'** hand, which is held against right side of face. Next, thumbs of **'MODIFIED 5'** hands, with palms toward the body and fingertips opposite, are placed at either side of upper chest. The wrists then rotate simultaneously to turn the hands so that the palms face away from the body and fingers point forward/upward.

(ASL CONCEPT—**bed - clothes**.) **Pyjamas** is frequently fingerspelled in the abbreviated form **PJ**.

pyramid: *n.* a structure with a square base and triangular sides. *The ancient **pyramids** in Egypt are an engineering wonder.*

SIGN: **'EXTENDED B'** hands, right palm facing left at a slight downward angle and left palm facing right at a slight downward angle, are held with fingertips of one hand touching those of the other hand. The hands are drawn apart and downward, and then rotated, the fingertips coming together once again and the right palm faces the body while the left palm faces forward at a slight downward angle. The hands are then drawn apart and down again.

Q

quadriplegic: *n.* someone who is paralyzed from the neck down. *The accident left him a* ***quadriplegic.***

SIGN: **'CROOKED 5'** hands are held parallel with palms down.They then jerk slightly forward/downward as they become **'SPREAD C'** hands. Next **'EXTENDED B'** hand is then brought up to touch upper chest with palm facing downward and fingertips pointing rightward. Right **'EXTENDED B'** hand, with palm facing down-ward and fingertips pointing leftward, is held just below left hand and then lowered to about waist level. (ASL CONCEPT—**paralyze - neck below**.)

qualification: *n.* a condition or ability that makes a person suitable for a specific under-taking. *He has the necessary* ***qualifications*** *for the job.*

SIGN: Edge of left **'EXTENDED B'** hand, palm facing right, is grasped by right **'OPEN A'** hand. Then right hand is pulled forward sharply and closed to form an **'A'** hand. (**QUALIFICATION** is frequently fingerspelled.)

qualified: *adj.* having the abilities or creden-tials necessary to do a particular job or task. *He is well* ***qualified*** *for his position.*

SIGN: Edge of left **'EXTENDED B'** hand, palm facing right, is grasped by right **'OPEN A'** hand. Then right hand is pulled forward sharply and closed to form an **'A'** hand. (**QUALIFIED** is fre-quently fingerspelled.)

qualify: *v.* to have or to meet the requirements which make one eligible or entitled to certain benefits. *He* ***qualifies*** *for social assistance.*

SIGN #1: Horizontal right **'F'** hand grasps the signer's shirt below the right shoulder between the thumb and forefinger, and is moved back and forth twice.

qualify: *v.* to prove oneself worthy, and thereby gain approval to enter competition. *The runner* ***qualified*** *for the Olympics.*

SIGN #2: **'A'** hands, palms down, are held slightly apart, and are then firmly pushed a very short distance downward. Horizontal right **'EXTENDED B'** hand, palm down, is then curved forward under horizontal left **'EXTENDED B'** palm to simulate 'entrance'. (ASL CONCEPT—**can - enter**.)

quality: *n.* degree of excellence. *They sell only the best* ***quality*** *of merchandise.*

SIGN #1: Fingerspell **QUALITY**.

quality: *n.* a character or feature of something. *The doll had a very lifelike* ***quality*** *about it.*

SIGN #2: Fingerspell **QUALITY**.

quality: *n.* a feature of personality. *The* ***quality*** *I enjoy most in him is his cheerful disposition.*

SIGN #3: Horizontal right **'C'** hand, palm facing the body, is twisted in a circular motion from the wrist so that it becomes upright with palm facing leftward as it is brought back against the left shoulder.

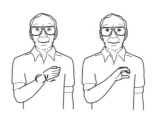

quarrel: *v.* to argue or to disagree angrily. *Even the best of friends sometimes quarrel.*

SIGN: **'BENT ONE'** hands, palms toward the chest, forefingers pointing toward each other, are either simultaneously or alternately moved up and down from the wrist.

quarter: *adj.* one-fourth. *The recipe called for a quarter teaspoon of salt.*

SIGN #1: Right **'ONE'** hand, palm toward the body, is held with forefinger pointing leftward/upward, and is then lowered slightly as it is changed to a **'4'** hand.

quarter: *n.* a 25-cent coin. *Could you give me two dimes and a nickel for this quarter please?*

SIGN #2: Tip of forefinger of vertical right **'BENT MIDFINGER 5'** hand, palm forward, touches right side of forehead. The bent middle finger then flutters as the hand moves slightly away from the forehead.

queasy: *adj.* nauseated. *The sight of so much blood made him feel queasy.*

SIGN: Right **'CLAWED C'** hand, palm toward the body, is circled in a clockwise direction (from the onlooker's perspective) in front of the stomach. Facial expression is important.

queen: *n.* a reigning female monarch, or the wife of a king. *Queen Victoria had nine children.*

SIGN: **'MODIFIED G'** hand is held with palm down and sides of thumb and forefinger against the left shoulder. Then the hand is moved diagonally downward so the hand comes to rest at the right side of the waist.

queer: *adj.* odd; strange. *She gave some queer answers to the questions on the test.*

SIGN: Vertical right **'C'** hand, palm facing left, is held at right side of face and is abruptly dropped leftward/downward from the wrist so the palm faces down.
REGIONAL VARIATION—**odd** #2

quench one's thirst: *v.* to satisfy one's thirst. *Some ice water will quench my thirst.*

SIGN: Right **'C'** hand is held in a horizontal position near the mouth with palm facing left. The hand is then tipped upward slightly. Then, tip of middle finger of right **'BENT MIDFINGER 5'** hand, palm toward the body, is brushed upward and off the chest. Finally, right **'BENT EXTENDED B'** hand, fingers on lips and pointing leftward, palm backward, is drawn rightward as the fingers bend to form an **'EXTENDED A'** hand with thumb pointing upward. (ASL CONCEPT—**drink - feel - better**.)

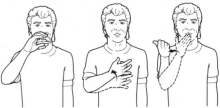

query: *n.* a question; something needing clarification. *The man had a query about bylaws so he phoned City Hall.*

SIGN: Forefinger of right **'ONE'** hand, palm forward, inscribes a question mark. As it does so, it takes on an **'X'** shape and finally a **'BENT ONE'** shape with the extended finger pointing forward.

quest: *n.* pursuit; search. *In her quest for perfection, she missed out on a lot of fun.*

SIGN: Vertical **'ONE'** hands, left palm facing right and right palm facing left, are held out in front of the face, with the left hand directly ahead of the right. The hands are then simultaneously moved forward.

question: *v.* to ask questions or to interrogate. *The police will question each suspect.*

SIGN #1: Vertical **'ONE'** hands, palms facing forward, are held apart, one at a slightly higher level than the other. The hands then alternately move forward and slightly downward in repeated circular motions. As the hands move forward, they take on the **'X'** handshape, and as they circle back toward the chest, they resume the **'ONE'** shape. ❖

question: *v.* to express doubt about something. *The player questioned the fairness of the referee's call.*

SIGN #2: Forefinger of right **'ONE'** hand, palm forward, inscribes a question mark. As it does so, it takes on an **'X'** shape and finally a **'BENT ONE'** shape with the tip of the extended finger thrust forward. Facial expression must clearly convey 'doubt'.

question: *n.* an expression intended to evoke a response; something that requires an answer. *The teacher asked the students to answer just one question for homework.*

SIGN #3: Forefinger of right **'ONE'** hand, palm forward, inscribes a question mark. As it does so, it takes on an **'X'** shape and finally a **'BENT ONE'** shape with the extended finger pointing forward.

questionnaire: *n.* questions set out in printed form, as in a survey. *Please complete this questionnaire and return it to me.*

SIGN: Vertical **'ONE'** hands are held apart with palms forward. As the hands move downward, they simultaneously alternate between **'ONE'** and **'X'** handshapes. Forefingers of **'ONE'** hands, palms down, are then placed side by side and are drawn apart, moved down, and brought together again to outline a sheet of paper. (ASL CONCEPT—**question - form.**)

queue: *n.* a line of people waiting in turn for something. *There was a long queue waiting for the show.*

SIGN: Vertical **'4'** hands, left palm facing forward/rightward and right palm facing backward/leftward, are held so that the right is slightly behind the left. Then the right hand is drawn back toward the right shoulder. (Signs vary according to 'what' forms the queue. To indicate that there is a queue of *cars*, the sign is made using horizontal **'3'** hands.)

quick: *adj.* fast. *The rabbit made a quick jump to escape from the fox.*

SIGN #1: Vertical **'COVERED T'** hands are held apart with palms facing, and are jerked forward as thumbs flick upward, resulting in horizontal **'CLAWED L'** hands, palms still facing.

OR

SIGN #2: Left horizontal **'L'** hand, palm facing right, is held apart from and slightly ahead of right horizontal **'L'** hand, whose palm faces left. The hands are then simultaneously jerked upward toward the body as they are changed to **'CLAWED L'** hands.

OR

SIGN #3 [ATLANTIC]: Thumb-tip of horizontal right **'FLAT C'** hand is held at the end of the nose, palm facing left, and the hand is closed to form a **'FLAT O'** shape.

quiet: *adj.* silent, calm; tranquil. *The evening was quiet and relaxing.*

SIGN: **'B'** (or **'EXTENDED B'**) hands are crossed in front of the mouth, left palm facing rightward/downward and right palm facing leftward/downward with the right hand just behind the left hand. Then they are drawn apart until the palms face completely downward.

quilt: *n.* a bed cover. *She made a beautiful patchwork quilt.*

SIGN: Fingerspell **QUILT**.

Q U I L T

quit: *v.* to give up or to stop doing something. *She finally quit smoking.*

SIGN: Extended fingers of horizontal right **'U'** hand are inserted into an opening created in the left horizontal **'S'** hand. Then the extended fingers of the right hand are withdrawn from the left hand, becoming more upright as they move back toward the chest. ❖

quite: *adv.* fairly; somewhat. *It is quite warm today, is it not?*

SIGN: Right **'BENT EXTENDED B'** hand with palm facing forward/left, is twisted slightly from the wrist so that it faces the right shoulder. Movement is repeated.

quiver: *v.* to tremble. *She quivers with fear whenever she thinks about spiders.*

SIGN: Horizontal **'CROOKED 5'** hands tremble as they are held parallel with palms down.

quiz: *n.* a set of questions designed to test knowledge. *The teacher gives a quiz every Friday.*

SIGN: Fingerspell **QUIZ**.

quote: *n.* words taken from someone else. *This **quote** is from the Prime Minister's speech.*

SIGN #1: Vertical **'V'** hands, palms facing forward, are held apart just above shoulder level, and are curved outward slightly from the wrists as they become **'CLAWED V'** hands. SAME SIGN—**quotation**, *n.*

quote: *v.* to use words originally used by someone else. *She **quoted** Stephen Leacock frequently in her talk on "Humour in Canadian Literature".*

SIGN #2: Parallel horizontal **'V'** hands are held with the left hand slightly ahead of the right and the extended fingertips of both hands pointing leftward/forward. The forearms then move simultaneously rightward and slightly upward as the hands take on **'CLAWED V'** shapes, and finally resume the **'V'** shape as they continue moving rightward and slightly downward.

R

rabbit: *n.* a burrowing mammal related to a hare. *Some people keep **rabbits** as pets.*

SIGN #1: **'CONTRACTED U'** (or **'BENT EXTENDED U'**) hands are held together in an almost vertical position, the right hand behind/above the left, with the left palm facing right and the right palm facing left. The extended fingers of each hand simultaneously flutter, thus alternating several times between **'CONTRACTED U'** and **'BENT U'** shapes.

OR

SIGN #2: Vertical **'CONTRACTED U'** (or **'BENT EXTENDED U'**) hands, palms facing backwards, are held at either side of the head as the extended fingers of each hand move up and down simultaneously.

rabies: *n.* an acute infectious disease passed on through an infected animal's saliva. *She made sure her dog had his injection for **rabies** annually.*

SIGN: Fingerspell **RABIES**.

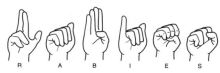

raccoon: *n.* a mammal easily recognized by the black band across its face. *The dog chased the **raccoon** out of the corn field.*

SIGN: Horizontal **'V'** hands, palms facing backward, are held so that the extended fingers frame the eyes. The hands are then drawn apart as the fingers close slightly to narrow the **'V'** shapes.

race: *v.* to compete to see who can finish first (or do something fastest). *Let us **race** from the school to your house.*

SIGN #1: **'A'** hands, palms facing, are held close to one another and moved alternately back and forth. This is a wrist movement.
SAME SIGN—**race**, *n.,* in this context.

race: *n.* a group of people of common ancestry. *A person's **race** is commonly distinguished by his or her skin colour.*

SIGN #2: **'SPREAD C'** hands are held upright and slightly apart with palms facing each other. The wrists then rotate forward, bringing the hands to a horizontal position. (**RACE** in this context may be fingerspelled.)

racism: *n.* discrimination based on a belief that people of certain races are inferior to others. *The Human Rights Act protects all citizens against **racism**.*

SIGN: Fingerspell **RACISM**.

racket: *n.* a noisy disturbance. *The neighbours made a lot of **racket** last night.*

SIGN #1: Thumbtips of vertical **'MODIFIED 5'** hands are held near either ear, palms facing forward but angled slightly toward each other, as forearms are simultaneously thrust outward/forward and back at least twice.

racket [*also spelled* **racquet**]: *n.* a light bat consisting of a handle and a network of strings in an oval frame. *A badminton **racket** is lighter in weight than a tennis **racket**.*

SIGN #2: Right **'A'** hand is swung back and forth with wrist action to simulate the motion of a racket in play.

radio: *n.* an electronic device used to transmit signals from broadcasting stations. *I like that song they are playing on the **radio**.*

SIGN #1: Vertical right **'SPREAD C'** hand, palm toward the head, is cupped over the right ear and is moved back and forth slightly several times. (Alternatively, the vertical right **'SPREAD C'** hand, palm left, is held near the right ear and twisted back and forth several times from the wrist.) **RADIO** is frequently fingerspelled.

SIGN #2 [ATLANTIC]: Vertical right **'MODIFIED 5'** hand, palm facing away from the head, is held near the right ear and is drawn toward it several times as the shape alternates between a **'FLAT O'** and a **'MODIFIED 5'**.

radio: *v.* to transmit a message by radio. *The pilot will* **radio** *the control tower to get clearance for landing.*

SIGN #3: Right **'A-INDEX'** hand, palm toward the body, is held up to the mouth as if the signer were speaking into a hand-held radio transmitter.

radiology: *n.* the use of x-rays and other radioactive substances in medical diagnosis and treatment. *Doctors rely on* **radiology** *extensively when diagnosing cancer.*

SIGN: Fingerspell **XRAY**.

radish: *n.* a pungent-tasting root vegetable that is eaten raw or used in salads. *Many people like the taste of* **radish** *in a tossed salad.*

SIGN: Fingerspell **RADISH**.

radius: *n.* a circular area of a specified extent. *The earthquake was felt within a 100-mile* **radius** *of Anchorage, Alaska.*

SIGN #1: Right **'5'** hand, palm down, is circled in a counter-clockwise motion.

radius: *n.* a straight line joining the centre of a circle with any point on its circumference. *The area of a circle may be calculated by squaring the* **radius** *and multiplying by 3.14.*

SIGN #2: Vertical **'C'** hands, palms facing each other, are held together with finger and thumb tips almost touching to form a circle. Then the right hand is changed to a **'BENT ONE'** shape, forefinger pointing forward at a slight leftward angle, as it moves back and forth along an imaginary radius from the centre to the right side of the imaginary circle originally formed.

rage: *n.* intense anger; fury. *The farmer was in a* **rage** *over losing his land.*

SIGN: **'CLAWED 5'** hands, palms toward body, fingertips touching chest, are swept vigorously upward/outward. Facial expression must clearly convey 'anger'.

raid: *n.* a sudden surprise attack or invasion. *A recent police* **raid** *resulted in several arrests for possession of stolen goods.*

SIGN: Right **'EXTENDED B'** hand, palm down and fingers pointing forward/leftward, is thrust under left **'STANDARD BASE'** hand to simulate forceful entry.

railroad [*or* **railway**]: *n.* a track on which trains travel. *The building of a* **railroad** *across Canada opened the west for settlement.*

SIGN: Horizontal **'U'** hands, palms down, are held so the extended fingers lie across each other with the right hand on top. Then the right hand is moved back and forth several times.

rain: *n.* drops of water that fall from clouds. *The farmers were hoping for more* **rain**.

SIGN: **'SPREAD EXTENDED C'** hands are held parallel with palms down, and are bounced up and down slightly at least twice. This is a wrist action.

rainbow: *n.* an arc that appears in the sky and displays the colours of the spectrum. *When the rain stopped, a beautiful* **rainbow** *appeared in the west.*

SIGN: Horizontal right **'4'** hand is held with palm facing the chest and fingers pointing leftward. The forearm is then drawn upward and the hand moved rightward in an arc formation.

raise: *v.* to bring up; rear. *She was* **raised** *in Cornerbrook, Newfoundland.*

SIGN #1: Right **'EXTENDED B'** hand is held palm-down with fingers pointing forward near right side of body. The hand is then moved directly upward. (Sign choice varies according to what is being raised. The raising of 'crops' would be indicated by the sign for **grow** but this would not be applicable to the raising of 'animals'.)

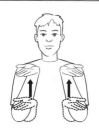

raise: *v.* to lift up to a higher position. *I need help to **raise** this window.*

SIGN #2: Horizontal **'EXTENDED B'** hands, palms up, are held slightly apart and are simultaneously lifted upward. (Sign choice varies according to the shape, size and weight of the object being raised. To indicate the raising of one's hand or head, natural gestures are used.)

raise: *n.* an increase in pay. *All employees will receive a five percent **raise**.*

SIGN #3: Vertical left **'BENT U'** hand is held in a fixed position with palm down and extended fingers pointing rightward/forward. Right **'U'** hand is held to the right of the left hand with palm left and extended fingers pointing forward. The right hand then moves in an upward/leftward arc as the wrist rotates leftward causing the palm to turn downward and the extended fingertips to come to rest on the backs of the extended fingers of the left hand.

rake: *n.* a hand implement with a row of teeth attached to a long handle. *A fan-shaped **rake** is often used to gather up leaves in the fall.*

SIGN #1: Horizontal **'A'** hands are held, right ahead of left, with left palm facing right and right palm facing left as if holding onto a rake handle. The hands are then simultaneously drawn toward the body a couple of times.

OR

SIGN #2: Right **'SPREAD EXTENDED C'** hand, palm down, is raked backward across the upturned palm of the left **'EXTENDED B'** hand at least twice.

ramp: *n.* a slope that joins two surfaces at different levels. *A **ramp** is needed to assure access for wheelchairs.*

SIGN: Horizontal right **'EXTENDED B'** hand, palm facing leftward/downward, is held aloft in front of the left side of the body and then moved straight downward/rightward. (**RAMP** may be fingerspelled.)

ranch: *n.* a large farm where cattle, horses or sheep are raised. *I grew up on a **ranch** in southern Alberta.*

SIGN: Fingerspell **RANCH**.

rancid: *adj.* rank; sour; spoiled (state of food or drink). *The butter is **rancid**.*

SIGN: Horizontal left **'X'** hand is held in a fixed position with palm rightward but slanted toward the body slightly while horizontal right **'X'** hand is held above/behind left hand with palm leftward. The right hand then slides briskly along the top of the left hand and continues to move in a forward/rightward direction.

random: *adj.* occurring without a definite plan, pattern or purpose. *This is a **random** selection of the complaints we received.*

SIGN: **'OPEN F'** (or **'OPEN 8'**) hands, palms forward, are held apart and alternately circled backward toward the chest several times as the thumbs and forefingers (or midfingers) close to form **'F'** (or **'8'**) hands with each backward rotation. A 'nonchalant' facial expression accompanies this sign. (Signs vary according to context.)

range: *v.* to vary or fluctuate within given limits. *Prices **range** from $40.00 to $85.00.*

SIGN #1: **'EXTENDED B'** hands are held so the edge of the vertical right, palm facing left, is placed against the thumb of the horizontal left of which the palm is facing backward and the fingers are pointing rightward. Then the right hand is moved back and forth between the thumb and the end of the left hand to indicate the limits of a certain range. (Sign choice varies according to context.)

range: *v.* to fluctuate. *The price of gas **ranges** throughout Canada.*

SIGN #2: Horizontal **'ONE'** hands, palms down and forefingers pointing forward, are held apart with one hand held slightly higher than the other. The hands are then moved further apart with alternating up and down movements. (This sign tends to be used when the limits of the 'range' are not specified.)

(a) range of: *adj.* the extent of variation that exists. *They sell **a range of** products.*

SIGN #3: **'ONE'** hands, palms forward/downward, are held so that the right forefinger is crossed over the left. The fingers then uncross and move apart. This movement is repeated several times as the hands simultaneously move from left to right. The head may swivel rightward.

rank: *n.* a position or standing within a social organization. *He holds the rank of Major in the military service.*

SIGN: Horizontal **'K'** hands are held out in front of the body with palms facing each other and tips of middle fingers touching. The hands then create a circle as they are drawn apart and brought toward the chest where they meet again. (For **high rank**, see **advanced**. For **low rank**, see **low class**.)

ransom: *n.* the price demanded to release someone from captivity. *The kidnappers demanded one million dollars in ransom.*

SIGN: Fingerspell **RANSOM**. (The circumstances surrounding the demand for ransom may be signed in various ways but the term itself is always fingerspelled for clarity.)

rap: *n.* a sharp sound made by knocking. *A Deaf person cannot hear a rap on the door.*

SIGN #1: Knuckles of right **'A'** hand, palm facing left, knock against right-facing palm of vertical left **'EXTENDED B'** hand.

rap: *v.* to strike with a sharp, quick blow. *We saw the judge rap his gavel on the bench.*

SIGN #2: Horizontal right **'CLOSED A-INDEX'** hand, palm facing left, is used to strike downward.

rap: *v.* to chat informally. *The lounge is where the students sit and rap.*

SIGN #3: Horizontal **'CROOKED 5'** hands are held apart with palms facing each other but slanted upward slightly. The hands are simultaneously moved up and down a few times. This is a wrist movement so that only the hands move up and down, as opposed to the arms.

rape: *n.* the forcing of a person to submit to sexual intercourse. *He was charged with statutory rape and sentenced to ten years in prison.*

SIGN: Fingerspell **RAPE**. (Various signs may also be used.)

rapid: *adj.* quick; fast. *He took several rapid strides across the room.*

SIGN: Left horizontal **'L'** hand, palm facing right, is held apart from and slightly ahead of right horizontal **'L'** hand, whose palm faces left. The hands are then simultaneously jerked upward toward the body as they are changed to **'CLAWED L'** hands.

rapport: *n.* a relationship of understanding and mutual trust. *The teacher has good rapport with his students.*

SIGN: Thumbs and forefingers of **'F'** hands interlock and the hands are moved back and forth together a couple of times.

rare: *adj.* uncommon; scarce. *A long-lasting friendship like theirs is rare.*

SIGN #1: Fingerspell **RARE**.

rare: *adj.* underdone; cooked only slightly (in reference to meat). *My favourite meal is a rare steak with a baked potato.*

SIGN #2: Fingerspell **RARE**.

rarely: *adv.* not often; seldom. *I rarely see him now that he has two jobs.*

SIGN: Right **'COVERED T'** hand is held with palm toward the body at a slight upward/leftward angle. Then the thumb is flicked out, thus forming an **'A-INDEX'** hand.

rash: *n.* a skin eruption (usually in the form of red spots). *The doctor diagnosed the baby's rash as measles.*

SIGN #1: Fingerspell **RASH**.

rash: *n.* a series of unpleasant occurrences. *There has been a rash of break-ins in our neighbourhood lately.*

SIGN #2: Horizontal right **'BENT EXTENDED B'** hand, palm left, is moved forward quickly in a series of small arcs.

rash: *adj.* too hasty; without thinking; impetuous. *His rash behaviour gets him into a lot of trouble.*

SIGN #3: Vertical right **'C'** hand, palm facing left, is held near the face and is abruptly dropped downward from the wrist so the palm faces down.

raspberry: *n.* a small, soft, sweet red fruit with many seeds. *This raspberry is too unripe to pick.*

SIGN: Fingerspell **RASPBERRY**.

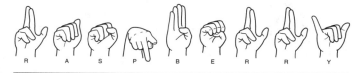

rat: *n.* a long-tailed rodent similar to but larger than a mouse. *Alberta is a province that is free of rats.*

SIGN: Crossed fingers of right **'R'** hand, palm facing left, are struck downward across the nose a couple of times.

ALTERNATE SIGN—**mouse** #1

rat race: *n.* a colloquial expression meaning a hectic routine or a chaotic and/or competitive situation. *I would like to get out of the 9 to 5 rat race and work on my hobbies.*

SIGN: Vertical **'BENT EXTENDED B'** hands are held with palms facing each other and finger-tips touching either side of forehead. Fingertips maintain contact with the forehead while the wrists rapidly twist back and forth several times in opposite directions.

rate: *n.* price; charge. *She inquired about the going rate for hotel rooms in Toronto.*

SIGN #1: Vertical **'F'** hands, palms facing forward, are brought together so the joined thumbs and forefingers touch each other twice.

rate: *n.* a measure given as part of a whole. *The employment rate is lower now than it was a year ago.*

SIGN #2: Vertical right **'O'** hand, palm forward/leftward, moves rightward and then downward at a slight leftward angle as if tracing the number '7' in the air. (Signs vary according to context.)

rate: *v.* to consider the comparative worth, importance or quality of something; evaluate; assess. *I would rate his skills much higher that those of his classmates.*

SIGN #3: **'F'** hands, with palms facing each other, are held apart in front of chest and are simultaneously lowered.

(at any) rate: *adv.* in any case; anyway. *I am not sure when they will return home; at any rate, they will be here before Christmas.*

SIGN #4: Fingers of horizontal **'BENT EXTENDED B'** hands, palms facing the chest, are alternately brushed back and forth against each other.

rather: *adv.* more willingly; preferably. *I would rather be sailing than surfing.*

SIGN #1: Tip of middle finger of right **'BENT MIDFINGER 5'** hand, palm toward the body, is tapped lightly against the chin a couple of times.

rather: *adv.* relatively; somewhat. *It is rather late so we had better stop working.*

SIGN #2: Right **'BENT EXTENDED B'** hand with palm facing forward/left, is twisted slightly from the wrist so that it faces the right shoulder.

ratify: *v.* to make something official by giving it formal approval. *The two countries will ratify their trade agreement this weekend.*

SIGN: Horizontal right **'S'** hand, palm toward the body and facing left slightly, is brought down firmly to rest on the upturned palm of the left **'EXTENDED B'** hand.

SAME SIGN—**ratification**, *n.*

ratio: *n.* a comparison between two amounts or measurements. *Our school has a high pupil/teacher ratio.*

SIGN: Fingerspell **RATIO**. (When a specific ratio is being quoted, the hands are held apart in an upright position with palms facing, and each hand taking on the form of a number to represent a ratio such as 3 to 1.)

rational: *adj.* having reasoning or logic in one's thinking. *From their parents' perspective, teenagers are not always rational.*

SIGN: Horizontal **'K'** (or **'V'**) hands are held with right hand resting on left hand and extended fingers pointing forward. Together the hands are circled forward a couple of times. Facial expression is important. Next, tip of forefinger of right **'ONE'** hand touches forehead. (ASL CONCEPT—**careful - think**.)

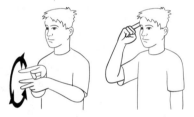

rationale: *n.* an account of the reasoning behind or justification for something. *The consultant explained the rationale behind the new policy.*

SIGN: Vertical right **'EXTENDED R'** (or **'R'**) hand, palm toward face, makes small circles (clockwise in the eyes of the onlooker) at right side of forehead.

raw: *adj.* uncooked. *I prefer to eat raw rather than cooked carrots.*

SIGN: Fingerspell **RAW**.

ray: *n.* a narrow beam of light. *A ray of light shone through the window warming the room.*

SIGN: Vertical right **'O'** hand, palm forward, is thrust ahead as it opens to form a **'CONTRACTED 5'** handshape with the palm eventually facing downward.

razor: *n.* a sharp instrument used for shaving. *He prefers to use a safety razor instead of an electric shaver.*

SIGN: Side of crooked forefinger of right **'X'** hand, palm forward, is used to scrape downward against the right cheek a couple of times. (**RAZOR** may be fingerspelled.)

RCMP: *n.* abbreviation for Royal Canadian Mounted Police. *The RCMP is a federal police force.*

SIGN: Fingerspell **RCMP**.

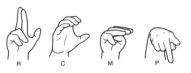

reach: *v.* to arrive at; get to. *We hope to reach home before dark.*

SIGN #1: Right **'BENT EXTENDED B'** hand, with palm facing the body, is brought down and laid palm-up on the upturned palm of the left **'EXTENDED B'** hand.
REGIONAL VARIATION—**arrive** #2

reach: *v.* to make contact or establish communication with someone. *We have been unable to reach them by telephone.*

SIGN #2: Vertical **'BENT MIDFINGER 5'** hands are held with palms facing each other. Then tips of middle fingers are tapped against one another a couple of times.

reach: *v.* to extend part of the body (usually a hand) as if to touch or grasp. *To reach across the dinner table is impolite.*

SIGN #3: Right **'CROOKED 5'** hand is held palm down at chest level and is thrust forward. ❖

react: *v.* to behave in a particular way as a result of something that happened. *How did he react when the boss fired him?*

NOTE—No illustration is provided as signs vary considerably. ASL is frequently more specific than English and sign choice for **react** when it appears in a question form depends specifically on what the signer means. The sample sentence in ASL is: *BOSS FIRE...WHAT DO HE (with questioning look on face)?* or *BOSS FIRE...WHAT FEEL HE (with questioning look on face)?* or *BOSS FIRE...WHAT SAY HE (with questioning look on face)?* However, when **react** appears in a declarative statement, it tends to be incorporated in the sign for the actual reaction. The English sentence *'He reacted with anger'* would be translated into ASL as: *'HE ANGRY'.*

react: *v.* to be made ill by something. *Many people react to penicillin.*

SIGN #2: Horizontal **'BENT ONE'** hands are held together, palms facing the body, and tips of forefingers almost touching. Then they are pulled apart with a short, firm motion.
SAME SIGN—**reaction**, *n.,* in this context.

read: *v.* to look at and understand the meaning of written material. *Have you read any stories or poems written by Deaf people?*

SIGN: Left **'EXTENDED B'** hand is held in a fixed position with palm facing the body and fingers pointing rightward while horizontal right **'V'** hand is held behind the left hand with palm down and extended fingers pointing forward. Right wrist then bends downward so that the tips of the extended fingers strike downward against the left palm.

ready: *adj.* prepared. *She is ready for her new job.*

SIGN #1: Vertical **'R'** hands are held apart with palms facing forward. The forearms then move further apart. (Alternatively, vertical **'R'** hands are held parallel with palms forward and are simultaneously thrust to the right. This involves a wrist action causing the extended fingers to eventually point rightward/upward.)

SIGN #2 [ATLANTIC]: Horizontal left **'SPREAD C'** hand is held in a fixed position in front of the chest with palm facing right while vertical right **'SPREAD C'** hand is held at the right cheek with palm facing left. The right wrist then rotates in a clockwise direction as the hand is lowered and the fingers close to form an **'S'** shape, the hand coming to rest, palm facing backward/upward, on the left hand which has also closed to form an **'S'** shape.

real: *adj.* genuine; actual; not artificial or fictitious. *She is wearing real diamond earrings.*

SIGN: Forefinger of vertical right **'ONE'** hand, palm facing left, is held against the lips and the hand is moved sharply forward. (For emphasis, the hand is very gradually moved upward and forward, eventually assuming a horizontal position.)

realize: *v.* to become aware of. *We did not realize how severe the blizzard was.*

SIGN: Vertical right **'EXTENDED R'** (or **'R'**) hand, palm toward face, makes small circles (clockwise in the eyes of the onlooker) at right side of forehead.

really: *adv.* in reality; truly. *She really made her own dress for her prom.*

SIGN: Forefinger of vertical right **'ONE'** hand, palm facing left, is held against the lips and the hand is moved sharply forward.

reap: *v.* to get as a reward. *He put a lot of effort into building a successful business, and now he is reaping the benefits.*

SIGN: Right **'SPREAD C'** hand, palm facing left and toward the body slightly, is transformed to an **'S'** hand, palm facing the body, as it is brushed left twice along the fixed, upturned palm of the left **'EXTENDED B'** hand and finally raised above it. (In contexts where **reap** means 'to harvest a crop', signs vary according to how the crop is cut and gathered.)

rear: *v.* (said of horses) to raise the front legs and become almost upright. *The horse began to rear and finally threw the rider.*

SIGN #1: **'CLAWED V'** hands are positioned one in front of the other with palms down and are then simultaneously raised so the palms are facing forward.

rear: *n.* the part that is farthest from the front; the back. *The driver asked the passengers to move to the rear of the bus.*

SIGN #2: Right **'EXTENDED A'** hand, palm facing left, is held upright and jabbed backward at least twice over the right shoulder.

rear [*or* **rear end**]: *n.* an informal word for buttocks. *He has a sore rear after falling on the ice.*

SIGN #3: Right **'EXTENDED B'** hand, fingers pointing downward, is used to tap the right buttock a couple of times.

rear end: *n.* the mechanism of an automobile that lies at the back of the vehicle. *He found the mechanical problem in the rear end.*

SIGN: Right **'EXTENDED A'** hand, palm facing left, is held upright and jabbed backward at least twice over the right shoulder.

rear-view mirror: *n.* a mirror (usually attached above the centre of the windshield in a vehicle) enabling the driver to see the traffic behind. *She could see the approaching police car in the rear-view mirror so she slowed down.*

SIGN: Horizontal **'BENT EXTENDED B'** hand is held aloft to the right with palm facing mainly backward and slightly to the left while the signer's eyes are both turned in that direction.

reason: *n.* a cause or motive for a belief or action. *Give me one good reason why you can not attend the meeting.*

SIGN #1: Vertical right **'EXTENDED R'** (or **'R'**) hand, palm toward face, makes small circles (clockwise in the eyes of the onlooker) at right side of forehead.

(it stands to) reason: *s.s.* It is logical, reasonable or obvious. *It stands to reason that she would like a better paying job.*

SIGN #2: Right **'ONE'** hand, palm facing left, is held above left **'ONE'** hand, palm facing right, with forefingers pointing relatively forward. Then right hand is tapped at least twice on left hand.

reasonable: *adj.* showing good judgment. *I thought it was a reasonable question.*

SIGN #1: Right **'ONE'** hand, palm facing left, is held above left **'ONE'** hand, palm facing right, with forefingers pointing relatively forward. Then right hand is tapped at least twice on left hand. (This sign is used to describe *things* rather than people.)
ALTERNATE SIGN—**good** #1

reasonable: *adj.* fair; sensible. *I am not afraid to ask my boss for the time off as he is a reasonable employer.*

SIGN #2: Horizontal **'CONTRACTED B'** hands, palms toward the body, are held slightly apart with the fingers of one hand pointing toward those of the other. Then they are alternately moved back and forth several times from the wrists. (This sign is used to describe *people* rather than things.)
ALTERNATE SIGN—**fair** #1

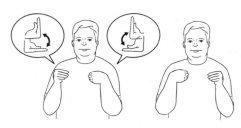

rebate: *n.* a partial return of payment. *We received a rebate on our property taxes.*

SIGN #1: Horizontal **'EXTENDED B'** hands, left palm up and right palm down, are positioned so the right is directly above the left. Then both hands are simultaneously contracted to form **'OPEN A'** handshapes as they firmly move a little closer to the chest.

OR

SIGN #2: Vertical **'ONE'** hands, palms toward the body, are positioned so the left is at a slightly lower level and closer to the body than the right hand. Then the forefingers are simultaneously contracted to form **'BENT ONE'** handshapes as they firmly move a little closer to the chest.

rebel: *v.* to resist authority. *Teenagers often rebel against their parents.*

SIGN: Vertical right **'S'** hand, palm facing backward, is held at or above shoulder level and is forcefully twisted a half turn so that palm faces forward. Alternatively, this sign may be made with two hands.
SAME SIGNS—**rebel**, *n.*, **rebellion**, *n.*, and **rebellious**, *adj.*

rebuke: *v.* to scold. *The judge* ***rebuked*** *the teenager for his attitude toward petty crime.*

SIGN: Vertical **'ONE'** hand is held with palm facing left. The forearm is then firmly thrust downward so that the hand is almost horizontal. Facial expression is stern. ❖

recall: *v.* to bring back to mind; remember. *We often* ***recall*** *the days of our youth.*

SIGN #1: Horizontal left **'EXTENDED A'** hand is held in a fixed position in front of the chest with palm toward the body. Right **'EXTENDED A'** hand is held palm down with thumbtip touching the centre of the forehead. Then the right hand is lowered and the thumbtip placed on that of the left hand.

recall: *v.* to order to be returned. *The manufacturer will* ***recall*** *all vehicles in which the defective seatbelts were installed.*

SIGN #2: Vertical **'L'** hands are held apart with palms facing backward and as the forearms are moved toward the chest slightly, the forefingers bend to form **'BENT L'** shapes.

receipt: *n.* a written acknowledgment of money or goods received. *You may return the dress within two days if you have the* ***receipt***.

SIGN: Fingerspell **RECEIPT**.

receive: *v.* to take into one's possession; get. *She* ***received*** *a letter from her sister in Germany.*

SIGN: Horizontal **'SPREAD C'** hands, right on top of left, are closed to form **'S'** hands as they are brought toward the chest.

recent: *adj.* happening a short time ago. *The Minister of Education made a* ***recent*** *announcement about changes in the curriculum.*

SIGN #1: Side of crooked forefinger of right **'X'** hand, palm facing right shoulder, is pressed into right cheek.

SIGN #2: Right **'BENT EXTENDED B'** hand is held with fingers and palm toward the right shoulder. The head is cocked to the right slightly, the eyes squint a bit and the teeth are visible and closed as if the signer is articulating the sound 'ee'.

reception: *n.* a formal party such as that held after a wedding ceremony. *They held their wedding* ***reception*** *in her parents' beautiful back yard.*

SIGN #1: **'FLAT O'** hands, palms facing the body, are circled alternately toward the mouth.

reception: *n.* the way in which a person or idea is received. *They were pleased with the warm* ***reception*** *they were given by the entire family.*

SIGN #2: Right **'BENT EXTENDED B'** hand is held out in front of the body with fingers pointing leftward and palm facing the body but angled upward slightly. The hand is then drawn in toward the chest. (**RECEPTION** may be fingerspelled.)

receptive: *adj.* able to take in. (Amongst Deaf people, this concept tends to mean 'able to take in *with the eyes*' specifically as Deaf people tend to perceive the world visually.) *It is important to have good* ***receptive*** *skills to communicate in ASL.*

SIGN #1: **'3'** hands, palms facing each other and extended fingers pointing forward/ upward, are held about a head's width apart and a little forward of the face. Then they are brought backward a couple of times toward the temples as the forefingers and middle fingers are retracted to form **'CROOKED EXTENDED V'** shapes.

receptive: *adj.* tending to receive suggestions favourably. *He seems quite* ***receptive*** *to our new proposal.*

SIGN #2: **'S'** hands, palms toward the body, are held at chest level with the left slightly above the right. Then the right is brought upward to strike the left a couple of times. (Facial expression is important.)

ALTERNATE SIGN—**accept** but facial expression is important. The movement is repeated and more gentle for **receptive** than for **accept**.

recess: *n.* a break in or cessation of customary activity. *Parliament adjourned for the summer recess.*

SIGN #1: Thumbs of horizontal **'MODIFIED 5'** hands, palms facing the body, are jabbed into either side of upper chest. (This sign connotes a *relatively long recess*, a week or more.)

recess: *n.* a break in or cessation of customary activity. *There will be a brief recess and court will resume at 10:30 a.m.*

SIGN #2: Left horizontal **'5'** hand is held with palm facing body while fingers of right palm-down **'EXTENDED B'** hand are inserted between forefinger and middle finger of left hand. (This sign connotes a *short recess*, of no more than an hour in duration. To refer to an extended period of time such as 'overnight', see **suspend**.)

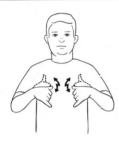

recess: *n.* a scheduled recreation period, usually in mid-morning and mid-afternoon in most schools. *The children prefer to go outdoors during their recess.*

SIGN #3: Horizontal **'Y'** hands are held parallel with palms facing each other but slanted slightly toward the body. The hands are then simultaneously bounced up and down twice. This is a wrist action. (This sign is sometimes followed by **time** #1.)

recession: *n.* a temporary decline in the economy. *We do not expect a salary increase during this recession.*

SIGN: Right **'BENT EXTENDED B'** hand is held with palm facing down and fingers pointing forward/downward. The forearm is then thrust downward/forward. (**DEPRESSION** is frequently fingerspelled.)

recipe: *n.* a list of ingredients and instructions for preparing a specific dish. *She asked for the recipe for the dessert.*

SIGN: Fingerspell **RECIPE**.

R E C I P E

reciprocal: *adj.* pertaining to the act of equal giving and receiving between two participants. *The two countries have a reciprocal trade agreement.*

SIGN: Horizontal **'F'** (or **'COVERED T'**) hands, left palm facing right and right palm facing left, are held so that the left is further from the chest than the right. Then their positions are simultaneously switched as the left hand moves back toward the body in an arc over the right hand while the right hand moves away from the body in an arc under the left hand. SAME SIGNS—**reciprocity**, *n.*, and **reciprocate**, *v.*

recite: *v.* to tell (a story) from memory. *At dinner time my father, who was Deaf, often recited the events of his day.*

SIGN #1: Left **'CONTRACTED C'** (or **'OPEN 8'**) hand is held horizontally with palm facing right while right **'CONTRACTED C'** (or **'OPEN 8'**) hand is held upright with palm facing left. The hands are held close enough together to be loosely interlocked. They are then drawn apart, closed and returned several times, thus alternating between **'CONTRACTED C'** (or **'OPEN 8'**) and **'FLAT O'** (or **'8'**) shapes with each movement. (This sign refers to the *recitation of a story or an accounting of events rendered in ASL specifically*. For the recitation of 'poetry' in ASL, see **recite** #2.)

recite: *v.* to tell (a story or poem) from memory. *The audience was fascinated as she recited several poems in ASL.*

SIGN #2: **'S'** hands, left palm facing right and right palm facing left, are held at about shoulder level and are alternately thrust forward as the fingers open to form **'MODIFIED 5'** hands. This is a very slow, deliberate movement which takes up a large signing space. The signer's eyes look pensively upward and forward. (This sign refers to the *recitation of a story or poem rendered in ASL specifically*.)

recite: *v.* to tell (a story or poem) from memory. *In a loud, clear voice he recited several passages from Shakespeare's The Tempest.*

SIGN #3: Tip of forefinger of vertical right **'4'** hand, palm facing left, is tapped a few times against the chin. (This sign refers to a *spoken recitation specifically*.)

reckless: *adj.* having no regard for danger; careless; rash. *We must watch out for reckless drivers.*

SIGN: Extended fingers of right **'V'** hand are waved up and down in front of the forehead with palm alternately facing leftward and downward. Facial expression is important.

reckon: *v.* an informal word for think, feel or suppose. *I reckon I will likely pass the exam.*

SIGN: Tip of middle finger of right **'BENT MIDFINGER 5'** hand, palm toward the body, is brushed upward and off the chest at least twice as the hand makes small circular-like movements in a clockwise direction.

recline: *v.* to lie down. *The nurse helped the patient to recline on the bed after his physical therapy session.*

SIGN: Left **'EXTENDED B'** hand is held in a fixed position with palm up and fingers pointing forward at a slight rightward angle. Right **'V'** hand is laid on the left palm with palm up and extended fingers pointing forward.

recognize: *v.* to perceive as familiar. *She thought she recognized the person.*

SIGN: Tip of forefinger of right **'CROOKED ONE'** hand is positioned at corner of right eye and brought down to rest on upturned palm of left **'EXTENDED B'** hand.
SAME SIGN—**recognition**, *n.*

recollect: *v.* to remember; recall from memory. *I can not recollect all the details of the accident.*

SIGN: Horizontal left **'EXTENDED A'** hand is held in a fixed position in front of the chest with palm toward the body. Right **'EXTENDED A'** hand is held palm down with thumbtip touching the centre of the forehead. Then the right hand is lowered and the thumbtip placed on that of the left hand.
SAME SIGN—**recollection**, *n.*

recommend: *v.* to suggest as being worthy or a good choice. *We asked them to recommend a suitable, reasonably priced hotel.*

SIGN: **'EXTENDED B'** hands, palms up and fingers pointing forward, are held slightly apart with the right just ahead of the left, and are simultaneously thrust forward and slightly upward in an arc formation.
SAME SIGN—**recommendation**, *n.*

recompense: *v.* to pay someone for his/her efforts. *We will recompense all volunteers for their travel expenses.*

SIGN: As the forearm is lowered slightly, the thumb of the horizontal right **'FLAT O'** hand, palm facing left, is slid across the bunched fingers until the handshape becomes an **'A'**. ❖

reconcile: *v.* to re-establish friendly relations after a period of estrangement. *After separating for six months, he and his wife decided to reconcile.*

SIGN #1: Vertical **'EXTENDED B'** hands are held quite far apart with palms facing each other at a forward angle and as they are drawn together, they simultaneously fingerspell the letters **ACK**. (This sign is *used only to refer to a couple who have lived together or had a romantic relationship.* See **reconcile** #2 for friends, relatives or associates who have reconciled.)
ALTERNATE SIGN—**join** #1

reconcile: *v.* to re-establish friendly relations after a period of estrangement. *After not speaking to each other for 25 years, the brothers finally decided to reconcile.*

SIGN #2: Left **'CROOKED ONE'** hand is held palm-up with forefinger pointing rightward/forward, while right **'CROOKED ONE'** hand is held palm-down with forefinger laid across left forefinger at right angles to it. The wrists then rotate so that the hands reverse positions. (This sign is *used to refer to friends, relatives or associates who have 'fallen out' and then reconciled.* See **reconcile** #1 for couples involved romantically.)

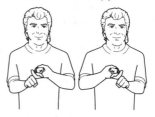

reconcile: *v.* to settle (an argument or disagreement). *I am glad that we were able to reconcile our differences.*

SIGN #3: **'FLAT O'** hands are held parallel with palms up and slanted slightly toward the body. As the hands are drawn apart the thumbs slide across the fingertips, causing the hands to assume **'A'** shapes.

reconcile: *v.* to bring oneself to accept (something unpleasant); to content oneself (albeit reluctantly). *I have finally reconciled myself to the fact that I will never succeed in this business.*

SIGN #4: Vertical right **'ONE'** hand is held with palm facing left and side of forefinger against the lips as the head and upper body droop slightly as if in defeat. (Alternatively, this sign may be followed by **accept** or **accept** may be used alone.)

record: *v.* to make a permanent account in writing. *The secretary will record the minutes of the meeting.*

SIGN #1: Horizontal left **'EXTENDED B'** hand is held in a fixed position with palm facing rightward/backward. Thumb and forefinger of right **'CLOSED X'** hand move forward/rightward along the palm of the left hand. Movement is repeated. (Sign choice depends on how the recording is being done. In certain contexts, **type** #3 would be more appropriate.)

record: *v.* to reproduce on video or audio tape. *Would you please record a two-hour movie for me tonight at 9:00 on Channel 4?*

SIGN #2: Left **'EXTENDED B'** hand is held in a fixed position with palm right and fingers pointing forward. Horizontal right **'CONTRACTED 5'** hand, palm left, is held with fingertips touching left palm. The right hand then moves rightward as the fingers close to form a **'FLAT O'** hand.

record: *n.* a thin disc of plastic material on which sound has been recorded. *The old-fashioned phonograph record has been replaced by the compact disc.*

SIGN #3: Horizontal **'C-INDEX'** hands are held parallel with palms facing each other. Next, **'BENT ONE'** (or **'BENT MIDFINGER 5'**) hands are held right above left, right palm facing downward and left palm facing upward as the hands both move in a counter-clockwise direction (from the signer's perspective) so that the extended fingers revolve around each other. (ASL CONCEPT—**disk - spin**.)

record: *n.* information collected methodically over a long period of time. *The judge will look at your record before he sentences you.*

SIGN #4: Fingerspell **RECORD**.

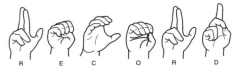

record: *n.* the best or most outstanding performance ever attained, as in a specific sport. *She holds a world record in diving.*

SIGN #5: Fingerspell **RECORD**.

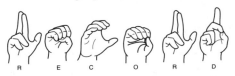

recover: *v.* to regain one's health. *He is expected to recover quickly after the surgery.*

SIGN #1: **'BENT 5'** hands, with fingertips on either side of chest and palms facing the body, are drawn forward to form **'S'** hands.
SAME SIGN—**recovery**, *n.*, in this context.
ALTERNATE SIGN—**improve**

recover: *v.* to find again or get back something that has been lost. *After the war, they tried to recover their possessions, which had been confiscated by the enemy.*

SIGN #2: Horizontal right **'SPREAD C'** hand is held with palm facing left. As the hand moves purposefully toward the chest, the fingers close to form an **'S'** hand. (If more than one thing is being recovered as in the sample sentence, two hands may be used, the hands alternately moving back toward the chest as if grabbing something and drawing it toward oneself.)

recreation: *n.* the refreshment of one's physical and/or mental health through relaxation and enjoyment. *Swimming is my favourite form of recreation.*

SIGN: Horizontal right **'EXTENDED B'** hand is held with palm against upper chest and fingers pointing left. Horizontal left **'EXTENDED B'** hand is held with palm against the body below the right hand and fingers pointing rightward. The hands then move in circles, the right hand appearing to the onlooker to be moving clockwise while the left hand moves counter-clockwise, palm on the chest, is moved in a circular motion, which appears to onlookers to be clockwise. The hands may not quite touch the body. (Alternatively, one hand may be used.)

rectangle: *n.* a parallelogram with four sides and four right angles. *A football field is shaped like a rectangle.*

SIGN: **'BENT ONE'** hands, palms down, are held side by side, then moved apart, drawn simultaneously toward the chest, and brought together again as they trace the outline of a rectangle.

recycle: *v.* to put something through a process that will result in its being used again. *We have very little garbage because we recycle most of our waste.*

SIGN: Fingerspell **RECYCLE**.

red: *adj.* the colour of blood. *He wore a red shirt and white shorts for Canada Day.*

SIGN: Vertical right **'ONE'** hand is held with palm facing the body and tip of forefinger touching the lower lip. As the hand is then drawn very firmly forward at a downward angle, the forefinger crooks to form an **'X'** shape.

redeem: *v.* to recover; get back. *He went to the pawnshop to redeem his watch.*

SIGN: Horizontal right **'SPREAD C'** hand is held with palm facing left. As the hand moves purposefully toward the chest, the fingers close to form an **'S'** hand.

reduce: *v.* to lessen; become smaller in size or amount. *She tried to reduce her expenditures.*

SIGN #1: Horizontal **'BENT EXTENDED B'** (or **'ONE'**) hands are held right above left with left palm up and right palm forward/downward. The right hand is then lowered toward the left hand.

reduce: *v.* to lose weight. *She is trying to reduce so she can wear a size 10 again.*

SIGN #2: Left **'BENT U'** hand is held in a fixed position with palm rightward/forward and extended fingers pointing rightward/forward. Right **'BENT U'** hand is held with palm leftward/forward and tips of extended fingers resting on those of the left hand at right angles. The right wrist then rotates rightward causing the hand to turn palm upward as it drops slightly.

refer to: *v.* to direct (someone) to a certain person or information source for help. *My doctor referred me to a specialist.*

SIGN #1: Vertical right **'ONE'** hand, palm toward the chest, is held with tip of forefinger on chin. The wrist then bends so that the forefinger drops to a horizontal position and touches the upper chest. Next, vertical right **'K'** hand, palm toward the face, is held with the tip of the middle finger touching the right cheekbone. The hand is then thrust forward. (ASL CONCEPT—**tell me - see**) This sign varies according to 'who' is being referred. See also **suggest**. (Sign choice depends on context.)

refer to: *v.* to relate to; apply to. *When he talks about his 'old man', he is referring to his father.*

SIGN #2: Horizontal left **'EXTENDED B'** hand is held in a fixed position with palm facing right while tip of forefinger of right palm-down **'BENT V'** hand is jabbed into the left palm. The right hand then moves away from the left hand as the right wrist rotates a quarter turn clockwise, and the middle fingertip is jabbed into the left palm.

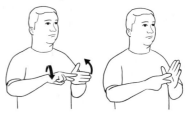

referee: *n.* an umpire or judge in various sports. *We need a referee for the hockey game.*

SIGN: Tips of crooked fingers of vertical right **'CLAWED V'** hand, palm toward the face, are tapped several times on the lips.

reference: *n.* a person referred to for a recommendation as to someone's character or ability. *She asked her teacher if he would be a reference for her application for a job.*

SIGN: Fingerspell **REFERENCE**.

refill: *n.* a replacement unit for use in a permanent container. *I need a refill for this pen.*

SIGN #1: Fingerspell **REFILL**.

R   E   F   I   L   L

refill: *v.* to fill something again, such as a gas tank. *I will lend you my car if you promise to refill the gas tank before you return it.*

SIGN #2: Left **'S'** hand is held, not in a tight fist but loosely, with palm down but slanted slightly rightward. Right **'EXTENDED A'** hand, palm down but slanted rightward as well, is positioned above and to the right of the left hand. The right hand then moves downward/leftward so that the extended thumb is inserted into the opening at the top of the left hand. (Handshapes for the right hand vary depending on the size and shape of the container being used.)

reflect: *v.* to redirect or throw back light. *The shiny chrome on the car reflects the sun.*

SIGN #1: Vertical right **'O'** hand is held at about shoulder level and thrust forward as it opens to form a **'CONTRACTED 5'** shape. The hand then turns around, resumes the **'O'** shape and is thrust toward the face as it again opens out into a **'CONTRACTED 5'** shape. SAME SIGN—**reflection**, *n.*, in this context. Signs vary depending mainly on the location of the light source and the object being lit.

reflect: *v.* to be manifested as a result of; to show. *His tears reflect great sorrow.*

SIGN #2: Tip of forefinger of horizontal right **'BENT ONE'** hand is placed against right facing palm of left **'EXTENDED B'** hand. Together, the hands are moved forward in a short arc.

reflect on: *v.* to contemplate; think seriously; ponder. *This is a good time to reflect on all the good things in life.*

SIGN #3: Vertical **'FLAT O'** hands are held just in front of either side of the forehead with palms facing backward and fingers rapidly fluttering as the hands move in small circles. From the signer's perspective, the left hand moves clockwise while the right hand moves counter-clockwise. (Alternatively, this sign may be made with one hand only.) SAME SIGN—**reflection**, *n.*, in this context. ALTERNATE SIGN—**consider**

reflection: *n.* a likeness; image. *I can see my reflection in the water.*

SIGN: Vertical right **'EXTENDED B'** hand is held with palm toward the face and is rapidly twisted back and forth from the wrist several times.

refrain: *v.* to hold back from (doing something). *He tried to refrain from eating too many sweets.*

SIGN: Right forearm with **'S'** hand, palm down, is thrust forward firmly away from the chest.

refrigerator [*or* **fridge**]: *n.* a chamber in which food and drink are kept cold. *After supper, please put the leftovers in the refrigerator immediately.*

SIGN: **'A'** (or **'S'**) hands are held apart, palms facing each other, and are shaken, along with the shoulders, as if the signer is shivering. (**Refrigerator** is frequently fingerspelled in the abbreviated form **REF.**)

refund: *v.* to give back part or all of the money paid for goods or services. *If you take the defective toaster to Customer Service, they will refund your money.*

SIGN #1: Vertical right **'S'** hand, palm forward, is thrust ahead as it opens to form a **'CONTRACTED 5'** hand. ❖

refund: *n.* money returned. *This toaster does not work so I would like a refund please.*

SIGN #2: Back of right **'CONTRACTED B'** (or **'BENT EXTENDED B'**) hand, palm up, is tapped two or three times on upturned palm of left **'EXTENDED B'** hand. Next, horizontal **'EXTENDED B'** hands, left palm up and right palm down, are positioned so the right is directly above the left. Then both hands are simultaneously contracted to form **'OPEN A'** handshapes as they firmly move a little closer to the chest. (ASL CONCEPT—**money - get back**.)

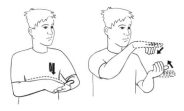

OR

SIGN #3: Back of right **'CONTRACTED B'** (or **'BENT EXTENDED B'**) hand, palm up, is tapped two or three times on upturned palm of left **'EXTENDED B'** hand. Next, vertical **'ONE'** hands, palms toward the body, are positioned so the left is at a slightly lower level and closer to the body than the right hand. Then the forefingers are simultaneously contracted to form **'BENT ONE'** handshapes as they firmly move a little closer to the chest. (ASL CONCEPT—**money - get back**.) Refund, *n.,* is frequently finger-spelled.

refurbish: *v.* to renovate; restore. *They are going to refurbish the historical mansion.*

SIGN: Horizontal right **'EXTENDED B'** hand, palm facing backward at a leftward angle, is circled in a clockwise direction a few times, brushing against the extended left forearm with each rotation.

refuse: *v.* to decline to accept. *I refuse to believe your story.*

SIGN #1: Right horizontal **'EXTENDED A'** hand, with palm facing leftward, is raised abruptly to an upright position so that the thumb points over the right shoulder. The facial expression is one of 'defiance'.
SAME SIGN—**refusal**, *n.*

refuse: *n.* trash; rubbish; anything thrown away. *The refuse in the bin was burned.*

SIGN #2: Forefinger of right **'ONE'** hand, palm facing forward/left, is moved in an arc in front of left arm from about mid-forearm to elbow. As the hand moves, it twists from the wrist so that the palm eventually faces the body.
REGIONAL VARIATION—**garbage** #2

regard: *v.* to consider. *I regard this as his best novel so far.*

SIGN: Tip of forefinger of right **'ONE'** hand touches forehead. (Sign choice depends on context.)

regarding [*or* **with regard to** *or* **in regard to**]: *prep.* concerning; in relation to; with respect to; in connection with. *He will call you regarding Saturday's game.*

SIGN: Left **'BENT ONE'** hand, palm facing right and forefinger pointing right, remains fixed while forefinger of right **'BENT ONE'** hand circles the left forefinger in a clockwise direction.
REGIONAL VARIATIONS—**about** #2 & #3

regardless of: *adv.* in spite of; taking no heed of. *Regardless of the hazards, he continues to weld without wearing goggles.*

SIGN: Fingers of horizontal **'BENT EXTENDED B'** hands, palms facing the chest, are alternately brushed back and forth against each other.

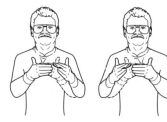

regards: *n.* good wishes or greetings. *Give my regards to your parents.*

SIGN: Side of forefinger of vertical right **'B'** hand, palm facing left, is placed against right side of forehead. The forearm is then moved forward/rightward as the hand tips forward/rightward from the wrist so that the fingers point in the same direction as if the signer is saluting someone.

regimen: See **schedule**.

region: *n.* an area considered as a unit. *They live in a mountainous region.*

SIGN: Horizontal left **'S'** hand is held in a fixed position with palm rightward/backward. Right **'EXTENDED B'** hand, fingers pointing forward and palm down, rubs the top of the left hand as it moves in several counter-clockwise circles. SAME SIGN—**regional**, *adj.* ALTERNATE SIGN—**area** #1

register: *v.* to enter one's name on a list. *I will register for the conference tomorrow.*

SIGN #1: Tips of extended fingers of right **'BENT U'** (or **'R'**) hand, palm down, are used to strike the upturned palm of the left **'EXTENDED B'** hand. (If more than one person is registering, the movement is repeated.)

register [*or* **registry**]: *n.* an official or formal list that records names, events or transactions. *The teacher marks the attendance in the class register.*

SIGN #2: Horizontal **'EXTENDED B'** hands, palms together, fingers pointing forward, are opened to the palms-up position. Next, left **'EXTENDED B'** hand is held in a fixed position with palm toward the body at a rightward and slightly upward angle. Right **'BENT EXTENDED B'** hand, palm leftward/backward, is placed against the fingers of the left hand and then slid down to the heel of the left hand. (ASL CONCEPT—**book - list**.)

(cash) register: *n.* a device used in a place of business to calculate the amount of money customers are required to pay as well as the amount of change they should receive. *Most cash registers are computerized.*

SIGN #3: Fingers of vertical right **'CLAWED 5'** hand, palm forward, flutter as the hand is circled in a counter-clockwise direction to simulate the ringing up of figures on a till or cash register.

registered mail: *n.* a postal service that guarantees delivery. *Please send me the documents by registered mail.*

SIGN: Right **'U'** hand, palm facing left and extended fingers pointing forward, is twisted from the wrist as it moves in a leftward arc so that the palm faces down and extended fingers come to rest in upturned palm of left **'EXTENDED B'** hand. Next, left **'EXTENDED B'** hand is held in a fixed position with palm facing backward/rightward and fingers pointing rightward/forward. Right **'EXTENDED A'** hand begins with palm toward the body and thumbtip on the lips, and is then lowered as the wrist twists to turn the palm down and the thumbtip is pressed into the left palm.

registration: *n.* the act of signing in or entering one's name on a list. *Registration for the conference will take place tomorrow.*

SIGN: Crossed fingertips of right **'R'** hand, palm down, are placed first on the fingers and then on the upturned palm of the left **'EXTENDED B'** hand. (Alternatively, the crossed fingertips of the right **'R'** hand, palm down, are tapped twice on the upturned palm of the left **'EXTENDED B'** hand.)

regress: *v.* to go back to a former or less desirable condition. *The patient's condition began to regress.*

SIGN: Edge of right **'EXTENDED B'** hand is placed in the crook between the left bicep and forearm. The right hand is then moved downward to the left wrist. SAME SIGN—**regression**, *n.* ALTERNATE SIGN—**deteriorate** #1

regret: *v.* to feel sorry or guilty; wish things had been different. *Now I regret my decision to quit school before graduating.*

SIGN #1: Vertical right **'Y'** hand is held with palm facing left and tip of thumb on the chin. The thumb maintains contact with the chin as the wrist slowly rotates until the palm faces down. (A slightly protruding but relaxed tongue is an important feature of this sign.)

(send) regrets: *v.* a polite expression meaning to inform (someone) of the inability to attend (something). *Everyone else attended the meeting but I sent my regrets.*

SIGN #2: Left **'MODIFIED O'** hand is held at about shoulder level with palm facing upward but angled slightly toward the body while right **'MODIFIED O'** hand is held upright just in front of the forehead with palm toward the face. The forearms then move simultaneously forward/downward as the hands open to assume **'MODIFIED 5'** shapes with palms facing upward. ❖ Next, left **'ONE'** hand is held palm-down with forefinger pointing forward/rightward. The forefinger of the right **'ONE'** hand is held above the left, then brought down sharply to strike the left forefinger. Finally, vertical right **'ONE'** hand is held with palm facing forward. The wrist then bends, causing the hand to fall forward so that the palm faces down. (Alternatively, this part of the sign may be made with two hands.) (ASL CONCEPT— **inform - can't go**.)

regular: *adj.* usual; normal; customary. *I do not really like herbal teas; I prefer regular tea.*

SIGN: Horizontal **'ONE'** hands are held, right just above left, with left palm facing rightward and right palm facing leftward/backward. Right hand is then lowered several times, striking the left hand each time in a circular movement.

regularly: *adv.* at fixed or established time intervals. *She has her car serviced regularly.*

SIGN: **'ONE'** hands are held right on top of left, with left palm facing rightward/backward and right palm facing leftward/backward while left forefinger points forward/rightward and right forefinger points leftward/forward at an upward angle. Together, the hands are lowered. (More specific signs are often used if actual time intervals are being stressed, *e.g.,* **every day, weekly, monthly, yearly**.)

regulate: *v.* to adjust as required; control. *It is difficult to regulate the air conditioning in this room.*

SIGN: Horizontal **'x'** hands are held slightly apart with left palm facing right and right palm facing left. Then they are alternately moved backward and forward.

regulation: *n.* a rule, principle, condition or law established to govern behaviour. *Construction workers must comply with safety regulations for their own protection.*

SIGN: Left **'EXTENDED B'** hand is held in a fixed position either vertically with palm facing right or horizontally with palm facing left at an upward angle. Right **'R'** hand, with palm facing that of the left hand, is positioned so that the tips of the crossed fingers touch the left hand at the end of the fingers. The right hand is then moved away from the left hand slightly and repositioned with tips of crossed fingers touching the palm of the left hand close to the heel.

rehabilitation: *n.* retraining and readaptation for the purpose of restoring someone to a productive, law-abiding life. *Rehabilitation of habitual criminals is rarely successful.*

SIGN: Fingerspell **REHAB**.

rehearse: *v.* to prepare oneself through practice. *We should rehearse daily for two weeks before the play opens.*

SIGN: Left **'ONE'** hand is held in a fixed position with palm down and forefinger pointing forward/rightward. With palm facing downward at a slight leftward/forward angle and knuckles lying along the left forefinger, the right **'A'** hand slides back and forth. SAME SIGN—**rehearsal**, *n.*

reign: *n.* the period during which a monarch is in power. *The Protestant Reformation took place during the reign of King Henry VIII.*

SIGN: Horizontal **'x'** hands are held slightly apart with left palm facing right and right palm facing left. Then they are alternately moved backward and forward.

reimburse: *v.* to repay or compensate (someone for money already spent). *The company will reimburse you for all your expenses when you get back from the conference.*

SIGN: As the forearm is lowered slightly, the thumb of the horizontal right **'FLAT O'** hand, palm facing left, is slid across the bunched fingers until the handshape becomes an **'A'**. ❖ SAME SIGN—**reimbursement**, *n.*

reinforce: *v.* to give extra strength or support to. *Your approval will reinforce our position on this issue.*

SIGN: **'S'** hands, palms toward the body, are held at chest level with the left slightly above the right. Then the right is brought upward to strike the left. SAME SIGN—**reinforcement**, *n.*, but the movement is repeated.

reins: *n.* a pair of leather straps used to control a horse. *The reins are made of leather.*

SIGN: Horizontal **'COVERED T'** hands, left palm facing right and right palm facing left, are positioned so that one hand is slightly ahead of the other and both are simultaneously shaken up and down to simulate the handling of a horse's reins.

reject: *v.* to refuse to accept. *The court might reject your testimony.*

SIGN: Fingertips of right **'BENT EXTENDED B'** hand, palm down, are placed on upturned palm of left **'EXTENDED B'** hand and brushed forward to form a straight **'EXTENDED B'** hand. ❖ SAME SIGN—**rejection**, *n.*

rejoice: *v.* to express great happiness. *My family will rejoice when they hear of my success.*

SIGN: Horizontal right **'EXTENDED B'** hand, palm toward the body, is slowly and deliberately brushed up and off the chest twice in a circular motion. ALTERNATE SIGN—**ecstatic** (In a religious context, **triumph** is often used.)

relapse: *n.* the return of an illness after an apparent recovery. *She had recovered from pneumonia but then she had a relapse.*

SIGN: Right **'BENT EXTENDED B'** hand, palm up, is overturned and brought downward so that the fingertips touch the upturned palm of the left **'EXTENDED B'** hand. Next, **'BENT MIDFINGER 5'** hands are then positioned so that the tip of the right middle finger is in the middle of the forehead and the tip of the left middle finger is on the stomach. (ASL CONCEPT—**again - sick**.) **Relapse** sometimes means 'the return to a state other than illness', in which case this sign would be inappropriate.

relate a story: *v.* to tell; narrate. *He related an interesting story that made everyone sit up and pay attention.*

SIGN: Left **'CONTRACTED C'** (or **'OPEN 8'**) hand is held horizontally with palm facing right while right **'CONTRACTED C'** (or **'OPEN 8'**) hand is held upright with palm facing left. The hands are held close enough together to be loosely interlocked. They are then drawn apart, closed and returned several times, thus alternating between **'CONTRACTED C'** (or **'OPEN 8'**) and **'FLAT O'** (or **'8'**) shapes with each movement.

(be) related to: *v.* to be connected with in terms of thought or meaning. *The report is related to the proposed tax reforms.*

SIGN #1: Thumbs and forefingers of both **'F'** hands interlock and are moved toward the person, place or thing to whom the situation pertains. ❖ ALTERNATE SIGN—**about** #1

(be) related to: *v.* to be connected through kinship or marriage. *Are you related to any famous people?*

SIGN #2: Thumbs and forefingers of both **'F'** hands interlock and are moved from side to side slightly a few times.

relationship: *n.* association; connection between people or things. *They have a very serious relationship built on love and trust.*

SIGN: Thumbs and forefingers of both **'F'** hands interlock and are moved from side to side slightly a few times.

relative: *n.* a person who is related by blood or marriage. *He is a distant relative of my mother.*

SIGN: Horizontal **'R'** hands, palms facing each other, are moved alternately up and down a few times, the crossed fingers of one hand striking those of the other with each motion.

relative to: *prep.* having significance in relation to something else. *Everyone on our staff is paid relative to his or her seniority.*

SIGN: Tips of forefingers of **'ONE'** hands are crossed slightly with the right on top of the left, and both palms facing down. Together, the hands are lowered as if the right forefinger is exerting downward pressure on the left forefinger.

relax: *v.* to lessen tension; take a rest from work. *Please relax and do not worry about anything.*

SIGN: **'EXTENDED B'** hands, palms toward the body, are crossed at the wrists and are then placed on the chest.
SAME SIGN—**relaxation**, *n.*

relay: *v.* to carry or pass on something to someone else. *She asked if I would relay her message to her boss.*

SIGN #1: Right **'FLAT O'** hand, palm up, is moved in arc formation from the vicinity of the person doing the passing to that of the person receiving the object. ❖

relay: *n.* a sports event between teams, each member of which covers a specified portion of the distance. *Our team won the swimming relay.*

SIGN #2: Vertical **'4'** hands are held, left in front of right, with left palm facing right and right palm facing left. The hands are then moved slightly apart and back together at least twice. (**RELAY** in this context may be finger-spelled.)

(Message) Relay Centre: *n.* a place where a hearing person's voice communication is typed on a TTY device to a Deaf person whose typewritten message is translated into voice for the hearing person. (This service is referred to in various ways throughout the country.) *I will call the loans officer at my bank through the Message Relay Centre.*

SIGN #3: Fingerspell **MRC**. (Fingerspelled abbreviations vary from place to place depending on what the service is called.)

M　　　　R　　　　C

release: *v.* to set free. *They will release the prisoner next week.*

SIGN #1: Fingers of right **'B'** hand, palm-down, are placed on and at right angles to fingers of upturned palm of left **'EXTENDED B'** hand. Right hand is then slid at a forward/rightward angle across and off the left hand. (Sign choice for **release**, meaning to 'let go of' something, depends on the size, shape and location of the object to which the signer is referring.)
ALTERNATE SIGN—**let go**

release: *v.* to issue for general circulation. *The press is not permitted to release the details of the case.*

SIGN #2: Horizontal **'CONTRACTED B'** hands are held with palms up and fingertips almost touching. The hands then move forward in an outward arc as the fingers spread to assume a **'SLANTED 5'** shape.

relevant: *adj.* related to the matter being discussed; pertinent. *This paragraph is very relevant to the plot of your story.*

SIGN: Thumbs and forefingers of both **'F'** hands interlock and are moved toward the person, place or thing to whom the situation pertains.
SAME SIGN—**relevance**, *n.*

reliable: *adj.* dependable. *He is a very reliable employee.*

SIGN: **'BENT EXTENDED B'** hands, palms facing the body, are tapped against the right shoulder a couple of times with the fingertips.

relieve: *v.* to lessen or alleviate pain or distress. *These pills will relieve your upset stomach.*

SIGN: **'FLAT O'** hands are held parallel with palms up and slanted slightly toward the body. As the hands are drawn apart the thumbs slide across the fingertips, causing the hands to assume **'A'** shapes.

SAME SIGN—**relief**, *n.*, in this context.

(be *or* feel) relieved: *v.* to experience relief from worry or anxiety. *I am sure my parents will be relieved when they hear the good news.*

SIGN: **'BENT B'** hands, right above left with left palm facing right and right palm facing left, are placed against the chest and simultaneously lowered. The face must register 'relief'.

SAME SIGN—**relief**, *n.*, in this context.

religion: *n.* the belief in and worship of a divine power. *The Christian religion is divided into many denominations.*

SIGN: The right wrist rotates toward the chest as the crossed fingertips of the horizontal **'R'** hand are brushed off the left shoulder in a slight downward arc.

SAME SIGN—**religious**, *adj.*

relinquish: *v.* to surrender; give up (something). *The police chief was forced to relinquish his job after he was found guilty of committing a serious crime.*

SIGN: **'OPEN A'** hands, held slightly apart at waist level, palms down, are thrust upward to form **'EXTENDED B'** hands with palms facing forward.

relocate: *v.* to move to a different location. *The company will pay us to relocate to Vancouver if I accept the position.*

SIGN: **'FLAT O'** hands are held parallel with palms down and are simultaneously flung forward/rightward/upward as they open to form **'MODIFIED 5'** hands.

reluctant: *adj.* hesitant; disinclined. *I am reluctant to leave the house in case they call while I am out.*

SIGN #1: **'S'** (or **'A'**) hands are held apart with palms down and are alternately raised and lowered.

SAME SIGN—**reluctance**, *n.*, in this context.

reluctant: *adj.* unwilling. *He is a reluctant reader.*

SIGN #2: Right **'A'** hand, palm facing left, is positioned with the thumb against the lips and is very slowly drawn downward and off the chin. Facial expression is important.

SAME SIGN—**reluctance**, *n.*, in this context.

ALTERNATE SIGN—**resist**

rely on: *v.* to depend on. *The majority of Deaf Canadians rely on the TTY for telephone communication.*

SIGN: Tips of forefingers of **'ONE'** hands are crossed slightly with the right on top of the left, and both palms facing down. Together, the hands are lowered as if the right forefinger is exerting downward pressure on the left forefinger. ❖

remain: *v.* to stay. *All the other students were allowed to leave but I was asked to remain in the classroom.*

SIGN #1: **'Y'** hands are held parallel with palms down but slanted slightly forward. The hands are then firmly pushed a very short distance downward.

remain: *v.* to continue to be. *They have remained friends after all these years.*

SIGN #2: **'EXTENDED A'** hands are held side by side with palms down and right thumbtip pressing against left thumbnail as the hands are moved purposefully forward.

remainder: *n.* the part or amount which is left. *You may spend the remainder of this money.*

SIGN: Horizontal **'5'** hands are held apart with palms facing each other. The forearms are then simultaneously lowered.

(be) remanded: *v.* to send a prisoner or accused person back into custody. *He was remanded until his lawyer could prepare his case with the new evidence.*

SIGN: Vertical right **'Y'**, palm facing forward/rightward is thrust forward at a rightward angle.

remark: *v.* to comment casually. *"It was a good movie but a little too long,"* **remarked** *Calvin.*

SIGN: Tip of forefinger of vertical right **'4'** hand, palm facing left, is tapped twice against the chin.

ALTERNATE SIGN—**say** #1

remarkable: *adj.* extraordinary; worthy of notice. *He has* **remarkable** *computer skills.*

SIGN: Vertical **'EXTENDED B'** hands, palms facing forward, are held apart near the face. Forearms are pushed purposefully forward a short distance.

remember: *v.* to bring back to one's mind; recall. *She* **remembered** *her first day at school.*

SIGN: Horizontal left **'EXTENDED A'** hand is held in a fixed position in front of the chest with palm toward the body. Right **'EXTENDED A'** hand is held palm down with thumbtip touching the centre of the forehead. Then the right hand is lowered and the thumbtip placed on that of the left hand.

remind: *v.* to cause someone to remember (to do something). *Please* **remind** *me to write a letter to the Minister of Education.*

SIGN #1: Fingertips of right **'BENT EXTENDED B'** hand, palm facing the body, are tapped against the right shoulder. ❖

remind: *v.* to bring to mind. *That* **reminds** *me that I should get some gas before I run out.*

SIGN #2: Vertical right **'ONE'** hand is purposefully raised so that the tip of the forefinger stabs the forehead as sudden realization is registered on the face.

reminisce: *v.* to think or talk about old times and past experiences. *Most people like to* **reminisce** *about their school days.*

SIGN: Right **'BENT V'** hand is held with palm backward and tip of middle finger just under/to the right of the right eye. The hand is then moved to the right and back so that it is just above the right shoulder.

remiss: *adj.* negligent in attending to duty; careless. *We were* **remiss** *in not sending them a special invitation.*

SIGN #1: Vertical right **'Y'** hand is held against the right side of the chin with palm facing left. The wrist then rotates to turn the hand so that the palm faces the body.

OR

SIGN #2: Vertical right **'Y'** hand, palm toward the body, is firmly tapped on the chin.

remit: *v.* to send (money for payment). *You must* **remit** *the balance before December 31st.*

SIGN: Vertical right **'S'** hand, palm forward, is thrust ahead as it opens to form a **'CONTRACTED 5'** hand. (This sign is sometimes preceded by the sign **money** #1 or **pay** #1.)

remnant: *n.* a part that is left over after something is completed. *She covered two cushions with a* **remnant** *of the material she had used to make the new drapes.*

SIGN: Horizontal **'5'** hands are held apart with palms facing each other. The forearms are then simultaneously lowered.

remorse: *n.* a sense of deep regret due to feelings of guilt. *The prisoner showed* **remorse** *throughout the trial.*

SIGN: Right **'A'** (or **'EXTENDED A'**) hand, palm facing the body, is rubbed on the chest with a circular motion that appears clockwise to onlookers.

SAME SIGN—**remorseful**, *adj.*

remote: *adj.* aloof; distant in manner. *He seemed* **remote** *and uninterested in our conversation.*

SIGN #1: Thumbs and forefingers of **'F'** hands, palms facing each other, are interlocked. The hands are then drawn apart to form **'OPEN F'** hands.

575

remote: *adj.* distant. *They live in a remote area of northern B.C.*

SIGN #2: Horizontal **'EXTENDED A'** hands are held together with palms facing each other. Then the right hand is moved forward in arc formation. Alternatively, this sign may be made without the left hand. The more slowly the sign is produced, the greater is the distance implied. (This sign means remote in terms of 'area' or 'space' specifically. To indicate remoteness in terms of 'time', see **(in the) distant future** and **(in the) distant past.**)

remote: *adj.* slight. *Our chances of winning the lottery are remote.*

SIGN #3: Tip of forefinger of the right **'COVERED T'** hand, palm toward the face, is held in front of the nose and the thumb is flicked out, thus forming an **'A-INDEX'** hand. (Alternatively, this sign may be made in front of the chest.)

remote control: *n.* a device used for controlling the functions of something like a television from a distance. *The batteries in my remote control need to be replaced.*

SIGN: Right **'A-INDEX'** hand, palm left, is held in a horizontal position and the thumb is flexed a few times as if pushing buttons on a remote control.

remove: *v.* to take away; take out of. *I can not remove this stain from my shirt.*

SIGN: Horizontal right **'A'** hand, palm facing left, is held against right-facing palm of horizontal left **'EXTENDED B'** hand, and is then moved rightward and downward as it opens to become a **'CROOKED 5'** hand with the palm facing down. (This sign is very context-specific. Signs vary according to 'what' is being removed and 'how' it is being removed. Natural gestures are often used with the hand(s) assuming whatever shape is necessary to take hold of a given object and remove it.)

remunerate: *v.* to pay for work or service. *He will be remunerated when he finishes the job.*

SIGN: Thumbtip of right **'EXTENDED A'** hand, palm down, is brushed forward across the upturned palm of the left **'EXTENDED B'** hand. ❖
SAME SIGN—**remuneration**, *n.*
ALTERNATE SIGN—**pay** #1

rendezvous: *n.* a social get-together at a specified time and place. *The graduates planned a rendezvous in ten years.*

SIGN: Both **'BENT 5'** hands, palms facing forward, are moved forward and slightly downward from shoulder level, fingers wiggling. (To refer to a **rendezvous** between two people only, see **meet** #1.)

renew: *v.* to repeat an action; restate a promise; regain validity for a continued period. *They plan to renew their wedding vows.*

SIGN: Right **'BENT EXTENDED B'** hand, palm up, is overturned and brought downward so that the fingertips touch the upturned palm of the left **'EXTENDED B'** hand. (**RENEW** may be fingerspelled.) Sign choices vary according to what is being renewed.

renounce: *v.* to give up formally a legal claim or right. *The king renounced his rights to the throne.*

SIGN: **'OPEN A'** hands, held slightly apart at waist level, palms down, are thrust upward to form **'EXTENDED B'** hands with palms facing forward.

renovate: *v.* to restore to good condition. *This year we plan to renovate our kitchen.*

SIGN: Horizontal right **'EXTENDED B'** hand, palm facing backward at a leftward angle, is circled in a clockwise direction a few times, brushing against the extended left forearm with each rotation.
SAME SIGN—**renovation**, *n.*

renowned: *adj.* of widespread fame or good reputation. *This soldier is renowned for his courage during battle.*

SIGN: **'BENT ONE'** hands, palms toward the body but slanted slightly toward each other, are positioned with tips of forefingers touching either side of chin. The arms then move forward/upward/outward simultaneously in two arcs.

rent: *v.* to be granted the use of certain goods or property in exchange for regular payments. *We plan to rent a computer for this office.*

SIGN: Fingerspell **RENT**. (When **rent** is used as a noun to refer to the amount of money paid monthly for the use of something, as in the following sentence, the sign for **monthly** is used: *The rent for my apartment is $700.*)

repair: *v.* to restore something broken or damaged to good condition. *He asked the mechanic to repair his car.*

SIGN: **'F'** hands, palms facing each other at a forward angle, are placed together with tips of thumbs and forefingers of each hand touching. The left hand remains steady while the right hand wobbles as the wrist twists back and forth slightly a few times.

ALTERNATE SIGNS—**fix** #1 & #3

repeat: *v.* to do, write, or say something again. *Please repeat your question.*

SIGN: Right **'BENT EXTENDED B'** hand, palm up, is overturned and brought downward so that the fingertips touch the upturned palm of the left **'EXTENDED B'** hand.

SAME SIGN—**repetition**, *n.*, but the movement is repeated.

repellent: *n.* a substance that drives (things) away. *We bought some insect repellent for our camping trip.*

SIGN #1: Right **'CLAWED L'** hand is held with palm forward and slightly downward and makes sweeping movements from side to side as if spraying with an aerosol can. (To refer to repellent in 'lotion' form, see **apply** #5.)

repellent: *adj.* able to keep (something) out or off; impervious to; resistant to. *This coat is water-repellent.*

SIGN #2: **'EXTENDED B'** hands are held at right angles to one another, the left hand in front of the right, with fingers of left hand pointing upward to the right and fingers of right hand pointing upward to the left. The hands are then pushed firmly forward.

repent: *v.* to feel remorse for; to regret or be sorry (for one's actions). *The accused man does not repent his actions.*

SIGN: Right **'A'** (or **'EXTENDED A'**) hand, palm facing the body, is rubbed on the chest with a circular motion that appears clockwise to onlookers.

replace: *v.* to take the place of; to substitute or put in the place of. *He will replace the secretary who was fired.*

SIGN: Horizontal **'F'** (or **'COVERED T'**) hands, left palm facing right and right palm facing left, are held so that the left is further from the chest than the right. Then their positions are simultaneously switched as the left hand moves back toward the body in an arc over the right hand while the right hand moves away from the body in an arc under the left hand.

reply: *v.* to answer; respond to. *I will reply to your question after I give it a little more thought.*

SIGN: Vertical **'ONE'** hands, palms facing forward, are held with the tip of the right forefinger near the mouth and the left hand slightly farther forward and downward. Both are moved forward and down, stopping with the palms facing downward.

SAME SIGN—**reply**, *n.*

report: *v.* to give an account of something. *The supervisor will report the incident to his employer.*

SIGN #1: Left **'MODIFIED O'** hand is held at about shoulder level with palm facing upward but angled slightly toward the body while right **'MODIFIED O'** hand is held upright just in front of the forehead with palm toward the face. The forearms then move simultaneously forward/downward as the hands open to assume **'MODIFIED 5'** shapes with palms facing upward. ❖

report: *v.* to present oneself at a specified place. *You must report to the manager's office at once.*

SIGN #2: Vertical **'ONE'** hands, palms forward, are staggered so that the right hand is held slightly closer to the chest than the left. The wrists then bend, causing the hands to fall forward so that the palms face downward. ❖ (Alternatively, this sign may be made with one hand only.)

report: *n.* a written (or typewritten) account of something that happened. *The police officer is typing up a report on the robbery.*

SIGN #3: Fingerspell **REPORT**.

repossess: *v.* to take back or seize property because of nonpayment of money due. *If you continue to be in arrears with your monthly payments, the loan company might repossess your car.*

SIGN: **'SPREAD C'** hands are held parallel with palms down and are then closed to form **'S'** hands as they are thrust forward.

represent: *v.* to act as an authorized delegate or agent for. *Members of Parliament represent the people in their constituencies.*

SIGN #1: Tip of forefinger of horizontal right **'BENT ONE'** hand is placed against right facing palm of left **'EXTENDED B'** hand. Together, the hands are moved forward in a short arc.

represent: *v.* to symbolize; stand for. *The dove is said to represent peace.*

SIGN #2: Horizontal left **'EXTENDED B'** hand is held in a fixed position with palm facing right while tip of forefinger of right palm-down **'BENT V'** hand is jabbed into the left palm. The right hand then moves away from the left hand as the right wrist rotates a quarter turn clockwise, and the middle fingertip is jabbed into the left palm.

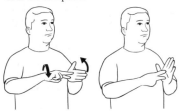

representative: *n.* a person who acts for another person or group. *The company will send a representative to the conference.*

SIGN: Tip of forefinger of horizontal right **'BENT ONE'** hand is placed against right facing palm of left **'EXTENDED B'** hand. Together, the hands are moved forward a couple of times.

repress: *v.* to suppress; hold back; keep under control. *He was able to repress his anger.*

SIGN: Right horizontal **'SPREAD C'** hand, palm up, is held at mid chest and is drawn down slightly as it closes to form an **'S'** hand. SAME SIGN—**repression**, *n.*, but the movement is repeated.

reprimand: *v.* to rebuke formally. *The principal will reprimand those students who broke the school rules.*

SIGN #1: Vertical **'ONE'** hand is held with palm facing left. The forearm is then firmly thrust downward so that the hand is almost horizontal. Movement is repeated. Facial expression is stern. ❖

OR

SIGN #2: **'EXTENDED B'** hands are held palms down, so that the right hand is above the left and is brought down so that the fingertips are tapped on the back of the left hand. Facial expression is stern. ❖

reproduce: *v.* to duplicate; make a copy of. *Many artists have tried to reproduce the Mona Lisa.*

SIGN #1: Left **'EXTENDED B'** hand is held in a fixed position with palm up and fingers pointing forward/rightward. Right **'CONTRACTED 5'** hand is positioned at the end of the left hand with palm facing forward. As the right hand is drawn backward toward the palm or heel of the left hand, it closes to form a **'FLAT O'** shape. SAME SIGN—**reproduction**, *n.*, in this context except that the movement is repeated.

reproduce: *v.* to cause the production of more of the same species. *Living things reproduce in different ways.*

SIGN #2: Horizontal **'EXTENDED B'** hands, palms facing the body, are positioned with the back of the right hand resting against the left palm. Then the right hand is curved down and under the left until its palm faces downward. Movement is repeated. Signs vary according to the species that is reproducing. SAME SIGN—**reproduction**, *n.*, in this context.

reptile: *n.* any cold-blooded vertebrate. *A rattlesnake is a reptile with a venomous bite.*

SIGN: Fingerspell **REPTILE**.

R E P T I L E

repulsive: *adj.* disgusting; causing strong dislike. *When he has too much to drink, his behaviour is repulsive.*

SIGN: Right **'CLAWED C'** hand, palm toward the body, is circled in a clockwise direction (from the onlooker's perspective) in front of the stomach. Facial expression is very important.

repugnant: See **repulsive**.

reputation: *n.* the public opinion that is generally held about a person. *A good reputation is essential to all politicians.*

SIGN: **'U'** hands are held horizontally with left palm facing right but angled slightly toward the body while right palm faces leftward at a slight angle toward the body. Right hand is positioned above the left at right angles to it. Right midfinger is then tapped twice on left forefinger. (In ASL a 'good' reputation is described as either *good* or *shiny* while a 'bad' reputation is described as either *bad* or *black*.)

request: *v.* to ask for or demand. *Our organization will request a grant from the government.*

SIGN: **'EXTENDED B'** hands are held with palms together and fingers pointing forward. Then they are tilted upward from the wrists so that the fingers are pointing upward.
SAME SIGN—**request**, *n.*

require: *v.* to demand or impose as something necessary. *This job requires shift work.*

SIGN: Tip of forefinger of right **'X'** hand is placed in right-facing palm of left **'EXTENDED B'** hand. Together the hands are moved firmly toward the chest, giving the impression that the left hand is being tugged by the right forefinger.
SAME SIGN—**requirement**, *n.*

rescind: See **cancel**.

rescue: *v.* to bring out of danger; save. *The firemen were able to rescue all the patients from the burning hospital.*

SIGN: **'S'** hands, left palm facing rightward/downward and right palm facing leftward/downward, are crossed at the wrists with the right hand nearer the body. Then they break apart so that they are held parallel with palms facing forward.

research: *n.* an investigation undertaken to collect information on a subject. *The information in this book is based on careful research.*

SIGN: Left **'EXTENDED B'** hand is held in a fixed position with palm turned upward but slanted slightly rightward and toward the body while fingers point rightward/forward. Right **'ONE'** hand is held palm down as tip of forefinger brushes forward a few times against palm of left hand.

resemble: *v.* to look like; have some similarity to. *The baby resembles her mother.*

SIGN: Tip of forefinger of right **'ONE'** hand touches cheekbone near right eye. The forearm then moves quickly forward a short distance as the wrist rotates and the hand takes on a vertical **'Y'** shape, the palm forward/leftward, and teeters from side to side several times. This is a wrist action.
SAME SIGN—**resemblance**, *n.*

resent: *v.* to feel bitter or indignant. *I resent being left out of the discussion.*

SIGN: Right **'5'** hand is held palm down with tip of thumb touching centre of chest. The wrist then rotates rightward as the hand moves away from the chest and turns so that the palm faces the body. Facial expression is important and must clearly convey a feeling that something is unjust.
ALTERNATE SIGN—**(don't) like**

(have) reservations: *v.* to be disinclined to accept, trust or have faith in someone/something. *I have reservations about certain conditions in this contract so I can not sign it.*

SIGN: Right forearm, with **'S'** hand palm down, is thrust forward firmly away from the chest.

reserve: *v.* to set aside for future use. *The recipe suggests that you reserve some of the mixture to sprinkle on top of the casserole.*

SIGN #1: Right **'S'** hand is clenched with palm upward but slanted toward the body and is moved, from the signer's perspective in small counter-clockwise circles.

reserve: *v.* to arrange to set aside for the use of a particular person or group of people; to book. *In popular restaurants, people need to reserve tables.*

SIGN #2: Extended fingers of right **'V'** hand are brought downward on either side of forefinger of vertical left **'ONE'** hand, which is held in a fixed position with palm facing right.
SAME SIGNS—**reservation**, *n.*, in this context or **to make a reservation**, *v.*

OR

SIGN #3: **'S'** hands are held palms down, right hand above left. Right hand is circled clockwise and brought down to rest on back of left hand.
SAME SIGNS—**reservation**, *n.*, in this context or **to make a reservation**, *v.*

reserve [*or* **reservation**]: *n.* an area of land set aside for aboriginal people. *Members of the Mohawk Nation live on that reserve [reservation].*

SIGN #4: Fingerspell **RESERVE** or **RESERVATION**.

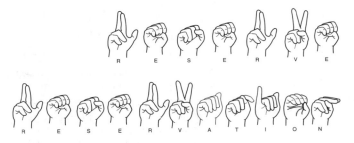

R E S E R V E

R E S E R V A T I O N

reserved: *adj.* not demonstrative; not outgoing in terms of speech or behaviour. *Being a very reserved woman, she was embarrassed by her husband's loud outbursts.*

SIGN: **'B'** (or **'EXTENDED B'**) hands are crossed in front of the mouth, left palm facing rightward/downward and right palm facing leftward/downward with the right hand just behind the left hand. Then the hands are simultaneously drawn apart and downward slightly a couple of times.

reside: *v.* to live (in a place) for an extended period of time. *When they retire, they will reside in Victoria.*

SIGN: Horizontal **'L'** hands are placed at either side, somewhere above the waist, with palms toward the body and forefingers pointing toward each other. They are then raised to a higher position on the chest.
ALTERNATE SIGN—**alive** #1

residence: *n.* a place in which one lives. *Our new residence is on Carter Street.*

SIGN #1: Fingertips of right **'MODIFIED O'** hand are placed against right cheek near the mouth, and the hand is then moved back to a position on the cheek that is nearer the right ear.

residence: *n.* a dormitory. *He lived in residence while attending the Manitoba School for the Deaf.*

SIGN #2: Right **'D'** hand, palm toward the face, is placed on the chin and then moved to the right cheek. (Alternatively, the abbreviation **DORM** may be fingerspelled.)

SIGN #3 [ONTARIO]: Horizontal right **'X'** hand, palm down, is held in front of the mid-forehead and is shaken up and down from the wrist.

residential school for Deaf children: *n.* a traditional school for Deaf students which usually combines living accommodations with academic and vocational education, as well as social and cultural development. *The residential school for Deaf children in Edmonton opened in 1955.*

SIGN: Vertical right **'ONE'** hand is held with tip of forefinger just in front of the right ear. The hand is then lowered so that the tip of the forefinger touches the right side of the mouth. Next, horizontal left **'I'** hand is held with palm facing the chest at a rightward angle while horizontal right **'I'** hand is held just above it with palm facing the chest at a leftward angle. The hands are then tapped together a couple of times. (ASL CONCEPT—**Deaf - school**.)

resign: *v.* to give up or relinquish in a formal way; quit. *The president was asked to resign his position.*

SIGN #1: Extended fingers of right **'CLAWED U'** hand, palm down, are inserted into an opening created in the left horizontal **'S'** hand. The right hand is then drawn back toward the body. SAME SIGN—**resignation**, *n.*

OR

SIGN #2: Extended fingers of horizontal right **'U'** hand are inserted into an opening created in the left horizontal **'S'** hand. Then the extended fingers of the right hand are withdrawn from the left hand, becoming more upright as they move back toward the chest. ❖ SAME SIGN—**resignation**, *n.*

resist: *v.* to oppose; stand firm against. *People often resist change.*

SIGN: Right forearm, with **'S'** hand palm down, is thrust forward firmly away from the chest. SAME SIGNS—**resistance**, *n.*, and **resistant**, *adj.*

resolute: *adj.* determined; strong in purpose. *She remains resolute in her belief that Deaf people can do anything hearing people can do except hear.*

SIGN: Thumb of vertical right **'EXTENDED B'** hand, palm forward, is placed near the right temple and the fingers are firmly lowered to form a **'BENT EXTENDED B'** hand. A look of fierce determination accompanies this sign.

resolution: *n.* a decision leading to a course of action; solution. *The City Council must find an appropriate resolution to the garbage problem.*

SIGN: **'FLAT O'** hands are held parallel with palms up and slanted slightly toward the body. As the hands are drawn apart the thumbs slide across the fingertips, causing the hands to assume **'A'** shapes. (**Resolution** has various connotations in English and sign choice depends on context. In certain contexts, the sign for **opinion** or **decide** would be more appropriate. When referring to a 'New Year's Resolution', **resolution** is fingerspelled.)

resolve: *v.* to find a solution; solve; settle. *They can not seem to resolve their problems.*

SIGN #1: **'FLAT O'** hands are held parallel with palms up and slanted slightly toward the body. As the hands are drawn apart the thumbs slide across the fingertips, causing the hands to assume **'A'** shapes.

resolve: *v.* to make a firm decision. *We resolve to complete the project before winter.*

SIGN #2: **'F'** hands, with palms facing each other, are held apart in front of chest and are purposefully lowered.

resolve: *v.* to separate into parts. *You can resolve certain chemicals into other components by applying heat.*

SIGN #3: Horizontal **'BENT EXTENDED B'** hands, palms facing chest and knuckles almost touching each other, are drawn apart.

resource: *n.* a source of economic wealth; a financial asset that can be used if needed. *Our forests are an important Canadian resource.*

SIGN #1: Fingerspell **RESOURCE**.

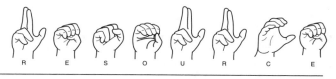

R E S O U R C E

resource: *n.* a source of help or support. *The public library provides a valuable resource within our community.*

SIGN #2: Fingerspell **RESOURCE**.

R E S O U R C E

respect: *v.* to have and/or show an attitude of admiration or esteem; to honour. *I respect him because he is so brave.*

SIGN #1: Vertical right **'R'** hand is held in front of the face with palm facing forward/leftward while vertical left **'R'** hand is held just below/in front of the right hand with palm facing forward/rightward. Both hands are then moved forward at a slight downward angle. Alternatively, the right hand only may be used. ❖ SAME SIGN—**respect**, *n.*, in this context.

respect: *n.* characteristic; feature; particular detail. *In what respect is the decision unfair?*

SIGN #2: Vertical left **'ONE'** hand is held in a fixed position with palm facing rightward/ forward. Horizontal right **'ONE'** hand is held behind left hand with palm facing left. The right hand then makes a slight but firm bounce as if intending to strike the tip of the left forefinger with that of the right forefinger but not quite touching it. (The sample sentence is translated into ASL as: *DECIDE...NOT FAIR...SPECIFIC...WHAT?*) Signs vary depending on the context.

(with) respect to: *prep.* concerning; in relation to; about. *He had not heard anything with respect to his application.*

SIGN #3: Left **'BENT ONE'** hand, palm facing right and forefinger pointing right, remains fixed while forefinger of right **'BENT ONE'** hand circles the left forefinger in a clockwise direction.

REGIONAL VARIATIONS—**about** #2 & #3

respiration: *n.* the process of breathing in and out. *The lungs are the main organs of respiration.*

SIGN: Horizontal **'5'** hands are held, right above left with palms facing the chest, and are moved forward and back.

respond: *v.* to answer; reply. *He thought carefully before responding to the teacher's question.*

SIGN: Vertical **'ONE'** hands, palms facing forward, are held with the tip of the right forefinger near the mouth and the left hand slightly farther forward and downward. Both are moved forward and down, stopping with the palms facing downward.

SAME SIGN—**response**, *n.*

Respond and **response** have various connotations in English and sign choice depends on context. This sign would be inappropriate in the following question: *How did the patient respond to the treatment?*

responsible: *adj.* reliable; dependable. *He is not a responsible person.*

SIGN #1: **'BENT EXTENDED B'** hands, palms facing the body, are tapped against the right shoulder a couple of times with the fingertips.

SAME SIGN—**responsibility**, *n.*, in this context.

responsible: *adj.* accountable (for something that has been done). *Who is responsible for this mess?*

SIGN #2: Fingertips of right **'BENT EXTENDED B'** hand, palm toward body, are placed against right shoulder. The wrist then rotates forward, causing the hand to drop while the fingertips maintain contact with the body. (If there is an implication that what has been done is something *positive* as in the following sentence, **DID** is fingerspelled. In English: *Who is responsible for this wonderful project?* In ASL: *WONDERFUL...WHO D-I-D?*)

rest: *v.* to relax after work or exertion. *They will rest when they finish the job.*

SIGN #1: **'EXTENDED B'** hands, palms toward the body, are crossed at the wrists and are then placed on the chest.

rest: *v.* to be finished with the presenting of evidence during a court case. *The defence rests.*

SIGN #2: Vertical **'5'** hands, palms facing the body, are held at chest level, and swung outward, away from the body so that the palms face down.

ALTERNATE SIGN—**cease**

rest: *n.* that which is left over or remaining, referring to objects only (not people). *You may eat the rest of the apples.*

SIGN #3: Horizontal **'5'** hands are held apart with palms facing each other. The forearms are then simultaneously lowered.

rest: *n.* those who are left; the others. *Two of you will stay here and the rest may come with me.*

SIGN #4: Horizontal right **'EXTENDED A'** hand, held in front of the left side of the body with palm facing left, is moved rightward.

rest: *n.* that which is left over or remaining, referring to time only. *He will need the medication for the rest of his life.*

SIGN #5: Horizontal **'BENT EXTENDED B'** hands, palms facing each other, are positioned so that the fingers of the right hand are just in front of the fingers of the left hand. The right hand is then moved forward briskly.

restaurant: *n.* a commercial establishment where meals are served. *The waiters in this restaurant know some ASL.*

SIGN: Crossed fingers of vertical right **'R'** hand, palm left, are placed first on the left and then on the right side of the chin. (As a variation, the crossed fingertips of the right **'EXTENDED R'** hand, palm toward the body, are used to stroked down against the left and then the right side of the chin.)

restless: *adj.* unable to sleep; tossing and turning in bed. *The children spent a restless night before Santa's arrival.*

SIGN #1: Right **'CROOKED V'** hand is placed palm-up on the upturned left palm and is wriggled back and forth from the wrist.

restless: *adj.* unable to sit quietly and relax. *The students were restless during the professor's lecture.*

SIGN #2: Extended fingers of right **'CROOKED V'** hand, palm down, are hooked over the extended fingers of the left horizontal **'U'** hand of which the palm is also facing down. Then the right hand is wriggled back and forth from the wrist.

restrain: *v.* to hold back from (some kind of action). *She tried to restrain her urge to laugh.*

SIGN: Right horizontal **'SPREAD C'** hand, palm up, is held at mid chest and is drawn down slightly as it closes to form an **'S'** hand. (In the following sentence, **control** is a more appropriate sign choice: *The police tried to restrain the angry crowd.*)

restrict: *v.* to confine; keep within certain limits. *The university will restrict its entrance requirements.*

SIGN: **'BENT EXTENDED B'** hands are held apart, right above left, with palms facing the body, but the left palm slanted slightly rightward while the right palm is slanted slightly leftward. The wrists then rotate to swing the hands into a position whereby the left palm faces forward at a rightward angle while the right hand faces forward at a leftward angle. SAME SIGN—**restriction**, *n.*

result: *n.* the outcome or consequence of an action. *What was the result of your discussion with your parents?*

SIGN #1: **'ONE'** hands, palms facing each other and forefingers pointing forward, are held apart and then turned over so that the palms face down.

result: *n.* the outcome of medical tests. *What was the result of your recent electrocardiogram?*

NOTE—Sign choice depends entirely on the situation—on whether or not the word is used in question or declarative form; on how well people involved in the conversation know each other; on how delicate the situation is deemed to be. If in doubt, it may be best to fingerspell **RESULT**.

resume: *n.* a summary of a person's educational and employment background, prepared for job applications. *I will update my resume before I apply for the position.*

SIGN #1: Fingerspell **RESUME**.

resume: *v.* to start again after an interruption. *The play will resume after a 15-minute intermission.*

SIGN #2: Left **'5'** hand is held with palm facing right while forefinger of right **'ONE'** hand is inserted between first two fingers of left hand and twisted 180 degrees either to the right or left. (Signs may vary according to context.)

retain: *v.* to keep; hold onto. *She was fortunate to retain her job when most of her colleagues were laid off.*

SIGN #1: Horizontal right **'K'** hand, with palm facing left, is held above horizontal left hand, which is held with palm facing right. Then right hand is brought purposefully down to strike left hand.

retain: *v.* to hold in a certain place. *Some medications cause the patient to retain fluids as an unwanted side effect.*

SIGN #2: Right **'S'** hand is clenched with palm upward but slanted toward the body and is moved in what appear from the signer's perspective to be small counter-clockwise circles in front of the abdomen. (The location of this sign varies. To refer to the 'retaining of knowledge', the sign is placed near the head.)

retaliate: *v.* to take retributory action; pay back; get even. *Our neighbour will retaliate by taking us to court.*

SIGN: Vertical **'BENT EXTENDED B'** hands are positioned so that the right hand is held close to the chest with palm facing forward/leftward while the left hand is held to the left and farther forward with the palm facing that of the right hand. The fingertips of one hand make contact with those of the other as the hands come forcefully together and then rebound. Facial expression is important.
SAME SIGN—**retaliation**, *n.*
ALTERNATE SIGN—**revenge**

retard: *v.* to delay or slow down a process. *Lack of communication may retard a child's linguistic development.*

SIGN: Right **'CROOKED 5'** hand is held palm down with fingertips touching the end of the left **'STANDARD BASE'** hand. The right hand is then drawn backward leftward along the back of the left hand as though petting it. (The ASL sentence is syntactically different than the English one. The sample sentence in ASL is: *NOT ENOUGH COMMUNICATE...CHILD LANGUAGE DEVELOP **SLOW**.*)

retire: *v.* to give up one's job when reaching pensionable age. *Some people are able to retire at the age of 55.*

SIGN #1 Horizontal **'MODIFIED 5'** (or **'CLAWED L'**) hands, palms facing each other, are held apart and simultaneously rotated backward from the wrists as the thumbs make contact with the chest just below each shoulder.
SAME SIGN—**retirement**, *n.*

retire: *v.* to go to bed. *I think I will retire early tonight because I am tired.*

SIGN #2: Left **'S'** hand is held loosely without actually forming a fist while the palm faces forward/rightward but is slanted slightly downward. Right **'U'** hand is held to the right of the left hand and closer to the body with palm facing upward but slanted leftward and toward the body while the extended fingers point forward/leftward. As the hands then move toward each other, the extended fingers of the right hand, which are meant to represent someone's legs, are inserted into the opening in the left hand. When making this sign, the signer generally closes his eyes as his head tilts rightward.
ALTERNATE SIGN—**bed**

retiring: See **shy**.

retract: *v.* to withdraw or take back an action, opinion, promise, charge, etc. *The politician was forced to retract his statement.*

SIGN: **'S'** hands are held parallel with palms down. Then they are simultaneously lowered slightly as the fingers open to form **'CROOKED 5'** hands. **Retract** may also mean to physically draw something backward or inward, as in the retracting of an airplane's landing gear or the retracting of a turtle's head as it disappears into its shell. Signs therefore vary considerably, depending on specifically what is retracting into what.
SAME SIGN—**retraction**, *n.*

retreat: *v.* to withdraw (from activity, especially in situations of danger). *The soldiers retreated when they realized that the opposing army could easily defeat them.*

SIGN #1: **'EXTENDED B'** hands are held parallel with palms down and fingers pointing forward. They are then drawn backward toward the shoulders as the fingers close to form **'EXTENDED A'** hands.

(go on a) retreat: *v.* to go away for a period of time to a safe, quiet, secluded place. *Our church group went on a retreat for a week.*

SIGN #2: Forefinger of right **'ONE'** hand, palm facing leftward/forward, is placed upright between the first two fingers of the left **'EXTENDED B'** hand which is held palm down with fingers pointing rightward/forward. Then the right forefinger is vigorously thrust forward/rightward. (**RETREAT** may be fingerspelled.)

retribution: See **revenge**.

retrieve: *v.* to recover; get back. *He was able to retrieve his bicycle from the flooded garage.*

SIGN: Horizontal right **'SPREAD C'** hand is held out in front of the chest with palm down. As the hand moves purposefully toward the chest, the fingers close to form an **'S'** hand. (If more than one thing is being retrieved, two hands may be used, the hands alternately moving back toward the chest as if grabbing something and drawing it toward oneself.)

retrospection: *n.* the act of looking back. *Retrospection makes me wish I could turn the clock back and do things differently.*

SIGN: Right **'BENT V'** hand is held with palm backward and tip of middle finger just under/to the right of the right eye. The hand is then moved to the right and back so that it is just above the right shoulder.

return: *v.* to come back to a former place or state. *He will return at 2 o'clock.*

SIGN #1: The right arm is extended in front of the body and as the hand is drawn back toward the chest, **BACK** is fingerspelled in one fluid motion.

OR

SIGN #2: Right forearm is extended to the right with the **'ONE'** (or **'CROOKED ONE'**) hand palm up but slanted slightly toward the body and forefinger pointing rightward/forward. The forearm then moves toward the chest as the wrist bends, causing the forefinger to arc so that it eventually points to the body.

return: *v.* to send, or take back. *She will return the dress to the store where she bought it.*

SIGN #3: Vertical right **'S'** hand, palm forward, is thrust ahead as it opens to form a **'CONTRACTED 5'** hand. ❖

return: *n.* profit; yield. *He is getting a low return on his investment.*

SIGN #4: Thumb and forefinger of right **'F'** hand, palm facing down, are brought slightly downward to be inserted into an imaginary pocket at waist level. Alternatively, the imaginary pocket is sometimes located at the left side of the chest.

return trip: *n.* travel both ways, *i.e.,* there and back. *The fare for a return trip was not much more than a one-way fare.*

SIGN #5: Horizontal left **'BENT ONE'** hand is held with forefinger pointing rightward. Horizontal right **'BENT ONE'** hand is held beside the left hand with forefinger pointing leftward so that the tips of the forefingers touch. The right arm then moves forward/rightward and back so that the tips of the forefingers are reunited. (Signs vary slightly.)

reunion: *n.* a gathering of relatives, friends, former associates or colleagues. *My graduating class will hold a reunion in 15 years.*

SIGN: Fingerspell **REUNION**. [Alternatively, an all-inclusive sign may be used for the verb as well as **reunion** which acts as the object of the verb. For **to have a reunion**, see **assemble** #1.]

R E U N I O N

reveal: *v.* to make known or to disclose (a secret). *Please do not reveal my secret to my parents.*

SIGN #1: Tip of forefinger of right **'BENT ONE'** hand, palm toward the body, is held just under the chin and flicked forward, thus creating a **'ONE'** hand. (This sign is appropriate when information is being *revealed to one or two people only*. If the information is being revealed to *many people*, see **disclose** #2.)

reveal: *v.* to show or expose to view (something that was previously hidden). *The bruises reveal that someone has abused him.*

SIGN #2: Tip of forefinger of horizontal right **'BENT ONE'** hand is placed against right facing palm of left **'EXTENDED B'** hand. Together, the hands are moved forward in a short arc.

revenge: *n.* the act of retaliating or getting even for hurtful acts such as insults. *They will seek revenge against the rival gang.*

SIGN: Left **'CLOSED X'** hand is held in a fixed position with palm upward at a slight rightward angle. Right **'CLOSED X'** hand is held closer to the chest and at a higher level than the left hand. Palms are facing each other. The right hand then moves purposefully toward the left hand and strikes it. Facial expression is important.

revenue: *n.* income. *The company's revenue is only slightly greater than its expenditures.*

SIGN: Horizontal right **'SPREAD EXTENDED C'** hand is moved across upturned palm of left **'EXTENDED B'** hand in a circular, counter-clockwise 'gathering' motion, with the palm toward the body.

revere: *v.* to regard with deep respect. *All her former students revere her as an outstanding professor.*

SIGN: **'V'** hands are held apart with one slightly ahead of the other and palms down. The hands then curve forward/upward so that the palms face forward and the extended fingers point upward at a slightly forward angle. ❖

reverend: *adj.* a title designating a clergy-man. *Reverend Schmidt is a Lutheran pastor.*

SIGN: Thumb and forefinger of vertical right **'MODIFIED G'** hand, palm leftward, are lightly brushed rightward several times across the throat.

reverse: *v.* to change to the opposite position. *The court of appeal may reverse the judge's decision.*

SIGN: **'A'** (or **'X'**) hands, palms facing each other, are twisted 180 degrees. (Sign choice depends on context as well as the nature of things being reversed.)

review: *v.* to study again, often in preparation for a test or examination. *We will review Lessons 14 to 20 for the test.*

SIGN #1: Left **'ONE'** hand is held in a fixed position with palm down and forefinger point-ing forward/rightward. With palm facing downward at a slight leftward/forward angle and knuckles lying along the left forefinger, the right **'A'** hand slides back and forth.

review: *v.* to look at or examine again. *I will review the figures before I recommend an investment.*

SIGN #2: Left **'EXTENDED B'** hand is held in a fixed position with palm turned upward but slanted slightly rightward and toward the body while fingers point rightward/forward. Right **'ONE'** hand is held palm down as tip of forefinger brushes forward several times against palm of left hand. (Signs vary accord-ing to context.)

review: *n.* a written commentary or critical evaluation (as of a play or a book). *The review of the play in the* Belleville Intelligencer *was quite favourable.*

SIGN #3: Horizontal left **'EXTENDED B'** hand is held in a fixed position with palm facing rightward/backward. Thumb and forefinger of right **'CLOSED X'** hand move forward/rightward along the palm of the left hand. Movement is repeated.

revise: *v.* to change; amend; prepare a new version. *They plan to revise the curriculum next year.*

SIGN: Vertical **'X'** hands are held slightly apart with palms facing. The hands are then simul-taneously lowered as rotations of the wrists cause the hands to alternately fall forward and back several times.

SAME SIGN—**revisions,** *n.*

revoke: *v.* to take back; withdraw; cancel. *The Medical Association will revoke the doctor's license to practise.*

SIGN #1: Horizontal right **'SPREAD C'** hand is held with palm facing left. As the hand moves abruptly toward the chest, the fingers close to form an **'S'** hand.

OR

SIGN #2: **'COVERED T'** hands are held side by side with palms down. The left hand remains fixed while the right hand is abruptly lowered.

revolt: *n.* rebellion against authority. *Gallaudet University was in a state of **revolt** for a week.*

SIGN: Vertical right **'S'** hand, palm facing backward, is held at or above shoulder level and is forcefully twisted a half turn so that palm faces forward. Alternatively, this sign may be made with two hands.

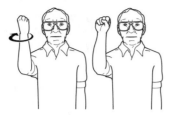

revolting: *adj.* unpleasant; repulsive; disgusting. *The scene of the crime was a **revolting** sight.*

SIGN: Right **'CLAWED C'** hand, palm toward the body, is circled in a clockwise direction (from the onlooker's perspective) in front of the stomach. Facial expression is very important. SAME SIGN—**revulsion**, *n.*

reward: *v.* to give something in return for worthy acts. *The teacher often **rewards** the children for good behaviour.*

SIGN #1: Vertical **'X'** hands, right palm facing left and left palm facing right, are offset so that one hand is a little higher than the other. The hands are then thrust forward simultaneously as they move to a horizontal position. ❖

reward: *n.* something given in return for something. *The police are offering a **reward** for information leading to an arrest.*

SIGN #2: Fingerspell **REWARD**.

rewind: *v.* to move an audio or video tape backward. *Please **rewind** the videotape after viewing it.*

SIGN: **'BENT ONE'** hands are held parallel with forefingers pointing downward and are simultaneously circled in a counter-clockwise direction.

rhinoceros: *n.* a large, thick-skinned, plant-eating African/Asian mammal with a horn on the nose. *A **rhinoceros** is an unusual animal.*

SIGN: Vertical right **'SPREAD C'** hand, palm left, is placed in front of the nose and is curved forward and slightly upward as it closes to form an **'S'** hand.

rhyme: *v.* to sound the same (often said of word endings at the ends of two lines of poetry). *"Moon" and "soon" **rhyme**.*

SIGN: Fingerspell **RHYME**. (This word may be fingerspelled but then is often followed by an explanation and a few examples of words which rhyme because it is not always easy for a Deaf person to distinguish rhyming words. The written forms of words such as 'wall' and 'ball' or 'feet' and 'beet' make it obvious that they are rhyming pairs, but it is a little more difficult to recognize rhyming words which are spelled differently at the end, *e.g.*, dim/hymn; wrestle/vessel; through/flew. It is equally difficult to recognize that some words which are spelled the same at the end do not in fact rhyme, *e.g.*, great/treat; where/here; word/sword.)

rhythm: *n.* a specific arrangement of beats, accents or metres in music, poetry, etc. *This music has a very pleasant **rhythm**.*

SIGN: Left **'EXTENDED B'** hand is held with palm facing right and fingers pointing forward. Right **'ONE'** hand, palm left and forefinger pointing forward, is rhythmically moved leftward several times so that the forefinger strikes the palm of the left hand with each movement.

rib: *n.* any one of 24 arched bones that form the human chest wall; a corresponding bone in other animals. *A broken **rib** can be very painful.*

SIGN: Fingerspell **RIB**.

ribbon: *n.* a narrow strip of fine fabric used for trimming or tying. *I need a ribbon to tie back my hair.*

SIGN: Extended fingers of horizontal **'DOUBLE MODIFIED G'** hands, palms toward body, are circled simultaneously forward around one another, pulled outward until fingertips are opposite, and then drawn apart as thumb and extended fingers of each hand come together to form **'CLOSED DOUBLE MODIFIED G'** hands. (Alternatively, **'N'** hands may be used throughout this sign.)

rice: *n.* an edible grain which is the staple food in many countries. *Brown rice becomes white when it is polished.*

SIGN: Fingerspell **RICE**.

rich: *adj.* having lots of money, property, etc. *Rich people are not always happy.*

SIGN #1: Left **'EXTENDED B'** hand is held with palm up and fingers pointing forward/rightward. Horizontal right **'S'** hand, palm left but slanted toward the chest, is held on the left palm, then raised abruptly as the fist opens to form a **'CROOKED 5'** shape and the left hand takes on a **'5'** shape.

SIGN #2 [ATLANTIC]: Right **'5'** hand is held with palm facing left and thumb against the chest. The hand then rises and moves forward in an arc formation.

rich: *adj.* in reference to food, having a large proportion of fatty ingredients which make the food flavourful. *This chocolate cake is moist and rich.*

SIGN #3: Fingerspell **RICH**.

rid [*or* **get rid of**]: *v.* to relieve from something undesirable. *Certain provinces have been able to rid themselves of rats.*

SIGN: Fingertips of right **'BENT EXTENDED B'** hand, palm down, are placed on upturned palm of left **'EXTENDED B'** hand and brushed forward to form a straight **'EXTENDED B'** hand. ❖

(good) riddance: *s.s.* an expression of happiness due to someone's departure. *We were so fed up with her attitude that when she resigned, we said, "Good riddance!"*

SIGN: Vertical right **'BENT B'** hand is held against the nose with palm forward/leftward and then thrust forward, the heel of the hand colliding forcefully with the side of the left **'STANDARD BASE'** hand.

ride: *v.* to be a passenger in a vehicle. *You should fasten your seatbelt when you ride in a car.*

SIGN #1: Right **'CLAWED U'** hand, palm down, is placed against the right facing palm of the left **'EXTENDED B'** hand and both are simultaneously moved forward.

OR

SIGN #2: Extended fingers of the right **'CLAWED U'** hand, palm down, are inserted into opening of the horizontal left **'S'** hand of which the palm is facing rightward/backward. Then the hands are moved forward together.

ride: *v.* to be carried along on the back of an animal. *This jockey will ride our horse in the next race.*

SIGN #3: Extended fingers of right **'EXTENDED K'** hand, palm down, are used to straddle the top of the left **'EXTENDED B'** hand which is held in a horizontal position with palm facing right. Together the hands move up and down in a circular fashion to simulate the gait of a horse.

ridicule: *v.* to humiliate; make fun of. *His classmates will probably ridicule his new hairstyle.*

SIGN: Horizontal **'BENT COMBINED I + ONE'** hands, palms down, are held slightly apart, with the right hand nearer the chest, and simultaneously make small jabbing motions. This sign is accompanied by a scornful facial expression. ❖

ALTERNATE SIGN—**insult**

ridiculous: *adj.* absurd; laughable; preposterous. *The children enjoyed the clown's ridiculous antics.*

SIGN: Vertical right **'Y'** hand, palm toward the nose, is twisted forward so that the palm faces left.

riding: *n.* a division of a city, province or the nation represented by an elected councillor, MLA, MPP or MP. *This riding has always been predominantly Liberal.*

SIGN: Right **'5'** hand, palm down, is circled in a counter-clockwise motion.
ALTERNATE SIGN—**region**

rifle: *n.* a firearm with a long barrel. *This is my father's favourite hunting rifle.*

SIGN: **'L'** hands are held, right slightly ahead of/ above the left, pointing forward/upward and right palm facing left while the left palm faces right. The forearms are then simultaneously moved slightly but firmly up and down a couple of times.

right: *n.* legal justification or freedom (to act). *Everyone has the right to demand justice.*

SIGN #1: The edge of the horizontal right **'EXTENDED B'** hand is placed on the upturned palm of the left **'EXTENDED B'** hand, and is pushed forward in a short, upward curving motion so that the fingers point upward.

right: *adj.* correct. *His answer is right.*

SIGN #2: Right **'ONE'** hand, palm left, is held above left hand, of which the palm faces right. Forefingers point forward. Right hand is then brought down firmly to rest on top of left hand.

right: *adj.* opposite to left. *I need to replace my right headlight.*

SIGN #3: Vertical right **'R'** hand, palm forward, is held out to the right and shaken slightly.

(turn) right: *v.* to move in a direction which is opposite to leftward. *Turn right at the next set of traffic lights.*

SIGN #4: Vertical right **'EXTENDED B'** (or **'R'**) hand is held with palm facing left. The wrist then rotates to turn the palm forward as the hand curves rightward.

right-handed: *adj.* able to use the right hand with more ease and skill than the left hand. *Most tools and sports equipment are designed for right-handed people.*

SIGN: Vertical right **'R'** hand, palm forward, is held out to the right and shaken slightly.

(self-)righteous: *adj.* having an exaggerated opinion of one's own morals, virtues, etc. *Most people can not tolerate a self-righteous individual.*

SIGN: Vertical right **'COMBINED U + Y'** hand, palm forward, is held in front of the right shoulder and the forearm is drawn firmly backward a short distance. This is essentially a jerking motion.

rigid: *adj.* stiff; not flexible. *The car's steering apparatus feels rigid because of the cold.*

SIGN #1: **'CROOKED 5'** hands are held parallel with palms down. They then jerk slightly forward/downward as the fingers retract to form **'CLAWED SPREAD C'** hands.

rigid: *adj.* very strict; harsh. *Some schools have very rigid rules.*

SIGN #2: Vertical right **'CLAWED V'** hand, palm left, is raised abruptly so the crooked forefinger strikes the nose.
ALTERNATE SIGN—**strict** #2

ring: *n.* a circular band worn on a finger as an ornament or a symbol of marriage, engagement or friendship. *My wedding ring is a plain gold band.*

SIGN #1: Thumb and forefinger of right **'OPEN F'** hand, palm down, are placed on either side of the 'ring' finger of the left **'5'** hand which is also held with palm facing down. The right hand then slides back and forth a little as if checking to see how loose or how tight the imaginary ring might be. (Sign choice must be made on the basis of context.)

ring: *v.* to make a resonant sound like that of a bell. *The phone is ringing.*

SIGN #2: Left side of forefinger of vertical right **'ONE'** hand, palm facing forward, is tapped against right facing palm of vertical left **'EXTENDED B'** hand at least twice.

rinse: *v.* to remove soap from something by using water only. *She washed her sweater by hand and rinsed it thoroughly.*

SIGN: **'CONTRACTED B'** hands are held parallel with palms down and fingers pointing downward. They are then simultaneously lowered at lease twice. (This sign may be preceded by the sign for **water**.) Signs vary considerably depending on 'what' is being rinsed and 'how' it is being rinsed.

riot: *n.* a disturbance made by unruly persons. *To protest the new law, citizens began a riot in the streets.*

SIGN: Left **'CROOKED 5'** hand is held palm-up with fingers pointing forward while right **'CROOKED 5'** hand is held apart and slightly higher with palm down and fingers pointing forward. The arms are then simultaneously moved upward/rightward as the hands are purposefully twisted rightward from the wrist so that the left palm faces right and the right palm faces left.

rip: *v.* to tear violently or roughly. *How did you rip your shirt?*

SIGN: **'F'** hands are held side by side with palms down. The left hand moves forward and slightly downward as the right hand moves back toward the chest, the wrist bending so that the palm faces forward.

rip-off: *n.* a colloquial term meaning grossly overpriced. *That is a real rip-off!*

SIGN: Fingerspell **RIP-OFF**.

ripe: *adj.* mature enough to be eaten or used. *The crop is ripe enough to harvest.*

SIGN: Vertical **'R'** hands are held apart with palms facing forward. The forearms then move further apart. (**RIPE** is frequently fingerspelled.)

ripple effect: *n.* the effects felt far beyond a specific situation. *The introduction of the new tax will have a ripple effect on the nation's economy.*

SIGN: **'FLAT O'** hands are held with tips of forefingers touching and palms forward/downward but slanted toward each other slightly. The hands are then flung forward/outward as the fingers flutter and spread to form **'CROOKED 5'** hands with the palms down.

rise: *v.* to increase in height or level. *The river water began to rise.*

SIGN #1: **'EXTENDED B'** hands are held parallel with palms down and fingers pointing forward. The hands are then raised simultaneously to a higher level. (Sign selection depends on 'what' is rising and 'how' it is rising.)

rise: *v.* to increase in amount or value. *If the price of houses continues to rise, we will sell our home.*

SIGN #2: Vertical left **'BENT U'** hand is held in a fixed position with palm down and extended fingers pointing rightward/forward. Right **'U'** hand is held to the right of the left hand with palm left and extended fingers pointing forward. The right hand then moves in an upward/leftward arc as the wrist rotates leftward causing the palm to turn downward and the extended fingertips to come to rest on the backs of the extended fingers of the left hand.

rise: *v.* to get up from a seated position; stand up. *Please rise when the judge enters the courtroom.*

SIGN #3: **'EXTENDED B'** hands are held parallel with palms up and fingers pointing forward. The hands are then simultaneously raised. (This sign is used only in the case of a *command* and only when *several people* are being told or asked to rise. If the command is issued to *one person* only, just one hand is used. If there are *several people* rising but there is *no command* involved, as in *'Everyone will rise when the judge enters the courtroom'*, vertical **'4'** hands are held parallel with palms forward and are simultaneously raised. If only *one person* is rising, left **'U'** hand is held palm down with extended fingers pointing forward/rightward. Right **'EXTENDED U'** hand is held palm down with extended fingers 'sitting' on those of the left hand at right angles to them. The right hand then moves forward/leftward as the extended fingers slide to a position whereby they are pointing downward as if they are two legs 'standing'. If you are referring to someone who is *rising from bed*, see **get up**.)

(sun) rise: *v.* to ascend or appear above the horizon (said of the sun). *The sun will rise at 6:06 a.m. tomorrow.*

SIGN #4: Left **'STANDARD BASE'** hand represents the horizon and right **'C'** (or **'O'** or **'F'**) hand, palm leftward/downward, represents the rising sun as it is held just ahead of/below the left hand and then raised to a level above the left hand.

risk: *n.* the possibility of danger or misfortune. *This is major surgery so there is some risk involved.*

SIGN: Left **'A'** hand is held in a fixed position with palm facing downward but slanted toward the chest. Right **'A'** hand is held just in front of the left hand with palm facing left and is circled in a clockwise direction a couple of times so that the thumb firmly brushes upward against the back of the left hand with each revolution. **RISK** is frequently fingerspelled.

REGIONAL VARIATION—**danger**

rival: *adj.* pertaining to an individual or group who tries to equal or surpass another; competitor. *Ford and General Motors are rival companies.*

SIGN: **'A'** hands, palms facing, are held close to one another and moved alternately back and forth. This is a wrist movement.

SAME SIGN—**rivalry**, *n.*

river: *n.* a large natural stream of fresh water that flows into a larger body of water such as a lake or an ocean. *The river is badly polluted and unsafe for swimming.*

SIGN: Forefinger of vertical right **'W'** hand, palm facing left, is tapped against the chin. Next, horizontal **'EXTENDED B'** hands, palms facing each other, are held slightly apart and are simultaneously moved forward in a meandering motion. (ASL CONCEPT—**water - way curve**.) This sign is used when **river** is first introduced into a conversation. After that, the sign may be abbreviated by using the second part of the sign only. Alternatively, **RIVER** is frequently fingerspelled, especially when the river is named, *e.g.*, **FRASER RIVER.**

road: *n.* an open way that provides passage from one place to another. *Which is the best road to the beach?*

SIGN: **'EXTENDED B'** hands, held parallel with palms facing one another and fingers pointing forward, are simultaneously moved forward. (When the road is named, the name of the road is fingerspelled followed by the fingerspelled abbreviation **RD**.)

roam: *v.* to wander about without purpose. *She roamed through the fields as if she did not have a care in the world.*

SIGN: Vertical right **'ONE'** hand, palm facing forward, is moved forward with a snakelike motion. (The **'ONE'** hand represents a *person*. If it is an *animal* which is roaming, the signer might assume a **'CLAWED V'** handshape with palm down. To indicate a *plural subject*, **'5'** hands, with palms down and fingers pointing forward and fluttering, simultaneously move inward, overlap and then move outward a couple of times as they progress forward.)

roar: *v.* to utter loud, deep cries as in anger or triumph. *When the score was tied, the fans began to roar.*

SIGN: Right vertical **'SPREAD C'** hand, palm toward the body, is held near the mouth and is forcefully drawn forward at an upward angle.

roast: *v.* to cook in an oven using dry heat. *I will roast the meat at 325 degrees.*

SIGN: Right **'EXTENDED B'** hand, palm up, with fingers pointing forward, slides under left palm-down **'EXTENDED B'** hand whose fingers point rightward. (When used as an adjective as in **roast beef**, ROAST is fingerspelled.)

rob: *v.* to take the property of another illegally and by force. *They planned to rob the bank.*

SIGN: Left arm is folded across in front of the chest. Horizontal right **'V'** hand is held with thumb against left forearm near the elbow and palm facing the arm. The right hand is then drawn rightward at a slight upward angle along the left forearm as the extended fingers retract to form a **'CLAWED V'** hand.
SAME SIGN—**robbery**, *n.* (If the robbery involves a gun, see **hold up**.)

robber: *n.* someone who steals another's property either by force or by threats of force. *The robber was wearing blue jeans and a striped shirt.*

SIGN: Extended fingers of right **'BENT U'** hand, palm facing downward, point leftward as they are drawn from left to right under the nose. Movement is repeated.

robe: *n.* a dressing gown, bathrobe, or any loose flowing garment such as that worn by a judge. *This flannel robe is warm and cozy in winter.*

SIGN: Fingerspell **ROBE**.

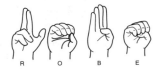

robot: *n.* a machine programmed to perform specific functions in the manner of a human. *They designed a robot to stock the warehouse shelves.*

SIGN: Fingerspell **ROBOT**.

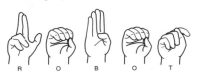

rock: *n.* a stone. *The girl threw a rock through the window.*

SIGN #1: **'A'** hands are held palms down, right above left. The right hand is lowered a couple of times, knocking firmly on the back of the left hand.
ALTERNATE SIGN—**stone** #1

rock [also **rock and roll** or **rock 'n' roll**]: *adj.* pertaining to a popular type of music that combines rhythm and blues and country and western and has a strong beat. *He loves to dance to rock music.*

SIGN #2: Fingerspell **ROCK**.

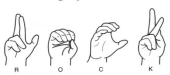

rocket: *n.* a spacecraft propelled by a rocket engine. *The rocket was programmed to circle the earth several times.*

SIGN: Heel of vertical right **'R'** hand, palm forward, rests on the back of the left **'STANDARD BASE'** hand. Then the right hand is raised slightly a couple of times.

rocking chair: *n.* a chair mounted on curving supports which allow the user to rock back and forth. *My grandmother has a beautiful old rocking chair.*

SIGN #1: **'3'** hands are held parallel with palms facing each other and are simultaneously curved up and down from the wrists.

OR

SIGN #2: Left **'BENT U'** hand is held with palm down and extended fingers pointing forward/rightward. Right **'CROOKED U'** hand is held palm down with extended fingers resting at right angles across those of the left hand. Together the hands are tilted back toward the chest and moved forward again a couple of times to simulate a rocking motion. This is a wrist action.

rod: *n.* a slim cylinder of metal, wood, etc. *The steel rod inside the beam will give added support.*

SIGN: Then horizontal **'F'** hands are held side by side, palms down and extended fingers pointing forward, and are drawn apart. (Sign choices vary according to context.)

rodeo: *n.* a show in which various skills of cowboys are displayed. *Rodeos are held in Alberta and Saskatchewan in the summer.*

SIGN: Downward-pointing forefinger and middle finger of **'EXTENDED K'** hand straddle horizontal left **'EXTENDED B'** hand of which the palm faces right. Then both hands are simultaneously circled forward several times.

role: *n.* the function performed by a person in a particular setting. *He explained his role in the school's administration.*

SIGN: **'BENT EXTENDED B'** hands, palms facing the body, are tapped against the right shoulder a couple of times with the fingertips.

roll: *v.* to move along by turning over and over. *The ball rolled across the floor.*

SIGN #1: Horizontal **'ONE'** hands, palms toward the chest, are positioned so the right forefinger is slightly in front of the left. The forearms then circle forward, the forefingers rotating around each other. ❖ (This sign is used only in situations where the object appears to be self-propelled. In cases where a person is rolling something, natural gestures are generally used.) Sign choice depends on context.

roll: *n.* a small, round portion of bread. *Would you like some butter for your roll?*

SIGN #2: Fingerspell **ROLL**.

roller blading [*more accurately called* **inline skating**]: *n.* a sport performed on blades that are specially fitted with small wheels. *Roller blading is fun but can cause serious injuries, especially if protective clothing is not worn.*

SIGN: Horizontal **'B'** hands, palms facing, are simultaneously circled in opposite directions, the left hand moving in a clockwise direction and the right hand moving in a counter-clockwise direction (from the signer's perspective). This is not a symmetrical movement. When the left hand is at the top of its circle, the right hand is at the bottom of its circle, and vice versa.

roller skating: *n.* gliding on skates that are fitted with four small wheels. *Roller skating is good exercise.*

SIGN: Left **'CLAWED V'** hand is held palm up and glides forward/leftward from the chest as the right **'CLAWED V'** hand, with palm up, glides backward/leftward toward the chest. The left hand then moves backward/rightward toward the chest as the right hand moves forward/rightward. Movement is repeated a few times. (Alternatively, this sign may be made with the palms down.)

(be) rolling in the aisles: *v.* a colloquial expression generally used in reference to an audience where everyone responds to an act with hilarious laughter. *We were rolling in the aisles when we heard the comedian's performance.*

SIGN: Right **'CROOKED V'** hand, palm up, is placed on the upturned palm of the left **'EXTENDED B'** hand and is circled a few times in a counter-clockwise direction as the crooked fingers, which represent legs, wiggle.

romance: *n.* a love affair. *Their romance continued for 50 years.*

SIGN: Horizontal **'EXTENDED A'** hands are held together with palms against left side of chest as the thumbs simultaneously flex and extend a few times. **ROMANCE** is frequently fingerspelled.

SAME SIGN—**romantic**, *adj.*

roof: *n.* a structure that covers the top of a building. *The roof of our house needs new shingles.*

SIGN: **'EXTENDED B'** hands are held with fingertips touching and palms facing each other at a downward angle. The hands are then drawn apart on a downward slant. (**ROOF** may be fingerspelled.)

rookie: *n.* an inexperienced newcomer; novice. *The best player on their team this year was a rookie.*

SIGN: Horizontal left **'EXTENDED B'** hand remains stationary with palm up and fingers pointing forward/rightward while right **'BENT EXTENDED B'** hand, palm facing upward, is brought leftward a couple of times across left palm using a scooping motion. (**ROOKIE** is frequently fingerspelled.) When this word is used with an emphasis on *lack of experience* or an implication that *skills and/or knowledge are underdeveloped*, **awkward** may be used.

room: *n.* an area in a building enclosed by a floor, ceiling and walls. *His office is the third room on the left.*

SIGN: With a slight but deliberate downward thrust horizontal **'EXTENDED B'** hands are held parallel, with palms facing each other and fingers pointing forward. Then the hands take on a **'BENT EXTENDED B'** shape as they are swung inward with a slight downward thrust again, and the right hand positioned ahead of the left, both palms facing the body.

room and board: *n.* an arrangement where sleeping accommodations as well as meals are provided. *My mother provides room and board for several university students.*

SIGN: Vertical right **'CONTRACTED 5'** hand, fingers pointing at forehead, is lowered to chin level as the fingers close to form a **'FLAT O'** shape. (ASL CONCEPT—**sleep - eat**.) Alternatively, use the signs for **bed + eat** or fingerspell **ROOM**, sign **and**, and fingerspell **BOARD**.

roommate: See **(room)mate**.

roomy: *adj.* spacious; having plenty of room. *The apartment is fairly roomy for that price.*

SIGN: **'S'** hands are held palms down in front of the chest with elbows out. The hands remain relatively fixed while the arms are simultaneously raised and lowered. Movement is repeated. (**ROOMY** may be fingerspelled.)

rooster: *n.* the male of the domestic fowl; cock. *I was awakened by the crow of a rooster.*

SIGN: Vertical right **'3'** hand, palm left, is placed with thumbtip on the nose. The hand is then raised so that the thumbtip makes contact with the forehead.

root: *n.* the part of a plant that anchors it in the ground. *Be careful not to damage the root when you transplant your fern.*

SIGN #1: Fingerspell **ROOT**. (Alternatively, this word may be signed but signs vary depending on the type and size of the root.)

root: *v.* to support a contestant or team; cheer. *She roots for the team that comes from her hometown.*

SIGN #2: **'S'** hands, palms toward the body, are held at chest level with the left slightly above the right. Then the right is brought upward to strike the left. (If their is an implication of actual *audible and/or visible cheering*, the right **'S'** hand is held at or above shoulder level and is jabbed into the air several times. If more than one person is rooting, both **'S'** hands are simultaneously jabbed into the air.)

rope: *n.* a thick cord made of intertwined fibres. *They threw a rope to the stranded swimmer.*

SIGN: Fingerspell **ROPE**.

rot: *v.* to decay as a result of bacterial or fungal action. *The old tree stump was beginning to rot.*

SIGN: **'A'** hands are held together with palms facing the chest. The hands then gradually rotate forward with fingers spreading until they take on a **'CROOKED 5'** shape with palms facing upward.

rotate: *v.* revolve; spin. *She began to feel dizzy as she watched the blades of the propeller rotate.*

SIGN: Horizontal right **'ONE'** hand, palm down and forefinger pointing forward, is rapidly rotated clockwise several times from the wrist. (Signs for **rotate**, *v.*, and **rotation**, *n.*, vary considerably depending on the context.)

rotten: *adj.* decayed; decomposed. *This old tree stump is rotten.*

SIGN #1: **'A'** hands are held together with palms facing the chest. The hands then gradually rotate forward with fingers spreading until they take on a **'CROOKED 5'** shape with palms facing upward.

rotten: *adj.* foul-smelling because of decay; stinking. *These old eggs are rotten!*

SIGN #2: Right **'5'** hand is held with palm facing leftward/downward and thumbtip touching or close to the tip of the nose. The hand is then firmly thrust a short distance forward at a slight downward angle. Meanwhile, a grimace appears on the signer's face and the lips appear to be articulating the syllable 'PO'. (**ROTTEN** in this context may be fingerspelled for emphasis.)

rotten: *adj.* a colloquial term meaning very bad; unsatisfactory. *It has been a rotten car ever since I bought it!*

SIGN #3: Vertical right **'3'** hand is held with palm facing left and tip of thumb touching the nose. The hand then moves forward/downward in an arc formation as the wrist rotates to turn the hand to a horizontal position. A look of displeasure accompanies this sign. (Signs vary. See also **awful** and **bad**.)

rough: *adj.* uneven; irregular; not smooth. *The gravel road is very rough.*

SIGN #1: Left **'EXTENDED B'** hand is held in a fixed position with fingers pointing forward/rightward and palm facing rightward but slanted toward the body and slightly upward. Fingertips of right **'SPREAD EXTENDED C'** hand, palm down, are brushed forward/rightward a few times along the left palm. This sign is accompanied by a lip pattern such that the upper teeth are resting on the lower lip as if articulating an 'F'.

SIGN #2 [ONTARIO]: Vertical right **'A'** hand, palm facing left, is placed on the right cheek and brushed forward firmly to a horizontal position.

rough: *adj.* approximate. *He asked for a rough estimate of the cost of the repair.*

SIGN #3: Vertical right **'5'** hand, palm forward, is circled in front of the right shoulder with a counter-clockwise motion.

round: *adj.* circular in shape. *Grandmother made a round braided rug.*

SIGN: Right **'ONE'** hand, palm down and with the forefinger pointing downward, is circled from the wrist in a counter-clockwise direction. (The positioning of this sign varies according to the location of the object being described.)

round trip: *n.* a journey to a place and back again. *We paid $500 for the round trip.*

SIGN: Horizontal left **'BENT ONE'** hand is held with forefinger pointing rightward. Horizontal right **'BENT ONE'** hand is held beside the left hand with forefinger pointing leftward so that the tips of the forefingers touch. The right arm then moves forward/rightward and back so that the tips of the forefingers are reunited. (Signs vary, depending particularly on the mode of transportation used.)

route: *n.* the road(s) taken to get from one place to another. *The bridge will be closed so we must take a different route to work.*

SIGN #1: Horizontal right **'ONE'** hand is held with forefinger pointing forward and the hand is moved forward in a zigzagging pattern which depends on how familiar the signer is with the particular route and how definite he wishes to be in specifying the route.

route: *v.* to send by a particular route; circulate; pass on. *The memo should be routed to all staff in this department.*

SIGN #2: Right **'CONTRACTED B'** hand is held, palm up, in front of the right side of the body and bounces slightly as it moves leftward in a semicircular pattern. (Each bounce represents the handing of something to someone.) ❖

routine: *n.* a regular procedure. *It is hard to follow a regular **routine** when you are vacationing.*

SIGN #1: Fingertips of right **'5'** hand, palm down, are stroked downward across palm of horizontal left **'5'** hand which is facing the chest, but angled rightward. Then the right wrist rotates forward a quarter turn so that the palm is turned toward the body at a leftward-facing angle as the fingertips are stroked across the left palm from left to right.

routine: *adj.* in accordance with a customary practice. *It is **routine** procedure to require post-operative patients to do breathing exercises.*

SIGN #2: Right **'BENT U'** hand, palm down, is circled clockwise over left **'STANDARD BASE'** hand, and the extended fingers are brought down to rest on it.

routinely: *adv.* at regular intervals. *He **routinely** has his car serviced every 6,000 kilometres.*

SIGN: **'ONE'** hands are held right on top of left, with left palm facing rightward/backward and right palm facing leftward/backward while left forefinger points forward/rightward and right forefinger points leftward/forward at an upward angle. Together, the hands are lowered. (More specific signs are often used if actual time intervals are being stressed, e.g., **every day**, **weekly**, **monthly**, **yearly**.)

row: *v.* to propel (a boat) by using oars. *I will **row** my boat across the lake.*

SIGN #1: Horizontal **'S'** hands, palms down, are positioned as if holding oars in a boat. Then they are simultaneously circled forward, up, and back toward the chest a couple of times.

row: *n.* the arrangement of things in a line. *Let us sit in the back **row**.*

SIGN #2: **'CLAWED V'** hands are held side by side with palms down and sides of forefingers touching. The hands are then moved apart. (Signs vary depending upon what/whom the 'row' consists of, the relative position of the row, and the number and length of the row(s).)

row: *n.* a noisy argument; quarrel. *They had a **row** with their neighbours over the continuous barking of their dog.*

SIGN #3: Vertical **'O'** hands, palms facing, are held slightly apart and are changed to **'5'** hands as they are brought together to strike each other firmly. Movement is repeated.

royal: *adj.* regal or related to a monarch. *The **royal** family is constantly in the newspaper headlines.*

SIGN: **'MODIFIED G'** hand is held with palm down and sides of thumb and forefinger against the left shoulder. Then the hand is moved diagonally downward so the hand comes to rest at the right side of the waist. (This sign is used to mean 'royal' when the reigning monarch is a *woman*. To refer to a *male* monarchy, see **king**.) ROYAL is frequently fingerspelled.

rub: *v.* to apply firmly. ***Rub** the lotion on the sunburned skin.*

SIGN #1: Right **'CROOKED EXTENDED B'** (or **'EXTENDED B'**) hand is moved back and forth on the relevant body part or object.

rub [*or* **rub off** *or* **rub out**]: *v.* to apply pressure to something with a backward and forward motion. *I will try to **rub** the black mark **off** the floor.*

SIGN #2: Right **'A'** hand is held palm down and is vigorously rubbed back and forth a few times along the upturned left palm. (Signs vary according to 'what' is being rubbed and 'how' it is being rubbed.)

rubber: *n.* an elastic substance made from the latex of the rubber tree. *Car tires are made of rubber.*

SIGN #1: Right **'x'** hand, palm forward at a slight leftward slant, is stroked downward several times against the lower right cheek.

OR

SIGN #2: Tip of the thumb of the right **'EXTENDED A'** hand, palm left, is placed below the upper teeth of the slightly open mouth and is flicked forward a couple of times.

rubber band: *n.* a continuous loop of thin rubber used to hold things together. *She placed a rubber band around the documents.*

SIGN: Horizontal **'CLAWED V'** hands, palms toward the body, are knocked together and drawn apart at least twice.

rubella: *n.* a contagious viral illness characterized by a red rash. *Rubella is sometimes called German measles and is often the cause of deafness in newborns if there has been maternal contact during early pregnancy.*

SIGN: Fingerspell **RUBELLA**.

rucksack: See **backpack**.

rude: *adj.* uncivil; discourteous; impolite. *She made a rude gesture toward her parents.*

SIGN: Vertical right **'A-INDEX'** hand, palm facing left, quivers as thumb and forefinger are used to grasp skin of right cheek. Facial expression is important.
SAME SIGN—**rudeness**, *n.*

rudimentary: See **basic**.

rug: *n.* a floor covering (usually not wall to wall) made of wool or synthetic materials. *They have a lovely patterned rug in their living room.*

SIGN: Fingerspell **RUG**.

rugged: *adj.* jagged; rocky; strong-featured. *Newfoundland's terrain is very rugged.*

SIGN #1: Horizontal right **'5'** hand, with palm down and fingers pointing forward, is held out in front of the left side of the body and as it moves rightward, the wrist rotates from side to side causing the hand to rock or wobble as it moves. (Signs vary depending on the specific context.)

rugged: *adj.* strong; very hardy; tough. *Early prairie pioneers were rugged people.*

SIGN #2: Wrist of right **'CLAWED V'** hand, palm facing the body, rotates turning the hand palm-downward as it is thrust downward, the knuckles of the forefinger and middle finger rapping the back of the left **'STANDARD BASE'** hand on the way past. Appropriate facial expression is essential.

ruin: *v.* to spoil or damage severely. *Drycleaning might ruin this sweater.*

SIGN #1: Horizontal left **'x'** hand is held in a fixed position with palm rightward but slanted toward the body slightly while horizontal right **'x'** hand is held above/behind left hand with palm leftward. The right hand then slides briskly along the top of the left hand and continues to move in a forward/rightward direction.

OR

SIGN #2: Right horizontal **'I'** hand, palm left but angled toward the body, is placed on upturned palm of left **'EXTENDED B'** hand and is then firmly pushed forward/rightward across it, the right wrist rotating so that the palm eventually faces downward.

ruins: *n.* the remains of a destroyed building or buildings. *The firemen sifted through the ruins to find clues as to what caused the fire.*

SIGN: Left **'CLAWED 5'** hand is held palm-up while right **'CLAWED 5'** hand is held palm-down to the right and above/ahead of left hand. The hands close to form **'A'** hands as they are brought together and just past each other, the knuckles of the right hand grazing those of the left. The knuckles brush against each other again as the left hand moves firmly backward/leftward and the right hand moves firmly rightward/forward. Movement is repeated. (Signs vary according to context.)

rule: *n.* an authoritative regulation governing behaviour and/or procedure. *Children find it easier to follow a rule if they understand the reason for it.*

SIGN #1: Left **'EXTENDED B'** hand is held in a fixed position either vertically with palm facing left or horizontally with palm facing left at an upward angle. Right **'R'** hand, with palm facing that of the left hand, is positioned so that the tips of the crossed fingers touch the left hand at the end of the fingers. The right hand is then moved away from the left hand slightly and repositioned with tips of crossed fingers touching the palm of the left hand close to the heel.

rule: *n.* the exercise of governmental authority or control. *The country prospered under Liberal rule.*

SIGN #2: Horizontal **'X'** hands are held slightly apart with left palm facing right and right palm facing left. Then they are alternately moved backward and forward.

SAME SIGNS—**rule**, *v.*, meaning *to govern* and **ruler**, *n.*, meaning *a person who rules or governs*, in which case it may be followed by the Agent Ending (see p. LIV).

ruler: *n.* a straight-edged strip of wood, metal or plastic used for measuring or drawing straight lines. *A ruler is a useful tool in math class.*

SIGN: **'MODIFIED G'** hands are held with palms facing forward and tips of forefingers and thumbs of one hand touching those of the other. The hands are then drawn apart about 15 centimetres each and the forefingers and thumbs close to form **'CLOSED MODIFIED G'** shapes.

rum: *n.* a form of alcohol made from sugar cane. *Rum is produced in Cuba and other Caribbean countries.*

SIGN: Fingerspell **RUM**.

rumour [*also spelled* **rumor**]: *n.* information passed around which is not based on definite knowledge and is often a mixture of truth and untruth. *It is unwise to spread rumours.*

SIGN #1: Vertical **'MODIFIED G'** hands, palms facing each other, are held apart in front of the mouth or upper chest and are rapidly alternated with **'CLOSED MODIFIED G'** handshapes as they are being moved simultaneously in a semicircular direction.

OR

SIGN #2: Vertical **'ONE'** hands are held apart with palms facing forward and are shaken slightly as they simultaneously move around in a counter-clockwise direction.

rump: *n.* a person's buttocks; rear end. *He fell on his rump.*

SIGN: Right **'EXTENDED B'** hand, fingers pointing downward, is used to tap the right buttock a couple of times. (When used as an adjective as in **rump roast**, **RUMP** is fingerspelled.)

run: *v.* to move on foot at a rapid pace. *The sprinter will run the 100 meter dash.*

SIGN #1: Left hand, palm facing right, is held in front of the right hand, of which the palm faces left. Forefinger of the right horizontal **'CLAWED L'** hand is hooked around the upright thumb of the left **'CLAWED L'** hand. Then both hands are thrust forward with curved motion. (Since there is an established distance for the 'run' in this context, repetition of the movement of the sign is unnecessary. Where the amount of running is not stated, the movement of the sign tends to be repeated in short, jabbing motions.) Sign choice depends on context.

run: *v.* to operate; cause to function. *I do not know how to run this machine.*

SIGN #2: Vertical right **'U'** hand, palm facing forward/leftward, is circled clockwise above left **'STANDARD BASE'** hand two or three times with the heel of its palm striking the back of the left hand each time. This sign may also be made without the left hand. (This sign is used for the running of *machines* only.)

run: *v.* to govern; administer; have control of. *He will run the meeting efficiently.*

SIGN #3: Horizontal **'x'** hands are held slightly apart with left palm facing right and right palm facing left. Then they are alternately moved backward and forward.

run: *v.* to discharge fluid. *Certain allergens cause his eyes and nose to run.*

SIGN #4: Horizontal right **'4'** hand, palm facing backward, is placed with tip of forefinger near the nose or eyes. Then the hand is moved downward slightly a few times.

run: *v.* to flow or drip. *The broken pipe caused the water to run through the ceiling.*

SIGN #5: Right **'4'** hand, palm facing left and fingers pointing forward, is held aloft and moved downward a few times from the wrist.

run: *v.* to flow freely. *The Bow River runs through Calgary.*

SIGN #6: **'5'** hands are held with palms down and fingers pointing forward, the left hand slightly ahead of the right. The hands then move simultaneously forward while the fingers flutter. ❖

run: *v.* to publish or print in a newspaper, magazine, etc. *The newspaper will run a notice offering a reward for the return of our dog.*

SIGN #7: Thumbnail of right **'MODIFIED G'** hand, palm forward/downward, is placed on upturned palm of left **'EXTENDED B'** hand. Right forefinger then moves downward to form a **'CLOSED MODIFIED G'** shape.

run: *v.* to continue for a sustained period of time. *The movie has run for five months and is still drawing crowds.*

SIGN #8: **'EXTENDED A'** hands are held side by side with palms down and right thumbtip pressing against left thumbnail as the hands are moved purposefully forward.

run: *v.* to recur persistently or be hereditary. *Curly hair runs in our family.*

SIGN #9: Tip of middle finger of right **'BENT MIDFINGER 5'** hand, palm toward the body, is placed on the right side of the chest and the hand is drawn away abruptly. An essential feature of this sign is the release of a puff of air from the lips as if whispering a 'P'. (The ASL sentence is syntactically different than the English one. The sample sentence is translated into ASL as: *CURLY HAIR, MY FAMILY TEND.*)

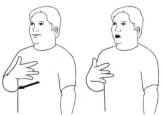

run: *v.* to be a candidate for political office. *She has decided to run for mayor.*

SIGN #10: **'A'** hands, palms facing, are held close to one another and moved alternately back and forth. This is a wrist movement.

run: *v.* to spread (said of the colour or dye in fabric). *You should wash this shirt separately because the colours might run.*

SIGN #11: **'FLAT O'** hands are held with tips of forefingers touching and palms forward/downward but slanted toward each other slightly. The hands are then flung forward/outward as the fingers spread to form **'5'** hands with the palms down.

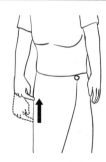

run: *n.* damage to fine material where stitches have come undone. *There is a big run in her pantyhose.*

SIGN #12: Tip of forefinger of right **'BENT ONE'** hand, palm toward the body, is used to trace on a 'run' on the signer's leg or thigh. (Signs vary according to the size and location of the 'run'.) **RUN**, in this context, may be fingerspelled.

(in the long) run: *adv.* pertaining to the final outcome; ultimately. *In the long run, it will not matter who wins the election.*

SIGN #13: Forefinger of vertical right **'ONE'** hand, palm facing left, is held against the lips and the hand is moved sharply forward.

(on the) run: *adv.* in a great hurry. *I eat most of my meals on the run.*

SIGN #14: Horizontal **'U'** hands are held apart with left palm facing right and right palm facing left, and the forearms are alternately circled forward repeatedly.

(on the) run: *adv.* having escaped from custody. *The convict is on the run from the law.*

SIGN #15: Forefinger of right **'ONE'** hand, palm facing leftward/forward, is placed upright between the first two fingers of the left **'EXTENDED B'** hand which is held palm down with fingers pointing rightward/forward. Then the right forefinger is vigorously thrust forward/rightward.

run across: *v.* to meet someone unexpectedly. *She did not run across anyone she knew at the party.*

SIGN: Vertical **'ONE'** hands are held slightly apart with palms facing and are then brought together so that they touch one another.

run after: *v.* to chase; follow closely. *The police officer ran after the suspect.*

SIGN: Horizontal left **'A'** hand, palm facing right, is held ahead of and to the left of horizontal right **'EXTENDED A'** hand, of which the palm faces the body at a leftward angle. Then the right is moved forward in a series of small clockwise circles to approach the left hand.

run away: *v.* to escape; run off. *The boy has run away from home.*

SIGN: Forefinger of right **'ONE'** hand, palm facing leftward/forward, is placed upright between the first two fingers of the left **'EXTENDED B'** hand which is held palm down with fingers pointing rightward/forward. Then the right forefinger is vigorously thrust forward/rightward.

run into: *v.* to meet by chance. *I often run into him at the mall.*

SIGN: Vertical **'ONE'** hands are held slightly apart with palms facing and are then brought together so that they touch one another.

run off: *v.* to run away; leave in haste. *If we do not accept their engagement, they might run off and get married without our blessing.*

SIGN #1: Forefinger of right **'ONE'** hand, palm facing leftward/forward, is placed upright between the first two fingers of the left **'EXTENDED B'** hand which is held palm down with fingers pointing rightward/forward. Then the right forefinger is vigorously thrust forward/rightward.

run off: *v.* to duplicate or make copies of. *The secretary will run off 100 copies.*

SIGN #2: Left **'EXTENDED B'** hand is held in a fixed position with palm down and fingers pointing forward/rightward while right **'CONTRACTED 5'** hand is held palm up with fingers touching left palm. The right hand is then drawn downward as it closes to form a **'FLAT O'** hand. Motion is repeated.

run out of: *v.* to completely deplete one's stock of something. *I hope we do not run out of food before we leave this campsite.*

SIGN: Right horizontal **'SPREAD C'** hand, palm toward the chest, is placed on the upturned palm of the left **'EXTENDED B'** hand. Then the right hand is drawn forward as it changes to an **'S'** handshape. (Sign choice varies depending on what one runs out of.)

run over: *v.* to knock down with a moving vehicle. *I think I ran over something.*

SIGN: Right horizontal **'3'** hand, palm left, is used to slide forward across the left **'STANDARD BASE'** hand. (The left hand varies in shape depending on what is being run over.)

rundown [*or* **run-down**]: *adj.* having fallen into disrepair. *They live in a rundown house across the railroad tracks.*

SIGN #1: **'EXTENDED A'** hands are held slightly apart in front of the chest with the palms facing each other, and are lowered slowly but simultaneously to waist level. (Signs vary according to context.)

rundown: *n.* a brief summary. *He will give you a rundown of the results of the election.*

SIGN #2: **'SPREAD C'** hands are held horizontally and slightly apart, right above left. Then both are closed to form **'S'** hands as the right is brought down to rest on top of the left.

(the) runs: *n.* a colloquial expression meaning 'diarrhea'. *I feel weak after having the runs all night.*

SIGN: Left **'EXTENDED C'** hand is held in a fixed position with palm at a rightward/backward angle and fingers pointing forward/rightward/upward. Horizontal right **'5'** hand is positioned just to the right of the left hand, and as the right wrist rotates leftward several times, the thumbtip is repeatedly brushed downward against the left palm.

runway: *n.* a hard, level roadway where aircraft take off and land. *We watched the jet taxi down the runway.*

SIGN: **'EXTENDED B'** hands, held parallel with palms facing one another and fingers pointing forward, are simultaneously moved forward.

rupture: *v.* to burst or break open. *Her appendix was about to rupture so it was surgically removed.*

SIGN: **'S'** hands are held with wrists crossed and palms down, the right hand nearest the body. Then both hands are thrust upward forcefully so that the palms face each other.

rural: *adj.* relating to country life. *They have always lived in a rural area.*

SIGN: Right **'EXTENDED B'** hand, with palm toward the body, is placed near the elbow of the bent left forearm, and is circled in a direction that appears to the onlooker to be clockwise.

rush: *v.* to proceed with haste. *We had to rush to get to the bank before it closed.*

SIGN #1: Horizontal **'U'** hands are held apart with left palm facing right and right palm facing left, and the forearms are alternately circled forward repeatedly.

rush: *v.* to cause to move quickly; hasten. *They had to rush him to the hospital by ambulance.*

SIGN #2: **'EXTENDED B'** hands are held parallel with palms up and fingers pointing forward. The hands are then simultaneously raised upward as they quickly move forward/rightward. (Sign choice depends on context.)

rust: *n.* a reddish brown substance that forms on iron or steel as a result of contact with water. *Most new cars are treated to prevent rust from forming.*

SIGN: Fingerspell **RUST**.

rustic: *adj.* characteristic of country life; simple; unsophisticated. *The inn provides rustic comfort and plain, wholesome food.*

SIGN: Right **'Y'** hand, with palm facing the body, is placed near the elbow of the bent left forearm, and is circled in a direction that appears to the onlooker to be clockwise. The sample sentence in ASL is: *HOTEL COMFORTABLE...FOOD HEALTHY...COUNTRY (head nods slightly).*
ALTERNATE SIGN—**country** #2

ruthless: *adj.* harsh; cruel; merciless; hard-hearted. *Several nations were being governed by ruthless dictators.*

SIGN: Right **'CROOKED 5'** hand is held with palm facing left and tip of forefinger touching or near end of nose while left **'CROOKED 5'** hand, palm facing right, is held just in front of/below right hand. The hands eventually assume **'A'** shapes as they brush past one another, the right hand moving downward/forward and the left hand moving upward/backward. Facial expression is important.

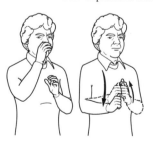

rye: *adj.* related to a cereal grain grown in the northern hemisphere and used for flour, animal fodder, etc. *I would like my sandwich on rye bread.*

SIGN #1: Fingerspell **RYE. Rye**, *n.,* meaning this type of cereal grain, is also fingerspelled.

rye: *n.* a type of whisky commonly produced in Canada. *Most of my friends drink Scotch but I prefer rye.*

SIGN #2: Fingerspell **RYE**.

S

sabotage: *n.* the deliberate disruption of a public service by enemy agents, disgruntled employees, etc. *The police investigation concluded that the bombing of the factory was a case of sabotage.*

SIGN: Left **'CROOKED 5'** hand is held palm-up with fingers pointing forward while right **'CROOKED 5'** hand is held apart and slightly higher with palm down and fingers pointing forward. The arms are then simultaneously moved upward/rightward as the hands are purposefully twisted rightward from the wrist so that the left palm faces right and the right palm faces left.

sack: *n.* a bag used as a container. *We took a sack of groceries to the Food Bank.*

SIGN #1: Horizontal **'C'** hands are held apart with palms facing each other. The hands are then simultaneously raised to indicate the height of the sack.

sack: *v.* to fire an employee. *The boss threatened to sack her if she continued arriving late for work.*

SIGN #2: Horizontal left **'S'** hand is held in a fixed position with palm facing the body at a slight rightward angle. Back of right **'BENT EXTENDED B'** hand, palm up, grazes the top of the left hand as it is firmly brought backward/leftward. (Handshapes for the left hand may vary.)

(hit the) sack: *v.* slang expression for 'go to bed'. *I am tired so I plan to hit the sack early tonight.*

SIGN #3: Left **'S'** hand is held loosely without actually forming a fist while the palm faces forward/rightward but is slanted slightly downward. Right **'U'** hand is held to the right of the left hand and closer to the body with palm facing upward but slanted leftward and toward the body while the extended fingers point forward/leftward. As the hands then move toward each other, the extended fingers of the right hand, which are meant to represent someone's legs, are inserted into the opening in the left hand. When making this sign, the signer closes his eyes as his head tilts rightward.

sacred: *adj.* regarded with reverence and awe. *In certain countries, cattle are considered sacred.*

SIGN: Knuckles of vertical right **'OPEN SPREAD O'** hand, palm toward the body, are placed on the chin and are firmly drawn downward, closing to form an **'S'** hand.

sacrifice: *v.* to give up or surrender something of value. *In order to reach your goals, you must be ready to sacrifice your time.*

SIGN: **'OPEN A'** hands, held slightly apart at waist level, palms down, are thrust upward to form **'EXTENDED B'** hands with palms facing forward.

sad: *adj.* unhappy; sorrowful. *Sad movies make her cry.*

SIGN: Vertical **'CROOKED 5'** hands are held slightly apart with palms toward the face. The hands are then simultaneously lowered somewhat and the head tilts to the right.
SAME SIGN—**sadness**, *n.*

saddle: *n.* a leather seat placed on a horse's back for a rider. *The equestrian uses a special saddle during a steeplechase.*

SIGN: Horizontal left **'B'** hand, palm toward the chest at a rightward angle, is held stationary while the right **'EXTENDED C'** hand, palm facing left palm, is fitted over its edge and is brushed lightly back and forth a couple of times. (Signs vary.) Alternatively, **SADDLE** may be fingerspelled.

sadistic: *adj.* related to the deriving of pleasure or gratification by inflicting pain and/or mental suffering on another person. *The criminal's cruel and sadistic behaviour towards the victim resulted in a longer sentence.*

SIGN: **'FLAT O'** hands, with palms up, are positioned so that the right hand is just in front of the mouth or chin while the left hand is a little lower and farther ahead. The thumbs slide across the fingers several times thus causing the handshapes to alternate between **'FLAT O'** and **'OFFSET O'**. Movement is repeated. Meanwhile, the signer's lips are protruded into a square shape with the closed teeth exposed. Facial expression is menacing.
SAME SIGN—**sadism**, *n.*

safe: *adj.* secure; protected from harm. *We found a safe place to wait until the blizzard was over.*

SIGN #1: '**S**' hands, left palm facing rightward/downward and right palm facing leftward/downward, are crossed at the wrists with the right hand nearer the body. Then they break apart so that they are held parallel with palms facing forward. (Alternatively, **SAFE** may be fingerspelled.)
SAME SIGN—**safety**, *n.*

safe: *n.* a strong, usually metal, container used for the secure storage of money and valuables. *Only the manager has access to the office safe.*

SIGN #2: Fingerspell **SAFE**.

safeguard: *v.* to protect. *The store has an alarm system to safeguard against burglary.*

SIGN: Horizontal '**S**' hands are held, the left just in front of the right, with palms down in front of the centre of the chest. The hands are then simultaneously moved emphatically forward a short distance.

safety pin: *n.* a wire clasp with a covered catch to shield the point when it is closed. *A safety pin is useful for repairing a broken strap.*

SIGN #1: Right '**MODIFIED G**' hand, palm leftward/downward, is held against the left side of the chest and is rapidly alternated with a '**CLOSED MODIFIED G**' handshape a couple of times. (The location of this sign varies depending on where the safety pin is actually used.)

OR

SIGN #2: Horizontal left '**ONE**' hand is held in a fixed position with palm facing right while and forefinger pointing forward/upward. Horizontal right '**X**' hand is held against the left hand with palm facing left and the tip of the forefinger scraping up and down against the end of the left forefinger.

sag: *v.* to hang down; curve downward. *As we age our skin begins to sag and wrinkle.*

SIGN: Fingertips of '**CONTRACTED 5**' hands are placed on either cheek and fingers are simultaneously drawn down, pulling the skin slightly. (Signs vary considerably depending very specifically on context.)

saga: *n.* a long story or a series of novels about several generations of a family or dynasty. *Most TV soap operas depict an ongoing family saga.*

SIGN: Left '**CONTRACTED C**' (or '**OPEN 8**') hand is held horizontally with palm facing right while right '**CONTRACTED C**' (or '**OPEN 8**') hand is held upright with palm facing left. The hands are held close enough together to be loosely interlocked. They are then drawn apart, closed and returned several times, thus alternating between '**CONTRACTED C**' (or '**OPEN 8**') and '**FLAT O**' (or '**8**') shapes with each movement.

sail: *v.* to glide over a body of water in a boat with sails. *They plan to sail around Vancouver Island.*

SIGN: '**CROOKED EXTENDED B**' hands, palms facing each other at a slight angle, are cupped together to form the hull of a boat. Together, the hands are moved forward.

sailboat: *n.* a water vessel propelled by the wind. *The sailboat is a three-masted schooner.*

SIGN: Right '**BENT EXTENDED B**' hand, palm facing the body, is placed on the upturned palm of the left '**EXTENDED B**' hand and together, the hands are moved forward and back a couple of times.

sailor: *n.* any member of a sailing crew. *If you join the navy, you will learn to be a sailor.*

SIGN: '**CONTRACTED B**' hands, palms toward the body, are placed side by side just below the right side of the waist, and are simultaneously moved across to the left side. (Signs vary.)

saint: *n.* a person of exceptional holiness. *A saint is a person who, after death, is canonized by certain Christian churches.*

SIGN: Fingerspell **SAINT**.

(for someone's) sake: *adv.* for the benefit or interest of. *For your sake, I hope the treatment will help.*

SIGN: Tip of forefinger of right '**ONE**' hand touches right side of forehead and left '**ONE**' hand is held palm-down at upper chest level with forefinger pointing forward and slightly to the right. Then both forefingers point this way as they move simultaneously forward.

salad: *n.* a dish of cold vegetables or fruit served with or without a dressing. *The restaurant is famous for its Caesar salad.*

SIGN: **'CROOKED SLANTED 5'** hands, palms facing upward but slanted toward each other slightly, are held apart and are lightly circled outward a few times as if tossing a salad. (**SALAD** may be fingerspelled.)

salary: *n.* a regular payment made by an employer. *She earns the same salary as her husband.*

SIGN: Horizontal right **'EXTENDED C'** hand, palm toward the body, is held on the upturned palm of the left **'EXTENDED B'** hand. The right hand then closes into an **'EXTENDED A'** shape as it is drawn across the left palm in a leftward arc toward the body. Movement is repeated. (**SALARY** may be fingerspelled.)

sale: *n.* the exchange of goods or property for an agreed amount of money. *Is your house for sale?*

SIGN #1: **'FLAT O'** hands, held parallel with palms down and fingers pointing down, are swung forward/upward from the wrists. (The ASL sentence is syntactically different than the English one. In ASL: *HOUSE (eyebrows raised) SELL?*)

sale: *n.* a special time when products are sold at reduced prices. *There is a sale on children's snow boots at the shoe store.*

SIGN #2: Fingerspell **SALE**.

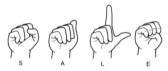

saliva: *n.* a liquid secreted from the salivary glands in the mouth. *Certain illnesses can be diagnosed by testing the saliva for the presence of bacteria.*

SIGN: Fingerspell **SALIVA**.

salmon: *n.* an edible fish having pinkish to red flesh and found in northern waters. *They liked to go fishing for salmon off the Queen Charlotte Islands.*

SIGN: Fingerspell **SALMON**.

saloon: *n.* a pub; bar. *The saloon offers live entertainment every night.*

SIGN: Tip of thumb of right **'Y'** (or **'EXTENDED A'**) hand, palm facing left, is tapped at least twice against the lower lip.

salt: *n.* sodium chloride used for seasoning and preserving food. *You will need salt to make dill pickles.*

SIGN #1: Horizontal **'V'** hands, palms down, are held so the right is just above the left at right angles to it. Then the right hand is lowered so that the extended fingers are tapped down on those of the left a couple of times. (**SALT** is frequently fingerspelled.)

OR

SIGN #2: Horizontal **'U'** hands, palms down, are held so the extended fingers of the right flutter as they rest on those of the left at right angles to them.

salty: *adj.* containing salt. (This sign is used to imply that there is an *excessive amount* of salt present.) *This soup is certainly salty!*

SIGN: Left **'V'** hand is held in a fixed position with palm down and extended fingers pointing forward/rightward. Vertical right **'V'** hand is held with palm facing forward/leftward. The right wrist then bends causing the hand to fall so that the extended fingers come to rest firmly on those of the left hand at right angles to them. This sign is accompanied by a grimace.

salute: *v.* to raise one's right hand to touch the forehead as a sign of respect as is done in the armed forces. *Soldiers usually salute their commanding officers.*

SIGN #1: Right **'B'** hand, palm left/forward, is raised stiffly to touch the right side of the forehead with the edge of the forefinger.

salute: *v.* to acknowledge with praise; commend; honour. *We salute you for your dedication and loyalty.*

SIGN #2: Right **'U'** hand, palm facing left, is held in a vertical position so that the side of the forefinger touches the middle of the forehead. The hand is curved downward slightly and moved forward. (Alternatively, this sign may be made with two hands, in which case the vertical left **'U'** hand, palm facing right, is held below the right hand and follows its movement.)

salutary: See **beneficial** under **benefit**.

salvage: *v.* to save or rescue goods or property from fire, flood or other dangers. *The firemen were able to salvage most of the contents of the house.*

SIGN: Left **'V'** hand is held in a fixed position with palm facing chest and extended fingers pointing upward/rightward. Right **'V'** hand is held just ahead of left hand with palm facing chest and extended fingers pointing upward/leftward while tapping against the fingers of the left hand.

(good) samaritan: *n.* a person who helps others when they are in distress or despair. *He is the good samaritan who came to my aid when my car stalled on the busy highway.*

SIGN: Horizontal **'BENT EXTENDED B'** hands, palms facing each other, are alternately circled forward around each other. (This sign is followed by **man** or **woman** as appropriate.)

same: *adj.* alike or identical. *Identical twins have the same features.*

SIGN #1: Vertical right **'Y'** hand is held with palm forward and appears to wobble from side to side as the wrist twists.

same: *adj.* alike or identical. *This is the same movie we saw yesterday.*

SIGN #2: **'ONE'** hands, palms down, forefingers pointing forward, are firmly brought together twice so that the sides of the forefingers strike each other. (This sign is used less frequently than **same** #1, and is generally not used when the things or people being compared are visible to the signer.)

same: *adj.* equal in quantity or amount. *Both of the accused were given the same sentence.*

SIGN #3: Vertical **'BENT EXTENDED B'** hands are held slightly apart with palms facing each other, and are then brought together so that the fingertips meet. Motion is repeated. (To translate the sample sentence into ASL, **same**, *adj.*, follows rather than precedes **sentence**, *n.*) This sign is generally used when there is an implication of 'fairness'.

same: *adj.* remaining unchanged. *She has looked the same ever since I have known her.*

SIGN #4: Vertical **'Y'** hands are held apart with palms facing forward and are simultaneously moved firmly forward a short distance.

sample: *n.* a part that is representative of the whole. *I would like you to see a sample of my work.*

SIGN: Tip of forefinger of horizontal right **'BENT ONE'** hand is placed against right facing palm of left **'EXTENDED B'** hand. Together, the hands are moved forward in a short arc.

sanction: *v.* to authorize; approve. *The prime minister will sanction the use of Canadian troops as peacekeepers.*

SIGN #1: **'K'** hands, palms down, are held apart, extended fingers pointing downward, and are then flicked upward from the wrists so that the hands are held in either a horizontal or upright position.
ALTERNATE SIGNS—**approve** #1 & #2

sanction: *n.* a coercive measure taken against a country guilty of violating international law. *Many nations placed sanctions on South African goods while apartheid was being practised by that government.*

SIGN #2: **'CLAWED L'** hands, palms forward, are held slightly apart and are simultaneously thrust ahead with a short, firm, abrupt movement.

sand: *n.* loose material consisting of fine grains of rock or minerals. *Some Caribbean islands are noted for their beaches of white sand.*

SIGN #1: **'FLAT O'** hands are held slightly apart with palms up. Then the fingers are slid across the thumbs a few times, thus alternating between **'FLAT O'** and **'OFFSET O'** hands.

sand: *v.* to spread sand on icy streets to prevent skidding. *The city crew will sand the streets because they are very icy.*

SIGN #2: With wrists bent, **'4'** hands are held parallel with palms and fingers pointing downward. The hands are then simultaneously moved forward.

sandals: *n.* open, light shoes with thongs or straps. *I usually wear **sandals** on the beach.*

SIGN: Tip of forefinger of inverted right **'ONE'** hand, palm facing backward/rightward, is slid between the forefinger and midfinger of the left **'5'** hand of which the palm faces down. Movement is repeated.

sandpaper: *n.* a strong paper coated with sand and used to smooth wood surfaces. *My father used fine **sandpaper** between coats of varnish when he refinished our table.*

SIGN: Right **'A'** hand, palm down, is placed on the upturned palm of the left **'EXTENDED B'** hand and is vigorously rubbed back and forth. (Alternatively, **SAND** may be fingerspelled, followed by the sign for **paper**.)

sandwich: *n.* two slices of bread with a filling. *I usually have a **sandwich** for lunch.*

SIGN #1: **'EXTENDED B'** hands are held, right slightly above left, in front of the upper chest with fingers pointing forward and right palm facing down while left palm faces upward. The hands are clapped lightly together as they move forward a little. Movement is repeated. (Signs vary considerably.)

OR

SIGN #2: Vertical right **'FLAT C'** hand, palm backward, is swung back and forth at least twice in front of the mouth.

sane: *adj.* having reasonably good judgment; rational; mentally healthy. *He was declared **sane** enough to stand trial for his crimes.*

SIGN: Tip of forefinger of right **'CROOKED ONE'** hand, palm toward the head, is tapped against right side of forehead. Next vertical right **'5'** hand, palm facing left, is held against the chest and dropped forward so that the fingers point forward. (ASL CONCEPT—**mind - fine**.)

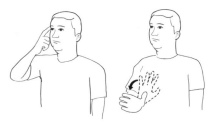

sanitary: *adj.* hygienic; clean. *The restaurant is well known for its **sanitary** kitchen.*

SIGN: Hands are held at right angles to one another as downturned palm of right **'EXTENDED B'** hand is smoothed rightward/forward across upturned palm of left **'EXTENDED B'** hand.

sanitary napkin: *n.* an absorbent pad worn externally by a woman during menstruation. *She preferred to use a **sanitary napkin** instead of a tampon.*

SIGN: Vertical right **'A'** hand, palm toward the face, is tapped lightly against the right cheek twice. Next, **'C-INDEX'** hands, palms down, are held side by side and moved apart to indicate the length of a sanitary napkin. (ASL CONCEPT—**period - pad**.)

Santa Claus: *n.* a mythical fat, white-bearded, jolly old man in a red suit who is said to bring gifts on Christmas Eve. *The children all wrote to **Santa Claus**.*

SIGN #1: Right **'SPREAD EXTENDED C'** hand, palm leftward/downward, is held with side of forefinger against the chin. The wrist then rotates forward to turn the hand palm-upward but slanted toward the body slightly as the hand is lowered to make contact with the chest. (Signs vary considerably.)

OR

SIGN #2: Vertical **'SPREAD EXTENDED C'** hands, palms facing each other, are placed with fingertips along the lower jawlines and outline a large beard as the wrists rotate forward to curve the hands downward and toward each other until they meet with the palms up.

OR

SIGN #3: Right horizontal **'C'** hand, palm backward, is placed first against the chin and then raised to the forehead.

sapling: *n.* a young tree. *Fifty years ago, this fine oak tree was a little **sapling**.*

SIGN: Fingers of palm-up right **'BENT EXTENDED B'** hand point leftward as they rest on rightward-pointing fingers of palm-up left **'BENT EXTENDED B'** hand. Together, the arms are then rocked from side to side. Next, elbow of upright right forearm is rested on the left **'STANDARD BASE'** hand and the right **'5'** hand, palm left, is twisted back and forth several times from the wrist. (ASL CONCEPT—**baby - tree**.)

sarcastic: *adj.* mocking; insulting; scornful; caustic. *She makes **sarcastic** remarks about every member of her staff.*

SIGN: **'BENT COMBINED I + ONE'** hands, left palm facing right and right palm facing left, are positioned so the tip of the right forefinger is at the end of the nose and the left hand is held slightly lower and to the left of the right hand. Then the right hand is curved forward/leftward, making contact with the left hand which is moving rightward so that the hands are eventually crossed at the wrists. The sign is accompanied by a sarcastic facial expression. SAME SIGN—**sarcasm**, *n.*

sassy: *adj.* impertinent; cheeky; saucy. *My parents would never tolerate **sassy** behaviour.*

SIGN: Forefinger and thumb of right palm-down **'A'** (or **'A-INDEX'**) hand grab tip of forefinger of left **'ONE'** hand, and give it a shake.

Satan: *n.* the devil. *The Bible sometimes refers to Satan as "Lucifer".*

SIGN: Thumb of vertical right **'CROOKED EXTENDED V'** hand is placed against the right side of the forehead, palm facing forward, and the two bent fingers are simultaneously wiggled up and down to alternate between a **'CROOKED EXTENDED V'** and **'CLAWED EXTENDED V'** shape. Alternatively, this sign may be made with two hands, one at either side of the forehead. SAME SIGN—**satanic**, *adj.*

satellite dish: *n.* a round, dish-shaped object that receives TV signals transmitted by a satellite in orbit. *The **satellite dish** provides us with dozens of TV channels.*

SIGN: Left horizontal **'ONE'** hand is held steady, palm down, with forefinger pointing at right wrist. Right **'MODIFIED 5'** hand, palm forward, is held beside and slightly in front of left hand and is drawn toward it and away from it a few times, intermittently touching the tip of the left forefinger. (**SATELLITE** may be fingerspelled.) Sign choice depends on context.

satisfy: *v.* to fulfil one's needs or desires. *A good salesman tries to **satisfy** his customers.*

SIGN: **'BENT B'** hands, right above left, with left palm facing right and right palm facing left, are placed firmly against the chest. SAME SIGN—**satisfaction**, *n.*

saturate: *v.* to soak; wet thoroughly. *We need a good rain that will **saturate** the ground.*

SIGN: Left **'CONTRACTED 5'** hand is held palm-up in front of chest while vertical right **'CONTRACTED 5'** hand is held with palm toward the body, and tip of middle finger touching the chin. Right hand is then lowered to a position parallel to the left hand as both hands are simultaneously closed to form **'FLAT O'** hands. (Alternatively, this sign may be made with the hands beginning in a parallel position rather than with the right hand beginning at the chin.) Facial expression is very important.

Saturday: *n.* the seventh day of the week. [See TIME CONCEPTS, p. LXX.] *Our office will be closed this **Saturday**.*

SIGN: Right vertical **'S'** hand, palm toward the shoulder, is held relatively upright as the forearm makes small counter-clockwise circles. (Alternatively, the hand is held steady as the thumb slides back and forth a few times along the clenched fingers.)

sauce: *n.* a liquid or semiliquid preparation used to enhance the flavour of other food. *He prepared a **sauce** to serve with the meat.*

SIGN: Horizontal right **'Y'** hand, with thumb pointing downward and palm facing away from the body, is circled in a counter-clockwise direction. (When **SAUCE** is qualified by an adjective, as in **tomato sauce**, it is usually fingerspelled.)

saucy: See **rude**.

sausage: *n.* a meat mixture packaged into a tube-shaped casing. *She asked the waitress for sausages with her pancakes.*

SIGN #1: **'c'** hands are held side by side with palms down. As the hands move apart they close to form **'s'** hands, open to resume the **'c'** shape, close to form **'s'** hands, and so on in a series of simultaneous motions.

SIGN #2 [PACIFIC/PRAIRIE]: **'CONTRACTED L'** hands, palms facing, are held so that the tips of the thumbs and forefingers meet. The hands are then moved apart as the thumbs and forefingers close and open several times, the handshapes thus alternating between **'CONTRACTED L'** and **'CLOSED MODIFIED G'**.

savage: *adj.* wild; ferocious; fierce. *The lion is a proud and savage beast.*

SIGN: Right **'CROOKED 5'** hand is held with palm facing left and tip of forefinger touching or near end of nose while left **'CROOKED 5'** hand, palm facing right, is held just in front of/below right hand. The hands eventually assume **'A'** shapes as they brush past one another, the right hand moving downward/forward and the left hand moving upward/backward. Appropriate facial expression is important.

save: *v.* to set aside for future use or enjoyment. *Their goal is to save the environment.*

SIGN #1: Left **'v'** hand is held in a fixed position with palm facing chest and extended fingers pointing upward/rightward. Right **'v'** hand is held just ahead of left hand with palm facing chest and extended fingers pointing upward/leftward while tapping against the fingers of the left hand.

save: *v.* to set (money) aside for future use. *It is a good idea to save your money for a rainy day.*

SIGN #2: Vertical left **'c'** hand is held with palm facing right. Then the forward-pointing fingertips of the right **'FLAT O'** hand are inserted into the opening in the left hand a couple of times.

save: *v.* to rescue from danger or harm. *He jumped into the water to save the drowning child.*

SIGN #3: **'s'** hands, left palm facing rightward/downward and right palm facing leftward/downward, are crossed at the wrists with the right hand nearer the body. Then they break apart so that they are held parallel with palms facing forward.

save: *v.* to keep or hold in reserve. *Will you save a front seat for me, please?*

SIGN #4: Right **'s'** hand is clenched with palm upward but slanted toward the body and is moved in a what appear from the signer's perspective to be small clockwise circles.

save: *n.* block; an action (in soccer or hockey) that prevents the opposing team from scoring a goal. *This goalie has an outstanding record for saves.*

SIGN #5: **'EXTENDED B'** hands are held at right angles to one another, the left hand in front of the right, with fingers of left hand pointing upward to the right and fingers of right hand pointing upward to the left. The hands are then pushed firmly forward.

savings: *adj.* a bank account that generally pays a higher rate of interest than a chequing account. *She deposited the cheque in her savings account.*

SIGN: Vertical left **'c'** hand is held with palm facing right. Then the forward-pointing fingertips of the right **'FLAT O'** hand are inserted into the opening in the left hand a couple of times.

savour [*also spelled* **savor**]: *v.* to relish; cherish; enjoy; appreciate. *A family photo album lets us savour memories of our youth.*

SIGN #1: Knuckles of vertical right **'OPEN SPREAD O'** hand, palm toward the body, are placed on the chin and are firmly drawn downward, closing to form an **'s'** hand.
ALTERNATE SIGN—**enjoy**

savour [*also spelled* **savor**] **one's food:** *v.* to eat slowly and appreciatively. *I like to see a dinner guest who savours his food.*

SIGN #2: Vertical right **'MODIFIED O'** hand, palm facing the body, is very slowly circled toward the mouth a couple of times as the signer moves his head slowly from side to side with his eyes squinted and tip of tongue visible as it moves from side to side between the otherwise closed lips.

savoury [*also spelled* **savory**]: *adj.* pleasant-tasting. *This spaghetti sauce is quite savoury.*

SIGN: Tip of middle finger of right **'BENT MIDFINGER 5'** hand (or tip of forefinger of right **'ONE'** hand), palm toward the body, is placed in the centre of the chin. Next, finger-tips of right **'BENT EXTENDED B'** hand are placed on the lips so that the palm is toward the body. Then the hand is moved forward a brief distance. (ASL CONCEPT—**taste - good**.)

saw: *n.* a cutting tool that has a blade with teeth along one edge. *I will use a saw to cut the board in half.*

SIGN: Left **'STANDARD BASE'** hand is held in a fixed position while horizontal **'S'** (or **'EXTENDED B'**) hand moves forward and back a couple of times beside it as if sawing a piece of wood. (Signs vary according to type.) For **saw,** *v.,* past tense of **to see**, please refer to **see**.

sawmill: *n.* an industrial plant where timber is processed. *New environmental legislation will affect every sawmill in Canada.*

SIGN: Vertical right **'4'** hand, palm facing left, is moved forward several times underneath the left **'STANDARD BASE'** hand.

say: *v.* to express in words. *What did you say?*

SIGN #1: Forefinger of right **'ONE'** hand is used to touch chin.

OR

SIGN #2: Tip of forefinger of vertical right **'4'** hand, palm facing left, is tapped twice against the chin.

say "no": *v.* to indicate an emphatic refusal or disagreement. *Stop asking me for a date because I will continue to say "no".*

SIGN #3: Vertical right **'CONTRACTED 3'** hand, palm forward, is changed to a **'CLOSED DOUBLE MODIFIED G'** hand as it is firmly thrust ahead. ❖

say "okay": *v.* to indicate agreement. *If you ask for permission to leave early, he will likely say "okay".*

SIGN #4: Fingerspell **O**, drop the wrist, and fingerspell **K**, which may resemble a **P** due to its unusual positioning. ❖

say "yes": *v.* to indicate emphatic agreement. *If you pester her long enough, your mother will finally say "yes".*

SIGN #5: Vertical right **'Y'** hand, palm forward, is thrust ahead firmly as it changes to an **'E'** and then an **'S'** hand.

OR

SIGN #6: Vertical right **'S'** hand, palm forward, bends at the wrist so that the palm turns downward, then quickly resumes its original position. In the process, the signer's head may nod forward and then resume its original position just like the hand. ❖

saying: *n.* an expression; proverb; maxim. *There is an old saying that "absence makes the heart grow fonder".*

SIGN: Vertical **'V'** hands, palms facing forward, are held apart just above shoulder level, and are curved outward slightly from the wrists as they become **'CLAWED V'** hands.

scab: *n.* the crust that forms over a wound while it is healing. *You should not be picking at that scab on your hand.*

SIGN: Fingerspell **SCAB**. (Signs vary.)

scald: *v.* to burn with hot liquid or steam. *If you upset the teapot, the hot tea will **scald** you.*

SIGN: **BURN** is emphatically fingerspelled with a pained expression on the face, sometimes followed by the hand(s) moving over the affected area(s) of the body.

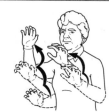

scale: *v.* to climb. *He wants to **scale** that mountain.*

SIGN #1: Vertical **'CROOKED 5'** hands alternately move upward in a succession of arcs.

scale: *n.* a sequence of intervals used in making measurements. *She converted the temperature from Fahrenheit to the Celsius **scale**.*

SIGN #2: **'Y'** hands are held parallel with palms forward/downward, and tips of thumbs are tapped together at least twice.

scale: *n.* a device for weighing. *The bathroom **scale** indicates that I am gaining weight.*

SIGN #3: Horizontal left **'U'** hand is held with palm facing rightward, but angled slightly toward the body while the fingers point forward/rightward. Extended fingers of horizontal right **'U'** hand are rested on extended fingers of left hand at right angles to them. The right hand then rocks up and down from the wrist a couple of times.

scales: *n.* the tiny, thin plates that cover the body of a fish. *The **scales** of most fish can be easily removed to prepare it for cooking.*

SIGN: Fingerspell **SCALES**.

S　C　A　L　E　S

scalpel: *n.* a surgical knife with a short, thin blade. *Surgeons must be very skilled in the use of a **scalpel**.*

SIGN: Horizontal right **'U'** hand, with palm facing left, is held above and at right angles to horizontal left **'U'** hand, of which fingers are angled forward/rightward. Extended fingers of right hand are then brushed forward/rightward twice off the end of extended fingers of left hand. (If the context is not mutually understood, the sign for **surgery** would precede this sign.)

scamper: *v.* to run quickly; dart. *We saw a mouse **scamper** through the kitchen.*

SIGN: Horizontal **'ONE'** hand, palm down and forefinger pointing forward, is moved forward in a hurried zigzag, darting manner.

scan: *v.* to glance over quickly in search of a specific item (usually printed material). *I always **scan** the obituaries to see if I recognize any of the names.*

SIGN #1: Left **'EXTENDED B'** hand is held in a fixed position with palm facing the body and fingers pointing rightward while horizontal right **'V'** hand is held behind the left hand with palm down and extended fingers pointing forward. Right wrist then bends downward so that the tips of the extended fingers strike downward against the left palm. (Facial expression is important.) Signs vary according to what is being scanned and how it is being scanned.

scan: *v.* to move a beam of light in a pattern that will produce information related to medical diagnosis. *The Magnetic Resonance Imaging machine will **scan** your body for possible tumours.*

SIGN #2: Horizontal right **'CONTRACTED 5'** hand is held with palm toward the face. The hand then moves downward to about stomach level and back to its original position as the fingers close to form a **'FLAT O'** shape.

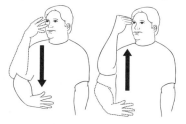

scandal: *n.* an improper act or circumstance that leads to disgrace. *The present government has lost support because of a recent **scandal**.*

SIGN: **'FLAT O'** hands are held with tips of forefingers touching and palms forward/downward but slanted toward each other slightly. The hands are then flung forward/outward as the fingers spread to form **'5'** hands with the palms down. Facial expression is important.

scapegoat: *n.* a person who is forced to take the blame for others. *The high-ranking officers made the young soldier their scapegoat in the scandal.*

SIGN: **'4'** hands are held apart at chest level with palms forward/downward and fingers pointing forward/upward. The hands then move slightly but emphatically forward/downward. The fingers represent the eyes of onlookers who are all looking simultaneously downward at one individual. Next, horizontal right **'EXTENDED A'** hand, palm facing left, is thrust forward twice across the back of the left **'A'** hand of which the palm faces downward. Facial expression must be accusatory. (ASL CONCEPT—**look down at - blame blame.**)

scar: *n.* a mark left on the skin after a wound has healed. *The injury will probably leave a scar on his face.*

SIGN: Vertical right **'ONE'** hand, palm facing left, is held with tip of forefinger against the right cheek near the nose. The hand then moves so that the forefinger slides downward/rightward across the cheek as if tracing the path of a scar. (The positioning of this sign varies according to the location of the scar being discussed.) **SCAR** is frequently fingerspelled.

scarce: *adj.* rare; not plentiful. *Sugar maple trees are scarce in Western Canada.*

SIGN: Right **'EXTENDED A'** hand, palm facing left, thumb under chin, is thrust forward. Next, **'S'** hands are held parallel with palms up and are thrust forward simultaneously as they are opened to form **'CROOKED 5'** hands. (ASL CONCEPT—**not - many.**)
ALTERNATE SIGN—**few**

scare: *v.* to fill with fear or alarm. *He tried to scare us by pretending to be a ghost.*

SIGN: Horizontal **'S'** hands, palms toward the body, are held near either side of the chest and are changed to **'5'** handshapes as they are thrust firmly toward each other. Facial expression must register fear. (For **scared**, *adj.*, and **scary**, *adj.*, see **afraid**.)

scarf: *n.* a rectangular or triangular piece of fabric worn around the neck, head or shoulders for warmth or decoration. *You need a colourful scarf to brighten up this plain-looking outfit.*

SIGN #1: Horizontal **'COVERED T'** hands, palms toward the body, are held just below the chin, quite near each other. Then they are simultaneously circled around each other and drawn slightly apart to simulate the tying of a scarf under the chin. (Signs vary according to the type of scarf and how/where it is worn.)

scarf: *n.* a long, narrow piece of fabric generally worn around the neck for warmth or decoration. *You should wear a warm scarf on a cold winter day.*

SIGN #2: Horizontal **'C'** hands are held at either side of the neck with palms facing the body and are simultaneously lowered. The left hand then opens to form an **'EXTENDED B'** shape and is held with the palm against the chest, the fingers pointing upward/rightward, as the right hand assumes a **'B'** shape and is swept upward so that it ends up against the left shoulder, palm facing the body. Alternatively, the right hand could end up with the back of the fingers against the left side of the neck as if tossing the end of a scarf over one's shoulder.

scarlet: *adj.* having a bright red colour. *The RCMP are recognized world-wide for their scarlet coats.*

SIGN: Vertical right **'ONE'** hand is held with palm facing the body and tip of forefinger touching the lower lip. As the hand is then drawn very firmly forward at a downward angle, the forefinger crooks to form an **'X'** shape.

scatter: *v.* to throw about in various directions. *Do not **scatter** your papers all over the room.*

SIGN #1: The arms gradually move forward as the hands, which are held apart with palms down, alternately change from **'S'** to **'CONTRACTED 5'** shapes several times as if dropping things on the floor.

scatter: *v.* to separate and move in various directions. *When they heard about the approaching storm, people **scattered** to their homes.*

SIGN #2: **'5'** hands are held parallel with palms down and fingers pointing forward. The hands then move outward/forward on a slight incline with fingers fluttering.

scene: *n.* a view. *Our first glimpse of the mountains was a breathtaking **scene**.*

SIGN #1: Right **'BENT V'** hand is held in front of left shoulder with palm facing left and extended fingers pointing left as well. The hand then makes a wide arc in a forward/rightward direction, coming to rest in front of the right side of the body with palm facing forward/rightward. Context must be considered when selecting signs. **Picture** #1 would be more appropriate in this example: *This painter is well known for his prairie **scenes**.* SAME SIGN—*scenery*, *n.*

scene: *n.* a subdivision of a stage performance in which the setting remains the same. *She will appear in the second **scene** in Act II of Romeo and Juliet.*

SIGN #2: Fingerspell **SCENE**.

scene: *n.* the place where something happens. *In mystery stories, the murderer often returns to the **scene** of the crime.*

SIGN #3: There is no general sign for **scene** in this context. Instead, a more specific sign would be used to indicate the location more precisely.

scent: *n.* a distinctive smell. *A bear can easily pick up the **scent** of a human.*

SIGN: Right **'EXTENDED B'** hand is held with palm facing the body, and fingertips just in front of the nose and pointing leftward/upward. The hand is then circled forward a few times in small clockwise circles.

schedule: *n.* a list of times and tasks to be performed within a set period. *The class **schedule** is ready for next term.*

SIGN: Fingertips of right **'5'** hand, palm down, are stroked downward across palm of horizontal left **'5'** hand which is facing the chest, but angled rightward. Then the right wrist rotates forward a quarter turn so that the palm is turned toward the body at a leftward-facing angle as the fingertips are stroked across the left palm from left to right.

scheme: *n.* a systematic plan; secret plan; plot. *Our **scheme** was to surprise our parents for their 50th anniversary.*

SIGN: Horizontal **'EXTENDED B'** hands, palms facing each other and fingers pointing forward, are held slightly apart at the left side of the body and are moved simultaneously toward the right.

schizophrenic: *adj.* related to a psychotic disorder characterized by emotional instability and withdrawal from reality. *The patient shows **schizophrenic** tendencies.*

SIGN: Vertical right **'B'** hand, palm left, is held in front of the forehead and is zigzagged downward to chest level.

scholar: *n.* a learned person or student possessing extensive academic knowledge. *He is a respected **scholar** noted for his thorough research.*

SIGN: Horizontal **'C'** hands, which are held with the left directly in front of the right, are pulled backward in a short jerking motion toward the forehead.

scholarship: *n.* money awarded to a student for academic excellence. *She was granted a **scholarship** during her training period.*

SIGN: Fingerspell **SCHOLARSHIP**.

school: *n.* a building in which students receive education. *He has attended* **school** *in several provinces.*

SIGN #1: Right **'EXTENDED B'** hand, palm down, fingers pointing forward and slightly to the left, is brought down twice on the upturned palm of the left **'EXTENDED B'** hand whose fingers point forward and slightly to the right.

SIGN #2 [ATLANTIC]: **'EXTENDED B'** hand, palm facing backwards and fingers pointing leftward/upward, is held with fingertips in front of the mouth and is moved up and down a couple of times.

school: *n.* a group of fish that swim together. *While snorkeling I saw a large* **school** *of fish.*

SIGN #3: **'SPREAD C'** hands are held upright and slightly apart with palms facing each other. The wrists then rotate forward, bringing the hands to a horizontal position.

school: *n.* an opinion or principle. *There is a new* **school of thought** *regarding bilingualism and biculturalism in the education of Deaf children.*

SIGN #4: Right **'K'** hand, palm down, is held in front of the forehead and is repeatedly moves up and down from the wrist.
ALTERNATE SIGN—**opinion** or **believe**

science: *n.* systematic study based on observation, experiment and measurement. *She studies* **science** *at the University of British Columbia.*

SIGN: **'EXTENDED A'** (or **'Y'**) hands, palms forward/downward, are held slightly apart and are alternately circled backward with the thumbs representing the spouts of beakers from which chemicals are being poured.
SAME SIGN—**scientific**, *adj.*

scissors: *n.* a cutting instrument used for cloth, paper, hair, etc. *I need these* **scissors** *to cut the ribbon at the official opening of the new school.*

SIGN: Extended fingers of horizontal right **'V'** hand, palm leftward/backward, are closed and opened at least twice, the handshapes thus alternating between **'V'** and **'U'** to simulate the action of cutting with scissors.

scoff at: *v.* to react to with derision. *He always* **scoffs at** *my suggestions.*

SIGN #1: Fingertip of vertical right **'ONE'** hand, palm left, touches the lips and the handshape then changes to an **'S'** as it is lowered to tap twice on the chest. Facial expression is important. (This sign is used to indicate a negative reaction to an idea or situation.)

scoff at: *v.* to mock; ridicule; deride; jeer at. *I* **scoffed at** *him because he was so arrogant.*

SIGN #2: Horizontal **'BENT COMBINED I + ONE'** hands, palms down, are held slightly apart, with the right hand nearer the chest, and simultaneously jabbed forward. This sign is accompanied by a mocking facial expression. ❖ (This sign is used to indicate a negative reaction to a *person* rather than an idea or a situation.)

scold: *v.* to rebuke or reprimand. *I will* **scold** *you for playing in the mud.*

SIGN: Vertical **'ONE'** hand is held with palm facing left. The forearm is then firmly thrust downward so that the hand is almost horizontal. Movement is repeated. Facial expression is stern. ❖
ALTERNATE SIGN—**bawl out**

scoop: *n.* a utensil with a small bowl at the end of a handle, used to take up various foods or ingredients. *I need to buy a new ice cream* **scoop.**

SIGN #1: Horizontal left **'C'** hand is held in a fixed position with palm facing right while right **'CLOSED A-INDEX'** hand is held to the right of it with palm facing downward. The right hand curves in a downward/leftward arc, the palm turning downward, then leftward before the hand curves upward/leftward, the palm now facing rightward/downward. Simply, the left hand represents a container while the right hand simulates the action of scooping something out of that container.
SAME SIGN—**scoop**, *v.*, depending on what kind of scooping is being referred to.

scoop: *n.* a portion (often rounded) of something which has been obtained by means of a digging motion. *I would like a small scoop of ice cream on my apple pie.*

SIGN #2: Left **'EXTENDED B'** hand is held in a fixed position with palm either up or down and fingers pointing forward/rightward while the right **'SPREAD C'** hand, palm down, is lowered and finally rests on the left hand. (The shape of the left hand varies according to size and shape of the object upon which the scoop is being placed.)

scoop: *n.* a colloquial term meaning news or gossip that one person finds out about before others do. *She told us the latest scoop in the neighbourhood.*

SIGN #3: Vertical **'MODIFIED G'** hands, palms facing each other, are held apart in front of the mouth or upper chest and are rapidly alternated with **'CLOSED MODIFIED G'** handshapes as they are being moved simultaneously in a semicircular direction.

scoot: *v.* to dart or go away quickly. *Please scoot to the mailbox and bring me today's mail.*

SIGN: Vertical right **'ONE'** hand is held with palm facing forward. The wrist then bends, causing the hand to fall forward so that the palm faces down. ❖

scooter: *n.* a light motorcycle with small wheels and an enclosed engine. *We rented scooters to travel around the island.*

SIGN: Horizontal **'S'** hands, palms down, are held side by side as if holding handlebars and are jiggled slightly while the signer is squinting and blowing a fine stream of air through drawn lips.

scope: *n.* the range, amount or area covered by a topic, activity, etc. *The scope of this course is limited.*

SIGN: **'EXTENDED B'** hands are held so the edge of the vertical right, palm facing left, is placed against the thumb of the horizontal left of which the palm is facing backward and the fingers are pointing rightward. Then the right hand is moved back and forth between the thumb and the end of the left hand to indicate the limits of a certain range. (This sign is used rarely as it is too general. The 'scope' of something is conveyed more specifically as either narrow or broad.) **Scope** has several connotations for which other sign choices would be more suitable.

scorch: *v.* to burn slightly, thus changing the colour or taste. *If the iron is too hot, you may scorch your blouse.*

SIGN: Fingerspell **BURN**.

score: *v.* to gain a point in a game. *He scored twice within five minutes.*

SIGN #1: Forefinger of horizontal right **'ONE'** hand, palm left, falls forward/downward until it lies between forefinger and midfinger of vertical left **'5'** hand, of which the palm is facing the body.
ALTERNATE SIGN—**goal** #3

score: *n.* the number of points earned by competitors in a game. *The score indicated that the home team was winning.*

SIGN #2: Fingerspell **SCORE**.

score: *n.* the final result of a quiz or test. *He wanted to know his score in the IQ test.*

SIGN #3: Vertical right **'O'** hand, palm forward/leftward, moves rightward and then downward at a slight leftward angle as if tracing the number '7' in the air.

score: *n.* a group or set of 20. *We have a score of problems to solve.*

SIGN #4: Vertical right **'MODIFIED G'** hand, palm forward, is alternated rapidly with a **'CLOSED MODIFIED G'** handshape several times as the forefinger moves up and down.

scorn: *n.* contempt. *She could only view him with scorn after he cheated her.*

SIGN: Right **'CLAWED C'** hand, palm toward the body, is circled in a clockwise direction (from the onlooker's perspective) in front of the stomach. Facial expression is very important.

scorpion: *n.* a large, spiderlike arthropod found in warm, dry regions. *If you are stung by a scorpion, it could be deadly.*

SIGN: Left arm with **'STANDARD BASE'** hand is held loosely so that fingertips are near the right elbow and the right **'CROOKED ONE'** hand, palm facing leftward/downward, is jiggled up and down a few times from the wrist.

(get off) scot-free: *v.* to get away without paying a price or penalty of any kind. *Our justice system sometimes allows culprits to get off scot-free.*

SIGN: Fingers of right **'B'** hand, palm-down, are placed on and at right angles to fingers of upturned palm of left **'EXTENDED B'** hand. Right hand is then slid at a forward/rightward angle across and off the left hand.

Scotch: *n.* whisky distilled in Scotland from fermented malted barley. *He ordered a single-malt Scotch.*

SIGN: Vertical right **'4'** hand, twisted at the wrist with palm rightward, is placed against the left shoulder with fingers pointed upward, and is drawn downward a short distance. Then it is changed to a horizontal **'4'** hand, palm toward the body, and the fingers are drawn rightward.

scour: *v.* to scrub vigorously. *I will scour the work surface until it shines.*

SIGN #1: Horizontal right **'A'** hand, palm down, is rubbed vigorously back and forth across the upturned palm of the left **'EXTENDED B'** hand. The teeth are visibly clenched as if articulating the sound 'ee'.

scour: *v.* to go over an area in search of someone or something. *The volunteers scoured the river banks in search of the lost child.*

SIGN #2: Vertical right **'C'** hand, palm facing left, is circled in front of the face several times in what appears to the signer as a counter-clockwise direction. (This sign is accompanied by a look of determination.)

scout: *v.* to observe someone in action in order to assess his/her capabilities as a potential future employee or player. *Major hockey teams usually scout the Junior League teams for potential players.*

SIGN #1: Horizontal **'BENT V'** hands are held slightly apart with fingers pointing forward and are circled in opposite directions (the left hand clockwise and the right hand counter-clockwise). Next, **'OPEN F'** (or **'OPEN 8'**) hands, palms forward, are held apart and alternately circled backward toward the chest several times as the thumbs and forefingers (or midfingers) close to form **'F'** (or **'8'**) hands with each backward rotation. (ASL CONCEPT— **look over - pick pick pick**.)

scout [*or* **boy scout**]: *n.* a young person who is a member of a world-wide organization founded in 1908 by Lord Baden-Powell. *A scout learns to be self-sufficient and to help others.*

SIGN #2: Vertical right **'CLOSED W'** hand, palm forward, is tapped against right side of forehead a couple of times.

SIGN #3 [PRAIRIE]: Right **'CONTRACTED 5'** hand is held, palm down, so the fingertips touch the top of the head. Then the hand rises rapidly as the fingers close to create a **'MODIFIED O'** shape. Motion is repeated at least once.

scowl: *v.* to frown angrily. *I scowled at her when she so rudely barged in front of me in the line.*

SIGN: Right **'BENT V'** hand is held with extended fingers pointing toward the person/ thing at whom/which the scowl is directed while the face very clearly expresses displeasure.

scramble: *v.* to mix in a haphazard way. *I will **scramble** the cards to make sure they are no longer in the same order.*

SIGN #1: **'5'** hands are held with palms down and are circled, the left hand moving in a clockwise direction while the right hand moves counter-clockwise. The hands move simultaneously but are offset rather than symmetrical in their respective positions. (Signs vary depending on what is being scrambled and how it is being scrambled.)

scramble: *v.* to cook eggs, the yolks and whites having been whisked together. *I will **scramble** some eggs for your breakfast.*

SIGN #2: Horizontal left **'c'** hand is held in a fixed position with palm facing rightward/downward as right **'COVERED T'** hand is inverted and rapidly circled clockwise from the wrist in a stirring motion within the opening created by the left hand.

scramble: *v.* to move hurriedly in a disorderly manner. *I had to **scramble** across the field to escape from the dog.*

SIGN #3: **'x'** hands are held at either side of the body and are alternately raised and lowered, thus alternating between being in a vertical position with palm forward and a horizontal position with palm down. (Signs vary according to context and whether the subject of the verb is singular or plural.)

scrambled: *adj.* refers to eggs whose yolks and whites have been mixed together. *I eat a **scrambled** egg every morning for breakfast.*

SIGN #1: Horizontal **'SPREAD EXTENDED C'** hands are held, right above left, with palms facing each other. Then right hand moves in a counter-clockwise direction while left hand moves in the opposite direction.

scrambled: *adj.* refers to a TTY message which is garbled. *I was unable to read your **scrambled** message on my TTY.*

SIGN #2: Vertical **'x'** hands, left palm facing right and right palm facing left at a slightly downward angle, are held together with the left hand in front of the right. Then the hands are simultaneously moved from left to right with the forefingers rapidly flexing as they represent the moving print on a TTY screen.

scrap: *v.* to discard as useless. *We plan to **scrap** our old car and buy a new one.*

SIGN #1: **'BENT 5'** hands are held parallel with palms down. The hands are then flung outward/forward at an upward angle as they take on **'5'** shapes. Facial expression is important. (Signs vary, depending on what is being scrapped and how it is being scrapped.)

scrap: *v.* to quarrel; argue. *Children often **scrap** about trivial matters.*

SIGN #2: **'BENT ONE'** hands, palms toward the chest, forefingers pointing toward each other, are either simultaneously or alternately moved up and down from the wrist.

scrap: *n.* a piece or fragment. *Please give those food **scraps** to the dog.*

SIGN #3: Horizontal **'5'** hands are held apart with palms facing each other. The forearms are then simultaneously lowered.

scrap paper: *n.* paper which is not valuable and can be used for rough notes as opposed to a formal piece of writing. *I need some scrap paper to jot down the shopping list.*

SIGN: Left **'EXTENDED B'** hand is held in a fixed position with fingers pointing forward/ rightward and palm facing rightward but slanted toward the body and slightly upward. Fingertips of right **'SPREAD EXTENDED C'** hand, palm down, are brushed forward/rightward a few times along the left palm. This sign is accompanied by a lip pattern such that the upper teeth are resting on the lower lip as if articulating an 'F'. Next, horizontal **'CROOKED 5'** hands, right palm down and left palm up, are positioned so that the right hand is slightly above the left. Then the right hand moves leftward/backward and the left hand moves rightward as the heels of each hand strike against each other at least twice. (ASL CONCEPT—**rough - paper.**)

scrape: *v.* to rub roughly against a surface. *We had to scrape the old varnish off the table.*

SIGN #1: Left **'EXTENDED B'** hand is held in a fixed position with palm up and fingers pointing forward while right **'EXTENDED B'** hand, palm down and fingertips pointing downward/ forward scrapes back and forth a few times on left palm. (Signs vary according to what is being scraped and how it is being done.)

scrape: *v.* to be very economical; scrimp. *They managed to scrape through the week without going to the Food Bank.*

SIGN #2: **'BENT MIDFINGER 5'** hands, palms toward the body, are alternately circled backward so that the tips of the middle fingers brush downward on either side of the chin with each revolution.

ALTERNATE SIGN—**scrimp** #2

scrape: *n.* a predicament; an embarrassing or problematic situation. *He has been in a lot of scrapes with the law.*

SIGN #3: Horizontal **'CLAWED V'** hands are held with palms facing the body and knuckles knocking against each other as the hands are alternately moved up and down.

scratch: *v.* to scrape with claws, fingernails or a sharp instrument or rough surface. *The bottom of that vase might scratch the table.*

SIGN #1: Fingertips of right **'CLAWED SPREAD C'** hand, palm down, are scraped across the upturned palm of the left **'EXTENDED B'** hand. (Signs vary according to what is being scratched and how it is being scratched. This sign is generally used when the scratches are *multiple*.)

scratch: *v.* to scrape with a claw, fingernail or sharp instrument. *Someone scratched my new car.*

SIGN #2: Tip of forefinger of right **'X'** hand, palm down, is placed on the upturned palm of the left **'EXTENDED B'** hand and is firmly drawn back toward the wrist. (This sign is generally used to refer to a *single* scratch.)

scratch the surface: *v.* to touch on but not to go into in depth. *In this course, we have only scratched the surface of Deaf Culture.*

SIGN #3: Right **'x'** hand is held palm toward the body with forefinger tightly crooked and tip of thumb repeatedly scraping downward against tip of forefinger. Next, right **'EXTENDED A'** hand, palm facing left, thumb under chin, is thrust forward. Finally, edge of downward-pointing forefinger of right **'BENT ONE'** hand is placed against right-facing palm of the left **'EXTENDED B'** hand. Then the right hand is pushed firmly downward. (ASL CONCEPT—**little bit - not - deep**.)

OR

SIGN #4: Tip of middle finger of right **'BENT MIDFINGER 5'** hand, palm down, touches down lightly on the back of the left **'STANDARD BASE'** hand a few times as the hands move rightward.

(start from) scratch: *v.* to start from the very beginning. *Since we lost all the data, we will have to start from scratch.*

SIGN #5: Left **'EXTENDED B'** hand is held in a fixed position with palm up and fingers pointing forward at a slight rightward angle. Right **'BENT EXTENDED B'** hand is held quite far to the right of the left hand with palm facing up. The right hand then moves leftward slowly in a wide arc as the palm gradually turns downward and the fingertips come to rest on the left palm.

(from) scratch: *adv.* from the beginning (in the case of cooking, without a commercially prepared mix). *She made the cake from scratch.*

SIGN #6: Forefinger of vertical right **'ONE'** hand, palm facing left, is held against the lips and the hand is moved sharply forward. (For emphasis, the hand is very gradually moved upward and forward, eventually assuming a horizontal position.)

scrawl: *v.* to write quickly and carelessly. *He scrawled a note to his parents and left it on the kitchen table.*

SIGN: Right **'CLOSED X'** hand, palm facing forward/leftward, moves rightward in a wavy line as if scrawling a message on a large writing surface. Facial expression is important and the signer appears to be producing a 'TH' sound with tongue protruding slightly between the teeth.

scrawny: *adj.* thin and bony. *The scrawny little girl developed into a beautiful woman.*

SIGN: Horizontal left **'I'** hand is held in a fixed position with palm toward the upper chest. Right **'I'** hand, palm upward, is positioned so that the tip of the little finger touches that of the left hand. Then the right hand is drawn downward. The signer's cheeks are hollowed.

scream: *v.* to emit a sharp, piercing cry. *We did not hear her scream for help.*

SIGN: Right vertical **'SPREAD C'** hand, palm toward the body, is held near the mouth and is forcefully drawn forward at an upward angle.

screen: *n.* the surface of a computer or TV set on which visible images appear. *He wanted a 17" screen for his computer.*

SIGN #1: **'ONE'** hands are held with palms forward and forefingers pointing upward/forward, the tips touching. The hands are then drawn apart, moved downward, and back together to outline the shape of a television screen. (Signs vary according to the type of screen due mainly to differences in size, shape and position.)

screen: *v.* to check out individuals or groups so as to determine suitability for a particular purpose. *The committee will screen the applicants and provide us with a short list.*

SIGN #2: **'ONE'** hands are held parallel with palms forward. As the forearms simultaneously move downward/forward, the forefingers retract to form **'x'** hands. Movement is repeated. Next, **'OPEN F'** (or **'OPEN 8'**) hands, palms forward, are held apart and alternately circled backward toward the chest several times as the thumbs and forefingers (or midfingers) close to form **'F'** (or **'8'**) hands with each backward rotation. (ASL CONCEPT—**test - pick pick pick**.)

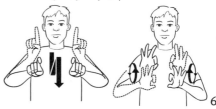

screening test: *n.* a test given in order to determine something. *The screening test revealed that only one person may have contracted tuberculosis.*

SIGN: **'ONE'** hands are held parallel with palms forward/downward. As the forearms simultaneously move downward/forward, the forefingers retract to form **'X'** hands. Movement is repeated.

screw: *n.* a threaded bolt used to fasten materials together. *A screw will hold the wood in place.*

SIGN #1: Tips of extended fingers of right **'U'** hand, palm down, are placed against right facing palm of horizontal left **'EXTENDED B'** hand. The right hand is then twisted forward and back a couple of times.

screw: *v.* to make a twisting movement. *Be sure to screw the lid on the jar tightly.*

SIGN #2: Right **'EXTENDED C'** hand is placed, palm down, over the horizontal left **'S'** hand, and twisted clockwise as if screwing a lid onto a jar. (Signs vary depending on what is being screwed and how it is being screwed.)

screw up: *v.* a colloquial term meaning to bungle or mishandle. *He will likely screw up the project.*

SIGN #1: Left **'CROOKED 5'** hand is held palm-up with fingers pointing forward while right **'CROOKED 5'** hand is held apart and slightly higher with palm down and fingers pointing forward. The arms are then simultaneously moved upward/rightward as the hands are purposefully twisted rightward from the wrist so that the left palm faces right and the right palm faces left.

OR

SIGN #2: Left **'V'** hand is held with palm up and extended fingers pointing forward at a slight rightward angle while right **'V'** hand is held just above the left hand with palm facing leftward at a downward/forward angle and extended fingers pointing leftward/upward at a slightly forward angle. Right hand is brought down to strike left hand, then bounces forward in arc formation as it takes on a **'K'** shape and the wrist rotates to turn the palm leftward at a downward angle.

screwdriver: *n.* a tool used for turning screws. *I need a screwdriver to tighten these screws.*

SIGN: Tips of extended fingers of right **'U'** hand, palm down, are placed against right facing palm of horizontal left **'EXTENDED B'** hand. The right hand is then twisted forward and back a couple of times.

scribble: *v.* to write or draw quickly in an illegible way. *My notes are hard to read because I had to scribble them quickly.*

SIGN: Right **'CLOSED X'** hand, palm facing forward/leftward, moves rightward in a wavy line as if scrawling a message on a large writing surface. Facial expression is important and the signer appears to be producing a 'TH' sound with tongue protruding slightly between the teeth.

scrimp: *v.* to be very economical, on a tight budget, or extremely frugal. *We had to scrimp to make ends meet.*

SIGN #1: **'BENT MIDFINGER 5'** hands, palms toward the body, are alternately circled backward so that the tips of the middle fingers brush downward on either side of the chin with each revolution.

OR

SIGN #2: **'CONTRACTED B'** hands, palms up, are circled backward around one another's fingertips. These are small, tight circles. The signer appears to be articulating the sound 'EE'.

script: *n.* the text of a play used by performers in film or theatre. *The director followed the script closely.*

SIGN #1: Fingerspell **SCRIPT**.

script: *n.* handwriting (not printing). *Her script is very neat and legible.*

SIGN #2: Horizontal left **'EXTENDED B'** hand is held in a fixed position with palm facing rightward/backward. Thumb and forefinger of right **'CLOSED X'** hand move forward/rightward twice along the palm of the left hand.

scrotum: *n.* the pouch of skin that contains the testes. *Testicular growths require examination of the scrotum.*

SIGN: **'OPEN SPREAD O'** hands are held a little apart and are very slightly moved up and down a couple of times.

scrub: *v.* to wash by rubbing hard; scour. *The sailors were ordered to scrub the deck of their ship.*

SIGN: **'A'** hands, palms down, are held slightly apart and are simultaneously circled in opposite directions, the left hand moving clockwise and the right hand moving counter-clockwise. (Signs vary according to what is being scrubbed and in what manner.)

scruples: *n.* moral integrity; principles. *Her scruples prevented her from lying under oath.*

SIGN: Vertical left **'EXTENDED B'** hand is held in a fixed position with palm facing right while horizontal right **'K'** hand is placed palm down against the fingers of the left hand, and then lowered to a position nearer the heel of the left hand.

scrupulous: *adj.* characterized by doing what is morally right; very honest. *The witness gave scrupulous testimony about his friend's involvement in the crime.*

SIGN: Left **'EXTENDED B'** hand is held in a fixed position with palm facing right but slanted upward slightly and fingers pointing forward as right **'U'** hand is held with palm facing left and tip of middle finger placed at heel of left hand. The right hand is then moved straight forward along the left palm until the tip of the right middle finger reaches the tip of the left middle finger.

scrutinize: *v.* to examine in minute detail. *My parents have promised me a reward if my marks improve so they will scrutinize my work closely.*

SIGN: Left **'EXTENDED B'** hand is held in a fixed position with palm turned upward but slanted slightly rightward and toward the body while fingers point rightward/forward. Right **'ONE'** hand is held palm down as tip of forefinger brushes forward several times against palm of left hand. Facial expression is important. Signs vary according to context.
SAME SIGN—**scrutiny**, *n.*

scuba diving: *n.* underwater swimming using a tank filled with compressed air for breathing. *Scuba diving is a very popular activity in many Caribbean resorts.*

SIGN: Right **'BENT V'** hand, palm toward the chest, is held under the left **'STANDARD BASE'** hand and is moved downward/forward diagonally with the extended fingers fluttering rapidly.

scuffle: *v.* to fight in a disorderly way. *The rowdy young men began to scuffle with the bouncers when they were evicted from the nightclub.*

SIGN: Vertical **'S'** hands, palms originally facing each other, are moved vigorously downward so that they come to rest side by side with palms facing down.

sculpture: *n.* a figure or design created by carving, moulding or casting various materials. *Michelangelo is widely known for his sculpture entitled "David".*

SIGN: Thumb of right **'EXTENDED A'** hand, palm down, is used to jab twice in an upward/backward direction at the fixed palm of the left **'EXTENDED B'** hand, which is held with fingers pointing forward/rightward, and palm facing rightward, but slanted slightly toward the body.
SAME SIGN—**sculptor**, *n.,* and may be followed by the Agent Ending (see p. LIV).

scurry: *v.* to move in a hurried, urgent manner. *The mouse scurried into its hole to escape the cat.*

SIGN: Horizontal **'ONE'** hand, palm down and forefinger pointing forward, is moved forward in a hurried zigzag, darting manner.

sea: *n.* the ocean or a smaller body of salt water; a large inland body of fresh water such as the Sea of Galilee. *I would love to live by the sea.*

SIGN: Forefinger of vertical right **'W'** hand, palm facing left, is tapped against the chin. Next, **'5'** hands are held slightly apart with palms down and fingers pointing forward/leftward. The hands are then moved simultaneously forward/leftward with a wave-like motion. (ASL CONCEPT—**water - wave**.) **SEA** is frequently fingerspelled. When the sea is specified, both **SEA** and the name of the sea are fingerspelled.

seal: *n.* an aquatic mammal with four flippers. *She watched the seals at the Vancouver Aquarium.*

SIGN #1: **'EXTENDED B'** hands are held with thumbtips against either side of the torso and are alternately pivoted to simulate the action of flippers. (**SEAL** is frequently fingerspelled.)

seal: *n.* a mark or stamp of authentication. *The document received the official seal of approval.*

SIGN #2: Horizontal right **'S'** hand, palm toward the body and facing left slightly, is brought down firmly to rest on the upturned palm of the left **'EXTENDED B'** hand.

seal: *v.* to close (an envelope) securely by moistening and pressing down a flap. *Be sure all the documents are enclosed before you seal the envelope.*

SIGN #3: With tongue protruding, the signer passes the horizontal right **'EXTENDED B'** hand, palm facing backward and fingers pointing leftward, from left to right in front of the mouth as if licking the flap of an envelope. (Signs vary depending on how the envelope is sealed.)

sealed: *adj.* airtight. *The food was placed in a sealed container to keep it fresh.*

SIGN #1: Horizontal right **'MODIFIED 5'** hand is held with palm facing left and thumbtip on the tightly closed lips. The fingers then close to form **'FLAT O'** as the signer's cheeks are drawn inward.

(my lips are) sealed: *s.s.* I will not tell anyone. *My lips are sealed so do not worry about anyone finding out about this.*

SIGN #2: Right **'F'** hand, palm facing backward, is held with joined thumb and forefinger touching the left corner of the mouth. The hand then moves rightward until the thumb and forefinger are touching the right corner of the mouth.

search: *v.* to look for. *When a plane crashes, the rescue squad will search for survivors.*

SIGN: Vertical right **'C'** hand, palm facing left, is circled in front of the face several times in what appears to the signer as a counter-clockwise direction.

seasick: *adj.* nausea and dizziness due to the motion of the sea. *We were seasick during the entire journey across the North Atlantic.*

SIGN: **'BENT MIDFINGER 5'** hands are positioned so that the tip of the right middle finger is in the middle of the forehead and the tip of the left middle finger is on the stomach. Sometimes this sign is made with the right hand only.

season: *n.* one of the four periods into which a year is divided. *Summer is my favourite season.*

SIGN #1: Fingerspell **SEASON**.

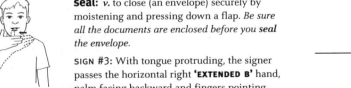

season: *v.* to enhance the flavour (of food) by adding such things as herbs, salt, pepper, or spices. *He will season the meat before putting it in the oven.*

SIGN #2: Vertical right **'C'** hand, palm forward, is tilted leftward from the wrist and is shaken up and down several times as if shaking a salt shaker.

seat: *n.* something to sit on; a chair. *Please save a seat for me in the front row.*

SIGN: Left **'U'** hand is held palm down with extended fingers pointing forward/rightward. Right **'U'** (or **'CROOKED U'**) hand is held palm down just above the left hand and at right angles to it. The extended fingers of the right hand are then tapped a couple of times on those of the left.

secluded: *adj.* kept apart from public view or from other people. *He lives in a secluded mountain cabin.*

SIGN: Thumbnail of right **'A'** hand, palm facing left, is placed against the lips and the hand is then lowered and concealed under the down-turned palm of the left **'CROOKED EXTENDED B'** hand.

SAME SIGN—**seclusion**, *n.*

second: *n.* 1/60 of a minute. *The runner completed the race one second ahead of the others.*

SIGN #1: Fingerspell **SEC.**

S   E   C

second: *adj.* denoting an instance that has occurred once before. [For an explanation of ordinals, see NUMBERS, p. LIX.] *That is the second time you have done that!*

SIGN #2: Horizontal right **'V'** hand is held palm down with extended fingers pointing forward. The wrist then rotates to turn the hand so that the palm faces leftward.

second: *adj.* coming after the first in terms of things which are numbered. *The second point I would like to discuss is this.*

SIGN #3: Left **'V'** hand is held with palm facing the body and extended fingers pointing rightward/upward while the tip of the forefinger of the right **'ONE'** hand is tapped a couple of times against the tip of the left midfinger.

(the) second [*or* **II**]: *adj.* a designation for someone, especially of royal blood, born after another. *Queen Elizabeth II is descended from the House of Hanover.*

SIGN #4: Horizontal right **'V'** hand, palm facing left and extended fingers pointing forward/upward, wobbles slightly.

second: *adv.* coming after the first position. *He finished second in the race.*

SIGN #5: Horizontal right **'V'** hand, palm facing left and extended fingers pointing forward, is drawn back firmly toward the body.

second: *v.* to express formal support for a motion already proposed. *I will second your motion.*

SIGN #6: Right **'L'** hand is extended from the body at about face level with palm facing left and forefinger pointing upward/forward. The wrist then bends to snap the hand downward slightly so that the forefinger points directly forward.

second: *v.* to transfer an employee temporarily to a different department. *We will second someone from Public Relations to help us with our advertising campaign.*

SIGN #7: Horizontal right **'S'** hand is held well out in front of the body with palm facing leftward and is then brought backward toward the body. ❖

secondary: *adj.* second in importance. *He drives a taxi at night as a secondary source of income.*

SIGN: Horizontal right **'V'** hand, palm left and fingers pointed forward, is shaken forward and back from the wrist.

secondary school: *n.* high school. *His marks were much better in secondary school than they were in elementary school.*

SIGN: Right **'U'** hand is held with palm facing the body and extended fingers pointing leftward at a slight upward angle. The hand is then firmly drawn rightward as the extended fingers are retracted so that the hand takes on an **'S'** shape with palm facing leftward.

secret: *adj.* kept hidden; not shared for general knowledge. *This is secret information.*

SIGN: Right **'A'** hand is brought to the lips with the thumb pointed upward and the palm facing left. Then the lips are touched twice with the thumbnail.

SAME SIGN—**secretive,** *adj.*

secretary: *n.* a person who handles correspondence, keeps records, and does clerical office work. *The secretary took notes at the meeting.*

SIGN #1: Left **'EXTENDED B'** hand is held in a fixed position with palm up and fingers pointing forward/rightward. Vertical right **'U'** hand is held with palm facing leftward/forward and tips of extended fingers touching the right cheek. The right hand is then lowered, the fingertips making contact with the left palm and sliding forward/rightward across the left hand and off.

OR

SIGN #2: Left **'EXTENDED B'** hand is held in a fixed position with palm up and fingers pointing forward/rightward. Vertical right **'K'** hand is held with palm facing leftward and tip of middle finger touching the right cheek. The right hand is then lowered, the tip of the middle finger making contact with the left palm and sliding forward/rightward across the left hand and off.

Secretary of State: *n.* the head of several government departments. *Many nonprofit organizations apply to the Secretary of State's department for grants.*

SIGN: Left **'EXTENDED B'** hand is held in a fixed position with palm up and fingers pointing forward/rightward. Vertical right **'U'** hand is held with palm facing leftward/forward and tips of extended fingers touching the right cheek. The right hand is then lowered, the fingertips making contact with the left palm and sliding forward/rightward across the left hand and off. After this, **STATE** is fingerspelled. (When it is understood that it is the **Secretary of State**, the abbreviation **SS** may be fingerspelled.)

sect: *n.* a religious denomination. *He joined a religious sect.*

SIGN: The right wrist rotates toward the chest as the crossed fingertips of the horizontal **'R'** hand are brushed off the left shoulder in a slight downward arc.

section: *n.* one of several parts. *The last section of the book is the most interesting part.*

SIGN: Horizontal left **'EXTENDED B'** hand is held in a fixed position with palm up but angled toward the body and fingers pointing rightward/forward while edge of horizontal right **'EXTENDED B'** hand, palm facing left, is placed on left palm and is drawn back toward the body. (Signs vary according to context.)

secular: *adj.* related to nonreligious matters. *Certain secluded monks have withdrawn from the secular world.*

SIGN: Right **'BENT U'** hand, palm down, is circled clockwise over left **'STANDARD BASE'** hand, and the extended fingers are brought down to rest on it.

secure: *adj.* free from danger or damage. *Please keep these records in a secure place until they can be placed in the vault.*

SIGN: **'S'** hands, left palm facing rightward/downward and right palm facing leftward/downward, are crossed at the wrists with the right hand nearer the body. Then they break apart so that they are held parallel with palms facing forward.

SAME SIGN—**security,** *n.,* in this context.

security guard: *n.* someone hired to protect buildings and people. *Many large supermarkets now hire security guards.*

SIGN: Horizontal **'S'** hands are held, the left just in front of the right, with palms down in front of the centre of the chest. The hands are then simultaneously moved emphatically forward a short distance.

sedative: *n.* a drug or medication that has a calming, soothing effect. *The doctor prescribed a mild sedative for her hyperactivity.*

SIGN: Tip of middle finger of right **'BENT MIDFINGER 5'** hand is placed on the upturned left palm, and maintains contact with the left palm as the right hand teeters back and forth a few times. Next, **'EXTENDED B'** hands are held parallel with palms down and fingers pointing forward. The forearms are then simultaneously moved slowly and deliberately down and up a couple of times.

(ASL CONCEPT—**medicine - calm down.**)

seduce: *v.* to tempt someone to engage in sexual intercourse. *He used all his charm to seduce her.*

SIGN: Horizontal **'EXTENDED B'** hands are held apart at about shoulder level with palms facing upward but slanted so that they are facing each other slightly as well. The forearms then move firmly downward/inward a short distance. Next, horizontal **'S'** hands are held side by side with palms down. Forefingers and midfingers are flipped forward simultaneously a couple of times to form horizontal **'BENT U'** hands. ❖ (ASL CONCEPT—**convince - sleep together**.)

see: *v.* to perceive with the eyes. *He will see the winter Olympic games on TV.*

SIGN #1: Vertical right **'K'** hand, palm toward the face, is held with the tip of the middle finger touching the right cheekbone. The hand is then thrust forward at a rightward/downward angle.

see: *v.* to make sure. *I will see that you are not disturbed.*

SIGN #2: Horizontal right **'S'** hand is placed on top of horizontal left **'S'** hand as both palms face the body. The right hand is then raised slightly and both wrists are bent causing the hands to turn so that the right palm faces left and the left palm faces right as the right hand re-establishes contact with the left hand. Next, forefinger of vertical right **'ONE'** hand, palm facing left, is held against the lips and the hand is moved sharply forward. Finally, right **'EXTENDED B'** hand, palm facing left, is held in a vertical position near the right side of the head. The forearm is then firmly moved forward a short distance so that the fingers eventually point forward/upward. This part of the sign is added to the end of the ASL sentence for emphasis. (ASL CONCEPT—**make - sure - will**.)
ALTERNATE SIGN—**ensure**

see: *v.* to accompany; go with. *I will see you to your car.*

SIGN #3: **'A'** hands are held together, palms facing each other, and knuckles touching. Then they are thrust forward/downward together from chest level. ❖

see: *v.* to understand. *I see your point.*

SIGN #4: Vertical right **'S'** hand, with knuckles near right side of forehead, is changed to a **'ONE'** hand as the forefinger is flicked upward. (See also **oh, I see**.)

(see) seen before: *v.* already seen. *I have seen that movie before.*

SIGN #5: Right **'BENT MIDFINGER 5'** hand is held with palm facing left and tip of middle finger flicking forward/upward at least twice off the right cheek. (The sample sentence in ASL is: *MOVIE...ME (understood so not signed)...SEEN BEFORE*.)

(see) not seen before: *v.* not seen yet. *I have not seen that movie before.*

SIGN #6: Vertical right **'BENT MIDFINGER 5'** hand is held with palm facing left and tip of middle finger brushing downward against the right cheek a few times. This movement is accompanied by a protruding tongue and the signer is likely to be shaking his head slowly. (The sample sentence in ASL is: *MOVIE... ME (understood so not signed)...NOT SEEN BEFORE*.)

seed: *n.* a mature, fertilized plant ovule from which new plants grow. *This plant grew from a seed.*

SIGN: Fingerspell **SEED**.

seek: *v.* to try to find by searching. *If it rains we can seek shelter at a nearby farm.*

SIGN: Vertical right **'C'** hand, palm facing left, is circled in front of the face several times in what appears to the signer as a counter-clockwise direction.

seem: *v.* to appear to be. *He does not **seem** worried.*

SIGN: Right **'BENT EXTENDED B'** hand with palm facing forward/left, is twisted slightly from the wrist so that it faces the right shoulder.

seep: *v.* to ooze or leak gradually. *Water began to **seep** into our basement.*

SIGN: Horizontal right **'4'** hand, palm left and fingers pointing forward, is held just under left **'STANDARD BASE'** hand near the fingertips and moves downward several times. This is a wrist movement.

seesaw: *n.* a teeter-totter. *Most children love to play on a **seesaw**.*

SIGN: **'CLAWED V'** hands, palms down and extended fingers toward each other, are alternately moved up and down.

seethe: *v.* to boil with anger or frustration. *Although she is always polite in public the politician often **seethes** with frustration.*

SIGN: Fingers of right **'CROOKED 5'** hand, palm toward body, are fluttered beneath left **'STANDARD BASE'** hand which is held close to the stomach. (Facial expression is important.)

segment: *n.* one of several parts or sections. *This legislation related to old age security benefits affects a large **segment** of our population.*

SIGN: Horizontal left **'EXTENDED B'** hand is held in a fixed position with palm up but angled toward the body and fingers pointing rightward/forward while edge of horizontal right **'EXTENDED B'** hand, palm facing left, is placed on left palm and is drawn back toward the body.

segregate: *v.* to set apart from the main group. *There will always be controversy about whether to **segregate** or integrate Deaf children for educational purposes.*

SIGN: Horizontal **'BENT EXTENDED B'** hands, palms facing chest and knuckles almost touching each other, are drawn apart.
SAME SIGN—**segregation**, *n.*

seize: *v.* to take legal possession of. *If you drive while your license is suspended, the police can **seize** your car.*

SIGN #1: **'SPREAD C'** hands are held parallel with palms down and are then closed to form **'S'** hands as they are thrust forward.

seize: *v.* to snatch or grab. *The thief **seized** the woman's purse and fled.*

SIGN #2: Horizontal right **'SPREAD C'** hand, palm facing left, is pulled backward as it closes to form an **'S'** hand. ❖

seizure: *n.* an epileptic convulsion. *Medication helps to control his **seizures**.*

SIGN: Edge of forefinger of right horizontal **'B'** hand, palm down, is placed between the lips as the wrist makes small twisting movements back and forth to rock the hand rapidly.

seldom: *adv.* rarely. *I **seldom** use that tool.*

SIGN: Both **'BENT EXTENDED B'** hands are held with palms toward the body. The left hand remains steady, while the fingertips of the right hand are brushed upward from the knuckles of the left. Next, right **'B'** (or **'EXTENDED B'**) hand, palm facing left, is held upright near the face and is vigorously curved downward. (ASL CONCEPT—**almost - never**.) Alternatively, **occasionally** or **often** #2 may be used but with the appearance of being made in painstakingly slow motion and without any repetition of the movement.

select: *v.* to choose in preference to others. *I need to **select** a suitable outfit for the dance.*

SIGN: Right **'FLAT OPEN F'** hand, palm forward, is drawn back toward the chest as it changes to an **'F'** hand. For **selection**, *n.*, the same basic sign is used but with two hands alternately moving backward a couple of times. ❖

self-: *prefix* autonomous; automatic; by or of itself or oneself. *I buy my gas at a self-serve station.*

SIGN: Horizontal right **'EXTENDED A'** hand, palm toward the body, is placed firmly against the chest. (For reflexive pronouns such as **myself**, **himself**, **herself**, and **ourselves**, see PRONOUNS, p. LXVI.)

self-assured: *adj.* having confidence in one-self. *They are looking for a manager who is competent and self-assured.*

SIGN: **'SPREAD EXTENDED C'** hands are held with palms toward the body at an upward angle, the left hand close to the chest and the right hand just above/ahead of the left. The hands are then thrust forward as they are snapped shut to form **'S'** hands.
SAME SIGN—**self-assurance**, *n.*

self-centred: *adj.* totally preoccupied with oneself. *She was an only child so she became self-centred.*

SIGN: Tip of forefinger of right **'CROOKED ONE'** hand, palm toward the head, is tapped against right side of forehead. Next, vertical right **'I'** hand, palm facing left, is thumped repeatedly against the centre of the chest.
(ASL CONCEPT—**think - self self self**.)

self-explanatory: *adj.* self-evident or under-standable without any explanation; obvious in meaning. *Our proposal is self-explanatory.*

SIGN: Vertical **'O'** (or **'FLAT O'**) hands are placed side by side, palms facing forward. Then they are moved apart and slightly upward as the fingers spread to form **'5'** hands. Next, right **'EXTENDED A'** hand, palm facing left, thumb under chin, is thrust forward. Then, right **'X'** hand, palm facing away from the body, is held in a vertical position in front of the chest and is sharply thrust downward from the wrist so that the palm faces down. Finally, **'F'** hands are held horizontally with palms facing each other, and are alternately moved backward and forward a few times.
(ASL CONCEPT—**clear - not - have to - explain**.)

self-righteous: *adj.* having an exaggerated opinion of one's own goodness or moral character. *Most people are offended by her self-righteous attitude.*

SIGN: Vertical right **'COMBINED U + Y'** hand, palm forward, is held in front of the right shoulder and the forearm is drawn firmly backward a short distance. This is essentially a jerking motion.
SAME SIGN—**self-righteousness**, *n.*

selfish: *adj.* overly concerned with one's own interest and advantage. *Some children are selfish with their toys.*

SIGN #1: Horizontal **'V'** hands, palms down, are held parallel and drawn firmly toward the chest as they change to **'CLAWED V'** hands. (Facial expression is important.)

OR

SIGN #2: Right **'S'** hand, palm downward/leftward, makes counter-clockwise (from the signer's perspective) circles as it is rubbed on the chin. (Facial expression is important.)

selfish (cont.)

OR

SIGN #3: Right **'SPREAD EXTENDED C'** hand is held palm down on the upturned palm of the left **'EXTENDED B'** hand and the fingertips scrape firmly backward toward the chest. (Facial expression is important.)
SAME SIGN—**selfishness**, n.

sell: v. to exchange for money. *They will sell their house and move to a condominium.*

SIGN: **'FLAT O'** hands, held parallel with palms down and fingers pointing down, are swung forward/upward from the wrists.

semantics: n. the branch of linguistics that deals with meaning. *The semantics of ASL and spoken English vary greatly.*

SIGN: Forefingers of **'ONE'** hands are crossed. The hands are then turned outward so that they become vertical with palms facing forward. Next, horizontal left **'EXTENDED B'** hand is held in a fixed position with palm facing right while tip of forefinger of right palm-down **'BENT V'** hand is jabbed into the left palm. The right hand then moves away from the left hand as the right wrist rotates a quarter turn clockwise, and the middle fingertip is jabbed into the left palm. (ASL CONCEPT—**different - meaning**.)

semen: n. whitish fluid ejaculated from the male genital tract. *It is the male's semen that fertilizes the female's egg.*

SIGN: Fingerspell **SEMEN**.

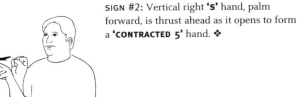

S E M E N

semester: n. a division of an academic year. *There are a variety of interesting courses offered this semester.*

SIGN: Vertical right **'S'** hand, palm facing forward at a leftward angle, is moved rightward, and then as the wrist bends, the hand drops to a palm-down position.

semi-: prefix half. *The choir formed a semi-circle on the stage.*

SIGN: Vertical **'4'** hands are held fairly close together with palms forward but angled toward each other slightly. The wrists then rotate outward to curve the hands forward so that the palms are directly facing each other. (Signs vary according to the concept that follows **semi-**.)

semicolon: n. a punctuation mark indicating a pause greater than that indicated by a comma but not as great as that of a period. *A semicolon is sometimes used to separate two related statements.*

SIGN: Wrist of vertical right **'CLOSED X'** hand, palm forward, bends to thrust the hand forward in a pecking manner as it simulates the making of first a dot, then a comma below the dot.

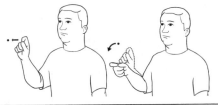

senate: n. the upper chamber of a legislature. *Many Canadians would prefer an elected rather than an appointed Senate.*

SIGN: Vertical right **'S'** hand, palm left, is placed first on the left side of the chest, below the shoulder, and is then transferred to the right side.

send: v. to cause something or someone to be taken or dispatched to another place. *I will send you a copy of the letter.*

SIGN #1: Fingertips of horizontal right **'BENT EXTENDED B'** hand are placed on the back of the left **'STANDARD BASE'** hand. The right hand then moves forward as the fingers straighten to form an **'EXTENDED B'** hand. ❖

OR

SIGN #2: Vertical right **'S'** hand, palm forward, is thrust ahead as it opens to form a **'CONTRACTED 5'** hand. ❖

senile: *adj.* mental deterioration due to old age. *When people get older, they sometimes become senile.*

SIGN: Tip of forefinger of right **'CROOKED ONE'** hand, palm toward the head, is tapped against right side of forehead. Next **'EXTENDED A'** hands are held parallel at about shoulder level with palms facing each other. Then they are lowered simultaneously to waist level. (ASL CONCEPT—**brain - go down**.) (**SENILE** may be fingerspelled.) SAME SIGN—**senility**, *n.*

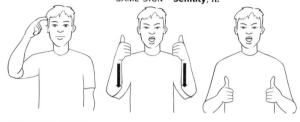

senior: *adj.* older in years. *She is five years my senior.*

SIGN #1: Right **'CROOKED 5'** hand is held at the chin with palm down. The hand then moves upward/rightward as the fingers close to form an **'S'** shape with palm facing leftward/downward. (ASL users tend to give the actual ages of the two people for further clarification.)

senior [*more frequently abbreviated* **Sr.**]: *adj.* the older of two people, usually a father as distinguished from his son. *Frank Smith Sr. works for a law firm downtown.*

SIGN #2: Fingerspell **SR**.

senior: *adj.* designating the last year of study at Gallaudet University. (This sign is not used to mean the senior year at any other university or high school in Canada—only at Gallaudet or American high schools.) *Nancy is in her senior year at Gallaudet University.*

SIGN #3: Horizontal left **'5'** hand is held stationary with palm rightward but angled slightly toward the body and fingers pointing forward/rightward. Right **'5'** hand, with palm down and fingers pointing forward/leftward, is used to tap several times on the thumbtip of the left hand.

senior citizens: *n.* people who are 65 years of age or older. *Senior citizens are given discounts in some stores and restaurants.*

SIGN: Right **'S'** hand, slightly open, palm facing left, is brought down firmly from the chin as it closes. Next, vertical **'K'** hands are held apart with palms forward but facing each other slightly, and are alternately circled backward. (ASL CONCEPT—**old - people**.) Signs vary. If just one senior citizen is being referred to, **old** alone is used.

seniority: *n.* precedence in rank due to holding senior status. *The company will lay off a few people but employees with seniority should be safe.*

SIGN: Horizontal left **'S'** hand is held in a stationary position with palm facing rightward/backward while the right **'S'** hand is held palm down above the left hand. The right wrist then twists so that the palm faces the chest as the fist is set down firmly on the left hand. Motion is repeated. (The sample sentence in ASL is: *COMPANY LAY OFF FEW PEOPLE WILL BUT WHO **YEAR YEAR** SAFE SHOULD*.)

sensation: *n.* a general feeling. *I have not experienced this sensation before.*

SIGN: Tip of middle finger of right **'BENT MIDFINGER 5'** hand, palm toward the body, is brushed upward and off the chest at least twice as the hand makes small circular-like movements in a clockwise direction.

sensational: *adj.* spectacular. *It is a sensational movie.*

SIGN: Fingertips of right **'BENT EXTENDED B'** hand are placed on the lips so that the palm is toward the body. Then the hand is moved purposefully forward a brief distance. Facial expression is important.

sense: *v.* to have a feeling. *I sense that you disapprove of my plans.*

SIGN #1: Tip of middle finger of right **'BENT MIDFINGER 5'** hand, palm toward the body, is brushed upward and off the chest at least twice as the hand makes small circular-like movements in a clockwise direction.

(have) sense: *v.* to have intelligence or good practical judgment. *The child had enough sense to avoid danger.*

SIGN #2: Fingertips of right **'EXTENDED B'** (or **'BENT EXTENDED B'**) hand, with palm facing body, are tapped against right side of forehead a couple of times.

sense: *n.* a faculty by which a person or animal receives information, *e.g.,* taste, smell, hearing, sight and touch. *Which sense is most important to someone who is Deaf?*

SIGN #3: Fingerspell **SENSE**. (In contexts where it is understood which sense is being referred to, it is not necessary to sign or fingerspell **SENSE** as in: *Vision is a sense which is very important to a Deaf person.*)

S   E   N   S   E

sense: *n.* a way of thinking; a specific meaning. *In what sense is it difficult?*

SIGN #4: Horizontal left **'EXTENDED B'** hand is held in a fixed position with palm facing right while tip of forefinger of right palm-down **'BENT V'** hand is jabbed into the left palm. The right hand then moves away from the left hand as the right wrist rotates a quarter turn clockwise, and the middle fingertip is jabbed into the left palm. (The sample sentence in ASL is: *HARD...MEAN (accompanied by a questioning look)?*)

sense of humour: *n.* an appreciation of or ability to express things which are funny. *He has a bizarre sense of humour.*

SIGN #5: The two extended fingers of the right **'BENT EXTENDED U'** hand, palm toward the face, stroke the nose at least twice in a downward motion.

sensible: *adj.* showing good sense or judgment. *It is sensible to dress warmly in sub-zero weather.*

SIGN: Left **'ONE'** hand, palm facing left, is held above left **'ONE'** hand, palm facing right, with forefingers pointing forward. Then right hand is tapped at least twice on left hand.

sensitive: *adj.* easily irritated. *My skin is sensitive to the hot sun.*

SIGN #1: Right **'BENT MIDFINGER 5'** hand is positioned so the midfinger touches the chest and the palm faces the body. The wrist then rotates in a counter-clockwise direction so that the hand moves forward and the palm faces forward/leftward. (Sign choice depends on context.)
SAME SIGN—**sensitivity**, *n.,* in this context.

sensitive: *adj.* easily offended. *She is a sensitive child.*

SIGN #2: Right **'BENT MIDFINGER 5'** hand is positioned so the midfinger touches the chest and the palm faces the body. The wrist then rotates in a counter-clockwise direction so that the hand moves forward and the palm faces forward/leftward.
SAME SIGN—**sensitivity**, *n.,* in this context.

sensitive: *adj.* touchy. *This is a very sensitive issue.*

SIGN #3: **'OPEN 8'** hands are held parallel with palms up as tips of middle fingers and thumbs tap together several times to form '8' shapes.
SAME SIGN—**sensitivity**, *n.,* in this context.

sentence: *n.* a group of words used to express a complete thought. *A sentence begins with a capital letter and usually ends with a period.*

SIGN #1: Joined fingertips of horizontal **'F'** hands, palms facing each other, are placed together. The hands are then drawn apart as the wrists rotate inward to turn the palms down.

sentence: *n.* the punishment assigned to a convicted person in a court of law. *He was given a 25-year sentence for his crimes.*

SIGN #2: Forefinger of right **'ONE'** hand, palm down, is used to strike downward across the bent elbow of the left arm.

separate: *v.* to part or become parted; divide. *My parents decided to **separate** when I was ten years old.*

SIGN: Horizontal **'BENT EXTENDED B'** hands, palms facing chest and knuckles almost touching each other, are drawn apart.

SAME SIGN—**separation**, *n.*, in this context. Signs vary depending on the context.

sequel: *n.* anything that follows from something else. *This novel was so good that I hope the author will write a **sequel**.*

SIGN: Horizontal right **'V'** hand, palm facing left and extended fingers pointing forward/upward, wobbles slightly. (This sign always appears *last* in the ASL sentence.)

sequence: *n.* the successive order of several items or things. *The biography is a chronological **sequence** of the main events in his life.*

SIGN: Horizontal right **'DOUBLE MODIFIED G'** hand, palm facing left, is held in front of the left side of the body and alternates between a **'DOUBLE MODIFIED G'** and a **'CLOSED DOUBLE MODIFIED G'** a few times as it moves rightward. Signs vary according to context.
SAME SIGN—**sequential**, *adj.*

sequester: *v.* to retire into seclusion. *The jury was **sequestered** for twelve hours before they reached a verdict.*

SIGN: Horizontal **'C'** hands are held quite far apart with palms facing. They are then brought firmly together so that the right hand fits into the left. Next, right **'A'** hand is brought to the lips with the thumb pointed upward and the palm facing left. Then the lips are touched twice with the thumbnail. Finally, forefinger of horizontal right **'ONE'** hand, palm toward the body, is tapped several times on the upturned palm of the left **'EXTENDED B'** hand, of which the fingers are pointing rightward/forward. (ASL CONCEPT—**get together - private - discuss**.)

sequins: *n.* small pieces of glittery, colourful metal used to decorate garments. *Country singers often wear costumes covered with **sequins**.*

SIGN: Vertical **'O'** hands are held close to the upper chest with palms facing each other and are simultaneously moved downward as the fingers flutter to simulate the sparkling effect of sequins. (The location of this sign may vary and sometimes only one hand is used depending on where the sequins are situated.)

serene: *adj.* calm and peaceful. *At dawn, the lake looks **serene** before it is taken over by boaters.*

SIGN: **'EXTENDED B'** hands are crossed in front of the chest, left palm facing rightward/downward and right palm facing leftward/downward with the right hand just behind the left hand. Then they are very slowly drawn apart until the palms face completely downward.
SAME SIGN—**serenity**, *n.*

sergeant: *n.* a noncommissioned officer in military service. *He is a **sergeant** in the army.*

SIGN #1: Fingertips of horizontal right **'4'** hand, palm facing backward, are placed on the upper left arm and used to outline a **'V'** from left to right, representing a sergeant's three stripes.

sergeant: *n.* an officer holding a certain rank in police administration. *He is a **sergeant** in the RCMP.*

SIGN #2: Horizontal right **'EXTENDED A'** hand, palm facing the body at a slight leftward angle, is raised purposefully upward to a level above the right shoulder.

serial killer: *n.* someone who kills several times. *The police were looking for him because they suspected that he was a **serial killer**.*

SIGN: Vertical left **'EXTENDED B'** hand is held in a fixed position in front of the left side of the body with palm facing rightward and slightly forward. Right **'ONE'** (or **'K'**) hand is held palm down as it moves forward/downward at a slight leftward angle, the forefinger firmly grazing the left palm. As the hands move rightward this sign is repeated a couple of times.

serial number: *n.* a number assigned to a vehicle, tool, machine, etc., for the purpose of identification. *The serial number of your vehicle appears on your registration certificate.*

SIGN: **'MODIFIED O'** hands are positioned so that the bunched fingertips of each hand are touching those of the other hand. Initially, left palm faces upward but is angled slightly toward the body while right palm faces downward but is angled forward slightly. Fingertips maintain contact as the hands then twist, thus reversing the palm orientations.

series: *n.* a succession of related things arranged in order. *I have had a series of accidents lately.*

SIGN #1: Horizontal **'ONE'** hands are held apart in front of the left side of the body with palms facing each other and forefingers pointing forward. The hands wobble as they are simultaneously moved rightward. (Signs vary considerably depending on the context. When it refers to a well known succession of games like the World Series, **SERIES** is always fingerspelled.)

series: *n.* a succession of programs shown at regular intervals. *This has been a very successful television series.*

NOTE—ASL users convey the concept of **series** by specifying the actual day on which the television program is regularly seen. See **every Monday**, **every Tuesday**, etc., in TIME CONCEPTS, p. LXIX–LXX. The sample sentence in ASL is: *(First specify name of program...)* *EVERY MONDAY SUCCESSFUL.*

series: *n.* a succession of literary works. *I am reading an interesting mystery series just now.*

SIGN #3: Left **'CONTRACTED C'** (or **'OPEN 8'**) hand is held horizontally with palm facing right while right **'CONTRACTED C'** (or **'OPEN 8'**) hand is held upright with palm facing left. The hands are held close enough together to be loosely interlocked. They are then drawn apart, closed and returned several times, thus alternating between **'CONTRACTED C'** (or **'OPEN 8'**) and **'FLAT O'** (or **'8'**) shapes with each movement. Next, **'ONE'** hands are held in front of the left side of the body with forefingers crossed and palms basically facing downward. The hands are then turned outward so that they become vertical with palms facing forward. The sign is repeated a couple of times as the hands move rightward. (ASL CONCEPT— **story - different different different**.)

serious: *adj.* solemn or grave in nature. *This is a serious problem.*

SIGN #1: Vertical right **'BENT ONE'** hand is held with tip of forefinger touching chin and palm facing leftward but slanted toward the body. The wrist then rotates, turning the hand so that the palm fully faces the body.

OR

SIGN #2: Vertical right **'B'** hand, palm facing left, is held directly in front of the face and thrust forward and slightly downward.

SIGN #3 [ONTARIO]: Right **'Y'** hand, palm downward, is positioned so that the thumbtip is touching the left side of the chin. The hand moves rightward as the thumbtip slides across the chin. The hand is then curved downward/ rightward away from the body as the wrist rotates slightly in a counter-clockwise direction.

sermon: *n.* a serious speech or one that gives religious instruction. *Today's sermon will be based on the Golden Rule.*

SIGN: Right arm is raised and the vertical **'EXTENDED B'** hand, palm facing left, is brought forward sharply from the wrist a couple of times.

ALTERNATE SIGN—**preach**

servant: *n.* a person employed to perform duties for another. *He has servants to do household tasks for him.*

SIGN #1: Horizontal **'EXTENDED B'** hands are held apart at about shoulder level with palms up and fingers pointing outward, and are alternately moved from side to side. (Agent Ending (see p. LIV) may follow.)

(civil *or* **public) servant:** *n.* a person employed by the government to perform duties for the public. *As a park ranger for Parks Canada he is a civil servant.*

SIGN #2: Wrist of right **'A'** (or **'S'**) hand, palm facing away from the body, strikes wrist of the left **'A'** (or **'S'**) hand, which is held in front of/below the right hand with palm facing downward. Motion is repeated. Finally, vertical right **'ONE'** hand is held near the right side of the forehead with palm forward and slightly leftward. The wrist then rotates forward to turn the hand as the forefinger tucks into a **'BENT ONE'** position with the fingertip coming to rest on the right side of the forehead. (ASL CONCEPT—**work - government**.)

serve: *v.* to render services; do work for; help. *People who serve royalty must follow certain protocol.*

SIGN #1: Horizontal **'EXTENDED B'** hands are held apart at about shoulder level with palms up and fingers pointing outward, and are alternately moved from side to side. (Sign choice depends on context.)

serve: *v.* to be enough for. *This recipe will serve eight people.*

SIGN #2: Horizontal right **'EXTENDED B'** hand is held palm down with fingers pointing forward/leftward and is brushed forward/rightward across the top of the left hand. Motion is repeated.

serve: *v.* to go through a period of imprisonment as ordered by a court of law. *The prisoner was sentenced to serve 15 years in the Kingston Penitentiary.*

SIGN #3: **'4'** (or **'5'**) hands are held with palms facing the body. Back of right hand, whose fingers point slightly upward to the left, is positioned behind palm of left hand at right angles, and is thrust against it. (The sample sentence in ASL is: *HE...JAIL 15 YEAR KINGSTON.*)

serve: *v.* to put the ball into play in tennis, volleyball, squash, etc. *It is your turn to serve the ball.*

SIGN #4: Horizontal **'EXTENDED B'** hands are held slightly apart at chest level with fingers pointing forward and palms facing upward but angled toward each other slightly. The hands are alternately moved forward and back a few times. (Alternatively, natural gestures may be used, varying according to which sport is being played.)

(it) serves (someone) right: *s.s.* It is something that is deserved or one's own fault. *It serves you right that your friends have abandoned you.*

SIGN #1: Left **'A'** hand is held in a fixed position with palm down. Horizontal right **'EXTENDED A'** hand, with palm facing left, is brought down firmly and decisively onto the back of the left hand and is then thrust forward in a slight arc toward the person being blamed. Facial expression is important. ❖

OR

SIGN #2: Vertical **'BENT EXTENDED B'** hands are positioned so that the right hand is held close to the chest with palm facing forward/leftward while the left hand is held to the left and farther forward with the palm facing that of the right hand. The fingertips of one hand make contact with those of the other as the hands are tapped together emphatically. (Facial expression is important.)

service: *n.* work done for guests or customers. *The restaurant is noted for its excellent service.*

SIGN #1: Horizontal **'EXTENDED B'** hands are held apart at about shoulder level with palms up and fingers pointing outward, and are alternately moved from side to side.

service: *n.* duty in one of the branches of the armed forces. *His years of service in the military will make him eligible for a veteran's pension.*

SIGN #2: Joined thumb and midfinger of right **'D'** hand are tapped down on the back of the left **'STANDARD BASE'** hand at least twice.

service: *n.* a ceremony, especially of a religious nature. *Funeral services will be held tomorrow at 2:00 p.m.*

SIGN #3: There is no direct ASL translation for **service** in this context. The concept is incorporated in the sign for the adjective which specifies the type of service. In the sample sentence, 'funeral service' is translated into ASL using the sign for **funeral** only.

service: *v.* to maintain equipment and machinery. *A local mechanic will service my car.*

SIGN #4: **'F'** hands, palms facing each other at a forward angle, are placed together with tips of thumbs and forefingers of each hand touching. The left hand remains steady while the right hand wobbles as the wrist twists back and forth slightly a few times.

ALTERNATE SIGN—**fix** #3

(be of) service: *v.* to assist; help. *May I be of service to you?*

SIGN #5: Horizontal left **'A'** (or **'EXTENDED A'**) hand, palm facing the body but turned slightly rightward, rests on the upturned palm of the right **'EXTENDED B'** hand. Both hands are moved forward in one motion toward the person receiving help. ❖

service station: *n.* a place that supplies fuel, oil, and service for motor vehicles. *I stopped at the service station on my way home.*

SIGN: Left **'S'** hand is held, not in a tight fist but loosely, with palm down but slanted slightly rightward. Right **'EXTENDED A'** hand, palm down but slanted rightward as well, is positioned above and to the right of the left hand. The right hand then moves downward/leftward so that the extended thumb is inserted into the opening at the top of the left hand. The motion is repeated.

serviette: *n.* a square of cloth or paper used to wipe the mouth while eating; napkin. *Do not forget to bring serviettes to the picnic.*

SIGN: Right **'EXTENDED B'** hand, palm toward the body and fingertips in front of the mouth, is circled in what appears to the signer to be a counter-clockwise direction.

session: *n.* a meeting. *We attended the morning session of the conference.*

SIGN: **'CONTRACTED 5'** hands are held virtually upright at a slight forward angle with palms facing each other. The fingers then come together to form **'FLAT O'** hands with fingertips of each hand touching those of the other. (Sign choice depends on context.)

set: *n.* the scenery and props used on stage for a play. *They built an elaborate set for their production of* Romeo and Juliet.

SIGN #1: Fingerspell SET. (ASL users would then specify what type of set it was, *e.g.*, a bedroom, living room, balcony, etc.)

S   E   T

set: *v.* to put or place. *You can set your things on this chair.*

SIGN #2: **'FLAT O'** hands are held parallel with palms relatively downward and are moved forward in arc formation. (This sign is frequently made with the right hand only. Signs vary considerably depending on the size and shape of the object and the manner in which it is being put somewhere.)

set: *v.* to turn into a firm or rigid state. *Do not walk on the new sidewalk until the cement has set firmly.*

SIGN #3: **'CROOKED 5'** hands are held parallel with palms down. They then jerk slightly forward/downward as the fingers retract to form **'CLAWED SPREAD C'** hands.

set: *v.* to prepare. *The professor will set an exam based on the novel we were asked to read.*

SIGN #4: Horizontal **'EXTENDED B'** hands, palms facing each other and fingers pointing forward, are held slightly apart at the left side of the body and are moved simultaneously toward the right.

set: *v.* to establish. *They set a date for their wedding.*

SIGN #5: **'F'** hands, with palms facing each other, are held apart in front of chest and are simultaneously lowered.

set aside: *v.* to put aside for the moment. *Please set aside your work for now.*

SIGN #1: Horizonal **'EXTENDED B'** hands are held right on top of left with palms facing rightward and fingers pointing forward. They are then simultaneously moved rightward as if pushing something out of the way.

set aside: *v.* to reserve for later or hold for a specific purpose. *They set aside enough money for a trip to Europe.*

SIGN #2: Vertical **'FLAT O'** hands, palms forward, are held side by side. The left remains stationary while the right is moved rightward in a slight downward arc formation. (This sign refers to the setting aside of *money* specifically.)

set fire to: *v.* to ignite either purposely or by accident. *The arsonist set fire to the house hoping to get money from the insurance company.*

SIGN: Left **'EXTENDED B'** hand is held in a fixed position with palm right and fingers pointing forward/upward. Right **'COVERED T'** hand, palm down, is held with forefinger against left palm. The right wrist then rotates clockwise as the forefinger resembles a match being struck against the left palm. The palm of the right hand eventually faces the body as the right hand moves away from the left.

set free: *v.* to allow to leave freely. *They decided the prisoner was innocent so they set him free.*

SIGN: **'CROOKED 5'** hands are held parallel with palms toward the body and fingers pointing downward. The hands are then flipped up so that the palms face downward. This is a wrist action.

ALTERNATE SIGN—**release** #1

set in one's ways: *adj.* inflexible and determined; not easily changed. *My parents are so set in their ways they refuse to accept modern standards.*

SIGN: Vertical right **'S'** hand, palm facing leftward/downward, is held with wrist against back of left **'S'** hand, which is held with palm down. Together, the hands are lowered slowly and emphatically.

set of objects: *n.* a number of objects grouped together that all have the same features or characteristics. *We gave our father a new set of golf clubs for his birthday.*

SIGN: Sign choice varies depending on what objects constitute the 'set'. Frequently, a sign for the specific object is used followed by a sign to indicate how the objects are contained or positioned within the set, or vice versa. For 'a set of golf clubs', **golf bag** is used first and then **golf** itself.

set out: *v.* to leave on a trip or journey. *We plan to set out at 5 a.m. on a fishing trip.*

SIGN: **'EXTENDED B'** hands are held parallel with palms down and fingers pointing forward/rightward. The hands are then drawn simultaneously leftward/backward as they change to **'A'** (or **'EXTENDED A'**) hands.

set the table: *v.* to put dishes, cutlery, glassware and serviettes on a table in readiness for a meal. *Please set the table with the best china and silverware as we are having guests.*

SIGN: **'FLAT O'** hands are held apart with palms either downward or facing each other at a forward angle, and are then simultaneously moved outward and forward in arc formation.

set up: *v.* to establish, organize, or arrange. *We will set up a display about Deaf Culture.*

SIGN: Right **'EXTENDED A'** hand is held palm down over left **'STANDARD BASE'** hand, then twisted so that it comes to rest on the back of the left hand with thumb pointing upward and palm facing leftward but slanted toward the body.

setback: *n.* anything that hinders or interferes. *Her husband's illness was a serious setback in their plans for the future.*

SIGN: Left **'EXTENDED B'** hand is held, palm down, in a fixed position. Right **'ONE'** hand, palm forward, is brought up underneath the left hand and the extended forefinger is thrust upward between the forefinger and middle finger of the left hand. Next, left **'CROOKED 5'** hand is held palm-up with fingers pointing forward while right **'CROOKED 5'** hand is held apart and slightly higher with palm down and fingers pointing forward. The arms are then simultaneously moved upward/rightward as the hands are purposefully twisted rightward from the wrist so that the left palm faces right and the right palm faces left. Signs vary according to context. (ASL CONCEPT—**pop up - unrest**.)

setting: *n.* the surroundings in which something is set or happens. *This is a beautiful setting for wedding photos.*

SIGN: Horizontal right **'5'** hand is held with palm down and fingers pointing forward. The hand then makes a wide arc leftward as it inscribes a circle in front of the body. (Signs vary depending on the context. Sometimes **place** is used or **time** or both.)

setting of the sun: *n.* the disappearance of the sun beneath the horizon. *The setting of the sun on the prairies is a beautiful sight.*

SIGN: Left **'STANDARD BASE'** hand is held in a fixed position while the right vertical **'C'** (or **'O'** or **'F'**) hand, palm facing left, is held in front of it and is slowly lowered out of sight.

settle: *v.* to come to a satisfactory solution (to a problem or disagreement). *They decided to settle the dispute without legal intervention.*

SIGN #1: **'FLAT O'** hands are held parallel with palms up and slanted slightly toward the body. As the hands are drawn apart the thumbs slide across the fingertips, causing the hands to assume **'A'** shapes.

settle: *v.* to stop moving and stay in a certain place. *They will settle in Zaire as medical missionaries.*

SIGN #2: **'EXTENDED B'** hands are held with palms downward/forward at a leftward angle and fingers pointing forward/leftward, the left hand a little ahead of/to the left of the right. The hands are then simultaneously lowered to a palms down position.

settle: *v.* to cause to become quiet and orderly. *They usually watch TV after they settle the children for the night.*

SIGN #3: **'EXTENDED B'** hands are held parallel at about shoulder level with palms down and fingers pointing forward. The hands are then simultaneously lowered.

settle down: *v.* to make someone calm. *The teacher asked the excited students to settle down.*

SIGN #4: **'EXTENDED B'** hands are held parallel with palms down and fingers pointing forward. The forearms are then simultaneously moved slowly and deliberately down and up a couple of times.

settle for: *v.* to accept; agree to. *If we can not have a salary raise, we will settle for two extra days off every year.*

SIGN #5: Both **'CONTRACTED 5'** hands, palms down, are brought toward the chest while they are being closed to form **'FLAT O'** hands, with fingertips touching the body. ALTERNATE SIGNS—**mind** #4 & **fine** #1

settlement: *n.* an agreement reached in matters of finance, employment, business, etc. *The company agreed to a $1,000,000 settlement for wrongful dismissal.*

SIGN #1: Left **'ONE'** hand is held at chest level with palm facing right, and forefinger pointing forward. Right **'ONE'** hand is held slightly higher with palm facing left, and is then turned downward to match the simultaneously downward turning left hand.

settlement: *n.* the colonization or establishment of a new region. *Many European immigrants came to the prairie settlements between 1900 and 1920.*

SIGN #2: Right **'EXTENDED A'** hand is held palm down over left **'STANDARD BASE'** hand in front of the left side of the body, then twisted so that it comes to rest on the back of the left hand with thumb pointing upward and palm facing leftward but slanted toward the body. This sign is repeated a few times as the hands move rightward in a slight forward arc formation.

seven: *n.* See NUMBERS, p. LX.

seventeen: *n.* See NUMBERS, p. LXI.

seventy: *n.* See NUMBERS, p. LXII.

sever: *v.* to break off, divide or separate. *During the Cold War, the U.S.A. decided to sever diplomatic relations with Cuba.*

SIGN: Thumbs and forefingers of **'F'** hands, palms facing each other, are interlocked. The hands are then drawn apart to form **'OPEN F'** hands. (Signs vary according to context.)

several: *adj.* more than a few. *I took several people on a tour of the buildings.*

SIGN: Right **'A'** hand, palm up, is moved slightly forward/rightward as each fingertip gradually slides forward off the thumbtip to create a **'4'** hand.

severe: *adj.* serious, critical, or dangerous. *An earthquake is a severe ground tremor.*

SIGN: Right **'COVERED 8'** hand, palm facing left, is held upright at about shoulder level. The hand is then thrust backward as the middle finger and thumb flick apart to form a **'MODIFIED 5'** hand. (Signs vary according to context.)

sew: *v.* to join or fasten by hand stitching. *He learned how to sew a button on his shirt.*

SIGN #1: Horizontal **'F'** hands are held slightly apart with palms facing each other. The left hand remains in a fixed position as the right hand is rotated clockwise at least twice so that the thumb and forefinger make contact with those of the left hand each time they brush past.

sew: *v.* to join, fasten or decorate by machine. *She has special machine attachments which she uses to sew draperies.*

SIGN #2: Horizontal left **'ONE'** hand is held in a fixed position with palm facing rightward and forefinger pointing forward at a slight rightward angle while the right **'CLOSED X'** hand, palm down, is brushed forward along the left forefinger at least twice.

sewer: *n.* an underground system used to carry away surface water and sewage. *During the rainstorm the sewer overflowed.*

SIGN: Fingerspell **SEWER**.

sex: *n.* the characteristics that distinguish organisms as either male or female. *People should not discriminate on the basis of sex.*

SIGN #1: Fingerspell **SEX**. (ASL users will often use **male**, **female**, **girl**, **boy** when they wish to specify.)

sex: *n.* sexual intercourse. *There is lots of sex in that movie.*

SIGN #2: Left **'V'** hand is held with palm up and extended fingers pointing forward at a slight rightward angle while right **'V'** hand is held just above the left hand with palm facing leftward at a downward/forward angle and extended fingers pointing leftward/upward at a slightly forward angle. The hands are brought together a few times so that the heels of the hands repeatedly collide. (**SEX** is frequently fingerspelled.)

sexism: *n.* discrimination on the basis of sex; exploitation of one sex by the other; rigid stereotyping of the sexes. *The military and police forces have strict policies against sexism.*

SIGN: Fingerspell **SEXISM**.

sexy: *adj.* exciting in a sexual way or intended to provoke sexual interest. *She always wears sexy clothes.*

SIGN: Fingerspell **SEXY**.

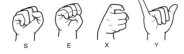

shabby: *adj.* threadbare, dilapidated or worn out. *She always wears shabby clothes.*

SIGN: Thumb and fingertips of right **'CONTRACTED 5'** hand grasp left elbow and close to form a **'FLAT O'** as they slide downward off the elbow. Motion is repeated. REGIONAL VARIATION—**poor** #3

shack: *n.* a crudely built house, cabin or hut. *The house is just an old shack now.*

SIGN: Fingertips of **'EXTENDED B'** hands, palms facing each other, are placed together at an angle in 'tent' fashion. The hands are then drawn apart, straightened to a more vertical posture, and lowered simultaneously. Next, **'EXTENDED A'** hands are held slightly apart in front of the chest with the palms facing each other, and are lowered slowly but simultaneously to waist level. (ASL CONCEPT—**house - not good condition**.) Signs vary depending on context.

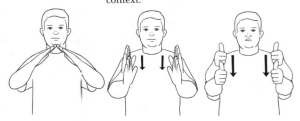

shack up: *v.* to live with one's lover. *When they decided to shack up, a scandal was created because of their notoriety.*

SIGN: Horizontal **'L'** (or **'EXTENDED A'**) hands are held above the waist with palms toward the body and forefingers pointing toward each other. They are then raised to a higher position on the chest. Next, **'A'** hands, palms facing, are simultaneously brought and held together. (ASL CONCEPT—**live - with**.)

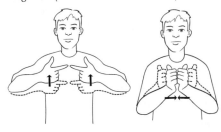

shackle: *v.* to secure a prisoner's wrists (and/or ankles) with metal bands. *They had to shackle the prisoner to prevent his escape.*

SIGN: Right **'C'** hand, palm down, is clamped onto the left wrist, then left **'C'** hand, palm down, is clamped onto the right wrist.

shade: *n.* the degree of darkness of a colour. *I like this shade of blue.*

SIGN #1: Fingerspell **SHADE**. (The concept of **shade** is generally incorporated in the sign for the colour itself rather than fingerspelled. 'A *light shade* of blue' would be indicated in the subtlety with which the sign for **blue** is formed while 'a *dark shade* of blue' is indicated by a more emphatic rendering of the sign for **blue**.)

shade: *n.* an area which is cooler and darker than its surroundings due to being cut off from the sun's rays. *Let us sit in the shade to eat our lunch.*

SIGN #2: Fingerspell **SHADE**. (ASL users usually sign rather than fingerspell this concept but signs vary considerably depending on what/who is in the shade of what, and where everything/everyone is positioned with respect to the sun.)

shade: *n.* a covering used to provide protection from the glare of direct lamplight. *This lamp needs a new shade.*

SIGN #3: **'CROOKED EXTENDED B'** hands, palms downward but facing each other slightly, are held near each other and are drawn slightly apart and down to outline the shape of a lampshade.

(window) shade: *n.* a window blind. *I need a window shade to keep my bedroom dark.*

SIGN #4: Right **'CLOSED X'** hand, with palm facing left, is brought down to simulate motion of lowering a blind.

shades: See **sunglasses**.

shadow: *n.* a dark image cast by something that intercepts light rays. *It is possible to calculate the height of a building by measuring its shadow.*

SIGN: Fingerspell **SHADOW**.

shake: *v.* to move up and down or back and forth with short, quick movements. *Shake this medication well before you take it.*

SIGN #1: Horizontal right **'C'** hand, palm facing left, is shaken up and down. (Signs vary according to the size and shape of the object being shaken and the way in which it is shaken.)

shake: *v.* to clasp hands either in greeting or in agreement. *Leaders often shake hands after signing an international pact or treaty.*

SIGN #2: Horizontal right **'CROOKED EXTENDED B'** hand, palm left, is used to reach forward and is lightly shaken up and down as if shaking hands with someone. ALTERNATE SIGN—**handshake**

shake: *v.* to tremble. *My hands shake when I am nervous.*

SIGN #3: Horizontal **'5'** hands are held parallel with fingers pointing forward and palms facing each other at a downward angle. The hands are then shaken as the wrists rapidly twist back and forth slightly. SAME SIGN—**shaky**, *adj.*

shake: *v.* to vibrate. *The force of the gale made the house shake.*

SIGN #4: The forearms represent opposite walls of a building as vertical **'EXTENDED B'** hands are held apart with palms facing each other. The arms then move from side to side a couple of times. (Signs vary according to context.)

Shakespeare: *n.* a well-known English playwright and poet. *Most high school English programs include the study of a work by Shakespeare.*

SIGN: Vertical right **'S'** hand, palm left, is shaken backward and forward slightly, then flung forward, the fingers opening to create a **'MODIFIED 5'** hand.

shall: *v.* an auxiliary verb that indicates future tense or shows intent or determination. *We shall succeed if we try hard enough.*

SIGN: Right **'EXTENDED B'** hand, palm facing left, is held in a vertical position near the right side of the head. The forearm is then moved forward a short distance so that the fingers eventually point forward/upward.

shallow: *adj.* not deep. *The water is shallow at this end of the pool.*

SIGN: Left **'EXTENDED B'** hand is held at about waist level with palm up and fingers pointing rightward while right **'EXTENDED B'** hand is held not far above the left hand with palm down and fingers pointing leftward/forward.

sham: *n.* something that seems genuine but is false. *After investing in shares they discovered the company was a sham.*

SIGN: Vertical right **'ONE'** hand, palm facing left, is held with forefinger just to the right of the mouth. The wrist bends, causing the forefinger to brush lightly leftward/downward against the lips with the palm eventually facing downward/leftward. (Context must be considered when selecting signs. Sometimes **sham** refers to a *decorative pillow covering*, in which case sign choice depends on what the actual pillow sham looks like.)

shambles: *n.* a place of chaos and disorder. *The teens left the place a shambles after their party.*

SIGN: Left **'CROOKED 5'** hand is held palm-up with fingers pointing forward while right **'CROOKED 5'** hand is held apart and slightly higher with palm down and fingers pointing forward. The arms are then simultaneously moved upward/rightward as the hands are purposefully twisted rightward from the wrist so that the left palm faces right and the right palm faces left.

shame: *n.* a painful feeling of regret or guilt resulting from doing something dishonourable. *She hung her head in shame.*

SIGN: The backs of the fingers of the right **'BENT EXTENDED B'** hand, palm facing right shoulder, are brushed forward against right cheek as palm faces up.
SAME SIGN—**shameful,** *adj.*

shampoo: *n.* a soap preparation used to wash the hair. *This shampoo contains a mild conditioner.*

SIGN: Vertical **'CLAWED 5'** hands are held at either side of the head and simultaneously moved back and forth to simulate the act of shampooing one's hair.

shape: *n.* the outward form or outline of an object. *The children are learning about shapes in math class.*

SIGN #1: First, **'ONE'** hands, palms forward, are used to outline the shapes of a square and a triangle. Next, **'BENT L'** hands are positioned with palms either downward or facing the body, and tips of forefingers touching each other, the right finger pointing leftward as the left finger points rightward. The hands are then moved apart with forefingers fluttering. (ASL CONCEPT—**square - triangle - etc.**) Sign selection is simply based on the actual shape of the object being discussed and the forefingers are generally used in the formation of the sign.

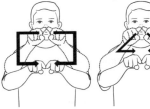

shape: *n.* the human form, especially the *female* body shape. *The clothing designer told her that she had a lovely shape.*

SIGN #2: **'A'** hands, palms facing each other, are held parallel just above shoulder level. Then they are simultaneously curved downward to outline the shape of an hourglass. (If it is a *man's body shape* being referred to, **'EXTENDED B'** hands are used to outline his body build.)

(in good) shape: *adj.* in good condition (as used in reference to inanimate *objects*.) *Your car is in good shape.*

SIGN #3: Fingertips of right **'BENT EXTENDED B'** hand are placed on the lips so that the palm is toward the body. Then the hand is moved purposefully forward a brief distance. (If you wish to describe something as being **in bad shape**, use **bad** #1 or **lousy**.)

(in good) shape: *adj.* in good condition (as used in reference to a *person's physical fitness* level). *He runs ten km. every morning so he should be in good shape.*

SIGN #4: Horizontal **'S'** hands are very firmly thrust into place in front of the chest with palms facing backward.

share: *v.* to divide equally. *We usually share the cost of our trips.*

SIGN: Right **'EXTENDED B'** hand, with palm facing left and fingers pointing forward, slides from side to side a few times along forefinger of horizontally held left **'EXTENDED B'** hand, whose palm is facing the body. As the right hand slides back and forth, the wrist rotates back and forth to slant the hand slightly with each twist.

shares: *n.* equal parts of a company's capital stock. *We decided to buy a few shares in that company.*

SIGN: Fingerspell **SHARES**.

sharp: *adj.* having a keen edge or point. *You will need a sharp knife to cut the meat.*

SIGN #1: Right **'BENT MIDFINGER 5'** hand is held with palm toward the body and tip of middle finger on the chin. The wrist is then rotated to turn the hand so that the palm faces leftward/forward. The eyes squint slightly. (Sign choice depends on context.)

sharp: *adj.* a colloquial expression meaning having a nice or smart appearance. *Your new suit looks really sharp.*

SIGN #2: Horizontal **'EXTENDED B'** hands are held, right on top of left, left palm facing upward and right palm facing downward, the fingers pointing basically forward. Together, the hands appear to jerk backward a short distance although the hands do not move any real distance at all. This is a twitchlike movement.

SIGN #3 [ONTARIO]: Right **'CROOKED EXTENDED B'** hand is held with side of forefinger against right side of chin and palm facing forward/leftward. The hand then curves downward and off the chin, the palm eventually facing downward. Facial expression is important.

sharp: *adj.* clever; quick-witted. *She has a very sharp mind.*

SIGN #4: Tip of middle finger of vertical right **'BENT MIDFINGER 5'** hand, palm toward the face, touches the forehead. Then the wrist is rotated so that the palm faces away from the body.

sharp: *adj.* chic and in fashionable good taste. *You look very sharp today.*

SIGN #5: Horizontal **'EXTENDED B'** hands are held, right on top of left, left palm facing upward and right palm facing downward, the fingers pointing basically forward. Together, the hands appear to jerk backward a short distance although the hands do not move any real distance at all. This is a twitchlike movement.

sharp: *adv.* exactly; precisely. *Please be there at 6 o'clock sharp.*

SIGN #6: Right **'CROOKED ONE'** (or **'X'**) hand is brought down sharply so the tip of the forefinger touches the wrist of the left **'STANDARD BASE'** hand ever so briefly (as if touching the face of a wristwatch) before the hand is raised again.

OR

SIGN #7: **'CLOSED X'** hands are held, right above left, with palms facing. The hands are then brought together sharply so that the joined thumbs and forefingers touch. Alternatively, the right hand sometimes moves in a small clockwise circle before making contact with the left hand.

sharp curve: *n.* a very sudden change in direction. *There was a sharp curve in the road.*

SIGN: Vertical right, slightly bent **'EXTENDED B'** hand, palm left, is moved forward and then sharply leftward as the wrist rotates to turn the palm to face the body. (In this particular context, the direction is leftward, but signs will vary according to the direction implied in the context.)

shatter: *v.* to break into many small pieces. *The force of the explosion was strong enough to shatter all the windows in the building.*

SIGN: **'S'** hands are placed side by side, palms down. Then they are wrenched apart so that palms face one another. Next, **'MODIFIED O'** hands are held side by side with palms down. The hands then move apart and downward as the fingers flutter. (ASL CONCEPT—**break - fall in little pieces**.)

shave: *v.* to remove hair with a razor. *He plans to shave off his beard.*

SIGN: Side of crooked forefinger of right **'x'** (or **'CLAWED V'**) hand, palm forward, is used to scrape downward against the right cheek. Alternatively, a **'MODIFIED Y'** hand may be used with the tip of the thumbnail scraping down against the cheek. (The location of this sign varies according to which part of the body is being shaved.)

she: *pron.* referring to a female previously named or whose identity is clear. [See PRONOUNS, p. LXIV.] *She is well-known in the Deaf Community.*

SIGN: Horizontal right **'BENT ONE'** hand is held with palm facing forward/rightward as the forefinger points at the person or animal being referred to.
SAME SIGN—**her,** *obj. pron.*

shears: *n.* a large pair of scissors. *I need to borrow your shears to cut the material.*

SIGN #1: Extended fingers of horizontal right **'V'** hand, palm leftward/backward, are closed and opened at least twice, the handshapes thus alternating between **'V'** and **'U'** to simulate the action of cutting with scissors.

shears: *n.* a large scissor-like, hand-held tool used for pruning hedges, trimming grass, etc. *You will need sturdy shears to trim the lilacs.*

SIGN #2: Horizontal **'S'** hands, palms facing upward but slanted toward each other slightly, are held a short distance apart as if holding a pair of shears and are simultaneously moved in and out to simulate the action of pruning.

shed: *n.* a small building of light construction used for storage or shelter. *The lawnmower is in the garden shed.*

SIGN #1: Fingerspell **SHED.**

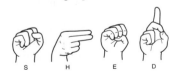

shed: *v.* to lose hair. *Some breeds of dogs shed almost continuously.*

SIGN #2: Horizontal **'V'** hands, palms facing the body, are held at either side of the chest and alternately move forward, the wrist rotating forward slightly, and then back so that the tips of the extended fingers make contact with the chest. Movement is repeated a few times. (The location of this sign varies according to context.)

642

sheep: *n.* a mammal usually raised for its wool. *They raise sheep on their ranch.*

SIGN: Right **'K'** hand, palm facing the body, is held in the crook of the left arm and circled twice in a clockwise direction.

sheer: *adj.* very thin so as to be transparent. *She wore a sheer black blouse.*

SIGN #1: **'A'** hands, palms down, are held slightly apart, and are then firmly pushed a very short distance downward. Next, vertical right **'K'** hand, palm toward the face, is held with the tip of the middle finger touching the right cheekbone. The hand is then thrust forward at a rightward/downward angle. Finally, vertical left **'5'** hand is held with palm facing the body as the horizontal right **'EXTENDED B'** hand with palm facing left is thrust forward between the forefinger and middle finger of the left hand. (ASL CONCEPT—**can - see - through.**) The sample sentence in ASL is: *HER BLOUSE BLACK CAN SEE THROUGH.*

sheer: *adj.* absolute; complete; pure. *That accusation is sheer nonsense.*

SIGN #2: Forefinger of vertical right **'ONE'** hand, palm facing left, is held against the lips and the hand is moved sharply forward. (For emphasis, the hand is very gradually moved upward and forward, eventually assuming a horizontal position.)

sheer: *adj.* very steep; almost perpendicular. *I get dizzy when I look down the sheer face of this mountain.*

SIGN #3: Right **'B'** hand, palm down but slanted toward the body slightly and fingers pointing downward and very slightly forward, moves almost straight downward to indicate steepness.

sheet: *n.* a large, rectangular piece of cloth used as part of a bed covering. *I need a new sheet for my bed.*

SIGN #1: Fingerspell **SHEET.**

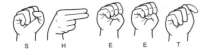

sheet of paper: *n.* a piece of paper. *I need a sheet of paper to write a letter.*

SIGN #2: Horizontal **'CROOKED 5'** hands, right palm down and left palm up, are positioned so that the right hand is slightly above the left. Then the right hand moves leftward/backward and the left hand moves rightward as the heels of each hand strike against each other at least twice. (Various signs are used for **sheet of ice**, **sheet of glass**, etc.)

shelf: *n.* a horizontal board on a wall or in a cabinet used to store or display things. *The keys are on the shelf.*

SIGN: **'B'** (or **'BENT B'** or **'EXTENDED B'** or **'BENT EXTENDED B'**) hands, positioned side by side, palms down, with fingers pointing forward, are moved apart in a straight line. To indicate that there are a number of shelves, the motion is repeated once or twice, each time at a lower position.

shell: *n.* a protective outer covering (of eggs, mollusks, turtles, nuts, etc.) *A robin's egg has a blue shell.*

SIGN #1: Fingerspell **SHELL**.

shell: *n.* a hollow tube containing explosive material shot from a gun. *The hunter had only one shell left.*

SIGN #2: Tips of forefinger and thumb of right **'A-INDEX'** hand, are brushed downward/forward at least twice against end of forefinger of left **'ONE'** hand, which is held with palm facing right and finger pointing forward/upward.

shelter: *n.* something that covers or protects. *We tried to find shelter from the storm.*

SIGN #1: Right **'CLAWED V'** hand, palm down, represents a person huddled under a protective covering represented by the left **'STANDARD BASE'** hand. (Signs vary depending on the context.)

shelter: *v.* to protect. *We will shelter the children from danger.*

SIGN #2: Horizontal **'S'** hands are held, the left just in front of the right, with palms down in front of the centre of the chest. The hands are then simultaneously moved emphatically forward a short distance.

sherbet: *n.* a frozen, fruit-flavoured dessert. *My favourite dessert after a heavy meal is a light sherbet.*

SIGN: Fingerspell **SHERBET**.

sheriff: *n.* the chief law enforcement officer of any county in the U.S.A. *The sheriff arrested the thief.*

SIGN: Vertical right **'C-INDEX'** hand, palm facing left, is tapped a couple of times against the left shoulder. (In *Canada*, **sheriff** refers to an *officer of the court*, but signs vary greatly, depending in particular on the specific act being carried out by the sheriff in a given context.)

shield: *v.* to protect from danger or harm. *I wear dark glasses to shield my eyes from the sun's glare.*

SIGN: Horizontal **'S'** hands are held, the left just in front of the right, with palms down in front of the centre of the chest. The hands are then simultaneously moved emphatically forward a short distance.

shift: *n.* a specific working period (usually of 8 hours duration). *Most nurses prefer to work a daytime shift.*

SIGN #1: Fingerspell **SHIFT**.

shift: *n.* a system for manually changing gears in a motor vehicle. *I prefer a car with a manual shift rather than an automatic.*

SIGN #2: Horizontal right **'S'** hand, palm left, is held at about waist level and is moved in a small counter-clockwise circle a couple of times.

shift: *v.* to move from one place, position or direction to another. *They will **shift** the furniture until they are satisfied with the way it is arranged.*

SIGN #3: **'CONTRACTED B'** hands are held apart with palms down and are circled, the left hand moving in a clockwise direction while the right hand moves counter-clockwise. The hands move simultaneously but are offset rather than symmetrical in their respective positions. (Signs vary depending on what is being shifted and how it is being shifted.)

shine: *v.* to give out light. *The street light **shines** on the bus stop.*

SIGN #1: Right **'MODIFIED O'** hand is held aloft with palm down. The fingers then open to form a **'CONTRACTED 5'** hand.

shine: *v.* to glow with reflected light. *This furniture polish made the table **shine**.*

SIGN #2: Tip of middle finger of right **'BENT MIDFINGER 5'** hand, palm down, is placed on back of left **'STANDARD BASE'** hand. The right hand wobbles as it moves upward/rightward. (Sometimes this sign is made without the left hand; instead the middle finger of the right hand is placed on the actual object or on the place where the object is imagined to be. Handshapes for the right hand may vary as well.)

SAME SIGN—**shiny**, *adj.*

shiner: *n.* a colloquial expression meaning a black eye. *He wore large dark glasses to cover up the **shiner** he had gotten during the fight.*

SIGN: Tip of forefinger of right **'BENT ONE'** hand, palm down, is drawn across forehead from left to right. In the process, the wrist turns so that the forefinger, which originally points leftward, eventually points backward. Next, forefinger of right **'BENT ONE'** hand touches face just under right eye. (ASL CONCEPT—**black - eye**.)

ship: *n.* a large sailing vessel. *The Bluenose was a famous clipper **ship**.*

SIGN #1: **'CROOKED EXTENDED B'** hands, palms facing each other at a slight angle, are cupped together to form the hull of a boat. Then they are moved up and down in a bobbing motion.

ship: *v.* to send or transport goods by vehicle. *They will **ship** the relief supplies by air.*

SIGN #2: Fingertips of horizontal right **'BENT EXTENDED B'** hand are placed on the back of the left **'STANDARD BASE'** hand. The right hand then moves forward as the fingers straighten to form an **'EXTENDED B'** hand. ❖

shirk: *v.* to neglect or avoid one's work. *Do not **shirk** your responsibilities.*

SIGN: Tip of forefinger of horizontal right **'4'** hand, palm facing downward, is placed on the nose and the hand is curved rightward from the wrist away from the face.

shirt: *n.* a garment worn on the upper part of the body. *He wore a brightly coloured silk **shirt**.*

SIGN #1: Horizontal right **'F'** hand grasps the signer's shirt below the right shoulder between the thumb and forefinger, and is moved back and forth twice.

OR

SIGN #2: Horizontal **'CROOKED 5'** hands are held with palms facing the body and fingertips touching either side of upper chest. Then the hands are simultaneously moved down to waist level.

shiver: *v.* to shake or tremble from fear or cold. *When he noticed the children begin to **shiver** he decided to build a fire.*

SIGN: **'A'** (or **'S'**) hands are held apart, palms facing each other, and are shaken, along with the shoulders, as if the signer is shivering.

shock: *n.* a sudden jolt caused by the passage of electricity throughout the body. *She got a **shock** when her wet fingers touched the prongs on the stove plug as she inserted it in the electrical socket.*

SIGN: Crooked forefingers of horizontal **'X'** hands, palms facing body, are abruptly tapped together at least twice. Facial expression is important.

shocked: *v.* to be in a state of extreme surprise, fright or emotional disturbance. *We were shocked when we heard the tragic news.*

SIGN: **'BENT 5'** hands are held apart, fingertips pointing downward, and are moved sharply downward. (This sign is used only in a passive voice situation or as an adjective. It may *not* be used in an active voice situation such as: *The tragic news shocked us.*)

SAME SIGN—**shock,** *n.,* in this context.

shoes: *n.* a matching pair of coverings shaped to fit the feet. *I need a new pair of gym shoes.*

SIGN #1: Horizontal right **'EXTENDED B'** hand, palm left, is placed against the thumb side of the left **'B'** hand of which the palm is facing down and the fingers pointing forward at a rightward angle. Then the right hand is curved forward and around the fingers to the opposite side of the left hand.

OR

SIGN #2: **'S'** hands, palms down, are held very near each other and are tapped together a couple of times.

SIGN #3 [ONTARIO]: Vertical right **'B'** hand is held with palm forward at a leftward angle as the hand is tapped against the right cheek.

shoot: *v.* to fire a gun. *He tried to shoot at the bull's eye in the target.*

SIGN #1: Horizontal right **'L'** hand represents a gun as it is held with palm left and forefinger pointing forward. The forearm then jerks backward slightly so that the forefinger points forward/upward as the thumb bends to form a **'BENT THUMB L'** hand. ❖ (Signs vary according to what kind of weapon is being shot.) Sign choice depends on context.

shoot: *v.* to photograph; take a picture of. *The photographer will shoot the cover picture beside the waterfall.*

SIGN #2: Vertical **'CROOKED L'** (or **'C-INDEX'**) hands are held so as to frame the eyes with a thumb touching either side of face, and palms facing each other, but angled forward slightly. The forefinger of the right hand then crooks as if depressing the button a camera in order to take a picture.

shop: *n.* a small store. *She manages a fashionable dress shop downtown.*

SIGN #1: **'FLAT O'** hands, held parallel with palms down and fingers pointing down, are swung forward/upward from the wrists a couple of times. (For **shop,** *v.,* see **(go) shopping.**)

shop: *n.* a course of study that prepares students for manual arts such as woodwork; industrial arts. *He will take shop and outdoor education as options this semester.*

SIGN #2: The bottom of the horizontal right **'S'** hand, palm facing leftward/backward, is brushed forward/rightward several times along the upturned palm of the left **'EXTENDED B'** hand of which the fingers point forward/rightward. (Signs vary.)

shoplifting: *n.* the act of stealing goods from a store. *She was arrested for shoplifting.*

SIGN: **'CROOKED 5'** hands, palms down, are held near each other in front of the chest and are moved slightly but firmly apart as they close to form **'A'** hands.

ALTERNATE SIGN—**steal** #1

(go) shopping: *v.* to go somewhere with the intention of buying something. *I am going shopping for a new coat this afternoon.*

SIGN #1: Left **'EXTENDED B'** hand is held in a fixed position with palm up and fingers pointing forward/rightward. Right **'FLAT O'** (or **'CONTRACTED B'**) hand, palm facing left, is brushed forward/rightward along the left hand a couple of times.

OR

SIGN #2: Horizontal **'X'** hands are held parallel with palms down are simultaneously moved up and down a few times.

shore: *n.* the land along the edge of a sea, lake, or river. *They built a cottage on the south shore of the lake.*

SIGN: Fingerspell **SHORE.**

short: *adj.* not long; of brief duration. *I will make my story* **short**.

SIGN #1: Left horizontal **'U'** hand is held steady with extended fingers pointing forward/rightward and palm facing backward/rightward. Right horizontal **'U'** hand is held at right angles to the left hand with extended fingers resting on those of the left hand. Extended fingers of right hand are then brushed forward/rightward off the fingers of the left hand.

short: *adj.* not long in terms of physical length. *The dog's tail is very* **short**.

SIGN #2: Horizontal **'ONE'** hands, palms facing each other, are held close together so that there is a short span between the tips of the forefingers.

short: *adj.* not tall. *The man is* **short** *and fat.*

SIGN #3: Right **'EXTENDED B'** hand is held out to the right side of the body with palm down and is moved up and down to indicate the shortness of stature.

short for: *adv.* an abbreviation for. *RCMP is* **short** *for Royal Canadian Mounted Police.*

SIGN #4: **'SPREAD C'** hands are held horizontally and slightly apart, right above left. Then both are closed to form **'S'** hands as the right is brought down to rest on top of the left.

short hair: *n.* hair which is not long. *Short hair is nice for the summer months.*

SIGN #5: **'BENT EXTENDED B'** hands are held against either side of the neck just under the ears with palms facing backward and fingers pointing backward as well. (A 'brush cut' or 'crew cut' such as that worn by military men is indicated by sliding the right **'MODIFIED G'** hand, palm left, from the top of the forehead to the crown of the head.)

short of: *adj.* not having enough (people, money, etc.). *We are* **short of** *money for our holiday.*

SIGN #6: Thumb of right **'EXTENDED A'** hand, palm facing left, is placed under the chin and is flicked forward firmly. Next, horizontal left **'S'** hand is held in a fixed position with palm facing right. Horizontal right **'EXTENDED B'** hand is held palm down with fingers pointing forward/leftward and is brushed forward/rightward a couple of times across the top of the left hand. (ASL CONCEPT—**not - enough**.)

shorten: *v.* to make shorter. *Please* **shorten** *your report.*

SIGN: **'SPREAD C'** hands are held horizontally and slightly apart, right above left. Then both are closed to form **'S'** hands as the right is brought down to rest on top of the left. (Signs vary depending on the context.)

shortly: *adv.* in a short time; soon. *I will be there* **shortly**.

SIGN #1: Horizontal left **'U'** hand is held in a fixed position with palm facing rightward/backward and extended fingers pointing forward/rightward. Horizontal right **'U'** hand, palm facing leftward/backward, is positioned with extended fingers pointing forward/leftward and resting on those of the left hand at right angles to them. The right hand then moves back and forth a few times, the extended fingers sliding along those of the left hand.

shortly: *adv.* a little. *I will be there* **shortly** *before noon.*

SIGN #2: Right **'X'** hand is held palm-up with forefinger tightly crooked and tip of thumb repeatedly scraping downward against tip of forefinger.

shorts: *n.* short trousers reaching partway to the knee; a man's underwear which looks like this. *We all wore shorts to the picnic.*

SIGN: **'BENT EXTENDED B'** hands are used to indicate the length of the shorts as the finger-tips brush outward across the thighs. This is a wrist action.

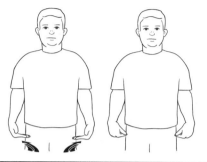

shot: *n.* an injection of vaccine or drug. *It is time for your cat to have a distemper shot.*

SIGN #1: Tip of forefinger of right **'BENT L'** hand is jabbed into upper left arm and thumb is repeatedly bent and extended as though depressing a plunger into a syringe. (Sign choice depends on context.)

(give it a) shot: *v.* to try; make an attempt. *I have never golfed before but I would like to give it a shot.*

SIGN #2: Horizontal **'EXTENDED A'** (or **'S'**) hands are held apart with palms facing the chest. The wrists then rotate toward the chest, causing the palms to turn downward as the hands curve downward and forward.

shotgun: *n.* a shoulder-held firearm used mainly for hunting small game but sometimes modified to be used in the commission of a crime. *I will trade in my handgun for a shotgun.*

SIGN: Horizontal **'V'** hands, palms down and extended fingers pointing forward, are staggered so that one hand is ahead of the other, and they are simultaneously jerked back slightly to simulate the recoil action of a shotgun.

ALTERNATE SIGN—**rifle**

shotput: *n.* a sport which involves the hurling of a heavy metal ball as far as possible. *He broke all records in the shotput.*

SIGN: Vertical right **'SPREAD C'** hand, palm forward, is held just in front of the right shoulder and then thrust forward twice.

should: *v.* the past tense of the *verb* 'shall' but used more commonly as an auxiliary verb to indicate obligation, duty or expectation. *You should inform your parents.*

SIGN: Right **'X'** hand, palm facing away from the body, is held in a vertical position in front of the chest and is sharply thrust downward from the wrist so that the palm faces down.

shoulder: *n.* the joint where the arm joins the trunk of the body. *I broke my shoulder.*

SIGN: Forefinger of right **'BENT ONE'** hand is used to touch the left shoulder. (To refer to the *right* shoulder, the signer will use the left hand to touch the right shoulder. To indicate that a shoulder or most any body part is *sore*, a flatter handshape such as a **'CROOKED EXTENDED B'** is used.) Context must be considered when selecting signs. When **shoulder** refers to the side of a road or highway where a car may pull over, the sign illustrated here is inappropriate. Signs in this context vary depending on several factors.

shout: *v.* to utter something in a loud voice. *We were talking from a distance so we had to shout.*

SIGN: Right vertical **'SPREAD C'** hand, palm toward the body, is held near the mouth and is forcefully drawn forward at an upward angle.

shove: *v.* to push with force. *I shoved him because he was in my way.*

SIGN: Vertical **'EXTENDED B'** hands, palms forward, are held slightly apart and are simultaneously shoved forward. ❖

shovel: *n.* an instrument for lifting and scooping loose material. *I need to go to the hardware store to buy a new shovel.*

SIGN #1: **'S'** hands are held apart, the left palm facing upward and the right palm facing downward. The wrists then bend so that the left palm faces backward and the right palm faces forward/leftward. Motion is repeated.

OR

SIGN #2: Horizontal left **'EXTENDED B'** hand is held with fingers pointing forward and palm facing rightward/upward. Horizontal right **'BENT EXTENDED B'** hand, palm facing backward/upward and slightly leftward, moves in a clockwise direction, the fingertips striking the left palm with each revolution.

shovel: *v.* to dig by lifting and scooping loose material with a shovel. *If you do not **shovel** the snow from your driveway, someone could slip and fall.*

SIGN #3: **'S'** hands are held apart, the left palm facing upward and the right palm facing downward. The arms then move backward so that the left palm faces backward and the right palm faces forward/leftward. Motion is repeated. The movement is like that of shoveling something over the left shoulder.

OR

SIGN #4: Horizontal left **'EXTENDED B'** hand is held with fingers pointing forward and palm facing rightward/upward. Horizontal right **'BENT EXTENDED B'** hand, palm facing backward/upward and slightly leftward, moves leftward so that the fingertips strike the left palm. The right hand then continues to move leftward/backward as it turns palm downward. Motion is repeated.

show: *v.* to display; exhibit. *Deaf artists will **show** their work at the upcoming conference.*

SIGN #1: Tip of forefinger of horizontal right **'BENT ONE'** hand is placed against right facing palm of left **'EXTENDED B'** hand. Together, the hands are moved forward in a short arc.

show: *v.* to escort someone to a certain place; conduct; guide. *My assistant will **show** you to the front door.*

SIGN #2: **'A'** hands are held together, palms facing each other, and knuckles touching. Then they are thrust forward/downward together from chest level. ❖

show: *v.* to prove; provide an explanation. *His behaviour **shows** that he did it.*

SIGN #3: Horizontal left **'EXTENDED B'** hand is held in a fixed position with palm up and fingers pointing forward/rightward. Horizontal right **'EXTENDED B'** hand is held palm up with fingers pointing forward/leftward and is brought down sharply onto the left palm.

show: *v.* to be visible or noticeable. *In spite of her makeup the scar on her face still **shows**.*

SIGN #4: **'A'** hands, palms down, are held slightly apart, and are then firmly pushed a very short distance downward. Next, vertical right **'K'** hand, palm toward the face, is held with the tip of the middle finger touching the right cheekbone. The hand is then thrust forward at a rightward/downward angle. (ASL CONCEPT—**can - see**.)

show: *v.* to come in third in a (horse) race. *We placed a bet that the horse would **show**.*

SIGN #5: Horizontal right **'3'** hand, palm left, is drawn back firmly toward the chest.

show: *n.* a film presented for public viewing. *We attended the **show** at the cinema downtown.*

SIGN #6: Horizontal left **'5'** hand is held with fingers pointing forward/rightward and palm facing rightward/backward. Vertical right **'5'** hand is held with heel in palm of left hand and is shaken back and forth. This is a wrist movement.
ALTERNATE SIGN—**movie** #2

show: *n.* a theatrical performance. *We went to see a Broadway **show** in New York City.*

SIGN #7: **'EXTENDED A'** hands, palms facing each other, are rotated alternately in small circles which are brought down against the chest.

show off: *v.* to make a display of one's abilities or possessions so as to invite admiration. *It embarrasses me when my brother **shows off**.*

SIGN #1: **'EXTENDED A'** hands, palms facing downward, are placed at either side of waist and are alternately moved away from the body and then toward the body so that the thumbs jab the signer in the sides. Facial expression is important.

SIGN #2 [ONTARIO]: Vertical right **'I'** hand, palm facing left, is thumped against the centre of the chest a few times. Facial expression is important.

show up: *v.* to appear. *I hope the interpreter will **show up** on time for the meeting.*

SIGN: Left **'EXTENDED B'** hand is held, palm down, in a fixed position. Right **'ONE'** hand, palm forward, is brought up underneath the left hand and the extended forefinger is thrust upward between the forefinger and middle finger of the left hand.

shower: *n.* a kind of bath in which a person stands and is sprayed with fine streams of water. *Most athletes have a **shower** after a game or workout.*

SIGN #1: Right **'S'** hand is held palm down above the head. The fingers then open to form a **'CONTRACTED 5'** shape. The motion is repeated.

shower: *n.* a short period of precipitation. *After a long dry spell, the **shower** came as a relief to local farmers.*

SIGN #2: **'SPREAD EXTENDED C'** hands are held parallel with palms down, and are bounced up and down slightly at least twice. This is a wrist action.

shower: *n.* a party held to celebrate a forthcoming event such as a wedding or a birth. *I want to buy a special gift for the baby **shower**.*

SIGN #3: Fingerspell **SHOWER**.

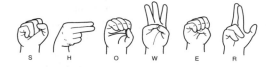

shred: *v.* to cut into narrow strips or fragments. *This gadget will **shred** the cabbage very finely.*

SIGN #1: Right **'A'** hand is placed palm-down on the upturned palm of the left **'EXTENDED B'** hand and is moved slowly and firmly rightward/forward a couple of times as if scraping against the left hand. This is more or less a circular movement as the right hand moves along the left hand, then into the air and back in a counter-clockwise direction to repeat the movement. (This sign is used mainly for the shredding of *vegetables*.)

shred: *v.* to cut into narrow strips or fragments. *This machine will **shred** the paper before we dispose of it.*

SIGN #2: Horizontal left **'5'** hand is held in a fixed position with palm facing the chest and fingers pointing rightward. Right **'5'** hand is held palm down with fingers pointing forward and fluttering as they move forward between the forefinger and midfinger of the left hand. (This sign is used mainly for the shredding of *paper*.)

shred: *n.* a little bit; a very small amount. *I do not think we can win the case based on that **shred** of evidence.*

SIGN #3: Right **'X'** hand is held palm-up with forefinger tightly crooked and tip of thumb repeatedly scraping downward against tip of forefinger.

shrewd: *adj.* sharp-witted, or clever, especially in business matters; astute. *The judge is a **shrewd** observer.*

SIGN: Tip of middle finger of vertical right **'BENT MIDFINGER 5'** hand, palm toward the face, touches the forehead. Then the wrist is rotated so that the palm faces away from the body.

shrimp: *n.* a marine crustacean with a slender body and a long tail. *You may use either fresh or frozen **shrimp** in this recipe.*

SIGN: Fingerspell **SHRIMP**.

shrink: *v.* to become smaller in size. *If you wash this sweater carefully, it will not **shrink**.*

SIGN #1: Vertical **'EXTENDED B'** hands, palms facing, are held about 30 centimetres apart and are moved simultaneously toward each other and slightly downward until they are very near one another but not touching.

shrink: *n.* a colloquial word for psychiatrist or psychologist. *Maybe you should go to a **shrink** for counselling.*

SIGN #2: Edge of right **'EXTENDED B'** hand, palm facing left, is tapped a couple of times between the thumb and forefinger of the vertical left **'CONTRACTED C'** hand of which the palm faces right.

shrub: *n.* a woody plant which has several stems and is lower in height than a tree. *They planted a lilac **shrub** in their backyard.*

SIGN: **'CROOKED 5'** hands, palms down, are held side by side and outline the shape of a shrub as they are simultaneously curved away from each other until the palms are almost facing upward. (**SHRUB** may be fingerspelled.)

shrug: *v.* to draw up and drop one's shoulders. (Usually the gesture expresses ignorance or indifference.) *He **shrugs** when he does not know the answers.*

SIGN: Natural gestures, accompanied by an appropriate facial expression, are used for this concept.

shudder: *v.* to tremble or shake violently from horror or fear. *Everyone **shuddered** in horror as the train hit the car.*

SIGN: A natural gesture, accompanied by an appropriate facial expression, is used to convey this concept.

shuffle: *v.* to move one's feet with a slow, dragging motion. *When people get old, they sometimes **shuffle** noticeably.*

SIGN #1: **'EXTENDED B'** hands, palms down and fingers pointing forward, are held apart and alternately moved back and forth very slowly and deliberately to simulate the action of a shuffling walk.

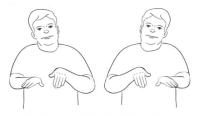

shuffle: *v.* to mix up or change the order of the cards in a deck. *It is your turn to **shuffle** the cards.*

SIGN #2: Horizontal right **'C'** hand, palm facing left but angled slightly toward the body, is held just above the upturned palm of the left **'EXTENDED B'** hand, which is held with fingers pointing forward/rightward. The right hand is then lowered into the left palm, raised, and lowered once again.

shuffle: *v.* to rearrange. *The Prime Minister **shuffled** his Cabinet.*

SIGN #3: Vertical **'FLAT O'** hands, palms forward, are circled several times, the left hand moving in a clockwise direction while the right hand moves counter-clockwise. The hands move simultaneously but are offset rather than symmetrical in their respective positions.

shun: *v.* to avoid deliberately. *The others **shun** him because he rebelled against the principles of their religion.*

SIGN: Fingertips of right **'BENT EXTENDED B'** hand, palm down, are placed on upturned palm of left **'EXTENDED B'** hand and brushed forward to form a straight **'EXTENDED B'** hand. ❖ (Signs vary depending on context.)

shut: *v.* to close. *Please **shut** the door when you leave the room.*

SIGN: Vertical left **'B'** hand is held in a fixed position with palm facing forward/rightward while vertical right **'B'** hand is held just to the right of it with palm facing leftward but angled backward slightly. The right wrist then rotates, turning the hand so that its palm faces forward/leftward and its forefinger comes to rest against the forefinger of the left hand, resulting in the creation of a **'V'** formation. (See also **close**.)

shut up [*or* **shut your mouth**]: *v.* to be quiet; cease talking; stop making a noise. *Shut up and listen to your father!*

SIGN: Horizontal right **'CONTRACTED 5'** hand, palm left is brought toward the mouth as it snaps closed to form a **'FLAT O'** at the lips.

shutout: *n.* a game in which the opposing team receives no points. *Our hockey team was happy to get a **shutout** last night.*

SIGN: Vertical right **'O'** hand, palm facing left, is moved firmly forward a short distance.

shy: *adj.* timid or uneasy in the company of others. *The students were not **shy** about performing on stage.*

SIGN: Backs of fingers of right **'BENT EXTENDED B'** hand are held against right cheek. The hand is then twisted forward slightly from the wrist.

SAME SIGN—**shyness**, *n.*

siblings: *n.* a person's brothers and/or sisters. *How many siblings do you have?*

SIGN: Horizontal left **'ONE'** hand is held in a fixed position with palm facing right, forefinger pointing forward and thumb extended so that it points forward/rightward. Right **'L'** hand, palm left, forefinger pointing forward/upward and thumb alongside the right cheek, is lowered so that it rests on top of the left hand. It is then quickly raised to forehead level and returned to rest on the left hand. (ASL CONCEPT—**sister - brother**.) When referring to a specific sibling, **brother** or **sister** is used.

sick: *adj.* ill. *Many people are sick with flu.*

SIGN #1: **'BENT MIDFINGER 5'** hands are then positioned so that the tip of the right middle finger is in the middle of the forehead and the tip of the left middle finger is on the stomach. Sometimes this sign is made with the right hand only.
SAME SIGN—**sickness**, *n.*

sick: *adj.* ill. (This sign is used specifically to indicate a *sudden attack of illness* that is especially incapacitating but not necessarily of long duration.) *Many who attended the banquet became violently sick from food poisoning.*

SIGN #2: **'BENT MIDFINGER 5'** hands are then positioned so that the tip of the right middle finger is in the middle of the forehead and the tip of the left middle finger is on the stomach. Next, **'V'** hands are held, left in front of right, in a semi-vertical position with extended fingers pointing forward/upward at a slight leftward angle as left palm faces right and right palm faces left. As the head turns to the right, the hands are simultaneously jerked backward/rightward to an entirely upright position and the extended fingers retract to form **'CLAWED V'** hands. (This part of the sign may begin and end with **'CLAWED V'** hands; alternatively, it may begin and end with **'V'** hands.) (ASL CONCEPT—**sick - very sick**.)

sick of: *adj.* disgusted with; tired of. *I am sick of your stupid behaviour.*

SIGN #3: Vertical right **'BENT MIDFINGER 5'** hand is held with palm left and tip of middle finger touching forehead. The wrist then rotates to turn the palm toward the face. Facial expression must clearly convey 'annoyance'.
ALTERNATE SIGNS—**disgusted** or **fed up**

side: *n.* a specific surface or area of an object. *The car went out of control and hit the side of the building.*

SIGN #1: The concept of **side** is generally communicated through an all-inclusive sign which incorporates many parts of the sentence. To translate the sample sentence into ASL, a single sign is used to convey 'car', 'hit', 'side' and 'building'. Signs vary considerably, depending on the sentence.

side: *n.* line of descent. *My father's side of the family comes from Ireland.*

SIGN #2: Fingerspell **SIDE**.

S   I   D   E

side with: *v.* to support. *He will naturally side with his friend in the argument.*

SIGN #3: **'S'** hands, palms toward the body, are held at chest level with the left slightly above the right. Then the right is brought upward to strike the left.

sideburns: *n.* a man's whiskers growing down either side of the face in front of the ears. *He went to the barber to have his sideburns trimmed.*

SIGN: Vertical **'A-INDEX'** hands, palms toward the face, are placed in front of the ears, and are simultaneously drawn down toward the lower jawlines.

sidestep: *v.* to dodge; evade. *During the interview, the premier was able to **sidestep** all the important issues.*

SIGN: Horizontal right **'EXTENDED A'** hand, palm facing left, is held directly behind horizontal left **'EXTENDED A'** hand whose palm faces right. Right hand then becomes vertical as it is brought back smartly toward the chest. (Sign selection depends on context. In a case where a person is physically moving out of the way, that person would be represented in ASL with a vertical **'ONE'** hand that moves rightward with palm facing forward.)

(be) sidetracked: *v.* to be distracted or caused to digress from the main subject or topic. *She began working on her homework assignment but **was sidetracked** by a television program.*

SIGN: Vertical left **'ONE'** hand is held in a fixed position with palm facing rightward/forward. Horizontal right **'BENT ONE'** hand, palm facing the body and forefinger pointing leftward, is held just to the right of the left hand and moves leftward behind the left hand, grazing the left forefinger on the way past. Meanwhile, the signer's tongue is visible between the teeth as if articulating a 'TH' sound.

sidewalk: *n.* a raised, paved walkway on either side of a city street. *You are not permitted to ride a bicycle on the **sidewalk**.*

SIGN: Fingerspell **SIDEWALK**.

(under) siege: *adj.* used in reference to offensive operations being carried out within a specific space or area. *The office was **under siege** until the miners' demands for safe working conditions were met.*

SIGN: **'SPREAD C'** hands are held parallel with palms down and are then closed to form **'S'** hands as they are thrust forward.

sift: *v.* to separate coarse matter from liquids or finer materials. *The prospector was able to **sift** several gold nuggets from the river silt.*

SIGN: Horizontal **'A'** hands, palms facing, are positioned as if holding a sieve. Then they are simultaneously shaken from side to side. Signs vary depending on what is being sifted and the type of sieve being used, such as a flour sieve, colander, etc.

SAME SIGN—**sieve**, *n.*

sight: *n.* vision; the power to see. *Sight is one of the five senses.*

SIGN: Vertical right **'K'** hand, palm toward the face, is held with the tip of the middle finger touching the right cheekbone. The hand is then thrust forward at a rightward/downward angle.

(go) sightseeing: *v.* to visit famous or interesting sights in a particular area. *If you plan **to go sightseeing** in London, I would recommend a walking tour.*

SIGN: Horizontal **'V'** hands are held parallel with palms down, fingers pointing forward, and are swept to the right in a succession of arcs.

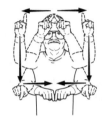

sign: *n.* a notice or placard intended to inform or warn. *You are required to obey every traffic **sign**.*

SIGN #1: **'ONE'** hands are held with palms forward and forefingers pointing upward/forward, the tips touching. The hands are then drawn apart, moved downward, and back together to outline the shape of a sign. (Signs vary depending on the shape of the sign.)

sign: *v.* to write one's name on (something). *Please **sign** this document before you leave.*

SIGN #2: Right **'U'** hand, palm facing left and extended fingers pointing forward, is twisted from the wrist as it moves in a leftward arc so that the palm faces down and extended fingers come to rest in upturned palm of left **'EXTENDED B'** hand.

sign: *v.* to communicate using sign language. *My Deaf brother taught me to **sign**.*

SIGN #3: Horizontal **'ONE'** hands are held slightly apart with palms facing the chest at a downward angle. As the wrists rotate backward toward the chest, the forefingers revolve around one another.

sign: *v.* to sign ASL very fluently. *She **signs** well!*

SIGN #4: The hands, held apart with palms up, alternately circle forward as the fingers rapidly open and close at least twice, thus alternating between **'S'** and **'SPREAD C'** shapes.

OR

SIGN #5: **'S'** hands, left palm facing right and right palm facing left, are held at about shoulder level and are alternately thrust forward as the fingers open to form **'MODIFIED 5'** hands.

sign language: *n.* a visual/manual communication system used by Deaf people. *The sign language shown in this book is ASL as it is used in Canada.*

SIGN: Horizontal **'ONE'** hands are held slightly apart with palms facing the chest at a downward angle. As the wrists rotate backward toward the chest, the forefingers revolve around one another. Next, **'L'** hands are held palms down with forefingers pointing forward and thumbtips touching each other. The hands are then drawn apart.

signal: *v.* to communicate a message through something representative such as a sign or symbol. *A white flag signals surrender.*

SIGN #1: Horizontal left **'EXTENDED B'** hand is held in a fixed position with palm facing right while tip of forefinger of right palm-down **'BENT V'** hand is jabbed into the left palm. The right hand then moves away from the left hand as the right wrist rotates a quarter turn clockwise, and the middle fingertip is jabbed into the left palm. (In contexts where **danger** is being signalled specifically, **warn** would be used for **signal**.)

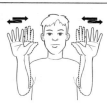

signal: *v.* to gesture in order to communicate certain information. *The RCMP officer signalled us to stop.*

SIGN #2: Vertical **'5'** hands are held apart, palms forward, and are simultaneously waved from side to side. (Natural gestures are used for this concept and may vary according to context.)

signal: *v.* to activate a flashing light which informs other drivers of an intention to turn in a certain direction. *He failed his driving test because he forgot to signal before he turned right.*

SIGN #3: Right hand is held upright with palm facing backward as the fingers open and close a few times, thus alternating between **'CONTRACTED 5'** and **'FLAT O'** shapes. The *left* hand is used to mean a *left-hand* signal. When referring specifically to a signal light at the *front* of a vehicle, the same basic sign is used but the hand is turned so that the palm faces forward.
SAME SIGN—**signal**, *n.,* in this context.

signature: *n.* a person's name written by him/herself. *I need your signature on this form.*

SIGN: Right **'U'** hand, palm facing left and extended fingers pointing forward, is twisted from the wrist as it moves in a leftward arc so that the palm faces down and extended fingers come to rest in upturned palm of left **'EXTENDED B'** hand.

signee: *n.* a person who watches to try to understand a message expressed in ASL (the equivalent of a listener in a spoken language). *The signee nodded to indicate that he understood the signer's message.*

SIGN: **'3'** hands, palms facing each other and extended fingers pointing forward/upward, are held about a head's width apart and a little forward of the face. Then they are brought backward a couple of times toward the temples as the forefingers and middle fingers are retracted to form **'CROOKED EXTENDED V'** shapes. This sign may be followed by the Agent Ending (see p. LIV).

signer: *n.* a person who expresses ideas using a signed language such as ASL. *The signer gave an eloquent presentation on Deaf Culture.*

SIGN: Horizontal **'ONE'** hands are held slightly apart with palms facing the chest at a downward angle. As the wrists rotate backward toward the chest, the forefingers revolve around one another. This sign must be followed by the Agent Ending (see p. LIV).

significant: *adj.* important; valuable; notable. *Many Canadians have made significant contributions to Deaf Culture.*

SIGN: Vertical **'F'** hands are held apart with palms facing forward. The hands are then brought purposefully together.
SAME SIGN—**significance**, *n.*
ALTERNATE SIGN—**important** #2

signify: *v.* to indicate or suggest. *The abbreviation ASL is used to **signify** American Sign Language.*

SIGN: Horizontal left **'EXTENDED B'** hand is held in a fixed position with palm facing right while tip of forefinger of right palm-down **'BENT V'** hand is jabbed into the left palm. The right hand then moves away from the left hand as the right wrist rotates a quarter turn clockwise, and the middle fingertip is jabbed into the left palm.

silent: *adj.* without sound; quiet. *Throughout the lecture, the audience was **silent**.*

SIGN: **'B'** (or **'EXTENDED B'**) hands are crossed in front of the mouth, left palm facing rightward/downward and right palm facing leftward/downward with the right hand just behind the left hand. Then they are drawn apart until the palms face completely downward. SAME SIGN—**silence**, *n.*

silhouette: *n.* an outline filled in with black. *Silhouettes of the heads of all the graduating students were used to decorate the auditorium.*

SIGN: Tip of forefinger of right **'BENT ONE'** hand, palm down, is drawn across forehead from left to right. In the process, the wrist turns so that the forefinger, which originally points leftward, eventually points backward. Next, tip of forefinger of right horizontal **'ONE'** hand, palm toward the face, is used to trace the outline of the signer's features from forehead to chin. (ASL CONCEPT—**black - line down face.**) Signs vary depending on the size and shape of what forms the silhouette.

silk: *n.* a fine, soft fabric made of threads produced by silkworms. *This blouse is made of silk.*

SIGN: Fingerspell **SILK.**

silly: *adj.* absurd; lacking in sense. *A clown does silly things to amuse his audience.*

SIGN: Vertical right **'Y'** hand, palm toward the nose, is twisted forward so that the palm faces left. SAME SIGN—**silliness**, *n.*

silver: *adj.* related to a brilliant metal which is greyish white in colour; having greyish-white colour. *She won a silver medal at the Olympics.*

SIGN: Right hand, held upright, is rapidly alternated between an **'COVERED 8'** and an **'OPEN 8'** handshape, with the palm facing left. (Signs vary.) **SILVER** is frequently finger-spelled.

similar: *adj.* showing resemblance in characteristics or appearance. *My new car is similar to yours.*

SIGN: Vertical right **'Y'** hand is held with palm forward and appears to wobble from side to side as the wrist twists. SAME SIGN—**similarity**, *n.*

simile: *n.* a figure of speech introduced by 'like' or 'as' and comparing one thing to another, e.g., *The boy ran like a deer. Our English teacher asked us to find a simile in the poem.*

SIGN: Fingerspell **SIMILE.**

simmer: *v.* to cook food slowly and gently just at or near the boiling point. *You can let the stew simmer until the flavours are well blended.*

SIGN: **'SPREAD EXTENDED C'** hands are held fairly close together with palms up and fingers fluttering gently. The signer appears to be blowing a narrow stream of air out of a small opening created by the lips.

simple: *adj.* easy to understand or do. *His instructions were very **simple** to follow.*

SIGN #1: Left **'BENT EXTENDED B'** hand is held in a fixed position with palm up. Palm of horizontal right **'EXTENDED B'** (or **'BENT EXTENDED B'**) hand faces left but is slanted slightly upward and toward the body as the fingers are brushed upward against the backs of the fingers of the left hand at least twice. SAME SIGN—**simplicity**, *n.*

OR

SIGN #2: Horizontal left **'F'** hand is held in a fixed position with palm facing right. Horizontal right **'F'** hand is held slightly above the left hand with palm facing the body at a leftward angle. As the right wrist then rotates in a counter-clockwise direction, the joined thumb and forefinger strike the joined thumb and forefinger of the left hand on the way past. The right palm eventually faces downward.

SIGN #3 [ATLANTIC/PRAIRIE]: Tip of forefinger of **'CROOKED ONE'** hand taps right cheek twice.

simultaneously: *adv.* happening at the same time. *An interpreter listens to a spoken message and signs **simultaneously**.*

SIGN: **'ONE'** hands, palms down and forefingers pointing forward, rise slightly as they are firmly brought together so that the sides of the forefingers strike each other, then bounce apart. Next, right **'CROOKED ONE'** hand, palm facing downward, is lowered so that the tip of the forefinger comes to rest on the back of the wrist of the left **'STANDARD BASE'** hand. (ASL CONCEPT—**same - time**.)

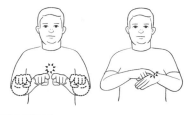

sin: *n.* a wrongdoing in terms of a religious or moral principle. *The sermon focussed on the forgiveness of **sin**.*

SIGN: **'CROOKED ONE'** hands, palms up, are held apart and are circled in opposite directions several times.

since: *conj.* during or throughout a certain period of time. *I have not seen him **since** he enlisted in the army two years ago.*

SIGN #1: Tips of forefingers of **'BENT ONE'** hands, palms facing the body, are placed slightly apart on the right shoulder. The hands then drop forward/downward from the wrists so that the palms are facing upward and the forefingers are pointing forward/upward. (**SINCE** may be fingerspelled.)

since: *conj.* because. ***Since** you are not free on Friday, perhaps we can have lunch together on Thursday.*

NOTE—**Since** in this context is generally conveyed through a pause rather than a specific sign. This pause occurs in the middle of the sentence rather than at the beginning. The sample sentence in ASL is: *YOU BUSY FRIDAY...**pause**...MAYBE YOU-AND-ME LUNCH THURSDAY.*

sincere: *adj.* genuine; honest; not hypocritical or deceitful. *I felt her apology was **sincere**.*

SIGN: Forefinger of vertical right **'ONE'** hand, palm facing left, is held against the lips and the hand is moved sharply forward. Next, left **'EXTENDED B'** hand is held in a fixed position with palm basically downward at a rightward/forward angle and fingers pointing basically upward at a rightward/forward angle. Right **'CONTRACTED U'** hand is held with palm toward the body and fingertips of forefinger and middle finger touching heel of left hand. The wrist of the right hand rotates clockwise as the extended fingers stroke the left hand in a straight line from the heel, along the palm and fingers and onward in an upward/rightward/forward direction. (ASL CONCEPT—**true - honest**.)
SAME SIGN—**sincerity**, *n.*

sing: *v.* to produce musical sounds with one's voice. *It is traditional to sing the national anthem at hockey games.*

SIGN: Horizontal right **'EXTENDED B'** hand is positioned above left forearm with palm facing leftward/backward. The right wrist makes slight back and forth rotations so that the palm alternates between being angled slightly upward and being angled slightly downward.

single: *adj.* existing alone; composed of one part only. (This sign is used to refer to single 'objects' rather than people.) *He placed a single rose on her desk every morning.*

SIGN #1: Right **'ONE'** hand is held upright with palm facing the chest. (Sign choice depends on context. This sign would not be appropriate for **single** when used as an adjective to describe the size of a bed.)

single: *adj.* lone; solitary; not accompanied by others. (This sign is used to refer to 'people' rather than objects.) *She finds it hard to make ends meet as a single parent.*

SIGN #2: Vertical right **'ONE'** hand, palm facing the body, is moved in a small counter-clockwise circle.

single: *adj.* unmarried. (This sign is used to refer specifically to one's marital status and cannot be used to mean 'just one person' in general.) *He wanted to know if she was married or single.*

SIGN #3: Vertical right **'S'** (or **'ONE'**) hand, palm left, is placed first on the left side of the chin and then on the right side.

singular: *adj.* denoting 'one' in number; not plural. *The singular form of the noun 'mice' is 'mouse'.*

SIGN: Right **'ONE'** hand is held upright with palm facing the chest.

sinister: *adj.* evil; wicked; harmful. *The gang had a sinister plan for revenge against their rivals.*

SIGN: Right **'CROOKED 5'** hand is held with palm facing left and tip of forefinger touching or near end of nose while left **'CROOKED 5'** hand, palm facing right, is held just in front of/below right hand. The hands eventually assume **'A'** shapes as they brush past one another, the right hand moving downward/forward and the left hand moving upward/backward. Appropriate facial expression is important.

sink: *n.* a fixed basin used for washing. *The sink is full of dirty dishes.*

SIGN #1: Fingerspell **SINK**.

sink: *v.* to descend below the surface of a liquid. *The crowd watched the ship sink.*

SIGN #2: Left **'5'** hand represents the surface of the water as it is held in a fixed position with palm down and fingers pointing forward/rightward. Horizontal right **'3'** hand, palm left and extended fingers pointing forward/leftward, is positioned at the end of the fingers of the left hand and is then lowered. (This sign applies to 'watercraft' only. Sign choice varies according to what/who is sinking.)

sinus: *adj.* relating to the spaces in the skull which open into the nasal region. *The doctor prescribed an antibiotic to clear her sinus infection.*

SIGN: Fingerspell **SINUS**. (When **sinus** is used as a noun, the plural form **SINUSES** is generally used and is fingerspelled.)

sip: *v.* to drink a liquid by taking small mouthfuls. *The little boy likes to* **sip** *apple juice from his cup.*

SIGN: Right **'C'** hand is held in a horizontal position near the mouth with palm facing left. The hand is then tipped upward slightly.

sissy: *n.* a person who is weak and/or cowardly. (In the case of a male, there may be an implication that he is effeminate.) *They called him a* **sissy** *because he refused to fight.*

SIGN: Vertical **'F'** hands, palms forward, are held apart at about shoulder level with elbows close but not touching the body. Then the hands are alternately moved forward/outward and back up several times. Facial expression is important. (**SISSY** is frequently fingerspelled.)

sister: *n.* a female person having the same parents as another person. *My* **sister** *is younger than I.*

SIGN #1: Horizontal right **'L'** hand, palm left, held with thumbtip touching the right side of the chin, is brought down to rest on the back of the thumb of the horizontal left **'L'** hand of which the palm faces right and forefinger points forward.

SIGN #2 [ATLANTIC]: Vertical right **'S'** hand, palm left, is placed on the nose and the forefinger is flicked out a couple of times so that it points leftward.

sit: *v.* to occupy a seat. *Please* **sit** *down and wait for me.*

SIGN: Left **'U'** hand is held in a fixed position with palm down and extended fingers pointing forward/rightward. Right **'U'** (or **'CROOKED U'**) hand is held palm down above the left hand with extended fingers pointing forward/leftward. The right hand is then lowered so that the extended fingers come to rest on those of the left hand.

site: *n.* the specific area where something is situated. *It was a perfect* **site** *for the new shopping mall.*

SIGN: Right **'5'** hand, palm down, is circled in a counter-clockwise motion.

ALTERNATE SIGNS—**place** #1 or #2

(be) situated: *v.* to be at or in (a certain place). *The Manitoba School for the Deaf is* **situated** *in Winnipeg.*

SIGN: Right **'BENT ONE'** hand, palm down and forefinger pointing forward, is used to point in a forward direction.

situation: *n.* a set of circumstances. *Their financial* **situation** *is critical.*

SIGN: It is not considered necessary to use a specific sign for **situation** as the fact that there is a situation is already made clear in the rest of the sentence.

six: *n.* See NUMBERS, p. LX.

sixteen: *n.* See NUMBERS, p. LXI.

sixty: *n.* See NUMBERS, p. LXII.

sizable [*also spelled* **sizeable**]: *adj.* fairly large. *They are looking for a* **sizable** *house for their family.*

SIGN: Horizontal **'CLAWED L'** hands, which are held slightly apart with palms facing, are simultaneously moved farther apart as the wrists rotate to turn the palms down. Facial expression is important and the syllable 'CHA' is formed on the lips. (Signs vary depending on context.)

size: *n.* the dimensions or extent of something. *This sweater is the wrong* **size** *for you.*

SIGN: Fingerspell **SIZE**.

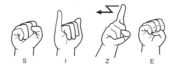

skateboard: *n.* roller skate wheels mounted under a board and usually ridden while standing up. *He got a new* **skateboard** *for Christmas.*

SIGN: Fingertips of right **'CLAWED V'** hand, palm down, are placed on the back of the left **'EXTENDED B'** hand of which the palm is facing down and the fingers are pointing forward/rightward. Together, the two hands are moved forward a couple of times.

ALTERNATE SIGN—**skateboarding**

skateboarding: *n.* a sport which involves standing and riding on a board with roller skate wheels attached underneath. *Some teenagers love skateboarding.*

SIGN: **'EXTENDED B'** hands are held left in front of right with palms down and fingers pointing forward as the hands simultaneously move forward in a wavy pattern.
ALTERNATE SIGN—**skateboard**

skates: *n.* boots with attached blades used to glide swiftly on ice. *If he wants to play hockey he will need a good pair of skates.*

SIGN: Horizontal **'x'** hands, are held apart with palms up and are alternately drawn back and forth, the left hand moving backward/rightward while the right hand moves forward/rightward, then the left hand moving forward/leftward while the right hand moves backward/leftward.
SAME SIGN—**(ice) skate,** *v.*
See also **roller skating**; also used for **(roller) skates,** *n.*

skeleton: *n.* the bony framework of the body. *He will dress up as a skeleton for the Halloween party.*

SIGN: **'CLAWED B'** hands, palms facing chest, are crossed at the wrists, with the right hand nearest the body. The back of the right wrist is tapped twice against the left wrist.

skeptical: *adj.* a state of being in doubt or distrustful of others. *People were skeptical about his theory that the earth was round.*

SIGN: Vertical **'CROOKED V'** hand is held near the face with palm facing leftward/backward. The crooked fingers simultaneously bend up and down slightly a few times as the head shakes slowly and the facial expression clearly shows doubtfulness.
SAME SIGN—**skepticism,** *n.*

sketch: *v.* to make a rough drawing of someone or something. *The police artist will sketch a profile of the suspect from the victim's description.*

SIGN: Left **'EXTENDED B'** hand is held in a fixed and relatively fixed position with palm facing the body. The tip of the little finger of the right **'I'** hand is stroked downward twice along the middle of the left palm. (Sign choice depends on context.)

(cross-country) ski [#1]: See **cross country skiing**.

(downhill) ski: *v.* to travel down a mountain slope on a pair of runners attached to one's boots. *We plan to ski at Lake Louise.*

SIGN #2: **'x'** hands, palms up, are held with the left slightly ahead of the right and are simultaneously bounced up and down slightly at least twice.

OR

SIGN #3: Horizontal **'s'** hands are held apart with palms facing each other and are simultaneously circled forward at least twice as if propelling oneself by poking ski poles repeatedly into the snow.

(water) ski [#4]: See **water-ski**.

skid: *v.* to slide sideways while in motion. *A car will easily skid on icy roads.*

SIGN: Horizontal right **'3'** hand, palm left, is placed on the upturned palm of the left **'EXTENDED B'** hand, moves from side to side a little, then slides straight forward/rightward along the length of the left hand and off. Facial expression is important.

skill: *n.* special talent or expertise. *Interpreting requires skill in two languages.*

SIGN: Left **'EXTENDED B'** hand, palm facing right and fingers pointing upward/forward, is grasped by right **'OPEN A'** hand. Then right hand is pulled forward sharply and closed to form an **'A'** hand.
SAME SIGN—**skillful,** *adj.*

skim: *v.* to remove something from the surface of a liquid either with a spoon or other utensil. *Skim the fat from the broth before you add the vegetables.*

SIGN #1: Horizontal right **'CROOKED EXTENDED B'** hand, palm facing left/backward, is drawn leftward/backward across the upturned palm of the left **'EXTENDED B'** hand and is then turned palm-downward to the left of the left hand. (Sign choice may vary according to what is being skimmed and the type of utensil used to do the skimming.)

skim: *v.* to read in a quick, relaxed way. *I only had time to skim through the newspaper this morning.*

SIGN #2: Horizontal left **'EXTENDED B'** hand, palm facing backward and fingers pointing rightward, is held in front of the left side of the body while horizontal right **'V'** hand is held behind the left hand with palm down and extended fingers pointing forward. As the hands move rightward, the right wrist bends repeatedly so that the tips of the extended fingers move up and down several times. (Facial expression is important.)

skim: *adj.* relating to milk from which the butterfat has been removed. *We use only skim milk because we are on a low-fat diet.*

SIGN #3: Fingerspell **SKIM**.

skin: *n.* the tissue forming the outer covering of the body. *A baby's skin is very soft.*

SIGN: Right cheek is pinched with thumb and forefinger of right **'A-INDEX'** hand. (**SKIN** is frequently fingerspelled.)

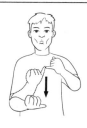

skinny: *adj.* very thin. *She was skinny as a child but she has a lovely figure now.*

SIGN: Horizontal left **'I'** hand is held in a fixed position with palm toward the upper chest. Right **'I'** hand, palm upward, is positioned so that the tip of the little finger touches that of the left hand. Then the right hand is drawn downward. The signer's cheeks are hollowed.

skip: *v.* to move by hopping from one foot to another. *The little girl skipped down the sidewalk.*

SIGN #1: The forefinger and midfinger of the right **'CROOKED V'** hand, palm down, represent legs as they alternately bounce up and down on the upturned palm of the left hand.

skip: *v.* to miss; leave out. *I am so busy today that I think I will skip lunch.*

SIGN #2: Tip of forefinger of horizontal right **'4'** hand, palm facing downward, is placed on the nose and the hand is curved rightward from the wrist away from the face.

skip: *v.* to be absent without permission (usually from school classes). *They agreed to skip English class and go to the mall instead.*

SIGN #3: Left **'BENT MIDFINGER 5'** hand is held in a fixed position with palm down while the forefinger of the right **'ONE'** hand is used to strike the midfinger of the left hand at a backward/leftward/downward angle. (If **skip** refers to someone unlawfully leaving the country to escape justice, **escape** is used.)

skirt: *n.* a garment that hangs from the waist. *She was wearing a black skirt.*

SIGN: **'CROOKED 5'** hands, palms down, are positioned with heels at either side of the waist, and are curved downward simultaneously.

skit: *n.* a short, usually funny, satirical play. *The students presented a skit about the faculty members.*

SIGN: **'EXTENDED A'** hands, palms facing each other, are rotated alternately in small circles which are brought down against the chest.

skull: *n.* the bony casing that encloses the brain. *The scientists examined the skull to see what they could determine about the age of the skeleton.*

SIGN: Fingerspell **SKULL**.

skunk: *n.* a black and white bushy-tailed mammal that ejects an unpleasant smelling fluid. *We could smell a skunk as we hiked along the trail.*

SIGN: Right horizontal **'K'** hand, palm down and fingers pointed forward, is placed near the front of the head and is curved back along the top of the head, the palm eventually facing upward. This is a wrist movement. (**SKUNK** is frequently fingerspelled.)

sky: *n.* the expanse extending upward from the horizon. *There is not a cloud in the sky.*

SIGN: Fingerspell **SKY**.

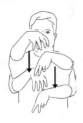

skydive: *v.* to jump from an airplane, using a parachute to slow down the descent. *When you skydive, the weather must be just right.*

SIGN: Right **'CLAWED SPREAD C'** hand, palm down, is used to represent an open parachute while the left **'V'** hand, palm down, represents the legs of the person below it. The hands are simultaneously lowered.

skyrocket: *v.* to rise very rapidly and often unexpectedly. (This sign is used when there is an intimation of *success*. It often refers to the sudden *prosperity of a business*.) *When oil was discovered the economy began to skyrocket.*

SIGN #1: Left **'EXTENDED B'** hand is held in a fixed position with palm facing right and fingers pointing upward/forward. Right **'B'** hand, palm forward/downward, is held against the left palm and shoots straight upward/forward.

skyrocket: *v.* to rise very rapidly and often unexpectedly. (This sign is used when there is *not necessarily any implication of success*.) *The price of gas began to skyrocket at that time.*

SIGN #2: Left **'ONE'** hand is held in a fixed position with palm downward/forward/rightward and forefinger pointing upward/forward/rightward. Right **'CONTRACTED L'** hand is held on the knuckle at the base of the left forefinger with palm facing forward/leftward. The right hand then moves along the left forefinger and out into the air as the finger and thumb close to form a **'CLOSED MODIFIED G'** shape.

slack: *adj.* not busy; having very little to do. *The hotel charges less during slack periods when there are few tourists in the area.*

SIGN: Right **'EXTENDED A'** hand, palm facing left, thumb under chin, is thrust forward. Next, wrist of vertical right **'B'** hand, palm facing forward/leftward, is brushed back and forth against wrist of left **'STANDARD BASE'** hand. (ASL CONCEPT—**not - busy**.) Signs vary according to context.

slacks: *n.* trousers, especially those worn on casual occasions. *He was wearing corduroy slacks.*

SIGN: **'EXTENDED B'** hands are held a thigh's width apart in front of the left side of the body at about hip level with palms facing each other and fingers pointed downward. The hands are simultaneously moved downward, then moved to the right side and moved downward once more.

ALTERNATE SIGN—**pants** #1

slam: *v.* to close noisily and with force. *Please leave quietly and do not slam the door.*

SIGN: Vertical left **'B'** hand is held in a fixed position with palm facing rightward/forward. Vertical right **'B'** hand, palm facing backward, is rotated from the wrist so the palm faces leftward/forward as its edge is slammed purposefully against the edge of the left hand, resulting in the creation of a **'V'** formation. (Signs vary according to context.)

slander: *n.* a false spoken statement that could damage someone's reputation. *If you say that in public, she can sue you for slander.*

SIGN: Vertical right **'BENT B'** (or **'BENT ONE'**) hand, palm left, is brushed leftward across the chin.

slang: *n.* language that is not appropriate in a formal context. *'Dunno' is slang meaning 'I do not know' and is often spoken with a shrug.*

SIGN: Fingerspell **SLANG**.

slap: *v.* to hit with the open hand. *She tried to slap his face.*

SIGN #1: A natural gesture is used as the right **'EXTENDED B'** hand, palm forward, is rotated sharply from the wrist so that the palm faces backwards. ❖

slap in the face: *n.* an insult. *After all her hard work, she thought his negative comments were a slap in the face.*

SIGN #2: Right **'ONE'** hand, palm facing left, is held in a horizontal position in front of the chest and is then curved upward from the wrist as it moves forward with a stabbing motion.

slash: *v.* to cut with a sweeping stroke, as with a blade of some kind. *The woman in the movie considered slashing her wrists, but decided it was a bad idea.*

SIGN #1: Right **'CLOSED A-INDEX'** hand is held palm down and makes a downward slashing motion against the left wrist. (The location of this sign varies according to context and an **'S'** handshape is used to indicate slashing which requires much effort.)

slash: *v.* to reduce prices significantly. *This department store will slash prices tomorrow.*

SIGN #2: Horizontal **'BENT EXTENDED B'** (or **'ONE'**) hands are held right above left with left palm up and right palm forward/downward. The right hand is then lowered toward the left hand.

slash: *n.* a symbol (/) used to set things off in print. *You will often see at least one slash in a web page address.*

SIGN #3: Right **'EXTENDED B'** hand, palm angled leftward/upward, is drawn down from left to right in a slanting manner.

slaughter: *v.* to kill in a cruel manner; to brutally kill several people. *He slaughtered a dozen innocent political prisoners.*

SIGN #1: Vertical left **'EXTENDED B'** hand is held in a fixed position with palm facing rightward and slightly forward. Right **'ONE'** (or **'K'**) hand is held palm down as it moves forward/downward at a slight leftward angle, the forefinger firmly grazing the left palm. Facial expression is important and the signer's lips are squared as if producing the 'SH' sound. ❖

slaughter: *v.* to kill animals for food. *The hogs will be slaughtered next week.*

SIGN #2: Right **'Y'** hand, palm forward/leftward, is thrust at the throat so the tip of the thumb touches it.

slave: *n.* a person who is legally owned by another and has no rights or freedom. *Many slaves escaped from the southern United States to Canada on the Underground Railroad.*

SIGN #1: **'S'** hands, left palm down and right palm forward/leftward, are positioned with the right wrist against the left hand. Together, the hands are swung from side to side.

SAME SIGN—**slavery**, *n.*

slave: *v.* to work like a slave. *All his employees slave from 9:00 a.m. to 5:00 p.m. because he is a strict boss.*

SIGN #2: Left **'S'** (or **'A'**) hand is held in a fixed position with palm down. Heel of right **'S'** (or **'A'**) hand, palm facing leftward/forward, strikes repeatedly against right side (or 'thumb' side) of left hand in a rightward/forward direction. The motion is laboured and appears as a series of counter-clockwise circles. Cheeks are puffed.

slay: *v.* to kill violently. *Soldiers were trained to slay the enemy.*

SIGN: Vertical left **'EXTENDED B'** hand is held in a fixed position with palm facing rightward and slightly forward. Right **'ONE'** (or **'K'**) hand is held palm down as it moves forward/downward at a slight leftward angle, the forefinger firmly grazing the left palm. Facial expression is important and the signer's lips are squared as if producing the 'SH' sound. ❖

sled: *n.* a vehicle mounted on runners and drawn by horses or dogs, or propelled by human power for recreational purposes. *He is training his dogs to pull a sled.*

SIGN: **'CLAWED V'** hands, palms facing upward/backward, are held slightly apart and are simultaneously curved downward and toward the chest.

sleek: *adj.* smooth and shiny. *She brushed the pony until his coat was sleek.*

SIGN: **'FLAT O'** hands are held parallel with palms up. The hands move simultaneously forward as the thumbs slowly slide across the fingers to form **'A'** hands.

sleep: *v.* to rest in a relatively unconscious state. *We should sleep an average of six to eight hours nightly.*

SIGN #1: Right **'CONTRACTED 5'** hand is held with palm toward the face. The hand is then drawn downward as the fingers close to form a **'FLAT O'** hand just in front of the chin or neck.

SIGN #2 [ATLANTIC]: Vertical right **'SPREAD C'** hand is held in front of right side of forehead with palm facing left. It is then moved leftward as it closes to form an **'S'** hand and the head tilts leftward.

sleepy: *adj.* drowsy; feeling the need to sleep. *We were sleepy when we got home after hiking from 6 a.m. to 6 p.m.*

SIGN: Right **'CONTRACTED 5'** hand is held with palm toward the face. Then it is moved downward as it closes to form a **'FLAT O'** hand. Motion is repeated as the head tilts downward to the right and the eyes gradually close.

sleet: *n.* partly frozen rain; a mixture of snow and rain. *The rain turned to sleet and made the highway very icy.*

SIGN: **'SPREAD EXTENDED C'** hands are held parallel with palms down, and are bounced up and down slightly at least twice. This is a wrist action. Next, **'CROOKED 5'** hands are held parallel with palms down. They then jerk slightly forward/downward as the fingers retract to form **'CLAWED SPREAD C'** hands. (ASL CONCEPT—rain - freeze.) SLEET may be fingerspelled.

sleeve: *n.* the part of a garment that covers the arm. *The blouse will be finished when the seamstress adds the left sleeve.*

SIGN: Right **'SPREAD C'** hand, palm down, is used to grasp the left bicep, then slides down the length of the left arm.

sleeveless: *adj.* having no sleeves. *She was wearing a sleeveless top with her shorts.*

SIGN: Horizontal **'BENT EXTENDED B'** hands, palms toward the body and the fingertips touching the shoulders at a point where a sleeve would normally begin. The wrists then rotate so that the fingertips brush downward against the shoulders a couple of times.

(long) sleeves: *n.* the parts of a garment that cover the arms from shoulder to wrist. *I want to buy a new blouse with long sleeves.*

SIGN #1: Edge of right horizontal **'EXTENDED B'** hand, palm left/backward, is brought down to touch the left arm at the wrist a couple of times to indicate the length of the sleeve.

(short) sleeves: *n.* the parts of a garment that cover only the biceps. *During the summer, I prefer to wear a shirt with short sleeves to keep cool.*

SIGN #2: Edge of right horizontal **'EXTENDED B'** hand, palm upward/backward, is brought down to touch the left bicep a couple of times to indicate the length of the sleeve.

sleigh: *n.* a sled. *A sleigh is a vehicle that usually has runners.*

SIGN: **'CLAWED V'** hands, palms facing upward/backward, are held slightly apart and are simultaneously curved downward and toward the chest. (Context may vary according to whether the sleigh is drawn by a human, a horse, or a team of dogs.)

slender: *adj.* of small width relative to height; slim; thin. *Competitive swimmers usually have slender bodies.*

SIGN: Right vertical **'I'** hand, palm toward the body, is drawn downward, the palm eventually facing upward. Meanwhile the signer appears to be emitting a very narrow stream of air between lips which are parted ever so slightly. ALTERNATE SIGN—**slim** #1

sleuth: *n.* an informal word for 'detective'. *Sherlock Holmes was a fictitious sleuth created by Sir Arthur Conan Doyle.*

SIGN: Joined midfinger and thumb of right **'D'** hand are placed against the upper left side of the chest and the hand is moved in a small, clockwise (from the onlooker's perspective) circle.

slice: *v.* to cut (usually in narrow pieces) from a larger piece or loaf. *She will slice the bread for sandwiches.*

SIGN: Left **'C'** hand is held palm down as the right horizontal **'EXTENDED B'** hand, palm left, chops downward a few times alongside the left hand, grazing it with each downward thrust. (For **slice**, *n.*, signs vary depending mainly on the size and shape of the slice.)

slide: *v.* to coast down a smooth surface. *Children love to slide downhill on a toboggan.*

SIGN #1: Right **'EXTENDED B'** hand, palm down and bent at the wrist, is held at the level of the right shoulder with fingers angled downward/forward. The hand is then moved straight downward/forward.

slide: *n.* play equipment on which children climb up a ladder and then slide down a smooth metal chute. *The children ran to the slide in the playground.*

SIGN #2: Right **'CLAWED V'** hand, palm down and bent at the wrist, is held at the level of the right shoulder and is moved straight downward/forward.

slide: *n.* the downward movement of a large mass of earth, rocks, snow, etc., usually on a mountain slope. *The highway was closed due to a snow slide near the mountain pass.*

SIGN #3: Horizontal **'5'** hands, bent at the wrists with palms down, are positioned so the left is slightly ahead of the right. Then both hands are simultaneously shoved downward at a forward angle with a very firm movement. (Signs vary according to whether the slide consists of rocks, mud, earth, etc.)

slide: *n.* a small photograph on a transparent base, mounted in a frame. *Our social studies teacher showed us a slide of the Parliament Buildings in Ottawa.*

SIGN #4: Fingerspell **SLIDE**.

slight: *adj.* small in extent. *I have a slight headache.*

SIGN #1: Right **'X'** hand is held palm-up with forefinger tightly crooked and tip of thumb repeatedly scraping downward against tip of forefinger.

slight: *adj.* slim and delicate. *He has a slight physique but is an excellent gymnast.*

SIGN #2: Horizontal left **'I'** hand is held in a fixed position with palm toward the upper chest. Right **'I'** hand, palm upward, is positioned so that the tip of the little finger touches that of the left hand. Then the right hand is drawn downward. The signer's cheeks are hollowed.

slim: *adj.* slender. *After he dieted, he was slim and trim.*

SIGN #1: **'EXTENDED B'** hands, palms facing each other, are placed at either side of the chest and are moved downward simultaneously along the sides of the body. The signer's eyes squint and the lips are parted only slightly to allow a narrow stream of air to escape.
ALTERNATE SIGN—**slender**

slim: *adj.* meager; poor (implying doubt). *The chances of his passing the final exams are very slim.*

SIGN #2: Vertical **'CROOKED V'** hand is held near the face with palm facing leftward/backward. The crooked fingers simultaneously bend up and down slightly a few times as the head shakes slowly and the facial expression clearly shows doubtfulness.

sling: *n.* a wide piece of cloth suspended from the neck to support an injured arm or hand. *After the accident he had his left arm in a sling for several weeks.*

SIGN: Horizontal **'EXTENDED B'** hands are held so the left is in a rigid, fixed position, bent at the elbow with palm toward the body. The right hand is placed just in front of the left shoulder, then brought down to circle the left forearm in the same way as a sling would cover it if it were injured.

slingshot: *n.* a simple, Y-shaped weapon with a band of rubber attached to the prongs for propelling small, stone-like objects. *He uses a slingshot to keep the birds away from the berry patch.*

SIGN: Vertical left **'V'** hand is held in a fixed position with palm toward the chest. Vertical right **'F'** (or **'S'**) hand, palm forward, is held just behind the left hand, then drawn back toward the chest as it changes to a **'FLAT OPEN F'** (or **'CONTRACTED 3'**) hand.

slip: *n.* an undergarment worn by a girl or woman as a lining for a skirt or dress. *You will need to wear a slip under that dress.*

SIGN #1: Fingerspell **SLIP**.

slip: *v.* to slide unexpectedly (often sideways). *If you **slip** on the icy sidewalk, you might fall and break some bones.*

SIGN #2: Right **'K'** hand is held palm down with tip of middle finger touching the upturned palm of the left **'EXTENDED B'** hand. The right hand then slides forward along the length of the left hand and curves slightly upward. Facial expression and body language are important. In addition, the teeth are visible as the signer appears to be articulating the vowel sound 'EE'.

slip one's mind: *v.* to escape from one's memory. *I meant to phone you but it **slipped my mind**.*

SIGN #3: Tip of forefinger of vertical right **'ONE'** hand, palm forward/leftward, touches centre of forehead. Then the hand drops so that the forefinger slips down between the forefinger and middle finger of the left **'EXTENDED B'** hand which is held palm down. (ASL CONCEPT—**think - disappear.**)

slip out: *v.* to leave quickly but stealthily. *He was able to **slip out** of the house undetected.*

SIGN #4: Forefinger of right **'ONE'** hand, palm facing leftward/forward, is placed upright between the first two fingers of the left **'EXTENDED B'** hand which is held palm down with fingers pointing rightward/forward. Then the right forefinger is vigorously thrust forward/rightward.

(make a) slip: *v.* to make an error. *If you **make a slip** in your calculations, the budget will not balance.*

SIGN #5: Vertical right **'Y'** hand, palm toward the body, is tapped a couple of times against the chin.

slipper: *n.* a light, comfortable shoe worn indoors. *The puppy chewed my **slipper**.*

SIGN #1: Head tilts slightly to the right, supported by right **'EXTENDED B'** hand, which is held against right side of face. Next, horizontal right **'EXTENDED B'** hand, palm left, is placed against the thumb side of the left **'B'** hand of which the palm is facing down and the fingers pointing forward at a rightward angle. Then the right hand is curved forward and around the fingers to the opposite side of the left hand. (ASL CONCEPT—**bed - shoe.**) Signs vary.

SIGN #2 [ONTARIO]: Horizontal **'CONTRACTED L'** hands are held right on top of left with the left palm facing right and the right palm facing left. Then the forefingers simultaneously flutter a few times so that the hands alternate rapidly between **'CONTRACTED L'** and **'BENT L'** shapes.

slippery: *adj.* causing objects to slip and slide. *The roads are **slippery** so drive carefully.*

SIGN: **'FLAT O'** hands are held with palms up, the left hand slightly ahead of the right hand. The hands move simultaneously forward while the hands close to form **'A'** hands. (Signs vary depending on what or who might be slipping on a given surface.)

slit: *v.* to make a long, narrow cut, opening, or incision. *He **slit the back of his hand** on the saw.*

SIGN: Tip of forefinger of right **'ONE'** hand, with palm facing leftward/backward, is drawn firmly backward across back of left **'STANDARD BASE'** hand. (Sign choice depends on context.)

sliver: *n.* a small thin piece of material (usually wood). *I have a sliver in my finger.*

SIGN: Horizontal right **'EXTENDED B'** hand, fingertips pointing forward/leftward and palm facing left, is placed on the left **'STANDARD BASE'** hand. Both hands then move back and forth in a sawing motion. Next, horizontal left **'ONE'** hand is held in a fixed position with palm toward the chest and forefinger pointing rightward. Horizontal right **'BENT ONE'** hand is held with palm toward the chest and tip of forefinger on the edge of the left forefinger and moving leftward along the finger to indicate the path of the sliver. (ASL CONCEPT—**wood - inside finger**.)

slobber: *v.* to dribble from the mouth. *Babies tend to slobber when they are teething.*

SIGN: Vertical right **'4'** hand, with palm left and tip of forefinger positioned at right side of mouth, is drawn downward.

slogan: *n.* a distinctive, catchy phrase used in advertising, politics, protests and other events. *Our new slogan will be: "Hire Deaf people; we deliver!"*

SIGN: Vertical **'V'** hands, palms facing forward, are held apart just above shoulder level, and are curved outward slightly from the wrists as they become **'CLAWED V'** hands.

slo-pitch: *n.* a popular sporting event that is similar to softball, the major difference being in the pitching style. *The tournament will include slo-pitch.*

SIGN: The wrist of the right **'SPREAD C'** hand bends up and down a couple of times so that the palm alternates between facing down and facing forward. (**SLO-PITCH** may be fingerspelled.)

sloppy: *adj.* messy; not neat and tidy. *He looks sloppy in those clothes.*

SIGN #1: Right **'MODIFIED 5'** hand is held under chin with palm down as the fingers flutter.

SIGN #2: Right **'MODIFIED 5'** hand is held with palm facing leftward at a slight downward slant and thumbtip at the left side of the chin. The hand is then drawn rightward until the thumbtip ends up at the right side of the chin. (This sign is used to describe someone's *appearance* specifically. **Sloppy** #1 may be used to describe anything/anyone as sloppy.)

slow: *adj.* not fast; lacking speed. *The slow traffic should stay in the right lane.*

SIGN #1: Right **'CROOKED 5'** hand is held palm down with fingertips touching the end of the left **'STANDARD BASE'** hand. The right hand is then drawn backward leftward along the back of the left hand as though petting it.

OR

SIGN #2: Right **'EXTENDED B'** hand is held to the right side of the body with fingers pointing downward and palm facing backward. Fingers simultaneously move back and forth.

SIGN #3 [ATLANTIC]: Tip of forefinger of horizontal right **'ONE'** hand, palm down, is placed on the back of the left hand and is drawn slowly up toward the left elbow.

slow down: *v.* to go less fast. *Please slow down because we can not keep up with you.*

SIGN: **'EXTENDED B'** hands are held parallel with palms down and fingers pointing forward. The forearms are then simultaneously moved slowly and deliberately down and up a couple of times.

slum: *n.* a squalid area of a city, where living conditions are inferior. *What was once a fashionable area of London is now a slum.*

SIGN: **'EXTENDED A'** hands are held slightly apart in front of the chest with the palms facing each other, and are lowered slowly but simultaneously to waist level. Facial expression is important. **SLUM** may be fingerspelled. ALTERNATE SIGN—**poor + area** #1

sly: *adj.* crafty. *He had a sly expression on his face.*

SIGN #1: Thumb and forefinger of the right **'FLAT OPEN F'** hand are laid flat against the left cheek with the palm facing leftward/backward. The forefinger moves rapidly up and down several times so that the hand alternates between a **'FLAT OPEN F'** shape and a **'FLAT F'**.

SIGN #2 [ATLANTIC]: Right **'A'** hand, palm leftward, is placed with thumbnail at about the right cheekbone and is drawn slowly down the cheek toward the lower jaw.

smack: *n.* a loud kiss. *After I won the race, my mother gave me a big smack on the cheek.*

SIGN #1: Fingertips of right **'FLAT O'** hand, palm facing left, are firmly planted against the right cheek while the lips smack as if kissing someone. (The location of this sign will vary according to context.)

smack: *v.* to slap with an open hand. *If you do not stop pestering me, I will smack you!*

SIGN #2: A natural gesture is used as the horizontal right **'EXTENDED B'** hand, palm forward, is rotated sharply from the wrist so that the palm faces backwards. ❖

smack: *v.* to make a sharp sound with the lips as if in enjoyment. *Do not smack your lips when you are eating.*

SIGN #3: The signer simply smacks his/her lips to convey this concept.

small: *adj.* little; not big. *They live in a small house in Eyebrow, Saskatchewan.*

SIGN #1: Horizontal **'EXTENDED B'** hands are held apart with palms facing each other and fingers pointing forward. They are then moved toward each other slightly a couple of times.

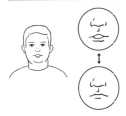

small: *adj.* limited in height. (This sign generally refers to the height of a person or a thing relative to the floor.) *She is too small to participate in the game.*

SIGN #2: Right **'EXTENDED B'** hand is held out to the right side of the body with palm down and is moved up and down to indicate the shortness of stature.

small: *adj.* little (in terms of the height of something such as a drink). *I will have a small root beer.*

SIGN #3: Horizontal **'BENT EXTENDED B'** hands are held right above left with left palm up and right palm forward/downward. The right hand is then lowered toward the left hand. The signer's lips appear to be articulating the syllable 'MO'.

small: *adj.* not large (in terms of clothing size). *She asked for the shirt in a small size.*

SIGN #4: Vertical right **'S'** hand, palm facing forward, appears to wobble from side to side slightly.

small: *adj.* little. (This sign is used to mean tiny or unusually small.) *There are many new small fish in the aquarium now.*

SIGN #5: Tips of extended fingers of right **'EXTENDED U'** hand, palm facing the body, are brushed downward on chin. This movement involves only the extended fingers, which bend in the process. The hand itself does not move. The signer's lips appear to be articulating the syllable 'MO'. (Alternatively, a **'MODIFIED G'** hand is used, with the gap between the thumb and forefinger indicating just how small a thing is.)

small: *adj.* trivial; petty; of little importance. *I will not let a small matter like that upset me.*

SIGN #6: Right **'COVERED T'** hand is held with palm upward/backward and the thumb is flicked out, thus forming an **'A-INDEX'** hand.

(feel) small: *v.* to feel humiliated, ashamed, or inferior. *She tried to make me feel small by questioning my credentials.*

SIGN #7: Right **'CONTRACTED C'** hand is positioned with palm facing leftward/forward and the thumb resting on the upturned palm of the left **'EXTENDED B'** hand. Then the right hand is purposefully snapped shut to form a **'FLAT O'** handshape.
ALTERNATE SIGN—humiliated

small-minded: *adj.* having very narrow views; intolerant. *Racists are often **small-minded** and mean toward new immigrants.*

SIGN #8: Tip of forefinger of right **'ONE'** hand, palm toward face, touches right side of forehead. Then tips of horizontal **'B'** hands are brought together at about chest level to form a **'V'** shape with the apex pointing forward. (ASL CONCEPT—**think - close**.)

smart: *adj.* intelligent. *He was **smart** enough to win a scholarship.*

SIGN #1: Tip of middle finger of right **'BENT MIDFINGER 5'** hand touches forehead and the hand is flung outward so that the palm faces away from face.

OR

SIGN #2: Vertical right **'ONE'** hand, palm leftward/forward, is positioned with the tip of the forefinger on the forehead and the hand is firmly thrust forward from the wrist so that the forefinger points forward.

smart: *adj.* well-dressed; neat. *That outfit looks **smart** on you.*

SIGN #3: Horizontal **'EXTENDED B'** hands are held, right on top of left, left palm facing upward and right palm facing downward, the fingers pointing basically forward. Together, the hands appear to jerk backward a short distance although the hands do not move any real distance at all. This is a twitchlike movement.

smart: *v.* to sting or feel sharply painful. *The doctor cautioned me that the medication would cause the wound to **smart** when it was applied.*

SIGN #4: Right **'OPEN SPREAD O'** hand is held over the area in question as the fingers wiggle to indicate the tingling sensation of the pain. The teeth are visible and give the impression that the signer is articulating the sound 'EE'.

smell: *v.* to perceive a scent. *I can **smell** the fresh bread in the bakery.*

SIGN: Right **'EXTENDED B'** hand is held with palm facing the body, and fingertips just in front of the nose and pointing leftward/upward. The hand is then circled forward a few times in small clockwise circles. SAME SIGN—**smell**, *n.*

smelly: *adj.* having a strong or nasty smell. *Please clean out your **smelly** locker.*

SIGN #1: Right **'5'** hand is held with palm facing leftward/downward and thumbtip touching or close to the tip of the nose. The hand is then firmly thrust a short distance forward at a slight downward angle. Meanwhile, a grimace appears on the signer's face and the lips appear to be articulating the syllable 'PO'. (In ASL the adjective follows rather than precedes the noun. In the sample sentence **locker** would come before **smelly**.)

OR

SIGN #2: Right horizontal **'OPEN F'** hand, palm facing backward, is positioned with forefinger and thumb holding the end of the nose. This sign is accompanied by a grimace.

smile: *v.* to show pleasure, fondness, or happiness by turning the corners of the mouth upward. *The baby is beginning to **smile**.*

SIGN: **'ONE'** hands, palms downward, are positioned so that the tips of the forefingers are touching either side of the chin and are curved upward slightly. SAME SIGN—**smile**, *n.*

smirk: *n.* a smile that shows scorn or smugness rather than pleasure. *The **smirk** on her face makes me distrust her.*

SIGN: Right **'BENT ONE'** hand, palm leftward, is positioned so that the tip of the forefinger is near the right corner of the mouth and is very slightly poked upward to give the lips a somewhat lopsided smile as the wrist rotates slightly to turn the hand so that the palm faces backward. Facial expression must clearly convey excessive self-satisfaction.

smog: *n.* a mixture of smoke, industrial and chemical fumes and fog. *The level of **smog** tends to be higher in cities where there is a lot of industry.*

SIGN: Fingerspell **SMOG**.

S   M   O   G

smoke: *n.* fumes produced by combustion. (This sign is used only for smoke which moves relatively sideways.) *Cars emit toxic smoke that pollutes the environment.*

SIGN #1: Left **'S'** hand is held out in front of the body with palm down. Right **'SPREAD C'** hand, palm forward/downward, is held just behind the left hand and spirals back toward the chest in a series of clockwise circles.

smoke: *n.* fumes produced by combustion. (This sign is used only for smoke which moves relatively upward.) *That factory emits smoke that pollutes the environment.*

SIGN #2: Horizontal left **'S'** hand is held out in front of the body with palm facing rightward/backward. Right **'SPREAD C'** hand, palm downward, is held just above the left hand and spirals upward in a series of counterclockwise circles.

smoke: *n.* fumes produced by combustion. (This sign is used only for smoke which tends to be concentrated in one area, especially an enclosed area, rather than travelling in a column.) *When I saw all the smoke in the kitchen, I ran next door right away to call the fire department.*

SIGN #3: **'5'** hands, palms facing backward, the left hand upright and the right hand inverted, revolve around each other as they both move in a clockwise direction. Cheeks are puffed out.

smoke: *v.* to draw in and exhale (the smoke from a cigarette). *If she continues to smoke, she will endanger her health.*

SIGN #4: Tips of extended fingers of vertical right **'SLANTED V'** hand, palm facing leftward/backward, are tapped against the lips several times.

smoke grass: *v.* to smoke cigarettes made of the dried leaves and flowers of the hemp plant. *During the 1960s and 1970s many young people smoked grass.*

SIGN: Joined thumb and forefinger of vertical right **'F'** (or **'CLOSED X'**) hand, palm left, are tapped a couple of times against the right side of the lips.

smooth: *adj.* even textured; not rough. *Velvet is smooth to the touch.*

SIGN: **'FLAT O'** hands are held with palms up, the left hand slightly ahead of the right hand. The hands move simultaneously forward while the hands close to form **'A'** hands.

smother: *v.* to stifle; suffocate. *He tried to smother his victim with a large pillow.*

SIGN: Horizontal **'A'** hands are held parallel with palms facing each other and are simultaneously thrust downward as if smothering someone with a pillow.

smuggle: *v.* to import or export prohibited goods or to bring in merchandise without paying the required duties. *He tried to smuggle cigarettes and alcohol across the U.S.A.-Canada border.*

SIGN: Right **'A'** hand is brought to the lips with the thumb pointed upward and the palm facing left. Then the lips are touched twice with the thumbnail. Next, **'EXTENDED B'** hands are held parallel with palms up in front of the left side of the body. Then they are simultaneously moved in a slight arc to the right. ❖ (ASL CONCEPT—**secret - bring**.)

snack: *n.* a light meal eaten between regular meals. *We will have some cheese and crackers for our snack.*

SIGN: Fingerspell **SNACK**.

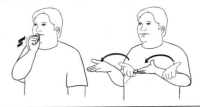

snake: *n.* a reptile with a scaly, cylindrical, limbless body. *The python is not a poisonous snake.*

SIGN #1: Right **'CROOKED V'** hand is held with the back against the mouth and is slithered forward to simulate the movement of a snake.

OR

SIGN #2: Horizontal right **'3'** hand is held with palm left and thumbtip against the lower lip. The hand is then slithered forward to simulate the movement of a snake.

snap: *v.* to bite at something by bringing the jaws together rapidly. *Do not go into their yard because their Rottweiler will snap at you.*

SIGN #1: Vertical right **'SPREAD C'** hand is held with palm facing forward and becomes a **'CLAWED SPREAD C'** hand as it is thrust forward short distance. Teeth are bared. ❖

snap: *v.* to break with a sharp sound. *They heard the cable snap as the chairlift descended.*

SIGN #2: Horizontal **'BENT ONE'** hands are positioned with palms toward the chest and tips of forefingers touching. The left hand remains fixed while the right hand abruptly moves upward from the wrist so that the forefinger points upward/leftward.

snap a picture: *v.* to take a snapshot with a camera. *He likes to snap pictures of his friends when they least expect it.*

SIGN #3: Vertical **'CROOKED L'** (or **'C-INDEX'**) hands are held so as to frame the eyes with a thumb touching either side of face, and palms facing each other, but angled forward slightly. The forefinger of the right hand then crooks as if depressing the button a camera in order to take a picture.

snap one's fingers: *v.* to rub one's thumb across the midfinger to create a sound. *He thinks he can make everyone jump to attention by merely snapping his fingers.*

SIGN #4: Tips of right thumb and midfinger are joined, palm facing leftward at an upward/backward angle, and the hand is then given a twist of the wrist as the thumb audibly slides off the middle finger to snap into an **'A'** handshape with the palm up.

snap (decision): *n.* a judgment made, suddenly, without giving it much thought. *It was a snap decision that fortunately paid off.*

SIGN #5: This concept would be included in the noun that follows it. The sign for **decision** would be made more quickly and emphatically than usual and the signer's facial expression would show determination.

(cold) snap: *n.* a short spell of severely cold weather. *The cold snap lasted longer than we expected.*

SIGN #6: **'A'** (or **'S'**) hands are held apart, palms facing each other, and are shaken, along with the shoulders, as if the signer is shivering.

snaps: *n.* fasteners that close by snapping two parts together. *Many babies' garments have snaps to make dressing them easier.*

SIGN: **'EXTENDED A'** hands are held together in front of the upper chest with palms down and thumbs almost touching. Then they are pushed toward each other as if fastening a snap on a garment. The hands are lowered at regular intervals several times and the motion is repeated. The location of this sign would depend on where the snaps are situated.

snatch: *v.* to seize or grasp suddenly. *The thief tried to snatch the old lady's handbag.*

SIGN: Sign choice for **snatch** depends on what is being snatched and where the snatching is taking place. The sign takes the form of a natural gesture, beginning with the hand open and fingers spread, and ending with a closed fist. ❖

sneak around: *v.* to move furtively or secretly. *The police caught him sneaking around our house while we were on vacation.*

SIGN #1: Vertical right **'ONE'** hand, palm forward, is zigzagged forward in a furtive manner.

sneak out: *v.* to leave unobtrusively. *He tried to sneak out of the house without his parents' permission.*

SIGN #2: Forefinger of right **'ONE'** hand, palm facing leftward/forward, is placed upright between the first two fingers of the left **'EXTENDED B'** hand which is held palm down with fingers pointing rightward/forward. Then the right forefinger is vigorously thrust forward/rightward.

sneak up on: *v.* to approach someone in a secretive manner. *He sneaked up on her in the dark and scared her half to death.*

SIGN #3: Vertical left **'ONE'** hand is held in a fixed position out in front of the body with palm forward/rightward while vertical right **'ONE'** hand, palm forward/leftward, is held close to the chest and moves forward with small bounces as if 'sneaking up on' the left hand.

sneaky: *adj.* underhanded; furtive; stealthy. *He is a sneaky person.*

SIGN: Thumb and forefinger of the right **'FLAT OPEN F'** hand are laid flat against the left cheek with the palm facing leftward/backward. The forefinger moves rapidly up and down several times so that the hand alternates between a **'FLAT OPEN F'** shape and a **'FLAT F'**.

sneer: *v.* to make a contemptuous or sarcastic facial expression, usually by raising one corner of the upper lip. *He sneered when his competitor made a mistake.*

SIGN: Vertical right **'BENT V'** hand is held at about shoulder level with palm facing forward and the extended fingers also pointing forward. A 'sneer' must be clearly visible on the face.

sneeze: *v.* to have air involuntarily escaping explosively from the nose. *Hay fever makes people sneeze.*

SIGN: Horizontal right **'BENT ONE'** hand is held with palm facing left and forefinger under the nose while the mouth is slightly open and the head tilted back a little. The head then abruptly falls forward as the mouth closes, thus simulating a sneeze.

sniff: *v.* to inhale through the nose in order to smell (something). *The children liked to sniff the aroma of fresh-baked cinnamon buns at the bakery.*

SIGN: Right **'EXTENDED B'** hand is held with palm facing the body, and fingertips just in front of the nose and pointing leftward/upward. The hand is then circled forward a few times in small clockwise circles. (If it is a *dog* doing the sniffing, the right **'CONTRACTED B'** hand with palm down represents the dog's head as it bobs along sniffing.)

snob: *n.* an arrogant person who behaves condescendingly toward others; someone who thinks s/he is better than other people. *Despite his wealth, he has never been a snob.*

SIGN: Right **'ONE'** hand is held under the nose with palm down and forefinger pointing left. The hand is then flicked upward to indicate a 'nose in the air' attitude.
SAME SIGN—**snobbish**, *adj.*

snooze: *v.* to nap or sleep lightly. *Sometimes I snooze while I am watching TV.*

SIGN: Right **'CONTRACTED 5'** hand is held with palm toward the face. The hand is then drawn downward as the fingers close to form a **'FLAT O'** hand just in front of the chin or neck.

snore: *v.* to make snorting sounds through the mouth and nose while sleeping. *When you snore, it keeps me awake.*

SIGN: Fingerspell **SNORE**.

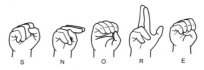

S N O R E

snorkel: *v.* to swim just under the water's surface, using a special breathing tube fitted into the mouth and projecting above the water. *We like to snorkel whenever we go to Hawaii.*

SIGN: Vertical right **'OPEN SPREAD O'** hand, palm facing backwards, is held in front of the mouth. The signer's cheeks are puffed and a fine stream of air is released through pursed lips as the hand takes on a **'COVERED O'** shape, moves slightly rightward, turns to a horizontal position as the elbow is raised, and moves straight upward. Next, the right **'BENT V'** hand, palm toward the body, is held under the left **'STANDARD BASE'** hand and is moved forward a short distance with the extended fingers fluttering. (ASL CONCEPT—**mouthpiece - tube - swim under water surface**.)

snow: *n.* precipitation in the form of flakes of frozen water. *The first snow of the season usually falls in November.*

SIGN: **'BENT EXTENDED B'** hands are positioned with palms toward the body and fingertips on either side of the upper chest and are simultaneously rotated forward from the wrists so that the fingers point forward and spread to form **'5'** hands with the palms facing down. The hands are then lowered delicately with the fingers fluttering. (Alternatively, the first part of this sign may be deleted so that the sign begins at the **'5'** hand stage.)

snowboarding: *n.* a winter activity in which a person moves down a snow-covered slope standing on a ski-like plank. *Snowboarding has become a very popular activity on many ski slopes.*

SIGN #1: **'5'** hands are held apart with palms facing down and fingers pointing forward. The hands are then lowered delicately with the fingers fluttering. Next, right **'CROOKED V'** hand is positioned palm down with tips of extended fingers resting on the left **'STANDARD BASE'**. Together, the hands move a short distance forward at a slight downward angle and back a couple of times. (In situations where the context is already understood, the first part of this sign may be omitted.)

OR

SIGN #2: **'5'** hands are held apart with palms facing down and fingers pointing forward. The hands are then lowered delicately with the fingers fluttering. Next, **'EXTENDED B'** hands are held left in front of right with palms down and fingers pointing forward as the hands simultaneously move forward and slightly downward in a wavy pattern. (In situations where the context is already understood, the first part of this sign may be omitted.)

snub: *n.* an insult. *I was hurt by her deliberate snub.*

SIGN: Right **'ONE'** hand, palm facing left, is held in a horizontal position in front of the chest and is then curved upward from the wrist as it moves forward with a stabbing motion.

SO: *adv.* very; to such an extent. *The house was so dirty and messy that it smelled terrible.*

SIGN #1: Horizontal **'CROOKED 5'** hands are held apart limply with palms facing the body and the fingers of one hand pointing toward those of the other hand. The hands then drop so that the fingers are pointing downward. The movement is repeated a few times. Facial expression is important. (Alternatively, this concept may be expressed by emphasizing the adjective, in this case **dirty**, rather than according a separate sign for **SO**.)

SO: *conj.* used to join two complete sentences that are separated with a pause. *We could not raise enough money, so we made other arrangements.*

SIGN #2: **'5'** hands are held apart with palms toward the body and fingertips of each hand pointing toward those of the other hand, yet angled slightly upward as well. Then as the head tilts to one side, the hands are simultaneously curved forward/downward from the wrists so the palms are facing up.

SO: *adj.* true. *If that is so, then how will we cope?*

SIGN #3: Forefinger of vertical right **'ONE'** hand, palm facing left, is held against the lips and the hand is moved sharply forward.

so far: *adv.* to date, or from a specific point in time until now. *I applied for the job but so far, I have had no reply.*

SIGN: Tips of forefingers of **'BENT ONE'** hands, palms facing the body, are placed slightly apart on the right shoulder. The hands then drop forward/downward from the wrists so that the palms are facing upward and the forefingers are pointing forward/upward.

(and) so forth [*or* **and so on**]: and other items, activities or miscellaneous things. *We will need to buy food, decorations, flowers, and so forth for our celebration.*

SIGN: **'BENT L'** hands are positioned with palms either downward or facing the body, and tips of forefingers touching each other, the right finger pointing leftward as the left finger points rightward. The hands are then moved apart with forefingers fluttering.

so long: *inter.* farewell; good-bye. *So long for now; I will see you tomorrow.*

SIGN: Vertical right **'BENT EXTENDED B'** hand is held with palm forward as the fingers are fluttered in unison.

so-so: *adj.* a colloquial expression meaning average or ordinary, neither excessively good or bad; mediocre. *The food in that restaurant is excellent but the service is only so-so.*

SIGN: Right **'5'** hand, palm down, is held with fingers pointing forward and is rocked as the wrist twists from side to side a few times. Facial expression is important.

soak: *v.* to make thoroughly wet by immersing in a liquid. *We only ran from the car to the house but we were completely soaked by the rain.*

SIGN: **'CONTRACTED 5'** hands, palms up, are held apart and are simultaneously drawn down heavily as they snap shut to form **'FLAT O'** handshapes. Facial expression is important.

soap: *n.* a cleaning substance. *Before handling food, wash your hands with soap and water.*

SIGN: Fingertips of right **'BENT EXTENDED B'** hand are brushed back twice against right-facing palm of left **'EXTENDED B'** hand. (**SOAP** may be fingerspelled.)

sob: *v.* to cry convulsively. *She sobs herself to sleep every night so she must be unhappy.*

SIGN: Vertical **'ONE'** (or **'L'**) hands, palms facing backwards, are held at either side of the face and are slowly and deliberately drawn to form **'X'** (or **'CLAWED L'**) handshapes. The motion is repeated several times with convulsive gasping shown through the signer's mouth and teeth.

sober: *adj.* not under the influence of alcohol. *It is important that a designated person remains sober in order to drive home after the party.*

SIGN #1: Vertical right **'B'** hand, palm facing left, is held directly in front of the face and thrust forward and slightly downward.

OR

SIGN #2: Right **'EXTENDED A'** hand, palm facing left, thumb under chin, is thrust forward. Next, right **'EXTENDED A'** hand is held in front of the mouth with palm facing left. The forearm is then tipped firmly downward/leftward causing the palm to face downward. (ASL CONCEPT—**not - drunk**.)

soccer: *n.* a team sport in which a ball is kicked or headed toward the opponent's goal. *Soccer is a popular sport in England.*

SIGN: Right **'B'** hand, fingers pointing down and palm facing left, is swung upward from the wrist to strike the underside of the left **'STANDARD BASE'** hand a couple of times.

sociable: *adj.* friendly. *Shy people often find it hard to be sociable.*

SIGN: **'5'** hands, palms facing backward, move backward with fingers fluttering until they come to rest close to either side of the face.

social: *adj.* related to human interaction. *He is involved with many social issues, especially saving the environment.*

SIGN #1: Fingerspell **SOCIAL**.

social: *n.* an informal gathering. *Most Deaf people like to attend socials sponsored by their various organizations.*

SIGN #2: Tips of midfingers of **'BENT MIDFINGER 5'** hands, palms toward the body, are placed slightly apart on the chest. The wrists then rotate forward as the hands move forward so that, while the palms still face the body, they are now angled upward slightly.

social insurance number: *n.* an identifying number issued to individuals by the government in connection with income tax and social insurance. *Your social insurance number will be required when you file your income tax.*

SIGN: Fingerspell **SIN**.

social worker: *n.* someone trained to alleviate conditions related to the welfare of the poor, aged, disabled, and especially the well-being of children and youth. *When the divorced mother had no source of income, a social worker was assigned to assist the family.*

SIGN: Horizontal right **'S'** hand, palm left, is dropped onto the upturned palm of the left **'EXTENDED B'** hand. Then the right hand bounces upward a short distance as is changed to a horizontal **'W'** hand and lowered to the left palm again.

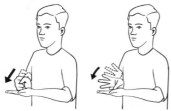

socialism: *n.* an economic system wherein production, distribution and exchange are controlled by the state. *Some historians consider T.C. Douglas the founder of socialism in Western Canada.*

SIGN: Fingerspell **SOCIALISM**.

socialize: *v.* to behave in a friendly, sociable manner. *Deaf people like to socialize.*

SIGN: Right **'EXTENDED A'** hand is held thumb-down above left **'EXTENDED A'** hand which is held thumb-up. The hands then revolve around each other in a counter-clockwise direction.
ALTERNATE SIGNS—**mingle** #1 & #2

society: *n.* a system of human organizations having distinctive cultures and institutions. *He is a member of the wealthier sector of society.*

SIGN: **'SPREAD C'** hands are held upright and slightly apart with palms facing each other. The wrists then rotate forward, bringing the hands to a horizontal position.

socket: *n.* a device into which an electric plug is inserted. *Plug the cord into this socket.*

SIGN: Horizontal **'V'** hands, palms facing each other but slanted a little toward the body, are held slightly apart. The right hand is then moved toward the left so that the forefinger of the right hand is thrust between the two extended fingers of the left hand.

socks: *n.* cloth coverings for the feet, worn inside the shoes. *You should wear warm socks for skating and skiing.*

SIGN #1: Right **'EXTENDED B'** hand is held palm down with fingers resting at right angles on those of the left **'STANDARD BASE'** hand. The right hand slides along the back of the left hand, then rises slightly as the wrist rotates to turn the hand so that the palm faces backward/leftward and the hand is brought down decisively to strike the back of the left wrist.

OR

SIGN #2: Forefingers of **'ONE'** hands, palms down, are held side by side and alternately moved back and forth so that the sides of the forefingers brush each other with each movement.

soda: *n.* a fizzy drink. *She ordered a soda with her hamburger.*

SIGN: The tip of the middle finger of the right **'BENT MIDFINGER 5'** hand, palm down, is inserted into the opening in the top of the horizontal left **'S'** hand. The right hand is then raised, changed to a **'5'** hand, and slapped palm-downward on the top of the left hand. (**Soda** is commonly used in the U.S., while **pop** or **soft drink** are used by Canadians.) Sign choice depends on context.

sofa: *n.* an upholstered couch. *We bought a new sectional sofa for our TV room.*

SIGN: Fingerspell **SOFA**.

soft: *adj.* pliable; smooth to touch; not hard or coarse. *Kittens usually have very soft fur.*

SIGN: **'CONTRACTED 5'** hands are held slightly apart with palms up and are drawn downward a few times as they are changed to **'FLAT O'** hands.

---

soft drink: See **soda**.

---

softhearted: *adj.* excessively kind, merciful, and easily moved to pity. *He is too softhearted to punish his children when they are rude.*

SIGN: Horizontal right **'BENT MIDFINGER 5'** hand is moved backward so that the tip of the middle finger makes very firm contact with the upper chest in the area of the heart. Next, **'CONTRACTED 5'** hands are held slightly apart in front of the left side of the chest with palms up and are drawn downward a few times as they are changed to **'FLAT O'** hands. During the production of this sign, the signer's tongue protrudes slightly as if articulating a 'TH' sound. (ASL CONCEPT—**heart - soft**.)

---

software: *n.* the programs which can be used by a specific computer. *This company specializes in educational software.*

SIGN: Fingerspell **SW**.

---

soggy: *adj.* moist and heavy. *The pastry in the pie is soggy.*

SIGN: **'CONTRACTED 5'** hands, palms up, are held apart and are simultaneously drawn down heavily as they snap shut to form **'FLAT O'** handshapes. Facial expression is important.

---

soil: *n.* the top layer of the earth's land surface. *The soil in the valley is very fertile.*

SIGN: **'FLAT O'** hands are held slightly apart with palms up. Then the fingers are slid across the thumbs a few times, thus alternating between **'FLAT O'** and **'OFFSET O'** hands.

soiled: *adj.* dirty and stained. *The child's clothes were soiled with mud.*

SIGN: Right **'MODIFIED 5'** hand is held under chin with palm down as the fingers flutter.

---

solar energy: *adj.* related to or using the energy of the sun. *Their new home will be heated by solar energy.*

SIGN: Fingerspell **SUN**.

solder: *v.* to join two metal surfaces or repair a hole in a metal surface by using a melted alloy. *He will solder the holes in the storage tank.*

SIGN: Horizontal **'ONE'** hands are held with palms facing one another and with tips of forefingers touching to form a **'V'** shape that points forward. Together, the hands are then shaken forward and back several times with short movements.

soldier: *n.* a member of the military service. *Canadian soldiers are often used for peace-keeping duties.*

SIGN: **'A'** hands are placed on the left side of the chest, palms facing the body, with the right hand above the left. Then they are simultaneously moved forward and back to tap twice against the body.

sole: *n.* the underside of the foot or of any footwear. *He had blisters on the soles of his feet after hiking 25 kilometres.*

SIGN #1: Left **'EXTENDED B'** hand is held in a fixed position with palm down and fingers pointing forward/rightward. Right **'EXTENDED B'** hand is held palm-up under the left hand at right angles to it and is slid back and forth a couple of times.

---

sole: *adj.* only; solitary. *She was granted sole custody of the children.*

SIGN #2: Vertical right **'ONE'** hand is held with palm forward. The wrist then rotates rightward to turn the hand so that the palm faces backward.

sole: *n.* a flatfish that is commonly used for food. *The chef prepared the fillet of sole with a special sauce.*

SIGN #3: Fingerspell **SOLE**.

S O L E

solemn: *adj.* serious; grave. *They made a solemn vow that they would never reveal the secret.*

SIGN: Vertical right **'BENT ONE'** hand is held with tip of forefinger touching chin and palm facing leftward but slanted toward the body. The wrist then rotates, turning the hand so that the palm fully faces the body.

solicit: *v.* to accost someone with an offer of sexual relations in exchange for money. *She will be charged if she solicits again.*

SIGN: Vertical right **'OPEN A'** hand is held with palm toward the face and backs of fingers (up to the second joint) touching the right cheek. The hand is then brushed forward off the cheek a couple of times. (**Solicit** may pertain to things other than sex, such as 'votes' or 'donations' and signs must be selected accordingly.)

solicitor: *n.* a lawyer. *You have the right to have your solicitor present when you make your statement to the police.*

SIGN: Vertical left **'EXTENDED B'** hand is held in a fixed position with palm facing right. Right **'L'** hand, palm facing left, is placed against the fingers of the left hand and then lowered to the heel of the left hand. (Agent Ending (see p. LIV) may follow.)
ALTERNATE SIGN—**attorney** #2

solid: *adj.* related to a physical state that resists changes in size or shape; firm. *The river ice is not solid enough for skating.*

SIGN #1: **'A'** hands are held palms down, right hand directly above the left. As the teeth clench, the hands come together and strike each other with force.

OR

SIGN #2: **'CROOKED 5'** hands are held parallel with palms down. They then jerk slightly forward/downward as the fingers retract to form **'CLAWED SPREAD C'** hands.

solid: *adj.* strong; substantial; having unity. *He has the solid support of his staff in this matter.*

SIGN #3: Right **'EXTENDED B'** hand, palm down with fingers pointing forward/leftward, grazes top of horizontal left **'S'** hand as the right hand is firmly swept leftward.
ALTERNATE SIGN—**strong**

solid: *adj.* without interruption; nonstop. *We worked four solid hours before we took a coffee break.*

SIGN #4: Left **'EXTENDED B'** hand is held in a fixed position with palm facing the body but slanted slightly upward and rightward. Vertical right **'4'** hand, palm leftward/forward and heel resting on the left palm, is circled slowly in a clockwise direction, returning with a firm tap to the left palm. The signer's cheeks are puffed while producing this sign. (Signs are very context specific.)

solitary: *adj.* without others; (done) alone. *He likes to go for a solitary walk along the riverbank.*

SIGN: Vertical right **'ONE'** hand, palm facing the body, is moved in a small counter-clockwise circle.

solitude: *n.* the state of being alone, in seclusion, having quietude. *We enjoy the solitude of living on an acreage outside the city.*

SIGN: **'B'** (or **'EXTENDED B'**) hands are crossed in front of the mouth, left palm facing rightward/downward and right palm facing leftward/downward with the right hand just behind the left hand. Then they are drawn apart until the palms face completely downward.

solo: *adj.* related to any performance by a person who is unaccompanied and unassisted. *The pilots in training will make their first solo flights today.*

SIGN: Vertical right **'ONE'** hand, palm facing the body, is moved in a small counter-clockwise circle.

solution: *n.* the answer to a problem. *They are trying to find a solution for the high rate of violent crime.*

SIGN #1: **'FLAT O'** hands are held parallel with palms up and slanted slightly toward the body. As the hands are drawn apart the thumbs slide across the fingertips, causing the hands to assume **'A'** shapes.

solution: *n.* a mixture of two or more substances. *A solution of four parts hot water and one part white vinegar is an excellent household cleanser.*

SIGN #2: Horizontal **'SPREAD EXTENDED C'** hands are held, right above left, with palms facing each other. Then right hand moves in a counter-clockwise direction while left hand moves in the opposite direction.

solve: *v.* to find an explanation, answer or solution. *Sherlock Holmes was able to solve all his cases by deductive reasoning.*

SIGN #1: **'FLAT O'** hands are held parallel with palms up and slanted slightly toward the body. As the hands are drawn apart the thumbs slide across the fingertips, causing the hands to assume **'A'** shapes.

solve: *v.* to work out the answer for a mathematical problem. *Can you solve this equation for the value of 'x'?*

SIGN #2: **'K'** hands are held, right above left, somewhere between horizontally and vertically with extended fingers pointing more or less forward, left palm facing right and right palm facing left yet both palms are angled slightly toward the body. The two hands brush against one another a few times as the right hand repeatedly moves leftward slightly, and the left hand moves rightward.

some: *adj.* a certain unknown or unspecified number or amount. *We plan to buy some land near the city.*

SIGN: Horizontal left **'EXTENDED B'** hand is held in a fixed position with palm up but angled toward the body and fingers pointing rightward/forward while edge of horizontal right **'EXTENDED B'** hand, palm facing left, is placed on left palm and is drawn back toward the body.

somebody: *pron.* an unknown or unnamed person; someone. [See also PRONOUNS, p. LXIII.] *Somebody left the door open.*

SIGN: Vertical right **'ONE'** hand, palm facing the body, is moved in a small counter-clockwise circle.

someday: *adv.* at some unspecified time in the distant future. *Someday you will be sorry you dropped out of school.*

SIGN: Right **'EXTENDED B'** hand, palm facing left, is held in a vertical position near the right side of the head. The forearm is then moved forward a short distance so that the fingers eventually point forward/upward. (The sample sentence in ASL is: *QUIT SCHOOL.... WILL SORRY...WILL.*)

someone: *pron.* an unknown or unnamed person; somebody. [See also PRONOUNS, p. LXIII.] *Someone will help me set up the display when I get there.*

SIGN: Vertical right **'ONE'** hand, palm facing the body, is moved in a small counter-clockwise circle.

something: *pron.* a certain, unspecified thing. [See also PRONOUNS, p. LXIII.] *You should eat something nourishing before the game.*

SIGN: Vertical right **'ONE'** hand, palm facing the body, is moved in a small counter-clockwise circle.

sometime: *adv.* at an unspecified time. *I hope we can get together sometime next week.*

NOTE—Because the concept is already understood, no sign is considered necessary for **sometime** in ASL.

sometimes: *adv.* once in a while; now and then. *Sometimes I really feel tired.*

SIGN: As right forearm slowly circles clockwise, tip of forefinger of horizontal right **'ONE'** hand strikes upward/rightward facing palm of horizontal left **'EXTENDED B'** hand each time it goes past. (The speed of movement and height of the arcs depends on the *frequency* implied. The *more frequent*, the smaller and faster the arcs; the less *frequent*, the higher and slower the arcs.)

somewhat: *adv.* rather; a little. *I am somewhat nervous about the surgery tomorrow.*

SIGN: Right **'X'** hand is held palm-up with forefinger tightly crooked and tip of thumb repeatedly scraping downward against tip of forefinger.

somewhere: *adv.* at, in or to some unspecified place; some place. *We only know that he lives somewhere in the Northwest Territories.*

SIGN: Right **'5'** hand, palm down, is circled in a counter-clockwise motion.

somnolent: See **sleepy**.

son: *n.* a male offspring. *His only son will inherit his fortune.*

SIGN: Right **'B'** hand is held with side of fore-finger touching forehead and palm facing leftward/downward. The right forearm then drops downward as the wrist rotates forward causing the palm to turn upward as the hand comes to rest on the left forearm.

song: *n.* a piece of music composed for the voice. *A song can be signed to the beat of a drum.*

SIGN: Horizontal right **'EXTENDED B'** hand is positioned above left forearm with palm facing leftward/backward. The right wrist makes slight back and forth rotations so that the palm alternates between being angled slightly upward and being angled slightly downward.

soon: *adv.* in a little while; after a short time. *He will be here soon.*

SIGN #1: Left horizontal **'U'** hand is held steady with extended fingers pointing forward/rightward and palm facing backward/rightward. Right horizontal **'U'** hand is held at right angles to the left hand with extended fingers resting on those of the left hand. Extended fingers of right hand are then brushed forward/rightward off the fingers of the left hand.

OR

SIGN #2: Joined forefinger and thumb of horizontal right **'F'** hand, palm facing backward, tap against the chin a few times. The signer's lips are pursed. (This is a very *small* movement.)

SIGN #3 [ATLANTIC]: Vertical right **'A'** hand, palm facing back, is placed on the right side of the chin, near the pursed lower lip, where it remains fixed while the forefinger and midfinger slowly (and somewhat surreptitiously) uncurl slightly a couple of times.

(very) soon [*or* **in the very near future**]: *adv.* in a very short time. *He is coming very soon.*

SIGN #4: Right **'5'** hand is held with palm left and thumbtip close to or touching the right cheek and is moved forward/downward slightly a few times. The teeth are visible and the signer appears to be articulating the sound 'EE'. (This sign is often used for emphasis.)

soothe: *v.* to make calm. *They tried to soothe the baby by changing her diaper and feeding her.*

SIGN #1: Left **'CROOKED EXTENDED B'** hand is held palm down with fingers pointing rightward/forward at a downward angle while right **'CROOKED EXTENDED B'** hand is held palm down on left hand at right angles to it. The right hand is drawn rightward/backward across the back of the left hand, which moves out from under the right hand to take up a position on top of it so that the positioning of the hands is the reverse of their original position. The left hand is then drawn leftward/backward across the back of the right hand, which moves out from under the left hand to take up a position on top of it. Movement is repeated.

soothe: *v.* to relieve (pain or discomfort). *This medication will soothe your nerves and help you sleep.*

SIGN #2: **'FLAT O'** hands are held parallel with palms up and slanted slightly toward the body. As the hands are drawn apart the thumbs slide across the fingertips, causing the hands to assume **'A'** shapes.

sophisticated: *adj.* refined; cultured. *She thinks she is so sophisticated.*

SIGN #1: Tip of forefinger of vertical right **'COMBINED I + ONE'** hand, palm left, is used to tilt the chin up ever so slightly. (Facial expression is important.) This sign is negative in its connotation. Sign choice for a more positive connotation varies considerably, depending on context.

sophisticated: *adj.* complex. *She uses a very sophisticated system of bookkeeping.*

SIGN #2: **'X'** hands are held apart and almost upright with left palm facing rightward/downward and right palm facing leftward/downward. The crooked forefingers wiggle up and down as the hands move toward one another in front of the face, coming to rest when they make contact in front of the nose with right hand directly behind left so that the hands appear to be crossed.

OR

SIGN #3: Vertical **'BENT EXTENDED B'** hands, held at shoulder level with palms facing each other, are moved upward simultaneously and thrust forward very slightly.

sophomore: *adj.* designating the second year of study at Gallaudet University. (This sign is not used to mean the sophomore year at any other university—only at Gallaudet.) *He is in his sophomore year at Gallaudet University.*

SIGN: Tip of forefinger of right **'ONE'** hand, palm facing left, taps the very end of the middle finger of the left **'5'** hand, which is held horizontally with palm facing right and angled slightly toward the body. The tapping is repeated a couple of times.

sordid: *adj.* dirty; squalid; foul. *He grew up in the sordid environment of an inner city slum.*

SIGN #1: Right **'MODIFIED 5'** hand is held under chin with palm down as the fingers flutter.

sordid: *adj.* degraded; vile. *The politician was unable to hide his sordid past from the media.*

SIGN #2: Thumb and forefinger of vertical right **'COVERED 8'** hand, which is held near right side of face with palm facing left, are snapped open and thrust slightly forward to form a **'MODIFIED 5'** hand. This sign can be made with either one or two hands, one at either side of the face.

sore: *adj.* painfully sensitive or tender. *His legs were sore after he cycled 25 kilometres.*

SIGN #1: Thumb of right **'A'** hand, palm facing left, is pressed against the chin as the wrist rotates to twist the hand so that the palm is toward the body. Facial expression is important.

OR

SIGN #2: Horizontal **'S'** hands, palms facing the chest, are circled forward around each other. Facial expression is important.

SIGN #3 [ONTARIO]: Right **'MODIFIED Y'** hand is placed palm down with thumbnail against left side of chin and is then drawn slowly across to the right side. Facial expression is important.

sorority: *n.* a social club or society for university women. *She was happy to become a member of the Phi Kappa Zeta sorority.*

SIGN: Fingerspell **SORORITY**.

sorrow: *n.* sadness; grief. *Our sorrow was great when we heard the tragic news.*

SIGN: Vertical **'CROOKED 5'** hands are held slightly apart with palms toward the face. The hands are then simultaneously lowered somewhat and the head tilts to the right. SAME SIGN—**sorrowful**, *adj.*

sorry: *adj.* regretful or sympathetic. *I am sorry to hear about your recent loss.*

SIGN #1: Right **'A'** (or **'EXTENDED A'**) hand, palm facing the body, is rubbed on the chest with a circular motion which, in the eyes of onlookers, appears clockwise.

(feel) sorry for: *v.* to be empathetic and/or sympathetic toward; to pity. *I feel sorry for the victim of that terrible crime.*

SIGN #2: Right **'BENT MIDFINGER 5'** hand is held upright with palm facing forward but slanted downward slightly. It is then moved forward with circular motions to simulate the stroking of an imaginary person with the middle finger. Appropriate facial expression is important. (Alternatively, this sign may be made with two hands.) ❖

sort: *n.* class, group or kind. *She did not know what sort of shoes to wear for the tour.*

SIGN #1: Right **'K'** hand, palm facing left and slightly toward the body, is held just above left **'K'** hand, which is held with palm facing right and slightly toward the body. Hands are then circled forward around one another one full turn, stopping with right hand resting on top of left.

sort: *v.* to arrange according to type or class. *Before you do the laundry, you should sort it according to colours and fabrics.*

SIGN #2: **'SPREAD C'** hands are held upright and slightly apart, palms facing each other. The wrists then rotate forward, bringing the hands to a horizontal position. The movement is repeated three times—to the left, in front of, and to the right of the body.

sort of: *adv.* somewhat; rather. *I am sort of scared.*

SIGN: Right **'5'** hand, palm down, is held with fingers pointing forward and is rocked as the wrist twists from side to side a few times. Facial expression is important.
ALTERNATE SIGN—**somewhat**

sort out: *v.* to clear up by organizing in an orderly and disciplined manner. *I must sort out what courses I want to take before I complete my application form.*

SIGN: With palms facing the body, **'CLAWED 5'** hands are held together so that little fingers interlock. As the hands are simultaneously lowered from the wrists, the corresponding fingers of each hand interlock to simulate the meshing of gears.

soul: *n.* the spiritual part of a person. *Followers of some faiths believe that a person's soul lives on after death.*

SIGN: Horizontal left **'F'** (or **'S'**) hand is held in a fixed position with palm facing the body at a rightward angle. Thumb and forefinger of right **'F'** hand, palm down, are inserted in the opening at the top of the left hand. Then the right hand is drawn upward with a wavy motion.

sound: *n.* anything that can be heard. *Musical instruments can produce a wide variety of sounds.*

SIGN #1: Tip of forefinger of right **'ONE'** hand, palm left, is tapped against right ear a couple of times.

sound: *adj.* wise; logical; showing good judgment. *You can rely on her to give you sound advice.*

SIGN #2: Fingertips of right **'BENT EXTENDED B'** hand are placed on the lips so that the palm is toward the body. Then the hand is moved purposefully forward a brief distance.

(of) sound mind: *adj.* sane; mentally healthy. *He made his will while he was of sound mind so it is perfectly valid.*

SIGN #3: Tip of forefinger of right **'CROOKED ONE'** hand, palm toward the head, is tapped against right side of forehead. Next, fingertips of right **'BENT EXTENDED B'** hand are placed on the lips so that the palm is toward the body. Then the hand is moved purposefully forward a brief distance. (ASL CONCEPT—**brain - good**.)

sound asleep: *adj.* deeply sleeping. *I was sound asleep by 10 p.m.*

SIGN #4: Vertical right **'CONTRACTED 5'** hand is positioned with the palm toward the face, eyes closed. The hand is slowly drawn downward as it closes to form an **'A'** handshape, turns palm downward and comes to rest on the left **'A'** hand which is held in a fixed position with palm up.

soup: *n.* a liquid food, either hot or cold, usually eaten with a spoon. *I would like a bowl of chicken soup.*

SIGN: Left **'EXTENDED U'** (or **'U'**) hand is held in a fixed position with palm up and extended fingers pointing forward/rightward. Right **'EXTENDED U'** (or **'U'**) hand, with palm up and extended fingers at right angles to those of the left hand, is raised toward the mouth and lowered toward the left hand a couple of times.

sour: *adj.* having a sharp, biting, acidic taste. *These pickles are very sour.*

SIGN: Tip of forefinger of right **'ONE'** hand is placed on chin and twisted a quarter turn to the right. Facial expression is important.

source: *n.* where something begins or originates. *The police traced the call to its source and found it was made from a local phone booth.*

SIGN #1: Vertical right **'ONE'** hand, palm forward, is held near the right shoulder and is waved from side to side a few times. The movement is from the wrist. Next, left **'5'** hand is held with palm facing right while forefinger of right **'ONE'** hand is inserted between first two fingers of left hand and twisted 180 degrees either to the right or left. (ASL CONCEPT—**where - start**.)

source: *n.* a person, book, or organization, from which information or evidence is obtained. *The news reporter refused to reveal the source of his information.*

SIGN #2: Vertical right **'ONE'** hand, palm forward, is held near the right shoulder and is waved from side to side a few times. The movement is from the wrist. Next, vertical left **'ONE'** hand, palm forward/rightward, is held in a fixed position in front of horizontal right **'ONE'** hand which is held with palm facing left and tip of forefinger touching the middle of the left forefinger. The right hand is then flicked backward/rightward to assume a vertical position as the forefinger retracts to take on an **'X'** shape. Alternatively, this part of the sign may be made with both hands beginning and ending with **'X'** shapes. (ASL CONCEPT— **where - from.**) Sign choices vary according to context.

south: *n.* one of the four cardinal points of a compass, at 180° from north. *I can you tell you which way is south.*

SIGN: Horizontal right **'S'** hand, palm left, is drawn downward. (While the positioning and movement of this sign may vary, the handshape remains the same.)

southpaw: *n.* a left-handed person. *Some of the greatest pitchers in baseball history were southpaws.*

SIGN: Vertical left **'L'** hand, palm forward, is held out to the left and shaken lightly.

souvenir: *n.* a memento or any object that reminds one of a certain place, person, or occasion. *They brought back a souvenir of their trip to Africa.*

SIGN: Fingerspell **SOUVENIR**.

SOW: *v.* to plant seeds in a section of ground. *In some areas farmers sow winter wheat.*

SIGN: Fingertips of right **'FLAT O'** hand, palm down, are repeatedly slid across the thumb to form an **'A'** shape as the hand moves forward a short distance. (This sign would not be appropriate when **SOW** refers to a female pig.)

space: *n.* a three-dimensional area, either empty or in which something is located. *I am looking for an apartment with more space.*

SIGN #1: **'S'** hands are held palms down in front of the chest with elbows out. The hands remain relatively fixed while the arms are simultaneously raised and lowered. Movement is repeated. (Alternatively, **SPACE** in this context may be fingerspelled.)

space: *n.* an area between or within things. *Make sure that the space between the words is uniform.*

SIGN #2: Vertical right **'BENT MIDFINGER 5'** hand, palm facing forward, is moved rightward a short distance.

space: *n.* the region beyond the earth's atmosphere. *Scientists have always been fascinated with the exploration of space.*

SIGN #3: Fingerspell **SPACE**.

spacious: *adj.* having a large capacity or area. *She lives in a spacious apartment overlooking the park.*

SIGN: Horizontal **'CLAWED L'** hands, which are held slightly apart with palms facing, are simultaneously moved farther apart as the wrists rotate to turn the palms down. Facial expression is important and the syllable 'CHA' is formed on the lips.

spade: *n.* a tool used for digging. *Every gardener needs a spade.*

SIGN #1: Horizontal left **'EXTENDED B'** hand is held with fingers pointing forward and palm facing rightward/upward. Horizontal **'BENT EXTENDED B'** hand, palm facing backward/upward and slightly leftward, moves in a clockwise direction, the fingertips striking the left palm with each revolution.

spade: *n.* the black symbol on a playing card that resembles a heart-shaped leaf with a stem. *I had only one spade in my hand.*

SIGN #2: Horizontal left **'EXTENDED B'** hand is held with fingers pointing forward and palm facing rightward/upward. Horizontal **'BENT EXTENDED B'** hand, palm facing backward/upward and slightly leftward, moves in a clockwise direction, the fingertips striking the left palm with each revolution.

spaghetti: *n.* pasta in the form of long strings. *My favourite Italian food is spaghetti with meatballs.*

SIGN: **'I'** hands, palms toward the chest, are held so the tips of the little fingers are touching each other. Then they are moved apart in a series of short arcs.

span: *n.* the extent of a period of time. *Over the span of ten years, he has had six different jobs.*

SIGN: **'EXTENDED B'** hands are purposefully set apart with palms facing each other and fingers pointing forward/upward. The right hand is then moved from side to side a couple of times in the space between where the hands were initially positioned.

spank: *v.* to slap the buttocks with an open hand. *Many parents do not spank their children.*

SIGN: Horizontal left **'EXTENDED B'** hand is held with palm facing basically rightward at an upward angle and fingers pointing forward while the horizontal right **'EXTENDED B'** hand is held with palm facing leftward at a downward angle and fingers pointing forward. The right hand moves in a series of clockwise circles, slapping the left palm with each revolution.

spare: *adj.* free (as in time); extra. *In his spare time my grandfather likes to help me with my homework.*

SIGN #1: **'F'** hands, left palm facing right and right palm facing left, are held upright with right hand directly behind left hand. Then they are simultaneously drawn apart as wrists rotate outward so that left palm faces rightward/forward while right palm faces leftward/forward. (**SPARE** in this context may be fingerspelled.)

spare: *adj.* a duplicate kept as a replacement in case of damage or loss. *She leaves a spare house key with her neighbours.*

SIGN #2: Horizontal left **'EXTENDED A'** hand is held in a fixed position with palm facing right. Right **'EXTENDED A'** hand, palm facing down, is twisted so that the palm faces left as it is brought forward to make contact with left hand just below the thumb. (**SPARE** in this context may be fingerspelled.)

spare: *n.* an extra tire carried in a motor vehicle in case of a flat occurring. *You will need a jack to remove the flat tire and put on the spare.*

SIGN #3: Horizontal left **'EXTENDED A'** hand is held in a fixed position with palm facing right. Right **'EXTENDED A'** hand, palm facing down, is twisted so that the palm faces left as it is brought forward to make contact with left hand just below the thumb. (**SPARE** in this context is frequently fingerspelled.)

spare: *n.* in bowling, the score achieved by knocking down all the pins in a single frame using only two balls. *He got a spare in the last frame.*

SIGN #4: Right **'EXTENDED B'** hand, held aloft with palm facing leftward/upward and fingers pointing forward, is lowered diagonally to the left.

spare: *v.* to be able to afford to give. *He was able to spare a dollar for the Girl Guides.*

SIGN #5: Horizontal right **'CONTRACTED B'** hand is held with palm facing leftward/upward and fingers pointing left. The hand then moves forward in a slight arc formation as if giving something to someone. (Handshapes for this sign vary according to the size and shape of the object being given; however, the basic movement remains the same.) ❖

sparkle: *v.* to reflect bright points of light; glitter. *Even at a distance we could see how her diamond tiara sparkled.*

SIGN: Tip of middle finger of right **'BENT MIDFINGER 5'** hand, palm down, is placed on back of left **'STANDARD BASE'** hand. The right hand wobbles as it moves upward/rightward. (Sometimes this sign is made without the left hand; instead the middle finger of the right hand is placed on the actual object or on the place where the object is imagined to be. Handshapes for the right hand may vary as well.)

sparse: *adj.* scanty; not dense. *Canada is a large land mass with a sparse population.*

SIGN: Right **'EXTENDED A'** hand, palm facing left, thumb under chin, is thrust forward. Next, **'S'** hands are held parallel with palms up and are thrust forward simultaneously as they are opened to form **'CROOKED 5'** hands. (ASL CONCEPT—**not - many.**)

spat: *n.* a minor quarrel. *She and her brother are having a spat about whose turn it is to load the dishwasher.*

SIGN: **'BENT ONE'** hands, palms toward the chest, forefingers pointing toward each other, are either simultaneously or alternately moved up and down from the wrist.

spay: *v.* to remove the ovaries from a female animal in order to prevent pregnancy. *The veterinarian will spay our cat so she will not have kittens.*

SIGN: Horizontal right **'A'** hand, palm facing left, is held against right-facing palm of horizontal left **'EXTENDED B'** hand, and is then moved rightward and downward as it opens to become a **'CROOKED 5'** hand with the palm facing down.

speak: *v.* to talk. *He speaks very clearly.*

SIGN #1: Tip of forefinger of vertical right **'4'** hand, palm facing left, is tapped twice against the chin.

speak: *v.* to give a speech. *He will speak at the conference next week.*

SIGN #2: Right arm is raised and the vertical **'EXTENDED B'** hand, palm facing left, is brought forward sharply from the wrist a couple of times

SAME SIGN—**speaker,** *n.*, and may be followed by the Agent Ending (see p. LIV).

speak out: *v.* to talk clearly and openly about one's views. *She will speak out against racial discrimination.*

SIGN: Tip of forefinger of vertical right **'4'** hand, palm left, is placed on the lower lip. Then the hand is thrust forward rigidly. This sign is accompanied by a look of determination.

spear: *v.* to pierce something with a spear. *They went to spear catfish in the river.*

SIGN #1: Vertical right **'S'** hand, palm facing left, is thrust forward/downward as if stabbing something.

spear: *n.* a throwing weapon with a long shaft and a sharp pointed end. *Natives in the African jungles often carry spears.*

SIGN #2: Vertical right **'S'** hand, palm facing left, is thrust forward as it opens to form a **'MODIFIED 5'** hand.

special: *adj.* distinguished from or set apart from others of its kind. *A birthday is always a special day.*

SIGN #1: Thumb and forefinger of right **'OPEN F'** (or **'A-INDEX'**) hand, palm facing down, grasp tip of forefinger of left **'ONE'** hand, which is held with palm toward body. Then right hand is used to pull left hand upward. (Sign choice depends on context.)

special: *adj.* different from others. *Diabetics must follow a special diet.*

SIGN #2: Forefingers of **'ONE'** hands are crossed. The hands are then turned outward so that they become vertical with palms facing forward.

special: *adj.* more dearly beloved than others. *She was always her father's special child.*

SIGN #3: Knuckles of vertical right **'OPEN SPREAD O'** hand, palm toward the body, are placed on the chin and are firmly drawn downward, closing to form an **'S'** hand.

special: *adj.* more important than others. *A special position was created for him in the premier's office.*

SIGN #4: Vertical **'F'** hands are held apart with palms facing forward. The hands are then brought purposefully together.
ALTERNATE SIGN—**important** #2

specialist: *n.* a person who specializes in a particular field. *A skin **specialist** will find the cause of your allergy.*

SIGN: Horizontal left **'ONE'** hand is held in a fixed position with palm facing right and forefinger pointing forward. Right **'ONE'** hand, palm facing leftward/backward, moves forward, the tip of the forefinger sliding along the forefinger of the left **'ONE'** hand. (Agent Ending (see p. LIV) may follow.)

specialize: *v.* to devote oneself to a particular area of study. *The medical student decided to **specialize** in surgery.*

SIGN: Horizontal left **'ONE'** hand is held in a fixed position with palm facing right and forefinger pointing forward. Right **'ONE'** hand, palm facing leftward/backward, moves forward, the tip of the forefinger sliding along the forefinger of the left **'ONE'** hand.

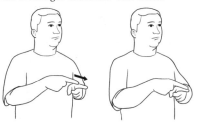

specialty: *n.* a major interest, skill, or service. *The restaurant's **specialty** is French cuisine.*

SIGN: Horizontal left **'ONE'** hand is held in a fixed position with palm facing right and forefinger pointing forward. Right **'ONE'** hand, palm facing leftward/backward, moves forward, the tip of the forefinger sliding along the forefinger of the left **'ONE'** hand.

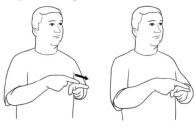

species: *n.* a group of specifically related plants or animals. *Lions, tigers and leopards are all carnivores of the feline **species**.*

SIGN: **'SPREAD C'** hands are held upright and slightly apart with palms facing each other. The wrists then rotate forward, bringing the hands to a horizontal position.

specific: *adj.* explicit; particular; definite. *Your response is not **specific** enough.*

SIGN: Vertical left **'ONE'** hand is held in a fixed position with palm facing rightward/forward. Horizontal right **'ONE'** hand is held behind left hand with palm facing left. The right hand then makes a slight but firm bounce as if intending to strike the tip of the left forefinger with that of the right forefinger but not quite touching it.

specify: *v.* to give particulars. *When you order the car, you can **specify** what colour you want.*

SIGN: Vertical left **'ONE'** hand is held in a fixed position with palm facing rightward/forward. Horizontal right **'ONE'** hand is held behind left hand with palm facing left. The right hand then makes a slight but firm bounce as if intending to strike the tip of the left forefinger with that of the right forefinger but not quite touching it.

spectacles: *n.* eyeglasses. *I need **spectacles** for reading.*

SIGN: **'CROOKED L'** hands, palms facing each other, are held in a vertical position beside each eye. The forearms then move outward and inward slightly a few times so that the thumb-tips tap against the cheeks. (Alternatively, the right hand only is frequently used.)

spectators: *n.* onlookers; observers. *There were 25,000 **spectators** at the game.*

SIGN: Vertical **'K'** hands are held apart with palms forward but facing each other slightly, and are alternately circled backward.

speculate: *v.* to conjecture without knowing all the facts. *We can only speculate about the potential value of this investment.*

SIGN: Vertical **'FLAT O'** hands are held just in front of either side of the forehead with palms facing backward and fingers rapidly fluttering as the hands move in small circles. From the signer's perspective, the left hand moves clockwise while the right hand moves counter-clockwise. (Alternatively, this sign may be made with one hand only.)
SAME SIGN—**speculation**, *n.*

speech: *n.* a talk or address delivered to an audience. *A speech by the British monarch is telecast every year on Christmas Day.*

SIGN #1: Right arm is raised and the vertical **'EXTENDED B'** hand, palm facing left, is brought forward sharply from the wrist a couple of times.

speech: *n.* that which is spoken. *To become an audiologist, you will require a course in the production of speech.*

SIGN #2: Right **'CLAWED V'** hand, held upright with the palm toward the body, is circled counter-clockwise in front of the lips.

speechless: *adj.* temporarily unable to speak, as from amazement or shock. *He was speechless when he won the award.*

SIGN: **'BENT 5'** hands are held apart, fingertips pointing downward, and are moved sharply downward.

speechreading: *n.* the art of understanding speech through observing the speaker's mouth, facial expression and body language. *Some deafened people practise speechreading to help them communicate.*

SIGN: Vertical right **'BENT V'** hand, palm facing backwards, is held with extended fingers pointing at the mouth and the hand is swung back and forth from the wrist several times.

speed: *n.* swiftness or rapidity of movement. *Excessive speed was definitely a factor that contributed to the fatal accident.*

SIGN #1: Left horizontal **'L'** hand, palm facing right, is held apart from and slightly ahead of right horizontal **'L'** hand, whose palm faces left. The hands are then rapidly alternated with **'CLAWED L'** handshapes as the forefingers flex and extend several times.
SAME SIGN—**speed**, *v.*, when it means to drive faster than the legal limit.

speed: *v.* to move quickly. *The paramedics will speed to the scene of the accident.*

SIGN #2: Vertical right **'ONE'** hand, palm forward, is held at about shoulder level, arcs rightward slightly, then quickly forward. (Context must be considered when selecting signs.)

speedometer: *n.* a device in a motor vehicle that measures and displays the rate of speed at which it is travelling. *Watch your speedometer carefully in school zones.*

SIGN: Horizontal left **'EXTENDED B'** hand is held in a fixed position with palm up but angled toward the body and fingers pointing rightward/forward. Right **'ONE'** hand, palm facing left, is placed on the left palm with forefinger pointing forward/rightward but slanted upward. The right wrist then bends up and down, causing the hand to pivot so that the forefinger moves back and forth to simulate the action of a compass needle.

spell: *v.* to write, say, or fingerspell the letters of a word in the right order. *She can spell "Tuktoyaktuk".*

SIGN #1: **'BENT 5'** hand, palm downward/forward and fingers pointing forward, is moved rightward with fingers fluttering. (Sign choice depends on context.)

spell: *v.* to indicate; to make clear. *Drinking and driving clearly spells trouble.*

SIGN #2: Horizontal left **'EXTENDED B'** hand is held in a fixed position with palm facing right while tip of forefinger of right palm-down **'BENT V'** hand is jabbed into the left palm. The right hand then moves away from the left hand as the right wrist rotates a quarter turn clockwise, and the middle fingertip is jabbed into the left palm.

(cast a) spell: *v.* to induce a state of mind through the use of magical force. *In folklore, witches often cast spells upon others.*

SIGN #3: Vertical **'S'** hands, palms forward, are held slightly apart and are simultaneously thrust forward, as they open into **'CONTRACTED 5'** handshapes with palms down.

spend: *v.* to pay out money. *I usually spend 75 percent of my salary and save the rest.*

SIGN #1: **'FLAT O'** hands are held with palms up, the left hand slightly ahead of the right hand. The hands move simultaneously forward while the hands close to form **'A'** hands.

spend: *v.* to pass (time). *We hope to spend the winter in Arizona.*

NOTE—There is no specific sign for this concept as it is always incorporated into the time frame signified by the context, *e.g.,* winter, morning, weekend, etc.

sperm: *n.* semen; male reproductive cell(s). *Some medical students donate sperm for 'in vitro' fertilization programs.*

SIGN: Fingerspell **SPERM**.

S P E R M

sphere: *n.* a three-dimensional solid figure that is globe-shaped. *The earth is a revolving sphere.*

SIGN: Vertical **'SPREAD C'** hands are held apart with palms facing each other.

spice: *n.* any vegetable substance used as flavouring such as cinnamon, nutmeg, cloves, paprika, etc. *Hot chili pepper is a spice commonly used in Cajun cooking.*

SIGN: Fingerspell **SPICE**.

S P I C E

spider: *n.* an arachnid; a bug-like creature with four pairs of legs and a rounded body. *A spider spun a web around the light fixture.*

SIGN: **'SPREAD C'** hands are held with palms down and wrists crossed as the fingers wiggle.

spill: *v.* unintentionally to allow to fall, flow or run out of a container. *Chris tried not to spill his drink on the white table cloth.*

SIGN: **'FLAT O'** hands are held with tips of forefingers touching and palms forward/downward but slanted toward each other slightly. The hands are then flung forward/outward as the fingers spread to form **'5'** hands with the palms down.

spin: *v.* to twirl around. *The back wheels of the car began to spin on the ice.*

SIGN: Horizontal **'BENT ONE'** hands, palms facing backward, and forefingers pointing toward each other, are held apart at chest level and are rapidly circled forward several times. The signer's cheeks are puffed out. (Signs vary according to context.)

spine: *n.* the backbone. *He injured his spine in a traffic accident and is now a paraplegic.*

SIGN: Fingerspell **SPINE**.

S P I N E

spiral: *adj.* winding or coiling (usually upward). *This mattress is filled with very firm spiral springs.*

SIGN: **'BENT ONE'** hands, are positioned so the left, palm up, remains fixed while the right, palm down, is slightly above it and is coiled upward a short distance.

spirit: *n.* a person's soul. *Many people believe that when you die your spirit goes to heaven.*

SIGN #1: Horizontal left **'F'** (or **'S'**) hand is held in a fixed position with palm facing the body at a rightward angle. Thumb and forefinger of right **'F'** hand, palm down, are inserted in the opening at the top of the left hand. Then the right hand is drawn upward with a wavy motion.

SAME SIGN—**spiritual**, *adj.*

spirit: *n.* a strong sense of loyalty or dedication. *They often hold rallies to boost school spirit.*

SIGN #2: Left **'FLAT OPEN F'** hand is held in a fixed position with palm up while the right **'FLAT OPEN F'** hand is held above it with palm down and thumb and forefinger loosely placed within the opening between the thumb and forefinger of the left hand. The hands then move apart abruptly as the thumb and forefinger of each hand snap shut to form **'FLAT F'** handshapes.

spirits: *n.* distilled alcoholic liquors such as whisky, gin, rum, or vodka. *The new store sells beer, wine and spirits.*

SIGN #1: Horizontal right **'COMBINED I + ONE'** hand is held above and at right angles to horizontal left **'COMBINED I + ONE'** hand, whose palm faces slightly to the right and slightly toward the body. The two hands are then tapped together twice.

(in good) spirits: *adj.* in a good mood; happy. *You seem to be in good spirits today.*

SIGN #2: Horizontal right **'EXTENDED B'** hand, palm toward the body, is brushed up and off the chest twice in a circular motion.

spit: *v.* to expel from the mouth. *The teacher told the students that it was not nice to spit on the playground.*

SIGN: Right **'S'** hand is positioned against the mouth with palm forward/downward and is then thrust forward as the forefinger flicks forward to form a **'ONE'** hand. (Signs vary according to context.)

spite: *v.* to act out of ill-will or malice; to vent frustration. *He did it to spite his parents.*

SIGN #1: Left **'CLOSED X'** hand is held in a fixed position with palm upward at a slight rightward angle. Right **'CLOSED X'** hand is held closer to the chest and at a higher level than the left hand. Palms are facing each other. The right hand then moves purposefully toward the left hand and strikes it. Facial expression is important. ❖
SAME SIGN—**spiteful**, *adj.*

(in) spite of: *conj.* even though; despite the fact that. *In spite of his hard work, he was not accepted into the Faculty of Medicine.*

SIGN #2: (To translate the sample sentence into ASL, two signs are required, one at the beginning of the sentence and one in the middle to join the two clauses. In ASL: *NO MATTER WORK HARD, STILL FACULTY MEDICINE NOT ACCEPT.*)
NO MATTER: Fingers of horizontal **'BENT B'** hands, palms facing the chest, are alternately brushed back and forth against each other.
STILL: Horizontal **'Y'** hands are held apart with palms facing chest, and are twisted smoothly from the wrists so that the palms face downward/forward. Sometimes only the right hand is used for this part of the sign.

(the) spitting image of: *adj.* resembling very closely. *You are the spitting image of your father!*

SIGN #1: Tip of forefinger of right **'ONE'** hand touches cheekbone near right eye. The forearm then moves quickly forward a short distance as the wrist rotates and the hand takes on a vertical **'Y'** shape, the palm forward/leftward, and teeters from side to side several times. This is a wrist action.

OR

SIGN #2: Forefinger of right **'ONE'** hand touches face just under right eye. Next, **'S'** hands are held parallel with palms facing the chest. The forearms are then simultaneously and purposefully lowered so that the palms, which still face the body, are slanted slightly upward. (ASL CONCEPT—**look - strong**.)

splash: *n.* a spattering of (liquid) in blobs. *She jumped into the pool with a big splash.*

SIGN: Horizontal **'S'** hands are held side by side with palms down and are moved upward/outward (at 45° angles) as they change to **'MODIFIED 5'** hands with palms forward. (Signs vary according to context.)

splendid: *adj.* magnificent. *The Canadian Cultural Society of the Deaf has a splendid display of work done by Deaf artists.*

SIGN: Vertical **'EXTENDED B'** hands, palms facing forward, are held apart near the face. Forearms are pushed purposefully forward a short distance.

split: *v.* to divide into roughly equal pieces or numbers. *She split the class into two groups.*

SIGN #1: Edge of right **'EXTENDED B'** hand is placed within the space between the thumb and forefinger of the left **'EXTENDED B'** hand, both palms facing the chest at a slight angle. Then they are separated with a downward curve so that both palms face down.

(in a) split second: *adv.* instantly; very quickly within a very short period of time. *In a split second, the child had disappeared.*

SIGN #2: Left horizontal **'L'** hand, palm facing right, is held apart from and slightly ahead of right horizontal **'L'** hand, whose palm faces left. The hands are then simultaneously jerked upward toward the body as they are changed to **'CLAWED L'** hands. This is a very small but firm movement accompanied by a startled facial expression.

splitting headache: *n.* a very severe headache. *I have a splitting headache and must go home now.*

SIGN: **'BENT ONE'** hands are held slightly apart in front of the forehead with palms facing each other at a downward angle and forefingers pointing toward each other. The hands are then sharply stabbed toward each other at least twice. (The face winces in obvious pain and the teeth are visible as the signer appears to be articulating the sound 'EE'.)

spoil: *v.* to damage; make unfit for use. *You will spoil this sweater if you wash it in hot water.*

SIGN #1: Horizontal left **'X'** hand is held in a fixed position with palm rightward but slanted toward the body slightly while horizontal right **'X'** hand is held above/behind left hand with palm leftward. The right hand then slides briskly along the top of the left hand and continues to move in a forward/rightward direction.

OR

SIGN #2: Right horizontal **'I'** hand, palm left but angled toward the body, is placed on upturned palm of left **'EXTENDED B'** hand and is then firmly pushed forward/rightward across it, the right wrist rotating so that the palm eventually faces downward.

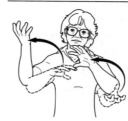

spoil: *v.* to disrupt; disturb. *He managed to spoil all our plans by arriving late.*

SIGN #3: Left **'CROOKED 5'** hand is held palm-up with fingers pointing forward while right **'CROOKED 5'** hand is held apart and slightly higher with palm down and fingers pointing forward. The arms are then simultaneously moved upward/rightward as the hands are purposefully twisted rightward from the wrist so that the left palm faces right and the right palm faces left.

spoiled: *adj.* overindulged. *A spoiled child likes to have his own way.*

SIGN: Horizontal right **'I'** hand, palm leftward/backward, is placed on the upturned palm of the left **'EXTENDED B'** hand and is circled several times in a counter-clockwise direction.

sponge: *n.* a light, porous object used in bathing and cleaning. *Makeup can be applied with a damp sponge.*

SIGN #1: Vertical **'SPREAD C'** hands are held fairly close with palms facing each other and fingers flexing repeatedly as if squeezing a sponge. The signer's cheeks are puffed out.

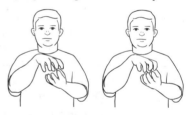

sponge off: *v.* to get things by taking advantage of others. *It is a well known fact that he constantly sponges off his friends.*

SIGN #2: Left **'BENT U'** hand is held in a fixed position with palm down and extended fingers pointing rightward/forward. Vertical right **'CONTRACTED 3'** hand is held above the level of the right shoulder with palm forward and is purposefully lowered so that the extended fingers and thumb snap shut on the extended fingers of the left hand. ❖

sponsor: *v.* to promote or support for profit or charity. *We are looking for a corporation to sponsor this project.*

SIGN: **'S'** hands, palms toward the body, are held at chest level with the left slightly above the right. Then the right is brought upward to strike the left.

SAME SIGN—**sponsor**, *n.*, except that the movement is repeated.

spoon: *n.* a utensil used in eating, serving, or stirring food. *I need a spoon to eat my dessert.*

SIGN: Left **'U'** hand is held with the palm facing the body and the extended fingers pointing rightward/upward. Right **'U'** hand, palm facing backward and the tips of the extended fingers touching the lips, is lowered so that the backs of the extended fingers come to rest on the extended fingers of the left hand at right angles to them.

sport: *n.* a person known for the way s/he reacts to losing or adversity (usually qualified by **good**, *adj.*, or **poor**, *adj.*, which will influence the definition). *Although he was disappointed, he was a good sport about losing the game.*

SIGN: Fingerspell **SPORT**.

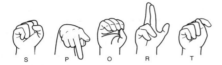

sports: *n.* recreational or competitive games; athletics. *Three popular sports in Canada are hockey, baseball and football.*

SIGN: **'A'** hands, palms facing, are held close to one another and moved alternately back and forth. This is a wrist movement. (**SPORTS** is frequently fingerspelled.)

spot: *n.* a mark or stain on something. *You have a spot of gravy on your tie.*

SIGN #1: Right **'F'** hand, palm left, is brought back firmly against the chest or wherever the spot happens to be.

spot: *n.* location. *This is a perfect spot to pitch our tent.*

SIGN #2: Horizontal **'K'** hands are held out in front of the body with palms facing each other and tips of middle fingers touching. The hands then create a circle as they are drawn apart and brought toward the chest where they meet again.

spot: *v.* to notice suddenly. *The birdwatchers spotted some nesting terns on the shore.*

SIGN #3: Right **'S'** hand, palm forward, is held against the right cheek near the eye, and is thrust forward a short distance as the forefinger flicks out to create to a **'BENT ONE'** handshape. Eyes are open wide.

(on the) spot: *adv.* immediately; right away. *When he admitted his guilt, he was fired on the spot.*

SIGN #4: Vertical **'COVERED T'** hands are held apart with palms facing, and are jerked forward as thumbs flick upward, resulting in horizontal **'CLAWED L'** hands, palms still facing.

(on the) spot: *adv.* in an awkward position. *By telling my parents, you are really putting me on the spot.*

SIGN #5: **'5'** hands are held apart with palms down and fingers pointing relatively forward as they are circled backward. This is not a symmetrical movement; rather, the hands are offset and circle backward in a staggered pattern. The signer is leaning backward slightly and the tongue is visibly relaxed between the teeth. (The sample sentence in ASL is: *YOU TELL MY PARENTS...ME AWKWARD.*)

spotless: See **immaculate**.

spotlight: *n.* a powerful light focussed so that it lights up a specific area. *The spotlight must be on the hero at this point.*

SIGN: Vertical right **'MODIFIED O'** hand, held up high with palm facing forward, is thrust forward/downward as the fingers open to create a **'CONTRACTED 5'** handshape.

spots: *n.* a skin blemish occurring through some kind of disease. *She suspected the child had measles when she saw some red spots.*

SIGN: Vertical **'F'** hands, with palms facing forward, are alternately tapped against each cheek. (The same basic sign is used for the verb phrase **break out in spots**, but **'S'** handshapes are used initially with the fingers uncurling to form **'F'** shapes as they make contact with the body.)

spouse: *n.* a person's husband or wife. *This invitation includes your* ***spouse***.

SIGN: Thumbtip of right **'EXTENDED C'** hand, palm down, is positioned at the centre of the forehead and the hand is brought downward to clasp left **'EXTENDED C'** hand, of which the palm faces upward. Then thumbtip of right **'EXTENDED C'** hand, palm down, is positioned at right cheek and the hand is brought downward to clasp left **'EXTENDED C'**, of which palm faces upward. (ASL CONCEPT—**husband - wife**.) When **spouse** refers specifically to a **husband**, the first part of this sign is used only; likewise, when the word refers specifically to a **wife**, the second part of this sign is used only.

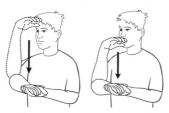

sprain: *v.* to injure a joint with a sudden twisting or wrenching of the muscles or ligaments. *He* ***sprained*** *his ankle while playing hockey.*

SIGN: Horizontal **'CLAWED V'** hands, left palm facing the chest and right palm down, are held with the knuckles of the forefinger and midfinger of one hand touching those of the other. The wrists then twist in opposite directions to turn the hands so that the left palm is facing down and the right palm is facing the chest.

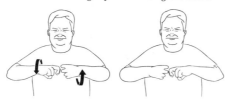

spray: *v.* to atomize, mist, or discharge a quantity of very fine liquid particles. *She* ***sprayed*** *the windows with a special cleaner before wiping them.*

SIGN: Right **'CLAWED L'** hand is held with palm forward and slightly downward and makes sweeping movements from side to side as if spraying with an aerosol can. (When **spray painting**, the same basic sign is used but with a horizontal **'L'** handshape, palm left and forefinger pointing forward.) For **spray**, *n.*, the vertical right **'CROOKED L'** hand is held in a fixed position with palm forward as forefinger and thumb flex a few times. Context must be considered when choosing signs.

spread: *v.* to distribute; disseminate. *He* ***spread*** *the news about their lottery win.*

SIGN #1: **'FLAT O'** hands are held with tips of forefingers touching and palms forward/downward but slanted toward each other slightly. The hands are then flung forward/outward as the fingers spread to form **'5'** hands with the palms down.

spread: *v.* to apply in a coating. *Cold butter does not* ***spread*** *easily.*

SIGN #2: Left **'EXTENDED B'** hand is held palm up in a fixed position while the undersides of the extended fingers of the right **'EXTENDED U'** hand, palm down, are stroked backward/leftward a couple of times along the left hand as if 'spreading' something on it.

spread: *n.* a top covering for a bed. *My aunt crocheted a beautiful* ***spread*** *for our bed.*

SIGN #3: **'BENT EXTENDED B'** hands are held apart just in front of the upper chest with palms down and fingers pointing forward but toward each other slightly. The hands are then turned inward from the wrists so that the fingertips touch the chest. Alternatively, this sign may be made with one hand only.

spreadsheet: *n.* a computer program used for charting information. ***Spreadsheets*** *help users create and analyze budgets.*

SIGN: Fingertips of right **'5'** hand, palm down, are stroked downward across palm of horizontal left **'5'** hand which is facing the chest, but angled rightward. Then the right wrist rotates forward a quarter turn so that the palm is turned toward the body at a leftward-facing angle as the fingertips are stroked across the left palm from left to right.

spring: *n.* the season between winter and summer. *Most Canadians welcome* **spring** *after a long, cold winter.*

SIGN #1: Right **'FLAT O'** hand is thrust upward through left **'C'** hand, as fingers open into a **'CONTRACTED 5'** hand. Movement is repeated. (Sign choice depends on context.)

spring: *n.* a flexible device such as a coil of wire which compresses when pressure is applied, then returns to its original position. *He counted the* **springs** *in the mattress when he could not sleep.*

SIGN #2: Horizontal **'C'** hands, palms facing each other, are held apart and are simultaneously lowered firmly to indicate the circumference of the coil. Then the right **'BENT ONE'** hand, forefinger pointing down, is held above the left **'C'** hand and is circled clockwise several times. Signs vary greatly according to the type of spring being referred to.

spring: *v.* to jump forward; leap. *The cougar will* **spring** *from the rock to devour the helpless animal.*

SIGN #3: **'CLAWED V'** hands represent the crouched legs of a springing animal as they are held palms down, left in front of right, and then simultaneously moved forward in an arc formation. ❖

sprinkle: *v.* to scatter in tiny particles. *I like to* **sprinkle** *a bit of brown sugar on my porridge.*

SIGN: Right **'O'** hand is held with palm down. Fingers flutter as the hand moves in a counter-clockwise circle.

sprint: *v.* to run a short distance at top speed. *I saw him* **sprint** *down the back lane away from the burning house.*

SIGN: Forefinger of the right horizontal **'CLAWED L'** hand is hooked around the upright thumb of the left **'CLAWED L'** hand, palms facing right and left. Then both hands are thrust forward with curved motion.

spruce: *n.* a coniferous tree found in the northern hemisphere. *The furniture is made of* **spruce.**

SIGN: Fingerspell **SPRUCE.**

spy: *v.* to keep a secret watch on others. *During World War II, he was sent to Germany to* **spy** *on military maneuvers.*

SIGN #1: Fingerspell **SPY**. (**SPY,** *n.,* is also fingerspelled.)

SIGN #2 [ATLANTIC]: Vertical right **'A'** hand, palm facing left and thumbtip just to the right of the nose, slides down the face until the thumbtip is touching the right side of the chin.

squabble: *v.* to quarrel over unimportant matters. *They always* **squabble** *while making holiday plans.*

SIGN: **'BENT ONE'** hands, palms toward the chest, forefingers pointing toward each other, are either simultaneously or alternately moved up and down from the wrist.

squander: *v.* to spend wastefully or extravagantly. *Do not* **squander** *your money on lottery tickets.*

SIGN: **'S'** hands are held, one at either hip, with palms up. The hands are then flung simultaneously upward/outward as they open to form **'CROOKED 5'** hands. Movement is repeated. (Alternatively, the hands may be flung alternately and repeatedly.)
ALTERNATE SIGN—waste

square: *adj.* having four equal sides. *The picture is* **square.**

SIGN #1: Tips of forefingers of vertical **'ONE'** hands, palms down, are held together, then simultaneously drawn apart, lowered, and brought together again. The movement should roughly outline a square.

square: *adj.* substantial; satisfying. *The lost hunters had not eaten a* **square** *meal for three days.*

SIGN #2: Fingertips of right **'BENT EXTENDED B'** hand are placed on the lips so that the palm is toward the body. Then the hand is moved purposefully forward a brief distance.

square: *n.* a colloquial term meaning a person who is old-fashioned in views, customs and appearance. *His classmates teased him and called him a square.*

SIGN #3: Right **'S'** hand, slightly open, palm facing left, is brought down firmly from the chin as it closes. Then right **'F'** hand, palm down, is moved from left to right in front of chest.

squash: *n.* any fruit of the gourd family, which is eaten as a vegetable. *We often have baked squash with roast chicken.*

SIGN #1: Fingerspell **SQUASH**.

squash: *n.* a sport played in an enclosed court with a light, long-handled racquet and a small rubber ball. *We will play squash together after work today.*

SIGN #2: Right **'CLOSED A-INDEX'** hand, palm left, is swung back and forth to simulate the swinging of a squash racquet in play.

squash: *v.* to crush; press down. *Your hat will get squashed if you put it in that suitcase.*

SIGN #3: Left **'EXTENDED B'** hand is held in a fixed position with palm up and fingers pointing forward/rightward. Right **'EXTENDED B'** hand is held quite a distance above the left hand with palm down and fingers pointing forward/leftward. The right hand then drops, landing forcefully on the left palm.

squat: *v.* to crouch with knees bent and body weight on the feet. *We saw the policeman squat beside his cruiser to avoid the shots being fired by the fleeing robbers.*

SIGN: Right **'V'** hand is positioned with palm down and tips of forefinger and midfinger on upturned palm of left **'EXTENDED B'** hand. Then the right hand collapses to form a **'CLAWED V'** handshape.

squeal: *v.* to utter a screaming sound, often in pain. *A dog will squeal if you step on its tail.*

SIGN: Right vertical **'SPREAD C'** hand, palm toward the body, is held near the mouth and is forcefully drawn forward at an upward angle.

squeeze: *v.* to grip firmly and apply pressure. *For this recipe you will need to squeeze the juice of two lemons.*

SIGN: Right **'SPREAD C'** hand is held with palm downward/rightward and is closed to form an **'S'** hand a couple of times. (Signs vary according to what is being squeezed and the manner in which it is being squeezed.)

squirrel: *n.* a rodent with a bushy tail. *Squirrels store food for the winter.*

SIGN: **'CLAWED V'** hands, left palm up and right palm forward/leftward and slightly downward, are positioned so the left remains fixed and the back of the right is in front of the mouth. Then the right is lowered a couple of times as the forefinger and midfinger tap down on those of the left hand.

stab: *v.* to pierce with a sharp pointed instrument. *She grabbed a kitchen knife and tried to stab her attacker.*

SIGN: Vertical right **'S'** hand, palm facing left, is thrust forward/downward as if stabbing something. ❖

stable: *n.* a farm building used for lodging livestock. *There are ten stalls in the stable.*

SIGN #1: Fingerspell **STABLE**. (The fingerspelled word is often followed by a more detailed explanation to set the word in context.)

stable: *adj.* reasonably strong; steady in position. *He has built up a stable business.*

SIGN #2: Vertical right **'BENT EXTENDED B'** hand is held just in front of the body with palm forward. The hand is then moved directly forward.

SAME SIGN—**stability**, *n.,* in this context.

691

stadium: *n.* a building, such as an arena, where sporting events are held. *The Grey Cup game will be played in the new stadium.*

SIGN: Fingerspell **STADIUM**.

staff: *n.* a group of people employed by one person or company. *The hospital staff has been greatly reduced due to recent layoffs.*

SIGN: Fingerspell **STAFF**.

stag: *n.* an all-male party or social evening (often held prior to the wedding of the guest of honour). *The groom's buddies planned an all-night stag for him.*

SIGN: Fingerspell **STAG**. (Sign selection depends on context.)

stage: *n.* a theatre setting where actors perform. *The cast returned to the stage for the final bow.*

SIGN: Fingerspell **STAGE**.

stagger: *v.* to walk unsteadily as if about to fall. *A drunk person will usually stagger.*

SIGN: Vertical right **'ONE'** hand, palm facing forward, represents a staggering person as it is bounced slightly forward in a wide zigzagging pattern. (Facial expression is important.) Sign choice depends on context. ❖

stain: *n.* a discoloured spot or patch. *The coffee left a stain on my sweater.*

SIGN: Right **'F'** hand, palm left, is brought back firmly against the chest or wherever the stain happens to be.

stairs: *n.* a flight of steps between two levels of a building. *In case of fire, use the stairs.*

SIGN #1: Right **'CLAWED EXTENDED V'** hand is held palm down with fingers pointing downward and fluttering (to simulate two legs walking) as the hand moves upward/forward.

OR

SIGN #2: Right **'BENT EXTENDED B'** hand is held with palm basically downward, the wrist twisting rapidly to make the hand quite noticeably wobble as it moves upward/forward.

stale: *adj.* no longer fresh or new. *After a few days, bread becomes stale.*

SIGN: Right **'S'** hand, slightly open, palm facing left, is brought down firmly from the chin as it closes. (Signs vary according to context.)

stalemate: *n.* a deadlock, when further action is impossible. *The government and the opposition had reached a stalemate in their talks.*

SIGN: Tips of extended fingers of right **'BENT V'** hand are thrust toward the throat.

stalk: *v.* to follow or pursue in a menacing way. *Her former husband has been ordered by the court to stop stalking her.*

SIGN #1: Horizontal left **'EXTENDED A'** hand is held with palm facing right while the horizontal right **'EXTENDED A'** hand, palm facing left, is held behind and appears to be pushing the left hand as the hands slowly move forward together in a zigzag pattern. The eyes squint and the signer is clearly concentrating very hard. (**STALK** may be fingerspelled.)

stalk: *n.* the main stem of a plant. *The plant has a rigid stalk.*

SIGN #2: Horizontal left **'COVERED F'** hand is held in a fixed position with palm facing right. Horizontal right **'COVERED F'** hand is held with palm facing left and thumb and forefinger resting on those of the left hand. Then the right hand is raised to indicate the length of the 'stalk'.

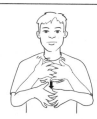

stall: *v.* to stop running. *If your car stalls often, you may need a new battery.*

SIGN #1: Fingers of horizontal **'CLAWED 5'** hands, palms toward the body, are interlocked and remain so as they are shaken up and down, ending with a rather abrupt downward movement. This is a wrist action.

stall: *v.* to make use of delaying tactics. *She is stalling for time hoping that we will forget all about the problem.*

SIGN #2: Left **'S'** hand is held with palm facing rightward/downward. Right **'S'** hand is held just in front of the left hand with palm facing leftward/downward. The left hand remains fixed while the right hand is firmly moved directly forward. (Signs vary considerably depending on the context. In general, more information is given in ASL than in English. The signer would probably explain exactly how someone is stalling for time rather than to say simply that s/he is stalling for time. Body shifts and facial expression are important.)

stall: *n.* a compartment (in a stable) designed for a single animal. *When I went to feed my horse, I found the stall empty.*

SIGN #3: Vertical **'EXTENDED B'** hands, palms toward the body, are held so their edges and pinky fingers are touching. Then they are drawn apart, turned so the palms are facing, and drawn back toward the shoulders, thus outlining a rectangular enclosure. (The same sign may be used for **cubicles** in washrooms.)

stamina: *n.* endurance; lasting strength, energy and resilience. *You need to have lots of stamina to interpret for three solid hours without a break.*

SIGN: **'S'** hands are held parallel with palms facing upward but angled toward the chest. The hands are then forcefully brought closer to the chest. Next, **'EXTENDED A'** hands are held side by side with palms down and right thumbtip pressing against left thumbnail as the hands are moved purposefully forward. (ASL CONCEPT—**strong - continue.**)

stamp: *n.* a small piece of gummed paper used for postage. *He has just purchased a valuable stamp for his collection.*

SIGN #1: Left **'EXTENDED B'** hand is held with palm toward the body at an upward angle and fingers pointing rightward. Tips of extended fingers of right **'U'** hand touch the lips. The right wrist then rotates to turn the hand palm downward as it is lowered so that the tips of the extended fingers come to rest on the left palm.

stamp: *v.* to mark with an official seal. *A customs official will stamp your passport.*

SIGN #2: Horizontal right **'S'** hand, palm toward the body and facing left slightly, is brought down firmly to rest on the upturned palm of the left **'EXTENDED B'** hand.

stamp: *v.* to walk with heavy, noisy footsteps. *We saw him stamp angrily into the principal's office.*

SIGN #3: **'EXTENDED B'** hands, palms down and fingers pointing forward, are alternately lifted and lowered with firm, deliberate movements.

stamp out: *v.* to stop; bring to an end. *This organization is trying to stamp out drunk driving.*

SIGN: Right **'EXTENDED B'** hand, palm facing left, is brought down sharply from a semi-vertical position to strike the upward/backward facing palm of the rigidly held left **'EXTENDED B'** hand, whose fingers point rightward/forward.

stampede: *n.* the sudden rush of a crowd (either human or animal). *The rumour that gold had been found created a stampede of prospectors to that area.*

SIGN #1: Both **'BENT 5'** hands, palms facing forward, are moved forward and slightly downward from shoulder level, fingers wiggling.

stampede: *n.* a rodeo. *The Calgary Stampede is an annual world-class event.*

SIGN #2: Downward-pointing forefinger and middle finger of **'EXTENDED K'** hand straddle horizontal left **'EXTENDED B'** hand of which the palm faces right. Then both hands are simultaneously circled forward several times.

stand: *v.* to be in an erect or upright position. *He will stand rather than sit while addressing the students.*

SIGN #1: Right **'BENT V'** hand is inverted so that the tips of the forefinger and midfinger are touching the upturned palm of the left **'EXTENDED B'** hand.

stand [*or* **stand up**]: *v.* to rise to an upright position. *The teacher asked the students to stand when answering questions.*

SIGN #2: Right **'CROOKED V'** hand, palm upward, is raised and overturned as it is brought downward, extended fingertips coming to rest on upturned palm of left **'EXTENDED B'** hand. (See also **rise** #3.)

stand: *v.* to tolerate; bear. *Kathy simply can not stand spiders.*

SIGN #3: Right **'A'** hand, with thumbnail touching closed lips and palm facing left, is moved slowly down chin.

stand: *v.* to continue; remain in effect. *Our agreement will still stand if the circumstances change.*

SIGN #4: **'EXTENDED A'** hands are held side by side with palms down and right thumbtip pressing against left thumbnail as the hands are moved purposefully forward.

stand: *n.* a resolute opinion, position or attitude. *She has a strong stand on the issue of human rights.*

SIGN #5: Vertical right **'MODIFIED O'** hand is held just in front of mid-forehead with palm facing left, and is bobbed slightly. (Facial expression is important. **Stand**, *n.*, has various connotations (*e.g.*, a wash stand, a music stand, a TV stand, etc.) and signs will vary accordingly.)

694

stand by: *v.* to be available and ready. *We will stand by in case you need our help.*

SIGN: **'BENT EXTENDED B'** hands are held apart with palms up and the right hand slightly ahead of the left while fingers simultaneously move back and forth. Motion may be repeated.

stand for: *v.* to represent or mean. *CCSD stands for the Canadian Cultural Society of the Deaf.*

SIGN: Horizontal left **'EXTENDED B'** hand is held in a fixed position with palm facing right while tip of forefinger of right palm-down **'BENT V'** hand is jabbed into the left palm. The right hand then moves away from the left hand as the right wrist rotates a quarter turn clockwise, and the middle fingertip is jabbed into the left palm.

stand out: *v.* to be conspicuous or noticeable. *Those black letters really stand out against the white background.*

SIGN: Vertical right **'CROOKED ONE'** hand is held with palm facing backward and tip of forefinger touching the face just under/to the right of the right eye. As the forearm moves forward, the wrist rotates to turn the hand so that the palm faces forward. This sign is formed quickly and emphatically.

stand up for: *v.* to support, side with, or defend. *Although they lose most of their games, the coach always stands up for his team.*

SIGN: **'S'** hands, palms toward the body, are held at chest level with the left slightly above the right. Then the right is brought upward to strike the left.

stand up to: *v.* to face; deal with in a brave way. *I will stand up to him because I am not afraid of him.*

SIGN: Vertical left **'EXTENDED B'** hand is held in a fixed position with palm toward face. Vertical right **'EXTENDED B'** hand, palm forward, is moved forward to stop near, but not touching the left hand. ❖

standard: *n.* an accepted or approved example against which others are measured. *What standard of work do you expect from me?*

SIGN: Vertical **'BENT EXTENDED B'** hands, palms facing each other and fingertips touching, are drawn apart. (A *'high* standard' is indicated when vertical **'BENT EXTENDED B'** hands are held apart with palms facing each other and are then raised; a *'low* standard' is indicated when vertical **'BENT EXTENDED B'** hands are held apart with palms facing each other and are then lowered.)

standardize: *v.* to make uniform throughout. *The Education professor thinks we should standardize the curricula throughout Canada.*

SIGN: **'Y'** hands are held parallel with palms down, and are simultaneously circled leftward in a wide arc so that they eventually return to their original position.
SAME SIGN—**standard**, *adj.,* in this context, but sign choice requires careful consideration.

standing ovation: *n.* a prolonged applause during which the audience or spectators rise to their feet. *The figure skaters were given a standing ovation.*

SIGN: Vertical **'A'** hands are held apart with palms forward and are simultaneously raised as the fingers open to form **'5'** hands. Next, **'EXTENDED B'** hands, palms facing each other, are clapped together. (ASL CONCEPT—**all stand - clap.**)

(at a) standstill: *adj.* having come to a complete stop. *Since we have run out of funds, the operation of the program is now at a standstill.*

SIGN: Right **'EXTENDED B'** hand, palm facing left, is brought down sharply from a semi-vertical position to strike the upward/backward facing palm of the rigidly held left **'EXTENDED B'** hand, whose fingers point rightward/forward. (If there is a definite intention of resuming whatever it is that has come to a standstill, **hold** #4 may be used.)

stanza: *n.* a unit of poetry with a certain number of lines and a definite metrical pattern; verse. *The third stanza of the poem contains a figure of speech.*

SIGN: Horizontal left **'EXTENDED B'** hand is held with fingers pointing rightward, and palm facing slightly upward yet angled toward the body, while thumb and forefinger of right **'C-INDEX'** hand are placed on left palm and drawn rightward across it.

stapler: *n.* a device that fastens staples to a surface. *I need to buy a new stapler for my office.*

SIGN: Right **'OPEN A'** hand, palm facing downward, is positioned with fingertips on the upturned palm of the left **'EXTENDED B'** hand. Then the right hand collapses to form an **'A'** handshape. Movement is repeated.

star: *n.* a celestial body visible in the clear night sky. *Early sailors were guided by the stars.*

SIGN #1: **'ONE'** hands, palms forward at a slight downward angle and fingers pointing upward at a slight forward angle, are held aloft and moved back and forth alternately so that the outer edges of the forefingers rub against each other.

star: *n.* a well known celebrity. *She is a popular movie star.*

SIGN #2: Fingerspell **STAR**.

S T A R

star: *v.* to feature as the leading actor. *They have not decided yet which actors will star in the production.*

SIGN #3: **'EXTENDED A'** hands, palms facing each other, are rotated alternately in small circles which are brought down against the chest.

star: *adj.* of outstanding ability or quality. *She is the star pupil in this class.*

SIGN #4: Left **'EXTENDED B'** hand is held in a semi-vertical position with palm facing right at a downward angle. Right **'EXTENDED B'** hand is held at a higher level in a semi-vertical position with palm facing left at a downward angle. The right forearm then moves downward so that the hand firmly strikes the fingertips of the left hand.

stare: *v.* to look at for a long period of time. *It is rude to stare at others.*

SIGN: Right **'BENT V'** hand, palm facing forward, is positioned near the right shoulder with extended fingers pointing forward, and the hand is circled forward several times. ❖

stark: *adj.* grim; desolate. *The landscape was stark after the forest fire.*

SIGN: Vertical right **'BENT MIDFINGER 5'** hand, palm forward, is held out in front of the left side of the body and moved rightward as the signer's lips are open only enough to allow a very narrow stream of air to be emitted. (Signs vary considerably depending on context.)

stark naked: *adj.* utterly or absolutely nude. *The streaker who was stark naked ran across the football field.*

SIGN: Tip of middle finger of right **'BENT MIDFINGER 5'** hand strokes forward/rightward across back of left **'STANDARD BASE'** hand. The signer's lips are open only enough to allow a very narrow stream of air to be emitted and the facial expression is clearly one of astonishment.

start: *v.* to commence; begin. *The race will start at noon.*

SIGN: Left **'5'** hand is held with palm facing right while forefinger of right **'ONE'** hand is inserted between first two fingers of left hand and twisted 180 degrees either to the right or left.

startled: *adj.* feeling surprise or sudden fright. *I was startled when something or someone touched my shoulder in the darkness.*

SIGN: With a jolt, horizontal **'CROOKED 5'** hands, palms facing the body, are positioned a short distance apart in front of the chest. The movement is sudden and appears to be involuntary while the signer's facial expression clearly conveys surprise. (This sign is used only in a passive voice situation or as an adjective to describe someone's feelings. It would *not* be possible to use this sign in an active voice situation such as: *You startled me when you touched my shoulder in the darkness.*)

starve: *v.* to be deprived of food. *Many people starve in developing nations.*

SIGN: Fingertips of horizontal right **'EXTENDED C'** hand, palm toward the body, are placed against middle of upper chest and the hand is drawn firmly downward. REGIONAL VARIATION—**hungry** #2

stash: *n.* a secret place where something is hidden. *The police found a stash of money when they searched the apartment.*

SIGN: Thumbnail of right **'A'** hand, palm facing left, is placed against the lips and the hand is then lowered and concealed under the down-turned palm of the left **'CROOKED EXTENDED B'** hand.

state: *n.* a political territory which is part of a federation. *Hawaii became a state in the U.S. in 1959.*

SIGN #1: Fingerspell **STATE**.

state: *n.* condition. *I am embarrassed about the state of this room.*

NOTE—Signs vary considerably depending on context. In the sample sentence, it is obvious that the room is in an *unsatisfactory state*. Rather than a sign for word translation, the ASL user would specify what kind of state the room is in. The sample sentence in ASL is: *THIS ROOM MESS...ME EMBARRASSED!*

state: *v.* to declare formally; express. *The witness stated that the suspect was seen in the area around the time of the robbery.*

SIGN #3: Tip of forefinger of vertical right **'4'** hand, palm facing left, is tapped twice against the chin. (Signs vary. If someone is stating something for the benefit of a *large group*, **announce** is used. If it is a *Deaf* person who is stating something, see **recite** #1.)

statement: *n.* a declaration; account; report. *The police need a statement from you about the accident.*

SIGN: Left **'MODIFIED O'** hand is held at about shoulder level with palm facing upward but angled slightly toward the body while right **'MODIFIED O'** hand is held upright just in front of the forehead with palm toward the face. The forearms then move simultaneously forward/downward as the hands open to assume **'MODIFIED 5'** shapes with palms facing upward. (Signs vary depending on context.) If it is a *Deaf* person who is giving a statement, see **recite** #1.

static: *adj.* inactive; unmoving; unchanging. *If we allow the industry to remain static, we will lose customers.*

SIGN #1: Horizontal **'Y'** hands are held slightly apart with palms down and are simultaneously circled slowly in opposite directions, the right hand appearing to the signer to be moving in a clockwise direction while the right hand is moving counter-clockwise. Facial expression must clearly convey 'boredom'.

static: *n.* electrical interference in the transmission of radio or television signals. *Radio reception was poor due to interference caused by static.*

SIGN #2: Vertical **'CLAWED SPREAD C'** hands are held with palms facing either ear and fingers rapidly flexing and relaxing several times. This sign is accompanied by a grimace, and the teeth are visible as if the signer is articulating an 'EE' sound.

static electricity: *n.* a build-up of electrical charge on an uninsulated object. *I got a slight shock from the static electricity when I touched the chair.*

SIGN: Crooked forefingers of horizontal **'X'** hands, palms facing body, are tapped together at least twice.

station: *n.* a place where public transportation carriers stop for loading and unloading of goods and passengers. *The train pulled into the station on time.*

SIGN: Fingerspell **STATION**.

S T A T I O N

stationary: *adj.* standing still; not moving. *The bus was stationary at the curb when it was struck by a speeding truck.*

SIGN: Right horizontal **'3'** hand is held with palm facing left. (Palm orientation varies according to context and other sign choices may apply depending on what is being described as stationary.)

stationery: *n.* writing materials such as paper and envelopes. *A box of stationery is always a welcome gift for anyone who writes a lot of letters.*

SIGN: Horizontal **'CROOKED 5'** hands, right palm down and left palm up, are positioned so that the right hand is slightly above the left. Then the right hand moves leftward/backward and the left hand moves rightward as the heels of each hand strike against each other at least twice.

statistics: *n.* the collection and interpretation of numerical data. *Statistics show that fifty percent of these people are unemployed.*

SIGN: Horizontal right **'S'** hand, palm facing upward/backward, is held just above horizontal left **'S'** hand. As the left hand moves slightly rightward a few times and the right hand moves leftward, the bottom of the right strikes across the top of the left with each movement.

SAME SIGN—**statistician**, *n.*, and may be followed by the Agent Ending (see p. LIV).

statue: *n.* a sculpture of a human or animal. *A statue of Queen Victoria stands on the Legislature grounds in Winnipeg.*

SIGN: **'A'** hands, palms facing each other, are held parallel just above shoulder level. Then they are simultaneously curved downward to outline the shape of an hourglass.

status: *n.* position; standing. *What is his status in the community?*

SIGN: Vertical **'BENT EXTENDED B'** hands, palms facing each other and fingertips touching, are drawn apart. (A 'high status' is indicated when vertical **'BENT EXTENDED B'** hands are held apart with palms facing each other and are then raised; a 'low status' is indicated when vertical **'BENT EXTENDED B'** hands are held apart with palms facing each other and are then lowered.) Sign choice depends on context.

statute: *n.* a law established by government. *This is an outdated statute which should be reviewed.*

SIGN: Vertical left **'EXTENDED B'** hand is held in a fixed position with palm facing right. Right **'L'** hand, palm facing left, is placed against the fingers of the left hand and then lowered to the heel of the left hand.

stay: *v.* to remain (in a certain place). *You stay in the car while I ask for directions.*

SIGN #1: **'Y'** hands are held parallel with palms down but slanted slightly forward. The hands are then firmly pushed a very short distance downward.

stay: *v.* a colloquial expression meaning to continue to be. *I hope you will stay interested in the project.*

SIGN #2: **'EXTENDED A'** hands are held side by side with palms down and right thumbtip pressing against left thumbnail as the hands are moved purposefully forward.

stay: *v.* to have lodgings at. *I do not know where I will stay during the convention.*

SIGN #3: Right **'CONTRACTED 5'** hand is held with palm toward the face. The hand is then drawn downward as the fingers close to form a **'FLAT O'** hand just in front of the chin or neck. REGIONAL VARIATION—**sleep** #2

stay: *n.* the suspension of a judicial proceeding. *A last minute stay of execution granted by the Governor-General saved the convict from the gallows.*

SIGN #4: **'ONE'** hands, palms down, are held so that the forefingers are crossed at right angles to one another, the right on top of the left. As the forefingers then retract to form **'X'** hands, the forefinger of the right hand hooks around the forefinger of the left hand, lifting it firmly upward.

steady: *adj.* constant; stable; regular. *He was glad to have a steady job.*

SIGN #1: **'EXTENDED A'** hands are held side by side with palms down and right thumbtip pressing against left thumbnail as the hands are moved purposefully forward.

steady: *v.* to make calm. *She takes deep breaths to steady her nerves.*

SIGN #2: **'EXTENDED B'** hands, palms downward but slanted forward slightly and fingers pointing upward/forward, are held apart and slowly lowered so that the palms face directly downward.

(go) steady: *v.* to date on a regular basis; to be sweethearts. *They have been going steady for several years.*

SIGN #3: **'A'** hands are held together, palms facing each other, and knuckles touching. Together, they are shaken or moved back and forth slightly.

steak: *n.* a cut of beef, pork, fish or other meat. *The steak was tender and tasty.*

SIGN: Fingerspell **STEAK**.

steal: *v.* to take something from someone else without permission. *Someone tried to steal my car but the burglar alarm frightened him away.*

SIGN #1: Left arm is folded across in front of the chest. Horizontal right **'V'** hand is held with thumb against left forearm near the elbow and palm facing the arm. The right hand is then drawn rightward at a slight upward angle along the left forearm as the extended fingers retract to form a **'CLAWED V'** hand.

steal: *v.* to plagiarize; illegally use the work of another author. *He might steal the plot for his new film from your book.*

SIGN #2: Parallel horizontal **'V'** hands are held with the left hand slightly ahead of the right and the extended fingertips of both hands pointing leftward/forward. The forearms then move simultaneously rightward and slightly upward as the hands take on **'CLAWED V'** shapes, and finally resume the **'V'** shape as they continue moving rightward and slightly downward.

steam: *n.* the gas or vapour formed when water boils. *I could see the* **steam** *rising from the tea kettle.*

SIGN: Horizontal left **'S'** hand is held in a fixed position with palm facing rightward/backward while right **'SPREAD C'** hand is held just above with palm down. The right hand is then moved upward with a wavy motion. The signer's cheeks are puffed out. (Signs vary according to context, in particular on the amount of area covered by the steam.)

steel: *n.* an alloy of iron and other elements. *Most Canadian* **steel** *comes from mills in southern Ontario.*

SIGN: Tip of forefinger of right **'CROOKED ONE'** hand, palm toward the body, is tapped against the upper front teeth. (**STEEL** may be fingerspelled.)

steer: *n.* a castrated male ox or bull. *The rancher sold only one* **steer** *at the livestock auction.*

SIGN #1: Fingerspell **STEER**.

steer: *v.* to direct the course of a vehicle. *The student driver found it hard to* **steer** *the car when it was in reverse.*

SIGN #2: **'S'** hands, with palms facing the body, are held in the steering wheel position and are moved up and down alternately to simulate the motion of steering a car. (Signs vary depending on what is being steered and how it is being steered.)

steer clear of: *v.* to avoid; try to stay away from. *The police advised us to* **steer clear** *of that part of town.*

SIGN #3: Horizontal right **'EXTENDED A'** hand, palm facing left, is held directly behind horizontal left **'EXTENDED A'** hand whose palm faces right. Right hand then becomes vertical as it is brought back smartly toward the chest.

stem: *n.* the stalk of a plant. *The* **stem** *of a sunflower might grow very tall.*

SIGN: Horizontal left **'COVERED F'** hand is held in a fixed position with palm facing right. Horizontal right **'COVERED F'** hand is held with palm facing left and thumb and forefinger resting on those of the left hand. Then the right hand is raised to indicate the length of the 'stem'.

stench: *n.* a strong, very unpleasant odour. *As soon as we entered the house we were overcome by the* **stench** *of decay.*

SIGN #1: Right **'5'** hand is held with palm facing leftward/downward and thumbtip touching or close to the tip of the nose. The hand is then firmly thrust a short distance forward at a slight downward angle. Meanwhile, a grimace appears on the signer's face and the lips appear to be articulating the syllable 'PO'.

OR

SIGN #2: Right horizontal **'OPEN F'** hand, palm facing backward, is positioned with forefinger and thumb holding the end of the nose. This sign is accompanied by a grimace.

stenographer: *n.* a typist who transcribes shorthand or dictated material into print. *She spent her entire career as a* **stenographer** *in a law office.*

SIGN: **'SPREAD C'** hands, palms facing down, are held parallel with fingers wiggling up and down to simulate the action of typing.

step: *n.* one of a sequence of foot movements that comprise walking. *A baby's first* **step** *is always an exciting occasion.*

SIGN #1: **'EXTENDED B'** hands are held parallel with palms down and fingers pointing forward. The left hand remains fixed as the right hand moves forward in arc formation. To indicate that a number of steps are taken, the hands alternately move forward a few times. Sign choice depends on context. If the steps are being taken quietly or furtively, the sign would be made using inverted **'BENT ONE'** hands. SAME SIGN—**step**, *v.*

step: *n.* one riser in a flight of stairs. *She was sitting on the bottom* **step** *of the basement stairs.*

SIGN #2: Vertical left **'BENT B'** hand is held in a fixed position with palm facing right while vertical right **'BENT B'** hand is held just in front of it with palm facing left. The right hand moves forward, the wrist then rotating to turn the hand to a horizontal position as it is lowered the depth of the step. (For **steps**, see **stairs** #2.)

step-: *prefix* indicating a relationship resulting from another marriage. *He became my stepfather when I was only two years old.*

SIGN #3: Fingerspell **STEP**.

step by step: *adv.* by degrees; methodically. *I will guide you through the procedure step by step.*

SIGN: Horizontal **'BENT EXTENDED B'** hands, with palms facing each other, are deliberately moved up and forward over each other in leapfrog fashion.

step down: *v.* to resign from one's position. *After 10 years as president of our organization, she decided to step down.*

SIGN: Extended fingers of right **'CLAWED U'** hand, palm down, are inserted into an opening created in the left horizontal **'S'** hand. The right hand is then drawn back toward the body. ❖

step on: *v.* to place one's foot on something. *I am sorry I stepped on your foot.*

SIGN: Left **'EXTENDED B'** hand is held palm down with fingers pointing forward/rightward while right **'EXTENDED B'** hand is held slightly above the left at right angles to it. Then the right is pressed down firmly across the back of the left, pushing it downward. (Signs vary according to context. To sign **step on the gas**, the right **'EXTENDED B'** hand is held with palm forward/downward and fingers pointing forward/upward. The wrist then bends to lower the hand to a palm down position to simulate the foot movement on the pedal of a car.)

step on it: *v.* a slang expression meaning to hurry and stop wasting time. *It is almost quitting time, so step on it!*

SIGN: Horizontal **'U'** hands are held parallel with palms facing and are slightly but firmly and rapidly moved up and down simultaneously as they move forward.

stereotype: *n.* a fixed, often over-generalized image of a group of people. *They are the stereotype of a suburban couple with 2.5 children, a dog, one car and a mortgaged house.*

SIGN: **'Y'** hands are held parallel with palms down, and are simultaneously circled leftward in a wide arc so that they eventually return to their original position.

sterile: *adj.* free from germs. *The surgeon's instruments must be sterile.*

SIGN #1: Horizontal **'EXTENDED B'** hands are held, right on top of left, left palm facing upward and right palm facing downward, the fingers pointing basically forward. Together, the hands appear to jerk backward a short distance although the hands do not move any real distance at all. This is a twitchlike movement.

sterile: *adj.* unable to produce offspring. *The obstetrician told the woman that the operation would make her sterile.*

SIGN #2: Left **'ONE'** hand is held palm-down with forefinger pointing forward/rightward. The forefinger of the right **'ONE'** hand is held above the left, then brought down sharply to strike the left forefinger. Next, horizontal **'5'** hands are held apart with palms facing each other but slanted slightly toward the body. The hands are then moved together so that the fingers interlock. (ASL CONCEPT—**can't - pregnant**.)

sterilize: *v.* to make free of germs. *The instruments must be sterilized before surgery.*

SIGN: **'BENT 5'** hands, held parallel with palms up and fingers fluttering, move in small circles, the left hand in a clockwise direction and the right hand in a counter-clockwise direction. (**Sterilize** sometimes means 'to render someone unable to reproduce', in which case sign choice depends on the method of sterilization.)

stern: *adj.* firm; strict. *Our father was a stern man but he was always fair.*

SIGN #1: Vertical right **'CLAWED V'** hand, palm left, is raised abruptly so the crooked forefinger strikes the nose.

stern: *n.* the rear part of a boat or ship. *The lifeboats are in the stern of the ocean liner.*

SIGN #2: Right **'EXTENDED A'** hand, palm facing left, is held upright and jabbed backward at least twice over the right shoulder.

stethoscope: *n.* a medical instrument used to listen to sounds inside the body. *The doctor took his stethoscope out of his bag.*

SIGN: Vertical **'CROOKED ONE'** hands are positioned with tips of forefingers in either ear. The right hand is then lowered as it takes on the form of a **'FLAT O'** hand, the bunched fingertips making contact with the centre of the chest.

stew: *n.* a dish usually made of meat, vegetables and gravy and cooked slowly by stewing or simmering. *I think I will make some stew with the leftovers.*

SIGN #1: Fingerspell **STEW**.

S T E W

stew: *v.* to be in a worried or troubled state. *I have stewed about it all night and still have not found a solution.*

SIGN #2: **'B'** hands are held apart in front of the face with palms facing forward and the fingers of the left hand pointing upward/rightward while the fingers of the right hand point upward/leftward. The hands are then alternately circled backward a few times. These are very small circles. Facial expression must clearly convey 'anxiety'.

steward/stewardess: See **flight attendant**.

stick: *n.* a thin piece of wood. *We need more sticks to start the campfire.*

SIGN #1: Horizontal right **'EXTENDED B'** hand, fingertips pointing forward/leftward and palm facing left, is placed on the left **'STANDARD BASE'** hand. Both hands then move back and forth in a sawing motion. (Alternatively, the left hand may take the shape of a horizontal **'EXTENDED B'** with fingertips pointing forward/rightward and palm facing right.) Next, horizontal **'F'** hands are held side by side with palms down and extended fingers pointing forward, and are drawn apart. (ASL CONCEPT—**wood - stick**.) This sign is used when **stick** is first introduced into a conversation. After that, the sign may be abbreviated by using the second part of the sign only.

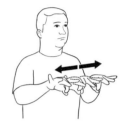

stick: *v.* to push one object through another; poke; thrust. *He tried to stick the cable through the hole in the wall.*

SIGN #2: **'CLOSED A-INDEX'** hand, palm up, is sharply thrust forward. Signs vary according to what kind of object is doing the sticking and the manner in which it is being done. ❖

stick out: *v.* to project or stand out from a surface. *Suddenly we saw a hand sticking out of the water.*

SIGN: Left **'STANDARD BASE'** hand is held in a fixed position while the vertical right **'5'** hand, palm facing forward, is positioned just behind the left hand at a rather low level. The right hand then rises so that the wrist is eventually touching the left hand. (Signs vary according to what is sticking out and from where.)

stick to: *v.* to abide by. *We will have to stick to our original agreement.*

SIGN: Horizontal left **'EXTENDED A'** hand is held with palm facing right while horizontal right **'EXTENDED A'** hand is held directly behind the left hand with palm facing left. Together, the hands are moved purposefully forward/downward. (Sign choice depends on context.)

stick with: *v.* to remain loyal to. *She promised to stick with me no matter what happened.*

SIGN: **'S'** hands, palms toward the body, are held at chest level with the left slightly above the right. Then the right is brought upward to strike the left. Facial expression is important. (Sign choice depends on context.)

sticky: *adj.* covered with an adhesive substance. *Caramel popcorn balls are very sticky.*

SIGN: **'OPEN 8'** hands are held parallel with palms up as tips of middle fingers and thumbs tap together several times to form **'8'** shapes.

stiff: *adj.* sore and hard to move (said of body parts after physical exertion). *I felt stiff after working all afternoon in the garden.*

SIGN #1: Fingerspell **STIFF**.

stiff: *adj.* rigid; inflexible. *My hands are stiff from the cold.*

SIGN #2: **'CROOKED 5'** hands are held parallel with palms down. They then jerk slightly forward/downward as the fingers retract to form **'CLAWED SPREAD C'** hands.

stiff: *adj.* harsh and severe. *We expect the judge will give him a stiff sentence for his violent crime.*

SIGN #3: Wrist of right **'CLAWED V'** hand, palm facing the body, rotates turning the hand palm-downward as it is thrust downward, the knuckles of the forefinger and middle finger rapping the back of the left **'STANDARD BASE'** hand on the way past. Facial expression is essential.

stiff: *n.* a slang expression meaning 'dead body'; corpse. *The unidentified stiff was taken to the morgue.*

SIGN #4: **'EXTENDED B'** hands are held with fingers pointing forward, left palm facing up and right palm facing down. Then they are flipped over simultaneously so that the palm positions are reversed. Next, horizontal **'EXTENDED B'** hands are placed slightly apart, fingertips opposite, with palms on upper chest. Then they are moved simultaneously to waist level. (ASL CONCEPT—**dead - body**.)

stifle: *v.* to crush or stamp out. *The administrators tried to stifle all complaints from their employees.*

SIGN #1: Left **'S'** hand is held with palm rightward/downward. Right **'EXTENDED B'** hand is held with fingers pointing forward/leftward/upward and palm forward/leftward/downward. With the palm of the right hand held against the top of the left hand, the right hand very firmly pushes the left hand forward/downward at a slight leftward angle. Facial expression is firm. ❖

stifle: *v.* to try to stop oneself from laughing, giggling, coughing, or yawning. *I had to stifle a laugh when I saw them trying to dance.*

SIGN #2: Horizontal right **'BENT EXTENDED B'** hand is held over the mouth while the signer obviously tries to refrain from giggling. (Signs vary depending on the context.)

still: *adv.* motionless or silent. *She sat still all afternoon.*

SIGN #1: **'B'** (or **'EXTENDED B'**) hands are crossed in front of the mouth, left palm facing rightward/downward and right palm facing leftward/downward with the right hand just behind the left hand. Then they are drawn apart until the palms face completely downward.

still: *adv.* yet; now as before. *He is still here.*

SIGN #2: Horizontal **'Y'** hands are held apart with palms facing chest, and are twisted smoothly from the wrists so that the palms face downward/forward. Sometimes only the right hand is used for this part of the sign.

still: *conj.* nevertheless. *I do not think it will work; still, we should give it a try.*

SIGN #3: Horizontal **'Y'** hands are held apart with palms facing chest, and are twisted smoothly from the wrists so that the palms face downward/forward. Sometimes only the right hand is used for this part of the sign. ALTERNATE SIGN—**but** #1

stillborn: *adj.* dead at birth. *She was devastated when she realized her baby was stillborn.*

SIGN: Horizontal **'EXTENDED B'** hands are held in front of the abdomen, palms facing the body, with the back of the right hand resting against the left palm. Then the right hand is curved down and under the left until its palm faces downward. Next, right **'EXTENDED B'** hand is held palm down with fingers pointing forward. The wrist then rotates rightward, turning the hand palm upward. (ASL CONCEPT—**born - die**.) Alternatively, **STILLBORN** may be fingerspelled.

stimulate: *v.* to rouse to activity; excite. *If you rub his feet, it will stimulate the blood circulation.*

NOTE—In the sample sentence and in most English sentences where **stimulate** appears, a specific sign would be considered redundant in ASL. Context must always be considered.

stingy: *adj.* unwilling to spend or give; miserly. *Scrooge was the stingy character in Dickens's A Christmas Carol.*

SIGN: Right **'SPREAD EXTENDED C'** hand is held palm down on the upturned palm of the left **'EXTENDED B'** hand and the fingertips scrape firmly backward toward the chest. (Facial expression is important.)

stink: *n.* a strong, foul smell. *If it is threatened, a skunk will create a terrible stink.*

SIGN #1: Right **'5'** hand is held with palm facing leftward/downward and thumbtip touching or close to the tip of the nose. The hand is then firmly thrust a short distance forward at a slight downward angle. Meanwhile, a grimace appears on the signer's face and the lips appear to be articulating the syllable 'PO'.

OR

SIGN #2: Right horizontal **'OPEN F'** hand, palm facing backward, is positioned with forefinger and thumb holding the end of the nose. This sign is accompanied by a grimace.

stir: *v.* to mix with a spoon or other utensil. *You need to stir the mixture until all the sugar is dissolved.*

SIGN: Left arm is extended as if curved around a large bowl. Right **'COVERED T'** hand, palm facing the body, is circled clockwise within the opening in a stirring motion. (Sign choice depends on context.)

stir up trouble: *v.* to create problems. *If you do that, you will stir up trouble.*

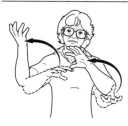

SIGN: Left **'CROOKED 5'** hand is held palm-up with fingers pointing forward while right **'CROOKED 5'** hand is held apart and slightly higher with palm down and fingers pointing forward. The arms are then simultaneously moved upward/rightward as the hands are purposefully twisted rightward from the wrist so that the left palm faces right and the right palm faces left.

stitch: *v.* to link by drawing a threaded needle through fabric or other material. *The doctor might want to stitch your wound.*

SIGN: Horizontal **'F'** hands are held slightly apart with palms facing each other. The left hand remains in a fixed position as the right hand is rotated clockwise at least twice so that the thumb and forefinger make contact with those of the left hand each time they brush past.

stock: *n.* shares in a business enterprise that will entitle the holder to dividends. *He holds a large amount of stock in several petroleum companies.*

SIGN #1: Fingerspell **STOCK**.

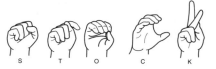

stock: *n.* a liquid or broth in which meat, bones, fish or vegetables are simmered for a long time. *We save the water when we drain cooked vegetables and add it to our soup stock.*

SIGN #2: Fingerspell **STOCK**.

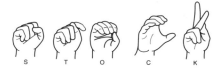

stock: *n.* a supply of materials, equipment, etc. that is stored for future use. *The clerk will take an inventory of the stock in the storage room.*

SIGN #3: Fingerspell **STOCK**.

stocking: *n.* one of a pair of garments worn over the foot and leg. *Hanging a Christmas stocking is a Canadian tradition.*

SIGN #1: Forefingers of **'ONE'** hands, palms down, are held side by side and alternately moved back and forth so that the sides of the forefingers brush each other with each movement.

OR

SIGN #2: Right **'5'** hand is held palm down with fingertips touching the back of the left wrist. The right hand then slides up to the crook in the left arm. Movement is repeated.

stomach: *n.* part of the abdominal area of the body. *The baby has an upset stomach.*

SIGN: Right **'EXTENDED B'** hand, fingertips pointing leftward and slightly downward, palm toward the body, pats the stomach a couple of times.

stone: *n.* a small piece of rock. *As I was walking through the field, I found an interesting stone.*

SIGN #1: Tip of forefinger of right **'CROOKED ONE'** hand, palm toward the body, is tapped against the upper front teeth.

ALTERNATE SIGN—**rock** #1

stone: *adj.* made of a hard compact material used in building. *They live in an old stone house.*

SIGN #2: Tip of forefinger of right **'CROOKED ONE'** hand, palm toward the body, is tapped against the upper front teeth.

stoned: *adj.* under the influence of drugs. *He became stoned from smoking marijuana.*

SIGN: Tip of forefinger of right **'ONE'** hand is used to touch the forehead. As the hand is lowered to about waist level, it takes on an **'S'** shape, then moves upward to strike the palm of the left **'STANDARD BASE'** hand with force. (ASL CONCEPT—**brain - hit top**.) Signs vary.

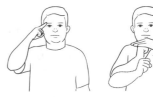

stool: *n.* waste material eliminated from the body through the bowel. *The doctor asked the mother to take a sample of the child's stool to the diagnostic laboratory.*

SIGN #1: Horizontal left **'A'** (or **'EXTENDED A'**) hand is held in a fixed position with palm facing backward/rightward. Thumb of horizontal right **'EXTENDED A'** hand is inserted in the base of the left hand. The right hand is then lowered from this position. Motion is repeated.

stool: *n.* a very simple piece of furniture that consists of a seat and either three or four legs. *My feet do not reach the floor when I sit on this high stool.*

SIGN #2: Fingerspell **STOOL**.

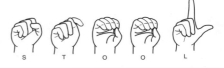

stool pigeon: *n.* someone who acts as an informer to the police. *He had many connections in the underworld so the police used him as a stool pigeon.*

SIGN: Vertical right **'S'** hand is held against the chin with palm forward. As the hand then moves forward, the forefinger flicks out so that it is pointing forward.

REGIONAL VARIATIONS—**tattle** #2 & #3

stoop: *v.* to bend forward and downward. *My back is so painful I can not **stoop** to tie my shoes.*

SIGN: Left **'C'** hand clasps forearm of right **'S'** hand which is held with palm facing forward at a slight leftward angle. Right hand is then lowered from the wrist so that palm faces downward. ❖

stop: *v.* to discontinue something. *Their father told them to **stop** shouting.*

SIGN: Right **'EXTENDED B'** hand, palm facing left, is brought down sharply from a semi-vertical position to strike the upward/backward facing palm of the rigidly held right **'EXTENDED B'** hand, whose fingers point rightward/forward.

stop keying: *v.* refers to the printed command which is used to terminate a TTY conversation. *Deaf people signal the end of a TTY conversation by typing SK which means '**stop keying**'.*

SIGN: Fingerspell **SK**.

stop sign: *n.* an octagonal red sign at an intersection that indicates to drivers that they must come to a full halt. *The collision occurred because one driver ignored the **stop sign**.*

SIGN: Right **'EXTENDED B'** hand, palm facing left, is brought down sharply from a semi-vertical position to strike the upward/backward facing palm of the rigidly held right **'EXTENDED B'** hand, whose fingers point rightward/forward. Next, tips of forefingers of vertical **'ONE'** hands, palms down, are held together, then simultaneously drawn apart, lowered, and brought together again. The movement should roughly outline a square.

stoplight: *n.* a traffic light, especially when it is red, to signal that drivers must halt. *You must turn right at the next **stoplight**.*

SIGN: Right **'COVERED 8'** hand is held upright, palm facing body, as middle finger flicks off thumb and strikes chin a couple of times. Next, vertical right **'FLAT O'** hand is held with the palm toward the body. The fingers are then opened to form a **'CONTRACTED 5'** and closed to resume the **'FLAT O'** shape. (ASL CONCEPT—**light - on off**.) Alternatively, the second part of this sign may be omitted.

stopover: *n.* a scheduled temporary interruption in a long flight. *We will have a 50-minute **stopover** in Toronto.*

SIGN: Right **'COMBINED LY'** hand is held with palm forward/leftward at a downward angle. The forearm is then lowered in a forward/leftward direction, so that the palm is eventually facing downward.

stopwatch: *n.* a device used for timing sporting events. *The **stopwatch** indicated he had completed the sprint in 57.9 seconds.*

SIGN: Horizontal right **'EXTENDED A'** hand, palm toward the chest, is moved up and down slightly as the thumb is depressed firmly several times.

storage: *n.* a space reserved for storing things. *We put our furniture in **storage** until our new house was built.*

SIGN: Fingerspell **STORAGE**.

store: *n.* a retail establishment that sells goods and services. *There are over 800 stores in the new mall.*

SIGN #1: **'FLAT O'** hands, held parallel with palms down and fingers pointing down, are swung forward/upward from the wrists a couple of times.

SIGN #2 [ATLANTIC]: **'CONTRACTED B'** hands, palms up, are alternately tapped against either side of the waist.

store: *v.* to set aside for future use. *We will store the camping equipment in the basement during the winter.*

SIGN #3: Horizontal **'S'** hands are held apart with palms facing leftward as the fingers open a couple of times, thus alternating between **'S'** and **'MODIFIED 5'** shapes. (Signs vary depending on context.)

storm: *n.* a violent weather condition. *The radio warned us about the coming storm.*

SIGN: Fingerspell **STORM**. (Signs vary. Sign choice depends on the type of storm.)

story: *n.* a narration of a chain of events, either written or told. *Children love a bedtime story.*

SIGN: Left **'CONTRACTED C'** (or **'OPEN 8'**) hand is held horizontally with palm facing right while right **'CONTRACTED C'** (or **'OPEN 8'**) hand is held upright with palm facing left. The hands are held close enough together to be loosely interlocked. They are then drawn apart, closed and returned several times, thus alternating between **'CONTRACTED C'** (or **'OPEN 8'**) and **'FLAT O'** (or **'8'**) shapes with each movement.

stout: *adj.* solidly built; fat; plump. *He is too stout to wear that costume.*

SIGN: **'SPREAD C'** hands are held one in front of either side of upper chest with palms toward the body but angled upward slightly. The forearms are then simultaneously and firmly moved a short distance forward at a slight downward angle. Cheeks are puffed out.

stout-hearted: See **brave**.

stove: *n.* an appliance used for cooking. *I prefer to cook on a gas stove.*

SIGN: Fingerspell **STOVE**.

S   T   O   V   E

straddle: *v.* to have a leg on either side of something. *The child's legs were too short to straddle the pony.*

SIGN: Left **'B'** hand is held in a fixed position with palm right and fingers pointing forward. Right **'V'** hand is held to the right of the left hand with palm toward the body and extended fingers pointing left at an upward angle. The right hand then moves leftward in an arc formation, coming to rest with the extended fingers straddling the left hand.

straight: *adj.* direct; not curved or crooked. *The highway between Edmonton and Calgary is very straight.*

SIGN #1: Vertical right **'B'** hand, palm facing left, is held directly in front of the face and thrust forward and slightly downward.

straight: *adj.* straightforward; forthright; candid. *If you do not like my idea, please give me a straight answer.*

SIGN #2: Left **'EXTENDED B'** hand is held in a fixed position with palm basically downward at a rightward/forward angle and fingers pointing basically upward at a rightward/forward angle. Right **'CONTRACTED U'** hand is held with palm toward the body and fingertips of forefinger and middle finger touching the heel of left hand. The wrist of the right hand rotates clockwise as the extended fingers stroke the left hand in a straight line from the heel, along the palm and fingers and onward in an upward/rightward/forward direction.
ALTERNATE SIGN—**honest** #1

straight: *adj.* a slang expression for heterosexual. *They used to hire only straight white males.*

SIGN #3: Vertical right **'B'** hand, palm facing left, is held directly in front of the face and thrust forward and slightly downward.

straight A's: *n.* continuous or uninterrupted A grades for school work. *She always has straight A's on her report cards.*

SIGN #4: Vertical right **'A'** hand, palm forward, is held fairly high and is lowered in a straight line. (This sign is very context specific. Context must always be considered when selecting signs.)

straight: *adv.* not deviating from one's course; directly. *Be sure to come straight home after school.*

SIGN #5: Vertical right **'EXTENDED B'** hand, palm left, is diagonally lowered to a horizontal position.

straighten: *v.* to make neat and tidy. *We should straighten up the house before our parents come home.*

SIGN: Hands are held at right angles to one another as downturned palm of right **'EXTENDED B'** hand is smoothed rightward/forward across upturned palm of left **'EXTENDED B'** hand. Motion is repeated a few times as the hands move around in a counter-clockwise direction.

straighten out: *v.* to resolve or make less confusing. *We have tried to straighten out the misunderstanding.*

SIGN: **'FLAT O'** hands are held parallel with palms up and slanted slightly toward the body. As the hands are drawn apart the thumbs slide across the fingertips, causing the hands to assume **'A'** shapes.

straightforward: *adj.* honest; frank. *You can count on him to give a straightforward opinion.*

SIGN #1: Left **'EXTENDED B'** hand is held in a fixed position with palm basically downward at a rightward/forward angle and fingers pointing basically upward at a rightward/forward angle. Right **'CONTRACTED U'** hand is held with palm toward the body and fingertips of forefinger and middle finger touching heel of left hand. The wrist of the right hand rotates clockwise as the extended fingers stroke the left hand in a straight line from the heel, along the palm and fingers and onward in an upward/rightward/forward direction.
ALTERNATE SIGN—**honest** #1

straightforward: *adj.* simple; clear. *The instructions are very straightforward.*

SIGN #2: **'O'** (or **'FLAT O'**) hands are placed side by side, palms facing forward. Then they are moved apart and upward as the fingers spread to form **'5'** hands, palms still facing away from the body.
ALTERNATE SIGNS—**easy** #1 & #2

strain: *n.* exertion; discomfort caused by excessive use. *Reading in poor light can cause eye strain.*

SIGN: Fingertips of **'BENT EXTENDED B'** hands are placed against either side of upper chest with palms facing the body. The wrists then rotate forward, causing the hands to drop while the fingertips maintain contact with the chest. The head may also tilt leftward a little. (Sign choice depends on context.)

stranded: *adj.* to be left helpless. *Many people were stranded during the snowstorm.*

SIGN: Tips of extended fingers of right **'BENT V'** hand are thrust toward the throat.

strange: *adj.* odd; unusual; peculiar. *His behaviour has been very strange lately.*

SIGN: Vertical right **'C'** hand, palm facing left, is held near the face and is abruptly dropped downward from the wrist so the palm faces down. (Signs for **stranger**, *n.*, vary according to context; however, this sign is definitely not appropriate.)

strangle: *v.* to kill by compressing the wind-pipe. *The medical examiner determined that the dead woman had been strangled.*

SIGN: Horizontal **'C'** hands, palms facing, are held so that the fingertips of one hand are touching those of the other. Together, the hands are shaken back and forth a few times as if strangling someone. Facial expression is important and the teeth are visible as if the signer is articulating an 'EE' sound.

strap: *v.* to beat with a leather strip as a punishment. *Teachers and principals are no longer permitted to strap children for misbehaviour.*

SIGN #1: Horizontal right **'CLOSED A-INDEX'** hand, is held with palm facing left. As the hand moves leftward at a slight downward angle, the wrist rotates to turn the hand so that the palm is slanted toward the body slightly. Movement is repeated.

strap: *n.* a strip such as that which forms part of a sandal. *The strap of my sandal is broken.*

SIGN #2: Tips of thumb and forefinger of right **'MODIFIED G'** hand, palm down, are drawn across, the back of the fingers of the left **'STANDARD BASE'** hand. (Signs vary considerably, depending mainly on the width and location of the strap.)

strategy: *n.* a plan for success. *She outlined her strategy for meeting the publisher's deadline.*

SIGN: Horizontal **'EXTENDED B'** hands, palms facing each other and fingers pointing forward, are held slightly apart at the left side of the body and are moved simultaneously toward the right.

straw: *n.* stalks of threshed grain used as fodder for livestock or to make hats, baskets, etc. *During the winter months ranchers often feed their cattle straw.*

SIGN #1: Back of right **'CROOKED 4'** hand, palm down, is held under the chin and the hand is moved briskly in small circular motions, brushing backward against the underside of the chin with each cycle. (**STRAW** is frequently fingerspelled.)

ALTERNATE SIGN—**grass** #2

straw: *n.* a long, thin, hollow tube used for sucking up a liquid. *I need a straw to drink this soda.*

SIGN #2: **'MODIFIED G'** hands, left palm facing right and right palm facing left, are positioned so the left is against the mouth and the right is slightly below it. Then the right is drawn forward/downward to indicate the length of a straw used for drinking.

strawberry: *n.* a red, edible fruit that grows on a plant spread by runners. *She likes to use fresh strawberries on her ice cream.*

SIGN #1: Vertical right **'ONE'** hand is held with palm facing the body and tip of forefinger touching the lower lip. As the hand is then drawn very firmly forward at a downward angle, the forefinger crooks to form an **'X'** shape. Next, thumbnail of right **'MODIFIED G'** hand, palm forward/downward, is placed on upturned palm of left **'EXTENDED B'** hand. Right forefinger then moves down to create a **'CLOSED MODIFIED G'** shape. (ASL CONCEPT—**red - pick**.)

OR

SIGN #2: Left **'ONE'** hand is held in a fixed position with palm facing the body at a downward angle and forefinger pointing rightward. Fingers of right **'OPEN SPREAD O'** hand grasp the end of the left forefinger as the right wrist twists back and forth several times. (Signs vary considerably.)

stray: *v.* to wander away. *Children can easily stray from their parents in a department store.*

SIGN #1: Vertical right **'ONE'** hand, palm forward, moves forward at a rightward angle. The tongue is visible between the teeth as if the signer is articulating the sound 'TH'. (Sign choice depends on context.)

stray: *adj.* lost. *Our son found a stray dog this afternoon.*

SIGN #2: Horizontal **'OPEN A'** hands, palms facing the body, are held together so that the knuckles of the bunched fingers are touching each other. The fingers are then unfurled so that the hands are swept apart, becoming horizontal **'CROOKED 5'** hands with palms facing each other and fingers pointing forward.

stream: *n.* a small river or brook. *The stream is stocked with rainbow trout.*

SIGN: Forefinger of vertical right **'W'** hand, palm facing left, is tapped against the chin. Next, horizontal **'EXTENDED B'** hands, palms facing each other, are held slightly apart and are simultaneously moved forward in a meandering motion. (ASL CONCEPT—**water - way curve**.) This sign is used when **stream** is first introduced into a conversation. After that, the sign may be abbreviated by using the second part of the sign only.

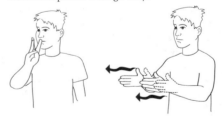

street: *n.* a public road, especially one which is lined with buildings and is in a town or city. *Every city has a main street.*

SIGN: **'EXTENDED B'** hands, held parallel with palms facing one another and fingers pointing forward, are simultaneously moved forward. (When the street is named, the name of the street is fingerspelled followed by the fingerspelled abbreviation **ST**.)

stress: *n.* mental, emotional or physical tension. *Stress can be hazardous to your health.*

SIGN #1: Palm of horizontal right **'EXTENDED B'** hand is placed on top of horizontal left **'S'** hand of which the palm is facing right, but is angled slightly toward the body. Together, the hands are pressed very firmly downward a few times. **STRESS** is frequently fingerspelled. SAME SIGN—**stressful**, *adj.*

stress: *v.* to emphasize or give special importance to something. *I want to stress that applicants must be at least 18 years of age.*

SIGN #2: Left **'EXTENDED B'** hand is held in a fixed position with palm right and fingers pointing forward/upward. Right **'EXTENDED A'** hand is held with palm down and thumbtip touching left palm. The right wrist then rotates forward, thus turning the hand so that the palm faces the body at a downward angle.

stretch: *v.* to extend (the limbs of the body). *I need to stretch after sitting here for so long.*

SIGN #1: **'S'** hands, palms facing forward, are held above shoulder level as the signer stretches.

stretch: *v.* to expand or extend in size or length. *Stretch the sweater after you wash it.*

SIGN #2: Horizontal **'S'** hands, palms toward the chest, are held together and then slowly drawn apart. There may be a repetition of this movement with the hands beginning in different locations depending on the context.

stretchy: *adj.* having the ability to expand or extend in size or length. *This bathing suit material is stretchy.*

SIGN: Horizontal **'S'** hands, palms toward the chest, are held together and drawn apart at least twice.

strict: *adj.* rigid in one's enforcement of rules or expectations. *Our instructor is strict but fair.*

SIGN #1: Vertical right **'CLAWED V'** hand, palm left, is raised abruptly so the crooked forefinger strikes the nose. (Sign choice depends on context.)

OR

SIGN #2: Horizontal left **'EXTENDED B'** hand is held with palm facing rightward/upward and fingers pointing forward. Right **'ONE'** hand is held above and to the right of the left hand and then moved purposefully so that the forefinger is jabbed into the left palm.

stride: *v.* to walk with a long step or pace. *We saw him stride along the path toward the footbridge.*

SIGN: Horizontal **'EXTENDED B'** (or **'3'**) hands, palms down, fingers pointing forward, are held slightly apart and are moved in a pattern whereby the right hand moves forward/rightward while the left hand moves backward/rightward. The left hand then moves forward/leftward while the right hand moves backward/leftward. The movement is repeated a few times to simulate the movement of one's feet while walking. This is done with long, purposeful movements.

(make) strides: *v.* to make good progress. *The organization is making strides with its fundraising.*

SIGN: Horizontal **'BENT EXTENDED B'** hands, left palm facing right and right palm facing left, are held with the right above the left. The hands then pass over and under each other as the forearms are slowly and purposefully circled forward a few times. Facial expression is important.

strike: *n.* a pitched ball which the umpire considers good and which was not swung at by the batter or was missed or hit into foul territory. *The umpire called it a strike even though it seemed wide of the plate.*

SIGN #1: Vertical right **'S'** hand is held with palm forward/leftward, and the forearm is thrust ahead very slightly.

strike: *n.* the knocking down of all the pins with one bowling ball. *He made a strike in nearly every frame.*

SIGN #2: Left **'ONE'** hand is held with palm facing the body at a rightward angle and fore-finger pointing rightward/forward. Right **'ONE'** hand is held slightly above and to the right of the left hand with palm facing the body at a leftward angle and forefinger point-ing leftward/forward. The right hand is then lowered so that the forefinger is placed firmly on the forefinger of the left hand at right angles to it.

strike: *v.* to stop work collectively as a way of protesting. *The employees decided to strike.*

SIGN #3: Vertical right **'S'** hand, palm facing backward, is held at or above shoulder level and is forcefully twisted a half turn so that palm faces forward. Alternatively, this sign may be made with two hands.
SAME SIGN—**strike**, *n.*, in this context.

strike: *v.* to hit. *He did not strike back in self-defence.*

SIGN #4: Horizontal right **'S'** hand, palm facing left, is moved forward forcefully to strike the forefinger of the vertical left **'ONE'** hand which is held with palm facing right. ❖

strike: *v.* to remove or erase. *Because of her involvement in the scandal, they will strike her name from the membership list.*

SIGN #5: Left **'ONE'** hand is held in a fixed position with palm rightward at a slight downward angle and forefinger pointing forward/ rightward. Right **'COVERED T'** hand is held to the right of the left hand with palm up and forefinger touching tip of left fore-finger. The right hand then moves rightward/ upward as the thumb is flicked out to form an **'EXTENDED A'** hand. Facial expression is important.

strike: *v.* to discover; come upon. *The prospector hoped to strike gold in that region.*

SIGN #6: Right **'OPEN F'** hand is held. The hand then moves upward as the thumb and forefinger are closed to form an **'F'** hand with palm facing forward.

strike it rich: *v.* an idiom meaning to have unexpected financial success. *Everyone who prospects for gold hopes to strike it rich.*

SIGN #7: Horizontal left **'EXTENDED B'** hand is held with fingers pointing forward and palm facing rightward at an upward angle. Right **'S'** hand is held higher and to the right of the left hand with palm facing backward at a slight leftward angle. The hands then quickly move toward each other and as the right hand makes firm contact with the left palm, the fingers of the left hand spread to form a **'5'** hand while those of the right hand open to form a **'CROOKED 5'** hand which bounces back to its original position.

strike out: *v.* (in a baseball game), to be retired as a batter because of having three strikes against. *We hoped he would not strike out when the bases were loaded.*

SIGN #8: Vertical left **'EXTENDED B'** hand is held in a fixed position with palm facing right. Right **'S'** hand, palm down, is held a short distance to the right of the left hand, then changes to a **'K'** hand as it is thrust left-ward against the left palm. (Sign choice depends on context.)

strike up: *v.* to initiate; start. *I am too shy to strike up conversations with strangers.*

SIGN #9: Left **'5'** hand is held with palm facing right while forefinger of right **'ONE'** hand is inserted between first two fingers of left hand and twisted 180 degrees to the right.

striking: *adj.* impressive in appearance. *She is a very striking woman.*

SIGN: Right **'CONTRACTED 5'** hand is slowly circled counter-clockwise (from the signer's perspective) around the face as the fingers close to form a **'FLAT O'** hand, with palm and fingers toward the chin. Facial expression is important. (**Striking** sometimes has the connotation of 'that which is very noticeable', in which case signs vary depending on the context. Rather than being accorded a specific sign, the concept is often incorporated, through emphasis, in the sign which indicates specif-ically what makes a certain person or thing striking.)

string: *n.* a thin length of cord. *I need some string to tie the package.*

SIGN: Horizontal 'I' hands are held with tips of little fingers touching each other and palms facing the body. The hands are then drawn apart. Movement is repeated.

strip: *v.* to take one's clothes off. *I am going to strip and have a shower after working out at the gym.*

SIGN #1: 'SPREAD EXTENDED C' hands, palms facing backward, are positioned with fingertips against the chest and are then drawn apart at an upward angle as they change to 'S' handshapes.

strip: *v.* to remove paint or varnish from a surface. *You will have to strip the table and sand it before applying the stain.*

SIGN #2: Right 'CONTRACTED B' hand, palm down and fingertips touching upturned palm of left 'EXTENDED B' hand, is rubbed back and forth.

strip: *n.* a relatively long, narrow piece of cloth wood, or other material. *He used a strip of wood to repair the picture frame.*

SIGN #3: 'MODIFIED G' hands are held with palms facing forward and tips of forefingers and thumbs of one hand touching those of the other. The hands are then drawn apart about 15 centimetres each and the forefingers and thumbs close to form 'CLOSED MODIFIED G' shapes.

strip mall: *n.* a long row of stores and other businesses under one roof. *Their hairdressing salon is situated in a suburban strip mall.*

SIGN: Horizontal 'EXTENDED B' hands are held apart with palms facing each other and fingers pointing forward and are then moved toward each other slightly a couple of times. Then **MALL** is fingerspelled. (ASL CONCEPT—small - mall.)

M   A   L   L

stripe: *n.* a band of material that differs in colour from that of the surrounding material. *She is wearing a white sweater with a red stripe down the front.*

SIGN: Tips of thumb and forefinger of right 'MODIFIED G' hand, palm toward the body, are placed on the chest and the hand is drawn downward. (Plurality is indicated by repeating the sign in a rightward progression.) Signs vary according to the width and location of the stripe.

striped: *adj.* having a series of stripes or bands of different colors. *He is wearing a striped shirt.*

SIGN: Right 'SLANTED 4' hand, palm facing upward/backward and fingertips touching chest, is drawn downward. (Signs vary mainly according to the width and location of the stripe.)

striptease: *n.* an erotic entertainment where a person gradually removes his/her clothing to music. *The dancer performed a striptease.*

SIGN: 'COVERED T' hands, palms toward the body, are held near either side of the chest and are alternately circled upward erotically as they switch between 'COVERED T' and 'A-INDEX' handshapes.

strive: *v.* to make a great effort; try very hard. *Their motto is to strive for excellence.*

SIGN: Vertical 'ONE' hands, left palm facing right and right palm facing left, are held out in front of the face, with the left hand directly ahead of the right. The hands are then simultaneously moved forward in a very purposeful way. A look of determination accompanies this sign.

stroke: *n.* the rupture of a blood vessel in the brain which may lead to paralysis or other cerebral problems. *My grandmother had to take speech therapy after she had a stroke.*

SIGN #1: Fingerspell **STROKE.**

S   T   R   O   K   E

stroke: *n.* a sudden, often unexpected occurrence. *Winning the contest was a stroke of luck for them.*

SIGN #2: Right 'S' hand, palm facing left, is moved forward forcefully to strike the forefinger of the left 'ONE' hand which is held upright with palm facing rightward/forward.

stroke: *n.* any one of the repeated movements used by a swimmer. I *can teach you that swimming stroke.*

SIGN #3: Signs vary as the arms are used to simulate whatever swimming pattern is specified in the context.

stroke: *v.* to brush lightly and gently with the hand. *She likes to sit in her rocking chair and stroke the cat on her lap.*

SIGN #4: **'EXTENDED B'** hands, palms down, are positioned so that the right is held above and at right angles to the left and is stroked backward a couple of times along the back of the left hand.

stroke (off *or* **out):** *v.* to draw a line through written information. *Please stroke off the names of those who have paid their dues.*

SIGN #5: Thumb and forefinger of right **'CLOSED X'** hand move left to right once across the right facing palm of the left **'EXTENDED B'** hand. Then fingerspell **OFF**.

stroll: *v.* to walk in an unhurried, leisurely manner. *We will stroll through the park after lunch.*

SIGN: **'EXTENDED B'** hands, palms down and fingers pointing forward, are alternately moved so that the right hand moves forward/rightward while the left hand moves backward/rightward. The left hand then moves forward/leftward while the right hand moves backward/leftward. The movement is repeated several times to simulate the act of walking. This sign is made slowly and with a flourish so that the palms slant slightly forward as the hands move forward, and the palms slant toward the body as the hands move backward.

strong: *adj.* vigorous, solid or robust. *You must eat properly to be strong and healthy.*

SIGN: **'S'** hands are held parallel with palms facing the chest. The forearms are then simultaneously and purposefully lowered so that the palms, which still face the body, are slanted slightly upward.
SAME SIGN—**strength**, *n.*

strong-minded: *adj.* firm or resolute in one's opinions; determined. *People respect him because he is a strong-minded but fair employer.*

SIGN: Tip of forefinger of right **'ONE'** hand, touches forehead. Next, vertical **'S'** hands are held parallel with palms facing backwards and are moved very firmly forward a very short distance. A look of determination accompanies this sign. (ASL CONCEPT—**think - strong.**)

structure: *n.* something that has been constructed; a building. *The school is a red brick structure.*

SIGN #1: Fingers of **'BENT EXTENDED U'** hands, palms facing each other, are alternately slid up from under to be placed on top of one another a few times.

structure: *n.* the arrangement of the parts of something. *The structure of ASL is much different than that of English.*

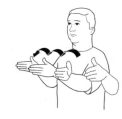

SIGN #2: Horizontal **'EXTENDED B'** hands are held apart in front of the left side of the body with palms facing each other and fingers pointing forward. The hands are then moved rightward in a series of small arcs.

struggle: *v.* the act of making a great effort; strife. *It was a long struggle but she finally completed her education.*

SIGN #1: Horizontal left **'BENT ONE'** hand is held out in front of the body with palm toward the body and forefinger pointing at an upward/rightward angle toward the body. Horizontal right **'BENT ONE'** hand, palm left, is held higher and closer to the body with forefinger pointing directly at tip of left forefinger. The hands then circle forward simultaneously a couple of times. This is a slow, painstaking movement, which is accompanied by an appropriate facial expression.
SAME SIGN—**struggle**, *v.*

SIGN #2 [ONTARIO]: Horizontal **'S'** hands, palms toward the body, are slowly and deliberately circled forward around each other a couple of times. Facial expression is important. (This sign is used when the **struggle** involves considerable *pain*, whether it be physical or emotional. This sign would not be appropriate in a context that simply involves hard work.)

stub: *n.* the part that remains after something has been cut off, removed, or worn down. *Save your **ticket stub** because you might win the door prize.*

SIGN: Extended fingers of the right **'CLAWED V'** hand, palm down, are used to grasp the outer edge of the vertical left **'EXTENDED B'** hand of which the palm is facing the body. Movement is repeated. Next, tips of forefingers and thumbs touch as **'CONTRACTED L'** hands are held together with palms facing forward/downward. The arms are then drawn apart and each forefinger and thumb come together to form **'CLOSED MODIFIED G'** shapes. (Signs vary according to the type of stub that remains and the manner in which the rest of the item was removed. 'Pencil stub', 'cigar stub', and 'cheque stub', would be signed differently.)

stub one's toe: *v.* to strike a toe painfully against a hard surface. *If you **stub your toe** you can cause a painful fracture.*

SIGN: Right **'5'** hand, palm down, is pushed forward/leftward so that the tip of the forefinger strikes the backward/rightward-facing palm of the horizontal left **'EXTENDED B'** hand making the signer wince.

stubborn: *adj.* obstinate; refusing to comply or give in. *Mules are **stubborn** animals.*

SIGN #1: Thumb of vertical right **'EXTENDED B'** hand, palm forward, is placed near the right temple and the fingers are firmly lowered to form a **'BENT EXTENDED B'** hand. A look of fierce determination accompanies this sign.
SAME SIGN—**stubbornness**, *n.*

stubborn: *adj.* difficult to remove. *Coffee can leave a **stubborn** stain on your clothes.*

SIGN #2: **'CLAWED V'** hands are held, right above left, at an angle somewhere between vertical and horizontal, with left palm facing right and right palm facing left. The hands then come together and strike each other with force. Next, **OFF** is fingerspelled as the hand is sharply moved to the right. (ASL CONCEPT—**hard - off**.) The sample sentence in ASL is: *COFFEE SPILL...HARD OFF.*

stuck: *adj.* in a difficult position which is difficult to get out of. *If nobody volunteers to help, I will be **stuck** with all the work.*

SIGN: Tips of extended fingers of right **'BENT V'** hand are thrust toward the throat.

student: *n.* a person following a course of study. *She is a **student** at Gallaudet University.*

SIGN: Right **'CONTRACTED 5'** hand is placed palm down on the upturned left palm and is closed to form a **'FLAT O'** shape as it is drawn upward, moved to the right, and flung open to resume a **'CONTRACTED 5'** shape.

studio: *n.* a room in which an artist, photographer or musician works. *A painter's **studio** requires good lighting.*

SIGN: Fingerspell **STUDIO**.

S T U D I O

studious: *adj.* serious and hardworking at one's studies. *She has always been more **studious** than her brother.*

SIGN: Left **'EXTENDED B'** hand is held in a fixed position with fingers pointing rightward and palm toward the body at a slight upward angle. Right **'BENT 5'** hand is held a little higher and closer to the chest with the palm down and the fingers pointing toward the left palm. The right hand then moves repeatedly and emphatically toward the left hand. A serious facial expression accompanies this sign.

study: *v.* to apply one's mind to learning. *You must study for the exam.*

SIGN: Left **'EXTENDED B'** hand is held in a fixed position with fingers pointing rightward and palm toward the body at a slight upward angle. Right **'BENT 5'** hand is held a little higher and closer to the chest with the palm down and the fingers fluttering as they point toward the left palm.

stuff: *n.* things in general. *She is packing up her stuff to move to a different office.*

SIGN #1: Right **'EXTENDED B'** hand, palm facing up, fingers pointing forward, is moved from left to right in a series of successive short arcs.

stuff: *v.* to cram or to pack fully and completely. *We stuffed the turkey and put it in the oven.*

SIGN #2: Vertical left **'C'** hand is held with palm facing right. Then the forward-pointing fingertips of the right **'FLAT O'** hand are inserted into the opening in the left hand a couple of times.

stuffed: *adj.* filled to capacity. *I feel stuffed after eating that enormous meal.*

SIGN: Right **'B'** hand, palm down, is held limp-wristed in front of the chest and is flicked upward from the wrist so that it strikes the underside of the chin with fingers pointing left. The cheeks are puffed out.

stuffy: *adj.* lacking fresh air. *This room is very stuffy so we should open some windows.*

SIGN: Right **'CLAWED 5'** hand is held with fingertips touching or close to the lips. The wrist then rotates briskly causing the palm to face leftward/downward. (Signs vary according to context. This sign would not apply to a 'stuffy' nose.)

stump: *n.* the base of a tree trunk that remains after the tree has been cut down. *There is a big oak stump in our backyard.*

SIGN: Left **'5'** hand is held upright to represent a tree while the edge of the right **'EXTENDED B'** hand, palm up and fingers pointing leftward/forward, is used to strike against the left forearm with a chopping motion. Next, horizontal **'C'** hands, palms facing, are held apart approximating the size of the 'stump' referred to in the context. Then they are simultaneously pushed forward slightly with a firm movement. (ASL CONCEPT—**tree - cut down - round-low**.) Signs vary according to the nature of the **stump**.

stumped: *adj.* perplexed; puzzled; at a loss as to what to say or do. *We were all stumped for a solution to the problem.*

SIGN: Tips of extended fingers of right **'BENT V'** hand are thrust toward the throat.

stunned: *adj.* shocked and overwhelmed. *We were all stunned by the jury's verdict.*

SIGN: **'BENT 5'** hands are held apart, fingertips pointing downward, and are moved sharply downward. (This sign is used only in a passive voice situation or as an adjective. It may *not* be used in an active voice situation such as: *The jury's verdict stunned all of us.*)

stunning: *adj.* remarkably attractive; impressive in beauty. *The bride was stunning in all her white finery.*

SIGN: Right **'CONTRACTED 5'** hand is slowly circled counter-clockwise (from the signer's perspective) around the face as the fingers close to form a **'FLAT O'** hand, with palm and fingers toward the chin. This is a slow, emphatic sign and facial expression is important.

stunt: *n.* a dangerous act, often in a film or TV production. *He performed a dangerous stunt on his motorcycle.*

SIGN #1: Fingerspell **STUNT**.

S T U N T

stunt: *v.* to impede (the growth and development of a plant, animal or human). *Small children are often told that smoking will stunt their growth.*

SIGN #2: **'EXTENDED B'** hands are held at right angles to one another, the left hand in front of the right, with fingers of left hand pointing upward to the right and fingers of right hand pointing upward to the left. The hands are then pushed firmly forward.

stupid: *adj.* showing a lack of intelligence or common sense. *It was a stupid thing to say.*

SIGN: Right **'A'** hand, with palm facing backward, is thumped against the forehead.
SAME SIGN—**stupidity**, *n.*
ALTERNATE SIGN—**ignorant**

sturdy: *adj.* strong; vigorous; durable. *We need some **sturdy** volunteers to move the furniture.*

SIGN: **'S'** hands are held parallel with palms facing the chest. The forearms are then simultaneously and purposefully lowered so that the palms, which still face the body, are slanted slightly upward.

style: *adj.* a form of design or production; fashion. *Our home is a ranch-**style** bungalow.*

SIGN: Fingerspell **STYLE**.

subconscious: *adj.* in the back of one's mind. *I have a **subconscious** feeling that she is not being honest with us.*

SIGN #1: Tip of forefinger of the right **'CROOKED ONE'** hand is used to tap the base of the skull on the right side a couple of times.

subconscious: *adj.* occurring without one's awareness. *When people are faced with calamity they often make incredible **subconscious** efforts to survive.*

SIGN #2: Horizontal **'BENT EXTENDED B'** hands are held parallel with palms facing, and are simultaneously moved forward. Next, right **'EXTENDED A'** hand, palm facing left, thumb under chin, is thrust forward. Finally, tip of forefinger of right **'ONE'** hand, palm toward face, touches right side of forehead. (ASL CONCEPT—**go ahead - not - think**.) The sample sentence in ASL is: *AWFUL HAPPEN... PEOPLE TEND GO AHEAD NOT THINK.* (In certain contexts there is no specific sign accorded **subconscious**; instead, the concept is conveyed through the sign for the verb and its accompanying facial expression.)

 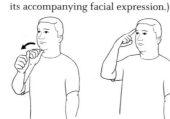

subdue: *v.* to bring under control. *The police tried to **subdue** the rioters.*

SIGN: **'EXTENDED B'** hands are held parallel with palms down and fingers pointing forward. The forearms are then simultaneously moved slowly and deliberately down and up a couple of times. If there is only one person being subdued, the hands are held closer together and closer to the chest. (Sign choice depends on context.)

subheading: *n.* the title of a section of written work that is subordinate to the main title. *You will find the information under the **subheading** 'TEENAGERS'.*

SIGN: Vertical **'V'** hands, palms facing forward, are held apart just above shoulder level, and are curved outward slightly from the wrists as they become **'CLAWED V'** hands. After this, the space between the hands is reduced and the hands are slightly lowered. The initial sign is then repeated in this position. (ASL CONCEPT—**title - small title under**.)

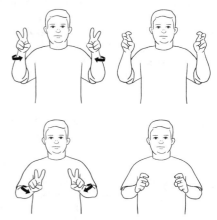

subject: *n.* any area of learning considered a course of study. *Her favourite school **subject** was science.*

SIGN #1: Left **'EXTENDED B'** hand is held in a fixed position with palm up and fingers pointing rightward/forward. Horizontal right **'BENT EXTENDED B'** hand, with palm facing left, is placed on the fingers of the left hand, then raised, moved backward, and placed on the heel of the left hand. (Signs vary considerably.)

subject: *n.* a main theme or topic. *Briefly outline the **subject** of the essay.*

SIGN #2: Vertical **'V'** hands, palms facing forward, are held apart just above shoulder level, and are curved outward slightly from the wrists as they become **'CLAWED V'** hands.

subject to: *prep.* on condition that; depending on. *She will be hired subject to the approval of the board.*

SIGN #3: Tips of forefingers of **'ONE'** hands are crossed slightly with the right on top of the left, and both palms facing down. Together, the hands are lowered a few times as if the right forefinger is exerting downward pressure on the left forefinger.

sublet: *v.* to rent out a dwelling under a secondary contract. *While we are in Europe, we plan to sublet our apartment to a university student.*

SIGN: Fingerspell **SUBLET**.

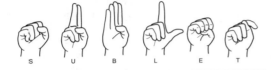

submarine: *n.* a vessel that operates beneath the water. *The submarine was called the Nautilus.*

SIGN: Horizontal right **'3'** hand, palm left, is moved forward a little a few times beneath the left **'STANDARD BASE'** hand.

submerge: *v.* to cause to go below the surface of a liquid. *The ship was soon completely submerged.*

SIGN: Left **'5'** hand represents the surface of the water as it is held in a fixed position with palm down and fingers pointing forward/rightward. Horizontal right **'3'** hand, palm left and extended fingers pointing forward/leftward, is positioned at the end of the fingers of the left hand and is then lowered. (This sign applies to **watercraft** but may also apply to an automobile or other motor vehicle. Sign choice varies according to 'what' is submerged.)

submit: *v.* to hand over for consideration. *He will submit his proposal to the board.*

SIGN #1: Right **'EXTENDED B'** hand, palm up and fingers pointing forward, is moved forward in an arc. ❖
SAME SIGN—**submission**, *n.*, in this context.

submit: *v.* to allow oneself to be subjected to certain treatment or investigation; give in. *She agreed to submit to an investigation of the validity of her claim.*

SIGN #2: Right **'EXTENDED B'** hand is held with palm against chest, and is brought forward so that the palm faces upward at a slight angle toward the body.

submit: *v.* to give as an opinion; to state; contend. *I submit that you had no intention of helping the victim.*

SIGN #3: Tip of forefinger of right **'BENT ONE'** hand, palm toward the body, is held just under the chin and firmly flicked forward, thus creating a **'ONE'** hand.

subordinate: *n.* a person of lower rank or position. *He supervises only one subordinate.*

SIGN: Horizontal **'EXTENDED A'** hands are held so the left is fixed with palm toward the chest. The right, palm left, is held apart but is curved leftward coming to rest just beneath the left hand with palm toward the chest.

subpoena: *n.* a legal document requiring a person to appear before a court of law at a specified time. *He was served with a subpoena to appear as a witness at his father's trial.*

SIGN: Fingerspell **SUBPOENA**.

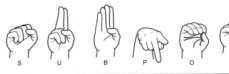

subscribe: *v.* to pay in advance for a publication received at regular intervals. *I subscribe to a monthly newsletter.*

SIGN: Right **'A-INDEX'** hand is held at an angle with palm facing partially upward and partially toward the body. The forearm is then brought smartly downward toward the body, with the hand taking on a **'CLOSED A-INDEX'** shape as the thumb and forefinger are retracted. Motion is repeated.
SAME SIGN—**subscription**, *n.*

subsequent: *adj.* following; succeeding. *The first issue is free but subsequent issues will cost $4 each.*

SIGN: Horizontal **'BENT EXTENDED B'** hands, palms facing each other, are positioned so that the fingers of the right hand are just in front of the fingers of the left hand. The right hand is then moved forward briskly.

subside: *v.* to become less intense. *My headache began to subside after I had some rest.*

SIGN: **'FLAT O'** hands are held parallel with palms up and slanted slightly toward the body. As the hands are drawn apart the thumbs slide across the fingertips, causing the hands to assume **'A'** shapes. (Signs vary according to context.)

subsidize: *v.* to give financial support (usually by government) as social assistance or public welfare. *The city will subsidize housing charges for low-income families.*

SIGN: **'S'** hands, palms toward the body, are held at chest level with the left slightly above the right. Then the right is brought upward to strike the left.

subsidy: *n.* a financial grant made (usually by government) for a special purpose. *Farmers will receive a subsidy through the Canadian Wheat Board.*

SIGN: Back of right **'CONTRACTED B'** (or **'BENT EXTENDED B'**) hand, palm up, is tapped two or three times on upturned palm of left **'EXTENDED B'** hand. Next, **'S'** hands, palms toward the body, are held at chest level with the left slightly above the right. Then the right is brought upward to strike the left. (ASL CONCEPT—**money - support.**)

substance: *n.* a specific material or element. *Ice and water are the same substance in different forms.*

SIGN: Right **'EXTENDED B'** hand, palm upward and fingers pointing forward, is moved rightward in an arc formation. (Sign choice depends on context.)

substantial: *adj.* of considerable size or value. *Canada has a substantial supply of grain.*

SIGN: **'EXTENDED A'** hands, palms slightly facing the body and slightly facing upward, are simultaneously circled outward in opposite directions. The cheeks are puffed out. (Sign choice depends on context.)

substitute: *n.* a person or thing that serves in the place of another. *Dieters often use a sugar substitute.*

SIGN: Horizontal **'F'** (or **'COVERED T'**) hands, left palm facing right and right palm facing left, are held so that the left is further from the chest than the right. Then their positions are simultaneously switched as the left hand moves back toward the body in an arc over the right hand while the right hand moves away from the body in an arc under the left hand.
SAME SIGN—**substitute**, *v.*

subterfuge: *n.* a means of concealing something by stealth. *Because they did not want their employers to know they were organizing a union, they had to resort to subterfuge.*

SIGN: Vertical **'A'** hands, right palm facing leftward/forward and left palm facing rightward/forward, are held close to the chin and alternately moved backward so that the thumb makes contact with the chin. The signer's mouth is tightly closed.

subtitles: *n.* a written translation which is superimposed on a screen showing a film with foreign dialogue. *Foreign films sometimes have English subtitles.*

SIGN: Horizontal **'F'** hands, palms facing each other, thumbs and forefingers touching, are moved apart with a slight rotation of the wrists so that palms face downward/forward. The movement is generally repeated as this word is usually used in a plural sense.

subtle: *adj.* not obvious or easily recognized. *The artist's use of straight lines in his landscape paintings is very subtle.*

SIGN: Vertical right **'EXTENDED B'** hand is held just to the right and in front of the face with the palm facing backward. The forearm then swings slowly downward past the face so that the hand is eventually positioned in front of the chest with fingers pointing leftward. (Signs vary considerably depending on the context.)

subtract: *v.* to remove part of something. *The payroll clerk will subtract this amount from your wages.*

SIGN: Horizontal left **'EXTENDED B'** hand is held in a fixed position with palm rightward/backward and fingers pointing forward/rightward. Fingertips of right **'SPREAD C'** hand are placed against the palm of the left hand. Then the right hand is pulled down and closed to form an **'S'** hand.

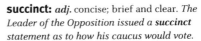

subtraction: *n.* a mathematical process for finding the difference between two amounts. *Subtraction is a basic computational function.*

SIGN: Edge of extended forefinger of right horizontal **'BENT ONE'** hand, palm down, is tapped a couple of times against forward-facing palm of vertical left **'EXTENDED B'** hand.

suburbs: *n.* a residential area located on the outskirts of a city. *I live in the suburbs.*

SIGN: Vertical **'EXTENDED B'** hands, left palm facing right and right palm facing left, are held so that their fingertips can be tapped together twice. Then, right **'BENT ONE'** hand, palm forward and forefinger pointing forward, is used to point to an imaginary area. Next, right **'5'** hand, palm down, is circled in a counter-clockwise motion.
(ASL CONCEPT—**city - around**.)

subway: *n.* an underground railway or tunnel for traffic. *She rides the subway to work every day.*

SIGN: Right **'ONE'** hand, palm down and forefinger pointing forward, is moved forward a few times under the left **'STANDARD BASE'** hand. (**SUBWAY** is frequently fingerspelled.)

succeed: *v.* to accomplish an aim or to do well. *We hope our Canadian team will succeed in winning a gold medal.*

SIGN: **'ONE'** hands, palms down, forefingers almost touching either side of forehead, are raised so that fingers point upward and palms face away from the body.
SAME SIGNS—**successful**, *adj.*, and **success**, *n.*

succession: *n.* things or people following one another in a specific order; series. *After the proposal was submitted, a succession of regional debates followed.*

SIGN: Horizontal right **'BENT EXTENDED B'** hand, palm left, is moved forward quickly in a series of small arcs.
SAME SIGN—**successive**, *adj.*

succinct: *adj.* concise; brief and clear. *The Leader of the Opposition issued a succinct statement as to how his caucus would vote.*

SIGN: Left horizontal **'U'** hand is held steady with extended fingers pointing forward/rightward and palm facing backward/rightward. Right horizontal **'U'** hand is held at right angles to the left hand with extended fingers resting on those of the left hand. Extended fingers of right hand are then brushed forward/rightward off the fingers of the left hand. Next, left **'CLOSED X'** hand is held in a fixed position with palm upward at a slight rightward angle. Right **'CLOSED X'** hand is held closer to the chest and at a higher level than the left hand. Palms are facing each other. The hands then abruptly come together, striking each other in the process.
(ASL CONCEPT—**short - exact**.)

succumb: *v.* to be forced to yield or give in. *The leader finally had to succumb to the wishes of the majority.*

SIGN #1: **'OPEN A'** hands, held slightly apart at waist level, palms down, are thrust upward to form **'EXTENDED B'** hands with palms facing forward. (Signs vary according to context.)

succumb: *v.* to die. *After a lengthy illness, the patient finally succumbed.*

SIGN #2: Right **'EXTENDED B'** hand is held palm down with fingers pointing forward. The wrist then rotates rightward, turning the hand palm upward.

such: *adv.* to such a great extent; so much. *I have never seen such a big lobster before.*

SIGN #1: Right **'CROOKED 5'** hand is held palm down in front of the right side of the body and is shaken back and forth from the wrist several times. Facial expression is important. (**SUCH** may be fingerspelled.)

such: *pron.* used as a substitute for 'that'. *We missed a golden opportunity but such is life.*

SIGN #2: Vertical right **'Y'** hand, palm forward, is held near the right shoulder and is curved downward to an abrupt stop, the palm eventually facing downward.

such as: *prep.* for example. *Deaf communities support organizations **such as** the CCSD, CAD, and many others.*

SIGN #3: This concept is generally conveyed very simply with a pause.

OR

SIGN #4: Tip of forefinger of horizontal right **'BENT ONE'** hand is placed against right facing palm of left **'EXTENDED B'** hand. Together, the hands are moved forward in a short arc.

suck: *v.* to draw in fluid through the mouth. *The patient was able to **suck** juice through a straw.*

SIGN: Right **'CLOSED MODIFIED G'** hand, palm facing left, is held with joined tips of forefinger and thumb near the mouth. The lips and cheeks of the signer are then used to simulate the drawing up of liquid through a straw. (Signs vary according to context. This sign is used only in contexts where the sucking is done through a 'straw'.)

sucker: *n.* a lollipop. *The barber gave the little boy a **sucker** to calm him down.*

SIGN #1: Vertical right **'COVERED T'** hand, palm facing left, is moved a short distance forward/downward and back several times while the lips smack as if licking a lollipop.

sucker: *n.* a colloquial term meaning a person who is easily deceived. *I felt like a **sucker** after buying a used car which immediately broke down .*

SIGN #2: Forefinger of right **'CROOKED ONE'** is poked toward the mouth a couple of times.

sudden: *adj.* happening quickly and without warning. *His death was very **sudden**.*

SIGN: Right **'BENT D'** hand, palm facing left, is twisted briskly from the wrist as it changes to an **'A'** handshape.

ALTERNATE SIGN—**quick** #2

suds: *n.* bubbles on the surface of a liquid or soapy water. *This detergent produces lots of **suds** in the washing machine.*

SIGN: **'SPREAD C'** hands are held parallel with palms down and are simultaneously moved upward a short distance as the fingers flutter. The signer's cheeks are puffed out.

sue: *v.* to initiate legal proceedings against. *We will **sue** our neighbours if they build their fence too high.*

SIGN #1: Horizontal left **'BENT EXTENDED B'** hand is held with palm facing rightward/backward and fingers pointing to the right. Right **'EXTENDED B'** (or **'B'**) hand is held upright very close to the chest with palm facing left. The right hand then drops from the wrist until it is horizontal with fingertips forcefully striking left hand between the palm and the fingers. ❖

OR

SIGN #2: Right **'S'** hand begins in a semi-vertical position with palm facing left as the forearm drops forward somewhat, the forefinger and midfinger flicking forward to form a **'U'** hand before the hand returns to its original position in an **'E'** shape. This is one fluid and very fast motion. ❖

suffer: *v.* to bear patiently. *He **suffered** from a debilitating disease for many years.*

SIGN: Thumb of right **'A'** hand, palm facing left, is pressed against the chin and the hand is twisted from the wrist several times. Facial expression must clearly convey 'suffering'.

sufficient: *adj.* enough to meet a need or purpose. *We now have **sufficient** funds for the project.*

SIGN: Horizontal left **'S'** hand, palm facing right, is covered with palm of right **'EXTENDED B'** hand. Then the right hand is brushed firmly forward and slightly to the right.

sugar: *n.* a sweetening agent used in food and drink. *I would like **sugar** in my tea.*

SIGN #1: Fingertips of the right **'DOUBLE MODIFIED G'** hand, palm facing backward, are brushed downward a few times on the chin as the handshape alternates between a **'DOUBLE MODIFIED G'** and a **'CLOSED DOUBLE MODIFIED G'**. (Signs vary.)

SIGN #2 [ONTARIO]: Horizontal left **'K'** hand is held in a fixed position in front of the left side of the chest with palm facing right while right **'K'** hand is held with tip of middle finger touching the mouth. The right hand is then lowered, the wrist twisting and the tip of the middle finger striking the tip of the middle finger on the left hand.

suggest: *v.* to put forward for consideration; propose. *I suggest that we have a coffee break now*

SIGN: **'EXTENDED B'** hands, palms up and fingers pointing forward, are held slightly apart with the right just ahead of the left, and are simultaneously thrust forward in an arc.
SAME SIGN—**suggestion**, *n.*

suicide: *n.* the act of killing oneself intentionally. *Many of his friends believe his death was a suicide.*

SIGN: Horizontal right **'EXTENDED A'** hand, palm leftward/forward, is firmly moved forward/rightward. (This part of the sign varies according to 'who' has committed suicide. Refer to reflexive pronouns in PRONOUNS, p. LXVI.) Next, vertical left **'EXTENDED B'** hand is held in a fixed position with palm facing rightward and slightly forward. Right **'ONE'** (or **'K'**) hand is held palm down as it moves forward/downward at a slight leftward angle, the forefinger firmly grazing the left palm. (ASL CONCEPT— **self - kill**.) Alternatively, **SUICIDE** may be fingerspelled.
SAME SIGN—**commit suicide**

suit: *n.* a set of clothes of the same or similar material. *He always wears a business suit to the office.*

SIGN #1: Vertical **'EXTENDED A'** hands are held parallel close to the upper chest with palms facing each other. They are then simultaneously lowered a few inches as palms turn downward. (**SUIT** is frequently fingerspelled.)

suit: *v.* to please or satisfy. *Your plan suits me.*

SIGN #2: Vertical right **'5'** hand, palm facing left, is tapped a couple of times against the chest. The head may nod in the process.

suit (someone): *v.* to look attractive or becoming (on someone). *The colour of your blouse really suits you.*

SIGN #3: Left **'ONE'** hand is held at chest level with palm facing right, and forefinger pointing forward. Right **'ONE'** hand is held slightly higher, palm facing left and forefinger pointing forward, and is then turned downward to match the simultaneously downward-turning left hand.

suit yourself: *v.* to follow your own inclination without considering the opinion of others. *It is your decision so suit yourself.*

SIGN: Right **'BENT L'** hand is held so the tip of the forefinger touches the forehead. Then the hand is drawn forward away from the face as it changes to a horizontal **'EXTENDED A'** hand. (ASL CONCEPT—**think - self**.)

suitable: *adj.* appropriate. *You should wear suitable clothes for skiing.*

SIGN: Right **'ONE'** hand, palm facing left, is held above left **'ONE'** hand, palm facing right, with forefingers pointing forward. Then right hand is tapped at least twice on left hand.

suitcase: *n.* a case used for carrying clothing while travelling. *Each student is allowed to bring only one suitcase.*

SIGN: Right **'S'** hand is held at one's side, with palm toward body, and the arm is moved up and down to simulate the carrying of a suitcase.

suite: *n.* an apartment or set of connected rooms sold or rented as one unit. *They live in a luxurious suite in a highrise tower.*

SIGN: Fingerspell **SUITE**. (For **suite of furniture**, no specific sign is accorded **suite**; instead **furniture** is used, sometimes followed by signs which specify the types of furniture included in the suite.)

sulk: *v.* to brood sullenly. *She was sent to her room where she sulked all day.*

SIGN: Vertical **'CROOKED 5'** hands are held slightly apart with palms toward the face. The hands are then simultaneously lowered somewhat and the head tilts to the right as the signer very clearly pouts.

sullen: *adj.* gloomy and unsociable; sulky. *Teenagers are often sullen when their privileges are withdrawn.*

SIGN: Vertical **'CROOKED 5'** hands are held slightly apart with palms toward the face. The hands are then simultaneously lowered somewhat and the head tilts to the right as the signer very clearly pouts.

sultry: *adj.* excessively hot and humid. *The weather here is usually sultry in July.*

SIGN: Right **'CLAWED 5'** hand is held with fingertips touching or close to the lips. The wrist then rotates briskly causing the palm to face leftward/downward.

sum: *n.* the result of adding numbers; total. *The sum of those figures is 812.*

SIGN #1: Horizontal **'CONTRACTED 5'** hands, palms facing each other, are brought together as the fingers close to form **'FLAT O'** hands with fingertips touching each other. REGIONAL VARIATION—**add** #2

(large) sum of: *adj.* a large quantity of; lots of. *You will need a large sum of money for a trip like that.*

SIGN #2: **'EXTENDED A'** hands, palms slightly facing the body and slightly facing upward, are simultaneously circled outward in opposite directions. The cheeks are puffed out.

sum up: *v.* to summarize. *The speaker will now sum up the main points to be discussed.*

SIGN #3: **'SPREAD C'** hands are held horizontally and slightly apart, right above left. Then both are closed to form **'S'** hands as the right is brought down to rest on top of the left.

summarize: *v.* to give a brief version of something by stating the main points only. *Please summarize the story for me.*

SIGN: **'SPREAD C'** hands are held horizontally and slightly apart, right above left. Then both are closed to form **'S'** hands as the right is brought down to rest on top of the left. SAME SIGN—**summary**, *n.*

summer: *n.* the warmest season of the year. *Summer officially begins in June and ends in September.*

SIGN: Right **'ONE'** hand is held in front of the forehead with palm down and forefinger pointing leftward. The forefinger then retracts to form an **'X'** shape as the hand moves to an upright position in front of the right side of the forehead with palm facing left. The movement is repeated once.

summit: *n.* the highest point of a mountain. *The climbers hoped to reach the summit of Mount Everest by the end of the day.*

SIGN #1: Left **'EXTENDED B'** hand is held in a semi-vertical position with palm facing right at a downward angle. Right **'EXTENDED B'** hand is held at a higher level in a semi-vertical position with palm facing left at a downward angle. The right forearm then moves downward so that the hand firmly strikes the fingertips of the left hand.

summit: *adj.* used in reference to heads of state or other highly placed officials. *The prime minister will attend a summit conference in Paris.*

SIGN #2: Fingerspell **SUMMIT**.

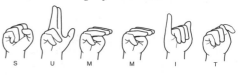

summon: *v.* to order to come; call. *They will summon the witnesses to testify in court.*

SIGN: Fingertips of right **'BENT EXTENDED B'** hand are placed on the back of the left **'STANDARD BASE'** hand. Then as the right hand is drawn slightly upward toward the body, the hand closes to form an **'EXTENDED A'** hand. ❖

summons: *n.* an official order for someone to come. *He received a summons to appear in court.*

SIGN: Tip of forefinger of vertical right **'ONE'** hand, palm forward, is placed on the lips and the hand is thrust forward.

sun: *n.* a star that provides the Earth with heat and light. *The sun is a star at the centre of our solar system.*

SIGN: Side of the vertical right **'C'** hand, palm forward, is tapped against the right side of the forehead at the temple.

sunburn: *n.* redness and inflammation of the skin caused by too much exposure to the sun. *If you stay out here much longer, you will get a sunburn.*

SIGN: Fingerspell **SUNBURN**.

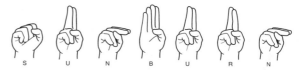

sundae: *n.* ice cream topped with a sauce and/or fruit, nuts, whipped cream, etc. *My favourite treat is a hot fudge sundae.*

SIGN: Fingerspell **SUNDAE**.

Sunday: *n.* the first day of the week, and the Christian day of worship. [See TIME CONCEPTS, p. LXIX.] *I will see you on Sunday.*

SIGN: Vertical **'EXTENDED B'** hands, palms forward, are held parallel and simultaneously moved back and forth slightly a few times.

sundown: *n.* the setting of the sun. *The flag was lowered at sundown.*

SIGN: Left **'STANDARD BASE'** hand is held in a fixed position while the right vertical **'C'** (or **'O'** or **'F'**) hand, palm facing left, is held just ahead of it and is slowly lowered to a position below the left hand.

sunglasses: *n.* eyeglasses with dark lenses that protect one's eyes from the sun's glare. *I wear sunglasses when I am driving on a sunny day.*

SIGN: Fingerspell **SUN**. Next, **'CROOKED L'** hands, palms facing each other, are held in a vertical position beside each eye. The forearms then move outward and inward slightly a few times so that the thumbtips tap against the cheeks. (Alternatively, the right hand only is frequently used.)

sunny: *adj.* bright; having lots of sunshine. *I hope it is a beautiful, sunny day for our picnic.*

SIGN: Vertical right **'MODIFIED O'** hand, held up high with palm facing forward, is thrust forward/downward as the fingers open to create a **'CONTRACTED 5'** handshape. (**SUNNY** is frequently fingerspelled.)

sunrise: *n.* the daily appearance of the sun above the horizon. *The rooster crows at sunrise.*

SIGN: Left **'STANDARD BASE'** hand represents the horizon and right **'C'** (or **'O'** or **'F'**) hand, palm leftward/downward, represents the rising sun as it is held just ahead of/below the left hand and then raised to a level above the left hand.

sunset: *n.* the daily disappearance of the sun below the horizon. *A prairie sunset is a beautiful sight.*

SIGN: Left **'STANDARD BASE'** hand is held in a fixed position while the right vertical **'C'** (or **'O'** or **'F'**) hand, palm facing left, is held just ahead of it and is slowly lowered to a position below the left hand.

sunshine: *n.* light emitted by the sun. *People enjoy the long hours of sunshine in the summer.*

SIGN: Vertical right **'FLAT O'** hand, palm toward the face, is held aloft and moved toward the face as the fingers open to form a **'CONTRACTED 5'** shape.

super: *adj.* outstanding; exceptional. *She always does a super job as an organizer.*

SIGN: Vertical **'EXTENDED B'** hands, palms facing forward, are held apart near the face. Forearms are pushed purposefully forward a short distance.

superb: *adj.* excellent; magnificent. *We have a superb view of the mountains from our living room window.*

SIGN: Vertical **'EXTENDED B'** hands, palms facing forward, are held apart near the face. Forearms are pushed purposefully forward a short distance.

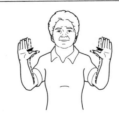

superficial: *adj.* showing a lack of thoroughness, care, or depth. *A superficial inspection of the crime scene gave the police several clues.*

SIGN: Left horizontal **'U'** hand is held steady with extended fingers pointing forward/rightward and palm facing backward/rightward. Right horizontal **'U'** hand is held at right angles to the left hand with extended fingers resting on those of the left hand. Extended fingers of right hand are then brushed forward/rightward off the fingers of the left hand. (Sign choice depends on context.)

superintendent: *n.* a person who is in charge of an organization, office, etc. *The chief executive officer of our organization is the superintendent.*

SIGN: Vertical **'MODIFIED 5'** hands, palms facing forward, are held near either temple and are simultaneously drawn outward as they close to become **'S'** hands. (The abbreviation **SUPT** is frequently fingerspelled.)

superior: *n.* a person who is higher in rank. *He reported to his superior.*

SIGN #1: Horizontal right **'EXTENDED A'** hand, palm facing the body at a slight leftward angle, is raised purposefully upward to a level above the right shoulder.

superior: *adj.* of extraordinary merit; of excellent quality. *She is a superior teacher.*

SIGN #2: Right **'BENT EXTENDED B'** hand, fingers on lips and pointing leftward, palm backward, is drawn upward to the right of the face as the fingers bend to form an **'EXTENDED A'** hand with thumb pointing upward. Appropriate facial expression is essential. Signs vary considerably according to context.

ALTERNATE SIGN—**best** #2

supermarket: *n.* a large store where groceries are sold. *We went to the supermarket to do our weekly food shopping.*

SIGN: Right **'MODIFIED O'** hand, palm toward body, is brought upward to the mouth, and fingertips are tapped against lips. Next, **'FLAT O'** hands, held parallel with palms down and fingers pointing down, are swung forward/upward from the wrists a couple of times.
(ASL CONCEPT—**food - store**.)

superstitious: *adj.* believing in irrational omens, charms and notions founded in ignorance and fear. *Some people are superstitious about broken mirrors bringing bad luck.*

SIGN: Fingerspell **SUPERSTITIOUS**.
(**SUPERSTITION**, *n.,* is also fingerspelled.)

supervise: *v.* to take charge of; direct; oversee. *She will supervise the children on the playground.*

SIGN: **'K'** hands are positioned horizontally with the right one resting on top of the left one. The hands are then moved together in a counter-clockwise motion.
SAME SIGNS—**supervision**, *n.,* and **supervisor**, *n.*

supper: *n.* an evening meal. *We usually eat supper at 5:00 p.m.*

SIGN: Fingertips of vertical right **'MODIFIED O'** hand, palm facing backwards, are tapped against the mouth twice.

supple: *adj.* bending easily; able to move with ease and agility. *If you want to become a gymnast, you must be very supple.*

SIGN: Horizontal **'CONTRACTED B'** hands, palms toward the body, are held slightly apart with the fingers of one hand pointing toward those of the other. Then they are alternately moved back and forth several times from the wrists. Next, horizontal **'EXTENDED B'** hands are placed slightly apart, fingertips opposite, with palms on upper chest. Then they are moved simultaneously to waist level.
(ASL CONCEPT—**flexible - body**.)

 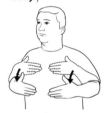

supplement: *n.* something that is added to make up for a deficiency. *She receives a supplement as part of her Old Age Pension.*

SIGN: Horizontal left **'FLAT O'** hand is held in a fixed position with palm toward the body while the right **'CONTRACTED 5'** hand is held palm-down to the right of and at a lower level than the left hand. The right wrist then rotates rightward/forward as the fingers close to form a **'FLAT O'** hand which is swung upward to touch the underside of the left hand.
SAME SIGN—**supplement**, *v.*

supplies: *n.* things that are needed. *The students will be provided with all the supplies required for the art class.*

SIGN: Right **'EXTENDED B'** hand, palm facing up, fingers pointing forward, is moved from left to right in a series of successive short arcs.

supply: *v.* to make available; provide. *I will* **supply** *the food for the party.*

SIGN: Horizontal **'CONTRACTED B'** hands are held with palms up and fingertips almost touching. The hands then move forward in an outward arc as the fingers spread to assume a **'SLANTED 5'** shape.

support: *v.* to endorse; advocate. *All organizations of the Deaf in Canada* **support** *the idea of keeping schools for the Deaf open.*

SIGN: **'S'** hands, palms toward the body, are held at chest level with the left slightly above the right. Then the right is brought upward to strike the left.
SAME SIGNS—**support**, *n.,* and **supportive**, *adj.,* but the motion is repeated.

suppose: *v.* to consider as possible. *Suppose I am laid off; then what will I do?*

SIGN #1: Tip of extended finger of vertical right **'I'** hand, palm facing backwards, is tapped against the right cheekbone two or three times.

suppose: *v.* to presume something to be true without certain knowledge. *I* **suppose** *the meeting will be cancelled.*

SIGN #2: Tip of forefinger of right **'ONE'** hand, palm toward face, touches right side of forehead.
ALTERNATE SIGN—**feel** #1

supposed to: *v.* expected to; required to. *Everyone* **is supposed to** *wear a seatbelt.*

SIGN: Vertical right **'X'** hand, palm facing forward, is bent forward smartly from the wrist so that the palm faces downward. Facial expression is important.

suppress: *v.* to hold in check; restrain. *He tried to* **suppress** *his anger.*

SIGN #1: Right horizontal **'SPREAD C'** hand, palm up, is held at mid chest and is drawn down slightly as it closes to form an **'S'** hand. In contexts where the activities of a 'group of people' are being quelled or held in check, **subdue** is used.
SAME SIGN—**suppression**, *n.,* but the movement is repeated.

suppress: *v.* to withhold information and not allow it to become public. *He tried to* **suppress** *the scandal.*

SIGN #2: Vertical **'C'** hands are held together, left ahead of right, in front of the mouth with left palm facing rightward and right palm facing leftward. The hands are then simultaneously closed to form **'S'** hands.

supreme: *adj.* having the highest power. *The case has been referred to the Supreme Court of Canada.*

SIGN: Vertical **'BENT EXTENDED B'** hands, held at shoulder level with palms facing each other, are moved upward simultaneously and thrust forward very slightly.

sure: *adj.* certain; without doubt. *Are you* **sure** *you do not mind helping me?*

SIGN #1: Forefinger of vertical right **'ONE'** hand, palm facing left, is held against the lips and the hand is moved sharply forward.

SIGN #2 [ATLANTIC]: **'EXTENDED B'** hands, left palm up and right palm angled left/back, are positioned so the left remains fixed while the right is firmly slid forward across the left palm a couple of times.

sure: *adj.* certain; bound. *If you continue skipping classes, you are* **sure** *to fail.*

SIGN #3: Right **'EXTENDED B'** hand, palm facing left, is held in a vertical position near the right side of the head. The forearm is then moved forward a short distance so that the fingers eventually point forward/upward.

surf: *v.* to ride a surfboard when the waves are high near the seashore. *They plan to surf, swim and scuba dive during their holidays.*

SIGN #1: Forefinger of vertical right **'W'** hand, palm facing left, is tapped against the chin. Then tips of extended fingers of right **'BENT V'** hand, palm down, are positioned on back of left **'STANDARD BASE'** hand as, together, the hands glide forward/rightward. (ASL CONCEPT—water - surf.)

(channel) surf: *v.* to switch television channels frequently. *I never see a whole television program because my husband is always channel surfing.*

SIGN #2: Right **'A-INDEX'** hand, palm left, is held in a horizontal position and the thumb is flexed a few times as if pushing buttons on a remote control.

surface: *n.* the exterior face or topmost part. *The road has a gravel surface.*

SIGN #1: Vertical **'BENT EXTENDED B'** hands are held together, right in front of left, close to the chest with the right palm facing left and the left palm facing right. The left hand remains fixed while the right hand moves directly forward. (Signs vary according to context.)

surface: *v.* to become evident or revealed. *Many clues began to surface as the investigation progressed.*

SIGN #2: Left **'EXTENDED B'** hand is held, palm down, in a fixed position. Right **'ONE'** hand, palm forward, is brought up underneath the left hand and the extended forefinger is thrust upward between the forefinger and middle finger of the left hand. As the hands move about, the sign is repeated a few times. (Signs vary according to context. Something rising to the surface of a body of water would require a sign related to whatever is 'surfacing'.)

(on the) surface: *adv.* superficially or to all appearances. *On the surface this looks like a good deal but you had better check it out carefully.*

SIGN #3: Right **'BENT EXTENDED B'** hand, palm facing forward/left, is twisted slightly from the wrist so that it faces the right shoulder.

surge: *n.* a sudden strong rush. *There was a sudden power surge after the near blackout.*

SIGN: **'FLAT O'** hands, palms down, are held apart above shoulder level when suddenly the fingers spread to form **'CONTRACTED 5'** hands. (Signs vary according to context.)

surgery: *n.* the branch of medicine requiring expertise in operating. *They performed emergency surgery to remove the bullet from his chest.*

SIGN: Thumbnail of horizontal right **'EXTENDED A'** (or **'Y'**) hand, palm down, is placed on the rightward facing palm of the left **'EXTENDED B'** hand. Then the right thumb is drawn downward across the left palm. (The positioning of this sign will vary according to which part of the body is undergoing surgery.) SAME SIGN—**surgeon,** *n.*

surly: *adj.* sullen, rude and in a bad mood. *His surly attitude makes him hard to work with.*

SIGN: Right vertical **'CROOKED 5'** hand is held with palm toward the face as the fingers rapidly alternate between a relaxed state (**'CROOKED 5'**) and a clawed state (**'CLAWED SPREAD C'**). This sign is accompanied by an appropriate facial expression.

surmise: *v.* to infer without sufficient evidence; guess. *Due to the circumstances, he could only surmise she was guilty.*

SIGN: Vertical right **'SPREAD C'** hand is held in front of right side of forehead with palm facing left, and is moved leftward as it closes to form an **'S'** hand.

surmount: *v.* to rise above; overcome. *You will need to surmount many obstacles if you hope to succeed.*

SIGN: Vertical right **'S'** hand, palm facing forward, is curved downward from the wrist across the extended finger of the left **'ONE'** hand, which is held horizontally with the palm facing downward.

surname: *n.* family name; last name. *Many women now retain their surnames when they marry.*

SIGN: Horizontal left **'I'** hand is held with palm facing the body at a rightward angle and little finger pointing forward/rightward. Vertical right **'I'** hand, with palm facing leftward/backward, is held to the right of and above the left hand. The right hand is then lowered so that the tip of the little finger strikes the tip of the little finger of the left hand. Next, **'U'** hands are held horizontally with left palm facing right but angled slightly toward the body while right palm faces leftward at a slight angle toward the body. Right hand is positioned above the left at right angles to it. Right midfinger is then tapped twice on left forefinger. (ASL CONCEPT—**last - name**.)

surpass: *v.* to be greater than or superior to in achievement or excellence. *Our team will surpass all others in the league.*

SIGN #1: Vertical left **'BENT EXTENDED B'** hand is held in a fixed position with palm facing right. Vertical right **'BENT EXTENDED B'** hand is held with palm facing left and fingertips resting on the ends of the fingers of the left hand. The right hand then moves rightward and upward in an arc so that it ends up directly above the left hand.

OR

SIGN #2: Vertical right **'S'** hand, palm facing forward, is curved downward from the wrist across the extended finger of the left **'ONE'** hand, which is held horizontally with the palm facing downward. ❖
ALTERNATE SIGN—**beat** #3

surplus: *n.* too much of what is required. *Her body manufactures a surplus of cholesterol.*

SIGN: Horizontal **'CROOKED 5'** hands are held with palms facing and fingertips touching. The hands are then simultaneously drawn apart. (If the items considered surplus are finite or countable, **many** is used.)

surprise: *v.* to cause amazement unexpectedly or suddenly. *The improvement in his grades will surprise you.*

SIGN: Thumbs and forefingers of **'CLOSED MODIFIED G'** (or **'CLOSED X'**) hands are placed at either cheek, and opened sharply to form **'L'** (or **'CONTRACTED L'**) hands as they move sharply away from the face.
SAME SIGN—**surprise**, *n.*

surrender: *v.* to give up. *The gunman was forced to surrender to the police.*

SIGN: **'OPEN A'** hands, held slightly apart at waist level, palms down, are thrust upward to form **'EXTENDED B'** hands with palms facing forward.

surrogate: *adj.* relating to someone who is used as a substitute. *She agreed to become a surrogate mother for her sister's child.*

SIGN: Tip of forefinger of right **'ONE'** hand touches right side of forehead and left **'ONE'** hand is held palm-down at upper chest level with forefinger pointing forward and slightly to the right. Then both forefingers point this way as they move simultaneously forward. (**SURROGATE** may be fingerspelled.)

surround: *v.* to encircle or enclose. *An island is surrounded by water.*

SIGN: Horizontal left **'C'** hand is held in a fixed position with palm facing right while the right **'5'** hand, palm down and fingers pointing forward is circled around it. (Signs vary considerably depending on the context.)

surveillance: *n.* close observation. *The police kept the house and its occupants under close surveillance.*

SIGN: **'BENT V'** hands, palms forward, are held at shoulder level in a slightly staggered position and are poked forward a little a few times. The eyes are squinted and a look of intense concentration appears on the signer's face.

survey: *v.* to examine or study in a comprehensive or general way. *They will survey the opinions of the Deaf Community.*

SIGN: Left **'EXTENDED B'** hand is held in a fixed position with palm turned upward but slanted slightly rightward and toward the body while fingers point rightward/forward. Right **'ONE'** hand is held palm down as tip of forefinger brushes forward several times against palm of left hand.

survive: *v.* to continue to exist after a period of time or adversity. *We could not **survive** long without water.*

SIGN: Horizontal **'EXTENDED A'** hands are placed at either side, somewhere above the waist, with palms toward the body. They are then raised to a higher position on the chest.
SAME SIGN—**survival**, *n.*
ALTERNATE SIGN—**alive** #2

susceptible: *adj.* easily affected by. *I am **susceptible** to environmental allergies.*

SIGN: Left **'BENT EXTENDED B'** hand is held in a fixed position with palm up. Palm of horizontal right **'EXTENDED B'** (or **'BENT EXTENDED B'**) hand faces left but is slanted slightly upward and toward the body as the fingers are brushed upward against the backs of the fingers of the left hand at least twice. Next, **'F'** hands, palms facing, are linked by thumbs and forefingers. The hands remain linked as they are brought back toward the body. (ASL CONCEPT—**easy - catch.**) Signs vary.

suspect: *v.* to think something is false or questionable. *I **suspect** the accused man is truly guilty.*

SIGN #1: Right **'CROOKED ONE'** hand, palm toward the head, is held with tip of forefinger stroking downward slightly against the right temple, then bouncing away a short distance as the finger retracts to form an **'X'** hand. Movement is repeated at least once. A look of suspicion accompanies this sign.

SIGN #2 [PACIFIC/PRAIRIE]: Tip of forefinger of vertical right **'V'** hand, palm left, is flicked forward off an upper front tooth as the hand is slowly moved forward a few times.

suspend: *v.* to delay temporarily; to exclude from work or school temporarily as punishment. *The principal will **suspend** those students for cheating.*

SIGN: **'ONE'** hands, palms down, are held so that the forefingers are crossed at right angles to one another, the right on top of the left. As the forefingers then retract to form **'X'** hands, the forefinger of the right hand hooks around the forefinger of the left hand, lifting it firmly upward. (Sign choice depends on context.)

suspense: *n.* excitement felt as the climax of a story, drama or film is being reached. *The **suspense** in the movie had us all on the edges of our seats.*

SIGN #1: Tips of midfingers of **'BENT MIDFINGER 5'** hands, palms toward the body, are placed slightly apart on the chest. The wrists then rotate forward as the hands move forward so that, while the palms still face the body, they are now angled upward slightly. (Facial expression must clearly indicate fear, horror or whatever emotion is required by the context.)

suspense: *n.* mental uncertainty and anxiety. *Tell us what happened and do not keep us in **suspense** any longer.*

SIGN #2: Thumb and forefinger of right **'F'** hand are held at the throat, as the hand wobbles due to a slight twisting of the wrist.

suspicious: *adj.* tending to question the truth (of something); distrustful or inclined to think something is wrong. *He became **suspicious** when he saw footprints in the snow below the window.*

SIGN: Right **'CROOKED ONE'** hand, palm toward the head, is held with tip of forefinger stroking downward slightly against the right temple, then bouncing away a short distance as the finger retracts to form an **'X'** hand. Movement is repeated at least once. A look of suspicion accompanies this sign.
SAME SIGN—**suspicion**, *n.*
REGIONAL VARIATION—**suspect**

sustain: *v.* to maintain; prolong; keep up. *If you **sustain** this level of stress, you may have a heart attack.*

SIGN #1: **'EXTENDED A'** hands are held side by side with palms down and right thumbtip pressing against left thumbnail as the hands are moved purposefully forward. (In the case of an 'injury being sustained', no specific sign is accorded the term 'sustained' because the concept is incorporated in the sign for **injury**.)

sustain: *v.* to support by supplying the necessities. *This machine is used to **sustain** the patient's life during major heart surgery.*

SIGN #2: **'S'** hands, palms toward the body, are held at chest level with the left slightly above the right. Then the right is brought upward to strike the left.

sustain: *v.* to uphold the justice or validity of something. *The judge will either overrule or sustain the objection.*

SIGN #3: Left **'ONE'** hand is held at chest level with palm facing right, and forefinger pointing forward. Right **'ONE'** hand is held slightly higher with palm facing left, and is then turned downward to match the simultaneously downward turning left hand.

swab: *v.* to clean or medicate with a small piece of cotton or gauze. *The nurse will swab your arm with alcohol before removing blood for the tests.*

SIGN: Hands are held at right angles to one another as downturned palm of right **'EXTENDED B'** hand is smoothed rightward/forward across upturned palm of left **'EXTENDED B'** hand. Motion is repeated a few times. (Signs vary according to context.)

swallow: *v.* to take food or drink in through the mouth to the stomach. *The child has difficulty swallowing pills.*

SIGN: Horizontal right **'ONE'** hand, palm left, is held with tip of forefinger touching the chin, then curved downward so that the fingertip slides down the throat.

swamp: *n.* ground that is permanently water-logged; marsh. *Everglades National Park in Florida was established to preserve the plant and animal life of the swamp.*

SIGN: Fingerspell **SWAMP**.

S   W   A   M   P

swamped: *adj.* overburdened; overwhelmed with work, calls, or commitments. *Every staff member is swamped with work right now.*

SIGN: Horizontal **'BENT EXTENDED B'** (or **'CROOKED 5'**) hands are held, one above each shoulder, with fingers pointing to neck. The arms are then moved upward so that the hands are level with the top of the head.

swan: *n.* a large, graceful aquatic bird with a long, curved neck. *The Ugly Duckling turned into a beautiful swan.*

SIGN: Elbow of the right arm with the palm of its vertical **'FLAT O'** hand facing forward, is placed on the back of the left **'STANDARD BASE'** hand. Then the right hand is slowly pushed forward to give the impression of a swimming swan. (**SWAN** is frequently fingerspelled.)

swanky: *adj.* expensive and stylish. *She wore a swanky dress to the party.*

SIGN: Horizontal right **'S'** hand, palm toward the body, is held on the chin and the forefinger is thrust out to form a **'ONE'** handshape. (This sign is formed along with the release of a slight puff of air from between the lips as the forefinger is flicked out.)

swap: *v.* to trade or exchange. *She suggested that we swap coats.*

SIGN: Horizontal **'CLOSED A-INDEX'** hands, palms facing the chest, are held so the right is nearer the chest than the left. Then their positions are reversed as the right is curved forward under the left and the left is curved backward over the right. (When the swapping involves *money* or something thin, like *sheets of paper*, the sign is made with **'FLAT O'** hands.)

swarm: *n.* a group of bees flying together. *We saw a swarm of bees coming toward us.*

SIGN #1: Vertical **'BENT 5'** hands, palms facing backward and fingers fluttering, are held apart and are simultaneously moved rightward/backward toward the signer. Facial expression is important. (The direction of this sign varies according to context.)

swarm: *v.* to move in large numbers. *People swarm to the beaches during hot weather.*

SIGN #2: Both **'BENT 5'** hands, palms facing forward, are moved forward and slightly downward from shoulder level, fingers wiggling. ❖

swear: *v.* to declare as true. *As a witness, you must swear that your evidence is true.*

SIGN #1: Tip of forefinger of vertical right **'ONE'** hand, palm facing left, is placed just under the lower lip. As the right hand is then brought purposefully forward/downward, it takes on a **'B'** handshape and is pressed onto the top of the left **'STANDARD BASE'** hand.

swear: *v.* to curse; use profane language. *Many people swear when they are angry or frustrated.*

SIGN #2: Left **'ONE'** hand is held in a fixed position with palm down and forefinger pointing forward/rightward. Right **'Y'** hand, with palm down, is moved forward/rightward along the length of the left forefinger.

sweat: *v.* to secrete moisture through the pores of the skin; perspire. *Hard work outdoors usually causes me to sweat.*

SIGN: **'SPREAD EXTENDED C'** hands, palms down, are held against either side of the face at about cheekbone level and are slowly and deliberately lowered. Teeth are visibly closed to show exertion.

sweater: *n.* a knitted or crocheted garment for the upper part of the body. *I have almost finished knitting a new sweater.*

SIGN #1: Horizontal **'A'** hands, palms facing the chest, are held against either side of upper chest near the shoulders and are simultaneously moved down in a slight arc formation to waist level.

SIGN #2 [ONTARIO]: Vertical **'3'** hands, palms facing each other and fingers pointing upward, are held so the wrists touch either side of the upper part of the chest. Then the hands are simultaneously curved downward to about waist level so that fingers are pointing relatively downward.

sweep: *v.* to clean with a broom. *I will sweep the leaves off the patio.*

SIGN: Horizontal right **'EXTENDED B'** hand, palm left but slanted toward the body, is brushed back and forth several times across upturned palm of right **'EXTENDED B'** hand, which is held with fingertips pointing forward/rightward.

sweet: *adj.* having a pleasant taste like sugar. *Eating too many sweet foods can lead to tooth decay.*

SIGN: Fingertips of right **'BENT EXTENDED B'** hand, palm toward the body, are brushed downward twice on the chin.

sweetheart: *n.* a person who is loved romantically by another (a term of endearment). *He married his high school sweetheart.*

SIGN: Horizontal **'EXTENDED A'** hands are held together with palms against left side of chest as the thumbs simultaneously flex and extend a few times.

swell: *v.* to increase in size or be puffed up. *If your hand continues to swell, see your doctor.*

SIGN #1: Right **'CROOKED 5'** hand, palm down and fingertips touching the left **'STANDARD BASE'** hand, moves upward a short distance. Signs vary considerably depending what it is that is swollen.
SAME SIGN—**swollen**, *adj.*

swell: *adj.* a slang expression for wonderful or super. *We had a swell time at the party.*

SIGN #2: Vertical **'EXTENDED B'** hands, palms facing forward, are held apart near the face. Forearms are pushed purposefully forward a short distance.

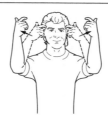

swelled head: *n.* an exaggerated view of oneself. *His success as a hockey player has given him a swelled head.*

SIGN: Horizontal **'CLAWED L'** hands are held with forefingers resting on either side of the forehead. The hands are then simultaneously thrust outward to indicate 'big-headedness'.

swift: *adj.* fast. *They were very swift to take revenge.*

SIGN: Left horizontal **'L'** hand, palm facing right, is held apart from and slightly ahead of right horizontal **'L'** hand, whose palm faces left. The hands are then simultaneously jerked upward toward the body as they are changed to **'CLAWED L'** hands.

swim: *v.* to move one's body along in the water. *If you can not swim, you should take some lessons.*

SIGN: **'EXTENDED B'** hands, palms down and fingers pointing forward, are circled away from each other several times to simulate a swimming motion.

swindle: *v.* to cheat or defraud. *They might try to swindle you if you are not careful.*

SIGN: Vertical right **'A'** hand, with palm forward and slightly leftward, is knocked against forefinger of vertical left **'ONE'** hand whose palm faces right. ❖

swing: *n.* a free-hanging seat suspended so that it can be moved back and forth. *The children are playing on the **swing** in the back yard.*

SIGN: Bent fingers of right **'CLAWED V'** hand, palm down, are hooked over extended fingers of left **'U'** hand, of which the palm is also facing down, as the hands are swung back and forth together. (Signs vary considerably depending on the context.)

switch: *v.* to replace with something else; change. *Our office will **switch** to a computerized system.*

SIGN #1: **'X'** hands, palms facing, are twisted 180 degrees.

switch: *n.* a device for opening and closing an electric circuit. *We could not find the light **switch** in the main auditorium.*

SIGN #2: Right **'CLOSED A-INDEX'** hand, palm facing backward, is placed against the right-facing palm of the left **'EXTENDED B'** hand and is slid up and down. (Signs vary depending on the type of switch. For, **switch on,** *v.,* and **switch off,** *v.,* natural gestures are used.)

sword: *n.* a weapon with a long blade that has either one or two cutting edges. *A special **sword** is used in the sport of fencing.*

SIGN: Horizontal right **'COVERED A-INDEX'** hand, palm facing left, is twisted clockwise from the wrist with a flourish, then jabbed forward as if brandishing a sword.

syllable: *n.* a unit of sound that may either constitute a spoken word, or a part of a word. *'Paper' and 'pencil' are words of two **syllables**.*

SIGN: Horizontal right **'EXTENDED B'** hand, palm left and fingers pointing forward, is moved rightward in a series of short arcs, depending upon the number of syllables indicated.

symbol: *n.* something used to represent something else. *The maple leaf is a **symbol** of Canada.*

SIGN: Tip of forefinger of horizontal right **'BENT ONE'** hand is placed against right facing palm of left **'EXTENDED B'** hand. Together, the hands are moved slightly forward a couple of times.

symbolize: *v.* to represent. *A poet uses word pictures to **symbolize** abstract ideas.*

SIGN: Tip of forefinger of horizontal right **'BENT ONE'** hand is placed against right facing palm of left **'EXTENDED B'** hand. Together, the hands are moved forward in a short arc.

symmetry: *n.* a balance, correspondence or sameness of parts. *The cathedral is a very impressive building because of the architect's use of **symmetry**.*

SIGN: Vertical right **'Y'** hand, palm forward, is held in front of the face and moved from side to side slightly a few times.
SAME SIGN—**symmetrical,** *adj.*

sympathize: *v.* to feel compassion. *I have had the same problems so I can **sympathize** with you.*

SIGN: Right **'BENT MIDFINGER 5'** hand is held upright with palm facing forward but slanted downward slightly. It is then moved forward with circular motions to simulate the stroking of an imaginary person with the middle finger. Facial expression is important. (Alternatively, this sign may be made with two hands.) ❖
SAME SIGN—**sympathetic,** *adj.*

sympathy: *n.* the sharing of another's sorrow or anguish. *I feel a great deal of **sympathy** for children in the Third World.*

SIGN #1: Right **'A'** (or **'EXTENDED A'**) hand, palm facing the body, is rubbed on the chest with a circular motion which, in the eyes of onlookers, appears clockwise.

OR

SIGN #2: Right **'BENT MIDFINGER 5'** hand is held upright with palm facing forward but slanted downward slightly. It is then moved forward with circular motions to simulate the stroking of an imaginary person with the middle finger. Facial expression is important. (Alternatively, this sign may be made with two hands.)

symposium: *n.* a meeting or conference planned to discuss a certain topic. *A symposium of medical experts was held in Paris to discuss world health problems.*

SIGN: **'CONTRACTED 5'** hands are held virtually upright at a slight forward angle with palms facing each other. The fingers then come together to form **'FLAT O'** hands with fingertips of each hand touching those of the other. Motion is repeated.

symptom: *n.* a sign or indication of something such as a particular disease. *Blurred vision, frequent urination and thirst are symptoms of diabetes.*

SIGN: Vertical right **'Y'** hand, palm forward, is held near the right shoulder and is curved downward to an abrupt stop, the palm eventually facing downward. Next, vertical right **'EXTENDED B'** hand, palm facing forward, is moved ever so slightly back and forth a few times. (ASL CONCEPT—**that - your way**.)

synchronize: *v.* to make things happen in unison at exactly the same time. *They all synchronized their wristwatches to make sure everyone returned on time.*

SIGN: **'Y'** hands are held parallel with palms down, and are simultaneously circled leftward in a wide arc so that they eventually return to their original position. (Signs vary according to context.)

syndicate: *n.* an association of business enterprises. *It used to be an independent newspaper but it was taken over by a syndicate.*

SIGN: Fingerspell **CO**.

c   o

syndrome: *n.* a combination of characteristics that define a specific medical condition. *Doctors finally agreed that Chronic Fatigue Syndrome actually exists.*

SIGN: Fingerspell **SYNDROME**.

S   Y   N   D   R   O   M   E

synonym: *n.* a word with the same meaning as another. *"Understand" is a synonym for the word "comprehend".*

SIGN: Vertical right **'Y'** hand is held with palm forward and appears to wobble from side to side as the wrist twists. Next, horizontal left **'EXTENDED B'** hand is held in a fixed position with palm facing right while tip of forefinger of right palm-down **'BENT V'** hand is jabbed into the left palm. The right hand then moves away from the left hand as the right wrist rotates a quarter turn clockwise, and the middle fingertip is jabbed into the left palm. (ASL CONCEPT—**same - meaning**.)

synopsis: *n.* a summary. *The speaker ended his talk with a synopsis of the main points he had covered.*

SIGN: **'SPREAD C'** hands are held horizontally and slightly apart, right above left. Then both are closed to form **'S'** hands as the right is brought down to rest on top of the left.

syntax: *n.* the grammatical arrangement of the components of a sentence in any language. *The syntax of English and ASL are very different.*

SIGN: Horizontal **'EXTENDED B'** hands are held apart in front of the left side of the body with palms facing each other and fingers pointing forward. The hands are then moved rightward in a series of small arcs.

synthetic: *adj.* made artificially by a chemical process. *Nylon is a synthetic fabric.*

SIGN: Side of forefinger of right **'ONE'** hand, palm facing leftward/forward, is lightly brushed forward/downward twice on the right cheek, forefinger either remaining upright or bending slightly to become a **'BENT ONE'**.

syphilis: *n.* a venereal disease that can have serious clinical developments if left untreated. *Antibiotics are used to treat infection caused by syphilis.*

SIGN: Fingerspell **SYPHILIS**. (Alternatively, the abbreviation **VD** meaning **venereal disease** is fingerspelled.)

S   Y   P   H   I   L   I   S

syringe: *n.* a hypodermic needle used for injecting fluids. *Hospitals use disposable syringes to reduce the chances of infection.*

SIGN: Tip of forefinger of right **'BENT L'** hand is jabbed into upper left arm and thumb is repeatedly bent and extended as though depressing a plunger into a syringe.

syrup: *n.* a thick, sticky, sweet liquid used in cooking or as a topping for waffles, pancakes, etc. *Canada is famous for its maple syrup.*

SIGN #1: Horizontal right **'Y'** hand, with thumb pointing downward and palm facing away from the body, is circled in a counter-clockwise direction.

OR

SIGN #2: Right **'MODIFIED G'** hand, palm facing left, is held in a vertical position at the left side of the chin and the thumb and forefinger are opened and closed rapidly several times as the hand is drawn to the right.

SIGN #3 [ONTARIO]: Tip of midfinger of right **'BENT MIDFINGER 5'** hand, palm facing backwards, is drawn across the chin from left to right. Then it is turned and dropped so the palm faces down. (Signs vary.)

system: *n.* a plan for how something will operate or be done. *Every province in Canada has its own education system.*

SIGN: **'EXTENDED B'** hands, held parallel with palms facing one another and fingers pointing forward, are simultaneously moved forward. (Signs vary according to context.)

T

table: *n.* a piece of furniture having a smooth, flat top supported by legs. *This dining room table can accommodate eight place settings.*

SIGN #1: Forearms are bent so that they are held parallel to and very close to the chest with the right arm directly above the left. Then the right arm is tapped down on the left forearm a couple of times.

OR

SIGN #2: **'CROOKED ONE'** hands are extended from the chest in a parallel position with palms down. Then they are simultaneously drawn toward the chest as the forefingers retract to form **'X'** hands.

table: *v.* to postpone discussion of a motion, report, or bill. *We will table the report until the next meeting.*

SIGN: Horizontal **'F'** hands are held parallel with palms facing each other and are simultaneously curved forward in a slight arc formation. ALTERNATE SIGN—**appointment** #1

table tennis: *n.* a game similar to tennis, played on a large table using wooden paddles and a small white ball. *Table tennis is a popular game in China.*

SIGN: Right **'CONTRACTED B'** hand, palm down and fingers pointing down, is held in front of the left side of the chest and is swung forward/upward from the wrist, then moved to a position in front of the right side of the chest and swung forward/upward again as if striking a ping-pong ball with a paddle.

tablecloth: *n.* material used for covering a table, especially during meals. *The tablecloth is made of lace.*

SIGN: Forearms are bent so that they are held parallel to and very close to the chest with the right arm directly above the left. Then the right arm is tapped down on the left forearm a couple of times. Next, **'CROOKED 5'** hands are held out from the body at about chest level with palms down. The hands are then drawn apart and curved downward so that the palms face each other. (ASL CONCEPT—**table - cover**.)

tablespoon: *n.* a large spoon used for eating soup, cereal, or other food in a bowl; a spoon with a capacity equal to that of three teaspoons. *The soup will taste better if you add a tablespoon of soy sauce.*

SIGN: Fingerspell **TBSP**. (Alternatively, the entire word **TABLESPOON** may be fingerspelled.)

T   B   S   P

tablet: *n.* a small, hard piece of medicine that you swallow; pill. *The doctor prescribed some tablets to help ease the pain.*

SIGN: Tip of middle finger of right **'BENT MIDFINGER 5'** hand is placed on the upturned left palm, and maintains contact with the left palm as the right hand teeters back and forth a few times.

tabloid: *n.* a small-sized newspaper with short articles and many photographs. *Tabloids always have sensational headlines.*

SIGN: Thumbnail of right **'MODIFIED G'** hand, palm forward/downward, is placed on upturned palm of left **'EXTENDED B'** hand. Right forefinger then moves up and down several times, thus alternately creating **'MODIFIED G'** and **'CLOSED MODIFIED G'** handshapes. REGIONAL VARIATION—**newspaper**

tack: *n.* a short nail with a broad, flat head. *I need a tack for this poster.*

SIGN: Left **'EXTENDED B'** hand is held in a fixed position with palm up but facing rightward slightly and fingers pointing forward. Thumb of right **'EXTENDED A'** hand, palm facing downward, is used to press against palm of left hand as if pushing on a tack. Movement is repeated. (**TACK** is frequently fingerspelled.)

tackle: *v.* to grab an opponent and prevent his progress. *The football player tackled his opponent.*

SIGN: Left **'U'** hand is held in a fixed position with fingers pointing downward. Then the horizontal right **'C'** hand, palm facing left, is used to grasp the extended fingers of the left hand, closing slightly to form an **'S'** shape in the process. (Sign choice depends on context.)

733

tacky: *adj.* without style; unpleasant to look at. *She wears cheap clothes and tacky jewellery.*

SIGN: Right **'5'** hand is placed on the upper part of the chest with fingers pointing leftward. Pressure is applied while the facial expression indicates the signer's distaste. (**TACKY** may be fingerspelled.)

tactful: *adj.* polite and inoffensive; careful not to hurt or upset anyone. *A diplomat must always be tactful.*

SIGN: Horizontal **'K'** (or **'ĸ'**) hands are held with right hand resting on left hand and extended fingers pointing forward. Together the hands are circled forward a couple of times. Facial expression is important. Next, right **'EXTENDED A'** hand, palm facing left, thumb under chin, is thrust forward. Finally, right **'ONE'** hand, palm facing left, is held in a horizontal position in front of the chest and is then curved upward from the wrist as it moves forward with a stabbing motion. Alternatively, this sign may be made with two hands alternately stabbing, either with or without the curving motion. ❖ (ASL CONCEPT—**careful - not - insult**.) This sign is also used for **tact**, *n.* For **tactless**, only the last part of this sign (i.e., **insult**) is used repetitively. Alternatively, **rude** may be used. When **tact** and **tactful** appear in negation, **insult** is used with repeated movement. In English: *She does not have much tact.* In ASL: *SHE INSULT INSULT.*

tactic: *n.* a method used to achieve whatever goal you have in mind. *This is a common tactic used by their coach.*

SIGN: **'EXTENDED B'** hands, held parallel with palms facing one another and fingers pointing forward, are simultaneously moved forward.

tadpole: *n.* a small water creature that develops into a frog or toad. *The pond was full of tadpoles.*

SIGN: Fingers of palm-up right **'BENT EXTENDED B'** hand point leftward as they rest on rightward-pointing fingers of palm-up left **'BENT EXTENDED B'** hand. The arms are simultaneously moved from side to side as if rocking a baby in one's arms. Next, right **'CLOSED V'** hand is held at the chin with palm down. Then the forefinger and middle finger are flicked forward/leftward to form a **'V'** hand. Movement is repeated. (ASL CONCEPT—**baby - frog**.)

tag: *n.* a small piece of paper that bears information about the object to which it is attached. *Be sure to put a tag on each piece of baggage.*

SIGN #1: Tips of forefingers and thumbs touch as **'CONTRACTED L'** hands are held together with palms facing forward/downward. The arms are then drawn apart and each forefinger and thumb come together to form **'CLOSED MODIFIED G'** shapes. (Signs vary slightly according to size, shape and location of the 'tag'.)

tag: *n.* a game in which one child chases other children and whoever s/he touches then becomes the chaser. *Many children like to play tag at recess.*

SIGN #2: **'EXTENDED B'** hands, palms toward the body, are alternately circled so the right palm brushes downward on the left side of the chest just below the shoulder and the left palm does likewise on the right side of the chest. (Signs may vary.)

tail: *n.* an elongated portion of the vertebral column at the rear of an animal's body. *The dog hurt his tail.*

SIGN: Right **'ONE'** hand is held with palm facing left and forefinger pointing forward. Left **'ONE'** hand is held with palm toward chest and tip of forefinger touching right wrist. Then the right hand sways from side to side several times. This is a wrist action. (Signs vary depending on the shape and length of the tail. Alternatively, **TAIL** may be fingerspelled. An all-inclusive sign is often used to incorporate **tail**, *n.*, as well as a verb telling what the tail is doing, *e.g.,* wagging. One sign may include the noun, verb and an adverb. One sign could be used to express all the italicized words in this sentence: *The dog's tail was wagging frantically*.)

taillight: *n.* a red light (usually one of a pair) at the rear of a vehicle. *Your right taillight is not working.*

SIGN: Vertical right **'MODIFIED O'** hand (or left, depending on context) is held with palm facing the upper right side (or left, as the case may be) of the chest. The fingers then open to form a **'CONTRACTED 5'** shape. (Two hands are used to refer to a set of *two* taillights.)

tailor: *n.* a person who makes, repairs, or alters clothing. *This suit was made by a European tailor.*

SIGN: Horizontal **'F'** hands are held slightly apart with palms facing each other. The left hand remains in a fixed position as the right hand is rotated clockwise at least twice so that the thumb and forefinger make contact with those of the left hand each time they brush past.

tainted: *adj.* spoiled or putrefied as a result of some undesirable condition. *Many of the diners became ill because the meat was tainted.*

SIGN: Right **'EXTENDED B'** hand, with fingertips on chin and palm facing body, is turned away, so that palm is facing down. Facial expression shows revulsion. (Signs vary depending on 'what' is tainted.)

take [*or* **take away**]: *v.* to gain possession of. *If you leave your coat here someone might take it.*

SIGN #1: Right **'SPREAD C'** hand is extended from the chest with palm down (or facing left) and is drawn rapidly toward the chest as the fingers close to form an **'S'** shape. ❖ (Signs vary depending on 'what' is being taken and 'how' it is being taken.)

take: *v.* to work at or study. *She plans to take a course in auto mechanics when she gets her new car.*

SIGN #2: **'SPREAD C'** hands, palms down, are held apart and are simultaneously raised as they change to **'S'** hands.

take: *v.* to require or be necessary. *It will take a lot of time to get it done.*

SIGN #3: Tip of forefinger of right **'X'** hand is placed in right-facing palm of left **'EXTENDED B'** hand. Together the hands are moved firmly toward the chest, giving the impression that the left hand is being tugged by the right forefinger.

take: *v.* to win. *She always takes first prize for her apple pies at the county fair.*

SIGN #4: **'SPREAD C'** hands are held horizontally and slightly apart, right above left. As the hands are then moved purposefully toward each other, they close to form **'S'** hands, the right hand grazing the top of the left hand, and the wrists eventually crossing.

take: *v.* to bear; endure; tolerate. *I can not take it any more!*

SIGN #5: Right **'A'** hand, with thumbnail touching closed lips and palm facing left, is moved slowly down chin.

take: *v.* to accept. *If he takes the job, he will do it well.*

SIGN #6: Both **'CONTRACTED 5'** hands, palms down, are brought toward the chest while they are being closed to form **'FLAT O'** hands, with fingertips touching the body.

take a picture: *v.* to photograph with a camera. *Smile while I take a picture of you.*

SIGN #7: Vertical **'CROOKED L'** (or **'C-INDEX'**) hands are held so as to frame the eyes with a thumb touching either side of face, and palms facing each other, but angled forward slightly. The forefinger of the right hand then retracts, thus taking on a **'CLAWED L'** shape as if clicking a camera.

OR

SIGN #8: Vertical right **'MODIFIED O'** hand is held with palm facing forward. The fingers then open to form a **'CONTRACTED 5'** shape as the hand makes a tight circle in a clockwise direction, the fingers closing to resume a **'MODIFIED O'** shape as the hand returns to its initial position.

take advantage of [#9]: See (take) advantage of.

take after: *v.* to resemble in terms of character or actions. *I am not surprised that he is a good worker because he **takes after** his father.*

SIGN #10: Vertical right **'Y'** hand is held with palm forward and appears to wobble from side to side as the wrist twists. (When **take after** means 'to resemble in terms of *appearance*', see **look like**.)

take away: *v.* to subtract. *Five **take away** three equals two.*

SIGN #11: Edge of extended forefinger of right horizontal **'BENT ONE'** hand, palm down, is tapped against forward-facing palm of vertical left **'EXTENDED B'** hand.
ALTERNATE SIGN—**deduct**
For **take away** meaning 'to take possession of', see **take** #1.

take back: *v.* to return merchandise. *The shirt is too small so I will **take** it **back** to the store.*

SIGN #12: Vertical right **'S'** hand, palm forward, is thrust ahead as it opens to form a **'CONTRACTED 5'** hand.

take back what one says: *v.* to admit something you said was wrong by withdrawing or retracting your words. *If I hurt your feelings, then I **take back what I said**.*

SIGN #13: Right **'A'** (or **'EXTENDED A'**) hand, palm facing the body, is rubbed on the chest with a circular motion which, in the eyes of onlookers, appears clockwise. Next, right **'EXTENDED A'** hand, palm facing left, thumb under chin, is thrust forward. Finally, horizontal left **'EXTENDED B'** hand is held in a fixed position with palm facing right while tip of forefinger of right palm-down **'BENT V'** hand is jabbed into the left palm. The right hand then moves away from the left hand as the right wrist rotates a quarter turn clockwise, and the middle fingertip is jabbed into the left palm. (ASL CONCEPT—**sorry - not - mean**.)

  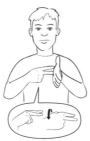

take care of: *v.* to handle; attend to; look after. *I will **take care of** all the arrangements.*

SIGN #14: Horizontal **'K'** (or **'V'**) hands are held, right above left, with extended fingers pointing forward, the left palm facing rightward and the right palm facing leftward. The hands are brought together to strike each other a couple of times.

take down: *v.* to remove from a vertical surface. *The caretaker will **take down** the posters from the walls in the corridor.*

SIGN #15: **'SPREAD C'** hands, palms forward, are held aloft and simultaneously drawn downward to form **'S'** shapes with the palms facing down. (Signs vary according to what is being taken down. This sign would not be appropriate for the 'taking down' of a flag.)

take down: *v.* to write down. *The secretary will **take down** the minutes of the meeting.*

SIGN #16: Horizontal left **'EXTENDED B'** hand is held in a fixed position with palm facing the chest. Vertical right **'CLOSED X'** hand is held with palm facing that of the left hand, and moves from side to side (from the wrist) as it moves downward. (To indicate that what is being taken down will be *brief*, see **jot down**.)

take in: *v.* to accept into one's home or household. *Her parents finally agreed to let the children **take in** the stray cat.*

SIGN #17: Horizontal right **'K'** hand, with palm facing left, is held above horizontal left hand, which is held with palm facing right. Then right hand is brought purposefully down to strike left hand. (Sign choice depends on context.)

take in: *v.* to consist of or be comprised of; include. *Our ranch **takes in** all the land between here and the U.S. border.*

SIGN #18: Right **'CONTRACTED 5'** hand is held palm down above horizontal left **'C'** hand of which the palm faces rightward/backward. The right hand is then closed to form a **'FLAT O'** hand as it plunges fingers first into the opening at the top of the left hand.

take it easy: *v.* to relax. *I think I will just **take it easy** this weekend.*

SIGN #19: **'EXTENDED B'** hands are held parallel with palms down and fingers pointing forward. The forearms are simultaneously lowered a short distance, then moved rightward in an arc formation, and back to their original position in a leftward arc. (In a context where someone is being *told* to **take it easy**, the sign for **calm down** would be used.)

take it easy *(cont.)*

OR

SIGN #20: **'EXTENDED B'** hands, palms toward the body, are crossed at the wrists and are then placed on the chest.

---

take off: *v.* to leave the ground and start flying. *The plane will take off in 10 seconds.*

SIGN #21: Right **'COMBINED LY'** hand is held palm down with extended fingers pointing forward/leftward. The forearm then moves upward at a forward/rightward angle, the palm of the hand eventually facing upward/rightward. (This sign is used in reference to the departure of an *airplane* only. The sign for **go** #4 is used in cases where 'take off' is used in a colloquial sense as in: *Look at the time; I should take off now!*)

---

take off: *v.* to remove. *Men used to be required to take off their hats in certain public places.*

SIGN #22: Right vertical **'COVERED T'** hand, palm facing left, is placed near the forehead and curved downward to simulate the doffing of one's hat or cap. (Sign choices vary according to the specific article of clothing or jewelry being taken off.)

---

take off: *v.* to deduct; subtract. *The clerk will take off 20 percent at the checkout.*

SIGN #23: Horizontal left **'EXTENDED B'** hand is held in a fixed position with palm rightward/backward and fingers pointing forward/rightward. Fingertips of right **'SPREAD C'** hand are placed against the palm of the left hand. Then the right hand is pulled down and closed to form an **'S'** hand.

---

take off: *v.* to lose (weight). *She is trying to take off 10 pounds.*

SIGN #24: Left **'BENT U'** hand is held in a fixed position with palm rightward/forward and extended fingers pointing rightward/forward. Right **'BENT U'** hand is held with palm leftward/forward and tips of extended fingers resting on those of the left hand at right angles. The right wrist then rotates rightward causing the hand to turn palm upward as it drops slightly.

---

take on: *v.* to hire. *The construction company will take on a new foreman.*

SIGN #25: Horizontal right **'SPREAD C'** hand is held well out in front of the body with palm facing leftward. As the hand is then brought back toward the body, it closes to assume an **'S'** shape. (Sign choice depends on context.)

---

take one's time: *v.* to go about something slowly and carefully. *It is important to take your time when presenting a new idea.*

SIGN #26: **'5'** hands are held parallel with palms down in front of the left side of the body and are simultaneously moved rightward in arc formation so that they are in front of the right side of the body. They are then moved leftward in arc formation to their original position. (Appropriate facial expression must accompany this sign. Cheeks are puffed and the face clearly appears to be at peace.)

---

take out: *v.* to remove. *The editor suggested that we take out one word.*

SIGN #27: Left **'ONE'** hand is held in a fixed position with palm rightward at a slight downward angle and forefinger pointing forward/rightward. Right **'COVERED T'** hand is held to the right of the left hand with palm up and forefinger touching tip of left forefinger. The right hand then moves rightward/upward as the thumb is flicked out to form an **'EXTENDED A'** hand. (Signs vary considerably depending on 'what' specifically is being taken out and 'how' it is being taken out. Sign choice depends on context.)

---

take over: *v.* to assume control; take charge. *I will take over for you if you do not feel well.*

SIGN #28: **'SPREAD C'** hands, palms down, are held apart and are simultaneously raised as they change to **'S'** hands.

---

take place: *v.* to occur; happen. *Where did the accident take place?*

SIGN #29: **'ONE'** hands, palms facing each other and forefingers pointing forward, are held apart and then turned over so that the palms face down.

take turns: *v.* to do something one after another in a regular sequence. *Let us take turns bringing the lunch for our meetings.*

SIGN #30: Right **'L'** hand is held in front of the left side of the body with the palm facing basically downward. As the hand moves rightward in a sweeping arc, the wrist rotates back and forth causing the hand to rock repeatedly. ❖ (If it is 'you and me' taking turns, the horizontal right **'L'** hand, forefinger pointing left and palm facing backwards, is drawn back toward the chest, as the wrist rotates to turn the palm downward and the thumbtip comes to rest against the chest. The wrist then rotates forward to return the hand to its original position. Movement is repeated.)

OR

SIGN #31: Horizontal right **'DOUBLE MODIFIED G'** hand is held in front of the left side of the body with palm facing left. As the hand moves rightward in a sweeping arc, the thumb and extended fingers snap open and shut a few times, thus alternating between the initial handshape and a **'CLOSED DOUBLE MODIFIED G'.** ❖ (If it's 'you and me' taking turns, the horizontal right **'DOUBLE MODIFIED G'** hand, extended fingers pointing left and palm facing backwards, is drawn back toward the chest, as the wrist rotates to turn the palm downward and close the fingers against the thumb to form a **'CLOSED DOUBLE MODIFIED G'** as the hand comes to rest against the chest. The wrist then rotates forward to return the hand to its original position. Movement is repeated.)

take up: *v.* to adopt (a new routine or practice). *He decided to take up stamp-collecting.*

SIGN #32: Left **'5'** hand is held with palm facing right while forefinger of right **'ONE'** hand is inserted between first two fingers of left hand and twisted 180 degrees either to the right or left.

(be) taken in: *v.* to be deceived by someone through the use of pretence. *We were taken in by his lies.*

SIGN #1: Left **'BENT EXTENDED B'** hand is held in a fixed position with palm toward the chest and fingers pointing rightward. Tongue protrudes as right **'ONE'** hand is placed at right angles on left hand with palm facing left and forefinger pointing forward. Tongue disappears into the mouth as the mouth closes and the right hand slides backward/downward behind the left hand so that the right forefinger eventually points upward.

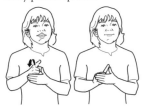

OR

SIGN #2: Tongue protrudes as vertical right **'BENT EXTENDED B'** hand, palm facing backward, is placed near the right cheek and is briskly shoved back toward the shoulder, the tongue disappearing into a closing mouth. (The ASL sentence is syntactically different than the English one. In ASL: *HE LIE...WE SWALLOW.*)

tale: *n.* a story. *That is an interesting tale!*

SIGN: Left **'CONTRACTED C'** (or **'OPEN 8'**) hand is held horizontally with palm facing right while right **'CONTRACTED C'** (or **'OPEN 8'**) hand is held upright with palm facing left. The hands are held close enough together to be loosely interlocked. They are then drawn apart, closed and returned several times, thus alternating between **'CONTRACTED C'** (or **'OPEN 8'**) and **'FLAT O'** (or **'8'**) shapes with each movement.

talent: *n.* a natural ability. *He has superior artistic talent.*

SIGN: Left **'EXTENDED B'** hand, palm facing right and fingers pointing upward/forward, is grasped by right **'OPEN A'** hand. Then right hand is pulled forward sharply and closed to form an **'A'** hand.
SAME SIGN—**talented,** *adj.*

talk: *v.* to have a conversation. *I will talk with you later.*

SIGN #1: Tip of forefinger of vertical right **'4'** hand, palm facing left, is tapped twice against the chin (When there is an implication that the talking will be informal or relaxed, **chat** is often used.)

(give a) talk: *v.* to lecture or give a speech. *At the conference, she will give a talk on this subject.*

SIGN #2: Right arm is raised and the vertical **'EXTENDED B'** hand, palm facing left, is brought forward sharply from the wrist a couple of times.

talk into: *v.* to persuade by continuous talk about the merits of something. *Try to talk your parents into letting you go to the party.*

SIGN: Horizontal **'EXTENDED B'** hands are held apart at about shoulder level with palms facing upward but slanted so that they are facing each other slightly as well. The forearms then move firmly downward/inward a short distance. ❖

talk to oneself: *v.* to have a conversation with oneself (in speech or in sign). *I was just talking to myself.*

SIGN: Vertical **'ONE'** hands are held with palms facing backward and the tips of the forefingers on the cheeks. The hands then take on an **'I'** shape as they are curved forward toward each other and tapped together a couple of times.

talkative: *adj.* (used with reference to ASL users only) having a tendency to talk a lot. *She is a very talkative person.*

SIGN #1: **'OPEN 8'** hands, palms facing, with right in a vertical position and left in a horizontal position, are rapidly linked and drawn apart several times as they alternate with **'8'** handshapes. Facial expression is important.

talkative: *adj.* (used with reference to users of spoken languages only) having a tendency to talk a lot. *She is a very talkative person.*

SIGN #2: **'CONTRACTED C'** hand, palm forward, is held in front of the mouth and is rapidly opened and closed several times, thus alternating between its original handshape and a **'FLAT O'**. Facial expression is important.

tall: *adj.* of more than average height. *My brother is the tall one in our family.*

SIGN: Vertical left **'EXTENDED B'** hand is held in a fixed position with palm facing right. Vertical right **'ONE'** hand, palm forward, is placed against the left palm and is pushed upward.

ALTERNATE SIGN—**giant**

tall tale: *n.* a story that is nonsensical or wildly exaggerated. *Stephen Leacock is an author famous for his tall tales.*

SIGN: Left **'CONTRACTED C'** (or **'OPEN 8'**) hand is held horizontally with palm facing right while right **'CONTRACTED C'** (or **'OPEN 8'**) hand is held upright with palm facing left. The hands are held close enough together to be loosely interlocked. They are then drawn apart, closed and returned several times, thus alternating between **'CONTRACTED C'** (or **'OPEN 8'**) and **'FLAT O'** (or **'8'**) shapes with each movement. Next, Right **'4'** hand is held upright in front of forehead with palm facing leftward. The hand is then moved forward (at a slight downward angle) in short jerky motions until the fingers are pointing forward.
(ASL CONCEPT—**story - nonsense.**)

tally: *v.* to add up; to total. *I will tally the scores in the bridge tournament.*

SIGN: **'CONTRACTED 5'** hands are held left above right with the left palm facing down and the right palm facing upward. The hands are then brought together as the fingers close to form **'FLAT O'** hands with fingertips touching each other. Movement is repeated.

tame: *adj.* domesticated; not wild. *The animal is no longer wild; he has become tame living with humans.*

SIGN: Fingerspell **TAME**.

T   A   M   E

tamper with: *v.* to interfere with something you have no right to touch. *All medicine should be kept out of the reach of children so they can not tamper with it.*

SIGN #1: Tip of middle finger of right **'BENT MIDFINGER 5'** hand, palm down, touches down on the back of the left **'STANDARD BASE'** hand.

tamper with: *v.* to try to change something when you have no right to do so. *The officials suspect someone tried to **tamper with** the statistics.*

SIGN #2: Left **'ONE'** hand is held in a fixed position with palm down and forefinger pointing rightward/forward while forefinger of right **'ONE'** hand, palm facing the body, is used to touch the nose and is then brought down to strike sharply against the tip of the left forefinger. This sign is accompanied by an appropriate facial expression and a lip pattern such as that used to produce an 'SH' sound. (For regional variation on this part of the sign, see **cheat**.) Next, **'A'** hands, palms facing each other, are twisted 180 degrees. (ASL CONCEPT—**cheat - change**.)

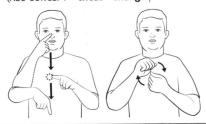

tampon: *n.* a firm, specially shaped absorbent object a woman places in her vagina to soak up menstrual flow. *She kept an extra **tampon** in her purse.*

SIGN: Vertical right **'A'** hand, palm toward the face, is tapped lightly against the right cheek twice. Next, horizontal **'COVERED F'** hands are held side by side, palms down and extended fingers pointing forward, and are drawn apart. (ASL CONCEPT—**period - tube**.) TAMPON is frequently fingerspelled.

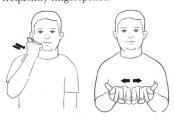

tan: *n.* skin that has become a brownish shade from exposure to the sun's rays. *She came back from Florida with a **tan**.*

SIGN #1: Vertical right **'T'** hand, palm forward, is placed high on the right cheekbone and is drawn down toward the jaw.

tan: *adj.* a coppery tone or yellowish-brown colour. *He was wearing a pair of **tan** coloured pants.*

SIGN #2: Fingerspell **TAN**.

tangible: *adj.* definite enough to be easily seen, felt or noticed. *The prosecution had little **tangible** evidence to present.*

SIGN: Forefinger of vertical right **'ONE'** hand, palm facing left, is held against the lips and the hand is moved sharply forward.

tangled: *adj.* twisted into an untidy mass that is difficult to unravel. *Please help me with this **tangled** rope.*

SIGN: **'OPEN SPREAD O'** hands are held close together, the left hand more or less in a horizontal position and the right hand vertical, with palms facing. The wrists then twist in opposite directions, thus moving the left hand backward and the right hand forward as the fingers retract so that they are tucked more tightly into the hands. Facial expression is important.

tank: *n.* an armored combat vehicle that moves on tracks. *The soldier ran when he saw the enemy **tanks** approaching.*

SIGN #1: Right **'ONE'** hand is held out from the body with palm facing left and forefinger pointing forward/upward. Left **'C'** hand grasps right forearm near the elbow, as right forearm jerks downward/backward, then jerks back to its original position to show the recoil action of a firearm.

tank: *n.* a large container used for holding liquids or gases. *We must get the propane **tank** filled.*

SIGN #2: Horizontal **'C'** hands are held apart with palms facing each other. Then they are moved upward simultaneously. (The distance between the hands depends on the diameter of the tank.) This sign is used for a tank which can be seen. If the 'tank' is not visible, as is the case with the gas tank in a vehicle, **TANK** is fingerspelled.)

tantrum: *n.* a noisy outburst of bad temper. *The child demonstrated his frustration by having **tantrums**.*

SIGN: Right **'CROOKED 5'** hand is placed palm down on the left horizontal **'S'** hand of which the palm faces the body. Then the right hand is forcefully raised a fair distance with the fingers fluttering and is returned to its original position. The motion may be repeated, particularly when referring to frequent tantrums.

tap: *v.* to strike with a series of quick, light blows. *Whenever you are ready to leave, please tap on the door.*

SIGN #1: Knuckles of right **'A'** hand, palm facing left, rap against right-facing palm of vertical left **'EXTENDED B'** hand.

tap: *v.* to touch lightly with the fingertips to get someone's attention. *Instead of calling my name, please tap me on the shoulder when the doctor is ready to see me.*

SIGN #2: Fingertips of right **'BENT EXTENDED B'** hand, palm facing the body, are tapped against the right shoulder a few times. ❖

tap: *n.* a faucet or spigot that controls the flow of a liquid or gas from a pipe or container. *The kitchen tap was dripping all night.*

SIGN #3: Right **'SPREAD C'** hand is held palm down and vigorously twisted back and forth several times as if turning a tap on and off a few times. (Signs vary according to the type of tap and how it is operated.)

tape: *n.* a long, thin strip of adhesive material used for binding. *Before I wrap the Christmas gifts, I need to buy some tape.*

SIGN #1: **'EXTENDED A'** hands are positioned with palms down and thumbtips touching. The hands are then drawn apart as the wrists rotate inward a bit. **TAPE** is frequently fingerspelled. SAME SIGN—**tape**, *v.*, in this context.

OR

SIGN #2: **'U'** hands, palms down, are held so the extended fingers of the right are resting across those of the left at right angles. The right hand is then moved downward, the extended fingers sliding rightward/backward across those of the left hand and slightly downward. SAME SIGN—**tape**, *v.*, in this context.

tape: *v.* to record (on tape). *Please tape the program on Channel 4 from 7:00 p.m. to 8:00 p.m. for me.*

SIGN #3: Left **'EXTENDED B'** hand is held in a fixed position with palm right and fingers pointing forward. Horizontal right **'CONTRACTED 5'** hand, palm left, is held with fingertips touching left palm. The right hand then moves rightward as the fingers close to form a **'FLAT O'** hand.

tape recorder: *n.* an electrical device used for recording and reproducing sound. *The news reporter used a tape recorder during the interview.*

SIGN: Vertical right **'ONE'** hand, palm left, is held with tip of forefinger at the right ear. Next, **'BENT ONE'** hands are held parallel with forefingers pointing downward and are simultaneously circled in a counter-clockwise direction. (ASL CONCEPT—**sound - spin**.)

tar: *n.* a thick, black substance used to pave roads. *Tar is applied while it is hot, but hardens as it cools.*

SIGN: Fingerspell **TAR**.

tardy: *adj.* late. *Please forgive this tardy response to your letter.*

SIGN: Right **'EXTENDED B'** hand is held to the right side of the body with fingers pointing downward and palm facing backward. Fingers simultaneously move back and forth.

target: *n.* something that is being aimed at. *See if you can hit the target.*

SIGN: Forefinger of right **'ONE'** hand is dropped forward smartly to strike horizontal forefinger of left **'ONE'** hand at right angles. (Signs vary according to context.)

tariff: *n.* a tax on goods imported into the country. *The Free Trade Agreement is supposed to reduce tariffs.*

SIGN: Forefinger of horizontal right **'X'** hand, palm toward the body at a leftward-facing angle, is brought down smartly across the palm of the horizontal left **'EXTENDED B'** hand, which is facing rightward but angled toward the body.

tart: *n.* a small pastry filled with something sweet. *I had a strawberry tart for dessert.*

SIGN: Fingerspell **TART**.

task: *n.* a specific piece of work required to be done. *Each child was given the responsibility of performing a simple task.*

SIGN: Wrist of right **'A'** (or **'S'**) hand, palm facing away from the body, strikes wrist of the left **'A'** (or **'S'**) hand, which is held in front of/below the right hand with palm facing downward. Motion is repeated.

tassel: *n.* a bunch of threads or strings tied together at one end and attached to something as a decoration. *The graduates wore green mortarboards with gold tassels.*

SIGN: Right **'N'** hand is held palm down near right side of face (where the tassel on a mortarboard would hang) and is shaken back and forth at least twice. (The location of this sign varies according to context.)

taste: *v.* to test the flavour of something by putting some in the mouth. *Taste the sauce to see if it needs more spices.*

SIGN: Tip of middle finger of right **'BENT MIDFINGER 5'** hand (or tip of forefinger of right **'ONE'** hand), palm toward the body, is placed in the centre of the chin.

tasty: *adj.* having a pleasant flavour. *The roast beef was tender and tasty.*

SIGN: Fingertips of right **'BENT EXTENDED B'** hand are placed on the lips so that the palm is toward the body. Then the hand is moved purposefully forward a brief distance. Facial expression must clearly show pleasure.

tattle: *v.* to gossip about the actions of others; to tell on. *He will likely tattle to his parents about his sister's mischievous behaviour.*

SIGN #1: Vertical right **'S'** hand is held against the chin with palm forward. As the hand then moves forward, the forefinger flicks out so that it is pointing forward/leftward.

SIGN #2 [PRAIRIE]: Vertical right **'CONTRACTED C'** hand is held in front of the nose and mouth with palm facing left and is then moved forward, as the fingers come together with the thumb to form a **'FLAT O'** handshape.

OR

SIGN #3 [PRAIRIE]: Vertical right **'CONTRACTED L'** is held in front of the mouth with palm facing left. As the hand moves forward, the thumb and forefinger close and open a few times, the handshape thus alternating between a **'CONTRACTED L'** and **'CLOSED MODIFIED G'**.

tattoo: *n.* a permanent, coloured picture or design made on someone's body by pricking the skin. *He had a tattoo of a snake on his left arm.*

SIGN: Right **'CLOSED X'** hand is placed on the upper left arm and tapped quickly in a circular pattern to simulate the process of pricking the skin with a needle. (This sign may be placed on whatever part of the body is indicated in the context.) **TATTOO** may be fingerspelled.

taunt: *v.* to say unkind, insulting things to someone in an aggressive manner; mock. *The other children often taunt her about her handicap.*

SIGN: Horizontal **'ONE'** hands, left palm facing right and right palm facing left, are alternately stabbed forward. Facial expression is important. ❖

tax: *n.* a compulsory contribution levied by government. *Canada's Goods and Services Tax was levied to help reduce the national debt.*

SIGN: Fingerspell **TAX**.

T   A   X

taxi: *n.* a car hired to carry passengers. *They went to the airport in a taxi.*

SIGN #1: Fingerspell **TAXI**.

T   A   X   I

SIGN #2 [ATLANTIC]: Right **'X'** hand, palm left, is held upright and is shaken forward from the wrist to a horizontal position at least twice.

SIGN #3 [ONTARIO]: Vertical right **'Y'** hand, palm toward the head, is tapped against the right side of the forehead a couple of times.

tea: *n.* a beverage made by infusion of dried leaves of various plants in boiling water. *Tea and coffee will be provided at the workshop.*

SIGN: Joined thumb and forefinger of the right **'F'** hand, palm down, are inserted into the opening of the horizontal left **'F'** hand of which the palm is facing right. The hands remain in this position while the right hand jiggles. (Signs vary. **TEA** is frequently fingerspelled.)

teach: *v.* to give instruction; give lessons. *What subject does he teach?*

SIGN: Vertical **'MODIFIED O'** hands are held parallel with palms facing each other and are moved slightly but firmly forward. ❖

teacher: *n.* a person who gives lessons or instruction. *My ASL teacher always makes the class interesting.*

SIGN: Vertical **'MODIFIED O'** hands are held parallel with palms facing each other and are moved slightly but firmly back and forth at least twice. (Agent Ending (see p. LIV) may follow.)

team: *n.* a group of people organized to work or play together. *Our team will organize and plan the workshop.*

SIGN: Vertical **'T'** hands are held slightly apart with palms basically facing forward. The wrists then rotate drawing the hands apart and curving them forward and together with palms eventually facing the body.
ALTERNATE SIGN—**group** #1

teamwork: *n.* the co-operative work done by a group of people. *Good teamwork enabled them to win the trophy.*

SIGN: **'F'** hands with thumbs and forefingers interlocked, and palms facing each other, are moved in a complete circle in front of the body using a counter-clockwise motion.

tear: *v.* to rip; pull apart. *She will tear up the letter.*

SIGN: **'CLOSED A-INDEX'** hands are held side by side with palms down. Right thumb and forefinger rub against those of the left hand as the left hand moves forward and the right hand moves backward toward the chest.

tear-jerker: *n.* a book, movie or drama that is excessively sentimental. *Last night we watched a movie that was a real tear-jerker.*

SIGN: Vertical **'X'** hands, palms forward, simultaneously stroke downward along the cheeks, then curve forward. Movement is repeated a few times. A sad facial expression must accompany this sign. (The ASL sentence is syntactically different than the English one. In ASL: *LAST NIGHT MOVIE ME CRY CRY CRY*.)

(have one's eyes fill with) tears: *v.* to be about to cry. *Her eyes filled with tears when she heard the verdict.*

SIGN #1: Vertical **'CLAWED 4'** hands, palms facing each other, are placed with tips of forefingers touching the face high on the cheekbones near each eye. As the wrists rotate inward, the hands slowly swivel so that the palms slant toward the face.

(shed) tears: *v.* to cry quietly. *Some people shed tears when they watch a sad movie or read a sad story.*

SIGN #2: Vertical **'L'** hands are held so that the tips of the forefingers are just below each eye and the palms are toward the face. The forefingers are then simultaneously stroked downward on the cheeks, thus taking on **'BENT L'** shapes. Motion is repeated.

tease: *v.* to poke fun at someone in a playful manner. *I like to tease you.*

SIGN: With palm facing left, horizontal right **'X'** hand is stroked forward at least twice across the top of horizontal left **'X'** hand, which is held with palm facing right. ❖ (**Tease** is sometimes used in a negative context, in which case **pick on** would be more appropriate.)

teaspoon: *n.* the measure contained in a spoon equal in capacity to 1/3 of a tablespoon. *The recipe calls for a teaspoon of salt.*

SIGN: Fingerspell **TEASPOON** or **TSP**.

technical: *adj.* relating to the applied sciences. *Many practical training programs are offered at technical institutes.*

SIGN: Tip of middle finger of right **'BENT MIDFINGER 5'** hand is used to tap lightly against the edge of the left **'EXTENDED B'** hand a couple of times.
SAME SIGN—**technology**, *n.*

technique: *n.* a particular method or means of doing something. *She showed us a number of techniques to improve our efficiency.*

SIGN: **'EXTENDED B'** hands, held parallel with palms facing one another and fingers pointing forward, are simultaneously moved forward.

tedious: *adj.* boring; uninteresting. *Housecleaning is tedious work.*

SIGN: Tip of forefinger of right **'ONE'** hand is placed against right side of nose, and is twisted half a turn clockwise. Facial expression must clearly convey 'boredom'.
SAME SIGN—**tedium**, *n.*
ALTERNATE SIGN—**bored/boring** #2

teenager: *n.* someone who is between 13 and 19 years of age inclusive. *Many teenagers are involved in sports activities.*

SIGN: Fingertips of **'BENT EXTENDED B'** hands, palms facing the body, are brushed upward against the chest. (**TEENAGER** may be finger-spelled.)

teeth: *n.* hard, bony projections set in the jaws and used for biting and chewing. *Many children require braces to straighten their teeth.*

SIGN: Vertical **'X'** hand, palm facing backward, is moved from side to side a couple of times in front of the mouth with the crooked fore-finger pointing toward the upper teeth.

telecast: *n.* a television broadcast. *We remember watching the telecast of the first moon landing.*

SIGN: Fingerspell **TV**.

telegram: *n.* a message sent by telegraph. *My relatives from Fort William sent a telegram wishing us happiness in our marriage.*

SIGN: Right **'BENT MIDFINGER 5'** hand is held with palm down as it bounces up and down a couple of times, the tip of the middle finger making contact with the upturned palm of the left **'EXTENDED B'** hand with each bounce.

telepathy: *n.* communication between two people through thoughts and feelings which cannot be explained scientifically. *The psychic identified the card she drew from the deck using the process of mental telepathy.*

SIGN: Tip of forefinger of right **'CROOKED ONE'** hand, palm toward the head, is tapped against right side of forehead. Next, vertical right **'S'** hand is held just in front of the forehead, with palm forward while vertical left **'S'** hand is held farther forward with palm facing that of the right hand. The hands then bend toward each other from the wrists as the forefingers are simultaneously flicked out toward each other to form **'BENT ONE'** hands. Motion is repeated a few times. ❖ (ASL CONCEPT—**brain - correspond**.)

telephone: *n.* an electronic device used to communicate over long distances. *She has a touch-tone telephone.*

SIGN: Right **'Y'** hand, with tip of little finger at the mouth and tip of thumb at the right ear, is tapped against the right jawline a couple of times. (For **telephone**, *v.*, see **phone** #1 and #2.)

telescope: *n.* an instrument used to make distant objects appear closer. *You need a telescope to study astronomy.*

SIGN: Vertical left **'C'** hand, palm facing right, is held in a fixed position in front of the right eye while the vertical right **'C'** hand, palm facing left, is held just in front of the left hand and is moved forward at an upward slant and then back to its initial position.

teletypewriter: *n.* an apparatus used by the Deaf to send a typewritten message to a print receiver. *Deaf people use a TTY to make phone calls.*

SIGN: Fingerspell **TTY**.

television: *n.* a device designed to receive and transmit visible images. *She watches television during the day.*

SIGN: Fingerspell **TV**.

tell: *v.* to inform, let know or notify. *The conductor can tell you how late the train will be.*

SIGN #1: Tip of forefinger of right **'BENT ONE'** hand, palm toward the body, is held just under the chin and flicked forward, thus creating a **'ONE'** hand. (Signs vary according to which person is being told. For **tell me**, the tip of the forefinger touches the chin first, then slides down to the upper chest.)

(be able to) tell: *v.* to be able to realize or recognize (something) through observation. *I am able to tell you are not paying attention.*

SIGN #2: Fingertips of right **'EXTENDED B'** hand, palm toward the head, are tapped against right side of forehead.

(be unable to) tell: *v.* to be unable to realize or recognize (something) through observation. *I am unable to tell if you are paying attention.*

SIGN #3: The fingertips of the right **'EXTENDED B'** (or **'BENT EXTENDED B'**) hand, palm toward the face, are placed on the forehead or in the area of the right cheekbone, and the hand is then curved to the right with the palm facing down.

teller: *n.* a bank cashier. *He works in the bank as a teller.*

SIGN: Fingerspell **TELLER**.

(have a bad) temper: *v.* to tend to become enraged easily. *I am afraid to tell him the truth because he has a bad temper.*

SIGN #1: Right **'CLAWED 5'** hand is held with fingertips touching or close to the lips. The wrist then rotates briskly causing the palm to face leftward/downward. Next, tip of forefinger of right **'CROOKED ONE'** hand, palm toward the head, is tapped against right side of forehead a couple of times.
(ASL CONCEPT—**hot - brain**.)

(lose one's) temper: *v.* to become enraged; show extreme anger. *He lost his temper when he found out that his tires were slashed.*

SIGN #2: Right **'CROOKED 5'** hand is placed palm down on the left horizontal **'S'** hand of which the palm faces the body. Then the right hand is forcefully raised a fair distance with the fingers fluttering and is returned to its original position.

temperature: *n.* the degree of warmth as measured on a standard scale. *During January the temperature is often well below 0°C.*

SIGN #1: Vertical right **'ONE'** hand, palm forward, is placed against right facing palm of vertical left **'EXTENDED B'** hand and is moved up and down a couple of times.
ALTERNATE SIGN—**thermometer** #1

temperature: *n.* a higher than normal body temperature; fever. *If the child has a temperature, you should phone the doctor.*

SIGN #2: Fingerspell **FEVER**.

temple: *n.* a church or building dedicated to worship. *They visited the Mormon Temple at Cardston.*

SIGN #1: Horizontal right **'T'** hand, palm facing forward/leftward, is tapped a couple of times on the back of the left **'S'** hand of which the palm is facing downward.

temple: *n.* the flat area on either side of the head between the forehead and the ear. *I can see the pulse beat in her right temple.*

SIGN #2: Vertical right **'CROOKED ONE'** hand, palm facing left and tip of forefinger touching the right temple, is moved back and forth slightly at least twice.

temporary: *adj.* provisional; lasting only for a while; not permanent. *It is just a temporary job.*

SIGN: Horizontal left **'U'** hand is held in a fixed position with palm facing rightward/backward and extended fingers pointing forward/rightward. Horizontal right **'U'** hand, palm facing leftward/backward, is positioned with extended fingers pointing forward/leftward and resting on those of the left hand at right angles to them. The right hand then moves back and forth a few times, the extended fingers sliding along those of the left hand.

tempt: *v.* to entice, allure or attract. *Do not tempt me to eat candy because I am trying to lose weight.*

SIGN: Tip of forefinger of right **'CROOKED ONE'** hand, palm toward the body, is tapped a couple of times on the bent left elbow.
SAME SIGN—**temptation**, *n.;* **tempting**, *adj.*

ten: *n.* See NUMBERS, p. LX.

tenacious: *adj.* holding firmly; stubborn; persistent. *She was tenacious in her opinion that it was not her fault.*

SIGN: Thumb of vertical right **'EXTENDED B'** hand, palm forward, is placed near the right temple and the fingers are firmly lowered to form a **'BENT EXTENDED B'** hand. A look of fierce determination accompanies this sign.
SAME SIGN—**tenacity**, *n.*

tenant: *n.* someone who occupies property owned by a landlord. *The owner of the house will evict the tenant for not paying the rent.*

SIGN: Fingerspell **TENANT**.

tend: *v.* to take care of; attend to. *Someone else will tend the baby while his parents are working.*

SIGN: Horizontal **'K'** (or **'V'**) hands are held, right above left, with extended fingers pointing forward, the left palm facing rightward and the right palm facing leftward. The hands are brought together to strike each other a couple of times.

tend to: *v.* to be inclined to. *Deaf people tend to socialize mainly with other Deaf people.*

SIGN: Tip of middle finger of right **'BENT MIDFINGER 5'** hand, palm toward the body, is placed on the right side of the chest and the hand is drawn away abruptly. An essential feature of this sign is the release of a puff of air from the lips as if whispering a 'P'. (Two hands may be used for this sign, with the left hand just below that of the right.)
SAME SIGN— **tendency**, *n.*

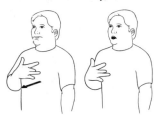

tender: *adj.* soft; gentle. *The baby has tender skin.*

SIGN #1: **'CONTRACTED 5'** hands are held slightly apart with palms up and are drawn downward a few times as they are changed to **'FLAT O'** hands. (Sign choice depends on context.)

tender: *adj.* sore; painful. *My broken arm has almost healed but it is still a bit tender.*

SIGN #2: Thumb of right **'A'** hand, palm facing left, is pressed against the chin as the wrist rotates to twist the hand so that the palm is toward the body.

tender: *n.* an offer to supply goods and/or service for a stated fee. *We got the job because our company made the most reasonable tender.*

SIGN #3: **'EXTENDED B'** hands, palms up and fingers pointing forward, are held slightly apart with the right just ahead of the left, and are simultaneously thrust forward in an arc.

tender one's resignation: *v.* to submit a letter indicating one's intention to resign. *I will tender my resignation at the end of the month.*

SIGN #4: Right **'EXTENDED B'** hand, with palm up and fingers pointing forward, is moved purposefully forward in a slight arc as if handing something to someone. Next, extended fingers of right **'CLAWED U'** hand, palm down, are inserted into an opening created in the left horizontal **'S'** hand. The right hand is then drawn back toward the body. (ASL CONCEPT— **hand in - quit**.)

tennis: *n.* a racquet sport played on a rectangular court. *They are going to play tennis this afternoon.*

SIGN: Right **'A'** (or **'S'**) hand, palm left, is swung back and forth to simulate the swinging of a tennis racquet in play.

tense: *adj.* under mental and/or emotional strain. *She was* **tense** *about taking her driver's test.*

SIGN #1: Horizontal **'5'** hands are held parallel with fingers pointing forward and palms facing each other at a downward angle. The hands are then shaken as the wrists rapidly twist back and forth slightly.
ALTERNATE SIGN—**nervous** #2

tense: *n.* a grammatical inflection of verbs that indicates time. *The past* **tense** *of the verb 'see' is 'saw'.*

SIGN #2: Fingerspell **TENSE**.

T E N S E

tension: *n.* intense emotional stress. *Their divorce has created a lot of emotional* **tension**.

SIGN #1: Palm of horizontal right **'EXTENDED B'** hand is placed on top of horizontal left **'S'** hand of which the palm is facing right, but is angled slightly toward the body. Together, the hands are pressed very firmly downward a few times.

tension: *n.* intense mental stress. *Their money worries are creating serious mental* **tension**.

SIGN #2: Vertical **'BENT EXTENDED B'** hands are held with palms facing each other and fingertips touching either side of forehead. Fingertips maintain contact with the forehead while the wrists rapidly twist back and forth several times in opposite directions.
ALTERNATE SIGN—**tension** #1

tent: *n.* a portable shelter made of canvas, nylon or other material and supported on poles. *We pitched our* **tent** *under the trees near the river.*

SIGN: **'COMBINED I + ONE'** hands are held with palms facing each other but angled downward slightly and extended fingertips of one hand touching the corresponding fingers of the other hand. The hands are then drawn apart with a downward curving motion. Movement is repeated.

tentative: *adj.* provisional; experimental. *Living with my aunt is only a* **tentative** *arrangement until I find a place of my own.*

SIGN #1: Horizontal left **'u'** hand is held in a fixed position with palm facing rightward/backward and extended fingers pointing forward/rightward. Horizontal right **'u'** hand, palm facing leftward/backward, is positioned with extended fingers pointing forward/leftward and resting on those of the left hand at right angles to them. The right hand then moves back and forth a few times, the extended fingers sliding along those of the left hand.

tentative: *adj.* as yet unconfirmed. *We have made* **tentative** *plans for the trip.*

SIGN #2: Fingerspell **TENTATIVE**. (Alternatively, various signs or sign combinations such as **(not) yet** #1 **+ decide** may be used for this concept. The face must convey indecision.)

T E N T A T I V E

tenuous: *adj.* flimsy; not strong. *There is only the most* **tenuous** *evidence that he is guilty.*

SIGN: Fingertips of right **'5'** hand, palm toward the body, are placed on upturned palm of left **'EXTENDED B'** hand. Then the fingers buckle so that the hand is transformed into a **'CLAWED 5'** shape.

tenure: *n.* the security of one's status as an employee. *All staff without* **tenure** *will be laid off.*

SIGN: Fingerspell **TENURE**.

T E N U R E

747

term: *n.* a period of time such as a division of an academic school year. *He has registered for the fall term.*

SIGN #1: Fingerspell **TERM**. (Alternatively, various signs may be used, depending on the context.)

term: *n.* a word with a specific meaning. *He was not familiar with this technical term.*

SIGN #2: Tips of forefinger and thumb of right **'MODIFIED G'** hand are tapped a couple of times against forward-pointing forefinger of left **'ONE'** hand, whose palm faces rightward/downward.

terminal: *n.* an access point for passengers or freight by various means of transport. *We will be flying into Terminal 2 at Pearson International Airport in Toronto.*

SIGN #1: Fingerspell **TERMINAL**. (It is unnecessary to fingerspell this word when it is already mutually understood in a given sentence. If both the signer and the signee are aware that the signee will be at the bus terminal at 4:00 p.m., the signer might say in English: *I will pick you up at the bus terminal at 4:00 p.m.,* but in ASL he would say *ME PICK-YOU-UP BUS 4:00 AFTERNOON.*)

terminal: *adj.* ending in death. *She was devastated when the doctor informed her that she had a terminal illness.*

SIGN #2: Right **'EXTENDED B'** hand, palm facing left, is held in a vertical position near the right side of the head. The forearm is then moved forward a short distance so that the fingers eventually point forward/upward. Next, right **'EXTENDED B'** hand is held palm down with fingers pointing forward. The wrist then rotates rightward, turning the hand palm upward. (ASL CONCEPT—**will - die.**)

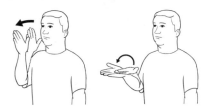

terminate: *v.* to conclude; put an end to. *The company will terminate your contract if your performance does not improve.*

SIGN: Left horizontal **'BENT EXTENDED B'** hand is held in a fixed position with palm facing the body and fingers pointing rightward. Right horizontal **'EXTENDED B'** hand, palm facing left and fingers pointing forward, makes a chopping motion near the fingertips of the left hand.
ALTERNATE SIGN—**stop**

terminology: *n.* specialized words related to a specific topic. *We could not understand the complex medical terminology in the report.*

SIGN: Tips of forefinger and thumb of right **'MODIFIED G'** hand are tapped a couple of times against forward-pointing forefinger of left **'ONE'** hand, whose palm faces rightward/downward.
ALTERNATE SIGN—**vocabulary**

terms: *n.* conditions of an agreement. *The lawyer explained the terms of the contract.*

SIGN #1: Vertical left **'ONE'** hand is held in a fixed position with palm facing rightward/forward. Horizontal right **'ONE'** hand is held behind left hand with palm facing left. The hands then move simultaneously downward.

(be on good) terms: *v.* to get along well together. *He is on good terms with his neighbour.*

SIGN #2: Horizontal **'BENT EXTENDED B'** hands are held parallel with palms facing, and are simultaneously moved forward.

terrible: *adj.* dreadful; severe; intense. *There was a terrible storm last night.*

SIGN: Thumb and forefinger of vertical right **'COVERED 8'** hand, which is held near right side of face with palm facing left, are snapped open and thrust slightly forward to form a **'MODIFIED 5'** hand. This sign can be made with either one or two hands, one at either side of the face.

terrific: *adj.* an informal expression for very good or excellent. *That was a terrific meal.*

SIGN: Vertical **'EXTENDED B'** hands, palms facing forward, are held apart near the face. Forearms are pushed purposefully forward a short distance.

terrified: *adj.* very frightened. *I am terrified of spiders.*

SIGN: Horizontal **'5'** hands, palms toward the body, are held out from either side of the chest, and are moved vigorously toward each other, stopping abruptly in front of the chest. Facial expression is important.

territory: *n.* a general geographical area or region. *The soldiers crossed the border into enemy territory.*

SIGN #1: Right **'5'** hand, palm down, is circled in a counter-clockwise motion.

Territory: *n.* a specific region of a country that has not yet achieved provincial status. (In this context, **Territory** is always capitalized.) *The Yukon Territory of Canada borders Alaska.*

SIGN #2: Fingerspell **TERRITORY**.

terror: *n.* great fear. *News of the convict's escape created terror in the community.*

SIGN: Horizontal **'5'** hands, palms toward the body, are held out from either side of the chest, and are moved vigorously toward each other, stopping abruptly in front of the chest. Facial expression is important.

terrorism: *n.* the systematic use of violent acts to achieve a goal. *Hijacking became a common act of terrorism during the 1970s.*

SIGN: Fingerspell **TERRORISM**. (**TERRORIST** is also fingerspelled.)

test: *n.* a set of questions or problems designed to determine one's knowledge or skill level; a method of checking for the presence of a certain substance or condition; an examination. *The students will have a Science test tomorrow.*

SIGN #1: **'ONE'** hands are held parallel with palms forward/downward. As the forearms simultaneously move downward/forward, the forefingers retract to form **'X'** hands. Movement is repeated.
SAME SIGN—**test**, *v.*

SIGN #2 [ATLANTIC]: Horizontal **'F'** hands, left palm facing right and right palm facing left, are positioned with the right hand slightly above the left. The left hand remains fixed while the right hand is circled forward 360 degrees with the joined thumb and forefinger eventually coming to rest on the thumb and forefinger of the left hand.
SAME SIGN—**test**, *v.*

SIGN #3 [ONTARIO]: Horizontal left **'5'** hand is held in a fixed position with palm facing right and fingers pointing forward/upward. Horizontal right **'5'** hand is held to the right of the left hand with palm toward the chest and fingers pointing leftward. The right hand moves leftward so that the fingertips poke into the top of the left palm. The right hand then moves rightward, downward and leftward once again so that the fingertips poke into the bottom of the left palm.
SAME SIGN—**test**, *v.*

SIGN #4 [PACIFIC]: Vertical **'ONE'** hands, palms toward the body, are held slightly apart and are alternately moved up and down a few times.
SAME SIGN—**test**, *v.*

SIGN #5 [PRAIRIE]: Left forearm is held parallel to the chest with the palm down as the right elbow is placed on the back of the left hand. The right hand assumes a vertical **'ONE'** shape with palm facing backward as the forearm is circled twice in a counter-clockwise direction.
SAME SIGN—**test**, *v.*

testicles: *n.* the two male reproductive glands. *Football players wear protective gear to prevent injury to the testicles.*

SIGN: **'OPEN SPREAD O'** hands are held a little apart and are very slightly moved up and down a couple of times.

testify: *v.* to make a statement under oath. *You will be required to testify in court that you witnessed the crime.*

SIGN: Tip of forefinger of right **'BENT ONE'** hand, palm toward the body, is held just under the chin and flicked forward, thus creating a **'ONE'** hand.
ALTERNATE SIGN—**explain**

testimony: *n.* a declaration of truth or fact. *Your testimony will be required during the trial.*

SIGN: **'F'** hands are held horizontally with palms facing each other, and are alternately moved backward and forward. Motion is repeated.

testy: *adj.* irritable; grouchy; touchy. *As he grew older, my grandfather became rather testy.*

SIGN: Right vertical **'CROOKED 5'** hand is held with palm toward the face as the fingers rapidly alternate between a relaxed state (**'CROOKED 5'**) and a clawed state (**'CLAWED SPREAD C'**). This sign is accompanied by an appropriate facial expression.

textbook: *n.* a book used as a standard source of information on a particular subject. *This is the authorized textbook for the course.*

SIGN: First, **TEXT** may be fingerspelled although this is not always the case. Then horizontal **'EXTENDED B'** hands, palms together, fingers pointing forward, are opened to the palms-up position.

texture: *n.* the composition or surface of something, usually perceived by touching it. *Her hair has a very fine texture.*

NOTE—No specific sign is used for **texture** as the concept is generally incorporated with the adjective used to describe it. In the sample sentence, **thin** would be used as a translation for the words 'fine texture'.

than: *conj.* a word used to introduce the second element of a comparison. *Canada is larger in size than the United States.*

SIGN: Left **'BENT EXTENDED B'** hand is held in a fixed position with palm down and fingers pointing forward/rightward. Right **'EXTENDED B'** hand is held above and to the right of the left hand in a relatively vertical position with palm forward/leftward. The right hand is then lowered from the wrist, the fingers striking the backs of the fingers of the left hand at right angles to them.

thank: *v.* to convey feelings of gratitude. *We can thank T.C. Douglas for Canadian Medicare.*

SIGN: Fingertips of right **'BENT EXTENDED B'** hand are placed on the lips so that the palm is toward the body. Then the hand is moved purposefully forward a brief distance.

thankful: *adj.* grateful; appreciative. *I am thankful for all your help.*

SIGN: Fingertips of vertical **'BENT EXTENDED B'** hands, palms toward the body, are placed on or just in front of the lips. The hands are then moved purposefully forward a brief distance. (Alternatively, this sign may be made with one hand only.)

thankless: *adj.* referring to an undesirable situation where no thanks are ever received; unappreciated. *Being a secretary is a thankless job.*

SIGN: Fingertips of right **'BENT EXTENDED B'** hand are placed on the lips so that the palm is toward the body. Then the hand is moved purposefully forward a brief distance. Next, vertical **'MODIFIED O'** hands are held apart with left palm facing forward/rightward and right palm facing forward/leftward. The hands are then thrust downward and outward to a horizontal position with palms facing. (ASL CONCEPT—**thank - no**.) The ASL sentence is syntactically different than the English one. In ASL: *SECRETARY WORK WORK...THANK NO.*

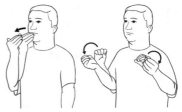

Thanksgiving: *n.* an annual holiday celebrated to give thanks for a bountiful harvest. *Canadians celebrate Thanksgiving in October.*

SIGN #1: Vertical right **'T'** hand, palm left, is held near the tip of the nose and is moved downward and forward in a wavy pattern.

OR

SIGN #2: Vertical right **'CONTRACTED 3'** hand is held with palm facing left and tip of forefinger touching the tip of the nose. The hand is then lowered to the chest as the fingers close to form a **'CLOSED DOUBLE MODIFIED G'** hand. (Signs vary.)

Thanksgiving *(cont.)*

SIGN #3 [ATLANTIC]: Right **'BENT EXTENDED B'** hand, fingertips pointing backward, strikes right side of neck a couple of times.
ALTERNATE SIGN—**turkey** #2

that: *pron.* referring to someone/something already mentioned or understood; referring to something further away as distinguished from 'this'; also used as an adjective to designate a specific person, place or thing. [See PRONOUNS, p. LXVII.] *That is your birthday present.*

SIGN #1: Horizontal right **'Y'** hand, palm down, is held in front of the right shoulder and is purposefully moved a short distance downward.

OR

SIGN #2: Right **'BENT ONE'** hand, is used to point at the person or thing being referred to.

that: *pron.* used to introduce a restrictive clause. [See PRONOUNS, p. LXVII.] *The book that you loaned me was on the best seller list for a long time.*

SIGN #3: Knuckles of right **'EXTENDED A'** hand, palm facing left, strike forefinger of vertical left **'ONE'** hand whose palm faces right. Motion is repeated.

thaw: *v.* to melt or defrost. *The meat in the freezer will thaw if the power fails.*

SIGN: **'FLAT O'** hands are held parallel with palms up and slanted slightly toward the body. As the hands are drawn apart the thumbs slide across the fingertips, causing the hands to assume **'A'** shapes.

theatre: *n.* the art of drama. *He is well known in the world of theatre.*

SIGN: **'EXTENDED A'** hands, palms facing each other, are rotated alternately in small circles which are brought down against the chest.
SAME SIGN—**theatre** meaning a building in which dramatic performances take place.

theft: *n.* the dishonest taking of someone else's property. *Theft is a criminal offence.*

SIGN: Left arm is folded across in front of the chest. Horizontal right **'V'** hand is held with thumb against left forearm near the elbow and palm facing the arm. The right hand is then drawn rightward at a slight upward angle along the left forearm as the extended fingers retract to form a **'CLAWED V'** hand.
ALTERNATE SIGN—**thief**

their/theirs: *pron.* used to refer to something belonging to or related to people, animals or things previously mentioned. [See PRONOUNS, p. LXVI.] *John and Mary introduced their friend* [or *a friend of theirs*].

SIGN: Vertical right **'EXTENDED B'** hand, palm facing forward, is held in front of the right shoulder and moved in a rightward arc so that the palm eventually faces more rightward.

them: *pron.* used to refer to people in general or to persons/objects/animals already named. [See PRONOUNS, p. LXIV.] *After meeting Steve's friends, I felt I had known them all my life.*

SIGN: Horizontal right **'ONE'** hand, palm facing leftward/forward and forefinger pointing forward/rightward, is swept rightward in an arc so that the palm faces more forward and the forefinger points more rightward.

theme: *n.* an idea that exists throughout; topic. *The underlying theme of the story is that crime does not pay.*

SIGN: Vertical **'V'** hands, palms facing forward, are held apart just above shoulder level, and are curved outward slightly from the wrists as they become **'CLAWED V'** hands.

themselves: *pron.* used to refer to the same people, animals or objects implied in the subject of the sentence. [See PRONOUNS, p. LXVI.] *They never asked for help; they did all the work themselves.*

SIGN: Horizontal right **'EXTENDED A'** hand, palm facing leftward, is swept rightward in an arc so that the palm faces more forward.

then: *adv.* at that time; after that. *The novel was then made into a movie.*

SIGN: Tip of forefinger of horizontal right **'ONE'** hand, palm down, is used to tap first the thumbtip and then the end of the forefinger of the horizontal left **'L'** hand of which the palm is facing rightward/backward. (Use of this sign is rare as it is felt to be unnecessary. The sample sentence in ASL is: *BOOK FINISH... MOVIE.*)

theology: *n.* the systematic study of God's nature and purpose. *She plans to major in* **theology**.

SIGN: The right wrist rotates toward the chest as the crossed fingertips of the horizontal **'R'** hand are brushed off the left shoulder in a slight downward arc.
SAME SIGN—**theological**, *adj.*

theory: *n.* an assumption; speculation; guess. *The scientist explained the* **theory** *behind his experiment.*

SIGN: Vertical right **'T'** hand, palm left, is held near the right side of the forehead and is moved forward/rightward in small arcs.
SAME SIGN—**theoretical**, *adj.*

therapy: *n.* treatment designed to improve a physical condition. *After injuring his leg, he had to go every day for physical* **therapy**.

SIGN #1: Horizontal left **'A'** (or **'EXTENDED A'**) hand is positioned with palm facing the body but turned slightly rightward. Right **'EXTENDED B'** hand is held with palm up and leftward/forward-pointing fingers just under the left hand. The right hand is then raised a couple of times so that the fingers make contact with the bottom of the left hand.
ALTERNATE SIGN—**exercise** #1

therapy: *n.* treatment of psychological or social disorders. *He was in* **therapy** *for his depression.*

SIGN #2: Fingertips of right **'FLAT O'** hand rest on back of left **'STANDARD BASE'** hand. Right hand is then thrust forward as it opens slightly to form a **'CONTRACTED 5'** hand. Movement is repeated.

there: *adv.* in or at that place. *Her husband was not* **there**.

SIGN #1: Horizontal right **'ONE'** hand, palm generally facing leftward, is thrust forward firmly in the direction of the place being pointed out. (**There** is often incorporated with the sign for the verb that precedes it rather than signed separately. **Go there** would be signed in one fluid motion, using the sign for **go** and moving it in the direction specified by 'there'.)

OR

SIGN #2: Horizontal right **'EXTENDED B'** hand, palm facing upward/leftward and fingers pointing forward, is held at about shoulder level and is thrust forward firmly in the direction of the place being pointed out.

(it's right) there: *s.s.* It is in this place. *I know you can not see it but* **it's right there!**

SIGN #3: Right **'BENT 5'** hand is held palm down but slightly forward with the fingers fluttering and pointing in the direction of the person/thing being pointed out. Meanwhile, the signer's upper teeth are resting on the lower lip as if articulating the word 'have'. (This sign is used when the object of discussion is hidden from view or is difficult to see.)

(it's right) there: *s.s.* It is in this place. *I do not know why you can not see it;* **it's right there!**

SIGN #4: The signer's teeth are visible and appear to be articulating the syllable 'ee' as the right forefinger is used to point to the object being discussed. (This sign is used when the object of discussion is in plain view.)

thereabout [*or* **thereabouts**]: *adv.* near that place, around that time, or about that amount; approximately. *I will be there at 7:00 p.m. or* **thereabouts**.

SIGN: Vertical right **'5'** hand, palm facing forward, is circled in front of the right shoulder in a counter-clockwise direction.

therefore: *conj.* thus; hence; consequently. *We know that X equals Y plus 3;* **therefore**, *if X equals 10, Y must equal 7.*

SIGN: Horizontal left **'EXTENDED B'** hand is held in a fixed position with palm facing right while tip of forefinger of right palm-down **'BENT V'** hand is jabbed into the left palm. The right hand then moves away from the left hand as the right wrist rotates a quarter turn clockwise, and the middle fingertip is jabbed into the left palm.
ALTERNATE SIGN—**hence**

thermometer: *n.* an instrument used to measure temperature. *Canadian thermometers use the Celsius scale.*

SIGN #1: Vertical left **'ONE'** hand is held in a fixed position with palm facing rightward/forward. Horizontal right **'ONE'** hand is held palm down and moves up and down as forefinger slides up and down against back of left forefinger.
ALTERNATE SIGN—temperature #1

thermometer: *n.* an instrument used to measure a person's body temperature. *My mother used to shake the thermometer before taking my temperature.*

SIGN #2: Forefinger of right **'BENT ONE'** hand represents a thermometer as it is poked toward the mouth a couple of times. (Signs vary depending on where on the body the temperature is taken. The forefinger of the right **'L'** hand could be poked into the right ear.)

thermos: *n.* a stoppered vacuum flask used to keep the contents at close to their original temperature. *I will bring a thermos of coffee.*

SIGN: Horizontal right **'C'** hand, palm facing left, is placed on upturned palm of left **'EXTENDED B'** hand. Right hand is then moved upward to outline the shape of a bottle. (This sign is used when it is clear in the ASL sentence that the container is a 'thermos'. Otherwise **THERMOS** is fingerspelled as in: *ME NEED NEW THERMOS.*)

these: *pron.* the plural form of 'this', used to refer to people/things already mentioned or understood, or things which are nearer as distinguished from 'those'; also used as an adjective to designate specific people, places or things. [See PRONOUNS, p. LXVII.] *These are your birthday presents.*

SIGN: Right **'BENT ONE'** hand sweeps rightward as the forefinger points at the people/things being referred to.

thesis: *n.* a dissertation based on original research and submitted for a degree or diploma. *She has completed her Master's thesis.*

SIGN: Fingerspell **THESIS**.

they: *pron.* used to refer to people in general or to persons/objects/animals already named. [See PRONOUNS, p. LXIV.] *When the committee finished the interviews, they selected Jane for the position.*

SIGN: Horizontal right **'ONE'** hand, palm facing leftward/forward and forefinger pointing forward/rightward, is swept rightward in an arc so that the palm faces more forward and the forefinger points more rightward.

thick: *adj.* dense. *The gravy is too thick.*

SIGN #1: Horizontal right **'CROOKED L'** hand is held, palm toward the body, with tips of forefinger and thumb at either side of the mouth. The wrist then bends slowly, causing the hand to move forward so that the palm is slanted upward.

thick: *adj.* of specific fatness; great in extent from one surface to the other; not thin. *We barbecued some thick steaks for dinner.*

SIGN #2: Right **'C-INDEX'** hand is held upright with palm facing forward at a slight leftward angle, and is moved very slightly forward. (The signer's lips are squared and appear to be articulating the syllable 'CHA'.)

(as) thick as thieves: *adj.* very friendly. *They used to hate each other, but now they are as thick as thieves.*

SIGN: Crooked fingers of **'X'** hands are interlocked so that palm of left hand, which is closest to the body, faces up while right palm faces down. Holding this position, the hands are simultaneously and firmly moved forward/downward slightly as interlocked fingers tighten.

thick-skinned: *adj.* not easily upset or offended; not sensitive to criticism. *Most people would feel insulted but he is very thick-skinned so he just laughed.*

SIGN: Wrist of right **'CLAWED V'** hand, palm facing the body, rotates turning the hand palm-downward as it is thrust downward, the knuckles of the forefinger and middle finger rapping the back of the left **'STANDARD BASE'** hand on the way past. Appropriate facial expression is essential.

thief: *n.* a person who steals. *The thief has been apprehended by the police.*

SIGN: Extended fingers of right **'BENT U'** hand, palm facing downward, point leftward as they are drawn from left to right under the nose.

thimble: *n.* a metal or plastic cap worn on the end of the finger that pushes the needle in sewing. *A thimble will protect your finger from needle pricks.*

SIGN: Vertical left **'ONE'** hand is held in a fixed position with palm toward the body. Right **'OPEN SPREAD O'** hand, palm down, is lowered slightly a couple of times so that the fingers encase the left forefinger.

thin: *adj.* slim; slender; lean. *If you lose more weight, you will look too thin.*

SIGN #1: Right **'MODIFIED G'** hand, palm toward the face, is held in a horizontal position with tips of thumb and forefinger touching either side of the mouth. The hand is then drawn downward to the bottom of the face. (This sign may be used to describe most things and/or people which are thin. The location of the sign may vary depending on the noun being described.)

OR

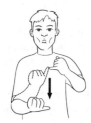

SIGN #2: Horizontal left **'I'** hand is held in a fixed position with palm toward the upper chest. Right **'I'** hand, palm upward, is positioned so that the tip of the little finger touches that of the left hand. Then the right hand is drawn downward. The signer's cheeks are hollowed. (This sign is used to describe a *person's body* only. It means *very thin.*)

OR

SIGN #3: Right vertical **'I'** hand, palm toward the body, is drawn downward, the palm eventually facing upward. The signer's cheeks are hollowed. (This sign is used to describe a *person's body* only. It means *very thin.*)

thin-skinned: *adj.* easily upset; very sensitive to insults or criticism. *She is so thin-skinned that she can not take a joke.*

SIGN: Right **'BENT MIDFINGER 5'** hand is positioned so the midfinger touches the chest and the palm faces the body. The wrist then rotates in a counter-clockwise direction so that the hand moves forward and the palm faces forward/leftward.

thing: *n.* an object; item; matter. *Each thing in the box has been numbered.*

SIGN: Right **'EXTENDED B'** hand, palm upward and fingers pointing forward, is moved rightward in an arc formation.

think: *v.* to have as a thought. *She did not think before she spoke.*

SIGN #1: Tip of forefinger of right **'ONE'** hand, palm toward face, touches right side of forehead.

think of [*or* **think about** *or* **think over**]: *v.* to use one's mind in order to reach a decision; contemplate; consider; ponder. *I am thinking of taking up golf next spring.*

SIGN #2: Vertical right **'ONE'** hand, palm toward the face, is held near right side of face and is circled clockwise with a small movement. (Alternatively, this sign may be made with two hands.)

OR

SIGN #3: Vertical **'FLAT O'** hands are held just in front of either side of the forehead with palms facing backward and fingers rapidly fluttering as the hands move in small circles. From the signer's perspective, the left hand moves clockwise while the right hand moves counter-clockwise. (Alternatively, this sign may be made with one hand only.)

third: *adj.* denoting an instance that has occurred twice previously. [For an explanation of ordinals, see NUMBERS, p. LIX.] *He succeeded on his third try.*

SIGN #1: Horizontal right **'3'** hand, palm down and extended fingers pointing forward, is twisted from the wrist so that the palm faces left.

third: *adj.* coming after the second in terms of things which are numbered. *The third point I would like to discuss is this.*

SIGN #2: Tip of forefinger of right **'ONE'** hand is used to tap lightly the tip of the midfinger of the horizontal left **'3'** hand, of which the palm is facing the chest and the fingers are pointing rightward. The tapping may be repeated.

third: *adv.* coming after the second in position. *He finished third in the race.*

SIGN #3: Horizontal right **'3'** hand, palm left, is drawn back firmly toward the chest.

thirst: *n.* a dryness of the throat or a craving to drink. *I have a* **thirst** *for a tall glass of ice water.*

SIGN: Tip of forefinger of right **'ONE'** hand is placed under the chin and is drawn downward slowly over the throat while the lips appear to be articulating an 'SH' sound.
SAME SIGN—**thirsty,** *adj.*

---

thirteen: *n.* See NUMBERS, p. LX.

---

thirty: *n.* See NUMBERS, p. LXII.

this: *pron.* referring to someone/something already mentioned or understood; referring to something nearer as distinguished from 'that'; also used as an adjective to designate a specific person, place or thing. [See PRONOUNS, p. LXVII.] *This is your birthday present.*

SIGN #1: Horizontal right **'Y'** hand, palm down, is held in front of the right shoulder and is purposefully moved a short distance downward.

OR

SIGN #2: Right **'BENT ONE'** hand, is used to point at the person or thing being referred to.

thongs: *n.* sandals that have a dividing strip between the big toe and the next one. *Thongs are open shoes worn at the beach.*

SIGN: Tip of forefinger of inverted right **'ONE'** hand, palm facing backward/rightward, is slid between the forefinger and midfinger of the left **'5'** hand of which the palm faces down. Movement is repeated.

thorough: *adj.* very complete. *His research was very thorough.*

SIGN: Edge of downward-pointing forefinger of right **'BENT ONE'** hand is placed against right-facing palm of the left **'EXTENDED B'** hand. Then the right hand is pushed firmly downward. (This sign is very context-specific. Signs vary considerably and are generally incorporated in the sign for the noun being described. A 'thorough investigation' would be signed using several repetitions of the sign for 'investigation', often creating a counter-clockwise pattern in front of the signer while the signer's eyes are squinting and the cheeks puffed out. **Thoroughly,** *adv.,* is often incorporated in the sign for the verb being modified. To say that he 'enjoyed something thoroughly', the signer, with lips protruding, would use **enjoy** but make the movement slower and larger.)

---

thoroughbred: *n.* any breed of horses whose ancestry can be traced and is considered pure or unmixed. *The rancher paid a lot of money for his new thoroughbred.*

SIGN: Fingerspell **THOROUGHBRED**.

those: *pron.* the plural form of 'that', used to refer to people/things already mentioned or understood, or things which are further away as distinguished from 'these'; also used as an adjective to designate specific people, places or things. [See PRONOUNS, p. LXVII.] *Those are your birthday presents.*

SIGN: Right **'BENT ONE'** hand sweeps rightward as the forefinger points at the people/things being referred to.

---

though: *conj.* despite the fact that. *Though we were very tired, we continued our journey.*

SIGN: (To translate the sample sentence into ASL, two signs are required, one at the beginning of the sentence and one in the middle to join the two clauses. In ASL: *NO MATTER WE VERY TIRED, STILL CONTINUE JOURNEY.*)
NO MATTER: Fingers of horizontal **'BENT B'** hands, palms facing the chest, are alternately brushed back and forth against each other.
STILL: Horizontal **'Y'** hands are held apart with palms facing chest, and are twisted smoothly from the wrists so that the palms face downward/forward. Sometimes only the right hand is used for this part of the sign.

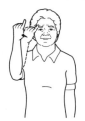

thought: *n.* the result of thinking or reasoning; idea; concept. *His thoughts about his future career were optimistic.*

SIGN: Tip of little finger of right **'I'** hand, palm toward the face, is placed on the right side of the forehead and is drawn forward/upward a brief distance. (For **thought** when used as a past tense verb form, see **think**.)

thoughtful: *adj.* considerate; showing regard for others. *Thank you for being so thoughtful.*

SIGN #1: Horizontal **'BENT EXTENDED B'** hands, palms facing each other, are alternately circled forward around each other.

755

thoughtful: *adj.* showing careful thought. *You seem very **thoughtful** this evening.*

SIGN #2: Vertical **'ONE'** hands are held, one at either side of the face with palms facing backward, and are alternately circled in front of the face. From the signer's perspective, the left hand appears to move clockwise while the right hand moves counter-clockwise. ALTERNATE SIGN—**contemplate**

thoughtless: *adj.* inconsiderate. *It was **thoughtless** of me to forget your birthday.*

SIGN: Right **'EXTENDED A'** hand, palm facing left, thumb under chin, is thrust forward. Next, hands are held at right angles to one another as downturned palm of right **'EXTENDED B'** hand is smoothed rightward/forward across upturned palm of left **'EXTENDED B'** hand. (ASL CONCEPT—**not - nice**.)

thousand: *adj.* ten hundred; 1,000. [See NUMBERS, p. LXII.] *We paid a one **thousand** dollar deposit on a holiday tour.*

SIGN: Fingertips of right **'BENT EXTENDED B'** hand, palm down, are used to strike the upturned palm of the left **'EXTENDED B'** hand.

thread: *n.* a fine strand or fibre of material. *You will need yellow **thread** to match this fabric.*

SIGN: Horizontal **'I'** hands are held with tips of little fingers touching each other and palms facing the body. The hands are then drawn apart. Movement is repeated.

threaten: *v.* to indicate an intention to hurt. *He **threatened** to hurt her if she did not do what he wanted.*

SIGN: Horizontal right **'C'** hand, palm facing the body, is firmly thrust toward the throat to encircle it. SAME SIGN—**threat**, *n.*

three: *n.* See NUMBERS, p. LX.

three-dimensional: *adj.* having or appearing to have depth. *A cube is a **three-dimensional** figure.*

SIGN: Right **'3'** hand is held with palm facing the chest. The wrist then rotates to turn the hand palm-forward as it takes on a **'D'** shape.

thrice: *adv.* threefold; three times. *They have three wonderful children so they feel **thrice** blessed.*

SIGN: Horizontal left **'EXTENDED B'** hand is held in a fixed position with palm facing upward and slightly rightward while the fingers point forward. Tip of midfinger of right horizontal **'EXTENDED K'** hand, palm down, is brushed firmly backward across the palm of the left hand. The right hand then moves upward, the palm turning to face backwards as the wrist rotates.

thrift (store): *adj.* related to a retail outlet that sells used items at very low cost. *She buys most of her clothes at the **thrift** store.*

SIGN: Side of forefinger of right palm-down **'B'** hand is brushed downward against right-facing palm of left **'EXTENDED B'** hand.

thrifty: *adj.* able to save money, shop wisely and not be wasteful. *If you are **thrifty**, you can get by on a student loan.*

SIGN: Left **'V'** hand is held in a fixed position with palm toward the chest and extended fingers pointing rightward/upward. Right **'V'** hand is held just a little further forward than the left hand with palm toward the chest and extended fingers pointing leftward/upward. Then the right hand is moved back and forth a few times so that extended fingers of the right hand are tapped against those of the left with small 'thrifty' movements.

thrill: *n.* a sudden feeling of excitement and pleasure. *It was a **thrill** to win the race.*

SIGN: Tips of midfingers of **'BENT MIDFINGER 5'** hands, palms toward the body, are placed slightly apart on the chest. The wrists then rotate forward as the hands move forward so that, while the palms still face the body, they are now angled upward slightly. See also **excited**.
SAME SIGN—**thrilled**, *adj.*, and **thrilling**, *adj.*

thrive: *v.* to do well; become successful; prosper. *Your business will **thrive** if you work hard at it.*

SIGN #1: Vertical left **'EXTENDED B'** hand is held in a fixed position with palm facing right. Right **'B'** hand is held against the left palm with palm forward/downward and fingers pointing forward/upward. The right hand is then thrust forward/upward. (Signs vary depending on context.)

OR

SIGN #2: **'ONE'** hands, palms down, forefingers almost touching either side of forehead, are raised so that fingers point upward and palms face away from the body. (For **thriving business**, see (**successful** *or* **profitable**) **business**.)

thrive: *v.* to become strong; flourish. *The plants will **thrive** if you follow these instructions.*

SIGN #3: Right **'FLAT O'** hand is thrust upward through horizontal left **'C'** hand, as fingers open into a **'CONTRACTED 5'** hand.

throat: *n.* the back of the mouth and the upper part of the tubes that go down to the stomach and lungs; the front of the neck. *She often has a sore **throat**.*

SIGN: Right **'MODIFIED G'** hand is positioned with palm toward the throat and thumb and forefinger lightly touching the throat just under the chin. The hand is then moved down the length of the throat a couple of times.

throb: *v.* to pulsate or vibrate, usually with pain. *My head is **throbbing**!*

SIGN: Vertical **'CROOKED 5'** hands are held out to either side of the head with palms facing the head and appear to pulsate as they are moved inward and outward a few times. (Signs vary according to the specific location of the throbbing and one hand is frequently used as opposed to two.)

throne: *n.* an elaborate chair used by a reigning monarch on state occasions. *The queen posed on her **throne** for her official portrait.*

SIGN #1: Left **'U'** hand is held palm down with extended fingers pointing forward/rightward. Right **'U'** (or **'CROOKED U'**) hand is held palm down just above the left hand and at right angles to it. The extended fingers of the right hand are then tapped a couple of times on those of the left.

(be on the) throne: *n.* to be the reigning monarch. *Queen Elizabeth II **was on the throne** at the turn of the century.*

SIGN #2: Horizontal **'X'** hands are held slightly apart with left palm facing right and right palm facing left. Then they are alternately moved backward and forward.

throng: *n.* a very large number of people. *A **throng of people** waited patiently for the Queen to appear.*

SIGN #1: **'SPREAD EXTENDED C'** hands are held one just in front of each shoulder, with palms down. The hands are then simultaneously moved forward.

throng: *v.* to move together in a very large group. *People **thronged** to the rock concert.*

SIGN #2: Both **'BENT 5'** hands, palms facing forward, are moved forward and slightly downward from shoulder level, fingers wiggling. ❖

throttle: *v.* to choke; strangle. *Sometimes when my sister pesters me, I could **throttle** her.*

SIGN: Horizontal **'SPREAD C'** hands are held together with palms facing each other and fingertips of one hand touching or almost touching those of the other. Together, the hands appear to vibrate as if actually choking someone. The signer's teeth are clenched.

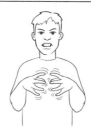

through: *prep.* in one side and out the other. *We drove **through** Calgary.*

SIGN #1: Vertical left **'5'** hand is held with palm facing the body as the horizontal right **'EXTENDED B'** hand with palm facing left is thrust forward between the forefinger and middle finger of the left hand. (Sign choice varies depending on whether it is a person or an object 'going through' and what is being 'gone through'.)

through: *prep.* from beginning to end. *The director went* **through** *the entire play with the cast suggesting improvements in several places.*

SIGN #2: Left **'5'** hand is held in a fixed position with palm facing the body. Edge of right **'EXTENDED B'** hand, palm leftward/downward and fingers pointing leftward/upward, is placed against the heel of the left hand. Then, as the wrist bends backward, the right hand is curved rightward across the palm of the left hand.

through: *adj.* finished; done. *The police were finally* **through** *with their investigation.*

SIGN #3: Vertical **'5'** hands, palms facing the body, are held at chest level, and swung outward, away from the body so that the palms face down.

(get) through: *v.* to make a telephone connection. *I was unable* **to get through** *to his office by phone.*

SIGN #4: Vertical **'BENT MIDFINGER 5'** hands are held with palms facing each other. Then tips of middle fingers are tapped against one another a couple of times. (If only one attempt is made to contact someone, this sign is appropriate, but if many attempts are made without success, the left hand remains fixed while the right hand is repeatedly circled toward the left hand, the tips of the middle fingers making contact with each rotation of the right hand. The facial expression clearly shows frustration.)

(get) through: *v.* to penetrate the comprehension of another person. *I have tried to explain it but I do not know how* **to get through** *to you.*

SIGN #5: Extended forefinger of right **'ONE'** hand, palm facing left, is forcefully thrust forward between the forefinger and middle finger of the left **'5'** hand which is held with palm toward the body.

throughout: *prep.* all the way through. *The storm raged* **throughout** *the night.*

SIGN: Fingertips of left horizontal **'EXTENDED B'** hand make contact with crook of right elbow as right **'EXTENDED B'** hand is held out from the body with palm down and fingers pointing forward. The right forearm is then curved leftward as the wrist rotates to make the palm face the body. (This sign is very context-specific but typical in that it represents a combined form of the preposition **throughout** and its object **night**. Signs vary considerably in that they are incorporated with the 'object of the preposition'.)

throw: *v.* to project something through the air. *I will* **throw** *the ball to you.*

SIGN: Vertical right **'S'** hand, palm forward, is thrust ahead as it opens to form a **'CONTRACTED 5'** hand. ❖ (Signs vary according to 'what' is being thrown and 'how' it is being thrown.)

throw (a party): *v.* to make plans to host a party. *I will* **throw** *a party for them to welcome them home.*

SIGN: **'SPREAD C'** hands, palms down, are held apart and are simultaneously raised as they change to **'S'** hands.

throw away [*or* **throw out**]: *v.* to discard or get rid of. *People are encouraged to recycle and to* **throw away** *less trash.*

SIGN: Vertical right **'S'** hand, palm forward, is flung downward from the wrist as it opens to form a **'CROOKED 5'** shape. Alternatively, this sign may be made with both hands.
ALTERNATE SIGN—**discard** #1

throw up: *v.* a colloquial expression meaning to vomit. *Patients sometimes* **throw up** *after being under anaesthetic for surgery.*

SIGN: Thumb of horizontal right **'MODIFIED 5'** hand, palm facing left, is held at chin while horizontal left **'MODIFIED 5'** hand is positioned just in front of right hand with palm facing right. The hands then move forward and downward in a slight arc.

thrust: *v.* to push with force. *During the fight, he* **thrust** *a knife into his opponent.*

SIGN: Vertical right **'S'** hand, palm facing left, is thrust forward/downward as if stabbing something. ❖ (Signs vary depending on what is being thrust and how it is being thrust.)

thumb: *n.* the short, thick, first digit of the hand. *She is a wonderful gardener and seems to have a green* **thumb**.

SIGN: Horizontal right **'EXTENDED A'** hand is held with palm facing backward and/or leftward, thus highlighting the thumb.

thunder: *n.* a loud rumbling atmospheric noise accompanied by lightning. **Thunder** *is often part of a summer storm.*

SIGN: Vertical left **'ONE'** hand is held to the left of the body with palm facing forward while vertical right **'ONE'** hand is held with palm forward and tip of forefinger touching the face just in front of the right ear. The hands both take on **'S'** shapes then as they simultaneously move from side to side a few times.

Thursday: *n.* the fifth day of the week, or fourth working day. [See TIME CONCEPTS, p. LXX.] *They hold their meetings on the first* **Thursday** *of each month.*

SIGN: Right **'CONTRACTED U'** hand, palm facing upward, is moved in what appear to the signer to be small counter-clockwise circles.

thus: *conj.* therefore; consequently. *He committed the crime;* **thus** *he must accept the punishment.*

SIGN: **'5'** hands are held apart with palms toward the body and fingertips of each hand pointing toward those of the other hand, yet angled slightly upward as well. Then as the head tilts to one side, the hands are simultaneously curved forward/downward from the wrists so the palms are facing up.

tick: *n.* a small, bloodsucking insect. *A* **tick** *is a parasite.*

SIGN #1: Fingerspell **TICK**.

tick: *v.* to make a short, clicking sound. *That clock seems to* **tick** *very loudly.*

SIGN #2: Left **'EXTENDED B'** hand is held in a fixed position with palm toward the body and fingers pointing rightward/upward. Right **'ONE'** hand, palm downward/leftward and forefinger pointing rightward/upward, is held against the left palm. Staying in place, the right hand then rotates rightward in spurts with the forefinger, which represents the big hand on a clock, appearing to mark off the seconds.

tick [*or* **tick off**]: *v.* to put a tick or check mark beside. *He will* **tick** *the item that he likes best.*

SIGN #3: Left **'EXTENDED B'** hand is held in a fixed position with palm facing rightward but slanted upward and toward the body slightly. Tip of forefinger of right **'ONE'** hand, palm down, is placed at the heel of the left hand, is stroked forward to the centre of the palm and deflected rightward/forward at an upward angle. (If more than one item is being ticked, see **mark** #2.)

ticked off: *adj.* annoyed; irritated. *He was* **ticked off** *with all his friends.*

SIGN: Middle finger of right **'K'** hand is brought up to touch the tip of the nose. The hand then turns forward and down as it forms an **'F'** hand. Facial expression must clearly convey 'annoyance'. (This sign is used only in a passive voice situation or as an adjective to describe someone's feelings. It would *not* be possible to use this sign in an active voice situation such as: *His friends* **ticked** *him* **off.**)

ticket: *v.* to give a ticket for a parking or traffic offence. *The police* **ticketed** *him for parking in a "No Parking" zone.*

SIGN #1: Extended fingers of the right **'CLAWED V'** hand, palm down, are used to grasp the outer edge of the vertical left **'EXTENDED B'** hand of which the palm is facing the body.

ticket: *n.* a summons given for a parking or traffic offence. *He got a* **ticket** *for speeding.*

SIGN #2: Extended fingers of the right **'CLAWED V'** hand, palm down, are used to grasp the outer edge of the vertical left **'EXTENDED B'** hand of which the palm is facing the body. Movement is repeated.

tickle: *v.* to touch (someone) in a way that produces a twitching sensation. *The baby always giggles when I* **tickle** *her.*

SIGN: Horizontal **'SPREAD C'** hands are held apart with palms facing and fingers repeatedly flexing as if tickling someone. (Signs vary according to the *type* of tickling and *where* it is being done.)

(high) tide: *n.* the cyclic rise of sea level caused by gravitational pull of sun and moon. *Ships usually leave the bay at* **high tide.**

SIGN #1: **'EXTENDED B'** hands are held parallel with palms down and fingers pointing forward. The hands are then raised simultaneously to a higher level.

(low) tide: *n.* the cyclic fall of sea level caused by gravitational pull of sun and moon. *Ships do not usually leave the bay at* **low tide.**

SIGN #2: **'EXTENDED B'** hands are held parallel at about shoulder level with palms down and fingers pointing forward. The hands are then simultaneously lowered.

tidings: *n.* information; news. *Everyone was excited when they heard the glad tidings that the war had ended.*

SIGN: Right **'FLAT O'** hand is held with fingertips touching or close to the centre of the forehead and palm toward the face while left **'FLAT O'** hand is held farther forward and slightly lower with palm toward the body as well. The right hand then drops to about the level of the left hand as the two hands are drawn outward and the fingers open to form **'CROOKED 5'** hands.

tidy: *adj.* neat and orderly. *Her desk is always tidy.*

SIGN: Hands are held at right angles to one another as downturned palm of right **'EXTENDED B'** hand is smoothed rightward/forward across upturned palm of left **'EXTENDED B'** hand.

tie: *v.* to fasten or bind with string, thread, ribbon, etc. *Please tie your shoelaces.*

SIGN #1: **'COVERED T'** hands, palms facing body, are held close together, circled forward around one another, and then drawn firmly apart as though tying something.

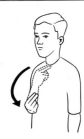

tie: *n.* a narrow length of material knotted close to the throat with the ends hanging down in front of the chest. *Men often wear a tie with a business suit.*

SIGN #2: Right **'BENT U'** hand, palm toward the body, is positioned so that the tips of the extended fingers are touching the base of the throat. The hand is then moved downward in a slight forward arc with the tips of the fingers re-establishing contact at about waist level.

tie: *n.* an equality in score or rating; a draw. *The score was a tie.*

SIGN #3: **'CONTRACTED C'** hands, palms down and fingers pointing forward, are held apart and then brought together.

OR

SIGN #4: Vertical **'BENT EXTENDED B'** hands, palms facing each other, are brought together with a bounce and then drawn apart slightly as they rebound.
ALTERNATE SIGN—**tie** #1

tiger: *n.* a large feline mammal having a brownish-yellow coat with black stripes. *The children like to watch the tigers at the zoo.*

SIGN: Horizontal **'CLAWED 5'** hands, palms facing backward, are placed with fingertips at either side of the mouth and are simultaneously drawn outward/backward a couple of times.

tight: *adj.* not loose; close-fitting. *This sweater is too tight since I washed it.*

SIGN #1: Fingerspell **TIGHT**. (Different sign choices may apply according to the context).

T I G H T

SIGN #2 [ONTARIO]: Horizontal **'ONE'** hands are held right on top of left with forefingers pointing forward and right palm facing left while the left palm faces right. Together, the hands are jerked toward the chest as the forefingers retract to take on **'X'** shapes.

tile: *n.* a flat, thin, usually square, piece of concrete, rubber, linoleum or plastic and used as floor, roof or wall covering. *They are putting new tile on their kitchen floor.*

SIGN: Fingerspell **TILE**.

T I L E

till: *prep.* an abbreviation for 'until'. *He starts at 9:00 a.m. and works till 5:00 p.m.*

SIGN #1: Vertical **'ONE'** hands, palms facing, are positioned so the right is near the chest and the left is a short distance in front of it. Then the right is curved forward until the palm faces down and the tips of the forefingers meet.

till: *n.* a cash register. *The cashier put the money in the till.*

SIGN #2: Fingers of vertical right **'CLAWED 5'** hand, palm forward, flutter as the hand is circled in a counter-clockwise direction to simulate the ringing up of figures on a till or cash register.

tilt: *v.* to incline at an angle. *Please tilt the mirror so I can see the hemline of my skirt.*

SIGN: Vertical right **'EXTENDED B'** hand, palm facing the body, is tilted toward the body so that the palm is slanted downward somewhat. (Signs vary considerably depending on what it is that is tilting and how it is tilting.)

timber: *n.* trees. *Environmentalists want to protect the timber in this area.*

SIGN #1: Both arms drift rightward as right elbow rests on left **'STANDARD BASE'** hand, and vertical right **'5'** hand shimmies or repeatedly twists back and forth in short, jerky movements.

timber: *n.* lumber or wood used for construction purposes. *Timber has become increasingly expensive.*

SIGN #2: Horizontal right **'EXTENDED B'** hand, fingertips pointing forward/leftward and palm facing left, is placed on the left **'STANDARD BASE'** hand. Both hands then move back and forth in a sawing motion. (Alternatively, the left hand may take the shape of a horizontal **'EXTENDED B'** with fingertips pointing forward/rightward and palm facing right.)
REGIONAL VARIATION—**wood** #2.

time: *n.* the duration of a given period, expressed in minutes, hours, days, etc. *The runner's official time in the marathon was 2:19:57.*

SIGN #1: Tip of forefinger of right **'CROOKED ONE'** hand, palm facing downward, is tapped at least twice on the back of the wrist of the left **'STANDARD BASE'** hand.

time: *n.* an era marked by specific events. *The 1940s were a time when many people began to travel to other countries.*

SIGN #2: Right **'T'** hand, palm left, is placed near the right-facing palm of the vertical left **'EXTENDED B'** hand. Then the right hand is circled clockwise and is brought to rest against the left palm.

time out: *n.* an interruption in play during a team sport. *The coach called for time out so his team could discuss tactics.*

SIGN #3: Left **'EXTENDED B'** hand is held in a fixed position with palm facing rightward and slightly downward and fingers pointing upward and slightly rightward. Horizontal right **'EXTENDED B'** hand is held palm down with fingers pointing leftward and is used to tap on the fingertips of the left hand a couple of times.

(behind the) times: *adj.* not up to date; old-fashioned. *The styles she wears are always behind the times.*

SIGN #4: Right **'S'** hand, slightly open, palm facing left, is brought down firmly from the chin as it closes. Then right **'F'** hand, palm down, is moved sharply from left to right in front of chest. (ASL CONCEPT—**old - fashioned**.)
REGIONAL VARIATION—**antique** #2
ALTERNATE SIGN—**behind** #3

(for the) time being: *adv.* for now; temporarily. *I will buy a new car eventually but this one will do for the time being.*

SIGN #5: **'Y'** hands, palms up, are held slightly apart and are simultaneously lowered.
ALTERNATE SIGN—**now** #2

(from) time to time: *adv.* occasionally; once in a while. *We go to California from time to time because we enjoy the climate.*

SIGN #6: As right forearm slowly circles clockwise, tip of forefinger of horizontal right **'ONE'** hand strikes upward/rightward facing palm of horizontal left **'EXTENDED B'** hand each time it goes past. (The speed of movement and height of the arcs depends on the *frequency* implied. The *more frequent*, the smaller and faster the arcs; the less *frequent*, the higher and slower the arcs.)

time-consuming: *adj.* taking up a great deal of time. *Writing long-hand is very time-consuming compared to typing.*

SIGN #7: Tip of forefinger of right **'CROOKED ONE'** hand, palm facing downward, is tapped at least twice on the back of the wrist of the left **'STANDARD BASE'** hand. Next, vertical right **'BENT EXTENDED B'** hand, palm facing backward, is placed near the right cheek and is briskly shoved back toward the shoulder.

timeless: *adj.* eternal; never-ending. *All of Shakespeare's plays are timeless classics.*

SIGN: **'EXTENDED A'** hands are held side by side with palms down and right thumbtip pressing against left thumbnail as the hands are moved purposefully forward. Next, vertical right **'ONE'** hand, palm facing backward, is held just in front of the right shoulder and is circled counter-clockwise. The hand is then changed to a **'Y'** shape with palm forward at a slight downward slant and the arm is extended in a forward/rightward direction. (ASL CONCEPT—**continue - forever**.)

timer: *n.* a device used to measure intervals of time. *He used a timer to roast the beef to perfection.*

SIGN: Tip of forefinger of right **'CROOKED ONE'** hand, palm facing downward, is tapped at least twice on the back of the wrist of the left **'STANDARD BASE'** hand. Next, vertical **'CLAWED L'** hands, palms forward but slanted toward each other slightly, are positioned a short distance apart with a short forward thrust. Representing the face of the timing device, the left hand remains in this position as the right hand, taking on an **'A-INDEX'** shape, appears to turn a dial on the face of the timer. (ASL CONCEPT—**time - clock - set**.)

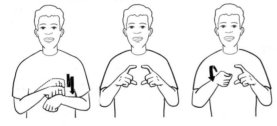

times: *prep.* multiplied by. *Four times four is sixteen.*

SIGN: Vertical **'V'** hands, palms facing each other but angled slightly toward the body, are held apart and are simultaneously thrust toward each other, ending with the wrists crossed

timetable: *n.* a table of events listed according to the times at which they will occur. *Every teacher must follow a timetable closely.*

SIGN: Fingertips of right **'5'** hand, palm down, are stroked downward across palm of horizontal left **'5'** hand which is facing the chest, but angled rightward. Then the right wrist rotates forward a quarter turn so that the palm is turned toward the body at a leftward-facing angle as the fingertips are stroked across the left palm from left to right.

timid: *adj.* fearful; shy. *I am too timid to ride the giant rollercoaster.*

SIGN: Horizontal **'5'** hands, palms toward the body, are held out from either side of the chest, and are simultaneously moved toward each other several times with short, staccato movements. Facial expression is important. (Context must always be considered when choosing signs. When **timid** relates to social situations, **shy** is a more appropriate choice.)

tin: *n.* a soft, silvery metallic element. *Tin is an alloy used in making bronze and pewter.*

SIGN: Fingerspell **TIN**. (Alternatively, **metal** may be used.)

tinnitus: *n.* a ringing, hissing or booming in one's ears due to a condition of the auditory nerve. *Tinnitus is often accompanied by hearing loss.*

SIGN: Vertical right **'U'** hand, palm forward, is held near the right ear and is moved away in a zigzag motion a couple of times.

tiny: *adj.* very small. *It is interesting to watch Deaf children signing with their tiny hands.*

SIGN: Horizontal **'EXTENDED B'** hands are held apart with palms facing each other and fingers pointing forward. They are then moved toward each other slightly a couple of times. (**TINY** may be fingerspelled.)
ALTERNATE SIGN—**small** #5

tip: *n.* a gratuity; money given for good service. *We left a large tip for the waiter.*

SIGN #1: Fingerspell **TIP**.

tip: *n.* the narrow or pointed end of something. *The tip of the arrow was embedded in the buffalo's hide.*

SIGN #2: Horizontal left **'ONE'** hand is held with palm facing rightward/backward and forefinger pointing forward/rightward. Horizontal right **'ONE'** hand, palm facing leftward/backward and forefinger pointing forward/leftward, is held with tip of forefinger close to that of the left hand and is moved leftward to touch it a couple of times. (Signs vary depending on context.)

tip: *n.* good advice; hint. *We gave her a few tips on how to do the job more efficiently.*

SIGN #3: Fingertips of right **'FLAT O'** hand rest on back of left **'STANDARD BASE'** hand. Right hand is then thrust forward as it opens slightly to form a **'CONTRACTED 5'** hand. Movement is repeated.

tip: *n.* inside information. *The police acted on a tip from an anonymous caller.*

SIGN #4: Left **'MODIFIED O'** hand is held at about shoulder level with palm facing upward but angled slightly toward the body while right **'MODIFIED O'** hand is held upright just in front of the forehead with palm toward the face. The forearms then move simultaneously forward/downward as the hands open to assume **'MODIFIED 5'** shapes with palms facing upward.

tip: *v.* to cause to overturn or fall. *Be careful not to tip your coffee mug.*

SIGN #5: Horizontal right **'C'** hand, palm left, is placed on back of left **'STANDARD BASE'** hand and is tipped forward from the wrist. (Signs vary depending on the context.)

tipsy: *adj.* slightly drunk. *He was a bit tipsy when he left the pub.*

SIGN: Vertical right **'SPREAD EXTENDED C'** hand is held near the head with the palm toward the face, and is moved in clockwise (from the onlooker's perspective) circles as the head lolls and the eyes are rolled slightly. (See also **drunk**.)

tiptoe: *v.* to walk silently and stealthily with one's heels off the ground. *He tiptoed so that he would not wake up his sleeping wife.*

SIGN: Bent **'ONE'** hands, palms down, are held close together, shoulders hunched and elbows drawn in, and are surreptitiously moved up and down alternately.

tire: *n.* the rubber covering placed over the rim of a road vehicle to provide traction and reduce shock. *This tire needs more air.*

SIGN: Fingerspell **TIRE**.

tired: *adj.* fatigued; weary. *He is tired after a long day of hard work.*

SIGN #1: Fingertips of **'BENT EXTENDED B'** hands are placed against either side of upper chest with palms facing the body. The wrists then rotate forward, causing the hands to drop while the fingertips maintain contact with the chest. (For **very tired**, see **exhausted**.)

SIGN #2 [ATLANTIC]: Fingertips of horizontal right **'SPREAD EXTENDED C'** hand, palm toward the body, are placed against middle of upper chest and the hand is drawn firmly downward. The signer slumps with fatigue. Head may tilt to one side. (Signs vary.)

tissue: *n.* a piece of thin, soft, absorbent paper used to blow one's nose. *The child needed a tissue for his runny nose.*

SIGN: Thumb and forefinger of right **'A-INDEX'** (or **'G'**) hand are used to cover the nostrils and close slightly toward the tip of the nose as the hand is brought downward/forward a short way. The movement is repeated to simulate the wiping of the nose with a handkerchief.

title: *n.* the name for a work of art, musical composition, or literary work. *The **title** of the book about Ann Sullivan is* The Miracle Worker.

SIGN: Vertical **'V'** hands, palms facing forward, are held apart just above shoulder level, and are curved outward slightly from the wrists as they become **'CLAWED V'** hands.

tits: *n.* female breasts. *Many women are offended when their breasts are referred to as "**tits**".*

SIGN: Fingerspell **TITS**.

to: *prep.* used to indicate a destination. *We are going **to** a movie.*

NOTE—**To** is generally not accorded a sign of its own but is incorporated in the sign for another word in the sentence, usually the verb. The sample sentence would be signed: *WE GO-TO MOVIE.*

toad: *n.* an amphibian similar to a frog but having a warty skin. ***Toads** are more common than frogs in dry regions.*

SIGN: Right **'CLOSED V'** hand is held at the chin with palm down. Then the forefinger and middle finger are flicked forward/leftward to form a **'V'** hand. Movement is repeated.

toast: *n.* bread that has been browned by heat. *She would like some jam with her **toast**.*

SIGN #1: Fingertips of the right **'CLAWED V'** hand, palm down, are placed on the upturned palm of the left **'EXTENDED B'** hand. Then the right hand is inverted so the palm is up and the fingertips are on the back of the left hand. (**TOAST** is frequently fingerspelled.)

OR

SIGN #2: Horizontal left **'EXTENDED B'** hand is held in a fixed position with palm facing right while tip of forefinger of right palm-down **'BENT V'** hand is jabbed into the left palm. The right hand then moves away from the left hand as the right wrist rotates a quarter turn clockwise, and the middle fingertip is jabbed into the left palm.

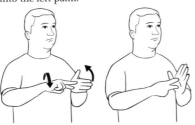

toast: *n.* a tribute marked by people raising their glasses and drinking together. *The Master of Ceremonies proposed a **toast** to the bride.*

SIGN #3: Horizontal right **'C'** (or **'C-INDEX'**) hand, palms facing left, is moved forward as if toasting someone.

toaster: *n.* an electrical device for browning bread. *We need a new **toaster**.*

SIGN: Fingerspell **TOASTER**.

tobacco: *n.* a plant, the leaves of which are used for smoking or chewing. *The pitcher had a big wad of chewing **tobacco** in his mouth.*

SIGN: Fingertips of vertical right **'EXTENDED C'** hand, palm facing left, maintain contact with the right cheek just above the jaw as the wrist pivots back and forth a couple of times.

toboggan: *n.* a long, narrow, runnerless sled curved upward at the front. *He uses a light, aluminum **toboggan** for racing.*

SIGN: Right **'EXTENDED C'** hand, palm up, is placed on the upturned palm of the left **'EXTENDED B'** hand and is pushed forward a couple of times.

today: *n.* the present day; this day. [See TIME CONCEPTS, p. LXXI.] *Today is Wednesday.*

SIGN #1: **'Y'** hands, palms up, are held slightly apart and are simultaneously lowered a couple of times.

OR

SIGN #2: Both **'BENT EXTENDED B'** hands, palms up, are held slightly apart and are simultaneously lowered a couple of times.

toe: *n.* any one of the digits of the foot. *He broke his **toe** when he kicked the football.*

SIGN: Fingerspell **TOE**.

together: *adv.* closely united for a mutual purpose. *If we work together we can finish quickly.*

SIGN: Horizontal **'A'** hands, palms facing each other, are placed together and circled clockwise a couple of times.

toil: *v.* to work or progress with slow painful movements. *The construction workers have toiled at this worksite for several months.*

SIGN: Wrist of right **'A'** (or **'S'**) hand, palm facing away from the body, strikes wrist of the left **'A'** (or **'S'**) hand, which is held in front of/below the right hand with palm facing downward. Motion is repeated several times with short, quick movements.

toilet: *n.* a bowl-shaped, bathroom fixture used for urination and defecation. *Please remember to flush the toilet.*

SIGN: Vertical right **'T'** hand is held with palm forward and is jiggled from side to side.
ALTERNATE SIGN—bathroom #1

token: *n.* a way of showing (something); indication; symbol. *Her students gave her a small gift as a token of their esteem.*

SIGN #1: Tip of forefinger of horizontal right **'BENT ONE'** hand is placed against right facing palm of left **'EXTENDED B'** hand. Together, the hands are moved forward in a short arc.

token: *adj.* simulated; not authentic. *Her chairmanship of the committee was just a token appointment.*

SIGN #2: Vertical right **'ONE'** hand, palm facing left, is held with forefinger just to the right of the mouth. The wrist bends, causing the forefinger to brush lightly leftward/downward against the lips with the palm eventually facing downward/leftward.

tolerable: *adj.* fairly good; adequate. *If you make a tolerable effort, you will likely succeed.*

SIGN #1: Fingertips of right **'BENT EXTENDED B'** hand are placed on the lips so that the palm is toward the body. Then the hand is moved purposefully forward a brief distance.

tolerable: *adj.* able to be endured; bearable. *I feel uncomfortable but the pain is tolerable.*

SIGN #2: **'A'** hands, palms down, are held slightly apart, and are then firmly pushed a very short distance downward. Next, right **'A'** hand, with thumbnail touching closed lips and palm facing left, is moved slowly down chin. (ASL CONCEPT—**can - patience**.)

tolerant: *adj.* inclined to accept differences in others. *His grandparents were prejudiced but he is very tolerant.*

SIGN: Both **'CONTRACTED 5'** hands, palms down, are brought toward the chest while they are being closed to form **'FLAT O'** hands, with fingertips touching the body. Motion is repeated. Facial expression is important.

tolerate: *v.* to put up with; bear. *I can not tolerate his moods.*

SIGN: Right **'A'** hand, with thumbnail touching closed lips and palm facing left, is moved slowly down chin.

toll: *n.* an amount of money charged for the use of certain bridges and roads. *Please have the exact change ready to pay the toll.*

SIGN #1: Fingerspell **TOLL**.

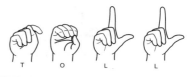

toll: *n.* the number (damaged, hurt or lost). *The death toll from the tornado was very high.*

SIGN #2: Vertical right **'CONTRACTED 5'** hand, palm facing forward/leftward, is held just in front of the right shoulder while the horizontal left **'CONTRACTED 5'** hand is held a little lower and to the left with palm facing right. As the two hands come together, the fingers close to form **'FLAT O'** hands. (Sign choice depends on context.)

765

toll: *v.* to ring slowly and repeatedly. *We could hear the church bells tolling every Sunday morning.*

SIGN #3: Vertical left **'EXTENDED B'** hand is held in a fixed position with palm facing right. Right **'S'** hand, palm down, strikes the left palm and moves slowly rightward. Movement is repeated. The signer's cheeks are puffed.

tomato: *n.* a red, fleshy, many-seeded fruit eaten as a vegetable. *You may use either canned or fresh tomatoes in this recipe.*

SIGN #1: Vertical right **'ONE'** hand is held with palm facing the body and tip of forefinger touching the lower lip. As the hand is then drawn very firmly forward at a downward angle, the forefinger crooks to form an **'X'** shape. Next, fingertips and thumbs of **'C'** (or **'C-INDEX'**) hands, palms facing, are tapped together at least twice. (ASL CONCEPT—**red - round**.)

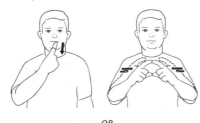

OR

SIGN #2: Vertical right **'ONE'** hand, is held with palm facing leftward/forward and tip of forefinger touching the lips. The right hand then falls forward from the wrist so that the forefinger strikes across the bunched fingertips of the vertical left **'O'** hand of which the palm faces right. (Signs vary.)

tomb: *n.* a vault used for the burial of a corpse. *The Egyptian pharaoh was buried in an elaborate tomb.*

SIGN: Fingerspell **TOMB**.

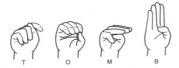

tomboy: *n.* a girl who acts and dresses in a boyish way. *Being the only girl in a family of boys, she was a tomboy.*

SIGN: Vertical right **'T'** hand, palm facing left, is positioned in front of the centre of the forehead and is quickly switched to a **'B'** shape. (**TOMBOY** is frequently fingerspelled.)

tomorrow: *adv.* on the day after today. [See TIME CONCEPTS, p. LXXI.] *We are starting our vacation tomorrow.*

SIGN: Vertical right **'EXTENDED A'** hand is held with palm facing left and tip of thumb against right cheek. As the thumbtip brushes forward against the cheek, the hand tilts downward to a horizontal position.

tongue: *n.* a mass of muscular tissue attached to the floor of the mouth and used in eating and speaking. *He had a sore tongue.*

SIGN #1: Tip of forefinger of right **'ONE'** hand, palm toward the chest, is used to tap the slightly protruding tongue once or twice.

(stick out one's) tongue: *v.* to make the tongue protrude. *The doctor asked him to stick out his tongue.*

SIGN #2: Vertical right **'S'** hand, palm forward/leftward, is held against the mouth and the forefinger and middle finger are flicked forward to create a **'BENT U'** shape as the signer sticks his/her tongue out. (Alternatively, the forefinger only may be flicked out to create a **'BENT ONE'** shape.)

tonight: *adv.* the evening or night of the present day. *We will watch the NHL game tonight.*

SIGN: Wrist of right **'BENT EXTENDED B'** hand, palm leftward/forward/downward, is tapped a couple of times against the back of the wrist of the left **'STANDARD BASE'** hand.

tonsillectomy: *n.* surgical removal of the tonsils. *I had a tonsillectomy when I was two years old.*

SIGN: Right **'BENT V'** hand is held with palm backward and tips of extended fingers touching the mouth. As the hand is then drawn forward, the extended fingers retract to form a **'CLAWED V'** handshape.

too: *adv.* as well; in addition; also. *I am delighted to meet the poet because I write poetry too.*

SIGN #1: Vertical right **'Y'** hand is held with palm forward and appears to wobble from side to side as the wrist twists.
ALTERNATE SIGN—**also** #1

too: *adv.* excessively; extremely; very. *I have too much work to do.*

NOTE—**Too** in this context is generally not accorded a sign of its own but is incorporated in the sign for the adjective it modifies. In the sample sentence, **much**, *adj.*, is signed relatively slowly using a larger signing space than usual for emphasis. Alternatively, **TOO** may be fingerspelled slowly and emphatically in this context. (ESL USERS: Although **too** may appear to be a positive word, in fact it is not. It means 'more than should be'. If you say that someone was 'too slow', you would mean that you think he should be faster. If you say that someone is 'too talkative', you would prefer that he did not talk so much. If you wish to use a superlative which is positive, use **so** or **very**. Saying that someone is 'so pretty' or 'very pretty' would be a positive comment whereas saying that someone is *'too* pretty' implies that you think they should be less pretty.)

too bad: *adj.* a negative expression that implies that you do not care. *If you do not like our plan, that is just too bad!*

SIGN #1: Vertical right '**F**' hand, palm forward, bends at the wrist so that the palm faces downward and in one fluid movement, the wrist rotates to turn the palm leftward as the hand moves rightward. Facial expression is important.

too bad: *adj.* an expression showing sympathy. *It is too bad you can not come with us.*

SIGN #2: Right '**A**' (or '**EXTENDED A**') hand, palm facing the body, is rubbed on the chest with a circular motion which, in the eyes of onlookers, appears clockwise. A look of sympathy accompanies this sign.

tool: *n.* an implement used to achieve a specific task, which may either be manually operated or power driven. *A hammer is a very useful tool.*

SIGN: Fingerspell **TOOL**.

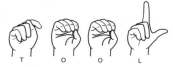

T O O L

toonie: *n.* a colloquial term meaning the Canadian coin that has a two dollar value. *He gave me eight quarters in exchange for a toonie.*

SIGN: Horizontal right '**V**' hand, palm facing left and extended fingers pointing forward/upward, wobbles slightly.

tooth: *n.* one of the bonelike structures set in the jaws and used for biting or chewing. *It is just a baby tooth.*

SIGN: Tip of forefinger of right '**CROOKED ONE**' hand, palm toward the chin, is tapped on one of the front teeth a couple of times. (The location of this sign varies to correspond with a specific tooth.)

toothache: *n.* a pain in or near a tooth. *If you have a toothache, you should see the dentist at once.*

SIGN: '**BENT ONE**' hands are held by the right cheek with palms facing each other and forefingers pointing toward one another. Then they are sharply stabbed toward each other at least twice.

toothbrush: *n.* a small brush with a long handle for cleaning teeth. *I always carry a toothbrush in my purse.*

SIGN: '**BENT ONE**' hand, palm leftward, is moved back and forth rapidly in front of the bared teeth.

toothpaste: *n.* a paste used for cleaning the teeth. *I will need some toothpaste for my trip.*

SIGN: Horizontal left '**ONE**' hand is held in a fixed position with palm toward the body and forefinger pointing rightward. Right '**A**' hand is held upside down with palm facing the body and tip of thumb sliding rightward along the left forefinger. Motion is repeated.

toothpick: *n.* a small, pointed sliver of wood or plastic used to remove food from between the teeth. *He needed a toothpick after eating corn on the cob.*

SIGN: Right '**CLOSED A-INDEX**' hand, palm facing backward, is moved up and down a few times in front of the teeth.

top: *adj.* the highest or uppermost of two or more. *Your socks are in the top drawer.*

SIGN #1: Right '**EXTENDED B**' hand, positioned at about shoulder level with palm down and fingers pointing forward, is waved upward a couple of times from the wrist.

top: *n.* the highest level or degree (of something). *He is always at the top of the class.*

SIGN #2: Left '**EXTENDED B**' hand is held in a semi-vertical position with palm facing right at a downward angle. Right '**EXTENDED B**' hand is held at a higher level in a semi-vertical position with palm facing left at a downward angle. The right forearm then moves downward so that the hand firmly strikes the fingertips of the left hand.

top: *n.* a child's cone-shaped toy that is spun on its pointed base. *They gave their young son a top for his birthday.*

SIGN #3: Right **'CLOSED A-INDEX'** hand is held in an inverted position with palm facing backward/rightward and is moved up and down a few times as if causing a top to spin.

top: *n.* a garment such as a blouse or sweater worn on the upper body. *I want to buy a new top to go with this skirt.*

SIGN #4: Horizontal **'CROOKED 5'** hands are held with palms facing the body and fingertips touching either side of upper chest. Then the hands are simultaneously moved down to waist level.

topic: *n.* the theme or subject of a speech, conversation, or piece of writing. *She explained the topic of the essay to her teacher.*

SIGN: Vertical **'V'** hands, palms facing forward, are held apart just above shoulder level, and are curved outward slightly from the wrists as they become **'CLAWED V'** hands.

(off) topic: *adj.* not relevant to a specific subject or theme. *Most of his arguments are off topic.*

SIGN: Left **'ONE'** hand, palm facing rightward/forward, is held upright and remains fixed as tip of forefinger of right **'BENT ONE'** hand flicks leftward/backward off tip of left forefinger.

toque: *n.* a knitted, round brimless hat fitted closely over the head and ears. *If you go skiing, be sure to wear a warm toque.*

SIGN: **'A'** hands, palms toward the head, are held against the sides of the head and are simultaneously drawn down toward the ears as if putting on a toque.

torch: *n.* a portable flame. *The Olympic torch shone brightly at the Opening Ceremonies.*

SIGN: Horizontal left **'S'** hand, palm facing right, is held against the left-facing right wrist as the fingers of the vertical right **'5'** hand flutter.

torment: *v.* to afflict with great pain, suffering, anguish, or torture. *The boy torments the cat by pulling its tail all the time.*

SIGN: **'FLAT O'** hands, with palms up, are positioned so that the right hand is just in front of the mouth or chin while the left hand is a little lower and farther ahead. The thumbs slide across the fingers several times thus causing the handshapes to alternate between **'FLAT O'** and **'OFFSET O'**. Movement is repeated. Meanwhile, the signer's lips are protruded into a square shape with the closed teeth exposed. Facial expression is menacing. ❖
ALTERNATE SIGN—**pick on**

(be) torn: *v.* to feel anxiety because you cannot decide between two alternatives. *She is torn between leaving her home in Newfoundland and accepting a job in New Brunswick.*

SIGN: **'5'** hands, palms up, are held apart and are alternately moved back and forth as if weights are resting on them. The head may swivel from side to side as a look of indecision appears on the signer's face.

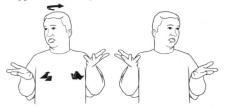

tornado: *n.* a violent storm characterized by funnel-shaped clouds and strong, whirling winds. *The tornado destroyed many homes.*

SIGN: **'BENT ONE'** hands are held right above left, the forefinger of the right hand pointing downward and that of the left hand pointing upward. Both hands move forward as they twirl in a counter-clockwise direction, the right forefinger revolving around the left as they spin.

torpedo: *n.* an explosive, cylindrical weapon launched from a plane, ship or submarine to follow an underwater path toward a target. *The German torpedo sank the Allied battleship.*

SIGN: Right **'ONE'** hand is held palm down with forefinger pointing forward and is thrust forward under left **'STANDARD BASE'** hand.

torrid: *adj.* scorching hot. *I would not want to live in a country with a torrid climate.*

SIGN #1: Right **'CLAWED 5'** hand is held with fingertips touching or close to the lips. The wrist then rotates briskly causing the palm to face leftward/downward.

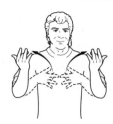

torrid: *adj.* very highly charged emotionally. *This movie has many **torrid** love scenes.*

SIGN #2: Tips of midfingers of **'BENT MIDFINGER 5'** hands, palms toward the body, are placed slightly apart on the chest. The wrists then rotate forward as the hands move forward so that, while the palms still face the body, they are now angled upward slightly.

torso: *n.* the trunk of the human body. *The sculpture will only show the head and **torso** of the prime minister.*

SIGN: Right **'B'** hand is held against the upper chest just at the base of the neck with palm down and fingers pointing leftward while left **'EXTENDED B'** hand is held against the abdomen at the top of the legs with palm up and fingers pointing rightward.

tortoise: *n.* a slow-moving reptile with a heavy, dome-shaped shell; a turtle. *A **tortoise** is a very slow-moving animal.*

SIGN #1: Horizontal right **'A'** hand, palm left, is held under the downfacing palm of the left **'EXTENDED C'** hand. The right thumb represents the turtle's head as it is wiggled up and down.

SIGN #2 [ONTARIO]: **'EXTENDED B'** hands, palms down and fingers pointing forward, are held so the right is resting on the left. The thumbs represent the turtle's legs as they are rotated forward a few times.

torture: *v.* to cause someone extreme physical pain or mental anguish. *They will **torture** the spy to force him to divulge information.*

SIGN: Horizontal **'BENT ONE'** hands are held apart with right palm down and left palm toward the body while forefingers point toward one another. The hands are then moved toward one another as the right hand twists forward and the left hand twists backward so that the right palm eventually faces the body and the left hand faces downward. The signer's mouth is square-lipped as if articulating a 'CH' sound and the facial expression is one of pain. (Signs vary widely for this concept, depending on the type of torture being inflicted and the body parts involved.)

toss: *v.* to throw lightly. *I will **toss** the ball to you.*

SIGN #1: Right **'CROOKED SLANTED 5'** is held with palm facing relatively upward and then moves forward as the hand relaxes into a **'CROOKED 5'** shape. (Signs vary depending on what is being tossed and how it is being tossed.)

toss a coin: *v.* to flip a coin in the air to decide between alternatives by guessing which side will fall uppermost. *Let us **toss** a coin to see who gets the first choice.*

SIGN #2: Horizontal right **'COVERED T'** hand, palm left, moves upward as the thumb is flipped up, forming an **'A-INDEX'** shape. The hand then changes to a **'CROOKED EXTENDED B'** which falls palm downward onto the back of the left **'STANDARD BASE'** hand at right angles to it.

toss a salad (with the hands): *v.* to mix a salad in a bowl using the hands. *I will **toss** the salad just before dinner.*

SIGN #3: **'CROOKED SLANTED 5'** hands, palms facing upward but slanted toward each other slightly, are held apart and are lightly circled outward a few times as if tossing a salad.

toss a salad (with utensils): *v.* to mix a salad using utensils. *The waiter will **toss** the salad after he adds the dressing.*

SIGN #4: Horizontal **'CLOSED A-INDEX'** hands, palms down, are held apart and are lightly twisted upward from the wrists several times to simulate the tossing of a salad.

total: *adj.* the complete sum of. *The **total** bill is over $50.00.*

SIGN #1: Vertical left **'CONTRACTED 5'** hand, palm facing forward/rightward, is held just in front of the left shoulder while the horizontal right **'CONTRACTED 5'** hand is held a little lower and to the right with palm facing left. As the two hands come together, the fingers close to form **'FLAT O'** hands.

total: *adj.* complete; absolute; utter. *He was acting like a **total** idiot!*

SIGN #2: Forefinger of vertical right **'ONE'** hand, palm facing left, is held against the lips and the hand is moved sharply forward. ALTERNATE SIGN—**absolute** #2.

(be) totalled: *v.* a slang expression for 'completely destroyed'. *His car **was totalled** when it rolled over.*

SIGN: Left **'CLAWED 5'** hand is held palm-up while right **'CLAWED 5'** hand is held palm-down to the right and above/ahead of left hand. The hands close to form **'A'** hands as they are slowly brought together and just past each other, the knuckles of the right hand grazing those of the left. The knuckles brush against each other again as the left hand moves firmly backward/leftward and the right hand moves firmly rightward/forward. (Facial expression is important.)

tote: *v.* to carry with one's hands or arms. *Will you please help me **tote** these things from the car.*

SIGN: **'EXTENDED B'** hands are held parallel with palms up in front of the right side of the body. Then they are simultaneously moved in a slight arc to the left. (Signs vary depending on what is being carried and how it is being carried.)

touch: *v.* to use the tips of the fingers to experience texture, temperature and other qualities of an object. *Do not **touch** the stove because it is still hot.*

SIGN #1: Tip of middle finger of right **'BENT MIDFINGER 5'** hand, palm down, touches down on the back of the left **'STANDARD BASE'** hand.

(a) touch of: *adj.* a very small amount or degree of. *We covered the tomato plants because the weatherman predicted **a touch of** frost.*

SIGN #2: Right **'X'** hand is held palm-up with forefinger tightly crooked and tip of thumb repeatedly scraping downward against tip of forefinger.

touchdown: *n.* a scoring play in North American football. *Our team made the first **touchdown**.*

SIGN: Horizontal **'EXTENDED B'** hands, palms facing each other, are held just in front of the shoulders and are raised to a vertical position. (See also **touch**. **Touchdown** is frequently fingerspelled in the abbreviated form **TD**.)

touched: *adj.* moved to sympathy or emotion. *We were **touched** by the boys' courage.*

SIGN: Horizontal right **'BENT MIDFINGER 5'** hand is moved backward so that the tip of the middle finger makes very firm contact with the upper chest in the area of the heart.

touching: *adj.* bringing about tender feelings. *There were many **touching** scenes in the movie.*

SIGN: Horizontal right **'BENT MIDFINGER 5'** hand is moved backward so that the tip of the middle finger makes very firm contact with the upper chest in the area of the heart.

touchy: *adj.* easily upset; very sensitive; irritable. *She is very **touchy** about her failed marriage.*

SIGN #1: Right **'BENT MIDFINGER 5'** hand is positioned so the midfinger touches the chest and the palm faces the body. The wrist then rotates in a counter-clockwise direction so that the hand moves forward and the palm faces forward/leftward.

touchy: *adj.* controversial; requiring tact. *We never discuss it because it is a **touchy** subject.*

SIGN #2: **'OPEN 8'** hands, palms up, are held apart and rapidly alternated with **'8'** hands several times.

tough: *adj.* hardened; strong; resilient. *He belongs to a **tough** gang.*

SIGN #1: Wrist of right **'CLAWED V'** hand, palm facing the body, rotates turning the hand palm-downward as it is thrust downward, the knuckles of the forefinger and middle finger rapping the back of the left **'STANDARD BASE'** hand on the way past. Appropriate facial expression is essential. (**TOUGH** may be fingerspelled for emphasis.)

tough: *adj.* hard to cut or chew; not tender. *This steak is hard to cut because it is so **tough**.*

SIGN #2: Horizontal left **'CLAWED V'** hand is held in a fixed position with palm toward the body while right **'CLAWED V'** hand is held above/to the right of the left hand with palm facing the body. The right hand is then thrust downward so that the knuckles of the forefinger and middle finger rap those of the left hand on the way past. Appropriate facial expression is essential.

tough: *adj.* very difficult. *That is really a tough question!*

SIGN #3: **'CLAWED V'** hands are held, right above left, at an angle somewhere between vertical and horizontal, with left palm facing right and right palm facing left. The hands then come together and strike each other with force.

tour: *n.* a trip arranged for the purpose of sightseeing or inspection. *The government offers a daily tour of the Legislature.*

SIGN: Right **'CROOKED V'** hand, palm down, is snaked forward. (**TOUR** is frequently finger-spelled.)

tournament: *n.* a competition involving a series of contests and resulting in one contestant or team being declared champion. *The Silver Broom is a national curling tournament.*

SIGN: **'CLAWED V'** hands, palms forward, are held slightly apart and are alternately moved up and down.

tow: *v.* to pull or drag by means of a rope, cable or chain. *This truck can tow your car out of the ditch.*

SIGN: Left **'X'** hand is held parallel to the chest with palm down. Horizontal right **'X'** hand is held with palm toward the chest and crooked forefinger interlocked with that of the left hand. Together, the hands then move right-ward as if the right hand is pulling the left.

toward: *prep.* in the direction of. *The child is walking toward the water.*

NOTE—**Toward** is generally not accorded a sign of its own but is incorporated in the sign for the verb. The sample sentence would be signed: *CHILD GO-TOWARD WATER.*

towel: *n.* an absorbent cloth used for drying the body. *You need a clean towel for your bath.*

SIGN: Vertical **'S'** hands, palms forward, are held above each shoulder, as if gripping a bath towel, and are moved from side to side to simulate the drying of one's back after a shower or bath. (Signs vary. Alternatively, **TOWEL** is frequently fingerspelled.)

tower: *n.* a tall structure which sometimes stands alone, or is part of another building. *She works in an office tower downtown.*

SIGN: Horizontal **'C'** hands are held apart with palms facing each other. Then they are moved upward simultaneously. (**TOWER** may be fingerspelled.)

town: *n.* an urban area smaller than a city but larger than a village. *They enjoy living in a small town.*

SIGN: Vertical **'EXTENDED B'** hands, left palm facing right and right palm facing left, are held so that their fingertips can be tapped together twice.

toxic: *adj.* harmful; deadly; poisonous. *The pulp mill is polluting the river with its toxic wastes.*

SIGN: **'S'** (or **'CLAWED V'**) hands, palms facing chest, are crossed at the wrists, with the right hand nearest the body. The back of the right wrist is tapped twice against the left wrist. SAME SIGN—**toxicity**, *n.*

toy: *n.* a plaything for children. *We bought our son a toy for his birthday.*

SIGN: Fingerspell **TOY**.

trace: *v.* to track down by following a trail of clues or information. *The police were able to trace the criminals by following their footprints.*

SIGN #1: Left **'EXTENDED B'** hand is held in a fixed position with palm turned upward but slanted slightly rightward and toward the body while fingers point rightward/forward. Right **'ONE'** hand is held palm down as tip of fore-finger brushes forward several times against palm of left hand. Next, right **'OPEN F'** hand is held palm down. The hand then moves upward as the thumb and forefinger are closed to form an **'F'** hand with palm facing forward. (ASL CONCEPT—**investigate - find**.)

trace: *v.* to copy an illustration by drawing over the lines of the original. *The little girl traced the picture and then coloured it.*

SIGN #2: Left **'EXTENDED B'** hand is held in a fixed position with palm down and fingers pointing forward. Right **'EXTENDED B'** hand is placed palm down on the left hand, then changed to a **'CLOSED X'** shape as it moves in a wavy line along the back of the left hand toward the body. (ASL CONCEPT—**hand on hand - draw**.)

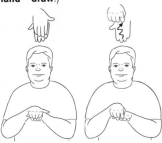

trace: *n.* a very small, almost unnoticeable amount of something. *There is just a trace of garlic in the casserole.*

SIGN #3: Right **'X'** hand is held palm-up with forefinger tightly crooked and tip of thumb repeatedly scraping downward against tip of forefinger.

track: *adj.* related to sports performed on a course for running or on the surrounding field. *He is on the Olympic track team.*

SIGN: Fingerspell **TRACK**.

track and field: *adj.* related to sports events that are done either on a track or a field. *Running, jumping and hurdling are major track and field events.*

SIGN: **'A'** hands, palms facing, are held close to one another and moved alternately back and forth. This is a wrist movement.

tracks: *n.* footprints. *We followed some animal tracks on the path.*

SIGN #1: **'EXTENDED B'** hands, palms down and fingers pointing forward, are alternately lifted and lowered. (Handshapes vary in order to specify the *type* of track.)

(railroad) tracks: *n.* the rails on which a train travels. *The train travelled along the railroad tracks.*

SIGN #2: **'MODIFIED G'** hands are held parallel with palms down and are moved forward.

tractor: *n.* a motor vehicle used to pull heavy loads, especially farm machinery. *My father used the tractor to move all the machinery to another farm.*

SIGN: **'A'** hands, palms together, are held so the left remains stationary while the right is circled clockwise against it several times. (**TRACTOR** may be fingerspelled.)

trade: *v.* to exchange one thing for something else. *I plan to trade my car for a new one.*

SIGN #1: Horizontal **'CLOSED A-INDEX'** hands, palms facing the chest, are held so the right is nearer the chest than the left. Then their positions are reversed as the right is curved forward under the left and the left is curved backward over the right. (When the trading involves *money or something thin like sheets of paper*, the sign is made with **'FLAT O'** hands.)

trade: *n.* commerce; the business of buying and selling. *Trade has improved since we began to advertise.*

SIGN #2: Wrist of vertical right **'B'** hand, palm facing forward/leftward, is brushed back and forth against wrist of left **'STANDARD BASE'** hand.

trade: *n.* skilled work; an occupation requiring skilled labour. *I plan to go into the plumbing trade after I graduate.*

SIGN #3: Horizontal left **'ONE'** hand is held in a fixed position with palm facing right and forefinger pointing forward. Right **'ONE'** hand, palm facing leftward/backward, moves forward, the tip of the forefinger sliding along the forefinger of the left **'ONE'** hand.

tradition: *n.* a custom carried on from generation to generation. *Attending church service on Christmas Eve is a family **tradition.***

SIGN: Vertical right **'S'** hand, palm facing leftward/downward, is held with wrist against back of left **'S'** hand, which is held with palm down. Together, the hands are lowered.

traffic: *n.* the movement of vehicles or people in a specific place. *The **traffic** is usually heavy during rush hour.*

SIGN #1: Vertical **'5'** hands are held with palms together and are alternately moved back and forth so that the palms and fingers of one hand rub against those of the other.

(stop and go) traffic: *n.* the unusually slow movement of vehicles. *I was late for my meeting because I was held up in **stop and go traffic** on the Whitemud Freeway.*

SIGN #2: **'5'** hands are held left in front of right with palms down and fingers pointing forward as they are simultaneously inched forward.

traffic light: *n.* a set of coloured lights placed at an intersection to control the flow of traffic. *If you turn left at the next **traffic light**, you will see the arena.*

SIGN: Right **'COVERED 8'** hand is held upright, palm facing body, as middle finger flicks off thumb and strikes chin a couple of times. Next, vertical right **'FLAT O'** hand is held with the palm toward the body. The fingers are rapidly opened and closed several times, thus alternating between a **'FLAT O'** and **'CONTRACTED 5'** shape. (ASL CONCEPT—**light - flash**.)

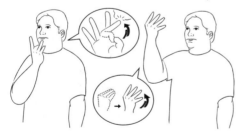

tragedy: *n.* a shocking or sad event or disaster. *The accident was a **tragedy**.*

SIGN: Vertical **'CROOKED 5'** hands are held slightly apart with palms toward the face. The hands are then simultaneously lowered somewhat and the head tilts to the right.
SAME SIGN—**tragic**, *adj.*

trail: *n.* a path; track; rough road. *We found a wonderful hiking **trail** through the Rockies.*

SIGN: Horizontal **'EXTENDED B'** hands, palms facing each other, are held slightly apart and are simultaneously moved forward in a meandering motion.

trailer: *n.* a road vehicle usually towed by a motor vehicle and used either for overnight accommodation or for transporting equipment, etc. *This **trailer** will sleep six people.*

SIGN: Fingerspell **TRAILER**. See also **(transport) truck**.

train: *n.* a line of connected coaches drawn by a railway locomotive. *The Deaf students went by **train** to attend the conference.*

SIGN #1: Horizontal **'U'** hands, palms down, are held so the extended fingers lie across each other with the right hand on top. Then the right hand is moved back and forth several times.

SIGN #2 [ATLANTIC]: Left horizontal **'U'** hand is held in a fixed position with palm facing right. Right horizontal **'U'** hand, palm facing left, is held to the right of the left hand but closer to the chest. Then the right forearm is circled forward a few times as if driving the wheels on a train.

train: *v.* to prepare for a specific purpose; take courses toward a specific end. *She plans to **train** as a nurse.*

SIGN #3: Left **'EXTENDED B'** hand is held in a fixed position with palm up and fingers pointing forward/rightward. Fingertips of right **'CONTRACTED 5'** hand, palm down, are placed on the left palm. Then the right hand is changed to a **'FLAT O'** handshape as it is raised slightly. Movement is rapidly repeated several times so that the right hand alternates between **'CONTRACTED O'** and **'FLAT O'**.

train: *v.* to teach; coach; give specific instruction and practice. *He will **train** all the new employees.*

SIGN #4: Vertical **'O'** hands are held parallel with palms facing each other and are simultaneously moved in deliberate circles which move forward over and over again in place. ❖

trait: *n.* a distinguishing quality or feature. *His most significant **trait** is his honesty.*

SIGN: Horizontal right **'C'** hand, palm facing the body, is twisted in a circular motion from the wrist so that it becomes upright with palm facing leftward as it is brought back against the left shoulder.

traitor: *n.* a person who is guilty of betrayal or treason. *He became a **traitor** to his company by selling information to their business competitors.*

SIGN: Fingerspell **TRAITOR**.

tramp: *n.* someone who gets around on foot and lives by begging and/or finding casual work; hobo. *There is an old **tramp** who lives in the woods near here.*

SIGN #1: Fingerspell **TRAMP**.

tramp: *n.* a slang expression for a promiscuous girl or woman; prostitute. *She is considered a **tramp** because of her lifestyle.*

SIGN #2: Side of forefinger of right palm-down **'B'** hand is brushed downward against right-facing palm of left **'EXTENDED B'** hand.
ALTERNATE SIGN—**prostitute**

tramp: *v.* to walk with firm, heavy steps. *I like to **tramp** through the woods in the fall.*

SIGN #3: **'EXTENDED B'** hands, palms down and fingers pointing forward, are alternately lifted and lowered with firm, deliberate movements.

trampoline: *n.* a piece of equipment on which people jump or bounce. *Using a **trampoline** incorrectly could cause injuries.*

SIGN: Tips of extended fingers of right **'V'** hand, are placed on upturned left palm, then raised quickly and retracted to form a **'CROOKED V'**. Motion is repeated.

tranquil: *adj.* quiet; calm; peaceful. *Walking in the woods is a **tranquil** experience.*

SIGN: **'B'** (or **'EXTENDED B'**) hands are crossed in front of the mouth, left palm facing rightward/downward and right palm facing leftward/downward with the right hand just behind the left hand. Then they are drawn apart until the palms face completely downward.
SAME SIGN—**tranquillity**, *n.*

tranquilizer: *n.* a drug that calms a person. *The doctor prescribed a mild **tranquilizer** for her nervousness.*

SIGN: Tip of middle finger of right **'BENT MIDFINGER 5'** hand is placed on the upturned left palm, and maintains contact with the left palm as the right hand teeters back and forth a few times. Next, **'EXTENDED B'** hands are held parallel with palms down and fingers pointing forward. The forearms are then simultaneously moved slowly and deliberately down and up a couple of times.
(ASL CONCEPT—**medicine - calm down.**)

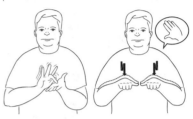

transaction: *n.* a business deal. *The bank's computer records every **transaction** made through the instant teller.*

NOTE—Although the concept of a **transaction** is generally used in connection with business, there is no specified sign because there are too many possible variations in the ways that business transactions could be made.

transcript: *n.* an official copy of a document, record or manuscript. *The university will provide a **transcript** of your record for a small fee.*

SIGN: **'ONE'** hands, palms down and fingers pointing forward, are placed side by side and are drawn apart, moved down, and brought together again to outline the printed page.
(**TRANSCRIPT** may be fingerspelled.)

transfer: *v.* to change or move from one place or thing to another. *The man asked if he could **transfer** to a different department.*

SIGN: Horizontal right **'CLAWED V'** hand is held with palm facing left. As the wrist rotates in a counter-clockwise direction, the hand moves rightward with the palm eventually facing downward.

transform: *v.* to alter in form and/or function. *A new hairstyle and more suitable clothes would* **transform** *her from an ordinary girl into a stunning beauty.*

SIGN: **'A'** (or **'X'**) hands, palms facing each other, are twisted 180 degrees. (For emphasis, the hands will be held farther apart and the movement will be larger to indicate a big change.)

transfusion: *n.* the injection of blood drawn from one person into the blood vessels of another person. *Some people were infected with HIV through blood* **transfusions**.

SIGN: Right **'CONTRACTED 5'** hand, palm leftward/forward, changes to a **'FLAT O'** shape as it is drawn to the crook of the extended left arm. Movement is repeated.

transient: *n.* a person who lives in a certain place only temporarily. *A person without a permanent home is a* **transient**.

SIGN: Right **'CLAWED V'** (or **'CONTRACTED B'**) hand, palm down, is moved forward with a zigzag motion in a series of small arcs.

transit: *n.* the movement of goods or people. *Every city should have good public* **transit** *system.*

SIGN: Right **'CROOKED V'** hand, palm down, is moved straight forward/rightward and back.

transition: *n.* the process of changing from one stage to another. *Canada's health care system is in a state of* **transition**.

SIGN: **'A'** (or **'X'**) hands, palms facing each other, are twisted 180 degrees. (For emphasis, the hands will be held farther apart and the movement will be larger to indicate a big change.)

translate: *v.* to express in another language. *It is sometimes difficult to* **translate** *ASL into English.*

SIGN: **'ONE'** hands are held together with palms facing one another, and are simultaneously twisted 180 degrees from the wrists.
SAME SIGN—**translation**, *n.*

transmit: *v.* to send. *A fax machine is a device that* **transmits** *messages quickly.*

SIGN #1: Fingertips of horizontal right **'BENT EXTENDED B'** hand are placed on the back of the left **'STANDARD BASE'** hand. The right hand then moves forward as the fingers straighten to form an **'EXTENDED B'** hand. (For contexts where a radio or television signal is being 'transmitted', see **broadcast**.)

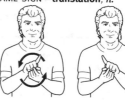

transmit: *v.* to spread; pass on. *This disease can be* **transmitted** *through close personal contact.*

SIGN #2: **'FLAT O'** hands are held with the palms down and sides of tips of forefingers touching. The hands are then opened to form **'5'** hands as they are moved apart in an outward/forward direction.
ALTERNATE SIGN—**contagious**

transparency: *n.* a transparent sheet on which writing and/or drawing can be viewed by means of a projector. *She used a* **transparency** *to present the agenda for the meeting.*

SIGN: **'ONE'** hands, palms down and fingers pointing forward, are placed side by side and are drawn apart, moved down, and brought together again to outline the printed page. (**TRANSPARENCY** may be fingerspelled.)

(be) transparent: *v.* to be easy to see through. *The shower curtain is transparent.*

SIGN: **'A'** hands, palms relatively downward, are held slightly apart, and are firmly pushed a very short distance downward. Next, vertical right **'K'** hand, palm toward the face, is held with the tip of the middle finger touching the right cheekbone. The hand is then thrust forward at a rightward/downward angle. Finally, vertical left **'5'** hand is held with palm facing the body as the horizontal right **'EXTENDED B'** hand with palm facing left is thrust forward between the forefinger and middle finger of the left hand. (ASL CONCEPT—**can - see - through**.)

transpire: See **happen**.

transplant: *v.* to transfer a body organ or tissue from one person to another; to uproot a plant and replant it somewhere else. *He is a surgeon who is highly skilled in transplanting hearts.*

SIGN #1: **'FLAT O'** hand, palm toward the chest, is moved toward the heart so that the thumb and bunched fingertips touch the chest in that area. (The movement and location of this sign vary according to which person and which part of his/her body is receiving the transplant.) ❖ The same handshape is used for **transplant** when it refers to the moving of *plants* but the hand is held palm down in front of the chest and moved from one location to another.

transplant: *n.* the transference of a body organ or tissue from one person to another. *He is scheduled for a heart transplant tomorrow morning.*

SIGN #2: Fingerspell **TRANSPLANT**.

transport: *v.* to carry from one place to another. *The van is used to transport people and baggage to the hotel.*

SIGN: **'EXTENDED B'** hands are held parallel with palms up in front of the right side of the body. Then they are simultaneously moved in a slight arc to the left.

transportation: *n.* a means or system of carrying things and/or people from one place to another. *He works for the Department of Transportation.*

SIGN: Right **'CROOKED V'** hand, palm down, is snaked forward.

transpose: *v.* to interchange the positions of words, paragraphs, figures, etc. *If we transpose these two pictures, we can improve the layout of the advertisement.*

SIGN: **'FLAT O'** hands are held apart with palms down and are drawn together so that the wrists cross. (Handshapes and positioning of the hands vary according to what specifically is being transposed.)

transvestite: *n.* a person who desires to or wears clothing of the opposite sex. *Some transvestites are referred to as 'Drag Queens'.*

SIGN: Right **'5'** hand is held with palm facing leftward/downward, fingers pointing upward/leftward, and tip of thumb touching the middle of the forehead. The hand is then lowered so that the tip of the thumb comes to rest at about mid-chest. Next, thumbs of **'MODIFIED 5'** hands, with palms toward the body and fingertips opposite, are placed at either side of upper chest. The wrists then rotate simultaneously to turn the hands so that the palms face down and fingers pointed forward. Next, vertical right **'Y'** hand is held with palm forward and appears to wobble from side to side as the wrist twists. Finally, thumbtip of vertical right **'5'** hand, palm left, is placed on chin and is lowered to mid-chest. (ASL CONCEPT—**man - dress - like - woman**. If the transvestite is female, the sign would be **woman - dress - like - man**.)

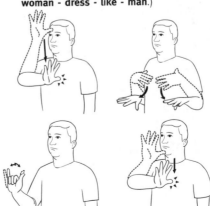

trap: *n.* a device used to capture an animal. *Many people think leg-hold **traps** are cruel and inhumane.*

SIGN #1: **'CROOKED ONE'** hands, palms angled downward, are held side by side, then brought together so that the sides of the forefingers are touching.

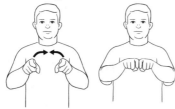

OR

SIGN #2: Heels of **'SPREAD EXTENDED C'** hands are placed together, with palms facing each other but held apart. Then the hands are brought together so that the fingers mesh, thus simulating the closing of the teeth of a metal trap.

trapped: *adj.* ensnared or entangled in such a way that escape is difficult or impossible; stuck. *She feels **trapped** in an unhappy marriage.*

SIGN: Tips of extended fingers of right **'BENT V'** hand are thrust toward the throat.

trash: *n.* worthless thing(s); garbage. *Much of our household **trash** can be recycled.*

SIGN: Forefinger of right **'ONE'** hand, palm facing forward/left, is moved in an arc in front of left arm from about mid-forearm to elbow. As the hand moves, it twists from the wrist so that the palm eventually faces the body.
REGIONAL VARIATION—**garbage** #2

travel: *v.* to journey from one place to another. *I plan to **travel** a lot when I retire.*

SIGN: Right **'CROOKED V'** hand, palm down, is snaked forward.

tray: *n.* a shallow, open receptacle used to carry things. *Please return your **tray** to the cafeteria when you finish eating.*

SIGN: Horizontal **'CLOSED A-INDEX'** hands, palms facing each other, are held apart as if carrying a tray. (Signs vary depending on the size and shape of the tray. Alternatively, **TRAY** may be fingerspelled.)

---

treacherous: *adj.* dangerous. *Crossing the river at this time of year can be **treacherous**.*

SIGN: Left **'A'** hand is held in a fixed position with palm facing downward but slanted toward the chest. Right **'A'** hand is held just in front of the left hand with palm facing left and is circled in a clockwise direction a couple of times so that the thumb firmly brushes upward against the back of the left hand with each revolution.
REGIONAL VARIATION—**dangerous**

tread: *n.* the outer grooved surface of a tire that makes contact with the road. *The **tread** on these tires is badly worn.*

SIGN: Right **'X'** hand, palm forward at a slight leftward slant, is stroked downward several times against the lower right cheek. (Alternatively, see **rubber** #2 for the first part of this sign.) Next, right **'MODIFIED G'** hand, palm forward/leftward is placed on back of left somewhat rounded **'STANDARD BASE'** hand near the wrist. Then the right hand is drawn forward/rightward to the end of the left hand. (ASL CONCEPT—**rubber - layer**)

treason: *n.* the betrayal of one's country. *The spies were charged with **treason**.*

SIGN: Fingerspell **TREASON**.

treasure: *v.* to value highly; cherish. *I have always **treasured** our friendship.*

SIGN: Knuckles of vertical right **'OPEN SPREAD O'** hand, palm toward the body, are placed on the chin and are firmly drawn downward, closing to form an **'S'** hand.
SAME SIGN—**treasure**, *n.*

treasurer: *n.* a person appointed to look after the funds of a society or governing body. *The **treasurer** is in charge of the funds for our organization.*

SIGN: Horizontal right **'EXTENDED C'** hand is moved across upturned palm of left **'EXTENDED B'** hand in a circular, counter-clockwise 'gathering' motion, with the palm toward the body. (Agent Ending (see p. LIV) may follow.)

treat: *v.* to pay for someone's food or entertainment. *I will treat you to lunch tomorrow.*

SIGN #1: As the forearm is lowered slightly, the thumb of the horizontal right **'FLAT O'** hand. palm facing left, is slid across the bunched fingers until the handshape becomes an **'A'**. ❖

treat: *v.* to provide medical care. *I wonder how my new doctor will treat my arthritis.*

SIGN #2: Fingerspell **TREAT**. (**TREATMENT**, *n.*, in this context is also fingerspelled.)

treat: *v.* to act in a certain way toward. *I do not like the way you treat him.*

SIGN #3: Fingerspell **TREAT**. (ASL users are generally more specific. Rather than use **treat** in this context, the signer would specify the actual behaviour. The sample sentence in ASL is: *ME NOT LIKE YOU CRUEL HIM* or *ME NOT LIKE YOU SARCASTIC HIM*, etc.)

treat: *n.* something considered special or delightful. *He always gives his dog a treat when she obeys his commands.*

SIGN #4: Fingerspell **TREAT**.

tree: *n.* any large, perennial, woody plant with a distinct trunk and branches. *This oak tree is very old.*

SIGN: Elbow of upright right forearm is rested on the left **'STANDARD BASE'** hand and the right **'5'** hand, palm left, is twisted back and forth several times from the wrist.

tremble: *v.* to shake; quiver. *When she heard the verdict she began to tremble.*

SIGN: Horizontal **'5'** hands are held parallel with fingers pointing forward and palms facing each other at a downward angle. The hands are then shaken as the wrists rapidly twist back and forth slightly.

tremendous: *adj.* wonderful; marvellous. *I think your promotion to general manager of the company is tremendous.*

SIGN #1: Vertical **'EXTENDED B'** hands, palms facing forward, are held apart near the face. Forearms are pushed purposefully forward a short distance. (Sign choice depends on context. In situations where **tremendous** means 'very large', the concept is often incorporated in the sign for the noun that it describes rather than accorded a 'sign for word' translation.)

tremendous: *adj.* dreadful; terrible; terrifying. *We had a tremendous storm here last night.*

SIGN #2: Thumb and forefinger of vertical right **'COVERED 8'** hand, which is held near right side of face with palm facing left, are snapped open and thrust slightly forward to form a **'MODIFIED 5'** hand. This sign can be made with either one or two hands, one at either side of the face.

tremor: *n.* a quick, shaking movement; vibration. *When the ship exploded in the Halifax harbour, tremors could be felt for many miles.*

SIGN: **'5'** hands vibrate in front of shoulders with palms down and fingers pointing forward. ALTERNATE SIGN—the second part of the sign for **earthquake.**
If the tremor refers to the involuntary shaking of human body parts, see **tremble**.

trench: See **ditch.**

trespass: *v.* to intrude upon the property or privacy of others without permission. *The farmer did not allow hunters to trespass on his land.*

SIGN #1: Right **'EXTENDED B'** hand, palm down, is curved under downturned palm of left **'EXTENDED B'** palm to simulate 'entrance'.

trespass: *v.* to sin; commit a wrong-doing. *Most children are taught not to trespass against others.*

SIGN #2: **'CROOKED ONE'** hands, palms up, are held apart and are circled in opposite directions several times.

trial: *n.* the judicial examination of evidence in a formal court procedure. *The murder trial is expected to last two weeks.*

SIGN #1: Horizontal **'F'** hands, palms facing each other, are alternately raised and lowered a few times.

trial: *n.* a test; an attempt to prove something. *New makes of cars must pass rigid trials before being declared roadworthy.*

SIGN #2: 'ONE' hands are held parallel with palms forward/downward. As the forearms simultaneously move downward/forward, the forefingers retract to form 'X' hands. Movement is repeated.

triangle: *n.* a figure having three sides and three angles. *The students had to find the area of the triangle.*

SIGN: Tips of forefingers of 'ONE' hands, palms forward, outline the shape of a triangle as they are placed together at an angle, drawn apart and downward diagonally, then brought together again.

tribute: *n.* something given, said or done to show gratitude, admiration or respect. *She funded the project as a tribute to her parents.*

SIGN: Right 'U' hand, palm facing left, is held in a vertical position so that the side of the forefinger touches the middle of the forehead. The hand is curved downward slightly and moved forward. (Alternatively, this sign may be made with two hands, in which case the vertical left 'U' hand, palm facing right, is held below the right hand and follows its movement.)

trick: *n.* a prank; joke. *Let us play a trick on him by putting a fake spider in his bed.*

SIGN #1: Fingerspell **TRICK**.

trick: *v.* to deceive; defraud. *I tricked you into giving me the money.*

SIGN #2: Vertical right 'A' hand, with palm forward and slightly leftward, is knocked against forefinger of vertical left 'ONE' hand whose palm faces right. ❖

tricycle: *n.* a three-wheeled cycle driven by pedals. *He wants a tricycle for his birthday.*

SIGN: 'S' hands are held palms down, and moved forward alternately in small circles to simulate the pedaling of a bicycle.
REGIONAL VARIATION—**bicycle** #2

trifle: *n.* a thing of little value or importance. *This problem is only a trifle; it is not worth worrying about.*

SIGN #1: Vertical 'F' hands, palms forward, are held slightly apart and simultaneously shaken from the wrists. (Appropriate facial expression is important.)

trifle: *adv.* a little; somewhat. *I am just a trifle confused about what I am supposed to do for homework.*

SIGN #2: Right 'X' hand is held palm-up with forefinger tightly crooked and tip of thumb repeatedly scraping downward against tip of forefinger.

(a) trifle of: *adv.* a little bit. *Just give me a trifle of your dessert so I can taste it.*

SIGN #3: Right 'X' hand is held palm-up with forefinger tightly crooked and tip of thumb repeatedly scraping downward against tip of forefinger.

trigger: *v.* set into motion; cause. *There are many allergens that can trigger an asthma attack.*

SIGN #1: Horizontal 'S' (or 'A') hands are held slightly apart with palms facing upward, the left hand slightly ahead of the right hand. The hands are then thrust forward slightly as the fingers open to form '5' hands.

(pull the) trigger: *v.* to activate a firearm. *She pointed the gun at the target and pulled the trigger.*

SIGN #2: Horizontal right 'L' hand is held with palm facing left and forefinger pointing forward. Then it is changed to a 'CLAWED L' hand, the forefinger retracting as if pulling a trigger.

trim: *v.* to decorate; adorn. *Every year we trim the balcony with Christmas lights.*

SIGN #1: Vertical 'SPREAD C' hands are held apart with palms forward and are simultaneously circled outward in opposite directions, the right hand moving clockwise and the left hand moving counter-clockwise.

trim: *v.* to cut to a desired size or shape. *I asked the barber to trim my hair.*

SIGN #2: Vertical **'V'** hands are held just in front of either side of the head with palms facing each other. The hands are then simultaneously moved backward toward the area of the ears as the extended fingers close to form **'U'** hands. Motion is repeated. (Sign choice varies according to what is being trimmed and how it is being trimmed.)

trim: *adj.* neat and tidy in appearance. *They live in a trim little bungalow on our street.*

SIGN #3: Hands are held at right angles to one another as downturned palm of right **'EXTENDED B'** hand is smoothed rightward/forward across upturned palm of left **'EXTENDED B'** hand.

trip: *n.* a journey; tour. *The class is raising funds for a trip to Ottawa.*

SIGN #1: Right **'CROOKED V'** hand, palm down, is snaked forward. (**TRIP** is frequently fingerspelled.)

trip: *v.* to stumble; fall (over something). *Many home accidents occur when people trip over objects left on floors or stairs.*

SIGN #2: Right **'SLANTED V'** hand is held behind left **'STANDARD BASE'** hand with extended fingers pointing downward. It then moves forward, colliding with the left hand, and bouncing forward over it in arc formation while the wrist twists causing the fingers to point leftward and the palm to face backward/leftward as the hand comes to rest firmly in front of the left hand.

triple: *adj.* threefold, or consisting of three. *I now receive triple the salary I was earning ten years ago.*

SIGN: Horizontal left **'EXTENDED B'** hand is held in a fixed position with palm facing upward and slightly rightward while the fingers point forward. Tip of midfinger of right horizontal **'EXTENDED K'** hand, palm down, is brushed firmly backward across the palm of the left hand. The right hand then moves upward, the palm turning to face backwards as the wrist rotates.

triplets: *n.* three children born at the same time to the same mother. *The birth of triplets is very rare.*

SIGN: Fingerspell **TRIPLETS**.

trite: *adj.* overused; common; dull. *Her essays are full of trite expressions.*

SIGN: With fingers pointing leftward, side of forefinger of right palm-down **'MODIFIED 5'** hand is held at left side of chin. As it is drawn rightward across the chin, it becomes a **'CLAWED 5'** hand, which is then flung forward/downward and becomes a **'5'** hand with palm down. Facial expression must clearly convey 'boredom'.

triumph: *n.* an outstanding success or achievement. *The election was a personal triumph for the new prime minister.*

SIGN: **'ONE'** hands, palms down, forefingers almost touching either side of forehead, are raised so that fingers point upward and palms face away from the body.

SAME SIGNS—**triumph**, *v.*, and **triumphant**, *adj.*

trivial: *adj.* commonplace and of little importance. *Everyone is tired of her trivial complaints.*

SIGN: Horizontal left **'F'** hand is held in a fixed position with palm facing right. Horizontal right **'F'** hand is held slightly above the left hand with palm facing the body at a leftward angle. As the right wrist then rotates in a counter-clockwise direction, the joined thumb and forefinger strike the joined thumb and forefinger of the left hand on the way past. The right palm eventually faces downward.

troll: *n.* a mythical creature in Scandinavian folklore, usually depicted as a homely dwarf. *In this folk tale, there was a **troll** living under the bridge.*

SIGN: Forefingers of **'ONE'** hands are crossed, left in front of right, in front of the nose. Palms are down, but the left palm is angled slightly rightward while the right palm is angled slightly leftward. The left forefinger points upward/rightward; the right forefinger points upward/leftward. The hands are then drawn apart as the forefingers curl to form **'X'** hands. (Facial expression is important.) Next, right **'5'** hand is held with palm facing leftward/downward, fingers pointing upward/leftward, and tip of thumb touching the middle of the forehead. The hand is then lowered so that the tip of the thumb comes to rest at about mid-chest. (ASL CONCEPT—**ugly - man**. If the troll is female, the sign would be: **ugly - woman**.)

troop: *n.* a large group. *A **troop** of Boy Scouts camped near the lake.*

SIGN: **'SPREAD C'** hands are held upright and slightly apart with palms facing each other. The wrists then rotate forward, bringing the hands to a horizontal position.

troops: *n.* armed forces; soldiers. *The prime minister sent **troops** to quell the riot.*

SIGN: **'A'** hands are placed on the left side of the chest, palms facing the body, with the right hand above the left. Then they are simultaneously moved forward and back to tap twice against the body.

trophy: *n.* an object that is presented as a symbol of victory or success. *The Stanley Cup is the most cherished **trophy** of all NHL teams.*

SIGN: **'Y'** hands, palms facing the chest, are held slightly apart and are brought together a few times so that the thumbs and little fingers touch each other.

trot: *v.* to move at a pace somewhere between a walk and a run (usually said with reference to a horse). *The horse **trotted** around the race-track.*

SIGN: **'CROOKED V'** hands, palms down, are positioned so one is slightly ahead of the other, and crooked fingers are simultaneously fluttered several times to simulate the movement of a horse's legs at a brisk trot. If the context suggests a more sedate pace, **'A'** hands are held side by side, palms down and are alternately raised and lowered.

trouble: *n.* a problem; difficulty. *I am having **trouble** with my computer.*

SIGN #1: Horizontal **'CLAWED V'** hands are held with palms facing the body and knuckles knocking against each other as the hands are alternately moved up and down.

trouble: *n.* a problem; difficulty. (This sign is used to indicate *frequent* or *continuous* trouble.) *I have been having **trouble** with this computer ever since I bought it.*

SIGN #2: Vertical **'B'** hands are held apart in front of the face, the left ahead of the right, with the right palm facing left and the left palm facing right. As the right hand moves leftward and back, the left hand moves rightward and back. Movement is repeated a few times. (The ASL sentence is syntactically different than the English one. In ASL: *BUY NEW COMPUTER...**TROUBLE TROUBLE TROUBLE EVER-SINCE**.*)

trouble: *n.* a state of distress, disorder, or misfortune. (This sign tends to be used most often to refer to problematic behaviour.) *If you continue to shoplift, you will be in **trouble** with the law.*

SIGN #3: Vertical **'B'** hands are held apart in front of the face, the left ahead of the right, with the right palm facing left and the left palm facing right. As the right hand moves leftward and back, the left hand moves rightward and back.

trouble: *v.* to bother; inconvenience. *Could I **trouble** you for a glass of water?*

SIGN #4: Edge of right **'EXTENDED B'** hand is brought down with a chopping motion between index and middle finger of left **'5'** hand. ❖

troubled: *adj.* agitated; worried. *They were troubled by their son's disappearance.*

SIGN: '**B**' (or '**EXTENDED B**') hands are held apart in front of the face at such an angle that the palms face each other but slant downward while the fingers of the left hand point upward/rightward and the fingers of the right hand point upward/leftward. The hands are then alternately circled toward each other a few times. Facial expression must clearly convey 'anxiety'.
ALTERNATE SIGN—**upset**

trout: *n.* fresh water fish which are considered a gourmet delicacy. *The chef prepared a sauce for the poached trout.*

SIGN: Fingerspell **TROUT**.

truck: *n.* a vehicle used for carrying things. *The truck will deliver the shipment today.*

SIGN #1: Fingerspell **TRUCK**.

(transport) truck: *n.* a large vehicle used for carrying freight/cargo. *He drives a transport truck for a large grocery chain.*

SIGN #2: Left '**EXTENDED B**' hand represents the cab of a large truck as it is held with palm down and fingers pointing forward. Right '**EXTENDED B**' hand is held with palm down and fingertips resting between the back of the left hand and the wrist. While the fingers of the right hand maintain contact with the left hand, the right hand moves from side to side a couple of times. This is essentially a wrist movement.

true: *adj.* factual; not fictional or false. *It is true that the Deaf are good employees.*

SIGN: Forefinger of vertical right '**ONE**' hand, palm facing left, is held against the lips and the hand is moved sharply forward.

trumpet: *n.* a brass musical instrument. *The music teacher ordered a new trumpet for the school band.*

SIGN: Vertical '**SPREAD C**' hands are held in front of the mouth or chin, the right hand just in front of the left, with the left palm facing right and the right palm facing left while the fingers flutter as if tapping on keys.

trunk: *n.* a large case or box in which articles can be packed for travelling or storage. *The trunk is full of blankets and tablecloths.*

SIGN #1: Fingerspell **TRUNK**.

trunk: *n.* the main stem of a tree. *Some animals live in the hollow trunk of that tree.*

SIGN #2: Left '**5**' hand with arm bent at the elbow, is held upright to represent a tree. The forearm twists slightly a couple of time. Right '**EXTENDED C**' hand is then moved down left forearm or tree trunk which it encloses.

trunk: *n.* the long nasal part of an elephant. *The elephant has a long trunk.*

SIGN #3: Vertical right '**C**' hand with the palm facing left, is positioned in front of the nose and is curved downward and forward.

trunk: *n.* an enclosed compartment at the rear of a car which is used for holding luggage, etc. *Leave the tools in the trunk of the car.*

SIGN #4: Vertical left '**BENT EXTENDED B**' hand is held in a fixed position with palm facing forward/rightward while fingertips rest against wrist of right '**SPREAD EXTENDED C**' hand whose palm faces downward and fingertips touch the back of the left hand. The right hand represents the 'trunk lid' as it moves up and down so that the palm alternates between facing downward and backward/leftward. (**TRUNK** in this context is frequently fingerspelled.)

trunks: *n.* a male garment worn for swimming. *My husband needs new swimming trunks.*

SIGN: '**BENT EXTENDED B**' hands are used to indicate the length of the swimming trunks as the fingertips brush outward across the thighs. This is a wrist action.

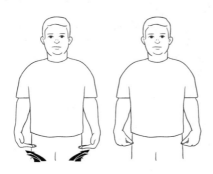

trust: *v.* to have confidence or faith in. *I trust you to put this key away safely.*

SIGN #1: **'SPREAD EXTENDED C'** hands are held with palms toward the body at an upward angle, the left hand close to the chest and the right hand just above/ahead of the left. The hands are then thrust forward as they are snapped shut to form **'S'** hands.
SAME SIGN—**trust,** *n.*

SIGN #2 [ATLANTIC]: Left **'X'** hand is held in a fixed position with palm up. Vertical right **'X'** hand is held in front of the face with palm facing forward and is then lowered so that the crooked forefinger of the right hand interlocks with that of the left hand.

trust account: *n.* a savings account controlled by a trustee. *My grandparents opened a trust account for me when I was born.*
SIGN: Fingerspell **TRUST ACCOUNT**.

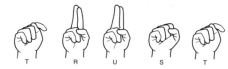

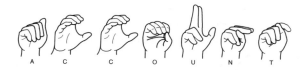

truth: *n.* the quality of being true, genuine, or factual. *Please tell me the truth.*

SIGN: Left **'EXTENDED B'** hand is held in a fixed position with palm basically downward at a rightward/forward angle and fingers pointing basically upward at a rightward/forward angle. Right **'CONTRACTED U'** hand is held with palm toward the body and fingertips of forefinger and middle finger touching heel of left hand. The wrist of the right hand rotates clockwise as the extended fingers stroke the left hand in a straight line from the heel, along the palm and fingers and onward in an upward/rightward/forward direction.
ALTERNATE SIGNS—**honest** #1 and **true**

try: *v.* to attempt; make an effort. *I will try to do my best.*

SIGN #1: Horizontal **'EXTENDED A'** (or **'S'**) hands are held apart with palms facing the chest. The wrists then rotate toward the chest, causing the palms to turn downward as the hands curve downward and forward.

try: *v.* to hear evidence in a court of law to determine guilt or innocence. *They will try him on a series of charges related to the crime.*

SIGN #2: Horizontal **'F'** hands, palms facing each other, are alternately raised and lowered a few times.

trying: *adj.* upsetting; difficult. *He went through a trying time while he was unemployed.*

SIGN: **'CLAWED V'** hands are held, right above left, at an angle somewhere between vertical and horizontal, with left palm facing right and right palm facing left. The hands then come together and strike each other with force.

tub: *n.* a porcelain or ceramic fixture used for bathing. *They installed a new tub in the main bathroom.*
SIGN: Fingerspell **TUB**.

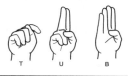

tuberculosis: *n.* a communicable disease affecting the lungs. *Long ago, tuberculosis was treated in special hospitals called sanatoriums.*
SIGN: Fingerspell **TB**.

tuck in: *v.* to place (something or someone) into a confined space. *His mother told him to tuck in his shirt.*

SIGN: Right **'EXTENDED B'** hand is inverted and held close to the waist with palm toward the body. The hand moves up and down as if tucking a shirt into one's pants. (Signs vary depending on the context. Natural gestures are generally used.)

Tuesday: *n.* the third day of the week; the second day of a work week. [See TIME CONCEPTS, p. LXIX.] *The assignment is due next Tuesday.*

SIGN: Vertical right **'T'** hand, palm facing backward, is circled a few times in what appears to the signer to be a counter-clockwise direction.

tuition: *n.* fee for instruction. *It cost his parents a lot of money for his university tuition.*

SIGN: Fingerspell **TUITION**.

tuna: *n.* a large marine fish usually caught in tropical waters. *Canned tuna is an excellent, economical source of protein.*

SIGN: Fingerspell **TUNA**.

tune: *n.* melody. *She will play her own tunes at the piano recital.*

SIGN: Horizontal right **'EXTENDED B'** hand is positioned above left forearm with palm facing leftward/backward. The right wrist makes slight back and forth rotations so that the palm alternates between being angled slightly upward and being angled slightly downward.

tune up: *v.* to adjust (a motor) in order to improve performance. *The mechanic agreed to tune up my car.*

SIGN: Fingerspell **TUNE UP**.

tunnel: *n.* any passageway through or under something. *The train passes through numerous tunnels in the Rockies.*

SIGN: Left **'CROOKED EXTENDED B'** hand is held in a fixed position with palm down as the right **'ONE'** hand, palm down and forefinger pointing forward, passes underneath in a forward motion. (**TUNNEL** may be fingerspelled.)

tunnel vision: *n.* a condition in which peripheral vision is very limited. *Tunnel vision is a symptom of Usher Syndrome.*

SIGN: Right **'BENT EXTENDED B'** hand is positioned against the forehead with the palm facing left while the left **'BENT EXTENDED B'** hand is just in front of the nose with palm facing right. The hands straighten to take on **'EXTENDED B'** shapes as they move outward to vertical positions at either side of the face with palms facing each other.

turban: *n.* a headdress made by swathing a length of fabric around the head. *Certain religions require males to wear turbans.*

SIGN: Right **'BENT EXTENDED B'** hand, palm down, is circled clockwise around the head a couple of times as if winding a turban around it.

turbine: *n.* an engine that produces mechanical energy when pressure is applied against rotating blades by steam, water, or air. *Several large turbines were installed at the damsite.*

SIGN: Fingers of horizontal **'CLAWED 5'** hands, palms toward the body, are interlocked and remain so as they are shaken up and down. This is a wrist action.

turbulent: *adj.* wild and unruly. *The 1960s were turbulent times on many university campuses.*

SIGN: Left **'CROOKED 5'** hand is held palm-up with fingers pointing forward while right **'CROOKED 5'** hand is held apart and slightly higher with palm down and fingers pointing forward. The arms are then simultaneously moved upward/rightward as the hands are purposefully twisted rightward from the wrist so that the left palm faces right and the right palm faces left.
SAME SIGN—**turbulence**, *n.*

turkey: *n.* a large, domesticated fowl raised for its meat. *People usually eat turkey at Thanksgiving.*

SIGN #1: Vertical right **'T'** (or **'MODIFIED G'**) hand, palm left, is held near the tip of the nose and is moved downward and forward in a wavy pattern.

turkey *(cont.)*

SIGN #2 [ATLANTIC]: **'CROOKED U'** hand is held under the chin with palm down and extended fingers pointing leftward as they move up and down. (Signs vary.)

turmoil: *n.* extreme confusion or agitation. *There was great turmoil after the tornado hit the town.*

SIGN: Left **'CROOKED 5'** hand is held palm-up with fingers pointing forward while right **'CROOKED 5'** hand is held apart and slightly higher with palm down and fingers pointing forward. The arms are then simultaneously moved upward/rightward as the hands are purposefully twisted rightward from the wrist so that the left palm faces right and the right palm faces left.

turn: *n.* the chance or scheduled time (to do something). *It is my turn to read aloud to the children.*

SIGN #1: Horizontal right **'L'** hand is held with palm facing left but angled slightly toward the body. The hand is then brought backward against the chest as the wrist rotates to turn the hand upright with palm facing leftward. (This sign always moves in a direction from the person whose turn it is now to the person whose turn it will be next.)

OR

SIGN #2: Horizontal right **'CONTRACTED 3'** hand is held with palm facing left. The hand is then brought backward against the chest as the wrist rotates to turn the palm downward and extended fingers and thumb close to form a **'CLOSED DOUBLE MODIFIED G'** hand with extended fingers pointing downward. (This sign always moves in a direction from the person whose turn it is now to the person whose turn it will be next.)

turn: *v.* to change in nature or character. *The weather is supposed to turn colder tonight.*

SIGN #3: **'A'** hands, palms facing each other, are twisted 180 degrees.

turn away: *v.* to send away or refuse to serve someone. *Potential customers who are inappropriately dressed will be turned away.*

SIGN: Fingertips of right **'BENT EXTENDED B'** hand, palm down, are placed on upturned palm of left **'EXTENDED B'** hand and brushed forward to form a straight **'EXTENDED B'** hand. ❖ (For other connotations of **turn away**, natural gestures may be used.)

turn back: *v.* to retrace one's steps or one's route. *I decided to turn back when I realized I was lost.*

SIGN: If it is a *person* who is turning back, the vertical right **'ONE'** hand, palm forward, is moved forward. The wrist is then rotated so that the palm is facing backward before the hand moves back toward the chest. If it is a *vehicle* which is turning back, the horizontal right **'3'** hand, palm leftward, is moved forward. The wrist is then rotated so that the palm is facing backward before the hand moves back toward the chest.

turn down: *v.* to refuse to accept; reject. *The board has turned down our proposal.*

SIGN #1: Horizontal right **'EXTENDED A'** hand, palm facing left, is overturned so that the thumb points downward. (Sign choice depends on context.)

turn down: *v.* to reduce the volume of a radio or TV, to dim the brightness of lights, or to reduce the power of something. *Please turn down the stereo so you will not awaken the children.*

SIGN #2: Thumb and forefinger of horizontal right **'CLOSED A-INDEX'** hand are used to simulate the grasping of a switch, knob or dial. Then the hand is twisted leftward from the wrist. (Sign choices will depend on what is being turned down and how it is being turned down. Natural gestures are generally used for the turning down of a *bed* or a *collar*.)

turn in: *v.* to hand in; return. *Do not forget to* **turn in** *your report before you go on holiday.*

SIGN #1: Horizontal right **'CONTRACTED B'** hand is held with palm facing leftward/upward and fingers pointing left. The hand then moves forward in a slight arc formation as if giving something to someone. ❖ (Signs vary depending on the size and shape of the object being turned in.)

turn in: *v.* to go to bed for the night. *I am tired tonight so I think I will* **turn in** *early.*

SIGN #2: Left **'S'** hand is held loosely without actually forming a fist while the palm faces downward but is slanted slightly downward. Right **'U'** hand is held to the right of the left hand and closer to the body with palm facing upward but slanted leftward and toward the body while the extended fingers point forward/leftward. As the hands then move toward each other, the extended fingers of the right hand, which are meant to represent someone's legs, are inserted into the opening in the left hand. When making this sign, the signer generally closes his eyes as his head tilts rightward. ALTERNATE SIGN—**bed**

turn into: *v.* to change from one form or condition to another. *If the wind increases, the snowfall may* **turn into** *a blizzard.*

SIGN: **'A'** hands, palms facing each other, are twisted 180 degrees.

turn left: *v.* to change direction so as to move leftward. *Turn left at the second light.*

SIGN: Vertical left **'EXTENDED B'** (or **'L'**) hand is held with palm facing right. The wrist then rotates to turn the palm forward as the hand curves leftward.

turn off: *v.* to leave a road and change direction. *They decided to* **turn off** *the main road onto a logging trail.*

SIGN: Horizontal right **'3'** hand, palm left, is moved forward and then veered either to right or left depending on context.

turn on/off: *v.* to cause something to start or stop operating by turning a switch, knob, dial, etc. *Do not forget to* **turn on** *the stove.*

SIGN: Thumb and forefinger of the right **'CLOSED A-INDEX'** hand, palm down, are used to simulate the grasping of a switch. Then the hand is twisted from the wrist, to the right for 'ON' and to the left for 'OFF'. (Signs vary depending on the type of switch and how it is operated.)

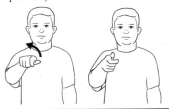

turn out: *v.* to come together (for an event). *A large group of people* **turned out** *to vote.*

SIGN: Both **'BENT 5'** hands, palms facing forward, are moved forward and slightly downward from shoulder level, fingers wiggling. ❖ (Sign choice depends on context.)

turn over: *v.* to change the position of something so that the top and bottom are reversed. *The teacher told the students to* **turn over** *their test papers and begin working.*

SIGN #1: Right **'EXTENDED B'** hand, palm down and fingers pointing forward, is flipped over so that the palm is facing up. (Signs vary depending on the size and shape of the object being turned over.)

turn over: *v.* to give; hand over. *You will have to* **turn over** *the evidence to the police.*

SIGN #2: Right **'EXTENDED B'** hand, with palm up and fingers pointing forward, is moved purposefully forward in a slight arc as if handing something to someone. (Signs vary depending on the context.)

turn right: *v.* to change direction so as to move rightward. *Turn right at the second light.*

SIGN: Vertical right **'EXTENDED B'** (or **'R'**) hand is held with palm facing left. The wrist then rotates to turn the palm forward as the hand curves rightward.

turn up/down: *v.* to increase/reduce the quantity of heat, electricity, volume, etc., by turning a knob or switch. *If you are cold, turn up the heat.*

SIGN: Thumb and forefinger of the right **'CLOSED A-INDEX'** hand, palm down, are used to simulate the grasping of a switch. Then the hand is twisted from the wrist, to the right for **up** and to the left for **down**. (Signs vary depending on the type of switch and how it is operated.)

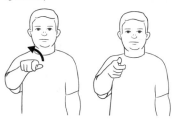

turnip: *n.* a roundish plant with a large, yellow or white, edible root. *Mashed turnip is my favorite vegetable.*

SIGN #1: Fingerspell **TURNIP**.

SIGN #2 [MANITOBA AND SASKATCHEWAN]: Right horizontal **'COVERED 8'** hand is held with palm down just above left **'STANDARD BASE'** hand. Then tip of middle finger of left hand is flicked against back of left hand, thus becoming an **'OPEN 8'** hand. Motion is repeated.

turtle: *n.* an aquatic reptile with a flat shell enclosing the body. *A turtle moves very slowly.*

SIGN #1: Horizontal right **'A'** hand, palm left, is held under the downfacing palm of the left **'EXTENDED C'** hand. The right thumb represents the turtle's head as it is wiggled up and down.

SIGN #2 [ONTARIO]: **'EXTENDED B'** hands, palms down and fingers pointing forward, are held so the right is resting on the left. The thumbs represent the turtle's legs as they are rotated forward a few times.

tusks: *n.* a pair of long toothlike projections hanging from the mouths of certain mammals such as the elephant, walrus, etc. *Tusks are valuable for their ivory.*

SIGN: **'O'** hands are held at either side of chin with palms facing one another, and are simultaneously lowered to chest level.

tutor: *n.* a teacher, usually instructing individual students. *His parents hired a tutor to help him with his French.*

SIGN: Vertical **'T'** (or **'FLAT O'**) hands, palms facing each other, are held parallel at about shoulder level and are simultaneously moved back and forth slightly a couple of times. (**TUTOR** may be fingerspelled.)

tuxedo: *n.* a man's formal evening attire. *Each man in the wedding party wore a tuxedo.*

SIGN: **'S'** hands, palms toward the body, are crossed at the wrists and placed on the upper chest just below the chin. The forefingers and middle fingers then flick outward to form **'U'** hands. (**Tuxedo** is frequently fingerspelled in the abbreviated form **TUX**.)

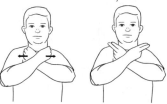

twelve: *n.* See NUMBERS, p. LX.

twenty: *n.* See NUMBERS, p. LXI.

twice: *adv.* two times; on two occasions. *Please check your work twice before you submit it for proofreading.*

SIGN: Left **'EXTENDED B'** hand is held in a fixed position with fingers pointing forward and palm facing right while tip of midfinger of horizontal right **'K'** hand is held against the left palm. As the wrist of the right hand rotates rightward, the tip of the midfinger of the right hand is flicked upward off the left palm.

twig: *n.* a small branch of a tree. *The twig snapped into two pieces when I stepped on it.*

SIGN: Fingerspell **TWIG**. (Signs vary. Sign choice depends on the size and shape of the twig as well as its location relative to other things.)

twilight: *n.* a period of faint light just after sundown. *We talked until* **twilight**.

SIGN: **'EXTENDED B'** hands are held near either side of the face with palms facing backward. The hands then move toward each other a little, then stop to indicate a loss of light but not total darkness. (When **twilight** refers to a period of subdued light just prior to sun*rise*, the same basic sign is used in reverse. **'EXTENDED B'** hands are held in front of the face with fingertips almost touching and palms facing backward and are then drawn apart as they become slightly more vertical.)

twine: *n.* a strong cord made by twisting fibres together. *I need some* **twine** *to tie the package.*

SIGN: Horizontal **'I'** hands are held with tips of little fingers touching each other and palms facing the body. The hands are then drawn apart. Movement is repeated.

twinkle: *n.* the reflection of flickering light. *We could see the* **twinkle** *of the city lights ahead of us.*

SIGN: Vertical **'O'** hands, palms toward the body, are held side by side and then drawn apart as the fingers are fluttered rapidly. The sign is accompanied by distinctive facial qualities where the eyes and lips are barely open and the signer appears to be smiling and blowing gently. (Specific movement and placement of this sign vary according to context.)

twins: *n.* two people conceived at the same time. *Twins can be identical or fraternal.*

SIGN #1: Vertical right **'T'** hand, palm left, is placed first on the left-hand side of the chin and then on the right. (**TWINS** is frequently fingerspelled.) Alternatively, this sign may be made using a **'CLAWED V'** hand, palm facing backward.

SIGN #2 [MANITOBA]: Fingertips of **'BENT EXTENDED B'** hands, palms facing body, are positioned at either side of chest and simultaneously slid up and down.

twirl: *v.* to move rapidly and repeatedly in a circle; spin. *The figure skater* **twirled** *gracefully across the ice.*

SIGN: **'BENT ONE'** hands are held right above left, the forefinger of the right hand pointing downward and that of the left hand pointing upward. Both hands move forward as they twirl in a counter-clockwise direction, the right forefinger revolving around the left as they spin. (Signs vary depending on the context.)

twist: *v.* to cause to be distorted or wrenched unnaturally. *The airplane was* **twisted** *into a mass of wreckage.*

SIGN #1: **'OPEN SPREAD O'** hands are held close together, the left hand more or less in a horizontal position and the right hand vertical, with palms facing. The wrists then twist in opposite directions, thus moving the left hand backward and the right hand forward as the fingers retract so that they are tucked more tightly into the hands. Facial expression is important. (Signs vary considerably, depending on context.)

twist: *v.* to distort the meaning of what someone has said. *Do not* **twist** *my words when you know that is not what I meant.*

SIGN #2: **'X'** hands, palms facing each other, are twisted 180 degrees.

twister: *n.* an informal word for tornado. *The* **twister** *destroyed an entire village.*

SIGN: **'BENT ONE'** hands are held right above left, the forefinger of the right hand pointing downward and that of the left hand pointing upward. Both hands move forward as they twirl in a counter-clockwise direction, the right forefinger revolving around the left as they spin.

two: *n.* See NUMBERS, p. LX.

two-faced: *adj.* deceitful; hypocritical. *A **two-faced** person often says one thing when he means another.*

SIGN: **'EXTENDED B'** hands are held, right on top of left, with palms down and fingers pointing forward. The fingers of both hands then bend so that they point downward.

twofold: *adj.* double; twice as much/many. *The benefits of owning real estate are **twofold**.*

SIGN: Left **'V'** hand is held upright with palm facing the left shoulder.

type: *n.* a classification; category; kind. *He did not know the **type** of computer he used.*

SIGN #1: Right **'K'** hand, palm facing left and slightly toward the body, is held just above left **'K'** hand, which is held with palm facing right and slightly toward the body. Hands are then circled forward around one another one full turn, stopping with right hand resting on top of left.

type: *n.* preferred kind. *He asked me to go to a movie but I decided he was not my **type**.*

SIGN #2: Tip of middle finger of right **'BENT MIDFINGER 5'** hand, palm toward the body, is tapped lightly against the chin a couple of times.

type: *v.* to operate a typewriter or computer keyboard. *Please **type** this letter for me.*

SIGN #3: **'SPREAD C'** hands, palms facing down, are held parallel with fingers wiggling up and down to simulate the action of typing.

typewriter: *n.* a writing machine with a keyboard used to print letters and numbers. ***Typewriters** have been almost replaced by computers.*

SIGN: **'SPREAD C'** hands, palms facing down, are held parallel with fingers wiggling up and down to simulate the action of typing.

typical: *adj.* having the characteristics of a specific group; conforming to a specific type. *He is a **typical** little boy who loves to play outdoors.*

SIGN #1: Right **'BENT U'** hand, palm down, is circled clockwise over left **'STANDARD BASE'** hand, and the extended fingers are brought down to rest on it.

typical: *adj.* characteristic. *That is **typical** of you!*

SIGN #2: Vertical right **'EXTENDED B'** hand is more or less pushed a couple of times toward the person to whom you are referring as the lips appear to articulate the syllable 'puh'. (This sign is generally preceded by the sign for **that** #1.) Signs vary.

tyrant: *n.* a person who exercises unfair control over others; a cruel, oppressive ruler. *Their father had been a **tyrant**.*

SIGN: Horizontal **'X'** hands are held slightly apart with left palm facing right and right palm facing left. Then they are alternately moved backward and forward. (Facial expression is essential.)

U

ugly: *adj.* having an unpleasant or unsightly appearance. *There is an **ugly** bruise on your leg.*

SIGN: Forefinger of right **'ONE'** hand, palm facing down, points leftward as it is held either under or in front of the nose. The hand is then drawn rightward as the forefinger curls into an **'X'** hand. Alternatively, this sign may be formed with two hands, beginning with the forefingers of the **'ONE'** hands crossed in front of the nose. The two-handed version is generally used for emphasis.

ulcer: *n.* an open sore on the skin or a mucous membrane such as the lining of the stomach, resulting in deterioration of the tissue. *The patient is being treated for a bleeding **ulcer**.*

SIGN: Fingerspell **ULCER**.

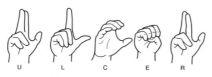

U   L   C   E   R

ultimate: *adj.* the highest or most significant aspect of something. *The model always wore the **ultimate** in women's fashion.*

SIGN: Right **'BENT EXTENDED B'** hand, fingers on lips and pointing left, palm toward body, is brought upward to right of face as it forms an **'EXTENDED A'** hand with thumb pointing upward. Right forearm is then lowered so that the palm of the **'EXTENDED B'** hand strikes the fingertips of the left **'EXTENDED B'** hand which is held with palm facing rightward/downward and fingertips pointing upward/rightward. (ASL CONCEPT—**best - top**.) Sign selection depends on context.

umbrella: *n.* a portable device with a collapsible canopy used to protect against rain/sun. *The girl wants an **umbrella** to match her raincoat.*

SIGN: Horizontal **'S'** hands, palms toward the chest, are held so the right is above the left and is moved up and down once or twice, thereby striking the top of the left hand as if opening or closing an umbrella.

umpire: *n.* an official who rules on the playing of a game such as baseball or cricket. *He has been a baseball **umpire** for 50 years.*

SIGN: Tips of crooked fingers of vertical right **'CLAWED V'** hand, palm toward the face, are tapped several times on the lips.

un-: *prefix* not. *She tried very hard to win the contract but she was **unsuccessful**.*

SIGN: Right **'EXTENDED A'** hand, palm facing left, thumb under chin, is thrust forward. The prefix **UN-** is frequently fingerspelled for emphasis. (When the prefix **un-** means *the reversal of a state or an action*, this sign is inappropriate. Even when **un-** means *not*, signs vary. Sign choice depends entirely on context.)

NOTE—Many words beginning with the prefix **'un-'**, meaning **not**, do not appear in this dictionary as they are simply conveyed using the sign for **not** followed by the sign for the root word.

unable to: *adj.* lacking the ability, power or opportunity to do something. *I am **unable to** attend the session.*

SIGN: **'ONE'** hands are held in front of chest with the right higher than the left, and both palms facing down. Then the right forefinger is brought down vigorously to strike the left forefinger at right angles to it.

unanimous: *adj.* in complete agreement. *He was installed as president by a **unanimous** vote.*

SIGN: **UNANIMOUS** is generally fingerspelled but may be signed in a variety of ways.

U   N   A   N   I   M   O   U   S

unaware: *adj.* having no prior knowledge. *I was **unaware** of the plan.*

SIGN: The fingertips of the right **'EXTENDED B'** (or **'BENT EXTENDED B'**) hand, palm toward the face, are placed on the forehead or in the area of the right cheekbone, and the hand is then curved to the right with the palm facing down.

ALTERNATE SIGNS—**know nothing** or **un- + aware**

uncertain: *adj.* not precisely determined or decided. *We are uncertain about going to the festival.*

SIGN #1: **'S'** (or **'A'**) hands are held apart with palms down and are alternately raised and lowered.

OR

SIGN #2: Tips of forefinger and middle finger of right **'BENT EXTENDED U'** hand, palm down, rest on forefinger of horizontal left **'B'** (or **'ONE'**) hand, of which the palm faces right and fingers point forward. The right hand then teeters from side to side as if trying to balance on left forefinger.
ALTERNATE SIGN—**un- + certain** #1

uncle: *n.* the brother of one's father or mother, or the husband of one's aunt. *Aunt Rachel's husband is my favourite uncle.*

SIGN: Vertical right **'U'** hand, palm forward, is held near right side of forehead and the arm is drawn downward once or twice.

unconscious: *adj.* lacking normal sensory awareness as when in a deep sleep or coma. *The driver was unconscious after the crash.*

SIGN: Tip of forefinger of right vertical **'ONE'** hand, palm toward face, is placed on forehead. **'SPREAD C'** hands are then held slightly apart with palms down and are simultaneously lowered a short distance with a rigid movement, stopping abruptly. (ASL CONCEPT—**think - shock**.) In cases where **unconscious** refers to an involuntary act, signs vary depending on the context.

under: *prep.* directly beneath or below. *The ball is under the table.*

SIGN #1: Vertical right **'EXTENDED A'** hand, palm facing left, is held behind left **'STANDARD BASE'** hand and is then curved forward underneath it.

under: *prep.* below (a certain amount). *Children under ten will be admitted free of charge.*

SIGN #2: Left **'EXTENDED B'** hand, palm down and fingers pointing rightward, is placed on the fingers of the right **'EXTENDED B'** hand of which the palm faces downward and the fingers point forward. The right hand is then moved sharply downward from the wrist.

underhanded: *adj.* deceptive, sneaky, or sly. *He got the contract in an underhanded way.*

SIGN: Right **'MODIFIED 5'** hand is held under chin, palm down, and the fingers flutter. Facial expression is important.
SAME SIGN—**underhandedness**, *n.*
ALTERNATE SIGN—**sly**

underline: *v.* to put a line below. *Please underline all the foreign words.*

SIGN: Right **'I'** hand is held in front of left side of body with palm down and little finger pointing leftward. The hand is then drawn straight rightward.

OR

SIGN: Vertical right **'CLOSED X'** hand is held in front of left side of body with palm forward and is drawn straight rightward.

underneath: *prep.* beneath or at a lower level. *They often play underneath the bridge.*

SIGN: Right **'EXTENDED B'** hand, palm down, fingers pointing slightly forward and to the left, is circled beneath left **'STANDARD BASE'** hand.

underpants: *n.* a pair of underwear (for women or girls mainly); panties. *I am going to the lingerie department to buy some underpants.*

SIGN: Fingertips of **'BENT MIDFINGER 5'** hands are placed just below either hip, palms toward the body. The hands are then raised and repositioned at the waist. (Signs vary.)

understand: *v.* to comprehend and know the meaning or nature of something. *The students **understand** what they are doing.*

SIGN: Vertical right **'s'** hand, with knuckles near right side of forehead, is changed to a **'ONE'** hand as the forefinger is flicked upward.

understanding: *adj.* sympathetic; having the insight and concern to relate to someone else's situation. *His boss was very **understanding** when he asked for time off to see a friend in the hospital.*

SIGN: Vertical **'s'** hands are held at either side of the forehead with palms facing backward. They are alternately transformed to **'ONE'** hands several times as the forefingers flick upward.

undertake: *v.* to commit oneself to do something. *He will **undertake** to inform all the members that the meeting has been postponed.*

SIGN: **'SPREAD C'** hands, palms down, are held apart and are simultaneously raised as they change to **'s'** hands.

undertaker: *n.* a person whose profession is the preparation of the dead for burial, and the management of funerals. *The **undertaker** directed the mourners to the cemetery.*

SIGN: Fingerspell **UNDERTAKER**.

underwear: *n.* clothing worn next to the skin under one's outer garments. *Please pack enough **underwear** for five days.*

SIGN: Fingertips of **'BENT EXTENDED B'** hands, palms toward the body, are held at the top of either leg and are simultaneously curved upward toward the waist. (Signs vary.)

unfair: *adj.* the state of being unequal or unjust. *It is **unfair** to expect me to do all the work.*

SIGN: Left **'F'** hand is held horizontally with palm facing right while tips of thumb and forefinger of horizontal right **'F'** hand are placed on chin. Then the joined thumb and forefinger of the right hand are used to strike down sharply across those of the left. The head moves from side to side to indicate negation.

ALTERNATE SIGN—**un- + fair** #1

unfortunate: *adj.* unlucky or unhappy. *The mishap was **unfortunate**.*

SIGN: Vertical **'CROOKED 5'** hands are held slightly apart with palms toward the face. The hands are then simultaneously lowered somewhat and the head tilts to the right.

ungainly: See **clumsy**.

uniform: *n.* a prescribed identifying set of clothes for the members of a specific group. *The RCMP **uniform** is very distinctive.*

SIGN #1: Palms of horizontal **'5'** hands are placed on upper part of chest and are simultaneously moved down to waist level. (**UNIFORM** is frequently fingerspelled.)

uniform: *adj.* the same; without variation. *The buildings in that part of town are quite **uniform** in design.*

SIGN #2: **'Y'** hands are held parallel with palms down, and are simultaneously circled leftward in a wide arc so that they eventually return to their original position.

union: *n.* a term used for labour or trade organizations. *The Auto Workers' **Union** is planning a strike.*

SIGN: Fingerspell **UNION**.

unique: *adj.* distinctive, or being the only one of a particular type. *Their new house has many **unique** features.*

SIGN: Thumb and forefinger of right **'OPEN F'** (or **'A-INDEX'**) hand, palm facing down, grasp tip of forefinger of left **'ONE'** hand, which is held with palm toward body. Then right hand is used to pull left hand upward.

unit: *n.* any group, individual or thing that is part of a larger whole. *Every **unit** in the apartment complex will be renovated.*

SIGN: Fingerspell **UNIT**.

unite: *v.* to join together to become an integrated whole. *The environmentalists will unite to fight against further destruction of the rainforest.*

SIGN: **'OPEN F'** hands are held slightly apart, palms facing each other, and are then brought together to form **'F'** hands, with thumbs and forefingers linked.

United Nations: *n.* an international organization formed in 1945 to promote world peace, co-operation and security. *Kofi Annan of Ghana is the seventh Secretary-General of the United Nations.*

SIGN: Fingerspell **UN**.

unity: *n.* a state of harmony or oneness. *Deaf leaders are working toward unity of purpose.*

SIGN: **'F'** hands with thumbs and forefingers interlocked, and palms facing each other, are moved in a complete circle in front of the body using a counter-clockwise motion.

universal: *adj.* typical of the whole of mankind or nature. *Poverty is a universal problem.*

SIGN: Horizontal right **'5'** hand is held with palm down and fingers pointing forward. The hand then makes a wide arc leftward as it inscribes a circle in front of the body.

universe: *n.* in astronomy, it represents all existing matter, energy and space. *Our Earth is only one small planet in the universe.*

SIGN: Fingerspell **UNIVERSE**. (Various signs may be used, but only after the meaning of the term has been clearly stated.)

university: *n.* an institution of higher learning having authority to grant degrees. *The Western Canadian Centre of Specialization in Deafness is situated at the University of Alberta.*

SIGN #1: Vertical right **'U'** hand, palm forward, is held in front of the right shoulder and circled clockwise.

OR

SIGN #2: Heel of right vertical **'U'** hand, palm facing forward, rests on back of left **'STANDARD BASE'** hand and is curved slightly to the left and upward.

unjust: *adj.* not in accordance with accepted standards of fairness. *Racial discrimination is unjust.*

SIGN: Right **'EXTENDED A'** hand, palm facing left, thumb under chin, is thrust forward. Vertical **'BENT EXTENDED B'** hands, palms facing each other, are then held slightly apart in front of the chest, and are brought together so that the fingertips tap against each other.

unless: *conj.* except under certain circumstances. *I will not go unless you come with me.*

SIGN: Fingerspell **UNLESS**.

unlike: *adj.* dissimilar or different. *Although they are identical, the twins are unlike in their behaviour.*

SIGN: Forefingers of **'ONE'** hands are crossed. Hands are then turned outward and swept apart so that they are parallel and both forefingers point straight up.

unrest: *n.* a troubled or rebellious state of discontent. *The employees in this department seem to be in a perpetual state of **unrest**.*

SIGN: Left **'CROOKED 5'** hand is held palm-up with fingers pointing forward while right **'CROOKED 5'** hand is held apart and slightly higher with palm down and fingers pointing forward. The arms are then simultaneously moved upward/rightward as the hands are purposefully twisted rightward from the wrist so that the left palm faces right and the right palm faces left.

until: *conj.* up to that time. *Let us wait **until** the results are in.*

SIGN: Vertical **'ONE'** hands, palms facing, are positioned so the right is near the chest and the left is a short distance in front of it. Then the right is curved forward until the palm faces down and the tips of the forefingers meet.

unusual: *adj.* not common; not ordinary. *It is very **unusual** for him to be late for work.*

SIGN: Right horizontal **'C'** hand is held just in front of the right side of the forehead with palm facing left. The wrist then relaxes as the hand drops, the palm finally facing downward. (**UNUSUAL** is frequently fingerspelled.)

unwind: *v.* to become relaxed. *I need a holiday to help me **unwind**.*

SIGN: **'EXTENDED B'** hands, palms toward the body, are crossed at the wrists and are then placed on the chest.

up: *prep.* indicating a higher position. *The office is **up** on the second floor.*

SIGN #1: Right vertical **'ONE'** hand, palm forward, is moved upward. (This sign is *not* used when **up** is conceptually involved with other words in English, as in cases like **warm up**, **get up**, **cheer up**, **fed up**, etc.)

up: *prep.* above; higher or greater in amount. *Only those aged twelve and **up** are eligible to participate.*

SIGN #2: Left **'EXTENDED B'** hand is held palm-down, with fingertips pointing right. Fingertips of right palm-down **'EXTENDED B'** hand rest on and at right angles to back of left hand and are then moved upward from the wrist.

update: *v.* to make current or to bring up to date. *The memo will **update** the members on the committee's findings.*

SIGN: Fingerspell **UPDATE**.

upgrade: *v.* to improve in value or importance. *He hopes to **upgrade** his skills for the job.*

SIGN: Edge of right **'EXTENDED B'** hand is placed on wrist of left forearm and moved upward in a small arc toward the elbow.

uphold: *v.* to maintain or defend against opposition. *As president, he promised to **uphold** our society's traditions.*

SIGN: **'S'** hands, palms toward the body, are held at chest level with the left slightly above the right. Then the hands come together to strike each other.

upholstery: *n.* the fitting of furniture with padding, springs, webbing and covering. *Many Deaf people used to work in **upholstery**.*

SIGN: Fingerspell **UPHOLSTERY**. (Signs vary.)

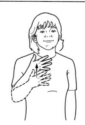

uplifting: *adj.* raising one's emotional or spiritual consciousness. *Her good nature and positive attitude are very **uplifting**.*

SIGN: Right **'5'** hand is held with palm on chest and fingertips pointing leftward/upward. The hand is then pushed purposefully upward. Alternatively, this sign may be made with two hands, one on either side of chest, especially for emphasis.

upon: *prep.* on. *They set the child **upon** Santa's knee.*

SIGN: Horizontal right **'EXTENDED B'** hand, palm down, is brought down at right angles onto the back of the left **'STANDARD BASE'** hand.

upset: *v.* to disturb mentally or emotionally. *News of his death will greatly **upset** the family.*

SIGN: Horizontal right **'EXTENDED B'** hand, palm on stomach and fingers pointing leftward, is turned 45° so the palm faces up. (**UPSET** is frequently fingerspelled.)

upstairs: *adv.* up the stairs, or on an upper floor. *Our bedroom is **upstairs**.*

SIGN: Right vertical **'ONE'** hand, palm forward, is moved upward once or twice.

urge: *v.* to advocate forcefully or recommend earnestly and persistently. *He **urged** his intoxicated friend to take a cab home from the party.*

SIGN #1: Horizontal **'X'** hands, are held apart with palms facing each other and the right hand slightly ahead of the left hand. The hands are then simultaneously moved forward and back at least twice with short deliberate movements as though prodding a reluctant individual. ❖

urge: *v.* to advocate, recommend or encourage. (The connotation of **urge** here is less emphatic than in the context above.) *He **urged** his son to read in his spare time.*

SIGN #2: Horizontal **'EXTENDED B'** hands are held apart with palms angled so that they partly face each other while partly facing forward. The hands then simultaneously make several small circles outward.

urgent: *adj.* requiring immediate action, as in an emergency or a very important situation. *The speaker received an **urgent** request for an interpreter from the Deaf people in the audience.*

SIGN: Fingerspell **URGENT**. (Signs vary.)

urine: *n.* a yellow-coloured liquid containing waste products collected in the kidneys and discharged through the urethra. *You must have your **urine** tested and a blood sample taken.*

SIGN: Vertical right **'T'** hand is held with palm forward and is jiggled from side to side. To refer to *male* urine only, **penis** may be used.
ALTERNATE SIGN—**bathroom**

us: *pron.* used to refer to the signer and one or more other person(s). [See PRONOUNS, p. LXIV & LXV.] *We waited for the receptionist to call **us**.*

SIGN: Horizontal right **'BENT ONE'** hand, tip of forefinger touching right shoulder, is moved leftward so that the forefinger touches the left shoulder.

use: *v.* to make use of; put into service or action. *She does not **use** a screwdriver very often.*

SIGN: Vertical right **'U'** hand, palm facing forward/leftward, is circled clockwise above left **'STANDARD BASE'** hand two or three times with the heel of its palm striking the back of the left hand each time. This sign may also be made without the left hand.

used: *adj.* second-hand, not new. *Our company sells both new and **used** cars.*

SIGN: Fingerspell **USED**.

used to: *adj.* an expression that indicates habitual or customary action. *Canadians are **used to** long, cold winters.*

SIGN #1: Right **'U'** hand is held upright with palm facing forward/leftward and its heel resting on the back of the left **'STANDARD BASE'** (or **'U'**) hand, which is horizontal with the palm down. Both hands maintain this position as they are simultaneously lowered.

used to: *v.* taking place in the past but not continuing into the present. *I **used to** think I would like to be a pilot when I grew up.*

SIGN #2: Vertical right **'5'** hand, palm facing forward/leftward, is circled backwards just in front of the right shoulder.

usher: *n.* a person who shows people to their seats or acts as a doorkeeper. *An **usher** escorted each wedding guest to an appropriate pew in the church.*

SIGN: Fingerspell **USHER**.

Usher Syndrome: *n.* a genetic condition characterized by deafness and visual impairment which is generally progressive and may lead to blindness. *Many children with Usher Syndrome have limited peripheral vision.*

SIGN: Side of forefinger of vertical right **'U'** hand, palm forward, is placed near right temple. Then the hand is drawn downward to the cheek as it changes to an **'S'** hand, palm remaining forward.

usual: *adj.* normal; occurring regularly. *Let us meet at the usual time.*

SIGN: Knuckles of the right **'A'** hand, with palm toward face, are brushed forward across the right cheek twice.
ALTERNATE SIGN—**normal**

utilize: *v.* to make practical or worthwhile use of. *We were able to utilize all our resources.*

SIGN: Vertical right **'U'** hand, palm facing forward/leftward, is circled clockwise above left **'STANDARD BASE'** hand two or three times with the heel of its palm striking the back of the left hand each time. This sign may also be made without the left hand.

V

vacant: *adj.* empty, or having no occupant. *The parking lot was vacant.*

SIGN: Tip of middle finger of right **'BENT MIDFINGER 5'** hand strokes forward/rightward across back of left **'STANDARD BASE'** hand. SAME SIGN—**vacancy**, *n.*

vacate: *v.* to leave; to give up tenure, possession, or occupancy. *He was asked to vacate the building at once.*

SIGN: **'EXTENDED B'** hands are held parallel with palms down and fingers pointing forward/rightward. The hands are then drawn simultaneously leftward/backward as they close to form **'A'** (or **'EXTENDED A'**) hands.

vacation: *n.* a holiday. *The family had a two-week vacation in California.*

SIGN: Thumbs of horizontal **'MODIFIED 5'** hands, palms facing the body, are jabbed into either side of upper chest.

vaccination: *n.* an inoculation that produces immunity to a specific disease. *If you travel to the tropics, you should have a vaccination for malaria.*

SIGN: Tip of forefinger of right **'BENT L'** hand is jabbed into upper left arm and thumb is repeatedly bent and extended as though depressing a plunger into a syringe.

vacuum cleaner: *n.* an electrical household appliance used for cleaning by suction. *Our vacuum cleaner needs repair.*

SIGN: Horizontal right **'CLOSED A-INDEX'** hand, palm facing left, is moved back and forth to simulate the action of operating a vacuum cleaner.

vagina: *n.* the passage in female mammals that leads from the opening on the outside of the body to the uterus. *Most babies are delivered through the vagina.*

SIGN: **'L'** hands, palms toward the body, are held slightly apart with forefingers pointing down. Then the thumbs and forefingers are tapped together twice.

vague: *adj.* hazy; not clear or precise. *His explanation about why he was late was quite vague.*

SIGN: Vertical **'5'** hands are held with palms either touching or at least close together. Left hand, palm facing body, is held steady while right hand faces forward and is circled counter-clockwise.

vain: *adj.* inordinately conceited and proud; showing too much pride in one's appearance. *She is so vain that she has an entire wall covered with mirrors.*

SIGN: **'V'** hands are held upright, palms facing either shoulder. The hands are then simultaneously bent backward from the wrists so that the extended fingers point backward. SAME SIGN—**vanity**, *n.*

valedictorian: *n.* a student, usually of high academic standing, who gives the farewell speech at a graduation ceremony. *The valedictorian gave an inspiring speech.*

SIGN: Fingerspell **VAL**.

valentine: *n.* a card expressing love and affection or a sweetheart selected for such a greeting. *February 14th is the day when we send valentines to those we love.*

SIGN: Tips of midfingers of **'BENT MIDFINGER 5'** hands (or tips of forefingers of **'BENT ONE'** hands), palms toward the chest, are placed together just below the left shoulder and are drawn apart to trace the outline of a heart, coming together again at a lower point.

valiant: *adj.* brave; fearless; courageous. *The soldier was awarded the Distinguished Service Order for the valiant rescue of his comrades.*

SIGN: **'BENT 5'** hands, with fingertips on either side of chest and palms facing the body, are drawn forward to form **'S'** hands. REGIONAL VARIATION—**brave** #2

valid: *adj.* having legal force or being legally acceptable; based on evidence or well-grounded reasoning. *For this job, you will need a **valid** driver's licence.*

SIGN: Fingerspell **VALID**.

valley: *n.* a long, broad depression in the land surface, usually containing a river. *Edmonton's river **valley** is one of its most attractive features.*

SIGN: Horizontal **'EXTENDED B'** (or **'B'**) hands, palms down and fingers pointing forward, are held apart and are then lowered and brought together, simulating the shape of a valley.

valuable: *adj.* highly regarded; of great importance; having considerable monetary worth. *Those documents contain **valuable** information.*

SIGN: Vertical **'F'** hands, palms facing forward, are held apart, and then are simultaneously curved toward each other until the joined thumbs and forefingers come together.

ALTERNATE SIGN—**important** #2

value: *n.* the price or monetary worth of property or goods. *The **value** of real estate in Toronto is high.*

SIGN #1: Vertical **'F'** hands, palms facing forward, are brought together so the joined thumbs and forefingers touch each other twice.

value: *n.* a quality or principle considered important. *The **values** shared by Deaf people are a significant part of their culture.*

SIGN #2: Knuckles of vertical right **'OPEN SPREAD O'** hand, palm toward the body, are placed on the chin and are firmly drawn downward, closing to form an **'S'** hand.

value: *v.* to cherish or regard very highly. *I really **value** his input.*

SIGN #3: Knuckles of vertical right **'OPEN SPREAD O'** hand, palm toward the body, are placed on the chin and are firmly drawn downward, closing to form an **'S'** hand.

vampire: *n.* in folklore, a corpse which comes to life to suck blood from sleeping people. *He drove a stake through the **vampire's** heart.*

SIGN: Extended fingertips of right **'CLAWED V'** hand are tapped twice against the neck just under the right jawbone.

van: *n.* a covered truck used to transport goods and/or passengers by road. *The tradesman's **van** was loaded with tools and equipment.*

SIGN: Fingerspell **VAN**.

vanilla: *n.* a flavour extracted from the seed pods of an orchid. *The recipe called for a tea-spoon of **vanilla**.*

SIGN: Fingerspell **VANILLA**.

vanish: *v.* to disappear suddenly or mysteriously. *The money **vanished** from the bank vault.*

SIGN: Right **'BENT MIDFINGER 5'** hand is held palm down with fingers pointing forward. The hand is then quickly moved backward toward the body and slightly upward so that the forearm becomes upright and the hand takes on an **'A'** shape. Lip pattern is important.

ALTERNATE SIGNS—**disappear** #1 & #2

vanquish: *v.* to defeat or overcome in a battle or contest. *We watched the West **vanquish** the East in the Grey Cup Classic.*

SIGN: Vertical right **'S'** hand, palm facing forward, is curved downward from the wrist across the extended finger of the left **'ONE'** hand, which is held horizontally with the palm facing downward.

variety: *n.* the quality or condition of being diversified; assortment. *Your daily diet should include a variety of foods.*

SIGN: **'BENT L'** hands are positioned palms-down with tips of forefingers touching each other, the right finger pointing leftward and the left finger pointing rightward. Then they are moved apart with forefingers fluttering.

various: *adj.* of several different kinds. *The book contains various recipes for chili con carne.*

SIGN: **'BENT L'** hands are positioned palms-down with tips of forefingers touching each other, the right finger pointing leftward and the left finger pointing rightward. Then they are moved apart with forefingers fluttering.

vary: *v.* to be different or subject to change. *Prices vary from store to store.*

SIGN: Horizontal **'ONE'** hands, palms down and forefingers pointing forward, are held apart with one hand held slightly higher than the other. The hands are then moved further apart with alternating up and down movements.

vase: *n.* a container, generally tall and cylindrical, used for holding and displaying flowers. *Please arrange the flowers in the vase.*

SIGN: Fingerspell **VASE**. (Signs vary based on the size and shape of the vase.)

vasectomy: *n.* a surgical procedure used to create sterility in males. *Some couples consider a vasectomy the safest method of birth control.*

SIGN: **'A'** (or **'COVERED T'**) hands, palms down, are held at waist level and alternately rotated forward in small circles and then firmly drawn apart.

vast: *adj.* unusually large in area, extent or number. *Bison once roamed freely across the vast Great Plains of North America.*

SIGN: Horizontal right **'5'** hand is held with palm down and fingers pointing forward. The hand then makes a wide arc leftward as it inscribes a circle in front of the body. (Sign selection depends on the context.)

vault: *n.* a room, often in a bank, used to store valuables. *All safety-deposit boxes are in a special vault at the bank.*

SIGN: Fingerspell **VAULT**.

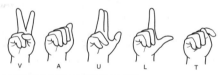

veal: *n.* the meat from a calf. *The veal was very tender.*

SIGN: Fingerspell **VEAL**.

vegetable: *n.* any of a large variety of edible plants. *My favourite vegetable is mashed turnip.*

SIGN: Fingerspell **VEG**.

vegetarian: *n.* a person who eats a diet consisting exclusively of vegetables, grains, nuts, and fruits. *A vegetarian does not eat meat.*

SIGN: Vertical right **'V'** hand, palm facing left, is held with tip of forefinger touching right side of chin. The hand is then reversed so the palm faces backward and the middle fingertip touches the chin. (**Vegetarian** is frequently fingerspelled **VEG**.)

vehicle: *n.* any wheeled conveyance by which people or goods are transported. *We finally passed the slow moving vehicle.*

SIGN #1: Right horizontal **'3'** hand is held with palm facing left. (This is a generic sign which is used when the specific type of vehicle being referred to is already understood and when that vehicle is in juxtaposition with another object.)

vehicle: *n.* any wheeled conveyance by which people or goods are transported. *Many vehicles are now equipped with air bags and other safety features.*

SIGN #2: **'S'** hands, with palms facing the body, are held in the steering wheel position and are alternately moved up and down to simulate the motion of steering a car. (This sign is used only when it refers specifically to a **car**, and only when that car is not juxtaposed with any other object.)

vein: *n.* a tubular vessel that carries blood to the heart. *Blood samples are usually taken from a vein on the inside of one's elbow.*

SIGN: Fingerspell **VEIN.**

V   E   I   N

velocity: *n.* speed; swiftness. *Successful operation of a sailboat depends on the velocity of the wind.*

SIGN: Left horizontal **'L'** hand, palm facing right, is held apart from and slightly ahead of right horizontal **'L'** hand, whose palm faces left. The hands are then simultaneously jerked upward toward the body as they are changed to **'CLAWED L'** hands.

vengeful: *adj.* desiring revenge, or characterized by a desire for revenge. *He became very vengeful toward his sister after she inherited their parents' entire estate.*

SIGN: **'X'** (or **'CLOSED X'**) hands, palms facing each other, are held slightly apart with the right nearer the chest, palm facing forward/downward. Then the hands are brought together so that they strike each other sharply. Alternatively, the left hand remains stationary as the right hand moves forward to strike the left.

SAME SIGN—**vengeance,** *n.*

venom: *n.* a poisonous fluid secreted by snakes and scorpions, usually through biting or stinging. *Hikers in snake-infested regions often carry a snake-bite kit to counteract snake venom.*

SIGN: **'S'** hands, palms facing chest, are crossed at the wrists, with the right hand nearest the body. The back of the right wrist is tapped twice against the left wrist.

SAME SIGN—**venomous,** *adj.*

ALTERNATE SIGN—**poison** #2

verbal: *adj.* oral rather than written. *They had a verbal agreement to support the motion.*

SIGN #1: Tip of forefinger of vertical right **'4'** hand, palm facing left, is tapped twice against the chin. (Signs vary in this context. Alternatively, **VERBAL** may be fingerspelled.)

verbal: *adj.* associated with words. *The verbal component of the test will assess how extensive the boy's vocabulary is.*

SIGN #2: Tips of forefinger and thumb of right **'MODIFIED G'** hand are tapped a couple of times against forefinger of left **'ONE'** hand, whose palm faces rightward/downward.

verdict: *n.* the findings of a jury. *The appeal court upheld the verdict.*

SIGN: **'F'** hands, with palms facing each other, are held apart in front of chest and are simultaneously lowered.

verify: *v.* to confirm or prove to be true. *Linguistic studies verify that American Sign Language is a bona fide and unique language.*

SIGN: Right **'EXTENDED B'** hand, palm facing upward/backward, is brought down sharply to lie at right angles to upturned palm of left **'EXTENDED B'** hand.

ALTERNATE SIGN—**confirm**

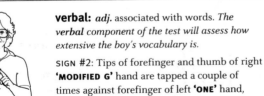

verse: *n.* a stanza of a poem. *The first grader memorized the first verse of the poem.*

SIGN: Horizontal left **'EXTENDED B'** hand is held with fingers pointing rightward, and palm facing slightly upward yet angled toward the body, while thumb and forefinger of right **'C-INDEX'** hand are placed on left palm and drawn rightward across it.

version: *n.* an account told, or description given by someone from his/her point of view; a translation or interpretation. *He told a different version of the story.*

SIGN: **'ONE'** hands are held together with palms facing one another, and are simultaneously twisted 180 degrees from the wrists.

ALTERNATE SIGN—**interpret**

versus: *prep.* in competition against. *Tonight's game will feature Montreal **versus** Toronto.*

SIGN: Horizontal **'EXTENDED A'** hands, palms toward the chest, are held slightly apart and are brought together so the knuckles strike each other.
ALTERNATE SIGN—**against**

vertical: *adj.* upright, or at right angles to the horizon. *The opposite of **vertical** is horizontal.*

SIGN: Right **'B'** (or **'EXTENDED B'**) hand, palm facing left and fingers pointing forward/upward, is held level with the forehead and brought straight down.

verticals: *n.* slatted window blinds that hang perpendicular to the sill. *Many people prefer **verticals** instead of heavy draperies.*

SIGN: Vertical **'B'** hands are positioned side by side with the left palm facing the body and the right palm facing forward. The forearms then twist simultaneously so that the left palm faces forward and the right palm faces the body. Motion is repeated.

very: *adv.* a word used to add emphasis or intensity. *It is **very** cold today.*

SIGN: Vertical **'V'** hands are held with palms facing and fingertips of left hand touching those of right hand. The hands are then drawn apart.

vessel: *n.* a ship that transports freight and/or passengers. *The **vessel** sank when it hit the reef.*

SIGN #1: **'CROOKED EXTENDED B'** hands, palms facing each other at a slight angle, are cupped together to form the hull of a boat. Then they are moved up and down in a bobbing motion.

vessel: *n.* a tubular structure that transports body fluids such as blood. *The broken glass severed a major blood **vessel** in his leg.*

SIGN #2: Fingerspell **VESSEL**.

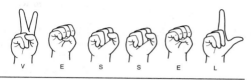

vest: *n.* a sleeveless undergarment or a waist-coat. *Most business suits include a **vest**.*

SIGN #1: Fingerspell **VEST**. (Signs vary.)

SIGN #2 [ONTARIO]: Thumb and forefinger of right **'C-INDEX'** hand are stroked downward twice on right side of chest with palm facing the body.

veteran: *n.* referring to someone who has lengthy experience in some capacity. *The **veteran** was honoured for his heroic acts.*

SIGN: Fingertips of right **'CONTRACTED 5'** hand are placed near the right temple and as the hand is drawn downward, the fingers are closed to form a **'FLAT O'** hand. Motion is repeated. (Sometimes the sign for **soldier** is used to mean a 'veteran with military experience'.)

veterinarian: *n.* a person practising in the field of medicine concerned with the health and treatment of animals. *We took our dog to the **veterinarian** for her annual checkup.*

SIGN: Fingerspell **VET**.

veto: *v.* to refuse consent to proposals or government bills. *An American president has the power to **veto** bills but can be overridden by a majority vote.*

SIGN: Horizontal right **'EXTENDED A'** hand, palm facing leftward-upward, is overturned so that the thumb points downward. (**VETO** is frequently fingerspelled.)

vibration: *n.* the act of moving back and forth rapidly. *Deaf people are usually very sensitive to vibration.*

SIGN: Horizontal **'5'** hands, palms down, fingers pointing forward, are held slightly apart and are moved in a rapid pattern whereby the right hand moves forward/rightward while the left hand moves backward/rightward. The hands then return to their original positions. The motion is repeated several times.
SAME SIGN—**vibrate,** *v.*

vice-president: *n.* an officer ranking immediately below a president and serving as his/her deputy. *She is the vice-president of the graduating class.*

SIGN: Tip of forefinger of vertical right **'v'** hand, palm facing forward, touches right side of forehead. Bending at the wrist, the hand then drops downward to form a **'K'** hand with the palm facing down.

vicinity: *n.* a surrounding area or neighbourhood. *She lives in a vicinity where a lot of crime occurs.*

SIGN: Right **'5'** hand, palm down, is circled in a counter-clockwise motion.

vicious: *adj.* wicked or cruel; unpleasantly severe or harsh. *A wolverine is one of the most vicious animals.*

SIGN: Horizontal **'CLAWED 5'** hands are held with the right slightly above the left and palms facing. The sign is accompanied by a fierce facial expression with the teeth bared.
ALTERNATE SIGN—**mean** #2

victim: *n.* a person or thing suffering harm, deception, or death. *Anne Frank was a victim of Hitler's holocaust.*

SIGN: Fingerspell VICTIM.

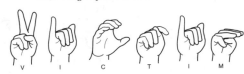

V I C T I M

victory: *n.* a triumph or final success in a contest or struggle. *The team is celebrating its latest victory.*

SIGN: Vertical right **'COVERED T'** hand, palm left, is held near the side of the head and forearm is circled clockwise.
SAME SIGN—**victorious,** *adj.*
ALTERNATE SIGN—**win** #1

videocamera: *n.* a piece of equipment used to record material on a videotape. *He will operate the videocamera at his sister's wedding.*

SIGN: Right horizontal **'3'** hand, palm facing left, is moved back and forth a couple of times from the wrist.

videotape: *n.* a magnetic tape used to record film for later transmission. *The teacher used a videotape to supplement her lecture.*

SIGN #1: Vertical right **'v'** hand, palm facing left, is held against right-facing palm of vertical left **'EXTENDED B'** hand. Then it is circled clockwise as it changes to a **'T'** hand.

videotape: *v.* to record a TV program on videotape. *She will videotape the soap operas while I am on vacation.*

SIGN #2: Horizontal **'v'** hands, palms down and extended fingers pointing forward, are held parallel and then curved rightward simultaneously in a small arc as they are changed to **'T'** hands.

OR

SIGN #3: Fingertips of right **'CONTRACTED 5'** hand, palm facing left, are held against right-facing palm of horizontal left **'EXTENDED B'** hand, whose fingers point forward. Right hand is then drawn rightward as it closes to form a **'FLAT O'** hand.

videotape: *v.* to record on videotape. *The bride's uncle will videotape the wedding.*

SIGN #4: Horizontal right **'3'** hand, palm facing left, is moved back and forth a couple of times from the wrist. ❖

view: *v.* to look at or inspect. *Did you view the exhibits?*

SIGN #1: Horizontal **'V'** hands are held parallel with palms down, fingers pointing forward, and are swept to the right in a succession of arcs. Sometimes only the right hand is used.

view: *n.* that which can be seen in one's field of vision. *There is a lovely view from our window.*

SIGN #2: Right **'BENT V'** hand is held in front of left shoulder with palm facing left and extended fingers pointing left as well. The hand then makes a wide arc in a forward/rightward direction, coming to rest in front of the right side of the body with palm facing forward/rightward. (**VIEW** in this context is frequently fingerspelled.)

view: *n.* one's perception or opinion. *He expressed his view of the Free Trade Act.*

SIGN #3: Tip of middle finger of right **'BENT V'** hand, palm toward the body, is held near the right eye. Then the hand is twisted clockwise from the wrist so that palm faces forward and extended fingers point at forefinger of vertical left **'ONE'** hand, whose palm faces rightward.

OR

SIGN #4: Vertical right **'MODIFIED O'** hand is held just in front of mid-forehead with palm facing left, and is bobbed slightly.

vile: *adj.* disagreeable; unpleasant. *He has a vile temper.*

SIGN: Right **'EXTENDED B'** hand, with fingertips on chin and palm facing body, is turned away, so that palm is facing down. (Sign selection depends on the context.)

village: *n.* an incorporated municipality smaller than a town. *That village has a general store and only a few houses.*

SIGN: Vertical **'EXTENDED B'** hands, left palm facing right and right palm facing left, are held so that their fingertips can be tapped together twice.

villain: *n.* a wicked or malevolent person. In literature or drama, the main evil character, or the antagonist. *He plays the villain in the movie.*

SIGN: Right **'EXTENDED B'** hand, with fingertips on chin and palm facing body, is turned away, so that palm is facing down.
ALTERNATE SIGN—**bad** #2

vine: *n.* a plant that has a long, flexible, creeping stem. *We picked several clusters of grapes from the vine.*

SIGN: Fingerspell **VINE**.

vinegar: *n.* a sour-tasting liquid, which results from the fermentation of wine, cider, etc. *I like vinegar on my french fries.*

SIGN: Tip of forefinger of vertical right **'V'** hand, palm facing left, is tapped at least twice against centre of chin.

violation: *n.* an infringement of a law or rule. *The penalty for a parking violation is $35.00.*

SIGN: Right **'L'** hand, palm facing left, is tapped smartly against palm of left **'EXTENDED B'** hand, which is held with palm facing right and fingers pointing upward/forward.

violent: *adj.* characterized by great physical force. *Murder is a violent crime.*

SIGN: Fingerspell **VIOLENT**. (**VIOLENCE**, *n.*, may be fingerspelled also. Alternatively, a detailed description of the violence is often given.)

violin: *n.* a bowed, stringed instrument. *A Stradivarius is a very rare and costly violin.*

SIGN: **'F'** hands are held so the left, palm up, simulates the holding of the neck of a violin, while the right, palm down, is drawn back and forth above the left forearm to simulate the bowing.

virgin: *n.* someone who has never had sexual intercourse. *He remained a virgin until his wedding night.*

SIGN: Tip of forefinger of vertical right **'V'** hand is placed against right cheek, with palm facing left, and is drawn downward.

virtue: *n.* a quality of moral excellence. *Patience is a virtue.*

SIGN: Forefinger of right **'ONE'** hand is brought forward smartly to strike horizontal forefinger of left **'ONE'** hand at right angles. Then horizontal right **'C'** hand, palm facing the body, is twisted in a circular motion from the wrist so that it becomes upright with palm facing leftward as it is brought back against the left shoulder. (ASL CONCEPT—**positive** (or **good**) - **characteristic**.)

virus: *n.* a microscopic entity that causes a variety of illnesses. *Influenza is a highly contagious disease caused by a virus.*

SIGN #1: Fingerspell **VIRUS**.

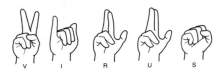

virus: *n.* an unauthorized computer program that inserts itself into a computer system with the intention of spreading to other programs and creating damage. *Our computer system was damaged by a virus.*

SIGN #2: Fingerspell **VIRUS**.

visa: *n.* an endorsement in a passport, signifying the holder is permitted to travel in the country of the government issuing it. *You will require a visa if you plan to tour that country.*

SIGN: Fingerspell **VISA**.

visible: *adj.* capable of being perceived by the eye. *The moon is visible on a clear night.*

SIGN: **'A'** hands, palms down, are held slightly apart, and are brought down firmly in front of the chest. Then tip of middle finger of vertical right **'K'** hand, palm facing left, touches right cheekbone and the forearm is moved purposefully a short distance outward from the face. (ASL CONCEPT—**can - see**.)

vision: *n.* eyesight or the act of perceiving with the eye. *Contact lenses should improve your vision.*

SIGN #1: Tip of middle finger of vertical right **'K'** hand, palm facing left, is tapped twice against right cheek bone. (This sign may be made with two hands, one at either cheek bone.)

vision: *n.* a vivid mental image produced by the imagination. *He had a clear vision of what the business would be like in 20 years.*

SIGN #2: Tip of forefinger of right **'ONE'** hand touches forehead. Then vertical **'S'** hands are held together, left in front of right, at centre of forehead with left palm facing right and right palm facing left. As the hands move apart, they open to form **'CROOKED 5'** hands.

visit: *v.* to call upon or to drop in on someone as a guest. *We will visit you tonight.*

SIGN: **'BENT V'** hands, palms toward the body and extended fingers pointing upward, are alternately circled forward. As a variation on this sign, the **'BENT V'** hands may be held with the right slightly ahead of the left. Both hands are then moved purposefully forward/ rightward a short distance. (The first sign described here may be used for **visitor**, *n.* Agent Ending (see p. LIV) may follow.) ❖

visual: *adj.* optical or capable of being seen. *It was a very visual presentation.*

SIGN: Vertical right **'K'** hand is held with palm facing left and tip of middle finger touching right cheekbone while vertical left **'K'** hand is held a short distance away from left cheekbone with palm facing right. Left hand is then moved toward the face so that tip of middle finger touches left cheek bone as right hand moves away from the face. The hands continue to alternate a few times in this way.

visualize: *v.* to form a mental image of something that cannot be seen at that moment. *I can not visualize my grandmother as a young woman.*

SIGN: Tip of forefinger of right **'ONE'** hand touches forehead. Then vertical **'S'** hands are held together, left in front of right, at centre of forehead with left palm facing right and right palm facing left. As the hands move apart, they open to form **'CROOKED 5'** hands.

vital: *adj.* essential or indispensable; absolutely necessary. *It is vital that you take your medicine.*

SIGN: Vertical right **'X'** hand, palm facing forward, is bent forward smartly from the wrist so that the palm faces downward. Facial expression is important.
ALTERNATE SIGNS—**important** #1 & #2

vitamin: *n.* a substance which is contained in food, and is essential to good health and well-being. *Fruits and vegetables are rich in vitamins.*

SIGN: Right **'V'** hand, palm forward, is held upright and shaken back and forth from the wrist.

vivid: *adj.* very bright, intense, or colorful. *She looked strikingly beautiful in a vivid red gown.*

SIGN: **'O'** (or **'FLAT O'**) hands are placed side by side, palms facing forward. Then they are moved apart and upward as the fingers spread to form **'5'** hands, palms still facing away from the body.

vocabulary: *n.* the lexicon, or words and phrases contained in a language. *This dictionary provides the essential vocabulary contained in ASL.*

SIGN: Tips of extended fingers of horizontal right **'V'** hand, palm down, are tapped down twice on forefinger of left horizontal **'ONE'** hand, of which the palm is facing downward.
ALTERNATE SIGN—**word** #1

vocational: *adj.* relating to educational courses concerned with skills needed for a trade. *Some high schools offer both vocational and academic programs.*

SIGN: Fingerspell **VOC**.

vodka: *n.* a colourless alcoholic beverage made from wheat, rye, corn or potatoes. *She ordered a vodka and orange juice.*

SIGN: Fingerspell **VODKA**.

voice: *n.* the sound made by the vibration of the vocal cords. *She has a very pleasant speaking voice.*

SIGN: Tips of extended fingers of right **'V'** hand, palm toward the body, are held near the throat and the hand is moved up and down from the wrist once or twice.

void: *adj.* invalid; not legally binding. *His failure to meet the requirements makes the contract void.*

SIGN #1: Tip of forefinger of right **'ONE'** hand draws an 'X' across palm of horizontal left **'EXTENDED B'** hand which faces the body at a slight rightward angle.
ALTERNATE SIGN—**(no) good**

void: *n.* emptiness of space, contents, or feelings. *The camels crossed the* **void** *of the Sahara Desert.*

SIGN #2: Right **'BENT MIDFINGER 5'** hand is held out in front of left side of chest with palm facing forward/downward. The hand then moves about 180 degrees in a wide rightward/forward arc.

volcano: *n.* an opening in the earth's crust from which molten lava is ejected. *Hot ashes from the* **volcano** *spread across the fields.*

SIGN: Right **'FLAT O'** hand, with palm up, is thrust upward through left **'C'** hand, as fingers open into a **'CONTRACTED 5'** hand.

volleyball: *n.* a team sport in which players hit a large ball back and forth over a high net with their hands. **Volleyball** *is my favourite sport.*

SIGN: Vertical **'CONTRACTED 3'** hands, palms forward, are held parallel above shoulder level and forearms are thrust apart and forward a short distance. Motion is repeated.

volume: *n.* the magnitude of a 3-dimensional space. *The student calculated the* **volume** *of water in the container.*

SIGN #1: **'Y'** hands are held parallel with palms forward/downward, and tips of thumbs are tapped together at least twice. (**VOLUME** is frequently fingerspelled.) In cases where the depth of a container is greater than its width, this sign is rotated a quarter turn so that the palms are facing rightward and the right hand is above the left.

volume: *n.* the loudness of sound, or the control for adjusting the loudness on a radio or TV. *You can adjust the* **volume** *of the TV to suit yourself.*

SIGN #2: Vertical right **'C-INDEX'** hand, palm forward, is twisted clockwise from the wrist. (Signs vary.)

volume: *n.* a book, or one of a set of books. *You can find the information you need in Volume 5.*

SIGN #3: **VOLUME** in this context is frequently fingerspelled but may be signed in a variety of ways.

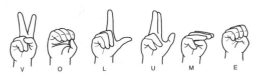

volunteer: *v.* to willingly offer to do something. *I will* **volunteer** *to do the work in my spare time.*

SIGN: Horizontal right **'F'** hand grasps the signer's shirt below the right shoulder between the thumb and forefinger, and is moved back and forth twice.

vomit: *v.* to eject the contents of the stomach through the mouth. *This medication might cause you to* **vomit.**

SIGN: Thumb of horizontal right **'MODIFIED 5'** hand, palm facing left, is held at chin while horizontal left **'MODIFIED 5'** hand is positioned just in front of right hand with palm facing right. The hands then move forward and downward in a slight arc.

vote: *v.* to indicate one's choice either by ballot or show of hands. *The general membership will* **vote** *on the proposal.*

SIGN: Joined thumb and forefinger of horizontal right **'F'** hand, palm down, appear to peck at the top of the horizontal left **'S'** hand, whose palm faces right.

vow: *n.* a solemn, earnest pledge. *The couple wrote their own marriage* **vows.**

SIGN: Tip of forefinger of vertical right **'ONE'** hand, palm facing left, is placed just under the lower lip. As the right hand is then brought purposefully forward/downward, it takes on a **'B'** handshape and is pressed onto the top of the left **'STANDARD BASE'** hand. (The handshapes for this sign vary.)

vowel: *n.* a letter representing a specific speech sound such as a, e, i, o, u. *A* **vowel** *can produce either a long or short voiced sound.*

SIGN: Fingerspell **VOWEL.**

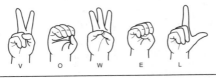

voyage: *n.* a long trip by land, sea, or air. *They visited more than 20 countries on their* **voyage** *around the world.*

SIGN: Right **'CROOKED V'** hand, palm down, is snaked forward.

vulgar: *adj.* extremely rude. *He used some vulgar expressions to describe his family.*

SIGN: Vertical right **'A-INDEX'** hand, palm facing left, quivers as thumb and forefinger are used to grasp skin of right cheek. Facial expression is important.
SAME SIGN—**vulgarity**, *n.*

vulnerable: *adj.* capable of being hurt, or open to attack. *With two of our best players injured, our team was in a vulnerable position.*

SIGN: Fingertips of right **'5'** hand, palm toward the body, are placed on upturned palm of left **'EXTENDED B'** hand. Then the fingers buckle so that the hand is transformed into a **'CLAWED 5'** shape. (Sign selection depends on the context.)

waffle: *n.* a crisp, golden-brown batter cake with deep indentations on both sides. *Sometimes I eat a **waffle** for brunch on Sunday.*

SIGN: Fingerspell **WAFFLE**.

wage: *n.* payment in return for work or services. *He expected to be paid the average **wage** for a carpenter.*

SIGN: Horizontal right **'EXTENDED C'** hand, palm toward the body, is held on the upturned palm of the left **'EXTENDED B'** hand. The right hand then closes into an **'EXTENDED A'** shape as it is drawn across the left palm in a leftward arc toward the body. Movement is repeated. (**WAGE** is frequently fingerspelled.)

wager: *v.* to bet or stake an amount on the outcome of an event. *I will **wager** $1,000 that our team will win.*

SIGN: **'B'** (or **'EXTENDED B'**) hands are held slightly apart, fingers pointing forward and palms facing upward. They are then turned over simultaneously so that palms are facing down. Alternatively, this sign may be made with one hand only.

wagon: *n.* a four-wheeled vehicle (often drawn by horses or a tractor) used to transport a load. *This is a special **wagon** for hauling hay.*

SIGN: Fingerspell **WAGON**. Alternatively, **wagon** may be signed, in which case, sign selection depends on the context.

waist: *n.* the part of the human body that is between the ribs and the hips. *The seamstress will need the measurement of your **waist**.*

SIGN: Fingertips of **'ONE'** hands are held together at the centre of the waist and are drawn apart along the waistline to either side of the body.

wait: *v.* to stay in one place or delay doing something until a certain time or until a certain event takes place. *You will have to **wait** for the next bus.*

SIGN #1: **'BENT EXTENDED B'** hands are held apart with palms up and the right hand slightly ahead of the left while fingers simultaneously move back and forth. Motion may be repeated.

SIGN #2 [ATLANTIC]: Horizontal **'C'** hands are clasped together and are simultaneously circled forward once or twice.

wait a minute: *v.* to ask someone to stay in one place or to delay doing something momentarily. ***Wait a minute!** You are not allowed to do that.*

SIGN: Forefinger of right **'ONE'** hand, palm forward, is held upright and very firmly moved forward a short distance. Appropriate facial expression is essential.

wait forever: *v.* to stay in one place or delay doing something for a long time. *It seemed like I had **waited forever** for the elevator to arrive at my floor.*

SIGN: Right **'Y'** hand is held upright with palm facing leftward and tip of thumb touching right side of forehead. The forearm is then moved sharply forward a short distance. Appropriate facial expression is essential. (The concept of 'waiting a long time' may be expressed in various ways.)

wait on: *v.* to serve; to act as a waiter or waitress. *He was assigned to **wait on** our table.*

SIGN: Horizontal **'EXTENDED B'** hands are held apart at about shoulder level with palms up and fingers pointing outward, and are alternately moved from side to side.

SAME SIGN—**waiter**, *n.*, and **waitress**, *n.* Agent Ending (see p. LIV) may follow.

waive: *v.* to agree to give up certain rights, or to agree not to insist on certain expectations. *Certain prerequisites were* **waived** *for her university entrance because she had already completed the courses at another university.*

SIGN: Fingers of right **'B'** hand, palm-down, are placed on and at right angles to fingers of upturned palm of left **'EXTENDED B'** hand. Right hand is then slid at a forward/rightward angle across and off the left hand.

wake up [*or* **awaken**]: *v.* to become roused from sleep. *He will* **wake up** *when the sun begins to shine through his window.*

SIGN #1: Thumbs of forefingers of **'CLOSED MODIFIED G'** (or **'CLOSED X'**) hands are placed at either cheek, and opened to form **'L'** (or **'CONTRACTED L'**) hands as they move outward a short distance from the face.

wake up [*or* **awaken**]: *v.* to rouse someone from sleep. *I will* **awaken** *you (or* **wake** *you* **up***) at 6:00 a.m.*

SIGN #2: Right **'BENT EXTENDED B'** hand, palm forward, taps in the air several times to simulate the act of rousing a sleeping person.

walk: *v.* to move or travel on foot. *I walk to work whenever possible.*

SIGN #1: Horizontal **'EXTENDED B'** (or **'3'**) hands, palms down, fingers pointing forward, are held slightly apart and are moved in a rapid pattern whereby the right hand moves forward/rightward while the left hand moves backward/rightward. The left hand then moves forward/leftward while the right hand moves backward/leftward. The movement is repeated several times to simulate the move-ment of one's feet while walking. This is often done with a flourish so that the palms slant slightly forward as the hands move forward, and the palms slant toward the body as the hands move backward.

OR

SIGN #2: Right **'EXTENDED K'** hand is held palm down with fingers pointing downward and fluttering to simulate two legs walking as the arm moves forward.

walk out: *v.* to strike or to leave one's place of employment due to a dispute with management. *If the workers are not happy with the new pay offer, I am afraid they might* **walk out***.*

SIGN: Right **'EXTENDED K'** hand is held palm down with fingers pointing downward and fluttering to simulate two legs walking as the arm moves briskly forward.

wall: *n.* a vertical side of a room. *The picture should be hung on this* **wall***.*

SIGN: Right **'EXTENDED B'** hand, palm facing left and fingers pointing forward, is held at about shoulder height and is firmly lowered. (**WALL** is frequently fingerspelled.)

wallet: *n.* a small folding case (usually leather) for holding money, credit cards and other documents. *He was looking in his* **wallet** *for appropriate identification.*

SIGN: Fingerspell **WALLET**.

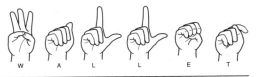

walrus: *n.* a big, seal-like marine mammal with large tusks and tough, wrinkled skin. *A* **walrus** *can be found in Arctic waters.*

SIGN: **'O'** hands are held at either side of chin with palms facing one another, and are simultaneously lowered to chest level.

wander: *v.* to go astray from a path or course. *She thought about happier times as she* **wandered** *through the field of daisies.*

SIGN: Vertical right **'ONE'** hand, palm facing forward, is moved forward with a snakelike motion. ❖

want: *v.* to feel a need or longing for. *Do you* **want** *me to stay with you?*

SIGN #1: **'CROOKED 5'** hands, palms up, are held slightly apart in front of the body. Then they retract to form **'CLAWED 5'** hands as they are simultaneously drawn toward the chest.

want *(cont.)*

SIGN #2 [ATLANTIC]: Tip of thumb of right horizontal **'MODIFIED 5'** hand, palm facing downward, is brushed downward once or twice on the right side of the chest.

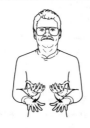

(don't) want: *v.* to have no need, want, or desire for. *I don't want help.*

SIGN: **'CROOKED 5'** hands, palms up, are held slightly apart and are simultaneously turned over as they open to become **'5'** hands with the palms facing downward. Facial expression is important.

war: *n.* an open armed conflict between two sides. *The war was fought in the Persian Gulf area.*

SIGN: **'BENT 4'** (or **'BENT 5'**) hands, are held slightly apart, palms facing downward, with right fingers pointing left and left fingers pointing right. Hands are then moved simultaneously to right and left twice. (**WAR** is frequently fingerspelled.)

ward: *n.* a large room or section in a hospital for patients requiring similar kinds of care. *The nurses in the children's ward all wear brightly coloured uniforms.*

SIGN #1: Tips of extended fingers of right **'BENT U'** hand, palm toward the body, are used to outline a small cross on the upper left arm. Right **'5'** hand, palm down and fingers pointing forward, is then circled in a counter-clockwise motion. (ASL CONCEPT—**hospital - area**.)

ward: *n.* an electoral district. *He is the alderman in our ward.*

SIGN #2: Fingerspell **WARD**.

ward: *n.* a person placed under the guardianship of a court or government. *Her child was made a ward of the court.*

SIGN #3: Fingerspell **WARD**.

wardrobe: *n.* the total collection of clothing belonging to one person. *Her wardrobe is extensive and stylish.*

SIGN: Thumbs of **'MODIFIED 5'** hands, with palms toward the body, are held at either side of upper chest and brushed downward a couple of times.

warm: *adj.* characterized by a moderate degree of heat. *Bread dough must be allowed to rise in a warm place.*

SIGN #1: Fingertips of right **'CLAWED 5'** hand, palm toward the face, are placed to the left of the mouth and then placed to the right of the mouth, the hand being drawn slowly across but not touching the lips.

OR

SIGN #2: Fingertips of vertical right **'CLAWED 5'** hand, palm toward the body, touch lower lip and then open to form a vertical **'CROOKED 5'** hand as the wrist bends, thus moving the hand forward a short distance.

warm-hearted: See kind #1 & #2.

warn: *v.* to caution or make aware of danger or harm. *Parents usually warn their children not to be too trusting of strangers.*

SIGN: **'EXTENDED B'** hands are held palms down, so that the right hand is above the left and is brought down so that the fingertips are tapped on the back of the left hand. Facial expression must clearly convey 'caution'. ❖

warrant: *n.* written authorization for a certain course of action. *The police showed up on her doorstep with a search warrant.*

SIGN: **'K'** hands, palms down, are held apart, extended fingers pointing downward, and are then flicked upward from the wrist so that the hands are held in either a horizontal or upright position. (**WARRANT** is frequently fingerspelled.)

warranty: *n.* a guarantee by a vendor or manufacturer that goods being sold meet specific requirements as to quality. *This microwave oven has a five-year warranty.*

SIGN: Fingerspell **WARRANTY**.

wart: *n.* a small, rounded skin growth caused by a virus. *Sometimes a doctor can remove a wart with liquid nitrogen.*

SIGN: Fingerspell **WART**.

wash (clothes): *v.* to clean (clothes) with water and detergent. *I am going to wash your clothes now.*

SIGN #1: **'SPREAD C'** hands, palms facing, are held apart with the right above the left and are simultaneously twisted back and forth (from the wrists) in opposite directions.

wash (dishes): *v.* to clean (dishes) with water and detergent. *It is your turn to wash the dishes.*

SIGN #2: Right **'EXTENDED B'** (or **'A'**) hand is held palm-down at right angles to left **'EXTENDED B'** hand which is held with the palm up but angled slightly towards the body as the right hand is circled counter-clockwise on it.

wash (face): *v.* to cleanse (face) with water and perhaps soap. *I would like to wash my face now.*

SIGN #3: Palms of **'A'** (or **'EXTENDED B'**) hands are positioned on either cheek and are rubbed simultaneously in circular motions.

wash (floor): *v.* to clean by applying water or other liquid, and generally detergent of some kind. *I will wash the floor on Saturday.*

SIGN #4: **'CLOSED A-INDEX'** hands are positioned left in front of right, with palms at a slight upward-facing angle, to simulate the holding of a mop handle and are drawn back and forth as if mopping a floor.

ALTERNATE SIGN—**wash (horizontal surfaces in general)** #7

wash (hair): *v.* to cleanse (hair) by applying water and shampoo. *After you wash your hair, do not forget to condition it.*

SIGN #5: Vertical **'CLAWED 5'** hands are held at either side of the head and simultaneously moved back and forth to simulate the act of shampooing one's hair.

wash (hands): *v.* to cleanse (hands) with soap and water. *I would like to wash my hands now.*

SIGN #6: **'EXTENDED C'** hands, palms together, simulate the motion of washing one's hands by rubbing and circling around each other.

wash (horizontal surfaces in general): *v.* to clean by applying water or other liquid, and generally soap or detergent of some kind. *The daycare worker washes the floor everyday.*

SIGN #7: **'A'** hands, palms down, are held slightly apart and are simultaneously circled in opposite directions, the left hand moving clockwise and the right hand moving counter-clockwise.

wash (vertical surfaces in general): *v.* to clean by applying water or other liquid, and generally soap or detergent of some kind. *He will wash the windows for you.*

SIGN #8: **'A'** hands, palms forward, are held slightly apart in a vertical position and are simultaneously circled in opposite directions, the left hand moving clockwise and the right hand moving counter-clockwise.

washcloth: *n.* a square of terry cloth used to wash one's body. *Please bring your own towel and washcloth.*

SIGN: Tips of forefingers of vertical **'ONE'** hands, palms down, are held together, then simultaneously drawn apart, lowered, and brought together again. The movement should roughly outline a square. Next, **'A'** hands or (palms of **'EXTENDED B'**) hands are positioned on either cheek and are rubbed simultaneously in circular motions.

(ASL CONCEPT—**square - wash**.)

washer [or **washing machine**]: *n.* an appliance used to wash clothes and linens. *Each apartment has its own washer and dryer.*

SIGN: **'SPREAD C'** hands, palms facing, are held apart with the right above the left and are simultaneously twisted back and forth (from the wrists) in opposite directions.

washroom: *n.* a public lavatory. *Every public building has a washroom.*

SIGN #1: Right **'A'** hand, with thumbnail on chin and palm facing left, is stroked downward twice.
ALTERNATE SIGNS—**bathroom** #2 & #3

SIGN #2 [ONTARIO]: Vertical right **'CONTRACTED C'** hand is held with palm facing left and fingertips touching right cheek. The fingertips brush downward against the cheek as they come together a few times to form a **'FLAT O'**.

wasp: *n.* a slender, winged insect, of which species the female has a vicious sting. *A wasp is attracted to sweet-smelling flowers.*

SIGN: Fingerspell **WASP**.

waste: *v.* to consume or expend carelessly. *Please do not waste any more time.*

SIGN: Right **'FLAT O'** hand, palm up, is placed on the upturned palm of the left **'EXTENDED B'** hand. Right hand is then flung forward/rightward as it opens to form a **'5'** hand with fingers pointing forward and palm facing leftward and slightly upward.
SAME SIGN—**wasteful**, *adj.*

watch: *n.* a small portable timepiece usually worn strapped to the wrist. *He is proud of his new gold watch.*

SIGN #1: Tip of forefinger of right **'CROOKED ONE'** hand, palm facing downward, is tapped at least twice on the back of the wrist of the left **'STANDARD BASE'** hand.

OR

SIGN #2: Right horizontal **'F'** hand, palm facing downward, is tapped at least twice on the back of the wrist of the left **'STANDARD BASE'** hand.

watch: *v.* to look at attentively. *We are going to watch television tonight.*

SIGN #3: Right **'BENT V'** hand, palm forward, is held at shoulder level or above and is moved forward a short distance. ❖

watch: *v.* to observe with continued interest, fascination and/or pleasure. *We watched the parade from our window.*

SIGN #4: Right **'CLAWED L'** hand is held palm up.
ALTERNATE SIGN—**watch** #3

watch out: *v.* to be careful; be alert. *Watch out! That car almost hit you!*

SIGN: Vertical right **'BENT V'** hand is held palm forward in front of the right shoulder and is jabbed forward. Facial expression is important. This sign may vary slightly depending on the location of the object of concern.

water: *n.* a clear, colourless, tasteless liquid that is essential to plant and animal life. *Canada contains one-third of all the fresh water on this planet.*

SIGN: Forefinger of vertical right **'W'** hand, palm facing left, is tapped against the chin.

watermelon: *n.* a large, edible fruit with a hard, green rind and rosy, sweet flesh. *A watermelon is elliptical in shape.*

SIGN #1: Vertical **'c'** hands, palms toward the body are held slightly apart and are simultaneously moved back and forth in front of the mouth to simulate the eating of a wedge of watermelon.

OR

SIGN #2: Right horizontal **'COVERED 8'** hand is held with palm down just above left **'STANDARD BASE'** hand. Then tip of middle finger of left hand is flicked against back of left hand, thus becoming an **'OPEN 8'** hand. Motion is repeated.

waterproof: *adj.* not penetrable by water. *Umbrellas are made of waterproof material.*

SIGN: Forefinger of vertical right **'w'** hand, palm facing left, is tapped against the chin. Next, **'EXTENDED B'** hands are held at right angles to one another, the left hand in front of the right, with fingers of left hand pointing upward to the right and fingers of right hand pointing upward to the left. The hands are then pushed firmly forward. (ASL CONCEPT— water - block.) Alternatively, the sign for **water** may be used and **PROOF** fingerspelled.

water-ski: *v.* to glide over the surface of a body of water on special skis while holding a rope towed by a boat. *After lunch we plan to water-ski on the lake.*

SIGN: Forefinger of vertical right **'w'** hand, palm facing left, is tapped against the chin. Then horizontal **'x'** hands are held parallel with palms up, and the right hand slightly ahead of the left. The hands are simultaneously moved forward in a straight line.

wave: *n.* an undulation that moves across the surface of a body of water. *We stood on the ship's deck and watched the ocean waves below.*

SIGN #1: Vertical **'5'** hands are held apart with palms facing forward/leftward, the left hand slightly ahead of the right. The hands are simultaneously curved downward so that the fingers point down, and then brought upward so that the fingers point up. The motion continues in a forward/leftward direction. It is a fluid motion, simulating that of ocean waves.

wave: *v.* to move the hand from side to side in greeting. *We saw the man wave to someone in the train as it was leaving the station.*

SIGN #2: Vertical right **'5'** hand is held upright with the palm forward and is moved back and forth from the wrist.

waver: *v.* to be irresolute or to hesitate between two possibilities. *Both arguments are convincing, so I am inclined to waver in my opinion.*

SIGN: Tips of index and middle fingers of right **'BENT EXTENDED U'** hand, palm down, rest on forefinger of horizontal left **'B'** (or **'ONE'**) hand, whose palm is facing right. Right hand then sways from side to side several times as though trying to balance on left forefinger. Appropriate facial expression is essential. ALTERNATE SIGN—**uncertain** #1

wax: *n.* a material that is water insoluble and sensitive to heat, consisting largely of fatty acids, and having a variety of domestic uses. *Candles are made of different types of wax.*

SIGN #1: Fingerspell **WAX**.

W　A　X

wax: *n.* a substance, also known as cerumen, found in the human ear. *The otologist removed the excess wax from her ears.*

SIGN #2: Fingerspell **WAX**.

W　A　X

wax: *v.* to apply wax to a surface and polish it. *He will wax his car this afternoon.*

SIGN #3: **'A'** hands, palms down, are held slightly apart and are simultaneously circled in opposite directions, the left hand moving clockwise and the right hand moving counter-clockwise. (Alternatively, only the right hand may be used.)

way: *n.* style, manner or method. *Let us try another way to solve the problem.*

SIGN: **'EXTENDED B'** hands, held parallel with palms facing one another and fingers pointing forward, are simultaneously moved forward.

(one-)way: *adj.* moving or allowing movement in one direction only, as in the case of a one-way street. *There are numerous one-way streets in the downtown area.*

SIGN: **'ONE'** hand is held vertically with palm facing body. Then the wrist rotates so that **WAY** may be fingerspelled with the palm facing forward.

one W A Y

we: *pron.* used to refer to the signer and one or more other person(s). [See Pronouns, p. LXIV.] *We waited for the receptionist to call us.*

SIGN: Horizontal right **'BENT ONE'** hand, tip of forefinger touching right shoulder, is moved leftward so that the forefinger touches the left shoulder.

weak: *adj.* lacking in strength or force. *She was very weak after her illness.*

SIGN: Fingertips of right **'5'** hand, palm toward the body, are placed on upturned palm of left **'EXTENDED B'** hand. Then the fingers buckle so that the hand is transformed into a **'CLAWED 5'** shape.

SAME SIGN—**weakness,** *n.*

wealth: *n.* a large amount of money or valuable possessions. *He inherited a great deal of wealth when his father passed away.*

SIGN: Left **'CROOKED 5'** hand is held with palm up while right **'CROOKED 5'** hand is held just above it with palm down. The hands are then moved apart, the right hand moving upward and back toward the body while the left hand is lowered slightly.

ALTERNATE SIGN (also for **wealthy**)—**rich**

weapon: *n.* a gun, knife, or any instrument that might be used in combat. *The police are still searching for the weapon used in the murder case.*

SIGN: Fingerspell **WEAPON**.

W E A P O N

wear: *v.* to have on one's body; to clothe oneself in. *I will wear a blue shirt to match my eyes.*

SIGN #1: Thumbs of **'5'** hands, with palms toward the body, are held at either side of upper chest and brushed downward a couple of times.

wear: *v.* to put (something other than a garment) on one's body. *I always wear sunglasses when I am driving.*

SIGN #2: Vertical right **'U'** hand, palm facing forward/leftward, is circled clockwise above left **'STANDARD BASE'** hand two or three times with the heel of its palm striking the back of the left hand each time. This sign may also be made without the left hand.

wear out: *v.* to become useless from too much use. *Car tires wear out faster if you drive at high speeds.*

SIGN: **'A'** hands are held together with palms facing the chest. The hands then gradually rotate forward with fingers spreading until they take on a **'CROOKED 5'** shape with palms facing upward.

weary: *adj.* tired, fatigued, or exhausted. *We were weary when we finally finished the job.*

SIGN: Horizontal right **'V'** hand, palm up, is laid across upturned palm of left **'EXTENDED B'** hand and is then drawn backward toward the body. Meanwhile, the cheeks are puffed.

weather: *n.* the day-to-day meteorological conditions affecting a specific place. *She hoped the weather would be good for the picnic.*

SIGN: Fingerspell **WEATHER**.

weave: *v.* to construct by interlacing fibres or other materials. *With practice, you can learn to weave neatly and evenly.*

SIGN: Left horizontal **'5'** hand is held with palm down and fingers pointing rightward/forward while right horizontal **'5'** hand is held just to the right of/behind the left hand with palm down and fingers pointing in a leftward/forward direction. With fingers fluttering, the right hand then proceeds to move leftward/forward while the left hand, with fingers similarly fluttering, passes under the right hand. Motion is repeated.

web: *n.* a structure formed by interweaving fibres or other materials. *The spider's web is a trap for insects.*

SIGN: Fingerspell **WEB**.

wedding: *n.* a marriage ceremony or celebration. *They had a small wedding with only a few guests.*

SIGN: **'CONTRACTED 5'** hands are held apart with wrists bent and palms down. The wrists then rotate inward, bringing the hands together as the right hand takes on a **'FLAT O'** shape, its fingers enveloped by those of the left hand which has taken the form of a **'FLAT C'**.

Wednesday: *n.* the fourth day of the week. [See TIME CONCEPTS, p. LXX.] *Wednesday is the third working day of the week.*

SIGN: Vertical right **'W'** hand, palm toward the body, is circled twice in a counter-clockwise direction.

weed: *n.* any unwanted plant that grows wild among cultivated plants. *Russian thistle is a common prairie weed.*

SIGN: Fingerspell **WEED**.

week: *n.* a period of seven consecutive days. [See TIME CONCEPTS, p. LXXI.] *My parents will visit us for a week.*

SIGN: Vertical right **'ONE'** hand, palm forward, is stroked rightward across palm of horizontal left **'EXTENDED B'** hand which is facing the chest.

weekend: *n.* the period from Friday night until Sunday night. *We went to our cottage for the weekend.*

SIGN #1: Vertical right **'ONE'** hand, palm forward, is stroked rightward across palm of horizontal left **'EXTENDED B'** hand which is facing the chest. As the right hand comes to the end of the left hand, it is transformed into a horizontal **'EXTENDED B'** hand with palm facing leftward, and it is moved straight downward.

OR

SIGN #2: Left horizontal **'EXTENDED B'** hand is held with fingers pointing rightward and palm facing the chest while horizontal right **'EXTENDED B'** hand is positioned between left thumb and forefinger with palm down and fingers pointing forward. The right hand slides rightward to the end of the left hand, then tips so that palm faces leftward as the forearm is moved straight downward.

weekly: *adj.* occurring every week or once a week. *They have weekly staff meetings on Tuesdays.*

SIGN: Vertical right **'ONE'** hand, palm forward, is stroked rightward across palm of horizontal left **'EXTENDED B'** hand which is facing the chest. Movement is repeated.

weep: *v.* to cry or shed tears. *Do you weep when you watch a sad movie?*

SIGN: **'BENT L'** hands are held so that the tips of the forefingers are just below each eye and the palms are toward the face. Forefingers are then stroked downward simultaneously on the cheeks at least twice. Facial expression is important.

weigh: *v.* to measure the heaviness of something or someone; to be of a certain weight or heaviness. *The postal clerk will* **weigh** *the package to determine how much postage is needed.*

SIGN: Horizontal left **'U'** hand is held with palm facing rightward, but angled slightly toward the body while the fingers point forward/rightward. Extended fingers of horizontal right **'U'** hand are rested on extended fingers of left hand at right angles to them. The right hand then rocks up and down from the wrist a couple of times. SAME SIGN—**weight**, *n.*

weightlifting: *n.* the sport of lifting barbells of specified weights in a prescribed way. *Weightlifting is a popular means of body-building.*

SIGN: Horizontal **'S'** hands are held parallel with palms up. The forearms are then simultaneously raised so that the hands become upright with palms facing the body. Movement is repeated.

weird: *adj.* unnatural, strange or bizarre. *His behaviour has been rather* **weird** *lately.*

SIGN: Vertical right **'W'** hand, palm left, is moved leftward in front of the face while the fingers are wiggling. Appropriate facial expression is essential. ALTERNATE SIGN—**odd** #1

welcome: *v.* to receive or invite gladly. *Welcome to our new home.*

SIGN: Right **'BENT EXTENDED B'** hand is held out in front of the body with fingers pointing leftward and palm facing the body but angled upward slightly. The hand is then drawn in toward the chest.

weld: *v.* to join (pieces of metal) by heating until soft. *He will* **weld** *the broken leg back onto the chair.*

SIGN: Horizontal **'ONE'** hands are held with palms facing one another and with tips of forefingers touching to form a **'V'** shape that points forward. Together, the hands are then shaken forward and back several times with short movements.

welfare: *n.* financial assistance given to people in need. *Many recipients of* **welfare** *use the Food Bank.*

SIGN #1: Right **'A-INDEX'** hand is held at an angle with palm facing partially upward and partially toward the body. The forearm is then brought smartly downward toward the body, with the hand taking on a **'CLOSED A-INDEX'** shape as the thumb and forefinger are retracted. Motion is repeated. (**WELFARE** is frequently fingerspelled.)

welfare: *n.* health, happiness, prosperity and general well-being. *This group works for the* **welfare** *of children.*

SIGN #2: Thumb and forefinger of right **'F'** hand, palm facing down, are brought slightly downward to be inserted into an imaginary pocket at waist level. Alternatively, the imaginary pocket is sometimes located at the left side of the chest.

well: *adv.* in a capable or skillful manner. *She signs* **well.**

SIGN #1: Fingertips of right **'BENT EXTENDED B'** hand are placed on the lips so that the palm is toward the body. Then the hand is moved purposefully forward a brief distance.

well: *adv.* in a state of good health. *If you follow the doctor's orders you will soon be* **well** *again.*

SIGN #2: **'BENT 5'** hands, with fingertips on either side of chest and palms facing the body, are drawn forward to form **'S'** hands.

well: *n.* a hole bored into the earth to tap a water supply. *Every farm in this area has its own* **well.**

SIGN #3: Forefinger of vertical right **'W'** hand, palm facing left, is tapped against the chin. Next, right **'BENT ONE'** hand, forefinger pointing downward, circles clockwise above horizontal left **'C'** hand, and then drops down through the opening created by the left hand. (ASL CONCEPT—**water - drill**.) Alternatively, **WELL** in this context may be fingerspelled.

well: *inter.* an expression used to preface a remark. *Well, I do not agree with you.*

SIGN #4: **'5'** hands are held apart with palms toward the body and fingertips of each hand pointing toward those of the other hand, yet angled slightly upward as well. Then as the head tilts to one side, the hands are simultaneously curved forward/downward from the wrists so the palms are facing up. (Alternatively, **WELL** may be fingerspelled in a forward direction with the right palm facing leftward.)

(as) well: *adv.* also, or in addition to. *While you are posting the letters, will you buy me some stamps as well?*

SIGN: Vertical right **'Y'** hand is held with palm forward and appears to wobble from side to side as the wrist twists.

ALTERNATE SIGN—**also** #1

west: *n.* the direction in which the sun sets. *The wind blew from the west.*

SIGN: Vertical right **'W'** hand, palm forward, is held near the right shoulder and the arm is extended rightward. (While the positioning and movement of this sign may vary, the handshape remains the same.)

wet: *adj.* saturated with water or other liquid. *The heavy rain left everything thoroughly wet.*

SIGN: Left **'CONTRACTED 5'** hand is held palm-up in front of chest while vertical right **'CONTRACTED 5'** hand is held with palm toward the body, and tip of middle finger touching the chin. Right hand is then lowered to a position parallel to the left hand as both hands are simultaneously closed to form **'FLAT O'** hands. The hands may then be simultaneously opened and closed a number of times, thus alternating between **'CONTRACTED 5'** and **'FLAT O'** shapes. (Alternatively, this sign may be made with the hands beginning in a parallel position rather than with the right hand beginning at the chin.)

whale: *n.* a large fishlike mammal. *From the deck of our cruise ship, we watched a whale in the distance.*

SIGN: Fingerspell **WHALE**.

what: *pron.* a pronoun used when asking for specification or identification of something. *What career are you planning after you graduate?*

SIGN #1: Horizontal left **'EXTENDED B'** hand is held with fingers pointing rightward/forward and palm facing rightward but angled slightly toward the body as tip of forefinger of right **'ONE'** hand, palm down, strikes downward across left palm.

OR

SIGN #2: Vertical right **'ONE'** hand, palm forward, is held near the right shoulder and is waved from side to side a few times. The movement is from the wrist. (The same sign is sometimes used to mean **where**. Knowing this can prevent confusion.)

OR

SIGN #3: **'CROOKED EXTENDED B'** hands are held parallel with palms up and are simultaneously moved toward each other and drawn apart several times very quickly. (The same sign is sometimes used to mean **where**. Knowing this can prevent confusion.)

SIGN #4 [ONTARIO]: Tip of protruding finger of right **'I'** hand is placed on right cheek and is brushed backward several times.

what: *inter.* an exclamation of surprise or strong feeling. *What!?*

SIGN #5: Right **'SLANTED 5'** hand is held with palm up, yet angled slightly toward the body. The fingers then close against the palm to form an **'A'** hand. Finally the forefinger rises just enough to allow the thumb to insert itself between the forefinger and middle finger, thus forming a **'T'** hand. (Appropriate facial expression is essential.)

what for?: *adv.* for what purpose? (or why?) *You asked me to come early. What for?*

SIGN: Tip of forefinger of right vertical **'ONE'** hand, palm toward face, is held near right side of forehead. The wrist is then twisted so that the palm faces leftward and/or forward. Motion may be repeated.

what if: (informal use of **suppose,** *v.*) suppose that; What would happen if...? *What if I run out of gas on the way there?*

SIGN: Tip of extended finger of vertical right **'I'** hand, palm facing backwards, is tapped against the right cheekbone two or three times.

what to do: *s.s.* This sign may be used as a direct translation of the phrase 'what to do' e.g., *You can not tell me what to do.* It is most often used to ask what someone 'did', 'was doing', 'does', 'is doing', or 'will do', *e.g., What were you doing?* or *What will you do?*

SIGN: Right **'BENT D'** hand is held with palm facing upward, but angled slightly towards the body. Tip of forefinger is then rapidly and repeatedly tapped against thumbtip, thus alternating between a **'BENT D'** and a **'CLOSED BENT D'**. (Two hands may be used for this sign.)

what's up?: *s.s.* What is going on? *When they saw the ambulance they asked, "What's up?"*

SIGN: Tips of middle fingers of **'BENT MIDFINGER 5'** hands are placed on either side of chest and quickly stroked upward so the palms are facing up. This sign may be made with one hand only. (Appropriate facial expression is essential.)

whatever: *pron.* anything that; no matter what. *Whatever he decides to do is fine with me.*

SIGN: Fingers of horizontal **'BENT EXTENDED B'** hands, palms facing the chest, are alternately brushed back and forth against each other.

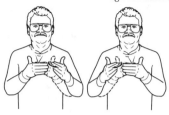

wheat: *n.* a cereal grass, from which the grain is used to make cereal, flour, and pasta. *Canada exports a lot of wheat.*

SIGN: Fingerspell **WHEAT**.

wheel: *n.* a disk on a circular frame mounted on an axle; anything that is like a wheel in shape or function. *The right rear wheel is slightly bent.*

SIGN: Right **'BENT ONE'** hand is held with palm facing the body and forefinger pointing leftward. It is then circled upward and forward. This is a wrist movement. To indicate plurality, two hands are used. (**WHEEL** is frequently fingerspelled.)

wheelchair: *n.* a chair with large wheels used by people who are unable to walk. *Office buildings should have ramps for wheelchairs.*

SIGN #1: **'A'** hands are held apart with palms down and are simultaneously moved forward as they take on the form of **'CROOKED 5'** hands. Motion is repeated.

OR

SIGN #2: **'BENT ONE'** hands, palms facing backwards and forefingers pointing toward one another, are held apart and simultaneously circled upward and forward.

when: *adv.* a word that asks: 'At what time?' or 'Over what period?' *When are we having dinner?*

SIGN #1: Left **'ONE'** hand is held with palm up and forefinger pointing forward, but angled rightward slightly. Right hand is held palm down with tip of forefinger touching tip of left forefinger. The right arm is then circled clockwise, the forefinger eventually returning to its original position.

OR

SIGN #2: **'MODIFIED G'** hands are held apart with palms facing the body and thumbs and forefingers pointing toward one other. Then they are simultaneously shaken up and down from the wrists.

where: *adv.* a word that asks the question: 'In, at, or to what place?' *Where are you going?*

SIGN #1: Vertical right **'ONE'** hand, palm forward, is held near the right shoulder and is waved from side to side a few times. The movement is from the wrist. (The same sign is sometimes used to mean **what**. Knowing this can prevent confusion.)

OR

SIGN #2: **'CROOKED EXTENDED B'** hands are held parallel with palms up and are simultaneously moved toward each other and drawn apart several times very quickly. (The same sign is sometimes used to mean **what**. Knowing this can prevent confusion.)

whereas: *conj.* used in formal or legal documents to mean 'It being the case that....' *Whereas the defendant has pleaded guilty, the judge will rule accordingly.*

SIGN #1: Fingerspell **WHEREAS**.

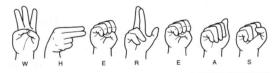

whereas: *conj.* a co-ordinating conjunction meaning 'but on the other hand'. *I enjoy reading whereas my husband prefers to watch T.V.*

SIGN #2: Horizontal **'BENT ONE'** hands are held together, palms facing the body, and tips of forefingers almost touching. Then they are pulled apart with a short, firm motion.
ALTERNATE SIGN—**but** #1

whether: *conj.* a word used to introduce an alternative in an indirect question. *He has not decided whether he will go to Edmonton or Calgary.*

SIGN: **'EXTENDED A'** hands, palms facing and thumbs pointing upward, are held parallel and are alternately moved up and down. This sign is accompanied by a lip pattern such as that used to produce a 'SH' sound.
ALTERNATE SIGN—**either** #2

which: *pron.* a word that asks the question: 'What particular one(s)?' *Which bus should I take to the Skydome?*

SIGN #1: **'EXTENDED A'** hands, palms facing and thumbs pointing upward, are held parallel and are alternately moved up and down. This sign is accompanied by a lip pattern such as that used to produce a 'SH' sound.

which: *pron.* to introduce a relative clause for which the antecedent refers to a thing or an animal. [See PRONOUNS, p. LXVII.] *The horse, which won the race, is owned by a rancher in southern Manitoba.*

SIGN #2: Knuckles of right **'EXTENDED A'** hand, palm facing left, strike forefinger of vertical left **'ONE'** hand whose palm faces right. Motion is repeated.

while: *conj.* at the same time that. *While they were on vacation, thieves broke into their house.*

SIGN: **'ONE'** hands are held apart close to the chest with palms down and forefingers pointing forward. The hands are then moved forward from the body in parallel lines.

whimper: *v.* to sob softly and intermittently. *The child began to whimper when his parents left him with the babysitter.*

SIGN: Tips of forefingers of vertical **'CONTRACTED L'** hands are placed high on each cheek near the eyes, palms toward the face, and are rapidly alternated with **'BENT L'** hands using short downward strokes. (Appropriate facial expression is important.)

whisky [*also spelled* **whiskey**]: *n.* alcoholic liquor. *Whisky is distilled from fermented barley or rye.*

SIGN: Horizontal right **'COMBINED I + ONE'** hand is held above and at right angles to horizontal left **'COMBINED I + ONE'** hand, whose palm faces slightly to the right and slightly toward the body. The two hands are then tapped together twice.

whisper: *v.* to sign in a secretive way so that only certain persons can see. *My friend and I sometimes whisper in sign language during class.*

SIGN #1: Right **'S'** hand, palm down, is placed against rightward/forward-facing palm of vertical left **'CROOKED EXTENDED B'** hand as its bunched fingers are rapidly opened and closed several times, thus alternating between an **'S'** and **'SPREAD C'** hand.

whisper: *v.* to speak in very soft, hushed tones, without full voice. *She whispered to her friend during the performance.*

SIGN #2: Vertical right **'B'** hand, palm facing left, is held near right side of mouth while lips are moved rapidly.

whistle: *v.* to make a shrill sound with pursed lips, or a small device used to make a shrill, high-pitched sound. *He whistled for his dog to come.*

SIGN: Tips of crooked fingers of vertical right **'CLAWED V'** hand, palm toward the body, are held on the lower lip as the head nods slightly but purposefully.

white: *adj.* the opposite of black; having no colour, or having the colour of milk or snow. *Bridal gowns are usually white.*

SIGN #1: Fingertips of right **'CONTRACTED 5'** hand, palm toward the body, are placed against the middle of the chest and the hand is then drawn forward as it closes to form a **'FLAT O'** hand. Motion is generally repeated.

white: *adj.* having light-coloured skin, such as that of a Caucasian. *His father was black, and his mother was white.*

SIGN #2: Fingertips of right **'FLAT O'** hand, palm toward the body, are placed in the middle of the chest. The hand is then raised to a position in front of the face where it opens to become a **'CONTRACTED 5'** hand with the palm toward the face.

white-out: *n.* a colloquial term used for 'correction fluid', a white substance which blots out errors in written or typewritten work so that corrections can be inserted. *Using white-out to make corrections in legal documents is not permitted.*

SIGN: Fingertips of right **'CONTRACTED 5'** hand, palm toward the body, are placed against the middle of the chest and the hand is then drawn forward as it closes to form a **'FLAT O'** hand. Next, tips of extended fingers of right **'BENT EXTENDED U'** hand, palm down, are brushed back and forth on palm of left **'EXTENDED B'** hand which is held with palm facing upward, but angled toward the body. (ASL CONCEPT—**white - paint on hand.**)

who: *pron.* a word used to introduce questions that ask: 'What or which person?' *Who will go swimming tomorrow?*

SIGN #1: Right **'CLAWED L'** hand is held with palm facing left and tip of thumb just under the lower lip while tip of forefinger flutters. Lips must be rounded.

OR

SIGN #2: Right **'BENT L'** hand is held with palm facing left and tip of thumb just under the lower lip while the forefinger flutters. Lips must be rounded.

OR

SIGN #3: Right **'BENT ONE'** hand is held with palm toward face and forefinger pointing to the mouth. The wrist is then rotated so that the forefinger inscribes a small clockwise circle. Lips must be rounded.

who: *pron.* a pronoun used to begin a relative clause in which the antecedent refers to a human. [See PRONOUNS, p. LXVII.] *The guest speaker, who is an expert on financial planning, has written several books on the subject.*

SIGN #4: Knuckles of right **'EXTENDED A'** hand, palm facing left, strike forefinger of vertical left **'ONE'** hand whose palm faces right. Motion is repeated.

whole: *adj.* complete or total quantity or amount. *We ate the whole chicken for dinner.*

SIGN: Left **'EXTENDED B'** hand is held with palm facing body and fingertips pointing to the right. Right **'EXTENDED B'** hand is circled around the left hand with the back of the right hand coming to rest in the palm of the left hand.

whore: *n.* a prostitute or promiscuous woman (usually used as a term of abuse). *She was upset because he called her a whore.*

SIGN: Vertical right **'OPEN A'** hand is held with palm toward the face and backs of fingers (up to the second joint) touching the right cheek. The hand is then brushed forward off the cheek a couple of times.

whose: *pron.* a word used to introduce questions that ask to whom something belongs. *Whose car is parked in my stall?*

SIGN: Right **'CLAWED L'** hand is held with palm facing left and tip of thumb just under the lower lip while tip of forefinger flutters. Lips must be rounded.

ALTERNATE SIGNS—**who** #2 & #3

why: *adv.* a word that asks for a reason, purpose or cause. *Why did he quit his job?*

SIGN #1: Vertical right **'BENT MIDFINGER 5'** hand is held with palm facing right side of forehead and middle finger repeatedly tapping gently in mid-air. This sign is generally used at the beginning of the ASL sentence and repeated at the end as well.

OR

SIGN #2: Fingertips of right **'EXTENDED B'** hand, palm toward right side of face, are placed on the forehead. The hand is then transformed into a **'Y'** shape as the forearm moves a short distance away from the body. This sign is generally used at the beginning of the ASL sentence and repeated at the end as well.

OR

SIGN #3: Tip of forefinger of right vertical **'ONE'** hand, palm toward face, is held near right side of forehead. The wrist is then twisted so that the palm faces leftward and/or forward. Motion may be repeated.

wicked: *adj.* morally bad or evil. *The wicked witch planned her revenge.*

SIGN: Right **'EXTENDED B'** hand, with fingertips on chin and palm facing body, is turned away, so that palm is facing down.

ALTERNATE SIGN—**bad** #2

wide: *adj.* having a great extent from side to side. *Winnipeg is known for its wide streets.*

SIGN: Fingertips of horizontal **'EXTENDED B'** hands point forward and palms face one another as the hands are held side by side, then moved apart.

wide-awake: *adj.* fully awake or alert. *He drank so much coffee that he was wide-awake all night.*

SIGN: **'C'** hands are held upright with palms facing each other and tips of thumbs touching either side of face at the cheek-bones. (A wide-eyed look accompanies this sign.)

widespread: *adj.* extending over a large area. *The flu epidemic was widespread and many seniors were hospitalized.*

SIGN: **'FLAT O'** hands are held with the palms down and sides of tips of forefingers touching. The hands are then opened to form **'5'** hands as they are moved apart in an outward/forward direction.

widow: *n.* a woman whose husband has died and she has not remarried. *My mother was a widow for many years.*

SIGN: Fingerspell **WIDOW**.

W   I   D   O   W

widower: *n.* a man whose wife has died and he has not remarried. *She married a widower who had several young children.*

SIGN: Fingerspell **WIDOWER**.

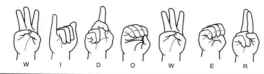

width: *n.* the measurement of something from side to side. *She measured the width of the queen-sized bed for her quilt.*

SIGN: Fingertips of horizontal **'EXTENDED B'** hands point forward and palms face one another as the hands are held side by side, then moved apart.

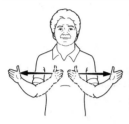

wiener: See **frankfurters**.

wife: *n.* a female partner in marriage. *They were pronounced "husband and wife" at the end of the wedding ceremony.*

SIGN: Thumbtip of right **'EXTENDED C'** hand, palm down, is positioned at right cheek and the hand is brought downward to clasp left **'EXTENDED C'** hand, of which palm faces upward.

wig: *n.* an artificial head of hair. *She wore a red wig for her role as Anne Shirley in the play, Anne of Green Gables.*

SIGN: Fingerspell **WIG**.

wild: *adj.* not domesticated or tamed. *Many wild creatures are in danger of becoming extinct.*

SIGN: Fingerspell **WILD**.

will: *v.* a word that indicates futurity. *There will be a holiday next week.*

SIGN #1: Right **'EXTENDED B'** hand, palm facing left, is held in a vertical position near the right side of the head. The forearm is then moved forward a short distance so that the fingers eventually point forward/upward.

will: *n.* a desire or intention. *The team has a strong will to win.*

SIGN #2: **'CROOKED 5'** hands, palms up, are held slightly apart in front of the body. Then they retract to form **'CLAWED 5'** hands as they are simultaneously drawn toward the chest. (Signs vary, depending upon the context. It may also be fingerspelled.)

will: *n.* a legal document stating someone's wishes as to what should become of his property and/or financial assets upon his death. *They made a will to leave their property to their children.*

SIGN #3: Fingerspell **WILL**.

will power: *n.* determination and self-control; strength of mind. *To resist temptation requires will power.*

SIGN #4: Forefinger of right **'CROOKED ONE'** hand, palm toward body, is tapped against right side of forehead. Next, horizontal right **'S'** hand is held palm-down in front of chest. The forearm is then jerked forcefully away from the body a short distance. Facial expression must clearly convey 'determination'. (ASL CONCEPT—**think - resist**.) (**WILL POWER** is frequently fingerspelled.)

willing: *adj.* cheerfully compliant; ready to do something happily. *He is always willing to help with the yard work.*

SIGN #1: Horizontal right **'EXTENDED B'** hand, palm toward the body, is brushed up and off the chest twice in a circular motion. (Appropriate facial expression is essential.)

willing: *adj.* compliant; agreeable to taking a certain course of action despite some reluctance. *It will not be easy, but he is willing to accept the responsibility.*

SIGN #2: Horizontal right **'EXTENDED B'** hand is held with palm against chest, and is brought forward so that the palm faces slightly upward, but still toward the body.

wily: See **cunning**.

win: *v.* to gain or succeed; to achieve first place in competition. *Our team hopes to win the competition tonight.*

SIGN #1: **'SPREAD C'** hands are held horizontally and slightly apart, right above left. As the hands are then moved purposefully toward each other, they close to form **'S'** hands, the right hand grazing the top of the left hand, and the wrists eventually crossing.

OR

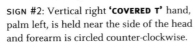

SIGN #2: Vertical right **'COVERED T'** hand, palm left, is held near the side of the head and forearm is circled counter-clockwise.

wind: *n.* moving air. *If there is no wind, we can not fly our kite today.*

SIGN #1: **'5'** hands, palms facing each other, are waved back and forth with a swaying motion.
SAME SIGN—**windy,** *adj.*

wind: *v.* to turn or coil around some object or point. *Do not forget to wind the clock.*

SIGN #2: Bent forefinger of right **'CLOSED A-INDEX'** hand, palm down, is placed against right-facing palm of horizontal left **'EXTENDED B'** hand. Then the right hand is twisted forward several times as if winding a clock.

window: *n.* an opening in a wall, which has glass to let in light. *My bedroom has a large window.*

SIGN #1: Horizontal **'BENT EXTENDED B'** hands, left palm facing right and right palm facing left, are held so that little finger of right hand is resting on forefinger of left hand. Then the right hand is moved up and down at least twice.

SIGN #2 [ATLANTIC]: Outer edge of vertical right **'X'** hand, palm facing leftward/forward, is tapped against the right cheek.
See also **close (a window)** and **open (a window).**

windshield wiper: *n.* an electrically operated blade with a rubber edge that wipes an automobile windshield clear of rain, snow, etc. *A windshield wiper can be set to move at various speeds.*

SIGN: Forearm or right **'ONE'** hand, palm forward, is moved back and forth from left to right to simulate the movement of a windshield wiper. (If the plural is indicated, both hands may be used, held parallel to one another, and moving simultaneously.)

windsurfing: *n.* the sport of moving along the surface of the water on a surfboard steered and propelled by a sail. *Windsurfing is a popular sport on Canada's west coast.*

SIGN: Forefinger of vertical right **'W'** hand, palm facing left, is tapped against the chin. Then tips of extended fingers of right **'BENT V'** hand, palm down, are positioned on back of left **'STANDARD BASE'** hand as, together, the hands glide forward/rightward. Next, vertical **'S'** hands, palms forward, are held above either shoulder and alternately moved backward and forward as if the signer is holding onto a horizontal bar while standing on a board which is bobbing about in rough waters. (ASL CONCEPT—**water - surf - handle**.)

wine: *n.* an alcoholic drink produced from grapes or other fruit. *There are many different types of wine produced in Canada.*

SIGN: The joined thumb and little finger of the right **'W'** hand, palm facing left, are placed on the right cheek and the hand is circled clockwise.

wing: *n.* a body part used by birds and insects for flying. *A blackbird's wing has red markings.*

SIGN: Right **'EXTENDED B'** hand, bent at the wrist with palm facing down, is held near the right shoulder and is flipped up and down. (When referring to a pair of wings, the signer uses both hands simultaneously.)

wing of an airplane: *n.* one of two armlike projections attached to either side of an airplane to provide lift. *She was seated by the wing of the airplane.*

SIGN: Horizontal right **'EXTENDED B'** hand is held palm down and straight out from the right side of the body with fingers pointing rightward. (Two hands are used to indicate plurality.)

wink: *v.* to close and open one eye quickly and deliberately. *He winked at the pretty girl.*

SIGN: Vertical right **'CONTRACTED L'** hand, palm facing leftward/forward, is held just to the right of the right eye. Forefinger taps down rapidly against the thumb to form a **'CLOSED MODIFIED G'** hand, and then moves upward just as fast to resume a **'CONTRACTED L'** shape. The signer should actually wink while making this sign.

winter: *n.* the season between fall and spring. *A Canadian winter can be long and very cold.*

SIGN: **'S'** (or **'A'**) hands are held apart, palms facing each other, and are shaken, along with the shoulders, as if the signer is shivering.

wipe: *v.* to rub a surface or object lightly, usually with a cloth or sponge. *Please wipe the table for me.*

SIGN: Right **'EXTENDED B'** hand is circled counter-clockwise. (Positioning of this sign varies according to what is being wiped.)

wire: *n.* a flexible strand of metal. *We strung some wire between the two posts.*

SIGN: Horizontal **'I'** hands are held with tips of little fingers touching each other and palms facing the body. The hands are then drawn apart. Movement is repeated. (**WIRE** is frequently fingerspelled.)

wise: *adj.* having wisdom, common sense and good judgment. *We always ask him for advice because he is so wise.*

SIGN: Horizontal right **'X'** hand, palm down, is held in front of the mid-forehead and is shaken up and down from the wrist.
SAME SIGN—**wisdom**, *n.*

wish: *v.* to desire or want something; to express a hope. *I wish I were 20 years younger.*

SIGN: Fingertips of horizontal right **'SPREAD EXTENDED C'** hand, palm toward the body, are placed against middle of upper chest and the hand is drawn firmly downward.

wit: *n.* speech or writing that has a clever or humorous effect. *The Canadian author, Stephen Leacock, was famous for his dry wit and satire.*

SIGN: Fingerspell **WIT**.

witch: *n.* a woman who has supernatural powers due to her association with evil spirits; a mean, ugly, old woman. *In the 1600s, a woman suspected of being a witch would be burned at the stake.*

SIGN #1: Forefinger of vertical right **'X'** hand, palm forward, is placed on the nose. The hand is then lowered so that the palm faces downward and the forefinger is tapped against that of the left **'X'** hand, of which the palm faces up. (Signs vary considerably.)

OR

SIGN #2: Back of forefinger of vertical right **'X'** hand, palm facing forward, taps against the nose a couple of times.

OR

SIGN #3: Side of forefinger of vertical right **'X'** hand, palm facing left, taps against the nose, as the hand is moved back and forth a couple of times from the wrist.

SIGN #4 [ONTARIO]: Horizontal right **'MODIFIED G'** hand is held against the bridge of the nose with palm facing left and is then lowered to make contact with the nose at a lower level.

with: *prep.* in the company of; alongside of. *She went skating with Paul.*

SIGN: **'A'** hands, palms facing, are simultaneously brought and held together. (The concept of 'being together' is frequently incorporated in a sign that represents the subject of a sentence and often the action performed by the subject as well. In such cases, no additional sign for **with** is required.)

withdraw: *v.* to remove from deposit or investment in a bank. *I plan to withdraw part of my savings to buy a new car.*

SIGN #1: Right **'CROOKED 5'** hand, palm down, is held so the wrist is directly below the left **'STANDARD BASE'** hand. Then the right hand is drawn back toward the chest as it closes to form an **'S'** hand.
SAME SIGN—**withdrawal**, *n.*, in this context.

withdraw: *v.* to remove oneself from a given situation. *He was asked to withdraw from the program.*

SIGN #2: Vertical right **'W'** hand, palm forward, is drawn back toward the right shoulder as it changes to a **'D'** hand.
SAME SIGN—**withdrawal**, *n.*, in this context.
ALTERNATE SIGN—**resign**

withdraw: *v.* to detach oneself socially, emotionally or mentally. *As his self-esteem diminished, he began to withdraw from society.*

SIGN #3: **'BENT EXTENDED B'** hands, palms down, are held slightly apart but close to the body. Then they are simultaneously drawn tightly toward the chest.
SAME SIGN—**withdrawal**, *n.*, in this context.

withdrawn: *adj.* unusually reserved or shy. *She has always been an introverted, withdrawn person.*

SIGN: Backs of fingers of right **'BENT EXTENDED B'** hand are held against right cheek. The hand is then twisted forward slightly from the wrist.

without: *prep.* not having; not accompanied by; not making use of. *I can not live without you.*

SIGN: **'A'** hands are held together with palms facing, and are changed to **'5'** hands as they are thrust apart.

witness: *n.* a person who has seen something happen and can give evidence. *As a witness to the accident he had to testify in court.*

SIGN: Vertical right **'BENT ONE'** hand, palm toward the face, is held with tip of forefinger just below the right eye. The head then tilts downward slightly, thus causing the face to exert pressure against the fingertip.

witty: *adj.* clever or humorous. *She is always making witty remarks.*

SIGN: The two extended fingers of the **'BENT EXTENDED U'** hand, palm toward the face, stroke the nose at least twice in a downward motion.

woe: *n.* deep sadness; intense affliction or misfortune. *His life seems to be a continuous tale of woe.*

SIGN: Vertical **'CROOKED 5'** hands are held slightly apart with palms toward the face. The hands are then simultaneously lowered somewhat and the head tilts to the right. (Appropriate facial expression is important.)

wolf: *n.* a wild, predatory canine mammal. *The wolf followed its prey silently.*

SIGN: Right **'CONTRACTED 5'** hand, palm toward the face, is held so the fingertips surround the nose. Then it is changed to a **'FLAT O'** hand as it is drawn forward, away from the face. Motion is repeated.

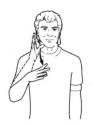

woman: *n.* an adult female human being. *The woman was driving a blue car.*

SIGN #1: Thumbtip of vertical right **'5'** hand, palm left, is placed on chin and is lowered to mid-chest.

OR

SIGN #2: Thumbtip of vertical right **'A'** hand, palm left, is placed on chin and as it is lowered to mid-chest, the hand opens out to assume a **'5'** shape.

womb: *n.* the nontechnical term for 'uterus', or the place where something is conceived. *The fetus can be treated in the womb before birth.*

SIGN: Fingerspell **WOMB**.

wonder: *v.* to have curiosity, sometimes mixed with puzzlement or doubt. *We often wonder how magicians do their tricks.*

SIGN #1: Vertical right **'ONE'** hand, palm toward the face, is held near right side of face and is circled clockwise with a small movement. (Sometimes this sign is made with two hands.)

wonder: *n.* a miracle or something that causes a feeling of awe. *The pyramids of Egypt are considered a wonder of the world.*

SIGN #2: Fingerspell **WONDER**.

wonderful: *adj.* marvelous; excellent; extremely fine. *The senior citizens enjoyed a wonderful cruise in the Caribbean.*

SIGN: Vertical **'EXTENDED B'** hands, palms facing forward, are held apart near the face. Forearms are pushed purposefully forward a short distance.

won't/wouldn't: *v.* contraction of 'will not', denoting refusal. *They won't help us.*

SIGN #1: Right horizontal **'EXTENDED A'** hand, with palm facing leftward, is raised abruptly to an upright position so that the thumb points over the right shoulder. (Alternatively, **WON'T** may be fingerspelled for emphasis. The facial expression is one of 'defiance'; **wouldn't**, however, is never fingerspelled.)

won't/wouldn't: *v.* contraction of 'will not', denoting unlikelihood. *We won't finish before noon.*

SIGN #2: Right **'EXTENDED A'** hand, palm facing left, thumb under chin, is thrust forward.

wood: *n.* the trunks of trees either to be used as fuel or prepared for use as building material. *The floor is made of wood.*

SIGN #1: Horizontal right **'EXTENDED B'** hand, fingertips pointing forward/leftward and palm facing left, is placed on the left **'STANDARD BASE'** hand. Both hands then move back and forth in a sawing motion. (Alternatively, the left hand may take the shape of a horizontal **'EXTENDED B'** with fingertips pointing forward/ rightward and palm facing right.)

SIGN #2 [ATLANTIC]: Right **'EXTENDED B'** hand, palm up and fingers pointing forward/leftward, is purposefully inserted between ring finger and little finger of left horizontal **'5'** hand, of which the palm is facing the body, but angled rightward. Motion is repeated.
SAME SIGN—**wooden**, *adj.*

woods: *n.* closely packed trees that form a forest. *We hiked on a path through the woods.*

SIGN: Both arms drift rightward as right elbow rests on left **'STANDARD BASE'** hand, and vertical right **'5'** hand shimmies or repeatedly twists back and forth in short, jerky movements.

wool: *n.* the outer coat of sheep and certain other mammals. *This jacket is made of pure wool.*

SIGN: Fingerspell **WOOL**.

word: *n.* the smallest meaningful unit of a language. *When I learn a new word, I try to use it so that I do not forget it.*

SIGN #1: Tips of forefinger and thumb of right **'C-INDEX'** (or **'MODIFIED G'**) hand are tapped a couple of times against forward-pointing forefinger of left **'ONE'** hand, whose palm faces rightward/downward.

(big) word: *n.* a long word. *'Erysipeloid' is a big word.*

SIGN #2: Left **'ONE'** hand is held in a fixed position with palm down and forefinger pointing rightward/forward. Right **'Y'** hand, palm down, is held very close to (just to the right of/behind) the left hand. It then firmly pokes at the left hand so that the thumbtip and the tip of the little finger span the length of the left forefinger. To indicate plurality, the motion is repeated several times as the hands are simultaneously lowered. Facial expression is important. (This sign is used to refer to a long word which is unfamiliar to the signer.)

word processing: *n.* a system for storage and organization of written text on a computer. *Word processing has simplified and improved business correspondence.*

SIGN: Fingerspell **WP**.

W P

work: *v.* to exert physical or mental effort in order to do or make something. *He has been working for that company for 20 years.*

SIGN #1: Wrist of right **'S'** (or **'A'**) hand, palm facing away from the body, strikes wrist of left **'S'** (or **'A'**) hand, which is held in front of/below right hand with palm facing downward. Motion is repeated.

OR

SIGN #2: **'SPREAD C'** hands, palms angled forward/downward, are held parallel and the arms are moved outward and back several times in short, rapid movements. (This sign is not appropriate in all contexts.)

workshop: *n.* an intensive seminar in a specialized field of study. *He attended a workshop on stress management.*

SIGN #1: Tips of forefingers of vertical **'W'** hands, palms forward but angled toward one another, are held together. Then the hands are drawn apart and curved outward/forward as they are changed to **'S'** hands and are rejoined with the palms facing the chest.

workshop: *n.* a room or building where industrial or manual work is done. *He makes fine furniture in his basement workshop.*

SIGN #2: Horizontal right **'S'** hand, palm left, is placed on the upturned palm of the left **'EXTENDED B'** hand, and is pushed forward across it several times.

OR

SIGN #3: Horizontal left **'X'** hand is held with palm facing right while horizontal right **'X'** hand is held above with palm facing left. Right hand is then brushed forward across the top of the left hand at least twice.

world: *n.* the planet Earth and its inhabitants. *Canada is the second largest country in the world.*

SIGN: Horizontal **'W'** hands, left palm facing right and right palm facing left, are held with the right above the left. The forearms are simultaneously circled forward 360 degrees with the right hand coming to rest on the left hand.

worm: *n.* an invertebrate with an elongated body and slow, sinuous movement. *I found a worm in my apple.*

SIGN: The edge of the forefinger of the right **'CROOKED ONE'** hand, palm down, is placed against the right-facing palm of the horizontal left **'EXTENDED B'** hand. Then the right hand is moved forward slowly with the crooked forefinger wiggling.

worn out: *adj.* used until threadbare, value-less, or useless. In reference to a person, it can mean completely exhausted or very weary. *He was worn out after his long trip.*

SIGN: **'A'** hands are held together with palms facing the chest. The hands then gradually rotate forward with fingers spreading until they take on a **'CROOKED 5'** shape with palms facing upward. (Appropriate facial expression is essential.)

worry: *v.* to be anxious or uneasy about something uncertain. *Many people worry about trivial things.*

SIGN: **'B'** (or **'EXTENDED B'**) hands are held apart in front of the face at such an angle that the palms face each other but slant downward while the fingers of the left hand point upward/rightward and the fingers of the right hand point upward/leftward. The hands are then alternately circled toward each other a few times. Facial expression must clearly convey 'anxiety'.

worse: *adj.* the comparative form of 'bad'. *His hair looks bad enough but mine is worse.*

SIGN #1: Vertical **'V'** (or **'K'**) hands, palms facing each other but angled slightly toward the body, are held apart and are simultane-ously thrust toward each other, ending with the wrists crossed.

(get) worse: *v.* to become more unfavorable, undesirable, or unpleasant. *The weather is getting worse.*

SIGN #2: Vertical **'V'** (or **'K'**) hands, palms fac-ing each other but angled slightly toward the body, are held apart and are simultaneously thrust toward each other, ending with the wrists crossed. Facial expression is important.

(get) worse: *v.* to deteriorate in quality, value or character. *The quality of her work is getting worse.*

SIGN #3: Right **'EXTENDED B'** hand, palm upward but slanted backward slightly, is held against middle of left arm and is lowered to the wrist. Facial expression is important.

(get) worse: *v.* to deteriorate in terms of *health. His medical condition is getting worse.*

SIGN #4: Horizontal **'EXTENDED A'** hands are held parallel with palms facing and are simultaneously lowered. Facial expression is important.

worship: *v.* to show profound devotion and respect for either God or another person or thing. *They worship God every Sunday.*

SIGN: Vertical right **'OPEN A'** hand, palm facing left, is cupped over the fingers of the vertical left **'A'** hand, of which the palm is facing right. The hands are then moved slightly downward together.

worth: *adj.* having value; deserving, meriting or justifying. *The old car was not worth the cost of the many repairs it needed.*

SIGN: Both vertical **'F'** hands, palms facing forward, are held apart, and then are simultaneously curved toward each other until the joined thumbs and forefingers come together.

worthless: *adj.* having no value or usefulness. *The antique coin was found to be worthless.*

SIGN: Vertical **'F'** hands, palms forward, are held so the joined thumbs and forefingers are touching each other. Then they are simultane-ously thrust apart and forward, ending with **'5'** handshapes.

worthwhile: *adj.* rewarding enough to justify time and effort spent. *All her volunteer work seems worthwhile.*

SIGN: Vertical **'F'** hands are held apart with palms facing forward. The hands are then brought purposefully together.

wound: *n.* an injury inflicted upon someone or something. *The soldiers sustained many wounds in battle.*

SIGN: Horizontal **'BENT ONE'** hands are held with palms facing the body and forefingers pointing toward each other. Then they are sharply stabbed toward each other several times. (Positioning of this sign often depends on the specific part of the body that has been afflicted.)

WOW: *inter.* an exclamation of admiration, pleasure or amazement. *Wow! That is a fantastic outfit!*

SIGN #1: Right **'CROOKED 5'** hand is held palm down in front of the right side of the body and is shaken back and forth from the wrist several times. Facial expression is important. (**WOW** is frequently fingerspelled.)

OR

SIGN #2: Right **'CROOKED 5'** hand, palm toward face, is held upright and tilted slightly leftward as it is waved leftward, then rightward in front of the face. Motion is repeated. Facial expression is important.

wrap: *v.* to fold or wind around so as to cover. *It is time to wrap the Christmas gifts.*

SIGN: Horizontal **'BENT EXTENDED B'** hands, left palm facing right and right palm facing left, are held with the right above the left. The hands then pass over and under each other as the forearms are simultaneously circled forward a few times.

wrath: *n.* intense or violent anger; rage. *It is difficult for some people to control their wrath.*

SIGN: **'CLAWED 5'** hands, palms toward body, fingertips touching chest, are swept vigorously upward/outward. Facial expression must clearly convey 'anger'.

wreath: *n.* a band of flowers or foliage intertwined into a ring. *The Christmas wreath is made of pine cones.*

SIGN: Vertical **'SPREAD C'** hands, palms forward, are held so the forefingers and thumbs are touching. Then they are simultaneously circled away from each other, ending with the palms up and tips of the little fingers touching each other.

wreck: *n.* the remains of something that has been ruined or destroyed. *His car is a total wreck as a result of the accident.*

SIGN: Left **'CROOKED 5'** hand is held palm-up with fingers pointing forward while right **'CROOKED 5'** hand is held apart and slightly higher with palm down and fingers pointing forward. The arms are then simultaneously moved upward/rightward as the hands are purposefully twisted rightward from the wrist so that the left palm faces right and the right palm faces left. (Sign selection depends on context.)

wrench: *n.* a tool with adjustable jaws. *The mechanic used a wrench to tighten the nuts on the wheel.*

SIGN: Extended fingers of horizontal right **'V'** hand, palm facing left and angled toward the body, are used to grasp and rock on horizontal forefinger of left **'ONE'** hand, thus simulating the function of a wrench.

wrestling: *n.* a sport in which two opponents try to throw each other without the use of fists. *Wrestling is now a popular Olympic event.*

SIGN #1: **'5'** hands are held so the fingers are interlocked, fingers of the left hand pointing upward/rightward and fingers of the right hand pointing upward/leftward. The hands are then moved back and forth together in short quick movements.

OR

SIGN #2: Horizontal **'5'** hands, palms facing, are held apart and are alternately circled forward.

wring: *v.* to twist and squeeze or compress to remove the liquid. *You should wring out the cloth before you wipe the table.*

SIGN: **'S'** hands are held side by side with palms down. The left hand remains stationary as the right hand twists forward/downward from the wrist as though wringing a wet garment.

wrinkles: *n.* creases in a normally smooth surface. *He needs to iron his shirt to get rid of the wrinkles.*

SIGN #1: **'SPREAD C'** hands, palms facing, are held apart with the right above the left and are simultaneously twisted clockwise from the wrists until the left is eventually above the right and the hands have taken on **'CLAWED SPREAD C'** shapes.

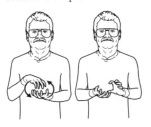

wrinkles: *n.* creases or lines in the skin such as those resulting from age. *She uses various creams to try to prevent* **wrinkles.**

SIGN #2: Fingertips of right **'BENT 4'** hand, palm facing backwards, are placed just under the right eye and moved along the contour of the cheek. Positioning of this sign depends on the exact location of the wrinkles.

wrist: *n.* the joint between the forearm and the hand. *He broke his* **wrist** *while playing hockey.*

SIGN: Right **'OPEN 8'** hand is held palm-up as midfinger and thumb enclose wrist of left **'STANDARD BASE'** hand.

write: *v.* to make symbols on paper or any other surface with a tool such as a pen, pencil, or chalk. *Please* **write** *a letter to your MLA about this issue.*

SIGN: Horizontal left **'EXTENDED B'** hand is held in a fixed position with palm facing rightward/backward. Thumb and forefinger of right **'CLOSED X'** hand move forward/ rightward along the palm of the left hand. (This sign may be varied according to whether the writing is being done on paper, a black-board, or any other surface simply by changing its location.) ❖

write down: *v.* to set down in writing. *She will* **write down** *the names of the committee members in attendance.*

SIGN: Bunched fingertips of right **'O'** hand, palm down, are placed on the upturned left palm. Right hand opens to form an **'EXTENDED B'** hand and is then tapped down smartly on the left palm.

write-off: *n.* something acknowledged as having become a total loss. *The insurance adjuster declared the car to be a complete* **write-off.**

SIGN: Thumb and forefinger of right **'CLOSED X'** hand move left to right once across the right facing palm of the left **'EXTENDED B'** hand. Then fingerspell **OFF.**

wrong: *adj.* not correct or truthful; judging erroneously. *You were* **wrong** *to assume everyone would agree.*

SIGN #1: Vertical right **'Y'** hand, palm toward the body, is firmly tapped on the chin.

SIGN #2 [ATLANTIC]: Fingertips of right **'5'** hand with palm toward the face, are fluttered on the lips.

X

Y

x-ray: *n.* a picture produced by a special process to be used in diagnostic medicine. *The x-ray showed that the bone was fractured.*

SIGN: Fingerspell **XRAY**. (Signs vary, but these generally depend on what is being x-rayed.)

yacht: *n.* a small ship used for racing or for cruises. *They have enjoyed many pleasure cruises on his yacht.*

SIGN: Fingerspell **YACHT**.

yard: *n.* a piece of enclosed ground around a building. *The children were playing in the yard.*

SIGN #1: Fingerspell **YARD**.

yard: *n.* a unit of length equal to three feet. *She needs another yard of fabric to make her dress.*

SIGN #2: Fingerspell **YARD**.

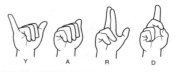

yawn: *v.* to open the mouth wide and take in air deeply. *People sometimes yawn if they are sleepy or bored.*

SIGN: Horizontal **'CROOKED V'** (or **CLAWED V'**) hands, left palm facing upward and right palm facing downward, are placed together. The right hand is curved upward in a small arc and then returns to its original position. The sign is generally accompanied by the yawning movement of the mouth. (Signs vary.)

year: *n.* a period of time consisting generally of 365 days. [See TIME CONCEPTS, p. LXXII.] *The year 1867 is significant in Canadian history.*

SIGN: Horizontal **'S'** hands, palms toward the body, are held so the right is slightly above the left. Then the right is circled forward around the left, coming to rest on top of it.

yearbook: *n.* a book published annually that contains information about the year before. *The yearbook committee met weekly.*

SIGN: Horizontal **'S'** hands, palms toward the body, are held so the right is slightly above the left. The right is circled forward around the left, coming to rest on top of it. Then **'EXTENDED B'** hands, palms together, fingers pointing forward, are opened to the palms-up position.

yearly: *adj.* occurring every year or annually. [See TIME CONCEPTS, p. LXXII.] *My cat had its yearly rabies shot last June.*

SIGN: Horizontal right **'S'** hand, palm facing left, is placed on top of horizontal left **'S'** hand whose palm faces right. Right forefinger is then flicked forward twice.
REGIONAL VARIATION—**annual** #2

yearn: *v.* to have a strong desire or longing. *He yearns to return to his childhood home in the mountains.*

SIGN: **'CLAWED SPREAD C'** hands are held parallel with palms up as fingers flex and relax several times.
SAME SIGN—**yearning**, *n.*
ALTERNATE SIGN—**long** #3

yell: *v.* to shout, scream, cheer, or utter a loud, piercing sound. *He was able to yell loudly enough to awaken everyone.*

SIGN: Right vertical **'SPREAD C'** hand, palm toward the body, is held near the mouth and is forcefully drawn forward at an upward angle.

yellow: *adj.* having a colour varying from a lemon hue to deep gold. *The yellow roses were pretty.*

SIGN: Right **'Y'** hand, palm left, is wiggled back and forth from the wrist several times.

yes: *s.s.* an expression of consent or agreement. *Yes, you may leave when your work is finished.*

SIGN: The horizontal right **'S'** hand, palm down, is shaken up and down from the wrist. (**YES** is frequently fingerspelled in one fluid motion backward toward the body.)

yesterday: *adv.* the day before today. [See TIME CONCEPTS, p. LXXI.] *He left for London yesterday and will return tomorrow.*

SIGN: Tip of thumb of vertical right **'EXTENDED A'** (or **'Y'**) hand, palm forward at a slight leftward angle, is placed near the chin along the right jawline and is moved back toward the ear.

yet: *conj.* however; nevertheless; in spite of that. *He does not really like milk, yet he drinks it every day.*

SIGN #1: Horizontal **'Y'** hands are held apart with palms facing chest, and are twisted smoothly from the wrists so that the palms face downward/forward. Sometimes only the right hand is used.

OR

SIGN #2: Forefingers of **'ONE'** hands are crossed. The hands are then turned outward so that they become vertical with palms facing forward. Next, horizontal **'Y'** hands are held apart with palms facing chest, and are twisted smoothly from the wrists so that the palms face downward/forward. Sometimes only the right hand is used for this part of the sign. (ASL CONCEPT—**but - still**.)

(not) yet: *adv.* so far; up until then or now. *He has **not yet** received the parcel.*

SIGN #1: Right **'EXTENDED B'** hand is held to the right side of the body with fingers pointing downward and palm facing backward. Fingers simultaneously move back and forth as though the hand is waving to an imaginary person who is standing on his head behind the signer. This movement is accompanied by a protruding tongue.

SIGN #2 [ATLANTIC]: Forearms simultaneously shake back and forth slightly as vertical **'CLAWED V'** hands are held apart with palms facing each other. This sign is accompanied by a lip pattern such as that used to produce an 'SH' sound.

(not) yet: *s.s.* so far; up until then or now. (This sign is used only as a short reply, and cannot be used in a regular statement or question.)

SIGN #3: Tip of thumb of right **'EXTENDED A'** hand, palm facing left, is placed under the chin and flicked forward so that thumb points upward. **YET** is then fingerspelled.

yield: *v.* to give way to other drivers. *In specific situations, we are required by law to **yield** to other drivers.*

SIGN: Fingerspell **YIELD**.

yogurt [*also spelled* **yoghurt**]: *n.* a semi-solid food prepared from milk that has curdled from bacteria. *He likes his **yogurt** mixed with honey.*

SIGN: Fingerspell **YOGURT** or **YOGHURT**.

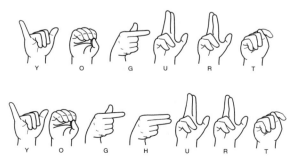

young: *adj.* having lived a relatively short time. *They have three **young** children.*

SIGN: Fingertips of both **'BENT EXTENDED B'** hands, palms facing the body, are brushed upward against the chest. Motion is repeated.

you *(sing.)*: *pron.* used to refer to the person being signed to. [See PRONOUNS, p. LXIV.] *You can help us.*

SIGN #1: Horizontal right **'BENT ONE'** hand is held with palm facing left and forefinger pointing forward at the person being referred to.

you *(pl.)*: *pron.* used to refer to the people being signed to. [See PRONOUNS, p. LXIV.] *You must all wear your life jackets.*

SIGN #2: Horizontal right **'BENT ONE'** hand is held in front of the right shoulder with palm facing forward/rightward and forefinger pointing in the same direction. The arm then sweeps leftward so that the forefinger eventually points forward/leftward.

your/yours *(sing.)*: *pron.* used to indicate something belonging to or related to the person being signed to. [See PRONOUNS, p. LXVI.] *Write **your** name at the top of the page.*

SIGN #1: Vertical right **'EXTENDED B'** hand, palm forward, is held in front of the right shoulder and moved forward a short distance.

your/yours *(pl.)*: *pron.* used to indicate something belonging to or related to more than one person being signed to. [See PRONOUNS, p. LXVI.] *The time is up, so please hand in **your** test papers.*

SIGN #2: Vertical right **'EXTENDED B'** hand, palm forward, is held in front of the right shoulder, then swept leftward so that it ends up in front of the left shoulder.

yourself: *pron.* used to emphasize the singular subject "you". [See PRONOUNS, p. LXVI.] *Did you build this house **yourself**?*

SIGN: Horizontal right **'EXTENDED A'** hand, palm facing left, is held in front of the right shoulder and jabbed forward a couple of times toward the person being referred to.

yourselves: *pron.* used to emphasize the plural subject "you". [See PRONOUNS, p. LXVI.] *Our club has no funds, so you will have to pay for the tickets yourselves.*

SIGN: Horizontal right **'EXTENDED A'** hand, palm facing left, is held in front of the right shoulder, then moved leftward as the wrist rotates so that the hand ends up in front of the left shoulder with the palm facing the body.

youth: *n.* the teenage period between childhood and maturity. *In his youth he dreamed of becoming a doctor.*

SIGN: Fingertips of both **'BENT EXTENDED B'** hands, palms facing the body, are brushed upward against the chest. Motion is repeated.

Z

Zamboni: *n.* a vehicle used to improve the condition of the ice surface for skaters. *Between periods, the hockey fans watched the man on the Zamboni do his job.*

SIGN: Fingerspell **ZAMBONI**.

zeal: *n.* eagerness; enthusiastic devotion. *His zeal for that political party is well known.*

SIGN: **'EXTENDED B'** hands, palms together and fingers pointing forward, are rubbed back and forth against each other. Facial expression must clearly convey 'enthusiasm'.

zebra: *n.* a striped black and white wild ass. *The children were fascinated with the zebra at the zoo.*

SIGN: Fingerspell **ZEBRA**.

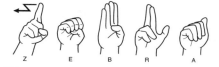

zero: *n.* the temperature indicated on a thermometer by the number 0. [See also NUMBERS, p. LX.] *The temperature went down to zero last night.*

SIGN #1: With palm facing left, vertical **'O'** hand wobbles.

zero: *n.* nothing; the numerical value of 0. *The teacher gave him zero on his essay because it was copied from a book.*

SIGN #2: Left **'EXTENDED B'** hand is held in a fixed position with palm facing upward but slanted slightly toward the body at a rightward angle. Vertical right **'O'** hand, palm facing left, is lowered so that it strikes the left palm.

zipper: *n.* a metal or plastic fastening device with teeth interlocked by a sliding tab. *The zipper on my parka is broken.*

SIGN: **'COVERED T'** hands, palms toward the body, are held at mid-waist so that the right is above the left. Then the right is drawn upward to simulate the zipping of a garment. (Positioning of this sign will vary according to the specific location of the zipper, but the handshapes remain standard.)

zit: *n.* a colloquial term meaning pimple or skin blemish. *The teenage boy felt self-conscious about the zit on his face.*

SIGN: Tip of forefinger of right **'CROOKED ONE'** hand taps twice on the place where the blemish has appeared. (**ZIT** may be fingerspelled.)

zone: *n.* a region; area; specific division. *The quarterback slid into the end zone to make the touchdown.*

SIGN: Fingerspell **ZONE**. (Signs vary depending on the context.)

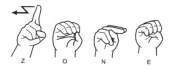

zoo: *n.* a place where live animals are exhibited to the public. *The kindergarten class visited the zoo yesterday.*

SIGN: Fingerspell **ZOO**.

zoom: *v.* to rush or move very rapidly. *The car zoomed down the road in a cloud of smoke.*

SIGN #1: The side of the thumb of the right **'CONTRACTED L'** hand, palm forward/leftward, is placed on the back of the left **'ONE'** hand which is held with palm facing down and forefinger pointing forward/rightward. Then the right hand is rapidly drawn across the left forefinger, as the right thumb and forefinger close to form a **'CLOSED MODIFIED G'** handshape.

zoom: *adj.* a system that allows a camera lens to vary its focal length so that the image appears close even though it may actually be far away. *You will need a zoom lens to photograph wild animals.*

SIGN #2: Vertical **'EXTENDED B'** hands are held with palms facing each other, the left facing forward and the right facing backward. Then the right is moved back and forth at least twice.

zucchini: *n.* an elongated squash which is white inside and has a smooth, dark green rind. *She sliced the zucchini into the casserole.*

SIGN: Fingerspell **ZUCCHINI**.

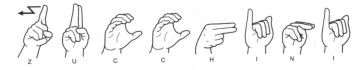